# FOOTBALL IN

# ENGLAND

## a statistical record

## 1872 to 1950

Alexander Graham

# INTRODUCTION

This book features a statistical history of football in England from 1872 (when the F.A. Cup was first played) until 1950. The F.A. Cup (or The Football Association Challenge Cup to give the full title) was the first major competition but the roots of organised English football predate this by almost 10 years. Organised football as we know it began with the formation of the Football Association in a meeting in the Freemason's Tavern in Great Queen Street, London on 26th October 1863. At that time there were no universally accepted rules for the playing of the game of football with a number of variations used in different areas of the country. The first revision of the rules for the modern game was drawn up during a series of six meetings held in the social room of this public house between October and December of 1863 and, with relatively minor alterations, these rules are used worldwide to this day!

The F.A. Cup itself was first suggested by C.W. Alcock, then Secretary of the Football Association, at a meeting on 20th July 1871 and the competition was embodied at a later meeting on 16th October 1871. The F.A. Cup remains the oldest and most prestigious domestic cup competition in the world and the 12 clubs who entered in 1872 could scarcely have believed that the Cup would grow to a record entry of 660 clubs for the 2004-2005 competition. The Cup is still played as a strict knock-out competition with no seeding of clubs and this book lists the F.A. Cup results from the Quarter-Final stage onwards including full line-ups and goalscorers for the Final matches themselves.

After the great success of the F.A. Cup, it was inevitable that a League competition would eventually begin and to this end William McGregor, a director of Aston Villa FC, arranged a preliminary meeting on 22nd March 1888 at Anderton's Hotel in Fleet Street. The Football League officially came into existence at a subsequent meeting on 17th April 1888 with 12 members. The Football League is, unsurprisingly, the oldest domestic League competition in the world. Since the first game was played on 8th September 1888, the League has expanded considerably and at it's height consisted of 4 separate divisions containing a total of 92 professional clubs. When the top division of clubs split off to form an independent F.A. Premier League in 1992, the remaining 3 divisions of the Football League continued to run as before and it is still commonplace to refer to the clubs in these two competitions as the "92 League Clubs."

Both the Football League and F.A. Cup were suspended during the two World Wars and a number of regional matches and championships were played in their stead. This book includes tables of the combined results of those wartime matches for each year they ran together with the results of games played in the 1939-40 Football League season which was abandoned due to the onset of War.

In addition to the results of all League matches, Final League tables and the F.A. Cup results, this book also lists the top goal-scorers for each season.

Most of the information in this book is taken from the now defunct "Statistical History of Football" series which were published by Skye Soccer Books. As in the original series, the full names of clubs are used whenever possible with name-changes, mergers etc. shown as and when they occur. The club names are listed in the following format:
    Club Name (Home Town/City/Village).

The information contained in this book has been gathered over a number of years and has come from myriad sources although most was collected through personal contacts. Other sources of information include newspapers, magazines, books etc. and in more recent times the internet. I would like to extend my thanks to all those who helped with the collection of this information. In an attempt to ensure accuracy, the information has been checked and collated. However, if any errors are found, readers are invited to notify the author care of the address below and if possible provide the corrected information.

Alex Graham

British Library Cataloguing in Publication Data

A catalogue record for this book is available from the British Library

ISBN 1-86223-133-8

**Printed by 4edge Ltd. www.4edge.co.uk**

# 1872

**F.A. CUP FINAL**    (Kennington Oval, London – 16/03/1872 – 2,000)

THE WANDERERS FC (LONDON)                 1-0                 Royal Engineers Regiment (Chatham)

*Betts*

Wanderers:  Welch, Bowen, Thompson, Lubbock, Crake, Wollaston, Alcock, Hooman, Betts, Vidal, Bonsor.

Royal Engineers:  Merriman, Marindin, Addison, Creswell, Mitchell, Renny-Tailyour, Rich, Goodwyn, Muirhead, Cotter, Bogle.

## Semi-finals

Royal Engineers Regiment (Chatham)          0-0,  3-0                 Crystal Palace FC (London)

The Wanderers FC (London)                    0-0,  w/o                 Queen's Park FC (Glasgow)

Queen's Park FC withdrew due to difficulty in meeting travel expenses for the replay.

## Round 3

Royal Engineers Regiment (Chatham)              3-0                 Hampstead Heathens FC (London)

The Wanderers FC (London)                       0-0                 Crystal Palace FC (London)

(Both teams qualified under rule 8.)

Queen's Park FC (Glasgow) received a bye.

# 1873

**F.A. CUP FINAL**    (Amateur Athletic Ground, Lillie Bridge, London – 29/03/1873 – 3,000)

THE WANDERERS FC (LONDON)                 2-0                 Oxford University FC (Oxford)

*Kinnaird, Wollaston*                        (H.T. 2-0)

Wanderers:  Welch, Howell, Bowen, Thompson, Kinnaird, Wollaston, Sturgis, Stewart, Kenyon-Slaney, Kingsford, Bonsor.

Oxford University:  Leach, Mackarness, Birley, Kirke-Smith, Ottaway, Longman, Chappell-Madison, Dixon, Paton, Vidal, Sumner.

## Semi-finals

Oxford University FC (Oxford)                   w/o                 Queen's Park FC (Glasgow)

The match was due to be played on the same day as an England vs Scotland international so Oxford decided they could not play. Instead of claiming the tie Queen's Park withdrew allowing Oxford to progress to the final.

The Wanderers FC (London) received a bye

## Quarter-finals

Oxford University FC (Oxford)                   4-0                 Maidenhead FC (Maidenhead)

Queen's Park FC (Glasgow) and The Wanderers FC (London) both received byes.

# 1874

**F.A. CUP FINAL**  (Kennington Oval, London – 14/04/1874 – 2,000)

OXFORD UNIVERSITY FC (OXFORD)  2-0  Royal Engineers Regiment (Chatham)
*Mackarness, Patton*

Oxford University:  Nepean, Mackarness, Birley, Green, Vidal, Ottaway, Benson, Patton, S.Rawson, Chappell-Madison, Johnson.

Royal Engineers:  Merriman, Marindin, Addison, Onslow, Digby, Oliver, Renny-Tailyour, E.Rawson, Blackburn, Wood von Donop.

## Semi-finals

Oxford University FC (Oxford)  1-0  Clapham Rovers FC (London)
Royal Engineers Regiment (Chatham)  2-0  The Swifts FC (London)

## Quarter-finals

Clapham Rovers FC (London)  2-1  Sheffield FC (Sheffield)
Royal Engineers Regiment (Chatham)  7-0  Maidenhead FC (Maidenhead)
The Wanderers FC (London)  1-1,  0-1  Oxford University FC (Oxford)
The Swifts FC (London) received a bye.


# 1875

**F.A. CUP FINAL**  (Kennington Oval, London – 16/03/1875 – 3,000)

ROYAL ENGINEERS REGIMENT  1-1  (aet)  Old Etonians FC (London)
*Renny-Tailyour*  *Bonsor*

Royal Engineers:  Merriman, Sim, Onslow, Ruck, von Donop, Wood, Rawson, Stafford, Renny-Tailyour, Mein, Wingfield-Stratford.

Old Etonians:  Farmer, Wilson, Thompson, E.Lubbock, Benson, Kenyon-Slaney, Patton, Bonsor, Ottaway, Kinnaird, Stronge.

**F.A. CUP FINAL REPLAY**  (Kennington Oval, London – 16/03/1875 – 3,000)

ROYAL ENGINEERS REGIMENT  2-0  Old Etonians FC (London)
*Renny-Tailyour, Stafford*

Old Etonians:  Drummond-Moray, Farrer, E.Lubbock, Wilson, Hamond, A.Lubbock, Patton, Farmer, Bonsor, Kinnaird, Stronge.

Royal Engineers:  Merriman, Sim, Onslow, Ruck, von Donop, Wood, Rawson, Stafford, Renny-Tailyour, Mein, Wingfield-Stratford.

## Semi-finals

Old Etonians FC (London)  1-0  Shropshire Wanderers FC (Shrewsbury)
Royal Engineers Regiment (Chatham)  1-1,  1-0 (aet)  Oxford University FC (Oxford)

## Quarter-finals

Old Etonians FC (London)  1-0  Maidenhead FC (Maidenhead)
Royal Engineers Regiment (Chatham)  3-2  Clapham Rovers FC (London)
Shropshire Wanderers FC (Shrewsbury)  1-1 (aet),  2-0  Woodford Wells FC
The Wanderers FC (London)  1-2  Oxford University FC (London)

# 1876

**F.A. CUP FINAL**   (Kennington Oval, London – 11/03/1876 – 3,000)

| THE WANDERERS FC (LONDON) | 1-1 (aet) | Old Etonians FC (London) |
|---|---|---|
| *Edwards* | *(H.T. 1-0)* | *Bonsor* |

Wanderers: Greig, Stratford, Lindsay, Maddison, Birley, Wollaston, GH Heron, F.Heron, Edwards. Kenrick, Hughes.

Old Etonians: Hogg, Wellson, C.Thompson, E.Lyttleton, A.Lyttleton, Kinnaird, Kenyon-Slaney, CM Thompson, Bonsor, Sturgis, Alleyne.

**F.A. CUP FINAL REPLAY**   (Kennington Oval, London – 18/03/1876 – 3,500)

| THE WANDERERS FC (LONDON) | 3-0 | Old Etonians FC (London) |
|---|---|---|
| *Hughes 2, Wollaston* | *(H.T. 2-0)* | |

Old Etonians: Hogg, Lubbock, Farrer, E.Lyttleton, Kinnaird, A.Lyttleton, Kenyon-Stanley, Bonsor, Sturgis, Alleyne, Stronge.

Wanderers: Greig, Stratford, Lindsay, Maddison, Birley, Wollaston, GH Heron, F.Heron, Edwards, Kenrick, Hughes.

## Semi-finals

| Oxford University FC (Oxford) | 0-1 | Old Etonians FC (London) |
|---|---|---|
| The Wanderers FC (London) | 2-1 | The Swifts FC (London) |

## Quarter-finals

| Cambridge University FC (Cambridge) | 0-4 | Oxford University FC (Oxford) |
|---|---|---|
| Old Etonians FC (London) | 1-0 | Clapham Rovers FC (London) |
| Royal Engineers Regiment (Chatham) | 1-3 | The Swifts FC (London) |
| The Wanderers FC (London) | 2-0 | Sheffield FC (Sheffield) |

# 1877

**F.A. CUP FINAL**   (Kennington Oval, London – 24/03/1877 – 3,000)

| THE WANDERERS FC (LONDON) | 2-1 (aet) | Oxford University FC (Oxford) |
|---|---|---|
| *Kenrick, Lindsay* | *(H.T. 0-1)* | *Waddington* |

Wanderers: Kinnaird, Lindsay, Stratford, Birley, Green, Hughes, Wollaston, GH Heron, Wace, Kenrick, Denton.

Oxford University: Alington, Dunell, Rawson, Waddington, Savory, Otter, Parry, Bain, Todd, Fernandez, Hills.

## Semi-finals

| The Wanderers FC (London) | 1-0 | Cambridge University FC (Cambridge) |
|---|---|---|
| Oxford University FC (Oxford) received a bye. | | |

## Quarter-finals

| Cambridge University FC (Cambridge) | 1-0 | Royal Engineers Regiment (Chatham) |
|---|---|---|
| Oxford University FC (Oxford) | 0-0, 1-0 | Upton Park FC (London) |
| The Wanderers FC (London) received a bye. | | |

# 1878

**F.A. CUP FINAL**   (Kennington Oval, London – 23/03/1878 – 4,500)

THE WANDERERS FC (LONDON)                3-1                Royal Engineers Regiment (Chatham)
*Kenrick 2, Kinnaird*                    *(H.T. 1-1)*                              *Scorer not known*

Wands.: Kirkpatrick, Stratford, Lindsay, Kinnaird, Green, Wollaston, GH.Heron, Wylie, Wace, Denton, Kenrick.
Royal Engineers: Friend, Cowan, Morris, Mayne, Heath, Lindsay, Barnet, Hedley, Haynes, Bond, Ruck.

## Semi-finals

Royal Engineers Regiment (Chatham)       2-1                        Old Harrovians FC (London)
The Wanderers FC (London) received a bye.

## Quarter-finals

Old Harrovians FC (London)               3-1                          Upton Park FC (London)
Royal Engineers Regiment (Chatham)   3-3, 2-2 (aet), 4-2          Oxford University FC (Oxford)
The Wanderers FC (London)                3-0                        Sheffield FC (Sheffield)

# 1879

**F.A. CUP FINAL**   (Kennington Oval, London – 29/03/1879 – 5,000)

OLD ETONIANS FC (LONDON)                 1-0                       Clapham Rovers FC (London)
*Clerke*                                 *(H.T. 0-0)*

Old Eton.: Hawtrey, Christian, Bury, Kinnaird, Lubbock, Clerke, Pares, Goodhart, Whitfield, Chevallier, Beaufoy
Clapham: Birkett, Ogilvie, Field, Bailey, Prinsep, Rawson, Stanley, Scott, Bevington, Growse, Keith-Falconer.

## Semi-finals

Old Etonians FC (London)                 2-1                  Nottingham Forest FC (Nottingham)
Clapham Rovers FC (London) received a bye.

## Quarter-finals

Clapham Rovers FC (London)               8-1                          The Swifts FC (London)
Nottingham Forest FC (Nottingham)        2-1                  Oxford University FC (Oxford)
Old Etonians FC (London)             5-5, 2-2 (aet), 6-2                Darwen FC (Darwen)

# 1880

**F.A. CUP FINAL**   (Kennington Oval, London – 10/04/1880 – 6,000)

CLAPHAM ROVERS FC (LONDON)               1-0                  Oxford University FC (Oxford)
*Lloyd-Jones*                            *(H.T. 0-0)*

Clapham Rovers: Birkett, Ogilvie, Field, Weston, Bailey, Brougham, Stanley, Barry, Sparks, Lloyd-Jones, Ram.
Oxford University: Parr, Wilson, King, Phillips, Rogers, Heygate, Childs, Eyre, Crowdy, Hill, Lubbock.

## Semi-finals

Oxford University FC (Oxford)            1-0                  Nottingham Forest FC (Nottingham)
Clapham Rovers FC (London) received a bye.

## Quarter-finals

Clapham Rovers FC (London)               1-0                          Old Etonians FC (London)
Oxford University FC (Oxford)        1-1 (aet), 1-0      Royal Engineers Regiment (Chatham)
Nottingham Forest FC (Nottingham) received a bye.

# 1881

**F.A. CUP FINAL**   (Kennington Oval, London – 09/04/1881 – 4,500)

OLD CARTHUSIANS FC (LONDON)          3-0          Old Etonians FC (London)

*Wynyard, Parry, Todd*                    *(H.T. 1-0)*

Old Carthusians: Gillett, Norris, Colvin, Prinsep, Vincent, Hensell, Richards, Page, Wynyard, Parry, Todd.

Old Etonians: Rawlinson, Foley, French, Kinnaird, Farrer, Chevallier, Anderson, Goodhart, Macaulay, Whitfield, Novelli.

## Semi-finals

Old Carthusians FC (London)          4-1          Darwen FC (Darwen)
Old Etonians FC (London) received a bye.

## Quarter-finals

Darwen FC (Darwen)                15-0          Romford FC (London)
Old Carthusians FC (London)        3-1          Clapham Rovers FC (London)
Stafford Road FC (Wolverhampton)   1-2          Old Etonians FC (London)


# 1882

**F.A. CUP FINAL**   (Kennington Oval, London – 25/03/1882 – 6,500)

OLD ETONIANS FC (LONDON)          1-0          Blackburn Rovers FC (Blackburn)

*Anderson*                          *(H.T. 1-0)*

Old Etonians: Rawlinson, French, de Paravicini, Kinnaird, Foley, Anderson, Chevallier, Macauley, Goodhart, Dunn, Novelli.

Blackburn: Howarth, McIntyre, Suter, F. Hargreaves, Sharples, Duckworth, Douglas, Brown, Strachan, Avery, J. Hargreaves,

## Semi-finals

Blackburn Rovers FC (Blackburn)     0-0,  5-1          The Wednesday FC (Sheffield)
Old Etonians FC (London)            5-0              Great Marlow FC (London)

## Quarter-finals

Blackburn Rovers FC (Blackburn)     3-1          Wednesbury Old Athletic FC (Wednesbury)
Old Foresters FC (London)           0-0,  0-1          Great Marlow FC (London)
The Wednesday FC (Sheffield)        6-0          Upton Park FC (London)
Old Etonians FC (London) received a bye.

# 1883

**F.A. CUP FINAL**   (Kennington Oval, London – 31/03/1883 – 8,000)

BLACKBURN OLYMPIC FC      2-1 (aet)      Old Etonians FC (London)

*Matthews, Crossley*      *(H.T. 0-1)*      *Goodhart*

Blackburn: Hacking, Ward, Warburton, Gibson, Hunter, Astley, Dewhurst, Matthews, Wilson, Crossley, Yates.

Old Etonians: Rawlinson, de Paravicini, French, Kinnaird, Foley, Anderson, Chevallier, Macaulay, Goodhart, Dunn, Bainbridge.

## Semi-finals

| | | |
|---|---|---|
| Blackburn Olympic FC (Blackburn) | 4-0 | Old Carthusians FC (London) |
| Old Etonians FC (London) | 2-1 | Notts County FC (Nottingham) |

## Quarter-finals

| | | |
|---|---|---|
| Blackburn Olympic FC (Blackburn) | 4-1 | Druids FC (Ruabon) |
| Hendon FC (London) | 2-4 | Old Etonians FC (London) |
| Old Carthusians FC (London) | 5-3 | Clapham Rovers FC (London) |
| Notts County FC (Nottingham) | 4-3 | Aston Villa FC (Birmingham) |

# 1884

**F.A. CUP FINAL**   (Kennington Oval, London – 29/03/1884 – 14,000)

BLACKBURN ROVERS FC (BLACKBURN)      2-1      Queen's Park FC (Glasgow)

*Brown, Forrest*      *(H.T. 2-1)*      *Christie*

Blackburn: Arthur, Beverley, Suter, McIntyre, Hargreaves, Forrest, Lofthouse, Douglas, Sowerbutts, Inglis, Brown.

Q.P.R.: Gillespie, Arnott, Macdonald, Campbell, Gow, Anderson, Watt, Smith, Harrower, Allan, Christie.

## Semi-finals

| | | |
|---|---|---|
| Blackburn Rovers FC (Blackburn) | 1-0 | Notts County FC (Nottingham) |
| Queen's Park FC (Glasgow) | 4-1 | Blackburn Olympic FC (Blackburn) |

## Quarter-finals

| | | |
|---|---|---|
| Blackburn Olympic FC (Blackburn) | 9-1 | Northwich Victoria FC (Northwich) |
| Notts County FC (Nottingham) | 1-1, 1-0 | The Swifts FC (London) |
| Old Westminsters FC (London) | 0-1 | Queen's Park FC (Glasgow) |
| Upton Park FC (London) | 0-3 | Blackburn Rovers FC (Blackburn) |

# 1885

**F.A. CUP FINAL**   (Kennington Oval, London – 04/04/1885 – 12,500)

BLACKBURN ROVERS FC (BLACKBURN)     2-0                    Queen's Park FC (Glasgow)
*Forrest, Brown*                    *(H.T. 1-0)*

Blackburn: Arthur, Turner, Suter, McIntyre, Haworth, Forrest, Lofthouse, Douglas, Brown, Fecitt, Sowerbutts.
QPR: Gillespie, Arnott, McLeod, Campbell, MacDonald, Hamilton, McWhannel, Anderson, Sellar, Gray, Allan.

## Semi-finals

| | | |
|---|---|---|
| Blackburn Rovers FC (Blackburn) | 5-1 | Old Carthusians FC (London) |
| Nottingham Forest FC (Nottingham) | 1-1, 0-3 | Queen's Park FC (Glasgow) |

## Quarter-finals

| | | |
|---|---|---|
| Church FC (Accrington) | 0-1 | Old Carthusians FC (London) |
| Notts County FC (Nottingham) | 2-2, 1-2 | Queen's Park FC (Glasgow) |
| Old Etonians FC (London) | 0-2 | Nottingham Forest FC (Nottingham) |
| West Bromwich Albion FC (West Bromwich) | 0-2 | Blackburn Rovers FC (Blackburn) |

# 1886

**F.A. CUP FINAL**   (Kennington Oval, London – 03/04/1886 – 15,000)

BLACKBURN ROVERS FC (BLACKBURN)     0-0     West Bromwich Albion FC (West Bromwich)

Blackburn: Arthur, Turner, Suter, Heyes, Forrest, McIntyre, Douglas, Strachan, Sowerbutts, Fecitt, Brown.
West Bromwich: Roberts, H.Green, H.Bell, Horton, Perry, Timmins, Woodhall, T.Green, Bayliss, Loach, G.Bell.

**F.A. CUP FINAL REPLAY**   (County Cricket Ground, Derby – 10/04/1886 – 12,000)

BLACKBURN ROVERS FC (BLACKBURN)     2-0     West Bromwich Albion FC (West Bromwich)
*Sowerbutts, Brown*                 *(H.T. 1-0)*

West Bromwich: Roberts, H.Green, H.Bell, Horton, Perry, Timming, Woodhall, T.Green, Bayliss, Loach, G.Bell.
Blackburn: Arthur, Turner, Suter, Douglas, Forest, McIntyre, Walton, Strachan, Brown, Fecitt, Sowerbutts.

## Semi-finals

| | | |
|---|---|---|
| Blackburn Rovers FC (Blackburn) | 2-1 | The Swifts FC (London) |
| West Bromwich Albion FC (West Bromwich) | 4-0 | Small Heath Alliance FC (Birmingham) |

## Quarter-finals

| | | |
|---|---|---|
| Brentwood FC (Brentwood) | 1-3 | Blackburn Rovers FC (Blackburn) |
| Small Heath Alliance FC (Birmingham) | 2-0 | Redcar & Coatham FC (Redcar) |
| South Shore FC (Blackpool) | 1-2 | The Swifts FC (London) |
| West Bromwich Albion FC (West Bromwich) | 6-0 | Old Westminsters FC (London) |

# 1887

**F.A. CUP FINAL** (Kennington Oval, London – 02/04/1887 – 15,534)

ASTON VILLA FC (BIRMINGHAM)   2-0   West Bromwich Albion FC (West Bromwich)

*Hodgetts, Hunter*   *(H.T. 0-0)*

Aston Villa: Warner, Coulton, Simmonds, Yates, Dawson, Burton, Davis, Brown, Hunter, Vaughton, Hodgetts.

West Bromwich: Roberts, Aldridge, H.Green, Horton, Perry, Timmins, Woodhall, T.Green, Bayliss, Pearson, Paddock.

## Semi-finals

| Aston Villa FC (Birmingham) | 3-1 | Rangers FC (Glasgow) |
| West Bromwich Albion FC (West Bromwich) | 3-1 | Preston North End FC (Preston) |

## Quarter-finals

| Aston Villa FC (Birmingham) | 3-2 | Darwen FC (Darwen) |
| Notts County FC (Nottingham) | 1-4 | West Bromwich Albion FC (West Bromwich) |
| Old Carthusians FC (London) | 1-2 (aet) | Preston North End FC (Preston) |
| Rangers FC (Glasgow) | 5-1 | Old Westminsters FC (London) |

# 1888

**F.A. CUP FINAL** (Kennington Oval, London – 24/03/1888 – 18,904)

WEST BROMWICH ALBION FC   2-1   Preston North End FC (Preston)

*Bayliss, Woodhall*   *(H.T. 1-0)*   *Dewhurst*

West Bromwich: Roberts, Aldridge, H.Green, Horton, Perry, Timmins, Bassett, Woodhall, Bayliss, Wilson, Pearson.

Preston: Mills-Roberts, Howarth, N.J. Ross, Holmes, Russell, Graham, Gordon, J.D. Ross, Goodall, Dewhurst, Drummond.

## Semi-finals

| Preston North End FC (Preston) | 4-0 | Crewe Alexandra FC (Crewe) |
| West Bromwich Albion FC (West Bromwich) | 3-0 | Derby Junction FC (Derby) |

## Quarter-finals

| Derby Junction FC (Derby) | 2-1 | Blackburn Rovers FC (Blackburn) |
| Middlesbrough FC (Middlesbrough) | 0-2 | Crewe Alexandra FC (Crewe) |
| The Wednesday FC (Sheffield) | 1-3 | Preston North End FC (Preston) |
| West Bromwich Albion FC (West Bromwich) | 4-2 | Old Carthusians FC (London) |

The Football League began in season 1888-89 with a single division of 12 clubs, this was extended to 14 clubs for season 1891-92, a 2nd division was introduced for season 1892-93.

# 1888-89

| Football League 1888-89 Season | Accrington | Aston Villa | Blackburn Rovers | Bolton Wanderers | Burnley | Derby County | Everton | Notts County | Preston North End | Stoke | W.B.A. | Wolves |
|---|---|---|---|---|---|---|---|---|---|---|---|---|
| Accrington FC | | 1-1 | 0-2 | 2-3 | 5-1 | 6-2 | 3-1 | 1-2 | 0-0 | 2-0 | 2-1 | 4-4 |
| Aston Villa FC | 4-3 | | 6-1 | 6-2 | 4-2 | 4-2 | 2-1 | 9-1 | 0-2 | 5-1 | 2-0 | 2-1 |
| Blackburn Rovers FC | 5-5 | 5-1 | | 4-4 | 4-2 | 3-0 | 3-0 | 5-2 | 2-2 | 5-2 | 6-2 | 2-2 |
| Bolton Wanderers FC | 4-1 | 2-3 | 3-2 | | 3-4 | 3-6 | 6-2 | 7-3 | 2-5 | 2-1 | 1-2 | 2-1 |
| Burnley FC | 2-2 | 4-0 | 1-7 | 4-1 | | 1-0 | 2-2 | 1-0 | 2-2 | 2-1 | 2-0 | 0-4 |
| Derby County FC | 1-1 | 5-2 | 0-2 | 2-3 | 1-0 | | 2-4 | 3-2 | 2-3 | 2-1 | 1-2 | 3-0 |
| Everton FC | 2-1 | 2-0 | 3-1 | 2-1 | 3-2 | 6-2 | | 2-1 | 0-2 | 2-1 | 1-4 | 1-2 |
| Notts County FC | 3-3 | 2-4 | 3-3 | 0-4 | 6-1 | 3-5 | 3-1 | | 0-7 | 0-3 | 2-1 | 3-0 |
| Preston North End FC | 2-0 | 1-1 | 1-0 | 3-1 | 5-2 | 5-0 | 3-0 | 4-1 | | 7-0 | 3-0 | 5-2 |
| Stoke FC | 2-4 | 1-1 | 2-1 | 2-2 | 4-3 | 1-1 | 0-0 | 3-0 | 0-3 | | 0-2 | 0-1 |
| West Bromwich Albion FC | 2-2 | 3-3 | 2-1 | 1-5 | 4-3 | 5-0 | 1-0 | 4-2 | 0-5 | 2-0 | | 1-3 |
| Wolverhampton Wanderers FC | 4-0 | 1-1 | 2-2 | 3-2 | 4-1 | 4-1 | 4-0 | 2-1 | 0-4 | 4-1 | 2-1 | |

## Football League

| | | Pd | Wn | Dw | Ls | GF | GA | Pts |
|---|---|---|---|---|---|---|---|---|
| 1. | PRESTON NORTH END FC (PRESTON) | 22 | 18 | 4 | - | 74 | 15 | 40 |
| 2. | Aston Villa FC (Birmingham) | 22 | 12 | 5 | 5 | 61 | 43 | 29 |
| 3. | Wolverhampton Wanderers FC (Wolverhampton) | 22 | 12 | 4 | 6 | 50 | 37 | 28 |
| 4. | Blackburn Rovers FC (Blackburn) | 22 | 10 | 6 | 6 | 66 | 45 | 26 |
| 5. | Bolton Wanderers FC (Bolton) | 22 | 10 | 2 | 10 | 63 | 59 | 22 |
| 6. | West Bromwich Albion FC (West Bromwich) | 22 | 10 | 2 | 10 | 40 | 46 | 22 |
| 7. | Accrington FC (Accrington) | 22 | 6 | 8 | 8 | 48 | 48 | 20 |
| 8. | Everton FC (Liverpool) | 22 | 9 | 2 | 11 | 35 | 46 | 20 |
| 9. | Burnley FC (Burnley) | 22 | 7 | 3 | 12 | 42 | 62 | 17 |
| 10. | Derby County FC (Derby) | 22 | 7 | 2 | 13 | 41 | 61 | 16 |
| 11. | Notts County FC (Nottingham) | 22 | 5 | 2 | 15 | 40 | 73 | 12 |
| 12. | Stoke FC (Stoke-upon-Trent) | 22 | 4 | 4 | 14 | 26 | 51 | 12 |
| | | 264 | 110 | 44 | 110 | 586 | 586 | 264 |

## Top Goalscorers

| | | | |
|---|---|---|---|
| 1) | John GOODALL | (Preston North End FC) | 21 |
| 2) | James D. ROSS | (Preston North End FC) | 18 |
| 3) | Albert ALLEN | (Aston Villa FC) | 17 |
| 4) | John SOUTHWORTH | (Blackburn Rovers FC) | 16 |
| | Harold WOOD | (Wolverhampton Wanderers FC) | 16 |

## F.A. CUP FINAL   (Kennington Oval, London – 30/03/1889 – 22,000)

PRESTON NORTH END FC (PRESTON)       3-0       Wolverhampton Wanderers FC

*Dewhurst, Ross, Thomson*                              *(H.T. 2-0)*

Preston: Mills-Roberts, Howarth, Holmes, Drummond, Russell, Graham, Gordon, J.D. Ross, Goodall, Dewhurst, Thomson.

Wolves: Baynton, Baugh, Mason, Fletcher, Allen, Lowder, Hunter, Wykes, Brodie, Wood, Knight.

## Semi-finals

| | | |
|---|---|---|
| Preston North End FC (Preston) | 1-0 | West Bromwich Albion FC (West Bromwich) |
| Wolverhampton Wanderers FC | 1-1 (aet), 3-1 | Blackburn Rovers FC (Blackburn) |

## Quarter-finals

| | | |
|---|---|---|
| Blackburn Rovers FC (Blackburn) | 8-1 | Aston Villa FC (Birmingham) |
| Chatham FC (Chatham) | 1-10 | West Bromwich Albion FC (West Bromwich) |
| Preston North End FC (Preston) | 2-0 | Birmingham St. George's FC (Birmingham) |
| Wolverhampton Wanderers FC (Wolverhampton) | 3-0 | The Wednesday FC (Sheffield) |

# 1889-90

| Football League 1889-90 Season | Accrington | Aston Villa | Blackburn Rovers | Bolton Wanderers | Burnley | Derby County | Everton | Notts County | Preston North End | Stoke | W.B.A. | Wolves |
|---|---|---|---|---|---|---|---|---|---|---|---|---|
| Accrington FC | | 4-2 | 2-2 | 3-1 | 2-2 | 6-1 | 5-3 | 1-8 | 2-2 | 2-1 | 0-0 | 6-3 |
| Aston Villa FC | 1-2 | | 3-0 | 1-2 | 2-2 | 7-1 | 1-2 | 1-1 | 5-3 | 6-1 | 1-0 | 2-1 |
| Blackburn Rovers FC | 3-2 | 7-0 | | 7-1 | 7-1 | 4-2 | 2-4 | 9-1 | 3-4 | 8-0 | 5-0 | 4-3 |
| Bolton Wanderers FC | 2-4 | 2-0 | 3-2 | | 2-2 | 7-1 | 3-4 | 0-4 | 2-6 | 5-0 | 7-0 | 4-1 |
| Burnley FC | 2-2 | 2-6 | 1-2 | 7-0 | | 2-0 | 0-1 | 3-0 | 0-3 | 1-3 | 1-2 | 1-2 |
| Derby County FC | 2-3 | 5-0 | 4-0 | 3-2 | 4-1 | | 2-2 | 2-0 | 2-1 | 2-0 | 3-1 | 3-3 |
| Everton FC | 2-2 | 7-0 | 3-2 | 3-0 | 2-1 | 3-0 | | 5-3 | 1-5 | 8-0 | 5-1 | 1-1 |
| Notts County FC | 3-1 | 1-1 | 1-1 | 3-5 | 1-1 | 3-1 | 4-3 | | 0-1 | 3-1 | 1-2 | 0-2 |
| Preston North End FC | 3-1 | 3-2 | 1-1 | 3-1 | 6-0 | 5-0 | 1-2 | 4-3 | | 10-0 | 5-0 | 0-2 |
| Stoke FC | 7-1 | 1-1 | 0-3 | 0-1 | 3-4 | 1-1 | 1-2 | 1-1 | 1-2 | | 1-3 | 2-1 |
| West Bromwich Albion FC | 4-1 | 3-0 | 3-2 | 6-3 | 6-1 | 2-3 | 4-1 | 4-2 | 2-2 | 2-1 | | 1-4 |
| Wolverhampton Wanderers FC | 2-1 | 1-1 | 2-4 | 5-1 | 9-1 | 2-1 | 2-1 | 2-0 | 0-1 | 2-2 | 1-1 | |

| | **Football League** | **Pd** | **Wn** | **Dw** | **Ls** | **GF** | **GA** | **Pts** | |
|---|---|---|---|---|---|---|---|---|---|
| 1. | PRESTON NORTH END FC (PRESTON) | 22 | 15 | 3 | 4 | 71 | 30 | 33 | |
| 2. | Everton FC (Liverpool) | 22 | 14 | 3 | 5 | 65 | 40 | 31 | |
| 3. | Blackburn Rovers FC (Blackburn) | 22 | 12 | 3 | 7 | 78 | 41 | 27 | |
| 4. | Wolverhampton Wanderers FC (Wolverhampton) | 22 | 10 | 5 | 7 | 51 | 38 | 25 | |
| 5. | West Bromwich Albion FC (West Bromwich) | 22 | 11 | 3 | 8 | 47 | 50 | 25 | |
| 6. | Accrington FC (Accrington) | 22 | 9 | 6 | 7 | 53 | 56 | 24 | |
| 7. | Derby County FC (Derby) | 22 | 9 | 3 | 10 | 43 | 55 | 21 | |
| 8. | Aston Villa FC (Birmingham) | 22 | 7 | 5 | 10 | 43 | 51 | 19 | |
| 9. | Bolton Wanderers FC (Bolton) | 22 | 9 | 1 | 12 | 54 | 65 | 19 | |
| 10. | Notts County FC (Nottingham) | 22 | 6 | 5 | 11 | 43 | 51 | 17 | |
| 11. | Burnley FC (Burnley) | 22 | 4 | 5 | 13 | 36 | 65 | 13 | |
| 12. | Stoke FC (Stoke-upon-Trent) | 22 | 3 | 4 | 15 | 27 | 69 | 10 | # |
| | | 264 | 109 | 46 | 109 | 611 | 611 | 264 | |

# Stoke FC (Stoke-upon-Trent) were not re-elected to the league for the next season and were replaced by the election of Sunderland AFC (Sunderland).

## Top Goalscorers

| | | | |
|---|---|---|---|
| 1) | James D. ROSS | (Preston North End FC) | 24 |
| 2) | John SOUTHWORTH | (Blackburn Rovers FC) | 22 |
| 3) | Frederick C. GEARY | (Everton FC) | 21 |
| 4) | Nicholas John ROSS | (Preston North End FC) | 16 |
| 5) | Harold CAMPBELL | (Blackburn Rovers FC) | 15 |
| | James OSWALD | (Notts County FC) | 15 |
| | David WYKES | (Wolverhampton Wanderers FC) | 15 |

## F.A. CUP FINAL  (Kennington Oval, London – 29/03/1890 – 20,000)

BLACKBURN ROVERS FC (BLACKBURN)  6-1  The Wednesday FC (Sheffield)

*Townley 3, John Southworth, Lofthouse, Walton*   (H.T. 4-0)   *Mumford*

Blackburn: Horne, James Southworth, Forbes, Barton, Dewar, Forrest, Lofthouse, Campbell, John Southworth, Walton, Townley.

Wednesday: Smith, Brayshaw, Morley, Dungworth, Betts, Walker, Ingram, Woodhouse, Bennett, Cawley, Mumford.

## Semi-finals

| | | |
|---|---|---|
| Blackburn Rovers FC (Blackburn) | 1-0 | Wolverhampton Wanderers FC (Wolverhampton) |
| The Wednesday FC (Sheffield) | 2-1 | Bolton Wanderers FC (Bolton) |

## Quarter-finals

| | | |
|---|---|---|
| Bootle FC (Bootle) | 0-7 | Blackburn Rovers FC (Blackburn) |
| Preston North End FC (Preston) | 2-3 | Bolton Wanderers FC (Bolton) |
| The Wednesday FC (Sheffield) | 5-0, 2-3, 2-1 | Notts County FC (Nottingham) |

(The first two games were replayed after protests.)

Wolverhampton Wanderers FC (Wolverhampton)  3-0, 8-0  Stoke FC (Stoke-upon-Trent)

(The first game was replayed after a protest.)

# 1890-91

| Football League 1890-91 Season | Accrington | Aston Villa | Blackburn Rovers | Bolton Wanderers | Burnley | Derby County | Everton | Notts County | Preston North End | Sunderland | W.B.A. | Wolves |
|---|---|---|---|---|---|---|---|---|---|---|---|---|
| Accrington FC | | 1-3 | 0-4 | 2-1 | 1-1 | 4-0 | 1-2 | 3-2 | 1-3 | 4-1 | 1-0 | 1-2 |
| Aston Villa FC | 3-1 | | 2-2 | 5-0 | 4-4 | 4-0 | 2-2 | 3-2 | 0-1 | 0-0 | 0-4 | 6-2 |
| Blackburn Rovers FC | 0-0 | 5-1 | | 0-2 | 5-2 | 8-0 | 2-1 | 1-7 | 1-0 | 3-2 | 2-1 | 2-3 |
| Bolton Wanderers FC | 6-0 | 4-0 | 2-0 | | 1-0 | 3-1 | 0-5 | 4-2 | 1-0 | 2-5 | 7-1 | 6-0 |
| Burnley FC | 2-0 | 2-1 | 1-6 | 1-2 | | 6-1 | 3-2 | 0-1 | 6-2 | 3-3 | 5-4 | 4-2 |
| Derby County FC | 1-2 | 5-4 | 8-5 | 1-1 | 2-4 | | 2-6 | 3-1 | 1-3 | 3-1 | 3-1 | 9-0 |
| Everton FC | 3-2 | 5-0 | 3-1 | 2-0 | 7-3 | 7-0 | | 4-2 | 0-1 | 1-0 | 2-3 | 5-0 |
| Notts County FC | 5-0 | 7-1 | 1-2 | 3-1 | 4-0 | 2-1 | 3-1 | | 2-1 | 2-1 | 3-2 | 1-1 |
| Preston North End FC | 1-1 | 4-1 | 1-2 | 1-0 | 7-0 | 6-0 | 2-0 | 0-0 | | 0-0 | 3-0 | 5-1 |
| Sunderland AFC | 2-2 | 5-1 | 3-1 | 2-0 | 2-3 | 5-1 | 1-0 | 4-0 | 3-0 | | 1-1 | 3-4 |
| West Bromwich Albion FC | 5-1 | 0-3 | 1-0 | 2-4 | 3-1 | 3-4 | 1-4 | 1-1 | 1-3 | 0-4 | | 0-1 |
| Wolverhampton Wanderers FC | 3-0 | 2-1 | 2-0 | 1-0 | 3-1 | 5-1 | 0-1 | 1-1 | 2-0 | 0-3 | 4-0 | |

| Football League | Pd | Wn | Dw | Ls | GF | GA | Pts | |
|---|---|---|---|---|---|---|---|---|
| 1. EVERTON FC (LIVERPOOL) | 22 | 14 | 1 | 7 | 63 | 29 | 29 | |
| 2. Preston North End FC (Preston) | 22 | 12 | 3 | 7 | 44 | 23 | 27 | |
| 3. Notts County FC (Nottingham) | 22 | 11 | 4 | 7 | 52 | 35 | 26 | |
| 4. Wolverhampton Wanderers FC (Wolverhampton) | 22 | 12 | 2 | 8 | 39 | 50 | 26 | |
| 5. Bolton Wanderers FC (Bolton) | 22 | 12 | 1 | 9 | 47 | 34 | 25 | |
| 6. Blackburn Rovers FC (Blackburn) | 22 | 11 | 2 | 9 | 52 | 43 | 24 | |
| 7. Sunderland AFC (Sunderland) | 22 | 10 | 5 | 7 | 51 | 31 | 23 | * |
| 8. Burnley FC (Burnley) | 22 | 9 | 3 | 10 | 52 | 63 | 21 | |
| 9. Aston Villa FC (Birmingham) | 22 | 7 | 4 | 11 | 45 | 58 | 18 | |
| 10. Accrington FC (Accrington) | 22 | 6 | 4 | 12 | 28 | 50 | 16 | |
| 11. Derby County FC (Derby) | 22 | 7 | 1 | 14 | 47 | 81 | 15 | |
| 12. West Bromwich Albion FC (West Bromwich) | 22 | 5 | 2 | 15 | 34 | 57 | 12 | |
| | 264 | 116 | 32 | 116 | 554 | 554 | 262 | |

\* Sunderland AFC had 2 points deducted for fielding Ned Doig (signed from Arbroath FC) against West Bromwich Albion FC on 20/10/1890 before his registration had been approved by the Football League.

Note: Darwen FC (Darwen) and Stoke FC (Stoke-upon-Trent) were elected to the league which was extended to 14 clubs from the next season.

## Top Goalscorers

| | | | |
|---|---|---|---|
| 1) | John SOUTHWORTH | (Blackburn Rovers FC) | 26 |
| 2) | Frederick C. GEARY | (Everton FC) | 20 |
| 3) | John M. CAMPBELL | (Sunderland AFC) | 18 |
| 4) | Claude LAMBIE | (Burnley FC) | 17 |
| 5) | Thomas PEARSON | (West Bromwich Albion FC) | 15 |

## F.A. CUP FINAL  (Kennington Oval, London – 21/03/1891 – 23,000)

BLACKBURN ROVERS FC (BLACKBURN)  3-1  Notts County FC (Nottingham)

*Dewar, Southworth, Townley*  (H.T. 3-0)  *Oswald*

Blackburn: Pennington, Brandon, Forbes, Barton, Dewar, Forrest, Lofthouse, Walton, John Southworth, Hall, Townley.

Notts County: Thraves, Ferguson, Hendry, Osborne, Calderhead, Shelton, McGregor, McInnes, Oswald, Locker, Daft.

## Semi-finals

| | | |
|---|---|---|
| Blackburn Rovers FC (Blackburn) | 3-2 | West Bromwich Albion FC (West Bromwich) |
| Notts County FC (Nottingham) | 3-3, 2-0 | Sunderland AFC (Sunderland) |

## Quarter-finals

| | | |
|---|---|---|
| Blackburn Rovers FC (Blackburn) | 2-0 | Wolverhampton Wanderers FC (Wolverhampton) |
| Notts County FC (Nottingham) | 1-0 | Stoke FC (Stoke-upon-Trent) |
| Sunderland AFC (Sunderland) | 4-0 | Nottingham Forest FC (Nottingham) |
| The Wednesday FC (Sheffield) | 0-2 | West Bromwich Albion FC (West Bromwich) |

# 1891-92

| Football League 1891-92 Season | Accrington | Aston Villa | Blackburn Rovers | Bolton Wanderers | Burnley | Darwen | Derby County | Everton | Notts County | Preston North End | Stoke | Sunderland | W.B.A. | Wolves |
|---|---|---|---|---|---|---|---|---|---|---|---|---|---|---|
| Accrington FC | | 3-2 | 1-0 | 0-3 | 1-0 | 1-1 | 1-1 | 1-1 | 2-0 | 1-3 | 3-0 | 3-5 | 4-2 | 3-2 |
| Aston Villa FC | 12-2 | | 5-1 | 1-2 | 6-1 | 7-0 | 6-0 | 3-4 | 5-1 | 3-1 | 2-1 | 5-3 | 5-1 | 3-6 |
| Blackburn Rovers FC | 2-2 | 4-3 | | 4-0 | 3-3 | 4-0 | 0-2 | 2-2 | 5-4 | 2-4 | 5-3 | 3-1 | 3-2 | 2-0 |
| Bolton Wanderers FC | 3-4 | 1-2 | 4-2 | | 2-0 | 1-0 | 3-1 | 1-0 | 2-0 | 3-0 | 1-1 | 4-3 | 1-1 | 3-0 |
| Burnley FC | 2-1 | 4-1 | 3-0 | 1-2 | | 9-0 | 2-4 | 1-0 | 1-0 | 2-0 | 4-1 | 1-2 | 3-2 | 1-1 |
| Darwen FC | 5-2 | 1-5 | 3-5 | 1-2 | 2-6 | | 2-0 | 3-1 | 2-3 | 0-4 | 9-3 | 1-7 | 1-1 | 1-4 |
| Derby County FC | 3-1 | 4-2 | 1-1 | 3-2 | 0-1 | 7-0 | | 0-3 | 3-0 | 1-2 | 3-3 | 0-1 | 1-1 | 2-1 |
| Everton FC | 3-0 | 5-1 | 3-1 | 2-5 | 1-1 | 5-3 | 1-2 | | 4-0 | 1-1 | 1-0 | 0-4 | 4-3 | 2-1 |
| Notts County FC | 9-0 | 5-2 | 2-2 | 2-0 | 5-1 | 5-0 | 2-1 | 1-3 | | 2-0 | 1-1 | 1-0 | 4-0 | 2-2 |
| Preston North End FC | 4-1 | 0-1 | 3-2 | 4-0 | 5-1 | 4-0 | 3-0 | 4-0 | 6-0 | | 3-2 | 3-1 | 1-0 | 2-0 |
| Stoke FC | 3-1 | 2-3 | 0-1 | 0-1 | 3-0 | 5-1 | 2-1 | 0-1 | 1-3 | 0-1 | | 1-3 | 1-0 | 1-3 |
| Sunderland AFC | 4-1 | 2-1 | 6-1 | 4-1 | 2-1 | 7-0 | 7-1 | 2-1 | 4-0 | 4-1 | 4-1 | | 4-0 | 5-2 |
| West Bromwich Albion FC | 3-1 | 0-3 | 2-2 | 0-2 | 1-0 | 12-0 | 4-2 | 4-0 | 2-2 | 1-2 | 2-2 | 2-5 | | 4-3 |
| Wolverhampton Wanderers FC | 5-0 | 2-0 | 6-1 | 1-2 | 0-0 | 2-2 | 1-3 | 5-1 | 2-1 | 3-0 | 4-1 | 1-3 | 2-1 | |

| | **Football League** | **Pd** | **Wn** | **Dw** | **Ls** | **GF** | **GA** | **Pts** | |
|---|---|---|---|---|---|---|---|---|---|
| 1. | SUNDERLAND AFC (SUNDERLAND) | 26 | 21 | - | 5 | 93 | 36 | 42 | |
| 2. | Preston North End FC (Preston) | 26 | 18 | 1 | 7 | 61 | 31 | 37 | |
| 3. | Bolton Wanderers FC (Bolton) | 26 | 17 | 2 | 7 | 51 | 37 | 36 | |
| 4. | Aston Villa FC (Birmingham) | 26 | 15 | - | 11 | 89 | 56 | 30 | |
| 5. | Everton FC (Liverpool) | 26 | 12 | 4 | 10 | 49 | 49 | 28 | |
| 6. | Wolverhampton Wanderers FC (Wolverhampton) | 26 | 11 | 4 | 11 | 59 | 46 | 26 | |
| 7. | Burnley FC (Burnley) | 26 | 11 | 4 | 11 | 49 | 45 | 26 | |
| 8. | Notts County FC (Nottingham) | 26 | 11 | 4 | 11 | 55 | 51 | 26 | |
| 9. | Blackburn Rovers FC (Blackburn) | 26 | 10 | 6 | 10 | 58 | 65 | 26 | |
| 10. | Derby County FC (Derby) | 26 | 10 | 4 | 12 | 46 | 52 | 24 | |
| 11. | Accrington FC (Accrington) | 26 | 8 | 4 | 14 | 40 | 78 | 20 | |
| 12. | West Bromwich Albion FC (West Bromwich) | 26 | 6 | 6 | 14 | 51 | 58 | 18 | |
| 13. | Stoke FC (Stoke-upon-Trent) | 26 | 5 | 4 | 17 | 38 | 61 | 14 | |
| 14. | Darwen FC (Darwen) | 26 | 4 | 3 | 19 | 38 | 112 | 11 | # |
| | | 364 | 159 | 46 | 159 | 777 | 777 | 364 | |

# Darwen FC (Darwen) were not re-elected to the League for the next season, but were elected to the newly-formed 12 club Division 2. Newton Heath FC (Manchester), Nottingham Forest FC (Nottingham) and The Wednesday FC (Sheffield) were elected to the re-titled Division 1 which was extended to 16 clubs from the next season.

Note: Royal Arsenal FC (London) changed their club name to Woolwich Arsenal FC (London).

## Top Goalscorers

| | | | |
|---|---|---|---|
| 1) | John M. CAMPBELL | (Sunderland AFC) | 32 |
| 2) | John Henry George DEVEY | (Aston Villa FC) | 25 |
| 3) | John SOUTHWORTH | (Blackburn Rovers FC) | 23 |
| 4) | James CASSIDY | (Bolton Wanderers FC) | 18 |
| 5) | James HANNAH | (Sunderland AFC) | 17 |
| | Alexander LATTA | (Everton FC) | 17 |

**F.A. CUP FINAL**   (Kennington Oval, London – 19/03/1892 – 32,810)

WEST BROMWICH ALBION FC                3-0                Aston Villa FC (Birmingham)
*Geddes, Nicholls, Reynolds*                (H.T. 2-0)

West Bromwich: Reader, Nicholson, McCulloch, Reynolds, Perry, Groves, Bassett, McLeod, Nicholls, Pearson, Geddes.

Aston Villa: Warner, Evans, Cox, HP Devey, Cowan, Baird, Athersmith, JH Devey, Dickson, Campbell, Hodgetts.

## Semi-finals

Aston Villa FC (Birmingham)                4-1                Sunderland AFC (Sunderland)
Nottingham Forest FC (Nottingham)    1-1 (aet), 1-1 (aet), 2-6    West Bromwich Albion FC

## Quarter-finals

Nottingham Forest FC (Nottingham)                2-0                Preston North End FC (Preston)
Stoke FC (Stoke-upon-Trent)                2-2 (aet), 0-4                Sunderland AFC (Sunderland)
West Bromwich Albion FC (West Bromwich)                2-1                The Wednesday FC (Sheffield)
Wolverhampton Wanderers FC (Wolverhampton)                1-3                Aston Villa FC (Birmingham)

# 1892-93

| Football League Division 1 1892-93 Season | Accrington | Aston Villa | Blackburn Rovers | Bolton Wanderers | Burnley | Derby County | Everton | Newton Heath | Nottingham Forest | Notts County | Preston North End | Stoke | Sunderland | Wednesday | W.B.A. | Wolves |
|---|---|---|---|---|---|---|---|---|---|---|---|---|---|---|---|---|
| Accrington FC | | 1-1 | 1-1 | 1-1 | 0-4 | 0-3 | 0-3 | 2-2 | 1-1 | 4-2 | 1-2 | 5-2 | 0-6 | 4-2 | 5-4 | 4-0 |
| Aston Villa FC | 6-4 | | 4-1 | 1-1 | 1-3 | 6-1 | 4-1 | 2-0 | 1-0 | 3-1 | 3-1 | 3-2 | 1-6 | 5-1 | 5-2 | 5-0 |
| Blackburn Rovers FC | 3-3 | 2-2 | | 3-0 | 2-0 | 2-2 | 2-2 | 4-3 | 0-1 | 1-0 | 0-0 | 3-3 | 2-2 | 0-2 | 2-1 | 3-3 |
| Bolton Wanderers FC | 5-2 | 5-0 | 2-1 | | 1-0 | 0-3 | 4-1 | 4-1 | 3-1 | 4-1 | 2-4 | 4-4 | 2-1 | 1-0 | 3-1 | 3-1 |
| Burnley FC | 1-3 | 0-2 | 0-0 | 3-0 | | 2-1 | 3-0 | 4-1 | 1-1 | 3-0 | 4-2 | 3-2 | 2-3 | 4-0 | 5-0 | 2-0 |
| Derby County FC | 3-3 | 2-1 | 3-0 | 1-1 | 1-0 | | 1-6 | 5-1 | 2-3 | 4-5 | 1-2 | 1-0 | 1-1 | 2-2 | 1-1 | 2-2 |
| Everton FC | 1-1 | 1-0 | 4-0 | 3-0 | 0-1 | 5-0 | | 6-0 | 2-2 | 6-0 | 6-0 | 2-2 | 1-4 | 3-5 | 1-0 | 3-2 |
| Newton Heath FC | 3-3 | 2-0 | 4-4 | 1-0 | 1-1 | 7-1 | 3-4 | | 1-3 | 1-3 | 2-1 | 1-0 | 0-5 | 1-5 | 2-4 | 10-1 |
| Nottingham Forest FC | 3-0 | 4-5 | 0-1 | 2-0 | 2-2 | 1-0 | 2-1 | 1-1 | | 3-1 | 1-2 | 3-4 | 0-5 | 2-0 | 3-4 | 3-1 |
| Notts County FC | 2-0 | 1-4 | 0-0 | 2-2 | 3-1 | 1-1 | 1-2 | 4-0 | 3-0 | | 3-1 | 0-1 | 3-1 | 0-1 | 8-1 | 3-0 |
| Preston North End FC | 0-0 | 4-1 | 2-1 | 2-1 | 2-0 | 0-1 | 5-0 | 2-1 | 1-0 | 4-0 | | 2-1 | 1-2 | 4-1 | 1-1 | 4-0 |
| Stoke FC | 2-2 | 0-1 | 2-2 | 6-0 | 4-1 | 1-3 | 0-1 | 7-1 | 3-0 | 1-0 | 2-1 | | 0-1 | 2-0 | 1-2 | 2-1 |
| Sunderland AFC | 4-2 | 6-0 | 5-0 | 3-3 | 2-0 | 3-1 | 4-3 | 6-0 | 1-0 | 2-2 | 2-0 | 3-1 | | 4-2 | 8-1 | 5-2 |
| The Wednesday FC | 5-2 | 5-3 | 0-3 | 4-2 | 2-0 | 3-3 | 0-2 | 1-0 | 2-2 | 3-2 | 0-5 | 0-1 | 3-2 | | 6-0 | 0-1 |
| West Bromwich Albion FC | 4-0 | 3-2 | 1-2 | 1-0 | 7-1 | 3-1 | 3-0 | 0-0 | 2-2 | 4-2 | 0-1 | 1-2 | 1-3 | 3-0 | | 2-1 |
| Wolverhampton Wanderers FC | 5-3 | 2-1 | 4-2 | 1-2 | 1-0 | 2-1 | 2-4 | 2-0 | 2-2 | 3-0 | 2-1 | 1-0 | 2-0 | 2-0 | 1-1 | |

## Division 1

| | | Pd | Wn | Dw | Ls | GF | GA | Pts | |
|---|---|---|---|---|---|---|---|---|---|
| 1. | SUNDERLAND AFC (SUNDERLAND) | 30 | 22 | 4 | 4 | 100 | 36 | 48 | |
| 2. | Preston North End FC (Preston) | 30 | 17 | 3 | 10 | 57 | 39 | 37 | |
| 3. | Everton FC (Liverpool) | 30 | 16 | 4 | 10 | 74 | 51 | 36 | |
| 4. | Aston Villa FC (Birmingham) | 30 | 16 | 3 | 11 | 73 | 62 | 35 | |
| 5. | Bolton Wanderers FC (Bolton) | 30 | 13 | 6 | 11 | 56 | 55 | 32 | |
| 6. | Burnley FC (Burnley) | 30 | 13 | 4 | 13 | 51 | 44 | 30 | |
| 7. | Stoke FC (Stoke-upon-Trent) | 30 | 12 | 5 | 13 | 58 | 48 | 29 | |
| 8. | West Bromwich Albion FC (West Bromwich) | 30 | 12 | 5 | 13 | 58 | 69 | 29 | |
| 9. | Blackburn Rovers FC (Blackburn) | 30 | 8 | 13 | 9 | 47 | 56 | 29 | |
| 10. | Nottingham Forest FC (Nottingham) | 30 | 10 | 8 | 12 | 48 | 52 | 28 | |
| 11. | Wolverhampton Wanderers FC (Wolverhampton) | 30 | 12 | 4 | 14 | 47 | 68 | 28 | |
| 12. | The Wednesday FC (Sheffield) | 30 | 12 | 3 | 15 | 55 | 65 | 27 | |
| 13. | Derby County FC (Derby) | 30 | 9 | 9 | 12 | 52 | 64 | 27 | |
| 14. | Notts County FC (Nottingham) | 30 | 10 | 4 | 16 | 53 | 61 | 24 | PO |
| 15. | Accrington FC (Accrington) | 30 | 6 | 11 | 13 | 57 | 81 | 23 | PO* |
| 16. | Newton Heath FC (Manchester) | 30 | 6 | 6 | 18 | 50 | 85 | 18 | PO |
| | | 480 | 194 | 92 | 194 | 936 | 936 | 480 | |

## Promotion/Relegation Play-offs

| | | |
|---|---|---|
| Darwen FC (Darwen) | 3-2 | Notts County FC (Nottingham) |
| Newton Heath FC (Manchester) | 1-1, 5-2 | Small Heath FC (Birmingham) |
| Sheffield United FC (Sheffield) | 1-0 | Accrington FC (Accrington) |

* Accrington FC (Accrington) resigned from the league after being relegated to Division 2.

## Top Goalscorers

| | | | |
|---|---|---|---|
| 1) | John M. CAMPBELL | (Sunderland AFC) | 31 |
| 2) | John Henry George DEVEY | (Aston Villa FC) | 20 |
| 3) | Frederick C. GEARY | (Everton FC) | 19 |
| | James HANNAH | (Sunderland AFC) | 19 |
| 5) | Robert DONALDSON | (Newton Heath FC) | 18 |
| | Alexander LATTA | (Everton FC) | 18 |
| | Harold WOOD | (Wolverhampton Wanderers FC) | 18 |

| Football League Division 2 1892-93 Season | Ardwick | Bootle | Burslem Port Vale | Burton Swifts | Crewe Alexandra | Darwen | Grimsby Town | Lincoln City | Northwich Victoria | Sheffield United | Small Heath | Walsall Town Swifts |
|---|---|---|---|---|---|---|---|---|---|---|---|---|
| Ardwick FC | ■ | 7-0 | 2-0 | 1-1 | 3-1 | 4-2 | 0-3 | 3-1 | 1-1 | 2-3 | 2-2 | 2-0 |
| Bootle FC | 5-3 | ■ | 1-1 | 3-2 | 2-1 | 5-1 | 3-1 | 4-1 | 2-5 | 2-0 | 1-4 | 7-1 |
| Burslem Port Vale FC | 1-2 | 0-0 | ■ | 1-0 | 4-1 | 2-4 | 0-1 | 1-2 | 4-0 | 0-10 | 0-3 | 3-0 |
| Burton Swifts FC | 2-0 | 2-1 | 3-3 | ■ | 7-1 | 0-2 | 5-1 | 4-2 | 2-0 | 0-3 | 2-3 | 3-2 |
| Crewe Alexandra FC | 4-1 | 2-1 | 5-0 | 2-4 | ■ | 2-2 | 1-0 | 4-1 | 4-2 | 0-4 | 1-3 | 5-6 |
| Darwen FC | 3-1 | 3-0 | 4-1 | 2-3 | 7-3 | ■ | 6-1 | 3-1 | 3-1 | 3-1 | 4-3 | 5-0 |
| Grimsby Town FC | 2-0 | 3-0 | 2-0 | 4-0 | 4-0 | 0-1 | ■ | 2-2 | 2-1 | 0-1 | 3-2 | 3-0 |
| Lincoln City FC | 2-1 | 5-1 | 3-4 | 5-1 | 1-1 | 1-1 | 1-3 | ■ | 5-1 | 1-0 | 3-4 | 3-1 |
| Northwich Victoria FC | 0-3 | 3-2 | 2-4 | 2-1 | 4-1 | 1-0 | 5-3 | 2-1 | ■ | 1-3 | 0-6 | 5-2 |
| Sheffield United FC | 2-1 | 8-3 | 4-0 | 3-1 | 4-0 | 2-0 | 2-0 | 4-2 | 1-1 | ■ | 2-0 | 3-0 |
| Small Heath FC | 3-2 | 6-2 | 5-1 | 3-2 | 6-0 | 3-2 | 8-3 | 4-1 | 6-2 | 1-1 | ■ | 12-0 |
| Walsall Town Swifts FC | 2-4 | 4-4 | 3-0 | 3-2 | 3-3 | 1-2 | 3-1 | 2-1 | 2-3 | 1-1 | 1-3 | ■ |

| Division 2 | Pd | Wn | Dw | Ls | GF | GA | Pts | |
|---|---|---|---|---|---|---|---|---|
| 1. Small Heath FC (Birmingham) | 22 | 17 | 2 | 3 | 90 | 35 | 36 | PO |
| 2. Sheffield United FC (Sheffield) | 22 | 16 | 3 | 3 | 62 | 19 | 35 | PO |
| 3. Darwen FC (Darwen) | 22 | 14 | 2 | 6 | 60 | 36 | 30 | POP |
| 4. Grimsby Town FC (Cleethorpes) | 22 | 11 | 1 | 10 | 42 | 41 | 23 | |
| 5. Ardwick FC (Manchester) | 22 | 9 | 3 | 10 | 45 | 40 | 21 | |
| 6. Burton Swifts FC (Burton-upon-Trent) | 22 | 9 | 2 | 11 | 47 | 47 | 20 | |
| 7. Northwich Victoria FC (Northwich) | 22 | 9 | 2 | 11 | 42 | 58 | 20 | |
| 8. Bootle FC (Liverpool) | 22 | 8 | 3 | 11 | 49 | 63 | 19 | # |
| 9. Lincoln City FC (Lincoln) | 22 | 7 | 3 | 12 | 45 | 51 | 17 | |
| 10. Crewe Alexandra FC (Crewe) | 22 | 6 | 3 | 13 | 42 | 69 | 15 | |
| 11. Burslem Port Vale FC (Burslem) | 22 | 6 | 3 | 13 | 30 | 57 | 15 | |
| 12. Walsall Town Swifts FC (Walsall) | 22 | 5 | 3 | 14 | 37 | 75 | 13 | |
| | 264 | 117 | 30 | 117 | 591 | 591 | 264 | |

\# Bootle FC (Liverpool) resigned from the league and later disbanded.

Liverpool FC (Liverpool), Middlesbrough Ironopolis FC (Middlesbrough), Newcastle United FC (Newcastle-upon-Tyne), Rotherham Town FC (Rotherham) and Woolwich Arsenal FC (London) were all elected to Division 2 which was extended to 16 clubs then reduced to 15 by the resignation of Bootle FC.

Note: Newcastle West End FC (Newcastle-upon-Tyne) and Newcastle East End FC (Newcastle-upon-Tyne) merged to become Newcastle United FC (Newcastle-upon-Tyne).

## F.A. CUP FINAL   (Manchester Athletic Club, Fallowfield, Manchester – 25/03/1893 – 45,000)

| WOLVERHAMPTON WANDERERS FC | 1-0 | Everton FC (Liverpool) |
|---|---|---|
| *Allen* | *(H.T. 0-0)* | |

Wolves: Rose, Baugh, Swift, Malpass, Allen, Kinsey, Topham, Wykes, Butcher, Wood, Griffin.
Everton: Williams, Kelso, Howarth, Boyle, Holt, Stewart, Latta, Gordon, Maxwell, Chadwick, Milward.

## Semi-finals

| Everton FC (Liverpool) | 2-2 (aet), 0-0 (aet), 2-1 | Preston North End FC (Preston) |
|---|---|---|
| Wolverhampton Wanderers FC (Wolverhampton) | 2-1 | Blackburn Rovers FC (Blackburn) |

## Quarter-finals

| Blackburn Rovers FC (Blackburn) | 3-0 | Sunderland AFC (Sunderland) |
|---|---|---|
| Everton FC (Liverpool) | 3-0 | The Wednesday FC (Sheffield) |
| Preston North End FC (Preston) | 2-2 (aet), 7-0 | Middlesbrough Ironopolis FC (Middlesbrough) |
| Wolverhampton Wanderers FC (Wolverhampton) | 5-0 | Darwen FC (Darwen) |

# 1893-94

| Football League Division 1 1893-94 Season | Aston Villa | Blackburn Rovers | Bolton Wanderers | Burnley | Darwen | Derby County | Everton | Newton Heath | Nottingham Forest | Preston North End | Sheffield United | Stoke | Sunderland | Wednesday | W.B.A. | Wolves |
|---|---|---|---|---|---|---|---|---|---|---|---|---|---|---|---|---|
| Aston Villa FC | ■ | 2-1 | 2-3 | 4-0 | 9-0 | 1-1 | 3-1 | 5-1 | 3-1 | 2-0 | 4-0 | 5-1 | 2-1 | 3-0 | 3-2 | 1-1 |
| Blackburn Rovers FC | 2-0 | ■ | 0-1 | 3-2 | 4-1 | 0-2 | 4-3 | 4-0 | 6-1 | 1-0 | 4-1 | 5-0 | 4-3 | 5-1 | 3-0 | 3-0 |
| Bolton Wanderers FC | 0-1 | 2-1 | ■ | 2-0 | 1-0 | 1-1 | 0-1 | 2-0 | 1-1 | 0-3 | 0-1 | 4-1 | 2-0 | 1-1 | 0-3 | 2-0 |
| Burnley FC | 3-6 | 1-0 | 2-1 | ■ | 5-1 | 3-1 | 2-1 | 4-1 | 3-1 | 4-1 | 4-1 | 4-0 | 1-0 | 0-1 | 3-0 | 4-2 |
| Darwen FC | 1-1 | 2-3 | 1-3 | 0-0 | ■ | 2-3 | 3-3 | 1-0 | 0-4 | 2-1 | 3-3 | 3-1 | 0-3 | 2-1 | 2-1 | 3-1 |
| Derby County FC | 0-3 | 5-2 | 6-1 | 3-3 | 2-1 | ■ | 7-3 | 2-0 | 3-4 | 2-1 | 2-1 | 5-2 | 1-4 | 3-3 | 2-3 | 4-1 |
| Everton FC | 4-2 | 2-2 | 3-2 | 4-3 | 8-1 | 1-2 | ■ | 2-0 | 4-0 | 2-3 | 2-3 | 6-2 | 7-1 | 8-1 | 7-1 | 3-0 |
| Newton Heath FC | 1-3 | 5-1 | 2-2 | 3-2 | 0-1 | 2-6 | 0-3 | ■ | 1-1 | 1-3 | 0-2 | 6-2 | 2-4 | 1-2 | 4-1 | 1-0 |
| Nottingham Forest FC | 1-2 | 0-0 | 1-0 | 5-0 | 4-1 | 4-2 | 3-2 | 2-0 | ■ | 4-2 | 1-1 | 2-0 | 1-2 | 1-0 | 2-3 | 7-1 |
| Preston North End FC | 2-5 | 0-1 | 1-0 | 1-2 | 4-1 | 1-0 | 2-4 | 2-0 | 0-2 | ■ | 3-0 | 3-3 | 1-2 | 1-0 | 3-1 | 1-3 |
| Sheffield United FC | 3-0 | 3-2 | 4-2 | 1-0 | 2-1 | 1-2 | 0-3 | 3-1 | 0-2 | 1-1 | ■ | 3-3 | 1-0 | 1-1 | 0-2 | 3-2 |
| Stoke FC | 3-3 | 3-1 | 5-0 | 4-2 | 3-1 | 3-1 | 3-1 | 3-1 | 2-1 | 2-1 | 5-0 | ■ | 2-0 | 4-1 | 3-1 | 0-3 |
| Sunderland AFC | 1-1 | 2-3 | 2-1 | 2-2 | 4-0 | 5-0 | 1-0 | 4-1 | 2-0 | 6-3 | 4-1 | 4-0 | ■ | 1-1 | 2-1 | 6-0 |
| The Wednesday FC | 2-2 | 4-2 | 2-1 | 0-1 | 5-0 | 4-0 | 1-1 | 0-1 | 1-0 | 3-0 | 1-2 | 4-1 | 2-2 | ■ | 2-4 | 1-4 |
| West Bromwich Albion FC | 3-6 | 2-1 | 5-2 | 1-1 | 2-2 | 0-1 | 3-1 | 3-1 | 3-0 | 2-0 | 3-1 | 4-2 | 2-3 | 2-2 | ■ | 0-0 |
| Wolverhampton Wanderers FC | 3-0 | 5-1 | 2-1 | 1-0 | 2-1 | 2-4 | 2-0 | 2-0 | 3-1 | 0-0 | 3-4 | 4-2 | 2-1 | 3-1 | 0-8 | ■ |

| | Division 1 | Pd | Wn | Dw | Ls | GF | GA | Pts | |
|---|---|---|---|---|---|---|---|---|---|
| 1. | ASTON VILLA FC (BIRMINGHAM) | 30 | 19 | 6 | 5 | 84 | 42 | 44 | |
| 2. | Sunderland AFC (Sunderland) | 30 | 17 | 4 | 9 | 72 | 44 | 38 | |
| 3. | Derby County FC (Derby) | 30 | 16 | 4 | 10 | 73 | 62 | 36 | |
| 4. | Blackburn Rovers FC (Blackburn) | 30 | 16 | 2 | 12 | 69 | 53 | 34 | |
| 5. | Burnley FC (Burnley) | 30 | 15 | 4 | 11 | 61 | 51 | 34 | |
| 6. | Everton FC (Liverpool) | 30 | 15 | 3 | 12 | 90 | 57 | 33 | |
| 7. | Nottingham Forest FC (Nottingham) | 30 | 14 | 4 | 12 | 57 | 48 | 32 | |
| 8. | West Bromwich Albion FC (West Bromwich) | 30 | 14 | 4 | 12 | 66 | 59 | 32 | |
| 9. | Wolverhampton Wanderers FC (Wolverhampton) | 30 | 14 | 3 | 13 | 52 | 63 | 31 | |
| 10. | Sheffield United FC (Sheffield) | 30 | 13 | 5 | 12 | 47 | 61 | 31 | |
| 11. | Stoke FC (Stoke-upon-Trent) | 30 | 13 | 3 | 14 | 65 | 79 | 29 | |
| 12. | The Wednesday FC (Sheffield) | 30 | 9 | 8 | 13 | 48 | 57 | 26 | |
| 13. | Bolton Wanderers FC (Bolton) | 30 | 10 | 4 | 16 | 38 | 52 | 24 | |
| 14. | Preston North End FC (Preston) | 30 | 10 | 3 | 17 | 44 | 56 | 23 | PO |
| 15. | Darwen FC (Darwen) | 30 | 7 | 5 | 18 | 37 | 83 | 19 | PO |
| 16. | Newton Heath FC (Manchester) | 30 | 6 | 2 | 22 | 36 | 72 | 14 | POR |
| | | 480 | 208 | 64 | 208 | 939 | 939 | 480 | |

## Promotion/Relegation Play-offs

| | | |
|---|---|---|
| Liverpool FC (Liverpool) | 2-0 | Newton Heath FC (Manchester) |
| Preston North End FC (Preston) | 4-0 | Notts County FC (Nottingham) |
| Small Heath FC (Birmingham) | 3-1 | Darwen FC (Darwen) |

## Top Goalscorers

1) John SOUTHWORTH         (Everton FC)     27
2) John Henry George DEVEY   (Aston Villa FC)   21
3) James MILLAR           (Sunderland AFC)   20
4) Stephen BLOOMER       (Derby County FC)   18
   Patrick TURNBULL        (Burnley FC)   18

| Football League Division 2 1893-94 Season | Ardwick | Burslem Port Vale | Burton Swifts | Crewe Alexandra | Grimsby Town | Lincoln City | Liverpool | Mid. Iron. | Newcastle United | Northwich Victoria | Notts County | Rotherham Town | Small Heath | Walsall Town Swifts | Woolwich Arsenal |
|---|---|---|---|---|---|---|---|---|---|---|---|---|---|---|---|
| Ardwick FC | ■ | 8-1 | 1-4 | 1-2 | 4-1 | 0-1 | 0-1 | 6-1 | 2-3 | 4-2 | 0-0 | 3-2 | 0-1 | 3-0 | 0-1 |
| Burslem Port Vale FC | 4-2 | ■ | 3-1 | 4-2 | 6-1 | 5-3 | 2-2 | 4-0 | 1-1 | 3-2 | 1-0 | 2-3 | 5-0 | 1-2 | 2-1 |
| Burton Swifts FC | 5-0 | 5-3 | ■ | 6-1 | 0-3 | 1-3 | 1-1 | 7-0 | 3-1 | 6-2 | 0-2 | 4-1 | 0-2 | 8-5 | 6-2 |
| Crewe Alexandra FC | 1-1 | 1-1 | 1-2 | ■ | 3-3 | 1-1 | 0-5 | 5-0 | 1-1 | 3-0 | 0-2 | 2-0 | 3-5 | 1-1 | 0-0 |
| Grimsby Town FC | 5-0 | 4-0 | 2-1 | 3-2 | ■ | 2-4 | 0-1 | 2-1 | 0-0 | 7-0 | 5-2 | 7-1 | 2-1 | 5-2 | 3-1 |
| Lincoln City FC | 6-0 | 2-2 | 1-1 | 6-1 | 1-2 | ■ | 1-1 | 2-3 | 2-1 | 4-1 | 0-2 | 1-1 | 2-5 | 0-2 | 3-0 |
| Liverpool FC | 3-0 | 2-1 | 3-1 | 2-0 | 2-0 | 4-0 | ■ | 6-0 | 5-1 | 4-0 | 2-1 | 5-1 | 3-1 | 3-0 | 2-0 |
| Middlesbrough Ironopolis FC | 2-0 | 3-1 | 2-1 | 2-0 | 2-6 | 0-0 | 0-2 | ■ | 1-1 | 2-1 | 0-0 | 6-1 | 3-0 | 1-1 | 3-6 |
| Newcastle United FC | 2-1 | 2-1 | 4-1 | 2-1 | 4-1 | 5-1 | 0-0 | 7-2 | ■ | 3-0 | 3-0 | 4-0 | 0-2 | 2-0 | 6-0 |
| Northwich Victoria FC | 1-4 | 1-5 | 1-1 | 1-2 | 0-1 | 0-3 | 2-3 | 2-1 | 5-3 | ■ | 0-1 | 1-1 | 0-7 | 1-0 | 2-2 |
| Notts County FC | 5-0 | 6-1 | 6-2 | 9-1 | 3-0 | 1-2 | 1-1 | 3-0 | 3-1 | 6-1 | ■ | 4-2 | 3-1 | 2-0 | 3-2 |
| Rotherham Town FC | 1-3 | 0-1 | 2-5 | 1-4 | 4-3 | 2-8 | 1-4 | 4-1 | 2-1 | 5-4 | 0-2 | ■ | 2-3 | 3-2 | 1-1 |
| Small Heath FC | 10-2 | 6-0 | 6-1 | 6-1 | 5-2 | 6-0 | 3-4 | 2-1 | 1-4 | 8-0 | 3-0 | 4-3 | ■ | 4-0 | 4-1 |
| Walsall Town Swifts FC | 5-2 | 0-5 | 3-4 | 5-1 | 5-0 | 5-2 | 1-1 | 1-0 | 1-2 | 3-0 | 2-1 | 3-0 | 1-3 | ■ | 1-2 |
| Woolwich Arsenal FC | 1-0 | 4-1 | 0-2 | 3-2 | 3-1 | 4-0 | 0-5 | 1-0 | 2-2 | 6-0 | 1-2 | 3-0 | 1-4 | 4-0 | ■ |

| | Division 2 | Pd | Wn | Dw | Ls | GA | GF | Pts | |
|---|---|---|---|---|---|---|---|---|---|
| 1. | Liverpool FC (Liverpool) | 28 | 22 | 6 | - | 77 | 18 | 50 | POP |
| 2. | Small Heath FC (Birmingham) | 28 | 21 | - | 7 | 103 | 44 | 42 | PO |
| 3. | Notts County FC (Nottingham) | 28 | 18 | 3 | 7 | 70 | 31 | 39 | PO |
| 4. | Newcastle United FC (Newcastle-upon-Tyne) | 28 | 15 | 6 | 7 | 66 | 39 | 36 | |
| 5. | Grimsby Town FC (Cleethorpes) | 28 | 15 | 2 | 11 | 71 | 58 | 32 | |
| 6. | Burton Swifts FC (Burton-upon-Trent) | 28 | 14 | 3 | 11 | 79 | 61 | 31 | |
| 7. | Burslem Port Vale FC (Burslem) | 28 | 13 | 4 | 11 | 66 | 64 | 30 | |
| 8. | Lincoln City FC (Lincoln) | 28 | 11 | 6 | 11 | 59 | 58 | 28 | |
| 9. | Woolwich Arsenal FC (London) | 28 | 12 | 4 | 12 | 52 | 55 | 28 | |
| 10. | Walsall Town Swifts FC (Walsall) | 28 | 10 | 3 | 15 | 51 | 61 | 23 | |
| 11. | Middlesbrough Ironopolis FC (Middlesbrough) | 28 | 8 | 4 | 16 | 37 | 72 | 20 | # |
| 12. | Crewe Alexandra FC (Crewe) | 28 | 6 | 7 | 15 | 42 | 73 | 19 | |
| 13. | Ardwick FC (Manchester) | 28 | 8 | 2 | 18 | 47 | 71 | 18 | |
| 14. | Rotherham Town FC (Rotherham) | 28 | 6 | 3 | 19 | 44 | 91 | 15 | |
| 15. | Northwich Victoria FC (Northwich) | 28 | 3 | 3 | 22 | 30 | 98 | 9 | # |
| | | 420 | 182 | 56 | 182 | 894 | 894 | 420 | |

# Middlesbrough Ironopolis FC (Middlesbrough) and Northwich Victoria FC (Northwich) resigned from the league at the end of the season.

Burton Wanderers FC (Burton-upon-Trent), Bury FC (Bury) and Leicester Fosse FC (Leicester) were elected to Division 2 which was extended to 16 clubs for next season.

**F.A. CUP FINAL**  (Goodison Park, Liverpool – 31/03/1894 – 37,000)

| NOTTS COUNTY FC (NOTTINGHAM) | 4-1 | Bolton Wanderers FC (Bolton) |
|---|---|---|

*Logan 3, Watson*  (H.T. 2-0)  *Cassidy*

Notts County: Toone, Harper, Hendry, Bramley, Calderhead, Shelton, Watson, Donnelly, Logan, Bruce, Daft.
Bolton: Sutcliffe, Somerville, Jones, Paton, Hughes, Gardiner, Tannahill, Wilson, Cassidy, Bentley, Dickenson.

## Semi-finals

| Bolton Wanderers FC (Bolton) | 2-1 | The Wednesday FC (Sheffield) |
|---|---|---|
| Notts County FC (Nottingham) | 1-0 | Blackburn Rovers FC (Blackburn) |

## Quarter-finals

| Bolton Wanderers FC (Bolton) | 3-0 | Liverpool FC (Liverpool) |
|---|---|---|
| Derby County FC (Derby) | 1-4 | Blackburn Rovers FC (Blackburn) |
| Nottingham Forest FC (Nottingham) | 1-1 (aet), 1-4 | Notts County FC (Nottingham) |
| The Wednesday FC (Sheffield) | 3-2 (aet) | Aston Villa FC (Birmingham) |

# 1894-95

| Football League Division 1 1894-95 Season | Aston Villa | Blackburn Rovers | Bolton Wanderers | Burnley | Derby County | Everton | Liverpool | Nottingham Forest | Preston North End | Sheffield United | Small Heath | Stoke | Sunderland | Wednesday | W.B.A. | Wolves |
|---|---|---|---|---|---|---|---|---|---|---|---|---|---|---|---|---|
| Aston Villa FC | | 3-0 | 2-1 | 5-0 | 4-0 | 2-2 | 5-0 | 4-1 | 4-1 | 5-0 | 2-1 | 6-0 | 1-2 | 3-1 | 3-1 | 2-2 |
| Blackburn Rovers FC | 1-3 | | 2-1 | 1-0 | 0-0 | 4-3 | 1-1 | 0-0 | 1-1 | 3-2 | 9-1 | 6-0 | 1-1 | 3-1 | 3-0 | 5-1 |
| Bolton Wanderers FC | 4-3 | 1-3 | | 1-1 | 6-0 | 1-3 | 1-0 | 4-1 | 1-2 | 6-2 | 1-2 | 2-2 | 4-1 | 2-2 | 5-0 | 6-1 |
| Burnley FC | 3-3 | 2-1 | 1-0 | | 2-0 | 2-4 | 3-3 | 0-1 | 2-1 | 2-4 | 3-1 | 1-2 | 0-3 | 3-0 | 2-0 | 2-1 |
| Derby County FC | 0-2 | 0-0 | 2-2 | 0-2 | | 2-2 | 0-1 | 4-2 | 2-1 | 4-1 | 4-1 | 1-1 | 1-2 | 1-2 | 1-1 | 1-3 |
| Everton FC | 4-2 | 2-1 | 3-1 | 3-2 | 2-3 | | 3-0 | 6-1 | 4-2 | 1-1 | 5-0 | 3-0 | 2-2 | 3-1 | 4-1 | 2-1 |
| Liverpool FC | 1-2 | 2-2 | 1-2 | 0-3 | 5-1 | 2-2 | | 5-0 | 2-5 | 2-2 | 3-1 | 2-0 | 2-3 | 4-2 | 4-0 | 3-3 |
| Nottingham Forest FC | 2-1 | 2-3 | 3-3 | 2-1 | 2-1 | 2-3 | 3-0 | | 0-2 | 3-0 | 2-0 | 3-1 | 2-1 | 2-1 | 5-3 | 0-2 |
| Preston North End FC | 0-1 | 1-1 | 2-2 | 4-0 | 3-2 | 1-2 | 2-2 | 3-1 | | 2-1 | 0-1 | 3-0 | 1-0 | 3-1 | 5-0 | 2-0 |
| Sheffield United FC | 2-1 | 3-0 | 5-0 | 2-2 | 1-4 | 4-2 | 2-2 | 3-2 | 0-1 | | 0-2 | 3-0 | 4-0 | 1-0 | 2-1 | 1-0 |
| Small Heath FC | 2-2 | 1-1 | 2-0 | 1-0 | 3-5 | 4-4 | 3-0 | 1-2 | 4-4 | 4-2 | | 4-2 | 1-1 | 0-0 | 1-2 | 4-3 |
| Stoke FC | 4-1 | 5-1 | 5-0 | 5-1 | 4-1 | 1-3 | 3-1 | 0-3 | 2-1 | 1-3 | 2-2 | | 2-5 | 0-2 | 1-1 | 0-0 |
| Sunderland AFC | 4-4 | 3-2 | 4-0 | 3-0 | 8-0 | 2-1 | 3-2 | 2-2 | 2-0 | 2-0 | 7-1 | 3-1 | | 3-1 | 3-0 | 2-0 |
| The Wednesday FC | 1-0 | 4-1 | 2-1 | 4-3 | 1-1 | 3-0 | 5-0 | 0-0 | 3-1 | 2-3 | 2-0 | 2-4 | 1-2 | | 3-2 | 3-1 |
| West Bromwich Albion FC | 3-2 | 2-0 | 1-1 | 0-1 | 2-2 | 1-4 | 5-0 | 1-0 | 4-5 | 1-0 | 4-1 | 3-2 | 0-2 | 6-0 | | 5-1 |
| Wolverhampton Wanderers FC | 0-4 | 3-3 | 4-2 | 1-0 | 2-2 | 1-0 | 3-1 | 1-1 | 1-3 | 0-3 | 2-1 | 0-0 | 1-4 | 2-0 | 3-1 | |

## Division 1

| | | Pd | Wn | Dw | Ls | GF | GA | Pts | |
|---|---|---|---|---|---|---|---|---|---|
| 1. | SUNDERLAND AFC (SUNDERLAND) | 30 | 21 | 5 | 4 | 80 | 37 | 47 | |
| 2. | Everton FC (Liverpool) | 30 | 18 | 6 | 6 | 82 | 50 | 42 | |
| 3. | Aston Villa FC (Birmingham) | 30 | 17 | 5 | 8 | 82 | 43 | 39 | |
| 4. | Preston North End FC (Preston) | 30 | 15 | 5 | 10 | 62 | 46 | 35 | |
| 5. | Blackburn Rovers FC (Blackburn) | 30 | 11 | 10 | 9 | 59 | 49 | 32 | |
| 6. | Sheffield United FC (Sheffield) | 30 | 14 | 4 | 12 | 57 | 55 | 32 | |
| 7. | Nottingham Forest FC (Nottingham) | 30 | 13 | 5 | 12 | 50 | 56 | 31 | |
| 8. | The Wednesday FC (Sheffield) | 30 | 12 | 4 | 14 | 50 | 55 | 28 | |
| 9. | Burnley FC (Burnley) | 30 | 11 | 4 | 15 | 44 | 56 | 26 | |
| 10. | Bolton Wanderers FC (Bolton) | 30 | 9 | 7 | 14 | 61 | 62 | 25 | |
| 11. | Wolverhampton Wanderers FC (Wolverhampton) | 30 | 9 | 7 | 14 | 43 | 63 | 25 | |
| 12. | Small Heath FC (Birmingham) | 30 | 9 | 7 | 14 | 50 | 74 | 25 | |
| 13. | West Bromwich Albion FC (West Bromwich) | 30 | 10 | 4 | 16 | 51 | 66 | 24 | |
| 14. | Stoke FC (Stoke-upon-Trent) | 30 | 9 | 6 | 15 | 50 | 67 | 24 | PO |
| 15. | Derby County FC (Derby) | 30 | 7 | 9 | 14 | 45 | 68 | 23 | PO |
| 16. | Liverpool FC (Liverpool) | 30 | 7 | 8 | 15 | 51 | 70 | 22 | POR |
| | | 480 | 192 | 96 | 192 | 917 | 917 | 480 | |

## Top Goalscorers

| | | | |
|---|---|---|---|
| 1) | John M. CAMPBELL | (Sunderland AFC) | 22 |
| 2) | William Henry HAMMOND | (Sheffield United FC) | 17 |
| 3) | Thomas Henry BRADSHAW | (Liverpool FC) | 16 |
| | Albert Frederick CARNELLY | (Nottingham Forest FC) | 16 |
| | Frank MOBLEY | (Small Heath FC) | 16 |

## Promotion/Relegation Play-offs

| | | |
|---|---|---|
| Bury FC (Bury) | 1-0 | Liverpool FC (Liverpool) |
| Derby County FC (Derby) | 2-1 | Notts County FC (Nottingham) |
| Stoke FC (Stoke-upon-Trent) | 3-0 | Newton Heath FC (Manchester) |

| Football League Division 2 1894-95 Season | Burslem Port Vale | Burton Swifts | Burton W. | Bury | Crewe Alexandra | Darwen | Grimsby Town | Leicester Fosse | Lincoln City | Manchester City | Newcastle United | Newton Heath | Notts County | Rotherham Town | Walsall Town Swifts | Woolwich Arsenal |
|---|---|---|---|---|---|---|---|---|---|---|---|---|---|---|---|---|
| Burslem Port Vale FC | ■ | 2-0 | 1-0 | 1-2 | 4-0 | 0-3 | 5-0 | 1-1 | 7-1 | 1-2 | 4-4 | 2-5 | 0-3 | 1-1 | 1-0 | 0-1 |
| Burton Swifts FC | 1-0 | ■ | 2-2 | 0-1 | 4-0 | 3-0 | 2-1 | 0-5 | 6-1 | 2-1 | 5-3 | 1-2 | 2-2 | 2-0 | 1-2 | 3-0 |
| Burton Wanderers FC | 4-0 | 1-2 | ■ | 1-2 | 4-0 | 2-2 | 0-0 | 1-1 | 4-1 | 8-0 | 9-0 | 1-0 | 1-0 | 4-0 | 7-0 | 2-1 |
| Bury FC | 4-0 | 2-0 | 4-0 | ■ | 4-1 | 1-0 | 5-1 | 4-1 | 4-1 | 4-2 | 4-1 | 2-1 | 2-1 | 2-1 | 4-1 | 2-0 |
| Crewe Alexandra FC | 2-2 | 1-3 | 1-2 | 1-5 | ■ | 2-2 | 2-1 | 2-2 | 1-4 | 2-3 | 2-1 | 0-2 | 0-3 | 2-1 | 2-3 | 0-0 |
| Darwen FC | 2-0 | 5-0 | 2-0 | 0-1 | 5-0 | ■ | 4-1 | 8-2 | 6-0 | 4-0 | 5-0 | 1-1 | 2-1 | 4-3 | 2-0 | 3-1 |
| Grimsby Town FC | 4-1 | 7-1 | 7-2 | 3-2 | 5-0 | 2-1 | ■ | 4-3 | 3-0 | 2-1 | 3-0 | 2-1 | 0-1 | 4-1 | 1-0 | 4-2 |
| Leicester Fosse FC | 2-1 | 2-2 | 1-2 | 1-0 | 4-0 | 2-1 | 1-0 | ■ | 2-1 | 3-1 | 4-4 | 2-3 | 5-1 | 4-2 | 9-1 | 3-1 |
| Lincoln City FC | 6-1 | 3-2 | 0-2 | 1-3 | 5-2 | 0-2 | 1-5 | 1-2 | ■ | 0-2 | 3-1 | 3-0 | 1-3 | 2-0 | 1-0 | 5-2 |
| Manchester City FC | 4-1 | 4-1 | 1-1 | 3-3 | 4-1 | 2-4 | 2-5 | 1-1 | 11-3 | ■ | 4-0 | 2-5 | 7-1 | 1-0 | 6-1 | 4-1 |
| Newcastle United FC | 1-2 | 6-3 | 3-1 | 1-0 | 6-0 | 3-2 | 1-4 | 2-0 | 4-2 | 5-4 | ■ | 3-0 | 2-2 | 5-2 | 7-2 | 2-4 |
| Newton Heath FC | 3-0 | 5-1 | 1-1 | 2-2 | 6-1 | 1-1 | 2-0 | 2-2 | 3-0 | 4-1 | 5-1 | ■ | 3-3 | 3-2 | 9-0 | 3-3 |
| Notts County FC | 10-0 | 5-1 | 2-0 | 2-1 | 5-1 | 2-1 | 3-2 | 3-0 | 3-0 | 1-3 | 2-1 | 1-1 | ■ | 4-2 | 5-0 | 2-2 |
| Rotherham Town FC | 2-1 | 4-1 | 1-3 | 2-3 | 2-0 | 4-1 | 3-2 | 0-1 | 5-2 | 3-2 | 1-0 | 2-1 | 1-2 | ■ | 6-1 | 1-2 |
| Walsall Town Swifts FC | 2-0 | 4-1 | 3-1 | 0-3 | 4-0 | 5-1 | 4-3 | 1-3 | 1-2 | 1-2 | 2-3 | 1-2 | 2-1 | 1-2 | ■ | 4-1 |
| Woolwich Arsenal FC | 7-0 | 3-0 | 1-1 | 4-2 | 7-0 | 4-0 | 1-3 | 3-3 | 5-2 | 4-2 | 3-2 | 3-2 | 2-1 | 1-1 | 6-1 | ■ |

## Division 2

| | Pd | Wn | Dw | Ls | GF | GA | Pts | |
|---|---|---|---|---|---|---|---|---|
| 1. Bury FC (Bury) | 30 | 23 | 2 | 5 | 78 | 33 | 48 POP | |
| 2. Notts County FC (Nottingham) | 30 | 17 | 5 | 8 | 75 | 45 | 39 PO | |
| 3. Newton Heath FC (Manchester) | 30 | 15 | 8 | 7 | 78 | 44 | 38 PO | |
| 4. Leicester Fosse FC (Leicester) | 30 | 15 | 8 | 7 | 72 | 53 | 38 | |
| 5. Grimsby Town FC (Cleethorpes) | 30 | 18 | 1 | 11 | 79 | 52 | 37 | |
| 6. Darwen FC (Darwen) | 30 | 16 | 4 | 10 | 74 | 43 | 36 | |
| 7. Burton Wanderers FC (Burton-upon-Trent) | 30 | 14 | 7 | 9 | 67 | 39 | 35 | |
| 8. Woolwich Arsenal FC (London) | 30 | 14 | 6 | 10 | 75 | 58 | 34 | |
| 9. Manchester City FC (Manchester) | 30 | 14 | 3 | 13 | 82 | 72 | 31 | * |
| 10. Newcastle United FC (Newcastle-upon-Tyne) | 30 | 12 | 3 | 15 | 72 | 84 | 27 | |
| 11. Burton Swifts FC (Burton-upon-Trent) | 30 | 11 | 3 | 16 | 52 | 74 | 25 | |
| 12. Rotherham Town FC (Rotherham) | 30 | 11 | 2 | 17 | 55 | 62 | 24 | |
| 13. Lincoln City FC (Lincoln) | 30 | 10 | - | 20 | 52 | 92 | 20 | |
| 14. Walsall Town Swifts FC (Walsall) | 30 | 10 | - | 20 | 47 | 92 | 20 | # |
| 15. Burslem Port Vale FC (Burslem) | 30 | 7 | 4 | 19 | 39 | 77 | 18 | |
| 16. Crewe Alexandra FC (Crewe) | 30 | 3 | 4 | 23 | 26 | 103 | 10 | |
| | 480 | 210 | 60 | 210 | 1023 | 1023 | 480 | |

* Ardwick FC (Manchester) were declared bankrupt in 1894 and re-formed as Manchester City FC (Manchester).

# Walsall Town Swifts FC (Walsall) were not re-elected to the league and changed their name to Walsall FC.

Loughborough Town FC (Loughborough) were elected to Division 2 for the next season.

## F.A. CUP FINAL   (Crystal Palace, London – 20/04/1895 – 42,560)

ASTON VILLA FC (BIRMINGHAM)              1-0     West Bromwich Albion FC (West Bromwich)
*Devey*                                        *(H.T. 1-0)*

Aston Villa: Wilkes, Spencer, Walford, Reynolds, Cowan, Russell, Athersmith, Chatt, Devey, Hodgetts, Smith.
West Bromwich: Reader, Horton, Williams, Perry, Higgins, Taggart, Bassett, McLeod, Richards, Hutchinson, Banks.

## Semi-finals

| Aston Villa FC (Birmingham) | 2-1 | Sunderland AFC (Sunderland) |
|---|---|---|
| West Bromwich Albion FC (West Bromwich) | 2-0 | The Wednesday FC (Sheffield) |

## Quarter-finals

| Aston Villa FC (Birmingham) | 6-2 | Nottingham Forest FC (Nottingham) |
|---|---|---|
| Sunderland AFC (Sunderland) | 2-1 | Bolton Wanderers FC (Bolton) |
| The Wednesday FC (Sheffield) | 2-0 | Everton FC (Liverpool) |
| West Bromwich Albion FC (West Bromwich) | 1-0 | Wolverhampton Wanderers FC (Wolverhampton) |

# 1895-96

| Football League Division 1 1895-96 Season | Aston Villa | Blackburn Rovers | Bolton Wanderers | Burnley | Bury | Derby County | Everton | Nottingham Forest | Preston North End | Sheffield United | Small Heath | Stoke | Sunderland | Wednesday | W.B.A. | Wolves |
|---|---|---|---|---|---|---|---|---|---|---|---|---|---|---|---|---|
| Aston Villa FC | ■ | 3-1 | 2-0 | 5-1 | 2-0 | 4-1 | 4-3 | 3-1 | 1-0 | 2-2 | 7-3 | 5-2 | 2-1 | 2-1 | 1-0 | 4-1 |
| Blackburn Rovers FC | 1-1 | ■ | 3-2 | 1-0 | 0-2 | 0-2 | 2-3 | 2-0 | 3-0 | 1-0 | 2-1 | 3-1 | 2-4 | 2-1 | 1-0 | 3-1 |
| Bolton Wanderers FC | 2-2 | 1-1 | ■ | 1-0 | 2-4 | 2-1 | 3-1 | 2-1 | 1-0 | 4-1 | 4-1 | 3-1 | 1-0 | 2-0 | 2-1 | 4-0 |
| Burnley FC | 3-4 | 6-0 | 1-2 | ■ | 3-0 | 2-2 | 1-1 | 0-0 | 1-0 | 5-0 | 1-1 | 2-0 | 0-0 | 2-0 | 3-0 | 3-1 |
| Bury FC | 5-3 | 2-0 | 0-3 | 3-4 | ■ | 1-2 | 1-1 | 1-0 | 1-2 | 1-0 | 4-5 | 0-1 | 1-2 | 6-1 | 3-0 | 3-0 |
| Derby County FC | 2-2 | 0-0 | 2-1 | 5-1 | 2-1 | ■ | 2-1 | 4-0 | 1-0 | 0-2 | 8-0 | 2-1 | 2-0 | 3-1 | 4-1 | 5-2 |
| Everton FC | 2-0 | 0-2 | 1-1 | 2-1 | 3-2 | 2-2 | ■ | 6-2 | 3-2 | 5-0 | 3-0 | 7-2 | 1-0 | 2-2 | 1-1 | 2-0 |
| Nottingham Forest FC | 0-2 | 4-2 | 0-0 | 2-1 | 5-0 | 2-5 | 2-1 | ■ | 0-1 | 3-1 | 3-0 | 4-0 | 3-1 | 1-0 | 2-0 | 3-2 |
| Preston North End FC | 4-3 | 1-1 | 1-0 | 1-1 | 1-1 | 1-0 | 1-1 | 6-0 | ■ | 4-3 | 3-2 | 0-1 | 4-1 | 0-1 | 0-0 | 4-3 |
| Sheffield United FC | 2-1 | 1-1 | 1-0 | 1-1 | 8-0 | 1-1 | 1-2 | 2-1 | 2-1 | ■ | 2-0 | 1-0 | 1-2 | 1-1 | 2-0 | 2-1 |
| Small Heath FC | 1-4 | 2-1 | 1-2 | 1-0 | 1-0 | 1-3 | 0-3 | 1-0 | 5-2 | 2-1 | ■ | 1-2 | 0-1 | 1-1 | 2-2 | 3-2 |
| Stoke FC | 1-2 | 3-0 | 2-0 | 2-1 | 0-2 | 2-1 | 1-2 | 1-0 | 4-0 | 4-0 | 6-1 | ■ | 5-0 | 5-0 | 3-1 | 4-1 |
| Sunderland AFC | 2-1 | 2-1 | 1-0 | 3-0 | 0-0 | 2-2 | 3-0 | 1-1 | 4-1 | 1-1 | 2-1 | 4-1 | ■ | 2-1 | 7-1 | 2-2 |
| The Wednesday FC | 1-3 | 3-0 | 1-1 | 1-0 | 1-3 | 0-4 | 3-1 | 3-0 | 1-1 | 1-0 | 3-0 | 2-1 | 3-0 | ■ | 5-3 | 3-1 |
| West Bromwich Albion FC | 1-1 | 3-2 | 2-3 | 0-2 | 1-3 | 0-0 | 0-3 | 3-1 | 1-2 | 1-0 | 0-0 | 1-0 | 1-1 | 2-3 | ■ | 2-1 |
| Wolverhampton Wanderers FC | 1-2 | 1-2 | 5-0 | 5-1 | 1-0 | 2-0 | 2-3 | 6-1 | 2-1 | 4-1 | 7-2 | 1-0 | 1-3 | 4-0 | 1-2 | ■ |

## Division 1

| | | Pd | Wn | Dw | Ls | GF | GA | Pts | |
|---|---|---|---|---|---|---|---|---|---|
| 1. | ASTON VILLA FC (BIRMINGHAM) | 30 | 20 | 5 | 5 | 78 | 45 | 45 | |
| 2. | Derby County FC (Derby) | 30 | 17 | 7 | 6 | 68 | 35 | 41 | |
| 3. | Everton FC (Liverpool) | 30 | 16 | 7 | 7 | 66 | 43 | 39 | |
| 4. | Bolton Wanderers FC (Bolton) | 30 | 16 | 5 | 9 | 49 | 37 | 37 | |
| 5. | Sunderland AFC (Sunderland) | 30 | 15 | 7 | 8 | 52 | 41 | 37 | |
| 6. | Stoke FC (Stoke-upon-Trent) | 30 | 15 | - | 15 | 56 | 47 | 30 | |
| 7. | The Wednesday FC (Sheffield) | 30 | 12 | 5 | 13 | 44 | 53 | 29 | |
| 8. | Blackburn Rovers FC (Blackburn) | 30 | 12 | 5 | 13 | 40 | 50 | 29 | |
| 9. | Preston North End FC (Preston) | 30 | 11 | 6 | 13 | 44 | 48 | 28 | |
| 10. | Burnley FC (Burnley) | 30 | 10 | 7 | 13 | 48 | 44 | 27 | |
| 11. | Bury FC (Bury) | 30 | 12 | 3 | 15 | 50 | 54 | 27 | |
| 12. | Sheffield United FC (Sheffield) | 30 | 10 | 6 | 14 | 40 | 50 | 26 | |
| 13. | Nottingham Forest FC (Nottingham) | 30 | 11 | 3 | 16 | 42 | 57 | 25 | |
| 14. | Wolverhampton Wanderers FC (Wolverhampton) | 30 | 10 | 1 | 19 | 61 | 65 | 21 | |
| 15. | Small Heath FC (Birmingham) | 30 | 8 | 4 | 18 | 39 | 79 | 20 | POR |
| 16. | West Bromwich Albion FC (West Bromwich) | 30 | 6 | 7 | 17 | 30 | 59 | 19 | PO |
| | | 480 | 201 | 78 | 201 | 807 | 807 | 480 | |

## Top Goalscorers

| 1) | Stephen BLOOMER | (Derby County FC) | 20 |
|---|---|---|---|
| | John CAMPBELL | (Aston Villa FC) | 20 |
| 3) | John Henry George DEVEY | (Aston Villa FC) | 19 |
| 4) | Thomas HYSLOP | (Stoke FC) | 18 |
| 5) | Alfred MILWARD | (Everton FC) | 17 |

| Football League Promotion/Relegation Play-offs 1895-96 Season | Liverpool | West Brom. Albion | Small Heath | Manchester City |
|---|---|---|---|---|
| Liverpool FC | | 2-0 | 4-0 | --- |
| West Bromwich Albion FC | 2-0 | | --- | 6-1 |
| Small Heath FC | 0-0 | --- | | 8-0 |
| Manchester City FC | 1-1 | 3-0 | * | |

## Prom/Relegation Play-offs

| | Pd | Wn | Dw | Ls | GF | GA | Pts | |
|---|---|---|---|---|---|---|---|---|
| 1. Liverpool FC (Liverpool) | 4 | 2 | 1 | 1 | 6 | 2 | 5 | P |
| 2. West Bromwich Albion FC (West Bromwich) | 4 | 2 | 1 | 1 | 9 | 4 | 5 | -- |
| 3. Small Heath FC (Birmingham) | 4 | 1 | 1 | 2 | 8 | 7 | 3 | R |
| 4. Manchester City FC (Manchester) | 4 | 1 | 1 | 2 | 5 | 15 | 3 | -- |
| | 16 | 6 | 4 | 6 | 28 | 28 | 16 | |

| Football League Division 2 1895-96 Season | Burslem Port Vale | Burton Swifts | Burton W. | Crewe Alexandra | Darwen | Grimsby Town | Leicester Fosse | Lincoln City | Liverpool | Loughborough Town | Manchester City | Newcastle United | Newton Heath | Notts County | Rotherham Town | Woolwich Arsenal |
|---|---|---|---|---|---|---|---|---|---|---|---|---|---|---|---|---|
| Burslem Port Vale FC | | 1-0 | 2-2 | 2-1 | 3-3 | 1-4 | 1-1 | 0-1 | 5-4 | 1-1 | 0-1 | 2-0 | 3-0 | 0-4 | 4-0 | 0-2 |
| Burton Swifts FC | 2-1 | | 0-2 | 1-1 | 1-2 | 2-1 | 0-2 | 4-0 | 0-7 | 1-2 | 1-4 | 3-1 | 4-1 | 0-0 | 2-0 | 3-2 |
| Burton Wanderers FC | 2-1 | 2-1 | | 4-0 | 3-0 | 2-1 | 0-0 | 4-1 | 2-1 | 4-0 | 4-1 | 0-3 | 5-1 | 1-3 | 6-1 | 4-1 |
| Crewe Alexandra FC | 3-2 | 1-3 | 0-1 | | 3-1 | 0-1 | 1-1 | 2-2 | 0-7 | 1-2 | 0-2 | 3-0 | 0-2 | 5-1 | 3-2 | 0-1 |
| Darwen FC | 8-2 | 3-0 | 3-0 | 6-1 | | 3-3 | 4-1 | 5-0 | 0-4 | 1-1 | 2-3 | 4-4 | 3-0 | 2-0 | 10-2 | 1-1 |
| Grimsby Town FC | 6-1 | 3-0 | 2-1 | 2-0 | 5-0 | | 7-1 | 4-2 | 1-0 | 2-0 | 5-0 | 2-1 | 4-2 | 3-0 | 4-0 | 1-1 |
| Leicester Fosse FC | 5-0 | 2-1 | 1-3 | 4-1 | 2-3 | 1-2 | | 1-3 | 2-0 | 5-0 | 1-2 | 2-0 | 3-0 | 2-1 | 8-0 | 1-0 |
| Lincoln City FC | 4-2 | 1-2 | 1-2 | 6-2 | 1-0 | 2-5 | 2-3 | | 0-1 | 4-1 | 1-2 | 4-0 | 2-0 | 2-3 | 5-0 | 1-1 |
| Liverpool FC | 5-1 | 6-1 | 4-1 | 6-1 | 0-0 | 3-1 | 3-1 | 6-1 | | 1-0 | 3-1 | 5-1 | 7-1 | 3-0 | 10-1 | 3-0 |
| Loughborough Town FC | 3-0 | 2-2 | 1-1 | 4-1 | 4-1 | 0-1 | 1-4 | 3-0 | 2-4 | | 2-4 | 1-0 | 3-3 | 1-3 | 3-0 | 2-1 |
| Manchester City FC | 1-0 | 1-1 | 1-1 | 4-0 | 4-1 | 2-1 | 2-0 | 4-0 | 1-1 | 5-1 | | 5-2 | 2-1 | 2-0 | 2-0 | 1-0 |
| Newcastle United FC | 4-2 | 5-0 | 4-0 | 6-0 | 7-2 | 1-5 | 1-0 | 5-0 | 1-0 | 3-0 | 4-1 | | 2-1 | 5-1 | 6-1 | 3-1 |
| Newton Heath FC | 2-1 | 5-0 | 1-2 | 5-0 | 4-0 | 3-2 | 2-0 | 5-5 | 5-2 | 2-0 | 1-1 | 2-1 | | 3-0 | 3-0 | 5-1 |
| Notts County FC | 7-2 | 5-0 | 1-4 | 6-0 | 4-1 | 5-3 | 1-2 | 2-0 | 2-3 | 2-0 | 3-0 | 0-1 | 0-2 | | 0-0 | 3-4 |
| Rotherham Town FC | 0-2 | 1-4 | 1-6 | 4-0 | 3-0 | 1-0 | 2-0 | 2-2 | 0-5 | 4-0 | 2-3 | 1-1 | 2-3 | 1-0 | | 3-0 |
| Woolwich Arsenal FC | 2-1 | 5-0 | 3-0 | 7-0 | 1-3 | 3-1 | 1-1 | 4-0 | 0-2 | 5-0 | 0-1 | 2-1 | 2-1 | 2-0 | 5-0 | |

| Division 2 | Pd | Wn | Dw | Ls | GF | GA | Pts | |
|---|---|---|---|---|---|---|---|---|
| 1. Liverpool FC (Liverpool) | 30 | 22 | 2 | 6 | 106 | 32 | 46 | POP |
| 2. Manchester City FC (Manchester) | 30 | 21 | 4 | 5 | 63 | 38 | 46 | PO |
| 3. Grimsby Town FC (Cleethorpes) | 30 | 20 | 2 | 8 | 82 | 38 | 42 | |
| 4. Burton Wanderers FC (Burton-upon-Trent) | 30 | 19 | 4 | 7 | 69 | 40 | 42 | |
| 5. Newcastle United FC (Newcastle-upon-Tyne) | 30 | 16 | 2 | 12 | 73 | 50 | 34 | |
| 6. Newton Heath FC (Manchester) | 30 | 15 | 3 | 12 | 66 | 57 | 33 | |
| 7. Woolwich Arsenal FC (London) | 30 | 14 | 4 | 12 | 59 | 42 | 32 | |
| 8. Leicester Fosse FC (Leicester) | 30 | 14 | 4 | 12 | 57 | 44 | 32 | |
| 9. Darwen FC (Darwen) | 30 | 12 | 6 | 12 | 72 | 67 | 30 | |
| 10. Notts County FC (Nottingham) | 30 | 12 | 2 | 16 | 57 | 54 | 26 | |
| 11. Burton Swifts FC (Burton-upon-Trent) | 30 | 10 | 4 | 16 | 39 | 69 | 24 | |
| 12. Loughborough Town FC (Loughborough) | 30 | 9 | 5 | 16 | 40 | 67 | 23 | |
| 13. Lincoln City FC (Lincoln) | 30 | 9 | 4 | 17 | 53 | 75 | 22 | |
| 14. Burslem Port Vale FC (Burslem) | 30 | 7 | 4 | 19 | 43 | 78 | 18 | # |
| 15. Rotherham Town FC (Rotherham) | 30 | 7 | 3 | 20 | 34 | 97 | 17 | # |
| 16. Crewe Alexandra FC (Crewe) | 30 | 5 | 3 | 22 | 30 | 95 | 13 | # |
| | 480 | 212 | 56 | 212 | 943 | 943 | 480 | |

# Burslem Port Vale FC (Burslem), Crewe Alexandra FC (Crewe) and Rotherham Town FC (Rotherham) were not re-elected to the league for next season.


Blackpool FC (Blackpool), Gainsborough Trinity FC (Gainsborough) and Walsall FC (Walsall) were elected to Division 2 for next season.


## F.A. CUP FINAL   (Crystal Palace, London – 18/04/1896 – 48,836)

THE WEDNESDAY FC (SHEFFIELD)                2-1                Wolverhampton Wanderers FC

*Spiksley 2*                                   *(H.T. 2-1)*                                   *Black*

Wednesday: Massey, Earp, Langley, Brandon, Crawshaw, Petrie, Brash, Brady, Bell, Davis, Spiksley.
Wolves: Tennant, Baugh, Dunn, Griffiths, Malpass, Owen, Tonks, Henderson, Beats, Wood, Black.


## Semi-finals

| The Wednesday FC (Sheffield) | 1-1 (aet), 3-1 | Bolton Wanderers FC (Bolton) |
|---|---|---|
| Wolverhampton Wanderers FC (Wolverhampton) | 2-1 | Derby County FC (Derby) |


## Quarter-finals

| Bolton Wanderers FC (Bolton) | 2-0 | Bury FC (Bury) |
|---|---|---|
| Derby County FC (Derby) | 1-0 | West Bromwich Albion FC (West Bromwich) |
| The Wednesday FC (Sheffield) | 4-0 | Everton FC (Liverpool) |
| Wolverhampton Wanderers FC (Wolverhampton) | 3-0 | Stoke FC (Stoke-upon-Trent) |

# 1896-97

| Football League Division 1 1896-97 Season | Aston Villa | Blackburn Rovers | Bolton Wanderers | Burnley | Bury | Derby County | Everton | Liverpool | Nottingham Forest | Preston North End | Sheffield United | Stoke | Sunderland | Wednesday | W.B.A. | Wolves |
|---|---|---|---|---|---|---|---|---|---|---|---|---|---|---|---|---|
| Aston Villa FC | | 3-0 | 6-2 | 0-3 | 1-1 | 2-1 | 1-2 | 0-0 | 3-2 | 3-1 | 2-2 | 2-1 | 2-1 | 4-0 | 2-0 | 5-0 |
| Blackburn Rovers FC | 1-5 | | 1-0 | 3-2 | 1-2 | 5-2 | 4-2 | 1-0 | 0-0 | 0-4 | 1-3 | 2-1 | 1-2 | 4-0 | 1-2 | 2-0 |
| Bolton Wanderers FC | 1-2 | 0-0 | | 2-1 | 2-0 | 1-3 | 2-0 | 1-4 | 0-0 | 3-1 | 0-2 | 4-0 | 1-0 | 2-1 | 2-2 | 1-2 |
| Burnley FC | 3-4 | 0-1 | 0-2 | | 1-0 | 2-3 | 2-1 | 4-1 | 2-2 | 2-2 | 1-1 | 1-3 | 1-1 | 1-1 | 5-0 | 0-3 |
| Bury FC | 0-2 | 3-0 | 2-2 | 1-1 | | 1-0 | 3-1 | 1-2 | 2-0 | 0-0 | 0-1 | 4-2 | 1-1 | 1-1 | 3-0 | 3-2 |
| Derby County FC | 1-3 | 6-0 | 1-0 | 3-2 | 7-2 | | 0-1 | 3-2 | 1-1 | 2-2 | 1-3 | 5-1 | 1-0 | 2-1 | 8-1 | 4-3 |
| Everton FC | 2-3 | 0-3 | 2-3 | 6-0 | 1-2 | 5-2 | | 2-1 | 3-1 | 3-4 | 1-2 | 4-2 | 5-2 | 2-1 | 6-3 | 0-0 |
| Liverpool FC | 3-3 | 4-0 | 0-2 | 1-2 | 3-1 | 2-0 | 0-0 | | 3-0 | 0-0 | 0-0 | 1-0 | 3-0 | 2-2 | 0-0 | 3-0 |
| Nottingham Forest FC | 2-4 | 2-1 | 2-0 | 4-1 | 3-0 | 1-2 | 3-0 | 2-0 | | 0-0 | 2-2 | 4-0 | 2-1 | 2-2 | 0-1 | 1-2 |
| Preston North End FC | 0-1 | 3-1 | 2-3 | 5-3 | 2-2 | 0-2 | 4-1 | 1-1 | 3-2 | | 1-0 | 3-0 | 5-3 | 2-2 | 0-0 | 4-0 |
| Sheffield United FC | 0-0 | 7-0 | 1-0 | 1-0 | 2-2 | 2-2 | 1-2 | 1-1 | 0-3 | 0-2 | | 1-0 | 3-0 | 2-0 | 0-1 | 1-3 |
| Stoke FC | 0-2 | 1-0 | 2-3 | 3-2 | 3-0 | 2-2 | 2-3 | 6-1 | 3-0 | 2-1 | 2-0 | | 0-1 | 0-0 | 2-2 | 2-1 |
| Sunderland AFC | 4-2 | 0-1 | 1-1 | 1-1 | 0-1 | 1-2 | 1-1 | 4-3 | 2-2 | 1-1 | 0-1 | 4-1 | | 0-0 | 2-1 | 0-3 |
| The Wednesday FC | 1-3 | 6-0 | 0-0 | 1-0 | 2-0 | 2-0 | 4-1 | 1-2 | 3-0 | 1-0 | 1-1 | 4-3 | 0-0 | | 3-1 | 0-0 |
| West Bromwich Albion FC | 3-1 | 1-0 | 1-0 | 3-0 | 0-0 | 1-4 | 1-4 | 0-1 | 4-0 | 1-1 | 0-1 | 1-2 | 1-0 | 0-2 | | 1-0 |
| Wolverhampton Wanderers FC | 1-2 | 1-1 | 4-0 | 2-0 | 1-1 | 1-0 | 0-1 | 1-2 | 4-1 | 1-1 | 1-1 | 2-0 | 1-2 | 0-1 | 6-1 | |

## Division 1

| | | Pd | Wn | Dw | Ls | GF | GA | Pts | |
|---|---|---|---|---|---|---|---|---|---|
| 1. | ASTON VILLA FC (BIRMINGHAM) | 30 | 21 | 5 | 4 | 73 | 38 | 47 | |
| 2. | Sheffield United FC (Sheffield) | 30 | 13 | 10 | 7 | 42 | 29 | 36 | |
| 3. | Derby County FC (Derby) | 30 | 16 | 4 | 10 | 70 | 50 | 36 | |
| 4. | Preston North End FC (Preston) | 30 | 11 | 12 | 7 | 55 | 40 | 34 | |
| 5. | Liverpool FC (Liverpool) | 30 | 12 | 9 | 9 | 46 | 38 | 33 | |
| 6. | The Wednesday FC (Sheffield) | 30 | 10 | 11 | 9 | 42 | 37 | 31 | |
| 7. | Everton FC (Liverpool) | 30 | 14 | 3 | 13 | 62 | 57 | 31 | |
| 8. | Bolton Wanderers FC (Bolton) | 30 | 12 | 6 | 12 | 40 | 43 | 30 | |
| 9. | Bury FC (Bury) | 30 | 10 | 10 | 10 | 39 | 44 | 30 | |
| 10. | Wolverhampton Wanderers FC (Wolverhampton) | 30 | 11 | 6 | 13 | 45 | 41 | 28 | |
| 11. | Nottingham Forest FC (Nottingham) | 30 | 9 | 8 | 13 | 44 | 49 | 26 | |
| 12. | West Bromwich Albion FC (West Bromwich) | 30 | 10 | 6 | 14 | 33 | 56 | 26 | |
| 13. | Stoke FC (Stoke-upon-Trent) | 30 | 11 | 3 | 16 | 48 | 59 | 25 | |
| 14. | Blackburn Rovers FC (Blackburn) | 30 | 11 | 3 | 16 | 35 | 62 | 25 | |
| 15. | Sunderland AFC (Sunderland) | 30 | 7 | 9 | 14 | 34 | 47 | 23 | PO |
| 16. | Burnley FC (Burnley) | 30 | 6 | 7 | 17 | 43 | 61 | 19 | POR |
| | | 480 | 184 | 112 | 184 | 751 | 751 | 480 | |

## Top Goalscorers

| | | | |
|---|---|---|---|
| 1) | Stephen BLOOMER | (Derby County FC) | 22 |
| 2) | George Frederick WHELDON | (Aston Villa FC) | 17 |
| 3) | George ALLAN | (Liverpool FC) | 16 |
| | John BELL | (Everton FC) | 16 |
| | John Henry George. DEVEY | (Aston Villa FC) | 16 |
| | James William STEVENSON | (Derby County FC) | 16 |

| Football League Promotion/Relegation Play-offs 1896-1897 Season | Notts County | Sunderland | Burnley | Newton Heath |
|---|---|---|---|---|
| Notts County FC | | 1-0 | 1-1 | --- |
| Sunderland AFC | 0-0 | | --- | 2-0 |
| Burnley FC | 0-1 | --- | | 2-0 |
| Newton Heath FC | --- | 1-1 | 2-0 | |

## Promotion/Relegation Play-offs

| | | Pd | Wn | Dw | Ls | GF | GA | Pts | |
|---|---|---|---|---|---|---|---|---|---|
| 1. | Notts County FC (Nottingham) | 4 | 2 | 2 | - | 3 | 1 | 6 | P |
| 2. | Sunderland AFC (Sunderland) | 4 | 1 | 2 | 1 | 3 | 2 | 4 | -- |
| 3. | Burnley FC (Burnley) | 4 | 1 | 1 | 2 | 3 | 4 | 3 | R |
| 4. | Newton Heath FC (Manchester) | 4 | 1 | 1 | 2 | 3 | 5 | 3 | -- |
| | | 16 | 5 | 6 | 5 | 12 | 12 | 16 | |

| Football League Division 2 1896-97 Season | Blackpool | Burton Swifts | Burton W. | Darwen | Gainsborough Trinity | Grimsby Town | Leicester Fosse | Lincoln City | Loughborough Town | Manchester City | Newcastle United | Newton Heath | Notts County | Small Heath | Walsall | Woolwich Arsenal |
|---|---|---|---|---|---|---|---|---|---|---|---|---|---|---|---|---|
| Blackpool FC | | 3-0 | 5-0 | 1-0 | 1-1 | 1-0 | 3-0 | 3-1 | 4-1 | 2-2 | 4-1 | 4-2 | 3-2 | 1-3 | 3-2 | 1-1 |
| Burton Swifts FC | 2-2 | | 1-1 | 2-0 | 4-0 | 0-0 | 2-1 | 4-0 | 3-1 | 5-0 | 3-0 | 3-5 | 1-4 | 1-1 | 1-3 | 1-2 |
| Burton Wanderers FC | 3-1 | 1-0 | | 1-0 | 3-2 | 5-1 | 2-1 | 2-0 | 0-1 | 1-1 | 0-1 | 1-2 | 0-3 | 2-6 | 1-0 | 0-3 |
| Darwen FC | 2-3 | 5-1 | 3-0 | | 3-2 | 3-1 | 4-1 | 4-1 | 5-1 | 3-1 | 2-1 | 0-2 | 2-1 | 2-0 | 12-0 | 4-1 |
| Gainsborough Trinity FC | 2-0 | 4-1 | 2-1 | 2-4 | | 1-1 | 0-2 | 7-0 | 2-0 | 1-1 | 2-0 | 2-0 | 3-2 | 1-3 | 2-0 | 4-1 |
| Grimsby Town FC | 2-2 | 3-0 | 3-0 | 4-2 | 1-1 | | 4-1 | 3-1 | 8-1 | 3-1 | 3-2 | 2-0 | 3-1 | 2-1 | 0-1 | 3-1 |
| Leicester Fosse FC | 2-1 | 3-0 | 2-1 | 4-1 | 0-0 | 4-2 | | 4-1 | 4-2 | 3-3 | 5-0 | 1-0 | 2-3 | 0-1 | 4-1 | 6-3 |
| Lincoln City FC | 3-1 | 1-1 | 2-3 | 1-0 | 0-2 | 0-3 | 2-1 | | 0-2 | 0-1 | 1-2 | 1-3 | 1-1 | 1-3 | 2-1 | 2-3 |
| Loughborough Town FC | 4-1 | 0-2 | 6-0 | 4-2 | 1-0 | 1-4 | 0-2 | 3-0 | | 2-0 | 3-0 | 2-0 | 0-1 | 2-0 | 1-2 | 8-0 |
| Manchester City FC | 4-2 | 3-1 | 2-1 | 4-1 | 4-1 | 3-1 | 4-0 | 3-0 | 1-1 | | 1-2 | 0-0 | 1-4 | 3-0 | 5-0 | 1-1 |
| Newcastle United FC | 4-1 | 2-1 | 3-0 | 5-1 | 1-2 | 3-0 | 3-1 | 2-1 | 4-1 | 3-0 | | 2-0 | 2-2 | 4-3 | 2-0 | 2-0 |
| Newton Heath FC | 2-0 | 1-1 | 3-0 | 3-1 | 2-0 | 4-2 | 2-1 | 3-1 | 6-0 | 2-1 | 4-0 | | 1-1 | 1-1 | 2-0 | 1-1 |
| Notts County FC | 3-1 | 6-1 | 5-0 | 4-0 | 2-0 | 1-3 | 6-0 | 8-0 | 3-1 | 3-3 | 3-1 | 3-0 | | 1-2 | 5-2 | 7-4 |
| Small Heath FC | 1-3 | 1-2 | 3-2 | 5-1 | 2-2 | 0-1 | 2-2 | 1-2 | 3-0 | 3-1 | 3-1 | 1-0 | 3-1 | | 3-3 | 5-2 |
| Walsall FC | 2-0 | 5-2 | 2-0 | 4-0 | 1-1 | 0-1 | 1-1 | 5-0 | 5-1 | 3-2 | 0-2 | 2-3 | 1-3 | 1-6 | | 5-3 |
| Woolwich Arsenal FC | 4-2 | 3-0 | 3-0 | 1-0 | 6-1 | 4-2 | 2-1 | 6-2 | 2-0 | 1-2 | 5-1 | 0-2 | 2-3 | 2-3 | 1-1 | |

| Division 2 | Pd | Wn | Dw | Ls | GF | GA | Pts | |
|---|---|---|---|---|---|---|---|---|
| 1. Notts County FC (Nottingham) | 30 | 19 | 4 | 7 | 92 | 43 | 42 POP | |
| 2. Newton Heath FC (Manchester) | 30 | 17 | 5 | 8 | 56 | 34 | 39 | |
| 3. Grimsby Town FC (Cleethorpes) | 30 | 17 | 4 | 9 | 66 | 45 | 38 | |
| 4. Small Heath FC (Birmingham) | 30 | 16 | 5 | 9 | 69 | 47 | 37 | |
| 5. Newcastle United FC (Newcastle-upon-Tyne) | 30 | 17 | 1 | 12 | 56 | 52 | 35 | |
| 6. Manchester City FC (Manchester) | 30 | 12 | 8 | 10 | 58 | 50 | 32 | |
| 7. Gainsborough Trinity FC (Gainsborough) | 30 | 12 | 7 | 11 | 50 | 47 | 31 | |
| 8. Blackpool FC (Blackpool) | 30 | 13 | 5 | 12 | 59 | 56 | 31 | |
| 9. Leicester Fosse FC (Leicester) | 30 | 13 | 4 | 13 | 59 | 56 | 30 | |
| 10. Woolwich Arsenal FC (London) | 30 | 13 | 4 | 13 | 68 | 70 | 30 | |
| 11. Darwen FC (Darwen) | 30 | 14 | - | 14 | 67 | 61 | 28 | |
| 12. Walsall FC (Walsall) | 30 | 11 | 4 | 15 | 53 | 69 | 26 | |
| 13. Loughborough Town FC (Loughborough) | 30 | 12 | 1 | 17 | 50 | 64 | 25 | |
| 14. Burton Swifts FC (Burton-upon-Trent) | 30 | 9 | 6 | 15 | 46 | 61 | 24 | |
| 15. Burton Wanderers FC (Burton-upon-Trent) | 30 | 9 | 2 | 19 | 31 | 67 | 20 | # |
| 16. Lincoln City FC (Lincoln) | 30 | 5 | 2 | 23 | 27 | 85 | 12 | |
| | 480 | 209 | 62 | 209 | 907 | 907 | 480 | |

# Burton Wanderers FC (Burton-upon-Trent) were not re-elected to the league and were replaced in Division 2 for next season by Luton Town FC (Luton).


**F.A. CUP FINAL**   (Crystal Palace, London – 10/04/1897 – 65,891)

| ASTON VILLA FC (BIRMINGHAM) | 3-2 | Everton FC (Liverpool) |
|---|---|---|
| *Devey, Campbell, Crabtree* | *(H.T. 3-2)* | *Bell, Hartley* |

Aston Villa: Whitehouse, Spencer, Evans, Reynolds, James Cowan, Crabtree, Athersmith, Devey, Campbell, Wheldon, John Cowan.

Everton: Menham, Meechan, Storrier, Boyle, Holt, Stewart, Taylor, Bell, Hartley, Chadwick, Milward.


## Semi-finals

| Aston Villa FC (Birmingham) | 3-0 | Liverpool FC (Liverpool) |
|---|---|---|
| Everton FC (Liverpool) | 3-2 | Derby County FC (Derby) |


## Quarter-finals

| Aston Villa FC (Birmingham) | 1-1 (aet), 0-0 (aet), 3-2 | Preston North End FC (Preston) |
|---|---|---|
| Derby County FC (Derby) | 2-0 | Newton Heath FC (Manchester) |
| Everton FC (Liverpool) | 2-0 | Blackburn Rovers FC (Blackburn) |
| Nottingham Forest FC (Nottingham) | 1-1 (aet), 0-1 | Liverpool FC (Liverpool) |

# 1897-98

| Football League Division 1 1897-98 Season | Aston Villa | Blackburn Rovers | Bolton Wanderers | Bury | Derby County | Everton | Liverpool | Nottingham Forest | Notts County | Preston North End | Sheffield United | Stoke | Sunderland | Wednesday | W.B.A. | Wolves |
|---|---|---|---|---|---|---|---|---|---|---|---|---|---|---|---|---|
| Aston Villa FC | | 5-1 | 3-2 | 3-1 | 4-1 | 3-0 | 3-1 | 2-0 | 4-2 | 4-0 | 1-2 | 1-1 | 4-3 | 5-2 | 4-3 | 1-2 |
| Blackburn Rovers FC | 4-3 | | 1-3 | 1-1 | 1-1 | 1-1 | 2-1 | 1-1 | 0-1 | 1-0 | 1-1 | 1-1 | 2-1 | 1-1 | 1-3 | 2-3 |
| Bolton Wanderers FC | 2-0 | 1-2 | | 0-0 | 3-3 | 1-0 | 0-2 | 2-0 | 1-0 | 1-0 | 0-1 | 2-1 | 1-0 | 0-3 | 2-0 | 2-1 |
| Bury FC | 1-2 | 1-0 | 2-1 | | 4-0 | 0-1 | 0-2 | 2-2 | 0-0 | 1-0 | 2-5 | 3-3 | 1-0 | 3-0 | 3-2 | 2-1 |
| Derby County FC | 3-1 | 3-1 | 1-0 | 2-2 | | 5-1 | 3-1 | 5-0 | 1-2 | 3-1 | 1-1 | 4-1 | 2-2 | 1-2 | 3-2 | 3-2 |
| Everton FC | 2-1 | 1-1 | 2-1 | 4-2 | 3-0 | | 3-0 | 2-0 | 1-0 | 1-1 | 1-4 | 1-1 | 2-0 | 1-0 | 6-1 | 3-0 |
| Liverpool FC | 4-0 | 0-1 | 1-1 | 2-2 | 4-2 | 3-1 | | 1-2 | 2-0 | 0-0 | 0-4 | 4-0 | 0-2 | 4-0 | 1-1 | 1-0 |
| Nottingham Forest FC | 3-1 | 3-1 | 2-0 | 3-1 | 3-4 | 2-2 | 2-3 | | 1-1 | 4-1 | 1-1 | 3-1 | 1-1 | 1-0 | 0-1 | 1-1 |
| Notts County FC | 2-3 | 0-0 | 1-2 | 2-1 | 1-1 | 3-2 | 3-2 | 1-3 | | 1-1 | 1-3 | 4-0 | 0-1 | 0-0 | 2-2 | 2-2 |
| Preston North End FC | 3-1 | 1-4 | 0-0 | 2-1 | 5-0 | 1-1 | 1-1 | 3-0 | 3-1 | | 1-3 | 0-0 | 2-0 | 2-0 | 1-1 | 1-2 |
| Sheffield United FC | 1-0 | 5-2 | 4-0 | 1-1 | 2-1 | 0-0 | 1-2 | 1-1 | 0-1 | 2-1 | | 4-3 | 1-0 | 1-1 | 2-0 | 2-1 |
| Stoke FC | 0-0 | 2-1 | 2-0 | 3-1 | 2-1 | 2-0 | 2-2 | 1-2 | 2-0 | 1-2 | 2-1 | | 0-1 | 2-1 | 0-0 | 0-2 |
| Sunderland AFC | 0-0 | 2-1 | 2-0 | 2-1 | 2-1 | 0-0 | 1-0 | 4-0 | 2-0 | 1-0 | 3-1 | 4-0 | | 1-0 | 0-2 | 3-2 |
| The Wednesday FC | 3-0 | 4-1 | 3-0 | 3-0 | 3-1 | 2-1 | 4-2 | 3-6 | 3-1 | 2-1 | 0-1 | 4-0 | 0-1 | | 3-0 | 2-0 |
| West Bromwich Albion FC | 1-1 | 1-1 | 2-0 | 1-0 | 3-1 | 2-2 | 2-1 | 2-0 | 0-3 | 3-1 | 2-0 | 2-0 | 2-2 | 0-2 | | 2-2 |
| Wolverhampton Wanderers FC | 1-1 | 3-2 | 2-0 | 3-0 | 2-0 | 2-3 | 2-1 | 0-0 | 3-1 | 3-0 | 1-1 | 4-2 | 4-2 | 5-0 | 1-1 | |

## Division 1

| | | Pd | Wn | Dw | Ls | GF | GA | Pts | |
|---|---|---|---|---|---|---|---|---|---|
| 1. | SHEFFIELD UNITED FC (SHEFFIELD) | 30 | 17 | 8 | 5 | 56 | 31 | 42 | |
| 2. | Sunderland AFC (Sunderland) | 30 | 16 | 5 | 9 | 43 | 30 | 37 | |
| 3. | Wolverhampton Wanderers FC (Wolverhampton) | 30 | 14 | 7 | 9 | 57 | 41 | 35 | |
| 4. | Everton FC (Liverpool) | 30 | 13 | 9 | 8 | 48 | 39 | 35 | |
| 5. | The Wednesday FC (Sheffield) | 30 | 15 | 3 | 12 | 51 | 42 | 33 | |
| 6. | Aston Villa FC (Birmingham) | 30 | 14 | 5 | 11 | 61 | 51 | 33 | |
| 7. | West Bromwich Albion FC (West Bromwich) | 30 | 11 | 10 | 9 | 44 | 45 | 32 | |
| 8. | Nottingham Forest FC (Nottingham) | 30 | 11 | 9 | 10 | 47 | 49 | 31 | |
| 9. | Liverpool FC (Liverpool) | 30 | 11 | 6 | 13 | 48 | 45 | 28 | |
| 10. | Derby County FC (Derby) | 30 | 11 | 6 | 13 | 57 | 61 | 28 | |
| 11. | Bolton Wanderers FC (Bolton) | 30 | 11 | 4 | 15 | 28 | 41 | 26 | |
| 12. | Preston North End FC (Preston) | 30 | 8 | 8 | 14 | 35 | 43 | 24 | |
| 13. | Notts County FC (Nottingham) | 30 | 8 | 8 | 14 | 36 | 46 | 24 | |
| 14. | Bury FC (Bury) | 30 | 8 | 8 | 14 | 39 | 51 | 24 | |
| 15. | Blackburn Rovers FC (Blackburn) | 30 | 7 | 10 | 13 | 39 | 54 | 24 | PO |
| 16. | Stoke FC (Stoke-upon-Trent) | 30 | 8 | 8 | 14 | 35 | 55 | 24 | PO |
| | | 480 | 183 | 114 | 183 | 724 | 724 | 480 | |

## Top Goalscorers

| | | | |
|---|---|---|---|
| 1) | George Frederick WHELDON | (Aston Villa FC) | 21 |
| 2) | Frederick SPIKESLEY | (Sheffield United FC) | 17 |
| 3) | Stephen BLOOMER | (Derby County FC) | 16 |
| 4) | Walter BENNETT | (The Wednesday FC) | 13 |
| | Harold WOOD | (Wolverhampton Wanderers FC) | 13 |

| Football League Promotion/Relegation Play-offs 1897-98 Season | Stoke City | Burnley | Newcastle United | Blackburn Rovers |
|---|---|---|---|---|
| Stoke FC | | 0-0 | 1-0 | --- |
| Burnley FC | 0-2 | | --- | 2-0 |
| Newcastle United FC | 2-1 | --- | | 4-0 |
| Blackburn Rovers FC | --- | 1-3 | 4-3 | |

## Promotion/Relegation Play-offs

| | | Pd | Wn | Dw | Ls | GF | GA | Pts |
|---|---|---|---|---|---|---|---|---|
| 1. | Stoke FC (Stoke-upon-Trent) | 4 | 2 | 1 | 1 | 4 | 2 | 5 |
| 2. | Burnley FC (Burnley) | 4 | 2 | 1 | 1 | 5 | 3 | 5 |
| 3. | Newcastle United FC (Newcastle/Tyne) | 4 | 2 | - | 2 | 9 | 6 | 4 |
| 4. | Blackburn Rovers FC (Blackburn) | 4 | 1 | - | 3 | 5 | 12 | 2 |
| | | 16 | 7 | 2 | 7 | 23 | 23 | 16 |

Division 1 was extended to 18 clubs for next season so all 4 clubs who entered the play-offs played in Division 1 the next season.

| Football League Division 2 1897-98 Season | Blackpool | Burnley | Burton Swifts | Darwen | Gainsborough Trinity | Grimsby Town | Leicester Fosse | Lincoln City | Loughborough Town | Luton Town | Manchester City | Newcastle United | Newton Heath | Small Heath | Walsall | Woolwich Arsenal |
|---|---|---|---|---|---|---|---|---|---|---|---|---|---|---|---|---|
| Blackpool FC | | 1-1 | 2-1 | 1-0 | 5-0 | 1-1 | 2-1 | 5-0 | 4-0 | 1-0 | 0-2 | 2-3 | 0-1 | 4-1 | 1-1 | 3-3 |
| Burnley FC | 5-1 | | 2-0 | 6-1 | 1-1 | 6-0 | 4-0 | 2-1 | 9-3 | 4-0 | 3-1 | 3-0 | 6-3 | 4-1 | 4-1 | 5-0 |
| Burton Swifts FC | 2-1 | 0-2 | | 2-0 | 1-1 | 4-0 | 2-3 | 1-1 | 3-0 | 2-1 | 0-0 | 3-1 | 0-4 | 1-3 | 3-2 | 1-2 |
| Darwen FC | 3-1 | 0-1 | 1-2 | | 2-4 | 1-0 | 1-2 | 3-2 | 2-1 | 0-2 | 2-4 | 1-3 | 2-3 | 1-1 | 1-2 | 1-4 |
| Gainsborough Trinity FC | 4-1 | 0-0 | 3-2 | 3-1 | | 2-0 | 1-0 | 4-0 | 4-0 | 3-3 | 1-0 | 1-3 | 2-1 | 0-0 | 1-1 | 1-0 |
| Grimsby Town FC | 3-0 | 2-1 | 7-2 | 5-0 | 4-2 | | 0-0 | 4-2 | 7-0 | 1-3 | 3-4 | 2-0 | 1-3 | 3-1 | 1-2 | 1-4 |
| Leicester Fosse FC | 4-1 | 0-1 | 1-1 | 0-1 | 3-1 | 1-0 | | 3-1 | 4-0 | 1-1 | 0-0 | 1-1 | 1-1 | 2-0 | 3-1 | 2-1 |
| Lincoln City FC | 3-2 | 1-1 | 3-0 | 2-2 | 2-1 | 1-1 | 1-4 | | 2-3 | 4-2 | 2-1 | 2-3 | 1-0 | 1-2 | 0-2 | 2-3 |
| Loughborough Town FC | 0-2 | 0-2 | 3-2 | 0-1 | 0-5 | 2-1 | 1-1 | 4-2 | | 2-0 | 0-3 | 0-1 | 0-0 | 0-2 | 2-1 | 1-3 |
| Luton Town FC | 3-1 | 2-0 | 1-1 | 3-0 | 4-0 | 6-0 | 0-1 | 9-3 | 7-0 | | 3-0 | 3-1 | 2-2 | 1-2 | 6-0 | 0-2 |
| Manchester City FC | 3-3 | 1-1 | 9-0 | 5-0 | 3-0 | 3-0 | 2-1 | 3-1 | 3-0 | 2-1 | | 1-1 | 0-1 | 3-3 | 3-2 | 4-1 |
| Newcastle United FC | 2-0 | 0-1 | 3-1 | 1-0 | 5-2 | 4-0 | 4-2 | 3-0 | 3-1 | 4-1 | 2-0 | | 2-0 | 4-0 | 2-1 | 4-1 |
| Newton Heath FC | 4-0 | 0-0 | 4-0 | 3-2 | 1-0 | 2-1 | 2-0 | 5-0 | 5-1 | 1-2 | 1-1 | 0-1 | | 3-1 | 6-0 | 5-1 |
| Small Heath FC | 2-3 | 2-2 | 2-1 | 5-1 | 4-3 | 0-2 | 2-1 | 4-0 | 1-0 | 4-2 | 0-1 | 1-0 | 2-1 | | 6-0 | 2-1 |
| Walsall FC | 6-0 | 1-2 | 4-0 | 5-0 | 3-0 | 1-1 | 2-1 | 3-1 | 3-0 | 5-0 | 2-2 | 2-3 | 1-1 | 1-2 | | 3-2 |
| Woolwich Arsenal FC | 2-1 | 1-1 | 3-0 | 3-1 | 4-0 | 4-1 | 0-3 | 2-2 | 4-0 | 3-0 | 2-2 | 0-0 | 5-1 | 4-2 | 4-0 | |

| Division 2 | Pd | Wn | Dw | Ls | GF | GA | Pts |
|---|---|---|---|---|---|---|---|
| 1. Burnley FC (Burnley) | 30 | 20 | 8 | 2 | 80 | 24 | 48 POP |
| 2. Newcastle United FC (Newcastle-upon-Tyne) | 30 | 21 | 3 | 6 | 64 | 32 | 45 POP |
| 3. Manchester City FC (Manchester) | 30 | 15 | 9 | 6 | 66 | 36 | 39 |
| 4. Newton Heath FC (Manchester) | 30 | 16 | 6 | 8 | 64 | 35 | 38 |
| 5. Woolwich Arsenal FC (London) | 30 | 16 | 5 | 9 | 69 | 49 | 37 |
| 6. Small Heath FC (Birmingham) | 30 | 16 | 4 | 10 | 58 | 50 | 36 |
| 7. Leicester Fosse FC (Leicester) | 30 | 13 | 7 | 10 | 46 | 35 | 33 |
| 8. Luton Town FC (Luton) | 30 | 13 | 4 | 13 | 68 | 50 | 30 |
| 9. Gainsborough Trinity FC (Gainsborough) | 30 | 12 | 6 | 12 | 50 | 54 | 30 |
| 10. Walsall FC (Walsall) | 30 | 12 | 5 | 13 | 58 | 58 | 29 |
| 11. Blackpool FC (Blackpool) | 30 | 10 | 5 | 15 | 49 | 61 | 25 |
| 12. Grimsby Town FC (Cleethorpes) | 30 | 10 | 4 | 16 | 52 | 62 | 24 |
| 13. Burton Swifts FC (Burton-upon-Trent) | 30 | 8 | 5 | 17 | 38 | 69 | 21 |
| 14. Lincoln City FC (Lincoln) | 30 | 6 | 5 | 19 | 43 | 82 | 17 |
| 15. Darwen FC (Darwen) | 30 | 6 | 2 | 22 | 31 | 76 | 14 |
| 16. Loughborough Town FC (Loughborough) | 30 | 6 | 2 | 22 | 24 | 87 | 14 |
| | 480 | 200 | 80 | 200 | 860 | 860 | 480 |

Barnsley St. Peter's FC (Barnsley), Burslem Port Vale FC (Burslem), Glossop North End FC (Glossop) and New Brighton Tower FC (Wallasey) were elected to Division 2 which was extended to 18 clubs for next season.

Automatic promotion/relegation started from the next season.


## F.A. CUP FINAL   (Crystal Palace, London – 16/04/1898 – 62,017)

NOTTINGHAM FOREST FC (NOTTINGHAM)          3-1                    Derby County FC (Derby)

*Capes 2, McPherson*                    *(H.T. 2-1)*                         *Bloomer*

Nottingham Forest: Allsop, Ritchie, Scott, Forman, McPherson, Wragg, McInnes, Richards, Benbow, Capes, Spouncer.

Derby: Fryer, Methven, Leiper, Cox, Goodall, Turner, Goodall, Bloomer, Boag, Stevenson, McQueen.


## Semi-finals

| Derby County FC (Derby) | 3-1 | Everton FC (Liverpool) |
|---|---|---|
| Southampton FC (Southampton) | 1-1 (aet), 0-2 | Nottingham Forest FC (Nottingham) |


## Quarter-finals

| Burnley FC (Burnley) | 1-3 | Everton FC (Liverpool) |
|---|---|---|
| Liverpool FC (Liverpool) | 1-1 (aet), 1-5 | Derby County FC (Derby) |
| Southampton FC (Southampton) | 0-0 (aet), 4-0 | Bolton Wanderers FC (Bolton) |
| West Bromwich Albion FC (West Bromwich) | 2-3 | Nottingham Forest FC (Nottingham) |

# 1898-99

| Football League Division 1 1898-99 Season | Aston Villa | Blackburn Rovers | Bolton Wanderers | Burnley | Bury | Derby County | Everton | Liverpool | Newcastle United | Nottingham Forest | Notts County | Preston North End | Sheffield United | Stoke | Sunderland | Wednesday | W.B.A. | Wolves |
|---|---|---|---|---|---|---|---|---|---|---|---|---|---|---|---|---|---|---|
| Aston Villa FC | ■ | 3-1 | 2-1 | 4-0 | 3-2 | 7-1 | 3-0 | 5-0 | 1-0 | 3-0 | 6-1 | 4-2 | 1-1 | 3-1 | 2-0 | 3-1 | 7-1 | 1-1 |
| Blackburn Rovers FC | 0-0 | ■ | 4-1 | 0-2 | 0-0 | 3-0 | 1-3 | 1-3 | 4-2 | 3-3 | 6-0 | 2-2 | 2-1 | 4-1 | 3-2 | 2-0 | 4-1 | 2-2 |
| Bolton Wanderers FC | 0-0 | 0-2 | ■ | 2-0 | 0-1 | 2-1 | 2-4 | 2-1 | 0-0 | 0-2 | 0-1 | 2-2 | 3-0 | 0-2 | 6-1 | 0-0 | 3-3 | 2-1 |
| Burnley FC | 2-4 | 2-0 | 2-0 | ■ | 2-1 | 2-1 | 0-0 | 2-1 | 2-1 | 0-0 | 0-0 | 3-1 | 1-0 | 1-1 | 1-0 | 5-0 | 1-1 | 4-2 |
| Bury FC | 2-1 | 3-2 | 3-1 | 1-1 | ■ | 0-0 | 3-1 | 3-0 | 1-1 | 2-0 | 2-0 | 3-1 | 1-3 | 5-2 | 1-2 | 0-0 | 1-1 | 0-2 |
| Derby County FC | 1-1 | 0-0 | 1-1 | 2-1 | 1-2 | ■ | 5-5 | 1-0 | 3-1 | 2-0 | 4-2 | 1-0 | 1-0 | 1-1 | 4-2 | 9-0 | 4-1 | 6-2 |
| Everton FC | 1-1 | 2-1 | 1-0 | 4-0 | 0-1 | 1-2 | ■ | 1-2 | 3-0 | 1-3 | 1-2 | 2-0 | 1-0 | 2-0 | 0-0 | 2-0 | 1-0 | 2-1 |
| Liverpool FC | 0-3 | 2-0 | 2-0 | 2-0 | 1-0 | 4-0 | 2-0 | ■ | 3-2 | 0-1 | 0-0 | 3-1 | 2-1 | 1-0 | 0-0 | 4-0 | 2-2 | 1-0 |
| Newcastle United FC | 1-1 | 1-0 | 4-1 | 4-1 | 2-0 | 2-0 | 2-2 | 3-0 | ■ | 0-1 | 1-2 | 2-1 | 1-2 | 3-0 | 0-1 | 2-2 | 3-0 | 2-4 |
| Nottingham Forest FC | 1-0 | 0-1 | 1-2 | 0-1 | 1-2 | 3-3 | 0-0 | 0-3 | 2-0 | ■ | 0-0 | 2-2 | 2-1 | 2-1 | 1-1 | 1-1 | 3-0 | 3-0 |
| Notts County FC | 1-0 | 5-3 | 2-1 | 2-2 | 4-1 | 2-2 | 0-1 | 1-1 | 3-1 | 2-2 | ■ | 1-0 | 2-2 | 2-0 | 5-2 | 1-0 | 0-0 | 0-2 |
| Preston North End FC | 2-0 | 1-1 | 0-1 | 1-1 | 3-1 | 3-1 | 0-0 | 1-2 | 1-0 | 1-0 | 2-0 | ■ | 1-0 | 4-2 | 2-3 | 1-1 | 4-0 | 2-1 |
| Sheffield United FC | 1-3 | 1-1 | 3-1 | 1-1 | 4-1 | 2-1 | 1-1 | 0-2 | 2-2 | 2-2 | 2-2 | 1-1 | ■ | 1-1 | 2-0 | 2-1 | 5-0 | 1-0 |
| Stoke FC | 3-0 | 0-1 | 2-3 | 4-1 | 1-1 | 0-0 | 2-1 | 2-1 | 0-0 | 2-1 | 1-1 | 2-1 | 4-1 | ■ | 1-0 | 1-0 | 2-1 | 2-4 |
| Sunderland AFC | 4-2 | 0-1 | 0-0 | 0-1 | 3-0 | 1-0 | 2-1 | 1-0 | 2-3 | 1-1 | 1-1 | 1-0 | 1-0 | 2-0 | ■ | 2-0 | 2-0 | 3-0 |
| The Wednesday FC | 4-1 | 1-2 | 1-0 | 1-0 | 3-2 | 3-1 | 1-2 | 0-3 | 1-3 | 2-1 | 1-1 | 2-1 | 1-1 | 1-3 | 0-1 | ■ | 1-2 | 3-0 |
| West Bromwich Albion FC | 0-1 | 6-2 | 1-0 | 0-1 | 2-0 | 1-1 | 3-0 | 0-1 | 2-0 | 2-0 | 2-0 | 2-0 | 3-0 | 0-1 | 1-0 | 2-0 | ■ | 1-2 |
| Wolverhampton Wanderers FC | 4-0 | 2-1 | 1-0 | 4-0 | 1-2 | 2-2 | 1-2 | 0-0 | 0-0 | 0-2 | 1-0 | 0-0 | 4-1 | 3-2 | 2-0 | 0-0 | 5-1 | ■ |

### Division 1

| | Division 1 | Pd | Wn | Dw | Ls | GF | GA | Pts | |
|---|---|---|---|---|---|---|---|---|---|
| 1. | ASTON VILLA FC (BIRMINGHAM) | 34 | 19 | 7 | 8 | 76 | 40 | 45 | |
| 2. | Liverpool FC (Liverpool) | 34 | 19 | 5 | 10 | 49 | 33 | 43 | |
| 3. | Burnley FC (Burnley) | 34 | 15 | 9 | 10 | 45 | 47 | 39 | |
| 4. | Everton FC (Liverpool) | 34 | 15 | 8 | 11 | 48 | 41 | 38 | |
| 5. | Notts County FC (Nottingham) | 34 | 12 | 13 | 9 | 47 | 51 | 37 | |
| 6. | Blackburn Rovers FC (Blackburn) | 34 | 14 | 8 | 12 | 60 | 52 | 36 | |
| 7. | Sunderland AFC (Sunderland) | 34 | 15 | 6 | 13 | 41 | 41 | 36 | |
| 8. | Wolverhampton Wanderers FC (Wolverhampton) | 34 | 14 | 7 | 13 | 54 | 48 | 35 | |
| 9. | Derby County FC (Derby) | 34 | 12 | 11 | 11 | 62 | 57 | 35 | |
| 10. | Bury FC (Bury) | 34 | 14 | 7 | 13 | 48 | 49 | 35 | |
| 11. | Nottingham Forest FC (Nottingham) | 34 | 11 | 11 | 12 | 42 | 42 | 33 | |
| 12. | Stoke FC (Stoke-upon-Trent) | 34 | 13 | 7 | 14 | 47 | 52 | 33 | |
| 13. | Newcastle United FC (Newcastle-upon-Tyne) | 34 | 11 | 8 | 15 | 49 | 48 | 30 | |
| 14. | West Bromwich Albion FC (West Bromwich) | 34 | 12 | 6 | 16 | 42 | 57 | 30 | |
| 15. | Preston North End FC (Preston) | 34 | 10 | 9 | 15 | 44 | 47 | 29 | |
| 16. | Sheffield United FC (Sheffield) | 34 | 9 | 11 | 14 | 45 | 51 | 29 | |
| 17. | Bolton Wanderers FC (Bolton) | 34 | 9 | 7 | 18 | 37 | 51 | 25 | R |
| 18. | The Wednesday FC (Sheffield) | 34 | 8 | 8 | 18 | 32 | 61 | 24 | R |
| | | 612 | 232 | 148 | 232 | 868 | 868 | 612 | |

# Top Goalscorers

| | | | |
|---|---|---|---|
| 1) | Stephen BLOOMER | (Derby County FC) | 23 |
| 2) | John Henry George DEVEY | (Aston Villa FC) | 21 |
| 3) | William S. MAXWELL | (Stoke FC) | 17 |
| | Jack H. PEDDIE | (Newcastle United FC) | 17 |
| 5) | Daniel J. HURST | (Blackburn Rovers FC) | 15 |

| Football League Division 2 1898-99 Season | Barnsley | Blackpool | Burslem Port Vale | Burton Swifts | Darwen | Gainsborough Trin. | Glossop | Grimsby Town | Leicester Fosse | Lincoln City | Loughborough Tn. | Luton Town | Manchester City | New Brighton | Newton Heath | Small Heath | Walsall | Woolwich Arsenal |
|---|---|---|---|---|---|---|---|---|---|---|---|---|---|---|---|---|---|---|
| Barnsley St. Peter's FC | ■ | 2-1 | 2-1 | 2-0 | 6-0 | 1-0 | 1-1 | 2-2 | 3-4 | 1-0 | 9-0 | 2-1 | 1-1 | 2-1 | 0-2 | 7-2 | 1-1 | 2-1 |
| Blackpool FC | 3-1 | ■ | 0-4 | 3-0 | 6-0 | 4-0 | 1-2 | 3-6 | 2-2 | 3-0 | 2-1 | 2-3 | 2-4 | 1-2 | 0-1 | 1-1 | 1-2 | 1-1 |
| Burslem Port Vale FC | 2-0 | 6-1 | ■ | 4-1 | 3-1 | 2-1 | 1-2 | 2-0 | 0-2 | 2-1 | 3-0 | 4-1 | 1-1 | 0-0 | 1-0 | 1-0 | 0-1 | 3-0 |
| Burton Swifts FC | 5-0 | 3-1 | 2-0 | ■ | 4-0 | 2-1 | 1-2 | 1-2 | 1-1 | 2-1 | 1-1 | 1-1 | 3-3 | 1-1 | 5-1 | 2-6 | 0-2 | 1-2 |
| Darwen FC | 1-1 | 0-2 | 1-3 | 0-2 | ■ | 0-3 | 0-2 | 0-2 | 3-0 | 1-2 | 0-1 | 4-1 | 0-2 | 2-4 | 1-1 | 1-1 | 1-1 | 1-4 |
| Gainsborough Trinity FC | 2-0 | 7-0 | 3-2 | 1-2 | 2-2 | ■ | 2-4 | 5-1 | 4-0 | 2-2 | 3-0 | 2-3 | 3-1 | 3-1 | 0-2 | 1-1 | 0-0 | 0-1 |
| Glossop FC | 1-0 | 4-1 | 0-0 | 5-0 | 5-0 | 5-1 | ■ | 4-2 | 1-3 | 2-0 | 4-0 | 5-0 | 1-2 | 5-0 | 1-2 | 1-2 | 2-0 | 2-0 |
| Grimsby Town FC | 0-1 | 2-1 | 3-1 | 1-3 | 9-2 | 0-2 | 1-1 | ■ | 1-0 | 1-1 | 5-0 | 5-0 | 1-2 | 2-2 | 3-0 | 2-0 | 2-1 | 1-0 |
| Leicester Fosse FC | 3-1 | 4-0 | 1-1 | 1-0 | 4-0 | 1-0 | 4-2 | 2-0 | ■ | 3-2 | 1-0 | 1-1 | 1-1 | 4-1 | 1-0 | 0-0 | 2-2 | 2-1 |
| Lincoln City FC | 1-0 | 0-0 | 1-0 | 1-1 | 2-0 | 1-0 | 2-2 | 1-6 | 3-1 | ■ | 6-0 | 2-0 | 3-1 | 1-2 | 2-0 | 2-2 | 1-1 | 2-0 |
| Loughborough Town FC | 2-0 | 1-3 | 0-3 | 1-0 | 10-0 | 0-0 | 1-3 | 1-3 | 0-3 | 2-4 | ■ | 4-1 | 1-3 | 6-0 | 0-1 | 1-1 | 1-1 | 0-0 |
| Luton Town FC | 4-1 | 3-2 | 0-1 | 3-0 | 8-1 | 4-2 | 0-2 | 3-1 | 1-6 | 2-0 | 2-2 | ■ | 0-3 | 2-3 | 0-1 | 2-3 | 3-2 | 0-1 |
| Manchester City FC | 5-0 | 4-1 | 3-1 | 6-0 | 10-0 | 4-0 | 0-2 | 7-2 | 3-1 | 3-1 | 5-0 | 2-0 | ■ | 1-1 | 4-0 | 2-0 | 2-0 | 3-1 |
| New Brighton Tower FC | 2-1 | 4-0 | 1-0 | 2-2 | 7-0 | 3-2 | 2-2 | 2-0 | 1-0 | 4-1 | 3-0 | 4-0 | 0-1 | ■ | 0-3 | 4-0 | 6-0 | 3-1 |
| Newton Heath FC | 0-0 | 3-1 | 2-1 | 2-2 | 9-0 | 6-1 | 3-0 | 3-2 | 2-2 | 1-0 | 6-1 | 5-0 | 3-0 | 1-2 | ■ | 2-0 | 1-0 | 2-2 |
| Small Heath FC | 3-1 | 5-0 | 1-2 | 4-1 | 8-0 | 6-1 | 1-1 | 2-1 | 0-3 | 4-1 | 6-0 | 9-0 | 4-1 | 3-2 | 4-1 | ■ | 2-1 | 4-1 |
| Walsall FC | 1-1 | 6-0 | 1-1 | 7-1 | 10-0 | 6-1 | 2-0 | 4-1 | 1-1 | 3-2 | 7-0 | 6-0 | 1-1 | 1-1 | 2-0 | 2-0 | ■ | 4-1 |
| Woolwich Arsenal FC | 3-0 | 6-0 | 1-0 | 2-1 | 6-0 | 5-1 | 3-0 | 1-1 | 4-0 | 4-2 | 3-1 | 6-2 | 0-1 | 4-0 | 5-1 | 2-0 | 0-0 | ■ |

| | Division 2 | Pd | Wn | Dw | Ls | GF | GA | Pts | |
|---|---|---|---|---|---|---|---|---|---|
| 1. | Manchester City FC (Manchester) | 34 | 23 | 6 | 5 | 92 | 35 | 52 | P |
| 2. | Glossop FC (Glossop) | 34 | 20 | 6 | 8 | 76 | 38 | 46 | P * |
| 3. | Leicester Fosse FC (Leicester) | 34 | 18 | 9 | 7 | 64 | 42 | 45 | |
| 4. | Newton Heath FC (Manchester) | 34 | 19 | 5 | 10 | 67 | 43 | 43 | |
| 5. | New Brighton Tower FC (Wallasey) | 34 | 18 | 7 | 9 | 71 | 52 | 43 | |
| 6. | Walsall FC (Walsall) | 34 | 15 | 12 | 7 | 79 | 36 | 42 | |
| 7. | Woolwich Arsenal FC (London) | 34 | 18 | 5 | 11 | 72 | 41 | 41 | |
| 8. | Small Heath FC (Birmingham) | 34 | 17 | 7 | 10 | 85 | 50 | 41 | |
| 9. | Burslem Port Vale FC (Burslem) | 34 | 17 | 5 | 12 | 56 | 34 | 39 | |
| 10. | Grimsby Town FC (Cleethorpes) | 34 | 15 | 5 | 14 | 71 | 60 | 35 | |
| 11. | Barnsley St. Peter's FC (Barnsley) | 34 | 12 | 7 | 15 | 52 | 56 | 31 | * |
| 12. | Lincoln City FC (Lincoln) | 34 | 12 | 7 | 15 | 51 | 56 | 31 | |
| 13. | Burton Swifts FC (Burton-upon-Trent) | 34 | 10 | 8 | 16 | 51 | 70 | 28 | |
| 14. | Gainsborough Trinity FC (Gainsborough) | 34 | 10 | 5 | 19 | 56 | 72 | 25 | |
| 15. | Luton Town FC (Luton) | 34 | 10 | 3 | 21 | 51 | 95 | 23 | |
| 16. | Blackpool FC (Blackpool) | 34 | 8 | 4 | 22 | 49 | 90 | 20 | # * |
| 17. | Loughborough Town FC (Loughborough) | 34 | 6 | 6 | 22 | 38 | 92 | 18 | |
| 18. | Darwen FC (Darwen) | 34 | 2 | 5 | 27 | 22 | 141 | 9 | # |
| | | 612 | 250 | 112 | 250 | 1103 | 1103 | 612 | |

# (# Blackpool FC (Blackpool) and Darwen FC (Darwen) were not re-elected to the league for next season and were replaced in Division 2 by Chesterfield FC (Chesterfield) and Middlesbrough FC (Middlesbrough).

\* Barnsley St. Peter's FC (Barnsley) changed the club name to Barnsley FC (Barnsley) and Blackpool FC (Blackpool) merged with South Shore FC (Blackpool) as Blackpool FC (Blackpool) for the next season. Glossop FC (Glossop) changed their club name from Glossop North End FC (Glossop) prior to the start of this season.

## F.A. CUP FINAL   (Crystal Palace, London – 15/04/1899 – 73,833)

SHEFFIELD UNITED FC (SHEFFIELD)          4-1          Derby County FC (Derby)

*Bennett, Beer, Almond, Priest*          *(H.T. 0-1)*          *Boag*

Sheffield United: Foulke, Thicket, Boyle, Johnson, Morren, Needham, Bennett, Beer, Hedley, Almond, Priest.
Derby: Fryer, Methven, Staley, Cox, Paterson, May, Arkesden, Bloomer, Boag, McDonald, Allan.

## Semi-finals

Derby County FC (Derby)          3-1          Stoke FC (Stoke-upon-Trent)
Sheffield United FC (Sheffield)          2-2 (aet), 4-4 (aet), 0-1, 1-0          Liverpool FC (Liverpool)
          (The third match was abandoned after the crowd encroached on the field of play.)

## Quarter-finals

Nottingham Forest FC (Nottingham)          0-1          Sheffield United FC (Sheffield)
Southampton FC (Southampton)          1-2          Derby County FC (Derby)
Stoke FC (Stoke-upon-Trent)          4-1          Tottenham Hotspur FC (London)
West Bromwich Albion FC (West Bromwich)          0-2          Liverpool FC (Liverpool)

# 1899-1900

| Football League Division 1 1899-1900 Season | Aston Villa | Blackburn Rovers | Burnley | Bury | Derby County | Everton | Glossop | Liverpool | Manchester City | Newcastle United | Nottingham Forest | Notts County | Preston North End | Sheffield United | Stoke | Sunderland | W.B.A. | Wolves |
|---|---|---|---|---|---|---|---|---|---|---|---|---|---|---|---|---|---|---|
| Aston Villa FC | | 3-1 | 2-0 | 2-1 | 3-2 | 1-1 | 9-0 | 1-0 | 2-1 | 2-1 | 2-2 | 6-2 | 3-1 | 1-1 | 4-1 | 4-2 | 0-2 | 0-0 |
| Blackburn Rovers FC | 0-4 | | 2-0 | 3-2 | 2-0 | 3-1 | 2-2 | 2-0 | 4-3 | 2-3 | 2-1 | 6-0 | 3-0 | 3-3 | 3-0 | 1-2 | 2-0 | 2-1 |
| Burnley FC | 1-2 | 1-0 | | 1-0 | 1-2 | 3-1 | 3-1 | 2-1 | 2-0 | 1-3 | 2-2 | 3-0 | 0-1 | 1-0 | 2-2 | 3-1 | 2-0 | 0-1 |
| Bury FC | 2-0 | 2-0 | 1-1 | | 1-1 | 4-1 | 2-1 | 2-1 | 1-4 | 2-1 | 2-1 | 0-1 | 2-0 | 2-1 | 0-1 | 2-0 | 1-0 | 3-0 |
| Derby County FC | 2-0 | 0-2 | 4-1 | 3-0 | | 2-1 | 4-1 | 3-2 | 0-0 | 2-1 | 2-2 | 0-1 | 2-0 | 0-1 | 2-0 | 2-0 | 4-1 | 0-2 |
| Everton FC | 1-2 | 0-0 | 2-0 | 2-0 | 3-0 | | 4-1 | 3-1 | 4-0 | 3-2 | 2-1 | 0-2 | 1-0 | 1-2 | 2-0 | 1-0 | 1-3 | 0-1 |
| Glossop FC | 1-0 | 4-2 | 2-0 | 0-0 | 1-3 | 1-1 | | 1-2 | 0-2 | 0-0 | 3-0 | 0-0 | 0-2 | 2-2 | 1-2 | 0-2 | 1-1 | 2-3 |
| Liverpool FC | 3-3 | 3-1 | 0-1 | 2-0 | 0-2 | 1-2 | 5-2 | | 5-2 | 2-0 | 1-0 | 3-1 | 1-0 | 2-2 | 0-0 | 0-2 | 2-0 | 1-1 |
| Manchester City FC | 0-2 | 1-1 | 1-0 | 2-2 | 4-0 | 1-2 | 4-1 | 0-1 | | 1-0 | 2-0 | 5-1 | 3-1 | 1-2 | 1-0 | 2-1 | 4-0 | 1-1 |
| Newcastle United FC | 3-2 | 4-1 | 2-0 | 2-1 | 2-0 | 2-0 | 1-0 | 1-1 | 0-0 | | 3-1 | 6-0 | 0-0 | 0-0 | 2-2 | 2-4 | 4-2 | 0-1 |
| Nottingham Forest FC | 1-1 | 3-2 | 4-0 | 2-2 | 4-1 | 4-2 | 5-0 | 1-0 | 2-0 | 1-0 | | 0-3 | 3-1 | 4-0 | 1-0 | 1-3 | 6-1 | 0-0 |
| Notts County FC | 1-4 | 5-1 | 6-1 | 2-2 | 0-0 | 2-2 | 0-0 | 2-1 | 1-1 | 0-0 | 1-2 | | 3-0 | 1-2 | 1-3 | 3-1 | 1-2 | 0-0 |
| Preston North End FC | 0-5 | 2-0 | 1-1 | 1-0 | 0-0 | 1-1 | 1-0 | 1-3 | 0-2 | 4-1 | 3-0 | 4-3 | | 0-1 | 3-0 | 0-1 | 5-2 | 2-0 |
| Sheffield United FC | 2-1 | 3-0 | 0-0 | 4-0 | 1-1 | 5-0 | 4-0 | 1-2 | 3-0 | 3-1 | 3-0 | 1-1 | 1-0 | | 1-0 | 2-2 | 1-1 | 5-2 |
| Stoke FC | 0-2 | 2-0 | 3-0 | 2-0 | 1-1 | 1-1 | 1-0 | 3-2 | 1-0 | 2-2 | 0-0 | 1-0 | 3-1 | 1-1 | | 1-2 | 1-0 | 1-3 |
| Sunderland AFC | 0-1 | 1-0 | 2-1 | 1-0 | 2-0 | 1-0 | 0-0 | 1-0 | 3-1 | 1-2 | 1-0 | 5-0 | 1-0 | 1-1 | 3-0 | | 3-1 | 1-2 |
| West Bromwich Albion FC | 0-2 | 1-0 | 2-0 | 0-1 | 0-0 | 0-0 | 3-3 | 2-0 | 0-0 | 1-1 | 8-0 | 0-0 | 1-0 | 1-2 | 4-0 | 1-0 | | 3-2 |
| Wolverhampton Wanderers FC | 0-1 | 4-0 | 3-0 | 1-0 | 3-0 | 2-1 | 4-0 | 0-1 | 1-1 | 1-1 | 2-2 | 2-2 | 1-3 | 1-2 | 0-2 | 1-0 | 2-0 | |

## Division 1

| | Pd | Wn | Dw | Ls | GF | GA | Pts | |
|---|---|---|---|---|---|---|---|---|
| 1. ASTON VILLA FC (BIRMINGHAM) | 34 | 22 | 6 | 6 | 77 | 35 | 50 | |
| 2. Sheffield United FC (Sheffield) | 34 | 18 | 12 | 4 | 63 | 33 | 48 | |
| 3. Sunderland AFC (Sunderland) | 34 | 19 | 3 | 12 | 50 | 35 | 41 | |
| 4. Wolverhampton Wanderers FC (Wolverhampton) | 34 | 15 | 9 | 10 | 48 | 37 | 39 | |
| 5. Newcastle United FC (Newcastle-upon-Tyne) | 34 | 14 | 10 | 11 | 53 | 43 | 36 | |
| 6. Derby County FC (Derby) | 34 | 14 | 8 | 12 | 45 | 43 | 36 | |
| 7. Manchester City FC (Manchester) | 34 | 13 | 8 | 13 | 50 | 44 | 34 | |
| 8. Nottingham Forest FC (Nottingham) | 34 | 13 | 8 | 13 | 56 | 55 | 34 | |
| 9. Stoke FC (Stoke-upon-Trent) | 34 | 13 | 8 | 13 | 37 | 45 | 34 | |
| 10. Liverpool FC (Liverpool) | 34 | 14 | 5 | 15 | 49 | 45 | 33 | |
| 11. Everton FC (Liverpool) | 34 | 13 | 7 | 14 | 47 | 49 | 33 | |
| 12. Bury FC (Bury) | 34 | 13 | 6 | 15 | 40 | 44 | 32 | |
| 13. West Bromwich Albion FC (West Bromwich) | 34 | 11 | 8 | 15 | 43 | 51 | 30 | |
| 14. Blackburn Rovers FC (Blackburn) | 34 | 13 | 4 | 17 | 49 | 61 | 30 | |
| 15. Notts County FC (Nottingham) | 34 | 9 | 11 | 14 | 46 | 60 | 29 | |
| 16. Preston North End FC (Preston) | 34 | 12 | 4 | 18 | 38 | 48 | 28 | |
| 17. Burnley FC (Burnley) | 34 | 11 | 5 | 18 | 34 | 54 | 27 | R |
| 18. Glossop FC (Glossop) | 34 | 4 | 10 | 20 | 31 | 74 | 18 | R |
| | 612 | 240 | 132 | 240 | 856 | 856 | 612 | |

## Top Goalscorers

| | | | |
|---|---|---|---|
| 1) | William GARRATY | (Aston Villa FC) | 27 |
| 2) | Stephen BLOOMER | (Derby County FC) | 19 |
| 3) | John CALVEY | (Nottingham Forest FC) | 17 |
| 4) | Walter BENNETT | (Sheffield United FC) | 15 |
| | Jack H. PEDDIE | (Newcastle United FC) | 15 |

**Football League Division 2 1899-1900 Season**

| | Barnsley | Bolton Wanderers | Burslem Port Vale | Burton Swifts | Chesterfield | Gainsborough Trinity | Grimsby Town | Leicester Fosse | Lincoln City | Loughborough Town | Luton Town | Middlesbrough | New Brighton | Newton Heath | Small Heath | Walsall | Wednesday | Woolwich Arsenal |
|---|---|---|---|---|---|---|---|---|---|---|---|---|---|---|---|---|---|---|
| Barnsley FC | | 1-6 | 3-0 | 4-1 | 0-0 | 5-0 | 0-1 | 1-2 | 0-4 | 7-0 | 2-1 | 5-2 | 1-1 | 0-0 | 1-1 | 2-2 | 1-0 | 3-2 |
| Bolton Wanderers FC | 2-0 | | 5-0 | 5-0 | 3-0 | 3-0 | 1-2 | 2-2 | 4-0 | 7-0 | 3-0 | 3-0 | 2-1 | 2-1 | 1-1 | 2-0 | 1-0 | 1-0 |
| Burslem Port Vale FC | 3-1 | 0-2 | | 2-1 | 2-0 | 1-0 | 2-3 | 0-2 | 2-0 | 3-1 | 1-0 | 3-1 | 1-1 | 1-0 | 3-0 | 1-0 | 0-3 | 1-1 |
| Burton Swifts FC | 4-0 | 2-5 | 2-2 | | 2-1 | 1-1 | 1-2 | 2-0 | 0-0 | 3-1 | 3-1 | 5-0 | 2-2 | 0-0 | 0-3 | 2-1 | 0-5 | 2-0 |
| Chesterfield FC | 2-1 | 3-3 | 0-4 | 0-4 | | 3-1 | 3-1 | 0-0 | 2-2 | 1-0 | 2-0 | 7-1 | 5-2 | 2-1 | 0-0 | 1-3 | 1-0 | 3-1 |
| Gainsborough Trinity FC | 1-0 | 1-1 | 4-0 | 4-1 | 3-5 | | 2-3 | 3-0 | 3-1 | 4-2 | 2-2 | 5-0 | 1-1 | 0-1 | 1-4 | 2-0 | 0-2 | 1-1 |
| Grimsby Town FC | 8-1 | 0-0 | 1-1 | 6-0 | 0-3 | 3-0 | | 6-1 | 5-2 | 3-0 | 3-3 | 2-0 | 1-2 | 0-7 | 2-0 | 4-2 | 1-2 | 1-0 |
| Leicester Fosse FC | 1-0 | 0-0 | 2-0 | 1-0 | 2-2 | 5-0 | 3-0 | | 2-0 | 5-0 | 2-2 | 4-1 | 1-2 | 2-0 | 2-1 | 0-0 | 0-0 | |
| Lincoln City FC | 1-1 | 1-0 | 1-1 | 3-0 | 2-0 | 2-1 | 1-1 | 2-0 | | 3-2 | 2-0 | 3-0 | 0-0 | 1-0 | 0-0 | 3-1 | 1-2 | 5-0 |
| Loughborough Town FC | 0-0 | 2-3 | 1-2 | 2-1 | 0-4 | 1-2 | 0-0 | 0-2 | 0-1 | | 1-1 | 1-1 | 1-2 | 0-2 | 1-2 | 0-0 | 0-0 | 2-3 |
| Luton Town FC | 3-0 | 0-2 | 1-1 | 5-2 | 0-3 | 4-0 | 0-4 | 0-0 | 0-2 | 4-0 | | 1-1 | 1-4 | 0-1 | 1-2 | 4-0 | 0-1 | 1-2 |
| Middlesbrough FC | 3-0 | 0-3 | 1-0 | 8-1 | 0-1 | 0-0 | 1-0 | 0-1 | 1-1 | 3-0 | 0-0 | | 5-2 | 2-0 | 1-3 | 1-1 | 1-2 | 1-0 |
| New Brighton Tower FC | 6-2 | 3-1 | 2-0 | 5-0 | 2-3 | 5-0 | 2-1 | 2-2 | 3-0 | 3-0 | 5-1 | 1-1 | | 1-4 | 2-2 | 0-1 | 2-2 | 0-2 |
| Newton Heath FC | 3-0 | 1-2 | 3-0 | 4-0 | 2-1 | 2-2 | 1-0 | 3-2 | 1-0 | 4-0 | 5-0 | 2-1 | 2-1 | | 3-2 | 5-0 | 1-0 | 2-0 |
| Small Heath FC | 5-0 | 0-0 | 2-1 | 2-0 | 5-3 | 8-1 | 0-1 | 4-1 | 5-0 | 6-0 | 3-0 | 5-1 | 2-0 | 1-0 | | 3-2 | 4-1 | 3-1 |
| Walsall FC | 4-2 | 2-2 | 0-1 | 2-0 | 6-3 | 1-0 | 1-1 | 1-2 | 3-1 | 1-0 | 7-3 | 1-1 | 2-1 | 0-0 | 1-0 | | 1-1 | 2-0 |
| The Wednesday FC | 5-1 | 2-1 | 4-0 | 6-0 | 5-1 | 5-1 | 2-1 | 2-0 | 1-0 | 5-0 | 6-0 | 3-0 | 4-0 | 2-1 | 4-0 | 2-0 | | 3-1 |
| Woolwich Arsenal FC | 5-1 | 0-1 | 1-0 | 1-1 | 2-0 | 2-1 | 2-0 | 0-2 | 2-1 | 12-0 | 3-1 | 3-0 | 5-0 | 2-1 | 3-0 | 3-1 | 1-2 | |

| Division 2 | Pd | Wn | Dw | Ls | GF | GA | Pts | |
|---|---|---|---|---|---|---|---|---|
| 1. The Wednesday FC (Sheffield) | 34 | 25 | 4 | 5 | 84 | 22 | 54 | P |
| 2. Bolton Wanderers FC (Bolton) | 34 | 22 | 8 | 4 | 79 | 25 | 52 | P |
| 3. Small Heath FC (Birmingham) | 34 | 20 | 6 | 8 | 78 | 38 | 46 | |
| 4. Newton Heath FC (Manchester) | 34 | 20 | 4 | 10 | 63 | 27 | 44 | |
| 5. Leicester Fosse FC (Leicester) | 34 | 17 | 9 | 8 | 53 | 36 | 43 | |
| 6. Grimsby Town FC (Cleethorpes) | 34 | 17 | 6 | 11 | 67 | 46 | 40 | |
| 7. Chesterfield FC (Chesterfield) | 34 | 16 | 6 | 12 | 65 | 60 | 38 | |
| 8. Woolwich Arsenal FC (London) | 34 | 16 | 4 | 14 | 61 | 43 | 36 | |
| 9. Lincoln City FC (Lincoln) | 34 | 14 | 8 | 12 | 46 | 43 | 36 | |
| 10. New Brighton Tower FC (Wallasey) | 34 | 13 | 9 | 12 | 66 | 58 | 35 | |
| 11. Burslem Port Vale FC (Burslem) | 34 | 14 | 6 | 14 | 39 | 49 | 34 | |
| 12. Walsall FC (Walsall) | 34 | 12 | 8 | 14 | 50 | 55 | 32 | |
| 13. Gainsborough Trinity FC (Gainsborough) | 34 | 9 | 7 | 18 | 47 | 75 | 25 | |
| 14. Middlesbrough FC (Middlesbrough) | 34 | 8 | 8 | 18 | 39 | 69 | 24 | |
| 15. Burton Swifts FC (Burton-upon-Trent) | 34 | 9 | 6 | 19 | 43 | 84 | 24 | |
| 6. Barnsley FC (Barnsley) | 34 | 8 | 7 | 19 | 46 | 79 | 23 | |
| 17. Luton Town FC (Luton) | 34 | 5 | 8 | 21 | 40 | 75 | 18 | # |
| 18. Loughborough Town FC (Loughborough) | 34 | 1 | 6 | 27 | 18 | 100 | 8 | # |
| | 612 | 246 | 120 | 246 | 984 | 984 | 612 | |

# Loughborough Town FC (Loughborough) and Luton Town FC (Luton) were not re-elected to the league for next season and were replaced by Blackpool FC (Blackpool) and Stockport County FC (Stockport).


## F.A. CUP FINAL   (Crystal Palace, London – 21/04/1900 – 68,945)

BURY FC (BURY)                    4-0                    Southampton FC (Southampton)

*McLuckie 2, Wood, Plant*

Bury: Thompson, Darroch, Davidson, Pray, Leeming, Ross, Richards, Wood, McLuckie, Sagar, Plant.
Southampton: Robinson, Meehan, Durber, Meston, Chadwick, Petrie, Turner, Yates, Farrell, Wood, Milward.


## Semi-finals

| Nottingham Forest FC (Nottingham) | 1-1 (aet), 2-3 (aet) | Bury FC (Bury) |
|---|---|---|
| Southampton FC (Southampton) | 0-0 (aet), 3-0 | Millwall Athletic FC (London) |


## Quarter-finals

| Millwall Athletic FC (London) | 1-1 (aet), 0-0 (aet), 2-1 | Aston Villa FC (Birmingham) |
|---|---|---|
| Preston North End FC (Preston) | 0-0 (aet), 0-1 | Nottingham Forest FC (Nottingham) |
| Sheffield United FC (Sheffield) | 2-2 (aet), 0-2 | Bury FC (Bury) |
| Southampton FC (Southampton) | 2-1 | West Bromwich Albion FC (West Bromwich) |

# 1900-01

| Football League Division 1 1900-1901 Season | Aston Villa | Blackburn Rovers | Bolton Wanderers | Bury | Derby County | Everton | Liverpool | Manchester City | Newcastle United | Nottingham Forest | Notts County | Preston North End | Sheffield United | Stoke | Sunderland | Wednesday | W.B.A. | Wolves |
|---|---|---|---|---|---|---|---|---|---|---|---|---|---|---|---|---|---|---|
| Aston Villa FC | ■ | 3-3 | 3-0 | 1-0 | 2-1 | 1-2 | 0-2 | 7-1 | 2-2 | 2-1 | 1-2 | 4-0 | 0-0 | 2-0 | 2-2 | 2-1 | 0-1 | 0-0 |
| Blackburn Rovers FC | 2-2 | ■ | 2-0 | 0-2 | 1-0 | 2-1 | 3-1 | 1-0 | 0-0 | 1-3 | 0-2 | 3-1 | 1-0 | 3-2 | 0-1 | 2-2 | 1-1 | 2-0 |
| Bolton Wanderers FC | 1-0 | 1-0 | ■ | 3-2 | 0-1 | 1-0 | 1-0 | 0-0 | 3-2 | 4-2 | 0-1 | 1-1 | 0-0 | 1-0 | 0-0 | 1-1 | 3-2 | 1-0 |
| Bury FC | 3-1 | 0-1 | 3-0 | ■ | 2-1 | 3-0 | 0-0 | 4-0 | 1-0 | 0-1 | 1-0 | 2-1 | 1-1 | 3-2 | 0-0 | 2-0 | 6-1 | 0-1 |
| Derby County FC | 3-0 | 4-0 | 4-2 | 5-2 | ■ | 0-1 | 2-3 | 2-0 | 1-1 | 0-0 | 2-1 | 0-0 | 4-0 | 4-1 | 1-1 | 3-1 | 4-0 | 4-5 |
| Everton FC | 2-1 | 0-0 | 2-3 | 3-3 | 2-0 | ■ | 1-1 | 5-2 | 0-1 | 4-1 | 0-1 | 4-1 | 3-1 | 3-0 | 1-0 | 1-1 | 1-0 | 5-1 |
| Liverpool FC | 5-1 | 3-0 | 2-1 | 1-0 | 0-0 | 1-2 | ■ | 3-1 | 3-0 | 2-0 | 1-0 | 3-2 | 1-2 | 3-1 | 1-2 | 1-1 | 5-0 | 1-0 |
| Manchester City FC | 4-0 | 1-3 | 1-1 | 1-0 | 2-0 | 1-0 | 3-4 | ■ | 2-1 | 1-0 | 2-0 | 3-1 | 2-1 | 2-0 | 1-1 | 2-2 | 1-0 | 3-2 |
| Newcastle United FC | 3-0 | 1-0 | 3-0 | 0-0 | 2-1 | 1-0 | 1-1 | 2-1 | ■ | 0-0 | 2-0 | 3-5 | 3-0 | 2-1 | 0-2 | 0-0 | 1-1 | 3-1 |
| Nottingham Forest FC | 3-1 | 0-1 | 3-0 | 1-1 | 1-0 | 2-1 | 0-0 | 4-2 | 1-2 | ■ | 5-0 | 4-1 | 2-0 | 1-1 | 0-0 | 1-0 | 2-3 | 2-1 |
| Notts County FC | 2-0 | 2-1 | 3-1 | 1-0 | 2-1 | 3-2 | 3-0 | 0-0 | 3-1 | 1-0 | ■ | 6-1 | 2-4 | 2-4 | 2-2 | 2-0 | 1-0 | 4-1 |
| Preston North End FC | 0-2 | 4-1 | 1-3 | 3-1 | 3-2 | 1-2 | 2-2 | 0-4 | 0-1 | 1-1 | 0-1 | ■ | 3-1 | 4-2 | 1-1 | 3-2 | 2-3 | 1-1 |
| Sheffield United FC | 2-2 | 2-1 | 0-2 | 0-3 | 2-1 | 2-1 | 0-2 | 1-1 | 2-0 | 0-1 | 4-2 | 2-1 | ■ | 0-4 | 2-0 | 1-0 | 1-1 | 1-1 |
| Stoke FC | 0-0 | 2-0 | 2-1 | 1-2 | 0-1 | 0-2 | 1-2 | 2-1 | 2-0 | 0-3 | 1-1 | 5-0 | 0-1 | ■ | 0-0 | 2-1 | 2-0 | 3-0 |
| Sunderland AFC | 0-0 | 2-0 | 5-1 | 4-1 | 2-1 | 2-0 | 0-1 | 3-0 | 1-1 | 0-1 | 1-1 | 3-1 | 3-0 | 6-1 | ■ | 1-0 | 3-0 | 7-2 |
| The Wednesday FC | 3-2 | 1-1 | 1-0 | 1-2 | 2-1 | 3-1 | 3-2 | 4-1 | 2-2 | 4-1 | 4-1 | 0-1 | 1-0 | 4-0 | 1-0 | ■ | 2-1 | 2-0 |
| West Bromwich Albion FC | 0-1 | 1-1 | 7-2 | 1-2 | 1-1 | 1-2 | 0-1 | 3-2 | 0-1 | 1-6 | 1-0 | 0-1 | 0-2 | 2-2 | 1-0 | 1-1 | ■ | 1-2 |
| Wolverhampton Wanderers FC | 0-0 | 2-2 | 1-1 | 1-1 | 0-0 | 1-1 | 2-1 | 1-0 | 1-0 | 1-0 | 3-2 | 2-2 | 3-0 | 0-2 | 2-2 | 1-1 | 0-0 | ■ |

## Division 1

| | Division 1 | Pd | Wn | Dw | Ls | GF | GA | Pts | |
|---|---|---|---|---|---|---|---|---|---|
| 1. | LIVERPOOL FC (LIVERPOOL) | 34 | 19 | 7 | 8 | 59 | 35 | 45 | |
| 2. | Sunderland AFC (Sunderland) | 34 | 15 | 13 | 6 | 57 | 26 | 43 | |
| 3. | Notts County FC (Nottingham) | 34 | 18 | 4 | 12 | 54 | 46 | 40 | |
| 4. | Nottingham Forest FC (Nottingham) | 34 | 16 | 7 | 11 | 53 | 36 | 39 | |
| 5. | Bury FC (Bury) | 34 | 16 | 7 | 11 | 53 | 37 | 39 | |
| 6. | Newcastle United FC (Newcastle-upon-Tyne) | 34 | 14 | 10 | 10 | 42 | 37 | 38 | |
| 7. | Everton FC (Liverpool) | 34 | 16 | 5 | 13 | 55 | 42 | 37 | |
| 8. | The Wednesday FC (Sheffield) | 34 | 13 | 10 | 11 | 52 | 42 | 36 | |
| 9. | Blackburn Rovers FC (Blackburn) | 34 | 12 | 9 | 13 | 39 | 47 | 33 | |
| 10. | Bolton Wanderers FC (Bolton) | 34 | 13 | 7 | 14 | 39 | 55 | 33 | |
| 11. | Manchester City FC (Manchester) | 34 | 13 | 6 | 15 | 48 | 58 | 32 | |
| 12. | Derby County FC (Derby) | 34 | 12 | 7 | 15 | 55 | 42 | 31 | |
| 13. | Wolverhampton Wanderers FC (Wolverhampton) | 34 | 9 | 13 | 12 | 39 | 55 | 31 | |
| 14. | Sheffield United FC (Sheffield) | 34 | 12 | 7 | 15 | 35 | 52 | 31 | |
| 15. | Aston Villa FC (Birmingham) | 34 | 10 | 10 | 14 | 45 | 51 | 30 | |
| 16. | Stoke FC (Stoke-upon-Trent) | 34 | 11 | 5 | 18 | 46 | 57 | 27 | |
| 17. | Preston North End FC (Preston) | 34 | 9 | 7 | 18 | 49 | 75 | 25 | R |
| 18. | West Bromwich Albion FC (West Bromwich) | 34 | 7 | 8 | 19 | 35 | 62 | 22 | R |
| | | 612 | 235 | 142 | 235 | 855 | 855 | 612 | |

* Burton Swifts FC (Burton-upon-Trent) merged with Burton Wanderers FC (Burton-upon-Trent) as Burton United FC (Burton-upon-Trent) for next season.

## Top Goalscorers

1) Stephen BLOOMER     (Derby County FC)   23
2) Samuel RAYBOULD     (Liverpool FC)   17
3) MORRIS     (Notts County FC)   16

**Football League Division 2 — 1900-1901 Season**

| | Barnsley | Blackpool | Burnley | Burslem Port Vale | Burton Swifts | Chesterfield | Gainsborough Trinity | Glossop | Grimsby Town | Leicester Fosse | Lincoln City | Middlesbrough | New Brighton | Newton Heath | Small Heath | Stockport County | Walsall | Woolwich Arsenal |
|---|---|---|---|---|---|---|---|---|---|---|---|---|---|---|---|---|---|---|
| Barnsley FC | ■ | 0-1 | 2-1 | 1-3 | 3-2 | 4-1 | 1-3 | 2-2 | 2-3 | 1-0 | 0-0 | 3-1 | 1-1 | 6-2 | 1-2 | 2-0 | 2-1 | 3-0 |
| Blackpool FC | 1-1 | ■ | 0-1 | 2-1 | 2-0 | 1-1 | 1-1 | 0-0 | 0-1 | 1-0 | 2-0 | 3-0 | 1-2 | 1-2 | 0-0 | 3-0 | 1-0 | 1-1 |
| Burnley FC | 4-0 | 4-0 | ■ | 1-0 | 2-1 | 5-1 | 2-1 | 5-1 | 3-0 | 0-0 | 1-0 | 2-0 | 2-1 | 1-0 | 1-0 | 3-1 | 0-0 | 3-0 |
| Burslem Port Vale FC | 3-2 | 4-0 | 1-0 | ■ | 4-0 | 5-1 | 1-1 | 0-0 | 0-0 | 0-0 | 2-0 | 0-2 | 1-3 | 2-0 | 2-2 | 0-1 | 2-2 | 1-0 |
| Burton Swifts FC | 1-1 | 1-2 | 1-0 | 0-2 | ■ | 0-4 | 1-0 | 1-3 | 1-2 | 0-1 | 0-0 | 0-0 | 1-0 | 3-1 | 0-2 | 3-2 | 2-1 | 1-0 |
| Chesterfield FC | 1-2 | 2-0 | 1-3 | 1-1 | 2-0 | ■ | 2-2 | 0-1 | 3-3 | 1-0 | 2-0 | 2-3 | 0-1 | 2-1 | 1-1 | 4-2 | 1-1 | 0-1 |
| Gainsborough Trinity FC | 4-2 | 1-3 | 3-0 | 2-1 | 2-1 | 2-3 | ■ | 1-1 | 0-1 | 0-0 | 1-1 | 1-1 | 4-1 | 0-1 | 1-2 | 2-0 | 1-0 | 1-0 |
| Glossop FC | 2-1 | 6-0 | 0-1 | 1-2 | 3-0 | 1-1 | 3-1 | ■ | 0-0 | 3-1 | 2-0 | 2-0 | 0-1 | 1-0 | 2-0 | 6-0 | 2-0 | 0-1 |
| Grimsby Town FC | 1-0 | 2-0 | 2-1 | 6-1 | 5-2 | 5-2 | 0-0 | 1-0 | ■ | 4-1 | 4-0 | 2-0 | 5-2 | 2-0 | 1-1 | 5-1 | 0-0 | 1-0 |
| Leicester Fosse FC | 2-0 | 3-1 | 1-1 | 0-0 | 5-2 | 1-3 | 1-0 | 1-2 | 4-0 | ■ | 0-2 | 1-0 | 1-1 | 1-0 | 1-1 | 2-2 | 5-0 | 1-0 |
| Lincoln City FC | 3-0 | 3-0 | 2-0 | 2-2 | 2-1 | 2-0 | 6-0 | 1-1 | 0-1 | 1-0 | ■ | 1-2 | 2-0 | 2-0 | 3-1 | 4-0 | 2-0 | 3-3 |
| Middlesbrough FC | 3-0 | 3-1 | 0-0 | 4-0 | 3-1 | 2-0 | 9-2 | 2-2 | 0-0 | 2-1 | 2-0 | ■ | 2-1 | 1-2 | 0-1 | 2-0 | 2-1 | 1-1 |
| New Brighton Tower FC | 2-0 | 0-0 | 2-1 | 1-1 | 3-1 | 1-1 | 3-2 | 1-0 | 5-0 | 0-0 | 2-0 | 3-1 | ■ | 2-0 | 0-0 | 3-0 | 5-1 | 1-0 |
| Newton Heath FC | 1-0 | 4-0 | 0-1 | 4-0 | 1-1 | 1-0 | 0-0 | 3-0 | 1-0 | 2-3 | 4-1 | 4-0 | 1-0 | ■ | 0-1 | 3-1 | 1-1 | 1-0 |
| Small Heath FC | 3-1 | 10-1 | 0-1 | 2-1 | 2-0 | 0-0 | 6-0 | 1-0 | 2-1 | 0-0 | 2-0 | 2-1 | 4-0 | 1-0 | ■ | 2-0 | 2-1 | 2-1 |
| Stockport County FC | 2-1 | 0-1 | 3-2 | 1-1 | 2-0 | 3-1 | 1-2 | 1-3 | 0-1 | 3-1 | 1-0 | 0-1 | 0-5 | 1-0 | 0-0 | ■ | 4-1 | 3-1 |
| Walsall FC | 3-0 | 1-2 | 2-0 | 2-1 | 1-5 | 2-2 | 3-3 | 2-1 | 0-0 | 2-0 | 3-0 | 0-0 | 3-3 | 1-1 | 2-2 | 1-3 | ■ | 1-0 |
| Woolwich Arsenal FC | 1-2 | 3-1 | 3-1 | 3-0 | 3-1 | 1-0 | 2-1 | 2-0 | 1-1 | 2-1 | 0-0 | 1-0 | 2-1 | 2-1 | 1-0 | 2-0 | 1-1 | ■ |

## Division 2

| | | Pd | Wn | Dw | Ls | GF | GA | Pts | |
|---|---|---|---|---|---|---|---|---|---|
| 1. | Grimsby Town FC (Cleethorpes) | 34 | 20 | 9 | 5 | 60 | 33 | 49 | P |
| 2. | Small Heath FC (Birmingham) | 34 | 19 | 10 | 5 | 57 | 24 | 48 | P |
| 3. | Burnley FC (Burnley) | 34 | 20 | 4 | 10 | 53 | 29 | 44 | |
| 4. | New Brighton Tower FC (Wallasey) | 34 | 17 | 8 | 9 | 57 | 38 | 42 | # |
| 5. | Glossop FC (Glossop) | 34 | 15 | 8 | 11 | 51 | 33 | 38 | |
| 6. | Middlesbrough FC (Middlesbrough) | 34 | 15 | 7 | 12 | 50 | 40 | 37 | |
| 7. | Woolwich Arsenal FC (London) | 34 | 15 | 6 | 13 | 39 | 35 | 36 | |
| 8. | Lincoln City FC (Lincoln) | 34 | 13 | 7 | 14 | 43 | 39 | 33 | |
| 9. | Burslem Port Vale FC (Burslem) | 34 | 11 | 11 | 12 | 45 | 47 | 33 | |
| 10. | Newton Heath FC (Manchester) | 34 | 14 | 4 | 16 | 42 | 38 | 32 | |
| 11. | Leicester Fosse FC (Leicester) | 34 | 11 | 10 | 13 | 39 | 37 | 32 | |
| 12. | Blackpool FC (Blackpool) | 34 | 12 | 7 | 15 | 33 | 58 | 31 | |
| 13. | Gainsborough Trinity FC (Gainsborough) | 34 | 10 | 10 | 14 | 45 | 60 | 30 | |
| 14. | Chesterfield FC (Chesterfield) | 34 | 9 | 10 | 15 | 46 | 58 | 28 | |
| 15. | Barnsley FC (Barnsley) | 34 | 11 | 5 | 18 | 47 | 60 | 27 | |
| 16. | Walsall FC (Walsall) | 34 | 7 | 13 | 14 | 40 | 56 | 27 | # |
| 17. | Stockport County FC (Stockport) | 34 | 11 | 3 | 20 | 38 | 68 | 25 | |
| 18. | Burton Swifts FC (Burton-upon-Trent) | 34 | 8 | 4 | 22 | 34 | 66 | 20 | * |
| | | 612 | 238 | 136 | 238 | 819 | 819 | 612 | |

# New Brighton Tower FC (Wallasey) resigned from the league at the end of the season.
Walsall FC (Walsall) were not re-elected to the league for the next season.


Bristol City FC (Bristol) and Doncaster Rovers FC (Doncaster) were elected to Division 2 for next season.


## F.A. CUP FINAL   (Crystal Palace, London – 20/04/1901 – 114,815)

TOTTENHAM HOTSPUR FC (LONDON)          2-2                          Sheffield United FC (Sheffield)

*Brown 2*                              *(H.T. 1-1)*                          *Priest, Bennett*

Tottenham:  Clawley, Erentz. Tait, Morris, Hughes, Jones, Smith, Cameron, Brown, Copeland, Kirwan.
Sheffield United:  Foulke, Thickett, Boyle, Johnson, Morren, Needham, Bennett, Field, Hedley, Priest, Lipsham.


## F.A. CUP FINAL REPLAY   (Burnden Park, Bolton – 27/04/1901 – 20,470)

TOTTENHAM HOTSPUR FC (LONDON)          3-1                          Sheffield United FC (Sheffield)

*Cameron, Smith, Brown*                *(H.T. 0-1)*                          *Priest*

Tottenham:  Clawley, Erentz. Tait, Morris, Hughes, Jones, Smith, Cameron, Brown, Copeland, Kirwan.
Sheffield United:  Foulke, Thickett, Boyle, Johnson, Morren, Needham, Bennett, Field, Hedley, Priest, Lipsham.


## Semi-finals

| | | |
|---|---|---|
| Sheffield United FC (Sheffield) | 2-2,  3-0 | Aston Villa FC (Birmingham) |
| Tottenham Hotspur FC (London) | 4-0 | West Bromwich Albion FC (West Bromwich) |


## Quarter-finals

| | | |
|---|---|---|
| Middlesbrough FC (Middlesbrough) | 0-1 | West Bromwich Albion FC (West Bromwich) |
| Reading FC (Reading) | 1-1,  0-3 | Tottenham Hotspur FC (London) |
| Small Heath FC (Birmingham) | 0-0,  0-1 | Aston Villa FC (Birmingham) |
| Wolverhampton Wanderers FC (Wolverhampton) | 0-4 | Sheffield United FC (Sheffield)1901-02 |

# 1901-02

| Football League Division 1 1901-1902 Season | Aston Villa | Blackburn Rovers | Bolton Wanderers | Bury | Derby County | Everton | Grimsby Town | Liverpool | Manchester City | Newcastle United | Nottingham Forest | Notts County | Sheffield United | Small Heath | Stoke | Sunderland | Wednesday | Wolves |
|---|---|---|---|---|---|---|---|---|---|---|---|---|---|---|---|---|---|---|
| Aston Villa FC | ■ | 1-1 | 1-0 | 2-0 | 3-2 | 1-1 | 4-1 | 0-1 | 2-2 | 0-0 | 3-0 | 2-0 | 1-2 | 1-0 | 0-0 | 0-1 | 4-1 | 2-1 |
| Blackburn Rovers FC | 4-0 | ■ | 2-0 | 0-3 | 3-1 | 3-1 | 2-0 | 1-1 | 1-4 | 0-0 | 1-0 | 4-2 | 2-1 | 3-1 | 6-1 | 0-1 | 2-0 | 2-0 |
| Bolton Wanderers FC | 2-2 | 4-0 | ■ | 2-2 | 2-1 | 1-3 | 4-0 | 1-0 | 3-3 | 3-1 | 3-0 | 1-1 | 1-0 | 4-0 | 2-1 | 0-0 | 3-1 | 2-2 |
| Bury FC | 0-0 | 2-0 | 2-2 | ■ | 2-0 | 1-0 | 1-1 | 0-0 | 3-0 | 4-0 | 1-1 | 3-0 | 1-2 | 2-0 | 4-2 | 1-0 | 2-0 | 2-1 |
| Derby County FC | 1-0 | 1-1 | 1-2 | 1-0 | ■ | 3-1 | 2-0 | 1-1 | 2-0 | 1-0 | 1-1 | 2-0 | 3-1 | 0-0 | 1-0 | 1-0 | 2-2 | 3-1 |
| Everton FC | 2-3 | 0-2 | 1-0 | 1-1 | 2-0 | ■ | 0-1 | 4-0 | 3-1 | 0-0 | 1-0 | 0-1 | 2-1 | 1-0 | 1-0 | 2-0 | 5-0 | 6-1 |
| Grimsby Town FC | 4-1 | 2-1 | 4-1 | 2-0 | 1-1 | 0-2 | ■ | 1-1 | 3-2 | 3-0 | 1-0 | 1-0 | 0-1 | 1-0 | 1-2 | 3-3 | 3-1 | 3-0 |
| Liverpool FC | 1-0 | 1-0 | 1-1 | 1-0 | 0-2 | 2-2 | 2-2 | ■ | 4-0 | 0-1 | 0-2 | 0-1 | 1-0 | 3-1 | 7-0 | 0-1 | 1-2 | 4-1 |
| Manchester City FC | 1-0 | 1-1 | 1-0 | 2-0 | 0-0 | 2-0 | 3-0 | 2-3 | ■ | 2-0 | 3-1 | 1-0 | 4-0 | 1-4 | 2-2 | 0-3 | 0-3 | 3-0 |
| Newcastle United FC | 2-1 | 0-3 | 4-1 | 1-1 | 0-1 | 1-1 | 5-1 | 1-0 | 3-0 | ■ | 3-0 | 8-0 | 1-1 | 2-0 | 5-1 | 0-1 | 2-1 | 3-1 |
| Nottingham Forest FC | 1-1 | 3-0 | 4-1 | 2-1 | 3-1 | 4-0 | 0-1 | 1-1 | 3-1 | 0-2 | ■ | 1-0 | 2-1 | 1-1 | 2-0 | 2-1 | 1-1 | 2-0 |
| Notts County FC | 0-3 | 3-0 | 2-1 | 2-1 | 3-2 | 0-2 | 3-0 | 2-2 | 2-0 | 0-2 | 3-0 | ■ | 4-0 | 6-1 | 1-1 | 2-0 | 6-1 | 5-3 |
| Sheffield United FC | 6-0 | 4-1 | 2-0 | 3-1 | 3-0 | 0-0 | 2-2 | 2-1 | 5-0 | 1-0 | 2-2 | 3-0 | ■ | 1-4 | 1-1 | 0-1 | 3-0 | 0-0 |
| Small Heath FC | 0-2 | 2-0 | 2-0 | 1-0 | 5-1 | 0-1 | 6-0 | 0-0 | 1-0 | 3-1 | 1-1 | 0-0 | 5-1 | ■ | 1-1 | 2-3 | 1-1 | 1-2 |
| Stoke FC | 1-0 | 2-2 | 4-0 | 1-2 | 1-1 | 1-2 | 2-0 | 1-0 | 3-0 | 0-0 | 1-1 | 3-0 | 3-2 | 1-0 | ■ | 3-0 | 1-2 | 3-0 |
| Sunderland AFC | 1-0 | 3-2 | 2-1 | 3-0 | 1-0 | 2-4 | 3-1 | 1-1 | 1-0 | 0-0 | 4-0 | 2-1 | 3-1 | 1-1 | 2-0 | ■ | 1-2 | 2-0 |
| The Wednesday FC | 1-0 | 0-1 | 5-1 | 4-1 | 2-0 | 1-1 | 3-1 | 1-1 | 2-1 | 0-0 | 0-2 | 4-0 | 1-0 | 1-2 | 3-1 | 1-1 | ■ | 1-1 |
| Wolverhampton Wanderers FC | 0-2 | 3-1 | 1-2 | 1-0 | 0-0 | 2-1 | 2-0 | 3-1 | 0-0 | 3-0 | 2-0 | 3-1 | 1-1 | 2-1 | 4-1 | 4-2 | 1-0 | ■ |

## Division 1

| | Division 1 | Pd | Wn | Dw | Ls | GF | GA | Pts | |
|---|---|---|---|---|---|---|---|---|---|
| 1. | SUNDERLAND AFC (SUNDERLAND) | 34 | 19 | 6 | 9 | 50 | 35 | 44 | |
| 2. | Everton FC (Liverpool) | 34 | 17 | 7 | 10 | 53 | 35 | 41 | |
| 3. | Newcastle United FC (Newcastle-upon-Tyne) | 34 | 14 | 9 | 11 | 48 | 34 | 37 | |
| 4. | Blackburn Rovers FC (Blackburn) | 34 | 15 | 6 | 13 | 52 | 48 | 36 | |
| 5. | Nottingham Forest FC (Nottingham) | 34 | 13 | 9 | 12 | 43 | 43 | 35 | |
| 6. | Derby County FC (Derby) | 34 | 13 | 9 | 12 | 39 | 41 | 35 | |
| 7. | Bury FC (Bury) | 34 | 13 | 8 | 13 | 44 | 38 | 34 | |
| 8. | Aston Villa FC (Birmingham) | 34 | 13 | 8 | 13 | 42 | 40 | 34 | |
| 9. | The Wednesday FC (Sheffield) | 34 | 13 | 8 | 13 | 48 | 52 | 34 | |
| 10. | Sheffield United FC (Sheffield) | 34 | 13 | 7 | 14 | 53 | 48 | 33 | |
| 11. | Liverpool FC (Liverpool) | 34 | 10 | 12 | 12 | 42 | 38 | 32 | |
| 12. | Bolton Wanderers FC (Bolton) | 34 | 12 | 8 | 14 | 51 | 56 | 32 | |
| 13. | Notts County FC (Nottingham) | 34 | 14 | 4 | 16 | 51 | 57 | 32 | |
| 14. | Wolverhampton Wanderers FC (Wolverhampton) | 34 | 13 | 6 | 15 | 46 | 57 | 32 | |
| 15. | Grimsby Town FC (Cleethorpes) | 34 | 13 | 6 | 15 | 44 | 60 | 32 | |
| 16. | Stoke FC (Stoke-upon-Trent) | 34 | 11 | 9 | 14 | 45 | 55 | 31 | |
| 17. | Small Heath FC (Birmingham) | 34 | 11 | 8 | 15 | 47 | 45 | 30 | R |
| 18. | Manchester City FC (Manchester) | 34 | 11 | 6 | 22 | 42 | 58 | 28 | R |
| | | 612 | 238 | 136 | 238 | 840 | 840 | 612 | |

## Top Goalscorer

1) James SETTLE      (Everton FC)    18

| Football League Division 2 1901-1902 Season | Barnsley | Blackpool | Bristol City | Burnley | Burslem Port Vale | Burton United | Chesterfield | Doncaster Rovers | Gainsborough Trinity | Glossop | Leicester Fosse | Lincoln City | Middlesbrough | Newton Heath | Preston North End | Stockport County | W.B.A. | Woolwich Arsenal |
|---|---|---|---|---|---|---|---|---|---|---|---|---|---|---|---|---|---|---|
| Barnsley FC | | 2-0 | 2-2 | 2-2 | 4-0 | 3-2 | 3-2 | 3-0 | 2-0 | 1-4 | 2-3 | 2-2 | 2-7 | 3-2 | 0-4 | 3-1 | 0-2 | 2-0 |
| Blackpool FC | 2-1 | | 0-2 | 2-1 | 1-0 | 1-0 | 0-0 | 3-1 | 3-0 | 1-1 | 4-0 | 3-0 | 0-2 | 2-4 | 1-4 | 1-0 | 2-2 | 1-3 |
| Bristol City FC | 3-1 | 3-0 | | 1-0 | 4-0 | 0-2 | 5-2 | 3-0 | 4-0 | 2-0 | 2-1 | 1-1 | 1-0 | 4-0 | 2-0 | 3-0 | 1-2 | 0-3 |
| Burnley FC | 2-0 | 2-0 | 0-1 | | 4-1 | 0-0 | 0-0 | 7-0 | 6-0 | 1-1 | 1-0 | 1-0 | 2-2 | 1-0 | 0-3 | 3-0 | 0-0 | 0-0 |
| Burslem Port Vale FC | 2-1 | 0-1 | 3-0 | 1-1 | | 2-1 | 4-2 | 2-2 | 1-1 | 1-0 | 3-0 | 1-2 | 1-1 | 1-1 | 0-0 | 1-1 | 2-3 | 1-0 |
| Burton United FC | 2-1 | 1-1 | 2-2 | 5-2 | 3-0 | | 0-1 | 1-1 | 5-0 | 1-1 | 2-0 | 0-6 | 3-2 | 0-0 | 1-1 | 3-2 | 1-3 | 2-0 |
| Chesterfield FC | 1-2 | 3-1 | 1-0 | 3-0 | 4-3 | 3-1 | | 0-0 | 2-0 | 1-0 | 3-3 | 0-1 | 0-0 | 3-0 | 2-0 | 8-1 | 0-3 | 1-3 |
| Doncaster Rovers FC | 0-1 | 4-3 | 3-0 | 3-0 | 3-3 | 2-0 | 4-1 | | 3-0 | 1-2 | 2-1 | 1-1 | 0-0 | 4-0 | 4-0 | 2-0 | 2-0 | 1-0 |
| Gainsborough Trinity FC | 0-0 | 3-0 | 2-0 | 1-1 | 2-3 | 1-4 | 0-0 | 4-1 | | 2-1 | 3-3 | 2-2 | 1-4 | 1-1 | 0-1 | 1-1 | 1-1 | 2-2 |
| Glossop FC | 1-1 | 3-1 | 1-2 | 0-0 | 0-1 | 2-1 | 3-1 | 3-1 | 0-0 | | 1-1 | 1-1 | 1-0 | 0-0 | 3-1 | 2-1 | 1-2 | 0-1 |
| Leicester Fosse FC | 2-0 | 1-0 | 0-1 | 2-1 | 0-1 | 4-0 | 3-0 | 1-0 | 2-0 | 1-1 | | 3-1 | 0-2 | 3-2 | 1-0 | 1-1 | 0-3 | 2-1 |
| Lincoln City FC | 1-1 | 0-0 | 1-0 | 1-0 | 1-1 | 0-0 | 4-0 | 0-0 | 3-0 | 1-0 | 2-0 | | 2-1 | 2-0 | 2-1 | 5-0 | 1-0 | 0-0 |
| Middlesbrough FC | 2-1 | 2-1 | 2-0 | 3-0 | 3-0 | 5-0 | 7-1 | 6-0 | 3-1 | 5-0 | 5-0 | 0-0 | | 5-0 | 2-1 | 6-0 | 1-2 | 1-0 |
| Newton Heath FC | 1-0 | 0-1 | 1-0 | 2-0 | 1-0 | 3-1 | 2-0 | 6-0 | 3-0 | 1-0 | 2-0 | 0-0 | 1-2 | | 0-2 | 3-3 | 1-2 | 0-1 |
| Preston North End FC | 4-0 | 1-1 | 0-0 | 3-1 | 2-0 | 1-0 | 5-0 | 3-0 | 4-1 | 2-2 | 5-0 | 8-0 | 0-3 | 5-1 | | 4-0 | 1-2 | 2-0 |
| Stockport County FC | 2-3 | 3-1 | 1-1 | 1-2 | 4-2 | 2-0 | 3-0 | 1-2 | 2-1 | 0-0 | 2-0 | 2-1 | 1-3 | 1-0 | 0-2 | | 0-2 | 0-0 |
| West Bromwich Albion FC | 3-1 | 7-2 | 2-2 | 3-0 | 3-1 | 2-1 | 4-0 | 2-2 | 7-0 | 0-1 | 1-0 | 4-1 | 2-0 | 4-0 | 3-1 | 3-0 | | 2-1 |
| Woolwich Arsenal FC | 2-1 | 0-0 | 2-0 | 4-0 | 3-1 | 0-1 | 3-2 | 1-0 | 5-0 | 4-0 | 2-0 | 2-0 | 0-3 | 2-0 | 0-0 | 3-0 | 2-1 | |

## Division 2

| | | Pd | Wn | Dw | Ls | GF | GA | Pts | |
|---|---|---|---|---|---|---|---|---|---|
| 1. | West Bromwich Albion FC (West Bromwich) | 34 | 25 | 5 | 4 | 82 | 29 | 55 | P |
| 2. | Middlesbrough FC (Middlesbrough) | 34 | 23 | 5 | 6 | 90 | 24 | 51 | P |
| 3. | Preston North End FC (Preston) | 34 | 18 | 6 | 10 | 71 | 32 | 42 | |
| 4. | Woolwich Arsenal FC (London) | 34 | 18 | 6 | 10 | 50 | 26 | 42 | |
| 5. | Lincoln City FC (Lincoln) | 34 | 14 | 13 | 7 | 45 | 35 | 41 | |
| 6. | Bristol City FC (Bristol) | 34 | 17 | 6 | 11 | 52 | 35 | 40 | |
| 7. | Doncaster Rovers FC (Doncaster) | 34 | 13 | 8 | 13 | 49 | 58 | 34 | |
| 8. | Glossop FC (Glossop) | 34 | 10 | 12 | 12 | 36 | 40 | 32 | |
| 9. | Burnley FC (Burnley) | 34 | 10 | 10 | 14 | 41 | 45 | 30 | |
| 10. | Burton United FC (Burton-upon-Trent) | 34 | 11 | 8 | 15 | 46 | 54 | 30 | |
| 11. | Barnsley FC (Barnsley) | 34 | 12 | 6 | 16 | 51 | 63 | 30 | |
| 12. | Burslem Port Vale FC (Burslem) | 34 | 10 | 9 | 15 | 43 | 59 | 29 | |
| 13. | Blackpool FC (Blackpool) | 34 | 11 | 7 | 16 | 40 | 56 | 29 | |
| 14. | Leicester Fosse FC (Leicester) | 34 | 12 | 5 | 17 | 38 | 56 | 29 | |
| 15. | Newton Heath FC (Manchester) | 34 | 11 | 6 | 17 | 38 | 53 | 28 | * |
| 16. | Chesterfield FC (Chesterfield) | 34 | 11 | 6 | 17 | 47 | 68 | 28 | |
| 17. | Stockport County FC (Stockport) | 34 | 8 | 7 | 19 | 36 | 72 | 23 | |
| 18. | Gainsborough Trinity FC (Gainsborough) | 34 | 4 | 11 | 19 | 30 | 80 | 19 | |
| | | 612 | 238 | 136 | 238 | 885 | 885 | 612 | |

* Newton Heath FC (Manchester) were declared bankrupt and re-formed as Manchester United FC (Manchester)

## F.A. CUP FINAL  (Crystal Palace, London – 19/04/1902 – 76,914)

| SHEFFIELD UNITED FC (SHEFFIELD) | 1-1 | Southampton FC (Southampton) |
|---|---|---|
| *Common* | *(H.T. 0-0)* | *Wood* |

Sheffield: Foulke, Thickett, Boyle, Johnson, Wilkinson, Needham, Bennett, Common, Hedley, Priest, Lipsham.
Southampton: Robinson, Fry, Molyneux, Meston, Bowman, Lee, A.Turner, Wood, Brown, Chadwick, J.Turner.

## F.A. CUP FINAL REPLAY  (Crystal Palace, London – 26/04/1902 – 33,068)

| SHEFFIELD UNITED FC (SHEFFIELD) | 2-1 | Southampton FC (Southampton) |
|---|---|---|
| *Hedley, Barnes* | *(H.T. 1-0)* | *Brown* |

Sheffield: Foulke, Thickett, Boyle, Johnson, Wilkinson, Needham, Barnes, Common, Hedley, Priest, Lipsham.
Southampton: Robinson, Fry, Molyneux, Meston, Bowman, Lee, A.Turner, Wood, Brown, Chadwick, J.Turner.

## Semi-finals

| Sheffield United FC (Sheffield) | 1-1, 1-1 (aet), 1-0 | Derby County FC (Derby) |
|---|---|---|
| Southampton FC (Southampton) | 3-1 | Nottingham Forest FC (Nottingham) |

## Quarter-finals

| Bury FC (Bury) | 2-3 | Southampton FC (Southampton) |
|---|---|---|
| Derby County FC (Derby) | 0-0, 6-3 | Portsmouth FC (Portsmouth) |
| Newcastle United FC (Newcastle-upon-Tyne) | 1-1, 1-2 | Sheffield United FC (Sheffield) |
| Nottingham Forest FC (Nottingham) | 2-0 | Stoke FC (Stoke-upon-Trent) |

# 1902-03

| Football League Division 1 1902-1903 Season | Aston Villa | Blackburn Rovers | Bolton Wanderers | Bury | Derby County | Everton | Grimsby Town | Liverpool | Middlesbrough | Newcastle United | Nottingham Forest | Notts County | Sheffield United | Stoke | Sunderland | Wednesday | W.B.A. | Wolves |
|---|---|---|---|---|---|---|---|---|---|---|---|---|---|---|---|---|---|---|
| Aston Villa FC | ■ | 5-0 | 4-2 | 2-2 | 0-0 | 2-1 | 2-2 | 1-2 | 5-0 | 7-0 | 3-1 | 2-1 | 4-2 | 2-0 | 0-1 | 1-0 | 0-3 | 3-1 |
| Blackburn Rovers FC | 0-2 | ■ | 4-2 | 0-3 | 2-4 | 3-2 | 2-0 | 3-1 | 0-1 | 3-1 | 2-2 | 1-2 | 2-0 | 1-1 | 0-2 | 2-1 | 1-0 | 1-0 |
| Bolton Wanderers FC | 0-1 | 1-2 | ■ | 1-0 | 2-0 | 1-3 | 0-1 | 1-1 | 2-1 | 0-2 | 1-1 | 0-1 | 1-0 | 2-3 | 2-0 | 0-2 | 0-1 | 4-1 |
| Bury FC | 0-1 | 1-1 | 3-0 | ■ | 1-0 | 4-2 | 2-1 | 3-1 | 3-1 | 1-0 | 3-1 | 3-1 | 3-1 | 2-1 | 3-1 | 4-0 | 1-2 | 4-0 |
| Derby County FC | 2-0 | 1-0 | 5-0 | 2-0 | ■ | 0-1 | 2-2 | 2-1 | 3-2 | 0-0 | 0-1 | 4-1 | 1-0 | 2-0 | 5-2 | 1-0 | 1-0 | 3-1 |
| Everton FC | 0-1 | 0-3 | 3-1 | 3-0 | 2-1 | ■ | 4-2 | 3-1 | 3-0 | 0-1 | 1-1 | 2-0 | 1-0 | 0-1 | 0-3 | 1-1 | 3-1 | 2-1 |
| Grimsby Town FC | 0-2 | 4-1 | 1-1 | 2-1 | 4-1 | 0-0 | ■ | 3-1 | 2-2 | 1-0 | 0-1 | 1-1 | 1-2 | 2-2 | 2-4 | 0-1 | 4-0 | 1-2 |
| Liverpool FC | 2-1 | 5-2 | 5-1 | 2-0 | 3-1 | 0-0 | 9-2 | ■ | 5-0 | 3-0 | 2-1 | 0-2 | 2-4 | 1-1 | 1-1 | 4-2 | 0-2 | 4-1 |
| Middlesbrough FC | 1-2 | 4-0 | 4-3 | 1-1 | 3-1 | 1-0 | 2-0 | 0-2 | ■ | 1-0 | 2-0 | 2-1 | 0-2 | 1-1 | 0-1 | 2-1 | 1-1 | 2-0 |
| Newcastle United FC | 2-0 | 1-0 | 2-0 | 1-0 | 2-1 | 3-0 | 1-0 | 1-2 | 0-1 | ■ | 0-2 | 6-1 | 0-0 | 5-0 | 1-0 | 3-0 | 1-0 | 2-4 |
| Nottingham Forest FC | 2-0 | 2-0 | 1-2 | 3-0 | 2-3 | 2-2 | 2-1 | 1-0 | 1-0 | 3-2 | ■ | 0-0 | 2-2 | 1-3 | 5-2 | 1-4 | 3-1 | 2-0 |
| Notts County FC | 2-1 | 4-0 | 1-3 | 1-0 | 1-2 | 2-0 | 0-1 | 1-2 | 2-0 | 2-2 | 1-1 | ■ | 1-1 | 3-0 | 0-0 | 0-3 | 3-1 | 0-0 |
| Sheffield United FC | 2-4 | 2-1 | 7-1 | 1-0 | 3-2 | 0-2 | 3-0 | 2-0 | 1-3 | 2-1 | 2-0 | 3-0 | ■ | 1-3 | 1-0 | 2-3 | 1-2 | 3-0 |
| Stoke FC | 1-0 | 0-2 | 2-0 | 1-0 | 2-0 | 2-0 | 1-1 | 1-0 | 0-2 | 5-0 | 3-2 | 0-2 | 0-1 | ■ | 1-1 | 4-0 | 3-0 | 3-0 |
| Sunderland AFC | 1-0 | 2-2 | 3-1 | 3-1 | 2-0 | 2-1 | 5-1 | 2-1 | 2-1 | 0-0 | 0-1 | 2-1 | 0-0 | 0-0 | ■ | 0-1 | 0-0 | 3-0 |
| The Wednesday FC | 4-0 | 0-0 | 3-0 | 2-0 | 0-1 | 4-1 | 1-1 | 3-1 | 2-0 | 3-0 | 1-0 | 2-0 | 0-1 | 1-0 | 1-0 | ■ | 3-1 | 1-1 |
| West Bromwich Albion FC | 1-2 | 5-3 | 2-1 | 1-3 | 3-0 | 2-1 | 1-0 | 1-2 | 1-0 | 6-1 | 2-0 | 3-2 | 3-3 | 2-1 | 0-3 | 2-3 | ■ | 2-2 |
| Wolverhampton Wanderers FC | 2-1 | 2-0 | 3-1 | 3-2 | 3-0 | 1-1 | 3-0 | 0-2 | 2-0 | 3-0 | 2-1 | 2-0 | 1-3 | 1-0 | 3-3 | 2-1 | 1-2 | ■ |

## Division 1

| | | Pd | Wn | Dw | Ls | GF | GA | Pts | |
|---|---|---|---|---|---|---|---|---|---|
| 1. | THE WEDNESDAY FC (SHEFFIELD) | 34 | 19 | 4 | 11 | 54 | 36 | 42 | |
| 2. | Aston Villa FC (Birmingham) | 34 | 19 | 3 | 12 | 61 | 40 | 41 | |
| 3. | Sunderland AFC (Sunderland) | 34 | 16 | 9 | 9 | 51 | 36 | 41 | |
| 4. | Sheffield United FC (Sheffield) | 34 | 17 | 5 | 12 | 58 | 44 | 39 | |
| 5. | Liverpool FC (Liverpool) | 34 | 17 | 4 | 13 | 68 | 49 | 38 | |
| 6. | Stoke FC (Stoke-upon-Trent) | 34 | 15 | 7 | 12 | 46 | 38 | 37 | |
| 7. | West Bromwich Albion FC (West Bromwich) | 34 | 16 | 4 | 14 | 54 | 53 | 36 | |
| 8. | Bury FC (Bury) | 34 | 16 | 3 | 15 | 54 | 43 | 35 | |
| 9. | Derby County FC (Derby) | 34 | 16 | 3 | 15 | 50 | 47 | 35 | |
| 10. | Nottingham Forest FC (Nottingham) | 34 | 14 | 7 | 13 | 49 | 47 | 35 | |
| 11. | Wolverhampton Wanderers FC (Wolverhampton) | 34 | 14 | 5 | 15 | 48 | 57 | 33 | |
| 12. | Everton FC (Liverpool) | 34 | 13 | 6 | 15 | 45 | 47 | 32 | |
| 13. | Middlesbrough FC (Middlesbrough) | 34 | 14 | 4 | 16 | 41 | 50 | 32 | |
| 14. | Newcastle United FC (Newcastle-upon-Tyne) | 34 | 14 | 4 | 16 | 41 | 51 | 32 | |
| 15. | Notts County FC (Nottingham) | 34 | 12 | 7 | 15 | 41 | 49 | 31 | |
| 16. | Blackburn Rovers FC (Blackburn) | 34 | 12 | 5 | 17 | 44 | 63 | 29 | |
| 17. | Grimsby Town FC (Cleethorpes) | 34 | 8 | 9 | 17 | 43 | 62 | 25 | R |
| 18. | Bolton Wanderers FC (Bolton) | 34 | 8 | 3 | 23 | 37 | 73 | 19 | R |
| | | 612 | 260 | 92 | 260 | 885 | 885 | 612 | |

## Top Goalscorer

1) Sam RAYBOULD      (Liverpool FC)    31

| Football League Division 2 1902-1903 Season | Barnsley | Blackpool | Bristol City | Burnley | Burslem Port Vale | Burton United | Chesterfield | Doncaster Rovers | Gainsborough Trinity | Glossop | Leicester Fosse | Lincoln City | Manchester City | Manchester United | Preston North End | Small Heath | Stockport County | Woolwich Arsenal |
|---|---|---|---|---|---|---|---|---|---|---|---|---|---|---|---|---|---|---|
| Barnsley FC | | 6-0 | 2-0 | 3-0 | 1-0 | 4-0 | 2-2 | 2-0 | 2-3 | 0-1 | 1-2 | 0-0 | 0-3 | 0-0 | 3-0 | 3-0 | 2-1 | 1-1 |
| Blackpool FC | 3-3 | | 0-1 | 2-0 | 2-5 | 3-3 | 2-1 | 4-0 | 4-0 | 2-2 | 2-0 | 2-3 | 0-3 | 2-0 | 2-2 | 0-1 | 2-0 | 0-0 |
| Bristol City FC | 3-3 | 0-1 | | 3-0 | 3-0 | 3-1 | 2-1 | 4-2 | 1-0 | 1-1 | 6-1 | 0-2 | 3-2 | 3-1 | 2-1 | 1-1 | 7-1 | 1-0 |
| Burnley FC | 1-2 | 1-1 | 0-0 | | 3-3 | 4-1 | 1-1 | 1-1 | 3-2 | 2-1 | 1-3 | 1-0 | 1-1 | 0-2 | 1-1 | 2-1 | 3-2 | 0-3 |
| Burslem Port Vale FC | 2-0 | 1-1 | 2-0 | 3-1 | | 4-2 | 2-1 | 3-0 | 3-1 | 1-0 | 2-0 | 5-1 | 1-4 | 1-1 | 0-0 | 2-2 | 3-1 | 1-1 |
| Burton United FC | 1-1 | 2-0 | 0-3 | 0-0 | 0-0 | | 1-0 | 1-0 | 3-0 | 2-1 | 2-3 | 2-2 | 0-5 | 3-1 | 2-1 | 0-1 | 5-1 | 2-1 |
| Chesterfield FC | 3-0 | 1-1 | 3-0 | 2-0 | 3-0 | 1-0 | | 1-1 | 0-1 | 10-0 | 5-0 | 1-0 | 0-1 | 2-0 | 4-2 | 1-1 | 4-1 | 2-2 |
| Doncaster Rovers FC | 2-0 | 3-0 | 0-0 | 2-1 | 3-2 | 1-1 | 3-4 | | 0-0 | 4-1 | 0-0 | 2-1 | 1-2 | 2-2 | 1-2 | 1-0 | 2-0 | 0-1 |
| Gainsborough Trinity FC | 1-2 | 0-0 | 2-1 | 3-0 | 1-1 | 3-1 | 3-2 | 3-0 | | 1-1 | 5-1 | 4-0 | 0-3 | 0-1 | 1-0 | 1-0 | 0-0 | 0-1 |
| Glossop FC | 2-2 | 1-0 | 0-2 | 2-0 | 2-1 | 3-0 | 0-3 | 3-0 | 4-2 | | 1-2 | 2-0 | 0-1 | 1-3 | 1-0 | 0-1 | 3-1 | 1-2 |
| Leicester Fosse FC | 1-2 | 2-1 | 2-2 | 2-1 | 2-0 | 0-1 | 0-2 | 0-1 | 4-1 | 3-2 | | 0-0 | 1-1 | 1-1 | 1-1 | 1-3 | 0-2 | 0-2 |
| Lincoln City FC | 1-3 | 0-2 | 1-1 | 4-1 | 4-1 | 4-0 | 0-0 | 4-2 | 1-0 | 1-0 | 1-2 | | 1-0 | 1-3 | 2-3 | 0-1 | 3-1 | 2-2 |
| Manchester City FC | 3-2 | 2-0 | 2-2 | 6-0 | 7-1 | 2-0 | 4-2 | 4-1 | 9-0 | 5-2 | 3-1 | 3-1 | | 0-2 | 1-0 | 4-0 | 5-0 | 4-1 |
| Manchester United FC | 2-1 | 2-2 | 1-2 | 4-0 | 2-1 | 1-0 | 2-1 | 4-0 | 3-1 | 1-1 | 5-1 | 1-2 | 1-1 | | 0-1 | 0-1 | 0-0 | 3-0 |
| Preston North End FC | 3-0 | 3-1 | 1-0 | 5-0 | 5-1 | 1-1 | 1-1 | 5-0 | 0-0 | 0-0 | 2-0 | 0-1 | 0-2 | 3-1 | | 2-1 | 6-1 | 2-2 |
| Small Heath FC | 2-1 | 5-1 | 2-0 | 3-0 | 5-1 | 2-0 | 2-1 | 12-0 | 1-0 | 3-1 | 4-3 | 3-1 | 4-0 | 2-1 | 3-1 | | 2-0 | 2-0 |
| Stockport County FC | 4-1 | 4-0 | 0-1 | 3-0 | 0-4 | 0-2 | 2-2 | 1-0 | 1-1 | 2-3 | 2-2 | 3-1 | 0-2 | 2-1 | 1-1 | 1-2 | | 0-1 |
| Woolwich Arsenal FC | 4-0 | 2-1 | 2-1 | 5-1 | 3-0 | 3-0 | 3-0 | 3-0 | 6-1 | 0-0 | 0-0 | 2-1 | 1-0 | 0-1 | 3-1 | 6-1 | 3-1 | |

| Division 2 | Pd | Wn | Dw | Ls | GF | GA | Pts | |
|---|---|---|---|---|---|---|---|---|
| 1. Manchester City FC (Manchester) | 34 | 25 | 4 | 5 | 95 | 29 | 54 | P |
| 2. Small Heath FC (Birmingham) | 34 | 24 | 3 | 7 | 74 | 36 | 51 | P |
| 3. Woolwich Arsenal FC (London) | 34 | 20 | 8 | 6 | 66 | 30 | 48 | |
| 4. Bristol City FC (Bristol) | 34 | 17 | 8 | 9 | 59 | 38 | 42 | |
| 5. Manchester United FC (Manchester) | 34 | 15 | 8 | 11 | 53 | 38 | 38 | |
| 6. Chesterfield FC (Chesterfield) | 34 | 14 | 9 | 11 | 67 | 40 | 37 | |
| 7. Preston North End FC (Preston) | 34 | 13 | 10 | 11 | 56 | 40 | 36 | |
| 8. Barnsley FC (Barnsley) | 34 | 13 | 8 | 13 | 55 | 51 | 34 | |
| 9. Burslem Port Vale FC (Burslem) | 34 | 13 | 8 | 13 | 57 | 62 | 34 | |
| 10. Lincoln City FC (Lincoln) | 34 | 12 | 6 | 16 | 46 | 53 | 30 | |
| 11. Glossop FC (Glossop) | 34 | 11 | 7 | 16 | 43 | 58 | 29 | |
| 12. Gainsborough Trinity FC (Gainsborough) | 34 | 11 | 7 | 16 | 41 | 59 | 29 | |
| 13. Burton United FC (Burton-upon-Trent) | 34 | 11 | 7 | 16 | 39 | 59 | 29 | |
| 14. Blackpool FC (Blackpool) | 34 | 9 | 10 | 15 | 44 | 59 | 28 | |
| 15. Leicester Fosse FC (Leicester) | 34 | 10 | 8 | 16 | 41 | 65 | 28 | |
| 16. Doncaster Rovers FC (Doncaster) | 34 | 9 | 7 | 18 | 35 | 72 | 25 | # |
| 17. Stockport County FC (Stockport) | 34 | 7 | 6 | 21 | 39 | 74 | 20 | |
| 18. Burnley FC (Burnley) | 34 | 6 | 8 | 20 | 30 | 77 | 20 | |
| | 612 | 240 | 132 | 240 | 940 | 940 | 612 | |

# Doncaster Rovers FC (Doncaster) were not re-elected to the league for the next season and were replaced in Division 2 by Bradford City AFC (Bradford).


## F.A. CUP FINAL   (Crystal Palace, London – 18/04/1903 – 63,102)

BURY FC (BURY)                                    6-0                    Derby County FC (Derby)

*Ross, Sagar, Leeming 2, Wood, Plant*          *(H.T. 1-0)*

Bury:  Monteith, Lindsay, McEwen, Johnston, Thorpe, Ross, W.Richards, Wood, Sagar, Leeming, Plant.
Derby:  Fryer, Methven, Morris, Warren, Goodall, May, Warrington, York, Boag, G. Richards, Davis.


## Semi-finals

| Aston Villa FC (Birmingham) | 0-3 | Bury FC (Bury) |
|---|---|---|
| Derby County FC (Derby) | 3-0 | Millwall Athletic FC (London) |


## Quarter-finals

| Bury FC (Bury) | 1-0 | Notts County FC (Nottingham) |
|---|---|---|
| Derby County FC (Derby) | 3-0 | Stoke FC (Stoke-upon-Trent) |
| Millwall Athletic FC (London) | 1-0 | Everton FC (Liverpool) |
| Tottenham Hotspur FC (London) | 2-3 | Aston Villa FC (Birmingham) |

# 1903-04

| Football League Division 1 1903-1904 Season | Aston Villa | Blackburn Rovers | Bury | Derby County | Everton | Liverpool | Manchester City | Middlesbrough | Newcastle United | Nottingham Forest | Notts County | Sheffield United | Small Heath | Stoke | Sunderland | Wednesday | W.B.A. | Wolves |
|---|---|---|---|---|---|---|---|---|---|---|---|---|---|---|---|---|---|---|
| Aston Villa FC | ■ | 2-3 | 0-2 | 3-0 | 3-1 | 2-1 | 0-1 | 2-1 | 3-1 | 3-1 | 4-0 | 6-1 | 1-1 | 3-1 | 2-0 | 2-1 | 3-1 | 2-0 |
| Blackburn Rovers FC | 0-3 | ■ | 2-2 | 2-1 | 0-2 | 2-3 | 2-5 | 1-1 | 4-0 | 3-1 | 3-0 | 3-0 | 1-1 | 2-0 | 1-3 | 0-0 | 2-0 | 1-1 |
| Bury FC | 2-2 | 3-0 | ■ | 2-2 | 0-0 | 2-2 | 1-3 | 1-1 | 0-3 | 2-2 | 3-0 | 0-1 | 1-0 | 2-2 | 3-1 | 1-0 | 2-1 | 0-0 |
| Derby County FC | 2-2 | 3-0 | 2-2 | ■ | 0-1 | 2-0 | 2-3 | 2-2 | 1-3 | 2-6 | 0-1 | 3-5 | 4-1 | 5-0 | 7-2 | 0-2 | 4-2 | 2-1 |
| Everton FC | 1-0 | 3-1 | 2-1 | 0-1 | ■ | 5-2 | 1-0 | 2-0 | 4-1 | 0-2 | 3-1 | 2-0 | 5-1 | 0-1 | 0-1 | 2-0 | 4-0 | 2-0 |
| Liverpool FC | 1-1 | 1-2 | 3-0 | 3-1 | 2-2 | ■ | 2-2 | 1-0 | 1-0 | 0-0 | 2-1 | 3-0 | 0-2 | 0-0 | 2-1 | 1-3 | 1-3 | 1-2 |
| Manchester City FC | 1-0 | 1-0 | 3-0 | 2-1 | 1-3 | 3-2 | ■ | 1-1 | 1-3 | 0-0 | 3-0 | 0-1 | 4-0 | 2-2 | 2-1 | 1-1 | 6-3 | 4-1 |
| Middlesbrough FC | 2-1 | 0-2 | 1-0 | 0-0 | 3-0 | 1-0 | 6-0 | ■ | 1-3 | 1-1 | 1-0 | 4-1 | 3-1 | 2-0 | 2-3 | 0-1 | 2-2 | 1-2 |
| Newcastle United FC | 1-1 | 2-1 | 3-2 | 0-0 | 1-0 | 1-1 | 1-0 | 2-1 | ■ | 3-1 | 4-1 | 0-1 | 3-1 | 1-0 | 1-3 | 4-0 | 1-0 | 3-0 |
| Nottingham Forest FC | 3-7 | 0-1 | 2-2 | 5-1 | 0-4 | 2-1 | 0-3 | 1-1 | 1-0 | ■ | 0-1 | 1-1 | 0-1 | 4-2 | 3-0 | 0-1 | 2-0 | 5-0 |
| Notts County FC | 0-0 | 4-2 | 0-0 | 2-2 | 0-3 | 4-2 | 0-3 | 3-2 | 3-2 | 1-3 | ■ | 2-1 | 2-0 | 1-0 | 2-1 | 1-0 | 2-3 | 0-2 |
| Sheffield United FC | 1-2 | 2-2 | 0-0 | 3-2 | 2-1 | 2-1 | 5-3 | 3-0 | 2-2 | 2-0 | 3-1 | ■ | 1-1 | 1-1 | 1-2 | 1-1 | 4-0 | 7-2 |
| Small Heath FC | 2-2 | 2-1 | 1-0 | 1-0 | 1-1 | 1-2 | 0-3 | 2-2 | 3-0 | 3-3 | 2-0 | 1-3 | ■ | 1-0 | 2-1 | 0-0 | 0-1 | 3-0 |
| Stoke FC | 2-0 | 6-2 | 4-1 | 1-1 | 2-3 | 5-2 | 1-2 | 0-0 | 2-3 | 2-3 | 0-2 | 3-4 | 1-0 | ■ | 3-1 | 3-1 | 5-0 | 5-1 |
| Sunderland AFC | 6-1 | 2-0 | 6-0 | 0-3 | 2-0 | 2-1 | 1-1 | 3-1 | 1-1 | 3-1 | 4-1 | 2-1 | 3-1 | 3-0 | ■ | 0-1 | 1-1 | 2-1 |
| The Wednesday FC | 4-2 | 3-1 | 1-1 | 1-0 | 1-0 | 2-1 | 1-0 | 4-1 | 1-1 | 2-1 | 2-0 | 3-0 | 3-2 | 1-0 | 0-0 | ■ | 1-0 | 4-0 |
| West Bromwich Albion FC | 1-3 | 2-1 | 3-2 | 0-0 | 0-0 | 2-2 | 2-1 | 0-0 | 1-2 | 1-1 | 0-0 | 2-2 | 0-1 | 3-0 | 1-1 | 0-1 | ■ | 1-2 |
| Wolverhampton Wanderers FC | 3-2 | 1-0 | 0-0 | 2-2 | 2-2 | 4-2 | 1-6 | 2-2 | 3-2 | 3-2 | 1-1 | 1-0 | 1-0 | 0-0 | 2-1 | 2-1 | 1-0 | ■ |

## Division 1

| | | Pd | Wn | Dw | Ls | GF | GA | Pts | |
|---|---|---|---|---|---|---|---|---|---|
| 1. | THE WEDNESDAY FC (SHEFFIELD) | 34 | 20 | 7 | 7 | 48 | 28 | 47 | |
| 2. | Manchester City FC (Manchester) | 34 | 19 | 6 | 9 | 71 | 45 | 44 | |
| 3. | Everton FC (Liverpool) | 34 | 19 | 5 | 10 | 59 | 32 | 43 | |
| 4. | Newcastle United FC (Newcastle-upon-Tyne) | 34 | 18 | 6 | 10 | 58 | 45 | 42 | |
| 5. | Aston Villa FC (Birmingham) | 34 | 17 | 7 | 10 | 70 | 48 | 41 | |
| 6. | Sunderland AFC (Sunderland) | 34 | 17 | 5 | 12 | 63 | 49 | 39 | |
| 7. | Sheffield United FC (Sheffield) | 34 | 15 | 8 | 11 | 62 | 57 | 38 | |
| 8. | Wolverhampton Wanderers FC (Wolverhampton) | 34 | 14 | 8 | 12 | 44 | 66 | 36 | |
| 9. | Nottingham Forest FC (Nottingham) | 34 | 11 | 9 | 14 | 57 | 57 | 31 | |
| 10. | Middlesbrough FC (Middlesbrough) | 34 | 9 | 12 | 13 | 46 | 47 | 30 | |
| 11. | Small Heath FC (Birmingham) | 34 | 11 | 8 | 15 | 39 | 52 | 30 | |
| 12. | Bury FC (Bury) | 34 | 7 | 15 | 12 | 40 | 53 | 29 | |
| 13. | Notts County FC (Nottingham) | 34 | 12 | 5 | 17 | 37 | 61 | 29 | |
| 14. | Derby County FC (Derby) | 34 | 9 | 10 | 15 | 58 | 60 | 28 | |
| 15. | Blackburn Rovers FC (Blackburn) | 34 | 11 | 6 | 17 | 48 | 60 | 28 | |
| 16. | Stoke FC (Stoke-upon-Trent) | 34 | 10 | 7 | 17 | 54 | 57 | 27 | |
| 17. | Liverpool FC (Liverpool) | 34 | 9 | 8 | 17 | 49 | 62 | 26 | R |
| 18. | West Bromwich Albion FC (West Bromwich) | 34 | 7 | 10 | 17 | 36 | 60 | 24 | R |
| | | 612 | 235 | 142 | 235 | 939 | 939 | 612 | |

## Top Goalscorer

1) Stephen BLOOMER      (Derby County FC)    20

| Football League Division 2 1903-1904 Season | Barnsley | Blackpool | Bolton Wanderers | Bradford City | Bristol City | Burnley | Burslem Port Vale | Burton United | Chesterfield | Gainsborough Trinity | Glossop | Grimsby Town | Leicester Fosse | Lincoln City | Manchester United | Preston North End | Stockport County | Woolwich Arsenal |
|---|---|---|---|---|---|---|---|---|---|---|---|---|---|---|---|---|---|---|
| Barnsley FC | | 2-2 | 1-0 | 1-2 | 2-0 | 1-1 | 1-0 | 2-1 | 0-0 | 2-0 | 4-0 | 3-1 | 1-1 | 2-1 | 0-2 | 1-0 | 0-0 | 2-1 |
| Blackpool FC | 0-2 | | 1-4 | 0-1 | 0-1 | 0-5 | 1-0 | 4-1 | 0-0 | 2-1 | 3-2 | 3-0 | 1-2 | 2-1 | 2-1 | 0-3 | 4-1 | 2-2 |
| Bolton Wanderers FC | 5-1 | 3-0 | | 1-0 | 1-1 | 1-1 | 5-0 | 3-0 | 4-0 | 5-0 | 0-1 | 4-0 | 3-1 | 1-2 | 0-0 | 0-2 | 0-1 | 2-1 |
| Bradford City AFC | 3-1 | 0-2 | 3-3 | | 1-0 | 3-0 | 1-1 | 3-0 | 2-6 | 1-3 | 2-1 | 1-0 | 4-0 | 2-1 | 3-3 | 1-1 | 0-0 | 0-3 |
| Bristol City FC | 2-0 | 5-0 | 2-0 | 1-1 | | 6-0 | 2-1 | 4-0 | 3-2 | 2-1 | 5-0 | 4-0 | 4-0 | 3-1 | 1-1 | 3-1 | 6-0 | 0-4 |
| Burnley FC | 2-2 | 1-4 | 0-0 | 3-2 | 2-3 | | 1-0 | 2-1 | 2-1 | 2-0 | 2-4 | 2-0 | 2-1 | 3-1 | 2-0 | 2-1 | 2-0 | 1-0 |
| Burslem Port Vale FC | 3-0 | 5-0 | 2-3 | 5-2 | 3-1 | 2-2 | | 3-1 | 3-0 | 3-0 | 1-1 | 1-2 | 6-2 | 2-2 | 1-0 | 0-1 | 2-0 | 2-3 |
| Burton United FC | 1-1 | 1-1 | 2-1 | 0-2 | 2-3 | 1-2 | 0-0 | | 4-0 | 2-1 | 2-0 | 1-0 | 0-0 | 5-2 | 2-2 | 0-0 | 7-0 | 3-1 |
| Chesterfield FC | 1-0 | 2-1 | 1-1 | 1-1 | 1-0 | 0-0 | 1-1 | 2-1 | | 6-1 | 0-0 | 0-1 | 2-0 | 0-1 | 0-2 | 0-1 | 4-1 | 1-0 |
| Gainsborough Trinity FC | 4-2 | 3-1 | 3-1 | 3-0 | 3-1 | 1-2 | 3-0 | 1-2 | 1-0 | | 0-1 | 4-2 | 4-0 | 0-0 | 0-1 | 2-0 | 2-2 | 0-2 |
| Glossop FC | 7-0 | 0-1 | 3-3 | 2-0 | 1-1 | 6-2 | 4-1 | 0-1 | 0-2 | 0-2 | | 1-1 | 5-0 | 5-0 | 0-5 | 2-2 | 5-1 | 1-3 |
| Grimsby Town FC | 5-1 | 4-0 | 0-0 | 2-0 | 2-0 | 0-0 | 3-1 | 4-0 | 1-0 | 3-1 | 2-0 | | 4-3 | 1-1 | 3-1 | 1-1 | 2-1 | 2-2 |
| Leicester Fosse FC | 2-0 | 5-1 | 2-2 | 1-2 | 1-0 | 0-0 | 1-1 | 1-3 | 0-0 | 2-2 | 4-2 | 1-1 | | 2-2 | 0-1 | 1-4 | 3-0 | 0-0 |
| Lincoln City FC | 0-0 | 0-0 | 1-0 | 1-0 | 2-6 | 3-1 | 3-2 | 1-0 | 0-2 | 0-1 | 3-1 | 2-1 | 6-1 | | 0-0 | 0-0 | 3-1 | 0-2 |
| Manchester United FC | 4-0 | 3-1 | 0-0 | 3-1 | 2-2 | 3-1 | 2-0 | 2-0 | 3-1 | 4-2 | 3-1 | 2-0 | 5-2 | 2-0 | | 0-2 | 3-1 | 1-0 |
| Preston North End FC | 1-1 | 1-0 | 3-1 | 4-0 | 3-0 | 2-0 | 3-1 | 4-0 | 2-1 | 2-0 | 3-0 | 2-0 | 4-3 | 2-1 | 1-1 | | 1-1 | 0-0 |
| Stockport County FC | 2-2 | 2-1 | 3-2 | 2-0 | 1-1 | 2-2 | 1-1 | 1-1 | 2-0 | 1-4 | 3-0 | 1-1 | 2-0 | 4-0 | 0-3 | 1-5 | | 0-0 |
| Woolwich Arsenal FC | 3-0 | 3-0 | 3-0 | 4-1 | 2-0 | 4-0 | 0-0 | 8-0 | 6-0 | 6-0 | 2-1 | 5-1 | 8-0 | 4-0 | 4-0 | 0-0 | 5-2 | |

| | Division 2 | Pd | Wn | Dw | Ls | GF | GA | Pts | |
|---|---|---|---|---|---|---|---|---|---|
| 1. | Preston North End FC (Preston) | 34 | 20 | 10 | 4 | 62 | 24 | 50 | P |
| 2. | Woolwich Arsenal FC (London) | 34 | 21 | 7 | 6 | 91 | 22 | 49 | P |
| 3. | Manchester United FC (Manchester) | 34 | 20 | 8 | 6 | 65 | 33 | 48 | |
| 4. | Bristol City FC (Bristol) | 34 | 18 | 6 | 10 | 73 | 41 | 42 | |
| 5. | Burnley FC (Burnley) | 34 | 15 | 9 | 10 | 50 | 55 | 39 | |
| 6. | Grimsby Town FC (Cleethorpes) | 34 | 14 | 8 | 12 | 50 | 49 | 36 | |
| 7. | Bolton Wanderers FC (Bolton) | 34 | 12 | 10 | 12 | 59 | 41 | 34 | |
| 8. | Barnsley FC (Barnsley) | 34 | 11 | 10 | 13 | 38 | 57 | 32 | |
| 9. | Gainsborough Trinity FC (Gainsborough) | 34 | 14 | 3 | 17 | 53 | 60 | 31 | |
| 10. | Bradford City AFC (Bradford) | 34 | 12 | 7 | 15 | 45 | 59 | 31 | |
| 11. | Chesterfield FC (Chesterfield) | 34 | 11 | 8 | 15 | 37 | 45 | 30 | |
| 12. | Lincoln City FC (Lincoln) | 34 | 11 | 8 | 15 | 41 | 58 | 30 | |
| 13. | Burslem Port Vale FC (Burslem) | 34 | 10 | 9 | 15 | 54 | 52 | 29 | |
| 14. | Burton United FC (Burton-upon-Trent) | 34 | 11 | 7 | 16 | 45 | 61 | 29 | |
| 15. | Blackpool FC (Blackpool) | 34 | 11 | 5 | 18 | 40 | 67 | 27 | |
| 16. | Stockport County FC (Stockport) | 34 | 8 | 11 | 15 | 40 | 72 | 27 | # |
| 17. | Glossop FC (Glossop) | 34 | 10 | 6 | 18 | 57 | 64 | 26 | |
| 18. | Leicester Fosse FC (Leicester) | 34 | 6 | 10 | 18 | 42 | 82 | 22 | |
| | | 612 | 235 | 142 | 235 | 942 | 942 | 612 | |

# Stockport County FC (Stockport) were not re-elected to the league for the next season and were replaced in Division 2 by Doncaster Rovers FC (Doncaster).

**F.A. CUP FINAL**   (Crystal Palace, London – 23/04/1904 – 61,374)

MANCHESTER CITY FC (MANCHESTER)          1-0          Bolton Wanderers FC (Bolton)

*Meredith*

Man. City: Hillman, McMahon, Burgess, Frost, Hynds, Ashworth, Meredith, Livingstone, Gillespie, Turnbull, Booth.

Bolton: Davies, Brown, Struthers, Clifford, Greenhaigh, Freebairn, Stokes, Marsh, Yenson, White, Taylor.

## Semi-finals

| | | |
|---|---|---|
| Bolton Wanderers FC (Bolton) | 1-0 | Derby County FC (Derby) |
| Manchester City FC (Manchester) | 3-0 | The Wednesday FC (Sheffield) |

## Quarter-finals

| | | |
|---|---|---|
| Derby County FC (Derby) | 2-1 | Blackburn Rovers FC (Blackburn) |
| Manchester City FC (Manchester) | 0-0, 3-1 | Middlesbrough FC (Middlesbrough) |
| Sheffield United FC (Sheffield) | 0-2 | Bolton Wanderers FC (Bolton) |
| Tottenham Hotspur FC (London) | 1-1, 0-2 | The Wednesday FC (Sheffield) |

# 1904-05

| Football League Division 1 1904-1905 Season | Aston Villa | Blackburn Rovers | Bury | Derby County | Everton | Manchester City | Middlesbrough | Newcastle United | Nottingham Forest | Notts County | Preston North End | Sheffield United | Small Heath | Stoke | Sunderland | Wednesday | Wolves | Woolwich Arsenal |
|---|---|---|---|---|---|---|---|---|---|---|---|---|---|---|---|---|---|---|
| Aston Villa FC | ■ | 3-0 | 2-0 | 0-2 | 1-0 | 3-2 | 0-0 | 0-1 | 2-0 | 4-2 | 1-2 | 3-0 | 2-1 | 3-0 | 2-2 | 0-2 | 3-0 | 3-1 |
| Blackburn Rovers FC | 4-0 | ■ | 0-2 | 3-1 | 1-0 | 3-1 | 0-2 | 2-0 | 0-0 | 1-0 | 1-1 | 2-4 | 1-4 | 4-0 | 2-1 | 0-1 | 3-0 | 1-1 |
| Bury FC | 2-3 | 0-2 | ■ | 2-0 | 1-2 | 2-4 | 1-0 | 2-4 | 5-1 | 2-0 | 0-1 | 7-1 | 1-1 | 3-1 | 1-0 | 1-4 | 3-1 | 1-1 |
| Derby County FC | 0-2 | 1-1 | 3-2 | ■ | 1-2 | 0-1 | 4-2 | 1-1 | 3-2 | 1-1 | 3-1 | 2-3 | 3-0 | 3-0 | 1-0 | 1-0 | 2-1 | 0-0 |
| Everton FC | 3-2 | 1-0 | 2-0 | 0-0 | ■ | 0-0 | 1-0 | 2-1 | 5-1 | 5-1 | 1-0 | 2-0 | 2-1 | 4-1 | 0-1 | 5-2 | 2-1 | 1-0 |
| Manchester City FC | 2-1 | 2-1 | 3-2 | 6-0 | 2-0 | ■ | 3-2 | 3-2 | 1-1 | 2-1 | 6-1 | 1-1 | 2-1 | 1-0 | 5-2 | 1-1 | 5-1 | 1-0 |
| Middlesbrough FC | 3-1 | 2-1 | 2-2 | 2-0 | 1-0 | 0-1 | ■ | 0-3 | 0-0 | 2-5 | 1-1 | 0-1 | 0-1 | 2-1 | 1-3 | 1-3 | 3-1 | 1-0 |
| Newcastle United FC | 2-0 | 1-0 | 3-1 | 2-0 | 3-2 | 2-0 | 3-0 | ■ | 5-1 | 1-0 | 1-0 | 1-1 | 0-1 | 4-1 | 1-3 | 6-2 | 3-0 | 3-0 |
| Nottingham Forest FC | 1-1 | 5-2 | 5-1 | 0-1 | 0-2 | 2-1 | 1-1 | 1-3 | ■ | 2-1 | 0-1 | 1-2 | 0-2 | 0-1 | 2-3 | 2-1 | 2-2 | 0-3 |
| Notts County FC | 1-2 | 2-1 | 0-1 | 0-0 | 1-2 | 1-1 | 0-0 | 0-3 | 1-2 | ■ | 1-3 | 1-5 | 0-0 | 0-0 | 2-2 | 2-2 | 3-4 | 1-5 |
| Preston North End FC | 2-3 | 0-0 | 0-0 | 2-0 | 1-1 | 0-1 | 2-0 | 1-0 | 0-1 | 3-1 | ■ | 4-0 | 2-2 | 2-1 | 3-1 | 1-0 | 2-2 | 3-0 |
| Sheffield United FC | 0-3 | 3-1 | 4-0 | 3-1 | 1-0 | 0-3 | 0-1 | 1-3 | 4-0 | 2-1 | 1-0 | ■ | 2-1 | 5-2 | 1-0 | 4-2 | 4-2 | 4-0 |
| Small Heath FC | 0-3 | 2-0 | 5-0 | 2-0 | 1-2 | 3-1 | 2-1 | 2-1 | 1-2 | 1-2 | 2-0 | 2-0 | ■ | 0-1 | 1-1 | 2-1 | 4-1 | 2-1 |
| Stoke FC | 1-4 | 4-0 | 2-0 | 1-2 | 2-2 | 1-0 | 3-1 | 1-0 | 0-0 | 0-2 | 1-1 | 2-1 | 1-0 | ■ | 1-3 | 2-1 | 2-1 | 2-0 |
| Sunderland AFC | 2-3 | 2-1 | 2-1 | 3-0 | 2-3 | 0-0 | 1-1 | 3-1 | 1-0 | 5-0 | 3-2 | 2-1 | 1-4 | 3-1 | ■ | 3-0 | 3-0 | 1-1 |
| The Wednesday FC | 3-2 | 1-2 | 4-0 | 1-1 | 5-5 | 2-1 | 5-0 | 1-3 | 2-0 | 1-0 | 2-0 | 1-3 | 3-1 | 3-0 | 1-1 | ■ | 4-0 | 0-3 |
| Wolverhampton Wanderers FC | 1-1 | 2-0 | 2-0 | 2-0 | 0-3 | 0-3 | 5-3 | 1-3 | 3-2 | 3-1 | 0-0 | 4-2 | 0-1 | 1-3 | 1-0 | 1-0 | ■ | 4-1 |
| Woolwich Arsenal FC | 1-0 | 2-0 | 2-1 | 0-0 | 2-1 | 1-0 | 1-1 | 0-2 | 0-3 | 1-2 | 0-0 | 1-0 | 1-1 | 2-1 | 0-0 | 3-0 | 2-0 | ■ |

## Division 1

| | | Pd | Wn | Dw | Ls | GF | GA | Pts |
|---|---|---|---|---|---|---|---|---|
| 1. | NEWCASTLE UNITED FC (NEWCASTLE/TYNE) | 34 | 23 | 2 | 9 | 72 | 33 | 48 |
| 2. | Everton FC (Liverpool) | 34 | 21 | 5 | 8 | 63 | 36 | 47 |
| 3. | Manchester City FC (Manchester) | 34 | 20 | 6 | 8 | 66 | 37 | 46 |
| 4. | Aston Villa FC (Birmingham) | 34 | 19 | 4 | 11 | 63 | 43 | 42 |
| 5. | Sunderland AFC (Sunderland) | 34 | 16 | 8 | 10 | 60 | 44 | 40 |
| 6. | Sheffield United FC (Sheffield) | 34 | 19 | 2 | 13 | 64 | 56 | 40 |
| 7. | Small Heath FC (Birmingham) | 34 | 17 | 5 | 12 | 54 | 38 | 39 |
| 8. | Preston North End FC (Preston) | 34 | 13 | 10 | 11 | 42 | 37 | 36 |
| 9. | The Wednesday FC (Sheffield) | 34 | 14 | 5 | 15 | 61 | 57 | 33 |
| 10. | Woolwich Arsenal FC (London) | 34 | 12 | 9 | 13 | 36 | 40 | 33 |
| 11. | Derby County FC (Derby) | 34 | 12 | 8 | 14 | 37 | 48 | 32 |
| 12. | Stoke FC (Stoke-upon-Trent) | 34 | 13 | 4 | 17 | 40 | 58 | 30 |
| 13. | Blackburn Rovers FC (Blackburn) | 34 | 11 | 5 | 18 | 40 | 51 | 27 |
| 14. | Wolverhampton Wanderers FC (Wolverhampton) | 34 | 11 | 4 | 19 | 47 | 73 | 26 |
| 15. | Middlesbrough FC (Middlesbrough) | 34 | 9 | 8 | 17 | 36 | 56 | 26 |
| 16. | Nottingham Forest FC (Nottingham) | 34 | 9 | 7 | 18 | 40 | 61 | 25 |
| 17. | Bury FC (Bury) | 34 | 10 | 4 | 20 | 47 | 67 | 24 |
| 18. | Notts County FC (Nottingham) | 34 | 5 | 8 | 21 | 36 | 69 | 18 |
| | | 612 | 254 | 104 | 254 | 904 | 904 | 612 |

Divisions 1 & 2 were both extended to 20 clubs for the next season. As a result of this, no clubs were relegated from Division 1 for this season.

## Top Goalscorer

1)   A. BROWN                                    (Sheffield United FC)      22

| Football League Division 2 1904-1905 Season | Barnsley | Blackpool | Bolton Wanderers | Bradford City | Bristol City | Burnley | Burslem Port Vale | Burton United | Chesterfield | Doncaster Rovers | Gainsborough Trinity | Glossop | Grimsby Town | Leicester Fosse | Lincoln City | Liverpool | Manchester United | W.B.A. |
|---|---|---|---|---|---|---|---|---|---|---|---|---|---|---|---|---|---|---|
| Barnsley FC | ■ | 2-1 | 2-1 | 1-0 | 1-0 | 1-2 | 3-0 | 7-0 | 1-0 | 2-1 | 2-1 | 0-0 | 2-2 | 2-1 | 2-1 | 0-2 | 0-0 | 1-1 |
| Blackpool FC | 6-0 | ■ | 0-2 | 2-0 | 2-4 | 2-0 | 3-0 | 1-0 | 1-1 | 1-0 | 2-2 | 4-1 | 1-1 | 0-0 | 1-0 | 0-3 | 0-1 | 0-0 |
| Bolton Wanderers FC | 2-1 | 3-0 | ■ | 2-0 | 3-1 | 4-0 | 3-1 | 7-1 | 4-3 | 2-0 | 5-1 | 4-0 | 4-1 | 0-1 | 4-1 | 2-0 | 2-4 | 2-1 |
| Bradford City AFC | 1-2 | 3-1 | 2-1 | ■ | 2-3 | 4-1 | 2-1 | 3-1 | 0-1 | 4-1 | 3-1 | 1-1 | 0-0 | 0-0 | 0-0 | 2-4 | 1-1 | 3-1 |
| Bristol City FC | 3-0 | 2-0 | 3-4 | 1-0 | ■ | 0-0 | 4-2 | 5-0 | 2-1 | 4-1 | 1-1 | 2-0 | 5-0 | 3-0 | 2-0 | 0-1 | 1-1 | 2-1 |
| Burnley FC | 3-0 | 0-1 | 0-1 | 2-1 | 2-3 | ■ | 5-0 | 1-1 | 2-0 | 4-3 | 1-3 | 3-1 | 1-0 | 2-0 | 2-1 | 0-2 | 2-0 | 1-4 |
| Burslem Port Vale FC | 0-2 | 2-2 | 1-2 | 1-1 | 3-2 | 3-1 | ■ | 4-2 | 0-0 | 2-0 | 3-2 | 0-1 | 2-0 | 1-3 | 0-1 | 1-2 | 2-2 | 3-2 |
| Burton United FC | 1-2 | 0-0 | 0-1 | 1-0 | 2-0 | 3-1 | 2-3 | ■ | 0-3 | 1-0 | 1-3 | 2-2 | 1-0 | 0-3 | 2-1 | 2-1 | 2-3 | 0-6 |
| Chesterfield FC | 2-0 | 2-0 | 1-0 | 0-0 | 0-3 | 1-1 | 2-1 | 6-0 | ■ | 4-1 | 3-2 | 1-2 | 0-0 | 0-0 | 0-0 | 1-1 | 2-0 | 1-0 |
| Doncaster Rovers FC | 2-0 | 0-0 | 0-4 | 0-1 | 0-2 | 0-2 | 2-2 | 1-3 | 0-2 | ■ | 1-5 | 2-1 | 0-2 | 3-0 | 0-2 | 1-4 | 0-1 | 0-1 |
| Gainsborough Trinity FC | 4-0 | 1-1 | 0-4 | 3-2 | 4-1 | 3-1 | 1-0 | 2-0 | 1-1 | 2-0 | ■ | 0-0 | 2-1 | 2-0 | 2-0 | 1-2 | 0-0 | 4-2 |
| Glossop FC | 5-0 | 0-0 | 1-2 | 3-1 | 0-1 | 0-0 | 0-0 | 1-1 | 0-1 | 2-0 | 3-1 | ■ | 2-0 | 0-0 | 3-2 | 0-2 | 1-2 | 2-1 |
| Grimsby Town FC | 0-0 | 2-0 | 2-2 | 0-2 | 4-0 | 1-0 | 0-3 | 1-0 | 3-1 | 2-1 | 0-0 | 3-0 | ■ | 2-0 | 1-0 | 0-1 | 0-1 | 1-3 |
| Leicester Fosse FC | 2-0 | 3-1 | 2-4 | 1-2 | 2-1 | 2-2 | 3-0 | 2-0 | 1-1 | 3-2 | 1-1 | 0-2 | 5-1 | ■ | 0-1 | 0-3 | 0-3 | 3-1 |
| Lincoln City FC | 2-0 | 1-0 | 0-2 | 1-1 | 1-3 | 2-0 | 3-3 | 3-1 | 0-0 | 3-0 | 4-1 | 3-0 | 0-0 | 5-1 | ■ | 0-2 | 3-0 | 0-2 |
| Liverpool FC | 2-1 | 5-0 | 1-1 | 4-1 | 3-1 | 3-0 | 8-1 | 2-0 | 6-1 | 1-0 | 6-1 | 2-2 | 5-0 | 4-0 | 1-1 | ■ | 4-0 | 3-2 |
| Manchester United FC | 4-0 | 3-1 | 1-2 | 7-0 | 4-1 | 1-0 | 6-1 | 5-0 | 3-0 | 6-0 | 3-1 | 4-1 | 2-1 | 4-1 | 2-0 | 3-1 | ■ | 2-0 |
| West Bromwich Albion FC | 4-1 | 4-2 | 0-1 | 0-2 | 0-0 | 1-1 | 0-1 | 4-0 | 0-2 | 6-1 | 4-3 | 1-0 | 0-2 | 2-0 | 2-0 | 0-2 | 0-2 | ■ |

| Division 2 | Pd | Wn | Dw | Ls | GF | GA | Pts | |
|---|---|---|---|---|---|---|---|---|
| 1. Liverpool FC (Liverpool) | 34 | 27 | 4 | 3 | 93 | 25 | 58 | P |
| 2. Bolton Wanderers FC (Bolton) | 34 | 27 | 2 | 5 | 87 | 32 | 56 | P |
| 3. Manchester United FC (Manchester) | 34 | 24 | 5 | 5 | 81 | 30 | 53 | |
| 4. Bristol City FC (Bristol) | 34 | 19 | 4 | 11 | 66 | 45 | 42 | |
| 5. Chesterfield FC (Chesterfield) | 34 | 14 | 11 | 9 | 44 | 35 | 39 | * |
| 6. Gainsborough Trinity FC (Gainsborough) | 34 | 14 | 8 | 12 | 61 | 58 | 36 | |
| 7. Barnsley FC (Barnsley) | 34 | 14 | 5 | 15 | 38 | 56 | 33 | |
| 8. Bradford City AFC (Bradford) | 34 | 12 | 8 | 14 | 45 | 49 | 32 | |
| 9. Lincoln City FC (Lincoln) | 34 | 12 | 7 | 15 | 42 | 40 | 31 | |
| 10. West Bromwich Albion FC (West Bromwich) | 34 | 13 | 4 | 17 | 56 | 48 | 30 | |
| 11. Burnley FC (Burnley) | 34 | 12 | 6 | 16 | 43 | 52 | 30 | |
| 12. Glossop FC (Glossop) | 34 | 10 | 10 | 14 | 37 | 46 | 30 | |
| 13. Grimsby Town FC (Cleethorpes) | 34 | 11 | 8 | 15 | 33 | 46 | 30 | |
| 14. Leicester Fosse FC (Leicester) | 34 | 11 | 7 | 16 | 40 | 55 | 29 | |
| 15. Blackpool FC (Blackpool) | 34 | 9 | 10 | 15 | 36 | 48 | 28 | |
| 16. Burslem Port Vale FC (Burslem) | 34 | 10 | 7 | 17 | 47 | 72 | 27 | |
| 17. Burton United FC (Burton-upon-Trent) | 34 | 8 | 4 | 22 | 30 | 84 | 20 | |
| 18. Doncaster Rovers FC (Doncaster) | 34 | 3 | 2 | 29 | 23 | 81 | 8 | # |
| | 612 | 250 | 112 | 250 | 902 | 902 | 612 | |

* Chesterfield FC (Chesterfield) changed their club name to Chesterfield Town FC (Chesterfield) for the next season.

# Doncaster Rovers FC (Doncaster) were not re-elected to the league for the next season.

Chelsea FC (London), Clapton Orient FC (London), Hull City AFC (Kingston-upon-Hull), Leeds City AFC (Leeds) and Stockport County FC (Stockport) were elected to Division 2 which was extended to 20 clubs for the next season.

## F.A. CUP FINAL  (Crystal Palace, London – 15/04/1905 – 101,117)

ASTON VILLA FC (BIRMINGHAM)          2-0     Newcastle United FC (Newcastle-upon-Tyne)

*Hampton 2*

Aston Villa: George, Spencer, Miles, Pearson, Leake, Windmill, Brown, Garratty, Hampton, Bache, Hall.

Newcastle: Lawrence, McCombie, Carr, Gardner, Aitken, McWilliam, Rutherford, Howie, Appleyard, Veitch, Gosnell.

## Semi-finals

| | | |
|---|---|---|
| Everton FC (Liverpool) | 1-1, 1-2 | Aston Villa FC (Birmingham) |
| Newcastle United FC (Newcastle-upon-Tyne) | 1-0 | The Wednesday FC (Sheffield) |

## Quarter-finals

| | | |
|---|---|---|
| Aston Villa FC (Birmingham) | 5-0 | Fulham FC (London) |
| Bolton Wanderers FC (Bolton) | 0-2 | Newcastle United FC (Newcastle-upon-Tyne) |
| Everton FC (Liverpool) | 4-0 | Southampton FC (Southampton) |
| Preston North End FC (Preston) | 1-1, 0-3 | The Wednesday FC (Sheffield) |

# 1905-06

| Football League Division 1 1905-1906 Season | Aston Villa | Birmingham | Blackburn Rvs. | Bolton Wands. | Bury | Derby County | Everton | Liverpool | Manchester City | Middlesbrough | Newcastle Utd. | Nottingham For. | Notts County | Preston N.E. | Sheffield United | Stoke | Sunderland | Wednesday | Wolves | Wool. Arsenal |
|---|---|---|---|---|---|---|---|---|---|---|---|---|---|---|---|---|---|---|---|---|
| Aston Villa FC | | 1-3 | 0-1 | 1-1 | 3-3 | 6-0 | 4-0 | 5-0 | 2-1 | 4-1 | 0-3 | 3-1 | 2-1 | 0-1 | 4-1 | 3-0 | 2-1 | 3-0 | 6-0 | 2-1 |
| Birmingham FC | 2-0 | | 3-0 | 2-5 | 0-3 | 3-1 | 1-0 | 1-0 | 3-2 | 7-0 | 0-1 | 5-0 | 4-2 | 1-1 | 2-0 | 2-0 | 3-0 | 5-1 | 3-3 | 2-1 |
| Blackburn Rovers FC | 1-1 | 5-1 | | 4-1 | 3-0 | 3-0 | 1-2 | 0-0 | 1-1 | 1-1 | 1-0 | 1-1 | 1-3 | 1-2 | 2-1 | 3-0 | 0-3 | 1-0 | 3-1 | 2-0 |
| Bolton Wanderers FC | 4-1 | 0-1 | 1-0 | | 4-0 | 5-0 | 3-2 | 3-2 | 1-3 | 2-1 | 1-1 | 6-0 | 2-0 | 1-2 | 1-2 | 1-2 | 6-2 | 1-0 | 3-2 | 6-1 |
| Bury FC | 0-1 | 1-0 | 5-0 | 2-1 | | 0-2 | 3-2 | 0-0 | 2-4 | 1-1 | 1-4 | 2-1 | 0-0 | 1-1 | 2-5 | 3-0 | 3-1 | 2-2 | 0-1 | 2-0 |
| Derby County FC | 1-0 | 0-0 | 1-2 | 0-1 | 3-1 | | 0-0 | 0-3 | 1-2 | 1-1 | 2-1 | 2-2 | 1-1 | 3-0 | 1-0 | 1-0 | 1-0 | 2-1 | 2-0 | 5-1 |
| Everton FC | 4-2 | 1-2 | 3-2 | 3-1 | 1-2 | 2-1 | | 4-2 | 0-3 | 4-1 | 1-2 | 4-1 | 6-2 | 1-0 | 3-2 | 0-3 | 3-1 | 2-0 | 2-2 | 0-1 |
| Liverpool FC | 3-0 | 2-0 | 1-3 | 2-2 | 3-1 | 4-1 | 1-1 | | 0-1 | 6-1 | 3-0 | 4-1 | 2-0 | 1-1 | 3-1 | 23-1 | 2-0 | 2-1 | 4-0 | 3-0 |
| Manchester City FC | 1-4 | 4-1 | 1-1 | 3-1 | 5-2 | 1-2 | 1-0 | 0-1 | | 4-0 | 1-4 | 5-0 | 5-1 | 0-0 | 1-2 | 2-0 | 5-1 | 2-1 | 4-0 | 1-2 |
| Middlesbrough FC | 1-2 | 1-0 | 1-1 | 4-4 | 5-1 | 0-1 | 0-0 | 1-5 | 6-1 | | 1-0 | 2-0 | 4-1 | 1-2 | 0-1 | 5-0 | 2-1 | 2-2 | 3-1 | 2-0 |
| Newcastle United FC | 3-1 | 2-2 | 3-0 | 2-1 | 3-1 | 0-1 | 4-2 | 2-3 | 2-2 | 4-1 | | 3-2 | 3-1 | 1-0 | 2-1 | 5-0 | 1-1 | 0-3 | 8-0 | 1-1 |
| Nottingham Forest FC | 2-2 | 2-1 | 1-2 | 4-0 | 3-2 | 0-0 | 4-3 | 1-2 | 0-1 | 2-1 | 2-1 | | 1-2 | 1-0 | 4-1 | 3-1 | 1-2 | 3-4 | 3-1 | 3-1 |
| Notts County FC | 2-1 | 0-0 | 1-1 | 3-3 | 2-2 | 1-0 | 0-0 | 3-0 | 3-0 | 1-1 | 1-0 | 1-1 | | 2-2 | 2-3 | 1-1 | 4-1 | 1-3 | 5-2 | 1-0 |
| Preston North End FC | 2-0 | 3-0 | 2-1 | 3-0 | 1-0 | 3-1 | 1-1 | 1-2 | 2-0 | 2-1 | 0-0 | 3-1 | 4-1 | | 1-1 | 2-0 | 1-1 | 0-1 | 3-2 | 2-2 |
| Sheffield United FC | 1-1 | 3-0 | 0-2 | 5-2 | 1-1 | 1-0 | 3-2 | 1-2 | 1-3 | 1-0 | 2-0 | 1-4 | 1-0 | 0-0 | | 1-1 | 4-1 | 0-2 | 4-1 | 3-1 |
| Stoke FC | 0-1 | 2-2 | 3-0 | 1-2 | 4-2 | 2-2 | 2-2 | 2-1 | 0-0 | 1-1 | 1-0 | 4-0 | 3-0 | 2-1 | 1-0 | | 1-0 | 4-0 | 4-0 | 2-1 |
| Sunderland AFC | 2-0 | 3-1 | 3-0 | 3-3 | 0-3 | 2-0 | 2-1 | 1-2 | 2-0 | 2-1 | 3-2 | 0-1 | 1-3 | 2-0 | 2-0 | 1-0 | | 2-0 | 7-2 | 2-2 |
| The Wednesday FC | 2-2 | 4-2 | 0-1 | 1-2 | 1-1 | 1-0 | 3-1 | 3-2 | 1-0 | 3-0 | 1-1 | 1-0 | 3-1 | 1-1 | 1-0 | 2-0 | 3-3 | | 5-1 | 4-2 |
| Wolverhampton Wanderers FC | 4-1 | 0-0 | 2-1 | 2-0 | 2-2 | 7-0 | 2-5 | 0-2 | 2-3 | 0-0 | 0-2 | 2-1 | 6-1 | 2-3 | 1-1 | 1-2 | 5-2 | 0-0 | | 0-2 |
| Woolwich Arsenal FC | 2-1 | 5-0 | 3-2 | 0-0 | 4-0 | 1-0 | 1-2 | 3-1 | 2-0 | 2-2 | 4-3 | 3-1 | 1-1 | 2-2 | 5-1 | 1-2 | 2-0 | 0-2 | 2-1 | |

## Division 1

| | | Pd | Wn | Dw | Ls | GF | GA | Pts | |
|---|---|---|---|---|---|---|---|---|---|
| 1. | LIVERPOOL FC (LIVERPOOL) | 38 | 23 | 5 | 10 | 79 | 46 | 51 | |
| 2. | Preston North End FC (Preston) | 38 | 17 | 13 | 8 | 54 | 39 | 47 | |
| 3. | The Wednesday FC (Sheffield) | 38 | 18 | 8 | 12 | 63 | 52 | 44 | |
| 4. | Newcastle United FC (Newcastle-upon-Tyne) | 38 | 18 | 7 | 13 | 74 | 48 | 43 | |
| 5. | Manchester City FC (Manchester) | 38 | 19 | 5 | 14 | 73 | 54 | 43 | |
| 6. | Bolton Wanderers FC (Bolton) | 38 | 17 | 7 | 14 | 81 | 67 | 41 | |
| 7. | Birmingham FC (Birmingham) | 38 | 17 | 7 | 14 | 65 | 59 | 41 | * |
| 8. | Aston Villa FC (Birmingham) | 38 | 17 | 6 | 15 | 72 | 56 | 40 | |
| 9. | Blackburn Rovers FC (Blackburn) | 38 | 16 | 8 | 14 | 54 | 52 | 40 | |
| 10. | Stoke FC (Stoke-upon-Trent) | 38 | 16 | 7 | 15 | 54 | 55 | 39 | |
| 11. | Everton FC (Liverpool) | 38 | 15 | 7 | 16 | 70 | 66 | 37 | |
| 12. | Woolwich Arsenal FC (London) | 38 | 15 | 7 | 16 | 62 | 64 | 37 | |
| 13. | Sheffield United FC (Sheffield) | 38 | 15 | 6 | 17 | 57 | 62 | 36 | |
| 14. | Sunderland AFC (Sunderland) | 38 | 15 | 5 | 18 | 61 | 70 | 35 | |
| 15. | Derby County FC (Derby) | 38 | 14 | 7 | 17 | 39 | 58 | 35 | |
| 16. | Notts County FC (Nottingham) | 38 | 11 | 12 | 15 | 55 | 71 | 34 | |
| 17. | Bury FC (Bury) | 38 | 11 | 10 | 17 | 57 | 74 | 32 | |
| 18. | Middlesbrough FC (Middlesbrough) | 38 | 10 | 11 | 17 | 56 | 71 | 31 | |
| 19. | Nottingham Forest FC (Nottingham) | 38 | 13 | 5 | 20 | 58 | 79 | 31 | R |
| 20. | Wolverhampton Wanderers FC (Wolverhampton) | 38 | 8 | 7 | 23 | 58 | 99 | 23 | R |
| | | 760 | 305 | 150 | 305 | 1242 | 1242 | 760 | |

* Birmingham FC (Birmingham) changed their club name pre-season from Small Heath FC (Birmingham).

# Top Goalscorer

1)   W. WHITE                         (Bolton Wanderers FC)    26

| Football League Division 2 1905-1906 Season | Barnsley | Blackpool | Bradford City | Bristol City | Burnley | Bursl. Port Vale | Burton United | Chelsea | Chesterfield | Clapton Orient | Gainsborough T. | Glossop | Grimsby Town | Hull City | Leeds City | Leicester Fosse | Lincoln City | Manchester Utd. | Stockport Co. | W.B.A. |
|---|---|---|---|---|---|---|---|---|---|---|---|---|---|---|---|---|---|---|---|---|
| Barnsley FC | ■ | 1-1 | 0-1 | 2-2 | 1-2 | 4-0 | 3-0 | 1-2 | 8-1 | 4-1 | 2-1 | 1-1 | 2-0 | 2-0 | 3-0 | 0-0 | 4-2 | 0-3 | 4-0 | 3-0 |
| Blackpool FC | 0-0 | ■ | 2-2 | 1-3 | 0-1 | 2-1 | 2-0 | 0-1 | 2-1 | 3-0 | 2-2 | 1-0 | 2-0 | 1-2 | 0-3 | 0-1 | 2-0 | 0-1 | 2-0 | 0-3 |
| Bradford City AFC | 0-0 | 2-1 | ■ | 1-2 | 0-1 | 2-0 | 1-0 | 1-1 | 1-0 | 3-0 | 1-2 | 2-0 | 0-1 | 0-2 | 1-0 | 3-3 | 2-2 | 1-5 | 0-1 | 0-1 |
| Bristol City FC | 3-0 | 2-1 | 1-0 | ■ | 2-0 | 4-0 | 4-0 | 2-1 | 3-1 | 1-0 | 2-0 | 2-1 | 2-0 | 2-1 | 2-0 | 1-2 | 1-0 | 1-1 | 7-0 | 1-0 |
| Burnley FC | 2-1 | 4-1 | 0-0 | 2-2 | ■ | 1-3 | 1-0 | 2-0 | 1-1 | 3-0 | 1-0 | 1-0 | 0-0 | 1-3 | 4-3 | 0-2 | 2-1 | 1-3 | 0-1 | 0-2 |
| Burslem Port Vale FC | 1-2 | 1-2 | 2-1 | 0-1 | 2-2 | ■ | 4-1 | 3-2 | 4-3 | 2-1 | 1-0 | 3-3 | 2-2 | 1-3 | 2-0 | 2-0 | 3-1 | 1-0 | 0-0 | 0-1 |
| Burton United FC | 4-1 | 1-1 | 0-1 | 0-1 | 1-3 | 1-0 | ■ | 2-4 | 4-0 | 1-0 | 3-1 | 1-0 | 1-0 | 0-3 | 1-1 | 0-0 | 2-0 | 0-2 | 2-0 | 2-2 |
| Chelsea FC | 6-0 | 6-0 | 4-2 | 0-0 | 1-0 | 7-0 | 3-0 | ■ | 0-1 | 6-1 | 1-3 | 0-0 | 2-0 | 5-1 | 4-0 | 3-3 | 4-2 | 1-1 | 4-2 | 1-0 |
| Chesterfield Town FC | 2-0 | 2-0 | 1-1 | 1-2 | 3-0 | 2-0 | 1-0 | 0-2 | ■ | 1-1 | 0-0 | 3-1 | 1-4 | 1-2 | 0-2 | 3-3 | 1-2 | 1-0 | 3-1 | 0-3 |
| Clapton Orient FC | 0-0 | 0-0 | 4-2 | 0-2 | 3-0 | 1-3 | 0-1 | 0-3 | 3-3 | ■ | 1-0 | 2-0 | 1-2 | 0-1 | 0-0 | 0-2 | 3-0 | 0-1 | 1-0 | 0-2 |
| Gainsborough Trinity FC | 1-0 | 0-1 | 2-3 | 1-3 | 0-1 | 4-0 | 5-2 | 0-2 | 4-0 | 2-1 | ■ | 2-0 | 1-0 | 3-1 | 4-1 | 0-1 | 2-3 | 2-2 | 0-0 | 2-1 |
| Glossop FC | 2-2 | 4-1 | 2-3 | 1-5 | 1-1 | 3-2 | 2-0 | 2-4 | 2-0 | 5-0 | 1-0 | ■ | 2-0 | 3-1 | 1-2 | 0-0 | 2-2 | 1-2 | 1-0 | 1-3 |
| Grimsby Town FC | 2-1 | 1-1 | 1-0 | 1-1 | 2-0 | 5-0 | 1-0 | 1-1 | 2-0 | 4-1 | 2-0 | 1-1 | ■ | 1-0 | 1-1 | 1-1 | 2-2 | 0-1 | 2-0 | 3-2 |
| Hull City AFC | 4-1 | 2-2 | 5-2 | 0-3 | 1-1 | 3-2 | 1-1 | 4-3 | 3-0 | 3-1 | 2-0 | 1-2 | 0-1 | ■ | 0-0 | 0-0 | 2-1 | 0-1 | 3-0 | 4-0 |
| Leeds City AFC | 3-2 | 3-0 | 0-2 | 1-1 | 1-1 | 3-1 | 2-1 | 0-0 | 3-0 | 6-1 | 1-0 | 1-0 | 3-0 | 3-1 | ■ | 4-1 | 2-2 | 1-3 | 1-1 | 0-2 |
| Leicester Fosse FC | 1-0 | 2-0 | 2-4 | 1-2 | 2-0 | 2-1 | 1-1 | 0-1 | 1-1 | 2-1 | 4-0 | 2-1 | 2-0 | 1-2 | 0-1 | ■ | 3-1 | 2-5 | 2-0 | 0-0 |
| Lincoln City FC | 4-1 | 1-1 | 5-0 | 0-3 | 5-0 | 3-1 | 5-1 | 1-4 | 0-1 | 2-3 | 3-0 | 4-1 | 3-1 | 1-4 | 1-2 | 3-1 | ■ | 2-3 | 2-0 | 1-2 |
| Manchester United FC | 5-1 | 2-1 | 0-0 | 5-1 | 1-0 | 3-0 | 6-0 | 0-0 | 4-1 | 4-0 | 2-0 | 5-2 | 5-0 | 5-0 | 0-3 | 3-2 | 2-1 | ■ | 3-1 | 0-0 |
| Stockport County FC | 0-0 | 2-1 | 1-0 | 2-3 | 3-1 | 3-0 | 2-0 | 1-0 | 0-0 | 3-3 | 2-2 | 5-0 | 2-2 | 2-1 | 2-1 | 1-1 | 3-0 | 0-1 | ■ | 2-2 |
| West Bromwich Albion FC | 5-3 | 5-0 | 6-1 | 1-3 | 1-2 | 4-1 | 3-0 | 1-1 | 3-0 | 1-1 | 4-0 | 6-0 | 2-0 | 1-1 | 2-1 | 3-0 | 1-1 | 1-0 | 3-1 | ■ |

| | Division 2 | Pd | Wn | Dw | Ls | GF | GA | Pts | |
|---|---|---|---|---|---|---|---|---|---|
| 1. | Bristol City FC (Bristol) | 38 | 30 | 6 | 2 | 83 | 28 | 66 | P |
| 2. | Manchester United FC (Manchester) | 38 | 28 | 6 | 4 | 90 | 28 | 62 | P |
| 3. | Chelsea FC (London) | 38 | 22 | 9 | 7 | 90 | 37 | 53 | |
| 4. | West Bromwich Albion FC (West Bromwich) | 38 | 22 | 8 | 8 | 79 | 36 | 52 | |
| 5. | Hull City FC (Kingston-upon-Hull) | 38 | 19 | 6 | 13 | 67 | 54 | 44 | |
| 6. | Leeds City AFC (Leeds) | 38 | 17 | 9 | 12 | 59 | 47 | 43 | |
| 7. | Leicester Fosse FC (Leicester) | 38 | 15 | 12 | 11 | 53 | 48 | 42 | |
| 8. | Grimsby Town FC (Cleethorpes) | 38 | 15 | 10 | 13 | 46 | 46 | 40 | |
| 9. | Burnley FC (Burnley) | 38 | 15 | 8 | 15 | 42 | 53 | 38 | |
| 10. | Stockport County FC (Stockport) | 38 | 13 | 9 | 16 | 44 | 56 | 35 | |
| 11. | Bradford City AFC (Bradford) | 38 | 13 | 8 | 17 | 46 | 60 | 34 | |
| 12. | Barnsley FC (Barnsley) | 38 | 12 | 9 | 17 | 60 | 62 | 33 | |
| 13. | Lincoln City FC (Lincoln) | 38 | 12 | 6 | 20 | 69 | 72 | 30 | |
| 14. | Blackpool FC (Blackpool) | 38 | 10 | 9 | 19 | 37 | 62 | 29 | |
| 15. | Gainsborough Trinity FC (Gainsborough) | 38 | 12 | 4 | 22 | 44 | 57 | 28 | |
| 16. | Glossop FC (Glossop) | 38 | 10 | 8 | 20 | 49 | 71 | 28 | |
| 17. | Burslem Port Vale FC (Burslem) | 38 | 12 | 4 | 22 | 49 | 82 | 28 | |
| 18. | Chesterfield Town FC (Chesterfield) | 38 | 10 | 8 | 20 | 40 | 72 | 28 | |
| 19. | Burton United FC (Burton-upon-Trent) | 38 | 10 | 6 | 22 | 34 | 67 | 26 | |
| 20. | Clapton Orient FC (London) | 38 | 7 | 7 | 24 | 35 | 78 | 21 | |
| | | 760 | 304 | 152 | 304 | 1116 | 1116 | 760 | |

**F.A. CUP FINAL**   (Crystal Palace, London – 21/04/1906 – 75,609)

EVERTON FC (LIVERPOOL)      1-0      Newcastle United FC (Newcastle-upon-Tyne)

*Young*

Everton: Scott, Crelley, Balmer, Makepeace, Taylor, Abbott, Sharp, Bolton, Young, Settle, Hardman.

Newcastle: Lawrence, McCombie, Carr, Gardner, Aitken, McWilliam, Rutherford, Howie, Orr, Veitch, Gosnell.

## Semi-finals

| | | |
|---|---|---|
| Everton FC (Liverpool) | 2-0 | Liverpool FC (Liverpool) |
| Woolwich Arsenal FC (London) | 0-2 | Newcastle United FC (Newcastle-upon-Tyne) |

## Quarter-finals

| | | |
|---|---|---|
| Birmingham FC (Birmingham) | 2-2, 0-3 | Newcastle United FC (Newcastle-upon-Tyne) |
| Everton FC (Liverpool) | 4-3 | The Wednesday FC (Sheffield) |
| Liverpool FC (Liverpool) | 3-0 | Southampton FC (Southampton) |
| Manchester United FC (Manchester) | 2-3 | Woolwich Arsenal FC (London) |

# 1906-07

| Football League Division 1 1906-1907 Season | Aston Villa | Birmingham | Blackburn Rovers | Bolton Wanderers | Bristol City | Bury | Derby County | Everton | Liverpool | Manchester City | Manchester United | Middlesbrough | Newcastle United | Notts County | Preston North End | Sheffield United | Stoke | Sunderland | Wednesday | Woolwich Arsenal |
|---|---|---|---|---|---|---|---|---|---|---|---|---|---|---|---|---|---|---|---|---|
| Aston Villa FC | ■ | 4-1 | 4-2 | 0-2 | 3-2 | 3-1 | 2-0 | 2-1 | 4-0 | 4-1 | 2-0 | 2-3 | 0-0 | 0-0 | 3-0 | 5-1 | 1-0 | 2-2 | 8-1 | 2-2 |
| Birmingham FC | 3-2 | ■ | 2-0 | 4-2 | 2-2 | 3-1 | 2-1 | 1-0 | 2-1 | 4-0 | 1-1 | 0-0 | 2-4 | 2-0 | 3-0 | 0-0 | 2-1 | 2-0 | 1-1 | 5-1 |
| Blackburn Rovers FC | 2-1 | 1-0 | ■ | 2-3 | 0-1 | 4-1 | 5-1 | 2-1 | 1-1 | 4-0 | 2-4 | 4-1 | 4-0 | 0-2 | 1-1 | 1-1 | 3-1 | 2-1 | 0-2 | 2-3 |
| Bolton Wanderers FC | 1-2 | 2-3 | 5-2 | ■ | 1-2 | 1-0 | 1-0 | 1-3 | 3-0 | 1-1 | 0-1 | 1-0 | 4-2 | 0-0 | 3-0 | 6-1 | 1-1 | 1-0 | 0-0 | 3-0 |
| Bristol City FC | 2-4 | 0-0 | 3-0 | 1-2 | ■ | 2-0 | 3-0 | 2-1 | 3-1 | 2-0 | 1-2 | 3-0 | 2-1 | 1-0 | 1-0 | 3-3 | 4-0 | 1-1 | 2-0 | 1-3 |
| Bury FC | 0-3 | 1-0 | 0-0 | 2-3 | 1-1 | ■ | 1-0 | 1-2 | 1-3 | 3-1 | 1-2 | 1-1 | 3-2 | 3-0 | 2-0 | 2-1 | 2-0 | 2-3 | 0-0 | 4-1 |
| Derby County FC | 0-1 | 1-1 | 2-3 | 0-1 | 1-3 | 2-1 | ■ | 5-2 | 0-1 | 2-2 | 2-2 | 1-0 | 0-0 | 3-0 | 3-0 | 3-0 | 2-1 | 1-1 | 1-0 | 0-0 |
| Everton FC | 1-2 | 3-0 | 2-0 | 1-0 | 2-0 | 1-0 | 2-0 | ■ | 0-0 | 9-1 | 3-0 | 5-1 | 3-0 | 2-2 | 1-0 | 4-2 | 3-0 | 4-1 | 2-0 | 2-1 |
| Liverpool FC | 5-2 | 2-0 | 0-2 | 0-2 | 2-4 | 2-2 | 2-0 | 1-2 | ■ | 5-4 | 0-1 | 2-4 | 4-1 | 5-1 | 6-1 | 2-2 | 1-0 | 1-2 | 1-2 | 4-0 |
| Manchester City FC | 4-2 | 1-0 | 0-0 | 1-1 | 0-1 | 2-2 | 2-2 | 3-1 | 1-0 | ■ | 3-0 | 3-1 | 1-1 | 2-1 | 1-1 | 0-2 | 2-2 | 2-3 | 0-1 | 1-4 |
| Manchester United FC | 1-0 | 2-1 | 1-1 | 1-2 | 0-0 | 2-4 | 1-1 | 3-0 | 0-0 | 1-1 | ■ | 3-1 | 1-3 | 0-0 | 3-0 | 2-0 | 4-1 | 2-0 | 5-0 | 1-0 |
| Middlesbrough FC | 1-0 | 1-0 | 0-1 | 0-0 | 1-0 | 3-1 | 4-1 | 2-2 | 0-1 | 2-3 | 2-0 | ■ | 0-3 | 2-0 | 2-1 | 0-1 | 5-0 | 2-1 | 1-3 | 5-3 |
| Newcastle United FC | 3-2 | 2-0 | 3-1 | 4-0 | 3-0 | 3-2 | 2-0 | 1-0 | 2-0 | 2-0 | 5-0 | 4-0 | ■ | 4-3 | 2-1 | 0-0 | 1-0 | 4-2 | 5-1 | 1-0 |
| Notts County FC | 1-1 | 2-2 | 1-2 | 0-0 | 2-3 | 1-2 | 4-0 | 0-1 | 2-0 | 0-0 | 3-0 | 2-2 | 1-0 | ■ | 0-0 | 4-0 | 2-2 | 0-0 | 2-2 | 4-1 |
| Preston North End FC | 2-0 | 2-0 | 1-0 | 3-1 | 3-1 | 3-2 | 1-0 | 1-1 | 3-1 | 1-3 | 2-0 | 4-2 | 2-2 | 0-0 | ■ | 2-1 | 2-2 | 2-0 | 1-0 | 0-3 |
| Sheffield United FC | 0-0 | 2-0 | 3-0 | 2-1 | 1-1 | 3-0 | 2-0 | 4-1 | 1-0 | 1-4 | 0-2 | 1-1 | 0-0 | 2-1 | 3-1 | ■ | 2-0 | 3-2 | 2-1 | 4-2 |
| Stoke FC | 0-2 | 3-0 | 1-1 | 3-0 | 0-3 | 3-1 | 2-1 | 2-0 | 1-1 | 3-0 | 1-2 | 0-2 | 1-2 | 1-1 | 0-2 | 1-1 | ■ | 2-2 | 1-1 | 2-0 |
| Sunderland AFC | 2-1 | 4-1 | 1-0 | 1-2 | 3-3 | 3-5 | 0-2 | 1-0 | 5-5 | 1-1 | 4-1 | 4-2 | 2-0 | 3-1 | 1-0 | 1-2 | 3-1 | ■ | 1-1 | 2-3 |
| The Wednesday FC | 2-1 | 0-1 | 3-1 | 2-0 | 3-0 | 1-2 | 1-1 | 1-1 | 2-3 | 3-1 | 5-2 | 0-2 | 2-2 | 1-3 | 2-1 | 2-2 | 0-1 | 2-1 | ■ | 1-1 |
| Woolwich Arsenal FC | 3-1 | 2-1 | 2-0 | 2-2 | 1-2 | 3-1 | 3-2 | 3-1 | 2-1 | 4-1 | 4-0 | 2-0 | 2-0 | 1-0 | 1-0 | 0-1 | 2-1 | 0-1 | 1-0 | ■ |

## Division 1

| | | Pd | Wn | Dw | Ls | GF | GA | Pts | |
|---|---|---|---|---|---|---|---|---|---|
| 1. | NEWCASTLE UNITED FC (NEWCASTLE/TYNE) | 38 | 22 | 7 | 9 | 74 | 46 | 51 | |
| 2. | Bristol City FC (Bristol) | 38 | 20 | 8 | 10 | 66 | 47 | 48 | |
| 3. | Everton FC (Liverpool) | 38 | 20 | 5 | 13 | 70 | 46 | 45 | |
| 4. | Sheffield United FC (Sheffield) | 38 | 17 | 11 | 10 | 57 | 55 | 45 | |
| 5. | Aston Villa FC (Birmingham) | 38 | 19 | 6 | 13 | 78 | 52 | 44 | |
| 6. | Bolton Wanderers FC (Bolton) | 38 | 18 | 8 | 12 | 59 | 47 | 44 | |
| 7. | Woolwich Arsenal FC (London) | 38 | 20 | 4 | 14 | 66 | 59 | 44 | |
| 8. | Manchester United FC (Manchester) | 38 | 17 | 8 | 13 | 53 | 56 | 42 | |
| 9. | Birmingham FC (Birmingham) | 38 | 15 | 8 | 15 | 52 | 52 | 38 | |
| 10. | Sunderland AFC (Sunderland) | 38 | 14 | 9 | 15 | 65 | 66 | 37 | |
| 11. | Middlesbrough FC (Middlesbrough) | 38 | 15 | 6 | 17 | 56 | 63 | 36 | |
| 12. | Blackburn Rovers FC (Blackburn) | 38 | 14 | 7 | 17 | 56 | 59 | 35 | |
| 13. | The Wednesday FC (Sheffield) | 38 | 12 | 11 | 15 | 49 | 60 | 35 | |
| 14. | Preston North End FC (Preston) | 38 | 14 | 7 | 17 | 44 | 57 | 35 | |
| 15. | Liverpool FC (Liverpool) | 38 | 13 | 7 | 18 | 64 | 65 | 33 | |
| 16. | Bury FC (Bury) | 38 | 13 | 6 | 19 | 58 | 68 | 32 | |
| 17. | Manchester City FC (Manchester) | 38 | 10 | 12 | 16 | 53 | 77 | 32 | |
| 18. | Notts County FC (Nottingham) | 38 | 8 | 15 | 15 | 46 | 50 | 31 | |
| 19. | Derby County FC (Derby) | 38 | 9 | 9 | 20 | 41 | 59 | 27 | R |
| 20. | Stoke FC (Stoke-upon-Trent) | 38 | 8 | 10 | 20 | 41 | 64 | 26 | R |
| | | 760 | 298 | 164 | 298 | 1148 | 1148 | 760 | |

## Top Goalscorer

1) A. YOUNG  (Everton FC)  28

| Football League Division 2 1906-1907 Season | Barnsley | Blackpool | Bradford City | Burnley | Burslem Port Vale | Burton United | Chelsea | Chesterfield | Clapton Orient | Gainsborough Trinity | Glossop | Grimsby Town | Hull City | Leeds City | Leicester Fosse | Lincoln City | Nottingham Forest | Stockport County | W.B.A. | Wolves |
|---|---|---|---|---|---|---|---|---|---|---|---|---|---|---|---|---|---|---|---|---|
| Barnsley FC | | 3-2 | 3-1 | 5-0 | 3-2 | 6-1 | 3-1 | 2-1 | 3-2 | 6-0 | 3-0 | 1-1 | 4-2 | 3-0 | 2-2 | 6-2 | 0-1 | 3-1 | 0-1 | 0-1 |
| Blackpool FC | 2-3 | | 1-0 | 2-0 | 0-1 | 1-1 | 0-0 | 0-0 | 1-3 | 1-0 | 4-1 | 4-3 | 1-1 | 1-0 | 1-0 | 2-0 | 1-2 | 0-1 | 2-1 | 1-2 |
| Bradford City AFC | 2-0 | 3-0 | | 3-1 | 3-2 | 2-3 | 6-3 | 1-0 | 5-2 | 1-1 | 2-1 | 1-0 | 1-0 | 2-2 | 3-1 | 3-0 | 1-2 | 1-0 | 4-0 | 2-3 |
| Burnley FC | 2-2 | 2-1 | 0-1 | | 6-0 | 4-0 | 1-1 | 0-0 | 3-0 | 1-0 | 1-1 | 2-0 | 4-2 | 1-2 | 5-0 | 5-1 | 2-1 | 3-0 | 0-1 | 3-0 |
| Burslem Port Vale FC | 2-2 | 3-0 | 2-3 | 4-4 | | 0-0 | 2-0 | 2-2 | 3-2 | 1-0 | 4-1 | 3-2 | 2-1 | 1-2 | 1-2 | 4-2 | 4-2 | 5-0 | 2-1 | 0-0 |
| Burton United FC | 1-1 | 0-0 | 1-0 | 0-1 | 2-0 | | 2-1 | 3-1 | 2-1 | 0-0 | 1-2 | 2-3 | 1-2 | 0-2 | 0-1 | 3-4 | 0-2 | 0-1 | 2-0 | 4-1 |
| Chelsea FC | 2-1 | 3-0 | 5-1 | 2-0 | 2-1 | 1-0 | | 7-1 | 2-1 | 4-1 | 9-2 | 3-0 | 2-0 | 1-0 | 2-0 | 0-2 | 2-0 | 2-0 | 2-0 | 4-0 |
| Chesterfield Town FC | 3-2 | 0-1 | 3-4 | 0-1 | 4-2 | 2-0 | 0-0 | | 2-1 | 7-0 | 1-3 | 1-3 | 3-1 | 1-0 | 2-1 | 1-0 | 1-1 | 0-2 | 2-2 | 3-2 |
| Clapton Orient FC | 1-0 | 0-0 | 1-1 | 2-1 | 1-1 | 1-0 | 0-1 | 1-2 | | 3-1 | 3-0 | 1-0 | 2-1 | 1-1 | 1-0 | 0-1 | 1-1 | 1-1 | 1-1 | 4-0 |
| Gainsborough Trinity FC | 1-1 | 2-0 | 4-1 | 0-2 | 2-0 | 2-0 | 1-1 | 1-0 | 3-1 | | 2-1 | 2-1 | 1-1 | 1-0 | 1-2 | 2-1 | 2-3 | 3-1 | 2-4 | 1-0 |
| Glossop FC | 2-1 | 0-0 | 1-2 | 1-0 | 4-0 | 2-2 | 0-1 | 3-1 | 3-0 | 3-1 | | 1-0 | 2-4 | 2-0 | 2-2 | 2-1 | 0-2 | 2-3 | 0-0 | 2-1 |
| Grimsby Town FC | 1-0 | 0-0 | 0-2 | 1-0 | 2-0 | 1-1 | 2-1 | 3-1 | 1-2 | 2-0 | 2-1 | | 1-3 | 4-0 | 0-1 | 4-0 | 3-1 | 3-1 | 2-1 | 2-1 |
| Hull City AFC | 2-0 | 3-0 | 0-3 | 1-1 | 4-1 | 3-0 | 0-1 | 2-0 | 2-0 | 2-4 | 5-0 | 4-2 | | 2-1 | 1-1 | 1-2 | 1-2 | 3-0 | 0-1 | 5-1 |
| Leeds City AFC | 2-1 | 1-1 | 1-1 | 0-1 | 2-0 | 3-1 | 0-1 | 1-0 | 3-2 | 4-0 | 1-4 | 4-3 | 2-2 | | 1-1 | 1-1 | 1-4 | 6-1 | 3-2 | 2-0 |
| Leicester Fosse FC | 2-1 | 5-1 | 1-0 | 2-0 | 4-1 | 3-0 | 1-1 | 2-1 | 2-1 | 3-1 | 2-2 | 2-0 | 3-0 | 2-2 | | 3-0 | 1-2 | 1-0 | 3-0 | 2-0 |
| Lincoln City FC | 1-0 | 0-1 | 0-2 | 1-2 | 4-0 | 2-0 | 0-5 | 1-0 | 3-0 | 4-0 | 2-1 | 2-1 | 0-1 | 1-1 | 2-2 | | 1-2 | 3-1 | 2-1 | 0-4 |
| Nottingham Forest FC | 0-0 | 3-0 | 3-0 | 2-0 | 2-2 | 2-0 | 3-1 | 3-1 | 4-0 | 3-1 | 2-0 | 0-3 | 2-1 | 3-0 | 2-1 | 3-1 | | 2-1 | 3-1 | 1-0 |
| Stockport County FC | 0-0 | 0-0 | 2-1 | 2-1 | 3-0 | 2-0 | 1-2 | 1-1 | 1-1 | 1-2 | 5-0 | 3-0 | 1-1 | 2-2 | 1-0 | 1-0 | 0-0 | | 0-1 | 0-0 |
| West Bromwich Albion FC | 3-1 | 3-0 | 3-0 | 3-2 | 3-0 | 5-1 | 1-2 | 5-2 | 5-0 | 5-0 | 5-1 | 6-1 | 3-0 | 5-0 | 0-1 | 2-1 | 3-1 | 1-1 | | 1-1 |
| Wolverhampton Wanderers FC | 5-1 | 1-1 | 1-1 | 3-0 | 6-2 | 3-0 | 1-2 | 2-1 | 6-1 | 1-0 | 4-0 | 5-0 | 1-1 | 3-2 | 1-0 | 3-0 | 2-0 | 1-1 | 0-3 | |

| | Division 2 | Pd | Wn | Dw | Ls | GF | GA | Pts | |
|---|---|---|---|---|---|---|---|---|---|
| 1. | Nottingham Forest FC (Nottingham) | 38 | 28 | 4 | 6 | 74 | 36 | 60 | P |
| 2. | Chelsea FC (London) | 38 | 26 | 5 | 7 | 80 | 34 | 57 | P |
| 3. | Leicester Fosse FC (Leicester) | 38 | 20 | 8 | 10 | 62 | 39 | 48 | |
| 4. | West Bromwich Albion FC (West Bromwich) | 38 | 21 | 5 | 12 | 83 | 45 | 47 | |
| 5. | Bradford City AFC (Bradford) | 38 | 21 | 5 | 12 | 70 | 53 | 47 | |
| 6. | Wolverhampton Wanderers FC (Wolverhampton) | 38 | 17 | 7 | 14 | 66 | 53 | 41 | |
| 7. | Burnley FC (Burnley) | 38 | 17 | 6 | 15 | 62 | 47 | 40 | |
| 8. | Barnsley FC (Barnsley) | 38 | 15 | 8 | 15 | 73 | 55 | 38 | |
| 9. | Hull City AFC (Kingston-upon-Hull) | 38 | 15 | 7 | 16 | 65 | 57 | 37 | |
| 10. | Leeds City AFC (Leeds) | 38 | 13 | 10 | 15 | 55 | 63 | 36 | |
| 11. | Grimsby Town FC (Cleethorpes) | 38 | 16 | 3 | 19 | 57 | 62 | 35 | |
| 12. | Stockport County FC (Stockport) | 38 | 12 | 11 | 15 | 42 | 52 | 35 | |
| 13. | Blackpool FC (Blackpool) | 38 | 11 | 11 | 16 | 33 | 51 | 33 | |
| 14. | Gainsborough Trinity FC (Gainsborough) | 38 | 14 | 5 | 19 | 45 | 72 | 33 | |
| 15. | Glossop FC (Glossop) | 38 | 13 | 6 | 19 | 53 | 79 | 32 | |
| 16. | Burslem Port Vale FC (Burslem) | 38 | 12 | 7 | 19 | 60 | 83 | 31 | # |
| 17. | Clapton Orient FC (London) | 38 | 11 | 8 | 19 | 45 | 67 | 30 | |
| 18. | Chesterfield Town FC (Chesterfield) | 38 | 11 | 7 | 20 | 50 | 66 | 29 | |
| 19. | Lincoln City FC (Lincoln) | 38 | 12 | 4 | 22 | 46 | 73 | 28 | |
| 20. | Burton United FC (Burton-upon-Trent) | 38 | 8 | 7 | 23 | 34 | 68 | 23 | # |
| | | 760 | 313 | 134 | 313 | 1155 | 1155 | 760 | |

# Burslem Port Vale FC (Burslem) resigned from the league at the end of the season.
Burton United (Burton-upon-Trent) were not re-elected to the league for next season.

Fulham FC (London) and Oldham Athletic AFC (Oldham) were elected to Division 2 for next season.

**F.A. CUP FINAL**   (Crystal Palace, London – 20/04/1907 – 84,594)

| THE WEDNESDAY FC (SHEFFIELD) | 2-1 | Everton FC (Liverpool) |
|---|---|---|
| *Stewart, Simpson* | | *Sharp* |

Wednesday: Lyall, Layton, Burton, Brittleton, Crawshaw, Bartlett, Chapman, Bradshaw, Wilson, Stewart, Simpson.

Everton: Scott, W.Balmer, R.Balmer, Makepeace, Taylor, Abbott, Sharp, Bolton, Young, Settle, Hardman.

## Semi-finals

| West Bromwich Albion FC (West Bromwich) | 1-2 | Everton FC (Liverpool) |
|---|---|---|
| Woolwich Arsenal FC (London) | 1-3 | The Wednesday FC (Sheffield) |

## Quarter-finals

| Barnsley FC (Barnsley) | 1-2 | Woolwich Arsenal FC (London) |
|---|---|---|
| Crystal Palace FC (London) | 1-1, 0-4 | Everton FC (Liverpool) |
| The Wednesday FC (Sheffield) | 1-0 | Liverpool FC (Liverpool) |
| West Bromwich Albion FC (West Bromwich) | 3-1 | Notts County FC (Nottingham) |

# 1907-08

| Football League Division 1 1907-1908 Season | Aston Villa | Birmingham | Blackburn Rovers | Bolton Wanderers | Bristol City | Bury | Chelsea | Everton | Liverpool | Manchester City | Manchester United | Middlesbrough | Newcastle United | Nottingham Forest | Notts County | Preston North End | Sheffield United | Sunderland | Wednesday | Woolwich Arsenal |
|---|---|---|---|---|---|---|---|---|---|---|---|---|---|---|---|---|---|---|---|---|
| Aston Villa FC | | 2-3 | 1-1 | 2-0 | 4-4 | 2-2 | 0-0 | 0-2 | 5-1 | 2-2 | 1-4 | 6-0 | 3-3 | 4-0 | 5-1 | 3-0 | 1-0 | 1-0 | 5-0 | 0-1 |
| Birmingham FC | 2-3 | | 1-1 | 2-1 | 0-4 | 0-1 | 1-1 | 2-1 | 1-1 | 2-1 | 3-4 | 1-4 | 1-1 | 1-0 | 0-0 | 2-0 | 0-0 | 0-2 | 2-1 | 1-2 |
| Blackburn Rovers FC | 2-0 | 1-0 | | 3-2 | 4-1 | 1-0 | 2-0 | 2-0 | 1-3 | 0-0 | 1-5 | 2-0 | 1-1 | 3-3 | 1-1 | 1-1 | 3-3 | 4-2 | 2-0 | 1-1 |
| Bolton Wanderers FC | 3-1 | 1-0 | 3-1 | | 1-2 | 3-6 | 1-2 | 3-0 | 0-4 | 2-0 | 2-2 | 1-1 | 4-0 | 1-0 | 0-1 | 2-0 | 1-1 | 2-3 | 2-1 | 3-1 |
| Bristol City FC | 2-2 | 0-0 | 2-2 | 2-0 | | 1-1 | 0-0 | 3-2 | 2-0 | 2-1 | 1-1 | 0-1 | 1-1 | 3-0 | 2-1 | 1-3 | 3-2 | 3-0 | 0-2 | 1-2 |
| Bury FC | 2-1 | 1-0 | 1-1 | 2-2 | 1-1 | | 1-1 | 3-0 | 3-1 | 0-0 | 0-1 | 1-4 | 1-2 | 0-0 | 0-0 | 5-1 | 3-2 | 2-1 | 0-2 | 3-2 |
| Chelsea FC | 1-3 | 2-2 | 1-0 | 1-3 | 4-1 | 3-4 | | 2-1 | 0-2 | 2-2 | 1-4 | 1-0 | 2-0 | 0-4 | 1-2 | 0-0 | 2-4 | 2-1 | 3-1 | 2-1 |
| Everton FC | 1-0 | 4-1 | 4-1 | 2-1 | 0-0 | 6-1 | 0-3 | | 2-4 | 3-3 | 1-3 | 2-1 | 2-0 | 1-0 | 1-0 | 2-1 | 2-1 | 0-3 | 0-0 | 1-1 |
| Liverpool FC | 5-0 | 3-4 | 2-0 | 1-0 | 3-1 | 2-1 | 1-4 | 0-0 | | 0-1 | 7-4 | 0-1 | 1-5 | 0-0 | 6-0 | 1-2 | 3-0 | 1-0 | 3-0 | 4-1 |
| Manchester City FC | 3-2 | 2-1 | 2-0 | 1-0 | 0-0 | 2-2 | 0-3 | 4-2 | 1-1 | | 0-0 | 2-1 | 1-0 | 4-2 | 2-1 | 5-0 | 0-2 | 0-0 | 3-2 | 4-0 |
| Manchester United FC | 1-2 | 1-0 | 1-2 | 2-1 | 2-1 | 2-1 | 1-0 | 4-3 | 4-0 | 3-1 | | 2-1 | 1-1 | 4-0 | 0-1 | 2-1 | 2-1 | 3-0 | 4-1 | 4-2 |
| Middlesbrough FC | 0-1 | 1-0 | 3-0 | 0-1 | 0-2 | 0-2 | 3-1 | 0-2 | 3-1 | 2-0 | 2-1 | | 2-1 | 1-1 | 3-1 | 1-0 | 2-0 | 3-1 | 6-1 | 0-0 |
| Newcastle United FC | 2-5 | 8-0 | 3-0 | 3-0 | 2-0 | 3-0 | 1-0 | 2-1 | 3-1 | 1-1 | 1-6 | 1-1 | | 3-0 | 1-1 | 0-0 | 2-3 | 1-3 | 2-1 | 2-1 |
| Nottingham Forest FC | 2-2 | 1-1 | 3-2 | 1-0 | 3-1 | 1-2 | 6-0 | 5-2 | 3-1 | 3-1 | 2-0 | 0-3 | 0-0 | | 2-0 | 2-2 | 1-1 | 4-1 | 2-2 | 1-0 |
| Notts County FC | 0-3 | 0-0 | 0-2 | 0-1 | 3-1 | 2-1 | 2-0 | 2-1 | 2-2 | 1-0 | 1-1 | 2-0 | 0-1 | 2-0 | | 0-1 | 0-3 | 4-0 | 1-2 | 2-0 |
| Preston North End FC | 3-0 | 1-1 | 1-1 | 2-0 | 3-0 | 3-1 | 2-4 | 2-2 | 3-0 | 2-4 | 0-0 | 1-1 | 2-0 | 0-1 | 1-0 | | 0-0 | 3-2 | 1-1 | 3-0 |
| Sheffield United FC | 1-1 | 1-0 | 4-2 | 1-0 | 2-0 | 0-2 | 0-3 | 0-0 | 1-2 | 2-0 | 0-1 | 1-1 | 2-2 | 0-1 | 2-0 | | | 5-3 | 1-3 | 2-2 |
| Sunderland AFC | 3-0 | 1-0 | 4-0 | 1-2 | 3-3 | 6-2 | 3-0 | 1-2 | 1-0 | 2-5 | 1-2 | 0-0 | 2-4 | 7-2 | 4-3 | 4-1 | 4-1 | | 1-2 | 5-2 |
| The Wednesday FC | 2-3 | 1-4 | 2-0 | 5-2 | 5-3 | 2-0 | 3-1 | 1-2 | 1-2 | 5-1 | 2-0 | 3-2 | 3-1 | 2-1 | 2-0 | 1-0 | 2-0 | 2-2 | | 6-0 |
| Woolwich Arsenal FC | 0-1 | 1-1 | 2-0 | 1-1 | 0-4 | 0-0 | 0-0 | 2-1 | 2-1 | 2-1 | 1-0 | 4-1 | 2-2 | 3-1 | 1-1 | 1-1 | 5-1 | 4-0 | 1-1 | |

## Division 1

| | | Pd | Wn | Dw | Ls | GF | GA | Pts | |
|---|---|---|---|---|---|---|---|---|---|
| 1. | MANCHESTER UNITED FC (MANCHESTER) | 38 | 23 | 6 | 9 | 81 | 48 | 52 | |
| 2. | Aston Villa FC (Birmingham) | 38 | 17 | 9 | 12 | 77 | 59 | 43 | |
| 3. | Manchester City FC (Manchester) | 38 | 16 | 11 | 11 | 62 | 54 | 43 | |
| 4. | Newcastle United FC (Newcastle-upon-Tyne) | 38 | 15 | 12 | 11 | 65 | 54 | 42 | |
| 5. | The Wednesday FC (Sheffield) | 38 | 19 | 4 | 15 | 73 | 64 | 42 | |
| 6. | Middlesbrough FC (Middlesbrough) | 38 | 17 | 7 | 14 | 54 | 45 | 41 | |
| 7. | Bury FC(Bury) | 38 | 14 | 11 | 13 | 58 | 61 | 39 | |
| 8. | Liverpool FC (Liverpool) | 38 | 16 | 6 | 16 | 68 | 61 | 38 | |
| 9. | Nottingham Forest FC (Nottingham) | 38 | 13 | 11 | 14 | 59 | 62 | 37 | |
| 10. | Bristol City FC (Bristol) | 38 | 12 | 12 | 14 | 58 | 61 | 36 | |
| 11. | Everton FC (Liverpool) | 38 | 15 | 6 | 17 | 58 | 64 | 36 | |
| 12. | Preston North End FC (Preston) | 38 | 12 | 12 | 14 | 47 | 53 | 36 | |
| 13. | Chelsea FC (London) | 38 | 14 | 8 | 16 | 53 | 62 | 36 | |
| 14. | Blackburn Rovers FC (Blackburn) | 38 | 12 | 12 | 14 | 51 | 63 | 36 | |
| 14. | Woolwich Arsenal FC (London) | 38 | 12 | 12 | 14 | 51 | 63 | 36 | |
| 16. | Sunderland AFC (Sunderland) | 38 | 16 | 3 | 19 | 78 | 75 | 35 | |
| 17. | Sheffield United FC (Sheffield) | 38 | 12 | 11 | 15 | 52 | 58 | 35 | |
| 18. | Notts County FC (Nottingham) | 38 | 13 | 8 | 17 | 39 | 51 | 34 | |
| 19. | Bolton Wanderers FC (Bolton) | 38 | 14 | 5 | 19 | 52 | 58 | 33 | R |
| 20. | Birmingham FC (Birmingham) | 38 | 9 | 12 | 17 | 40 | 60 | 30 | R |
| | | 760 | 291 | 178 | 291 | 1176 | 1176 | 760 | |

# Top Goalscorer

1)  E. WEST                    (Nottingham Forest FC)    27

| Football League Division 2 1907-1908 Season | Barnsley | Blackpool | Bradford City | Burnley | Chesterfield | Clapton Orient | Derby County | Fulham | Gainsborough T. | Glossop | Grimsby Town | Hull City | Leeds City | Leicester Fosse | Lincoln City | Oldham Athletic | Stockport Co. | Stoke | W.B.A. | Wolves |
|---|---|---|---|---|---|---|---|---|---|---|---|---|---|---|---|---|---|---|---|---|
| Barnsley FC | ■ | 0-0 | 1-2 | 2-3 | 5-2 | 2-2 | 2-4 | 6-0 | 1-2 | 4-1 | 2-1 | 4-2 | 1-3 | 1-3 | 2-1 | 2-1 | 0-0 | 0-1 | 1-3 | 5-0 |
| Blackpool FC | 1-1 | ■ | 2-1 | 1-0 | 2-0 | 5-0 | 1-0 | 2-1 | 0-1 | 4-0 | 3-0 | 1-1 | 2-3 | 2-2 | 4-3 | 1-0 | 1-3 | 1-0 | 0-1 | 0-2 |
| Bradford City AFC | 2-0 | 3-0 | ■ | 2-0 | 8-1 | 1-0 | 3-1 | 1-3 | 7-1 | 2-1 | 1-1 | 2-1 | 5-0 | 1-5 | 2-0 | 1-0 | 5-0 | 6-0 | 0-0 | 6-2 |
| Burnley FC | 4-1 | 2-1 | 2-1 | ■ | 1-1 | 3-0 | 2-2 | 0-1 | 2-0 | 1-0 | 5-1 | 5-0 | 1-0 | 4-1 | 1-2 | 2-1 | 4-0 | 3-1 | 1-1 | 1-0 |
| Chesterfield Town FC | 1-3 | 3-2 | 1-1 | 2-4 | ■ | 1-1 | 0-2 | 1-1 | 2-2 | 3-7 | 0-0 | 1-2 | 4-3 | 2-2 | 2-1 | 1-2 | 4-1 | 2-4 | 1-0 | 2-0 |
| Clapton Orient FC | 2-0 | 1-1 | 0-3 | 0-1 | 5-1 | ■ | 1-0 | 0-1 | 2-0 | 0-0 | 2-1 | 1-0 | 0-0 | 0-1 | 2-0 | 2-0 | 4-1 | 3-0 | 2-2 | 1-1 |
| Derby County FC | 3-0 | 2-1 | 2-3 | 1-0 | 0-0 | 4-0 | ■ | 0-1 | 5-2 | 2-0 | 4-0 | 4-1 | 6-1 | 1-2 | 4-0 | 1-0 | 3-0 | 3-0 | 2-0 | 3-2 |
| Fulham FC | 2-0 | 3-0 | 0-2 | 2-1 | 5-0 | 4-0 | 0-0 | ■ | 6-0 | 6-1 | 0-1 | 0-1 | 2-0 | 5-1 | 6-1 | 1-2 | 0-1 | 5-1 | 1-1 | 2-1 |
| Gainsborough Trinity | 0-1 | 2-1 | 1-5 | 2-0 | 2-1 | 0-0 | 1-4 | 3-3 | ■ | 1-0 | 3-2 | 1-2 | 2-1 | 1-1 | 5-1 | 1-1 | 3-2 | 2-0 | 1-2 | 0-1 |
| Glossop FC | 3-1 | 2-2 | 2-2 | 3-1 | 3-2 | 2-1 | 2-3 | 1-2 | 1-0 | ■ | 1-2 | 5-1 | 0-2 | 2-3 | 3-1 | 0-0 | 1-1 | 2-0 | 2-1 | 1-1 |
| Grimsby Town FC | 4-1 | 2-2 | 0-1 | 0-1 | 4-3 | 0-0 | 1-0 | 0-4 | 1-4 | 4-0 | ■ | 1-1 | 2-0 | 1-1 | 0-2 | 2-0 | 2-1 | 1-0 | 2-2 | 0-1 |
| Hull City AFC | 2-0 | 3-2 | 0-2 | 3-1 | 2-0 | 5-0 | 4-0 | 1-2 | 0-1 | 3-2 | 4-2 | ■ | 4-1 | 3-2 | 5-3 | 3-2 | 0-0 | 2-1 | 4-2 | 2-0 |
| Leeds City AFC | 1-1 | 1-1 | 0-1 | 2-2 | 0-0 | 5-2 | 5-1 | 0-1 | 0-0 | 2-1 | 4-1 | 3-2 | ■ | 0-0 | 2-1 | 1-2 | 3-0 | 0-1 | 1-0 | 3-1 |
| Leicester Fosse FC | 4-0 | 2-1 | 2-1 | 3-1 | 3-1 | 0-2 | 1-3 | 2-3 | 3-0 | 3-1 | 1-1 | 3-2 | 2-2 | ■ | 1-0 | 4-1 | 2-1 | 1-0 | 3-0 | 1-0 |
| Lincoln City FC | 0-2 | 2-0 | 2-4 | 1-3 | 4-0 | 2-2 | 1-0 | 2-4 | 2-0 | 1-0 | 0-1 | 1-0 | 5-0 | 0-3 | ■ | 0-2 | 1-1 | 1-2 | 0-2 | 3-1 |
| Oldham Athletic AFC | 1-0 | 3-2 | 4-0 | 1-1 | 4-0 | 4-1 | 3-1 | 3-3 | 4-1 | 0-0 | 2-0 | 3-0 | 4-2 | 1-1 | 4-0 | ■ | 5-0 | 3-1 | 2-1 | 2-0 |
| Stockport County FC | 2-0 | 1-1 | 1-1 | 1-3 | 1-0 | 6-1 | 2-1 | 2-0 | 1-1 | 3-2 | 3-0 | 2-3 | 2-1 | 2-1 | 1-1 | 2-3 | ■ | 1-2 | 1-2 | 1-3 |
| Stoke FC | 4-0 | 3-1 | 3-0 | 0-0 | 1-1 | 3-0 | 0-3 | 6-1 | 5-0 | 4-0 | 5-0 | 1-1 | 2-1 | 0-1 | 3-0 | 1-3 | 1-0 | ■ | 1-1 | 0-0 |
| West Bromwich Albion FC | 1-1 | 3-0 | 3-2 | 5-0 | 4-0 | 3-0 | 1-0 | 3-1 | 0-1 | 1-1 | 1-2 | 1-0 | 1-0 | 1-1 | 5-2 | 1-2 | 2-0 | 1-0 | ■ | 1-0 |
| Wolverhampton Wanderers FC | 0-1 | 1-0 | 0-0 | 5-1 | 0-0 | 2-0 | 2-2 | 2-0 | 1-0 | 5-0 | 5-1 | 1-2 | 2-0 | 0-0 | 3-0 | 2-1 | 0-1 | 2-0 | 1-2 | ■ |

## Division 2

| | | Pd | Wn | Dw | Ls | GF | GA | Pts | |
|---|---|---|---|---|---|---|---|---|---|
| 1. | Bradford City AFC (Bradford) | 38 | 24 | 6 | 8 | 90 | 42 | 54 | P |
| 2. | Leicester Fosse FC (Leicester) | 38 | 21 | 10 | 7 | 72 | 47 | 52 | P |
| 3. | Oldham Athletic AFC (Oldham) | 38 | 22 | 6 | 10 | 76 | 42 | 50 | |
| 4. | Fulham FC (London) | 38 | 22 | 5 | 11 | 82 | 49 | 49 | |
| 5. | West Bromwich Albion FC (West Bromwich) | 38 | 19 | 9 | 10 | 61 | 39 | 47 | |
| 6. | Derby County FC (Derby) | 38 | 21 | 4 | 13 | 77 | 45 | 46 | |
| 7. | Burnley FC (Burnley) | 38 | 20 | 6 | 12 | 67 | 50 | 46 | |
| 8. | Hull City AFC (Kingston-upon-Hull) | 38 | 21 | 4 | 13 | 73 | 62 | 46 | |
| 9. | Wolverhampton Wanderers FC (Wolverhampton) | 38 | 15 | 7 | 16 | 50 | 45 | 37 | |
| 10. | Stoke FC (Stoke-upon-Trent) | 38 | 16 | 5 | 17 | 57 | 52 | 37 | # |
| 11. | Gainsborough Trinity FC (Gainsborough) | 38 | 14 | 7 | 17 | 47 | 71 | 35 | |
| 12. | Leeds City AFC (Leeds) | 38 | 12 | 8 | 18 | 53 | 65 | 32 | |
| 13. | Stockport County FC (Stockport) | 38 | 12 | 8 | 18 | 48 | 67 | 32 | |
| 14. | Clapton Orient FC (London) | 38 | 11 | 10 | 17 | 40 | 65 | 32 | |
| 15. | Blackpool FC (Blackpool) | 38 | 11 | 9 | 18 | 51 | 58 | 31 | |
| 16. | Barnsley FC (Barnsley) | 38 | 12 | 6 | 20 | 54 | 68 | 30 | |
| 17. | Glossop FC (Glossop) | 38 | 11 | 8 | 19 | 54 | 74 | 30 | |
| 18. | Grimsby Town FC (Cleethorpes) | 38 | 11 | 8 | 19 | 43 | 71 | 30 | |
| 19. | Chesterfield Town FC (Chesterfield) | 38 | 6 | 11 | 21 | 46 | 92 | 23 | |
| 20. | Lincoln City FC (Lincoln) | 38 | 9 | 3 | 26 | 46 | 83 | 21 | # |
| | | 760 | 310 | 140 | 310 | 1187 | 1187 | 760 | |

\# Stoke FC (Stoke-upon-Trent) resigned from the league at the end of the season.
Lincoln City FC (Lincoln) were not re-elected to the league for next season.

Bradford Park Avenue FC (Bradford) & Tottenham Hotspur FC (London) were elected to Division 2 for next season.

## F.A. CUP FINAL   (Crystal Palace, London – 25/04/1908 – 74,697)

WOLVERHAMPTON WANDERERS FC        3-1     Newcastle United FC (Newcastle-upon-Tyne)

*Hunt, Hedley, Harrison*                                                                                      *Howie*

Wolves: Lunn, Jones, Collins, Hunt, Wooldridge, Bishop, Harrison, Shelton, Hedley, Radford, Pedley.

Newcastle: Lawrence, McCracken, Pudan, Gardner, Veitch, McWilliam, Rutherford, Howie, Appleyard, Speedie, Wilson.

## Semi-finals

| | | |
|---|---|---|
| Newcastle United FC (Newcastle-upon-Tyne) | 6-0 | Fulham FC (London) |
| Wolverhampton Wanderers FC (Wolverhampton) | 2-0 | Southampton FC (Southampton) |

## Quarter-finals

| | | |
|---|---|---|
| Everton FC (Liverpool) | 0-0, 2-3 | Southampton FC (Southampton) |
| Fulham FC (London) | 2-1 | Manchester United FC (Manchester) |
| Newcastle United FC (Newcastle-upon-Tyne) | 5-1 | Grimsby Town FC (Cleethorpes) |
| Stoke FC (Stoke-upon-Trent) | 0-1 | Wolverhampton Wanderers FC (Wanderers) |

# 1908-09

| Football League Division 1 1908-1909 Season | Aston Villa | Blackburn Rvs. | Bradford City | Bristol City | Bury | Chelsea | Everton | Leicester Fosse | Liverpool | Manchester City | Manchester Utd. | Middlesbrough | Newcastle United | Nottingham For. | Notts County | Preston N.E. | Sheffield United | Sunderland | Wednesday | Woolw. Arsenal |
|---|---|---|---|---|---|---|---|---|---|---|---|---|---|---|---|---|---|---|---|---|
| Aston Villa FC | | 1-1 | 1-3 | 1-1 | 3-0 | 0-0 | 3-1 | 1-1 | 1-1 | 2-1 | 3-1 | 0-3 | 3-0 | 1-2 | 1-1 | 2-4 | 3-0 | 2-0 | 1-1 | 2-1 |
| Blackburn Rovers FC | 3-1 | | 1-1 | 1-1 | 0-1 | 2-0 | 0-0 | 3-0 | 1-0 | 3-2 | 1-3 | 0-0 | 2-4 | 0-3 | 0-2 | 1-1 | 0-1 | 8-1 | 2-2 | 1-3 |
| Bradford City AFC | 1-1 | 0-2 | | 0-1 | 4-1 | 3-0 | 1-1 | 4-1 | 0-2 | 0-0 | 1-0 | 0-2 | 1-2 | 1-1 | 2-2 | 2-0 | 3-1 | 0-2 | 0-0 | 4-1 |
| Bristol City FC | 0-0 | 1-4 | 0-1 | | 4-2 | 1-0 | 0-2 | 1-1 | 1-0 | 1-0 | 0-0 | 1-1 | 3-3 | 2-1 | 1-0 | 2-3 | 1-1 | 2-4 | 1-1 | 2-1 |
| Bury FC | 1-2 | 1-1 | 2-1 | 1-2 | | 2-1 | 2-2 | 2-2 | 2-1 | 1-0 | 2-2 | 2-1 | 1-1 | 3-2 | 3-1 | 0-1 | 1-2 | 4-2 | 4-2 | 1-1 |
| Chelsea FC | 0-2 | 1-1 | 1-1 | 3-1 | 4-1 | | 3-3 | 1-0 | 3-0 | 1-2 | 1-1 | 3-0 | 1-2 | 2-1 | 3-2 | 0-0 | 1-1 | 2-0 | 2-2 | 1-2 |
| Everton FC | 3-1 | 4-4 | 0-1 | 5-2 | 4-0 | 3-2 | | 4-2 | 5-0 | 6-3 | 3-2 | 1-1 | 0-1 | 3-3 | 0-1 | 0-1 | 5-1 | 4-0 | 1-0 | 0-3 |
| Leicester Fosse FC | 4-2 | 2-4 | 1-4 | 1-1 | 2-5 | 5-2 | 0-2 | | 3-2 | 3-1 | 3-2 | 1-1 | 0-4 | 0-3 | 0-2 | 0-0 | 1-1 | 4-3 | 1-1 | 1-1 |
| Liverpool FC | 3-2 | 1-1 | 4-0 | 1-2 | 2-2 | 2-1 | 0-1 | 4-1 | | 1-3 | 3-1 | 1-2 | 2-1 | 1-1 | 1-1 | 2-1 | 2-1 | 3-0 | 1-2 | 2-2 |
| Manchester City FC | 2-0 | 3-3 | 4-3 | 5-1 | 6-1 | 1-2 | 4-0 | 5-2 | 4-0 | | 1-2 | 0-0 | 0-2 | 2-1 | 1-0 | 4-1 | 1-3 | 1-0 | 4-0 | 2-2 |
| Manchester United FC | 0-2 | 0-3 | 2-0 | 0-1 | 2-1 | 0-1 | 2-2 | 4-2 | 3-2 | 3-1 | | 6-3 | 1-0 | 2-2 | 4-3 | 0-2 | 2-1 | 2-2 | 3-1 | 1-4 |
| Middlesbrough FC | 1-0 | 1-0 | 1-0 | 4-0 | 0-1 | 1-4 | 2-3 | 6-2 | 1-0 | 3-0 | 5-0 | | 0-0 | 4-0 | 1-2 | 4-2 | 1-2 | 0-3 | 2-1 | 1-1 |
| Newcastle United FC | 0-2 | 2-0 | 1-0 | 2-1 | 3-1 | 1-3 | 3-0 | 2-0 | 0-1 | 2-0 | 2-1 | 1-0 | | 1-1 | 1-0 | 2-0 | 4-0 | 1-9 | 1-0 | 3-1 |
| Nottingham Forest FC | 1-2 | 2-1 | 2-1 | 1-1 | 0-2 | 2-1 | 1-2 | 12-0 | 5-1 | 0-2 | 2-0 | 4-1 | 0-4 | | 1-0 | 1-1 | 0-2 | 4-0 | 1-2 | 0-1 |
| Notts County FC | 1-1 | 2-3 | 1-1 | 0-1 | 3-2 | 3-0 | 0-0 | 2-3 | 1-2 | 5-1 | 0-1 | 3-2 | 0-4 | 3-0 | | 1-0 | 3-1 | 0-0 | 1-0 | 2-1 |
| Preston North End FC | 3-2 | 2-0 | 0-0 | 2-1 | 0-2 | 6-0 | 3-3 | 0-1 | 2-0 | 3-0 | 0-3 | 1-1 | 0-1 | 1-1 | 0-0 | | 1-1 | 1-0 | 4-1 | 0-0 |
| Sheffield United FC | 3-1 | 0-0 | 3-0 | 3-1 | 2-2 | 1-3 | 1-5 | 2-1 | 0-2 | 4-0 | 0-0 | 2-0 | 1-1 | 1-2 | 3-2 | 2-1 | | 0-2 | 2-1 | 1-1 |
| Sunderland AFC | 4-3 | 0-1 | 2-1 | 0-2 | 3-1 | 1-2 | 2-0 | 3-1 | 1-4 | 2-0 | 6-1 | 2-0 | 3-1 | 2-1 | 0-1 | 2-1 | 3-1 | | 4-2 | 1-0 |
| The Wednesday FC | 4-2 | 1-2 | 0-2 | 2-0 | 4-3 | 5-1 | 2-0 | 3-1 | 2-3 | 3-1 | 2-0 | 3-2 | 2-0 | 3-0 | 2-0 | 1-0 | 1-0 | 2-5 | | 6-2 |
| Woolwich Arsenal FC | 0-1 | 0-1 | 1-0 | 1-1 | 4-0 | 0-0 | 0-4 | 2-1 | 5-0 | 3-0 | 0-1 | 1-1 | 1-2 | 1-2 | 1-0 | 1-0 | 1-0 | 0-4 | 2-0 | |

| | Division 1 | Pd | Wn | Dw | Ls | GF | GA | Pts | |
|---|---|---|---|---|---|---|---|---|---|
| 1. | NEWCASTLE UNITED FC (NEWCASTLE/TYNE) | 38 | 24 | 5 | 9 | 65 | 41 | 53 | |
| 2. | Everton FC (Liverpool) | 38 | 18 | 10 | 10 | 82 | 57 | 46 | |
| 3. | Sunderland AFC (Sunderland) | 38 | 21 | 2 | 15 | 78 | 63 | 44 | |
| 4. | Blackburn Rovers FC (Blackburn) | 38 | 14 | 13 | 11 | 61 | 50 | 41 | |
| 5. | The Wednesday FC (Sheffield) | 38 | 17 | 6 | 15 | 67 | 61 | 40 | |
| 6. | Woolwich Arsenal FC (London) | 38 | 14 | 10 | 14 | 52 | 49 | 38 | |
| 7. | Aston Villa FC (Birmingham) | 38 | 14 | 10 | 14 | 58 | 56 | 38 | |
| 8. | Bristol City FC (Bristol) | 38 | 13 | 12 | 13 | 45 | 58 | 38 | |
| 9. | Middlesbrough FC (Middlesbrough) | 38 | 14 | 9 | 15 | 59 | 53 | 37 | |
| 10. | Preston North End FC (Preston) | 38 | 13 | 11 | 14 | 48 | 44 | 37 | |
| 11. | Chelsea FC (London) | 38 | 14 | 9 | 15 | 56 | 61 | 37 | |
| 12. | Sheffield United FC (Sheffield) | 38 | 14 | 9 | 15 | 51 | 59 | 37 | |
| 13. | Manchester United FC (Manchester) | 38 | 15 | 7 | 16 | 58 | 68 | 37 | |
| 14. | Nottingham Forest FC (Nottingham) | 38 | 14 | 8 | 16 | 66 | 57 | 36 | |
| 15. | Notts County FC (Nottingham) | 38 | 14 | 8 | 16 | 51 | 48 | 36 | |
| 16. | Liverpool FC (Liverpool) | 38 | 15 | 6 | 17 | 57 | 65 | 36 | |
| 17. | Bury FC (Bury) | 38 | 14 | 8 | 16 | 63 | 77 | 36 | |
| 18. | Bradford City AFC (Bradford) | 38 | 12 | 10 | 16 | 47 | 47 | 34 | |
| 19. | Manchester City FC (Manchester) | 38 | 15 | 4 | 19 | 67 | 69 | 34 | R |
| 20. | Leicester Fosse FC (Leicester) | 38 | 8 | 9 | 21 | 54 | 102 | 25 | R |
| | | 760 | 297 | 166 | 297 | 1185 | 1185 | 760 | |

## Top Goalscorer

1) B. FREEMAN — (Everton FC) — 38

| Football League Division 2 1908-1909 Season | Barnsley | Birmingham | Blackpool | Bolton Wanderers | Bradford Park Ave. | Burnley | Chesterfield | Clapton Orient | Derby County | Fulham | Gainsborough Tr. | Glossop | Grimsby Town | Hull City | Lincoln City | Oldham Athletic | Stockport County | Tottenham Hotspur | W.B.A. | Wolves |
|---|---|---|---|---|---|---|---|---|---|---|---|---|---|---|---|---|---|---|---|---|
| Barnsley FC | | 3-1 | 4-0 | 0-1 | 3-1 | 1-2 | 4-0 | 3-0 | 1-0 | 1-2 | 2-2 | 1-3 | 3-1 | 2-1 | 2-1 | 2-0 | 2-0 | 1-1 | 0-2 | 1-1 |
| Birmingham FC | 2-1 | | 2-2 | 2-0 | 3-1 | 2-0 | 3-0 | 1-0 | 1-1 | 1-3 | 2-2 | 1-2 | 3-1 | 1-2 | 1-0 | 2-0 | 4-2 | 3-3 | 0-0 | 1-1 |
| Blackpool FC | 1-1 | 2-0 | | 1-2 | 2-1 | 0-0 | 2-2 | 1-3 | 2-2 | 2-0 | 3-0 | 2-1 | 2-2 | 2-3 | 1-0 | 1-0 | 2-1 | 1-1 | 0-2 | 3-1 |
| Bolton Wanderers FC | 3-0 | 2-1 | 3-1 | | 0-1 | 2-1 | 4-0 | 2-0 | 1-0 | 0-0 | 4-0 | 2-0 | 2-0 | 1-0 | 2-0 | 3-0 | 4-1 | 0-1 | 1-1 | 1-1 |
| Bradford Park Avenue | 3-2 | 1-2 | 4-3 | 1-2 | | 2-3 | 1-0 | 0-1 | 2-0 | 1-1 | 4-1 | 1-0 | 0-2 | 1-0 | 2-0 | 3-4 | 0-1 | 0-2 | 0-0 | 4-1 |
| Burnley FC | 3-2 | 1-1 | 1-1 | 1-2 | 3-3 | | 0-1 | 0-1 | 2-0 | 1-3 | 5-2 | 3-2 | 2-0 | 1-0 | 0-0 | 1-0 | 5-1 | 1-2 | 0-2 | 3-5 |
| Chesterfield Town FC | 1-0 | 4-2 | 3-1 | 0-2 | 2-1 | 1-0 | | 2-0 | 2-4 | 2-1 | 2-1 | 2-1 | 1-2 | 0-4 | 2-0 | 1-1 | 1-2 | 1-3 | 2-2 | 1-1 |
| Clapton Orient FC | 1-1 | 3-2 | 1-1 | 0-2 | 2-0 | 0-1 | 1-1 | | 2-0 | 1-1 | 2-2 | 0-2 | 2-1 | 1-2 | 0-0 | 2-0 | 5-0 | 0-0 | 1-0 | 1-3 |
| Derby County FC | 0-0 | 1-2 | 1-1 | 1-0 | 3-1 | 1-0 | 1-1 | 1-0 | | 2-1 | 5-0 | 4-0 | 2-1 | 0-0 | 5-1 | 1-0 | 5-0 | 1-1 | 2-1 | 2-1 |
| Fulham FC | 2-2 | 1-1 | 3-0 | 1-2 | 3-1 | 3-0 | 0-0 | 1-2 | 1-2 | | 4-0 | 2-3 | 5-2 | 0-3 | 0-1 | 3-2 | 5-1 | 2-3 | 2-0 | 1-1 |
| Gainsborough Trinity | 4-1 | 1-3 | 1-0 | 2-1 | 2-1 | 1-0 | 3-0 | 2-0 | 0-0 | 1-1 | | 3-1 | 0-3 | 2-0 | 1-1 | 1-4 | 3-2 | 0-2 | 2-0 | 1-0 |
| Glossop FC | 3-0 | 3-1 | 3-0 | 0-2 | 1-1 | 1-2 | 2-0 | 4-0 | 3-1 | 0-0 | 2-2 | | 1-0 | 2-1 | 0-0 | 2-1 | 3-0 | 1-1 | 1-3 | 3-2 |
| Grimsby Town FC | 0-0 | 0-3 | 2-1 | 1-0 | 1-1 | 0-1 | 1-0 | 1-0 | 2-0 | 2-2 | 1-2 | 2-0 | | 0-0 | 0-1 | 2-0 | 3-0 | 1-2 | 1-1 | 3-0 |
| Hull City AFC | 4-0 | 4-1 | 2-0 | 2-0 | 2-3 | 3-2 | 1-0 | 3-2 | 4-0 | 2-0 | 5-1 | 0-0 | 0-1 | | 4-1 | 1-0 | 4-1 | 1-0 | 2-2 | 0-1 |
| Leeds City AFC | 2-0 | 2-0 | 1-0 | 1-2 | 0-3 | 1-1 | 3-0 | 0-0 | 2-5 | 2-0 | 0-2 | 3-1 | 4-1 | 2-0 | | 3-0 | 2-1 | 1-0 | 1-1 | 5-2 |
| Oldham Athletic AFC | 0-0 | 2-0 | 3-1 | 1-1 | 2-0 | 4-1 | 2-0 | 2-0 | 1-1 | 1-0 | 2-0 | 2-1 | 4-0 | 2-2 | 6-0 | | 0-1 | 1-0 | 2-0 | 2-1 |
| Stockport County FC | 2-1 | 3-2 | 1-0 | 1-0 | 0-1 | 2-1 | 2-0 | 1-1 | 1-0 | 1-2 | 0-1 | 4-2 | 0-1 | 3-1 | 1-0 | 1-3 | | 1-3 | 0-0 | 1-0 |
| Tottenham Hotspur FC | 4-0 | 4-0 | 4-1 | 2-1 | 3-0 | 4-2 | 4-0 | 0-1 | 0-0 | 1-0 | 1-1 | 3-3 | 2-0 | 0-0 | 3-0 | 3-0 | 0-0 | | 1-3 | 3-0 |
| West Bromwich Albion FC | 1-1 | 1-1 | 5-1 | 2-0 | 1-0 | 0-0 | 2-2 | 1-0 | 2-0 | 1-1 | 2-0 | 1-0 | 7-0 | 1-0 | 2-1 | 1-0 | 3-0 | | | 0-2 |
| Wolverhampton Wanderers FC | 2-0 | 2-0 | 2-2 | 1-2 | 1-1 | 2-1 | 3-0 | 5-1 | 1-1 | 0-1 | 4-0 | 0-0 | 0-0 | 3-0 | 2-1 | 1-1 | 2-0 | 1-0 | 0-1 | |

| Division 2 | Pd | Wn | Dw | Ls | GF | GA | Pts | |
|---|---|---|---|---|---|---|---|---|
| 1. Bolton Wanderers FC (Bolton) | 38 | 24 | 4 | 10 | 59 | 28 | 52 | P |
| 2. Tottenham Hotspur FC (London) | 38 | 20 | 11 | 7 | 67 | 32 | 51 | P |
| 3. West Bromwich Albion FC (West Bromwich) | 38 | 19 | 13 | 6 | 56 | 27 | 51 | |
| 4. Hull City AFC (Kingston-upon-Hull) | 38 | 19 | 6 | 13 | 63 | 39 | 44 | |
| 5. Derby County FC (Derby) | 38 | 16 | 11 | 11 | 55 | 41 | 43 | |
| 6. Oldham Athletic AFC (Oldham) | 38 | 17 | 6 | 15 | 55 | 43 | 40 | |
| 7. Wolverhampton Wanderers FC (Wolverhampton) | 38 | 14 | 11 | 13 | 56 | 48 | 39 | |
| 8. Glossop FC (Glossop) | 38 | 15 | 8 | 15 | 57 | 53 | 38 | |
| 9. Gainsborough Trinity FC (Gainsborough) | 38 | 15 | 8 | 15 | 49 | 70 | 38 | |
| 10. Fulham FC (London) | 38 | 13 | 11 | 14 | 58 | 48 | 37 | |
| 11. Birmingham FC (Birmingham) | 38 | 14 | 9 | 15 | 58 | 61 | 37 | |
| 12. Leeds City AFC (Leeds) | 38 | 14 | 7 | 17 | 43 | 53 | 35 | |
| 13. Grimsby Town FC (Cleethorpes) | 38 | 14 | 7 | 17 | 41 | 54 | 35 | |
| 14. Burnley FC (Burnley) | 38 | 13 | 7 | 18 | 51 | 58 | 33 | |
| 15. Clapton Orient FC (London) | 38 | 12 | 9 | 17 | 37 | 49 | 33 | |
| 16. Bradford Park Avenue FC (Bradford) | 38 | 13 | 6 | 19 | 51 | 59 | 32 | |
| 17. Barnsley FC (Barnsley) | 38 | 11 | 10 | 17 | 48 | 57 | 32 | |
| 18. Stockport County FC (Stockport) | 38 | 14 | 3 | 21 | 39 | 71 | 31 | |
| 19. Chesterfield Town FC (Chesterfield) | 38 | 11 | 8 | 19 | 37 | 67 | 30 | # |
| 20. Blackpool FC (Blackpool) | 38 | 9 | 11 | 18 | 46 | 68 | 29 | |
| | 760 | 297 | 166 | 297 | 1026 | 1026 | 760 | |

# Chesterfield Town FC (Chesterfield) were not re-elected to the league for next season and subsequently changed their club name to Chesterfield FC (Chesterfield).

Lincoln City FC (Lincoln) were elected to Division 2 for next season.

## F.A. CUP FINAL (Crystal Palace, London – 24/04/1909 – 71,401)

MANCHESTER UNITED FC (MANCHESTER) 1-0 Bristol City FC (Bristol)

*A.Turnbull*

Man. United: Moger, Stacey, Hayes, Duckworth, Roberts, Bell, Meredith, Halse, J.Turnbull, A.Turnbull, Wall.
Bristol City: Clay, Annan, Cottle, Hanlin, Wedlock, Spear, Staniforth, Hardy, Gilligan, Burton, Hilton.

## Semi-finals

| Bristol City FC (Bristol) | 1-1, 2-1 | Derby County FC (Derby) |
|---|---|---|
| Manchester United FC (Manchester) | 1-0 | Newcastle United FC (Newcastle-upon-Tyne) |

## Quarter-finals

| Burnley FC (Burnley) | 1-0, 2-3 | Manchester United FC (Manchester) |
|---|---|---|
| | (The first match was abandoned after 72 minutes.) | |
| Derby County FC (Derby) | 3-0 | Nottingham Forest FC (Nottingham) |
| Glossop FC (Glossop) | 0-0, 0-1 | Bristol City FC (Bristol) |
| Newcastle United FC (Newcastle-upon-Tyne) | 2-2, 3-0 | Sunderland AFC (Sunderland) |

# 1909-10

| Football League Division 1 1909-1910 Season | Aston Villa | Blackburn Rovers | Bolton Wanderers | Bradford City | Bristol City | Bury | Chelsea | Everton | Liverpool | Manchester United | Middlesbrough | Newcastle United | Nottingham Forest | Notts County | Preston North End | Sheffield United | Sunderland | Wednesday | Tottenham Hotspur | Woolwich Arsenal |
|---|---|---|---|---|---|---|---|---|---|---|---|---|---|---|---|---|---|---|---|---|
| Aston Villa FC | ■ | 4-3 | 3-1 | 3-1 | 1-0 | 4-1 | 4-1 | 3-1 | 3-1 | 7-1 | 4-2 | 4-0 | 0-0 | 1-1 | 3-0 | 2-1 | 3-2 | 5-0 | 3-2 | 5-1 |
| Blackburn Rovers FC | 3-2 | ■ | 4-2 | 2-0 | 5-2 | 5-1 | 1-0 | 2-1 | 1-1 | 3-2 | 1-1 | 2-0 | 2-2 | 2-0 | 2-2 | 3-1 | 0-0 | 0-0 | 2-0 | 7-0 |
| Bolton Wanderers FC | 1-2 | 1-2 | ■ | 1-1 | 4-2 | 1-3 | 5-2 | 0-1 | 1-2 | 2-3 | 1-1 | 0-4 | 2-1 | 3-4 | 3-1 | 1-0 | 2-1 | 0-1 | 0-2 | 3-0 |
| Bradford City AFC | 1-2 | 2-0 | 1-0 | ■ | 3-1 | 0-0 | 4-1 | 2-0 | 1-2 | 0-2 | 4-1 | 3-3 | 1-1 | 2-1 | 2-0 | 2-0 | 3-1 | 2-0 | 5-1 | 0-1 |
| Bristol City FC | 0-0 | 2-2 | 1-0 | 2-0 | ■ | 1-1 | 1-0 | 3-1 | 0-1 | 2-1 | 4-1 | 0-3 | 4-0 | 3-1 | 2-0 | 0-2 | 2-3 | 1-1 | 0-0 | 0-1 |
| Bury FC | 0-2 | 2-1 | 1-2 | 3-4 | 1-2 | ■ | 4-2 | 2-2 | 1-2 | 1-1 | 2-1 | 1-2 | 4-1 | 1-1 | 3-1 | 2-0 | 0-1 | 3-2 | 3-1 | 1-2 |
| Chelsea FC | 0-0 | 3-1 | 3-2 | 0-3 | 4-1 | 2-0 | ■ | 0-1 | 2-1 | 1-1 | 2-1 | 2-1 | 0-1 | 2-2 | 2-0 | 2-2 | 1-4 | 4-1 | 2-1 | 0-1 |
| Everton FC | 0-0 | 0-2 | 3-1 | 1-1 | 1-0 | 3-0 | 2-2 | ■ | 2-3 | 3-3 | 1-1 | 1-4 | 0-4 | 2-0 | 2-1 | 1-2 | 2-1 | 1-1 | 4-2 | 1-0 |
| Liverpool FC | 2-0 | 3-1 | 3-0 | 1-0 | 0-1 | 2-2 | 5-1 | 0-1 | ■ | 3-2 | 0-0 | 6-5 | 7-3 | 2-1 | 2-0 | 0-0 | 1-4 | 3-1 | 2-0 | 5-1 |
| Manchester United FC | 2-0 | 2-0 | 5-0 | 1-0 | 2-1 | 2-0 | 2-0 | 3-2 | 3-4 | ■ | 4-1 | 1-1 | 2-6 | 2-1 | 1-1 | 1-0 | 2-0 | 0-3 | 5-0 | 1-0 |
| Middlesbrough FC | 3-2 | 1-3 | 1-2 | 3-7 | 0-0 | 0-5 | 0-1 | 1-1 | 2-2 | 1-2 | ■ | 1-1 | 2-1 | 2-0 | 1-0 | 0-2 | 3-2 | 4-0 | 4-3 | 5-2 |
| Newcastle United FC | 1-0 | 4-1 | 1-0 | 1-0 | 3-1 | 2-2 | 1-0 | 1-2 | 1-3 | 3-4 | 2-0 | ■ | 1-2 | 1-3 | 5-2 | 0-0 | 1-0 | 3-1 | 1-0 | 1-1 |
| Nottingham Forest FC | 1-4 | 0-4 | 2-0 | 1-1 | 0-0 | 3-3 | 0-0 | 1-0 | 1-4 | 2-0 | 0-1 | 0-1 | ■ | 2-1 | 0-0 | 2-3 | 1-3 | 0-6 | 2-2 | 1-1 |
| Notts County FC | 2-3 | 2-2 | 0-0 | 3-2 | 0-2 | 3-1 | 2-1 | 2-3 | 3-1 | 3-2 | 2-1 | 2-2 | 4-1 | ■ | 3-1 | 1-2 | 1-1 | 0-0 | 3-0 | 5-1 |
| Preston North End FC | 1-0 | 3-2 | 1-0 | 2-2 | 3-0 | 2-1 | 2-0 | 0-1 | 2-0 | 1-0 | 1-0 | 4-0 | 0-1 | 4-0 | ■ | 1-1 | 1-0 | 1-0 | 4-1 | 3-4 |
| Sheffield United FC | 0-1 | 3-0 | 2-2 | 1-2 | 4-0 | 2-0 | 0-0 | 3-0 | 4-2 | 0-1 | 2-0 | 4-0 | 1-4 | 2-2 | 5-1 | ■ | 3-0 | 3-3 | 1-1 | 2-0 |
| Sunderland AFC | 1-1 | 0-0 | 3-0 | 3-0 | 4-0 | 2-3 | 4-0 | 0-1 | 2-1 | 3-0 | 2-2 | 0-2 | 2-1 | 0-3 | 2-1 | 1-0 | ■ | 2-0 | 3-1 | 6-2 |
| The Wednesday FC | 3-2 | 2-1 | 0-0 | 2-1 | 2-0 | 1-4 | 4-1 | 1-3 | 3-0 | 4-1 | 1-5 | 3-1 | 4-3 | 0-0 | 4-1 | 1-3 | 1-0 | ■ | 1-1 | 1-1 |
| Tottenham Hotspur FC | 1-1 | 4-0 | 1-1 | 0-0 | 3-2 | 1-0 | 2-1 | 3-0 | 1-0 | 2-2 | 1-3 | 0-4 | 2-2 | 1-3 | 2-1 | 2-1 | 5-1 | 3-0 | ■ | 1-1 |
| Woolwich Arsenal FC | 1-0 | 0-1 | 2-0 | 0-1 | 2-2 | 0-0 | 3-2 | 1-0 | 1-1 | 0-0 | 3-0 | 0-3 | 0-1 | 1-2 | 1-3 | 0-0 | 1-2 | 0-1 | 1-0 | ■ |

### Division 1

| | | Pd | Wn | Dw | Ls | GF | GA | Pts | |
|---|---|---|---|---|---|---|---|---|---|
| 1. | ASTON VILLA FC (BIRMINGHAM) | 38 | 23 | 7 | 8 | 84 | 42 | 53 | |
| 2. | Liverpool FC (Liverpool) | 38 | 21 | 6 | 11 | 78 | 57 | 48 | |
| 3. | Blackburn Rovers FC (Blackburn) | 38 | 18 | 9 | 11 | 73 | 55 | 45 | |
| 4. | Newcastle United FC (Newcastle-upon-Tyne) | 38 | 19 | 7 | 12 | 70 | 56 | 45 | |
| 5. | Manchester United FC (Manchester) | 38 | 19 | 7 | 12 | 69 | 61 | 45 | |
| 6. | Sheffield United FC (Sheffield) | 38 | 16 | 10 | 12 | 62 | 41 | 42 | |
| 7. | Bradford City AFC (Bradford) | 38 | 17 | 8 | 13 | 64 | 47 | 42 | |
| 8. | Sunderland AFC (Sunderland) | 38 | 18 | 5 | 15 | 66 | 51 | 41 | |
| 9. | Notts County FC (Nottingham) | 38 | 15 | 10 | 13 | 67 | 59 | 40 | |
| 10. | Everton FC (Liverpool) | 38 | 16 | 8 | 14 | 51 | 56 | 40 | |
| 11. | The Wednesday FC (Sheffield) | 38 | 15 | 9 | 14 | 60 | 63 | 39 | |
| 12. | Preston North End FC (Preston) | 38 | 15 | 5 | 18 | 52 | 58 | 35 | |
| 13. | Bury FC (Bury) | 38 | 12 | 9 | 17 | 62 | 66 | 33 | |
| 14. | Nottingham Forest FC (Nottingham) | 38 | 11 | 11 | 16 | 54 | 72 | 33 | |
| 15. | Tottenham Hotspur FC (London) | 38 | 11 | 10 | 17 | 53 | 69 | 32 | |
| 16. | Bristol City FC (Bristol) | 38 | 12 | 8 | 18 | 45 | 60 | 32 | |
| 17. | Middlesbrough FC (Middlesbrough) | 38 | 11 | 9 | 18 | 56 | 73 | 31 | |
| 18. | Woolwich Arsenal FC (London) | 38 | 11 | 9 | 18 | 37 | 67 | 31 | |
| 19. | Chelsea FC (London) | 38 | 11 | 7 | 20 | 47 | 70 | 29 | R |
| 20. | Bolton Wanderers FC (Bolton) | 38 | 9 | 6 | 23 | 44 | 71 | 24 | R |
| | | 760 | 300 | 160 | 300 | 1194 | 1194 | 760 | |

## Top Goalscorer

1)  J. PARKINSON  (Liverpool FC)  30

| Football League Division 2 1909-1910 Season | Barnsley | Birmingham | Blackpool | Bradford Park Ave. | Burnley | Clapton Orient | Derby County | Fulham | Gainsborough Trin. | Glossop | Grimsby Town | Hull City | Leeds City | Leicester Fosse | Lincoln City | Manchester City | Oldham Athletic | Stockport County | W.B.A. | Wolves |
|---|---|---|---|---|---|---|---|---|---|---|---|---|---|---|---|---|---|---|---|---|
| Barnsley FC | | 5-1 | 1-0 | 4-0 | 0-0 | 2-1 | 5-1 | 2-1 | 4-1 | 3-0 | 2-1 | 1-2 | 1-1 | 3-1 | 2-1 | 1-1 | 2-1 | 1-0 | 2-1 | 7-1 |
| Birmingham FC | 2-1 | | 1-2 | 0-1 | 2-1 | 1-2 | 1-3 | 1-1 | 5-0 | 2-2 | 2-4 | 0-2 | 1-2 | 2-1 | 1-0 | 1-1 | 2-2 | 3-0 | 0-1 | 1-0 |
| Blackpool FC | 0-0 | 2-0 | | 0-0 | 2-3 | 2-2 | 1-1 | 1-1 | 0-2 | 1-1 | 1-0 | 1-2 | 3-1 | 0-1 | 3-0 | 0-0 | 1-3 | 2-0 | 2-1 | 2-0 |
| Bradford Park Avenue | 2-0 | 5-0 | 2-1 | | 3-1 | 3-1 | 1-2 | 3-0 | 2-0 | 3-3 | 6-1 | 0-1 | 4-2 | 1-3 | 4-0 | 2-0 | 1-6 | 2-4 | 1-0 | 2-3 |
| Burnley FC | 2-0 | 2-0 | 5-1 | 1-0 | | 2-0 | 1-2 | 2-0 | 2-1 | 0-1 | 3-1 | 0-1 | 3-0 | 5-2 | 3-0 | 3-3 | 1-2 | 2-2 | 2-3 | 4-2 |
| Clapton Orient FC | 4-0 | 3-0 | 2-1 | 1-0 | 2-1 | | 0-2 | 0-0 | 2-0 | 0-0 | 0-0 | 0-2 | 3-0 | 1-2 | 3-2 | 1-2 | 2-0 | 1-3 | 1-0 | |
| Derby County FC | 2-1 | 3-1 | 2-1 | 1-2 | 5-2 | 1-0 | | 3-1 | 2-2 | 2-1 | 6-0 | 4-0 | 1-0 | 0-1 | 2-0 | 3-1 | 1-1 | 1-0 | 2-1 | 5-0 |
| Fulham FC | 3-0 | 0-0 | 0-1 | 3-1 | 2-1 | 0-0 | 0-0 | | 0-1 | 2-0 | 3-2 | 3-1 | 5-1 | 2-0 | 1-1 | 1-1 | 1-1 | 2-0 | 0-2 | 0-0 |
| Gainsborough Trinity | 0-0 | 1-0 | 3-1 | 3-1 | 2-0 | 0-1 | 2-4 | 2-0 | | 1-3 | 1-1 | 0-1 | 2-0 | 0-1 | 0-0 | 1-3 | 0-2 | 1-0 | 3-1 | 0-2 |
| Glossop FC | 3-0 | 4-1 | 2-3 | 3-1 | 2-0 | 3-1 | 1-1 | 0-1 | 4-0 | | 3-1 | 2-1 | 2-1 | 1-0 | 0-1 | 0-3 | 6-2 | 1-0 | 3-2 | 2-0 |
| Grimsby Town FC | 7-0 | 0-2 | 0-1 | 0-1 | 5-3 | 2-0 | 1-1 | 0-2 | 2-1 | 4-0 | | 2-3 | 3-1 | 0-0 | 1-2 | 0-1 | 0-0 | 0-1 | 3-0 | 1-0 |
| Hull City AFC | 1-0 | 7-0 | 1-2 | 2-1 | 3-2 | 3-0 | 0-0 | 3-2 | 5-1 | 4-2 | 5-1 | | 3-1 | 2-1 | 0-0 | 1-2 | 4-0 | 1-1 | 5-1 | 2-2 |
| Leeds City AFC | 0-7 | 2-1 | 3-2 | 2-3 | 1-0 | 2-1 | 2-1 | 2-2 | 0-0 | 1-2 | 3-1 | 1-1 | | 1-1 | 5-0 | 1-3 | 3-5 | 0-2 | 0-1 | 1-0 |
| Leicester Fosse FC | 1-1 | 3-1 | 3-2 | 3-0 | 1-1 | 4-0 | 6-0 | 2-3 | 9-1 | 3-1 | 3-1 | 3-1 | 6-2 | | 4-1 | 1-3 | 3-0 | 1-0 | 2-1 | 2-1 |
| Lincoln City FC | 2-1 | 3-2 | 2-2 | 1-1 | 0-0 | 4-0 | 2-3 | 2-2 | 4-0 | 1-2 | 0-0 | 1-3 | 0-0 | 3-1 | | 0-2 | 0-2 | 1-0 | 0-3 | 1-0 |
| Manchester City FC | 0-0 | 3-0 | 1-2 | 3-1 | 4-0 | 2-1 | 2-1 | 3-1 | 3-3 | 3-2 | 2-0 | 3-0 | 3-0 | 2-0 | 6-2 | | 0-2 | 2-1 | 3-2 | 6-0 |
| Oldham Athletic AFC | 5-0 | 1-1 | 2-0 | 1-1 | 1-0 | 5-0 | 4-0 | 0-1 | 2-0 | 1-0 | 4-1 | 3-0 | 2-1 | 2-1 | 6-1 | 1-0 | | 3-0 | 1-2 | 3-0 |
| Stockport County FC | 5-0 | 1-1 | 2-0 | 2-1 | 1-1 | 3-0 | 1-1 | 0-2 | 3-0 | 5-0 | 2-1 | 1-5 | 0-0 | 6-2 | 1-1 | 1-2 | 2-0 | | 0-2 | 1-1 |
| West Bromwich Albion FC | 4-3 | 3-1 | 0-3 | 1-0 | 1-2 | 3-0 | 0-0 | 3-2 | 5-0 | 0-0 | 4-3 | 0-2 | 3-1 | 1-2 | 1-1 | 0-0 | 1-1 | 0-1 | | 0-1 |
| Wolverhampton Wanderers FC | 1-0 | 4-2 | 2-1 | 0-2 | 3-1 | 3-1 | 2-3 | 1-1 | 0-0 | 3-1 | 8-1 | 2-2 | 5-0 | 4-1 | 4-2 | 3-2 | 1-0 | 2-1 | 3-1 | |

## Division 2

| | | Pd | Wn | Dw | Ls | GF | GA | Pts | |
|---|---|---|---|---|---|---|---|---|---|
| 1. | Manchester City FC (Manchester) | 38 | 23 | 8 | 7 | 81 | 40 | 54 | P |
| 2. | Oldham Athletic FC (Oldham) | 38 | 23 | 7 | 8 | 79 | 39 | 53 | P |
| 3. | Hull City AFC (Kingston-upon-Hull) | 38 | 23 | 7 | 8 | 80 | 46 | 53 | |
| 4. | Derby County FC (Derby) | 38 | 22 | 9 | 7 | 72 | 47 | 53 | |
| 5. | Leicester Fosse FC (Leicester) | 38 | 20 | 4 | 14 | 79 | 58 | 44 | |
| 6. | Glossop FC (Glossop) | 38 | 18 | 7 | 13 | 64 | 57 | 43 | |
| 7. | Fulham FC (London) | 38 | 14 | 13 | 11 | 51 | 43 | 41 | |
| 8. | Wolverhampton Wanderers FC (Wolverhampton) | 38 | 17 | 6 | 15 | 64 | 63 | 40 | |
| 9. | Barnsley FC (Barnsley) | 38 | 16 | 7 | 15 | 62 | 59 | 39 | |
| 10. | Bradford Park Avenue FC (Bradford) | 38 | 17 | 4 | 17 | 64 | 59 | 38 | |
| 11. | West Bromwich Albion FC (West Bromwich) | 38 | 16 | 5 | 17 | 58 | 56 | 37 | |
| 12. | Blackpool FC (Blackpool) | 38 | 14 | 9 | 16 | 50 | 52 | 36 | |
| 13. | Stockport County FC (Stockport) | 38 | 13 | 8 | 17 | 50 | 47 | 34 | |
| 14. | Burnley FC (Burnley) | 38 | 14 | 6 | 18 | 62 | 61 | 34 | |
| 15. | Lincoln City FC (Lincoln) | 38 | 10 | 11 | 17 | 42 | 69 | 31 | |
| 16. | Clapton Orient FC (London) | 38 | 12 | 6 | 20 | 37 | 60 | 30 | |
| 17. | Leeds City AFC (Leeds) | 38 | 10 | 7 | 21 | 46 | 80 | 27 | |
| 18. | Gainsborough Trinity FC (Gainsborough) | 38 | 10 | 6 | 22 | 33 | 75 | 26 | |
| 19. | Grimsby Town FC (Cleethorpes) | 38 | 9 | 6 | 23 | 50 | 77 | 24 | # |
| 20. | Birmingham FC (Birmingham) | 38 | 8 | 7 | 23 | 42 | 78 | 23 | |
| | | 760 | 309 | 142 | 309 | 1166 | 1166 | 760 | |

\# Grimsby Town FC (Cleethorpes) were not re-elected to the league for the next season and were replaced in Division 2 by Huddersfield Town AFC (Huddersfield).

## F.A. CUP FINAL   (Crystal Palace, London – 23/04/1910 – 77,747)

| NEWCASTLE UNITED FC | 1-1 | Barnsley FC (Barnsley) |
|---|---|---|
| *Rutherford* | | *Tuffnell* |

Newcastle: Lawrence, McCracken, Carr, Veitch, Low, McWilliam, Rutherford, Howie, Shepherd, Wilson, Higgins.
Barnsley: Mearns, Downs, Ness, Glendinning, Boyle, Utley, Bartrop, Gadsby, Lilycrop, Tuffnell, Forman.

## F.A. CUP FINAL REPLAY   (Goodison Park, Liverpool – 28/04/1910 – 69,000)

| NEWCASTLE UNITED FC | 2-0 | Barnsley FC (Barnsley) |
|---|---|---|
| *Shepherd 2 (1 pen)* | | |

Newcastle: Lawrence, McCracken, Carr, Veitch, Low, McWilliam, Rutherford, Howie, Shepherd, Wilson, Whitson.
Barnsley: Mearns, Downs, Ness, Glendinning, Boyle, Utley, Bartrop, Gadsby, Lilycrop, Tuffnell, Forman.

## Semi-finals

| Barnsley FC (Barnsley) | 0-0,  3-0 | Everton FC (Liverpool) |
|---|---|---|
| Newcastle United FC (Newcastle-upon-Tyne) | 2-0 | Swindon Town FC (Swindon) |

## Quarter-finals

| Barnsley FC (Barnsley) | 1-0 | Queen's Park Rangers FC (London) |
|---|---|---|
| Coventry City FC (Coventry) | 0-2 | Everton FC (Liverpool) |
| Newcastle United FC (Newcastle-upon-Tyne) | 3-0 | Leicester Fosse FC (Leicester) |
| Swindon Town FC (Swindon) | 2-0 | Manchester City FC (Manchester) |

# 1910-11

| Football League Division 1 1910-1911 Season | Aston Villa | Blackburn Rovers | Bradford City | Bristol City | Bury | Everton | Liverpool | Manchester City | Manchester United | Middlesbrough | Newcastle United | Nottingham Forest | Notts County | Oldham Athletic | Preston North End | Sheffield United | Sunderland | Wednesday | Tottenham Hotspur | Woolwich Arsenal |
|---|---|---|---|---|---|---|---|---|---|---|---|---|---|---|---|---|---|---|---|---|
| Aston Villa FC | ■ | 2-2 | 4-1 | 2-0 | 4-1 | 2-1 | 1-1 | 2-1 | 4-2 | 5-0 | 3-2 | 3-1 | 3-1 | 1-1 | 0-2 | 3-0 | 2-1 | 4-0 | 2-1 | 3-0 |
| Blackburn Rovers FC | 0-0 | ■ | 3-0 | 2-0 | 6-2 | 0-1 | 1-2 | 2-0 | 1-0 | 5-1 | 3-1 | 4-1 | 1-1 | 1-0 | 0-1 | 1-2 | 0-1 | 3-0 | 6-1 | 1-0 |
| Bradford City AFC | 1-2 | 1-0 | ■ | 3-1 | 2-2 | 3-1 | 1-3 | 1-0 | 1-0 | 1-0 | 1-0 | 2-1 | 0-1 | 1-2 | 1-0 | 0-1 | 3-0 | 3-0 | 5-2 | 3-0 |
| Bristol City FC | 1-2 | 1-0 | 0-2 | ■ | 2-0 | 0-1 | 1-1 | 2-1 | 0-1 | 3-2 | 1-0 | 5-1 | 1-0 | 3-2 | 0-0 | 0-2 | 1-1 | 0-2 | 2-2 | 0-1 |
| Bury FC | 1-0 | 2-2 | 0-1 | 2-1 | ■ | 0-0 | 3-0 | 5-2 | 0-3 | 4-2 | 1-1 | 1-0 | 0-0 | 2-2 | 1-0 | 1-1 | 0-0 | 2-1 | 1-1 | 1-1 |
| Everton FC | 0-1 | 6-1 | 0-0 | 4-3 | 2-1 | ■ | 0-1 | 1-0 | 0-1 | 2-0 | 1-5 | 2-1 | 5-0 | 1-0 | 2-0 | 1-0 | 2-2 | 2-0 | 1-1 | 2-0 |
| Liverpool FC | 3-1 | 2-2 | 1-2 | 4-0 | 2-0 | 0-2 | ■ | 1-1 | 3-2 | 3-0 | 3-0 | 2-3 | 2-1 | 1-0 | 3-0 | 2-0 | 1-2 | 1-2 | 3-0 | 1-1 |
| Manchester City FC | 1-1 | 0-0 | 1-3 | 1-2 | 5-1 | 2-1 | 1-2 | ■ | 1-1 | 2-1 | 2-0 | 1-0 | 0-1 | 2-0 | 0-2 | 0-4 | 3-3 | 2-1 | 1-2 | 1-1 |
| Manchester United FC | 2-0 | 3-2 | 1-0 | 3-1 | 3-2 | 2-2 | 2-0 | 2-1 | ■ | 1-2 | 2-0 | 4-2 | 0-0 | 0-0 | 5-0 | 1-1 | 5-1 | 3-2 | 3-2 | 5-0 |
| Middlesbrough FC | 0-1 | 2-3 | 3-2 | 3-0 | 2-1 | 1-0 | 2-2 | 0-0 | 2-2 | ■ | 0-2 | 2-2 | 4-1 | 1-2 | 2-0 | 3-1 | 1-0 | 2-0 | 0-1 | 1-1 |
| Newcastle United FC | 1-0 | 2-2 | 6-1 | 0-1 | 5-1 | 1-0 | 6-1 | 3-3 | 0-1 | 0-0 | ■ | 4-1 | 2-0 | 3-0 | 1-1 | 1-1 | 1-1 | 1-1 | 0-2 | 0-1 |
| Nottingham Forest FC | 3-1 | 5-2 | 0-2 | 3-3 | 1-2 | 1-1 | 2-0 | 0-0 | 2-1 | 1-1 | 0-1 | ■ | 0-2 | 4-1 | 1-3 | 1-2 | 1-3 | 1-2 | 0-1 | 2-3 |
| Notts County FC | 1-2 | 2-0 | 1-1 | 2-0 | 1-0 | 0-1 | 1-0 | 0-1 | 1-0 | 1-0 | 2-2 | 1-1 | ■ | 1-0 | 3-3 | 0-3 | 1-1 | 1-0 | 2-0 | 0-2 |
| Oldham Athletic AFC | 1-1 | 2-0 | 1-0 | 1-0 | 0-0 | 2-0 | 3-1 | 1-1 | 1-3 | 1-1 | 0-2 | 2-0 | 2-1 | ■ | 2-1 | 3-0 | 2-1 | 2-0 | 1-0 | 3-0 |
| Preston North End FC | 0-1 | 0-0 | 2-0 | 4-0 | 2-0 | 0-2 | 2-1 | 1-1 | 0-2 | 1-1 | 2-1 | 0-2 | 2-0 | 1-1 | ■ | 1-1 | 0-2 | 2-0 | 1-3 | 4-1 |
| Sheffield United FC | 2-1 | 1-1 | 0-1 | 0-4 | 3-0 | 0-1 | 2-0 | 2-2 | 2-0 | 2-1 | 0-0 | 0-1 | 0-2 | 1-2 | 5-0 | ■ | 1-2 | 3-0 | 0-1 | 3-2 |
| Sunderland AFC | 3-2 | 2-2 | 1-1 | 3-1 | 4-1 | 4-0 | 4-0 | 4-0 | 1-2 | 3-1 | 2-1 | 2-2 | 1-1 | 2-1 | 1-1 | 0-2 | ■ | 4-0 | 1-2 | 2-2 |
| The Wednesday FC | 3-2 | 2-1 | 2-1 | 2-0 | 1-4 | 1-3 | 3-0 |  | 4-1 | 1-5 | 3-1 | 4-3 | 0-0 |  | 4-1 | 1-3 | 1-0 | ■ | 1-1 | 1-1 |
| Tottenham Hotspur FC | 1-0 | 1-0 | 0-1 | 2-1 | 1-0 | 0-2 | 1-0 | 4-1 | 0-0 | 1-1 | 0-2 | 5-2 | 1-3 | 2-0 | 0-0 | 2-0 | 1-1 | 2-1 | ■ | 0-0 |
| Woolwich Arsenal FC | 1-1 | 4-1 | 0-0 | 3-0 | 3-2 | 1-0 | 0-0 | 0-1 | 1-2 | 0-2 | 1-2 | 3-2 | 2-1 | 0-0 | 2-0 | 0-0 | 0-0 | 2-0 | 1-0 | ■ |

## Division 1

| | | Pd | Wn | Dw | Ls | GF | GA | Pts | |
|---|---|---|---|---|---|---|---|---|---|
| 1. | MANCHESTER UNITED FC (MANCHESTER) | 38 | 22 | 8 | 8 | 72 | 40 | 52 | |
| 2. | Aston Villa FC (Birmingham) | 38 | 22 | 7 | 9 | 69 | 41 | 51 | |
| 3. | Sunderland AFC (Sunderland) | 38 | 15 | 15 | 8 | 67 | 48 | 45 | |
| 4. | Everton FC (Liverpool) | 38 | 19 | 7 | 12 | 50 | 36 | 45 | |
| 5. | Bradford City AFC (Bradford) | 38 | 20 | 5 | 13 | 51 | 42 | 45 | |
| 6. | The Wednesday FC (Sheffield) | 38 | 17 | 8 | 13 | 47 | 48 | 42 | |
| 7. | Oldham Athletic AFC (Oldham) | 38 | 16 | 9 | 13 | 44 | 41 | 41 | |
| 8. | Newcastle United FC (Newcastle-upon-Tyne) | 38 | 15 | 10 | 13 | 61 | 43 | 40 | |
| 9. | Sheffield United FC (Sheffield) | 38 | 15 | 8 | 15 | 49 | 43 | 38 | |
| 10. | Woolwich Arsenal FC (London) | 38 | 13 | 12 | 13 | 41 | 49 | 38 | |
| 11. | Notts County FC (Nottingham) | 38 | 14 | 10 | 14 | 37 | 45 | 38 | |
| 12. | Blackburn Rovers FC (Blackburn) | 38 | 13 | 11 | 14 | 62 | 54 | 37 | |
| 13. | Liverpool FC (Liverpool) | 38 | 15 | 7 | 16 | 53 | 53 | 37 | |
| 14. | Preston North End FC (Preston) | 38 | 12 | 11 | 15 | 40 | 49 | 35 | |
| 15. | Tottenham Hotspur FC (London) | 38 | 13 | 6 | 19 | 52 | 63 | 32 | |
| 16. | Middlesbrough FC (Middlesbrough) | 38 | 11 | 10 | 17 | 49 | 63 | 32 | |
| 17. | Manchester City FC (Manchester) | 38 | 9 | 13 | 16 | 43 | 58 | 31 | |
| 18. | Bury FC (Bury) | 38 | 9 | 11 | 18 | 43 | 71 | 29 | |
| 19. | Bristol City FC (Bristol) | 38 | 11 | 5 | 22 | 43 | 66 | 27 | R |
| 20. | Nottingham Forest FC (Nottingham) | 38 | 9 | 7 | 22 | 55 | 75 | 25 | R |
| | | 760 | 290 | 180 | 290 | 1028 | 1028 | 760 | |

64

# Top Goalscorer

1) A. SHEPHERD       (Newcastle United FC)    25

| Football League Division 2 1910-1911 Season | Barnsley | Birmingham | Blackpool | Bolton Wanderers | Bradford Park Ave. | Burnley | Chelsea | Clapton Orient | Derby County | Fulham | Gainsborough Trin. | Glossop | Huddersfield Town | Hull City | Leeds City | Leicester Fosse | Lincoln City | Stockport County | W.B.A. | Wolves |
|---|---|---|---|---|---|---|---|---|---|---|---|---|---|---|---|---|---|---|---|---|
| Barnsley FC | ■ | 2-3 | 1-2 | 0-0 | 7-0 | 0-1 | 3-2 | 1-2 | 0-2 | 4-2 | 2-2 | 4-0 | 1-2 | 0-1 | 4-0 | 1-1 | 2-2 | 1-1 | 1-1 | 2-2 |
| Birmingham FC | 1-0 | ■ | 2-0 | 2-1 | 1-0 | 1-1 | 2-1 | 0-1 | 2-0 | 1-1 | 1-1 | 1-2 | 2-1 | 1-0 | 2-1 | 1-0 | 0-1 | 1-3 | 1-1 | 1-3 |
| Blackpool FC | 1-0 | 3-1 | ■ | 1-1 | 4-1 | 1-0 | 0-2 | 1-1 | 0-1 | 1-2 | 1-1 | 1-0 | 1-1 | 2-0 | 1-2 | 2-0 | 5-1 | 2-1 | 0-0 | 2-0 |
| Bolton Wanderers FC | 4-0 | 5-1 | 1-0 | ■ | 1-0 | 1-1 | 2-0 | 2-0 | 2-1 | 2-0 | 3-0 | 4-0 | 3-1 | 2-1 | 3-0 | 6-2 | 3-1 | 2-2 | 3-1 | 4-1 |
| Bradford Park Avenue | 2-3 | 2-2 | 1-0 | 1-1 | ■ | 1-1 | 2-1 | 3-0 | 2-1 | 1-0 | 5-0 | 6-0 | 0-1 | 2-0 | 0-2 | 3-1 | 6-0 | 3-2 | 3-3 | 1-0 |
| Burnley FC | 0-0 | 2-2 | 1-1 | 1-3 | 1-1 | ■ | 1-1 | 2-0 | 2-1 | 1-0 | 1-1 | 0-0 | 2-1 | 0-0 | 4-1 | 2-1 | 3-1 | 5-3 | 2-0 | 1-1 |
| Chelsea FC | 3-1 | 2-2 | 0-0 | 3-0 | 3-0 | 3-0 | ■ | 1-0 | 3-2 | 2-0 | 2-0 | 2-0 | 2-0 | 2-0 | 4-1 | 2-0 | 7-0 | 2-0 | 2-1 | 2-0 |
| Clapton Orient FC | 3-0 | 2-1 | 2-1 | 0-0 | 1-0 | 0-2 | 0-0 | ■ | 1-0 | 1-0 | 1-0 | 4-0 | 2-0 | 1-1 | 1-0 | 3-1 | 2-0 | 1-0 | 0-0 | 3-1 |
| Derby County FC | 5-1 | 1-0 | 1-1 | 2-2 | 4-2 | 3-0 | 1-4 | 3-1 | ■ | 2-2 | 4-0 | 2-1 | 1-1 | 2-3 | 2-2 | 3-0 | 5-0 | 4-1 | 1-3 | 2-0 |
| Fulham FC | 0-2 | 3-0 | 2-1 | 2-0 | 4-0 | 3-0 | 1-0 | 1-1 | 3-1 | ■ | 1-0 | 2-2 | 2-1 | 0-1 | 2-1 | 3-0 | 0-0 | 6-2 | 0-1 | 0-1 |
| Gainsborough Trinity | 1-1 | 1-0 | 2-0 | 1-0 | 1-2 | 1-2 | 3-1 | 3-1 | 0-0 | 0-1 | ■ | 3-0 | 3-1 | 1-1 | 1-2 | 2-0 | 1-0 | 0-0 | 1-1 | 1-3 |
| Glossop FC | 1-1 | 2-1 | 3-1 | 1-2 | 0-1 | 1-1 | 2-1 | 1-3 | 2-2 | 2-1 | 3-1 | ■ | 5-2 | 0-0 | 2-1 | 1-0 | 2-0 | 3-0 | 0-2 | 5-1 |
| Huddersfield Town AFC | 2-0 | 7-1 | 2-2 | 1-1 | 0-0 | 0-1 | 3-1 | 2-0 | 0-3 | 1-2 | 2-1 | 1-0 | ■ | 2-0 | 3-2 | 1-2 | 1-1 | 4-1 | 0-2 | 3-1 |
| Hull City AFC | 5-1 | 4-1 | 1-1 | 1-1 | 2-2 | 3-0 | 1-1 | 1-2 | 2-0 | 0-0 | 3-2 | 1-0 | 2-2 | ■ | 1-1 | 2-2 | 2-1 | 4-1 | 1-1 | 2-2 |
| Leeds City AFC | 0-0 | 1-1 | 1-2 | 1-0 | 0-0 | 0-0 | 3-3 | 1-0 | 3-2 | 3-1 | 4-0 | 0-2 | 5-2 | 1-0 | ■ | 2-3 | 0-1 | 4-0 | 3-1 | 1-0 |
| Leicester Fosse FC | 1-1 | 2-0 | 2-0 | 5-0 | 0-1 | 1-1 | 1-0 | 2-1 | 1-2 | 3-2 | 1-0 | 1-1 | 2-1 | 0-2 | 2-1 | ■ | 2-0 | 5-1 | 2-3 | 2-3 |
| Lincoln City FC | 1-0 | 0-1 | 0-1 | 1-3 | 0-0 | 1-0 | 0-0 | 0-0 | 0-2 | 1-0 | 0-0 | 2-2 | 2-2 | 1-4 | 1-1 | 2-0 | ■ | 2-0 | 1-2 | 1-5 |
| Stockport County FC | 2-2 | 3-1 | 1-3 | 0-1 | 1-0 | 4-2 | 2-2 | 0-3 | 3-2 | 1-1 | 1-0 | 2-1 | 1-0 | 1-1 | 0-4 | 1-0 | 3-2 | ■ | 0-1 | 1-0 |
| West Bromwich Albion FC | 3-3 | 1-0 | 0-1 | 2-0 | 3-0 | 2-1 | 1-3 | 3-0 | 1-1 | 2-1 | 2-1 | 3-1 | 1-0 | 0-2 | 2-0 | 5-1 | 3-0 | 4-2 | ■ | 2-1 |
| Wolverhampton Wanderers FC | 1-0 | 3-1 | 0-3 | 3-0 | 1-0 | 1-0 | 0-0 | 1-0 | 1-2 | 5-1 | 1-1 | 2-0 | 0-3 | 0-0 | 3-1 | 1-0 | 2-1 | 0-0 | 2-3 | ■ |

## Division 2

| | | Pd | Wn | Dw | Ls | GF | GA | Pts | |
|---|---|---|---|---|---|---|---|---|---|
| 1. | West Bromwich Albion FC (West Bromwich) | 38 | 22 | 9 | 7 | 67 | 41 | 53 | P |
| 2. | Bolton Wanderers FC (Bolton) | 38 | 21 | 9 | 8 | 69 | 40 | 51 | P |
| 3. | Chelsea FC (London) | 38 | 20 | 9 | 9 | 71 | 35 | 49 | |
| 4. | Clapton Orient FC (London) | 38 | 19 | 7 | 12 | 44 | 35 | 45 | |
| 5. | Hull City AFC (Kingston-upon-Hull) | 38 | 14 | 16 | 8 | 55 | 39 | 44 | |
| 6. | Derby County FC (Derby) | 38 | 17 | 8 | 13 | 73 | 52 | 42 | |
| 7. | Blackpool FC (Blackpool) | 38 | 16 | 10 | 12 | 49 | 38 | 42 | |
| 8. | Burnley FC (Burnley) | 38 | 13 | 15 | 10 | 45 | 45 | 41 | |
| 9. | Wolverhampton Wanderers FC (Wolverhampton) | 38 | 15 | 8 | 15 | 51 | 52 | 38 | |
| 10. | Fulham FC (London) | 38 | 15 | 7 | 16 | 52 | 48 | 37 | |
| 11. | Leeds City AFC (Leeds) | 38 | 15 | 7 | 16 | 58 | 56 | 37 | |
| 12. | Bradford Park Avenue FC (Bradford) | 38 | 14 | 9 | 15 | 53 | 55 | 37 | |
| 13. | Huddersfield Town AFC (Huddersfield) | 38 | 13 | 8 | 17 | 57 | 58 | 34 | |
| 14. | Glossop FC (Glossop) | 38 | 13 | 8 | 17 | 48 | 62 | 34 | |
| 15. | Leicester Fosse FC (Leicester) | 38 | 14 | 5 | 19 | 52 | 62 | 33 | |
| 16. | Birmingham FC (Birmingham) | 38 | 12 | 8 | 18 | 42 | 64 | 32 | |
| 17. | Stockport County FC (Stockport) | 38 | 11 | 8 | 19 | 47 | 79 | 30 | |
| 18. | Gainsborough Trinity FC (Gainsborough) | 38 | 9 | 11 | 18 | 37 | 55 | 29 | |
| 19. | Barnsley FC (Barnsley) | 38 | 7 | 14 | 17 | 52 | 62 | 28 | |
| 20. | Lincoln City FC (Lincoln) | 38 | 7 | 10 | 21 | 28 | 72 | 24 | # |
| | | 760 | 287 | 186 | 287 | 1050 | 1050 | 760 | |

\# Lincoln City FC (Lincoln) were not re-elected to the league for the next season and were replaced in Division 2 by Grimsby Town FC (Cleethorpes).

Burslem Port Vale FC (Burslem) re-formed as a Limited Company under the name of Port Vale FC (Stoke-on-Trent) the town of Burslem having been merged in 1910 with the towns of Fenton, Hanley, Longton, Stoke-upon-Trent and Tunstall as the city of Stoke-on-Trent.

## F.A. CUP FINAL    (Crystal Palace, London – 22/04/1911 – 69,098)

BRADFORD CITY AFC (BRADFORD)          0-0     Newcastle United FC (Newcastle-upon-Tyne)

Bradford: Mellors, Campbell, Taylor, Robinson, Gildea, McDonald, Logan, Spiers, O'Rourke, Devine, Thompson.
Newcastle: Lawrence, McCracken, Whitson, Veitch, Low, Willis, Rutherford, Jobey, Stewart, Higgins, Wilson.

## F.A. CUP FINAL REPLAY    (Old Trafford, Manchester – 26/04/1911 – 58,000)

BRADFORD CITY AFC (BRADFORD)          1-0     Newcastle United FC (Newcastle-upon-Tyne)
*Speirs*

Bradford: Mellors, Campbell, Taylor, Robinson, Torrance, McDonald, Logan, Spiers, O'Rourke, Devine, Thompson.
Newcastle: Lawrence, McCracken, Whitson, Veitch, Low, Willis, Rutherford, Jobey, Stewart, Higgins, Wilson.

## Semi-finals

| Bradford City AFC (Bradford) | 3-0 | Blackburn Rovers FC (Blackburn) |
| Newcastle United FC (Newcastle-upon-Tyne) | 3-0 | Chelsea FC (London) |

## Quarter-finals

| Bradford City AFC (Bradford) | 1-0 | Burnley FC (Burnley) |
| Chelsea FC (London) | 3-1 | Swindon Town FC (Swindon) |
| Newcastle United FC (Newcastle-upon-Tyne) | 4-0 | Derby County FC (Derby) |
| West Ham United FC (London) | 2-3 | Blackburn Rovers FC (Blackburn) |

# 1911-12

| Football League Division 1 1911-1912 Season | Aston Villa | Blackburn Rovers | Bolton Wanderers | Bradford City | Bury | Everton | Liverpool | Manchester City | Manchester United | Middlesbrough | Newcastle United | Notts County | Oldham Athletic | Preston North End | Sheffield United | Sunderland | Wednesday | Tottenham Hotspur | W.B.A. | Woolwich Arsenal |
|---|---|---|---|---|---|---|---|---|---|---|---|---|---|---|---|---|---|---|---|---|
| Aston Villa FC | | 0-3 | 0-1 | 0-0 | 5-2 | 3-0 | 5-0 | 3-1 | 6-0 | 2-1 | 2-0 | 5-1 | 6-1 | 1-0 | 1-0 | 2-3 | 1-3 | 2-2 | 0-3 | 4-1 |
| Blackburn Rovers FC | 3-1 | | 2-0 | 3-1 | 2-0 | 2-1 | 1-0 | 2-0 | 2-2 | 2-1 | 1-1 | 0-0 | 1-0 | 3-0 | 1-0 | 2-2 | 0-0 | 0-0 | 4-1 | 4-0 |
| Bolton Wanderers FC | 3-0 | 2-0 | | 2-0 | 1-0 | 1-2 | 2-1 | 2-1 | 1-1 | 1-0 | 0-2 | 3-0 | 2-1 | 3-0 | 0-3 | 3-0 | 4-2 | 1-0 | 2-0 | 2-2 |
| Bradford City AFC | 2-1 | 1-0 | 1-0 | | 1-0 | 1-0 | 0-2 | 4-1 | 0-1 | 2-1 | 1-1 | 2-3 | 0-0 | 0-1 | 1-0 | 2-1 | 5-1 | 3-0 | 4-1 | 1-1 |
| Bury FC | 1-1 | 1-2 | 1-3 | 2-0 | | 1-2 | 2-2 | 1-2 | 0-1 | 0-2 | 2-1 | 0-1 | 1-1 | 0-0 | 3-1 | 0-2 | 2-2 | 2-1 | 1-0 | 3-1 |
| Everton FC | 1-1 | 1-3 | 1-0 | 1-0 | 1-1 | | 2-1 | 1-0 | 4-0 | 1-0 | 2-0 | 1-1 | 1-1 | 1-0 | 3-2 | 1-0 | 1-0 | 2-2 | 3-0 | 1-0 |
| Liverpool FC | 1-2 | 1-2 | 1-0 | 1-0 | 1-1 | 1-3 | | 2-2 | 3-2 | 1-1 | 0-1 | 3-0 | 1-0 | 0-1 | 2-0 | 2-1 | 1-1 | 1-2 | 1-3 | 4-1 |
| Manchester City FC | 2-6 | 3-0 | 3-1 | 4-0 | 2-0 | 4-0 | 2-3 | | 0-0 | 2-0 | 1-1 | 4-0 | 1-3 | 0-0 | 0-0 | 2-0 | 4-0 | 2-1 | 0-2 | 3-3 |
| Manchester United FC | 3-1 | 3-1 | 2-0 | 0-1 | 0-0 | 2-1 | 1-1 | 0-0 | | 3-4 | 0-2 | 2-0 | 3-1 | 0-0 | 1-0 | 2-2 | 3-1 | 1-2 | 1-2 | 2-0 |
| Middlesbrough FC | 1-2 | 2-1 | 1-0 | 1-0 | 1-1 | 0-0 | 3-2 | 3-1 | 3-0 | | 1-1 | 4-0 | 3-0 | 4-2 | 1-1 | 3-3 | 1-1 | 2-0 | 1-0 | 0-2 |
| Newcastle United FC | 6-2 | 4-2 | 5-2 | 0-2 | 3-2 | 2-0 | 1-1 | 1-0 | 2-3 | 0-1 | | 3-2 | 1-1 | 1-0 | 2-2 | 3-1 | 0-2 | 2-0 | 0-0 | 1-1 |
| Notts County FC | 2-0 | 1-3 | 3-2 | 0-0 | 2-0 | 0-1 | 0-0 | 0-1 | 0-1 | 2-1 | 1-4 | | 1-1 | 1-2 | 2-0 | 3-1 | 1-0 | 2-2 | 2-0 | 3-1 |
| Oldham Athletic AFC | 1-2 | 0-1 | 3-1 | 3-0 | 2-0 | 3-0 | 0-1 | 4-1 | 2-2 | 2-0 | 2-4 | 1-2 | | 1-0 | 2-3 | 0-0 | 1-0 | 2-3 | 3-1 | 0-0 |
| Preston North End FC | 4-1 | 2-2 | 1-2 | 2-2 | 1-0 | 2-1 | 2-1 | 2-1 | 0-0 | 0-3 | 2-1 | 2-1 | 0-1 | | 3-0 | 0-3 | 2-3 | 0-1 | 1-1 | 0-1 |
| Sheffield United FC | 0-1 | 1-1 | 0-5 | 7-3 | 4-0 | 2-1 | 3-1 | 6-2 | 6-1 | 1-1 | 2-1 | 1-3 | 4-0 | 4-2 | | 1-2 | 1-1 | 1-2 | 1-1 | 2-1 |
| Sunderland AFC | 2-2 | 3-0 | 0-1 | 1-1 | 1-0 | 4-0 | 1-2 | 1-1 | 5-0 | 1-0 | 1-2 | 5-0 | 4-2 | 3-0 | 0-0 | | 0-0 | 1-1 | 3-2 | 1-0 |
| The Wednesday FC | 3-0 | 1-1 | 0-1 | 4-2 | 2-1 | 1-3 | 2-2 | 3-0 | 3-0 | 0-2 | 1-2 | 3-0 | 1-0 | 0-1 | 1-1 | 8-0 | | 4-0 | 4-1 | 3-0 |
| Tottenham Hotspur FC | 2-1 | 0-2 | 1-0 | 2-3 | 2-1 | 0-1 | 2-0 | 0-2 | 1-1 | 2-1 | 1-2 | 2-2 | 4-0 | 6-2 | 1-1 | 0-0 | 3-1 | | 1-0 | 5-0 |
| West Bromwich Albion FC | 2-2 | 2-0 | 0-0 | 0-0 | 2-0 | 1-0 | 1-0 | 1-1 | 1-0 | 3-1 | 3-1 | 2-1 | 0-0 | 0-2 | 0-1 | 1-0 | 1-5 | 2-0 | | 1-1 |
| Woolwich Arsenal FC | 2-2 | 5-1 | 3-0 | 2-0 | 1-0 | 0-1 | 2-2 | 2-0 | 2-1 | 3-1 | 2-0 | 0-3 | 1-1 | 4-1 | 3-1 | 3-0 | 0-2 | 3-1 | 0-2 | |

## Division 1

| | | Pd | Wn | Dw | Ls | GF | GA | Pts | |
|---|---|---|---|---|---|---|---|---|---|
| 1. | BLACKBURN ROVERS FC (BLACKBURN) | 38 | 20 | 9 | 9 | 60 | 43 | 49 | |
| 2. | Everton FC (Liverpool) | 38 | 20 | 6 | 12 | 46 | 42 | 46 | |
| 3. | Newcastle United FC (Newcastle-upon-Tyne) | 38 | 18 | 8 | 12 | 64 | 50 | 44 | |
| 4. | Bolton Wanderers FC (Bolton) | 38 | 20 | 3 | 15 | 54 | 43 | 43 | |
| 5. | The Wednesday FC (Sheffield) | 38 | 16 | 9 | 13 | 69 | 49 | 41 | |
| 6. | Aston Villa FC (Birmingham) | 38 | 17 | 7 | 14 | 76 | 63 | 41 | |
| 7. | Middlesbrough FC (Middlesbrough) | 38 | 16 | 8 | 14 | 56 | 45 | 40 | |
| 8. | Sunderland AFC (Sunderland) | 38 | 14 | 11 | 13 | 58 | 51 | 39 | |
| 9. | West Bromwich Albion FC (West Bromwich) | 38 | 15 | 9 | 14 | 43 | 47 | 39 | |
| 10. | Woolwich Arsenal FC (London) | 38 | 15 | 8 | 15 | 55 | 59 | 38 | |
| 11. | Bradford City AFC (Bradford) | 38 | 15 | 8 | 15 | 46 | 50 | 38 | |
| 12. | Tottenham Hotspur FC (London) | 38 | 14 | 9 | 15 | 53 | 53 | 37 | |
| 13. | Manchester United FC (Manchester) | 38 | 13 | 11 | 14 | 45 | 60 | 37 | |
| 14. | Sheffield United FC (Sheffield) | 38 | 13 | 10 | 15 | 63 | 56 | 36 | |
| 15. | Manchester City FC (Manchester ) | 38 | 13 | 9 | 16 | 56 | 58 | 35 | |
| 16. | Notts County FC (Nottingham) | 38 | 14 | 7 | 17 | 46 | 63 | 35 | |
| 17. | Liverpool FC (Liverpool) | 38 | 12 | 10 | 16 | 49 | 55 | 34 | |
| 18. | Oldham Athletic AFC (Oldham) | 38 | 12 | 10 | 16 | 46 | 54 | 34 | |
| 19. | Preston North End FC (Preston) | 38 | 13 | 7 | 18 | 40 | 57 | 33 | R |
| 20. | Bury FC (Bury) | 38 | 6 | 9 | 23 | 32 | 59 | 21 | R |
| | | 760 | 296 | 168 | 296 | 1057 | 1057 | 760 | |

# Top Goalscorers

1)  H. HAMPTON      (Aston Villa FC)    25
    G. HOLLEY       (Sunderland AFC)    25
    D. McLEAN      (The Wednesday FC)    25

| Football League Division 2 1911-1912 Season | Barnsley | Birmingham | Blackpool | Bradford Park Avenue | Bristol City | Burnley | Chelsea | Clapton Orient | Derby County | Fulham | Gainsborough Trinity | Glossop | Grimsby Town | Huddersfield Town | Hull City | Leeds City | Leicester Fosse | Nottingham Forest | Stockport County | Wolves |
|---|---|---|---|---|---|---|---|---|---|---|---|---|---|---|---|---|---|---|---|---|
| Barnsley FC | ■ | 1-0 | 1-0 | 1-0 | 4-1 | 1-1 | 0-2 | 2-1 | 0-2 | 2-2 | 4-0 | 1-0 | 2-2 | 0-0 | 1-2 | 3-4 | 0-0 | 1-0 | 2-1 | 2-1 |
| Birmingham FC | 1-3 | ■ | 2-1 | 2-3 | 0-0 | 4-0 | 1-4 | 4-0 | 0-4 | 1-3 | 2-2 | 2-0 | 2-2 | 1-0 | 5-1 | 4-3 | 4-0 | 4-2 | 2-0 | 3-1 |
| Blackpool FC | 0-0 | 1-0 | ■ | 0-4 | 1-0 | 0-0 | 1-0 | 1-0 | 1-0 | 3-1 | 0-0 | 2-0 | 1-2 | 3-1 | 3-2 | 3-0 | 1-1 | 2-0 | 0-1 | 1-0 |
| Bradford Park Avenue | 1-0 | 3-0 | 0-0 | ■ | 0-1 | 2-1 | 1-1 | 2-1 | 0-1 | 0-2 | 5-0 | 1-1 | 4-1 | 3-1 | 3-1 | 1-1 | 1-1 | 2-1 | 1-0 | 0-1 |
| Bristol City FC | 0-1 | 2-1 | 2-0 | 1-0 | ■ | 0-3 | 1-1 | 1-0 | 1-1 | 1-0 | 2-0 | 2-0 | 3-0 | 3-2 | 0-0 | 4-1 | 0-1 | 2-2 | 2-1 | 0-3 |
| Burnley FC | 3-0 | 1-1 | 1-1 | 3-1 | 4-2 | ■ | 2-2 | 1-0 | 0-0 | 5-1 | 2-0 | 4-0 | 1-1 | 3-0 | 5-1 | 4-2 | 3-0 | 2-0 | 4-1 | 2-1 |
| Chelsea FC | 2-1 | 0-2 | 4-1 | 1-0 | 2-2 | 0-2 | ■ | 3-0 | 1-0 | 1-0 | 1-0 | 1-0 | 4-1 | 3-1 | 1-0 | 4-2 | 2-1 | 2-0 | 0-0 | 4-0 |
| Clapton Orient FC | 2-0 | 2-0 | 2-0 | 2-0 | 4-0 | 1-2 | 1-4 | ■ | 3-0 | 4-0 | 3-0 | 2-1 | 1-0 | 2-1 | 4-0 | 2-1 | 4-1 | 0-2 | 4-2 | 1-0 |
| Derby County FC | 0-0 | 0-1 | 5-1 | 1-0 | 3-0 | 2-0 | 2-0 | 5-1 | ■ | 6-1 | 4-0 | 5-0 | 2-1 | 4-2 | 2-3 | 5-2 | 5-0 | 1-0 | 2-0 | 1-1 |
| Fulham FC | 2-2 | 2-1 | 3-0 | 2-0 | 2-1 | 3-4 | 0-1 | 0-2 | 0-0 | ■ | 7-1 | 0-2 | 1-3 | 3-1 | 0-1 | 7-2 | 41 | 2-0 | 3-1 | 1-1 |
| Gainsborough Trinity | 1-2 | 0-0 | 0-0 | 0-0 | 2-3 | 1-0 | 0-2 | 0-2 | 1-1 | 0-1 | ■ | 1-1 | 2-3 | 5-0 | 0-3 | 2-1 | 0-1 | 1-2 | 0-0 | 1-0 |
| Glossop FC | 0-2 | 2-0 | 1-1 | 0-0 | 3-0 | 1-3 | 1-2 | 3-3 | 3-1 | 1-1 | 1-1 | ■ | 5-2 | 2-3 | 1-1 | 2-1 | 6-0 | 0-0 | 1-1 | 0-1 |
| Grimsby Town FC | 0-0 | 1-0 | 1-0 | 0-0 | 3-0 | 1-0 | 2-1 | 2-1 | 0-3 | 1-0 | 3-3 | 0-0 | ■ | 1-2 | 1-0 | 1-2 | 4-0 | 1-4 | 2-2 | 0-0 |
| Huddersfield Town AFC | 2-1 | 3-2 | 4-0 | 3-1 | 1-2 | 1-1 | 1-3 | 0-0 | 0-0 | 2-0 | 2-2 | 3-1 | 2-0 | ■ | 0-2 | 1-2 | 1-2 | 1-2 | 2-0 | 1-1 |
| Hull City AFC | 0-0 | 4-0 | 3-0 | 5-1 | 3-0 | 4-1 | 1-0 | 0-2 | 0-0 | 2-3 | 1-1 | 2-0 | 1-0 | 0-1 | ■ | 1-0 | 4-1 | 2-1 | 0-2 | 3-0 |
| Leeds City AFC | 3-2 | 0-0 | 1-0 | 1-2 | 3-1 | 1-5 | 0-0 | 0-2 | 0-1 | 0-2 | 0-0 | 2-1 | 1-2 | 2-0 | 0-0 | ■ | 2-1 | 3-1 | 1-1 | 1-1 |
| Leicester Fosse FC | 0-0 | 5-2 | 4-0 | 3-0 | 2-0 | 3-2 | 2-0 | 0-1 | 2-5 | 2-0 | 1-0 | 0-2 | 0-2 | 3-0 | 2-1 |  | ■ | 1-1 | 1-1 | 1-1 |
| Nottingham Forest FC | 0-2 | 0-1 | 2-1 | 2-1 | 2-0 | 0-1 | 2-3 | 3-0 | 1-3 | 1-1 | 2-0 | 0-1 | 1-0 | 3-0 | 0-0 | 2-1 | 4-1 | ■ | 1-2 | 0-0 |
| Stockport County FC | 1-1 | 2-0 | 1-2 | 1-0 | 1-0 | 0-1 | 0-1 | 1-1 | 4-0 | 2-1 | 0-3 | 3-0 | 3-0 | 3-1 | 1-1 | 3-3 | 2-3 | 2-2 | ■ | 1-2 |
| Wolverhampton Wanderers FC | 5-0 | 1-0 | 3-0 | 1-1 | 3-1 | 2-0 | 3-1 | 0-1 | 0-1 | 0-0 | 1-0 | 1-1 | 1-2 | 1-2 | 8-0 | 5-0 | 1-0 | 1-0 | 4-0 | ■ |

| Division 2 | | Pd | Wn | Dw | Ls | GF | GA | Pts | |
|---|---|---|---|---|---|---|---|---|---|
| 1. | Derby County FC (Derby) | 38 | 23 | 8 | 7 | 74 | 28 | 54 | P |
| 2. | Chelsea FC (London) | 38 | 24 | 6 | 8 | 64 | 34 | 54 | P |
| 3. | Burnley FC (Burnley) | 38 | 22 | 8 | 8 | 77 | 41 | 52 | |
| 4. | Clapton Orient FC (London) | 38 | 21 | 3 | 14 | 61 | 44 | 45 | |
| 5. | Wolverhampton Wanderers FC (Wolverhampton) | 38 | 16 | 10 | 12 | 57 | 33 | 42 | |
| 6. | Barnsley FC (Barnsley) | 38 | 15 | 12 | 11 | 45 | 42 | 42 | |
| 7. | Hull City AFC (Kingston-upon-Hull) | 38 | 17 | 8 | 13 | 54 | 51 | 42 | |
| 8. | Fulham FC (London) | 38 | 16 | 7 | 15 | 66 | 58 | 39 | |
| 9. | Grimsby Town FC (Cleethorpes) | 38 | 15 | 9 | 14 | 48 | 55 | 39 | |
| 10. | Leicester Fosse FC (Leicester) | 38 | 15 | 7 | 16 | 49 | 66 | 37 | |
| 11. | Bradford Park Avenue FC (Bradford) | 38 | 13 | 9 | 16 | 44 | 45 | 35 | |
| 12. | Birmingham FC (Birmingham) | 38 | 14 | 6 | 18 | 55 | 59 | 34 | |
| 13. | Bristol City FC (Bristol) | 38 | 14 | 6 | 18 | 41 | 60 | 34 | |
| 14. | Blackpool FC (Blackpool) | 38 | 13 | 8 | 17 | 32 | 52 | 34 | |
| 15. | Nottingham Forest FC (Nottingham) | 38 | 13 | 7 | 18 | 46 | 48 | 33 | |
| 16. | Stockport County FC (Stockport) | 38 | 11 | 11 | 16 | 47 | 54 | 33 | |
| 17. | Huddersfield Town AFC (Huddersfield) | 38 | 13 | 6 | 19 | 50 | 64 | 32 | |
| 18. | Glossop FC (Glossop) | 38 | 8 | 12 | 18 | 42 | 56 | 28 | |
| 19. | Leeds City AFC (Leeds) | 38 | 10 | 8 | 20 | 50 | 78 | 28 | |
| 20. | Gainsborough Trinity FC (Gainsborough) | 38 | 5 | 13 | 20 | 30 | 64 | 23 | # |
| | | 760 | 298 | 164 | 298 | 1032 | 1032 | 760 | |

\# Gainsborough Trinity FC (Gainsborough) were not re-elected to the league for next season and were replaced in Division 2 by Lincoln City FC (Lincoln).

## F.A. CUP FINAL    (Crystal Palace, London – 20/04/1912 – 54,556)

BARNSLEY FC (BARNSLEY)                 0-0  (aet)                 West Bromwich Albion FC

Barnsley: Copper, Downs, Taylor, Glendinning, Bratley, Utley, Bartrop, Tuffnell, Lillycrop, Travers, Moore.

West Bromwich: Pearson, Cook, Pennington, Baddeley, Buck, McNeal, Jephcott, Wright, Pailor, Bowser, Shearman.

## F.A. CUP FINAL REPLAY    (Bramall Lane, Sheffield – 24/04/1912 – 38,555)

BARNSLEY FC (BARNSLEY)                 1-0      West Bromwich Albion FC (West Bromwich)

*Tuffnell*

Barnsley: Copper, Downs, Taylor, Glendinning, Bratley, Utley, Bartrop, Tuffnell, Lillycrop, Travers, Moore.

West Bromwich: Pearson, Cook, Pennington, Baddeley, Buck, McNeal, Jephcott, Wright, Pailor, Bowser, Shearman.

## Semi-finals

| | | |
|---|---|---|
| Blackburn Rovers FC (Blackburn) | 0-0, 0-1 | West Bromwich Albion FC (West Bromwich) |
| Swindon Town FC (Swindon) | 0-0, 0-1 | Barnsley FC (Barnsley) |

## Quarter-finals

| | | |
|---|---|---|
| Barnsley FC (Barnsley) | 0-0, 0-0, 0-0, 3-2 | Bradford City AFC (Bradford) |
| Manchester United FC (Manchester) | 1-1, 2-4 | Blackburn Rovers FC (Blackburn) |
| Swindon Town FC (Swindon) | 2-1 | Everton FC (Liverpool) |
| West Bromwich Albion FC (West Bromwich) | 3-0 | Fulham FC (London) |

# 1912-13

| Football League Division 1 1912-1913 Season | Aston Villa | Blackburn Rovers | Bolton Wanderers | Bradford City | Chelsea | Derby County | Everton | Liverpool | Manchester City | Manchester United | Middlesbrough | Newcastle United | Notts County | Oldham Athletic | Sheffield United | Sunderland | Wednesday | Tottenham Hotspur | W.B.A. | Woolwich Arsenal |
|---|---|---|---|---|---|---|---|---|---|---|---|---|---|---|---|---|---|---|---|---|
| Aston Villa FC | | 1-1 | 1-1 | 3-1 | 1-0 | 5-1 | 1-1 | 1-3 | 2-0 | 4-2 | 5-1 | 3-1 | 1-0 | 7-1 | 4-2 | 1-1 | 10-0 | 1-0 | 2-4 | 4-1 |
| Blackburn Rovers FC | 2-2 | | 6-0 | 5-0 | 1-1 | 0-1 | 1-2 | 5-1 | 2-2 | 0-0 | 5-2 | 2-0 | 2-1 | 7-1 | 3-1 | 4-0 | 0-1 | 6-1 | 2-4 | 1-1 |
| Bolton Wanderers FC | 2-3 | 1-1 | | 2-0 | 1-0 | 1-1 | 0-0 | 1-1 | 2-2 | 2-1 | 3-2 | 1-2 | 0-0 | 3-0 | 4-2 | 1-3 | 3-0 | 2-0 | 2-1 | 5-1 |
| Bradford City AFC | 1-1 | 0-2 | 4-1 | | 2-2 | 2-3 | 4-1 | 2-0 | 2-1 | 1-0 | 1-2 | 2-0 | 1-0 | 0-0 | 3-1 | 1-5 | 0-0 | 3-1 | 1-1 | 3-1 |
| Chelsea FC | 1-2 | 1-6 | 2-3 | 0-3 | | 3-1 | 1-3 | 1-2 | 2-1 | 1-4 | 2-3 | 1-0 | 5-1 | 1-1 | 4-2 | 2-0 | 0-4 | 1-0 | 0-2 | 1-1 |
| Derby County FC | 0-1 | 1-1 | 3-3 | 4-0 | 3-1 | | 1-4 | 4-2 | 2-0 | 2-1 | 0-2 | 2-1 | 1-0 | 1-2 | 5-1 | 0-3 | 1-4 | 5-0 | 1-2 | 4-1 |
| Everton FC | 0-1 | 2-1 | 2-3 | 2-1 | 1-0 | 2-2 | | 0-2 | 0-0 | 4-1 | 1-0 | 0-6 | 4-0 | 2-3 | 0-1 | 0-4 | 3-1 | 1-2 | 1-3 | 3-0 |
| Liverpool FC | 2-0 | 4-1 | 5-0 | 2-1 | 1-2 | 2-1 | 0-2 | | 1-2 | 0-2 | 4-2 | 2-1 | 0-0 | 2-0 | 2-2 | 2-5 | 2-1 | 4-1 | 2-1 | 3-0 |
| Manchester City FC | 1-0 | 3-1 | 2-0 | 1-3 | 2-0 | 1-1 | 1-0 | 4-1 | | 0-2 | 3-0 | 0-1 | 4-0 | 2-0 | 3-0 | 1-0 | 2-2 | 2-2 | 2-1 | 0-1 |
| Manchester United FC | 4-0 | 1-1 | 2-1 | 2-0 | 4-2 | 4-0 | 2-0 | 3-1 | 0-1 | | 2-3 | 3-0 | 2-1 | 0-0 | 4-0 | 1-3 | 2-0 | 2-0 | 1-1 | 2-0 |
| Middlesbrough FC | 1-1 | 0-0 | 4-0 | 1-1 | 0-3 | 4-1 | 0-0 | 3-4 | 0-0 | 3-2 | | 0-0 | 1-1 | 2-2 | 4-1 | 0-2 | 0-2 | 1-1 | 3-1 | 2-0 |
| Newcastle United FC | 2-3 | 0-1 | 2-1 | 1-1 | 3-2 | 2-4 | 2-0 | 0-0 | 0-1 | 1-3 | 3-1 | | 0-0 | 4-1 | 1-2 | 1-1 | 1-0 | 3-0 | 1-1 | 3-1 |
| Notts County FC | 1-1 | 3-1 | 1-0 | 1-1 | 0-0 | 0-1 | 0-1 | 3-0 | 0-1 | 1-2 | 1-3 | 0-1 | | 2-1 | 0-1 | 2-1 | 1-2 | 0-1 | 1-1 | 2-1 |
| Oldham Athletic AFC | 2-2 | 0-0 | 2-3 | 0-0 | 3-2 | 2-2 | 2-0 | 3-1 | 2-1 | 0-0 | 1-0 | 1-0 | 4-0 | | 2-0 | 3-0 | 2-0 | 4-1 | 0-0 | 0-0 |
| Sheffield United FC | 3-2 | 0-0 | 0-2 | 3-2 | 3-3 | 4-1 | 4-1 | 4-1 | 1-1 | 2-1 | 1-0 | 1-1 | 2-0 | 1-1 | | 1-3 | 0-2 | 4-0 | 1-0 | 1-3 |
| Sunderland AFC | 3-1 | 2-4 | 2-1 | 1-0 | 4-0 | 0-2 | 3-1 | 7-0 | 1-0 | 3-1 | 4-0 | 2-0 | 4-0 | 1-1 | 1-0 | | 0-2 | 2-2 | 3-1 | 4-1 |
| The Wednesday FC | 1-1 | 2-1 | 2-2 | 6-0 | 3-2 | 3-3 | 1-2 | 1-0 | 1-0 | 3-3 | 3-1 | 1-2 | 3-1 | 5-0 | 1-0 | 1-2 | | 2-1 | 3-2 | 2-0 |
| Tottenham Hotspur FC | 3-3 | 0-1 | 0-1 | 2-1 | 1-0 | 1-2 | 0-2 | 1-0 | 4-0 | 1-1 | 5-3 | 1-0 | 0-3 | 1-0 | 1-0 | 1-2 | 2-4 | | 3-1 | 1-1 |
| West Bromwich Albion FC | 2-2 | 1-1 | 2-2 | 1-1 | 0-1 | 0-0 | 0-0 | 3-1 | 0-2 | 1-2 | 2-0 | 1-0 | 2-0 | 2-3 | 3-1 | 3-1 | 1-1 | 4-1 | | 2-1 |
| Woolwich Arsenal FC | 0-3 | 0-1 | 1-2 | 1-1 | 0-1 | 1-2 | 0-0 | 1-1 | 0-4 | 0-0 | 1-1 | 1-1 | 0-0 | 0-0 | 1-3 | 1-3 | 2-5 | 0-3 | 1-0 | |

## Division 1

| | | Pd | Wn | Dw | Ls | GF | GA | Pts | |
|---|---|---|---|---|---|---|---|---|---|
| 1. | SUNDERLAND AFC (SUNDERLAND) | 38 | 25 | 4 | 9 | 86 | 43 | 54 | |
| 2. | Aston Villa FC (Birmingham) | 38 | 19 | 12 | 7 | 86 | 52 | 50 | |
| 3. | The Wednesday FC (Sheffield) | 38 | 21 | 7 | 10 | 75 | 55 | 49 | |
| 4. | Manchester United FC (Manchester) | 38 | 19 | 8 | 11 | 69 | 43 | 46 | |
| 5. | Blackburn Rovers FC (Blackburn) | 38 | 16 | 13 | 9 | 79 | 43 | 45 | |
| 6. | Manchester City FC (Manchester) | 38 | 18 | 8 | 12 | 53 | 37 | 44 | |
| 7. | Derby County FC (Derby) | 38 | 17 | 8 | 13 | 69 | 66 | 42 | |
| 8. | Bolton Wanderers FC (Bolton) | 38 | 16 | 10 | 12 | 62 | 63 | 42 | |
| 9. | Oldham Athletic AFC (Oldham) | 38 | 14 | 14 | 10 | 50 | 55 | 42 | |
| 10. | West Bromwich Albion FC (West Bromwich) | 38 | 13 | 12 | 13 | 57 | 50 | 38 | |
| 11. | Everton FC (Liverpool) | 38 | 15 | 7 | 16 | 48 | 54 | 37 | |
| 12. | Liverpool FC (Liverpool) | 38 | 16 | 5 | 17 | 61 | 71 | 37 | |
| 13. | Bradford City AFC (Bradford) | 38 | 12 | 11 | 15 | 50 | 60 | 35 | |
| 14. | Newcastle United FC (Newcastle-upon-Tyne) | 38 | 13 | 8 | 17 | 47 | 47 | 34 | |
| 15. | Sheffield United FC (Sheffield) | 38 | 14 | 6 | 18 | 56 | 70 | 34 | |
| 16. | Middlesbrough FC (Middlesbrough) | 38 | 11 | 10 | 17 | 55 | 69 | 32 | |
| 17. | Tottenham Hotspur FC (London) | 38 | 12 | 6 | 20 | 45 | 72 | 30 | |
| 18. | Chelsea FC (London) | 38 | 11 | 6 | 21 | 51 | 73 | 28 | |
| 19. | Notts County FC (Nottingham) | 38 | 7 | 9 | 22 | 28 | 56 | 23 | R |
| 20. | Woolwich Arsenal FC (London) | 28 | 3 | 12 | 23 | 26 | 74 | 18 | R |
| | | 760 | 292 | 176 | 292 | 1153 | 1153 | 760 | |

# Top Goalscorer

1) D. McLEAN       (The Wednesday FC)     30

| Football League Division 2 1912-1913 Season | Barnsley | Birmingham | Blackpool | Bradford Park A. | Bristol City | Burnley | Bury | Clapton Orient | Fulham | Glossop | Grimsby Town | Huddersfield T. | Hull City | Leeds City | Leicester Fosse | Lincoln City | Nottingham For. | Preston N.E. | Stockport County | Wolves |
|---|---|---|---|---|---|---|---|---|---|---|---|---|---|---|---|---|---|---|---|---|
| Barnsley FC | ■ | 1-0 | 5-3 | 4-0 | 7-1 | 1-4 | 4-3 | 0-0 | 2-1 | 2-1 | 3-0 | 2-0 | 2-1 | 2-0 | 1-0 | 4-0 | 1-0 | 1-1 | 1-1 | 3-2 |
| Birmingham FC | 3-1 | ■ | 3-2 | 1-1 | 3-0 | 3-0 | 1-2 | 1-1 | 2-1 | 0-0 | 2-1 | 3-2 | 3-1 | 2-2 | 5-1 | 4-1 | 2-0 | 0-1 | 1-1 | 0-0 |
| Blackpool FC | 0-1 | 2-0 | ■ | 0-2 | 1-1 | 0-2 | 2-1 | 2-0 | 2-0 | 1-1 | 2-1 | 2-1 | 1-2 | 0-3 | 2-1 | 1-1 | 2-1 | 0-1 | 1-1 | 1-2 |
| Bradford Park Avenue | 0-0 | 0-0 | 4-2 | ■ | 4-1 | 2-3 | 3-1 | 3-0 | 2-3 | 5-0 | 3-0 | 2-1 | 2-0 | 0-1 | 2-2 | 3-0 | 3-1 | 0-0 | 4-2 | 5-1 |
| Bristol City FC | 3-0 | 0-3 | 0-0 | 0-0 | ■ | 3-3 | 1-5 | 1-0 | 2-1 | 3-3 | 2-2 | 0-0 | 1-1 | 1-1 | 1-0 | 2-0 | 1-2 | 1-1 | 7-2 | 3-1 |
| Burnley FC | 0-1 | 3-0 | 4-0 | 5-1 | 2-2 | ■ | 3-1 | 5-0 | 5-0 | 2-1 | 3-2 | 4-0 | 0-0 | 2-2 | 5-1 | 3-1 | 3-5 | 2-2 | 3-2 | 4-2 |
| Bury FC | 2-0 | 3-0 | 1-1 | 2-0 | 0-1 | 1-1 | ■ | 0-0 | 1-0 | 4-1 | 4-2 | 0-2 | 3-0 | 1-1 | 2-2 | 0-3 | 2-0 | 0-0 | 2-0 | 1-0 |
| Clapton Orient FC | 2-2 | 0-2 | 1-0 | 1-0 | 0-0 | 2-0 | 1-2 | ■ | 2-1 | 1-0 | 1-3 | 1-1 | 2-1 | 2-0 | 1-1 | 1-2 | 2-2 | 1-2 | 4-1 | 0-0 |
| Fulham FC | 1-1 | 3-2 | 4-2 | 3-1 | 0-0 | 4-2 | 3-1 | 1-1 | ■ | 2-0 | 0-1 | 2-0 | 4-0 | 1-1 | 3-1 | 0-0 | 3-1 |  | 7-0 | 4-2 |
| Glossop FC | 1-0 | 0-2 | 2-0 | 4-3 | 3-1 | 1-3 | 1-1 | 3-0 | 2-0 | ■ | 2-0 | 1-0 | 0-3 | 2-1 | 3-0 | 0-1 | 4-3 | 2-3 | 2-2 | 1-3 |
| Grimsby Town FC | 1-1 | 2-2 | 1-1 | 3-0 | 3-0 | 2-0 | 4-0 | 1-2 | 2-1 | 0-0 | ■ | 0-0 | 2-0 | 3-2 | 2-0 | 0-0 | 0-0 | 0-0 | 4-1 | 2-1 |
| Huddersfield Town AFC | 2-0 | 0-0 | 3-0 | 2-0 | 5-0 | 1-0 | 4-0 | 0-0 | 5-1 | 6-0 | 0-2 | ■ | 5-2 | 1-0 | 3-0 | 5-1 | 1-1 | 1-1 | 3-3 | 2-1 |
| Hull City AFC | 0-1 | 1-2 | 4-1 | 5-0 | 3-1 | 0-0 | 2-0 | 2-1 | 0-1 | 2-0 | 5-0 | 1-3 | ■ | 6-2 | 2-1 | 2-0 | 2-1 | 2-2 | 3-2 | 0-1 |
| Leeds City AFC | 2-0 | 4-0 | 0-2 | 2-0 | 1-1 | 4-1 | 4-2 | 3-1 | 2-3 | 4-0 | 1-2 | 0-3 | 1-0 | ■ | 5-1 | 2-2 | 1-0 | 5-1 | 2-1 | 2-2 |
| Leicester Fosse FC | 1-0 | 1-2 | 5-1 | 3-0 | 3-1 | 2-3 | 3-0 | 1-0 | 1-0 | 1-4 | 1-0 | 0-0 | 3-2 | 1-1 | ■ | 1-0 | 3-1 | 0-3 | 4-1 | 0-1 |
| Lincoln City AFC | 2-0 | 0-1 | 1-0 | 1-1 | 2-0 | 1-3 | 0-1 | 1-1 | 3-0 | 0-0 | 3-0 | 3-1 | 1-1 | 3-3 | 3-0 | ■ | 2-1 | 0-0 | 3-2 | 2-1 |
| Nottingham Forest FC | 2-0 | 3-1 | 1-1 | 1-2 | 4-1 | 2-1 | 1-1 | 0-0 | 2-4 | 3-2 | 1-2 | 0-1 | 5-0 | 1-2 | 4-2 | 1-2 | ■ | 0-2 | 2-1 | 2-0 |
| Preston North End FC | 4-0 | 1-0 | 2-1 | 4-2 | 5-1 | 1-1 | 2-0 | 0-1 | 1-0 | 2-0 | 2-0 | 2-1 | 1-0 | 3-2 | 1-0 | 0-0 | 1-1 | ■ | 1-1 | 1-1 |
| Stockport County FC | 0-3 | 0-1 | 2-0 | 1-0 | 0-1 | 0-1 | 1-2 | 2-0 | 1-0 | 1-1 | 1-1 | 3-1 | 3-3 | 6-0 | 1-2 | 2-4 | 2-1 | 1-1 | ■ | 5-1 |
| Wolverhampton Wanderers FC | 3-0 | 2-2 | 4-0 | 0-0 | 1-1 | 0-2 | 3-1 | 1-1 | 2-1 | 3-1 | 3-0 | 2-0 | 0-1 | 2-2 | 1-1 | 2-0 | 2-3 | 2-0 | 1-0 | ■ |

## Division 2

| | | Pd | Wn | Dw | Ls | GF | GA | Pts | |
|---|---|---|---|---|---|---|---|---|---|
| 1. | Preston North End FC (Preston) | 38 | 19 | 15 | 4 | 56 | 33 | 53 | P |
| 2. | Burnley FC (Burnley) | 38 | 21 | 8 | 9 | 88 | 53 | 50 | P |
| 3. | Birmingham FC (Birmingham) | 38 | 18 | 10 | 10 | 59 | 44 | 46 | |
| 4. | Barnsley FC (Barnsley) | 38 | 19 | 7 | 12 | 57 | 47 | 45 | |
| 5. | Huddersfield Town AFC (Huddersfield) | 38 | 17 | 9 | 12 | 66 | 40 | 43 | |
| 6. | Leeds City AFC (Leeds) | 38 | 15 | 10 | 13 | 70 | 64 | 40 | |
| 7. | Grimsby Town FC (Cleethorpes) | 38 | 15 | 10 | 13 | 51 | 50 | 40 | |
| 8. | Lincoln City FC (Lincoln) | 38 | 15 | 10 | 13 | 50 | 52 | 40 | |
| 9. | Fulham FC (London) | 38 | 17 | 5 | 16 | 65 | 55 | 39 | |
| 10. | Wolverhampton Wanderers FC (Wolverhampton) | 38 | 14 | 10 | 14 | 56 | 54 | 38 | |
| 11. | Bury FC (Bury) | 38 | 15 | 8 | 15 | 53 | 57 | 38 | |
| 12. | Hull City AFC (Kingston-upon-Hull) | 38 | 15 | 6 | 17 | 60 | 56 | 36 | |
| 13. | Bradford Park Avenue FC (Bradford) | 38 | 14 | 8 | 16 | 60 | 60 | 36 | |
| 14. | Clapton Orient FC (London) | 38 | 10 | 14 | 14 | 34 | 47 | 34 | |
| 15. | Leicester Fosse FC (Leicester) | 38 | 13 | 7 | 18 | 50 | 65 | 33 | |
| 16. | Bristol City FC (Bristol) | 38 | 9 | 15 | 14 | 46 | 72 | 33 | |
| 17. | Nottingham Forest FC (Nottingham) | 38 | 12 | 8 | 18 | 58 | 59 | 32 | |
| 18. | Glossop FC (Glossop) | 38 | 12 | 8 | 18 | 49 | 68 | 32 | |
| 19. | Stockport County FC (Stockport) | 38 | 8 | 10 | 20 | 56 | 78 | 26 | |
| 20. | Blackpool FC (Blackpool) | 38 | 9 | 8 | 21 | 39 | 69 | 26 | |
| | | 760 | 287 | 186 | 287 | 1123 | 1123 | 760 | |

**F.A. CUP FINAL**  (Crystal Palace, London – 19/04/1913 – 121,919)

| ASTON VILLA FC (BIRMINGHAM) | 1-0 | Sunderland AFC (Sunderland) |
|---|---|---|

*Barber*

Aston Villa:  Hardy, Lyons, Weston, Barber, Harrop, Leach, Wallace, Halse, Hampton, Stephenson, Bache.
Sunderland:  Butler, Gladwin, Ness, Cuggy, Thomson, Low, Mordue, Buchan, Richardson, Holley, Martin.

## Semi-finals

| Aston Villa FC (Birmingham) | 1-0 | Oldham Athletic AFC (Oldham) |
|---|---|---|
| Sunderland AFC (Sunderland) | 0-0,  3-2 | Burnley FC (Burnley) |

## Quarter-finals

| Blackburn Rovers FC (Blackburn) | 0-1 | Burnley FC (Burnley) |
|---|---|---|
| Bradford Park Avenue FC (Bradford) | 0-5 | Aston Villa FC (Birmingham) |
| Everton FC (Liverpool) | 0-1 | Oldham Athletic AFC (Oldham) |
| Sunderland AFC (Sunderland) | 0-0,  2-2,  3-0 | Newcastle United FC (Newcastle-upon-Tyne) |

# 1913-14

| Football League Division 1 1913-1914 Season | Aston Villa | Blackburn Rovers | Bolton Wanderers | Bradford City | Burnley | Chelsea | Derby County | Everton | Liverpool | Manchester City | Manchester United | Middlesbrough | Newcastle United | Oldham Athletic | Preston North End | Sheffield United | Sunderland | Wednesday | Tottenham Hotspur | W.B.A. |
|---|---|---|---|---|---|---|---|---|---|---|---|---|---|---|---|---|---|---|---|---|
| Aston Villa FC | | 1-3 | 1-0 | 0-1 | 1-0 | 1-2 | 3-2 | 3-1 | 2-1 | 1-1 | 3-1 | 1-3 | 1-3 | 0-0 | 3-0 | 3-0 | 5-0 | 2-0 | 3-3 | 2-0 |
| Blackburn Rovers FC | 0-0 | | 3-2 | 0-0 | 0-0 | 3-1 | 3-1 | 6-0 | 6-2 | 2-1 | 0-1 | 6-0 | 3-0 | 2-1 | 5-0 | 3-2 | 3-1 | 3-2 | 1-1 | 2-0 |
| Bolton Wanderers FC | 3-0 | 1-0 | | 3-0 | 0-0 | 1-1 | 3-1 | 0-0 | 2-1 | 3-0 | 6-1 | 1-1 | 3-1 | 6-2 | 0-3 | 3-1 | 2-1 | 0-1 | 3-0 | 1-0 |
| Bradford City AFC | 0-0 | 0-2 | 5-1 | | 1-1 | 0-0 | 0-0 | 0-1 | 1-0 | 3-2 | 1-1 | 2-3 | 2-0 | 0-1 | 0-0 | 2-1 | 0-2 | 3-1 | 2-1 | 1-0 |
| Burnley FC | 4-0 | 1-2 | 2-2 | 2-2 | | 6-1 | 5-1 | 2-0 | 5-2 | 2-0 | 1-2 | 1-2 | 1-0 | 2-0 | 3-4 | 0-0 | 0-1 | 3-0 | 3-1 | 0-0 |
| Chelsea FC | 0-3 | 2-0 | 2-1 | 2-1 | 0-0 | | 2-1 | 2-0 | 3-0 | 1-0 | 0-2 | 3-2 | 0-1 | 2-1 | 2-0 | 2-0 | 1-1 | 2-1 | 1-3 | 1-1 |
| Derby County FC | 0-2 | 2-3 | 3-3 | 3-1 | 3-1 | 0-1 | | 1-0 | 1-1 | 2-4 | 4-2 | 2-2 | 2-0 | 1-2 | 0-1 | 3-5 | 1-1 | 1-1 | 4-0 | 1-2 |
| Everton FC | 1-4 | 0-0 | 1-1 | 1-1 | 1-1 | 0-0 | 5-0 | | 1-2 | 1-0 | 5-0 | 2-0 | 2-0 | 0-2 | 2-0 | 5-0 | 1-5 | 1-1 | 1-1 | 2-0 |
| Liverpool FC | 0-1 | 3-3 | 2-1 | 0-1 | 1-1 | 3-0 | 1-0 | 1-2 | | 4-2 | 1-2 | 2-1 | 0-0 | 0-3 | 3-1 | 1-1 | 1-3 | 1-2 | 2-1 | 0-0 |
| Manchester City FC | 3-1 | 1-2 | 0-1 | 1-0 | 4-1 | 2-1 | 1-2 | 1-1 | 1-0 | | 0-2 | 1-1 | 0-1 | 2-1 | 1-1 | 2-1 | 3-1 | 1-2 | 2-1 | 2-3 |
| Manchester United FC | 0-6 | 0-0 | 0-1 | 1-1 | 0-1 | 0-1 | 3-3 | 0-1 | 3-0 | 0-1 | | 0-1 | 2-2 | 4-1 | 3-0 | 2-1 | 3-1 | 2-1 | 3-1 | 1-0 |
| Middlesbrough FC | 5-2 | 3-0 | 2-3 | 1-1 | 2-1 | 2-0 | 3-2 | 2-0 | 4-0 | 2-0 | 3-1 | | 3-0 | 0-0 | 4-1 | 2-3 | 3-4 | 5-2 | 6-0 | 3-0 |
| Newcastle United FC | 2-2 | 0-0 | 4-3 | 0-0 | 3-1 | 1-0 | 1-1 | 0-1 | 1-2 | 0-1 | 0-1 | 1-0 | | 0-0 | 2-0 | 2-1 | 2-1 | 3-1 | 2-0 | 3-3 |
| Oldham Athletic AFC | 0-1 | 1-1 | 2-0 | 3-1 | 1-1 | 3-2 | 0-0 | 2-0 | 2-2 | 1-3 | 2-2 | 3-0 | 3-0 | | 1-0 | 1-2 | 2-1 | 2-0 | 3-0 | 2-0 |
| Preston North End FC | 3-2 | 1-5 | 1-1 | 2-1 | 2-1 | 3-3 | 2-0 | 1-0 | 0-1 | 2-2 | 4-2 | 4-1 | 4-1 | 0-1 | | 2-4 | 2-2 | 5-0 | 1-2 | 0-2 |
| Sheffield United FC | 3-0 | 1-1 | 2-0 | 1-1 | 5-0 | 3-2 | 2-2 | 4-1 | 0-1 | 1-3 | 2-0 | 3-1 | 2-0 | 2-1 | 2-0 | | 1-0 | 0-1 | 1-4 | 1-1 |
| Sunderland AFC | 2-0 | 2-1 | 3-2 | 0-1 | 1-1 | 2-0 | 1-0 | 5-2 | 1-2 | 0-0 | 2-0 | 4-2 | 1-2 | 2-0 | 3-1 | 1-2 | | 0-1 | 2-0 | 0-0 |
| The Wednesday FC | 2-3 | 3-1 | 1-1 | 1-3 | 2-6 | 3-0 | 1-3 | 2-2 | 4-1 | 2-2 | 1-3 | 2-0 | 0-0 | 1-2 | 2-1 | 2-1 | 2-1 | | 2-0 | 1-4 |
| Tottenham Hotspur FC | 0-2 | 3-3 | 3-0 | 0-0 | 2-0 | 1-2 | 1-1 | 4-1 | 0-0 | 3-1 | 2-1 | 0-0 | 3-1 | 1-0 | 3-1 | 1-0 | 1-4 | 1-1 | | 3-0 |
| West Bromwich Albion FC | 1-0 | 2-0 | 1-1 | 2-1 | 4-1 | 3-1 | 2-1 | 1-1 | 0-1 | 0-0 | 2-1 | 2-1 | 1-1 | 2-2 | 1-0 | 2-1 | 2-1 | 1-1 | 1-1 | |

| | Division 1 | Pd | Wn | Dw | Ls | GF | GA | Pts | |
|---|---|---|---|---|---|---|---|---|---|
| 1. | BLACKBURN ROVERS FC (BLACKBURN) | 38 | 20 | 11 | 7 | 78 | 42 | 51 | |
| 2. | Aston Villa FC (Birmingham) | 38 | 19 | 6 | 13 | 65 | 50 | 44 | |
| 3. | Middlesbrough FC (Middlesbrough) | 38 | 19 | 5 | 14 | 77 | 60 | 43 | |
| 4. | Oldham Athletic AFC (Oldham) | 38 | 17 | 9 | 12 | 55 | 45 | 43 | |
| 5. | West Bromwich Albion FC (West Bromwich) | 38 | 15 | 13 | 10 | 46 | 42 | 43 | |
| 6. | Bolton Wanderers FC (Bolton) | 38 | 16 | 10 | 12 | 65 | 52 | 42 | |
| 7. | Sunderland AFC (Sunderland) | 38 | 17 | 6 | 15 | 63 | 52 | 40 | |
| 8. | Chelsea FC (London) | 38 | 16 | 7 | 15 | 46 | 55 | 39 | |
| 9. | Bradford City AFC (Bradford) | 38 | 12 | 14 | 12 | 40 | 40 | 38 | |
| 10. | Sheffield United FC (Sheffield) | 38 | 16 | 5 | 17 | 63 | 60 | 37 | |
| 11. | Newcastle United FC (Newcastle-upon-Tyne) | 38 | 13 | 11 | 14 | 39 | 48 | 37 | |
| 12. | Burnley FC (Burnley) | 38 | 12 | 12 | 14 | 61 | 53 | 36 | |
| 13. | Manchester City FC (Manchester) | 38 | 14 | 8 | 16 | 51 | 53 | 36 | |
| 14. | Manchester United FC (Manchester) | 38 | 15 | 6 | 17 | 52 | 62 | 36 | |
| 15. | Everton FC (Liverpool) | 38 | 12 | 11 | 15 | 46 | 55 | 35 | |
| 16. | Liverpool FC (Liverpool) | 38 | 14 | 7 | 17 | 46 | 62 | 35 | |
| 17. | Tottenham Hotspur FC (London) | 38 | 12 | 10 | 16 | 50 | 62 | 34 | |
| 18. | The Wednesday FC (Sheffield) | 38 | 13 | 8 | 17 | 53 | 70 | 34 | |
| 19. | Preston North End FC (Preston) | 38 | 12 | 6 | 20 | 52 | 69 | 30 | R |
| 20. | Derby County FC (Derby) | 38 | 8 | 11 | 19 | 55 | 71 | 27 | R |
| | | 760 | 292 | 176 | 292 | 1103 | 1103 | 760 | |

## Top Goalscorer

1) G. ELLIOTT  (Middlesbrough FC)  32

| Football League Division 2 1913-1914 Season | Barnsley | Birmingham | Blackpool | Bradford Park Ave. | Bristol City | Bury | Clapton Orient | Fulham | Glossop | Grimsby Town | Huddersfield Town | Hull City | Leeds City | Leicester Fosse | Lincoln City | Nottingham Forest | Notts County | Stockport County | Wolves | Woolwich Arsenal |
|---|---|---|---|---|---|---|---|---|---|---|---|---|---|---|---|---|---|---|---|---|
| Barnsley FC | | 1-1 | 2-1 | 1-2 | 3-0 | 2-0 | 2-1 | 1-0 | 2-0 | 3-1 | 2-1 | 0-2 | 1-4 | 3-0 | 1-0 | 5-0 | 0-1 | 1-0 | 2-1 | 1-0 |
| Birmingham FC | 0-0 | | 0-0 | 1-2 | 2-2 | 1-0 | 2-0 | 0-1 | 6-0 | 1-2 | 1-4 | 1-1 | 0-2 | 1-0 | 2-0 | 2-0 | 2-1 | 3-2 | 4-1 | 2-0 |
| Blackpool FC | 3-1 | 2-2 | | 2-1 | 0-1 | 0-1 | 0-0 | 1-1 | 1-1 | 1-1 | 0-1 | 2-2 | 2-2 | 1-0 | 2-1 | 2-1 | 0-0 | 2-2 | 2-0 | 1-1 |
| Bradford Park Avenue | 1-1 | 5-1 | 4-1 | | 4-3 | 3-1 | 1-0 | 1-0 | 2-1 | 3-0 | 2-1 | 2-0 | 3-1 | 3-2 | 3-0 | 4-0 | 0-3 | 0-2 | 1-0 | 2-3 |
| Bristol City FC | 1-1 | 1-2 | 1-0 | 2-0 | | 2-0 | 3-0 | 0-1 | 4-1 | 1-0 | 1-0 | 2-1 | 1-1 | 1-0 | 4-1 | 1-0 | 1-1 | 5-0 | 0-0 | 1-1 |
| Bury FC | 4-0 | 3-1 | 1-0 | 0-0 | 3-1 | | 0-0 | 1-0 | 1-0 | 3-1 | 2-1 | 2-0 | 1-1 | 1-1 | 1-0 | 1-0 | 3-3 | 1-0 | 1-4 | 1-1 |
| Clapton Orient FC | 1-0 | 2-2 | 2-0 | 1-0 | 5-2 | 1-0 | | 1-0 | 5-1 | 0-0 | 0-0 | 3-0 | 3-1 | 1-0 | 5-1 | 3-1 | 1-0 | 1-1 | 2-2 | 1-0 |
| Fulham FC | 1-2 | 1-0 | 0-0 | 1-6 | 3-1 | 1-1 | 2-0 | | 2-1 | 2-2 | 1-0 | 0-1 | 0-1 | 1-2 | 4-0 | 2-0 | 1-2 | 2-0 | 1-0 | 6-1 |
| Glossop FC | 5-1 | 4-1 | 1-2 | 2-1 | 1-1 | 2-1 | 0-3 | 0-1 | | 3-0 | 2-3 | 2-1 | 1-1 | 0-2 | 4-0 | 3-0 | 0-1 | 1-1 | 1-2 | 0-2 |
| Grimsby Town FC | 1-1 | 0-2 | 2-0 | 0-0 | 1-0 | 1-0 | 2-0 | 0-3 | 3-0 | | 2-1 | 1-3 | 0-1 | 3-0 | 1-3 | 3-0 | 0-0 | 2-0 | 1-0 | 1-1 |
| Huddersfield Town AFC | 3-1 | 7-0 | 1-0 | 0-1 | 1-2 | 1-1 | 1-0 | 3-1 | 2-1 | 1-2 | | 0-3 | 1-1 | 1-2 | 2-1 | 1-1 | 2-1 | 0-2 | 0-0 | 1-2 |
| Hull City AFC | 0-1 | 0-0 | 0-0 | 1-3 | 0-1 | 0-1 | 2-0 | 1-1 | 3-0 | 2-1 | 4-1 | | 1-0 | 0-0 | 1-1 | 1-0 | 2-0 | 3-0 | 7-1 | 1-2 |
| Leeds City AFC | 3-0 | 3-2 | 2-1 | 5-1 | 1-0 | 2-1 | 0-0 | 2-1 | 3-0 | 4-1 | 5-1 | 1-2 | | 2-1 | 1-0 | 8-0 | 2-4 | 5-1 | 5-0 | 0-0 |
| Leicester Fosse FC | 0-2 | 0-0 | 0-1 | 2-3 | 3-0 | 0-0 | 1-0 | 3-0 | 1-3 | 2-0 | 0-1 | 0-4 | 5-1 | | 2-0 | 5-1 | 0-2 | 2-5 | 2-3 | 1-2 |
| Lincoln City AFC | 2-2 | 1-1 | 1-2 | 0-3 | 2-1 | 1-0 | 0-0 | 0-1 | 1-5 | 1-3 | 3-0 | 0-0 | 1-0 | 3-0 | | 1-0 | 0-0 | 0-3 | 1-0 | 5-2 |
| Nottingham Forest FC | 0-2 | 3-1 | 3-0 | 1-0 | 1-1 | 1-1 | 1-1 | 1-1 | 1-2 | 4-1 | 1-1 | 1-2 | 2-1 | 1-3 | 2-1 | | 1-0 | 2-2 | 1-3 | 0-0 |
| Notts County FC | 3-1 | 5-1 | 2-0 | 2-3 | 4-0 | 2-0 | 3-0 | 4-0 | 2-2 | 4-0 | 3-0 | 4-1 | 4-0 | 4-1 | 2-1 | 2-2 | | 2-1 | 2-0 | 1-0 |
| Stockport County FC | 1-1 | 2-0 | 0-0 | 3-1 | 5-1 | 3-0 | 0-1 | 1-3 | 1-1 | 2-2 | 0-0 | 2-1 | 2-1 | 3-0 | 2-3 | 2-1 | 1-2 | | 0-0 | 2-0 |
| Wolverhampton Wanderers FC | 0-1 | 1-0 | 1-0 | 1-0 | 0-2 | 3-0 | 2-1 | 1-0 | 1-0 | 4-1 | 2-2 | 1-0 | 1-3 | 2-1 | 1-0 | 4-1 | 4-1 | 3-1 | | 1-2 |
| Woolwich Arsenal FC | 1-0 | 1-0 | 2-1 | 2-0 | 1-1 | 0-1 | 2-2 | 2-0 | 2-0 | 2-0 | 0-1 | 0-0 | 1-0 | 2-1 | 3-0 | 3-2 | 3-0 | 4-0 | 3-1 | |

| Division 2 | Pd | Wn | Dw | Ls | GF | GA | Pts | |
|---|---|---|---|---|---|---|---|---|
| 1. Notts County FC (Nottingham) | 38 | 23 | 7 | 8 | 77 | 36 | 53 | P |
| 2. Bradford Park Avenue FC (Bradford) | 38 | 23 | 3 | 12 | 71 | 47 | 49 | P |
| 3. Woolwich Arsenal FC (London) | 38 | 20 | 9 | 9 | 54 | 38 | 49 | * |
| 4. Leeds City AFC (Leeds) | 38 | 20 | 7 | 11 | 76 | 46 | 47 | |
| 5. Barnsley FC (Barnsley) | 38 | 19 | 7 | 12 | 51 | 45 | 45 | |
| 6. Clapton Orient FC (London) | 38 | 16 | 11 | 11 | 47 | 35 | 43 | |
| 7. Hull City AFC (Kingston-upon-Hull) | 38 | 16 | 9 | 13 | 53 | 37 | 41 | |
| 8. Bristol City FC (Bristol) | 38 | 16 | 9 | 13 | 52 | 50 | 41 | |
| 9. Wolverhampton Wanderers FC (Wolverhampton) | 38 | 18 | 5 | 15 | 51 | 52 | 41 | |
| 10. Bury FC (Bury) | 38 | 15 | 10 | 13 | 39 | 40 | 40 | |
| 11. Fulham FC (London) | 38 | 16 | 6 | 16 | 46 | 43 | 38 | |
| 12. Stockport County FC (Stockport) | 38 | 13 | 10 | 15 | 55 | 57 | 36 | |
| 13. Huddersfield Town AFC (Huddersfield) | 38 | 13 | 8 | 17 | 47 | 53 | 34 | |
| 14. Birmingham FC (Birmingham) | 38 | 12 | 10 | 16 | 48 | 60 | 34 | |
| 15. Grimsby Town FC (Cleethorpes) | 38 | 13 | 8 | 17 | 42 | 58 | 34 | |
| 16. Blackpool FC (Blackpool) | 38 | 9 | 14 | 15 | 33 | 44 | 32 | |
| 17. Glossop FC (Glossop) | 38 | 11 | 6 | 21 | 51 | 67 | 28 | |
| 18. Leicester Fosse FC (Leicester) | 38 | 11 | 4 | 23 | 45 | 61 | 26 | |
| 19. Lincoln City FC (Lincoln) | 38 | 10 | 6 | 22 | 36 | 66 | 26 | |
| 20. Nottingham Forest FC (Nottingham) | 38 | 7 | 9 | 22 | 37 | 76 | 23 | |
| | 760 | 301 | 158 | 301 | 1011 | 1011 | 760 | |

* Woolwich Arsenal FC (London) changed their club name to The Arsenal FC (London) for next season.

## F.A. CUP FINAL    (Crystal Palace, London – 25/04/1914 – 72,778)

BURNLEY FC (BURNLEY)                    1-0                    Liverpool FC (Liverpool)

*Freeman*

Burnley: Sewell, Bamford, Taylor, Halley, Boyle, Watson, Nesbitt, Lindley, Freeman, Hodgson, Mosscrop.

Liverpool: Campbell, Longworth, Pursell, Fairfoul, Ferguson, MacKinlay, Sheldon, Metcalfe, Miller, Lacey, Nicholl.

## Semi-finals

| Aston Villa FC (Birmingham) | 0-2 | Liverpool FC (Liverpool) |
|---|---|---|
| Sheffield United FC (Sheffield) | 0-0, 0-1 | Burnley FC (Burnley) |

## Quarter-finals

| Liverpool FC (Liverpool) | 2-1 | Queen's Park Rangers FC (London) |
|---|---|---|
| Manchester City FC (Manchester) | 0-0, 0-0 (aet), 0-1 | Sheffield United FC (Sheffield) |
| Sunderland AFC (Sunderland) | 0-0, 1-2 | Burnley FC (Burnley) |
| The Wednesday FC (Sheffield) | 0-1 | Aston Villa FC (Birmingham) |

# 1914-15

| Football League Division 1 1914-1915 Season | Aston Villa | Blackburn Rovers | Bolton Wanderers | Bradford City | Bradford Park Avenue | Burnley | Chelsea | Everton | Liverpool | Manchester City | Manchester United | Middlesbrough | Newcastle United | Notts County | Oldham Athletic | Sheffield United | Sunderland | Wednesday | Tottenham Hotspur | W.B.A. |
|---|---|---|---|---|---|---|---|---|---|---|---|---|---|---|---|---|---|---|---|---|
| Aston Villa FC | ■ | 2-1 | 1-7 | 0-0 | 1-2 | 3-3 | 2-1 | 1-5 | 6-2 | 4-1 | 3-3 | 5-0 | 2-1 | 2-1 | 0-0 | 1-0 | 1-3 | 0-0 | 3-1 | 2-1 |
| Blackburn Rovers FC | 1-2 | ■ | 2-2 | 2-1 | 2-2 | 6-0 | 3-2 | 2-1 | 4-2 | 0-1 | 3-3 | 4-0 | 2-3 | 5-1 | 4-1 | 1-2 | 3-1 | 1-1 | 4-1 | 2-1 |
| Bolton Wanderers FC | 2-2 | 3-2 | ■ | 3-5 | 3-2 | 3-1 | 3-1 | 0-0 | 0-1 | 2-3 | 3-0 | 4-0 | 0-0 | 1-2 | 2-0 | 0-1 | 1-1 | 0-3 | 4-2 | 1-1 |
| Bradford City AFC | 3-0 | 3-0 | 4-2 | ■ | 3-2 | 0-0 | 2-2 | 0-1 | 3-2 | 0-0 | 4-2 | 1-1 | 1-1 | 3-1 | 1-0 | 1-1 | 3-1 | 1-0 | 2-2 | 5-0 |
| Bradford Park Avenue | 2-2 | 1-2 | 1-2 | 3-0 | ■ | 2-2 | 3-0 | 1-2 | 1-0 | 3-1 | 5-0 | 2-0 | 1-0 | 3-1 | 1-1 | 2-0 | 2-1 | 1-1 | 5-1 | 1-4 |
| Burnley FC | 2-1 | 3-2 | 5-0 | 0-1 | 2-0 | ■ | 2-0 | 1-0 | 3-0 | 1-2 | 3-0 | 4-0 | 2-0 | 0-0 | 2-3 | 1-2 | 2-1 | 2-3 | 3-1 | 0-2 |
| Chelsea FC | 3-1 | 1-3 | 2-1 | 2-0 | 0-1 | 1-4 | ■ | 2-0 | 3-1 | 0-0 | 1-3 | 2-2 | 0-3 | 4-1 | 2-2 | 1-1 | 3-0 | 0-0 | 1-1 | 4-1 |
| Everton FC | 0-0 | 1-3 | 5-3 | 1-1 | 4-1 | 0-2 | 2-2 | ■ | 1-3 | 4-1 | 4-2 | 2-3 | 3-0 | 4-0 | 3-4 | 0-0 | 7-1 | 0-1 | 1-1 | 2-1 |
| Liverpool FC | 3-6 | 3-0 | 4-3 | 2-1 | 2-1 | 3-0 | 3-3 | 0-5 | ■ | 3-2 | 1-1 | 1-1 | 2-2 | 1-1 | 1-2 | 2-1 | 2-1 | 2-1 | 7-2 | 3-1 |
| Manchester City FC | 1-0 | 1-3 | 2-1 | 4-1 | 2-3 | 1-0 | 2-1 | 0-1 | 1-1 | ■ | 1-1 | 1-1 | 1-1 | 0-0 | 0-0 | 0-0 | 2-0 | 4-0 | 2-1 | 4-0 |
| Manchester United FC | 1-0 | 2-0 | 4-1 | 1-0 | 1-2 | 0-2 | 2-2 | 1-2 | 2-0 | 0-0 | ■ | 2-2 | 1-0 | 2-2 | 1-3 | 1-2 | 3-0 | 2-0 | 1-1 | 0-0 |
| Middlesbrough FC | 1-1 | 1-4 | 0-0 | 3-0 | 1-3 | 1-1 | 3-0 | 5-1 | 3-0 | 1-0 | 1-1 | ■ | 1-1 | 4-1 | 2-2 | 2-3 | 3-1 | 7-5 | 3-1 | 2-0 |
| Newcastle United FC | 3-0 | 2-1 | 1-2 | 1-1 | 1-0 | 1-2 | 2-0 | 0-1 | 0-0 | 2-1 | 2-0 | 1-2 | ■ | 1-1 | 1-2 | 4-3 | 2-5 | 0-0 | 4-0 | 1-2 |
| Notts County FC | 1-1 | 1-1 | 0-0 | 0-0 | 1-2 | 0-0 | 2-0 | 0-0 | 3-1 | 0-2 | 4-2 | 5-1 | 1-0 | ■ | 2-1 | 3-1 | 2-1 | 1-2 | 1-2 | 1-1 |
| Oldham Athletic AFC | 3-3 | 3-2 | 5-3 | 1-0 | 6-2 | 1-2 | 0-0 | 1-1 | 0-2 | 0-0 | 1-0 | 5-1 | 1-0 | 2-0 | ■ | 3-0 | 4-5 | 5-2 | 4-1 | 1-1 |
| Sheffield United FC | 3-0 | 1-2 | 3-1 | 1-1 | 3-2 | 1-0 | 1-1 | 1-0 | 2-1 | 0-0 | 3-1 | 0-1 | 1-0 | 1-0 | 3-0 | ■ | 1-1 | 0-1 | 1-1 | 2-0 |
| Sunderland AFC | 4-0 | 5-1 | 4-3 | 1-1 | 3-3 | 2-1 | 2-1 | 0-3 | 2-2 | 1-0 | 4-1 | 2-4 | 3-1 | 1-2 | 3-2 |  | ■ | 3-1 | 5-0 | 1-2 |
| The Wednesday FC | 5-2 | 1-1 | 7-0 | 3-3 | 6-0 | 0-0 | 3-2 | 1-4 | 2-1 | 2-1 | 1-0 | 3-1 | 2-1 | 0-0 | 2-2 | 1-1 | 1-2 | ■ | 3-2 | 0-0 |
| Tottenham Hotspur FC | 0-2 | 0-4 | 4-2 | 0-0 | 3-0 | 1-3 | 1-1 | 1-3 | 1-1 | 2-2 | 2-0 | 3-3 | 0-0 | 2-0 | 1-0 | 1-1 | 0-6 | 6-1 | ■ | 2-0 |
| West Bromwich Albion FC | 2-0 | 0-0 | 3-0 | 3-0 | 1-0 | 3-0 | 2-0 | 1-2 | 4-0 | 0-1 | 0-0 | 1-0 | 2-0 | 4-1 | 0-0 | 1-1 | 1-2 | 0-0 | 3-2 | ■ |

## Division 1

| | | Pd | Wn | Dw | Ls | GF | GA | Pts | |
|---|---|---|---|---|---|---|---|---|---|
| 1. | EVERTON FC (LIVERPOOL) | 38 | 19 | 8 | 11 | 76 | 47 | 46 | |
| 2. | Oldham Athletic AFC (Oldham) | 38 | 17 | 11 | 10 | 70 | 56 | 45 | |
| 3. | Blackburn Rovers FC (Blackburn) | 38 | 18 | 7 | 13 | 83 | 61 | 43 | |
| 4. | Burnley FC (Burnley) | 38 | 18 | 7 | 13 | 61 | 47 | 43 | |
| 5. | Manchester City FC (Manchester) | 38 | 15 | 13 | 10 | 49 | 39 | 43 | |
| 6. | Sheffield United FC (Sheffield) | 38 | 15 | 13 | 10 | 49 | 41 | 43 | |
| 7. | The Wednesday FC (Sheffield) | 38 | 15 | 13 | 10 | 61 | 54 | 43 | |
| 8. | Sunderland AFC (Sunderland) | 38 | 18 | 5 | 15 | 81 | 72 | 41 | |
| 9. | Bradford Park Avenue FC (Bradford) | 38 | 17 | 7 | 14 | 69 | 65 | 41 | |
| 10. | Bradford City AFC (Bradford) | 38 | 13 | 14 | 11 | 55 | 49 | 40 | |
| 11. | West Bromwich Albion FC (West Bromwich) | 38 | 15 | 10 | 13 | 49 | 43 | 40 | |
| 12. | Middlesbrough FC (Middlesbrough) | 38 | 13 | 12 | 13 | 62 | 74 | 38 | |
| 13. | Aston Villa FC (Birmingham) | 38 | 13 | 11 | 14 | 62 | 72 | 37 | |
| 14. | Liverpool FC (Liverpool) | 38 | 14 | 9 | 15 | 65 | 75 | 37 | |
| 15. | Newcastle United FC (Newcastle-upon-Tyne) | 38 | 11 | 10 | 17 | 46 | 48 | 32 | |
| 16. | Notts County FC (Nottingham) | 38 | 9 | 13 | 16 | 41 | 57 | 31 | |
| 17. | Bolton Wanderers FC (Bolton) | 38 | 11 | 8 | 19 | 68 | 84 | 30 | |
| 18. | Manchester United FC (Manchester) | 38 | 9 | 12 | 17 | 46 | 62 | 30 | |
| 19. | Chelsea FC (London) | 38 | 8 | 13 | 17 | 51 | 65 | 29 | # |
| 20. | Tottenham Hotspur FC (London) | 38 | 8 | 12 | 18 | 57 | 90 | 28 | # |
| | | 760 | 276 | 208 | 276 | 1201 | 1201 | 760 | |

# Top Goalscorer

1) Robert PARKER         (Everton FC)    35

| Football League Division 2 1914-1915 Season | Barnsley | Birmingham | Blackpool | Bristol City | Bury | Clapton Orient | Derby County | Fulham | Glossop | Grimsby Town | Huddersfield Town | Hull City | Leeds City | Leicester Fosse | Lincoln City | Nottingham Forest | Preston North End | Stockport County | The Arsenal | Wolves |
|---|---|---|---|---|---|---|---|---|---|---|---|---|---|---|---|---|---|---|---|---|
| Barnsley FC | | 2-1 | 1-2 | 2-1 | 2-0 | 1-0 | 1-0 | 2-2 | 2-0 | 0-0 | 1-0 | 1-0 | 2-1 | 1-0 | 3-1 | 3-0 | 2-1 | 2-0 | 1-0 | 2-1 |
| Birmingham FC | 2-0 | | 3-0 | 1-1 | 1-0 | 1-0 | 0-2 | 1-0 | 11-1 | 3-0 | 1-0 | 2-2 | 6-3 | 2-0 | 2-0 | 3-0 | 1-1 | 0-1 | 3-0 | 1-2 |
| Blackpool FC | 1-1 | 3-1 | | 2-0 | 3-4 | 5-1 | 2-1 | 2-2 | 3-0 | 5-0 | 3-2 | 1-2 | 1-0 | 1-2 | 0-0 | 3-0 | 0-2 | 4-2 | 0-2 | 1-0 |
| Bristol City FC | 3-1 | 2-3 | 2-1 | | 1-0 | 3-0 | 2-3 | 0-0 | 3-1 | 7-0 | 0-1 | 5-2 | 1-0 | 1-0 | 2-1 | 1-2 | 4-0 | 0-2 | 1-1 | 0-1 |
| Bury FC | 1-2 | 1-3 | 2-2 | 2-1 | | 3-0 | 2-0 | 1-0 | 5-0 | 2-2 | 3-1 | 0-1 | 0-0 | 3-1 | 1-1 | 4-2 | 0-0 | 2-1 | 3-1 | 4-1 |
| Clapton Orient FC | 4-2 | 1-1 | 2-0 | 2-0 | 2-2 | | 0-1 | 2-1 | 5-2 | 2-1 | 3-1 | 0-3 | 2-0 | 2-0 | 3-1 | 0-0 | 1-1 | 3-0 | 1-0 | 1-1 |
| Derby County FC | 7-0 | 1-0 | 5-0 | 1-0 | 2-1 | 0-3 | | 1-1 | 1-1 | 1-1 | 1-0 | 4-1 | 1-2 | 1-0 | 3-0 | 1-0 | 2-0 | 1-0 | 4-0 | 3-1 |
| Fulham FC | 2-0 | 2-3 | 0-1 | 1-2 | 6-3 | 4-0 | 2-0 | | 2-0 | 2-1 | 2-3 | 4-1 | 1-0 | 1-0 | 3-1 | 2-1 | 0-2 | 1-0 | 0-1 | 0-1 |
| Glossop FC | 0-1 | 3-3 | 1-3 | 2-1 | 3-0 | 3-1 | 1-1 | 1-0 | | 0-0 | 2-2 | 0-5 | 0-3 | 2-3 | 1-2 | 1-0 | 0-1 | 1-1 | 0-4 | 0-2 |
| Grimsby Town FC | 2-3 | 1-0 | 2-0 | 2-3 | 1-0 | 2-1 | 1-2 | 1-1 | 1-0 | | 0-0 | 1-1 | 2-5 | 1-0 | 5-1 | 4-0 | 2-2 | 6-1 | 1-0 | 1-4 |
| Huddersfield Town AFC | 1-0 | 0-0 | 5-0 | 5-3 | 0-1 | 1-1 | 0-0 | 2-2 | 0-1 | 3-1 | | 1-0 | 1-0 | 3-1 | 0-1 | 4-0 | 3-1 | 2-1 | 3-0 | 2-0 |
| Hull City AFC | 2-1 | 0-0 | 1-3 | 1-1 | 3-1 | 0-1 | 1-0 | 2-0 | 2-0 | 4-1 | 0-4 | | 2-6 | 2-1 | 6-1 | 3-1 | 0-1 | 1-0 | 1-0 | 5-1 |
| Leeds City AFC | 0-2 | 2-0 | 2-0 | 1-1 | 2-1 | 0-1 | 3-5 | 0-1 | 3-0 | 5-0 | 1-0 | 2-3 | | 7-2 | 3-1 | 4-0 | 0-0 | 1-3 | 2-2 | 2-3 |
| Leicester Fosse FC | 0-1 | 1-0 | 2-2 | 1-3 | 1-3 | 1-1 | 0-6 | 0-2 | 3-2 | 2-0 | 1-2 | 1-1 | 5-1 | | 2-2 | 3-1 | 2-3 | 5-4 | 1-4 | 0-3 |
| Lincoln City AFC | 3-0 | 0-1 | 0-1 | 3-1 | 2-3 | 1-0 | 0-0 | 3-1 | 2-1 | 2-1 | 1-1 | 0-3 | 0-1 | 2-3 | | 2-1 | 3-1 | 2-2 | 1-0 | 2-2 |
| Nottingham Forest FC | 2-1 | 1-1 | 2-1 | 0-1 | 1-1 | 0-1 | 2-2 | 2-2 | 1-0 | 4-2 | 3-2 | 1-0 | 3-1 | 1-3 | 3-2 | | 1-1 | 1-1 | 1-1 | 3-1 |
| Preston North End FC | 5-2 | 2-0 | 1-0 | 4-1 | 2-0 | 2-2 | 1-3 | 2-1 | 1-0 | 3-0 | 1-1 | 2-1 | 2-0 | 1-0 | 0-0 | 2-2 | | 2-0 | 3-0 | 5-3 |
| Stockport County FC | 1-2 | 3-1 | 0-2 | 2-2 | 1-0 | 2-0 | 3-2 | 0-2 | 2-1 | 1-1 | 2-1 | 3-0 | 3-1 | 3-0 | 1-0 | 1-0 | 2-1 | | 1-1 | 2-2 |
| The Arsenal FC | 1-0 | 1-0 | 2-0 | 3-0 | 3-1 | 2-1 | 1-2 | 3-0 | 3-0 | 6-0 | 0-3 | 2-1 | 2-0 | 6-0 | 1-1 | 7-0 | 1-2 | 3-1 | | 5-1 |
| Wolverhampton Wanderers FC | 4-1 | 0-0 | 2-0 | 2-2 | 1-1 | 0-0 | 0-1 | 2-0 | 4-0 | 0-1 | 4-1 | 1-2 | 5-1 | 7-0 | 3-1 | 5-1 | 2-0 | 4-1 | 1-0 | |

| | Division 2 | Pd | Wn | Dw | Ls | GF | GA | Pts | |
|---|---|---|---|---|---|---|---|---|---|
| 1. | Derby County FC (Derby) | 38 | 23 | 7 | 8 | 71 | 33 | 53 | P |
| 2. | Preston North End FC (Preston) | 38 | 20 | 10 | 8 | 61 | 42 | 50 | P |
| 3. | Barnsley FC (Barnsley) | 38 | 22 | 3 | 13 | 51 | 51 | 47 | |
| 4. | Wolverhampton Wanderers FC (Wolverhampton) | 38 | 19 | 7 | 12 | 77 | 52 | 45 | |
| 5. | Birmingham FC (Birmingham) | 38 | 17 | 9 | 12 | 62 | 39 | 43 | |
| 6. | The Arsenal FC (London) | 38 | 19 | 5 | 14 | 69 | 41 | 43 | # |
| 7. | Hull City AFC (Kingston-upon-Hull) | 38 | 19 | 5 | 14 | 65 | 54 | 43 | |
| 8. | Huddersfield Town AFC (Huddersfield) | 38 | 17 | 8 | 13 | 61 | 42 | 42 | |
| 9. | Clapton Orient FC (London) | 38 | 16 | 9 | 13 | 50 | 48 | 41 | |
| 10. | Blackpool FC (Blackpool) | 38 | 17 | 5 | 16 | 58 | 57 | 39 | |
| 11. | Bury FC (Bury) | 38 | 15 | 8 | 15 | 61 | 56 | 38 | |
| 12. | Fulham FC (London) | 38 | 15 | 7 | 16 | 53 | 47 | 37 | |
| 13. | Bristol City FC (Bristol) | 38 | 15 | 7 | 16 | 62 | 56 | 37 | |
| 14. | Stockport County FC (Stockport) | 38 | 15 | 7 | 16 | 54 | 60 | 37 | |
| 15. | Leeds City AFC (Leeds) | 38 | 14 | 4 | 20 | 65 | 64 | 32 | |
| 16. | Lincoln City FC (Lincoln) | 38 | 11 | 9 | 18 | 46 | 65 | 31 | |
| 17. | Grimsby Town FC (Cleethorpes) | 38 | 11 | 9 | 18 | 48 | 76 | 31 | |
| 18. | Nottingham Forest FC (Nottingham) | 38 | 10 | 9 | 19 | 43 | 77 | 29 | |
| 19. | Leicester Fosse FC (Leicester) | 38 | 10 | 4 | 24 | 47 | 88 | 24 | |
| 20. | Glossop FC (Glossop) | 38 | 6 | 6 | 26 | 31 | 87 | 18 | ## |
| | | 760 | 311 | 138 | 311 | 1135 | 1135 | 760 | |

76

## Glossop FC (Glossop) resigned from the league at the end of the season.

# The league was suspended due to World War 1 and did not resume until season 1919-20 when Divisions 1 & 2 were both extended to 22 clubs. As a result of this Chelsea FC (London) and The Arsenal FC (London) were both elected to Division 1 for season 1919-20, however Tottenham Hotspur FC (London) were relegated to Division 2.

Coventry City FC (Coventry), Rotherham County FC (Rotherham), South Shields FC (South Shields), Stoke FC (Stoke-on-Trent) and West Ham United FC (London) were elected to Division 2 for the 1919-20 season.

## F.A. CUP FINAL   (Old Trafford, Manchester – 24/04/1915 – 49,557)

SHEFFIELD UNITED FC (SHEFFIELD)          3-0                              Chelsea FC (London)

*Simmons, Fazackerley, Kitchen*

Sheffield United: Gough, Cook, English, Sturgess, Brelsford, Utley, Simmons, Fazackerley, Kitchen, Masterman, Evans.

Chelsea: Molyneux, Bettridge, Harrow, Taylor, Logan, Walker, Ford, Halse, Thompson, Croal, McNeil.

## Semi-finals

| | | |
|---|---|---|
| Chelsea FC (London) | 2-0 | Everton FC (Liverpool) |
| Sheffield United FC (Sheffield) | 2-1 | Bolton Wanderers FC (Bolton) |

## Quarter-finals

| | | |
|---|---|---|
| Bolton Wanderers FC (Bolton) | 4-2 | Hull City AFC (Kingston-upon-Hull) |
| Bradford City AFC (Bradford) | 0-2 | Everton FC (Liverpool) |
| Chelsea FC (London) | 1-1 (aet), 1-0 | Newcastle United FC (Newcastle-upon-Tyne) |
| Oldham Athletic AFC (Oldham) | 0-0 (aet), 0-3 | Sheffield United FC (Sheffield) |

# 1915-16

| | Lancashire (Principal) | Pd | Wn | Dw | Ls | GF | GA | Pts |
|---|---|---|---|---|---|---|---|---|
| 1. | Manchester City FC (Manchester) | 26 | 16 | 3 | 7 | 61 | 35 | 35 |
| 2. | Burnley FC (Burnley) | 26 | 14 | 5 | 7 | 71 | 43 | 33 |
| 3. | Blackpool FC (Blackpool) | 26 | 14 | 3 | 9 | 54 | 41 | 31 |
| 4. | Everton FC (Liverpool) | 25 | 15 | - | 10 | 59 | 42 | 30 |
| 5. | Oldham Athletic AFC (Oldham) | 25 | 13 | 3 | 9 | 52 | 44 | 29 |
| 6. | Liverpool FC (Liverpool) | 26 | 11 | 7 | 8 | 48 | 42 | 29 |
| 7. | Stockport County FC (Stockport) | 26 | 13 | 3 | 10 | 47 | 43 | 29 |
| 8. | Stoke FC (Stoke-on-Trent) | 26 | 10 | 7 | 9 | 43 | 46 | 27 |
| 9. | Southport Central FC (Southport) | 26 | 9 | 6 | 11 | 41 | 41 | 24 |
| 10. | Bury FC (Bury) | 26 | 10 | 3 | 13 | 46 | 52 | 23 |
| 11. | Manchester United FC (Manchester) | 26 | 7 | 8 | 11 | 41 | 51 | 22 |
| 12. | Bolton Wanderers FC (Bolton) | 26 | 9 | 3 | 14 | 48 | 65 | 21 |
| 13. | Rochdale AFC (Rochdale) | 26 | 7 | 5 | 14 | 34 | 56 | 19 |
| 14. | Preston North End FC (Preston) | 26 | 4 | 2 | 20 | 23 | 67 | 10 |
| | | 362 | 152 | 58 | 152 | 668 | 668 | 362 |

| | Lancashire (Subsidiary – North) | Pd | Wn | Dw | Ls | GF | GA | Pts |
|---|---|---|---|---|---|---|---|---|
| 1. | Burnley FC (Burnley) | 10 | 8 | - | 2 | 29 | 12 | 16 |
| 2. | Blackpool FC (Blackpool) | 10 | 8 | - | 2 | 24 | 13 | 16 |
| 3. | Preston North End FC (Preston) | 10 | 4 | 2 | 4 | 22 | 19 | 10 |
| 4. | Bolton Wanderers FC (Bolton) | 10 | 4 | 1 | 5 | 16 | 22 | 9 |
| 5. | Bury FC (Bury) | 10 | 3 | - | 7 | 17 | 26 | 6 |
| 6. | Southport Central FC (Southport) | 10 | 1 | 1 | 8 | 12 | 28 | 3 |
| | | 60 | 28 | 4 | 28 | 120 | 120 | 60 |

## Lancashire (Subsidiary – South)

| | | Pd | Wn | Dw | Ls | GF | GA | Pts |
|---|---|---|---|---|---|---|---|---|
| 1. | Manchester City FC (Manchester) | 10 | 5 | 3 | 2 | 23 | 19 | 13 |
| 2. | Everton FC (Liverpool) | 10 | 6 | 1 | 3 | 19 | 16 | 13 |
| 3. | Liverpool FC (Liverpool) | 10 | 4 | 2 | 4 | 21 | 13 | 10 |
| 4. | Oldham Athletic AFC (Oldham) | 10 | 4 | 2 | 4 | 17 | 21 | 10 |
| 5. | Stockport County FC (Stockport) | 10 | 4 | 1 | 5 | 19 | 18 | 9 |
| 6. | Manchester United FC (Manchester) | 10 | 2 | 1 | 7 | 12 | 24 | 5 |
| | | 60 | 25 | 10 | 25 | 111 | 111 | 60 |

## Midland (Principal)

| | | Pd | Wn | Dw | Ls | GF | GA | Pts |
|---|---|---|---|---|---|---|---|---|
| 1. | Nottingham Forest FC (Nottingham) | 26 | 15 | 5 | 6 | 48 | 25 | 35 |
| 2. | Sheffield United FC (Sheffield) | 26 | 12 | 7 | 7 | 51 | 36 | 31 |
| 3. | Huddersfield Town AFC (Huddersfield) | 26 | 12 | 5 | 9 | 43 | 36 | 29 |
| 4. | Bradford City AFC (Bradford) | 26 | 12 | 4 | 10 | 52 | 32 | 28 |
| 5. | Leicester Fosse FC (Leicester) | 26 | 11 | 6 | 9 | 42 | 34 | 28 |
| 6. | Barnsley FC (Barnsley) | 26 | 12 | 4 | 10 | 46 | 55 | 28 |
| 7. | The Wednesday FC (Sheffield) | 26 | 11 | 5 | 10 | 46 | 43 | 27 |
| 8. | Notts County FC (Nottingham) | 26 | 10 | 6 | 10 | 39 | 36 | 26 |
| 9. | Lincoln City FC (Lincoln) | 26 | 12 | 2 | 12 | 54 | 54 | 26 |
| 10. | Leeds City AFC (Leeds) | 26 | 10 | 5 | 11 | 39 | 43 | 25 |
| 11. | Hull City AFC (Kingston-upon-Hull) | 26 | 10 | 3 | 13 | 42 | 58 | 23 |
| 12. | Bradford Park Avenue FC (Bradford) | 26 | 9 | 4 | 13 | 46 | 46 | 22 |
| 13. | Grimsby Town FC (Cleethorpes) | 26 | 7 | 6 | 13 | 31 | 46 | 20 |
| 14. | Derby County FC (Derby) | 26 | 7 | 2 | 17 | 39 | 74 | 16 |
| | | 364 | 150 | 64 | 150 | 618 | 618 | 364 |

## Midland (Subsidiary – North)

| | | Pd | Wn | Dw | Ls | GF | GA | Pts |
|---|---|---|---|---|---|---|---|---|
| 1. | Leeds City AFC (Leeds) | 10 | 7 | 1 | 2 | 21 | 13 | 15 |
| 2. | Bradford Park Avenue FC (Bradford) | 10 | 6 | - | 4 | 27 | 17 | 12 |
| 3. | Huddersfield Town AFC (Huddersfield) | 10 | 4 | 3 | 3 | 19 | 15 | 11 |
| 4. | Bradford City AFC (Bradford) | 10 | 4 | 1 | 5 | 18 | 20 | 9 |
| 5. | Rochdale AFC (Rochdale) | 10 | 4 | 1 | 5 | 15 | 21 | 9 |
| 6. | Barnsley FC (Barnsley) | 10 | 2 | - | 8 | 13 | 27 | 4 |
| | | 60 | 27 | 6 | 27 | 113 | 113 | 60 |

## Midland (Subsidiary – Midland)

| | | Pd | Wn | Dw | Ls | GF | GA | Pts |
|---|---|---|---|---|---|---|---|---|
| 1. | Grimsby Town FC (Cleethorpes) | 10 | 5 | 2 | 3 | 25 | 10 | 12 |
| 2. | Sheffield United FC (Sheffield) | 10 | 4 | 3 | 3 | 17 | 11 | 11 |
| 3. | Rotherham County FC (Rotherham) | 10 | 5 | 1 | 4 | 20 | 24 | 11 |
| 4. | Hull City AFC (Kingston-upon-Hull) | 10 | 5 | - | 5 | 18 | 27 | 10 |
| 5. | The Wednesday FC (Sheffield) | 10 | 3 | 3 | 4 | 10 | 13 | 9 |
| 6. | Lincoln City FC (Lincoln) | 10 | 2 | 3 | 5 | 17 | 22 | 7 |
| | | 60 | 24 | 12 | 24 | 107 | 107 | 60 |

## Midland (Subsidiary – South)

| | | Pd | Wn | Dw | Ls | GF | GA | Pts |
|---|---|---|---|---|---|---|---|---|
| 1. | Nottingham Forest FC (Nottingham) | 10 | 7 | - | 3 | 28 | 12 | 14 |
| 2. | Notts County FC (Nottingham) | 10 | 5 | 3 | 2 | 16 | 12 | 13 |
| 3. | Leicester Fosse FC (Leicester) | 10 | 3 | 3 | 4 | 15 | 19 | 9 |
| 4. | Stoke FC (Stoke-on-Trent) | 10 | 4 | - | 6 | 21 | 18 | 8 |
| 5. | Derby County FC (Derby) | 10 | 4 | - | 6 | 23 | 28 | 8 |
| 6. | Chesterfield FC (Chesterfield) | 10 | 3 | 2 | 5 | 15 | 29 | 8 |
| | | 60 | 26 | 8 | 26 | 118 | 118 | 60 |

## London (Principal)

| | | Pd | Wn | Dw | Ls | GF | GA | Pts |
|---|---|---|---|---|---|---|---|---|
| 1. | Chelsea FC (London) | 22 | 17 | 3 | 2 | 71 | 18 | 37 |
| 2. | Millwall Athletic FC (London) | 22 | 12 | 6 | 4 | 46 | 24 | 30 |
| 3. | The Arsenal FC (London) | 22 | 10 | 5 | 7 | 43 | 46 | 25 |
| 4. | West Ham United FC (London) | 22 | 10 | 4 | 8 | 47 | 35 | 24 |
| 5. | Fulham FC (London) | 22 | 10 | 4 | 8 | 45 | 37 | 24 |
| 6. | Tottenham Hotspur FC (London) | 22 | 8 | 8 | 6 | 38 | 35 | 24 |
| 7. | Brentford FC (London) | 22 | 6 | 8 | 8 | 36 | 40 | 20 |
| 8. | Queen's Park Rangers FC (London) | 22 | 8 | 3 | 11 | 27 | 41 | 19 |
| 9. | Crystal Palace FC (London) | 22 | 8 | 3 | 11 | 35 | 55 | 19 |
| 10. | Watford FC (Watford) | 22 | 8 | 1 | 13 | 37 | 46 | 17 |
| 11. | Clapton Orient FC (London) | 22 | 4 | 6 | 12 | 22 | 44 | 14 |
| 12. | Croydon Common FC (London) | 22 | 3 | 5 | 14 | 24 | 50 | 11 |
| | | 264 | 104 | 56 | 104 | 471 | 471 | 264 |

## London (Principal)

| | | Pd | Wn | Dw | Ls | GF | GA | Pts |
|---|---|---|---|---|---|---|---|---|
| 1. | Chelsea FC (London) | 14 | 10 | 1 | 3 | 50 | 15 | 21 |
| 2. | West Ham United FC (London) | 14 | 9 | 2 | 3 | 32 | 16 | 20 |
| 3. | Tottenham Hotspur FC (London) | 14 | 8 | 3 | 3 | 32 | 22 | 19 |
| 4. | Fulham FC (London) | 14 | 9 | - | 5 | 38 | 19 | 18 |
| 5. | Millwall Athletic FC (London) | 14 | 8 | 2 | 4 | 30 | 22 | 18 |
| 6. | Crystal Palace FC (London) | 14 | 8 | 2 | 4 | 41 | 29 | 18 |
| 7. | Watford FC (Watford) | 14 | 5 | 3 | 6 | 22 | 20 | 13 |
| 8. | Brentford FC (London) | 14 | 5 | 2 | 7 | 29 | 33 | 12 |
| 9. | Croydon Common FC (London) | 14 | 4 | 3 | 7 | 28 | 27 | 11 |
| 10. | Clapton Orient FC (London) | 14 | 3 | 4 | 7 | 17 | 27 | 10 |
| 11. | The Arsenal FC (London) | 14 | 3 | 4 | 7 | 19 | 31 | 10 |
| 12. | Luton Town FC (Luton) | 14 | 4 | 1 | 9 | 31 | 44 | 9 |
| 13. | Queen's Park Rangers FC (London) | 14 | 2 | 5 | 7 | 14 | 37 | 9 |
| 14. | Reading FC (Reading) | 14 | 2 | 4 | 8 | 23 | 64 | 8 |
| | | 196 | 80 | 36 | 80 | 406 | 406 | 196 |

## South-West Combination

| | | Pd | Wn | Dw | Ls | GF | GA | Pts |
|---|---|---|---|---|---|---|---|---|
| 1. | Portsmouth FC (Portsmouth) | 12 | 9 | - | 3 | 29 | 11 | 18 |
| 2. | Southampton FC (Southampton) | 12 | 8 | 1 | 3 | 37 | 19 | 17 |
| 3. | Cardiff City AFC (Cardiff) | 12 | 7 | - | 5 | 21 | 18 | 14 |
| 4. | Bristol Rovers FC (Bristol) | 12 | 5 | 3 | 4 | 17 | 20 | 13 |
| 5. | Bristol City FC (Bristol) | 12 | 5 | 1 | 6 | 13 | 16 | 11 |
| 6. | Swindon Town FC (Swindon) | 11 | 2 | 2 | 7 | 12 | 17 | 6 |
| 7. | Newport County AFC (Newport) | 11 | 1 | 1 | 9 | 8 | 32 | 3 |
| | | 82 | 37 | 8 | 37 | 138 | 133 | 82 |

# 1916-17

## Lancashire  (Principal)

| | | Pd | Wn | Dw | Ls | GF | GA | Pts |
|---|---|---|---|---|---|---|---|---|
| 1. | Liverpool FC (Liverpool) | 30 | 19 | 8 | 3 | 62 | 26 | 46 |
| 2. | Stockport County FC (Stockport) | 30 | 18 | 7 | 5 | 61 | 31 | 43 |
| 3. | Stoke FC (Stoke-on-Trent) | 30 | 16 | 7 | 7 | 64 | 36 | 39 |
| 4. | Manchester City FC (Manchester) | 30 | 14 | 9 | 7 | 49 | 29 | 37 |
| 5. | Everton FC (Liverpool) | 30 | 15 | 7 | 8 | 62 | 41 | 37 |
| 6. | Burnley FC (Burnley) | 30 | 15 | 4 | 11 | 73 | 56 | 34 |
| 7. | Manchester United FC (Manchester) | 30 | 13 | 6 | 11 | 48 | 54 | 32 |
| 8. | Rochdale AFC (Rochdale) | 30 | 12 | 5 | 13 | 47 | 54 | 29 |
| 9. | Southport Central FC (Southport) | 30 | 10 | 8 | 12 | 40 | 43 | 28 |
| 10. | Bolton Wanderers FC (Bolton) | 30 | 9 | 6 | 15 | 59 | 65 | 24 |
| 11. | Blackburn Rovers FC (Blackburn) | 30 | 10 | 4 | 16 | 52 | 66 | 24 |
| 12. | Preston North End FC (Preston) | 30 | 8 | 7 | 15 | 47 | 65 | 23 |
| 13. | Bury FC (Bury) | 30 | 7 | 8 | 15 | 40 | 63 | 22 |
| 14. | Oldham Athletic AFC (Oldham) | 30 | 8 | 6 | 16 | 36 | 65 | 22 |
| 15. | Port Vale FC (Stoke-on-Trent) | 30 | 7 | 7 | 16 | 50 | 60 | 21 |
| 16. | Blackpool FC (Blackpool) | 30 | 6 | 7 | 17 | 44 | 80 | 19 |
| | | 480 | 187 | 106 | 187 | 834 | 834 | 480 |

## Lancashire – Subsidiary – Group "A"

| | | Pd | Wn | Dw | Ls | GF | GA | Pts |
|---|---|---|---|---|---|---|---|---|
| 1. | Burnley FC (Burnley) | 6 | 4 | 1 | 1 | 14 | 9 | 9 |
| 2. | Preston North End FC (Preston) | 6 | 2 | 2 | 2 | 8 | 7 | 6 |
| 3. | Blackpool FC (Blackpool) | 6 | 2 | 1 | 3 | 10 | 12 | 5 |
| 4. | Blackburn Rovers FC (Blackburn) | 6 | 2 | - | 4 | 11 | 15 | 4 |
| | | 24 | 10 | 4 | 10 | 43 | 43 | 24 |

## Lancashire – Subsidiary – Group "B"

| | | Pd | Wn | Dw | Ls | GF | GA | Pts |
|---|---|---|---|---|---|---|---|---|
| 1. | Rochdale AFC (Rochdale) | 6 | 5 | 1 | - | 15 | 6 | 11 |
| 2. | Bolton Wanderers FC (Bolton) | 6 | 3 | - | 3 | 12 | 12 | 6 |
| 3. | Oldham Athletic AFC (Oldham) | 6 | 2 | 1 | 3 | 9 | 8 | 5 |
| 4. | Bury FC (Bury) | 6 | 1 | - | 5 | 6 | 16 | 2 |
| | | 24 | 11 | 2 | 11 | 42 | 42 | 24 |

## Lancashire – Subsidiary – Group "C"

| | | Pd | Wn | Dw | Ls | GF | GA | Pts |
|---|---|---|---|---|---|---|---|---|
| 1. | Manchester United FC (Manchester) | 6 | 4 | - | 2 | 15 | 9 | 8 |
| 2. | Stoke FC (Stoke-on-Trent) | 6 | 3 | - | 3 | 11 | 6 | 6 |
| 3. | Port Vale FC (Stoke-on-Trent) | 6 | 2 | 1 | 3 | 9 | 12 | 5 |
| 4. | Manchester City FC (Manchester) | 6 | 2 | 1 | 3 | 3 | 11 | 5 |
| | | 24 | 11 | 2 | 11 | 38 | 38 | 24 |

## Lancashire – Subsidiary – Group "D"

| | | Pd | Wn | Dw | Ls | GF | GA | Pts |
|---|---|---|---|---|---|---|---|---|
| 1. | Everton FC (Liverpool) | 6 | 4 | 1 | 1 | 16 | 5 | 9 |
| 2. | Stockport County FC (Stockport) | 6 | 2 | 3 | 1 | 6 | 10 | 7 |
| 3. | Liverpool FC (Liverpool) | 6 | 2 | 1 | 3 | 13 | 10 | 5 |
| 4. | Southport Central FC (Southport) | 6 | 1 | 1 | 4 | 5 | 15 | 3 |
| | | 24 | 9 | 6 | 9 | 40 | 40 | 24 |

## London (Combination)

| | | Pd | Wn | Dw | Ls | GF | GA | Pts |
|---|---|---|---|---|---|---|---|---|
| 1. | West Ham United FC (London) | 40 | 30 | 5 | 5 | 110 | 45 | 65 |
| 2. | Millwall Athletic FC (London) | 40 | 26 | 6 | 8 | 85 | 48 | 58 |
| 3. | Chelsea FC (London) | 40 | 24 | 5 | 11 | 93 | 48 | 53 |
| 4. | Tottenham Hotspur FC (London) | 40 | 24 | 5 | 11 | 112 | 64 | 53 |
| 5. | The Arsenal FC (London) | 40 | 19 | 10 | 11 | 62 | 47 | 48 |
| 6. | Fulham FC (London) | 40 | 21 | 3 | 16 | 102 | 63 | 45 |
| 7. | Luton Town FC (Luton) | 39 | 20 | 3 | 16 | 101 | 82 | 43 |
| 8. | Crystal Palace FC (London) | 38 | 14 | 7 | 17 | 68 | 72 | 35 |
| 9. | Southampton FC (Southampton) | 39 | 13 | 8 | 18 | 57 | 80 | 34 |
| 10. | Queen's Park Rangers FC (London) | 39 | 10 | 9 | 20 | 48 | 86 | 29 |
| 11. | Watford FC (Watford) | 39 | 8 | 9 | 22 | 69 | 115 | 25 |
| 12. | Brentford FC (London) | 40 | 9 | 7 | 24 | 56 | 99 | 25 |
| 13. | Portsmouth FC (Portsmouth) | 40 | 9 | 4 | 27 | 58 | 117 | 22 |
| 14. | Clapton Orient FC (London) | 40 | 6 | 7 | 27 | 49 | 104 | 19 |
| | | 554 | 233 | 88 | 233 | 1070 | 1070 | 554 |

## Midland (Principal)

| | | Pd | Wn | Dw | Ls | GF | GA | Pts |
|---|---|---|---|---|---|---|---|---|
| 1. | Leeds City AFC (Leeds) | 30 | 18 | 10 | 2 | 68 | 29 | 46 |
| 2. | Barnsley FC (Barnsley) | 30 | 15 | 8 | 7 | 65 | 41 | 38 |
| 3. | Birmingham FC (Birmingham) | 30 | 14 | 9 | 7 | 56 | 38 | 37 |
| 4. | Huddersfield Town AFC (Huddersfield) | 30 | 15 | 6 | 9 | 41 | 31 | 36 |
| 5. | Bradford Park Avenue FC (Bradford) | 30 | 14 | 6 | 10 | 51 | 32 | 34 |
| 6. | Nottingham Forest FC (Nottingham) | 30 | 14 | 5 | 11 | 57 | 39 | 33 |
| 7. | Notts County FC (Nottingham) | 30 | 13 | 6 | 11 | 47 | 52 | 32 |
| 8. | Bradford City FC (Bradford) | 30 | 12 | 7 | 11 | 41 | 41 | 31 |
| 9. | Rotherham County FC (Rotherham) | 30 | 12 | 6 | 12 | 53 | 52 | 30 |
| 10. | Sheffield United FC (Sheffield) | 30 | 11 | 7 | 12 | 43 | 47 | 29 |
| 11. | Hull City AFC (Kingston-upon-Hull) | 30 | 10 | 7 | 13 | 36 | 57 | 27 |
| 12. | Chesterfield FC (Chesterfield) | 30 | 11 | 4 | 15 | 59 | 62 | 26 |
| 13. | The Wednesday FC (Sheffield) | 30 | 9 | 6 | 15 | 36 | 48 | 24 |
| 14. | Grimsby Town FC (Cleethorpes) | 30 | 8 | 6 | 16 | 38 | 71 | 22 |
| 15. | Leicester Fosse FC (Leicester) | 30 | 6 | 7 | 17 | 29 | 53 | 19 |
| 16. | Lincoln City FC (Lincoln) | 30 | 5 | 6 | 19 | 38 | 65 | 16 |
| | | 480 | 187 | 106 | 187 | 758 | 758 | 480 |

## Midland (Subsidiary – Group "A")

| | | Pd | Wn | Dw | Ls | GF | GA | Pts |
|---|---|---|---|---|---|---|---|---|
| 1. | Sheffield United FC (Sheffield) | 6 | 4 | - | 2 | 12 | 7 | 8 |
| 2. | The Wednesday FC (Sheffield) | 6 | 2 | 2 | 2 | 12 | 12 | 6 |
| 3. | Barnsley FC (Barnsley) | 6 | 1 | 3 | 2 | 8 | 9 | 5 |
| 4. | Rotherham County FC (Rotherham) | 6 | 2 | 1 | 3 | 9 | 13 | 5 |
| | | 24 | 9 | 6 | 9 | 41 | 41 | 24 |

## Midland (Subsidiary – Group "B")

| | | Pd | Wn | Dw | Ls | GF | GA | Pts |
|---|---|---|---|---|---|---|---|---|
| 1. | Birmingham FC (Birmingham) | 6 | 3 | 2 | 1 | 17 | 12 | 8 |
| 2. | Leicester Fosse FC (Leicester) | 6 | 4 | - | 2 | 12 | 12 | 8 |
| 3. | Notts County FC (Nottingham) | 6 | 1 | 2 | 3 | 9 | 12 | 4 |
| 4. | Nottingham Forest FC (Nottingham) | 6 | 1 | 2 | 3 | 12 | 14 | 4 |
| | | 24 | 9 | 6 | 9 | 50 | 50 | 24 |

## Midland (Subsidiary – Group "C")

| | | Pd | Wn | Dw | Ls | GF | GA | Pts |
|---|---|---|---|---|---|---|---|---|
| 1. | Bradford Park Avenue FC (Bradford) | 6 | 3 | 2 | 1 | 10 | 5 | 8 |
| 2. | Huddersfield Town AFC (Huddersfield) | 6 | 3 | 1 | 2 | 6 | 4 | 7 |
| 3. | Leeds City AFC (Leeds) | 6 | 2 | 2 | 2 | 8 | 7 | 6 |
| 4. | Bradford City AFC (Bradford) | 6 | - | 3 | 3 | 5 | 13 | 3 |
| | | 24 | 8 | 8 | 8 | 29 | 29 | 24 |

## Midland (Subsidiary – Group "D")

| | | Pd | Wn | Dw | Ls | GF | GA | Pts |
|---|---|---|---|---|---|---|---|---|
| 1. | Chesterfield FC (Chesterfield) | 6 | 4 | - | 2 | 15 | 16 | 8 |
| 2. | Grimsby Town FC (Cleethorpes) | 6 | 2 | 2 | 2 | 12 | 11 | 6 |
| 3. | Hull City AFC (Kingston-upon-Hull) | 6 | 2 | 2 | 2 | 13 | 12 | 6 |
| 4. | Lincoln City FC (Lincoln) | 6 | 1 | 2 | 3 | 11 | 12 | 4 |
| | | 24 | 9 | 6 | 9 | 51 | 51 | 24 |

# 1917-18

## Lancashire (Principal)

| | | Pd | Wn | Dw | Ls | GF | GA | Pts |
|---|---|---|---|---|---|---|---|---|
| 1. | Stoke FC (Stoke-on-Trent) | 30 | 22 | 4 | 4 | 109 | 27 | 48 |
| 2. | Liverpool FC (Liverpool) | 30 | 21 | 6 | 3 | 101 | 26 | 48 |
| 3. | Everton FC (Liverpool) | 30 | 19 | 6 | 5 | 92 | 36 | 44 |
| 4. | Manchester City FC (Manchester) | 30 | 15 | 8 | 7 | 57 | 28 | 38 |
| 5. | Stockport County FC (Stockport) | 30 | 17 | 3 | 10 | 59 | 32 | 37 |
| 6. | Rochdale AFC (Rochdale) | 30 | 14 | 9 | 7 | 78 | 51 | 37 |
| 7. | Bolton Wanderers FC (Bolton) | 30 | 13 | 4 | 13 | 68 | 70 | 30 |
| 8. | Manchester United FC (Manchester) | 30 | 11 | 8 | 11 | 45 | 49 | 30 |
| 9. | Oldham Athletic AFC (Oldham) | 30 | 11 | 6 | 13 | 50 | 59 | 28 |
| 10. | Preston North End FC (Preston) | 30 | 12 | 3 | 15 | 38 | 53 | 27 |
| 11. | Port Vale FC (Stoke-on-Trent) | 30 | 9 | 8 | 13 | 47 | 58 | 26 |
| 12. | Blackpool FC (Blackpool) | 30 | 10 | 5 | 15 | 46 | 70 | 25 |
| 13. | Southport Central FC (Southport) | 30 | 8 | 6 | 16 | 33 | 69 | 22 |
| 14. | Bury FC (Bury) | 30 | 8 | 5 | 17 | 46 | 64 | 21 |
| 15. | Burnley FC (Burnley) | 30 | 5 | 4 | 21 | 32 | 104 | 14 |
| 16. | Blackburn Rovers FC (Blackburn) | 30 | 2 | 1 | 27 | 22 | 127 | 5 |
| | | 480 | 197 | 86 | 197 | 923 | 923 | 480 |

## Lancashire (Subsidiary – Group "A")

| | | Pd | Wn | Dw | Ls | GF | GA | Pts |
|---|---|---|---|---|---|---|---|---|
| 1. | Preston North End FC (Preston) | 6 | 4 | 1 | 1 | 10 | 8 | 9 |
| 2. | Blackpool FC (Blackpool) | 6 | 4 | - | 2 | 18 | 9 | 8 |
| 3. | Burnley FC (Burnley) | 6 | 2 | 1 | 3 | 10 | 11 | 5 |
| 4. | Blackburn Rovers FC (Blackburn) | 6 | 1 | - | 5 | 3 | 13 | 2 |
| | | 24 | 11 | 2 | 11 | 41 | 41 | 24 |

## Lancashire (Subsidiary – Group "B")

| | | Pd | Wn | Dw | Ls | GF | GA | Pts |
|---|---|---|---|---|---|---|---|---|
| 1. | Bolton Wanderers FC (Bolton) | 6 | 3 | 1 | 2 | 11 | 9 | 7 |
| 2. | Oldham Athletic AFC (Oldham) | 6 | 3 | 1 | 2 | 9 | 9 | 7 |
| 3. | Rochdale AFC (Rochdale) | 6 | 3 | - | 3 | 13 | 8 | 6 |
| 4. | Bury FC (Bury) | 6 | 1 | 2 | 3 | 8 | 15 | 4 |
| | | 24 | 10 | 4 | 10 | 41 | 41 | 24 |

## Lancashire (Subsidiary – Group "C")

| | Pd | Wn | Dw | Ls | GF | GA | Pts |
|---|---|---|---|---|---|---|---|
| 1. Manchester City FC (Manchester) | 6 | 4 | 1 | 1 | 11 | 4 | 9 |
| 2. Manchester United FC (Manchester) | 6 | 3 | 1 | 2 | 6 | 7 | 7 |
| 3. Stoke FC (Stoke-on-Trent) | 6 | 2 | 2 | 2 | 10 | 5 | 6 |
| 4. Port Vale FC (Stoke-on-Trent) | 6 | 1 | - | 5 | 4 | 15 | 2 |
| | 24 | 10 | 4 | 10 | 31 | 31 | 24 |

## Lancashire (Subsidiary – Group "D")

| | Pd | Wn | Dw | Ls | GF | GA | Pts |
|---|---|---|---|---|---|---|---|
| 1. Liverpool FC (Liverpool) | 6 | 5 | - | 1 | 24 | 7 | 10 |
| 2. Everton FC (Liverpool) | 6 | 5 | - | 1 | 19 | 7 | 10 |
| 3. Stockport County FC (Stockport) | 6 | 2 | - | 4 | 6 | 13 | 4 |
| 4. Southport Central FC (Southport) | 6 | - | - | 6 | 1 | 23 | - |
| | 24 | 12 | - | 12 | 50 | 50 | 24 |

## London (Combination)

| | Pd | Wn | Dw | Ls | GF | GA | Pts |
|---|---|---|---|---|---|---|---|
| 1. Chelsea FC (London) | 36 | 21 | 8 | 7 | 82 | 39 | 50 |
| 2. West Ham United FC (London) | 36 | 20 | 9 | 7 | 103 | 51 | 49 |
| 3. Fulham FC (London) | 36 | 20 | 7 | 9 | 75 | 60 | 47 |
| 4. Tottenham Hotspur FC (London) | 36 | 22 | 2 | 12 | 86 | 56 | 46 |
| 5. The Arsenal FC (London) | 36 | 16 | 5 | 15 | 76 | 57 | 37 |
| 6. Brentford FC (London) | 36 | 16 | 3 | 17 | 81 | 94 | 35 |
| 7. Crystal Palace FC (London) | 36 | 13 | 4 | 19 | 54 | 83 | 30 |
| 8. Queen's Park Rangers FC (London) | 36 | 14 | 2 | 20 | 48 | 73 | 30 |
| 9. Millwall Athletic FC (London) | 36 | 12 | 4 | 20 | 52 | 74 | 28 |
| 10. Clapton Orient FC (London) | 36 | 2 | 4 | 30 | 34 | 104 | 8 |
| | 360 | 156 | 48 | 156 | 691 | 691 | 360 |

## Midland (Principal)

| | Pd | Wn | Dw | Ls | GF | GA | Pts |
|---|---|---|---|---|---|---|---|
| 1. Leeds City AFC (Leeds) | 28 | 23 | 1 | 4 | 75 | 23 | 47 |
| 2. Sheffield United FC (Sheffield) | 28 | 20 | 1 | 7 | 66 | 27 | 41 |
| 3. Birmingham FC (Birmingham) | 28 | 14 | 6 | 8 | 59 | 38 | 34 |
| 4. Hull City AFC (Kingston-upon-Hull) | 28 | 15 | 4 | 9 | 67 | 50 | 34 |
| 5. Nottingham Forest FC (Nottingham) | 28 | 13 | 4 | 11 | 41 | 28 | 30 |
| 6. Bradford Park Avenue FC (Bradford) | 28 | 13 | 4 | 11 | 40 | 29 | 30 |
| 7. Leicester Fosse FC (Leicester) | 28 | 13 | 3 | 12 | 52 | 43 | 29 |
| 8. Huddersfield Town AFC (Huddersfield) | 28 | 12 | 2 | 14 | 49 | 46 | 26 |
| 9. Rotherham County FC (Rotherham) | 28 | 8 | 9 | 11 | 42 | 52 | 25 |
| 10. Notts County FC (Nottingham) | 28 | 7 | 9 | 12 | 43 | 54 | 23 |
| 11. The Wednesday FC (Sheffield) | 28 | 9 | 5 | 14 | 45 | 59 | 23 |
| 12. Grimsby Town FC (Cleethorpes) | 28 | 5 | 11 | 12 | 24 | 62 | 21 |
| 13. Bradford City AFC (Bradford) | 28 | 8 | 4 | 16 | 34 | 55 | 20 |
| 14. Lincoln City FC (Lincoln) | 28 | 7 | 5 | 16 | 25 | 62 | 19 |
| 15. Barnsley FC (Barnsley) | 28 | 8 | 2 | 18 | 40 | 74 | 18 |
| | 420 | 175 | 70 | 175 | 702 | 702 | 420 |

## Midland (Subsidiary – Group "A")

| | Pd | Wn | Dw | Ls | GF | GA | Pts |
|---|---|---|---|---|---|---|---|
| 1. The Wednesday FC (Sheffield) | 6 | 3 | 2 | 1 | 15 | 8 | 8 |
| 2. Barnsley FC (Barnsley) | 6 | 3 | 1 | 2 | 14 | 12 | 7 |
| 3. Sheffield United FC (Sheffield) | 6 | 2 | 1 | 3 | 9 | 12 | 5 |
| 4. Rotherham County FC (Rotherham) | 6 | 1 | 2 | 3 | 4 | 10 | 4 |
| | 24 | 9 | 6 | 9 | 42 | 42 | 24 |

| Midland (Subsidiary – Group "B") | Pd | Wn | Dw | Ls | GF | GA | Pts |
|---|---|---|---|---|---|---|---|
| 1. Notts County FC (Nottingham) | 6 | 4 | - | 2 | 19 | 9 | 8 |
| 2. Birmingham FC (Birmingham) | 6 | 2 | 2 | 2 | 6 | 9 | 6 |
| 3. Leicester Fosse FC (Leicester) | 6 | 2 | 1 | 3 | 6 | 10 | 5 |
| 4. Nottingham Forest FC (Nottingham) | 6 | 2 | 1 | 3 | 4 | 7 | 5 |
| | 24 | 10 | 4 | 10 | 35 | 35 | 24 |

| Midland (Subsidiary – Group "C") | Pd | Wn | Dw | Ls | GF | GA | Pts |
|---|---|---|---|---|---|---|---|
| 1. Leeds City AFC (Leeds) | 6 | 3 | 2 | 1 | 8 | 6 | 8 |
| 2. Huddersfield Town AFC (Huddersfield) | 6 | 3 | 1 | 2 | 13 | 11 | 7 |
| 3. Bradford City AFC (Bradford) | 6 | 1 | 4 | 1 | 8 | 8 | 6 |
| 4. Bradford Park Avenue FC (Bradford) | 6 | 1 | 1 | 4 | 8 | 12 | 3 |
| | 24 | 8 | 8 | 8 | 37 | 37 | 24 |

| Midland (Subsidiary – Group "D") | Pd | Wn | Dw | Ls | GF | GA | Pts |
|---|---|---|---|---|---|---|---|
| 1. Grimsby Town FC (Cleethorpes) | 6 | 4 | 1 | 1 | 13 | 3 | 9 |
| 2. Hull City AFC (Kingston-upon-Hull) | 6 | 3 | 2 | 1 | 12 | 9 | 8 |
| 3. Lincoln City FC (Lincoln) | 6 | 3 | 1 | 2 | 11 | 8 | 7 |
| 4. Gainsborough Trinity FC (Gainsborough) | 6 | - | - | 6 | 3 | 19 | - |
| | 24 | 10 | 4 | 10 | 39 | 39 | 24 |

# 1918-19

## Football League Championship Play-off

Nottingham Forest FC (Nottingham)　　　0-0, 1-0　　　Everton FC (Liverpool)

| Lancashire (Principal) | Pd | Wn | Dw | Ls | GF | GA | Pts |
|---|---|---|---|---|---|---|---|
| 1. Everton FC (Liverpool) | 30 | 27 | 2 | 1 | 108 | 26 | 56 |
| 2. Stoke FC (Stoke-on-Trent) | 30 | 20 | 3 | 7 | 84 | 36 | 43 |
| 3. Liverpool FC (Liverpool) | 30 | 19 | 4 | 7 | 82 | 33 | 42 |
| 4. Bolton Wanderers FC (Bolton) | 30 | 15 | 6 | 9 | 58 | 58 | 36 |
| 5. Manchester City FC (Manchester) | 30 | 15 | 3 | 12 | 57 | 36 | 33 |
| 6. Southport Vulcan FC (Southport) | 30 | 15 | 3 | 12 | 49 | 53 | 33 |
| 7. Preston North End FC (Preston) | 30 | 12 | 6 | 12 | 41 | 51 | 30 |
| 8. Stockport County FC (Stockport) | 30 | 11 | 7 | 12 | 48 | 52 | 29 |
| 9. Manchester United FC (Manchester) | 30 | 11 | 5 | 14 | 51 | 50 | 27 |
| 10. Rochdale AFC (Rochdale) | 30 | 11 | 5 | 14 | 56 | 61 | 27 |
| 11. Blackpool FC (Blackpool) | 30 | 10 | 5 | 15 | 45 | 61 | 25 |
| 12. Port Vale FC (Stoke-on-Trent) | 30 | 10 | 4 | 16 | 39 | 77 | 24 |
| 13. Burnley FC (Burnley) | 30 | 10 | 3 | 17 | 54 | 76 | 23 |
| 14. Bury FC (Bury) | 30 | 7 | 6 | 17 | 27 | 58 | 20 |
| 15. Oldham Athletic AFC (Oldham) | 30 | 7 | 4 | 19 | 39 | 62 | 18 |
| 16. Blackburn Rovers FC (Blackburn) | 30 | 5 | 4 | 21 | 35 | 83 | 14 |
| | 480 | 205 | 70 | 205 | 873 | 873 | 480 |

| Lancashire (Subsidiary – Group "A") | Pd | Wn | Dw | Ls | GF | GA | Pts |
|---|---|---|---|---|---|---|---|
| 1. Blackpool FC (Blackpool) | 6 | 3 | 2 | 1 | 13 | 7 | 8 |
| 2. Burnley FC (Burnley) | 6 | 3 | 1 | 2 | 15 | 8 | 7 |
| 3. Preston North End FC (Preston) | 6 | 3 | 1 | 2 | 6 | 7 | 7 |
| 4. Blackburn Rovers FC (Blackburn) | 6 | - | 2 | 4 | 6 | 18 | 2 |
| | 24 | 9 | 6 | 9 | 40 | 40 | 24 |

| Lancashire (Subsidiary – Group "B") | Pd | Wn | Dw | Ls | GF | GA | Pts |
|---|---|---|---|---|---|---|---|
| 1. Oldham Athletic AFC (Oldham) | 6 | 5 | - | 1 | 17 | 4 | 10 |
| 2. Bolton Wanderers FC (Bolton) | 6 | 5 | - | 1 | 16 | 9 | 10 |
| 3. Rochdale AFC (Rochdale) | 6 | 1 | - | 5 | 5 | 13 | 2 |
| 4. Bury FC (Bury) | 6 | 1 | - | 5 | 4 | 16 | 2 |
| | 24 | 12 | - | 12 | 42 | 42 | 24 |

| Lancashire (Subsidiary – Group "C") | Pd | Wn | Dw | Ls | GF | GA | Pts |
|---|---|---|---|---|---|---|---|
| 1. Manchester City FC (Manchester) | 6 | 5 | 1 | - | 14 | 4 | 11 |
| 2. Stoke FC (Stoke-on-Trent) | 6 | 2 | 2 | 2 | 9 | 10 | 6 |
| 3. Manchester United FC (Manchester) | 6 | 2 | - | 4 | 9 | 14 | 4 |
| 4. Port Vale FC (Stoke-on-Trent) | 6 | 1 | 1 | 4 | 9 | 13 | 3 |
| | 24 | 10 | 4 | 10 | 41 | 41 | 24 |

| Lancashire (Subsidiary – Group "D") | Pd | Wn | Dw | Ls | GF | GA | Pts |
|---|---|---|---|---|---|---|---|
| 1. Liverpool FC (Liverpool) | 6 | 4 | 2 | - | 13 | 6 | 10 |
| 2. Stockport County FC (Stockport) | 6 | 3 | 1 | 2 | 7 | 6 | 7 |
| 3. Southport Vulcan FC (Southport) | 6 | 2 | - | 4 | 9 | 12 | 4 |
| 4. Everton FC (Liverpool) | 6 | 1 | 1 | 4 | 5 | 10 | 3 |
| | 24 | 10 | 4 | 10 | 34 | 34 | 24 |

# Lancashire Cup Final

| Liverpool FC (Liverpool) | 3-0 | Oldham Athletic AFC (Oldham) |
|---|---|---|

## Semi-finals

| Blackpool FC (Blackpool) | 0-1 | Liverpool FC (Liverpool) |
|---|---|---|
| Manchester City FC (Manchester) | 0-1 | Oldham Athletic AFC (Oldham) |

# London Victory Cup

| Chelsea FC (London) | 3-0 | Fulham FC (London) |
|---|---|---|

## Semi-finals

| Chelsea FC (London) | 4-0 | Crystal Palace FC (London) |
|---|---|---|
| Tottenham Hotspur FC (London) | 0-2 | Fulham FC (London) |

| Midland (Principal) | Pd | Wn | Dw | Ls | GF | GA | Pts |
|---|---|---|---|---|---|---|---|
| 1. Nottingham Forest FC (Nottingham) | 30 | 18 | 6 | 6 | 59 | 31 | 42 |
| 2. Birmingham FC (Birmingham) | 30 | 20 | 1 | 9 | 72 | 36 | 41 |
| 3. Notts County FC (Nottingham) | 30 | 16 | 9 | 5 | 65 | 38 | 41 |
| 4. Leeds City AFC (Leeds) | 30 | 17 | 4 | 9 | 53 | 38 | 38 |
| 5. Bradford Park Avenue FC (Bradford) | 30 | 15 | 7 | 8 | 53 | 41 | 37 |
| 6. Huddersfield Town AFC (Huddersfield) | 30 | 13 | 8 | 9 | 45 | 45 | 34 |
| 7. Hull City AFC (Kingston-upon-Hull) | 30 | 12 | 7 | 11 | 48 | 42 | 31 |
| 8. Sheffield United FC (Sheffield) | 30 | 12 | 6 | 12 | 56 | 47 | 30 |
| 9. Coventry City FC (Coventry) | 30 | 13 | 4 | 13 | 55 | 59 | 30 |
| 10. Leicester Fosse FC (Leicester) | 30 | 13 | 3 | 14 | 53 | 53 | 29 |
| 11. The Wednesday FC (Sheffield) | 30 | 11 | 6 | 13 | 49 | 49 | 28 |
| 12. Lincoln City FC (Lincoln) | 30 | 10 | 4 | 16 | 38 | 59 | 24 |
| 13. Bradford City AFC (Bradford) | 30 | 9 | 4 | 17 | 48 | 56 | 22 |
| 14. Barnsley FC (Barnsley) | 30 | 9 | 3 | 18 | 45 | 79 | 21 |
| 15. Grimsby Town FC (Cleethorpes) | 30 | 7 | 6 | 17 | 40 | 69 | 20 |
| 16. Rotherham County FC (Rotherham) | 30 | 2 | 8 | 20 | 23 | 60 | 12 |
| | 480 | 197 | 86 | 197 | 802 | 802 | 480 |

## Midland (Subsidiary – Group "A")

| | | Pd | Wn | Dw | Ls | GF | GA | Pts |
|---|---|---|---|---|---|---|---|---|
| 1. | Sheffield United FC (Sheffield) | 6 | 5 | 1 | - | 14 | 3 | 11 |
| 2. | The Wednesday FC (Sheffield) | 6 | 3 | 1 | 2 | 11 | 10 | 7 |
| 3. | Barnsley FC (Barnsley) | 6 | 1 | 1 | 4 | 13 | 18 | 3 |
| 4. | Rotherham County FC (Rotherham) | 6 | 1 | 1 | 4 | 11 | 18 | 3 |
| | | 24 | 10 | 4 | 10 | 49 | 49 | 24 |

## Midland (Subsidiary – Group "B")

| | | Pd | Wn | Dw | Ls | GF | GA | Pts |
|---|---|---|---|---|---|---|---|---|
| 1. | Birmingham FC (Birmingham) | 6 | 5 | - | 1 | 13 | 7 | 10 |
| 2. | Leicester Fosse FC (Leicester) | 6 | 3 | - | 3 | 10 | 13 | 6 |
| 3. | Notts County FC (Nottingham) | 6 | 2 | - | 4 | 13 | 13 | 4 |
| 4. | Nottingham Forest FC (Nottingham) | 6 | 2 | - | 4 | 7 | 10 | 4 |
| | | 24 | 12 | - | 12 | 43 | 43 | 24 |

## Midland (Subsidiary – Group "C")

| | | Pd | Wn | Dw | Ls | GF | GA | Pts |
|---|---|---|---|---|---|---|---|---|
| 1. | Bradford Park Avenue FC (Bradford) | 6 | 3 | 2 | 1 | 13 | 6 | 8 |
| 2. | Huddersfield Town AFC (Huddersfield) | 6 | 2 | 3 | 1 | 7 | 4 | 7 |
| 3. | Leeds City AFC (Leeds) | 6 | 3 | - | 3 | 10 | 9 | 6 |
| 4. | Bradford City FC (Bradford) | 6 | 1 | 1 | 4 | 4 | 15 | 3 |
| | | 24 | 9 | 6 | 9 | 34 | 34 | 24 |

## Midland (Subsidiary – Group "D")

| | | Pd | Wn | Dw | Ls | GF | GA | Pts |
|---|---|---|---|---|---|---|---|---|
| 1. | Hull City AFC (Kingston-upon-Hull) | 6 | 4 | - | 2 | 11 | 7 | 8 |
| 2. | Coventry City FC (Coventry) | 6 | 3 | 2 | 1 | 7 | 6 | 8 |
| 3. | Grimsby Town FC (Cleethorpes) | 6 | 2 | 1 | 3 | 8 | 10 | 5 |
| 4. | Lincoln City FC (Lincoln) | 6 | 1 | 1 | 4 | 6 | 9 | 3 |
| | | 24 | 10 | 4 | 10 | 32 | 32 | 24 |

## London (Combination)

| | | Pd | Wn | Dw | Ls | GF | GA | Pts |
|---|---|---|---|---|---|---|---|---|
| 1. | Brentford FC (London) | 36 | 20 | 9 | 7 | 94 | 48 | 49 |
| 2. | The Arsenal FC (London) | 36 | 20 | 5 | 11 | 85 | 56 | 45 |
| 3. | West Ham United FC (London) | 36 | 17 | 7 | 12 | 65 | 51 | 41 |
| 4. | Fulham FC (London) | 36 | 17 | 6 | 13 | 70 | 55 | 40 |
| 5. | Queen's Park Rangers FC (London) | 36 | 16 | 7 | 13 | 69 | 60 | 39 |
| 6. | Chelsea FC (London) | 36 | 13 | 11 | 12 | 70 | 53 | 37 |
| 7. | Crystal Palace FC (London) | 36 | 14 | 6 | 16 | 66 | 73 | 34 |
| 8. | Tottenham Hotspur FC (London) | 36 | 13 | 8 | 15 | 52 | 72 | 34 |
| 9. | Millwall Athletic FC (London) | 36 | 10 | 9 | 17 | 50 | 67 | 29 |
| 10. | Clapton Orient FC (London) | 36 | 3 | 6 | 27 | 35 | 123 | 12 |
| | | 360 | 143 | 74 | 143 | 656 | 658 | 360 |

# 1919-20

| Football League Division 1 1919-1920 Season | Aston Villa | Blackburn R. | Bolton Wands. | Bradford City | Bradford P.A. | Burnley | Chelsea | Derby County | Everton | Liverpool | Man. City | Man. United | Middlesbro' | Newcastle U. | Notts County | Oldham Ath. | Preston N.E. | Sheffield U. | Sunderland | The Arsenal | Wednesday | W.B.A. |
|---|---|---|---|---|---|---|---|---|---|---|---|---|---|---|---|---|---|---|---|---|---|---|
| Aston Villa FC | ■ | 1-2 | 3-6 | 3-1 | 1-0 | 2-2 | 5-2 | 2-2 | 2-2 | 0-1 | 0-1 | 2-0 | 5-3 | 4-0 | 3-1 | 3-0 | 2-4 | 4-0 | 0-3 | 2-1 | 3-1 | 2-4 |
| Blackburn Rovers FC | 5-1 | ■ | 2-2 | 4-1 | 3-3 | 2-3 | 3-1 | 2-0 | 3-2 | 0-2 | 1-4 | 5-0 | 0-2 | 2-0 | 1-1 | 0-1 | 4-0 | 4-0 | 3-0 | 2-2 | 1-0 | 1-5 |
| Bolton Wanderers FC | 2-1 | 2-1 | ■ | 1-1 | 1-2 | 1-1 | 1-2 | 3-0 | 0-2 | 0-3 | 6-2 | 3-5 | 2-1 | 0-3 | 1-0 | 1-0 | 4-1 | 1-0 | 1-0 | 2-2 | 2-0 | 1-2 |
| Bradford City AFC | 3-1 | 3-1 | 0-1 | ■ | 0-0 | 2-1 | 3-1 | 3-1 | 3-3 | 1-3 | 1-0 | 2-1 | 0-1 | 1-0 | 3-4 | 1-1 | 2-2 | 1-2 | 2-0 | 1-1 | 1-1 | 3-0 |
| Bradford Park Avenue | 6-1 | 5-2 | 2-0 | 0-0 | ■ | 0-1 | 1-0 | 1-1 | 0-2 | 1-2 | 2-1 | 1-4 | 1-1 | 0-1 | 0-1 | 2-0 | 3-3 | 1-0 | 2-2 | 0-0 | 3-0 | 0-4 |
| Burnley FC | 0-0 | 3-1 | 2-1 | 1-1 | 2-6 | ■ | 2-3 | 2-0 | 5-0 | 1-2 | 2-0 | 2-1 | 5-3 | 1-0 | 2-1 | 2-1 | 1-1 | 2-2 | 2-1 | 2-1 | 2-0 | 2-2 |
| Chelsea FC | 2-1 | 2-1 | 2-3 | 1-0 | 4-0 | 0-1 | ■ | 0-0 | 0-1 | 1-0 | 1-0 | 1-0 | 3-1 | 0-0 | 2-0 | 1-0 | 4-0 | 1-1 | 2-0 | 3-1 | 1-1 | 2-0 |
| Derby County FC | 1-0 | 0-0 | 1-2 | 3-0 | 0-0 | 0-2 | 5-0 | ■ | 2-1 | 3-0 | 0-0 | 1-1 | 1-2 | 1-0 | 3-1 | 1-1 | 2-0 | 5-1 | 3-1 | 2-1 | 2-1 | 0-4 |
| Everton FC | 1-1 | 3-0 | 3-3 | 4-1 | 2-0 | 2-2 | 2-3 | 4-0 | ■ | 0-0 | 2-0 | 0-0 | 5-2 | 4-0 | 1-2 | 0-2 | 0-1 | 3-0 | 1-3 | 2-3 | 1-1 | 2-5 |
| Liverpool FC | 2-1 | 3-0 | 2-0 | 2-1 | 3-3 | 0-1 | 0-1 | 3-0 | 3-1 | ■ | 1-0 | 0-0 | 1-0 | 1-1 | 3-0 | 2-2 | 1-2 | 2-0 | 3-2 | 2-3 | 1-0 | 0-0 |
| Manchester City FC | 2-2 | 8-2 | 1-4 | 1-0 | 4-1 | 3-1 | 1-0 | 3-1 | 1-1 | 2-1 | ■ | 3-3 | 1-0 | 0-0 | 4-1 | 3-1 | 1-0 | 3-3 | 1-0 | 4-1 | 4-2 | 2-3 |
| Manchester United FC | 1-2 | 1-1 | 1-1 | 0-0 | 0-1 | 0-1 | 0-2 | 0-2 | 1-0 | 0-0 | 1-0 | ■ | 1-1 | 2-1 | 0-0 | 1-1 | 5-1 | 3-0 | 2-0 | 0-1 | 0-0 | 1-2 |
| Middlesbrough FC | 1-4 | 2-2 | 1-3 | 4-0 | 1-2 | 4-0 | 0-0 | 2-0 | 1-1 | 3-2 | 0-2 | 1-1 | ■ | 0-1 | 5-2 | 1-0 | 4-1 | 1-0 | 0-2 | 1-0 | 3-0 | 0-0 |
| Newcastle United FC | 2-0 | 0-0 | 0-1 | 0-1 | 4-0 | 0-0 | 3-0 | 0-0 | 3-0 | 3-0 | 2-1 | 0-0 | 0-0 | ■ | 2-1 | 0-1 | 1-0 | 2-1 | 2-3 | 3-1 | 1-1 | 0-2 |
| Notts County FC | 2-1 | 5-0 | 2-2 | 5-2 | 0-2 | 2-0 | 0-1 | 2-2 | 1-0 | 4-1 | 0-0 | 2-1 | 1-1 | 0-0 | ■ | 2-1 | 1-2 | 2-2 | 2-2 | 2-2 | 3-1 | 2-0 |
| Oldham Athletic AFC | 0-3 | 0-0 | 2-0 | 0-1 | 2-2 | 1-0 | 1-0 | 3-0 | 4-1 | 1-1 | 1-3 | 0-3 | 1-2 | 1-0 | 0-0 | ■ | 4-1 | 4-0 | 2-1 | 3-0 | 1-0 | 2-1 |
| Preston North End FC | 3-0 | 0-0 | 1-1 | 1-5 | 0-3 | 0-1 | 3-1 | 1-1 | 1-1 | 2-1 | 1-1 | 2-3 | 3-1 | 2-3 | 2-0 | 2-1 | ■ | 2-0 | 5-2 | 1-1 | 3-0 | 0-1 |
| Sheffield United FC | 1-2 | 2-0 | 3-2 | 0-0 | 2-2 | 1-3 | 3-1 | 0-0 | 1-1 | 3-2 | 3-1 | 2-2 | 5-1 | 2-1 | 3-0 | 1-0 | 2-1 | ■ | 3-1 | 2-0 | 3-0 | 1-0 |
| Sunderland AFC | 2-1 | 2-0 | 2-0 | 2-0 | 2-0 | 3-0 | 3-2 | 2-1 | 2-3 | 0-1 | 2-1 | 3-0 | 1-1 | 2-0 | 3-1 | 3-0 | 1-0 | 3-2 | ■ | 1-1 | 2-1 | 4-1 |
| The Arsenal FC | 0-1 | 0-1 | 2-2 | 1-2 | 3-0 | 2-0 | 1-1 | 1-0 | 1-1 | 1-0 | 2-2 | 0-3 | 2-1 | 0-1 | 3-1 | 3-2 | 0-0 | 3-0 | 3-2 | ■ | 3-1 | 1-0 |
| The Wednesday FC | 0-1 | 0-1 | 0-2 | 1-0 | 0-1 | 3-1 | 0-2 | 2-0 | 1-0 | 2-2 | 0-0 | 1-3 | 0-1 | 0-0 | 1-0 | 0-1 | 2-1 | 0-2 | 1-2 | 1-2 | ■ | 0-3 |
| West Bromwich Albion FC | 1-2 | 5-2 | 4-1 | 4-1 | 3-1 | 4-1 | 4-0 | 3-0 | 4-3 | 1-1 | 2-0 | 2-1 | 4-1 | 3-0 | 8-0 | 3-1 | 4-1 | 0-2 | 4-0 | 1-0 | 1-3 | ■ |

## Division 1

| | | Pd | Wn | Dw | Ls | GF | GA | Pts | |
|---|---|---|---|---|---|---|---|---|---|
| 1. | WEST BROMWICH ALBION FC (W. BROMWICH) | 42 | 28 | 4 | 10 | 104 | 47 | 60 | |
| 2. | Burnley FC (Burnley) | 42 | 21 | 9 | 12 | 65 | 59 | 51 | |
| 3. | Chelsea FC (London) | 42 | 22 | 5 | 15 | 56 | 51 | 49 | |
| 4. | Liverpool FC Liverpool) | 42 | 19 | 10 | 13 | 59 | 44 | 48 | |
| 5. | Sunderland AFC (Sunderland) | 42 | 22 | 4 | 16 | 72 | 59 | 48 | |
| 6. | Bolton Wanderers FC (Bolton) | 42 | 19 | 9 | 14 | 72 | 65 | 47 | |
| 7. | Manchester City FC (Manchester) | 42 | 18 | 9 | 15 | 71 | 62 | 45 | |
| 8. | Newcastle United FC (Newcastle-upon-Tyne) | 42 | 17 | 9 | 16 | 44 | 39 | 43 | |
| 9. | Aston Villa FC (Birmingham) | 42 | 18 | 6 | 18 | 75 | 73 | 42 | |
| 10. | The Arsenal FC (London) | 42 | 15 | 12 | 15 | 56 | 58 | 42 | |
| 11. | Bradford Park Avenue FC (Bradford) | 42 | 15 | 12 | 15 | 60 | 63 | 42 | |
| 12. | Manchester United FC (Manchester) | 42 | 13 | 14 | 15 | 54 | 50 | 40 | |
| 13. | Middlesbrough FC (Middlesbrough) | 42 | 15 | 10 | 17 | 61 | 65 | 40 | |
| 14. | Sheffield United FC (Sheffield) | 42 | 16 | 8 | 18 | 59 | 69 | 40 | |
| 15. | Bradford City AFC (Bradford) | 42 | 14 | 11 | 17 | 54 | 63 | 39 | |
| 16. | Everton FC (Liverpool) | 42 | 12 | 14 | 16 | 69 | 68 | 38 | |
| 17. | Oldham Athletic AFC (Oldham) | 42 | 15 | 8 | 19 | 49 | 52 | 38 | |
| 18. | Derby County FC (Derby) | 42 | 13 | 12 | 17 | 47 | 57 | 38 | |
| 19. | Preston North End FC (Preston) | 42 | 14 | 10 | 18 | 57 | 73 | 38 | |
| 20. | Blackburn Rovers FC (Blackburn) | 42 | 13 | 11 | 18 | 64 | 77 | 37 | |
| 21. | Notts County FC (Nottingham) | 42 | 12 | 12 | 18 | 56 | 74 | 36 | R |
| 22. | The Wednesday FC (Sheffield) | 42 | 7 | 9 | 26 | 28 | 64 | 23 | R |
| | | 924 | 358 | 208 | 358 | 1332 | 1332 | 924 | |

# Grimsby Town FC (Cleethorpes) and Lincoln City FC (Lincoln) were not re-elected to the league for next season and were replaced in Division 2 by Cardiff City AFC (Cardiff) and Leeds United AFC (Leeds) (who were founded after Leeds City AFC was disbanded – see below for further details of this).

## Top Goalscorer

1)   Fred MORRIS                    (West Bromwich Albion FC)        37

A new Division 3 began the next season and was formed by the promotion of Southern League Division 1 clubs plus Grimsby Town FC

| Football League Division 2 1919-1920 Season | Barnsley | Birmingham | Blackpool | Bristol City | Bury | Clapton Orient | Coventry City | Fulham | Grimsby Town | Huddersfield Town | Hull City | Leeds City | Leicester City | Lincoln City | Nottingham Forest | Port Vale | Rotherham County | South Shields | Stockport County | Stoke | Tottenham Hotspur | West Ham United | Wolves |
|---|---|---|---|---|---|---|---|---|---|---|---|---|---|---|---|---|---|---|---|---|---|---|---|
| Barnsley FC | ■ | 0-5 | 1-1 | 0-0 | 1-3 | 2-1 | 1-0 | 4-1 | 0-1 | 3-3 | 2-3 | --- | 0-1 | 5-2 | 2-2 | 1-0 | 4-0 | 0-1 | 0-0 | 1-2 | 3-0 | 7-0 | 4-1 |
| Birmingham FC | 0-0 | ■ | 4-2 | 1-0 | 0-2 | 2-1 | 4-1 | 2-0 | 4-0 | 4-2 | 4-1 | --- | 0-1 | 7-0 | 8-0 | 3-0 | 2-2 | 4-0 | 1-1 | 2-1 | 0-1 | 0-1 | 2-0 |
| Blackpool FC | 0-2 | 3-0 | ■ | 0-0 | 1-0 | 3-0 | 2-0 | 1-1 | 2-0 | 0-3 | 2-1 | 4-2 | 3-0 | 6-0 | 3-2 | --- | 5-1 | 0-3 | 1-0 | 3-1 | 0-1 | 0-0 | 1-1 |
| Bristol City FC | 3-1 | 1-1 | 0-0 | ■ | 1-0 | 1-1 | 1-0 | 0-3 | 3-1 | 2-1 | 2-2 | --- | 0-0 | 6-0 | 0-0 | 1-1 | 2-1 | 3-1 | 1-0 | 1-2 | 1-2 | 0-0 | 1-1 |
| Bury FC | 2-0 | 1-0 | 1-2 | 0-1 | ■ | 3-0 | 2-2 | 2-2 | 1-1 | 2-0 | 2-0 | --- | 1-0 | 3-0 | 1-1 | 2-1 | 4-1 | 2-1 | 0-2 | 1-0 | 2-1 | 1-0 | 2-0 |
| Clapton Orient FC | 2-0 | 2-1 | 3-0 | 1-0 | 2-1 | ■ | 2-2 | 0-1 | 3-0 | 0-1 | 2-2 | --- | 3-0 | 1-0 | 1-0 | 2-1 | 1-2 | 4-0 | 2-1 | 2-1 | 0-4 | 1-0 | 0-0 |
| Coventry City FC | 1-0 | 1-3 | 0-0 | 0-0 | 2-1 | 0-0 | ■ | 0-1 | 2-0 | 0-2 | 0-1 | 0-4 | 1-2 | 2-0 | 4-2 | --- | 1-1 | 1-1 | 1-1 | 3-2 | 0-5 | 0-0 | 1-0 |
| Fulham FC | 1-1 | 1-2 | 1-2 | 1-1 | 1-0 | 2-1 | 0-0 | ■ | 2-1 | 2-2 | 1-0 | --- | 5-0 | 3-0 | 1-0 | 4-0 | 3-0 | 1-0 | 4-1 | 0-0 | 1-4 | 1-2 | 1-1 |
| Grimsby Town FC | 1-1 | 0-3 | 1-1 | 2-2 | 1-2 | 2-0 | 0-1 | 0-2 | ■ | 1-0 | 2-1 | --- | 1-2 | 2-2 | 1-0 | 2-0 | 0-1 | 3-1 | 0-3 | 2-0 | 2-0 | 0-1 | 0-1 |
| Huddersfield Town AFC | 4-1 | 0-0 | 1-3 | 1-0 | 5-0 | 2-1 | 5-0 | 3-0 | 3-0 | ■ | 2-0 | --- | 0-0 | 4-2 | 2-1 | 4-1 | 7-1 | 2-2 | 5-0 | 3-0 | 1-1 | 2-0 | 2-0 |
| Hull City AFC | 3-1 | 0-0 | 0-1 | 0-0 | 4-2 | 3-1 | 0-1 | 2-0 | 4-1 | 1-4 | ■ | 1-1 | 5-1 | 5-2 | 2-0 | --- | 1-0 | 3-0 | 4-1 | 3-0 | 1-3 | 1-1 | 10-3 |
| Leeds City AFC | --- | --- | 1-0 | --- | --- | --- | 3-0 | --- | --- | --- | 1-2 | ■ | --- | --- | --- | --- | --- | --- | --- | --- | --- | --- | 1-1 |
| Leicester City FC | 0-0 | 1-0 | 2-3 | 2-1 | 0-5 | 1-1 | 1-0 | 3-2 | 2-0 | 0-4 | 3-2 | --- | ■ | 4-0 | 0-0 | 0-1 | 1-1 | 0-0 | 0-2 | 3-1 | 2-4 | 0-0 | 1-2 |
| Lincoln City AFC | 0-4 | 2-2 | 0-3 | 0-0 | 2-1 | 2-1 | 4-1 | 0-1 | 2-0 | 1-3 | 2-0 | --- | 0-3 | ■ | 1-4 | 0-0 | 0-0 | 1-1 | 2-0 | 2-1 | 1-1 | 1-4 | 4-0 |
| Nottingham Forest FC | 0-1 | 1-2 | 2-0 | 1-2 | 1-0 | 2-1 | 2-1 | 0-3 | 2-0 | 1-2 | 0-2 | --- | 0-0 | 2-1 | ■ | 0-1 | 4-1 | 0-0 | 1-1 | 0-2 | 1-1 | 2-1 | 1-0 |
| Port Vale FC | 0-2 | 1-3 | --- | 3-1 | 2-2 | 4-2 | --- | 3-4 | 2-1 | 0-0 | --- | --- | 1-2 | 1-0 | 4-1 | ■ | 4-2 | 1-0 | 2-0 | 0-3 | 0-1 | 1-0 | |
| Rotherham County FC | 1-0 | 0-3 | 1-2 | 2-2 | 1-2 | 3-1 | 4-3 | 1-1 | 3-1 | 1-3 | 1-2 | --- | 1-0 | 3-0 | 2-0 | 2-2 | ■ | 1-0 | 1-0 | 1-3 | 1-1 | 0-1 | 2-0 |
| South Shields FC | 0-0 | 1-0 | 6-0 | 0-2 | 0-0 | 2-0 | 1-0 | 2-0 | 2-0 | 1-2 | 7-1 | --- | 2-0 | 2-2 | 5-2 | 2-0 | 6-2 | ■ | 3-2 | 2-2 | 0-3 | 3-0 | 0-0 |
| Stockport County FC | 1-0 | 2-1 | 0-0 | 2-3 | 1-1 | 3-1 | 1-1 | 2-1 | 1-2 | 1-2 | 3-1 | --- | 0-2 | 3-0 | 0-0 | 0-4 | 4-1 | 1-0 | ■ | 3-1 | 1-2 | 1-0 | 4-1 |
| Stoke FC | 2-0 | 0-1 | 2-0 | 2-0 | 1-1 | 2-0 | 6-1 | 1-0 | 3-0 | 0-1 | 3-1 | --- | 3-0 | 1-3 | 0-2 | 0-0 | 3-0 | 0-0 | 2-1 | ■ | 1-3 | 2-1 | 3-0 |
| Tottenham Hotspur FC | 4-0 | 0-0 | 2-2 | 2-0 | 2-1 | 2-1 | 4-1 | 4-0 | 3-1 | 2-0 | 4-0 | --- | 4-0 | 6-1 | 5-2 | 2-0 | 2-0 | 2-0 | 2-0 | 2-0 | ■ | 2-0 | 4-2 |
| West Ham United FC | 0-2 | 1-2 | 1-0 | 2-0 | 1-0 | 0-1 | 2-0 | 0-1 | 1-0 | 1-1 | 2-1 | --- | 1-0 | 1-1 | 5-1 | 3-1 | 2-1 | 1-0 | 3-0 | 1-1 | 2-1 | ■ | 4-0 |
| Wolverhampton Wands. | 2-4 | 0-2 | 0-3 | 3-1 | 0-1 | 1-2 | 2-0 | 2-1 | 6-1 | 2-3 | 4-2 | 2-4 | 1-1 | 4-0 | 4-0 | --- | 0-1 | 0-0 | 2-2 | 4-0 | 1-3 | 1-1 | ■ |

| | Division 2 | Pd | Wn | Dw | Ls | GF | GA | Pts | |
|---|---|---|---|---|---|---|---|---|---|
| 1. | Tottenham Hotspur FC (London) | 42 | 32 | 6 | 4 | 102 | 32 | 70 | P |
| 2. | Huddersfield Town AFC (Huddersfield) | 42 | 28 | 8 | 6 | 97 | 38 | 64 | P |
| 3. | Birmingham FC (Birmingham) | 42 | 24 | 8 | 10 | 85 | 34 | 56 | |
| 4. | Blackpool FC (Blackpool) | 42 | 21 | 10 | 11 | 65 | 47 | 52 | |
| 5. | Bury FC (Bury) | 42 | 20 | 8 | 14 | 60 | 44 | 48 | |
| 6. | Fulham FC (London) | 42 | 19 | 9 | 14 | 61 | 50 | 47 | |
| 7. | West Ham United FC (London) | 42 | 19 | 9 | 14 | 47 | 40 | 47 | |
| 8. | Bristol City FC (Bristol) | 42 | 13 | 17 | 12 | 46 | 43 | 43 | |
| 9. | South Shields FC (South Shields) | 42 | 15 | 12 | 15 | 58 | 48 | 42 | |
| 10. | Stoke FC (Stoke-on-Trent) | 42 | 18 | 6 | 18 | 60 | 54 | 42 | |
| 11. | Hull City AFC (Kingston-upon-Hull) | 42 | 18 | 6 | 18 | 78 | 72 | 42 | |
| 12. | Barnsley FC (Barnsley) | 42 | 15 | 10 | 17 | 61 | 55 | 40 | |
| 13. | Port Vale FC (Stoke-on-Trent) | 42 | 16 | 8 | 18 | 59 | 62 | 40 | * |
| 14. | Leicester City FC (Leicester) | 42 | 15 | 10 | 17 | 41 | 61 | 40 | |
| 15. | Clapton Orient FC (London) | 42 | 16 | 6 | 20 | 51 | 59 | 38 | |
| 16. | Stockport County FC (Stockport) | 42 | 14 | 9 | 19 | 52 | 61 | 37 | |
| 17. | Rotherham County FC (Rotherham) | 42 | 13 | 8 | 21 | 51 | 83 | 34 | |
| 18. | Nottingham Forest FC (Nottingham) | 42 | 11 | 9 | 22 | 43 | 73 | 31 | |
| 19. | Wolverhampton Wanderers FC (Wolverhampton) | 42 | 10 | 10 | 22 | 55 | 80 | 30 | |
| 20. | Coventry City FC (Coventry) | 42 | 9 | 11 | 22 | 35 | 73 | 29 | |
| 21. | Lincoln City FC (Lincoln) | 42 | 9 | 9 | 24 | 44 | 101 | 27 | |
| 22. | Grimsby Town FC (Cleethorpes) | 42 | 10 | 5 | 27 | 34 | 75 | 25 | |
| | | 924 | 365 | 194 | 365 | 1285 | 1285 | 924 | |

* Port Vale FC (Stoke-on-Trent) took the place of Leeds City AFC (Leeds) who were expelled from the league for refusing to submit their club accounts to Football League inspection after allegations of financial misconduct.

| | | | | | | | |
|---|---|---|---|---|---|---|---|
| Leeds City AFC (Leeds) playing record | 8 | 4 | 2 | 2 | 17 | 10 | 10 |
| Port Vale FC (Stoke-on-Trent) playing record | 34 | 12 | 6 | 16 | 42 | 52 | 30 |

## F.A. CUP FINAL   (Stamford Bridge, London – 24/04/1920 – 50,018)

ASTON VILLA FC (BIRMINGHAM)          1-0 (aet)          Huddersfield Town AFC (Huddersfield)

*Kirton*

Aston Villa:  Hardy, Smart, Weston, Ducat, Barson, Moss, Wallace, Kirton, Walker, Stephenson, Dorrell.

Huddersfield:  Mutch, Wood, Bullock, Slade, Wilson, Watson, Richardson, Mann, Taylor, Swan, Islip.

## Semi-finals

| Aston Villa FC (Birmingham) | 3-1 | Chelsea FC (London) |
|---|---|---|
| Bristol City FC (Bristol) | 1-2 | Huddersfield Town AFC (Huddersfield) |

## Quarter-finals

| Bristol City FC (Bristol) | 2-0 | Bradford City AFC (Bradford) |
|---|---|---|
| Chelsea FC (London) | 4-1 | Bradford Park Avenue FC (Bradford) |
| Huddersfield Town AFC (Huddersfield) | 2-1 | Liverpool FC (Liverpool) |
| Tottenham Hotspur FC (London) | 0-1 | Aston Villa FC (Birmingham) |

| Football League Division 1 1920-1921 Season | Aston Villa | Blackburn R. | Bolton Wands. | Bradford City | Bradford P.A. | Burnley | Chelsea | Derby County | Everton | Liverpool | Huddersfield T. | Man. City | Man. United | Middlesbro' | Newcastle Utd. | Oldham Ath. | Preston N.E. | Sheffield Utd. | Sunderland | The Arsenal | Tottenham H. | W.B.A. |
|---|---|---|---|---|---|---|---|---|---|---|---|---|---|---|---|---|---|---|---|---|---|---|
| Aston Villa FC | | 3-0 | 2-0 | 1-2 | 4-1 | 0-0 | 3-0 | 1-0 | 1-3 | 0-0 | 0-2 | 3-1 | 3-4 | 0-1 | 0-0 | 3-0 | 1-0 | 4-0 | 1-5 | 5-0 | 4-2 | 0-0 |
| Blackburn Rovers FC | 0-1 | | 2-2 | 2-3 | 1-0 | 1-3 | 0-0 | 2-0 | 0-0 | 1-2 | 1-1 | 0-2 | 2-0 | 3-2 | 3-3 | 5-1 | 2-2 | 1-1 | 2-0 | 2-2 | 1-1 | 5-1 |
| Bolton Wanderers FC | 5-0 | 2-1 | | 1-1 | 2-0 | 1-1 | 3-1 | 1-0 | 4-2 | 3-1 | 1-0 | 3-0 | 1-1 | 6-2 | 3-1 | 1-1 | 3-0 | 2-2 | 6-2 | 1-1 | 1-0 | 3-0 |
| Bradford City AFC | 3-0 | 3-4 | 2-2 | | 2-1 | 2-0 | 1-1 | 2-2 | 2-2 | 0-2 | 0-0 | 1-2 | 1-1 | 0-1 | 1-1 | 1-3 | 6-2 | 4-0 | 2-2 | 3-1 | 1-0 | 1-1 |
| Bradford Park Avenue | 4-0 | 1-1 | 2-1 | 1-2 | | 1-3 | 0-2 | 2-1 | 3-3 | 1-1 | 1-3 | 1-2 | 2-4 | 3-0 | 0-2 | 2-1 | 1-3 | 2-0 | 1-1 | 0-1 | 1-1 | 0-3 |
| Burnley FC | 7-1 | 4-1 | 3-1 | 1-4 | 1-0 | | 4-0 | 2-1 | 1-1 | 3-0 | 1-0 | 2-1 | 1-0 | 2-1 | 3-1 | 7-1 | 2-0 | 6-0 | 2-2 | 1-0 | 2-0 | 1-1 |
| Chelsea FC | 5-1 | 1-2 | 1-0 | 3-1 | 4-1 | 1-1 | | 1-1 | 0-1 | 1-1 | 1-1 | 2-1 | 1-2 | 1-1 | 2-0 | 1-1 | 1-1 | 2-1 | 3-1 | 1-2 | 0-4 | 3-0 |
| Derby County FC | 2-3 | 0-1 | 0-0 | 1-1 | 1-0 | 0-0 | 0-0 | | 2-4 | 2-1 | 0-0 | 3-0 | 1-1 | 0-1 | 0-1 | 3-3 | 1-1 | 1-1 | 0-1 | 1-1 | 2-2 | 1-1 |
| Everton FC | 1-1 | 2-1 | 2-3 | 2-2 | 1-1 | 1-1 | 5-1 | 3-1 | | 0-0 | 0-3 | 3-0 | 2-0 | 2-1 | 3-1 | 5-2 | 0-1 | 3-0 | 1-1 | 2-4 | 0-0 | 2-2 |
| Huddersfield Town AFC | 1-0 | 0-0 | 0-0 | 1-0 | 0-0 | 1-0 | 2-0 | 2-0 | 0-1 | | 1-2 | 0-1 | 5-2 | 0-1 | 1-3 | 3-1 | 1-0 | 1-0 | 0-0 | 0-45 | 2-0 | 5-1 |
| Liverpool FC | 4-1 | 2-0 | 2-3 | 2-1 | 0-1 | 0-0 | 2-1 | 1-1 | 1-0 | 4-1 | | 4-2 | 2-0 | 0-0 | 0-1 | 5-2 | 6-0 | 2-2 | 0-0 | 3-0 | 1-1 | 0-0 |
| Manchester City FC | 3-1 | 0-0 | 3-1 | 1-0 | 1-0 | 3-0 | 1-0 | 0-0 | 2-0 | 3-2 | 3-2 | | 3-0 | 3-1 | 3-1 | 5-1 | 3-1 | 3-1 | 3-1 | 2-0 | 3-1 | 4-0 |
| Manchester United FC | 1-3 | 0-1 | 2-3 | 1-1 | 5-1 | 0-3 | 3-1 | 3-0 | 1-2 | 2-0 | 1-1 | 1-1 | | 0-1 | 2-0 | 4-1 | 1-0 | 2-1 | 3-0 | 1-1 | 0-1 | 1-4 |
| Middlesbrough FC | 1-4 | 1-1 | 4-1 | 2-1 | 2-1 | 0-0 | 0-0 | 1-0 | 3-1 | 2-0 | 0-1 | 3-1 | 2-4 | | 0-0 | 1-2 | 0-0 | 2-2 | 2-0 | 2-1 | 1-0 | 0-1 |
| Newcastle United FC | 2-1 | 1-2 | 1-0 | 4-0 | 2-1 | 1-2 | 1-0 | 0-1 | 2-0 | 1-0 | 2-0 | 1-1 | 6-3 | 2-0 | | 1-2 | 4-2 | 3-0 | 6-1 | 1-0 | 1-1 | 1-1 |
| Oldham Athletic AFC | 1-1 | 1-0 | 0-0 | 2-0 | 1-0 | 2-2 | 1-2 | 2-1 | 0-1 | 1-2 | 0-0 | 2-0 | 2-2 | 3-3 | 0-0 | | 0-2 | 0-0 | 2-1 | 1-1 | 2-5 | 0-3 |
| Preston North End FC | 6-1 | 4-2 | 1-2 | 1-1 | 3-3 | 0-3 | 0-1 | 2-1 | 1-0 | 0-1 | 2-3 | 0-1 | 0-0 | 2-0 | 3-2 | 4-0 | | 2-0 | 1-1 | 0-1 | 4-1 | 2-1 |
| Sheffield United FC | 0-0 | 1-1 | 2-2 | 4-1 | 2-0 | 1-1 | 0-1 | 0-1 | 2-0 | 1-1 | 0-1 | 1-1 | 1-0 | 1-1 | 0-3 | 3-0 | 1-0 | | 1-1 | 1-1 | 1-1 | 0-2 |
| Sunderland AFC | 0-1 | 2-0 | 0-0 | 0-0 | 5-1 | 0-0 | 3-0 | 0-2 | 2-1 | 2-1 | 1-0 | 2-3 | 0-2 | 1-1 | 2-2 | 3-1 | 1-1 | 2-2 | | 5-1 | 0-1 | 3-1 |
| The Arsenal FC | 0-1 | 2-0 | 0-0 | 1-2 | 2-1 | 1-1 | 1-1 | 2-0 | 1-1 | 2-0 | 0-0 | 2-1 | 2-0 | 2-2 | 1-1 | 2-2 | 2-1 | 2-6 | 1-2 | | 3-2 | 2-1 |
| Tottenham Hotspur FC | 1-2 | 1-2 | 5-2 | 2-0 | 1-2 | 0-1 | 5-0 | 2-0 | 2-0 | 1-0 | 1-0 | 2-0 | 4-1 | 2-2 | 2-0 | 5-1 | 1-2 | 4-1 | 0-0 | 2-1 | | 1-0 |
| West Bromwich Albion FC | 2-1 | 1-1 | 2-1 | 2-0 | 0-1 | 2-0 | 1-1 | 3-0 | 1-2 | 3-0 | 1-1 | 2-2 | 0-2 | 0-1 | 0-0 | 0-0 | 0-3 | 1-1 | 4-1 | 3-4 | 3-1 | |

## Division 1

| | | Pd | Wn | Dw | Ls | GF | GA | Pts | |
|---|---|---|---|---|---|---|---|---|---|
| 1. | BURNLEY FC (BURNLEY) | 42 | 23 | 13 | 6 | 79 | 36 | 59 | |
| 2. | Manchester City FC (Manchester) | 42 | 24 | 6 | 12 | 70 | 50 | 54 | |
| 3. | Bolton Wanderers FC (Bolton) | 42 | 19 | 14 | 9 | 77 | 53 | 52 | |
| 4. | Liverpool FC (Liverpool) | 42 | 18 | 15 | 9 | 63 | 35 | 51 | |
| 5. | Newcastle United FC (Newcastle-upon-Tyne) | 42 | 20 | 10 | 12 | 66 | 45 | 50 | |
| 6. | Tottenham Hotspur FC (London) | 42 | 19 | 9 | 14 | 70 | 48 | 47 | |
| 7. | Everton FC (Liverpool) | 42 | 17 | 13 | 12 | 66 | 55 | 47 | |
| 8. | Middlesbrough FC (Middlesbrough) | 42 | 17 | 12 | 13 | 53 | 53 | 46 | |
| 9. | The Arsenal FC (London) | 42 | 15 | 14 | 13 | 59 | 63 | 44 | |
| 10. | Aston Villa FC (Birmingham) | 42 | 18 | 7 | 17 | 63 | 70 | 43 | |
| 11. | Blackburn Rovers FC (Blackburn) | 42 | 13 | 15 | 14 | 57 | 59 | 41 | |
| 12. | Sunderland AFC (Sunderland) | 42 | 14 | 13 | 15 | 57 | 60 | 41 | |
| 13. | Manchester United FC (Manchester) | 42 | 15 | 10 | 17 | 64 | 68 | 40 | |
| 14. | West Bromwich Albion FC (West Bromwich) | 42 | 13 | 14 | 15 | 54 | 58 | 40 | |
| 15. | Bradford City AFC (Bradford) | 42 | 12 | 15 | 15 | 61 | 63 | 39 | |
| 16. | Preston North End FC (Preston) | 42 | 15 | 9 | 18 | 61 | 65 | 39 | |
| 17. | Huddersfield Town AFC (Huddersfield) | 42 | 15 | 9 | 18 | 42 | 49 | 39 | |
| 18. | Chelsea FC (London) | 42 | 13 | 13 | 16 | 48 | 58 | 39 | |
| 19. | Oldham Athletic AFC (Oldham) | 42 | 9 | 15 | 18 | 49 | 86 | 33 | |
| 20. | Sheffield United FC (Sheffield) | 42 | 6 | 18 | 18 | 42 | 68 | 30 | |
| 21. | Derby County FC (Derby) | 42 | 5 | 16 | 21 | 32 | 58 | 26 | R |
| 22. | Bradford Park Avenue FC (Bradford) | 42 | 8 | 8 | 26 | 43 | 76 | 24 | R |
| | | 924 | 328 | 268 | 328 | 1276 | 1276 | 924 | |

# Top Goalscorer

1)   Joe SMITH                                   (Bolton Wanderers FC)        38

| Football League Division 2 1920-1921 Season | Barnsley | Birmingham | Blackpool | Bristol City | Bury | Cardiff City | Clapton Orient | Coventry City | Fulham | Hull City | Leeds United | Leicester City | Nottingham Forest | Notts County | Port Vale | Rotherham County | South Shields | Stockport County | Stoke | Wednesday | West Ham United | Wolves |
|---|---|---|---|---|---|---|---|---|---|---|---|---|---|---|---|---|---|---|---|---|---|---|
| Barnsley FC | ■ | 1-1 | 0-1 | 1-1 | 5-0 | 0-2 | 1-0 | 2-2 | 3-1 | 0-0 | 1-1 | 2-1 | 0-0 | 2-2 | 3-0 | 2-1 | 1-1 | 2-0 | 1-0 | 0-0 | 1-1 | 3-2 |
| Birmingham FC | 1-3 | ■ | 3-0 | 0-0 | 4-0 | 1-1 | 0-0 | 3-2 | 1-0 | 5-1 | 1-0 | 5-0 | 3-0 | 2-1 | 4-0 | 3-2 | 1-1 | 5-0 | 3-0 | 4-0 | 2-1 | 4-1 |
| Blackpool FC | 1-0 | 3-0 | ■ | 1-2 | 0-1 | 2-4 | 2-2 | 4-0 | 1-0 | 1-2 | 1-0 | 2-0 | 1-0 | 0-2 | 1-0 | 0-1 | 3-2 | 1-1 | 3-1 | 1-1 | 1-0 | 3-0 |
| Bristol City FC | 1-0 | 0-1 | 1-1 | ■ | 1-0 | 0-0 | 2-0 | 2-0 | 2-0 | 2-1 | 0-0 | 1-0 | 1-0 | 0-1 | 3-0 | 2-4 | 4-2 | 5-1 | 5-0 | 0-1 | 1-0 | 2-0 |
| Bury FC | 0-0 | 0-1 | 2-2 | 2-0 | ■ | 3-1 | 0-1 | 2-0 | 1-1 | 0-0 | 1-1 | 4-0 | 2-2 | 0-1 | 1-0 | 1-0 | 1-0 | 1-1 | 3-0 | 1-1 | 1-0 | 3-1 |
| Cardiff City AFC | 3-2 | 2-1 | 0-0 | 1-0 | 2-1 | ■ | 0-0 | 0-1 | 3-0 | 0-0 | 1-0 | 2-0 | 3-0 | 1-1 | 1-2 | 1-0 | 1-0 | 3-0 | 0-1 | 1-0 | 0-0 | 2-0 |
| Clapton Orient FC | 3-2 | 1-1 | 0-0 | 0-0 | 1-0 | 2-0 | ■ | 0-0 | 3-0 | 1-1 | 1-0 | 2-0 | 2-1 | 3-0 | 0-0 | 2-0 | 1-0 | 5-0 | 3-2 | 1-0 | 0-1 | 0-1 |
| Coventry City FC | 3-1 | 0-4 | 0-2 | 2-1 | 1-0 | 2-4 | 1-1 | ■ | 0-2 | 3-2 | 1-1 | 1-0 | 0-0 | 1-1 | 0-0 | 0-1 | 1-0 | 1-1 | 1-0 | 2-3 | 0-1 | 4-0 |
| Fulham FC | 1-0 | 5-0 | 1-2 | 3-0 | 0-0 | 0-3 | 1-0 | 2-0 | ■ | 3-0 | 1-0 | 1-1 | 2-1 | 3-1 | 1-0 | 0-0 | 3-1 | 1-3 | 2-0 | 0-0 | 2-0 |  |
| Hull City AFC | 3-0 | 1-0 | 2-1 | 2-0 | 1-1 | 2-0 | 3-0 | 1-1 | 0-0 | ■ | 0-1 | 1-1 | 0-3 | 1-1 | 1-1 | 1-1 | 0-2 | 1-1 | 1-1 | 1-1 | 2-1 | 0-1 |
| Leeds United AFC | 0-0 | 1-0 | 2-0 | 0-1 | 1-0 | 1-2 | 2-1 | 4-0 | 0-0 | 1-1 | ■ | 3-1 | 1-1 | 3-0 | 3-1 | 1-0 | 1-2 | 0-2 | 0-0 | 2-0 | 1-2 | 3-0 |
| Leicester City FC | 2-0 | 3-0 | 0-1 | 0-0 | 4-0 | 2-0 | 2-1 | 0-1 | 1-1 | 0-0 | 1-1 | ■ | 2-0 | 0-3 | 0-0 | 1-1 | 2-0 | 0-0 | 3-1 | 2-1 | 1-0 | 0-0 |
| Nottingham Forest FC | 0-0 | 1-1 | 3-1 | 0-1 | 4-2 | 1-2 | 0-0 | 0-2 | 5-1 | 2-0 | 1-0 | 1-2 | ■ | 1-0 | 1-4 | 6-1 | 1-2 | 1-1 | 2-2 | 4-2 | 1-0 | 1-1 |
| Notts County FC | 1-0 | 0-0 | 1-2 | 2-2 | 2-1 | 1-2 | 3-1 | 1-1 | 2-1 | 4-1 | 1-2 | 1-1 | 2-0 | ■ | 0-1 | 1-0 | 2-0 | 3-0 | 3-0 | 3-0 | 1-1 | 2-1 |
| Port Vale FC | 1-1 | 0-2 | 0-1 | 0-2 | 3-0 | 0-0 | 4-0 | 0-0 | 0-0 | 4-0 | 2-0 | 0-0 | 0-1 | 1-2 | ■ | 1-1 | 0-2 | 6-1 | 2-1 | 1-0 | 1-2 | 2-3 |
| Rotherham County FC | 1-0 | 1-1 | 0-2 | 0-0 | 0-5 | 2-0 | 0-0 | 2-3 | 2-0 | 1-1 | 0-2 | 1-1 | 0-0 | 0-0 | 1-1 | ■ | 5-4 | 1-0 | 1-1 | 2-0 | 2-0 | 1-0 |
| South Shields FC | 3-2 | 3-0 | 1-0 | 0-0 | 2-0 | 0-1 | 3-0 | 4-1 | 3-0 | 0-0 | 3-0 | 4-3 | 0-1 | 1-0 | 6-1 | 1-0 | ■ | 3-1 | 1-1 | 2-3 | 0-0 | 1-2 |
| Stockport County FC | 3-2 | 0-3 | 2-2 | 0-2 | -2 | 2-5 | 6-0 | 3-0 | 1-1 | 2-2 | 3-1 | 0-0 | 1-0 | 1-0 | 0-0 | 0-1 | 0-0 | ■ | 2-0 | 0-1 | 2-0 | 1-2 |
| Stoke FC | 3-2 | 1-2 | 1-1 | 0-0 | 0-1 | 0-0 | 0-1 | 4-1 | 1-2 | 1-3 | 4-0 | 1-1 | 4-0 | 1-0 | 0-1 | 2-0 | 0-0 | 1-0 | ■ | 0-1 | 1-0 | 1-0 |
| The Wednesday FC | 0-0 | 1-2 | 0-1 | 2-2 | 2-0 | 0-1 | 1-1 | 3-0 | 3-0 | 3-0 | 2-0 | 0-0 | 0-0 | 1-1 | 2-0 | 1-1 | 2-1 | 1-3 |  | ■ | 0-1 | 6-0 |
| West Ham United FC | 2-1 | 1-1 | 1-1 | 1-0 | 0-1 | 1-1 | 1-0 | 7-0 | 2-0 | 1-1 | 3-0 | 0-1 | 3-0 | 0-2 | 1-1 | 1-0 | 2-1 | 5-0 | 1-0 | 4-0 | ■ | 1-0 |
| Wolverhampton Wanderers FC | 1-1 | 0-3 | 3-1 | 0-0 | 2-1 | 1-3 | 0-2 | 1-0 | 1-0 | 1-3 | 3-0 | 3-0 | 2-1 | 1-0 | 2-2 | 3-0 | 3-0 | 2-0 | 3-3 | 1-2 | 1-2 | ■ |

## Division 2

| | | Pd | Wn | Dw | Ls | GF | GA | Pts | |
|---|---|---|---|---|---|---|---|---|---|
| 1. | Birmingham FC (Birmingham) | 42 | 24 | 10 | 8 | 79 | 38 | 58 | P |
| 2. | Cardiff City AFC (Cardiff) | 42 | 24 | 10 | 8 | 59 | 32 | 58 | P |
| 3. | Bristol City FC (Bristol) | 42 | 19 | 13 | 10 | 49 | 29 | 51 | |
| 4. | Blackpool FC (Blackpool) | 42 | 20 | 10 | 12 | 54 | 42 | 50 | |
| 5. | West Ham United FC (London) | 42 | 19 | 10 | 13 | 51 | 30 | 48 | |
| 6. | Notts County FC (Nottingham) | 42 | 18 | 11 | 13 | 55 | 40 | 47 | |
| 7. | Clapton Orient FC (London) | 42 | 16 | 13 | 13 | 43 | 42 | 45 | |
| 8. | South Shields FC (South Shields) | 42 | 17 | 10 | 15 | 61 | 46 | 44 | |
| 9. | Fulham FC (London) | 42 | 16 | 10 | 16 | 43 | 47 | 42 | |
| 10. | The Wednesday FC (Sheffield) | 42 | 15 | 11 | 16 | 48 | 48 | 41 | |
| 11. | Bury FC (Bury) | 42 | 15 | 10 | 17 | 45 | 49 | 40 | |
| 12. | Leicester City FC (Leicester) | 42 | 12 | 16 | 14 | 39 | 46 | 40 | |
| 13. | Hull City AFC (Kingston-upon-Hull) | 42 | 10 | 20 | 12 | 43 | 53 | 40 | |
| 14. | Leeds United AFC (Leeds) | 42 | 14 | 10 | 18 | 40 | 45 | 38 | |
| 15. | Wolverhampton Wanderers FC (Wolverhampton) | 42 | 16 | 6 | 20 | 49 | 66 | 38 | |
| 16. | Barnsley FC (Barnsley) | 42 | 10 | 16 | 16 | 48 | 50 | 36 | |
| 17. | Port Vale FC (Stoke-on-Trent) | 42 | 11 | 14 | 17 | 43 | 49 | 36 | |
| 18. | Nottingham Forest FC (Nottingham) | 42 | 12 | 12 | 18 | 48 | 55 | 36 | |
| 19. | Rotherham County FC (Rotherham) | 42 | 12 | 12 | 18 | 37 | 53 | 36 | |
| 20. | Stoke FC (Stoke-on-Trent) | 42 | 12 | 11 | 19 | 46 | 56 | 35 | |
| 21. | Coventry City FC (Coventry) | 42 | 12 | 11 | 19 | 39 | 70 | 35 | |
| 22. | Stockport County FC (Stockport) | 42 | 9 | 12 | 21 | 42 | 75 | 30 | R |
| | | 924 | 333 | 258 | 333 | 1061 | 1061 | 924 | |

| Football League Division 3 1920-1921 Season | Brentford | Brighton | Bristol Rovers | Crystal Palace | Exeter City | Gillingham | Grimsby Town | Luton Town | Merthyr Town | Millwall Athletic | Newport County | Northampton | Norwich City | Plymouth Argyle | Portsmouth | Q.P.R. | Reading | Southampton | Southend United | Swansea Town | Swindon Town | Watford |
|---|---|---|---|---|---|---|---|---|---|---|---|---|---|---|---|---|---|---|---|---|---|---|
| Brentford FC | ■ | 2-0 | 0-0 | 0-4 | 0-0 | 3-3 | 5-0 | 1-0 | 0-0 | 1-0 | 2-2 | 1-1 | 3-1 | 0-0 | 1-2 | 0-2 | 3-2 | 1-1 | 2-2 | 1-2 | 0-1 | 1-0 |
| Brighton & Hove Albion | 4-0 | ■ | 2-0 | 0-2 | 1-1 | 1-0 | 1-3 | 1-1 | 0-0 | 1-0 | 1-0 | 3-2 | 2-0 | 1-0 | 3-0 | 2-1 | 2-2 | 1-1 | 1-0 | 1-1 | 0-3 | 0-3 |
| Bristol Rovers FC | 2-1 | 3-1 | ■ | 2-1 | 5-0 | 2-0 | 2-0 | 5-0 | 1-1 | 1-2 | 3-2 | 4-2 | 2-2 | 2-0 | 2-2 | 3-0 | 3-2 | 1-2 | 2-1 | 1-2 | 3-1 | 2-0 |
| Crystal Palace FC | 4-2 | 3-2 | 3-0 | ■ | 2-1 | 4-1 | 2-0 | 2-1 | 3-0 | 3-2 | 2-0 | 5-1 | 1-0 | 0-0 | 3-0 | 0-0 | 2-0 | 1-1 | 2-3 | 0-1 | 1-0 | 2-2 |
| Exeter City FC | 3-0 | 1-0 | 1-0 | 1-1 | ■ | 2-1 | 1-1 | 1-0 | 3-3 | 4-0 | 0-1 | 4-0 | 1-1 | 1-1 | 0-0 | 0-1 | 0-1 | 1-0 | 0-0 | 1-2 | 1-0 | 1-2 |
| Gillingham FC | 1-3 | 1-0 | 1-0 | 0-1 | 2-1 | ■ | 2-1 | 0-0 | 0-0 | 0-0 | 1-4 | 2-5 | 0-0 | 0-1 | 1-1 | 1-2 | 1-0 | 1-1 | 1-1 | 2-1 | 1-1 | 1-1 |
| Grimsby Town FC | 2-0 | 2-2 | 3-1 | 1-0 | 2-0 | 2-0 | ■ | 0-1 | 1-1 | 0-2 | 1-1 | 2-0 | 1-1 | 1-1 | 0-3 | 2-1 | 2-0 | 3-0 | 1-0 | 0-2 | 3-0 | 3-0 |
| Luton Town FC | 2-0 | 3-2 | 1-2 | 2-2 | 3-0 | 5-0 | 3-1 | ■ | 1-0 | 0-0 | 2-2 | 3-1 | 4-0 | 1-1 | 2-2 | 2-1 | 6-0 | 1-1 | 4-0 | 3-0 | 2-0 | 1-0 |
| Merthyr Town FC | 3-1 | 4-1 | 2-2 | 2-1 | 7-1 | 6-1 | 3-1 | 4-1 | ■ | 0-1 | 1-2 | 1-0 | 0-0 | 0-0 | 2-1 | 3-1 | 1-0 | 1-1 | 2-0 | 0-3 | 2-2 | 1-0 |
| Millwall Athletic FC | 0-0 | 0-1 | 2-0 | 0-1 | 2-0 | 4-0 | 1-0 | 0-0 | 0-0 | ■ | 1-0 | 1-0 | 2-0 | 0-0 | 1-0 | 0-0 | 2-0 | 0-1 | 4-2 | 0-2 | 5-0 | 1-0 |
| Newport County AFC | 3-1 | 0-4 | 0-2 | 0-1 | 2-0 | 1-0 | 2-1 | 2-0 | 0-3 | 3-1 | ■ | 1-1 | 2-0 | 0-0 | 1-0 | 1-3 | 0-1 | 0-0 | 1-1 | 1-1 | 0-1 | 0-2 |
| Northampton Town | 6-2 | 1-0 | 1-2 | 2-2 | 3-3 | 2-0 | 4-1 | 1-0 | 2-2 | 0-2 | 0-2 | ■ | 1-0 | 1-1 | 1-0 | 0-3 | 1-0 | 2-0 | 1-0 | 2-0 | 1-2 | 0-1 |
| Norwich City FC | 0-0 | 3-0 | 1-1 | 0-1 | 0-0 | 2-1 | 0-0 | 3-0 | 0-0 | 2-0 | 3-0 | 3-3 | ■ | 0-0 | 2-2 | 2-0 | 2-0 | 0-1 | 3-1 | 1-1 | 3-2 | 1-1 |
| Plymouth Argyle FC | 1-0 | 5-0 | 2-1 | 0-1 | 0-0 | 3-1 | 0-0 | 1-0 | 2-1 | 0-2 | 5-1 | 0-2 | 1-1 | ■ | 2-0 | 1-0 | 1-1 | 0-0 | 0-0 | 1-0 | 0-0 | 0-2 |
| Portsmouth FC | 0-2 | 3-0 | 1-0 | 0-0 | 2-1 | 2-2 | 2-1 | 3-0 | 0-0 | 0-0 | 0-2 | 2-0 | 2-1 | 1-1 | ■ | 0-0 | 2-2 | 0-1 | 3-0 | 3-0 | 1-1 | 1-0 |
| Queen's Park Rangers | 1-0 | 4-0 | 2-1 | 3-0 | 2-1 | 0-1 | 2-0 | 4-1 | 4-2 | 0-0 | 2-0 | 1-2 | 2-0 | 4-0 | 0-0 | ■ | 2-0 | 0-0 | 2-0 | 1-1 | 1-0 | 1-2 |
| Reading FC | 2-1 | 0-1 | 2-1 | 1-0 | 0-1 | 1-2 | 4-1 | 0-1 | 2-0 | 0-1 | 4-0 | 4-0 | 0-1 | 1-1 | 1-0 | 0-0 | ■ | 0-4 | 1-1 | 1-3 | 2-3 | 1-1 |
| Southampton FC | 3-0 | 1-0 | 4-0 | 1-1 | 3-0 | 3-0 | 0-1 | 1-1 | 5-0 | 1-1 | 0-0 | 3-1 | 1-0 | 1-0 | 2-0 | 2-2 | 1-2 | ■ | 3-0 | 3-0 | 4-0 | 4-1 |
| Southend United FC | 4-1 | 2-0 | 1-0 | 0-2 | 0-0 | 1-0 | 3-1 | 1-1 | 0-1 | 1-2 | 2-1 | 1-2 | 3-1 | 2-1 | 2-1 | 1-0 | 1-0 | 1-0 | ■ | 1-2 | 1-3 | 4-1 |
| Swansea Town AFC | 1-1 | 0-0 | 2-2 | 0-0 | 2-1 | 2-0 | 3-1 | 1-1 | 1-0 | 0-0 | 1-2 | 2-2 | 5-2 | 3-0 | 0-0 | 1-3 | 2-1 | 1-1 | 2-0 | ■ | 1-1 | 2-1 |
| Swindon Town FC | 1-0 | 2-0 | 2-1 | 1-3 | 1-1 | 1-1 | 0-0 | 9-1 | 3-0 | 4-1 | 5-0 | 2-1 | 4-2 | 1-1 | 5-2 | 0-1 | 2-0 | 3-2 | 3-0 | 0-0 | ■ | 2-0 |
| Watford FC | 1-0 | 1-0 | 2-1 | 1-1 | 0-0 | 3-1 | 4-2 | 1-0 | 1-0 | 5-1 | 7-1 | 2-0 | 1-1 | 3-2 | 0-2 | 1-2 | 0-0 | 3-0 | 3-0 | 0-1 | | ■ |

| | Division 3 | Pd | Wn | Dw | Ls | GF | GA | Pts | |
|---|---|---|---|---|---|---|---|---|---|
| 1. | Crystal Palace FC (London) | 42 | 24 | 11 | 7 | 70 | 34 | 59 | P |
| 2. | Southampton FC (Southampton) | 42 | 19 | 16 | 7 | 64 | 28 | 54 | |
| 3. | Queen's Park Rangers FC (London) | 42 | 22 | 9 | 11 | 61 | 32 | 53 | |
| 4. | Swindon Town FC (Swindon) | 42 | 21 | 10 | 11 | 73 | 49 | 52 | |
| 5. | Swansea Town AFC (Swansea) | 42 | 18 | 15 | 9 | 56 | 45 | 51 | |
| 6. | Watford FC (Watford) | 42 | 20 | 8 | 14 | 59 | 44 | 48 | |
| 7. | Millwall Athletic FC (London) | 42 | 18 | 11 | 13 | 42 | 30 | 47 | |
| 8. | Merthyr Town FC (Merthyr Tydfil) | 42 | 15 | 15 | 12 | 60 | 49 | 45 | |
| 9. | Luton Town FC (Luton) | 42 | 16 | 12 | 14 | 61 | 56 | 44 | |
| 10. | Bristol Rovers FC (Bristol) | 42 | 18 | 7 | 17 | 68 | 57 | 43 | |
| 11. | Plymouth Argyle FC (Plymouth) | 42 | 11 | 21 | 10 | 35 | 34 | 43 | |
| 12. | Portsmouth FC (Portsmouth) | 42 | 12 | 15 | 15 | 46 | 48 | 39 | |
| 13. | Grimsby Town FC (Cleethorpes) | 42 | 15 | 9 | 18 | 49 | 59 | 39 | T |
| 14. | Northampton Town FC (Northampton) | 42 | 15 | 8 | 19 | 59 | 75 | 38 | |
| 15. | Newport County AFC (Newport) | 42 | 14 | 9 | 19 | 43 | 64 | 37 | |
| 16. | Norwich City FC (Norwich) | 42 | 10 | 16 | 16 | 44 | 53 | 36 | |
| 17. | Southend United FC (Southend-on-Sea) | 42 | 14 | 8 | 20 | 44 | 61 | 36 | |
| 18. | Brighton & Hove Albion FC (Hove) | 42 | 14 | 8 | 20 | 42 | 61 | 36 | |
| 19. | Exeter City FC (Exeter) | 42 | 10 | 15 | 17 | 39 | 54 | 35 | |
| 20. | Reading FC (Reading) | 42 | 12 | 7 | 23 | 42 | 59 | 31 | |
| 21. | Brentford FC (London) | 42 | 8 | 12 | 21 | 42 | 67 | 30 | |
| 22. | Gillingham FC (Gillingham) | 42 | 8 | 12 | 22 | 34 | 74 | 28 | |
| | | 924 | 335 | 254 | 335 | 1133 | 1133 | 924 | |

T: Grimsby Town FC (Cleethorpes) were transferred to the newly-formed Division 3 (North) for next season

Promoted: Charlton Athletic FC (London), Aberdare Athletic FC (Aberdare)

Division 3 was changed to Division 3 (South) for the next season and a new Division 3 (North) was inaugurated with the following clubs as members: Accrington Stanley FC, Ashington FC, Barrow AFC, Chesterfield FC, Crewe Alexandra FC, Darlington FC, Durham City FC, Halifax Town AFC, Hartlepools United FC, Lincoln City FC, Nelson FC, Rochdale AFC, Southport FC, Stalybridge Celtic FC, Tranmere Rovers FC, Walsall FC, Wigan Borough FC, Wrexham AFC + Grimsby Town FC (Cleethorpes) transferred from Division 3 + Stockport County FC relegated from Division 2.

## F.A. CUP FINAL  (Stamford Bridge, London – 23/04/1921 – 72,805)

TOTTENHAM HOTSPUR FC (LONDON)  1-0  Wolverhampton Wanderers FC (Wolverhampton)

*Dimmock*

Tottenham: Hunter, Clay, McDonald, Smith, Walters, Grimsdell, Banks, Seed, Cantrell, Bliss, Dimmock.

Wolves: George, Woodward, Marshall, Gregory, Hodnett, Riley, Lea, Burrill, Edmonds, Potts, Brooks.

## Semi-finals

| | | |
|---|---|---|
| Tottenham Hotspur FC (London) | 2-1 | Preston North End FC (Preston) |
| Wolverhampton Wanderers FC | 0-0, 3-1 | Cardiff City AFC (Cardiff) |

## Quarter-finals

| | | |
|---|---|---|
| Cardiff City AFC (Cardiff) | 1-0 | Chelsea FC (London) |
| Everton FC (Liverpool) | 0-1 | Wolverhampton Wanderers FC (Wolverhampton) |
| Hull City AFC (Kingston-upon-Hull) | 0-0, 0-1 | Preston North End FC (Preston) |
| Tottenham Hotspur FC (London) | 1-0 | Aston Villa FC (Birmingham) |

# 1921-22

Football League Division 1 — 1921-1922 Season

| | Aston Villa | Birmingham | Blackburn R. | Bolton Wands. | Bradford City | Burnley | Cardiff City | Chelsea | Everton | Huddersfield T. | Liverpool | Man. City | Man. United | Middlesbro' | Newcastle Utd. | Oldham Ath. | Preston N.E. | Sheffield Utd. | Sunderland | The Arsenal | Tottenham H. | W.B.A. |
|---|---|---|---|---|---|---|---|---|---|---|---|---|---|---|---|---|---|---|---|---|---|---|
| Aston Villa FC | ■ | 1-1 | 1-1 | 2-1 | 7-1 | 2-0 | 2-1 | 1-4 | 2-1 | 2-0 | 1-1 | 4-0 | 3-1 | 6-2 | 1-0 | 2-0 | 2-0 | 5-3 | 2-0 | 2-0 | 2-1 | 0-1 |
| Birmingham FC | 1-0 | ■ | 1-0 | 1-1 | 1-0 | 2-3 | 0-1 | 5-1 | 1-1 | 0-2 | 0-2 | 3-1 | 0-1 | 4-3 | 0-4 | 3-0 | 0-2 | 2-1 | 1-0 | 0-1 | 0-3 | 0-2 |
| Blackburn Rovers FC | 1-2 | 1-1 | ■ | 1-2 | 3-1 | 3-2 | 1-3 | 1-1 | 2-2 | 2-0 | 0-0 | 3-1 | 3-0 | 2-2 | 0-2 | 3-2 | 3-0 | 2-3 | 1-2 | 0-1 | 1-1 | 2-3 |
| Bolton Wanderers FC | 1-0 | 1-2 | 1-1 | ■ | 3-3 | 0-1 | 1-2 | 0-2 | 1-0 | 3-1 | 1-3 | 5-0 | 1-0 | 4-2 | 3-2 | 5-1 | 2-2 | 3-1 | 1-1 | 1-0 | 1-0 | 2-0 |
| Bradford City AFC | 3-2 | 1-2 | 1-1 | 4-3 | ■ | 0-4 | 1-0 | 0-1 | 3-1 | 4-0 | 0-0 | 1-2 | 2-1 | 0-2 | 2-3 | 3-0 | 1-0 | 1-1 | 0-0 | 0-2 | 0-4 | 1-1 |
| Burnley FC | 2-1 | 3-1 | 1-2 | 2-0 | 4-0 | ■ | 1-1 | 5-0 | 2-0 | 1-0 | 1-1 | 5-2 | 4-2 | 3-1 | 2-0 | 0-1 | 3-3 | 2-1 | 2-0 | 1-0 | 1-0 | 4-2 |
| Cardiff City AFC | 0-4 | 3-1 | 1-3 | 1-2 | 6-3 | 4-2 | ■ | 2-0 | 0-0 | 2-0 | 0-2 | 3-1 | 3-1 | 1-0 | 0-1 | 3-0 | 1-1 | 2-0 | 4-3 | 0-1 | 2-0 | |
| Chelsea FC | 1-0 | 1-2 | 1-0 | 0-3 | 1-0 | 4-1 | 1-0 | ■ | 1-0 | 1-0 | 0-0 | 0-0 | 1-1 | 1-1 | 1-0 | 0-0 | 0-2 | 1-0 | 0-2 | 1-2 | 1-1 | |
| Everton FC | 3-2 | 2-1 | 2-0 | 1-0 | 2-0 | 2-0 | 0-1 | 2-3 | ■ | 6-2 | 1-1 | 2-2 | 5-0 | 4-1 | 2-3 | 2-2 | 0-0 | 1-1 | 3-0 | 1-1 | 0-0 | 1-2 |
| Huddersfield Town AFC | 1-0 | 1-0 | 3-0 | 3-0 | 1-2 | 1-0 | 0-1 | 2-0 | 1-2 | ■ | 0-1 | 2-0 | 1-1 | 2-1 | 1-2 | 1-0 | 6-0 | 1-1 | 1-2 | 2-0 | 1-1 | 2-0 |
| Liverpool FC | 2-0 | 1-0 | 2-0 | 0-2 | 2-1 | 2-1 | 5-1 | 1-1 | 1-1 | 2-0 | ■ | 3-2 | 2-1 | 4-0 | 1-0 | 2-0 | 4-0 | 1-1 | 2-1 | 4-0 | 1-1 | 1-2 |
| Manchester City FC | 2-1 | 1-0 | 1-1 | 2-3 | 3-2 | 2-0 | 1-1 | 0-0 | 2-1 | 2-1 | 1-1 | ■ | 4-1 | 2-2 | 1-0 | 2-1 | 2-0 | 2-2 | 3-0 | 2-0 | 3-3 | 6-1 |
| Manchester United FC | 1-0 | 1-1 | 0-1 | 0-1 | 1-1 | 2-0 | 1-1 | 0-0 | 2-1 | 1-1 | 0-0 | 3-1 | ■ | 3-5 | 0-1 | 0-3 | 1-1 | 3-2 | 3-1 | 1-0 | 2-1 | 2-3 |
| Middlesbrough FC | 5-0 | 1-1 | 0-1 | 4-2 | 1-2 | 4-1 | 0-0 | 0-1 | 3-1 | 5-1 | 3-1 | 4-1 | 2-0 | ■ | 1-1 | 1-1 | 1-0 | 1-1 | 3-0 | 4-2 | 0-0 | 3-2 |
| Newcastle United FC | 1-2 | 0-1 | 2-0 | 2-1 | 1-2 | 2-1 | 0-0 | 1-0 | 3-0 | 1-2 | 1-1 | 5-1 | 3-0 | 0-0 | ■ | 1-1 | 3-1 | 2-1 | 2-2 | 3-1 | 0-2 | 3-0 |
| Oldham Athletic AFC | 3-1 | 0-1 | 1-1 | 0-0 | 0-0 | 0-1 | 2-1 | 0-3 | 0-0 | 4-0 | 0-1 | 1-1 | 0-1 | 0-0 | | ■ | 2-0 | 0-2 | 3-0 | 2-1 | 1-0 | 1-0 |
| Preston North End FC | 1-0 | 2-2 | 2-1 | 3-1 | 2-1 | 2-1 | 1-1 | 2-0 | 1-0 | 1-1 | 1-1 | 1-0 | 3-2 | 1-1 | 2-0 | 0-0 | ■ | 3-0 | 1-1 | 3-2 | 1-2 | 0-3 |
| Sheffield United FC | 2-3 | 1-2 | 0-1 | 1-0 | 1-0 | 0-1 | 0-2 | 1-2 | 1-1 | 0-1 | 1-0 | 1-0 | 3-0 | 6-1 | 1-1 | 1-0 | 3-0 | ■ | 4-1 | 4-1 | 1-0 | 0-0 |
| Sunderland AFC | 1-4 | 2-1 | 3-1 | 6-2 | 0-0 | 3-2 | 4-1 | 1-2 | 1-2 | 1-2 | 1-2 | 3-0 | 2-3 | 2-1 | 1-1 | 5-1 | 1-0 | 1-0 | ■ | 1-0 | 2-0 | 1-0 |
| The Arsenal FC | 2-0 | 5-2 | 1-1 | 1-1 | 1-0 | 0-0 | 0-0 | 1-0 | 1-0 | 1-3 | 1-0 | 0-1 | 3-1 | 2-2 | 2-1 | 0-1 | 1-0 | 1-2 | 1-2 | ■ | 1-0 | 2-2 |
| Tottenham Hotspur FC | 3-1 | 2-1 | 2-1 | 1-2 | 1-0 | 1-1 | 4-1 | 0-0 | 2-0 | 1-0 | 0-1 | 3-1 | 2-2 | 2-4 | 4-0 | 3-1 | 5-0 | 2-1 | 1-0 | 2-0 | ■ | 2-0 |
| West Bromwich Albion FC | 0-1 | 1-0 | 0-2 | 0-1 | 1-1 | 2-0 | 2-2 | 2-2 | 1-1 | 3-2 | 1-4 | 2-0 | 0-0 | 0-0 | 1-2 | 0-1 | 2-0 | 3-0 | 2-1 | 0-3 | 3-0 | ■ |

## Division 1

| | | Pd | Wn | Dw | Ls | GF | GA | Pts | |
|---|---|---|---|---|---|---|---|---|---|
| 1. | LIVERPOOL FC (LIVERPOOL) | 42 | 22 | 13 | 7 | 63 | 36 | 57 | |
| 2. | Tottenham Hotspur FC (London) | 42 | 21 | 9 | 12 | 65 | 39 | 51 | |
| 3. | Burnley FC (Burnley) | 42 | 22 | 5 | 15 | 72 | 54 | 49 | |
| 4. | Cardiff City AFC (Cardiff) | 42 | 19 | 10 | 13 | 61 | 53 | 48 | |
| 5. | Aston Villa FC (Birmingham) | 42 | 22 | 3 | 17 | 74 | 55 | 47 | |
| 6. | Bolton Wanderers FC (Bolton) | 42 | 20 | 7 | 15 | 68 | 59 | 47 | |
| 7. | Newcastle United FC (Newcastle-upon-Tyne) | 42 | 18 | 10 | 14 | 59 | 45 | 46 | |
| 8. | Middlesbrough FC (Middlesbrough) | 42 | 16 | 14 | 12 | 79 | 69 | 46 | |
| 9. | Chelsea FC (London) | 42 | 17 | 12 | 13 | 40 | 43 | 46 | |
| 10. | Manchester City FC (Manchester) | 42 | 18 | 9 | 15 | 65 | 70 | 45 | |
| 11. | Sheffield United FC (Sheffield) | 42 | 15 | 10 | 17 | 59 | 54 | 40 | |
| 12. | Sunderland AFC (Sunderland) | 42 | 16 | 8 | 18 | 60 | 62 | 40 | |
| 13. | West Bromwich Albion FC (West Bromwich) | 42 | 15 | 10 | 17 | 51 | 63 | 40 | |
| 14. | Huddersfield Town AFC (Huddersfield) | 42 | 15 | 9 | 18 | 53 | 54 | 39 | |
| 15. | Blackburn Rovers FC (Blackburn) | 42 | 13 | 12 | 17 | 54 | 57 | 38 | |
| 16. | Preston North End FC (Preston) | 42 | 13 | 12 | 17 | 42 | 65 | 38 | |
| 17. | The Arsenal FC (London) | 42 | 15 | 7 | 20 | 47 | 56 | 37 | |
| 18. | Birmingham FC (Birmingham) | 42 | 15 | 7 | 20 | 48 | 60 | 37 | |
| 19. | Oldham Athletic AFC (Oldham) | 42 | 13 | 11 | 18 | 38 | 50 | 37 | |
| 20. | Everton FC (Liverpool) | 42 | 12 | 12 | 18 | 57 | 55 | 36 | |
| 21. | Bradford City AFC (Bradford) | 42 | 11 | 10 | 21 | 48 | 72 | 32 | R |
| 22. | Manchester United FC (Manchester) | 42 | 8 | 12 | 22 | 41 | 73 | 28 | R |
| | | 924 | 356 | 212 | 356 | 1244 | 1244 | 924 | |

# Top Goalscorer

1)   Andrew WILSON                    (Middlesbrough FC)      31

| Football League Division 2 1921-1922 Season | Barnsley | Blackpool | Bradford Park Avenue | Bristol City | Bury | Clapton Orient | Coventry City | Crystal Palace | Derby County | Fulham | Hull City | Leeds United | Leicester City | Nottingham Forest | Notts County | Port Vale | Rotherham County | South Shields | Stoke | Wednesday | West Ham United | Wolves |
|---|---|---|---|---|---|---|---|---|---|---|---|---|---|---|---|---|---|---|---|---|---|---|
| Barnsley FC | | 3-2 | 2-0 | 1-1 | 3-0 | 4-0 | 0-1 | 3-1 | 2-1 | 2-1 | 4-1 | 2-2 | 0-0 | 2-0 | 3-0 | 3-2 | 0-1 | 2-1 | 2-2 | 2-0 | 1-1 | 2-1 |
| Blackpool FC | 1-0 | | 1-1 | 2-0 | 0-1 | 2-0 | 2-1 | 1-3 | 4-2 | 0-2 | 0-1 | 1-3 | 2-0 | 2-1 | 1-2 | 0-1 | 3-1 | 4-0 | 3-2 | 0-2 | 3-1 | 1-3 |
| Bradford Park Avenue | 2-3 | 0-0 | | 2-1 | 1-1 | 3-1 | 1-2 | 0-0 | 5-1 | 1-2 | 1-1 | 0-1 | 0-1 | 1-0 | 2-1 | 2-0 | 4-2 | 1-0 | 2-4 | 2-1 | 2-0 | 0-0 |
| Bristol City FC | 3-0 | 0-1 | 1-0 | | 2-0 | 2-1 | 0-2 | 1-2 | 1-2 | 1-0 | 1-0 | 0-0 | 1-1 | 0-1 | 2-2 | 2-1 | 1-2 | 0-1 | 2-0 | 3-1 | 0-1 | 2-0 |
| Bury FC | 1-2 | 3-0 | 2-2 | 5-0 | | 0-0 | 3-2 | 1-2 | 2-0 | 1-0 | 4-0 | 2-1 | 0-1 | 1-2 | 1-0 | 5-2 | 0-0 | 1-0 | 0-1 | 1-2 | 0-1 | 2-1 |
| Clapton Orient FC | 2-1 | 3-0 | 1-0 | 0-1 | 3-1 | | 4-0 | 0-0 | 3-2 | 4-2 | 0-2 | 4-2 | 0-0 | 1-2 | 2-1 | 2-0 | 1-2 | 0-1 | 1-0 | 1-1 | 0-0 | 1-0 |
| Coventry City FC | 0-1 | 0-1 | 2-2 | 1-1 | 1-2 | 1-2 | | 1-1 | 1-2 | 2-0 | 2-0 | 1-0 | 0-0 | 0-1 | 4-2 | 4-1 | 4-0 | 0-1 | 0-1 | 2-2 | 2-0 | 3-1 |
| Crystal Palace FC | 0-1 | 1-0 | 1-1 | 1-1 | 4-1 | 1-0 | 1-1 | | 3-1 | 2-0 | 0-2 | 1-2 | 1-0 | 4-1 | 0-0 | 2-0 | 1-2 | 0-2 | 2-2 | 1-2 | 1-1 | |
| Derby County FC | 1-0 | 1-0 | 1-3 | 5-1 | 1-0 | 3-0 | 1-0 | 2-0 | | 1-1 | 0-0 | 2-0 | 0-1 | 1-2 | 1-1 | 3-2 | 4-0 | 0-2 | 2-4 | 0-1 | 3-1 | 2-3 |
| Fulham FC | 0-0 | 1-0 | 2-1 | 0-0 | 0-1 | 2-0 | 5-0 | 1-1 | 2-2 | | 6-0 | 0-1 | 0-0 | 2-0 | 4-0 | 1-0 | 4-0 | 3-0 | 2-1 | 3-1 | 2-0 | 1-0 |
| Hull City AFC | 1-3 | 2-0 | 3-0 | 1-0 | 1-1 | 2-1 | 2-0 | 1-0 | 1-1 | 2-1 | | 1-0 | 5-2 | 0-1 | 2-0 | 2-0 | 0-1 | 1-1 | 7-1 | 0-0 | 0-0 | 2-0 |
| Leeds United AFC | 4-0 | 0-0 | 3-0 | 3-0 | 2-0 | 2-0 | 5-2 | 0-0 | 2-1 | 2-0 | 0-2 | | 3-0 | 0-0 | 1-1 | 2-1 | 0-2 | 0-0 | 1-2 | 1-1 | 0-0 | 0-0 |
| Leicester City FC | 1-0 | 1-0 | 2-1 | 4-1 | 0-0 | 1-0 | 1-1 | 2-0 | 1-1 | 1-2 | 0-1 | 0-0 | | 2-2 | 3-0 | 3-0 | 1-0 | 1-0 | 3-4 | 1-1 | 2-1 | 0-1 |
| Nottingham Forest FC | 1-1 | 0-0 | 4-1 | 1-0 | 1-2 | 2-0 | 1-0 | 2-1 | 3-0 | 0-0 | 3-2 | 1-0 | 0-0 | | 0-0 | 1-1 | 1-0 | 1-0 | 3-1 | 2-0 | 2-0 | 0-0 |
| Notts County FC | 1-4 | 2-1 | 3-0 | 0-2 | 1-1 | 0-0 | 1-1 | 3-2 | 1-2 | 3-0 | 2-0 | 4-1 | 0-0 | 1-1 | | 1-2 | 2-0 | 0-0 | 2-0 | 1-1 | 4-0 | |
| Port Vale FC | 2-3 | 1-0 | 1-0 | 3-1 | 5-2 | 3-0 | 1-2 | 3-0 | 1-1 | 1-1 | 1-0 | 0-1 | 1-1 | 0-2 | 0-0 | | 1-0 | 1-1 | 0-1 | 1-0 | 2-1 | 0-2 |
| Rotherham County FC | 0-0 | 0-1 | 2-0 | 0-0 | 1-1 | 2-0 | 0-0 | 1-1 | 2-0 | 1-0 | 2-0 | 1-0 | 0-0 | 0-1 | 3-0 | 0-1 | | 1-1 | 0-0 | 0-0 | 0-1 | 1-0 |
| South Shields FC | 5-2 | 2-1 | 1-0 | 2-0 | 1-1 | 1-1 | 2-1 | 1-1 | 3-1 | 1-0 | 1-0 | 0-1 | 1-0 | 0-0 | 0-0 | 0-1 | 2-0 | | 1-1 | 0-0 | 1-0 | 0-2 |
| Stoke FC | 1-0 | 1-1 | 0-1 | 3-0 | 1-0 | 0-0 | 2-2 | 5-1 | 1-1 | 3-0 | 0-0 | 3-0 | 1-1 | 1-1 | 0-0 | 0-0 | 1-1 | 2-1 | | 1-1 | 2-0 | 3-0 |
| The Wednesday FC | 2-3 | 5-1 | 2-1 | 1-0 | 4-1 | 0-0 | 3-2 | 1-0 | 1-1 | 1-4 | 0-0 | 2-1 | 1-0 | 0-4 | 0-0 | 2-0 | 1-0 | 0-3 | 0-1 | | 2-1 | 3-1 |
| West Ham United FC | 4-0 | 0-2 | 1-0 | 3-0 | 3-2 | 1-2 | 3-0 | 2-0 | 3-1 | 1-0 | 1-1 | 1-1 | 1-0 | 2-1 | 3-0 | 1-2 | 1-1 | 3-0 | 2-0 | | | 2-0 |
| Wolverhampton Wanderers FC | 2-0 | 4-0 | 5-0 | 2-2 | 1-1 | 0-2 | 1-0 | 0-1 | 0-3 | 0-0 | 0-2 | 0-0 | 1-1 | 2-0 | 1-2 | 2-0 | 3-1 | 3-2 | 1-1 | 0-0 | 0-1 | |

## Division 2

| | | Pd | Wn | Dw | Ls | GF | GA | Pts | |
|---|---|---|---|---|---|---|---|---|---|
| 1. | Nottingham Forest FC (Nottingham) | 42 | 22 | 12 | 8 | 51 | 30 | 56 | P |
| 2. | Stoke FC (Stoke-on-Trent) | 42 | 18 | 16 | 8 | 60 | 44 | 52 | P |
| 3. | Barnsley FC (Barnsley) | 42 | 22 | 8 | 12 | 67 | 52 | 52 | |
| 4. | West Ham United FC (London) | 42 | 20 | 8 | 14 | 52 | 39 | 48 | |
| 5. | Hull City AFC (Kingston-upon-Hull) | 42 | 19 | 10 | 13 | 51 | 41 | 48 | |
| 6. | South Shields FC (South Shields) | 42 | 17 | 12 | 13 | 43 | 38 | 46 | |
| 7. | Fulham FC (London) | 42 | 18 | 9 | 15 | 57 | 38 | 45 | |
| 8. | Leeds United AFC (Leeds) | 42 | 16 | 13 | 13 | 48 | 38 | 45 | |
| 9. | Leicester City FC (Leicester) | 42 | 14 | 17 | 11 | 39 | 34 | 45 | |
| 10. | The Wednesday FC (Sheffield) | 42 | 15 | 14 | 13 | 47 | 50 | 44 | |
| 11. | Bury FC (Bury) | 42 | 15 | 10 | 17 | 54 | 55 | 40 | |
| 12. | Derby County FC (Derby) | 42 | 15 | 9 | 18 | 60 | 64 | 39 | |
| 13. | Notts County FC (Nottingham) | 42 | 12 | 15 | 15 | 47 | 51 | 39 | |
| 14. | Crystal Palace FC (London) | 42 | 13 | 13 | 16 | 45 | 51 | 39 | |
| 15. | Clapton Orient FC (London) | 42 | 15 | 9 | 18 | 43 | 50 | 39 | |
| 16. | Rotherham County FC (Rotherham) | 42 | 14 | 11 | 17 | 32 | 43 | 39 | |
| 17. | Wolverhampton Wanderers FC (Wolverhampton) | 42 | 13 | 11 | 18 | 44 | 49 | 37 | |
| 18. | Port Vale FC (Stoke-on-Trent) | 42 | 14 | 8 | 20 | 43 | 57 | 36 | |
| 19. | Blackpool FC (Blackpool) | 42 | 15 | 5 | 22 | 44 | 57 | 35 | |
| 20. | Coventry City FC (Coventry) | 42 | 12 | 10 | 20 | 51 | 60 | 34 | |
| 21. | Bristol City FC (Bristol) | 42 | 12 | 9 | 21 | 37 | 58 | 33 | R |
| 22. | Bradford Park Avenue FC (Bradford) | 42 | 12 | 9 | 21 | 46 | 62 | 33 | R |
| | | 924 | 343 | 238 | 343 | 1061 | 1061 | 924 | |

| Football League Division 3 (N) 1921-1922 Season | Accrington Stanley | Ashington | Barrow | Chesterfield | Crewe Alexandra | Darlington | Durham City | Grimsby Town | Halifax Town | Hartlepools United | Lincoln City | Nelson | Rochdale | Southport | Stalybridge Celtic | Stockport County | Tranmere Rovers | Walsall | Wigan Borough | Wrexham |
|---|---|---|---|---|---|---|---|---|---|---|---|---|---|---|---|---|---|---|---|---|
| Accrington Stanley FC | | 3-0 | 3-0 | 3-1 | 2-0 | 1-0 | 5-1 | 1-0 | 1-2 | 4-1 | 2-0 | 4-1 | 4-0 | 1-2 | 4-1 | 1-3 | 3-0 | 3-3 | 4-0 | 1-0 |
| Ashington FC | 2-1 | | 0-2 | 1-0 | 0-1 | 1-0 | 1-0 | 1-0 | 3-1 | 4-1 | 4-2 | 4-0 | 7-3 | 2-2 | 2-3 | 2-0 | 1-0 | 2-3 | 3-1 | 2-2 |
| Barrow AFC | 3-1 | 2-0 | | 1-0 | 1-2 | 0-2 | 0-1 | 2-2 | 1-1 | 0-1 | 2-0 | 0-2 | 1-0 | 2-1 | 2-1 | 0-2 | 2-0 | 3-0 | 2-0 | 5-2 |
| Chesterfield FC | 0-1 | 0-1 | 2-0 | | 1-1 | 0-3 | 2-1 | 4-1 | 2-0 | 2-1 | 3-0 | 1-2 | 2-1 | 2-1 | 4-0 | 0-1 | 3-0 | 1-0 | 1-1 | 3-0 |
| Crewe Alexandra FC | 2-1 | 1-2 | 2-1 | 1-2 | | 7-3 | 3-2 | 1-2 | 2-1 | 2-0 | 0-2 | 2-1 | 2-0 | 1-0 | 5-1 | 0-1 | 1-1 | 2-0 | 2-1 | 3-0 |
| Darlington FC | 3-0 | 5-0 | 3-0 | 7-0 | 0-1 | | 2-2 | 2-0 | 2-0 | 0-0 | 4-2 | 0-1 | 2-1 | 3-0 | 3-0 | 1-0 | 4-0 | 5-0 | 3-0 | 3-0 |
| Durham City FC | 3-1 | 1-0 | 3-1 | 3-1 | 4-2 | 3-7 | | 1-2 | 3-1 | 1-0 | 2-0 | 0-2 | 2-0 | 3-1 | 0-2 | 3-0 | 3-0 | 2-0 | 6-0 | 3-0 |
| Grimsby Town FC | 2-1 | 6-1 | 4-0 | 2-2 | 3-0 | 3-1 | 5-2 | | 4-1 | 2-0 | 3-1 | 3-1 | 3-0 | 0-0 | 1-1 | 2-1 | 5-1 | 3-1 | 1-1 | 2-0 |
| Halifax Town AFC | 2-1 | 2-0 | 3-2 | 1-2 | 5-5 | 5-1 | 3-2 | 2-0 | | 3-0 | 1-2 | 3-1 | 1-1 | 1-1 | 2-3 | 1-0 | 0-2 | 1-3 | 1-2 | 0-0 |
| Hartlepools United FC | 2-1 | 2-1 | 3-1 | 7-0 | 1-0 | 0-0 | 0-1 | 0-0 | 4-0 | | 1-1 | 6-1 | 5-3 | 1-0 | 0-1 | 0-0 | 0-0 | 1-0 | 0-0 | 0-1 |
| Lincoln City FC | 1-1 | 4-1 | 1-0 | 2-1 | 2-3 | 0-2 | 3-0 | 0-2 | 3-1 | 1-1 | | 0-2 | 1-2 | 3-1 | 2-1 | 0-1 | 4-1 | 1-0 | 3-0 | 1-0 |
| Nelson FC | 0-1 | 0-2 | 1-1 | 2-0 | 1-2 | 1-1 | 3-5 | 3-0 | 0-0 | 0-4 | 0-0 | | 4-1 | 3-2 | 1-0 | 2-2 | 0-0 | 1-0 | 1-2 | 4-0 |
| Rochdale AFC | 6-3 | 2-1 | 0-1 | 0-1 | 2-0 | 0-2 | 1-0 | 0-2 | 3-3 | 0-1 | 0-2 | 2-2 | | 0-1 | 2-1 | 0-1 | 2-1 | 7-0 | 4-2 | 3-0 |
| Southport FC | 1-1 | 0-0 | 1-0 | 3-0 | 2-0 | 3-1 | 1-1 | 7-1 | 3-0 | 3-0 | 0-0 | 0-1 | 2-1 | | 5-1 | 2-1 | 1-1 | 3-0 | 1-1 | 1-2 |
| Stalybridge Celtic FC | 3-1 | 2-0 | 3-0 | 6-0 | 2-2 | 1-0 | 4-3 | 3-0 | 2-1 | 1-3 | 2-0 | 2-0 | 1-0 | 0-0 | | 0-4 | 4-0 | 2-0 | 0-0 | 4-1 |
| Stockport County FC | 2-1 | 3-2 | 2-0 | 2-1 | 1-1 | 1-0 | 4-0 | 0-1 | 0-0 | 1-0 | 2-2 | 3-0 | 3-0 | 2-1 | 4-0 | | 0-0 | 3-1 | 3-0 | 0-0 |
| Tranmere Rovers FC | 2-4 | 2-3 | 2-2 | 2-0 | 4-1 | 0-1 | 3-3 | 2-2 | 2-2 | 1-2 | 4-0 | 4-0 | 7-0 | 0-1 | 4-1 | 0-2 | | 0-1 | 2-0 | 0-0 |
| Walsall FC | 6-1 | 6-2 | 3-1 | 2-1 | 1-0 | 0-1 | 2-0 | 2-1 | 4-1 | 3-1 | 3-0 | 2-0 | 4-0 | 4-1 | 2-2 | 0-2 | 2-0 | | 4-1 | 2-2 |
| Wigan Borough FC | 0-1 | 1-1 | 1-2 | 1-2 | 2-0 | 3-3 | 2-0 | 1-1 | 4-3 | 1-0 | 3-1 | 1-4 | 3-2 | 3-2 | 0-2 | 0-1 | 0-0 | 4-2 | | 2-1 |
| Wrexham AFC | 2-1 | 2-0 | 0-0 | 6-1 | 1-0 | 1-1 | 3-1 | 0-1 | 5-1 | 0-2 | 3-1 | 4-2 | 1-1 | 2-0 | 2-0 | 0-0 | 1-3 | 4-0 | 3-2 | |

## Division 3 (North)

| | | Pd | Wn | Dw | Ls | GF | GA | Pts | |
|---|---|---|---|---|---|---|---|---|---|
| 1. | Stockport County FC (Stockport) | 38 | 24 | 8 | 6 | 60 | 21 | 56 | P |
| 2. | Darlington FC (Darlington) | 38 | 22 | 6 | 10 | 81 | 37 | 50 | |
| 3. | Grimsby Town FC (Cleethorpes) | 38 | 21 | 8 | 9 | 72 | 47 | 50 | |
| 4. | Hartlepools United FC (Hartlepool) | 38 | 17 | 8 | 13 | 52 | 39 | 42 | |
| 5. | Accrington Stanley FC (Accrington) | 38 | 19 | 3 | 16 | 73 | 57 | 41 | |
| 6. | Crewe Alexandra FC (Crewe) | 38 | 18 | 5 | 15 | 60 | 56 | 41 | |
| 7. | Stalybridge Celtic FC (Stalybridge) | 38 | 18 | 5 | 15 | 62 | 63 | 41 | |
| 8. | Walsall FC (Walsall) | 38 | 18 | 3 | 17 | 66 | 65 | 39 | |
| 9. | Southport FC (Southport) | 38 | 14 | 10 | 14 | 55 | 44 | 38 | |
| 10. | Ashington FC (Ashington) | 38 | 17 | 4 | 17 | 59 | 66 | 38 | |
| 11. | Durham City FC (Durham) | 38 | 17 | 3 | 18 | 68 | 67 | 37 | |
| 12. | Wrexham AFC (Wrexham) | 38 | 14 | 9 | 15 | 51 | 56 | 37 | |
| 13. | Chesterfield FC (Chesterfield) | 38 | 16 | 3 | 19 | 48 | 67 | 35 | |
| 14. | Lincoln City FC (Lincoln) | 38 | 14 | 6 | 18 | 48 | 59 | 34 | |
| 15. | Barrow AFC (Barrow-in-Furness) | 38 | 14 | 5 | 19 | 42 | 54 | 33 | |
| 16. | Nelson FC (Nelson) | 38 | 13 | 7 | 18 | 48 | 66 | 33 | |
| 17. | Wigan Borough FC (Wigan) | 38 | 11 | 9 | 18 | 46 | 72 | 31 | |
| 18. | Tranmere Rovers FC (Birkenhead) | 38 | 9 | 11 | 18 | 51 | 61 | 29 | |
| 19. | Halifax Town AFC (Halifax) | 38 | 10 | 9 | 19 | 56 | 76 | 29 | |
| 20. | Rochdale AFC (Rochdale) | 38 | 11 | 4 | 23 | 52 | 77 | 26 | |
| | | 760 | 317 | 126 | 317 | 1150 | 1150 | 760 | |

| Football League Division 3 (S) 1921-1922 Season | Aberdare Athletic | Brentford | Brighton | Bristol Rovers | Charlton Athletic | Exeter City | Gillingham | Luton Town | Merthyr Town | Millwall Athletic | Newport County | Northampton | Norwich City | Plymouth Argyle | Portsmouth | Q.P.R. | Reading | Southampton | Southend United | Swansea Town | Swindon Town | Watford |
|---|---|---|---|---|---|---|---|---|---|---|---|---|---|---|---|---|---|---|---|---|---|---|
| Aberdare Athletic FC | | 2-0 | 2-0 | 2-0 | 3-3 | 0-2 | 6-1 | 2-0 | 0-0 | 0-0 | 3-0 | 4-2 | 1-2 | 0-0 | 0-0 | 4-2 | 0-1 | 0-1 | 1-1 | 2-1 | 3-2 | 3-0 |
| Brentford FC | 2-1 | | 4-0 | 4-2 | 0-2 | 5-2 | 0-1 | 0-2 | 0-1 | 1-0 | 1-0 | 1-0 | 2-1 | 3-1 | 2-2 | 5-1 | 2-0 | 1-0 | 1-0 | 3-0 | 3-0 | 1-1 |
| Brighton & Hove Albion | 1-2 | 2-1 | | 3-1 | 2-0 | 3-1 | 0-1 | 1-1 | 1-3 | 0-1 | 3-0 | 7-0 | 0-2 | 1-1 | 3-0 | 2-1 | 1-1 | 0-1 | 0-0 | 0-0 | 2-1 | 1-1 |
| Bristol Rovers FC | 5-1 | 0-0 | 1-2 | | 4-2 | 1-3 | 0-3 | 2-0 | 2-0 | 0-0 | 3-4 | 2-0 | 4-2 | 1-3 | 1-1 | 1-1 | 2-0 | 1-0 | 0-0 | 1-1 | 1-1 | 1-1 |
| Charlton Athletic FC | 2-1 | 1-1 | 1-0 | 2-0 | | 1-0 | 0-0 | 0-1 | 1-0 | 2-1 | 1-1 | 2-2 | 2-1 | 0-0 | 1-2 | 1-1 | 0-1 | 1-2 | 4-0 | 1-0 | 4-5 | 1-0 |
| Exeter City FC | 0-1 | 1-0 | 0-3 | 2-2 | 1-0 | | 1-1 | 0-1 | 1-0 | 1-0 | 2-2 | 2-0 | 2-0 | 0-2 | 1-4 | 0-1 | 1-3 | 0-0 | 4-1 | 1-1 | 1-4 | 1-3 |
| Gillingham FC | 3-1 | 0-0 | 1-0 | 3-2 | 2-0 | 3-0 | | 0-1 | 5-0 | 0-1 | 0-2 | 3-2 | 5-2 | 1-2 | 1-2 | 2-0 | 2-0 | 1-0 | 0-0 | 2-2 | 1-1 | |
| Luton Town FC | 1-2 | 3-0 | 2-0 | 1-2 | 2-0 | 4-0 | 7-0 | | 3-0 | 1-0 | 4-0 | 2-0 | 3-1 | 1-0 | 1-0 | 3-1 | 0-1 | 1-0 | 3-0 | 3-0 | 2-1 | 1-1 |
| Merthyr Town FC | 0-1 | 2-0 | 2-1 | 0-2 | 1-0 | 0-0 | 2-0 | 2-0 | | 3-1 | 2-1 | 2-1 | 3-0 | 0-1 | 2-1 | 2-0 | 2-0 | 0-1 | 2-2 | 1-0 | 4-1 | 1-2 |
| Millwall Athletic FC | 0-0 | 1-1 | 2-0 | 4-1 | 0-1 | 1-0 | 1-0 | 1-1 | 4-0 | | 1-1 | 0-0 | 2-2 | 1-1 | 1-1 | 0-0 | 3-0 | 1-1 | 0-1 | 1-0 | 0-0 | 0-0 |
| Newport County AFC | 1-0 | 2-1 | 0-1 | 0-1 | 2-1 | 1-1 | 1-1 | 2-2 | 0-2 | 1-0 | | 2-2 | 1-0 | 0-0 | 0-1 | 1-0 | 2-1 | 2-1 | 2-3 | 4-0 | 0-0 | |
| Northampton Town | 2-0 | 2-0 | 2-0 | 2-2 | 1-0 | 2-3 | 3-1 | 2-0 | 2-0 | 0-3 | 2-0 | | 3-0 | 1-3 | 0-0 | 2-1 | 0-0 | 0-2 | 0-1 | 2-1 | 1-0 | |
| Norwich City FC | 0-0 | 2-0 | 1-1 | 0-1 | 2-0 | 0-0 | 2-0 | 0-1 | 2-0 | 3-1 | 2-2 | 2-0 | | 1-1 | 2-1 | 0-0 | 4-1 | 2-2 | 1-1 | 3-2 | 1-2 | 1-1 |
| Plymouth Argyle FC | 3-0 | 4-2 | 3-1 | 1-0 | 3-0 | 0-0 | 3-0 | 2-0 | 0-0 | 2-0 | 1-0 | 2-0 | 1-1 | | 0-0 | 4-0 | 2-0 | 1-0 | 4-0 | 3-1 | 1-0 | 3-0 |
| Portsmouth FC | 2-2 | 1-0 | 0-0 | 1-0 | 1-0 | 2-0 | 4-1 | 1-1 | 2-1 | 2-2 | 4-3 | 1-1 | 0-1 | 3-1 | | 1-0 | 1-0 | 0-2 | 6-0 | 3-0 | 1-3 | 2-0 |
| Queen's Park Rangers | 1-0 | 1-1 | 3-0 | 1-2 | 3-1 | 2-1 | 1-0 | 1-0 | 0-0 | 6-1 | 2-1 | 4-0 | 2-0 | 2-0 | 1-1 | | 1-1 | 2-2 | 1-0 | 1-0 | 0-0 | 1-1 |
| Reading FC | 0-1 | 0-3 | 0-0 | 4-0 | 1-2 | 0-2 | 2-1 | 2-1 | 5-0 | 1-0 | 1-0 | 0-0 | 2-1 | 0-1 | 1-1 | 0-1 | | 0-1 | 4-0 | 2-0 | 1-1 | 2-1 |
| Southampton FC | 1-0 | 0-0 | 3-0 | 1-0 | 6-0 | 2-0 | 2-0 | 2-1 | 1-1 | 4-2 | 5-0 | 8-0 | 2-0 | 0-0 | 1-1 | 1-1 | 0-0 | | 5-0 | 1-1 | 3-1 | 2-0 |
| Southend United FC | 3-2 | 1-1 | 1-2 | 3-0 | 1-1 | 0-1 | 2-0 | 0-1 | 2-1 | 1-1 | 0-1 | 1-1 | 0-1 | 1-0 | 1-2 | 1-2 | 2-0 | 0-0 | | 1-0 | 1-2 | 1-4 |
| Swansea Town AFC | 1-2 | 1-0 | 2-1 | 8-1 | 0-0 | 2-1 | 2-0 | 1-1 | 3-2 | 3-0 | 2-2 | 2-2 | 1-1 | 3-0 | 2-2 | 1-0 | 0-0 | 1-0 | 1-1 | | 1-3 | 3-0 |
| Swindon Town FC | 2-2 | 2-1 | 1-0 | 0-1 | 0-0 | 1-1 | 0-0 | 1-1 | 3-0 | 1-1 | 3-2 | 4-2 | 6-1 | 1-2 | 0-0 | 2-0 | 4-0 | 2-3 | 6-1 | 1-0 | | 0-3 |
| Watford FC | 3-0 | 0-0 | 1-0 | 1-0 | 2-2 | 0-0 | 1-0 | 4-1 | 4-1 | 0-1 | 1-0 | 2-2 | 4-2 | 0-1 | 0-3 | 2-2 | 2-2 | 1-1 | 4-1 | 0-0 | 2-2 | |

| Division 3 (South) | | Pd | Wn | Dw | Ls | GF | GA | Pts | |
|---|---|---|---|---|---|---|---|---|---|
| 1. | Southampton FC (Southampton) | 42 | 23 | 15 | 4 | 68 | 21 | 61 | P |
| 2. | Plymouth Argyle FC (Plymouth) | 42 | 25 | 11 | 6 | 63 | 24 | 61 | |
| 3. | Portsmouth FC (Portsmouth) | 42 | 18 | 17 | 7 | 62 | 39 | 53 | |
| 4. | Luton Town FC (Luton) | 42 | 22 | 8 | 12 | 64 | 35 | 52 | |
| 5. | Queen's Park Rangers FC (London) | 42 | 18 | 13 | 11 | 53 | 44 | 49 | |
| 6. | Swindon Town FC (Swindon) | 42 | 16 | 13 | 13 | 72 | 60 | 45 | |
| 7. | Watford FC (Watford) | 42 | 13 | 18 | 11 | 54 | 48 | 44 | |
| 8. | Aberdare Athletic FC (Aberdare) | 42 | 17 | 10 | 15 | 57 | 51 | 44 | |
| 9. | Brentford FC (London) | 42 | 16 | 11 | 15 | 52 | 43 | 43 | |
| 10. | Swansea Town AFC (Swansea) | 42 | 13 | 15 | 14 | 50 | 47 | 41 | |
| 11. | Merthyr Town FC (Merthyr Tydfil) | 42 | 17 | 6 | 19 | 45 | 56 | 40 | |
| 12. | Millwall Athletic FC (London) | 42 | 10 | 18 | 14 | 38 | 42 | 38 | |
| 13. | Reading FC (Reading) | 42 | 14 | 10 | 18 | 40 | 47 | 38 | |
| 14. | Bristol Rovers FC (Bristol) | 42 | 14 | 10 | 18 | 52 | 67 | 38 | |
| 15. | Norwich City FC (Norwich) | 42 | 12 | 13 | 17 | 50 | 62 | 37 | |
| 16. | Charlton Athletic FC (London) | 42 | 13 | 11 | 18 | 43 | 56 | 37 | |
| 17. | Northampton Town FC (Northampton) | 42 | 13 | 11 | 18 | 47 | 71 | 37 | |
| 18. | Gillingham FC (Gillingham) | 42 | 14 | 8 | 20 | 47 | 60 | 36 | |
| 19. | Brighton & Hove Albion FC (Hove) | 42 | 13 | 9 | 20 | 45 | 51 | 35 | |
| 20. | Newport County AFC (Newport) | 42 | 11 | 12 | 19 | 44 | 61 | 34 | |
| 21. | Exeter City FC (Exeter) | 42 | 11 | 12 | 19 | 38 | 59 | 34 | |
| 22. | Southend United FC (Southend-on-Sea) | 42 | 8 | 11 | 23 | 34 | 74 | 27 | |
| | | 924 | 331 | 262 | 331 | 1118 | 1118 | 924 | |

## F.A. CUP FINAL   (Stamford Bridge, London – 29/04/1922 – 53,000)

HUDDERSFIELD TOWN AFC                    1-0                    Preston North End FC (Preston)
*Smith*

Huddersfield: Mutch, Wood, Wadsworth, Slade, Wilson, Watson, Richardson, Mann, Islip, Stephenson, W.H. Smith.

Preston: J.F. Mitchell, Hamilton, Doolan, Duxbury, McCall, Williamson, Rawlings, Jefferies, Roberts, Woodhouse, Quinn.


## Semi-finals

| | | |
|---|---|---|
| Huddersfield Town AFC (Huddersfield) | 3-1 | Notts County FC (Nottingham) |
| Preston North End FC (Preston) | 2-1 | Tottenham Hotspur FC (London) |


## Quarter-finals

| | | |
|---|---|---|
| Cardiff City AFC (Cardiff) | 1-1, 1-2 | Tottenham Hotspur FC (London) |
| Huddersfield Town AFC (Huddersfield) | 3-0 | Millwall Athletic FC (London) |
| Notts County FC (Nottingham) | 2-2, 4-3 | Aston Villa FC (Birmingham) |
| The Arsenal FC (London) | 1-1, 1-2 | Preston North End FC (Preston) |

# 1922-23

| Football League Division 1 1922-1923 Season | Aston Villa | Birmingham | Blackburn R. | Bolton Wands. | Burnley | Cardiff City | Chelsea | Everton | Huddersfield T. | Liverpool | Man. City | Middlesbro' | Newcastle Utd. | Nottingham F. | Oldham Ath. | Preston N.E. | Sheffield Utd. | Stoke | Sunderland | The Arsenal | Tottenham H. | W.B.A. |
|---|---|---|---|---|---|---|---|---|---|---|---|---|---|---|---|---|---|---|---|---|---|---|
| Aston Villa FC | | 3-0 | 2-0 | 2-0 | 3-1 | 1-3 | 1-0 | 3-0 | 2-1 | 0-1 | 2-0 | 2-2 | 1-1 | 4-0 | 3-0 | 1-0 | 0-1 | 6-0 | 1-0 | 1-1 | 2-0 | 2-0 |
| Birmingham FC | 1-0 | | 1-1 | 2-0 | 1-0 | 0-0 | 0-1 | 1-1 | 0-0 | 0-1 | 0-1 | 2-0 | 0-2 | 2-0 | 2-3 | 1-0 | 4-2 | 2-0 | 1-2 | 3-2 | 2-1 | 0-2 |
| Blackburn Rovers FC | 4-2 | 1-1 | | 1-0 | 2-1 | 3-1 | 0-0 | 5-1 | 0-0 | 1-0 | 0-0 | 2-0 | 1-1 | 2-0 | 1-0 | 1-1 | 1-0 | 1-5 | 0-0 | 0-5 | 1-0 | 5-1 |
| Bolton Wanderers FC | 3-0 | 3-0 | 3-0 | | 2-1 | 0-0 | 1-1 | 0-2 | 1-0 | 1-1 | 2-1 | 1-1 | 1-0 | 4-2 | 3-1 | 1-1 | 1-1 | 1-1 | 1-1 | 4-1 | 0-2 | 3-0 |
| Burnley FC | 1-1 | 0-2 | 3-1 | 2-1 | | 1-5 | 1-0 | 0-1 | 0-2 | 2-0 | 2-0 | 3-0 | 0-0 | 8-2 | 1-1 | 2-0 | 1-4 | 3-2 | 2-0 | 4-1 | 0-1 | 3-0 |
| Cardiff City AFC | 3-0 | 1-1 | 5-0 | 1-0 | 2-2 | | 6-1 | 0-2 | 0-1 | 3-0 | 3-1 | 2-0 | 5-0 | 3-1 | 2-0 | 1-0 | 1-0 | 2-1 | 2-4 | 4-1 | 2-3 | 3-0 |
| Chelsea FC | 1-1 | 1-1 | 1-1 | 3-0 | 0-1 | 1-1 | | 3-1 | 2-2 | 0-0 | 1-1 | 1-1 | 3-0 | 2-2 | 4-0 | 0-1 | 0-0 | 3-2 | 1-3 | 0-0 | 0-0 | 2-2 |
| Everton FC | 2-1 | 2-1 | 2-0 | 1-1 | 1-0 | 3-1 | 3-1 | | 0-3 | 0-1 | 0-0 | 5-3 | 3-2 | 4-2 | 0-0 | 1-1 | 5-1 | 4-0 | 1-1 | 1-0 | 3-1 | 0-1 |
| Huddersfield Town AFC | 3-5 | 4-0 | 0-2 | 0-2 | 2-0 | 1-0 | 3-0 | 1-0 | | 0-0 | 0-0 | 0-2 | 2-0 | 2-1 | 3-0 | 2-0 | 2-1 | 1-0 | 0-1 | 4-0 | 1-0 | 4-1 |
| Liverpool FC | 3-0 | 0-0 | 3-0 | 3-0 | 3-0 | 3-1 | 1-0 | 5-1 | 1-1 | | 2-0 | 2-0 | 0-2 | 2-1 | 2-1 | 5-2 | 2-1 | 1-0 | 5-1 | 5-2 | 0-0 | 2-0 |
| Manchester City FC | 1-1 | 0-1 | 2-1 | 2-0 | 1-0 | 5-1 | 3-0 | 2-1 | 3-1 | 1-0 | | 2-1 | 0-0 | 1-1 | 3-2 | 2-1 | 3-3 | 2-1 | 1-0 | 0-0 | 3-0 | 1-1 |
| Middlesbrough FC | 2-2 | 2-1 | 1-2 | 1-2 | 4-1 | 0-1 | 2-1 | 2-4 | 2-2 | 0-2 | 5-0 | | 1-1 | 4-0 | 2-1 | 1-1 | 3-2 | 3-1 | 2-0 | 2-0 | 2-0 | 0-1 |
| Newcastle United FC | 0-0 | 0-0 | 5-1 | 1-0 | 0-2 | 3-1 | 0-0 | 2-0 | 1-0 | 0-1 | 3-1 | 1-1 | | 1-0 | 1-0 | 3-1 | 3-0 | 1-0 | 2-1 | 1-1 | 1-1 | 2-0 |
| Nottingham Forest FC | 3-1 | 1-1 | 1-0 | 1-1 | 1-0 | 3-2 | 0-4 | 2-1 | 0-1 | 1-3 | 2-0 | 2-1 | 0-1 | | 1-0 | 3-0 | 1-0 | 0-1 | 1-0 | 2-1 | 0-1 | 0-4 |
| Oldham Athletic AFC | 0-2 | 2-0 | 1-0 | 3-1 | 1-1 | 3-1 | 2-0 | 1-0 | 0-3 | 0-2 | 0-3 | 0-0 | 0-0 | 2-0 | | 2-1 | 0-2 | 4-1 | 0-0 | 0-0 | 0-3 | 0-0 |
| Preston North End FC | 3-2 | 2-3 | 1-0 | 3-1 | 3-1 | 3-0 | 2-0 | 2-2 | 1-0 | 1-3 | 0-2 | 1-2 | 1-0 | 2-2 | 5-1 | | 2-3 | 4-2 | 2-0 | 1-2 | 2-0 | 0-0 |
| Sheffield United FC | 1-1 | 7-1 | 1-1 | 2-2 | 2-1 | 0-0 | 0-2 | 0-1 | 0-2 | 4-1 | 2-0 | 4-1 | 2-0 | 0-0 | 2-2 | 2-2 | | 2-0 | 3-1 | 2-1 | 2-0 | 3-1 |
| Stoke FC | 1-1 | 0-0 | 1-1 | 2-0 | 0-1 | 3-1 | 1-2 | 4-1 | 2-2 | 0-0 | 1-1 | 0-0 | 0-1 | 2-2 | 4-2 | 4-0 | | | 1-2 | 1-0 | 0-0 | 0-2 |
| Sunderland AFC | 2-0 | 5-3 | 4-3 | 5-1 | 3-1 | 2-1 | 0-0 | 3-1 | 1-1 | 1-1 | 2-0 | 2-0 | 0-0 | 2-2 | 3-5 | 2-0 | | 2-0 | | 3-3 | 2-0 | 3-2 |
| The Arsenal FC | 2-0 | 1-0 | 1-1 | 5-0 | 1-1 | 2-1 | 3-1 | 1-2 | 1-1 | 1-0 | 1-0 | 3-0 | 1-2 | 2-0 | 2-0 | 1-1 | 2-0 | 3-0 | 2-3 | | 0-2 | 3-1 |
| Tottenham Hotspur FC | 1-2 | 2-0 | 2-0 | 0-1 | 1-3 | 1-1 | 3-1 | 2-0 | 0-0 | 2-4 | 3-1 | 2-0 | 0-1 | 2-1 | 3-0 | 1-1 | 2-1 | 3-1 | 0-1 | 1-2 | | 3-1 |
| West Bromwich Albion FC | 3-0 | 1-0 | 3-0 | 1-1 | 2-1 | 3-0 | 0-0 | 0-0 | 0-2 | 0-0 | 2-0 | 2-1 | 0-0 | 1-0 | 2-2 | 4-0 | 0-1 | 1-1 | 7-0 | 5-1 | 3-1 | |

## Division 1

| | | Pd | Wn | Dw | Ls | GF | GA | Pts | |
|---|---|---|---|---|---|---|---|---|---|
| 1. | LIVERPOOL FC (LIVERPOOL) | 42 | 26 | 8 | 8 | 70 | 31 | 60 | |
| 2. | Sunderland AFC (Sunderland) | 42 | 22 | 10 | 10 | 72 | 54 | 54 | |
| 3. | Huddersfield Town AFC (Huddersfield) | 42 | 21 | 11 | 10 | 60 | 32 | 53 | |
| 4. | Newcastle United FC (Newcastle-upon-Tyne) | 42 | 18 | 12 | 12 | 45 | 37 | 48 | |
| 5. | Everton FC (Liverpool) | 42 | 20 | 7 | 15 | 63 | 59 | 47 | |
| 6. | Aston Villa FC (Birmingham) | 42 | 18 | 10 | 14 | 64 | 51 | 46 | |
| 7. | West Bromwich Albion FC (West Bromwich) | 42 | 17 | 11 | 14 | 58 | 49 | 45 | |
| 8. | Manchester City FC (Manchester) | 42 | 17 | 11 | 14 | 50 | 49 | 45 | |
| 9. | Cardiff City AFC (Cardiff) | 42 | 18 | 7 | 17 | 73 | 59 | 43 | |
| 10. | Sheffield United FC (Sheffield) | 42 | 16 | 10 | 16 | 68 | 64 | 42 | |
| 11. | The Arsenal FC (London) | 42 | 16 | 10 | 16 | 61 | 62 | 42 | |
| 12. | Tottenham Hotspur FC (London) | 42 | 17 | 7 | 18 | 50 | 50 | 41 | |
| 13. | Bolton Wanderers FC (Bolton) | 42 | 14 | 12 | 16 | 50 | 58 | 40 | |
| 14. | Blackburn Rovers FC (Blackburn) | 42 | 14 | 12 | 16 | 47 | 62 | 40 | |
| 15. | Burnley FC (Burnley) | 42 | 16 | 6 | 20 | 58 | 59 | 38 | |
| 16. | Preston North End FC (Preston) | 42 | 13 | 11 | 18 | 60 | 64 | 37 | |
| 17. | Birmingham FC (Birmingham) | 42 | 13 | 11 | 18 | 41 | 57 | 37 | |
| 18. | Middlesbrough FC (Middlesbrough) | 42 | 13 | 10 | 19 | 57 | 63 | 36 | |
| 19. | Chelsea FC (London) | 42 | 9 | 18 | 15 | 45 | 53 | 36 | |
| 20. | Nottingham Forest FC (Nottingham) | 42 | 13 | 8 | 21 | 41 | 70 | 34 | |
| 21. | Stoke FC (Stoke-on-Trent) | 42 | 10 | 10 | 22 | 47 | 67 | 30 | R |
| 22. | Oldham Athletic AFC (Oldham) | 42 | 10 | 10 | 22 | 35 | 65 | 30 | R |
| | | 924 | 351 | 222 | 351 | 1215 | 1215 | 924 | |

1) Charles BUCHAN (Sunderland AFC) 30

| Football League Division 2 1922-1923 Season | Barnsley | Blackpool | Bradford City | Bury | Clapton Orient | Coventry City | Crystal Palace | Derby County | Fulham | Hull City | Leeds United | Leicester City | Manchester United | Notts County | Port Vale | Rotherham County | Southampton | South Shields | Stockport County | Wednesday | West Ham United | Wolves |
|---|---|---|---|---|---|---|---|---|---|---|---|---|---|---|---|---|---|---|---|---|---|---|
| Barnsley FC | ■ | 2-2 | 3-1 | 2-1 | 2-1 | 6-2 | 1-2 | 5-0 | 0-1 | 1-0 | 1-0 | 0-1 | 2-2 | 1-0 | 0-1 | 2-2 | 3-0 | 5-0 | 1-1 | 2-4 | 2-0 | 1-0 |
| Blackpool FC | 0-1 | ■ | 3-0 | 5-1 | 0-0 | 0-1 | 4-0 | 3-2 | 3-0 | 0-0 | 1-0 | 1-2 | 1-0 | 1-1 | 0-2 | 1-0 | 1-2 | 3-0 | 0-0 | 3-0 | 4-1 | 3-1 |
| Bradford City AFC | 2-0 | 0-2 | ■ | 4-0 | 1-2 | 4-0 | 1-1 | 0-0 | 2-1 | 2-1 | 0-2 | 2-2 | 1-1 | 1-2 | 2-0 | 0-1 | 0-0 | 1-0 | 2-0 | 1-1 | 0-1 | 1-1 |
| Bury FC | 2-1 | 3-0 | 1-0 | ■ | 5-1 | 1-1 | 2-1 | 4-1 | 0-1 | 1-0 | 1-1 | 2-0 | 2-2 | 2-2 | 2-0 | 1-0 | 0-0 | 1-0 | 2-0 | 4-0 | 2-5 | 3-0 |
| Clapton Orient FC | 0-1 | 0-1 | 1-0 | 0-2 | ■ | 0-0 | 3-1 | 0-0 | 0-2 | 2-0 | 3-0 | 2-0 | 1-1 | 2-1 | 0-0 | 5-1 | 1-0 | 0-0 | 0-2 | 2-2 | 0-2 | 4-1 |
| Coventry City FC | 3-0 | 1-2 | 2-1 | 3-0 | 2-1 | ■ | 2-1 | 1-0 | 1-0 | 0-1 | 1-2 | 1-1 | 2-0 | 1-2 | 1-2 | 2-1 | 2-0 | 0-2 | 1-0 | 1-1 | 1-3 | 7-1 |
| Crystal Palace FC | 2-0 | 1-1 | 2-0 | 1-1 | 2-0 | 0-0 | ■ | 2-2 | 0-0 | 1-1 | 1-0 | 0-1 | 2-3 | 0-1 | 2-0 | 4-0 | 1-0 | 1-1 | 3-0 | 2-0 | 1-5 | 5-0 |
| Derby County FC | 0-1 | 1-0 | 0-2 | 1-0 | 0-0 | 4-0 | 6-0 | ■ | 2-0 | 0-2 | 0-1 | 2-0 | 1-1 | 0-0 | 1-2 | 1-0 | 0-2 | 1-0 | 1-2 | 1-1 | 2-1 | 1-1 |
| Fulham FC | 0-1 | 1-1 | 0-0 | 3-0 | 0-0 | 4-0 | 2-1 | 3-1 | ■ | 0-0 | 3-0 | 2-0 | 0-0 | 2-1 | 1-1 | 1-2 | 1-1 | 0-1 | 3-0 | 1-0 | 0-2 | 2-0 |
| Hull City AFC | 2-1 | 0-0 | 0-0 | 2-2 | 2-1 | 1-1 | 1-1 | 4-2 | 1-0 | ■ | 3-1 | 1-3 | 2-1 | 0-2 | 3-0 | 2-3 | 1-3 | 2-0 | 1-0 | 0-0 | 1-1 | 0-0 |
| Leeds United AFC | 1-1 | 1-1 | 1-0 | 0-0 | 0-0 | 1-0 | 4-1 | 1-0 | 1-1 | 2-2 | ■ | 0-0 | 0-1 | 3-0 | 2-1 | 2-0 | 1-0 | 0-1 | 2-0 | 0-0 | 3-1 | 1-0 |
| Leicester City FC | 2-2 | 1-2 | 2-0 | 2-0 | 2-0 | 2-1 | 3-0 | 0-1 | 1-1 | 0-1 | 2-1 | ■ | 0-1 | 2-1 | 3-0 | 3-0 | 2-1 | 3-0 | 2-0 | 3-1 | 0-6 | 7-0 |
| Manchester United FC | 1-0 | 2-1 | 1-1 | 0-1 | 0-0 | 2-1 | 2-1 | 0-0 | 1-1 | 3-2 | 0-0 | 0-2 | ■ | 1-1 | 1-2 | 3-0 | 1-2 | 3-0 | 1-0 | 1-0 | 1-2 | 1-0 |
| Notts County FC | 1-0 | 2-0 | 0-0 | 1-0 | 3-1 | 2-0 | 0-4 | 1-2 | 1-0 | 0-1 | 1-0 | 1-0 | 1-6 | ■ | 1-0 | 2-0 | 1-0 | 2-0 | 2-0 | 1-0 | 2-0 | 4-1 |
| Port Vale FC | 1-1 | 2-0 | 1-2 | 2-0 | 3-1 | 0-1 | 2-0 | 2-3 | 0-1 | 1-0 | 1-2 | 0-0 | 1-0 | 0-0 | ■ | 0-0 | 0-0 | 3-0 | 0-2 | 2-2 | 1-3 | 1-0 |
| Rotherham County FC | 1-1 | 1-0 | 0-2 | 0-0 | 0-0 | 2-0 | 4-1 | 3-0 | 1-3 | 0-1 | 3-1 | 0-0 | 1-1 | 1-0 | 3-1 | ■ | 0-0 | 2-1 | 2-1 | 1-2 | 2-2 | 3-2 |
| Southampton FC | 2-2 | 1-1 | 2-0 | 0-3 | 2-0 | 3-0 | 0-2 | 0-4 | 2-0 | 2-1 | 0-1 | 0-0 | 0-0 | 0-1 | 3-1 | 4-2 | ■ | 0-2 | 1-0 | 1-1 | 2-0 | 3-0 |
| South Shields FC | 2-0 | 1-0 | 0-0 | 0-2 | 3-0 | 0-0 | 2-0 | 3-1 | 2-0 | 0-0 | 0-2 | 2-1 | 0-3 | 1-0 | 3-1 | 2-0 | 0-0 | ■ | 3-0 | 1-1 | 0-0 | 1-1 |
| Stockport County FC | 3-1 | 2-2 | 1-0 | 1-0 | 0-2 | 5-1 | 2-2 | 2-1 | 0-2 | 1-1 | 2-1 | 4-5 | 1-0 | 0-0 | 0-2 | 1-0 | 3-0 | 1-1 | ■ | 0-1 | 2-1 | 1-1 |
| The Wednesday FC | 2-3 | 2-3 | 2-2 | 2-0 | 4-1 | 3-0 | 3-1 | 0-0 | 1-0 | 1-0 | 3-1 | 2-1 | 1-0 | 0-1 | 2-0 | 1-0 | 0-0 | 2-0 | 4-1 | ■ | 0-2 | 1-0 |
| West Ham United FC | 0-0 | 2-0 | 1-2 | 0-0 | 1-0 | 1-0 | 1-1 | 0-0 | 1-0 | 3-0 | 0-0 | 2-2 | 0-2 | 0-1 | 0-0 | 4-0 | 1-1 | 1-0 | 0-1 | 2-1 | ■ | 1-0 |
| Wolverhampton Wanderers FC | 3-3 | 3-4 | 4-1 | 1-1 | 1-3 | 1-2 | 1-0 | 0-1 | 0-0 | 3-0 | 0-1 | 1-2 | 0-1 | 1-0 | 3-0 | 3-2 | 0-0 | 1-0 | 3-1 | 2-0 | 1-4 | ■ |

| Division 2 | Pd | Wn | Dw | Ls | GF | GA | Pts | |
|---|---|---|---|---|---|---|---|---|
| 1. Notts County FC (Nottingham) | 42 | 23 | 7 | 12 | 46 | 34 | 53 | P |
| 2. West Ham United FC (London) | 42 | 20 | 11 | 11 | 63 | 38 | 51 | P |
| 3. Leicester City FC (Leicester) | 42 | 21 | 9 | 12 | 65 | 44 | 51 | |
| 4. Manchester United FC (Manchester) | 42 | 17 | 14 | 11 | 51 | 36 | 48 | |
| 5. Blackpool FC (Blackpool) | 42 | 18 | 11 | 13 | 60 | 43 | 47 | |
| 6. Bury FC (Bury) | 42 | 18 | 11 | 13 | 55 | 46 | 47 | |
| 7. Leeds United AFC (Leeds) | 42 | 18 | 11 | 13 | 43 | 36 | 47 | |
| 8. The Wednesday FC (Sheffield) | 42 | 17 | 12 | 13 | 54 | 47 | 46 | |
| 9. Barnsley FC (Barnsley) | 42 | 17 | 11 | 14 | 62 | 51 | 45 | |
| 10. Fulham FC (London) | 42 | 16 | 12 | 14 | 43 | 32 | 44 | |
| 11. Southampton FC (Southampton) | 42 | 14 | 14 | 14 | 40 | 40 | 42 | |
| 12. Hull City AFC (Kingston-upon-Hull) | 42 | 14 | 14 | 14 | 43 | 45 | 42 | |
| 13. South Shields FC (South Shields) | 42 | 15 | 10 | 17 | 35 | 44 | 40 | |
| 14. Derby County FC (Derby) | 42 | 14 | 11 | 17 | 46 | 50 | 39 | |
| 15. Bradford City AFC (Bradford) | 42 | 12 | 13 | 17 | 41 | 45 | 37 | |
| 16. Crystal Palace FC (London) | 42 | 13 | 11 | 18 | 54 | 62 | 37 | |
| 17. Port Vale FC (Stoke-on-Trent) | 42 | 14 | 9 | 19 | 39 | 51 | 37 | |
| 18. Coventry City FC (Coventry) | 42 | 15 | 7 | 20 | 46 | 63 | 37 | |
| 19. Clapton Orient FC (London) | 42 | 12 | 12 | 18 | 40 | 50 | 36 | |
| 20. Stockport County FC (Stockport) | 42 | 14 | 8 | 20 | 43 | 58 | 36 | |
| 21. Rotherham County FC (Rotherham) | 42 | 13 | 9 | 20 | 44 | 63 | 35 | R |
| 22. Wolverhampton Wanderers FC (Wolverhampton) | 42 | 9 | 9 | 24 | 42 | 77 | 27 | R |
| | 924 | 344 | 236 | 344 | 1055 | 1055 | 924 | |

| Football League Division 3 (N) 1922-1923 Season | Accrington Stanley | Ashington | Barrow | Bradford P.A. | Chesterfield | Crewe Alexandra | Darlington | Durham City | Grimsby Town | Halifax Town | Hartlepools United | Lincoln City | Nelson | Rochdale | Southport | Stalybridge Celtic | Tranmere Rovers | Walsall | Wigan Borough | Wrexham |
|---|---|---|---|---|---|---|---|---|---|---|---|---|---|---|---|---|---|---|---|---|
| Accrington Stanley FC | | 4-1 | 3-4 | 4-3 | 0-4 | 0-0 | 2-1 | 3-1 | 4-0 | 4-1 | 2-1 | 1-0 | 0-1 | 2-1 | 3-1 | 1-0 | 4-1 | 2-1 | 0-0 | 1-0 |
| Ashington FC | 2-5 | | 2-6 | 2-1 | 2-0 | 2-4 | 3-1 | 0-0 | 2-1 | 3-2 | 4-2 | 0-2 | 0-2 | 2-0 | 1-1 | 0-3 | 3-1 | 3-0 | 2-1 | 1-1 |
| Barrow AFC | 5-2 | 3-0 | | 1-2 | 3-1 | 2-0 | 0-1 | 2-1 | 2-0 | 0-1 | 0-0 | 1-3 | 1-0 | 4-1 | 2-0 | 0-1 | 2-1 | 0-0 | 2-3 | 1-0 |
| Bradford Park Avenue | 5-1 | 3-0 | 3-0 | | 1-0 | 3-0 | 2-1 | 4-1 | 2-1 | 2-2 | 1-1 | 4-1 | 6-2 | 3-0 | 5-1 | 1-0 | 3-0 | 2-2 | 1-1 | 0-1 |
| Chesterfield FC | 3-1 | 2-2 | 2-1 | 2-2 | | 2-1 | 0-0 | 3-1 | 3-2 | 3-0 | 1-1 | 3-3 | 1-2 | 4-0 | 3-0 | 1-0 | 5-0 | 6-0 | 3-1 | 2-1 |
| Crewe Alexandra FC | 1-1 | 3-1 | 1-0 | 0-1 | 2-0 | | 3-0 | 4-0 | 3-0 | 2-1 | 2-1 | 3-1 | 1-0 | 0-1 | 1-0 | 4-1 | 2-0 | 0-0 | 0-1 | 0-0 |
| Darlington FC | 4-0 | 1-1 | 3-2 | 2-0 | 4-1 | 5-0 | | 1-0 | 1-3 | 0-1 | 4-0 | 0-0 | 2-3 | 1-1 | 2-1 | 1-0 | 4-0 | 2-0 | 2-0 | 4-1 |
| Durham City FC | 4-1 | 1-1 | 4-1 | 0-0 | 1-1 | 2-0 | 0-0 | | 0-3 | 2-2 | 3-2 | 7-1 | 0-1 | 1-1 | 1-1 | 0-0 | 1-0 | 0-2 | 2-2 | 2-0 |
| Grimsby Town FC | 7-1 | 7-4 | 2-0 | 0-1 | 3-1 | 2-3 | 0-1 | 1-0 | | 0-1 | 1-0 | 1-0 | 0-2 | 1-1 | 2-1 | 3-0 | 0-0 | 1-2 | 0-0 | 4-0 |
| Halifax Town AFC | 0-0 | 0-0 | 3-0 | 3-0 | 2-0 | 1-0 | 2-1 | 1-3 | 1-0 | | 3-0 | 3-1 | 2-2 | 1-0 | 0-1 | 2-1 | 3-1 | 1-2 | 0-1 | 1-1 |
| Hartlepools United FC | 0-0 | 3-1 | 2-0 | 0-1 | 5-0 | 1-1 | 1-0 | 2-1 | 2-0 | 3-2 | | 2-0 | 5-1 | 0-2 | 1-1 | 4-0 | 0-1 | 2-2 | 0-0 | 1-1 |
| Lincoln City FC | 0-0 | 2-0 | 1-1 | 0-0 | 0-0 | 1-0 | 1-1 | 3-1 | 1-2 | 0-0 | 2-1 | | 1-0 | 0-1 | 2-0 | 1-1 | 2-0 | 0-2 | 2-1 | 2-0 |
| Nelson FC | 2-1 | 1-3 | 2-1 | 1-0 | 4-0 | 0-0 | 3-0 | 4-0 | 1-1 | 2-0 | 4-1 | 2-1 | | 1-2 | 2-0 | 1-0 | 1-0 | 3-0 | 1-0 | 2-0 |
| Rochdale AFC | 1-1 | 2-0 | 3-1 | 0-3 | 0-2 | 1-1 | 2-2 | 2-0 | 0-1 | 0-1 | 4-0 | 1-1 | 0-3 | | 3-2 | 2-0 | 0-0 | 0-2 | 3-2 | 5-0 |
| Southport FC | 1-2 | 1-0 | 2-0 | 0-0 | 0-2 | 2-0 | 2-1 | 1-0 | 3-1 | 1-3 | 1-0 | 3-0 | 0-1 | 0-1 | | 0-0 | 0-0 | 2-1 | 1-0 | 1-0 |
| Stalybridge Celtic FC | 1-0 | 2-1 | 2-0 | 1-0 | 1-2 | 0-1 | 4-2 | 1-0 | 3-2 | 4-3 | 1-1 | 0-1 | 2-0 | 0-0 | 1-0 | | 4-1 | 2-0 | 0-2 | 3-2 |
| Tranmere Rovers FC | 4-1 | 1-0 | 3-0 | 0-0 | 2-3 | 1-2 | 2-2 | 5-1 | 3-2 | 2-1 | 1-1 | 2-0 | 0-2 | 2-0 | 2-0 | 1-1 | | 2-3 | 4-2 | 4-0 |
| Walsall FC | 0-2 | 2-1 | 3-1 | 1-0 | 0-1 | 1-1 | 2-2 | 2-0 | 1-0 | 2-1 | 2-2 | 2-0 | 5-0 | 0-0 | 1-0 | 2-1 | 2-1 | | 3-1 | 1-0 |
| Wigan Borough FC | 2-0 | 6-1 | 2-1 | 3-2 | 1-0 | 1-1 | 3-0 | 0-2 | 1-0 | 0-1 | 2-0 | 9-1 | 3-1 | 6-0 | 1-0 | 3-0 | 0-0 | 1-0 | | 1-1 |
| Wrexham AFC | 2-0 | 0-0 | 0-0 | 3-0 | 3-1 | 2-1 | 0-0 | 1-0 | 1-1 | 2-1 | 2-0 | 0-2 | 2-1 | 3-1 | 1-1 | 2-1 | 2-1 | 1-0 | 2-1 | |

101

| | Division 3 (North) | Pd | Wn | Dw | Ls | GF | GA | Pts | |
|---|---|---|---|---|---|---|---|---|---|
| 1. | Nelson FC (Nelson) | 38 | 24 | 3 | 11 | 61 | 41 | 51 | P |
| 2. | Bradford Park Avenue FC (Bradford) | 38 | 19 | 9 | 10 | 67 | 38 | 47 | |
| 3. | Walsall FC (Walsall) | 38 | 19 | 8 | 11 | 51 | 44 | 46 | |
| 4. | Chesterfield FC (Chesterfield) | 38 | 19 | 7 | 12 | 68 | 52 | 45 | |
| 5. | Wigan Borough FC (Wigan) | 38 | 18 | 8 | 12 | 64 | 39 | 44 | |
| 6. | Crewe Alexandra FC (Crewe) | 38 | 17 | 9 | 12 | 48 | 38 | 43 | |
| 7. | Halifax Town AFC (Halifax) | 38 | 17 | 7 | 14 | 53 | 46 | 41 | |
| 8. | Accrington Stanley FC (Accrington) | 38 | 17 | 7 | 14 | 59 | 65 | 41 | |
| 9. | Darlington FC (Darlington) | 38 | 15 | 10 | 13 | 59 | 46 | 40 | |
| 10. | Wrexham AFC (Wrexham) | 38 | 14 | 10 | 14 | 38 | 48 | 38 | |
| 11. | Stalybridge Celtic FC (Stalybridge) | 38 | 15 | 6 | 17 | 42 | 47 | 36 | # |
| 12. | Rochdale AFC (Rochdale) | 38 | 13 | 10 | 15 | 42 | 53 | 36 | |
| 13. | Lincoln City FC (Lincoln) | 38 | 13 | 10 | 15 | 39 | 55 | 36 | |
| 14. | Grimsby Town FC (Cleethorpes) | 38 | 14 | 5 | 19 | 55 | 52 | 33 | |
| 15. | Hartlepools United FC (Hartlepool) | 38 | 10 | 12 | 16 | 48 | 54 | 32 | |
| 16. | Tranmere Rovers FC (Birkenhead) | 38 | 12 | 8 | 18 | 49 | 59 | 32 | |
| 17. | Southport FC (Southport) | 38 | 12 | 7 | 19 | 32 | 46 | 31 | |
| 18. | Barrow AFC (Barrow-in-Furness) | 38 | 13 | 4 | 21 | 50 | 60 | 30 | |
| 19. | Ashington FC (Ashington) | 38 | 11 | 8 | 19 | 51 | 77 | 30 | |
| 20. | Durham City FC (Durham) | 38 | 9 | 10 | 19 | 43 | 59 | 28 | |
| | | 760 | 301 | 158 | 301 | 1019 | 1019 | 760 | |

# Stalybridge Celtic FC (Stalybridge) resigned from the league at the end of the season.

Elected: Doncaster Rovers FC (Doncaster) and New Brighton FC (Wallasey)

Division 3 (North) was extended to 22 clubs for next season

## Football League Division 3 (S) 1922-1923 Season

| | Aberdare Athletic | Brentford | Brighton | Bristol City | Bristol Rovers | Charlton Athletic | Exeter City | Gillingham | Luton Town | Merthyr Town | Millwall Athletic | Newport County | Northampton | Norwich City | Plymouth Argyle | Portsmouth | Q.P.R. | Reading | Southend United | Swansea Town | Swindon Town | Watford |
|---|---|---|---|---|---|---|---|---|---|---|---|---|---|---|---|---|---|---|---|---|---|---|
| Aberdare Athletic FC | ▓ | 0-0 | 0-1 | 0-1 | 0-0 | 3-1 | 3-1 | 2-0 | 2-1 | 0-0 | 0-1 | 6-2 | 0-2 | 0-3 | 2-2 | 0-2 | 0-0 | 0-0 | 1-1 | 0-1 | 3-3 | 3-1 |
| Brentford FC | 0-1 | ▓ | 1-2 | 4-0 | 0-1 | 0-3 | 0-1 | 2-0 | 3-2 | 3-1 | 1-1 | 0-0 | 2-1 | 1-4 | 2-0 | 1-0 | 1-3 | 1-1 | 0-0 | 0-1 | 3-0 | 2-1 |
| Brighton & Hove Albion | 3-1 | 2-1 | ▓ | 2-1 | 2-1 | 1-0 | 3-0 | 3-0 | 0-1 | 0-0 | 2-0 | 2-1 | 1-0 | 0-0 | 1-0 | 7-1 | 2-0 | 3-1 | 0-1 | 1-3 | 1-1 | 3-0 |
| Bristol City FC | 0-0 | 1-1 | 3-1 | ▓ | 0-1 | 3-1 | 1-1 | 2-1 | 1-0 | 3-0 | 1-1 | 2-0 | 1-0 | 4-0 | 2-0 | 2-1 | 3-2 | 2-1 | 5-0 | 1-0 | 3-1 | 3-1 |
| Bristol Rovers FC | 1-0 | 1-1 | 0-0 | 1-2 | ▓ | 1-1 | 3-3 | 1-0 | 1-1 | 3-0 | 0-0 | 3-1 | 0-0 | 3-2 | 0-1 | 0-1 | 1-3 | 1-1 | 2-0 | 0-0 | 2-0 | 1-2 |
| Charlton Athletic FC | 1-1 | 1-1 | 0-1 | 1-0 | 0-0 | ▓ | 0-0 | 3-1 | 2-1 | 0-1 | 0-2 | 6-0 | 2-0 | 3-0 | 1-0 | 0-2 | 1-1 | 1-0 | 5-1 | 3-1 | 3-1 | 0-0 |
| Exeter City FC | 1-0 | 0-2 | 1-0 | 0-0 | 0-0 | 0-0 | ▓ | 0-1 | 1-2 | 2-1 | 2-1 | 4-0 | 1-2 | 2-0 | 0-0 | 2-3 | 1-2 | 4-0 | 2-1 | 1-0 | 2-1 | 1-2 |
| Gillingham FC | 4-0 | 2-0 | 2-0 | 1-1 | 0-1 | 2-2 | 2-1 | ▓ | 1-0 | 2-0 | 3-0 | 3-0 | 0-3 | 5-0 | 1-0 | 4-2 | 0-1 | 2-1 | 1-0 | 2-2 | 0-0 | 1-4 |
| Luton Town FC | 4-1 | 4-0 | 1-1 | 1-1 | 1-0 | 2-2 | 6-0 | 2-0 | ▓ | 2-1 | 2-2 | 1-0 | 2-1 | 4-0 | 2-1 | 0-2 | 1-0 | 1-2 | 2-0 | 6-1 | 3-2 | 0-1 |
| Merthyr Town FC | 0-2 | 1-0 | 2-0 | 0-1 | 1-1 | 3-0 | 3-1 | 1-0 | 0-1 | ▓ | 1-1 | 1-0 | 3-0 | 0-1 | 0-1 | 3-0 | 0-1 | 1-1 | 2-1 | 2-1 | 1-1 | 2-3 |
| Millwall Athletic FC | 1-0 | 1-1 | 2-1 | 1-1 | 1-0 | 1-1 | 3-0 | 3-1 | 0-0 | 1-0 | ▓ | 0-0 | 2-0 | 3-0 | 0-0 | 1-3 | 0-0 | 0-0 | 1-1 | 0-2 | 1-1 | 5-1 |
| Newport County AFC | 0-0 | 0-1 | 1-0 | 0-1 | 4-1 | 4-0 | 6-2 | 2-1 | 0-3 | 1-1 | 0-0 | ▓ | 1-1 | 1-3 | 1-0 | 0-0 | 1-0 | 3-0 | 0-2 | 1-2 | 2-2 | 0-1 |
| Northampton Town FC | 3-1 | 1-1 | 0-0 | 2-1 | 1-0 | 0-0 | 3-0 | 1-0 | 2-0 | 1-1 | 2-1 | 2-1 | ▓ | 1-1 | 1-0 | 3-0 | 4-2 | 5-0 | 5-2 | 1-3 | 1-2 | 1-1 |
| Norwich City FC | 1-4 | 0-2 | 1-0 | 2-2 | 0-0 | 2-3 | 6-0 | 1-1 | 1-2 | 1-1 | 3-2 | 1-1 | 1-0 | ▓ | 1-0 | 0-2 | 1-1 | 2-0 | 2-1 | 1-4 | 0-0 | 2-0 |
| Plymouth Argyle FC | 2-0 | 3-0 | 2-2 | 5-1 | 3-0 | 2-0 | 5-1 | 2-0 | 4-0 | 2-0 | 1-0 | 1-0 | 1-0 | 1-1 | ▓ | 2-0 | 2-0 | 3-0 | 1-1 | 2-0 | 2-0 | 1-0 |
| Portsmouth FC | 1-0 | 3-0 | 1-2 | 1-2 | 0-0 | 3-0 | 3-4 | 6-1 | 1-2 | 1-1 | 2-0 | 2-0 | 0-0 | 2-1 | 1-2 | ▓ | 1-1 | 1-0 | 0-0 | 0-3 | 4-1 | 1-0 |
| Queen's Park Rangers | 4-1 | 1-1 | 0-0 | 1-2 | 3-1 | 1-2 | 2-0 | 2-1 | 4-0 | 1-1 | 2-3 | 1-1 | 3-2 | 2-0 | 2-3 | 0-1 | ▓ | 1-0 | 1-0 | 2-1 | 0-2 | 1-2 |
| Reading FC | 1-0 | 1-1 | 0-0 | 0-0 | 0-1 | 2-1 | 1-3 | 1-1 | 3-0 | 1-0 | 1-2 | 2-0 | 0-0 | 4-1 | 0-1 | 0-0 | 0-0 | ▓ | 1-1 | 4-4 | 1-0 | 1-0 |
| Southend United FC | 4-0 | 1-2 | 0-0 | 0-3 | 0-0 | 0-0 | 5-0 | 1-1 | 1-3 | 1-0 | 4-0 | 3-1 | 3-1 | 2-1 | 0-0 | 2-0 | 3-1 |  | ▓ | 0-1 | 2-0 | 2-1 |
| Swansea Town AFC | 5-1 | 0-0 | 0-0 | 4-1 | 0-1 | 3-2 | 5-1 | 1-0 | 1-0 | 1-1 | 0-1 | 5-1 | 4-0 | 3-1 | 1-1 | 2-1 | 3-0 | 2-2 | 1-0 | ▓ | 5-0 | 0-0 |
| Swindon Town FC | 5-4 | 3-0 | 3-0 | 0-1 | 1-0 | 2-1 | 2-1 | 0-1 | 1-1 | 4-0 | 0-0 | 2-2 | 2-0 | 1-2 | 2-1 | 3-0 | 1-0 | 3-1 | 3-0 | 2-1 | ▓ | 1-1 |
| Watford FC | 6-0 | 2-0 | 1-2 | 1-1 | 0-1 | 2-2 | 4-0 | 5-2 | 2-1 | 1-1 | 0-0 | 2-1 | 0-0 | 2-1 | 1-0 | 2-3 | 0-3 | 1-0 | 1-1 | 2-1 | 0-3 | ▓ |

### Division 3 (South)

| | | Pd | Wn | Dw | Ls | GF | GA | Pts | |
|---|---|---|---|---|---|---|---|---|---|
| 1. | Bristol City FC (Bristol) | 42 | 24 | 11 | 7 | 66 | 40 | 59 | P |
| 2. | Plymouth Argyle FC (Plymouth) | 42 | 23 | 7 | 12 | 61 | 29 | 53 | |
| 3. | Swansea Town AFC (Swansea) | 42 | 22 | 9 | 11 | 78 | 45 | 53 | |
| 4. | Brighton & Hove Albion FC (Brighton) | 42 | 20 | 11 | 11 | 52 | 34 | 51 | |
| 5. | Luton Town FC (Luton) | 42 | 21 | 7 | 14 | 68 | 49 | 49 | |
| 6. | Portsmouth FC (Portsmouth) | 42 | 19 | 8 | 15 | 58 | 52 | 46 | |
| 7. | Millwall Athletic FC (London) | 42 | 14 | 18 | 10 | 45 | 40 | 46 | |
| 8. | Northampton Town FC (Northampton) | 42 | 17 | 11 | 14 | 54 | 44 | 45 | |
| 9. | Swindon Town FC (Swindon) | 42 | 17 | 11 | 14 | 62 | 56 | 45 | |
| 10. | Watford FC (Watford) | 42 | 17 | 10 | 15 | 57 | 54 | 44 | |
| 11. | Queen's Park Rangers FC (London) | 42 | 16 | 10 | 16 | 54 | 49 | 42 | |
| 12. | Charlton Athletic FC (London) | 42 | 14 | 14 | 14 | 55 | 51 | 42 | |
| 13. | Bristol Rovers FC (Bristol) | 42 | 13 | 16 | 13 | 35 | 36 | 42 | |
| 14. | Brentford FC (London) | 42 | 13 | 12 | 17 | 41 | 51 | 38 | |
| 15. | Southend United FC (Southend-on-Sea) | 42 | 12 | 13 | 17 | 49 | 54 | 37 | |
| 16. | Gillingham FC (Gillingham) | 42 | 15 | 7 | 20 | 51 | 59 | 37 | |
| 17. | Merthyr Town FC (Merthyr Tydfil) | 42 | 11 | 14 | 17 | 39 | 48 | 36 | |
| 18. | Norwich City FC (Norwich) | 42 | 13 | 10 | 19 | 51 | 71 | 36 | |
| 19. | Reading FC (Reading) | 42 | 10 | 14 | 18 | 36 | 55 | 34 | |
| 20. | Exeter City FC (Exeter) | 42 | 13 | 7 | 22 | 47 | 84 | 33 | |
| 21. | Aberdare Athletic FC (Aberdare) | 42 | 9 | 11 | 22 | 42 | 70 | 29 | |
| 22. | Newport County AFC (Newport) | 42 | 8 | 11 | 23 | 40 | 70 | 27 | |
| | | 924 | 341 | 242 | 341 | 1141 | 1141 | 924 | |

## F.A. CUP FINAL  (Wembley Stadium, London – 28/04/1923 – 126,047)

| BOLTON WANDERERS FC (BOLTON) | 2-0 | West Ham United FC (London) |

*Jack, JR Smith*

Bolton: Pym, Haworth, Finney, Nuttall, Seddon, Jennings, Butler, Jack, JR Smith, J.Smith, Vizard.

West Ham: Hufton, Henderson, Young, Bishop, Kay, Tresadern, Richards, Brown, V.Watson, Moore, Ruffell.

## Semi-finals

| Bolton Wanderers FC (Bolton) | 1-0 | Sheffield United FC (Sheffield) |
| West Ham United FC (London) | 5-2 | Derby County FC (Derby) |

## Quarter-finals

| Charlton Athletic FC (London) | 0-1 | Bolton Wanderers FC (Bolton) |
| Queen's Park Rangers FC (London) | 0-1 | Sheffield United FC (Sheffield) |
| Southampton FC (Southampton) | 1-1, 1-1, 0-1 | West Ham United FC (London) |
| Tottenham Hotspur FC (London) | 0-1 | Derby County FC (Derby) |

# 1923-24

| Football League Division 1 1923-1924 Season | Aston Villa | Birmingham | Blackburn Rovers | Bolton Wanderers | Burnley | Cardiff City | Chelsea | Everton | Huddersfield Town | Liverpool | Manchester City | Middlesbrough | Newcastle United | Nottingham Forest | Notts County | Preston North End | Sheffield United | Sunderland | The Arsenal | Tottenham Hotspur | W.B.A. | West Ham United |
|---|---|---|---|---|---|---|---|---|---|---|---|---|---|---|---|---|---|---|---|---|---|---|
| Aston Villa FC | | 0-0 | 1-0 | 1-0 | 1-1 | 2-1 | 0-0 | 1-1 | 3-1 | 0-0 | 2-0 | 0-0 | 6-1 | 2-0 | 0-0 | 5-1 | 2-2 | 0-1 | 2-1 | 0-0 | 4-0 | 1-1 |
| Birmingham FC | 3-0 | | 1-1 | 0-3 | 2-1 | 0-0 | 1-0 | 0-1 | 0-1 | 2-1 | 3-0 | 2-1 | 4-1 | 0-2 | 0-0 | 2-0 | 0-1 | 0-2 | 0-2 | 3-2 | 0-0 | 2-0 |
| Blackburn Rovers FC | 3-1 | 4-1 | | 3-1 | 1-1 | 2-1 | 3-0 | 2-0 | 1-0 | 0-0 | 0-1 | 2-0 | 2-1 | 1-1 | 4-1 | 2-0 | 1-1 | 3-2 | 2-0 | 0-1 | 4-0 | 0-0 |
| Bolton Wanderers FC | 1-0 | 1-1 | 3-0 | | 0-0 | 2-2 | 4-0 | 2-0 | 3-1 | 4-1 | 0-0 | 2-0 | 0-1 | 4-0 | 7-1 | 0-0 | 4-2 | 1-0 | 1-2 | 3-1 | 2-0 | 1-1 |
| Burnley FC | 1-2 | 1-2 | 1-2 | 1-0 | | 1-2 | 2-0 | 2-2 | 1-1 | 2-0 | 3-2 | 0-0 | 3-2 | 2-4 | 1-1 | 1-0 | 2-0 | 0-3 | 4-1 | 2-2 | 4-0 | 5-1 |
| Cardiff City AFC | 0-2 | 2-0 | 2-0 | 3-2 | 2-0 | | 1-1 | 0-0 | 0-0 | 2-0 | 1-1 | 1-0 | 1-0 | 4-1 | 0-2 | 1-1 | 3-1 | 2-1 | 4-0 | 2-1 | 3-0 | 1-0 |
| Chelsea FC | 0-0 | 1-1 | 2-0 | 0-0 | 3-2 | 1-2 | | 1-1 | 0-1 | 2-1 | 3-1 | 2-0 | 1-0 | 1-1 | 0-6 | 1-2 | 1-1 | 4-1 | 0-0 | 0-1 | 0-0 | 0-0 |
| Everton FC | 2-0 | 2-0 | 0-0 | 2-2 | 3-3 | 0-0 | 2-0 | | 1-1 | 1-0 | 6-1 | 1-0 | 2-2 | 2-1 | 3-0 | 1-1 | 2-0 | 2-3 | 3-1 | 4-2 | 2-0 | 2-1 |
| Huddersfield Town AFC | 1-0 | 1-0 | 1-0 | 1-0 | 1-0 | 2-0 | 0-1 | 2-0 | | 3-1 | 1-1 | 1-0 | 1-1 | 3-0 | 0-0 | 4-0 | 1-0 | 3-2 | 6-1 | 2-1 | 0-0 | 1-1 |
| Liverpool FC | 0-1 | 6-2 | 0-0 | 3-1 | 1-0 | 0-2 | 3-1 | 1-2 | 1-1 | | 0-0 | 3-1 | 0-1 | 4-2 | 1-0 | 3-1 | 2-3 | 4-2 | 0-0 | 1-0 | 0-0 | 2-0 |
| Manchester City FC | 1-2 | 1-0 | 3-1 | 1-1 | 2-2 | 1-1 | 1-0 | 2-1 | 1-1 | 0-1 | | 3-2 | 1-1 | 1-3 | 1-0 | 2-2 | 2-1 | 4-1 | 1-0 | 1-0 | 3-3 | 3-1 |
| Middlesbrough FC | 0-2 | 0-1 | 2-0 | 1-2 | 3-0 | 0-1 | 2-0 | 1-1 | 2-0 | 1-1 | 1-1 | | 1-0 | 5-2 | 2-3 | 1-2 | 0-1 | 1-3 | 0-0 | 0-1 | 0-1 | 0-1 |
| Newcastle United FC | 4-1 | 2-1 | 2-1 | 1-0 | 2-0 | 1-1 | 2-1 | 3-1 | 0-1 | 2-1 | 4-1 | 3-2 | | 4-0 | 1-2 | 3-1 | 2-2 | 0-2 | 1-0 | 2-2 | 1-1 | 1-1 |
| Nottingham Forest FC | 0-0 | 1-1 | 0-0 | 1-0 | 0-0 | 0-1 | 2-0 | 1-0 | 0-1 | 1-2 | 3-1 | 0-0 | | | 1-0 | 1-1 | 1-2 | 1-2 | 2-1 | 0-0 | 1-1 | 2-1 |
| Notts County FC | 0-1 | 1-1 | 3-0 | 1-1 | 2-1 | 1-0 | 0-0 | 1-1 | 1-0 | 1-2 | 2-0 | 1-0 | 1-0 | 2-1 | | 0-0 | 0-2 | 1-2 | 1-2 | 0-0 | 1-0 | 1-1 |
| Preston North End FC | 2-2 | 1-0 | 0-1 | 0-2 | 5-0 | 3-1 | 1-1 | 0-1 | 1-3 | 0-1 | 4-1 | 4-0 | 1-2 | 3-1 | 2-1 | | 1-1 | 1-2 | 0-2 | 2-2 | 1-2 | 2-1 |
| Sheffield United FC | 2-1 | 0-2 | 4-0 | 0-0 | 2-1 | 1-1 | 1-0 | 4-0 | 0-1 | 1-1 | 3-0 | 0-1 | 2-1 | 0-0 | 3-1 | 4-0 | | 1-1 | 3-1 | 6-2 | 2-0 | 0-0 |
| Sunderland AFC | 2-0 | 1-1 | 5-1 | 2-2 | 0-1 | 0-3 | 2-0 | 3-0 | 2-1 | 0-0 | 5-2 | 3-2 | 3-2 | 1-0 | 1-1 | 2-1 | 2-2 | | 1-1 | 1-0 | 2-0 | 0-0 |
| The Arsenal FC | 0-1 | 0-0 | 2-2 | 0-0 | 2-0 | 1-2 | 1-0 | 0-1 | 1-3 | 3-1 | 1-2 | 2-1 | 1-4 | 1-0 | 0-0 | 1-2 | 1-3 | 2-0 | | 1-1 | 1-0 | 4-1 |
| Tottenham Hotspur FC | 2-3 | 1-1 | 2-1 | 0-0 | 1-0 | 1-1 | 0-1 | 2-5 | 1-1 | 1-1 | 4-1 | 2-1 | 2-0 | 3-0 | 1-3 | 2-0 | 1-1 | 1-1 | 3-0 | | 0-0 | 0-1 |
| West Bromwich Albion FC | 1-0 | 0-0 | 3-3 | 0-5 | 0-3 | 2-4 | 2-2 | 5-0 | 2-4 | 2-0 | 2-1 | 1-1 | 0-0 | 3-2 | 5-0 | 1-2 | 3-1 | 3-1 | 4-0 | 4-1 | | 0-0 |
| West Ham United FC | 1-0 | 4-1 | 0-1 | 0-1 | 0-0 | 0-0 | 2-0 | 2-1 | 2-3 | 1-0 | 1-2 | 1-1 | 1-0 | 3-2 | 1-1 | 3-1 | 2-2 | 0-1 | 1-0 | 0-0 | 1-0 | |

| | Division 1 | Pd | Wn | Dw | Ls | GF | GA | Pts | |
|----|----------------------------------------------|-----|-----|-----|-----|------|------|-----|---|
| 1. | HUDDERSFIELD TOWN AFC (HUDDERSFIELD) | 42 | 23 | 11 | 8 | 60 | 33 | 57 | |
| 2. | Cardiff City AFC (Cardiff) | 42 | 22 | 13 | 7 | 61 | 34 | 57 | |
| 3. | Sunderland AFC (Sunderland) | 42 | 22 | 9 | 11 | 71 | 54 | 53 | |
| 4. | Bolton Wanderers FC (Bolton) | 42 | 18 | 14 | 10 | 68 | 34 | 50 | |
| 5. | Sheffield United FC (Sheffield) | 42 | 19 | 12 | 11 | 69 | 49 | 50 | |
| 6. | Aston Villa FC (Birmingham) | 42 | 18 | 13 | 11 | 52 | 37 | 49 | |
| 7. | Everton FC (Liverpool) | 42 | 18 | 13 | 11 | 62 | 53 | 49 | |
| 8. | Blackburn Rovers FC (Blackburn) | 42 | 17 | 11 | 14 | 54 | 50 | 45 | |
| 9. | Newcastle United FC (Newcastle-upon-Tyne) | 42 | 17 | 10 | 15 | 60 | 54 | 44 | |
| 10. | Notts County FC (Nottingham) | 42 | 14 | 14 | 14 | 44 | 49 | 42 | |
| 11. | Manchester City FC (Manchester) | 42 | 15 | 12 | 15 | 54 | 71 | 42 | |
| 12. | Liverpool FC (Liverpool) | 42 | 15 | 11 | 16 | 49 | 48 | 41 | |
| 13. | West Ham United FC (London) | 42 | 13 | 15 | 14 | 40 | 43 | 41 | |
| 14. | Birmingham FC (Birmingham) | 42 | 13 | 13 | 16 | 41 | 49 | 39 | |
| 15. | Tottenham Hotspur FC (London) | 42 | 12 | 14 | 16 | 50 | 56 | 38 | |
| 16. | West Bromwich Albion FC (West Bromwich) | 42 | 12 | 14 | 16 | 51 | 62 | 38 | |
| 17. | Burnley FC (Burnley) | 42 | 12 | 12 | 18 | 55 | 60 | 36 | |
| 18. | Preston North End FC (Preston) | 42 | 12 | 10 | 20 | 52 | 67 | 34 | |
| 19. | The Arsenal FC (London) | 42 | 12 | 9 | 21 | 40 | 63 | 33 | |
| 20. | Nottingham Forest FC (Nottingham) | 42 | 10 | 12 | 20 | 42 | 64 | 32 | |
| 21. | Chelsea FC (London) | 42 | 9 | 14 | 19 | 31 | 53 | 32 | R |
| 22. | Middlesbrough FC (Middlesbrough) | 42 | 7 | 8 | 27 | 37 | 60 | 22 | R |
| | | 924 | 330 | 264 | 330 | 1143 | 1143 | 924 | |

## Top Goalscorer

| | | | |
|----|-------------|--------------|----|
| 1) | W. CHADWICK | (Everton FC) | 28 |

| Football League Division 2 1923-1924 Season | Barnsley | Blackpool | Bradford City | Bristol City | Bury | Clapton Orient | Coventry City | Crystal Palace | Derby County | Fulham | Hull City | Leeds United | Leicester City | Man. United | Nelson | Oldham Ath. | Port Vale | Southampton | South Shields | Stockport Co. | Stoke | Wednesday |
|---|---|---|---|---|---|---|---|---|---|---|---|---|---|---|---|---|---|---|---|---|---|---|
| Barnsley FC | ■ | 3-1 | 2-1 | 3-1 | 2-0 | 1-0 | 1-1 | 5-2 | 1-3 | 2-1 | 0-0 | 1-3 | 3-1 | 1-0 | 0-0 | 4-1 | 3-0 | 1-1 | 1-0 | 0-0 | 0-0 | 0-0 |
| Blackpool FC | 0-2 | ■ | 2-1 | 2-0 | 3-1 | 3-0 | 5-0 | 2-0 | 4-0 | 3-0 | 0-0 | 1-1 | 3-1 | 1-0 | 1-1 | 2-2 | 6-1 | 2-0 | 1-1 | 0-0 | 1-1 | 1-0 |
| Bradford City AFC | 3-2 | 0-2 | ■ | 1-1 | 2-2 | 0-0 | 0-0 | 0-1 | 1-2 | 1-0 | 2-1 | 0-0 | 2-2 | 0-0 | 0-2 | 2-1 | 2-0 | 2-1 | 0-1 | 0-1 | 2-1 | 4-1 |
| Bristol City FC | 1-1 | 1-1 | 0-1 | ■ | 4-1 | 0-2 | 2-2 | 0-0 | 0-8 | 0-1 | 1-0 | 0-1 | 0-1 | 1-2 | 1-0 | 0-0 | 0-0 | 1-1 | 1-0 | 3-0 | 1-1 | 2-3 |
| Bury FC | 1-1 | 2-0 | 3-0 | 6-0 | ■ | 0-0 | 5-0 | 1-1 | 1-0 | 2-1 | 1-0 | 3-0 | 2-0 | 2-0 | 2-0 | 2-2 | 0-0 | 1-0 | 0-1 | 2-1 | 1-0 | 5-0 |
| Clapton Orient FC | 2-1 | 1-0 | 1-1 | 2-0 | 1-0 | ■ | 4-0 | 1-0 | 2-0 | 0-0 | 0-1 | 1-0 | 1-0 | 5-1 | 1-2 | 1-1 | 0-0 | 3-0 | 1-1 | 0-2 | 0-0 | |
| Coventry City FC | 2-3 | 3-1 | 1-0 | 1-1 | 1-0 | 1-1 | ■ | 0-0 | 0-1 | 3-0 | 0-2 | 2-1 | 2-4 | 1-1 | 4-0 | 5-2 | 1-3 | 0-0 | 1-0 | 0-0 | 1-2 | 5-1 |
| Crystal Palace FC | 3-1 | 3-1 | 3-0 | 1-0 | 1-0 | 2-1 | 3-1 | ■ | 0-1 | 1-1 | 0-0 | 1-1 | 4-3 | 1-1 | 1-1 | 2-3 | 1-2 | 0-0 | 1-0 | 1-1 | 5-1 | 3-0 |
| Derby County FC | 2-1 | 2-0 | 0-0 | 2-3 | 0-2 | 1-0 | 1-0 | 5-0 | ■ | 3-3 | 4-1 | 2-0 | 4-0 | 3-0 | 6-0 | 2-1 | 2-0 | 1-0 | 6-1 | 4-1 | 1-1 | 1-1 |
| Fulham FC | 3-0 | 2-3 | 1-1 | 1-1 | 0-2 | 0-0 | 1-1 | 1-0 | 3-2 | ■ | 1-1 | 0-2 | 1-0 | 3-1 | 0-0 | 0-0 | 0-0 | 3-2 | 2-3 | 1-0 | 3-0 | 4-1 |
| Hull City AFC | 1-2 | 2-1 | 2-0 | 5-0 | 0-1 | 2-2 | 3-2 | 2-2 | 0-1 | 4-2 | ■ | 1-2 | 1-1 | 1-1 | 2-1 | 0-0 | 1-2 | 0-0 | 1-0 | 1-2 | 2-0 | 1-1 |
| Leeds United AFC | 3-1 | 0-0 | 1-0 | 0-0 | 1-2 | 1-0 | 3-1 | 3-0 | 1-1 | 3-0 | 5-2 | ■ | 1-2 | 0-0 | 1-0 | 5-0 | 3-0 | 3-0 | 2-1 | 4-0 | 0-0 | 1-0 |
| Leicester City FC | 2-0 | 1-2 | 0-1 | 5-1 | 3-0 | 1-2 | 2-0 | 1-0 | 3-0 | 2-1 | 1-1 | 2-0 | ■ | 2-2 | 3-1 | 1-1 | 2-0 | 0-1 | 4-1 | 1-1 | 5-0 | 2-1 |
| Manchester United FC | 1-2 | 0-0 | 3-0 | 2-1 | 0-1 | 2-2 | 1-2 | 5-1 | 0-0 | 0-0 | 1-1 | 3-1 | 3-0 | ■ | 0-1 | 2-0 | 5-0 | 1-0 | 1-1 | 3-0 | 2-2 | 2-0 |
| Nelson FC | 4-3 | 2-3 | 1-1 | 2-1 | 0-5 | 1-1 | 3-0 | 4-2 | 2-1 | 1-1 | 1-1 | 3-1 | 1-1 | 0-2 | ■ | 2-1 | 1-3 | 0-0 | 0-2 | 1-1 | 2-0 | 1-1 |
| Oldham Athletic AFC | 1-1 | 1-1 | 0-0 | 0-0 | 0-0 | 1-0 | 1-1 | 1-0 | 2-0 | 2-1 | 0-0 | 2-2 | 0-0 | 3-2 | 1-0 | ■ | 2-0 | 1-3 | 1-0 | 3-1 | 0-0 | 2-0 |
| Port Vale FC | 4-1 | 2-6 | 2-2 | 0-2 | 2-1 | 1-0 | 1-1 | 3-4 | 2-0 | 3-1 | 2-2 | 0-1 | 2-1 | 0-1 | 0-0 | 3-0 | ■ | 1-0 | 1-1 | 0-1 | 2-4 | 2-1 |
| Southampton FC | 6-0 | 3-2 | 2-0 | 1-0 | 3-0 | 5-0 | 1-3 | 1-0 | 0-0 | 1-0 | 2-0 | 0-1 | 1-0 | 0-0 | 3-0 | 3-1 | 1-1 | ■ | 0-0 | 0-0 | 0-1 | 3-0 |
| South Shields FC | 2-0 | 1-0 | 0-0 | 1-1 | 1-0 | 1-1 | 4-2 | 2-0 | 3-2 | 1-0 | 0-1 | 3-0 | 1-2 | 1-0 | 3-0 | 2-0 | 3-3 | 1-2 | ■ | 3-1 | 1-0 | 1-1 |
| Stockport County FC | 1-1 | 2-1 | 1-2 | 0-0 | 3-2 | 2-0 | 0-0 | 2-2 | 0-0 | 2-1 | 5-1 | 1-1 | 3-1 | 3-2 | 1-0 | 0-1 | 0-0 | 2-3 | 3-2 | ■ | 0-1 | 1-0 |
| Stoke FC | 2-0 | 2-2 | 2-0 | 3-0 | 0-0 | 0-1 | 2-1 | 1-1 | 1-1 | 0-0 | 1-0 | 1-1 | 1-0 | 3-0 | 4-0 | 1-1 | 1-0 | 1-1 | 0-0 | 0-0 | ■ | 1-1 |
| The Wednesday FC | 1-0 | 2-2 | 0-0 | 1-0 | 1-1 | 1-0 | 2-0 | 6-0 | 1-0 | 2-1 | 1-0 | 0-0 | 2-1 | 2-0 | 5-0 | 1-2 | 2-1 | 1-1 | 5-0 | 3-0 | 3-0 | ■ |

| | Division 2 | Pd | Wn | Dw | Ls | GF | GA | Pts | |
|---|---|---|---|---|---|---|---|---|---|
| 1. | Leeds United AFC (Leeds) | 42 | 21 | 12 | 9 | 61 | 35 | 54 | P |
| 2. | Bury FC (Bury) | 42 | 21 | 9 | 12 | 63 | 35 | 51 | P |
| 3. | Derby County FC (Derby) | 42 | 21 | 9 | 12 | 75 | 42 | 51 | |
| 4. | Blackpool FC (Blackpool) | 42 | 18 | 13 | 11 | 72 | 47 | 49 | |
| 5. | Southampton FC (Southampton) | 42 | 17 | 14 | 11 | 52 | 31 | 48 | |
| 6. | Stoke FC (Stoke-on-Trent) | 42 | 14 | 18 | 10 | 44 | 42 | 46 | |
| 7. | Oldham Athletic AFC (Oldham) | 42 | 14 | 17 | 11 | 45 | 52 | 45 | |
| 8. | The Wednesday FC (Sheffield) | 42 | 16 | 12 | 14 | 54 | 51 | 44 | |
| 9. | South Shields FC (South Shields) | 42 | 17 | 10 | 15 | 49 | 50 | 44 | |
| 10. | Clapton Orient FC (London) | 42 | 14 | 15 | 13 | 40 | 36 | 43 | |
| 11. | Barnsley FC (Barnsley) | 42 | 16 | 11 | 15 | 57 | 61 | 43 | |
| 12. | Leicester City FC (Leicester) | 42 | 17 | 8 | 17 | 64 | 54 | 42 | |
| 13. | Stockport County FC (Stockport) | 42 | 13 | 16 | 13 | 44 | 52 | 42 | |
| 14. | Manchester United FC (Manchester) | 42 | 13 | 14 | 15 | 52 | 44 | 40 | |
| 15. | Crystal Palace FC (London) | 42 | 13 | 13 | 16 | 53 | 65 | 39 | |
| 16. | Port Vale FC (Stoke-on-Trent) | 42 | 13 | 12 | 17 | 50 | 66 | 38 | |
| 17. | Hull City AFC (Kingston-upon-Hull) | 42 | 10 | 17 | 15 | 46 | 51 | 37 | |
| 18. | Bradford City AFC (Bradford) | 42 | 11 | 15 | 16 | 35 | 48 | 37 | |
| 19. | Coventry City FC (Coventry) | 42 | 11 | 13 | 18 | 52 | 68 | 35 | |
| 20. | Fulham FC (London) | 42 | 10 | 14 | 18 | 45 | 56 | 34 | |
| 21. | Nelson FC (Nelson) | 42 | 10 | 13 | 19 | 40 | 74 | 33 | R |
| 22. | Bristol City FC (Bristol) | 42 | 7 | 15 | 20 | 32 | 65 | 29 | R |
| | | 924 | 317 | 290 | 317 | 1125 | 1125 | 924 | |

| Football League Division 3 (N) 1923-1924 Season | Accrington S. | Ashington | Barrow | Bradford P.A. | Chesterfield | Crewe Alex. | Darlington | Doncaster R. | Durham City | Grimsby Town | Halifax Town | Hartlepools Utd. | Lincoln City | New Brighton | Rochdale | Rotherham Co. | Southport | Tranmere Rvrs. | Walsall | Wigan Boro' | Wolves | Wrexham |
|---|---|---|---|---|---|---|---|---|---|---|---|---|---|---|---|---|---|---|---|---|---|---|
| Accrington Stanley FC | | 0-1 | 3-1 | 2-2 | 2-0 | 1-1 | 2-0 | 0-0 | 5-4 | 2-0 | 1-2 | 2-0 | 3-1 | 0-0 | 0-1 | 3-2 | 2-0 | 3-1 | 0-3 | 2-2 | 1-0 | 1-0 |
| Ashington FC | 1-1 | | 2-0 | 1-0 | 1-1 | 3-0 | 2-1 | 3-1 | 2-1 | 1-0 | 4-0 | 0-0 | 2-1 | 5-0 | 1-0 | 1-2 | 2-0 | 3-3 | 3-1 | 3-0 | 1-7 | 0-2 |
| Barrow AFC | 0-0 | 2-2 | | 1-1 | 2-0 | 1-2 | 1-0 | 0-0 | 1-2 | 3-1 | 1-0 | 1-2 | 2-1 | 2-1 | 1-2 | 1-2 | 1-3 | 1-1 | 0-1 | 2-1 | 2-2 | 0-0 |
| Bradford Park Avenue FC | 1-1 | 3-1 | 3-0 | | 2-1 | 1-1 | 1-0 | 4-2 | 3-0 | 2-1 | 1-0 | 4-0 | 3-1 | 1-1 | 4-2 | 2-0 | 2-0 | 2-0 | 5-0 | 4-0 | 0-1 | 2-0 |
| Chesterfield FC | 3-0 | 2-0 | 2-1 | 2-3 | | 2-1 | 5-1 | 2-1 | 1-1 | 4-2 | 1-1 | 5-1 | 2-1 | 1-0 | 1-1 | 3-1 | 4-0 | 5-0 | 7-0 | 1-0 | 0-0 | 1-0 |
| Crewe Alexandra FC | 1-2 | 1-3 | 2-0 | 1-1 | 0-1 | | 2-1 | 0-2 | 0-2 | 0-0 | 2-2 | 2-1 | 1-2 | 2-0 | 0-2 | 1-0 | 1-1 | 1-1 | 2-0 | 0-2 | 0-0 | 1-1 |
| Darlington FC | 2-1 | 3-2 | 5-1 | 3-1 | 2-1 | 1-1 | | 1-1 | 3-2 | 1-0 | 0-0 | 5-0 | 1-0 | 3-1 | 2-2 | 1-0 | 3-1 | 4-1 | 4-2 | 3-1 | 1-1 | 3-0 |
| Doncaster Rovers FC | 1-2 | 2-1 | 2-2 | 1-1 | 0-2 | 4-1 | 1-0 | | 2-1 | 2-1 | 7-0 | 3-1 | 3-2 | 2-0 | 0-0 | 0-1 | 3-0 | 4-0 | 3-0 | 0-0 | 0-2 | 1-0 |
| Durham City FC | 3-0 | 4-0 | 1-2 | 2-0 | 1-1 | 3-1 | 3-2 | 2-1 | | 0-1 | 2-2 | 3-0 | 1-0 | 2-1 | 0-0 | 3-2 | 0-1 | 1-1 | 1-0 | 2-2 | 2-3 | 4-3 |
| Grimsby Town FC | 2-0 | 4-0 | 5-0 | 2-0 | 0-0 | 2-0 | 3-0 | 1-1 | 1-0 | | 1-1 | 0-1 | 2-2 | 0-0 | 1-0 | 1-1 | 1-0 | 0-0 | 1-0 | 1-1 | 2-0 | 0-0 |
| Halifax Town AFC | 3-0 | 3-0 | 1-0 | 0-0 | 2-0 | 2-0 | 1-4 | 0-1 | 2-1 | 1-3 | | 1-0 | 1-0 | 2-1 | 0-1 | 0-2 | 1-0 | 0-0 | 3-0 | 1-2 | 2-2 | 0-0 |
| Hartlepools United FC | 3-0 | 0-1 | 1-0 | 0-0 | 2-3 | 2-2 | 0-1 | 1-1 | 0-0 | 1-1 | 1-3 | | 1-1 | 0-1 | 1-2 | 2-5 | 1-0 | 2-1 | 0-1 | 0-0 | 0-1 | 1-0 |
| Lincoln City FC | 0-2 | 2-0 | 4-1 | 2-3 | 0-1 | 0-0 | 2-0 | 1-1 | 3-1 | 1-3 | 1-1 | 1-1 | | 1-0 | 0-2 | 2-1 | 1-1 | 1-1 | 2-0 | 1-1 | 0-0 | 4-2 |
| New Brighton FC | 1-2 | 1-1 | 5-0 | 1-0 | 0-0 | 2-1 | 1-1 | 2-0 | 2-0 | 0-0 | 2-0 | 0-0 | 3-1 | | 1-1 | 1-2 | 0-0 | 0-0 | 1-0 | 5-0 | 0-1 | 0-0 |
| Rochdale AFC | 4-1 | 1-0 | 3-1 | 3-0 | 3-0 | 1-0 | 0-0 | 2-0 | 2-0 | 4-2 | 3-0 | 1-0 | 1-0 | 6-2 | | 1-0 | 2-2 | 1-0 | 1-0 | 1-0 | 0-0 | 0-0 |
| Rotherham County FC | 2-0 | 1-0 | 2-0 | 1-0 | 1-2 | 1-0 | 2-0 | 3-0 | 5-1 | 2-1 | 3-2 | 5-0 | 2-0 | 3-1 | 0-0 | | 1-1 | 5-1 | 0-2 | 4-0 | 1-1 | 2-1 |
| Southport FC | 1-0 | 2-0 | 2-0 | 1-0 | 1-0 | 1-0 | 1-0 | 2-2 | 1-0 | 3-0 | 3-0 | 2-2 | 3-2 | 3-0 | 0-1 | 0-0 | | 1-1 | 1-1 | 1-1 | 0-0 | 1-0 |
| Tranmere Rovers FC | 2-0 | 2-4 | 3-0 | 2-1 | 0-0 | 1-1 | 1-4 | 3-0 | 1-0 | 2-1 | 3-0 | 1-3 | 1-2 | 2-1 | 0-1 | 1-1 | 1-1 | | 3-1 | 1-0 | 0-0 | 1-1 |
| Walsall FC | 2-0 | 1-1 | 1-1 | 2-3 | 0-1 | 1-0 | 2-1 | 5-2 | 1-1 | 2-0 | 2-0 | 2-0 | 0-0 | 3-0 | 0-1 | 1-1 | 0-0 | 0-4 | | 3-0 | 2-1 | 1-2 |
| Wigan Borough FC | 2-0 | 1-1 | 4-0 | 0-1 | 3-1 | 3-0 | 2-2 | 1-0 | 0-1 | 4-0 | 0-1 | 4-1 | 0-0 | 1-0 | 3-0 | 3-1 | 1-1 | 1-2 | 2-1 | | 1-1 | 3-1 |
| Wolverhampton Wanderers | 5-1 | 1-0 | 3-0 | 2-0 | 2-1 | 1-0 | 2-0 | 1-0 | 2-1 | 4-1 | 4-0 | 2-1 | 3-0 | 5-1 | 0-0 | 3-0 | 2-1 | 3-0 | 0-0 | 3-3 | | 3-0 |
| Wrexham AFC | 1-0 | 4-0 | 2-0 | 2-2 | 0-0 | 1-0 | 0-1 | 2-2 | 0-0 | 1-1 | 0-1 | 1-0 | 2-1 | 0-0 | 1-1 | 1-0 | 3-0 | 1-1 | 0-0 | 0-0 | 2-2 | |

### Division 3 (North)

| | | Pd | Wn | Dw | Ls | GF | GA | Pts | |
|---|---|---|---|---|---|---|---|---|---|
| 1. | Wolverhampton Wanderers FC (Wolverhampton) | 42 | 24 | 15 | 3 | 76 | 27 | 63 | P |
| 2. | Rochdale AFC (Rochdale) | 42 | 25 | 12 | 5 | 60 | 26 | 62 | |
| 3. | Chesterfield FC (Chesterfield) | 42 | 22 | 10 | 10 | 70 | 39 | 54 | |
| 4. | Rotherham County FC (Rotherham) | 42 | 23 | 6 | 13 | 70 | 43 | 52 | |
| 5. | Bradford Park Avenue FC (Bradford) | 42 | 21 | 1- | 11 | 69 | 43 | 52 | |
| 6. | Darlington FC (Darlington) | 42 | 20 | 8 | 14 | 70 | 53 | 48 | |
| 7. | Southport FC (Southport) | 42 | 16 | 14 | 12 | 44 | 42 | 46 | |
| 8. | Ashington FC (Ashington) | 42 | 18 | 8 | 16 | 59 | 61 | 44 | |
| 9. | Doncaster Rovers FC (Doncaster) | 42 | 15 | 12 | 15 | 59 | 53 | 42 | |
| 10. | Wigan Borough FC (Wigan) | 42 | 14 | 14 | 14 | 55 | 53 | 42 | |
| 11. | Grimsby Town FC (Cleethorpes) | 42 | 14 | 13 | 15 | 49 | 47 | 41 | |
| 12. | Tranmere Rovers FC (Birkenhead) | 42 | 13 | 15 | 14 | 51 | 60 | 41 | |
| 13. | Accrington Stanley FC (Accrington) | 42 | 16 | 8 | 18 | 48 | 61 | 40 | |
| 14. | Halifax Town AFC (Halifax) | 42 | 15 | 10 | 17 | 42 | 59 | 40 | |
| 15. | Durham City FC (Durham) | 42 | 15 | 9 | 18 | 59 | 60 | 39 | |
| 16. | Wrexham AFC (Wrexham) | 42 | 10 | 18 | 14 | 37 | 44 | 38 | |
| 17. | Walsall FC (Walsall) | 42 | 14 | 8 | 20 | 44 | 59 | 36 | |
| 18. | New Brighton FC (Wallasey) | 42 | 11 | 13 | 18 | 40 | 53 | 35 | |
| 19. | Lincoln City FC (Lincoln) | 42 | 10 | 12 | 20 | 48 | 59 | 32 | |
| 20. | Crewe Alexandra FC (Crewe) | 42 | 7 | 13 | 22 | 32 | 58 | 27 | |
| 21. | Hartlepools United FC (Hartlepool) | 42 | 7 | 11 | 24 | 33 | 70 | 25 | |
| 22. | Barrow AFC (Barrow-in-Furness) | 42 | 8 | 9 | 25 | 35 | 80 | 25 | |
| | | 924 | 338 | 248 | 338 | 1150 | 1150 | 924 | |

**Football League Division 3 (S) 1923-1924 Season**

| | Aberdare Athletic | Bournemouth | Brentford | Brighton | Bristol Rovers | Charlton Athletic | Exeter City | Gillingham | Luton Town | Merthyr Town | Millwall Athletic | Newport County | Northampton | Norwich City | Plymouth Argyle | Portsmouth | Q.P.R. | Reading | Southend United | Swansea Town | Swindon Town | Watford |
|---|---|---|---|---|---|---|---|---|---|---|---|---|---|---|---|---|---|---|---|---|---|---|
| Aberdare Athletic FC | | 1-0 | 1-2 | 3-1 | 2-0 | 4-1 | 0-0 | 1-1 | 0-1 | 0-0 | 1-1 | 2-0 | 2-2 | 0-0 | 1-2 | 0-0 | 1-1 | 1-0 | 5-2 | 4-2 | 2-2 | 4-0 |
| Bournemouth & B. Athletic | 0-1 | | 2-4 | 1-0 | 0-1 | 1-0 | 1-0 | 0-0 | 2-3 | 3-3 | 2-0 | 0-1 | 2-1 | 1-2 | 0-0 | 0-0 | 3-1 | 0-0 | 0-1 | 0-0 | 0-0 | 1-1 |
| Brentford FC | 1-1 | 2-0 | | 1-2 | 1-2 | 0-0 | 1-0 | 3-2 | 2-1 | 0-0 | 1-3 | 0-0 | 1-0 | 3-0 | 1-1 | 1-1 | 0-1 | 4-1 | 3-1 | 2-2 | 2-2 | 4-1 |
| Brighton & Hove Albion | 5-0 | 5-0 | 2-0 | | 2-1 | 3-0 | 1-0 | 2-2 | 4-0 | 0-0 | 2-2 | 4-0 | 2-0 | 3-0 | 4-1 | 0-4 | 3-0 | 4-0 | 2-0 | 4-1 | 1-1 | 3-0 |
| Bristol Rovers FC | 2-0 | 3-4 | 2-0 | 2-0 | | 2-0 | 0-0 | 2-0 | 1-1 | 0-0 | 4-1 | 0-0 | 1-1 | 3-1 | 1-1 | 0-1 | 2-1 | 0-0 | 3-1 | 2-0 | 0-1 | 4-2 |
| Charlton Athletic FC | 3-1 | 1-2 | 3-1 | 0-2 | 1-3 | | 1-0 | 0-0 | 1-1 | 1-0 | 0-1 | 2-1 | 0-0 | 0-0 | 0-1 | 1-1 | 3-0 | 0-0 | 4-1 | 1-3 | 3-1 | 1-1 |
| Exeter City FC | 1-1 | 0-2 | 1-0 | 0-1 | 3-1 | 0-0 | | 2-1 | 2-1 | 1-0 | 2-0 | 5-0 | 2-1 | 1-2 | 0-4 | 0-0 | 3-0 | 3-2 | 2-0 | 1-0 | 3-1 | 1-0 |
| Gillingham FC | 3-1 | 1-0 | 6-0 | 1-1 | 1-0 | 0-1 | 1-1 | | 0-0 | 2-1 | 0-2 | 2-1 | 1-1 | 3-1 | 1-0 | 0-2 | 0-0 | 1-0 | 3-2 | 0-1 | 1-0 | 0-0 |
| Luton Town FC | 1-0 | 6-2 | 2-1 | 0-0 | 0-0 | 0-1 | 1-0 | 1-1 | | 1-1 | 2-0 | 2-0 | 1-1 | 2-1 | 0-2 | 4-1 | 2-0 | 2-0 | 4-4 | 1-2 | 3-2 | 0-0 |
| Merthyr Town FC | 0-0 | 4-2 | 2-0 | 2-1 | 1-1 | 2-1 | 3-0 | 0-2 | 0-0 | | 1-0 | 3-3 | 0-0 | 2-3 | 1-0 | 2-2 | 2-0 | 1-1 | 3-2 | 0-0 | 2-0 | 2-1 |
| Millwall Athletic FC | 2-0 | 4-2 | 4-1 | 0-0 | 1-0 | 1-0 | 3-1 | 5-0 | 0-1 | 6-0 | | 2-1 | 4-3 | 2-1 | 1-0 | 2-0 | 3-0 | 0-0 | 0-0 | 2-1 | 1-0 | 2-0 |
| Newport County AFC | 0-0 | 2-0 | 3-2 | 0-0 | 1-0 | 0-0 | 2-0 | 2-1 | 1-0 | 4-4 | 2-1 | | 1-1 | 1-0 | 1-2 | 2-1 | 2-1 | 0-0 | 5-0 | 4-1 | 3-0 | 1-0 |
| Northampton Town | 1-2 | 3-1 | 2-3 | 3-0 | 0-0 | 1-0 | 1-0 | 2-0 | 2-0 | 3-0 | 2-1 | 0-0 | | 1-0 | 1-0 | 0-4 | 3-0 | 3-1 | 8-0 | 2-0 | 1-1 | 1-2 |
| Norwich City FC | 5-0 | 1-1 | 2-3 | 1-0 | 3-1 | 2-2 | 4-0 | 1-0 | 2-0 | 2-0 | 1-1 | 3-1 | 1-4 | | 0-1 | 3-1 | 5-0 | 2-2 | 3-1 | 2-0 | 2-0 | 0-0 |
| Plymouth Argyle FC | 2-0 | 4-0 | 4-1 | 3-0 | 2-2 | 1-1 | 4-0 | 3-0 | 0-0 | 1-1 | 1-1 | 3-2 | 0-0 | 2-0 | | 1-2 | 2-0 | 2-1 | 7-1 | 2-0 | 1-3 | 1-0 |
| Portsmouth FC | 4-0 | 3-0 | 3-0 | 1-3 | 1-1 | 0-0 | 4-0 | 3-0 | 3-0 | 1-0 | 0-1 | 5-0 | 1-3 | 4-0 | 2-1 | | 7-0 | 1-1 | 3-0 | 3-0 | 4-1 | 4-0 |
| Queen's Park Rangers | 3-0 | 0-1 | 1-0 | 1-0 | 1-2 | 0-0 | 2-0 | 1-1 | 2-0 | 3-0 | 1-1 | 0-3 | 3-2 | 2-1 | 3-2 | 0-2 | | 1-4 | 0-0 | 2-2 | 2-2 | 2-1 |
| Reading FC | 0-1 | 1-2 | 1-0 | 0-1 | 3-2 | 3-1 | 1-0 | 4-0 | 0-1 | 3-0 | 2-0 | 1-1 | 1-0 | 3-0 | 1-2 | 1-4 | 4-0 | | 1-0 | 3-4 | 1-0 | 1-1 |
| Southend United FC | 1-1 | 1-1 | 3-1 | 1-0 | 1-0 | 2-2 | 0-0 | 3-2 | 1-1 | 3-1 | 0-0 | 2-0 | 5-1 | 3-1 | 0-2 | 0-1 | 4-2 | 2-1 | | 0-0 | 0-2 | 3-0 |
| Swansea Town AFC | 1-0 | 1-0 | 4-0 | 1-0 | 3-1 | 1-0 | 1-0 | 3-1 | 1-0 | 5-1 | 1-2 | 2-1 | 2-1 | 1-0 | 1-0 | 0-0 | 2-0 | 5-1 | 2-1 | | 1-1 | 1-0 |
| Swindon Town FC | 3-1 | 3-1 | 2-1 | 4-0 | 0-0 | 1-1 | 0-1 | 4-1 | 3-2 | 3-0 | 1-0 | 3-0 | 4-2 | 0-1 | 0-0 | 0-0 | 1-0 | 3-0 | 1-0 | 1-0 | | 0-0 |
| Watford FC | 2-0 | 0-0 | 0-1 | 0-0 | 4-0 | 1-0 | 4-1 | 1-1 | 0-0 | 4-0 | 1-1 | 8-2 | 0-2 | 0-0 | 0-1 | 2-3 | 0-2 | 2-1 | 4-1 | 2-2 | 0-0 | |

## Division 3 (South)

| | | Pd | Wn | Dw | Ls | GF | GA | Pts | |
|---|---|---|---|---|---|---|---|---|---|
| 1. | Portsmouth FC (Portsmouth) | 42 | 24 | 11 | 7 | 87 | 30 | 59 | P |
| 2. | Plymouth Argyle FC (Plymouth) | 42 | 23 | 9 | 10 | 70 | 34 | 55 | |
| 3. | Millwall Athletic FC (London) | 42 | 22 | 10 | 10 | 64 | 38 | 54 | |
| 4. | Swansea Town AFC (Swansea) | 42 | 22 | 8 | 12 | 60 | 48 | 52 | |
| 5. | Brighton & Hove Albion FC (Hove) | 42 | 21 | 9 | 12 | 68 | 37 | 51 | |
| 6. | Swindon Town FC (Swindon) | 42 | 17 | 13 | 12 | 58 | 44 | 47 | |
| 7. | Luton Town FC (Luton) | 42 | 16 | 14 | 12 | 50 | 44 | 46 | |
| 8. | Northampton Town FC (Northampton) | 42 | 17 | 11 | 14 | 64 | 47 | 45 | |
| 9. | Bristol Rovers FC (Bristol) | 42 | 15 | 13 | 14 | 52 | 46 | 43 | |
| 10. | Newport County AFC (Newport) | 42 | 17 | 9 | 16 | 56 | 64 | 43 | |
| 11. | Norwich City FC (Norwich) | 42 | 16 | 8 | 18 | 60 | 59 | 40 | |
| 12. | Aberdare Athletic FC (Aberdare) | 42 | 12 | 14 | 16 | 45 | 58 | 38 | |
| 13. | Merthyr Town FC (Merthyr Tydfil) | 42 | 11 | 16 | 15 | 45 | 65 | 38 | |
| 14. | Charlton Athletic FC (London) | 42 | 11 | 15 | 16 | 38 | 45 | 37 | |
| 15. | Gillingham FC (Gillingham) | 42 | 12 | 13 | 17 | 43 | 58 | 37 | |
| 16. | Exeter City FC (Exeter) | 42 | 15 | 7 | 20 | 37 | 52 | 37 | |
| 17. | Brentford FC (London) | 42 | 14 | 8 | 20 | 54 | 71 | 36 | |
| 18. | Reading FC (Reading) | 42 | 13 | 9 | 20 | 51 | 57 | 35 | |
| 19. | Southend United FC (Southend-on-Sea) | 42 | 12 | 10 | 20 | 53 | 84 | 34 | |
| 20. | Watford FC (Watford) | 42 | 9 | 15 | 18 | 45 | 54 | 33 | |
| 21. | Bournemouth & Boscombe Athletic FC (Bournemouth) | 42 | 11 | 11 | 20 | 40 | 65 | 33 | |
| 22. | Queen's Park Rangers FC (London) | 42 | 11 | 9 | 22 | 37 | 77 | 31 | |
| | | 924 | 341 | 242 | 341 | 1177 | 1177 | 924 | |

# F.A. CUP FINAL   (Wembley Stadium, London – 26/04/1924 – 91,695)

| NEWCASTLE UNITED FC | 2-0 | Aston Villa FC (Birmingham) |
|---|---|---|

*Harris, Seymour*

Newcastle: Gradle, Hampson, Hudspeth, Mooney, Spencer, Gibson, Low, Cowan, Harris, McDonald, Seymour.
Aston Villa: Jackson, Smart, Mort, Moss, Milne, Blackburn, York, Kirton, Capewell, Walker, Dorrell.

## Semi-finals

| Aston Villa FC (Birmingham) | 3-0 | Burnley FC (Burnley) |
|---|---|---|
| Newcastle United FC (Newcastle-upon-Tyne) | 2-0 | Manchester City FC (Manchester) |

## Quarter-finals

| Manchester City FC (Manchester) | 0-0, 1-0 (aet) | Cardiff City AFC (Cardiff) |
|---|---|---|
| Newcastle United FC (Newcastle-upon-Tyne) | 1-0 | Liverpool FC (Liverpool) |
| Swindon Town FC (Swindon) | 1-1, 1-3 | Burnley FC (Burnley) |
| West Bromwich Albion FC (West Bromwich) | 0-2 | Aston Villa FC (Birmingham) |

# 1924-25

| Football League Division 1 1924-1925 Season | Aston Villa | Birmingham | Blackburn Rovers | Bolton Wanderers | Burnley | Bury | Cardiff City | Everton | Huddersfield Town | Leeds United | Liverpool | Manchester City | Newcastle United | Nottingham Forest | Notts County | Preston North End | Sheffield United | Sunderland | The Arsenal | Tottenham Hotspur | W.B.A. | West Ham United |
|---|---|---|---|---|---|---|---|---|---|---|---|---|---|---|---|---|---|---|---|---|---|---|
| Aston Villa FC | | 1-0 | 4-3 | 2-2 | 3-0 | 3-3 | 1-2 | 3-1 | 1-1 | 2-1 | 1-4 | 2-1 | 0-0 | 2-0 | 0-0 | 1-0 | 1-1 | 1-4 | 4-0 | 0-1 | 1-0 | 1-1 |
| Birmingham FC | 1-0 | | 1-1 | 1-0 | 1-0 | 0-1 | 2-1 | 2-2 | 0-1 | 0-0 | 5-2 | 2-1 | 1-1 | 1-1 | 1-0 | 3-0 | 1-1 | 2-1 | 2-1 | 0-2 | 0-0 | 1-1 |
| Blackburn Rovers FC | 1-1 | 7-1 | | 0-2 | 0-3 | 0-1 | 3-1 | 3-0 | 2-3 | 2-3 | 3-1 | 3-1 | 1-1 | 0-0 | 0-2 | 0-1 | 2-2 | 1-1 | 1-0 | 1-1 | 1-0 | 0-1 |
| Bolton Wanderers FC | 4-0 | 3-0 | 6-0 | | 5-0 | 3-3 | 3-0 | 1-0 | 1-0 | 1-0 | 2-0 | 4-2 | 3-2 | 1-0 | 1-0 | 6-1 | 3-1 | 1-2 | 4-1 | 3-0 | 1-1 | 5-0 |
| Burnley FC | 1-1 | 3-2 | 3-5 | 0-0 | | 4-0 | 0-0 | 0-0 | 1-5 | 1-1 | 2-1 | 1-0 | 1-3 | 0-0 | 1-1 | 1-0 | 1-1 | 1-2 | 1-0 | 1-4 | 0-1 | 5-4 |
| Bury FC | 4-3 | 1-4 | 1-1 | 1-0 | 1-0 | | 4-1 | 1-0 | 0-1 | 1-0 | 0-0 | 0-2 | 0-0 | 3-0 | 2-1 | 1-1 | 1-0 | 3-0 | 2-0 | 5-2 | 0-2 | 4-2 |
| Cardiff City AFC | 2-1 | 1-0 | 3-0 | 1-2 | 4-0 | 4-1 | | 2-1 | 2-2 | 3-0 | 1-3 | 0-2 | 3-0 | 2-0 | 1-1 | 0-0 | 1-1 | 2-0 | 1-1 | 0-2 | 0-1 | 2-1 |
| Everton FC | 2-0 | 2-1 | 1-0 | 2-2 | 3-2 | 0-0 | 1-2 | | 0-2 | 1-0 | 0-1 | 3-1 | 0-1 | 3-1 | 1-0 | 0-0 | 1-1 | 0-3 | 2-3 | 1-0 | 1-0 | 1-0 |
| Huddersfield Town AFC | 4-1 | 0-1 | 0-0 | 0-0 | 2-0 | 2-0 | 0-0 | 2-0 | | 2-0 | 1-1 | 1-1 | 0-0 | 3-0 | 1-0 | 2-1 | 4-0 | 1-2 | 1-1 | 1-2 | | |
| Leeds United AFC | 6-0 | 0-1 | 1-1 | 2-1 | 0-2 | 1-0 | 0-0 | 2-0 | 1-1 | | 4-1 | 0-3 | 1-1 | 1-1 | 4-0 | 1-1 | 1-1 | 0-1 | 2-1 | | | |
| Liverpool FC | 2-4 | 1-1 | 0-0 | 0-0 | 3-0 | 4-0 | 1-2 | 3-1 | 2-3 | 1-0 | | 5-3 | 1-1 | 3-0 | 1-0 | 3-1 | 4-1 | 3-1 | 2-1 | 1-0 | 1-1 | 2-0 |
| Manchester City FC | 1-0 | 2-2 | 1-3 | 2-2 | 3-3 | 0-0 | 2-2 | 2-2 | 1-1 | 4-2 | 5-0 | | 3-1 | 4-2 | 2-1 | 2-1 | 2-1 | 1-3 | 2-0 | 1-2 | | 3-1 |
| Newcastle United FC | 4-1 | 4-0 | 4-0 | 0-1 | 3-0 | 2-2 | 1-2 | 1-1 | 1-3 | 4-1 | 0-0 | 2-0 | | 4-1 | 1-0 | 3-1 | 0-0 | 2-0 | 2-2 | 1-1 | 0-1 | 4-1 |
| Nottingham Forest FC | 0-2 | 1-1 | 0-2 | 1-1 | 0-0 | 2-0 | 2-1 | 0-1 | 0-1 | 4-0 | 0-1 | 0-3 | 1-1 | | 0-0 | 0-1 | 2-3 | 1-1 | 0-2 | 1-0 | 1-0 | 2-1 |
| Notts County FC | 0-0 | 0-1 | 0-0 | 0-1 | 2-0 | 1-1 | 3-0 | 3-1 | 1-1 | 1-0 | 1-2 | 2-0 | 2-0 | 0-0 | | 1-0 | 2-0 | 4-1 | 2-1 | 0-0 | 0-2 | 4-1 |
| Preston North End FC | 3-2 | 1-0 | 3-2 | 1-0 | 0-2 | 1-1 | 1-3 | 1-1 | 1-4 | 1-4 | 4-0 | 2-3 | 0-1 | 3-1 | 0-1 | | 0-1 | 1-2 | 2-0 | 0-3 | 1-2 | 3-2 |
| Sheffield United FC | 2-2 | 4-3 | 2-3 | 2-0 | 4-0 | 0-1 | 1-0 | 1-1 | 1-1 | 1-1 | 0-1 | 0-5 | 1-2 | 1-2 | 2-0 | 3-0 | | 2-1 | 2-1 | 2-0 | 2-0 | 1-1 |
| Sunderland AFC | 1-1 | 4-0 | 1-0 | 1-0 | 1-1 | 1-1 | 1-0 | 4-1 | 1-1 | 2-1 | 3-0 | 3-2 | 1-1 | 3-1 | 0-1 | 2-0 | 0-1 | | 2-0 | 4-1 | 3-0 | 1-1 |
| The Arsenal FC | 1-1 | 0-1 | 1-0 | 1-0 | 5-0 | 0-1 | 1-1 | 3-1 | 0-5 | 6-1 | 2-0 | 1-0 | 0-2 | 2-1 | 0-1 | 4-0 | 2-0 | 0-0 | | 1-0 | 2-0 | 1-2 |
| Tottenham Hotspur FC | 1-3 | 0-1 | 5-0 | 3-0 | 1-1 | 1-1 | 1-1 | 0-0 | 1-2 | 2-1 | 1-1 | 1-1 | 3-0 | 1-0 | 1-1 | 2-0 | 4-1 | 1-0 | 2-0 | | 0-1 | 1-1 |
| West Bromwich Albion FC | 4-1 | 1-1 | 1-1 | 0-0 | 1-4 | 1-1 | 1-0 | 3-0 | 1-0 | 3-1 | 0-0 | 3-1 | 2-0 | 5-1 | 1-2 | 1-1 | 2-1 | 2-1 | 2-0 | 2-0 | | 4-1 |
| West Ham United FC | 2-0 | 0-1 | 2-0 | 1-1 | 2-0 | 1-1 | 3-2 | 4-1 | 0-0 | 0-0 | 0-1 | 4-0 | 0-0 | 0-0 | 3-0 | 1-0 | 6-2 | 4-1 | 1-0 | 1-1 | 2-1 | |

| | Division 1 | Pd | Wn | Dw | Ls | GF | GA | Pts | |
|---|---|---|---|---|---|---|---|---|---|
| 1. | HUDDERSFIELD TOWN AFC (HUDDERSFIELD) | 42 | 21 | 16 | 5 | 69 | 28 | 58 | |
| 2. | West Bromwich Albion FC (West Bromwich) | 42 | 23 | 10 | 9 | 58 | 34 | 56 | |
| 3. | Bolton Wanderers FC (Bolton) | 42 | 22 | 11 | 9 | 76 | 34 | 55 | |
| 4. | Liverpool FC Liverpool) | 42 | 20 | 10 | 12 | 63 | 55 | 50 | |
| 5. | Bury FC (Bury) | 42 | 17 | 15 | 10 | 54 | 51 | 49 | |
| 6. | Newcastle United FC (Newcastle-upon-Tyne) | 42 | 16 | 16 | 10 | 61 | 42 | 48 | |
| 7. | Sunderland AFC (Sunderland) | 42 | 19 | 10 | 13 | 64 | 51 | 48 | |
| 8. | Birmingham FC (Birmingham) | 42 | 17 | 12 | 13 | 49 | 53 | 46 | |
| 9. | Notts County FC (Nottingham) | 42 | 16 | 13 | 13 | 42 | 31 | 45 | |
| 10. | Manchester City FC (Manchester) | 42 | 17 | 9 | 16 | 76 | 68 | 43 | |
| 11. | Cardiff City AFC (Cardiff) | 42 | 16 | 11 | 15 | 56 | 51 | 43 | |
| 12. | Tottenham Hotspur FC (London) | 42 | 15 | 12 | 15 | 52 | 43 | 42 | |
| 13. | West Ham United FC (London) | 42 | 15 | 12 | 15 | 62 | 60 | 42 | |
| 14. | Sheffield United FC (Sheffield) | 42 | 13 | 13 | 16 | 55 | 63 | 39 | |
| 15. | Aston Villa FC (Birmingham) | 42 | 13 | 13 | 16 | 58 | 71 | 39 | |
| 16. | Blackburn Rovers FC (Blackburn) | 42 | 11 | 13 | 18 | 53 | 66 | 35 | |
| 17. | Everton FC (Liverpool) | 42 | 12 | 11 | 19 | 40 | 60 | 35 | |
| 18. | Leeds United AFC (Leeds) | 42 | 11 | 12 | 19 | 46 | 59 | 34 | |
| 19. | Burnley FC (Burnley) | 42 | 11 | 12 | 19 | 46 | 75 | 34 | |
| 20. | The Arsenal FC (London) | 42 | 14 | 5 | 23 | 46 | 58 | 33 | |
| 21. | Preston North End FC (Preston) | 42 | 10 | 6 | 26 | 37 | 74 | 26 | R |
| 22. | Nottingham Forest FC (Nottingham) | 42 | 6 | 12 | 24 | 29 | 65 | 24 | R |
| | | 924 | 335 | 254 | 335 | 1192 | 1192 | 924 | |

## Top Goalscorer

1)   F. ROBERTS                      (Manchester City FC)    31

## Football League Division 2 — 1924-1925 Season

| | Barnsley | Blackpool | Bradford City | Chelsea | Clapton Orient | Coventry City | Crystal Palace | Derby County | Fulham | Hull City | Leicester City | Man. United | Middlesbro' | Oldham Ath. | Portsmouth | Port Vale | Southampton | South Shields | Stockport Co. | Stoke | Wednesday | Wolves |
|---|---|---|---|---|---|---|---|---|---|---|---|---|---|---|---|---|---|---|---|---|---|---|
| Barnsley FC | ■ | 2-4 | 3-1 | 3-3 | 1-1 | 3-1 | 3-0 | 3-0 | 1-0 | 1-2 | 1-1 | 0-0 | 1-0 | 0-0 | 1-4 | 1-3 | 1-1 | 1-0 | 0-1 | 1-1 | 3-0 | 0-0 |
| Blackpool FC | 1-2 | ■ | 1-2 | 1-2 | 1-0 | 3-1 | 0-1 | 5-1 | 4-1 | 0-0 | 2-1 | 1-1 | 1-1 | 1-2 | 1-1 | 4-1 | 1-0 | 5-0 | 0-1 | 1-2 | 2-2 | 2-4 |
| Bradford City AFC | 1-0 | 1-0 | ■ | 2-0 | 0-0 | 1-0 | 0-0 | 0-3 | 1-1 | 4-1 | 1-1 | 0-1 | 0-1 | 1-1 | 2-0 | 1-1 | 1-2 | 1-0 | 3-0 | 1-0 | 2-0 | 3-1 |
| Chelsea FC | 0-1 | 3-0 | 3-0 | ■ | 1-1 | 1-0 | 2-2 | 1-1 | 0-0 | 1-0 | 4-0 | 0-0 | 2-0 | 4-1 | 2-3 | 1-0 | 1-0 | 1-1 | 1-1 | 2-1 | 0-0 | 1-0 |
| Clapton Orient FC | 0-0 | 1-0 | 0-0 | 0-0 | ■ | 1-2 | 3-0 | 0-1 | 3-0 | 0-0 | 0-1 | 0-1 | 0-1 | 5-1 | 1-1 | 3-1 | 1-0 | 0-0 | 1-1 | 0-2 | 1-0 | 2-1 |
| Coventry City FC | 3-2 | 2-1 | 0-0 | 0-3 | 1-0 | ■ | 1-4 | 0-0 | 0-1 | 0-0 | 4-2 | 1-0 | 2-2 | 5-1 | 2-1 | 0-0 | 1-0 | 0-1 | 4-2 | 3-1 | 1-1 | 2-4 |
| Crystal Palace FC | 0-1 | 1-2 | 4-1 | 1-0 | 0-1 | 0-0 | ■ | 2-0 | 1-2 | 1-0 | 0-2 | 2-1 | 2-2 | 0-1 | 1-2 | 0-0 | 3-1 | 0-0 | 3-0 | 0-1 | 0-1 | 2-1 |
| Derby County FC | 1-1 | 2-2 | 2-0 | 1-0 | 3-0 | 5-1 | 3-0 | ■ | 5-1 | 4-0 | 0-3 | 1-0 | 3-1 | 1-0 | 6-1 | 4-1 | 3-0 | 0-0 | 2-0 | 1-2 | 2-1 | 0-1 |
| Fulham FC | 1-2 | 1-0 | 1-1 | 1-2 | 0-2 | 2-0 | 3-1 | 0-2 | ■ | 4-0 | 2-2 | 1-0 | 0-0 | 1-0 | 0-0 | 1-1 | 1-0 | 1-1 | 2-0 | 1-0 | 2-1 | 1-0 |
| Hull City AFC | 5-2 | 1-1 | 0-0 | 1-0 | 2-1 | 4-1 | 5-0 | 1-1 | 3-0 | ■ | 2-1 | 0-1 | 0-0 | 1-0 | 5-0 | 2-1 | 1-1 | 0-1 | 3-0 | 0-0 | 4-2 | 0-1 |
| Leicester City FC | 6-0 | 0-2 | 1-0 | 4-0 | 4-2 | 5-1 | 3-1 | 0-0 | 4-0 | 1-0 | ■ | 3-0 | 0-3 | 0-0 | 4-0 | 7-0 | 0-0 | 1-1 | 4-0 | 0-1 | 6-1 | 2-0 |
| Manchester United FC | 1-0 | 0-0 | 3-0 | 1-0 | 4-2 | 5-1 | 1-0 | 1-1 | 2-0 | 2-0 | 1-0 | ■ | 2-0 | 0-1 | 2-0 | 4-0 | 1-1 | 1-0 | 2-0 | 2-0 | 2-0 | 3-0 |
| Middlesbrough FC | 2-0 | 4-1 | 1-0 | 1-1 | 1-1 | 1-1 | 0-0 | 1-3 | 1-3 | 0-1 | 1-5 | 1-1 | ■ | 0-0 | 1-1 | 0-1 | 0-0 | 1-1 | 1-1 | 1-0 | 2-0 | 2-0 |
| Oldham Athletic AFC | 2-0 | 4-1 | 1-3 | 0-5 | 2-1 | 5-0 | 0-2 | 0-1 | 0-0 | 1-0 | 0-1 | 0-3 | 0-0 | ■ | 0-2 | 2-0 | 1-1 | 1-0 | 0-0 | 2-1 | 1-1 | 2-0 |
| Portsmouth FC | 0-0 | 1-1 | 5-0 | 0-0 | 0-2 | 1-0 | 0-0 | 1-1 | 3-0 | 2-0 | 1-1 | 1-1 | 3-1 | 2-2 | ■ | 2-0 | 1-1 | 1-0 | 1-1 | 0-0 | 1-1 | 2-2 |
| Port Vale FC | 2-0 | 1-2 | 1-0 | 1-1 | 4-2 | 4-0 | 3-0 | 2-1 | 0-1 | 1-1 | 1-2 | 2-1 | 2-1 | 1-0 | 0-2 | ■ | 1-1 | 0-0 | 4-1 | 2-0 | 1-0 | 1-3 |
| Southampton FC | 3-1 | 2-1 | 2-0 | 0-0 | 2-0 | 3-0 | 2-0 | 2-0 | 1-0 | 2-2 | 0-0 | 0-2 | 1-1 | 0-0 | 0-0 | 1-0 | ■ | 1-1 | 2-1 | 3-0 | 1-0 | 1-1 |
| South Shields FC | 5-2 | 1-3 | 1-0 | 1-1 | 2-0 | 4-1 | 1-1 | 1-0 | 2-1 | 2-0 | 1-1 | 1-2 | 0-1 | 0-0 | 0-2 | 3-0 | 1-1 | ■ | 0-1 | 4-0 | 0-1 | 3-3 |
| Stockport County FC | 1-0 | 1-0 | 3-0 | 4-0 | 0-1 | 1-1 | 1-0 | 0-0 | 4-1 | 0-2 | 0-2 | 2-1 | 1-1 | 2-0 | 1-2 | 0-2 | 1-1 | 0-0 | ■ | 2-0 | 1-0 | 1-1 |
| Stoke FC | 1-1 | 3-1 | 0-0 | 1-0 | 0-1 | 4-1 | 1-1 | 1-1 | 1-1 | 2-0 | 1-1 | 0-0 | 0-1 | 2-1 | 0-1 | 2-0 | 0-0 | 3-0 | | ■ | 0-2 | 0-3 |
| The Wednesday FC | 1-0 | 2-6 | 3-3 | 2-1 | 0-0 | 2-0 | 0-1 | 0-1 | 3-1 | 5-0 | 1-4 | 1-1 | 2-0 | 1-0 | 5-2 | 0-1 | 1-0 | 0-1 | 3-0 | 2-1 | ■ | 2-0 |
| Wolverhampton Wanderers FC | 0-1 | 2-0 | 2-0 | 0-1 | 1-2 | 3-1 | 3-1 | 0-4 | 2-1 | 2-1 | 0-1 | 0-0 | 1-0 | 2-0 | 0-5 | 1-0 | 3-0 | 2-1 | 3-0 | 1-0 | 1-0 | ■ |

## Division 2

| | | Pd | Wn | Dw | Ls | GF | GA | Pts | |
|---|---|---|---|---|---|---|---|---|---|
| 1. | Leicester City FC (Leicester) | 42 | 24 | 11 | 7 | 90 | 32 | 59 | P |
| 2. | Manchester United FC (Manchester) | 42 | 23 | 11 | 8 | 57 | 23 | 57 | P |
| 3. | Derby County FC (Derby) | 42 | 22 | 11 | 9 | 71 | 36 | 55 | |
| 4. | Portsmouth FC (Portsmouth) | 42 | 15 | 18 | 9 | 58 | 50 | 48 | |
| 5. | Chelsea FC (London) | 42 | 16 | 15 | 11 | 51 | 37 | 47 | |
| 6. | Wolverhampton Wanderers FC (Wolverhampton) | 42 | 20 | 6 | 16 | 55 | 51 | 46 | |
| 7. | Southampton FC (Southampton) | 42 | 13 | 18 | 11 | 40 | 36 | 44 | |
| 8. | Port Vale FC (Stoke-on-Trent) | 42 | 17 | 8 | 17 | 48 | 56 | 42 | |
| 9. | South Shields FC (South Shields) | 42 | 12 | 17 | 13 | 42 | 38 | 41 | |
| 10. | Hull City AFC (Kingston-upon-Hull) | 42 | 15 | 11 | 16 | 50 | 49 | 41 | |
| 11. | Clapton Orient FC (London) | 42 | 14 | 12 | 16 | 42 | 42 | 40 | |
| 12. | Fulham FC (London) | 42 | 15 | 10 | 17 | 41 | 56 | 40 | |
| 13. | Middlesbrough FC (Middlesbrough) | 42 | 10 | 19 | 13 | 36 | 44 | 39 | |
| 14. | The Wednesday FC (Sheffield) | 42 | 15 | 8 | 19 | 50 | 56 | 38 | |
| 15. | Barnsley FC (Barnsley) | 42 | 13 | 12 | 17 | 46 | 59 | 38 | |
| 16. | Bradford City AFC (Bradford) | 42 | 13 | 12 | 17 | 37 | 50 | 38 | |
| 17. | Blackpool FC (Blackpool) | 42 | 14 | 9 | 19 | 65 | 61 | 37 | |
| 18. | Oldham Athletic AFC (Oldham) | 42 | 13 | 11 | 18 | 35 | 51 | 37 | |
| 19. | Stockport County FC (Stockport) | 42 | 13 | 11 | 18 | 37 | 57 | 37 | |
| 20. | Stoke FC (Stoke-on-Trent) | 42 | 12 | 11 | 19 | 34 | 46 | 35 | * |
| 21. | Crystal Palace FC (London) | 42 | 12 | 10 | 20 | 38 | 54 | 34 | R |
| 22. | Coventry City FC (Coventry) | 42 | 11 | 9 | 22 | 45 | 84 | 31 | R |
| | | 924 | 332 | 260 | 332 | 1068 | 1068 | 924 | |

* Stoke FC (Stoke-on-Trent) changed their club name to Stoke City FC (Stoke-on-Trent) from the next season.

| Football League Division 3 (N) 1924-1925 Season | Accrington St. | Ashington | Barrow | Bradford P.A. | Chesterfield | Crewe Alex. | Darlington | Doncaster R. | Durham City | Grimsby Town | Halifax Town | Hartlepools U. | Lincoln City | Nelson | New Brighton | Rochdale | Rotherham U. | Southport | Tranmere R. | Walsall | Wigan Boro' | Wrexham |
|---|---|---|---|---|---|---|---|---|---|---|---|---|---|---|---|---|---|---|---|---|---|---|
| Accrington Stanley FC | | 2-2 | 1-2 | 2-2 | 2-2 | 1-0 | 2-0 | 3-2 | 6-0 | 0-3 | 2-0 | 4-1 | 0-2 | 2-0 | 0-1 | 2-2 | 2-0 | 5-1 | 2-1 | 1-1 | 3-1 | 1-0 |
| Ashington FC | 1-2 | | 5-2 | 1-0 | 2-1 | 1-1 | 4-2 | 2-0 | 0-2 | 0-2 | 2-0 | 0-3 | 2-1 | 1-1 | 1-1 | 4-3 | 3-1 | 2-0 | 1-0 | 6-1 | 1-1 | 2-0 |
| Barrow AFC | 3-1 | 3-2 | | 2-1 | 1-0 | 2-0 | 0-4 | 4-0 | 2-0 | 3-2 | 2-1 | 1-1 | 1-2 | 3-0 | 1-1 | 1-0 | 3-1 | 1-0 | 1-1 | 3-2 | 0-1 | 2-2 |
| Bradford Park Avenue FC | 3-0 | 7-1 | 1-1 | | 3-0 | 6-1 | 0-0 | 4-1 | 4-1 | 0-1 | 2-1 | 3-0 | 4-0 | 1-1 | 5-2 | 0-0 | 3-0 | 1-0 | 5-1 | 2-0 | 2-2 | 3-0 |
| Chesterfield FC | 1-0 | 1-1 | 1-1 | 1-1 | | 1-0 | 0-1 | 2-1 | 6-0 | 2-0 | 1-3 | 4-0 | 2-0 | 0-1 | 3-0 | 2-0 | 3-2 | 1-2 | 4-1 | 1-0 | 3-1 | 3-0 |
| Crewe Alexandra FC | 4-2 | 1-0 | 3-1 | 2-1 | 1-1 | | 0-5 | 1-1 | 3-0 | 3-1 | 1-1 | 3-1 | 1-1 | 2-1 | 1-0 | 2-0 | 3-1 | 1-1 | 0-2 | 1-1 | 1-1 | 1-2 |
| Darlington FC | 2-1 | 2-1 | 3-0 | 2-1 | 3-3 | 5-1 | | 1-1 | 0-0 | 0-0 | 3-0 | 2-0 | 0-1 | 3-1 | 3-1 | 2-0 | 4-0 | 2-1 | 2-1 | 3-0 | 5-0 | 3-1 |
| Doncaster Rovers FC | 4-1 | 7-3 | 0-0 | 1-0 | 0-1 | 1-1 | 0-2 | | 0-0 | 2-2 | 0-1 | 1-0 | 2-1 | 1-1 | 1-0 | 2-1 | 4-1 | 0-1 | 2-0 | 2-1 | 5-0 | 1-0 |
| Durham City FC | 2-0 | 0-0 | 6-0 | 1-0 | 1-1 | 4-1 | 2-1 | 1-0 | | 6-1 | 1-2 | 0-1 | 5-0 | 3-1 | 0-0 | 3-2 | 1-1 | 0-0 | 0-3 | 0-2 | 1-1 | 1-0 |
| Grimsby Town FC | 4-0 | 1-3 | 2-1 | 2-0 | 0-0 | 0-0 | 0-2 | 1-1 | 1-1 | | 1-1 | 2-1 | 1-2 | 2-0 | 2-3 | 1-1 | 3-1 | 3-1 | 6-1 | 2-1 | 4-0 | 0-1 |
| Halifax Town AFC | 2-2 | 0-0 | 2-0 | 1-3 | 1-0 | 2-2 | 1-1 | 2-0 | 3-0 | 1-0 | | 2-0 | 1-0 | 2-4 | 1-2 | 3-1 | 4-0 | 2-0 | 1-3 | 1-1 | 1-2 | 3-1 |
| Hartlepools United FC | 3-0 | 0-1 | 1-0 | 2-2 | 1-0 | 2-0 | 1-1 | 2-2 | 1-0 | 2-1 | 1-1 | | 1-1 | 2-4 | 0-2 | 1-1 | 0-0 | 1-2 | 2-1 | 3-1 | 1-0 | 1-1 |
| Lincoln City FC | 3-0 | 5-0 | 2-1 | 0-4 | 3-1 | 4-1 | 0-1 | 2-0 | 3-0 | 0-0 | 1-1 | 2-1 | | 2-1 | 2-0 | 1-2 | 3-1 | 1-1 | 3-2 | 0-1 | 1-0 | 1-1 |
| Nelson FC | 4-1 | 4-0 | 2-0 | 2-2 | 1-0 | 7-0 | 1-1 | 3-0 | 7-1 | 1-0 | 2-1 | 2-0 | 1-0 | | 5-0 | 1-0 | 4-1 | 2-1 | 4-1 | 2-1 | 1-0 | 2-4 |
| New Brighton FC | 4-0 | 4-4 | 3-0 | 0-0 | 2-1 | 3-0 | 1-0 | 0-2 | 4-0 | 3-2 | 3-1 | 2-0 | 4-1 | 5-0 | | 5-0 | 3-1 | 1-1 | 1-0 | 3-2 | 3-0 | 2-1 |
| Rochdale AFC | 0-1 | 0-0 | 5-1 | 2-2 | 2-1 | 5-0 | 2-1 | 5-2 | 3-0 | 2-0 | 3-1 | 3-1 | 3-0 | 0-1 | 2-0 | | 4-1 | 1-0 | 2-1 | 3-0 | 3-2 | 3-1 |
| Rotherham United FC | 1-1 | 1-4 | 0-1 | 1-1 | 1-3 | 1-3 | 1-1 | 3-0 | 1-2 | 3-0 | 0-0 | 1-2 | 1-1 | 1-0 | 2-1 | 1-3 | | 1-3 | 2-0 | 2-0 | 3-4 | 0-1 |
| Southport FC | 3-1 | 3-0 | 5-0 | 3-0 | 0-2 | 2-0 | 1-0 | 3-0 | 1-1 | 3-1 | 3-1 | 2-0 | 4-0 | 1-0 | 2-0 | 0-0 | 2-0 | | 1-0 | 1-0 | 0-1 | 1-0 |
| Tranmere Rovers FC | 2-1 | 5-4 | 4-1 | 2-0 | 5-1 | 2-2 | 0-1 | 1-2 | 1-1 | 2-3 | 0-2 | 4-3 | 0-0 | 2-0 | 1-3 | 3-1 | 1-0 | 1-0 | | 0-1 | 2-3 | 2-0 |
| Walsall FC | 1-1 | 1-0 | 1-0 | 0-2 | 0-0 | 0-0 | 2-1 | 4-0 | 2-2 | 2-0 | 1-1 | 2-0 | 1-2 | 2-1 | 0-2 | 0-1 | 0-0 | 2-0 | | | 3-1 | 3-0 |
| Wigan Borough FC | 1-2 | 2-0 | 2-0 | 1-0 | 0-0 | 3-4 | 1-1 | 2-2 | 0-0 | 3-1 | 2-0 | 0-0 | 4-0 | 1-1 | 0-1 | 2-3 | 4-1 | 2-0 | 4-0 | 0-0 | | 5-0 |
| Wrexham AFC | 1-0 | 3-1 | 3-0 | 1-3 | 0-0 | 2-1 | 0-2 | 2-0 | 3-1 | 1-2 | 0-0 | 3-1 | 0-1 | 1-1 | 0-0 | 1-0 | 3-1 | 2-3 | 4-0 | 1-1 | 6-2 | |

## Division 3 (North)

| | | Pd | Wn | Dw | Ls | GF | GA | Pts | |
|---|---|---|---|---|---|---|---|---|---|
| 1. | Darlington FC (Darlington) | 42 | 24 | 10 | 8 | 78 | 33 | 58 | P |
| 2. | Nelson FC (Nelson) | 42 | 23 | 7 | 12 | 79 | 50 | 53 | |
| 3. | New Brighton FC (Wallasey) | 42 | 23 | 7 | 12 | 75 | 50 | 53 | |
| 4. | Southport FC (Southport) | 42 | 22 | 7 | 13 | 59 | 37 | 51 | |
| 5. | Bradford Park Avenue FC (Bradford) | 42 | 19 | 12 | 11 | 84 | 42 | 50 | |
| 6. | Rochdale AFC (Rochdale) | 42 | 21 | 7 | 14 | 75 | 53 | 49 | |
| 7. | Chesterfield FC (Chesterfield) | 42 | 17 | 11 | 14 | 60 | 44 | 45 | |
| 8. | Lincoln City FC (Lincoln) | 42 | 18 | 8 | 16 | 53 | 58 | 44 | |
| 9. | Halifax Town AFC (Halifax) | 42 | 16 | 11 | 15 | 56 | 52 | 43 | |
| 10. | Ashington FC (Ashington) | 42 | 16 | 10 | 16 | 68 | 76 | 42 | |
| 11. | Wigan Borough FC (Wigan) | 42 | 15 | 11 | 16 | 62 | 65 | 41 | |
| 12. | Grimsby Town FC (Cleethorpes) | 42 | 15 | 9 | 18 | 60 | 60 | 39 | |
| 13. | Durham City FC (Durham) | 42 | 13 | 13 | 16 | 50 | 68 | 39 | |
| 14. | Barrow AFC (Barrow-in-Furness) | 42 | 16 | 7 | 19 | 51 | 74 | 39 | |
| 15. | Crewe Alexandra FC (Crewe) | 42 | 13 | 13 | 16 | 53 | 78 | 39 | |
| 16. | Wrexham AFC (Wrexham) | 42 | 15 | 8 | 19 | 53 | 61 | 38 | |
| 17. | Accrington Stanley FC (Accrington) | 42 | 15 | 8 | 19 | 60 | 72 | 38 | |
| 18. | Doncaster Rovers FC (Doncaster) | 42 | 14 | 10 | 18 | 54 | 65 | 38 | |
| 19. | Walsall FC (Walsall) | 42 | 13 | 11 | 18 | 44 | 53 | 37 | |
| 20. | Hartlepools United FC (Hartlepool) | 42 | 12 | 11 | 19 | 45 | 63 | 35 | |
| 21. | Tranmere Rovers FC (Birkenhead) | 42 | 14 | 4 | 24 | 59 | 78 | 32 | |
| 22. | Rotherham County FC (Rotherham) | 42 | 7 | 7 | 28 | 42 | 88 | 21 | * |
| | | 924 | 361 | 202 | 361 | 1320 | 1320 | 924 | |

| Football League Division 3 (S) 1924-1925 Season | Aberdare Ath. | Bournemouth | Brentford | Brighton | Bristol City | Bristol Rovers | Charlton Ath. | Exeter City | Gillingham | Luton Town | Merthyr Town | Millwall Ath. | Newport Co. | Northampton | Norwich City | Plymouth A. | Q.P.R. | Reading | Southend U. | Swansea Town | Swindon Town | Watford |
|---|---|---|---|---|---|---|---|---|---|---|---|---|---|---|---|---|---|---|---|---|---|---|
| Aberdare Athletic FC | | 4-2 | 2-1 | 1-2 | 1-2 | 2-1 | 2-0 | 3-1 | 2-1 | 1-1 | 2-0 | 0-1 | 1-3 | 1-1 | 2-1 | 3-1 | 1-1 | 3-0 | 3-0 | 3-1 | 1-1 | 2-0 |
| Bournemouth & B. Athletic | 3-1 | | 2-0 | 0-0 | 1-3 | 0-1 | 2-1 | 1-1 | 3-0 | 2-1 | 2-0 | 0-1 | 0-0 | 1-2 | 0-0 | 0-1 | 0-2 | 0-0 | 1-0 | 0-2 | 0-0 | 2-1 |
| Brentford FC | 2-2 | 1-2 | | 2-4 | 1-0 | 1-1 | 1-0 | 2-5 | 2-1 | 3-0 | 2-2 | 1-0 | 2-0 | 1-3 | 1-1 | 1-0 | 0-1 | 0-1 | 2-2 | 3-1 | 0-0 | 0-0 |
| Brighton & Hove Albion | 4-1 | 0-1 | 4-1 | | 1-0 | 1-0 | 0-0 | 2-0 | 2-0 | 2-1 | 3-1 | 3-3 | 4-1 | 0-1 | 3-1 | 2-3 | 5-0 | 0-1 | 2-1 | 0-0 | 3-1 | 2-0 |
| Bristol City FC | 0-1 | 2-1 | 3-0 | 2-1 | | 2-0 | 1-1 | 0-1 | 2-1 | 2-0 | 1-0 | 4-1 | 2-0 | 1-0 | 2-0 | 2-2 | 5-0 | 3-0 | 5-0 | 0-0 | 0-0 | 1-1 |
| Bristol Rovers FC | 1-0 | 1-0 | 2-0 | 1-2 | 0-0 | | 4-0 | 0-1 | 0-0 | 1-1 | 1-0 | 1-1 | 0-1 | 0-2 | 3-0 | 1-1 | 3-0 | 1-0 | 1-3 | 3-0 | 0-1 | 2-0 |
| Charlton Athletic FC | 5-1 | 2-2 | 3-0 | 1-0 | 0-1 | 1-1 | | 1-0 | 2-0 | 2-0 | 3-0 | 0-2 | 1-0 | 0-0 | 3-2 | 2-1 | 1-2 | 0-0 | 1-0 | 1-1 | 0-1 | 1-1 |
| Exeter City FC | 3-1 | 2-1 | 5-1 | 2-0 | 0-2 | 1-1 | 2-1 | | 3-3 | 0-1 | 2-1 | 0-0 | 4-3 | 0-0 | 1-0 | 3-0 | 1-3 | 1-0 | 0-1 | 2-0 | 1-0 | 4-0 |
| Gillingham FC | 2-0 | 0-0 | 1-0 | 2-0 | 1-1 | 0-0 | 2-0 | 1-1 | | 4-1 | 2-1 | 1-0 | 0-1 | 3-1 | 0-3 | 1-0 | 0-0 | 3-1 | 1-0 | 0-1 | 1-1 | 0-0 |
| Luton Town FC | 0-0 | 0-2 | 3-1 | 3-1 | 3-0 | 1-1 | 1-0 | 1-1 | 0-0 | | 6-0 | 1-1 | 2-2 | 2-0 | 0-0 | 1-1 | 3-0 | 1-0 | 4-0 | 0-0 | 2-2 | 0-3 |
| Merthyr Town FC | 3-1 | 3-1 | 4-0 | 1-2 | 2-3 | 1-0 | 2-1 | 0-1 | 0-0 | 0-0 | | 2-1 | 1-0 | 0-2 | 0-2 | 1-2 | 2-3 | 0-0 | 1-0 | 0-2 | 1-5 | 0-1 |
| Millwall Athletic FC | 2-1 | 3-1 | 3-0 | 1-1 | 3-1 | 0-0 | 1-0 | 2-0 | 2-0 | 2-2 | 3-1 | | 3-0 | 3-1 | 0-0 | 0-0 | 3-0 | 0-1 | 2-0 | 1-2 | 1-2 | 0-1 |
| Newport County AFC | 1-0 | 2-0 | 1-0 | 0-0 | 0-2 | 4-1 | 2-1 | 2-1 | 2-0 | 1-1 | 3-0 | 2-3 | | 1-0 | 3-0 | 0-0 | 0-0 | 1-1 | 1-1 | 3-0 | 3-1 | 3-0 |
| Northampton Town | 5-0 | 3-0 | 0-2 | 1-0 | 1-2 | 5-0 | 2-1 | 2-1 | 1-0 | 1-0 | 2-0 | 0-2 | 0-2 | | 1-1 | 5-2 | 1-0 | 2-0 | 0-1 | 1-3 | 0-0 | 1-1 |
| Norwich City FC | 1-1 | 6-3 | 3-0 | 2-2 | 0-0 | 1-1 | 2-1 | 0-1 | 0-0 | 1-1 | 1-0 | 2-2 | 2-1 | 4-0 | | 1-1 | 5-0 | 0-2 | 0-1 | 2-0 | 4-0 | 2-1 |
| Plymouth Argyle FC | 2-0 | 2-0 | 7-1 | 1-0 | 7-1 | 3-2 | 3-2 | 1-1 | 2-0 | 4-0 | 2-0 | 1-1 | 0-2 | 2-1 | 5-0 | | 1-0 | 2-0 | 6-0 | 1-1 | 2-0 | 1-0 |
| Queen's Park Rangers | 4-1 | 0-2 | 1-0 | 2-0 | 3-0 | 1-2 | 0-0 | 1-4 | 1-1 | 2-1 | 1-1 | 0-0 | 4-3 | 2-0 | 1-2 | 0-1 | | 1-0 | 3-1 | 0-0 | 0-0 | 0-0 |
| Reading FC | 2-0 | 0-1 | 3-1 | 0-0 | 0-1 | 4-1 | 0-0 | 1-1 | 0-1 | 3-0 | 2-1 | 1-2 | 0-1 | 0-1 | 2-0 | 0-0 | 2-1 | | 2-2 | 2-0 | 1-1 | 3-0 |
| Southend United FC | 2-1 | 3-0 | 6-1 | 2-0 | 2-0 | 2-1 | 0-3 | 3-0 | 4-0 | 2-1 | 2-1 | 1-0 | 0-1 | 0-1 | 0-1 | 0-3 | 1-0 | 3-0 | | 1-0 | 0-0 | 0-4 |
| Swansea Town AFC | 2-2 | 1-0 | 7-0 | 1-1 | 1-1 | 2-2 | 6-1 | 2-1 | 2-1 | 4-1 | 2-0 | 2-2 | 1-0 | 2-1 | 2-0 | 2-0 | 2-0 | 1-0 | 4-0 | | 2-0 | 3-1 |
| Swindon Town FC | 2-0 | 4-0 | 2-0 | 3-0 | 3-0 | 3-0 | 2-2 | 1-0 | 2-0 | 4-1 | 5-1 | 1-0 | 2-2 | 5-0 | 1-0 | 1-0 | 5-3 | 2-1 | 3-0 | 0-2 | | 0-1 |
| Watford FC | 0-0 | 2-1 | 3-1 | 0-1 | 1-0 | 1-0 | 0-0 | 3-0 | 1-2 | 1-1 | 3-1 | 1-0 | 0-5 | 1-0 | 0-2 | 1-0 | 1-0 | 1-0 | 0-3 | 1-3 | 1-0 | |

## Division 3 (South)

| | | Pd | Wn | Dw | Ls | GF | GA | Pts | |
|---|---|---|---|---|---|---|---|---|---|
| 1. | Swansea Town AFC (Swansea) | 42 | 23 | 11 | 8 | 68 | 35 | 57 | P |
| 2. | Plymouth Argyle FC (Plymouth) | 42 | 23 | 10 | 9 | 77 | 38 | 56 | |
| 3. | Bristol City FC (Bristol) | 42 | 22 | 9 | 11 | 60 | 41 | 53 | |
| 4. | Swindon Town FC (Swindon) | 42 | 20 | 11 | 11 | 66 | 38 | 51 | |
| 5. | Millwall Athletic FC (London) | 42 | 18 | 13 | 11 | 58 | 38 | 49 | * |
| 6. | Newport County AFC (Newport) | 42 | 20 | 9 | 13 | 62 | 42 | 49 | |
| 7. | Exeter City FC (Exeter) | 42 | 19 | 9 | 14 | 59 | 48 | 47 | |
| 8. | Brighton & Hove Albion FC (Hove) | 42 | 19 | 8 | 15 | 59 | 45 | 46 | |
| 9. | Northampton Town FC (Northampton) | 42 | 20 | 6 | 16 | 51 | 44 | 46 | |
| 10. | Southend United FC (Southend-on-Sea) | 42 | 19 | 5 | 18 | 51 | 61 | 43 | |
| 11. | Watford FC (Watford) | 42 | 17 | 9 | 16 | 38 | 47 | 43 | |
| 12. | Norwich City FC (Norwich) | 42 | 14 | 13 | 15 | 53 | 51 | 41 | |
| 13. | Gillingham FC (Gillingham) | 42 | 13 | 14 | 15 | 35 | 44 | 40 | |
| 14. | Reading FC (Reading) | 42 | 14 | 10 | 18 | 37 | 38 | 38 | |
| 15. | Charlton Athletic FC (London) | 42 | 13 | 12 | 17 | 46 | 48 | 38 | |
| 16. | Luton Town FC (Luton) | 42 | 10 | 17 | 15 | 49 | 57 | 37 | |
| 17. | Bristol Rovers FC (Bristol) | 42 | 12 | 13 | 17 | 42 | 49 | 37 | |
| 18. | Aberdare Athletic FC (Aberdare) | 42 | 14 | 9 | 19 | 54 | 67 | 37 | |
| 19. | Queen's Park Rangers FC (London) | 42 | 14 | 8 | 20 | 42 | 63 | 36 | |
| 20. | Bournemouth & Boscombe Athletic FC (Bournemouth) | 42 | 13 | 8 | 21 | 40 | 58 | 34 | |
| 21. | Brentford FC (London) | 42 | 9 | 7 | 26 | 38 | 91 | 25 | |
| 22. | Merthyr Town FC (Merthyr Tydfil) | 42 | 8 | 5 | 29 | 35 | 77 | 21 | |
| | | 924 | 354 | 216 | 354 | 1120 | 1120 | 924 | |

\* Millwall Athletic FC (London) changed their club name to Millwall FC (London) from the next season.

## F.A. CUP FINAL  (Wembley Stadium, London – 25/04/1925 – 91,763)

SHEFFIELD UNITED FC (SHEFFIELD)            1-0            Cardiff City AFC (Cardiff)
*Tunstall*

Sheffield United: Sutcliffe, Cook, Milton, Pantling, King, Green, Mercer, Boyle, Johnson, Gillespie, Tunstall.
Cardiff City: Farqurharson, Nelson, Blair, Wake, Keenor, Hardy, W.Davies, Gill, Nicholson, Beadles, J.Evans.

## Semi-finals

| | | |
|---|---|---|
| Cardiff City AFC (Cardiff) | 3-1 | Blackburn Rovers FC (Blackburn) |
| Sheffield United FC (Sheffield) | 2-0 | Southampton FC (Southampton) |

## Quarter-finals

| | | |
|---|---|---|
| Blackburn Rovers FC (Blackburn) | 1-0 | Blackpool FC (Blackpool) |
| Cardiff City AFC (Cardiff) | 2-1 | Leicester City FC (Leicester) |
| Sheffield United FC (Sheffield) | 2-0 | West Bromwich Albion FC (West Bromwich) |
| Southampton FC (Southampton) | 1-0 | Liverpool FC (Liverpool) |

# 1925-26

| Football League Division 1 1925-1926 Season | Aston Villa | Birmingham | Blackburn Rovers | Bolton Wanderers | Burnley | Bury | Cardiff City | Everton | Huddersfield Town | Leeds United | Leicester City | Liverpool | Manchester City | Manchester United | Newcastle United | Notts County | Sheffield United | Sunderland | The Arsenal | Tottenham Hotspur | W.B.A. | West Ham United |
|---|---|---|---|---|---|---|---|---|---|---|---|---|---|---|---|---|---|---|---|---|---|---|
| Aston Villa FC | | 3-3 | 1-2 | 2-2 | 10-0 | 1-1 | 0-2 | 3-1 | 3-0 | 3-1 | 2-2 | 3-0 | 3-1 | 2-2 | 2-2 | 2-1 | 2-2 | 4-2 | 3-0 | 3-0 | 2-1 | 2-0 |
| Birmingham FC | 2-1 | | 2-0 | 0-1 | 1-7 | 2-3 | 3-2 | 3-1 | 1-3 | 2-1 | 1-1 | 2-0 | 1-0 | 2-1 | 1-1 | 0-1 | 2-0 | 2-1 | 1-0 | 3-1 | 3-0 | 1-0 |
| Blackburn Rovers FC | 3-1 | 4-4 | | 3-0 | 6-3 | 1-2 | 6-3 | 2-2 | 2-1 | 2-2 | 0-0 | 1-1 | 3-3 | 7-0 | 1-2 | 4-1 | 3-1 | 3-0 | 2-3 | 4-2 | 1-2 | 1-0 |
| Bolton Wanderers FC | 1-3 | 5-3 | 2-2 | | 4-2 | 3-2 | 0-1 | 0-2 | 6-1 | 1-0 | 2-2 | 0-1 | 5-1 | 3-1 | 2-2 | 2-1 | 2-1 | 3-2 | 1-1 | 1-1 | 2-2 | 1-0 |
| Burnley FC | 2-3 | 3-1 | 1-3 | 1-1 | | 2-2 | 4-1 | 1-3 | 1-1 | 6-3 | 4-0 | 2-1 | 1-2 | 0-1 | 1-0 | 0-0 | 1-1 | 5-2 | 2-2 | 1-2 | 3-4 | 2-2 |
| Bury FC | 2-3 | 2-1 | 3-1 | 0-5 | 8-1 | | 4-1 | 1-0 | 0-0 | 0-2 | 4-0 | 0-1 | 6-5 | 1-3 | 1-1 | 3-1 | 7-4 | 2-2 | 2-2 | 3-0 | 2-0 | 4-1 |
| Cardiff City AFC | 2-0 | 2-0 | 4-1 | 0-1 | 2-3 | 3-2 | | 2-1 | 1-2 | 0-0 | 5-2 | 2-2 | 2-2 | 0-2 | 0-0 | 2-1 | 0-1 | 0-1 | 0-0 | 0-1 | 3-2 | 0-1 |
| Everton FC | 1-1 | 2-2 | 3-0 | 2-1 | 1-1 | 1-1 | 1-1 | | 2-3 | 4-2 | 1-0 | 3-3 | 1-1 | 1-3 | 3-0 | 3-0 | 2-2 | 2-1 | 2-3 | 1-1 | 4-0 | 2-0 |
| Huddersfield Town AFC | 5-1 | 4-1 | 3-1 | 3-0 | 2-1 | 2-1 | 1-1 | 3-0 | | 3-1 | 3-0 | 0-0 | 2-2 | 5-0 | 0-1 | 2-0 | 4-1 | 1-1 | 2-2 | 2-1 | 1-1 | 2-1 |
| Leeds United AFC | 2-2 | 0-0 | 2-1 | 2-1 | 2-2 | 2-3 | 1-0 | 1-1 | 0-4 | | 1-0 | 1-1 | 3-4 | 2-0 | 2-0 | 2-1 | 2-0 | 0-2 | 4-2 | 4-1 | 0-1 | 5-2 |
| Leicester City FC | 1-2 | 1-0 | 2-1 | 5-2 | 3-2 | 0-2 | 1-2 | 1-1 | 2-0 | 1-3 | | 3-1 | 2-3 | 1-3 | 3-2 | 1-0 | 2-2 | 4-1 | 0-1 | 5-3 | 3-0 | 1-1 |
| Liverpool FC | 3-1 | 2-2 | 2-2 | 2-2 | 3-2 | 0-1 | 0-2 | 5-1 | 1-2 | 1-1 | 0-3 | | 2-1 | 5-0 | 6-3 | 2-0 | 2-2 | 2-2 | 3-0 | 0-0 | 2-0 | 0-0 |
| Manchester City FC | 4-2 | 2-4 | 0-1 | 1-1 | 8-3 | 0-2 | 3-2 | 4-4 | 1-5 | 2-1 | 5-1 | 1-1 | | 1-1 | 2-2 | 1-1 | 2-4 | 4-1 | 2-5 | 0-0 | 3-1 | 3-2 |
| Manchester United FC | 3-0 | 3-1 | 2-0 | 2-1 | 6-1 | 0-1 | 1-0 | 0-0 | 1-1 | 2-1 | 3-2 | 3-3 | 1-6 | | 2-1 | 0-1 | 1-2 | 5-1 | 0-1 | 0-0 | 3-2 | 2-1 |
| Newcastle United FC | 2-2 | 1-3 | 1-7 | 5-1 | 1-3 | 4-0 | 0-1 | 3-3 | 0-2 | 3-0 | 3-2 | 3-0 | 3-2 | 4-1 | | 6-3 | 3-1 | 0-0 | 7-0 | 3-1 | 3-0 | 4-1 |
| Notts County FC | 1-0 | 3-0 | 1-1 | 3-0 | 0-1 | 4-1 | 2-4 | 0-3 | 4-2 | 1-0 | 2-2 | 1-2 | 1-0 | 0-3 | 1-3 | | 2-0 | 2-0 | 4-1 | 4-2 | 0-0 | 1-1 |
| Sheffield United FC | 4-1 | 4-1 | 1-1 | 2-0 | 6-1 | 3-1 | 11-2 | 1-1 | 2-3 | 2-0 | 2-4 | 3-1 | 8-3 | 2-0 | 4-3 | 3-0 | | 4-1 | 4-0 | 2-3 | 3-2 | 1-1 |
| Sunderland AFC | 3-2 | 3-1 | 6-2 | 2-1 | 2-2 | 1-0 | 1-3 | 7-3 | 4-1 | 1-3 | 3-0 | 3-2 | 5-3 | 2-1 | 2-2 | 3-1 | 6-1 | | 2-1 | 3-0 | 4-0 | 4-1 |
| The Arsenal FC | 2-0 | 3-0 | 4-2 | 2-3 | 1-2 | 6-1 | 5-0 | 4-1 | 3-1 | 4-1 | 2-2 | 1-1 | 1-0 | 3-2 | 3-0 | 3-0 | 4-0 | 2-0 | | 0-1 | 1-0 | 3-2 |
| Tottenham Hotspur FC | 2-2 | 2-1 | 4-2 | 2-3 | 0-2 | 4-2 | 1-2 | 1-1 | 5-5 | 3-2 | 1-3 | 3-1 | 1-0 | 0-1 | 1-0 | 4-0 | 3-2 | 0-2 | 1-1 | | 3-2 | 4-2 |
| West Bromwich Albion FC | 1-1 | 5-1 | 1-1 | 0-3 | 5-3 | 4-0 | 3-0 | 1-1 | 2-2 | 3-0 | 3-1 | 0-3 | 4-1 | 5-1 | 4-0 | 4-4 | 2-0 | 2-5 | 2-1 | 1-0 | | 7-1 |
| West Ham United FC | 5-2 | 2-2 | 2-1 | 6-0 | 2-0 | 0-2 | 3-1 | 1-0 | 2-3 | 4-2 | 1-1 | 1-2 | 3-1 | 1-0 | 1-0 | 1-0 | 1-3 | 3-2 | 0-4 | 3-1 | 3-0 | |

| Division 1 | Pd | Wn | Dw | Ls | GF | GA | Pts | |
|---|---|---|---|---|---|---|---|---|
| 1. HUDDERSFIELD TOWN AFC (HUDDERSFIELD) | 42 | 23 | 11 | 8 | 92 | 60 | 57 | |
| 2. The Arsenal FC (London) | 42 | 22 | 8 | 12 | 87 | 63 | 52 | |
| 3. Sunderland AFC (Sunderland) | 42 | 21 | 6 | 15 | 96 | 80 | 48 | |
| 4. Bury FC (Bury) | 42 | 20 | 7 | 15 | 85 | 77 | 47 | |
| 5. Sheffield United FC (Sheffield) | 42 | 19 | 8 | 15 | 102 | 82 | 46 | |
| 6. Aston Villa FC (Birmingham) | 42 | 16 | 12 | 14 | 86 | 76 | 44 | |
| 7. Liverpool FC (Liverpool) | 42 | 14 | 16 | 12 | 70 | 63 | 44 | |
| 8. Bolton Wanderers FC (Bolton) | 42 | 17 | 10 | 15 | 75 | 76 | 44 | |
| 9. Manchester United FC (Manchester) | 42 | 19 | 6 | 17 | 66 | 73 | 44 | |
| 10. Newcastle United FC (Newcastle-upon-Tyne) | 42 | 16 | 10 | 16 | 84 | 75 | 42 | |
| 11. Everton FC (Liverpool) | 42 | 12 | 18 | 12 | 72 | 70 | 42 | |
| 12. Blackburn Rovers FC (Blackburn) | 42 | 15 | 11 | 16 | 91 | 80 | 41 | |
| 13. West Bromwich Albion FC (West Bromwich) | 42 | 16 | 8 | 18 | 79 | 78 | 40 | |
| 14. Birmingham FC (Birmingham) | 42 | 16 | 8 | 18 | 66 | 81 | 40 | |
| 15. Tottenham Hotspur FC (London) | 42 | 15 | 9 | 18 | 66 | 79 | 39 | |
| 16. Cardiff City AFC (Cardiff) | 42 | 16 | 7 | 19 | 61 | 76 | 39 | |
| 17. Leicester City FC (Leicester) | 42 | 14 | 10 | 18 | 70 | 80 | 38 | |
| 18. West Ham United FC (London) | 42 | 15 | 7 | 20 | 63 | 76 | 37 | |
| 19. Leeds United AFC (Leeds) | 42 | 14 | 8 | 20 | 64 | 76 | 36 | |
| 20. Burnley FC (Burnley) | 42 | 13 | 10 | 19 | 85 | 108 | 36 | |
| 21. Manchester City FC (Manchester) | 42 | 12 | 11 | 19 | 89 | 100 | 35 | R |
| 22. Notts County FC (Nottingham) | 42 | 13 | 7 | 22 | 54 | 74 | 33 | R |
| | 924 | 358 | 208 | 358 | 1703 | 1703 | 924 | |

## Top Goalscorer

1) Ted HARPER        (Blackburn Rovers FC)     43

| Football League Division 2 1925-1926 Season | Barnsley | Blackpool | Bradford City | Chelsea | Clapton Orient | Darlington | Derby County | Fulham | Hull City | Middlesbrough | Nottingham Forest | Oldham Athletic | Portsmouth | Port Vale | Preston North End | Southampton | South Shields | Stockport County | Stoke | Swansea Town | Wednesday | Wolves |
|---|---|---|---|---|---|---|---|---|---|---|---|---|---|---|---|---|---|---|---|---|---|---|
| Barnsley FC | ▓ | 2-0 | 0-0 | 2-3 | 3-1 | 1-1 | 0-1 | 2-2 | 2-1 | 0-1 | 4-1 | 3-4 | 2-2 | 3-0 | 2-0 | 2-0 | 2-1 | 1-1 | 2-1 | 2-0 | 1-1 | 1-1 |
| Blackpool FC | 4-0 | ▓ | 3-0 | 0-0 | 3-0 | 0-1 | 1-2 | 2-0 | 2-2 | 2-3 | 3-0 | 2-1 | 2-2 | 2-2 | 3-1 | 2-1 | 1-0 | 4-1 | 0-0 | 0-0 | 1-0 | 4-0 |
| Bradford City AFC | 4-1 | 1-0 | ▓ | 4-2 | 0-3 | 2-0 | 0-0 | 0-0 | 0-1 | 2-0 | 0-1 | 1-1 | 0-1 | 2-0 | 2-0 | 0-5 | 1-1 | 2-2 | 2-1 | 3-1 | 1-4 | 1-2 |
| Chelsea FC | 3-2 | 2-3 | 2-0 | ▓ | 1-3 | 5-2 | 2-1 | 4-0 | 4-0 | 0-1 | 0-0 | 3-0 | 0-0 | 3-1 | 5-0 | 0-0 | 0-0 | 3-2 | 1-1 | 1-3 | 0-0 | 3-3 |
| Clapton Orient FC | 4-0 | 2-2 | 3-1 | 1-2 | ▓ | 1-2 | 0-1 | 1-1 | 0-0 | 1-0 | 0-1 | 1-2 | 1-1 | 1-2 | 1-1 | 2-1 | 1-2 | 2-1 | 4-0 | 2-0 | 0-0 | 2-1 |
| Darlington FC | 2-2 | 1-3 | 1-3 | 1-1 | 6-0 | ▓ | 3-0 | 1-2 | 1-2 | 0-2 | 0-0 | 1-0 | 7-1 | 4-0 | 1-1 | 3-1 | 4-1 | 3-2 | 1-2 | 3-3 | 5-1 | 3-4 |
| Derby County FC | 4-0 | 5-2 | 0-0 | 4-2 | 3-1 | 0-2 | ▓ | 3-1 | 3-1 | 2-0 | 1-0 | 0-2 | 2-0 | 2-2 | 2-0 | 4-0 | 7-3 | 5-0 |  | 4-1 | 2-0 |  |
| Fulham FC | 2-2 | 1-1 | 2-0 | 0-3 | 0-2 | 4-0 | 1-1 | ▓ | 1-1 | 2-0 | 0-2 | 2-1 | 2-3 | 3-3 | 2-1 | 1-1 | 2-1 | 1-0 | 2-4 | 0-1 | 3-0 | 1-2 |
| Hull City AFC | 2-2 | 1-2 | 5-0 | 0-1 | 2-0 | 1-1 | 0-0 | 1-0 | ▓ | 1-2 | 4-1 | 1-2 | 1-0 | 3-0 | 1-1 | 4-0 | 1-3 | 4-0 | 1-0 | 4-2 | 0-1 | 3-1 |
| Middlesbrough FC | 5-0 | 3-2 | 2-5 | 1-2 | 1-2 | 3-2 | 1-2 | 4-0 | 3-3 | ▓ | 1-0 | 2-1 | 4-1 | 3-1 | 5-1 | 3-0 | 1-2 | 4-0 | 3-0 | 0-3 | 3-0 | 4-1 |
| Nottingham Forest FC | 4-2 | 1-1 | 0-0 | 1-5 | 1-0 | 2-0 | 1-2 | 2-2 | 4-0 | 1-0 | ▓ | 1-1 | 3-1 | 2-0 | 4-0 | 1-2 | 4-1 | 1-2 | 0-2 | 1-2 | 2-0 | 1-4 |
| Oldham Athletic AFC | 2-1 | 3-2 | 3-0 | 1-1 | 1-1 | 0-1 | 2-0 | 4-0 | 2-1 | 4-1 | 8-3 | ▓ | 1-3 | 3-2 | 3-2 | 1-0 | 2-1 | 3-0 | 7-2 | 0-0 | 1-1 | 1-2 |
| Portsmouth FC | 1-2 | 2-0 | 3-1 | 4-0 | 3-2 | 2-0 | 2-2 | 0-0 | 2-2 | 1-5 | 5-1 | 0-2 | ▓ | 3-2 | 5-2 | 1-2 | 4-2 | 4-0 | 2-0 | 0-0 | 1-2 | 3-0 |
| Port Vale FC | 3-0 | 5-0 | 2-0 | 0-6 | 4-2 | 6-1 | 0-1 | 0-1 | 3-1 | 4-0 | 1-0 | 3-0 | 1-1 | ▓ | 3-0 | 1-1 | 2-0 | 2-0 | 3-0 | 3-0 | 4-3 | 3-0 |
| Preston North End FC | 4-2 | 6-4 | 3-1 | 3-1 | 4-1 | 0-0 | 2-1 | 2-1 | 4-0 | 1-0 | 2-0 | 2-1 | 3-2 | 4-0 | ▓ | 2-2 | 0-4 | 5-3 | 2-0 | 4-2 | 0-3 | 1-0 |
| Southampton FC | 0-0 | 2-2 | 1-2 | 0-1 | 2-0 | 4-1 | 2-1 | 2-0 | 0-2 | 3-1 | 2-0 | 3-1 | 1-3 | 2-3 | 2-0 | ▓ | 0-1 | 3-0 | 1-2 | 4-1 | 1-2 | 4-2 |
| South Shields FC | 3-0 | 3-4 | 1-3 | 0-0 | 1-0 | 2-4 | 0-0 | 5-2 | 1-3 | 2-2 | 3-1 | 0-0 | 5-1 | 5-2 | 1-1 | 2-0 | ▓ | 4-2 | 5-1 | 3-1 | 1-1 | 3-1 |
| Stockport County FC | 1-1 | 4-3 | 1-1 | 0-0 | 3-2 | 1-1 | 3-0 | 1-2 | 0-1 | 1-2 | 3-0 | 1-0 | 3-3 | 2-2 | 1-1 | 1-2 | 4-1 | ▓ | 2-1 | 1-3 | 0-2 | 1-0 |
| Stoke FC | 1-2 | 1-3 | 1-0 | 1-3 | 0-0 | 6-1 | 0-1 | 5-0 | 3-1 | 4-0 | 1-1 | 1-0 | 2-1 | 0-3 | 1-3 | 1-1 | 0-1 | 3-0 | ▓ | 1-1 | 0-1 | 0-0 |
| Swansea Town AFC | 3-0 | 6-1 | 1-0 | 0-0 | 1-1 | 2-0 | 6-0 | 4-0 | 3-0 | 3-3 | 1-0 | 1-0 | 4-1 | 3-1 | 1-2 | 4-0 | 1-1 |  |  | ▓ | 2-2 | 2-4 |
| The Wednesday FC | 3-0 | 2-0 | 5-1 | 4-1 | 3-0 | 4-0 | 1-4 | 3-0 | 2-0 | 2-0 | 2-0 | 5-1 | 4-2 | 0-2 | 5-1 | 2-1 | 1-0 | 6-2 | 2-0 | 3-1 | ▓ | 2-1 |
| Wolverhampton Wanderers FC | 7-1 | 0-0 | 1-1 | 0-0 | 3-0 | 1-0 | 2-0 | 0-0 | 3-1 | 3-1 | 4-0 | 2-1 | 4-1 | 3-1 | 3-0 | 4-1 | 2-0 | 5-1 | 5-1 | 2-3 | 1-2 | ▓ |

## Division 2

| | | Pd | Wn | Dw | Ls | GF | GA | Pts | |
|---|---|---|---|---|---|---|---|---|---|
| 1. | The Wednesday FC (Sheffield) | 42 | 27 | 6 | 9 | 88 | 48 | 60 | P |
| 2. | Derby County FC (Derby) | 42 | 25 | 7 | 10 | 77 | 42 | 57 | P |
| 3. | Chelsea FC (London) | 42 | 19 | 14 | 9 | 76 | 49 | 52 | |
| 4. | Wolverhampton Wanderers FC (Wolverhampton) | 42 | 21 | 7 | 14 | 84 | 60 | 49 | |
| 5. | Swansea Town AFC (Swansea) | 42 | 19 | 11 | 12 | 84 | 57 | 49 | |
| 6. | Blackpool FC (Blackpool) | 42 | 17 | 11 | 14 | 76 | 69 | 45 | |
| 7. | Oldham Athletic AFC (Oldham) | 42 | 18 | 8 | 16 | 74 | 62 | 44 | |
| 8. | Port Vale FC (Stoke-on-Trent) | 42 | 19 | 6 | 17 | 79 | 69 | 44 | |
| 9. | South Shields FC (South Shields) | 42 | 18 | 8 | 16 | 74 | 65 | 44 | |
| 10. | Middlesbrough FC (Middlesbrough) | 42 | 21 | 2 | 19 | 77 | 68 | 44 | |
| 11. | Portsmouth FC (Portsmouth) | 42 | 17 | 10 | 15 | 79 | 74 | 44 | |
| 12. | Preston North End FC (Preston) | 42 | 18 | 7 | 17 | 71 | 84 | 43 | |
| 13. | Hull City AFC (Kingston-upon-Hull) | 42 | 16 | 9 | 17 | 63 | 61 | 41 | |
| 14. | Southampton FC (Southampton) | 42 | 15 | 8 | 19 | 63 | 63 | 38 | |
| 15. | Darlington FC (Darlington) | 42 | 14 | 10 | 18 | 72 | 77 | 38 | |
| 16. | Bradford City AFC (Bradford) | 42 | 13 | 10 | 19 | 47 | 66 | 36 | |
| 17. | Nottingham Forest FC (Nottingham) | 42 | 14 | 8 | 20 | 51 | 73 | 36 | |
| 18. | Barnsley FC (Barnsley) | 42 | 12 | 12 | 18 | 58 | 84 | 36 | |
| 19. | Fulham FC (London) | 42 | 11 | 12 | 19 | 46 | 77 | 34 | |
| 20. | Clapton Orient FC (London) | 42 | 12 | 9 | 21 | 50 | 65 | 33 | |
| 21. | Stoke City FC (Stoke-on-Trent) | 42 | 12 | 8 | 22 | 54 | 77 | 32 | R |
| 22. | Stockport County FC (Stockport) | 42 | 8 | 9 | 25 | 51 | 97 | 25 | R |
| | | 924 | 366 | 192 | 366 | 1487 | 1487 | 924 | |

| Football League Division 3 (N) 1925-1926 Season | Accrington St. | Ashington | Barrow | Bradford P.A. | Chesterfield | Coventry City | Crewe Alexandra | Doncaster Rovers | Durham City | Grimsby Town | Halifax Town | Hartlepools Utd. | Lincoln City | Nelson | New Brighton | Rochdale | Rotherham Utd. | Southport | Tranmere Rovers | Walsall | Wigan Borough | Wrexham |
|---|---|---|---|---|---|---|---|---|---|---|---|---|---|---|---|---|---|---|---|---|---|---|
| Accrington Stanley FC | | 2-1 | 2-0 | 1-4 | 2-0 | 3-1 | 2-0 | 2-3 | 3-1 | 1-0 | 0-1 | 1-2 | 3-1 | 3-2 | 0-2 | 1-3 | 2-3 | 4-3 | 4-3 | 5-2 | 4-0 | 4-2 |
| Ashington FC | 3-1 | | 1-4 | 1-1 | 0-0 | 2-0 | 2-0 | 6-1 | 0-1 | 4-2 | 0-1 | 2-0 | 4-1 | 5-1 | 1-1 | 0-1 | 4-2 | 1-1 | 1-0 | 2-0 | 3-3 | 2-2 |
| Barrow AFC | 1-2 | 2-3 | | 0-1 | 0-3 | 1-4 | 0-1 | 0-2 | 1-4 | 0-3 | 1-2 | 1-4 | 3-0 | 1-0 | 2-3 | 1-3 | 1-2 | 0-3 | 3-3 | 5-2 | 1-1 | 4-3 |
| Bradford Park Avenue | 3-0 | 1-0 | 3-0 | | 1-0 | 3-0 | 3-0 | 2-0 | 2-1 | 0-1 | 2-2 | 4-0 | 4-1 | 3-0 | 1-0 | 3-1 | 6-1 | 6-1 | 3-0 | 8-0 | 6-1 | 1-1 |
| Chesterfield FC | 7-2 | 6-1 | 3-1 | 1-1 | | 4-3 | 4-2 | 2-2 | 2-0 | 2-0 | 1-0 | 5-2 | 2-0 | 3-1 | 3-0 | 1-2 | 6-1 | 3-0 | 4-0 | 4-0 | 4-0 | 3-1 |
| Coventry City FC | 2-1 | 2-0 | 2-0 | 2-2 | 2-4 | | 2-1 | 4-0 | 3-1 | 1-1 | 4-1 | 5-2 | 3-2 | 1-0 | 0-0 | 2-2 | 7-0 | 0-0 | 1-2 | 2-0 | 0-0 | 2-0 |
| Crewe Alexandra FC | 3-0 | 2-1 | 4-1 | 1-2 | 2-0 | 2-1 | | 2-2 | 2-0 | 1-1 | 0-1 | 2-1 | 3-1 | 1-4 | 4-1 | 3-2 | 3-1 | 0-1 | 1-1 | 2-1 | 3-1 | 2-0 |
| Doncaster Rovers FC | 6-2 | 2-1 | 0-1 | 0-3 | 3-0 | 8-1 | 5-2 | | 4-1 | 1-4 | 2-2 | 2-1 | 1-0 | 1-1 | 2-0 | 2-2 | 0-0 | 6-1 | 4-0 | 1-1 | 1-1 | 1-1 |
| Durham City FC | 5-1 | 0-0 | 2-1 | 2-1 | 5-2 | 4-1 | 1-1 | 3-0 | | 0-0 | 2-0 | 0-0 | 3-2 | 0-2 | 0-0 | 0-2 | 5-1 | 3-2 | 2-1 | 4-1 | 2-0 | 2-1 |
| Grimsby Town FC | 5-2 | 3-1 | 4-0 | 3-0 | 1-0 | 2-0 | 2-0 | 3-0 | 3-1 | | 1-0 | 2-0 | 4-0 | 3-0 | 1-0 | 3-0 | 3-0 | 3-2 | 8-0 | 5-1 | 1-1 | 1-0 |
| Halifax Town AFC | 1-1 | 0-0 | 3-2 | 1-2 | 2-0 | 1-0 | 1-0 | 0-3 | 2-1 | 0-2 | | 2-1 | 0-2 | 1-1 | 1-0 | 1-1 | 5-1 | 3-0 | 1-1 | 5-0 | 2-0 | 2-1 |
| Hartlepools United FC | 5-1 | 2-1 | 2-0 | 0-3 | 2-1 | 3-2 | 0-0 | 2-1 | 1-1 | 1-1 | 1-1 | | 4-2 | 2-0 | 6-1 | 4-2 | 2-1 | 5-0 | 3-2 | 9-3 | 0-0 | 5-0 |
| Lincoln City FC | 3-1 | 2-0 | 4-3 | 1-1 | 2-1 | 0-3 | 2-2 | 3-1 | 1-0 | 4-1 | 0-1 | 2-1 | | 1-0 | 3-1 | 0-2 | 0-3 | 3-0 | 1-3 | 5-1 | 2-1 | 3-2 |
| Nelson FC | 1-0 | 2-2 | 3-3 | 2-2 | 3-3 | 4-1 | 2-1 | 5-3 | 4-0 | 1-1 | 1-1 | 5-2 | 5-2 | | 1-1 | 1-3 | 3-0 | 3-3 | 7-0 | 2-0 | 7-0 | 5-1 |
| New Brighton FC | 4-1 | 1-1 | 2-1 | 1-1 | 1-2 | 5-1 | 2-3 | 2-1 | 1-2 | 1-4 | 2-1 | 3-2 | 5-0 | 0-0 | | 3-0 | 5-1 | 1-0 | 3-2 | 3-2 | 4-2 | 2-2 |
| Rochdale AFC | 3-2 | 1-3 | 2-1 | 2-0 | 2-4 | 4-1 | 0-4 | 4-1 | 5-0 | 5-2 | 2-1 | 6-0 | 0-1 | 2-0 | 2-1 | | 2-2 | 3-1 | 3-2 | 2-0 | 2-1 | 1-2 |
| Rotherham United FC | 3-1 | 5-1 | 2-1 | 2-3 | 0-1 | 2-1 | 2-2 | 1-1 | 2-0 | 2-1 | 1-1 | 1-0 | 1-3 | 1-3 | 1-0 | 0-4 | | 5-2 | 2-0 | 4-1 | 1-0 | 6-2 |
| Southport FC | 1-3 | 1-1 | 2-0 | 2-1 | 1-3 | 1-2 | 0-0 | 3-3 | 6-1 | 0-1 | 3-1 | 1-1 | 3-2 | 2-1 | 3-2 | 1-7 | 1-1 | | 2-1 | 1-1 | 3-1 | 0-1 |
| Tranmere Rovers FC | 2-2 | 1-4 | 3-0 | 3-2 | 0-4 | 2-1 | 2-0 | 1-0 | 2-1 | 0-0 | 2-1 | 2-0 | 4-2 | 0-1 | 3-5 | 3-1 | 1-0 | | | 2-1 | 5-1 | 4-1 |
| Walsall FC | 3-3 | 2-0 | 1-2 | 3-1 | 3-1 | 4-1 | 0-3 | 2-1 | 0-1 | 2-2 | 3-1 | 1-2 | 0-0 | 0-2 | 3-1 | 1-5 | 4-1 | 2-2 | 1-3 | | 0-1 | 5-1 |
| Wigan Borough FC | 5-0 | 0-2 | 4-1 | 1-3 | 2-0 | 5-1 | 3-1 | 0-1 | 4-1 | 2-2 | 0-0 | 1-0 | 3-3 | 5-0 | 3-1 | 2-2 | 0-1 | 3-1 | 2-2 | 2-0 | | 6-0 |
| Wrexham AFC | 5-6 | 2-3 | 0-0 | 4-2 | 1-1 | 3-1 | 1-1 | 0-2 | 3-0 | 4-1 | 2-0 | 2-2 | 1-1 | 3-2 | 1-2 | 1-0 | 2-2 | 3-2 | 0-2 | 0-1 | 1-0 | |

## Division 3 (North)

| | | Pd | Wn | Dw | Ls | GF | GA | Pts | |
|---|---|---|---|---|---|---|---|---|---|
| 1. | Grimsby Town FC (Cleethorpes) | 42 | 26 | 9 | 7 | 91 | 40 | 61 | P |
| 2. | Bradford Park Avenue FC (Bradford) | 42 | 26 | 8 | 8 | 101 | 43 | 60 | |
| 3. | Rochdale AFC (Rochdale) | 42 | 27 | 5 | 10 | 104 | 58 | 59 | |
| 4. | Chesterfield FC (Chesterfield) | 42 | 25 | 5 | 12 | 100 | 54 | 55 | |
| 5. | Halifax Town AFC (Halifax) | 42 | 17 | 11 | 14 | 53 | 50 | 45 | |
| 6. | Hartlepools United FC (Hartlepool) | 42 | 18 | 8 | 16 | 82 | 73 | 44 | |
| 7. | Tranmere Rovers FC (Birkenhead) | 42 | 19 | 6 | 17 | 73 | 83 | 44 | |
| 8. | Nelson FC (Nelson) | 42 | 16 | 11 | 15 | 89 | 71 | 43 | |
| 9. | Ashington FC (Ashington) | 42 | 16 | 11 | 15 | 70 | 62 | 43 | |
| 10. | Doncaster Rovers FC (Doncaster) | 42 | 16 | 11 | 15 | 80 | 72 | 43 | |
| 11. | Crewe Alexandra FC (Crewe) | 42 | 17 | 9 | 16 | 63 | 61 | 43 | |
| 12. | New Brighton FC (Wallasey) | 42 | 17 | 8 | 17 | 69 | 67 | 42 | |
| 13. | Durham City FC (Durham) | 42 | 18 | 6 | 18 | 63 | 70 | 42 | |
| 14. | Rotherham United FC (Rotherham) | 42 | 17 | 7 | 18 | 69 | 92 | 41 | |
| 15. | Lincoln City FC (Lincoln) | 42 | 17 | 5 | 20 | 66 | 82 | 39 | |
| 16. | Coventry City FC (Coventry) | 42 | 16 | 6 | 20 | 73 | 82 | 38 | T |
| 17. | Wigan Borough FC (Wigan) | 42 | 13 | 11 | 18 | 68 | 74 | 37 | |
| 18. | Accrington Stanley FC (Accrington) | 42 | 17 | 3 | 22 | 81 | 105 | 37 | |
| 19. | Wrexham AFC (Wrexham) | 42 | 11 | 10 | 21 | 63 | 92 | 32 | |
| 20. | Southport FC (Southport) | 42 | 11 | 10 | 21 | 62 | 92 | 32 | |
| 21. | Walsall FC (Walsall) | 42 | 10 | 6 | 26 | 58 | 107 | 26 | |
| 22. | Barrow AFC (Barrow-in-Furness) | 42 | 7 | 4 | 31 | 50 | 98 | 18 | |
| | | 924 | 377 | 170 | 377 | 1628 | 1628 | 924 | |

T: Coventry City FC (Coventry) were transferred to Division 3 (South) from the next season.

| Football League Division 3 (S) 1925-1926 Season | Aberdare Ath. | Bournemouth | Brentford | Brighton | Bristol City | Bristol Rovers | Charlton Ath. | Crystal Palace | Exeter City | Gillingham | Luton Town | Merthyr Town | Millwall | Newport Co. | Northampton | Norwich City | Plymouth Arg. | Q.P.R. | Reading | Southend Utd. | Swindon Town | Watford |
|---|---|---|---|---|---|---|---|---|---|---|---|---|---|---|---|---|---|---|---|---|---|---|
| Aberdare Athletic FC | | 3-3 | 3-0 | 2-2 | 3-3 | 0-1 | 3-1 | 2-0 | 5-0 | 0-1 | 2-5 | 0-0 | 1-2 | 2-0 | 1-0 | 3-1 | 6-1 | 1-0 | 2-2 | 2-0 | 1-1 | 8-1 |
| Bournemouth & B. Athletic | 3-0 | | 3-2 | 0-3 | 1-1 | 2-0 | 4-1 | 6-1 | 2-1 | 1-2 | 2-2 | 2-1 | 0-0 | 0-2 | 4-2 | 2-2 | 1-2 | 4-1 | 1-1 | 1-2 | 2-0 | 3-4 |
| Brentford FC | 1-0 | 0-2 | | 1-6 | 2-1 | 4-1 | 4-0 | 3-2 | 2-0 | 0-0 | 1-0 | 1-1 | 2-0 | 3-3 | 3-4 | 5-1 | 2-2 | 1-2 | 1-0 | 1-3 | 3-1 | 4-3 |
| Brighton & Hove Albion | 6-2 | 3-4 | 3-2 | | 0-0 | 2-3 | 1-0 | 3-2 | 1-3 | 1-2 | 2-0 | 3-1 | 3-1 | 2-1 | 2-2 | 1-1 | 1-2 | 2-1 | 2-2 | 3-2 | 3-1 | 3-1 |
| Bristol City FC | 1-0 | 5-0 | 3-0 | 1-0 | | 0-0 | 4-0 | 1-0 | 1-0 | 4-0 | 5-1 | 2-1 | 1-1 | 1-2 | 1-1 | 0-1 | 2-1 | 3-1 | 0-1 | 1-4 | 5-1 | 1-0 |
| Bristol Rovers FC | 0-3 | 7-2 | 1-2 | 4-0 | 0-1 | | 4-1 | 3-1 | 0-1 | 2-0 | 2-2 | 0-0 | 0-1 | -2 | 1-2 | 2-2 | 2-3 | 5-0 | 4-2 | 2-0 | 1-2 | 2-1 |
| Charlton Athletic FC | 1-0 | 5-0 | 0-2 | 1-1 | 3-1 | 0-1 | | 1-1 | 1-0 | 1-0 | 2-1 | 0-0 | 1-4 | 0-0 | 3-3 | 3-0 | 0-5 | 1-1 | 1-2 | 5-0 | 2-0 | 1-1 |
| Crystal Palace FC | 0-1 | 3-1 | 2-0 | 2-1 | 5-2 | 0-2 | 4-1 | | 3-2 | 0-2 | 3-0 | 3-0 | 1-2 | 4-2 | 1-0 | 2-0 | 5-5 | 1-0 | 3-0 | 3-0 | 1-0 | 4-0 |
| Exeter City FC | 4-0 | 0-1 | 6-1 | 2-4 | 1-1 | 3-0 | 5-3 | 0-1 | | 2-1 | 2-2 | 6-2 | 3-1 | 2-1 | 1-0 | 0-1 | 4-0 | 3-0 | 3-2 | 0-1 | 1-2 | 6-1 |
| Gillingham FC | 0-1 | 1-2 | 1-3 | 3-1 | 0-1 | 6-3 | 0-0 | 1-1 | 2-0 | | 2-1 | 3-1 | 0-0 | 2-0 | 1-1 | 2-0 | 2-0 | 3-0 | 4-1 | 3-1 | 0-1 | 0-1 |
| Luton Town FC | 2-1 | 4-1 | 4-2 | 3-3 | 4-1 | 1-0 | 1-0 | 3-2 | 1-1 | 5-3 | | 4-0 | 2-2 | 4-2 | 3-2 | 3-2 | 1-1 | 4-0 | 0-1 | 2-0 | 4-1 | 5-0 |
| Merthyr Town FC | 1-1 | 0-2 | 6-0 | 0-1 | 3-2 | 2-3 | 0-1 | 4-0 | 3-1 | 0-0 | 2-1 | | 0-2 | 4-1 | 5-3 | 3-1 | 1-1 | 1-0 | 5-2 | 5-1 | 2-1 | 4-1 |
| Millwall FC | 4-2 | 0-1 | 2-1 | 2-0 | 3-0 | 0-0 | 1-0 | 3-0 | 0-0 | 7-0 | 1-1 | | | 3-3 | 4-1 | 3-1 | 0-0 | 3-0 | 1-0 | 8-1 | 3-0 | 3-0 |
| Newport County AFC | 0-0 | 1-2 | 2-3 | 4-3 | 1-0 | 3-1 | 0-0 | 2-3 | 3-0 | 4-0 | 2-1 | 3-1 | 1-0 | | 3-0 | 1-1 | 0-3 | 4-1 | 1-1 | 1-0 | 0-4 | 3-3 |
| Northampton Town | 3-2 | 1-1 | 6-1 | 1-2 | 1-2 | 2-0 | 2-1 | 4-0 | 2-1 | 1-2 | 0-1 | 4-1 | 3-1 | 2-0 | | 3-2 | 2-1 | 3-2 | 0-1 | 3-3 | 2-0 | 2-2 |
| Norwich City FC | 2-3 | 3-1 | 1-0 | 1-2 | 1-3 | 1-0 | 3-0 | 4-3 | 3-1 | 1-0 | 2-0 | 2-2 | 1-0 | 0-0 | 2-1 | | 0-3 | 1-1 | 3-1 | 1-2 | 2-2 | 1-1 |
| Plymouth Argyle FC | 7-2 | 7-2 | 4-0 | 5-3 | 3-1 | 1-2 | 1-0 | 6-2 | 2-2 | 2-1 | 4-3 | 3-0 | 2-0 | 3-0 | 2-4 | 6-3 | | 3-1 | 1-3 | 6-2 | 1-1 | 2-1 |
| Queen's Park Rangers FC | 1-3 | 2-2 | 1-1 | 0-2 | 0-2 | 2-1 | 2-2 | 1-3 | 0-0 | 0-1 | 1-0 | 1-1 | 3-0 | 0-2 | 3-2 | 0-1 | 0-4 | | 1-2 | 2-2 | 1-1 | 2-0 |
| Reading FC | 2-1 | 5-2 | 7-1 | 0-0 | 1-1 | 3-0 | 1-1 | 2-1 | 3-2 | 1-0 | 3-0 | 1-1 | 2-1 | 4-2 | 2-0 | 1-1 | 2-1 | | | 1-0 | 2-0 | 4-1 |
| Southend United FC | 0-1 | 3-0 | 3-1 | 4-0 | 1-2 | 3-1 | 1-2 | 5-1 | 3-1 | 1-1 | 5-1 | 0-2 | 4-1 | 6-1 | 0-1 | 2-0 | 2-1 | 2-2 | | | 3-0 | 0-1 |
| Swindon Town FC | 2-1 | 8-2 | 2-1 | 1-0 | 1-3 | 4-2 | 3-0 | 3-1 | 2-1 | 1-0 | 2-0 | 0-2 | 1-1 | 2-1 | 1-2 | 3-1 | 2-0 | 2-0 | 1-1 | 2-0 | | 5-3 |
| Watford FC | 2-0 | 0-0 | 2-2 | 3-3 | 2-2 | 2-1 | 1-1 | 3-0 | 3-1 | 3-1 | 2-0 | 6-1 | 0-1 | 5-1 | 3-2 | 3-1 | 0-1 | 3-1 | 0-1 | 1-4 | 3-2 | |

## Division 3 (South)

| | | Pd | Wn | Dw | Ls | GF | GA | Pts | |
|---|---|---|---|---|---|---|---|---|---|
| 1. | Reading FC (Reading) | 42 | 23 | 11 | 8 | 77 | 52 | 57 | P |
| 2. | Plymouth Argyle FC (Plymouth) | 42 | 24 | 8 | 10 | 107 | 67 | 56 | |
| 3. | Millwall FC (London) | 42 | 21 | 11 | 10 | 73 | 39 | 53 | |
| 4. | Bristol City FC (Bristol) | 42 | 21 | 9 | 12 | 72 | 51 | 51 | |
| 5. | Brighton & Hove Albion FC (Hove) | 42 | 19 | 9 | 14 | 84 | 73 | 47 | |
| 6. | Swindon Town FC (Swindon) | 42 | 20 | 6 | 16 | 69 | 64 | 46 | |
| 7. | Luton Town FC (Luton) | 42 | 18 | 7 | 17 | 80 | 75 | 43 | |
| 8. | Bournemouth & Boscombe Athletic FC (Bournemouth) | 42 | 17 | 9 | 16 | 75 | 91 | 43 | |
| 9. | Aberdare Athletic FC (Aberdare) | 42 | 17 | 8 | 17 | 74 | 66 | 42 | |
| 10. | Gillingham FC (Gillingham) | 42 | 17 | 8 | 17 | 53 | 49 | 42 | |
| 11. | Southend United FC (Southend-on-Sea) | 42 | 19 | 4 | 19 | 78 | 73 | 42 | |
| 12. | Northampton Town FC (Northampton) | 42 | 17 | 7 | 18 | 82 | 80 | 41 | |
| 13. | Crystal Palace FC (London) | 42 | 19 | 3 | 20 | 75 | 79 | 41 | |
| 14. | Merthyr Town FC (Merthyr Tydfil) | 42 | 14 | 11 | 17 | 69 | 75 | 39 | |
| 15. | Watford FC (Watford) | 42 | 15 | 9 | 18 | 73 | 89 | 39 | |
| 16. | Norwich City FC (Norwich) | 42 | 15 | 9 | 18 | 58 | 73 | 39 | |
| 17. | Newport County AFC (Newport) | 42 | 14 | 10 | 18 | 64 | 74 | 38 | |
| 18. | Brentford FC (London) | 42 | 16 | 6 | 20 | 69 | 94 | 38 | |
| 19. | Bristol Rovers FC (Bristol) | 42 | 15 | 6 | 21 | 66 | 69 | 36 | |
| 20. | Exeter City FC (Exeter) | 42 | 15 | 5 | 22 | 72 | 70 | 35 | |
| 21. | Charlton Athletic FC (London) | 42 | 11 | 13 | 18 | 48 | 68 | 35 | |
| 22. | Queen's Park Rangers FC (London) | 42 | 6 | 9 | 27 | 37 | 84 | 21 | |
| | | 924 | 373 | 178 | 373 | 1155 | 1155 | 924 | |

# F.A. CUP FINAL   (Wembley Stadium, London – 24/04/1926 – 91,447)

BOLTON WANDERERS FC (BOLTON)          1-0          Manchester City FC (Manchester)

*Jack*

Bolton:  Pym, Haworth, Greenhaugh, Nuttall, Seddon, Jennings, Butler, Jack, JR Smith, J.Smith, Vizard.

Man. City:  Goodchild, Cookson, McCloy, Pringle, Cowen, McMullan, Austin, Browell, Roberts, Johnson, Hicks.

## Semi-finals

| | | |
|---|---|---|
| Bolton Wanderers FC (Bolton) | 3-0 | Swansea Town AFC (Swansea) |
| Manchester City FC (Manchester) | 3-0 | Manchester United FC (Manchester) |

## Quarter-finals

| | | |
|---|---|---|
| Clapton Orient FC (London) | 1-6 | Manchester City FC (Manchester) |
| Fulham FC (London) | 1-2 | Manchester United FC (Manchester) |
| Nottingham Forest FC (Nottingham) | 2-2, 0-0, 0-1 | Bolton Wanderers FC (Bolton) |
| Swansea Town AFC (Swansea) | 2-1 | The Arsenal FC (London) |

# 1926-27

Football League Division 1 1926-1927 Season

| | Aston Villa | Birmingham | Blackburn Rovers | Bolton Wanderers | Burnley | Bury | Cardiff City | Derby County | Everton | Huddersfield Town | Leeds United | Leicester City | Liverpool | Manchester United | Newcastle United | Sheffield United | Sunderland | The Arsenal | The Wednes. | Tottenham Hotspur | W.B.A. | West Ham United |
|---|---|---|---|---|---|---|---|---|---|---|---|---|---|---|---|---|---|---|---|---|---|---|
| Aston Villa FC | ■ | 4-2 | 4-3 | 3-4 | 1-1 | 1-2 | 0-0 | 3-1 | 5-3 | 3-0 | 5-1 | 2-0 | 1-1 | 2-0 | 1-2 | 4-0 | 3-1 | 2-3 | 2-2 | 2-3 | 2-0 | 1-5 |
| Birmingham FC | 1-2 | ■ | 3-1 | 6-1 | 1-0 | 2-2 | 1-2 | 1-0 | 1-0 | 1-3 | 2-0 | 2-1 | 3-0 | 4-0 | 2-0 | 2-3 | 2-0 | 0-0 | 0-0 | 1-0 | 1-0 | 0-2 |
| Blackburn Rovers FC | 0-2 | 3-2 | ■ | 0-3 | 1-5 | 2-2 | 1-0 | 4-4 | 3-3 | 4-2 | 4-1 | 2-1 | 2-1 | 2-1 | 1-2 | 3-4 | 0-2 | 1-2 | 2-2 | 1-0 | 0-0 | 4-1 |
| Bolton Wanderers FC | 0-2 | 1-0 | 5-1 | ■ | 3-1 | 2-2 | 2-0 | 3-1 | 5-0 | 4-0 | 3-0 | 2-0 | 2-1 | 4-0 | 2-1 | 4-1 | 2-2 | 2-2 | 3-2 | 2-2 | 1-1 | 2-0 |
| Burnley FC | 6-3 | 0-2 | 3-1 | 4-3 | ■ | 0-0 | 4-3 | 1-0 | 5-1 | 2-2 | 3-2 | 1-1 | 4-0 | 1-0 | 3-3 | 2-5 | 4-2 | 2-0 | 1-0 | 5-0 | 2-1 | 2-1 |
| Bury FC | 0-1 | 3-1 | 0-2 | 2-0 | 3-3 | ■ | 2-3 | 1-2 | 5-2 | 2-2 | 4-2 | 0-0 | 0-2 | 0-3 | 3-2 | 4-4 | 1-2 | 3-2 | 0-0 | 7-3 | 1-2 | |
| Cardiff City AFC | 2-3 | 1-0 | 0-1 | 1-0 | 0-0 | 2-1 | ■ | 2-0 | 1-0 | 2-0 | 3-1 | 0-1 | 2-0 | 0-2 | 1-1 | 3-0 | 3-0 | 2-0 | 3-2 | 1-2 | 1-1 | 1-2 |
| Derby County FC | 2-3 | 4-1 | 4-5 | 2-0 | 4-1 | 2-0 | 6-3 | ■ | 0-0 | 4-4 | 1-0 | 4-1 | 2-1 | 2-2 | 1-1 | 1-0 | 4-2 | 0-2 | 8-0 | 4-1 | 2-1 | 3-0 |
| Everton FC | 2-2 | 3-1 | 1-0 | 1-1 | 3-2 | 2-2 | 0-1 | 3-2 | ■ | 0-0 | 2-1 | 3-4 | 1-0 | 0-0 | 1-3 | 2-0 | 5-4 | 3-1 | 2-1 | 1-2 | 0-0 | 0-3 |
| Huddersfield Town AFC | 0-0 | 0-2 | 5-0 | 1-0 | 2-0 | 3-1 | 0-0 | 4-2 | 0-0 | ■ | 4-1 | 5-3 | 1-0 | 0-0 | 1-0 | 0-2 | 0-0 | 3-3 | 4-3 | 2-0 | 4-1 | 2-1 |
| Leeds United AFC | 3-1 | 2-1 | 4-1 | 2-5 | 0-2 | 4-1 | 0-0 | 1-0 | 1-3 | 1-1 | ■ | 1-1 | 0-0 | 2-3 | 1-2 | 1-1 | 2-2 | 4-1 | 4-1 | 1-1 | 3-1 | 6-3 |
| Leicester City FC | 5-1 | 5-2 | 4-0 | 0-1 | 0-3 | 1-1 | 3-1 | 1-1 | 6-2 | 2-4 | 3-2 | ■ | 3-2 | 2-3 | 2-1 | 2-2 | 2-1 | 2-1 | 5-3 | 2-2 | 5-0 | 3-0 |
| Liverpool FC | 2-1 | 2-1 | 2-2 | 3-2 | 2-2 | 2-2 | 5-0 | 3-2 | 1-0 | 2-3 | 2-4 | 1-0 | ■ | 4-2 | 1-2 | 5-1 | 1-2 | 3-0 | 3-0 | 1-0 | 2-1 | 0-0 |
| Manchester United FC | 2-1 | 0-1 | 2-0 | 0-0 | 2-1 | 1-2 | 1-1 | 2-2 | 2-1 | 0-0 | 0-2 | 1-0 | 0-1 | ■ | 3-1 | 5-0 | 0-0 | 2-2 | 0-0 | 2-1 | 2-0 | 0-3 |
| Newcastle United FC | 4-0 | 5-1 | 6-1 | 1-0 | 1-5 | 3-1 | 5-0 | 3-0 | 7-3 | 1-0 | 1-0 | 1-1 | 1-0 | 4-2 | ■ | 2-0 | 1-0 | 6-1 | 2-1 | 3-2 | 5-2 | 2-0 |
| Sheffield United FC | 3-1 | 4-3 | 5-3 | 1-1 | 2-2 | 2-0 | 3-1 | 1-0 | 3-3 | 3-3 | 1-0 | 0-3 | 1-4 | 2-2 | 2-1 | ■ | 2-0 | 4-0 | 2-0 | 3-3 | 2-1 | 0-2 |
| Sunderland AFC | 1-1 | 4-1 | 2-5 | 6-2 | 7-1 | 3-0 | 2-2 | 3-2 | 1-1 | 6-2 | 3-0 | 2-1 | 6-0 | 2-0 | 3-0 | | ■ | 5-1 | 4-1 | 3-2 | 4-1 | 2-3 |
| The Arsenal FC | 2-1 | 3-0 | 2-2 | 2-1 | 6-2 | 1-0 | 3-2 | 2-1 | 1-2 | 0-2 | 1-0 | 2-2 | 2-0 | 1-0 | 2-2 | 1-1 | 2-3 | ■ | 6-2 | 2-4 | 4-1 | 2-2 |
| The Wednesday FC | 3-1 | 4-4 | 0-3 | 2-1 | 2-1 | 1-3 | 3-0 | 2-1 | 4-0 | 1-1 | 1-0 | 2-2 | 3-2 | 2-0 | 3-2 | 2-3 | 4-1 | 4-2 | ■ | 3-1 | 2-1 | 1-0 |
| Tottenham Hotspur FC | 0-1 | 6-1 | 1-1 | 1-0 | 4-1 | 1-0 | 4-1 | 3-2 | 2-1 | 3-3 | 4-1 | 2-2 | 1-2 | 1-1 | 1-3 | 3-1 | 0-2 | 0-4 | 7-3 | ■ | 3-0 | 1-3 |
| West Bromwich Albion FC | 6-2 | 1-2 | 2-0 | 1-1 | 4-2 | 3-1 | 1-2 | 3-1 | 3-2 | 2-2 | 2-4 | 0-1 | 0-1 | 2-2 | 4-2 | 1-0 | 3-0 | 1-3 | 2-2 | 5-0 | ■ | 1-3 |
| West Ham United FC | 5-1 | 1-0 | 1-5 | 4-4 | 2-1 | 1-2 | 2-2 | 1-2 | 2-1 | 3-2 | 3-2 | 3-3 | 3-3 | 4-0 | 1-1 | 3-0 | 1-2 | 7-0 | 1-1 | 1-2 | 1-2 | ■ |

## Division 1

| | | Pd | Wn | Dw | Ls | GF | GA | Pts | |
|---|---|---|---|---|---|---|---|---|---|
| 1. | NEWCASTLE UNITED FC (NEWCASTLE/TYNE) | 42 | 25 | 6 | 11 | 96 | 58 | 56 | |
| 2. | Huddersfield Town AFC (Huddersfield) | 42 | 17 | 17 | 8 | 76 | 60 | 51 | |
| 3. | Sunderland AFC (Sunderland) | 42 | 21 | 7 | 14 | 98 | 70 | 49 | |
| 4. | Bolton Wanderers FC (Bolton) | 42 | 19 | 10 | 13 | 84 | 62 | 48 | |
| 5. | Burnley FC (Burnley) | 42 | 19 | 9 | 14 | 91 | 80 | 47 | |
| 6. | West Ham United FC (London) | 42 | 19 | 8 | 15 | 86 | 70 | 46 | |
| 7. | Leicester City FC (Leicester) | 42 | 17 | 12 | 13 | 85 | 70 | 46 | |
| 8. | Sheffield United FC (Sheffield) | 42 | 17 | 10 | 15 | 74 | 86 | 44 | |
| 9. | Liverpool FC (Liverpool) | 42 | 18 | 7 | 17 | 69 | 61 | 43 | |
| 10. | Aston Villa FC (Birmingham) | 42 | 18 | 7 | 17 | 81 | 83 | 43 | |
| 11. | The Arsenal FC (London) | 42 | 17 | 9 | 16 | 77 | 86 | 43 | * |
| 12. | Derby County FC (Derby) | 42 | 17 | 7 | 18 | 86 | 73 | 41 | |
| 13. | Tottenham Hotspur FC (London) | 42 | 16 | 9 | 17 | 76 | 78 | 41 | |
| 14. | Cardiff City AFC (Cardiff) | 42 | 16 | 9 | 17 | 55 | 65 | 41 | |
| 15. | Manchester United FC (Manchester) | 42 | 13 | 14 | 15 | 52 | 64 | 40 | |
| 16. | The Wednesday FC (Sheffield) | 42 | 15 | 9 | 18 | 75 | 92 | 39 | |
| 17. | Birmingham FC (Birmingham) | 42 | 17 | 4 | 21 | 64 | 73 | 38 | |
| 18. | Blackburn Rovers FC (Blackburn) | 42 | 15 | 8 | 19 | 77 | 96 | 38 | |
| 19. | Bury FC (Bury) | 42 | 12 | 12 | 18 | 68 | 77 | 36 | |
| 20. | Everton FC (Liverpool) | 42 | 12 | 10 | 20 | 64 | 90 | 34 | |
| 21. | Leeds United AFC (Leeds) | 42 | 11 | 8 | 23 | 69 | 88 | 30 | R |
| 22. | West Bromwich Albion FC (West Bromwich) | 42 | 11 | 8 | 23 | 65 | 86 | 30 | R |
| | | 924 | 362 | 200 | 362 | 1668 | 1668 | 924 | |

* The Arsenal FC (London) changed their club name to Arsenal FC (London) from the next season.

## Top Goalscorer

1) James TROTTER                    (The Wednesday FC)      37

| Football League Division 2 1926-1927 Season | Barnsley | Blackpool | Bradford City | Chelsea | Clapton Orient | Darlington | Fulham | Grimsby Town | Hull City | Man. City | Middlesbrough | Nottingham For. | Notts County | Oldham Ath. | Portsmouth | Port Vale | Preston N.E. | Reading | Southampton | South Shields | Swansea Town | Wolves |
|---|---|---|---|---|---|---|---|---|---|---|---|---|---|---|---|---|---|---|---|---|---|---|
| Barnsley FC | ■ | 6-1 | 1-0 | 3-0 | 4-2 | 3-2 | 5-0 | 2-1 | 1-2 | 1-1 | 1-1 | 0-2 | 4-4 | 0-1 | 2-0 | 2-0 | 3-0 | 2-2 | 5-1 | 6-1 | 1-1 | 4-1 |
| Blackpool FC | 6-1 | ■ | 3-0 | 3-1 | 6-0 | 1-1 | 0-0 | 6-2 | 4-0 | 2-4 | 2-2 | 2-2 | 5-0 | 2-0 | 2-0 | 2-2 | 2-3 | 3-1 | 3-2 | 6-1 | 3-1 | 2-3 |
| Bradford City AFC | 1-1 | 4-1 | ■ | 0-1 | 1-3 | 0-1 | 1-0 | 2-2 | 1-2 | 4-3 | 0-1 | 1-1 | 1-2 | 0-1 | 1-2 | 1-2 | 0-1 | 1-1 | 2-0 | 3-1 | 5-0 | 1-2 |
| Chelsea FC | 4-2 | 1-1 | 5-2 | ■ | 2-1 | 2-2 | 2-2 | 2-0 | 1-0 | 0-0 | 3-0 | 2-0 | 2-0 | 1-0 | 0-0 | 2-0 | 2-1 | 0-0 | 2-3 | 4-1 | 2-2 | 1-0 |
| Clapton Orient FC | 0-1 | 1-0 | 1-1 | 3-0 | ■ | 0-4 | 2-3 | 2-4 | 1-2 | 2-4 | 2-3 | 2-2 | 2-1 | 3-1 | 4-5 | 1-2 | 1-1 | 5-1 | 1-0 | 1-0 | 1-0 | 2-0 |
| Darlington FC | 3-3 | 1-3 | 3-0 | 2-2 | 2-1 | ■ | 5-0 | 2-3 | 1-3 | 2-2 | 1-4 | 4-2 | 4-2 | 0-1 | 0-4 | 4-3 | 0-1 | 4-2 | 1-2 | 8-2 | 3-1 | 3-1 |
| Fulham FC | 1-0 | 1-0 | 1-1 | 1-2 | 2-0 | 2-1 | ■ | 0-5 | 3-1 | 2-5 | 0-3 | 2-1 | 3-0 | 1-1 | 0-0 | 6-2 | 0-1 | 1-2 | 3-0 | 2-2 | 4-3 | 4-1 |
| Grimsby Town FC | 1-3 | 2-1 | 4-2 | 0-0 | 2-2 | 2-1 | 2-0 | ■ | 0-1 | 2-2 | 4-7 | 1-1 | 1-4 | 2-5 | 0-0 | 4-4 | 5-2 | 0-1 | 0-1 | 1-1 | 0-1 | 6-0 |
| Hull City AFC | 5-1 | 3-0 | 4-0 | 0-1 | 4-0 | 2-1 | 2-0 | 2-3 | ■ | 3-2 | 3-3 | 1-2 | 2-0 | 1-2 | 2-1 | 0-0 | 3-1 | 1-1 | 0-0 | 2-0 | 2-1 | 1-0 |
| Manchester City FC | 1-1 | 2-1 | 8-0 | 1-0 | 6-1 | 7-0 | 4-2 | 2-0 | 2-2 | ■ | 3-5 | 1-1 | 4-1 | 3-0 | 4-0 | 4-1 | 1-0 | 3-0 | 3-4 | 1-2 | 3-1 | 2-1 |
| Middlesbrough FC | 5-1 | 4-4 | 4-3 | 0-0 | 6-0 | 4-1 | 6-1 | 3-0 | 2-0 | 2-1 | ■ | 1-0 | 4-2 | 3-1 | 7-3 | 5-2 | 0-2 | 5-0 | 3-1 | 5-0 | 7-1 | 2-0 |
| Nottingham Forest FC | 3-1 | 2-0 | 3-0 | 4-1 | 1-1 | 5-1 | 2-0 | 1-1 | 3-1 | 3-3 | 4-3 | ■ | 2-0 | 1-1 | 1-0 | 0-3 | 7-0 | 5-1 | 3-1 | 4-2 | 2-2 | 1-1 |
| Notts County FC | 1-1 | 2-3 | 4-0 | 5-0 | 3-1 | 3-1 | 4-0 | 3-0 | 1-0 | 1-0 | 2-2 | 1-2 | ■ | 1-2 | 2-3 | 2-1 | 1-1 | 2-0 | 0-1 | 4-1 | 1-3 | 2-2 |
| Oldham Athletic AFC | 0-4 | 1-3 | 2-1 | 1-2 | 5-2 | 3-2 | 2-3 | 3-1 | 1-1 | 1-2 | 2-1 | 3-3 | 5-2 | ■ | 1-0 | 1-3 | 5-1 | 3-1 | 1-1 | 3-2 | 5-2 | 2-0 |
| Portsmouth FC | 1-2 | 5-0 | 1-0 | 2-3 | 1-1 | 0-0 | 2-0 | 5-2 | 2-0 | 2-1 | 0-1 | 0-0 | 9-1 | 7-2 | ■ | 4-0 | 5-1 | 5-0 | 3-1 | 1-1 | 1-0 | 2-1 |
| Port Vale FC | 3-2 | 2-4 | 0-0 | 0-0 | 3-0 | 3-2 | 7-1 | 6-1 | 0-0 | 0-2 | 3-1 | 0-2 | 6-2 | 3-0 | 2-3 | ■ | 2-0 | 1-1 | 3-1 | 4-2 | 1-1 | 1-1 |
| Preston North End FC | 2-1 | 4-1 | 3-2 | 0-2 | 2-2 | 4-1 | 2-2 | 3-2 | 1-0 | 2-4 | 2-2 | 1-0 | 4-1 | 5-2 | 1-2 | 4-4 | ■ | 3-1 | 1-0 | 4-0 | 4-0 | 2-0 |
| Reading FC | 3-2 | 0-1 | 2-3 | 2-1 | 0-1 | 4-2 | 2-0 | 1-1 | 0-1 | 1-0 | 2-1 | 4-0 | 7-1 | 6-1 | 1-2 | 2-0 | 3-0 | ■ | 1-0 | 2-1 | 3-0 | 1-2 |
| Southampton FC | 3-1 | 5-3 | 0-0 | 1-1 | 1-2 | 3-1 | 4-1 | 0-0 | 0-1 | 1-1 | 2-1 | 1-0 | 2-0 | 0-1 | 0-2 | 2-2 | 1-1 | 1-1 | ■ | 6-2 | 1-1 | 1-0 |
| South Shields FC | 7-1 | 2-2 | 3-3 | 5-1 | 2-1 | 1-0 | 1-1 | 3-2 | 3-1 | 2-2 | 0-0 | 1-1 | 5-0 | 4-1 | 1-0 | 3-3 | 1-1 | 3-0 | 1-2 | ■ | 0-1 | 1-2 |
| Swansea Town AFC | 5-2 | 2-0 | 1-0 | 2-1 | 3-2 | 5-1 | 4-2 | 1-1 | 1-0 | 1-3 | 0-1 | 2-1 | 0-1 | 3-0 | 1-1 | 2-2 | 0-0 | 3-0 | 2-2 | 2-0 | ■ | 4-1 |
| Wolverhampton Wanderers FC | 9-1 | 4-1 | 7-2 | 0-3 | 5-0 | 2-1 | 2-1 | 3-4 | 5-2 | 4-1 | 1-2 | 2-0 | 0-1 | 1-1 | 0-1 | 1-2 | 1-2 | 1-1 | 2-2 | 2-0 | 2-2 | ■ |

### Division 2

| | | Pd | Wn | Dw | Ls | GF | GA | Pts | |
|---|---|---|---|---|---|---|---|---|---|
| 1. | Middlesbrough FC (Middlesbrough) | 42 | 27 | 8 | 7 | 122 | 60 | 62 | P |
| 2. | Portsmouth FC (Portsmouth) | 42 | 23 | 8 | 11 | 87 | 49 | 54 | P |
| 3. | Manchester City FC (Manchester) | 42 | 22 | 10 | 10 | 108 | 61 | 54 | |
| 4. | Chelsea FC (London) | 42 | 20 | 12 | 10 | 62 | 52 | 50 | |
| 5. | Nottingham Forest FC (Nottingham) | 42 | 18 | 14 | 10 | 80 | 55 | 50 | |
| 6. | Preston North End FC (Preston) | 42 | 20 | 9 | 13 | 74 | 72 | 49 | |
| 7. | Hull City AFC (Kingston-upon-Hull) | 42 | 20 | 7 | 15 | 63 | 52 | 47 | |
| 8. | Port Vale FC (Stoke-on-Trent) | 42 | 16 | 13 | 13 | 88 | 78 | 45 | |
| 9. | Blackpool FC (Blackpool) | 42 | 18 | 8 | 16 | 95 | 80 | 44 | |
| 10. | Oldham Athletic AFC (Oldham) | 42 | 19 | 6 | 17 | 74 | 84 | 44 | |
| 11. | Barnsley FC (Barnsley) | 42 | 17 | 9 | 16 | 88 | 87 | 43 | |
| 12. | Swansea Town AFC (Swansea) | 42 | 16 | 11 | 15 | 68 | 72 | 43 | |
| 13. | Southampton FC (Southampton) | 42 | 15 | 12 | 15 | 60 | 62 | 42 | |
| 14. | Reading FC (Reading) | 42 | 16 | 8 | 18 | 64 | 72 | 40 | |
| 15. | Wolverhampton Wanderers FC (Wolverhampton) | 42 | 14 | 7 | 21 | 73 | 75 | 35 | |
| 16. | Notts County FC (Nottingham) | 42 | 15 | 5 | 22 | 70 | 96 | 35 | |
| 17. | Grimsby Town FC (Cleethorpes) | 42 | 11 | 12 | 19 | 74 | 91 | 34 | |
| 18. | Fulham FC (London) | 42 | 13 | 8 | 21 | 58 | 92 | 34 | |
| 19. | South Shields FC (South Shields) | 42 | 11 | 11 | 20 | 71 | 96 | 33 | |
| 20. | Clapton Orient FC (London) | 42 | 12 | 7 | 23 | 60 | 96 | 31 | |
| 21. | Darlington FC (Darlington) | 42 | 12 | 6 | 24 | 79 | 98 | 30 | R |
| 22. | Bradford City AFC (Bradford) | 42 | 7 | 9 | 26 | 50 | 88 | 23 | R |
| | | 924 | 362 | 200 | 362 | 1668 | 1668 | 924 | |

121

## Football League Division 3 (N) 1926-1927 Season

| | Accrington St. | Ashington | Barrow | Bradford P.A. | Chesterfield | Crewe Alexandra | Doncaster R. | Durham City | Halifax Town | Hartlepools Utd. | Lincoln City | Nelson | New Brighton | Rochdale | Rotherham Utd. | Southport | Stockport Co. | Stoke City | Tranmere R. | Walsall | Wigan Borough | Wrexham |
|---|---|---|---|---|---|---|---|---|---|---|---|---|---|---|---|---|---|---|---|---|---|---|
| Accrington Stanley FC | | 3-0 | 0-1 | 2-3 | 2-1 | 3-1 | 2-0 | 3-0 | 4-2 | 7-2 | 1-1 | 0-5 | 2-3 | 0-1 | 3-1 | 2-2 | 2-4 | 0-1 | 2-3 | 3-5 | 3-1 | 1-1 |
| Ashington FC | 2-1 | | 3-0 | 2-2 | 2-1 | 4-1 | 1-1 | 3-1 | 3-0 | 1-0 | 1-2 | 1-1 | 2-3 | 2-2 | 4-4 | 4-1 | 1-1 | 0-2 | 4-3 | 0-2 | 1-1 | 1-1 |
| Barrow AFC | 1-1 | 2-2 | | 0-3 | 1-0 | 3-1 | 0-1 | 2-1 | 1-1 | 1-3 | 0-3 | 0-1 | 0-3 | 2-3 | 2-2 | 1-4 | 1-3 | 0-0 | 2-1 | 1-0 | 2-2 | 0-5 |
| Bradford Park Avenue | 6-1 | 2-0 | 1-0 | | 5-0 | 2-0 | 7-3 | 3-0 | 2-1 | 4-1 | 3-1 | 2-2 | 1-1 | 5-1 | 2-2 | 6-2 | 3-1 | 3-0 | 5-3 | 5-1 | 2-1 | 5-0 |
| Chesterfield FC | 1-1 | 4-1 | 8-1 | 3-2 | | 3-0 | 1-1 | 7-1 | 2-0 | 1-0 | 4-2 | 1-1 | 3-1 | 2-3 | 5-2 | 5-1 | 3-0 | 1-1 | 3-1 | 2-0 | 5-2 | 1-3 |
| Crewe Alexandra FC | 4-0 | 2-1 | 5-0 | 1-1 | 0-0 | | 1-3 | 2-1 | 1-2 | 0-1 | 3-3 | 2-1 | 3-2 | 4-0 | 2-2 | 1-0 | 3-2 | 0-2 | 4-1 | 1-1 | 2-4 | 5-1 |
| Doncaster Rovers FC | 2-0 | 3-1 | 7-0 | 4-1 | 0-3 | 0-2 | | 5-1 | 2-0 | 2-0 | 1-3 | 6-0 | 2-2 | 3-2 | 2-2 | 3-1 | 1-2 | 3-1 | 4-1 | 2-2 | 4-1 | 2-2 |
| Durham City FC | 2-0 | 0-2 | 1-1 | 2-1 | 2-1 | 1-2 | 2-2 | | 0-1 | 2-1 | 4-2 | 3-3 | 2-2 | 1-3 | 0-1 | 4-2 | 1-5 | 1-2 | 0-3 | 3-0 | 3-1 | 1-0 |
| Halifax Town AFC | 4-3 | 1-1 | 5-1 | 2-0 | 3-1 | 3-1 | 2-1 | 1-2 | | 2-1 | 2-1 | 4-1 | 2-2 | 1-0 | 4-2 | 1-1 | 4-1 | 2-2 | 2-0 | 1-1 | 0-0 | 0-1 |
| Hartlepools United FC | 3-1 | 0-1 | 1-1 | 2-4 | 1-2 | 1-1 | 3-0 | 4-0 | 0-1 | | 1-1 | 3-2 | 4-0 | 3-2 | 3-1 | 2-0 | 1-2 | 1-3 | 2-1 | 2-2 | 2-1 | 4-0 |
| Lincoln City FC | 4-0 | 4-0 | 3-1 | 5-1 | 3-1 | 3-3 | 0-0 | 5-0 | 3-1 | 1-2 | | 1-4 | 4-1 | 2-3 | 1-2 | 1-1 | 1-3 | 1-3 | 1-2 | 3-3 | 2-0 | 2-2 |
| Nelson FC | 7-0 | 4-0 | 3-0 | 1-0 | 0-3 | 7-1 | 5-1 | 1-1 | 0-0 | 6-2 | 2-1 | | 2-0 | 3-1 | 5-3 | 1-2 | 6-1 | 1-0 | 0-2 | 3-2 | 4-0 | 3-1 |
| New Brighton FC | 0-1 | 4-0 | 3-1 | 3-1 | 1-0 | 3-0 | 0-2 | 3-1 | 0-3 | 2-1 | 1-1 | 7-2 | | 1-2 | 3-0 | 4-1 | 1-2 | 5-0 | 0-0 | 3-1 | 3-1 | 2-1 |
| Rochdale AFC | 2-1 | 5-0 | 5-1 | 3-0 | 8-1 | 3-1 | 7-2 | 1-3 | 2-0 | 3-0 | 7-3 | 2-1 | 1-1 | | 2-1 | 1-0 | 2-0 | 4-0 | 3-1 | 4-4 | 4-1 | 3-1 |
| Rotherham United FC | 1-1 | 5-0 | 2-0 | 1-1 | 0-4 | 2-1 | 1-3 | 3-1 | 2-4 | 5-3 | 2-4 | 2-3 | 0-0 | 1-1 | | 1-2 | 1-2 | 2-2 | 2-2 | 4-1 | 2-0 | 4-0 |
| Southport FC | 2-1 | 4-1 | 3-0 | 2-1 | 2-1 | 2-2 | 2-0 | 4-5 | 0-0 | 1-0 | 2-3 | 3-4 | 7-2 | 1-1 | 2-0 | | 2-2 | 0-3 | 1-3 | 6-1 | 2-2 | 6-0 |
| Stockport County FC | 3-3 | 6-2 | 7-0 | 1-2 | 4-0 | 3-1 | 1-0 | 4-0 | 1-3 | 3-3 | 3-3 | 4-1 | 1-0 | 3-0 | 3-1 | 2-4 | | 2-2 | 2-1 | 0-2 | 4-1 | 3-2 |
| Stoke City FC | 1-0 | 7-0 | 4-0 | 0-0 | 3-2 | 2-1 | 0-0 | 4-0 | 5-1 | 3-1 | 2-0 | 4-1 | 1-1 | 3-1 | 4-1 | 4-0 | 0-1 | | 2-0 | 4-1 | 2-0 | 2-0 |
| Tranmere Rovers FC | 2-1 | 2-1 | 7-2 | 1-2 | 3-2 | 1-0 | 1-1 | 8-3 | 0-0 | 2-0 | 1-2 | 4-1 | 0-1 | 4-0 | 3-0 | 0-0 | 1-1 | | | 6-0 | 3-1 | 2-0 |
| Walsall FC | 5-1 | 0-0 | 1-0 | 1-0 | 0-1 | 2-3 | 1-0 | 1-1 | 0-1 | 2-2 | 1-2 | 4-1 | 0-1 | 4-1 | 3-2 | 1-1 | 1-0 | 0-1 | 5-1 | | 3-2 | 0-1 |
| Wigan Borough FC | 3-0 | 1-4 | 8-0 | 1-2 | 1-2 | 2-2 | 1-1 | 3-0 | 1-1 | 3-0 | 3-2 | 2-1 | 3-2 | 0-3 | 0-0 | 3-1 | 2-0 | 0-3 | 1-1 | 5-2 | | 1-1 |
| Wrexham AFC | 5-0 | 1-1 | 0-2 | 1-0 | 3-1 | 3-1 | 0-1 | 3-1 | 1-2 | 4-0 | 1-1 | 2-2 | 2-2 | 2-2 | 3-0 | 3-0 | 2-1 | 2-6 | 0-1 | 1-2 | 2-0 | |

### Division 3 (North)

| | | Pd | Wn | Dw | Ls | GF | GA | Pts | |
|---|---|---|---|---|---|---|---|---|---|
| 1. | Stoke City FC (Stoke-on-Trent) | 42 | 27 | 9 | 6 | 92 | 40 | 63 | P |
| 2. | Rochdale AFC (Rochdale) | 42 | 26 | 6 | 10 | 105 | 65 | 58 | |
| 3. | Bradford Park Avenue FC (Bradford) | 42 | 24 | 7 | 11 | 101 | 59 | 55 | |
| 4. | Halifax Town AFC (Halifax) | 42 | 21 | 11 | 10 | 70 | 53 | 53 | |
| 5. | Nelson FC (Nelson) | 42 | 22 | 7 | 13 | 104 | 75 | 51 | |
| 6. | Stockport County FC (Stockport) | 42 | 22 | 7 | 13 | 93 | 69 | 49 | -2 |
| 7. | Chesterfield FC (Chesterfield) | 42 | 21 | 5 | 16 | 92 | 68 | 47 | |
| 8. | Doncaster Rovers FC (Doncaster) | 42 | 18 | 11 | 13 | 81 | 65 | 47 | |
| 9. | Tranmere Rovers FC (Birkenhead) | 42 | 19 | 8 | 15 | 85 | 67 | 46 | |
| 10. | New Brighton FC (Wallasey) | 42 | 18 | 10 | 14 | 79 | 67 | 46 | |
| 11. | Lincoln City FC (Lincoln) | 42 | 15 | 12 | 15 | 90 | 78 | 42 | |
| 12. | Southport FC (Southport) | 42 | 15 | 9 | 18 | 80 | 85 | 39 | |
| 13. | Wrexham AFC (Wrexham) | 42 | 14 | 10 | 18 | 65 | 73 | 38 | |
| 14. | Walsall FC (Walsall) | 42 | 14 | 10 | 18 | 68 | 81 | 38 | T |
| 15. | Crewe Alexandra FC (Crewe) | 42 | 14 | 9 | 19 | 71 | 81 | 37 | |
| 16. | Ashington FC (Ashington) | 42 | 12 | 12 | 18 | 60 | 90 | 36 | |
| 17. | Hartlepools United FC (Hartlepool) | 42 | 14 | 6 | 22 | 66 | 81 | 34 | |
| 18. | Wigan Borough FC (Wigan) | 42 | 11 | 10 | 21 | 66 | 83 | 32 | |
| 19. | Rotherham United FC (Rotherham) | 42 | 10 | 12 | 20 | 70 | 92 | 32 | |
| 20. | Durham City FC (Durham) | 42 | 12 | 6 | 24 | 58 | 105 | 30 | |
| 21. | Accrington Stanley FC (Accrington) | 42 | 10 | 7 | 25 | 62 | 98 | 27 | |
| 22. | Barrow AFC (Barrow-in-Furness) | 42 | 7 | 8 | 27 | 34 | 117 | 22 | |
| | | 924 | 366 | 192 | 366 | 1692 | 1692 | 922 | |

Note: Stockport County FC had 2 points deducted for fielding ineligible player Joe Smith on 26/03/1927 during the away match against Rotherham United FC.  T: Walsall FC were transferred to Division 3 (South) from next season.

| Football League Division 3 (S) 1926-1927 Season | Aberdare Ath. | Bournemouth | Brentford | Brighton | Bristol City | Bristol Rovers | Charlton Ath. | Coventry City | Crystal Palace | Exeter City | Gillingham | Luton Town | Merthyr Town | Millwall | Newport Co. | Northampton | Norwich City | Plymouth Arg. | Q.P.R. | Southend Utd. | Swindon Town | Watford |
|---|---|---|---|---|---|---|---|---|---|---|---|---|---|---|---|---|---|---|---|---|---|---|
| Aberdare Athletic FC | ■ | 2-1 | 3-1 | 2-2 | 3-7 | 2-1 | 0-0 | 0-7 | 2-3 | 3-1 | 2-1 | 0-1 | 1-2 | 1-3 | 0-1 | 6-1 | 1-2 | 5-6 | 0-2 | 1-0 | 1-4 | 3-2 |
| Bournemouth & B. Athletic | 3-0 | ■ | 3-1 | 1-0 | 2-0 | 0-1 | 0-3 | 1-2 | 1-1 | 4-3 | 4-2 | 2-0 | 1-1 | 0-1 | 2-1 | 3-1 | 0-1 | 6-2 | 6-2 | 3-0 | 1-2 | 6-0 |
| Brentford FC | 1-4 | 0-0 | ■ | 4-0 | 3-0 | 0-2 | 2-0 | 7-3 | 3-0 | 6-1 | 0-0 | 2-2 | 1-1 | 0-0 | 1-1 | 1-1 | 3-0 | 0-0 | 4-2 | 3-1 | 2-2 | 3-0 |
| Brighton & Hove Albion | 3-1 | 0-2 | 1-1 | ■ | 3-0 | 7-0 | 3-2 | 1-1 | 1-1 | 5-2 | 3-2 | 1-1 | 4-0 | 3-1 | 1-0 | 2-0 | 3-2 | 1-2 | 4-1 | 2-1 | 9-3 | 4-1 |
| Bristol City FC | 2-1 | 2-0 | 1-0 | 0-2 | ■ | 3-1 | 4-1 | 3-0 | 5-4 | 3-2 | 9-4 | 6-0 | 3-0 | 4-1 | 4-1 | 4-3 | 1-1 | 4-2 | 1-0 | 5-1 | 2-0 | 5-0 |
| Bristol Rovers FC | 4-0 | 2-1 | 1-3 | 0-0 | 0-5 | ■ | 1-1 | 1-2 | 4-1 | 3-1 | 2-1 | 1-2 | 2-1 | 1-1 | 4-0 | 5-2 | 1-0 | 2-2 | 4-1 | 5-1 | 3-1 | 0-2 |
| Charlton Athletic FC | 5-1 | 1-3 | 1-1 | 1-0 | 0-1 | 3-1 | ■ | 4-2 | 1-2 | 1-0 | 3-0 | 2-2 | 3-2 | 1-1 | 3-0 | 5-2 | 2-0 | 1-1 | 2-0 | 1-0 | 2-2 | 2-1 |
| Coventry City FC | 1-0 | 6-2 | 3-1 | 1-2 | 2-5 | 2-2 | 1-0 | ■ | 3-1 | 0-0 | 0-2 | 4-1 | 5-1 | 1-4 | 3-1 | 0-3 | 1-0 | 3-3 | 1-0 | 1-1 | 1-3 | 5-1 |
| Crystal Palace FC | 0-0 | 2-2 | 4-3 | 2-0 | 4-2 | 7-4 | 2-1 | 1-2 | ■ | 1-0 | 2-2 | 1-1 | 1-1 | 1-6 | 6-2 | 3-0 | 7-1 | 1-1 | 2-1 | 5-3 | 5-0 | 0-1 |
| Exeter City FC | 2-1 | 4-0 | 3-1 | 0-0 | 1-1 | 1-1 | 1-0 | 8-1 | 3-1 | ■ | 5-1 | 1-2 | 3-0 | 1-1 | 2-1 | 3-2 | 1-0 | 0-2 | 0-2 | 2-0 | 3-1 | 2-1 |
| Gillingham FC | 2-1 | 1-0 | 1-2 | 2-3 | 1-1 | 2-0 | 1-1 | 2-0 | 2-1 | 3-2 | ■ | 0-0 | 0-1 | 2-1 | 0-1 | 1-2 | 4-1 | 2-2 | 2-3 | 4-4 |  | 3-0 |
| Luton Town FC | 3-3 | 4-0 | 2-1 | 4-0 | 0-0 | 1-1 | 1-0 | 4-1 | 1-0 | 2-2 | 2-1 | ■ | 2-1 | 6-0 | 4-1 | 2-0 | 2-2 | 3-3 | 2-0 | 0-0 | 1-1 | 2-2 |
| Merthyr Town FC | 2-2 | 4-6 | 1-0 | 1-0 | 1-1 | 3-2 | 3-0 | 1-0 | 1-2 | 3-3 | 2-0 | 4-1 | ■ | 1-0 | 1-2 | 2-0 | 1-1 | 5-1 | 4-0 | 0-1 | 1-2 | 1-1 |
| Millwall FC | 1-0 | 1-1 | 3-0 | 1-1 | 0-1 | 2-3 | 3-0 | 1-0 | 1-0 | 4-2 | 7-0 | 3-1 |  | ■ | 4-1 | 4-2 | 6-1 | 1-3 | 2-1 | 2-0 | 4-1 | 3-1 |
| Newport County AFC | 5-2 | 2-1 | 0-0 | 0-1 | 0-0 | 1-0 | 2-1 | 4-1 | 2-1 | 2-0 | 1-0 | 3-2 | 4-3 | 1-1 | ■ | 1-0 | 0-0 | 2-1 | 0-2 | 3-0 | 5-3 | 2-1 |
| Northampton Town | 2-1 | 2-2 | 2-3 | 0-0 | 2-0 | 3-0 | 0-1 | 2-1 | 1-1 | 2-2 | 2-1 | 2-1 | 2-0 | 1-4 | 1-2 | ■ | 3-0 | 2-1 | 1-0 | 2-1 | 1-0 | 3-2 |
| Norwich City FC | 2-2 | 4-1 | 2-1 | 0-2 | 1-1 | 2-0 | 2-3 | 3-0 | 0-1 | 4-4 | 0-0 | 3-2 | 4-0 | 0-2 | 1-0 | 6-1 | ■ | 0-2 | 0-1 | 1-1 | 2-1 | 4-0 |
| Plymouth Argyle FC | 2-0 | 1-1 | 2-1 | 2-0 | 4-2 | 3-2 | 3-1 | 3-0 | 7-1 | 2-0 | 1-0 | 1-1 | 1-1 | 4-1 | 3-0 | 2-1 |  | ■ | 2-0 | 2-1 | 3-1 | 4-0 |
| Queen's Park Rangers FC | 3-0 | 1-1 | 1-1 | 2-2 | 1-2 | 2-2 | 2-1 | 1-1 | 0-2 | 1-1 | 1-1 | 1-0 | 5-1 | 1-1 | 2-0 | 4-2 | 4-0 | 4-2 | ■ | 3-2 | 0-1 | 2-4 |
| Southend United FC | 5-1 | 0-3 | 3-1 | 0-1 | 0-1 | 2-1 | 5-0 | 3-1 | 3-1 | 1-2 | 1-0 | 2-1 | 3-1 | 1-1 | 5-0 | 2-0 | 3-3 | 1-2 | 0-3 | ■ | 2-2 | 2-0 |
| Swindon Town FC | 3-2 | 2-0 | 4-2 | 2-2 | 2-2 | 3-5 | 2-0 | 2-2 | 6-1 | 4-2 | 1-0 | 2-0 | 3-2 | 3-0 | 3-1 | 3-1 | 3-2 | 1-2 | 6-2 | 5-1 | ■ | 4-2 |
| Watford FC | 2-2 | 1-2 | 0-0 | 1-0 | 0-1 | 3-3 | 1-0 | 1-0 | 1-2 | 1-0 | 4-0 | 2-1 | 4-1 | 2-4 | 0-0 | 4-0 | 1-1 | 1-4 | 1-2 | 4-2 | 2-2 | ■ |

## Division 3 (South)

| | | Pd | Wn | Dw | Ls | GF | GA | Pts | |
|---|---|---|---|---|---|---|---|---|---|
| 1. | Bristol City FC (Bristol) | 42 | 27 | 8 | 7 | 104 | 54 | 62 | P |
| 2. | Plymouth Argyle FC (Plymouth) | 42 | 25 | 10 | 7 | 95 | 61 | 60 | |
| 3. | Millwall FC (London) | 42 | 23 | 10 | 9 | 89 | 51 | 56 | |
| 4. | Brighton & Hove Albion FC (Hove) | 42 | 21 | 11 | 10 | 79 | 50 | 53 | |
| 5. | Swindon Town FC (Swindon) | 42 | 21 | 9 | 12 | 100 | 85 | 51 | |
| 6. | Crystal Palace FC (London) | 42 | 18 | 9 | 15 | 84 | 81 | 45 | |
| 7. | Bournemouth & Boscombe Athletic FC (Bournemouth) | 42 | 18 | 8 | 16 | 78 | 66 | 44 | |
| 8. | Luton Town FC (Luton) | 42 | 15 | 14 | 13 | 68 | 66 | 44 | |
| 9. | Newport County AFC (Newport) | 42 | 19 | 6 | 17 | 57 | 71 | 44 | |
| 10. | Bristol Rovers FC (Bristol) | 42 | 16 | 9 | 17 | 78 | 80 | 41 | |
| 11. | Brentford FC (London) | 42 | 13 | 14 | 15 | 70 | 61 | 40 | |
| 12. | Exeter City FC (Exeter) | 42 | 15 | 10 | 17 | 76 | 73 | 40 | |
| 13. | Charlton Athletic FC (London) | 42 | 16 | 8 | 18 | 60 | 61 | 40 | |
| 14. | Queen's Park Rangers FC (London) | 42 | 15 | 9 | 18 | 65 | 71 | 39 | |
| 15. | Coventry City FC (Coventry) | 42 | 15 | 7 | 20 | 71 | 86 | 37 | |
| 16. | Norwich City FC (Norwich) | 42 | 12 | 11 | 19 | 59 | 71 | 35 | |
| 17. | Merthyr Town FC (Merthyr Tydfil) | 42 | 13 | 9 | 20 | 63 | 80 | 35 | |
| 18. | Northampton Town FC (Northampton) | 42 | 15 | 5 | 22 | 59 | 87 | 35 | |
| 19. | Southend United FC (Southend-on-Sea) | 42 | 14 | 6 | 22 | 64 | 77 | 34 | |
| 20. | Gillingham FC (Gillingham) | 42 | 11 | 10 | 21 | 54 | 72 | 32 | |
| 21. | Watford FC (Watford) | 42 | 12 | 8 | 22 | 57 | 87 | 32 | |
| 22. | Aberdare Athletic FC (Aberdare) | 42 | 9 | 7 | 26 | 62 | 101 | 25 | # |
| | | 924 | 363 | 198 | 363 | 1592 | 1592 | 924 | |

# Aberdare Athletic FC were not re-elected to the league for next season. The club merged pre-season with Welsh League club Aberaman AFC with the 1st XI playing in the Football League as Aberdare Athletic FC and the 2nd XI in the Welsh League as Aberdare & Aberaman AFC.    Elected:  Torquay United FC

## F.A. CUP FINAL    (Wembley Stadium, London – 23/04/1927 – 91,206)

CARDIFF CITY AFC (CARDIFF)                    1-0                    The Arsenal FC (London)

*Ferguson*

Cardiff:  Farqurharson, Nelson, Watson, Keenor, Sloan, Hardy, Curtis, Irving, Ferguson, L.Davies, McLachlan.
Arsenal:  Lewis, Parker, Kennedy, Baker, Butler, John, Hulme, Buchan, Brain, Blyth, Hoar.

## Semi-finals

| | | |
|---|---|---|
| Cardiff City AFC (Cardiff) | 3-0 | Reading FC (Reading) |
| The Arsenal FC (London) | 2-1 | Southampton FC (Southampton) |

## Quarter-finals

| | | |
|---|---|---|
| Chelsea FC (London) | 0-0, 2-3 | Cardiff City AFC (Cardiff) |
| Millwall FC (London) | 0-0, 0-2 | Southampton FC (Southampton) |
| Swansea Town AFC (Swansea) | 1-3 | Reading FC (Reading) |
| The Arsenal FC (London) | 2-1 | Wolverhampton Wanderers FC (Wolverhampton) |

# 1927-28

| Football League Division 1 1927-1928 Season | Arsenal | Aston Villa | Birmingham | Blackburn Rovers | Bolton Wands. | Burnley | Bury | Cardiff City | Derby County | Everton | Huddersfield T. | Leicester City | Liverpool | Man. United | Middlesbrough | Newcastle United | Portsmouth | Sheffield United | Sunderland | The Wednes. | Tottenham H. | West Ham United |
|---|---|---|---|---|---|---|---|---|---|---|---|---|---|---|---|---|---|---|---|---|---|---|
| Arsenal FC | | 0-3 | 2-2 | 3-2 | 1-2 | 4-1 | 3-1 | 3-0 | 3-4 | 3-2 | 0-0 | 2-2 | 6-3 | 0-1 | 3-1 | 4-1 | 0-2 | 6-1 | 2-1 | 1-1 | 1-1 | 2-2 |
| Aston Villa FC | 2-2 | | 1-1 | 2-0 | 2-2 | 3-1 | 1-0 | 3-1 | 0-1 | 2-3 | 3-0 | 0-3 | 3-4 | 3-1 | 5-1 | 3-0 | 7-2 | 1-0 | 4-2 | 5-4 | 1-2 | 1-0 |
| Birmingham FC | 1-1 | 1-1 | | 2-1 | 1-1 | 4-0 | 2-2 | 1-3 | 2-1 | 2-2 | 3-1 | 0-2 | 2-0 | 0-0 | 3-2 | 0-2 | 2-0 | 4-1 | 1-1 | 1-0 | 3-2 | 1-2 |
| Blackburn Rovers FC | 4-1 | 0-1 | 4-4 | | 1-6 | 2-1 | 0-1 | 0-0 | 3-2 | 4-2 | 1-1 | 0-0 | 2-1 | 3-0 | 3-0 | 1-0 | 6-0 | 1-0 | 0-0 | 3-1 | 2-1 | 1-0 |
| Bolton Wanderers FC | 1-1 | 3-1 | 3-2 | 3-1 | | 7-1 | 2-1 | 2-1 | 1-3 | 1-1 | 0-1 | 3-3 | 2-1 | 3-2 | 0-0 | 1-2 | 3-1 | 1-1 | 1-2 | 2-0 | 4-1 | 4-0 |
| Burnley FC | 1-2 | 4-2 | 2-1 | 3-1 | 2-2 | | 2-3 | 2-1 | 4-2 | 3-5 | 0-1 | 5-1 | 2-2 | 4-0 | 1-1 | 5-1 | 2-0 | 5-3 | 3-0 | 3-1 | 2-2 | 0-0 |
| Bury FC | 5-1 | 0-0 | 2-3 | 2-3 | 1-0 | 2-0 | | 3-0 | 3-0 | 2-3 | 2-3 | 2-1 | 5-2 | 4-3 | 1-4 | 1-4 | 4-0 | 1-0 | 5-3 | 4-2 | 1-2 | 3-1 |
| Cardiff City AFC | 2-2 | 2-1 | 2-1 | 1-1 | 2-1 | 3-2 | 0-1 | | 4-4 | 2-0 | 4-0 | 3-0 | 1-1 | 2-0 | 1-1 | 3-1 | 3-1 | 2-2 | 3-1 | 1-1 | 2-1 | 1-5 |
| Derby County FC | 4-0 | 5-0 | 4-1 | 6-0 | 1-0 | 3-4 | 5-2 | 7-1 | | 0-3 | 0-0 | 2-1 | 2-3 | 5-0 | 2-1 | 1-1 | 2-2 | 2-1 | 1-0 | 4-6 | 1-1 | 2-3 |
| Everton FC | 3-3 | 3-2 | 5-2 | 4-1 | 2-2 | 4-1 | 1-1 | 2-1 | 2-2 | | 2-2 | 7-1 | 1-1 | 5-2 | 3-1 | 3-0 | 0-0 | 0-0 | 0-1 | 4-0 | 2-5 | 7-0 |
| Huddersfield Town AFC | 2-1 | 1-1 | 2-0 | 3-1 | 1-0 | 1-2 | 3-0 | 8-2 | 2-1 | 4-1 | | 3-1 | 2-4 | 4-2 | 2-4 | 1-3 | 4-1 | 0-1 | 4-2 | 1-0 | 4-2 | 5-2 |
| Leicester City FC | 3-2 | 3-0 | 3-0 | 6-0 | 4-2 | 5-0 | 2-2 | 4-1 | 4-0 | 1-0 | 1-2 | | 1-1 | 1-0 | 3-3 | 3-0 | 6-2 | 3-1 | 3-3 | 2-2 | 6-1 | 2-3 |
| Liverpool FC | 0-2 | 0-0 | 2-3 | 4-2 | 4-2 | 2-2 | 5-1 | 1-2 | 5-2 | 3-3 | 4-2 | 1-1 | | 2-0 | 1-1 | 0-0 | 8-2 | 2-1 | 2-5 | 5-2 | 2-0 | 1-3 |
| Manchester United FC | 4-1 | 5-1 | 1-1 | 1-1 | 2-1 | 4-3 | 0-1 | 2-2 | 5-0 | 1-0 | 0-0 | 5-2 | 6-1 | | 3-0 | 1-7 | 2-0 | 2-3 | 2-1 | 1-1 | 3-0 | 1-1 |
| Middlesbrough FC | 2-2 | 0-0 | 1-1 | 2-0 | 2-5 | 2-3 | 6-1 | 1-2 | 3-3 | 4-2 | 3-1 | 1-1 | 1-1 | 1-2 | | 1-1 | 5-1 | 3-0 | 0-3 | 3-3 | 3-1 | 2-2 |
| Newcastle United FC | 1-1 | 7-5 | 1-1 | 0-1 | 2-2 | 1-1 | 2-3 | 2-0 | 4-3 | 2-2 | 2-3 | 1-5 | 1-1 | 4-1 | 3-3 | | 1-3 | 1-0 | 3-1 | 4-3 | 4-1 | 3-1 |
| Portsmouth FC | 2-3 | 3-1 | 2-2 | 2-2 | 1-0 | 1-0 | 1-0 | 3-0 | 2-2 | 1-3 | 2-1 | 2-0 | 1-0 | 1-0 | 4-1 | 0-1 | | 4-1 | 3-5 | 0-0 | 3-0 | 2-1 |
| Sheffield United FC | 6-4 | 0-3 | 3-1 | 2-3 | 4-3 | 5-2 | 3-1 | 3-4 | 1-0 | 1-3 | 1-1 | 1-1 | 1-7 | 1-1 | 2-1 | 4-1 | 1-1 | 3-2 | 5-1 | 1-1 | 3-1 | 6-2 |
| Sunderland AFC | 5-1 | 2-3 | 4-2 | 1-0 | 1-1 | 2-3 | 1-0 | 0-2 | 0-1 | 0-2 | 3-0 | 2-2 | 2-1 | 4-1 | 1-0 | 1-1 | 3-3 | 0-1 | | 2-3 | 0-0 | 3-2 |
| The Wednesday FC | 1-1 | 2-0 | 2-3 | 4-1 | 3-0 | 5-0 | 4-0 | 3-3 | 2-2 | 1-2 | 0-5 | 1-2 | 4-0 | 0-2 | 2-3 | 0-0 | 2-0 | 3-3 | 0-0 | | 4-2 | 2-0 |
| Tottenham Hotspur FC | 2-0 | 2-1 | 1-0 | 1-1 | 1-2 | 5-0 | 1-4 | 1-0 | 1-2 | 1-3 | 2-2 | 2-1 | 3-1 | 4-1 | 4-2 | 5-2 | 0-3 | 2-2 | 3-1 | 1-3 | | 5-3 |
| West Ham United FC | 2-2 | 0-0 | 3-3 | 4-3 | 2-0 | 2-0 | 1-2 | 2-0 | 2-2 | 0-0 | 4-2 | 4-0 | 3-1 | 1-2 | 4-5 | 5-2 | 4-2 | 1-1 | 2-4 | 1-2 | 1-1 | |

| Division 1 | Pd | Wn | Dw | Ls | GF | GA | Pts | |
|---|---|---|---|---|---|---|---|---|
| 1. EVERTON FC (LIVERPOOL) | 42 | 20 | 13 | 9 | 102 | 66 | 53 | |
| 2. Huddersfield Town AFC (Huddersfield) | 42 | 22 | 7 | 13 | 91 | 68 | 51 | |
| 3. Leicester City FC (Leicester) | 42 | 18 | 12 | 12 | 96 | 72 | 48 | |
| 4. Derby County FC (Derby) | 42 | 17 | 10 | 15 | 96 | 83 | 44 | |
| 5. Bury FC (Bury) | 42 | 20 | 4 | 18 | 80 | 80 | 44 | |
| 6. Cardiff City AFC (Cardiff) | 42 | 17 | 10 | 15 | 70 | 80 | 44 | |
| 7. Bolton Wanderers FC (Bolton) | 42 | 16 | 11 | 15 | 81 | 66 | 43 | |
| 8. Aston Villa FC (Birmingham) | 42 | 17 | 9 | 16 | 78 | 73 | 43 | |
| 9. Newcastle United FC (Newcastle-upon-Tyne) | 42 | 15 | 13 | 14 | 79 | 81 | 43 | |
| 10. Arsenal FC (London) | 42 | 13 | 15 | 14 | 82 | 86 | 41 | |
| 11. Birmingham FC (Birmingham) | 42 | 13 | 15 | 14 | 70 | 75 | 41 | |
| 12. Blackburn Rovers FC (Blackburn) | 42 | 16 | 9 | 17 | 66 | 78 | 41 | |
| 13. Sheffield United FC (Sheffield) | 42 | 15 | 10 | 17 | 79 | 86 | 40 | |
| 14. The Wednesday FC (Sheffield) | 42 | 13 | 13 | 16 | 81 | 78 | 39 | |
| 15. Sunderland AFC (Sunderland) | 42 | 15 | 9 | 18 | 74 | 76 | 39 | |
| 16. Liverpool FC (Liverpool) | 42 | 13 | 13 | 16 | 84 | 87 | 39 | |
| 17. West Ham United FC (London) | 42 | 14 | 11 | 17 | 81 | 88 | 39 | |
| 18. Manchester United FC (Manchester) | 42 | 16 | 7 | 19 | 72 | 80 | 39 | |
| 19. Burnley FC (Burnley) | 42 | 16 | 7 | 19 | 82 | 98 | 39 | |
| 20. Portsmouth FC (Portsmouth) | 42 | 16 | 7 | 19 | 66 | 90 | 39 | |
| 21. Tottenham Hotspur FC (London) | 42 | 15 | 8 | 19 | 74 | 86 | 38 | R |
| 22. Middlesbrough FC (Middlesbrough) | 42 | 11 | 15 | 16 | 81 | 88 | 37 | R |
| | 924 | 348 | 228 | 348 | 1765 | 1765 | 924 | |

## Top Goalscorer

| 1) | William "Dixie" DEAN | (Everton FC) | 60 |
|---|---|---|---|

| Football League Division 2 1927-1928 Season | Barnsley | Blackpool | Bristol City | Chelsea | Clapton Orient | Fulham | Grimsby Town | Hull City | Leeds United | Man. City | Nottingham F. | Notts County | Oldham Ath. | Port Vale | Preston N.E. | Reading | Southampton | South Shields | Stoke City | Swansea Town | W.B.A. | Wolves |
|---|---|---|---|---|---|---|---|---|---|---|---|---|---|---|---|---|---|---|---|---|---|---|
| Barnsley FC | | 2-1 | 2-3 | 3-1 | 4-2 | 8-4 | 1-4 | 1-1 | 2-1 | 0-3 | 2-1 | 0-0 | 0-1 | 4-2 | 2-1 | 2-0 | 0-1 | 0-0 | 3-1 | 3-3 | 2-4 | 2-2 |
| Blackpool FC | 1-3 | | 6-2 | 2-4 | 0-1 | 4-0 | 4-5 | 2-1 | 0-2 | 2-2 | 5-3 | 3-3 | 1-2 | 1-6 | 4-1 | 3-1 | 1-0 | 4-1 | 3-1 | 2-2 | 4-3 | 3-0 |
| Bristol City FC | 2-0 | 2-2 | | 1-1 | 5-1 | 3-0 | 0-0 | 0-1 | 1-2 | 2-0 | 0-0 | 1-2 | 2-1 | 4-0 | 1-3 | 4-1 | 3-0 | 1-1 | 4-0 | 2-1 | 0-1 | 4-1 |
| Chelsea FC | 1-2 | 3-0 | 5-2 | | 1-0 | 2-1 | 4-0 | 2-0 | 2-3 | 0-1 | 2-1 | 5-0 | 2-1 | 1-0 | 2-1 | 0-0 | 0-2 | 6-0 | 1-0 | 4-0 | 1-1 | 2-0 |
| Clapton Orient FC | 2-0 | 2-5 | 4-2 | 2-1 | | 3-2 | 1-2 | 0-0 | 2-1 | 0-2 | 2-2 | 0-1 | 2-0 | 0-1 | 1-1 | 3-0 | 2-0 | 2-2 | 3-2 | 1-1 | 0-0 | 0-0 |
| Fulham FC | 3-1 | 2-2 | 5-0 | 1-1 | 2-0 | | 2-2 | 0-2 | 1-1 | 1-1 | 2-0 | 2-1 | 1-1 | 4-0 | 2-2 | 1-0 | 1-0 | 2-0 | 1-5 | 3-2 | 3-1 | 7-0 |
| Grimsby Town FC | 3-1 | 3-3 | 1-4 | 1-1 | 2-2 | 1-0 | | 1-1 | 3-2 | 4-1 | 2-1 | 1-0 | 1-2 | 3-0 | 4-6 | 3-3 | 2-2 | 4-1 | 1-2 | 1-2 | 0-6 | 0-1 |
| Hull City AFC | 2-1 | 2-2 | 1-1 | 0-2 | 2-2 | 3-2 | 0-1 | | 3-1 | 0-0 | 2-0 | 1-1 | 2-2 | 1-0 | 0-0 | 0-1 | 1-0 | 1-0 | 1-0 | 0-2 | 1-1 | 2-0 |
| Leeds United AFC | 2-2 | 4-0 | 3-2 | 5-0 | 4-0 | 2-1 | 0-0 | 2-0 | | 0-1 | 4-0 | 6-0 | 1-0 | 3-0 | 2-4 | 6-2 | 2-0 | 3-0 | 5-1 | 5-0 | 1-2 | 3-0 |
| Manchester City FC | 7-3 | 4-1 | 4-2 | 0-1 | 5-3 | 2-1 | 2-0 | 2-1 | 2-1 | | 3-3 | 3-1 | 3-1 | 1-0 | 2-2 | 4-1 | 6-1 | 3-0 | 4-0 | 7-4 | 3-1 | 3-0 |
| Nottingham Forest FC | 1-1 | 4-1 | 1-1 | 2-2 | 4-3 | 7-0 | 5-2 | 1-1 | 2-2 | 4-5 | | 2-1 | 2-1 | 0-2 | 3-1 | 5-3 | 1-1 | 7-2 | 0-2 | 0-2 | 0-2 | 3-2 |
| Notts County FC | 9-0 | 3-1 | 1-2 | 0-1 | 3-0 | 0-1 | 3-2 | 1-1 | 2-2 | 2-1 | 1-2 | | 2-1 | 2-4 | 6-2 | 1-1 | 0-0 | 4-1 | 1-2 | 2-0 | 3-0 | 1-2 |
| Oldham Athletic AFC | 0-1 | 6-0 | 4-1 | 2-1 | 5-0 | 4-2 | 1-0 | 5-0 | 0-1 | 3-2 | 4-1 | 0-0 | | 4-1 | 0-0 | 3-2 | 3-1 | 2-2 | 3-1 | 0-1 | 3-1 | 6-0 |
| Port Vale FC | 2-1 | 3-0 | 5-1 | 1-1 | 0-0 | 4-1 | 2-2 | 1-2 | 1-2 | 1-2 | 2-2 | 3-0 | 1-0 | | 2-0 | 3-0 | 4-0 | 2-3 | 0-0 | 2-0 | 4-1 | 2-2 |
| Preston North End FC | 1-2 | 2-1 | 5-1 | 0-3 | 0-0 | 1-0 | 3-0 | 4-2 | 5-1 | 1-0 | 5-0 | 4-0 | 1-1 | 4-0 | | 4-0 | 1-2 | 7-2 | 2-0 | 4-2 | 3-3 | 5-4 |
| Reading FC | 1-1 | 1-0 | 3-2 | 1-2 | 4-0 | 2-1 | 2-2 | 3-0 | 0-1 | 1-1 | 0-2 | 2-2 | 1-0 | 0-0 | 2-1 | | 0-0 | 5-1 | 1-1 | 0-0 | 1-4 | 2-1 |
| Southampton FC | 6-1 | 2-0 | 3-2 | 2-4 | 1-3 | 5-2 | 5-0 | 2-0 | 1-4 | 1-1 | 2-1 | 5-1 | 5-2 | 1-3 | 0-0 | 0-0 | | 3-5 | 3-6 | 0-2 | 3-2 | 4-1 |
| South Shields FC | 0-0 | 2-2 | 1-3 | 2-1 | 2-2 | 2-1 | 1-2 | 1-0 | 1-5 | 0-1 | 3-4 | 2-3 | 0-3 | 0-1 | 2-3 | 0-0 | 2-1 | | 2-3 | 3-1 | 2-3 | 2-2 |
| Stoke City FC | 0-0 | 2-2 | 1-0 | 1-0 | 2-0 | 5-1 | 0-0 | 3-1 | 5-1 | 1-3 | 3-0 | 3-0 | 0-2 | 3-2 | 4-1 | 2-1 | 3-1 | | | 1-1 | 1-1 | 2-2 |
| Swansea Town AFC | 3-0 | 1-0 | 1-1 | 0-0 | 5-0 | 2-1 | 3-2 | 2-0 | 1-1 | 5-3 | 2-0 | 1-1 | 0-0 | 2-0 | 0-1 | 0-1 | 2-0 | 6-3 | 1-1 | | 3-2 | 6-0 |
| West Bromwich Albion FC | 1-1 | 6-3 | 0-0 | 3-0 | 4-1 | 4-0 | 3-1 | 1-1 | 0-1 | 1-1 | 2-3 | 2-2 | 0-0 | 0-0 | 2-4 | 5-3 | 2-1 | 3-0 | 2-4 | 5-2 | | 4-0 |
| Wolverhampton Wanderers FC | 2-1 | 2-4 | 5-2 | 1-2 | 5-3 | 3-1 | 0-1 | 1-1 | 0-0 | 2-2 | 1-0 | 2-2 | 3-1 | 2-1 | 2-3 | 2-1 | 2-1 | 2-1 | 1-2 | 1-1 | 4-1 | |

## Division 2

| | | Pd | Wn | Dw | Ls | GF | GA | Pts | |
|---|---|---|---|---|---|---|---|---|---|
| 1. | Manchester City FC (Manchester) | 42 | 25 | 9 | 8 | 100 | 59 | 59 | P |
| 2. | Leeds United AFC (Leeds) | 42 | 25 | 7 | 10 | 98 | 49 | 57 | P |
| 3. | Chelsea FC (London) | 42 | 23 | 8 | 11 | 75 | 45 | 54 | |
| 4. | Preston North End FC (Preston) | 42 | 22 | 9 | 11 | 100 | 66 | 53 | |
| 5. | Stoke City FC (Stoke-on-Trent) | 42 | 22 | 8 | 12 | 78 | 59 | 52 | |
| 6. | Swansea Town AFC (Swansea) | 42 | 18 | 12 | 12 | 75 | 63 | 48 | |
| 7. | Oldham Athletic AFC (Oldham) | 42 | 19 | 8 | 15 | 75 | 51 | 46 | |
| 8. | West Bromwich Albion FC (West Bromwich) | 42 | 17 | 12 | 13 | 90 | 70 | 46 | |
| 9. | Port Vale FC (Stoke-on-Trent) | 42 | 18 | 8 | 16 | 68 | 57 | 44 | |
| 10. | Nottingham Forest FC (Nottingham) | 42 | 15 | 10 | 7 | 83 | 84 | 40 | |
| 11. | Grimsby Town FC (Cleethorpes) | 42 | 14 | 12 | 16 | 69 | 83 | 40 | |
| 12. | Bristol City FC (Bristol) | 42 | 15 | 9 | 18 | 76 | 79 | 39 | |
| 13. | Hull City AFC (Kingston-upon-Hull) | 42 | 12 | 15 | 15 | 41 | 54 | 39 | |
| 14. | Barnsley FC (Barnsley) | 42 | 14 | 11 | 17 | 65 | 85 | 39 | |
| 15. | Notts County FC (Nottingham) | 42 | 13 | 12 | 17 | 68 | 74 | 38 | |
| 16. | Wolverhampton Wanderers FC (Wolverhampton) | 42 | 13 | 10 | 19 | 63 | 91 | 36 | |
| 17. | Southampton FC (Southampton) | 42 | 14 | 7 | 21 | 68 | 77 | 35 | |
| 18. | Reading FC (Reading) | 42 | 11 | 13 | 18 | 53 | 75 | 35 | |
| 19. | Blackpool FC (Blackpool) | 42 | 13 | 8 | 21 | 83 | 101 | 34 | |
| 20. | Clapton Orient FC (London) | 42 | 11 | 12 | 19 | 55 | 85 | 34 | |
| 21. | Fulham FC (London) | 42 | 13 | 7 | 22 | 68 | 89 | 33 | R |
| 22. | South Shields FC (South Shields) | 42 | 7 | 9 | 26 | 56 | 111 | 23 | R |
| | | 924 | 354 | 216 | 354 | 1607 | 1607 | 924 | |

| Football League Division 3 (N) 1927-1928 Season | Accrington St. | Ashington | Barrow | Bradford City | Bradford P.A. | Chesterfield | Crewe Alexandra | Darlington | Doncaster Rovers | Durham City | Halifax Town | Hartlepools Utd. | Lincoln City | Nelson | New Brighton | Rochdale | Rotherham United | Southport | Stockport County | Tranmere Rovers | Wigan Borough | Wrexham |
|---|---|---|---|---|---|---|---|---|---|---|---|---|---|---|---|---|---|---|---|---|---|---|
| Accrington Stanley FC | ■ | 3-1 | 5-1 | 1-1 | 2-1 | 0-0 | 5-0 | 0-0 | 1-3 | 2-0 | 3-2 | 2-2 | 1-0 | 7-1 | 2-1 | 1-0 | 3-1 | 4-1 | 1-0 | 2-3 | 2-4 | 2-0 |
| Ashington FC | 1-1 | ■ | 1-0 | 2-2 | 0-3 | 0-0 | 0-2 | 2-3 | 1-2 | 2-2 | 3-3 | 3-1 | 4-5 | 5-1 | 3-2 | 5-1 | 6-0 | 1-3 | 4-1 | 3-0 | 6-3 | 2-1 |
| Barrow AFC | 1-0 | 1-1 | ■ | 0-0 | 0-0 | 2-0 | 1-1 | 2-0 | 0-0 | 1-2 | 6-2 | 2-0 | 3-3 | 3-1 | 2-1 | 1-3 | 1-1 | 3-1 | 2-3 | 2-1 | 6-2 | 2-2 |
| Bradford City FC | 2-0 | 5-0 | 4-1 | ■ | 2-3 | 3-3 | 4-1 | 0-1 | 1-0 | 4-0 | 0-0 | 2-1 | 3-1 | 9-1 | 3-1 | 2-2 | 3-1 | 2-0 | 2-2 | 3-1 | 3-0 | 2-0 |
| Bradford Park Avenue | 3-3 | 5-0 | 1-1 | 5-0 | ■ | 1-0 | 2-0 | 6-3 | 0-2 | 4-0 | 3-2 | 3-0 | 3-0 | 3-2 | 2-1 | 4-1 | 3-1 | 5-3 | 2-0 | 6-2 | 5-1 | 2-0 |
| Chesterfield FC | 3-1 | 3-0 | 6-0 | 2-0 | 0-0 | ■ | 3-2 | 1-3 | 1-0 | 4-2 | 3-0 | 1-3 | 0-1 | 6-0 | 2-3 | 1-3 | 2-5 | 5-2 | 1-1 | 2-2 | 0-0 | 0-1 |
| Crewe Alexandra FC | 2-3 | 3-0 | 4-1 | 2-1 | 1-3 | 4-1 | ■ | 3-3 | 4-1 | 5-2 | 1-1 | 4-0 | 0-0 | 6-1 | 1-1 | 1-1 | 3-2 | 0-1 | 3-0 | 2-3 | 1-2 | 1-1 |
| Darlington FC | 3-0 | 5-1 | 1-1 | 1-2 | 1-3 | 4-2 | 1-3 | ■ | 3-0 | 5-0 | 2-0 | 5-0 | 9-2 | 4-1 | 3-0 | 1-0 | 4-1 | 3-1 | 3-1 | 3-7 | 1-0 | 1-3 |
| Doncaster Rovers FC | 0-0 | 3-2 | 4-0 | 2-1 | 2-0 | 4-0 | 3-1 | 5-0 | ■ | 5-0 | 1-1 | 1-1 | 3-0 | 4-2 | 5-1 | 5-2 | 2-0 | 0-1 | 0-2 | 5-2 | 4-1 | 1-1 |
| Durham City FC | 2-1 | 0-0 | 4-1 | 3-2 | 0-1 | 2-0 | 5-1 | 3-3 | 1-3 | ■ | 1-1 | 1-0 | 0-4 | 3-0 | 2-1 | 3-2 | 1-4 | 0-0 | 1-2 | 1-3 | 3-0 | 1-1 |
| Halifax Town AFC | 3-1 | 6-1 | 5-2 | 2-1 | 1-1 | 1-2 | 0-0 | 2-1 | 0-1 | 3-1 | ■ | 4-1 | 3-1 | 5-1 | 1-1 | 1-1 | 0-0 | 1-0 | 1-3 | 2-2 | 2-2 | 4-1 |
| Hartlepools United FC | 0-2 | 4-1 | 6-2 | 2-3 | 1-1 | 1-0 | 4-3 | 0-1 | 1-0 | 2-1 | 0-1 | ■ | 1-2 | 4-5 | 3-3 | 0-2 | 1-3 | 2-1 | 2-1 | 2-0 | 1-1 | 4-2 |
| Lincoln City FC | 3-1 | 3-1 | 5-0 | 2-2 | 2-0 | 0-0 | 5-2 | 1-0 | 2-0 | 2-1 | 5-2 | 1-5 | ■ | 0-0 | 1-2 | 3-1 | 4-1 | 2-0 | 2-0 | 1-1 | 4-1 | 5-0 |
| Nelson FC | 1-4 | 1-5 | 4-0 | 0-3 | 1-2 | 3-3 | 3-3 | 4-0 | 0-1 | 2-1 | 3-2 | 4-2 | 1-3 | ■ | 0-3 | 6-3 | 6-1 | 1-1 | 0-4 | 3-5 | 3-3 | 4-0 |
| New Brighton FC | 3-1 | 6-0 | 3-3 | 1-1 | 1-2 | 3-3 | 5-1 | 0-0 | 3-1 | 4-0 | 3-1 | 2-1 | 2-3 | 4-0 | ■ | 2-1 | 1-1 | 0-1 | 0-0 | 0-1 | 2-1 | 0-0 |
| Rochdale AFC | 3-2 | 2-2 | 3-0 | 3-3 | 0-4 | 5-1 | 4-0 | 4-1 | 1-0 | 1-0 | 2-2 | 0-1 | 0-3 | 1-0 | 0-0 | ■ | 2-1 | 5-1 | 2-1 | 1-2 | 3-0 | 3-0 |
| Rotherham United FC | 2-1 | 1-1 | 3-0 | 0-0 | 1-0 | 1-2 | 2-0 | 3-1 | 2-1 | 1-1 | 0-0 | 5-0 | 2-4 | 4-3 | 0-0 | 3-1 | ■ | 1-1 | 0-1 | 2-1 | 6-0 | 0-1 |
| Southport FC | 5-0 | 3-3 | 4-0 | 5-1 | 2-1 | 2-1 | 3-2 | 2-0 | 1-2 | 3-1 | 3-1 | 0-2 | 3-1 | 1-2 | 4-2 | 3-1 | 1-1 | ■ | 4-0 | 0-1 | 2-1 | 4-1 |
| Stockport County FC | 3-3 | 3-0 | 4-0 | 3-0 | 2-2 | 3-0 | 1-0 | 4-0 | 2-1 | 2-1 | 3-0 | 2-2 | 2-0 | 8-0 | 0-0 | 5-1 | 2-0 | 6-3 | ■ | 1-0 | 1-1 | 5-0 |
| Tranmere Rovers FC | 3-2 | 5-3 | 5-0 | 2-1 | 2-2 | 6-3 | 3-3 | 3-1 | 0-0 | 11-1 | 2-2 | 1-2 | 2-2 | 1-1 | 4-0 | 3-0 | 2-0 | 1-0 | 5-2 | ■ | 5-2 | 2-1 |
| Wigan Borough FC | 2-0 | 0-0 | 1-0 | 2-2 | 1-3 | 3-2 | 2-1 | 0-3 | 1-1 | 3-0 | 1-3 | 0-2 | 1-3 | 4-2 | 2-2 | 1-2 | 0-0 | 1-3 | 1-3 | 1-0 | ■ | 3-0 |
| Wrexham AFC | 0-1 | 5-1 | 5-0 | 1-0 | 1-1 | 1-2 | 2-0 | 1-2 | 1-2 | 4-0 | 2-0 | 3-2 | 1-0 | 5-2 | 0-2 | 2-1 | 3-2 | 3-0 | 1-0 | 2-0 | 5-1 | ■ |

## Division 3 (North)

| | | Pd | Wn | Dw | Ls | GF | GA | Pts | |
|---|---|---|---|---|---|---|---|---|---|
| 1. | Bradford Park Avenue FC (Bradford) | 42 | 27 | 9 | 6 | 101 | 45 | 63 | P |
| 2. | Lincoln City FC (Lincoln) | 42 | 24 | 7 | 11 | 91 | 64 | 55 | |
| 3. | Stockport County FC (Stockport) | 42 | 23 | 8 | 11 | 89 | 51 | 54 | |
| 4. | Doncaster Rovers FC (Doncaster) | 42 | 23 | 7 | 12 | 80 | 44 | 53 | |
| 5. | Tranmere Rovers FC (Birkenhead) | 42 | 22 | 9 | 11 | 105 | 72 | 53 | |
| 6. | Bradford City AFC (Bradford) | 42 | 18 | 12 | 12 | 85 | 60 | 48 | |
| 7. | Darlington FC (Darlington) | 42 | 21 | 5 | 16 | 89 | 74 | 47 | |
| 8. | Southport FC (Southport) | 42 | 20 | 5 | 17 | 79 | 70 | 45 | |
| 9. | Accrington Stanley FC (Accrington) | 42 | 18 | 8 | 16 | 76 | 67 | 44 | |
| 10. | New Brighton FC (Wallasey) | 42 | 14 | 14 | 14 | 72 | 62 | 42 | |
| 11. | Wrexham AFC (Wrexham) | 42 | 18 | 6 | 18 | 64 | 67 | 42 | |
| 12. | Halifax Town AFC (Halifax) | 42 | 13 | 15 | 14 | 73 | 71 | 41 | |
| 13. | Rochdale AFC (Rochdale) | 42 | 17 | 7 | 18 | 74 | 77 | 41 | |
| 14. | Rotherham United FC (Rotherham) | 42 | 14 | 11 | 17 | 65 | 69 | 39 | |
| 15. | Hartlepools United FC (Hartlepool) | 42 | 16 | 6 | 20 | 69 | 81 | 38 | |
| 16. | Chesterfield FC (Chesterfield) | 42 | 13 | 10 | 19 | 71 | 78 | 36 | |
| 17. | Crewe Alexandra FC (Crewe) | 42 | 12 | 10 | 20 | 77 | 86 | 34 | |
| 18. | Ashington FC (Ashington) | 42 | 11 | 11 | 20 | 77 | 103 | 33 | |
| 19. | Barrow AFC (Barrow-in-Furness) | 42 | 10 | 11 | 21 | 54 | 102 | 31 | |
| 20. | Wigan Borough FC (Wigan) | 42 | 10 | 10 | 22 | 56 | 97 | 30 | |
| 21. | Durham City FC (Durham) | 42 | 11 | 7 | 24 | 53 | 100 | 29 | # |
| 22. | Nelson FC (Nelson) | 42 | 10 | 6 | 26 | 76 | 136 | 26 | |
| | | 924 | 365 | 194 | 365 | 1676 | 1676 | 924 | |

| Football League Division 3 (S) 1927-1928 Season | Bournemouth | Brentford | Brighton | Bristol Rovers | Charlton Ath. | Coventry City | Crystal Palace | Exeter City | Gillingham | Luton Town | Merthyr Town | Millwall Ath. | Newport Co. | Northampton | Norwich City | Plymouth A. | Q.P.R. | Southend Utd. | Swindon Town | Torquay United | Walsall | Watford |
|---|---|---|---|---|---|---|---|---|---|---|---|---|---|---|---|---|---|---|---|---|---|---|
| Bournemouth & B. Athletic | ■ | 1-0 | 3-1 | 4-3 | 3-1 | 2-3 | 2-2 | 2-0 | 3-0 | 2-2 | 2-1 | 5-0 | 0-0 | 1-1 | 2-1 | 2-2 | 1-2 | 2-3 | 2-0 | 1-1 | 3-1 | 1-0 |
| Brentford FC | 2-1 | ■ | 1-3 | 5-1 | 1-1 | 4-1 | 2-1 | 1-1 | 2-0 | 4-2 | 4-0 | 6-1 | 3-1 | 3-0 | 3-1 | 0-2 | 0-3 | 2-2 | 1-4 | 1-2 | 3-2 | 1-1 |
| Brighton & Hove Albion | 3-2 | 5-2 | ■ | 5-0 | 2-2 | 3-0 | 4-2 | 0-2 | 0-0 | 3-1 | 5-0 | 3-1 | 1-4 | 2-1 | 1-0 | 4-1 | 1-3 | 1-0 | 4-2 | 3-0 | 0-0 | 1-1 |
| Bristol Rovers FC | 3-0 | 1-3 | 1-0 | ■ | 2-1 | 1-1 | 1-1 | 1-2 | 2-4 | 1-2 | 2-1 | 1-6 | 2-1 | 2-2 | 3-0 | 3-1 | 0-4 | 1-3 | 1-0 | 5-1 | 5-2 | 3-1 |
| Charlton Athletic FC | 1-1 | 3-2 | 3-0 | 2-1 | ■ | 2-1 | 0-4 | 0-0 | 1-0 | 4-3 | 0-0 | 1-1 | 3-2 | 2-2 | 3-2 | 2-0 | 1-0 | 1-2 | 3-1 | 1-0 | 1-3 | 0-2 |
| Coventry City FC | 3-2 | 0-0 | 2-2 | 2-3 | 3-3 | ■ | 2-2 | 0-0 | 1-2 | 4-2 | 1-2 | 0-3 | 0-2 | 2-4 | 2-2 | 1-1 | 0-0 | 6-1 | 4-0 | 5-1 | 0-1 | 2-3 |
| Crystal Palace FC | 6-1 | 0-2 | 1-1 | 3-2 | 5-0 | 1-0 | ■ | 2-0 | 2-2 | 3-2 | 2-0 | 0-4 | 2-0 | 1-0 | 2-1 | 0-2 | 1-1 | 4-1 | 1-0 | 3-2 | 5-1 | 2-1 |
| Exeter City FC | 4-1 | 0-1 | 0-3 | 4-1 | 2-1 | 0-1 | 2-2 | ■ | 2-2 | 3-2 | 2-0 | 2-4 | 5-1 | 1-1 | 2-2 | 2-0 | 4-0 | 3-2 | 0-0 | 5-0 | 3-0 | 3-3 |
| Gillingham FC | 2-1 | 2-1 | 0-1 | 3-1 | 1-1 | 1-2 | 3-1 | 1-1 | ■ | 0-4 | 1-1 | 0-1 | 4-0 | 1-3 | 3-0 | 3-1 | 1-2 | 1-0 | 0-1 | 4-1 | 2-0 | 0-3 |
| Luton Town FC | 3-3 | 5-2 | 2-5 | 2-0 | 2-1 | 3-1 | 6-1 | 2-1 | 6-1 | ■ | 5-1 | 1-1 | 1-1 | 2-0 | 1-3 | 1-1 | 0-1 | 0-0 | 2-1 | 5-0 | 4-1 | 3-2 |
| Merthyr Town FC | 1-1 | 3-1 | 4-2 | 2-3 | 0-0 | 3-2 | 2-2 | 0-3 | 3-1 | 0-0 | ■ | 0-0 | 0-2 | 1-3 | 1-1 | 1-4 | 0-4 | 2-3 | 8-2 | 1-3 | 3-2 | 3-1 |
| Millwall FC | 2-0 | 3-0 | 6-0 | 1-0 | 5-0 | 9-1 | 1-1 | 2-0 | 6-0 | 3-2 | 3-0 | ■ | 5-1 | 3-0 | 2-1 | 2-0 | 6-1 | 5-1 | 3-3 | 9-1 | 7-1 | 4-2 |
| Newport County AFC | 4-3 | 3-0 | 3-1 | 3-1 | 4-3 | 3-0 | 0-3 | 1-0 | 1-1 | 7-2 | 1-1 | 1-3 | ■ | 4-1 | 2-2 | 1-1 | 1-6 | 3-2 | 1-3 | 2-2 | 4-1 | 3-2 |
| Northampton Town | 1-1 | 3-2 | 1-0 | 2-0 | 2-1 | 2-1 | 1-1 | 5-0 | 1-0 | 6-5 | 6-0 | 5-2 | 1-2 | ■ | 4-2 | 2-1 | 1-0 | 2-1 | 3-0 | 4-4 | 10-0 | 5-0 |
| Norwich City FC | 3-3 | 1-1 | 0-0 | 4-2 | 0-0 | 0-2 | 4-1 | 2-2 | 0-0 | 3-0 | 4-0 | 2-0 | 1-1 | 3-4 | ■ | 2-0 | 3-1 | 2-1 | 1-3 | 4-0 | 1-4 | 1-1 |
| Plymouth Argyle FC | 3-1 | 1-0 | 2-0 | 4-1 | 2-0 | 4-0 | 5-1 | 1-2 | 2-2 | 4-0 | 5-0 | 3-2 | 2-0 | 3-3 | 4-2 | ■ | 3-0 | 3-2 | 3-0 | 4-1 | 2-1 | 0-1 |
| Queen's Park Rangers FC | 2-0 | 2-3 | 5-0 | 4-2 | 3-3 | 1-5 | 2-0 | 0-1 | 3-3 | 3-2 | 0-0 | 0-1 | 4-2 | 0-4 | 0-0 | 0-1 | ■ | 3-2 | 0-1 | 2-3 | 1-1 | 2-1 |
| Southend United FC | 3-0 | 3-2 | 0-1 | 2-1 | 1-2 | 3-2 | 6-1 | 1-2 | 1-2 | 1-0 | 2-1 | 0-1 | 5-1 | 2-0 | 1-1 | 3-0 | 7-0 | ■ | 1-1 | 1-0 | 2-1 | 3-0 |
| Swindon Town FC | 3-2 | 1-1 | 4-3 | 2-1 | 2-2 | 6-0 | 3-3 | 3-0 | 6-1 | 4-2 | 1-2 | 3-0 | 4-1 | 4-0 | 1-1 | 2-2 | 0-2 | 0-1 | ■ | 2-2 | 5-0 | 4-0 |
| Torquay United FC | 2-2 | 2-1 | 1-1 | 0-0 | 1-2 | 2-3 | 0-2 | 1-1 | 1-1 | 0-4 | 2-2 | 0-1 | 1-1 | 1-5 | 4-2 | 1-2 | 1-0 | 3-3 | 2-1 | ■ | 1-1 | 1-1 |
| Walsall FC | 2-3 | 4-2 | 3-3 | 1-2 | 1-0 | 7-0 | 1-1 | 5-1 | 7-4 | 4-1 | 2-2 | 2-5 | 0-3 | 1-1 | 1-1 | 2-1 | 2-2 | 0-1 | 1-2 | 4-0 | ■ | 2-0 |
| Watford FC | 2-0 | 1-1 | 3-3 | 2-1 | 1-2 | 3-1 | 2-1 | 3-2 | 5-3 | 1-0 | 1-1 | 0-3 | 2-3 | 2-0 | 2-0 | 1-2 | 3-3 | 1-1 | 2-5 | 1-2 | 4-0 | ■ |

## Division 3 (South)

| | | Pd | Wn | Dw | Ls | GF | GA | Pts | |
|---|---|---|---|---|---|---|---|---|---|
| 1. | Millwall FC (London) | 42 | 30 | 5 | 7 | 127 | 50 | 65 | P |
| 2. | Northampton Town FC (Northampton) | 42 | 23 | 9 | 10 | 102 | 64 | 55 | |
| 3. | Plymouth Argyle FC (Plymouth) | 42 | 23 | 7 | 12 | 85 | 54 | 53 | |
| 4. | Brighton & Hove Albion FC (Hove) | 42 | 19 | 10 | 13 | 81 | 69 | 48 | |
| 5. | Crystal Palace FC (London) | 42 | 18 | 12 | 12 | 79 | 72 | 48 | |
| 6. | Swindon Town FC (Swindon) | 42 | 19 | 9 | 14 | 90 | 69 | 47 | |
| 7. | Southend United FC (Southend-on-Sea) | 42 | 20 | 6 | 16 | 80 | 64 | 46 | |
| 8. | Exeter City FC (Exeter) | 42 | 17 | 12 | 13 | 70 | 60 | 46 | |
| 9. | Newport County AFC (Newport) | 42 | 18 | 9 | 15 | 81 | 84 | 45 | |
| 10. | Queen's Park Rangers FC (London) | 42 | 17 | 9 | 16 | 72 | 71 | 43 | |
| 11. | Charlton Athletic FC (London) | 42 | 15 | 13 | 14 | 60 | 70 | 43 | |
| 12. | Brentford FC (London) | 42 | 16 | 8 | 18 | 76 | 74 | 40 | |
| 13. | Luton Town FC (Luton) | 42 | 16 | 7 | 19 | 94 | 87 | 39 | |
| 14. | Bournemouth & Boscombe Athletic FC (Bournemouth) | 42 | 13 | 12 | 17 | 72 | 79 | 38 | |
| 15. | Watford FC (Watford) | 42 | 14 | 10 | 18 | 68 | 78 | 38 | |
| 16. | Gillingham FC (Gillingham) | 42 | 13 | 11 | 18 | 62 | 81 | 37 | |
| 17. | Norwich City FC (Norwich) | 42 | 10 | 16 | 16 | 66 | 70 | 36 | |
| 18. | Walsall FC (Walsall) | 42 | 12 | 9 | 21 | 75 | 101 | 33 | |
| 19. | Bristol Rovers FC (Bristol) | 42 | 14 | 4 | 24 | 67 | 93 | 32 | |
| 20. | Coventry City FC (Coventry) | 42 | 11 | 9 | 22 | 67 | 96 | 31 | |
| 21. | Merthyr Town FC (Merthyr Tydfil) | 42 | 9 | 13 | 20 | 53 | 91 | 31 | |
| 22. | Torquay United FC (Torquay) | 42 | 8 | 14 | 20 | 53 | 103 | 30 | |
| | | 924 | 355 | 214 | 355 | 1680 | 1680 | 924 | |

# F.A. CUP FINAL   (Wembley Stadium, London – 21/04/1928 – 92,041)

**BLACKBURN ROVERS FC (BLACKBURN)**   3-1   Huddersfield Town AFC (Huddersfield)

*Roscamp 2, McLean*                                                                 *Jackson*

Blackburn: Crawford, Hutton, Jones, Healless, Rankin, Campbell, Thornewell, Puddefoot, Roscamp, McLean, Rigby.

Huddersfield: Mercer, Goodall, Barkas, Redfern, Wilson, Steele, A.Jackson, Kelly, Brown, Stephenson, WH Smith.

## Semi-finals

| | | |
|---|---|---|
| Blackburn Rovers FC (Blackburn) | 1-0 | Arsenal FC (London) |
| Huddersfield Town AFC (Huddersfield) | 2-2, 0-0, 1-0 | Sheffield United FC (Sheffield) |

## Quarter-finals

| | | |
|---|---|---|
| Arsenal FC (London) | 4-1 | Stoke City FC (Stoke-on-Trent) |
| Blackburn Rovers FC (Blackburn) | 2-0 | Manchester United FC (Manchester) |
| Huddersfield Town AFC (Huddersfield) | 6-1 | Tottenham Hotspur FC (London) |
| Sheffield United FC (Sheffield) | 3-0 | Nottingham Forest FC (Nottingham) |

# 1928-29

| Football League Division 1 1928-1929 Season | Arsenal | Aston Villa | Birmingham | Blackburn Rovers | Bolton Wanderers | Burnley | Bury | Cardiff City | Derby County | Everton | Huddersfield Town | Leeds United | Leicester City | Liverpool | Manchester City | Manchester United | Newcastle United | Portsmouth | Sheffield United | Sunderland | Wednesday | West Ham United |
|---|---|---|---|---|---|---|---|---|---|---|---|---|---|---|---|---|---|---|---|---|---|---|
| Arsenal FC | ■ | 2-5 | 0-0 | 1-0 | 2-0 | 3-1 | 7-1 | 2-1 | 1-3 | 2-0 | 2-0 | 1-0 | 1-1 | 4-4 | 0-0 | 3-1 | 1-2 | 4-0 | 2-0 | 1-1 | 2-2 | 2-3 |
| Aston Villa FC | 4-2 | ■ | 1-2 | 2-1 | 3-5 | 4-2 | 7-1 | 1-0 | 2-3 | 2-0 | 4-1 | 1-0 | 4-2 | 3-1 | 5-1 | 0-0 | 1-1 | 3-2 | 3-2 | 3-1 | 4-1 | 5-2 |
| Birmingham FC | 1-1 | 2-4 | ■ | 4-0 | 0-2 | 3-6 | 3-2 | 0-0 | 1-4 | 1-3 | 1-2 | 5-1 | 1-0 | 0-0 | 4-1 | 1-1 | 0-0 | 1-0 | 2-2 | 1-0 | 4-1 | 2- |
| Blackburn Rovers FC | 5-2 | 2-5 | 4-1 | ■ | 1-3 | 1-1 | 1-1 | 2-0 | 3-1 | 2-1 | 1-1 | 0-1 | 1-1 | 2-1 | 2-2 | 0-3 | 2-0 | 4-0 | 1-1 | 2-0 | 4-1 | 2-0 |
| Bolton Wanderers FC | 1-2 | 3-1 | 6-2 | 0-3 | ■ | 0-1 | 0-1 | 1-0 | 3-0 | 2-3 | 1-1 | 4-1 | 5-0 | 0-0 | 1-1 | 1-1 | 1-0 | 4-2 | 3-1 | 2-2 | 2-2 | 4-1 |
| Burnley FC | 3-3 | 4-1 | 4-0 | 2-2 | 3-1 | ■ | 0-0 | 3-0 | 2-2 | 2-0 | 3-2 | 5-0 | 0-1 | 3-2 | 2-3 | 3-4 | 4-3 | 4-1 | 2-1 | 3-1 | 0-2 | 3-3 |
| Bury FC | 1-0 | 2-2 | 3-1 | 1-0 | 3-4 | 2-1 | ■ | 4-1 | 3-3 | 1-2 | 2-1 | 2-2 | 3-1 | 2-2 | 1-2 | 1-3 | 2-0 | 0-0 | 4-0 | 1-3 | 0-4 | 0-3 |
| Cardiff City AFC | 1-1 | 0-2 | 1-4 | 1-1 | 1-1 | 7-0 | 4-0 | ■ | 3-0 | 0-2 | 0-0 | 2-1 | 1-2 | 1-2 | 1-3 | 2-2 | 2-0 | 1-1 | 0-0 | 0-1 | 3-1 | 3-2 |
| Derby County FC | 0-0 | 1-0 | 2-2 | 5-1 | 2-1 | 4-0 | 3-1 | 2-0 | ■ | 3-0 | 1-2 | 3-4 | 5-2 | 2-5 | 1-1 | 6-1 | 1-2 | 1-0 | 2-2 | 0-0 | 6-0 | 6-0 |
| Everton FC | 4-2 | 0-1 | 0-2 | 5-2 | 3-0 | 2-0 | 1-0 | 1-0 | 4-0 | ■ | 0-3 | 0-1 | 3-1 | 1-0 | 2-6 | 2-4 | 5-2 | 4-0 | 1-3 | 0-0 | 0-0 | 0-4 |
| Huddersfield Town AFC | 0-1 | 3-0 | 0-0 | 0-2 | 4-1 | 7-1 | 0-2 | 1-1 | 0-0 | 3-1 | ■ | 6-1 | 1-1 | 1-3 | 2-2 | 1-2 | 2-1 | 3-1 | 6-1 | 1-2 | 0-0 | 4-0 |
| Leeds United AFC | 1-1 | 4-1 | 0-1 | 0-1 | 2-2 | 2-1 | 3-1 | 3-0 | 1-1 | 3-1 | 1-2 | ■ | 4-3 | 2-2 | 4-1 | 3-2 | 0-0 | 3-2 | 2-0 | 0-3 | 0-2 | 4-1 |
| Leicester City FC | 1-1 | 4-1 | 5-3 | 2-1 | 6-1 | 1-1 | 5-2 | 2-0 | 1-0 | 4-1 | 4-1 | 4-4 | ■ | 2-0 | 3-2 | 2-1 | 1-1 | 10-0 | 3-1 | 1-0 | 1-1 | 5-0 |
| Liverpool FC | 2-4 | 4-0 | 1-2 | 1-1 | 3-0 | 8-0 | 3-0 | 2-0 | 3-0 | 1-2 | 2-3 | 1-1 | 6-3 | ■ | 1-1 | 2-3 | 2-1 | 0-0 | 1-2 | 5-2 | 3-2 | 2-1 |
| Manchester City FC | 4-1 | 3-0 | 2-3 | 1-2 | 5-1 | 4-1 | 6-4 | 1-1 | 2-3 | 5-1 | 3-2 | 3-0 | 2-3 | 2-3 | ■ | 2-2 | 2-4 | 2-1 | 3-1 | 5-3 | 2-2 | 4-2 |
| Manchester United FC | 4-1 | 2-2 | 1-0 | 1-4 | 1-1 | 1-0 | 1-0 | 1-1 | 0-1 | 1-1 | 1-0 | 1-2 | 1-1 | 2-2 | 1-2 | ■ | 5-0 | 0-0 | 1-1 | 3-0 | 2-1 | 2-3 |
| Newcastle United FC | 0-3 | 2-1 | 1-0 | 0-2 | 4-1 | 2-7 | 2-1 | 1-1 | 4-1 | 2-0 | 4-1 | 3-2 | 1-0 | 2-2 | 4-0 | 5-0 | ■ | 0-1 | 4-2 | 4-3 | 2-1 | 1-0 |
| Portsmouth FC | 2-0 | 3-2 | 3-1 | 2-2 | 4-4 | 3-1 | 4-1 | 0-1 | 1-5 | 3-0 | 1-0 | 0-2 | 1-0 | 0-1 | 3-0 | 0-1 | 3-0 | ■ | 2-3 | 4-0 | 3-2 | 3-0 |
| Sheffield United FC | 2-2 | 1-3 | 3-2 | 2-1 | 1-1 | 10-0 | 6-1 | 3-1 | 2-1 | 2-1 | 1-0 | 1-1 | 1-4 | 1-3 | 1-3 | 6-1 | 3-1 | 3-0 | ■ | 4-0 | 1-1 | 3-3 |
| Sunderland AFC | 5-1 | 1-3 | 3-4 | 3-1 | 4-0 | 2-1 | 3-1 | 1-0 | 4-0 | 2-2 | 4-1 | 2-1 | 1-2 | 2-1 | 3-1 | 5-1 | 5-2 | 5-0 | 4-4 | ■ | 4-3 | 4-1 |
| The Wednesday FC | 3-2 | 4-1 | 3-0 | 1-0 | 0-0 | 1-1 | 3-1 | 1-0 | 5-0 | 1-0 | 1-1 | 4-2 | 1-0 | 3-2 | 4-0 | 2-1 | 3-1 | 2-1 | 5-2 | 2-1 | ■ | 6-0 |
| West Ham United FC | 3-4 | 4-1 | 2-1 | 3-3 | 3-0 | 4-0 | 2-3 | 1-1 | 2-2 | 2-4 | 1-1 | 8-2 | 2-1 | 1-1 | 3-0 | 3-1 | 1-0 | 0-1 | 4-0 | 3-3 | 3-2 | ■ |

| | Division 1 | Pd | Wn | Dw | Ls | GF | GA | Pts | |
|---|---|---|---|---|---|---|---|---|---|
| 1. | THE WEDNESDAY FC (SHEFFIELD) | 42 | 21 | 10 | 11 | 86 | 62 | 52 | * |
| 2. | Leicester City FC (Leicester) | 42 | 21 | 9 | 12 | 96 | 67 | 51 | |
| 3. | Aston Villa FC (Birmingham) | 42 | 23 | 4 | 15 | 98 | 81 | 50 | |
| 4. | Sunderland AFC (Sunderland) | 42 | 20 | 7 | 15 | 93 | 75 | 47 | |
| 5. | Liverpool FC (Liverpool) | 42 | 17 | 12 | 13 | 90 | 64 | 46 | |
| 6. | Derby County FC (Derby) | 42 | 18 | 10 | 14 | 86 | 71 | 46 | |
| 7. | Blackburn Rovers FC (Blackburn) | 42 | 17 | 11 | 14 | 72 | 63 | 45 | |
| 8. | Manchester City FC (Manchester) | 42 | 18 | 9 | 15 | 95 | 86 | 45 | |
| 9. | Arsenal FC (London) | 42 | 16 | 13 | 13 | 77 | 72 | 45 | |
| 10. | Newcastle United FC (Newcastle-upon-Tyne) | 42 | 19 | 6 | 17 | 70 | 72 | 44 | |
| 11. | Sheffield United FC (Sheffield) | 42 | 15 | 11 | 16 | 86 | 85 | 41 | |
| 12. | Manchester United FC (Manchester) | 42 | 14 | 13 | 15 | 66 | 76 | 41 | |
| 13. | Leeds United AFC (Leeds) | 42 | 16 | 9 | 17 | 71 | 84 | 41 | |
| 14. | Bolton Wanderers FC (Bolton) | 42 | 14 | 12 | 16 | 73 | 80 | 40 | |
| 15. | Birmingham FC (Birmingham) | 42 | 15 | 10 | 17 | 68 | 77 | 40 | |
| 16. | Huddersfield Town AFC (Huddersfield) | 42 | 14 | 11 | 17 | 70 | 61 | 39 | |
| 17. | West Ham United FC (London) | 42 | 15 | 9 | 18 | 86 | 96 | 39 | |
| 18. | Everton FC (Liverpool) | 42 | 17 | 4 | 21 | 63 | 75 | 38 | |
| 19. | Burnley FC (Burnley) | 42 | 15 | 8 | 19 | 81 | 103 | 38 | |
| 20. | Portsmouth FC (Portsmouth) | 42 | 15 | 6 | 21 | 56 | 80 | 36 | |
| 21. | Bury FC (Bury) | 42 | 12 | 7 | 23 | 62 | 99 | 31 | R |
| 22. | Cardiff City AFC (Cardiff) | 42 | 8 | 13 | 21 | 43 | 59 | 29 | R |
| | | 924 | 360 | 204 | 360 | 1688 | 1688 | 924 | |

*  The Wednesday FC (Sheffield) changed their club name to Sheffield Wednesday FC (Sheffield) from the next season.

## Top Goalscorer

1)  David HALLIDAY                     (Sunderland AFC)     43

| Football League Division 2 1928-1929 Season | Barnsley | Blackpool | Bradford P.A. | Bristol City | Chelsea | Clapton Orient | Grimsby Town | Hull City | Middlesbrough | Millwall | Nottingham F. | Notts County | Oldham Ath. | Port Vale | Preston N.E. | Reading | Southampton | Stoke City | Swansea Town | Tottenham H. | W.B.A. | Wolves |
|---|---|---|---|---|---|---|---|---|---|---|---|---|---|---|---|---|---|---|---|---|---|---|
| Barnsley FC | | 3-1 | 1-2 | 4-2 | 0-1 | 2-0 | 0-2 | 2-2 | 2-2 | 2-2 | 1-2 | 2-0 | 2-1 | 6-0 | 4-1 | 2-3 | 4-1 | 4-2 | 2-1 | 4-1 | 2-0 | 2-2 |
| Blackpool FC | 0-1 | | 3-0 | 2-1 | 0-1 | 0-1 | 1-1 | 2-1 | 3-0 | 3-0 | 2-2 | 3-2 | 4-0 | 4-0 | 3-2 | 7-0 | 3-0 | 2-0 | 2-2 | 2-2 | 0-2 | 3-0 |
| Bradford Park Avenue | 2-1 | 5-2 | | 3-2 | 1-2 | 2-1 | 1-0 | 5-1 | 3-2 | 4-0 | 1-1 | 2-2 | 2-0 | 2-0 | 7-2 | 1-0 | 4-1 | 2-1 | 3-1 | 4-1 | 4-1 | 4-1 |
| Bristol City FC | 3-1 | 3-2 | 1-0 | | 0-0 | 1-0 | 2-2 | 0-0 | 0-1 | 5-0 | 2-5 | 0-4 | 6-0 | 2-1 | 1-0 | 0-0 | 1-1 | 1-1 | 2-1 | 2-1 | 2-3 | 3-2 |
| Chelsea FC | 1-0 | 2-3 | 3-1 | 3-0 | | 2-2 | 3-2 | 0-0 | 2-0 | 0-3 | 3-0 | 1-1 | 2-3 | 3-3 | 2-1 | 2-1 | 1-1 | 3-1 | 4-0 | 1-1 | 2-5 | 0-2 |
| Clapton Orient FC | 3-1 | 2-4 | 1-0 | 0-1 | 1-0 | | 3-1 | 0-2 | 3-0 | 1-1 | 1-4 | 2-2 | 2-0 | 1-0 | 1-0 | 1-1 | 1-1 | 1-0 | 1-2 | 2-3 | 0-2 | 2-0 |
| Grimsby Town FC | 2-1 | 1-4 | 4-2 | 3-2 | 1-0 | 6-1 | | 0-1 | 1-4 | 3-0 | 2-2 | 2-2 | 1-0 | 3-1 | 1-0 | 4-0 | 2-1 | 2-1 | 4-1 | 2-3 | 2-0 | |
| Hull City AFC | 0-0 | 1-3 | 1-0 | 5-1 | 2-2 | 0-0 | 2-3 | | 1-1 | 4-0 | 0-1 | 1-1 | 1-0 | 2-0 | 5-1 | 3-0 | 2-2 | 1-3 | 1-1 | 1-1 | 4-1 | 1-3 |
| Middlesbrough FC | 1-0 | 4-1 | 5-3 | 3-1 | 4-5 | 4-0 | 3-0 | 1-1 | | 3-0 | 1-0 | 3-1 | 1-0 | 5-1 | 2-3 | 0-0 | 1-2 | 1-0 | 0-0 | 3-0 | 1-1 | 8-3 |
| Millwall FC | 0-2 | 2-1 | 1-3 | 3-1 | 2-1 | 2-0 | 4-1 | 0-0 | 2-3 | | 1-1 | 0-1 | 3-3 | 2-1 | 3-1 | 5-1 | 2-4 | 1-3 | 3-0 | 5-1 | 2-2 | 0-5 |
| Nottingham Forest FC | 1-3 | 2-0 | 3-2 | 1-1 | 3-0 | 0-0 | 0-1 | 3-1 | 1-1 | 0-4 | | 1-2 | 3-1 | 2-2 | 4-1 | 1-2 | 1-1 | 1-5 | 2-1 | 2-2 | 1-2 | 2-1 |
| Notts County FC | 4-1 | 3-1 | 3-3 | 2-0 | 4-3 | 2-0 | 1-2 | 6-0 | 0-3 | 4-5 | 1-1 | | 2-0 | 3-0 | 0-1 | 1-1 | 1-1 | 1-0 | 5-1 | 2-0 | 3-1 | 3-0 |
| Oldham Athletic AFC | 1-0 | 4-2 | 2-1 | 1-0 | 1-0 | 1-1 | 0-3 | 0-1 | 1-3 | 4-1 | 2-0 | 3-2 | | 1-1 | 2-1 | 3-1 | 1-0 | 2-1 | 3-1 | 3-0 | 0-4 | |
| Port Vale FC | 3-0 | 1-0 | 0-1 | 5-0 | 1-0 | 3-0 | 0-3 | 4-1 | 2-3 | 5-2 | 4-2 | 3-0 | 2-1 | | 3-2 | 4-0 | 1-2 | 1-2 | 0-0 | 2-1 | 8-1 | 1-4 |
| Preston North End FC | 2-1 | 3-1 | 2-0 | 2-2 | 3-0 | 5-2 | 5-2 | 1-0 | 0-0 | 3-4 | 3-2 | 0-1 | 3-2 | 7-1 | | 7-0 | 0-1 | 2-2 | 2-2 | 2-2 | 1-1 | 5-1 |
| Reading FC | 1-0 | 4-1 | 4-0 | 2-1 | 3-3 | 4-2 | 1-3 | 3-0 | 2-3 | 0-2 | 0-3 | 1-2 | 6-1 | 2-1 | 0-0 | | 0-1 | 1-1 | 2-0 | 4-3 | 5-3 | 3-0 |
| Southampton FC | 1-2 | 8-2 | 2-2 | 2-1 | 1-2 | 2-0 | 3-1 | 3-2 | 1-1 | 3-0 | 2-1 | 4-0 | 2-1 | 1-2 | 4-0 | 2-2 | | 0-0 | 3-0 | 1-1 | 1-1 | 2-1 |
| Stoke City FC | 0-0 | 1-1 | 2-0 | 2-0 | 0-1 | 3-1 | 1-2 | 1-1 | 3-2 | 0-0 | 1-1 | 5-0 | 1-1 | 2-1 | 1-1 | 5-0 | 3-0 | | 5-0 | 2-0 | 4-1 | 4-3 |
| Swansea Town AFC | 2-1 | 5-5 | 3-1 | 0-2 | 0-1 | 0-1 | 2-1 | 0-1 | 2-0 | 2-0 | 3-5 | 1-0 | 3-2 | 2-0 | 5-0 | 0-1 | 1-1 | 3-3 | | 4-0 | 6-1 | 2-0 |
| Tottenham Hotspur FC | 2-0 | 1-2 | 3-2 | 1-1 | 4-1 | 2-1 | 2-1 | 4-1 | 2-5 | 2-1 | 2-1 | 3-0 | 4-1 | 4-2 | 2-0 | 2-2 | 3-2 | 1-0 | 1-1 | | 2-0 | 3-2 |
| West Bromwich Albion FC | 6-2 | 2-2 | 1-2 | 1-1 | 3-0 | 3-1 | 1-0 | 2-0 | 1-1 | 3-2 | 3-0 | 1-3 | 1-0 | 3-1 | 1-1 | 5-0 | 2-3 | 5-1 | 3-2 | | | 0-2 |
| Wolverhampton Wanderers FC | 3-1 | 1-5 | 3-1 | 2-1 | 1-1 | 3-2 | 2-2 | 2-4 | 3-3 | 0-1 | 2-3 | 3-1 | 0-0 | 4-0 | 1-2 | 2-0 | 1-1 | 4-0 | 0-0 | 4-2 | 0-1 | |

## Division 2

| | | Pd | Wn | Dw | Ls | GF | GA | Pts | |
|---|---|---|---|---|---|---|---|---|---|
| 1. | Middlesbrough FC (Middlesbrough) | 42 | 22 | 11 | 9 | 92 | 57 | 55 | P |
| 2. | Grimsby Town FC (Cleethorpes) | 42 | 24 | 5 | 13 | 82 | 61 | 53 | P |
| 3. | Bradford Park Avenue FC (Bradford) | 42 | 22 | 4 | 16 | 88 | 70 | 48 | |
| 4. | Southampton FC (Southampton) | 42 | 17 | 14 | 11 | 74 | 60 | 48 | |
| 5. | Notts County FC (Nottingham) | 42 | 19 | 9 | 14 | 78 | 65 | 47 | |
| 6. | Stoke City FC (Stoke-on-Trent) | 42 | 17 | 12 | 13 | 74 | 51 | 46 | |
| 7. | West Bromwich Albion FC (West Bromwich) | 42 | 19 | 8 | 15 | 80 | 79 | 46 | |
| 8. | Blackpool FC (Blackpool) | 42 | 19 | 7 | 16 | 92 | 76 | 45 | |
| 9. | Chelsea FC (London) | 42 | 17 | 10 | 15 | 64 | 65 | 44 | |
| 10. | Tottenham Hotspur FC (London) | 42 | 17 | 9 | 16 | 75 | 81 | 43 | |
| 11. | Nottingham Forest FC (Nottingham) | 42 | 15 | 12 | 15 | 71 | 70 | 42 | |
| 12. | Hull City AFC (Kingston-upon-Hull) | 42 | 13 | 14 | 15 | 58 | 63 | 40 | |
| 13. | Preston North End FC (Preston) | 42 | 15 | 9 | 18 | 78 | 79 | 39 | |
| 14. | Millwall FC (London) | 42 | 16 | 7 | 19 | 71 | 86 | 39 | |
| 15. | Reading FC (Reading) | 42 | 15 | 9 | 18 | 63 | 86 | 39 | |
| 16. | Barnsley FC (Barnsley) | 42 | 16 | 6 | 20 | 69 | 66 | 38 | |
| 17. | Wolverhampton Wanderers FC (Wolverhampton) | 42 | 15 | 7 | 20 | 77 | 81 | 37 | |
| 18. | Oldham Athletic AFC (Oldham) | 42 | 16 | 5 | 21 | 54 | 75 | 37 | |
| 19. | Swansea Town AFC (Swansea) | 42 | 13 | 10 | 19 | 58 | 72 | 36 | |
| 20. | Bristol City FC (Bristol) | 42 | 13 | 10 | 19 | 58 | 72 | 36 | |
| 21. | Port Vale FC (Stoke-on-Trent) | 42 | 15 | 4 | 23 | 71 | 86 | 34 | R |
| 22. | Clapton Orient FC (London) | 42 | 12 | 8 | 22 | 45 | 72 | 32 | R |
| | | 924 | 367 | 190 | 367 | 1576 | 1576 | 924 | |

**Football League Division 3 (N) 1928-1929 Season**

| | Accrington St. | Ashington | Barrow | Bradford City | Carlisle United | Chesterfield | Crewe Alex. | Darlington | Doncaster R. | Halifax Town | Hartlepools Utd. | Lincoln City | Nelson | New Brighton | Rochdale | Rotherham Utd. | Southport | South Shields | Stockport Co. | Tranmere R. | Wigan Borough | Wrexham |
|---|---|---|---|---|---|---|---|---|---|---|---|---|---|---|---|---|---|---|---|---|---|---|
| Accrington Stanley FC | ■ | 0-1 | 1-0 | 0-1 | 2-3 | 0-0 | 2-0 | 4-0 | 6-0 | 1-1 | 2-2 | 0-1 | 4-4 | 3-1 | 2-2 | 1-3 | 2-0 | 2-0 | 2-0 | 2-0 | 2-0 | 4-3 |
| Ashington FC | 2-2 | ■ | 1-0 | 2-8 | 0-4 | 0-2 | 0-5 | 4-2 | 4-7 | 0-3 | 3-1 | 1-1 | 3-2 | 1-1 | 2-1 | 0-1 | 1-3 | 1-3 | 0-1 | 3-2 | 1-1 | 2-2 |
| Barrow AFC | 2-1 | 3-0 | ■ | 1-3 | 1-1 | 1-2 | 2-4 | 3-1 | 2-2 | 1-3 | 2-1 | 2-3 | 7-2 | 0-0 | 3-3 | 4-0 | 1-2 | 1-1 | 2-4 | 1-2 | 1-0 | 2-2 |
| Bradford City AFC | 4-1 | 2-0 | 8-0 | ■ | 4-2 | 6-1 | 4-1 | 3-0 | 3-0 | 2-2 | 4-1 | 2-3 | 0-2 | 5-2 | 0-0 | 11-1 | 5-0 | 3-1 | 2-1 | 8-0 | 1-0 | 5-0 |
| Carlisle United FC | 4-3 | 5-1 | 4-1 | 2-2 | ■ | 1-2 | 1-0 | 3-0 | 1-2 | 2-1 | 8-0 | 3-1 | 4-0 | 2-1 | 4-2 | 1-1 | 4-2 | 5-0 | 0-5 | 4-1 | 2-1 | 1-1 |
| Chesterfield FC | 4-1 | 4-1 | 3-0 | 0-5 | 1-2 | ■ | 1-0 | 2-1 | 0-1 | 3-2 | 4-1 | 1-1 | 3-2 | 0-2 | 2-1 | 1-2 | 6-0 | 3-2 | 1-2 | 4-1 | 0-0 | 3-1 |
| Crewe Alexandra FC | 4-0 | 7-0 | 3-1 | 0-0 | 1-1 | 6-1 | ■ | 2-0 | 1-1 | 3-0 | 4-2 | 1-3 | 1-1 | 3-0 | 1-1 | 3-0 | 1-1 | 1-5 | 2-0 | 0-1 | 0-4 | 3-1 |
| Darlington FC | 0-0 | 4-0 | 1-2 | 3-3 | 0-0 | 2-2 | 4-2 | ■ | 1-0 | 2-0 | 4-1 | 2-1 | 3-2 | 3-1 | 5-3 | 2-1 | 3-1 | 2-2 | 2-3 | 1-2 | 3-0 | 0-0 |
| Doncaster Rovers FC | 4-1 | 2-1 | 1-0 | 1-1 | 3-0 | 2-0 | 0-1 | 3-1 | ■ | 1-0 | 4-1 | 0-0 | 2-2 | 1-2 | 4-2 | 1-0 | 4-2 | 2-1 | 0-2 | 2-1 | 1-2 | 1-1 |
| Halifax Town AFC | 4-2 | 1-0 | 2-0 | 1-1 | 5-2 | 1-1 | 2-2 | 5-1 | 2-2 | ■ | 2-0 | 4-2 | 1-2 | 1-1 | 1-1 | 3-1 | 2-1 | 0-2 | 1-1 | 2-0 | 1-0 | 1-2 |
| Hartlepools United FC | 1-3 | 1-3 | 1-0 | 1-3 | 1-0 | 0-2 | 2-1 | 2-0 | 2-2 | 3-1 | ■ | 3-2 | 2-2 | 5-2 | 0-2 | 1-1 | 4-2 | 0-5 | 1-1 | 4-1 | 1-3 | 0-2 |
| Lincoln City FC | 3-1 | 3-1 | 5-0 | 3-4 | 3-0 | 1-0 | 1-0 | 0-0 | 2-1 | 3-0 | 7-1 | ■ | 5-1 | 4-0 | 2-0 | 1-1 | 4-1 | 5-0 | 1-2 | 3-1 | 1-1 | 1-1 |
| Nelson FC | 0-2 | 5-0 | 3-4 | 0-1 | 1-0 | 4-1 | 2-1 | 2-4 | 3-1 | 1-0 | 3-4 | | ■ | 3-0 | 3-0 | 4-1 | 1-1 | 1-0 | 4-1 | 4-2 | 2-1 | 1-3 |
| New Brighton FC | 2-1 | 3-2 | 1-3 | 0-3 | 1-0 | 2-3 | 2-3 | 1-0 | 1-1 | 1-0 | 1-3 | 6-1 | 0-1 | ■ | 6-1 | 0-0 | 3-1 | 1-0 | 4-1 | 1-2 | 2-2 | 2-0 |
| Rochdale AFC | 2-1 | 5-0 | 4-2 | 1-3 | 4-0 | 2-1 | 2-1 | 5-0 | 1-3 | 2-2 | 7-4 | 0-2 | 2-1 | 4-2 | ■ | 2-1 | 1-1 | 1-2 | 1-3 | 5-1 | 0-0 | 4-4 |
| Rotherham United FC | 2-1 | 0-0 | 2-1 | 2-2 | 4-0 | 2-0 | 1-2 | 2-0 | 1-2 | 0-0 | 3-2 | 3-2 | 4-0 | 3-1 | 5-0 | ■ | 0-2 | 1-1 | 3-3 | 0-1 | 4-2 | 2-1 |
| Southport FC | 3-1 | 2-1 | 2-2 | 0-3 | 4-3 | 1-0 | 6-2 | 3-1 | 3-3 | 1-0 | 6-2 | 2-1 | 5-1 | 0-0 | 1-1 | 2-0 | ■ | 5-0 | 1-1 | 1-2 | 3-0 | 1-3 |
| South Shields FC | 3-0 | 0-0 | 2-2 | 1-1 | 5-0 | 6-3 | 3-0 | 1-3 | 1-0 | 2-1 | 1-1 | 1-0 | 3-2 | 0-2 | 5-2 | 10-1 | 4-0 | ■ | 0-1 | 4-1 | 2-2 | 3-2 |
| Stockport County FC | 6-1 | 4-0 | 3-2 | 2-1 | 2-2 | 3-1 | 2-2 | 7-3 | 3-0 | 3-0 | 7-3 | 3-0 | 2-1 | 4-0 | 1-0 | 2-1 | 7-1 | | ■ | 4-1 | 2-1 | 6-2 |
| Tranmere Rovers FC | 1-1 | 3-2 | 2-1 | 1-0 | 1-2 | 3-0 | 1-2 | 4-0 | 1-1 | 2-1 | 3-0 | 2-1 | 6-1 | 1-3 | 5-1 | 3-0 | 6-1 | 4-0 | 2-1 | ■ | 3-2 | 1-1 |
| Wigan Borough FC | 5-2 | 5-1 | 2-1 | 2-0 | 2-2 | 5-1 | 4-2 | 2-0 | 4-2 | 1-1 | 2-0 | 4-0 | 1-0 | 1-1 | 4-1 | 1-0 | 1-0 | 4-0 | 4-0 | 0-1 | ■ | 1-1 |
| Wrexham AFC | 4-1 | 4-0 | 5-0 | 2-1 | 5-1 | 4-3 | 1-2 | 4-3 | 4-2 | 2-2 | 3-1 | 2-1 | 3-1 | 1-1 | 3-0 | 2-0 | 3-1 | 1-0 | 2-1 | 3-1 | 1-3 | ■ |

## Division 3 (North)

| | | Pd | Wn | Dw | Ls | GF | GA | Pts | |
|---|---|---|---|---|---|---|---|---|---|
| 1. | Bradford City AFC (Bradford) | 42 | 27 | 9 | 6 | 128 | 43 | 63 | P |
| 2. | Stockport County FC (Stockport) | 42 | 28 | 6 | 8 | 111 | 58 | 62 | |
| 3. | Wrexham AFC (Wrexham) | 42 | 21 | 10 | 11 | 91 | 69 | 52 | |
| 4. | Wigan Borough FC (Wigan) | 42 | 21 | 9 | 12 | 82 | 49 | 51 | |
| 5. | Doncaster Rovers FC (Doncaster) | 42 | 20 | 10 | 12 | 76 | 66 | 50 | |
| 6. | Lincoln City FC (Lincoln) | 42 | 21 | 6 | 15 | 91 | 67 | 48 | |
| 7. | Tranmere Rovers FC (Birkenhead) | 42 | 22 | 3 | 17 | 79 | 77 | 47 | |
| 8. | Carlisle United FC (Carlisle) | 42 | 19 | 8 | 15 | 86 | 77 | 46 | |
| 9. | Crewe Alexandra FC (Crewe) | 42 | 18 | 8 | 16 | 80 | 68 | 44 | |
| 10. | South Shields FC (South Shields) | 42 | 18 | 8 | 16 | 83 | 74 | 44 | |
| 11. | Chesterfield FC (Chesterfield) | 42 | 18 | 5 | 19 | 71 | 77 | 41 | |
| 12. | Southport FC (Southport) | 42 | 16 | 8 | 18 | 75 | 85 | 40 | |
| 13. | Halifax Town AFC (Halifax) | 42 | 13 | 13 | 16 | 63 | 62 | 39 | |
| 14. | New Brighton FC (Wallasey) | 42 | 15 | 9 | 18 | 64 | 71 | 39 | |
| 15. | Nelson FC (Nelson) | 42 | 17 | 5 | 20 | 77 | 90 | 39 | |
| 16. | Rotherham United FC (Rotherham) | 42 | 15 | 9 | 18 | 60 | 77 | 39 | |
| 17. | Rochdale AFC (Rochdale) | 42 | 13 | 10 | 19 | 79 | 96 | 36 | |
| 18. | Accrington Stanley FC (Accrington) | 42 | 13 | 8 | 21 | 68 | 82 | 34 | |
| 19. | Darlington FC (Darlington) | 42 | 13 | 7 | 22 | 64 | 88 | 33 | |
| 20. | Barrow AFC (Barrow-in-Furness) | 42 | 10 | 8 | 24 | 64 | 93 | 28 | |
| 21. | Hartlepools United FC (Hartlepool) | 42 | 10 | 6 | 26 | 59 | 112 | 26 | |
| 22. | Ashington FC (Ashington) | 42 | 8 | 7 | 27 | 45 | 115 | 23 | # |
| | | 924 | 376 | 172 | 376 | 1696 | 1696 | 924 | |

| Football League Division 3 (S) 1928-1929 Season | Bournemouth | Brentford | Brighton | Bristol Rovers | Charlton Ath. | Coventry City | Crystal Palace | Exeter City | Fulham | Gillingham | Luton Town | Merthyr Town | Newport Co. | Northampton | Norwich City | Plymouth Arg. | Q.P.R. | Southend Utd. | Swindon T. | Torquay Utd. | Walsall | Watford |
|---|---|---|---|---|---|---|---|---|---|---|---|---|---|---|---|---|---|---|---|---|---|---|
| Bournemouth & B. Athletic | ■ | 1-1 | 3-2 | 6-2 | 4-2 | 2-1 | 2-0 | 3-1 | 1-0 | 4-3 | 3-3 | 3-0 | 0-1 | 2-0 | 2-0 | 4-1 | 2-3 | 2-2 | 2-1 | 4-3 | 1-2 | 3-3 |
| Brentford FC | 0-0 | ■ | 5-1 | 2-0 | 1-0 | 1-0 | 2-4 | 4-2 | 1-2 | 4-1 | 0-1 | 2-1 | 1-3 | 2-2 | 4-0 | 0-2 | 1-1 | 1-0 | 2-0 | 0-0 | 1-0 | 0-1 |
| Brighton & Hove Albion | 1-0 | 3-2 | ■ | 4-0 | 2-3 | 0-1 | 1-5 | 3-2 | 2-0 | 3-1 | 1-0 | 2-1 | 2-1 | 0-3 | 3-0 | 2-1 | 2-1 | 2-1 | 2-2 | 1-2 | 2-1 | 1-1 |
| Bristol Rovers FC | 1-2 | 2-0 | 3-0 | ■ | 3-0 | 1-1 | 1-1 | 1-1 | 5-3 | 2-4 | 1-1 | 3-0 | 0-3 | 1-2 | 2-0 | 0-1 | 1-1 | 4-1 | 1-4 | 2-1 | 4-1 | 1-1 |
| Charlton Athletic FC | 6-2 | 1-0 | 3-0 | 1-2 | ■ | 3-1 | 1-3 | 3-1 | 0-0 | 1-1 | 4-1 | 2-2 | 2-2 | 3-1 | 1-0 | 2-1 | 2-2 | 3-2 | 4-1 | 2-0 | 5-0 | 2-0 |
| Coventry City FC | 1-2 | 1-0 | 3-0 | 2-0 | 0-1 | ■ | 1-3 | 1-1 | 1-2 | 2-0 | 1-1 | 6-1 | 3-1 | 0-2 | 3-0 | 1-4 | 0-0 | 1-1 | 4-1 | 2-1 | 1-1 | 1-1 |
| Crystal Palace FC | 1-3 | 1-0 | 1-0 | 5-2 | 0-2 | 0-3 | ■ | 1-0 | 2-1 | 3-0 | 3-0 | 2-0 | 1-1 | 1-0 | 2-1 | 1-4 | 1-4 | 3-2 | 6-1 | 2-0 | 1-1 | 3-0 |
| Exeter City FC | 6-3 | 2-3 | 4-1 | 2-2 | 2-5 | 2-3 | 1-2 | ■ | 1-4 | 4-2 | 1-1 | 5-0 | 6-1 | 2-0 | 3-1 | 1-2 | 1-1 | 1-2 | 1-1 | 1-3 | 1-1 | 2-2 |
| Fulham FC | 3-0 | 1-0 | 3-1 | 6-1 | 2-5 | 2-2 | 2-2 | 0-0 | ■ | 4-2 | 4-2 | 4-0 | 2-3 | 2-1 | 2-1 | 5-2 | 5-0 | 2-4 | 2-0 | 2-1 | 5-1 | 2-3 |
| Gillingham FC | 2-2 | 1-2 | 1-1 | 1-0 | 1-0 | 1-1 | 0-1 | 1-3 | 2-2 | ■ | 1-0 | 1-0 | 0-4 | 2-1 | 4-0 | 2-0 | 0-0 | 0-2 | 0-0 | 1-1 | 1-4 | 0-0 |
| Luton Town FC | 2-1 | 2-1 | 1-0 | 4-2 | 3-0 | 1-1 | 5-3 | 4-0 | 1-3 | 8-0 | ■ | 2-0 | 5-2 | 4-0 | 2-1 | 2-2 | 3-2 | 4-2 | 5-3 | 1-2 | 3-1 | 2-2 |
| Merthyr Town FC | 1-0 | 2-2 | 1-0 | 4-0 | 2-3 | 2-2 | 2-2 | 2-1 | 4-1 | 2-3 | 3-4 | ■ | 2-1 | 2-2 | 2-1 | 2-2 | 1-2 | 2-1 | 0-0 | 3-0 | 1-0 | 2-1 |
| Newport County AFC | 0-2 | 1-1 | 1-2 | 2-0 | 2-0 | 2-1 | 1-3 | 1-1 | 3-3 | 5-0 | 1-2 | 6-1 | ■ | 0-3 | 2-2 | 1-0 | 0-0 | 2-2 | 0-1 | 4-1 | 3-1 | 0-2 |
| Northampton Town FC | 2-0 | 1-1 | 1-1 | 3-1 | 4-1 | 3-3 | 8-1 | 4-0 | 3-3 | 1-0 | 2-2 | 4-1 | 7-0 | ■ | 2-0 | 3-0 | 4-2 | 2-3 | 1-1 | 6-1 | 4-2 | 3-0 |
| Norwich City FC | 5-1 | 2-4 | 3-1 | 2-1 | 0-1 | 3-0 | 0-1 | 5-0 | 2-2 | 1-2 | 3-0 | 3-1 | 3-1 | 1-1 | ■ | 0-3 | 3-1 | 2-5 | 1-1 | 3-0 | 2-1 | 5-2 |
| Plymouth Argyle FC | 2-0 | 4-0 | 1-0 | 2-0 | 2-2 | 3-0 | 1-1 | 0-0 | 4-2 | 3-0 | 2-0 | 4-0 | 5-2 | 1-1 | 4-0 | ■ | 1-2 | 1-1 | 3-0 | 4-0 | 2-2 | 2-0 |
| Queen's Park Rangers FC | 0-0 | 2-2 | 3-2 | 0-3 | 2-2 | 3-1 | 1-1 | 1-0 | 2-1 | 1-0 | 1-1 | 8-0 | 0-0 | 4-1 | 3-0 | 2-0 | ■ | 3-1 | 4-2 | 5-1 | 2-2 | 3-2 |
| Southend United FC | 4-4 | 1-1 | 1-1 | 1-0 | 1-3 | 0-0 | 3-0 | 1-0 | 0-1 | 2-0 | 5-0 | 5-1 | 4-2 | 2-2 | 5-3 | 1-1 | 0-3 | ■ | 1-1 | 3-0 | 3-1 | 1-3 |
| Swindon Town FC | 3-3 | 3-1 | 2-2 | 2-1 | 1-1 | 1-2 | 3-2 | 2-0 | 1-2 | 2-1 | 4-2 | 2-1 | 5-2 | 0-1 | 1-2 | 0-0 | 2-1 | 3-1 | ■ | 1-1 | 5-1 | 5-0 |
| Torquay United FC | 4-1 | 4-1 | 5-1 | 0-1 | 3-1 | 0-2 | 1-2 | 1-3 | 1-1 | 2-1 | 2-2 | 6-2 | 4-1 | 0-1 | 0-3 | 2-2 | 3-4 | 2-1 | 2-4 | ■ | 3-2 | 1-0 |
| Walsall FC | 2-1 | 2-0 | 1-2 | 1-3 | 0-2 | 0-0 | 3-1 | 7-2 | 2-2 | 4-0 | 0-0 | 1-1 | 3-1 | 4-3 | 3-3 | 1-1 | 3-1 | 4-1 | 1-1 | 1-0 | ■ | 4-0 |
| Watford FC | 0-3 | 2-0 | 2-1 | 1-0 | 3-1 | 4-2 | 3-3 | 3-0 | 2-6 | 1-0 | 3-2 | 4-0 | 3-0 | 1-1 | 2-2 | 6-3 | 4-1 | 4-1 | 3-2 | 0-2 | 4-1 | ■ |

## Division 3 (South)

| | | Pd | Wn | Dw | Ls | GF | GA | Pts | |
|---|---|---|---|---|---|---|---|---|---|
| 1. | Charlton Athletic FC (London) | 42 | 23 | 8 | 11 | 86 | 60 | 54 | P |
| 2. | Crystal Palace FC (London) | 42 | 23 | 8 | 11 | 81 | 67 | 54 | |
| 3. | Northampton Town FC (Northampton) | 42 | 20 | 12 | 10 | 96 | 57 | 52 | |
| 4. | Plymouth Argyle FC (Plymouth) | 42 | 20 | 12 | 10 | 83 | 51 | 52 | |
| 5. | Fulham FC (London) | 42 | 21 | 10 | 11 | 107 | 71 | 52 | |
| 6. | Queen's Park Rangers FC (London) | 42 | 19 | 14 | 9 | 82 | 61 | 52 | |
| 7. | Luton Town FC (Luton) | 42 | 19 | 11 | 12 | 89 | 73 | 49 | |
| 8. | Watford FC (Watford) | 42 | 19 | 10 | 13 | 79 | 74 | 48 | |
| 9. | Bournemouth & Boscombe Athletic FC (Bournemouth) | 42 | 19 | 9 | 14 | 84 | 77 | 47 | |
| 10. | Swindon Town FC (Swindon) | 42 | 15 | 13 | 14 | 75 | 72 | 43 | |
| 11. | Coventry City FC (Coventry) | 42 | 14 | 14 | 14 | 62 | 57 | 42 | |
| 12. | Southend United FC (Southend-on-Sea) | 42 | 15 | 11 | 16 | 80 | 75 | 41 | |
| 13. | Brentford FC (London) | 42 | 14 | 10 | 18 | 56 | 60 | 38 | |
| 14. | Walsall FC (Walsall) | 42 | 13 | 12 | 17 | 73 | 79 | 38 | |
| 15. | Brighton & Hove Albion FC (Hove) | 42 | 16 | 6 | 20 | 58 | 76 | 38 | |
| 16. | Newport County AFC (Newport) | 42 | 13 | 9 | 20 | 69 | 86 | 35 | |
| 17. | Norwich City FC (Norwich) | 42 | 14 | 6 | 22 | 69 | 81 | 34 | |
| 18. | Torquay United FC (Torquay) | 42 | 14 | 6 | 22 | 66 | 84 | 34 | |
| 19. | Bristol Rovers FC (Bristol) | 42 | 13 | 7 | 33 | 60 | 79 | 33 | |
| 20. | Merthyr Town FC (Merthyr Tydfil) | 42 | 11 | 8 | 23 | 55 | 103 | 30 | |
| 21. | Exeter City FC (Exeter) | 42 | 9 | 11 | 22 | 67 | 88 | 29 | |
| 22. | Gillingham FC (Gillingham) | 42 | 10 | 9 | 23 | 43 | 83 | 29 | |
| | | 924 | 354 | 216 | 354 | 1614 | 1614 | 924 | |

## F.A. CUP FINAL  (Wembley Stadium, London – 27/03/29 – 92,576)

BOLTON WANDERERS FC (BOLTON)  2-0  Portsmouth FC (Portsmouth)
*Butler, Blackmore*

Bolton: Pym, Haworth, Finney, Kean, Seddon, Nuttall, Butler, McClelland, Blackmore, Gibson, W.Cook.
Portsmouth: Gilfillan, Mackie, Bell, Nichol, McIlwaine, Thackeray, Forward, J.Smith, Weddle, Watson, F.Cook

## Semi-finals

Bolton Wanderers FC (Bolton)  2-1  Huddersfield Town AFC (Huddersfield)
Portsmouth FC (Portsmouth)  1-0  Aston Villa FC (Birmingham)

## Quarter-finals

Aston Villa FC (Birmingham)  1-0  Arsenal FC (London)
Blackburn Rovers FC (Blackburn)  1-1, 1-2  Bolton Wanderers FC (Bolton)
Portsmouth FC (Portsmouth)  3-2  West Ham United FC (London)
West Bromwich Albion FC (West Bromwich)  1-1, 1-2  Huddersfield Town AFC (Huddersfield)

# 1929-30

| Football League Division 1 1929-1930 Season | Arsenal | Aston Villa | Birmingham | Blackburn Rovers | Bolton Wanderers | Burnley | Derby County | Everton | Grimsby Town | Huddersfield Town | Leeds United | Leicester City | Liverpool | Manchester City | Manchester United | Middlesbrough | Newcastle United | Portsmouth | Sheffield United | Sheffield Wednesday | Sunderland | West Ham United |
|---|---|---|---|---|---|---|---|---|---|---|---|---|---|---|---|---|---|---|---|---|---|---|
| Arsenal FC | | 2-4 | 1-0 | 4-0 | 1-2 | 6-1 | 1-1 | 4-0 | 4-1 | 2-0 | 4-0 | 1-1 | 0-1 | 3-2 | 4-2 | 1-2 | 0-1 | 1-2 | 8-1 | 2-3 | 0-1 | 0-1 |
| Aston Villa FC | 5-2 | | 2-1 | 3-0 | 2-0 | 1-2 | 2-2 | 5-2 | 4-1 | 5-3 | 3-4 | 3-0 | 2-3 | 0-2 | 1-0 | 4-2 | 2-0 | 0-1 | 5-1 | 1-3 | 2-1 | 2-3 |
| Birmingham FC | 2-3 | 1-1 | | 1-2 | 3-1 | 2-0 | 2-4 | 0-0 | 0-2 | 4-1 | 1-0 | 3-0 | 1-0 | 3-0 | 0-1 | 1-1 | 5-1 | 1-0 | 2-1 | 1-0 | 3-1 | 4-2 |
| Blackburn Rovers FC | 1-1 | 2-0 | 7-5 | | 3-1 | 8-3 | 0-3 | 3-1 | 4-1 | 5-2 | 2-1 | 3-1 | 1-0 | 1-3 | 5-4 | 7-0 | 4-2 | 1-0 | 0-1 | 0-1 | 5-3 | 3-3 |
| Bolton Wanderers FC | 0-0 | 3-0 | 0-0 | 2-1 | | 1-1 | 1-2 | 5-0 | 2-3 | 7-1 | 4-2 | 1-0 | 0-2 | 1-2 | 4-1 | 2-2 | 1-1 | 2-1 | 2-1 | 1-3 | 3-0 | 4-1 |
| Burnley FC | 2-2 | 1-4 | 3-1 | 3-2 | 2-2 | | 6-2 | 1-1 | 3-1 | 1-3 | 0-3 | 1-1 | 4-1 | 4-2 | 4-0 | 4-1 | 0-3 | 4-0 | 5-0 | 2-4 | 2-0 | 1-1 |
| Derby County FC | 4-1 | 4-0 | 3-1 | 4-3 | 2-1 | 1-3 | | 2-1 | 5-4 | 2-2 | 3-0 | 2-2 | 2-2 | 4-2 | 1-1 | 3-1 | 3-1 | 3-2 | 2-1 | 4-1 | 3-0 | 4-3 |
| Everton FC | 1-1 | 3-4 | 2-4 | 2-2 | 3-3 | 3-0 | 4-0 | | 2-4 | 0-2 | 1-1 | 4-5 | 3-3 | 2-3 | 0-0 | 3-2 | 5-2 | 1-1 | 3-2 | 1-4 | 4-1 | 1-2 |
| Grimsby Town FC | 1-1 | 0-2 | 2-1 | 5-3 | 1-1 | 4-0 | 1-3 | 0-3 | | 4-2 | 1-2 | 1-4 | 3-2 | 2-2 | 2-2 | 0-3 | 4-0 | 1-1 | 4-1 | 0-5 | 0-1 | 0-1 |
| Huddersfield Town AFC | 2-2 | 1-1 | 1-1 | 0-0 | 0-2 | 3-0 | 0-1 | 1-2 | 0-1 | | 1-0 | 3-2 | 3-0 | 1-1 | 2-2 | 1-0 | 2-0 | 2-1 | 2-2 | 4-1 | 0-2 | 3-0 |
| Leeds United AFC | 2-0 | 4-1 | 1-0 | 4-2 | 2-1 | 3-0 | 2-1 | 2-1 | 6-0 | 0-1 | | 1-2 | 1-1 | 3-2 | 3-1 | 1-2 | 5-2 | 1-0 | 2-2 | 3-0 | 5-0 | 1-3 |
| Leicester City FC | 6-6 | 4-3 | 2-1 | 1-1 | 5-2 | 4-3 | 0-0 | 5-4 | 1-0 | 1-2 | 2-2 | | 2-1 | 3-1 | 4-1 | 4-1 | 6-1 | 0-5 | 3-3 | 2-1 | 1-2 | 1-2 |
| Liverpool FC | 1-0 | 2-0 | 1-1 | 1-1 | 3-0 | 1-3 | 2-2 | 0-3 | 2-0 | 3-0 | 1-0 | 1-1 | | 1-6 | 1-0 | 5-2 | 0-0 | 2-0 | 2-0 | 1-3 | 0-6 | 3-1 |
| Manchester City FC | 3-1 | 1-2 | 1-4 | 1-1 | 2-0 | 2-2 | 3-0 | 1-2 | 3-1 | 1-1 | 4-1 | 3-2 | 4-3 | | 0-1 | 3-1 | 3-0 | 5-2 | 2-1 | 3-3 | 2-2 | 4-3 |
| Manchester United FC | 1-0 | 2-3 | 0-0 | 1-0 | 1-1 | 1-0 | 3-2 | 3-3 | 2-5 | 1-0 | 3-1 | 2-1 | 1-2 | 1-3 | | 0-3 | 5-0 | 3-0 | 1-5 | 2-2 | 2-1 | 4-2 |
| Middlesbrough FC | 1-1 | 2-3 | 5-1 | 2-4 | 3-1 | 3-1 | 4-0 | 1-2 | 1-5 | 1-3 | 1-1 | 0-2 | 5-0 | 1-0 | 2-3 | | 2-2 | 2-0 | 3-1 | 4-1 | 3-0 | 2-0 |
| Newcastle United FC | 1-1 | 2-2 | 1-1 | 5-1 | 2-3 | 2-1 | 2-3 | 1-0 | 3-1 | 5-2 | 2-1 | 2-1 | 3-1 | 2-2 | 4-1 | 3-2 | | 4-1 | 3-5 | 1-3 | 3-0 | 1-0 |
| Portsmouth FC | 0-1 | 1-2 | 2-1 | 4-0 | 3-0 | 7-1 | 3-1 | 1-4 | 1-1 | 0-1 | 0-0 | 3-0 | 3-3 | 2-2 | 3-0 | 1-1 | 2-0 | | 3-1 | 0-4 | 1-1 | 3-1 |
| Sheffield United FC | 4-1 | 3-3 | 4-2 | 5-7 | 2-3 | 3-1 | 2-0 | 2-0 | 2-3 | 0-1 | 3-2 | 7-1 | 4-0 | 1-2 | 3-1 | 1-3 | 1-0 | 2-3 | | 2-2 | 4-2 | 4-2 |
| Sheffield Wednesday FC | 0-2 | 3-0 | 1-1 | 4-0 | 1-0 | 4-1 | 6-3 | 4-0 | 1-0 | 3-1 | 1-2 | 4-0 | 2-1 | 5-1 | 7-2 | 1-0 | 4-2 | 1-1 | 1-1 | | 1-1 | 2-1 |
| Sunderland AFC | 0-1 | 4-1 | 2-0 | 3-1 | 4-1 | 3-3 | 3-1 | 2-2 | 2-0 | 1-0 | 1-4 | 2-1 | 2-3 | 5-2 | 2-4 | 3-2 | 1-0 | 1-1 | 3-2 | 2-4 | | 4-2 |
| West Ham United FC | 3-2 | 5-2 | 0-1 | 2-3 | 5-3 | 1-0 | 2-0 | 3-1 | 2-0 | 2-3 | 3-0 | 1-2 | 4-1 | 3-0 | 2-1 | 5-3 | 5-1 | 0-1 | 1-0 | 1-1 | 1-1 | |

## Division 1

| | | Pd | Wn | Dw | Ls | GF | GA | Pts | |
|---|---|---|---|---|---|---|---|---|---|
| 1. | SHEFFIELD WEDNESDAY FC (SHEFFIELD) | 42 | 26 | 8 | 8 | 105 | 57 | 60 | |
| 2. | Derby County FC (Derby) | 42 | 21 | 8 | 13 | 90 | 82 | 50 | |
| 3. | Manchester City FC (Manchester) | 42 | 19 | 9 | 14 | 91 | 81 | 47 | |
| 4. | Aston Villa FC (Birmingham) | 42 | 21 | 5 | 16 | 92 | 83 | 47 | |
| 5. | Leeds United AFC (Leeds) | 42 | 20 | 6 | 16 | 79 | 63 | 46 | |
| 6. | Blackburn Rovers FC (Blackburn) | 42 | 19 | 7 | 16 | 99 | 93 | 45 | |
| 7. | West Ham United FC (London) | 42 | 19 | 5 | 18 | 86 | 79 | 43 | |
| 8. | Leicester City FC (Leicester) | 42 | 17 | 9 | 16 | 86 | 90 | 43 | |
| 9. | Sunderland AFC (Sunderland) | 42 | 18 | 7 | 17 | 76 | 80 | 43 | |
| 10. | Huddersfield Town AFC (Huddersfield) | 42 | 17 | 9 | 16 | 63 | 69 | 43 | |
| 11. | Birmingham FC (Birmingham) | 42 | 16 | 9 | 17 | 67 | 62 | 41 | |
| 12. | Liverpool FC (Liverpool) | 42 | 16 | 9 | 17 | 63 | 79 | 41 | |
| 13. | Portsmouth FC (Portsmouth) | 42 | 15 | 10 | 17 | 66 | 62 | 40 | |
| 14. | Arsenal FC (London) | 42 | 14 | 11 | 17 | 78 | 66 | 39 | |
| 15. | Bolton Wanderers FC (Bolton) | 42 | 15 | 9 | 18 | 74 | 74 | 39 | |
| 16. | Middlesbrough FC (Middlesbrough) | 42 | 16 | 6 | 20 | 82 | 84 | 38 | |
| 17. | Manchester United FC (Manchester) | 42 | 15 | 8 | 19 | 67 | 88 | 38 | |
| 18. | Grimsby Town FC (Cleethorpes) | 42 | 15 | 7 | 20 | 73 | 89 | 37 | |
| 19. | Newcastle United FC (Newcastle-upon-Tyne) | 42 | 15 | 7 | 20 | 71 | 92 | 37 | |
| 20. | Sheffield United FC (Sheffield) | 42 | 15 | 6 | 21 | 91 | 96 | 36 | |
| 21. | Burnley FC (Burnley) | 42 | 14 | 8 | 20 | 79 | 97 | 36 | R |
| 22. | Everton FC (Liverpool) | 42 | 12 | 11 | 19 | 80 | 92 | 35 | R |
| | | 924 | 375 | 174 | 375 | 1758 | 1758 | 924 | |

## Top Goalscorer

| | | | |
|---|---|---|---|
| 1) | Victor WATSON | (West Ham United FC) | 41 |

| Football League Division 2 1929-1930 Season | Barnsley | Blackpool | Bradford City | Bradford P.A. | Bristol City | Bury | Cardiff City | Charlton Ath. | Chelsea | Hull City | Millwall | Nottingham F. | Notts County | Oldham Ath. | Preston N.E. | Reading | Southampton | Stoke City | Swansea Town | Tottenham H. | W.B.A. | Wolves |
|---|---|---|---|---|---|---|---|---|---|---|---|---|---|---|---|---|---|---|---|---|---|---|
| Barnsley FC | | 2-4 | 2-1 | 1-1 | 3-1 | 2-1 | 2-2 | 2-0 | 1-1 | 3-0 | 1-2 | 1-1 | 2-2 | 2-1 | 0-0 | 1-0 | 3-1 | 3-1 | 1-0 | 2-0 | 2-2 | 3-1 |
| Blackpool FC | 2-1 | | 3-0 | 1-0 | 7-1 | 2-1 | 3-0 | 6-0 | 1-1 | 1-2 | 4-3 | 5-1 | 1-2 | 3-0 | 5-1 | 4-2 | 5-1 | 0-2 | 3-0 | 3-2 | 1-0 | 3-2 |
| Bradford City AFC | 0-1 | 1-1 | | 1-2 | 3-0 | 2-1 | 0-1 | 4-1 | 0-1 | 2-1 | 1-1 | 1-1 | 2-0 | 2-4 | 1-1 | 1-0 | 2-5 | 3-0 | 3-3 | 0-2 | 2-2 | 2-2 |
| Bradford Park Avenue | 4-4 | 5-0 | 0-2 | | 3-1 | 2-1 | 2-0 | 4-0 | 1-3 | 4-2 | 6-0 | 5-1 | 3-3 | 2-2 | 5-2 | 5-2 | 1-1 | 3-2 | 3-0 | 2-1 | 5-1 | 0-0 |
| Bristol City FC | 2-1 | 0-1 | 1-3 | 0-0 | | 1-2 | 2-0 | 1-1 | 2-1 | 4-0 | 1-0 | 4-1 | 0-0 | 0-4 | 2-2 | 5-3 | 3-1 | 2-6 | 2-1 | 1-0 | 2-1 | 1-2 |
| Bury FC | 2-1 | 0-1 | 2-4 | 5-1 | 2-0 | | 4-2 | 2-2 | 1-0 | 2-1 | 5-1 | 0-0 | 2-0 | 0-2 | 1-2 | 2-4 | 4-2 | 2-0 | 1-0 | 2-1 | 3-2 | 3-1 |
| Cardiff City AFC | 1-0 | 4-2 | 0-1 | 2-0 | 1-1 | 5-1 | | 1-0 | 1-0 | 0-1 | 3-1 | 1-1 | 3-1 | 5-0 | 2-0 | 2-1 | 5-2 | 1-2 | 0-0 | 1-0 | 3-2 | 0-0 |
| Charlton Athletic FC | 2-0 | 1-4 | 1-3 | 2-0 | 3-1 | 1-2 | 4-1 | | 1-1 | 4-0 | 1-1 | 5-0 | 1-0 | 1-1 | 1-1 | 0-0 | 4-1 | 4-4 | 0-2 | 1-0 | 0-1 | 2-0 |
| Chelsea FC | 2-0 | 4-0 | 3-2 | 1-2 | 2-1 | 5-3 | 1-0 | 1-1 | | 3-0 | 3-0 | 2-0 | 3-1 | 1-1 | 5-0 | 1-0 | 2-0 | 3-2 | 1-0 | 3-0 | 2-0 | 1-1 |
| Hull City AFC | 2-0 | 0-3 | 0-0 | 0-2 | 0-1 | 1-3 | 2-2 | 0-2 | 1-3 | | 3-2 | 1-2 | 0-0 | 1-0 | 2-0 | 4-2 | 2-0 | 3-0 | 1-0 | 2-0 | 3-2 | 2-0 |
| Millwall FC | 2-1 | 3-1 | 2-2 | 1-2 | 1-1 | 2-4 | 2-0 | 1-1 | 0-0 | 0-0 | | 2-2 | 2-0 | 2-1 | 2-0 | 3-1 | 1-1 | 2-1 | 0-2 | 2-5 | 2-1 | 4-0 |
| Nottingham Forest FC | 4-0 | 0-0 | 2-1 | 1-1 | 5-2 | 1-2 | 3-1 | 0-2 | 0-0 | 2-1 | 1-1 | | 1-1 | 1-2 | 2-4 | 5-0 | 0-5 | 2-1 | 1-0 | 0-0 | 0-2 | 5-2 |
| Notts County FC | 3-0 | 0-2 | 2-0 | 1-1 | 3-1 | 1-3 | 2-1 | 4-0 | 2-2 | 4-1 | 1-1 | 0-0 | | 1-1 | 0-3 | 3-0 | 1-2 | 3-3 | 0-0 | 0-1 | 2-1 | 0-3 |
| Oldham Athletic AFC | 3-2 | 1-2 | 6-1 | 5-1 | 2-2 | 2-0 | 4-1 | 1-0 | 4-2 | 3-1 | 2-2 | 0-0 | 2-2 | | 0-2 | 0-0 | 3-2 | 5-0 | 4-1 | 2-0 | 5-0 | 6-0 |
| Preston North End FC | 3-1 | 4-6 | 2-2 | 4-1 | 2-2 | 1-1 | 2-3 | 0-3 | 1-2 | 1-2 | 3-1 | 1-2 | 3-1 | 0-3 | | 2-1 | 1-1 | 5-1 | 0-0 | 4-0 | 2-2 | 1-1 |
| Reading FC | 1-0 | 1-1 | 1-1 | 1-0 | 1-6 | 0-1 | 2-0 | 3-1 | 3-1 | 1-1 | 0-1 | 0-1 | 2-0 | 1-1 | 2-0 | | 1-1 | 0-0 | 3-1 | 3-0 | 2-2 | 3-1 |
| Southampton FC | 4-0 | 4-2 | 2-1 | 2-2 | 3-0 | 0-0 | 1-1 | 2-0 | 4-2 | 2-2 | 0-0 | 2-0 | 2-2 | 2-0 | 1-2 | 4-3 | | 2-1 | 2-1 | 1-0 | 3-2 | 1-1 |
| Stoke City FC | 3-0 | 0-1 | 2-0 | 2-1 | 6-2 | 1-0 | 1-1 | 2-1 | 1-1 | 3-1 | 1-0 | 6-0 | 1-1 | 0-2 | 2-3 | 2-2 | 4-0 | | 0-1 | 1-0 | 0-3 | 3-0 |
| Swansea Town AFC | 0-2 | 3-0 | 5-0 | 2-4 | 1-1 | 2-4 | 1-0 | 2-0 | 3-0 | 2-0 | 3-1 | 1-1 | 3-2 | 3-0 | 4-0 | 0-1 | 2-2 | 2-2 | | 0-1 | 1-0 | 2-2 |
| Tottenham Hotspur FC | 2-1 | 6-1 | 1-1 | 1-1 | 2-1 | 2-2 | 1-2 | 3-0 | 3-3 | 2-2 | 1-1 | 1-1 | 2-0 | 2-1 | 1-0 | 0-0 | 3-2 | 3-1 | 3-0 | | 0-2 | 4-2 |
| West Bromwich Albion FC | 4-2 | 5-1 | 4-2 | 5-0 | 2-0 | 5-1 | 0-2 | 1-1 | 2-0 | 7-1 | 6-1 | 1-3 | 4-2 | 0-3 | 2-0 | 1-0 | 5-1 | 2-3 | 6-2 | 4-3 | | 7-3 |
| Wolverhampton Wanderers FC | 3-0 | 1-2 | 6-0 | 4-4 | 1-0 | 2-0 | 4-0 | 0-4 | 0-1 | 4-2 | 1-1 | 2-1 | 5-1 | 1-1 | 4-0 | 2-1 | 2-0 | 2-1 | 4-1 | 3-0 | 2-4 | |

## Division 2

| | | Pd | Wn | Dw | Ls | GF | GA | Pts | |
|---|---|---|---|---|---|---|---|---|---|
| 1. | Blackpool FC (Blackpool) | 42 | 27 | 4 | 11 | 98 | 67 | 58 | P |
| 2. | Chelsea FC (London) | 42 | 22 | 11 | 9 | 74 | 46 | 55 | P |
| 3. | Oldham Athletic AFC (Oldham) | 42 | 21 | 11 | 10 | 90 | 51 | 53 | |
| 4. | Bradford Park Avenue FC (Bradford) | 42 | 19 | 12 | 11 | 91 | 70 | 50 | |
| 5. | Bury FC (Bury) | 42 | 22 | 5 | 15 | 78 | 67 | 49 | |
| 6. | West Bromwich Albion FC (West Bromwich) | 42 | 21 | 5 | 16 | 105 | 73 | 47 | |
| 7. | Southampton FC (Southampton) | 42 | 17 | 11 | 14 | 77 | 76 | 45 | |
| 8. | Cardiff City AFC (Cardiff) | 42 | 18 | 8 | 16 | 61 | 59 | 44 | |
| 9. | Wolverhampton Wanderers FC (Wolverhampton) | 42 | 16 | 9 | 17 | 77 | 79 | 41 | |
| 10. | Nottingham Forest FC (Nottingham) | 42 | 13 | 15 | 14 | 55 | 69 | 41 | |
| 11. | Stoke City FC (Stoke-on-Trent) | 42 | 16 | 8 | 18 | 74 | 72 | 40 | |
| 12. | Tottenham Hotspur FC (London) | 42 | 15 | 9 | 18 | 59 | 61 | 39 | |
| 13. | Charlton Athletic FC (London) | 42 | 14 | 11 | 17 | 59 | 63 | 39 | |
| 14. | Millwall FC (London) | 42 | 12 | 15 | 15 | 57 | 73 | 39 | |
| 15. | Swansea Town AFC (Swansea) | 42 | 14 | 9 | 19 | 57 | 61 | 37 | |
| 16. | Preston North End FC (Preston) | 42 | 13 | 11 | 19 | 65 | 80 | 37 | |
| 17. | Barnsley FC (Barnsley) | 42 | 14 | 8 | 20 | 56 | 71 | 36 | |
| 18. | Bradford City AFC (Bradford) | 42 | 12 | 12 | 18 | 60 | 77 | 36 | |
| 19. | Reading FC (Reading) | 42 | 12 | 11 | 19 | 54 | 67 | 35 | |
| 20. | Bristol City FC (Bristol) | 42 | 13 | 9 | 20 | 61 | 83 | 35 | |
| 21. | Hull City AFC (Kingston-upon-Hull) | 42 | 14 | 7 | 21 | 51 | 78 | 35 | R |
| 22. | Notts County FC (Nottingham) | 42 | 9 | 15 | 18 | 54 | 70 | 33 | R |
| | | 924 | 354 | 216 | 354 | 1513 | 1513 | 924 | |

| Football League Division 3 (N) 1929-1930 Season | Accrington St. | Barrow | Carlisle United | Chesterfield | Crewe Alexandra | Darlington | Doncaster R. | Halifax Town | Hartlepools Utd. | Lincoln City | Nelson | New Brighton | Port Vale | Rochdale | Rotherham Utd. | Southport | South Shields | Stockport Co. | Tranmere Rovers | Wigan Borough | Wrexham | York City |
|---|---|---|---|---|---|---|---|---|---|---|---|---|---|---|---|---|---|---|---|---|---|---|
| Accrington Stanley FC | ■ | 3-1 | 7-2 | 3-0 | 0-3 | 3-1 | 3-3 | 7-1 | 3-0 | 0-3 | 3-0 | 5-0 | 0-2 | 6-2 | 2-0 | 1-1 | 1-2 | 0-1 | 3-3 | 3-1 | 1-3 | 1-1 |
| Barrow AFC | 3-1 | ■ | 0-2 | 0-1 | 1-0 | 0-1 | 1-0 | 0-4 | 3-0 | 2-1 | 0-2 | 3-0 | 1-1 | 2-0 | 5-1 | 0-2 | 1-3 | 1-4 | 1-1 | 4-1 | 3-3 | 0-0 |
| Carlisle United FC | 2-1 | 7-1 | ■ | 6-0 | 2-0 | 1-4 | 1-1 | 2-0 | 5-2 | 2-4 | 2-2 | 2-2 | 1-4 | 2-0 | 3-1 | 4-0 | 4-1 | 1-5 | 4-3 | 5-0 | 5-1 | 2-2 |
| Chesterfield FC | 4-2 | 2-1 | 3-1 | ■ | 5-1 | 4-1 | 2-1 | 2-0 | 2-0 | 2-1 | 3-0 | 1-0 | 1-1 | 2-0 | 2-1 | 2-0 | 1-2 | 1-3 | 1-0 | 5-0 | 5-0 | 3-0 |
| Crewe Alexandra FC | 2-1 | 0-0 | 1-2 | 2-1 | ■ | 1-2 | 4-0 | 4-1 | 5-2 | 1-1 | 4-0 | 2-3 | 0-2 | 6-1 | 6-1 | 5-4 | 2-2 | 1-1 | 3-1 | 2-1 | 2-0 | 2-2 |
| Darlington FC | 2-4 | 4-0 | 3-0 | 1-4 | 3-0 | ■ | 6-2 | 3-2 | 0-0 | 1-1 | 6-1 | 1-2 | 0-1 | 3-0 | 8-1 | 2-1 | 8-3 | 1-2 | 7-2 | 2-0 | 5-1 | 5-2 |
| Doncaster Rovers FC | 3-1 | 4-0 | 1-4 | 2-1 | 2-1 | 3-1 | ■ | 1-0 | 0-0 | 0-0 | 3-0 | 1-1 | 0-2 | 3-1 | 2-0 | 3-1 | 1-0 | 1-1 | 1-1 | 4-2 | 4-2 | 0-3 |
| Halifax Town AFC | 1-1 | 0-1 | 1-0 | 3-2 | 1-3 | 3-1 | 1-0 | ■ | 0-0 | 1-1 | 1-1 | 4-0 | 1-2 | 2-3 | 1-1 | 1-1 | 0-2 | 0-3 | 0-1 | 2-1 | 2-0 | 2-2 |
| Hartlepools United FC | 2-2 | 2-0 | 1-0 | 0-0 | 5-1 | 2-5 | 3-0 | 3-0 | ■ | 4-0 | 1-2 | 1-1 | 2-0 | 2-8 | 5-1 | 1-1 | 2-1 | 0-1 | 2-0 | 4-0 | 5-0 | 3-1 |
| Lincoln City FC | 3-3 | 3-0 | 4-1 | 2-1 | 2-2 | 2-2 | 3-1 | 0-1 | 2-2 | ■ | 4-1 | 5-3 | 3-2 | 0-0 | 1-1 | 1-1 | 2-2 | 1-0 | 8-0 | 2-0 | 3-0 | 3-0 |
| Nelson FC | 2-1 | 2-0 | 2-2 | 0-2 | 1-1 | 0-1 | 4-1 | 1-0 | 3-2 | 0-0 | ■ | 2-1 | 2-3 | 1-0 | 0-1 | 2-2 | 0-1 | 1-2 | 0-1 | 1-3 | 4-0 | 3-1 |
| New Brighton FC | 5-0 | 5-0 | 2-1 | 1-1 | 3-1 | 1-3 | 1-0 | 4-0 | 1-4 | 2-1 |  | ■ | 0-1 | 2-0 | 2-2 | 1-3 | 4-1 | 3-2 | 3-0 | 5-0 | 2-1 | 1-1 |
| Port Vale FC | 5-2 | 5-0 | 4-0 | 4-1 | 2-0 | 0-2 | 2-1 | 3-0 | 2-1 | 5-2 | 3-1 | 5-1 | ■ | 3-3 | 7-1 | 1-0 | 3-0 | 1-2 | 1-0 | 4-0 | 3-0 | 1-1 |
| Rochdale AFC | 4-0 | 6-1 | 2-0 | 2-1 | 3-1 | 4-1 | 2-4 | 0-3 | 1-1 | 3-4 | 4-1 | 5-0 | 0-0 | ■ | 1-2 | 2-2 | 2-0 | 3-1 | 2-1 | 2-1 | 5-4 | 4-2 |
| Rotherham United FC | 2-4 | 7-0 | 4-1 | 1-1 | 2-1 | 1-4 | 1-0 | 2-0 | 0-4 | 1-0 | 1-2 | 2-2 | 2-2 | 0-4 | ■ | 6-3 | 0-1 | 2-2 | 5-0 | 4-1 | 1-3 | 2-5 |
| Southport FC | 2-0 | 0-2 | 4-3 | 5-1 | 0-3 | 3-0 | 1-1 | 4-0 | 1-1 | 3-2 | 0-0 | 2-1 | 1-2 | 2-3 | 7-1 | ■ | 2-1 | 1-2 | 4-4 | 1-1 | 5-3 | 1-0 |
| South Shields FC | 2-2 | 2-0 | 5-2 | 3-1 | 1-0 | 3-3 | 2-1 | 1-0 | 3-5 | 3-1 | 2-1 | 1-2 | 0-0 | 2-2 | 5-0 | 4-0 | ■ | 2-3 | 1-5 | 2-2 | 1-1 | 4-1 |
| Stockport County FC | 1-0 | 5-0 | 7-1 | 1-0 | 2-3 | 4-0 | 3-0 | 6-0 | 5-1 | 1-1 | 6-1 | 2-0 | 4-2 | 4-2 | 6-1 | 2-2 | 2-0 | ■ | 3-1 | 1-1 | 0-1 | 2-3 |
| Tranmere Rovers FC | 2-2 | 5-2 | 3-0 | 1-2 | 1-2 | 2-1 | 3-3 | 7-1 | 0-1 | 2-3 | 3-1 | 1-5 | 2-2 | 5-4 | 3-1 | 3-0 | 2-0 |  | ■ | 3-0 | 3-0 | 4-4 |
| Wigan Borough FC | 2-1 | 2-0 | 8-0 | 2-1 | 2-2 | 3-2 | 3-2 | 2-1 | 1-3 | 4-1 | 2-0 | 5-0 | 0-3 | 3-1 | 1-1 | 1-1 | 1-1 | 0-1 | 0-2 | ■ | 2-1 | 0-2 |
| Wrexham AFC | 0-1 | 3-0 | 3-3 | 1-1 | 1-0 | 2-2 | 0-2 | 2-1 | 3-5 | 3-1 | 5-1 | 2-1 | 0-2 | 8-0 | 1-0 | 1-2 | 1-3 | 1-1 | 2-0 | 2-1 | ■ | 1-1 |
| York City FC | 2-0 | 3-1 | 2-2 | 1-1 | 4-2 | 1-1 | 2-2 | 3-0 | 4-1 | 1-0 | 1-0 | 3-0 | 0-2 | 6-0 | 3-0 | 0-4 | 2-2 | 1-2 | 4-0 | 4-0 | 0-0 | ■ |

### Division 3 (North)

|  |  | Pd | Wn | Dw | Ls | GF | GA | Pts |  |
|---|---|---|---|---|---|---|---|---|---|
| 1. | Port Vale FC (Stoke-on-Trent) | 42 | 30 | 7 | 5 | 103 | 37 | 67 | P |
| 2. | Stockport County FC (Stockport) | 42 | 28 | 7 | 7 | 106 | 44 | 63 |  |
| 3. | Darlington FC (Darlington) | 42 | 22 | 6 | 14 | 108 | 73 | 50 |  |
| 4. | Chesterfield FC (Chesterfield) | 42 | 22 | 6 | 14 | 76 | 56 | 50 |  |
| 5. | Lincoln City FC (Lincoln) | 42 | 17 | 14 | 11 | 83 | 61 | 48 |  |
| 6. | York City FC (York) | 42 | 15 | 16 | 11 | 77 | 64 | 46 |  |
| 7. | South Shields FC (South Shields) | 42 | 18 | 10 | 14 | 77 | 74 | 46 | * |
| 8. | Hartlepools United FC (Hartlepool) | 42 | 17 | 11 | 14 | 81 | 74 | 45 |  |
| 9. | Southport FC (Southport) | 42 | 15 | 13 | 14 | 81 | 74 | 43 |  |
| 10. | Rochdale AFC (Rochdale) | 42 | 18 | 7 | 17 | 89 | 91 | 43 |  |
| 11. | Crewe Alexandra FC (Crewe) | 42 | 17 | 8 | 17 | 82 | 71 | 42 |  |
| 12. | Tranmere Rovers FC (Birkenhead) | 42 | 16 | 9 | 17 | 83 | 86 | 41 |  |
| 13. | New Brighton FC (Wallasey) | 42 | 16 | 8 | 18 | 69 | 79 | 40 |  |
| 14. | Doncaster Rovers FC (Doncaster) | 42 | 15 | 9 | 18 | 62 | 69 | 39 |  |
| 15. | Carlisle United FC (Carlisle) | 42 | 16 | 7 | 19 | 90 | 101 | 39 |  |
| 16. | Accrington Stanley FC (Accrington) | 42 | 14 | 9 | 19 | 84 | 81 | 37 |  |
| 17. | Wrexham AFC (Wrexham) | 42 | 13 | 8 | 21 | 67 | 88 | 34 |  |
| 18. | Wigan Borough FC (Wigan) | 42 | 13 | 7 | 22 | 60 | 88 | 33 |  |
| 19. | Nelson FC (Nelson) | 42 | 13 | 7 | 22 | 51 | 80 | 33 |  |
| 20. | Rotherham United FC (Rotherham) | 42 | 11 | 8 | 23 | 67 | 113 | 30 |  |
| 21. | Halifax Town AFC (Halifax) | 42 | 10 | 8 | 24 | 44 | 79 | 28 |  |
| 22. | Barrow AFC (Barrow-in-Furness) | 42 | 11 | 5 | 26 | 41 | 98 | 27 |  |
|  |  | 924 | 367 | 190 | 367 | 1681 | 1681 | 924 |  |

* South Shields FC (South Shields) moved to the town of Gateshead and changed their name to Gateshead FC.

| Football League Division 3 (S) 1929-1930 Season | Bournemouth | Brentford | Brighton | Bristol Rovers | Clapton Orient | Coventry City | Crystal Palace | Exeter City | Fulham | Gillingham | Luton Town | Merthyr Town | Newport County | Northampton | Norwich City | Plymouth Arg. | Q.P.R. | Southend Utd. | Swindon Town | Torquay United | Walsall | Watford |
|---|---|---|---|---|---|---|---|---|---|---|---|---|---|---|---|---|---|---|---|---|---|---|
| Bournemouth & B. Athletic | ■ | 1-2 | 1-1 | 3-1 | 5-1 | 1-0 | 2-1 | 3-0 | 5-0 | 1-2 | 5-1 | 4-2 | 1-1 | 3-1 | 2-3 | 1-1 | 0-0 | 0-0 | 1-3 | 4-1 | 1-1 | 3-2 |
| Brentford FC | 1-0 | ■ | 5-2 | 2-1 | 3-1 | 3-1 | 2-0 | 2-0 | 5-1 | 2-1 | 2-0 | 6-0 | 1-0 | 2-0 | 3-0 | 3-0 | 3-0 | 2-1 | 3-2 | 5-0 | 6-2 | 5-0 |
| Brighton & Hove Albion | 4-3 | 2-0 | ■ | 1-0 | 1-0 | 1-1 | 1-2 | 1-1 | 5-0 | 2-0 | 4-1 | 4-1 | 3-2 | 2-1 | 6-3 | 0-1 | 2-3 | 1-0 | 3-0 | 5-0 | 4-0 | 2-1 |
| Bristol Rovers FC | 2-1 | 4-1 | 1-0 | ■ | 0-0 | 1-3 | 2-3 | 1-0 | 4-1 | 3-0 | 2-2 | 2-2 | 2-3 | 2-3 | 0-1 | 2-3 | 4-1 | 4-2 | 3-2 | 2-0 | 3-1 | 1-2 |
| Clapton Orient FC | 0-0 | 1-1 | 4-1 | 3-0 | ■ | 3-1 | 2-1 | 3-0 | 2-4 | 2-0 | 6-1 | 1-0 | 3-1 | 0-0 | 0-0 | 0-2 | 2-4 | 1-1 | 2-1 | 1-1 | 1-1 | 1-1 |
| Coventry City FC | 0-2 | 2-1 | 0-2 | 1-0 | 5-2 | ■ | 1-0 | 3-3 | 3-1 | 5-0 | 5-1 | 2-2 | 2-0 | 2-2 | 3-1 | 1-0 | 2-3 | 5-1 | 1-2 | 4-1 | 4-0 | 3-1 |
| Crystal Palace FC | 1-1 | 2-1 | 2-2 | 3-0 | 3-0 | 4-3 | ■ | 1-1 | 4-3 | 5-1 | 4-1 | 6-1 | 1-0 | 1-3 | 3-2 | 3-0 | 1-1 | 1-2 | 1-0 | 4-2 | 5-1 | 1-1 |
| Exeter City FC | 1-2 | 0-0 | 1-4 | 5-2 | 4-0 | 1-1 | 6-1 | ■ | 2-1 | 3-0 | 2-2 | 1-1 | 0-4 | 6-4 | 3-0 | 1-1 | 0-2 | 3-1 | 5-1 | 0-0 | 0-2 | 1-0 |
| Fulham FC | 3-3 | 2-0 | 5-1 | 6-2 | 2-2 | 2-0 | 1-2 | 2-2 | ■ | 2-1 | 1-1 | 5-4 | 2-1 | 1-0 | 3-3 | 1-3 | 0-2 | 2-2 | 4-1 | 1-0 | 3-2 | 6-1 |
| Gillingham FC | 1-5 | 1-3 | 2-2 | 3-3 | 2-0 | 0-3 | 1-1 | 2-0 | 0-1 | ■ | 2-0 | 6-0 | 5-0 | 5-2 | 1-2 | 0-0 | 3-1 | 1-0 | 0-0 | 0-2 | 2-1 | 1-2 |
| Luton Town FC | 1-0 | 2-1 | 1-0 | 3-0 | 1-2 | 2-2 | 2-2 | 0-4 | 4-1 | 2-0 | ■ | 4-0 | 4-2 | 1-0 | 1-1 | 5-2 | 2-1 | 0-3 | 1-1 | 3-1 | 2-3 | 2-0 |
| Merthyr Town FC | 0-1 | 2-3 | 2-8 | 1-1 | 0-1 | 2-2 | 5-2 | 0-2 | 3-4 | 1-1 | 3-1 | ■ | 5-1 | 1-0 | 1-5 | 0-3 | 1-4 | 2-2 | 3-3 | 3-0 | 2-3 | 1-0 |
| Newport County AFC | 1-1 | 1-3 | 2-2 | 2-2 | 0-0 | 4-2 | 0-0 | 4-1 | 1-1 | 5-1 | 0-0 | 10-0 | ■ | 2-1 | 4-4 | 0-2 | 4-5 | 0-0 | 2-1 | 2-1 | 3-2 | 1-0 |
| Northampton Town FC | 2-0 | 1-1 | 1-3 | 6-1 | 3-0 | 2-2 | 2-0 | 2-2 | 3-1 | 3-1 | 4-1 | 2-0 | 2-0 | ■ | 4-0 | 1-1 | 2-1 | 5-1 | 3-3 | 2-2 | 1-0 | 2-0 |
| Norwich City FC | 1-0 | 2-2 | 2-0 | 4-2 | 1-0 | 10-2 | 2-2 | 3-1 | 0-4 | 2-0 | 1-1 | 5-1 | 4-1 | 4-3 | ■ | 1-2 | 3-0 | 1-1 | 1-5 | 2-0 | 3-0 | 3-1 |
| Plymouth Argyle FC | 2-1 | 1-1 | 1-1 | 3-0 | 3-0 | 6-1 | 4-1 | 3-1 | 3-0 | 6-1 | 2-1 | 3-1 | 1-0 | 4-1 |  | ■ | 4-0 | 1-0 | 5-0 | 5-0 | 1-1 | 2-1 |
| Queen's Park Rangers FC | 3-1 | 2-1 | 3-1 | 2-1 | 1-1 | 3-1 | 4-1 | 20 | 0-0 | 2-1 | 1-0 | 2-0 | 4-1 | 0-2 | 3-2 | 1-2 | ■ | 2-5 | 8-3 | 1-1 | 2-2 | 0-0 |
| Southend United FC | 4-1 | 2-0 | 0-0 | 6-0 | 4-1 | 1-2 | 3-2 | 1-0 | 1-2 | 0-0 | 1-1 | 6-0 | 2-1 | 1-2 | 1-1 | 1-1 | 1-0 | ■ | 3-1 | 1-1 | 1-0 | 1-3 |
| Swindon Town FC | 1-1 | 0-2 | 0-1 | 2-2 | 0-0 | 1-1 | 3-1 | 1-0 | 1-1 | 3-0 | 1-1 | 6-3 | 5-1 | 2-0 | 2-1 | 1-2 | 2-2 | 5-1 | ■ | 2-1 | 3-1 | 1-3 |
| Torquay United FC | 7-0 | 2-1 | 5-2 | 2-1 | 0-5 | 1-3 | 2-2 | 2-1 | 2-4 | 1-1 | 2-2 | 4-0 | 3-2 | 0-1 | 2-2 | 3-4 | 1-3 | 1-1 | 1-1 | ■ | 5-2 | 4-0 |
| Walsall FC | 2-2 | 1-2 | 2-0 | 0-0 | 0-1 | 3-2 | 0-0 | 5-2 | 2-2 | 1-2 | 1-0 | 6-0 | 2-1 | 1-2 | 1-0 | 1-3 | 4-0 | 1-3 | 4-0 | 7-0 | ■ | 1-2 |
| Watford FC | 0-0 | 1-2 | 3-0 | 4-3 | 3-0 | 1-3 | 1-1 | 2-1 | 0-0 | 4-1 | 0-4 | 2-3 | 2-3 | 1-2 | 2-1 | 0-2 | 1-1 | 2-1 | 4-1 | 2-0 | 2-1 | ■ |

## Division 3 (South)

| | | Pd | Wn | Dw | Ls | GF | GA | Pts | |
|---|---|---|---|---|---|---|---|---|---|
| 1. | Plymouth Argyle FC (Plymouth) | 42 | 30 | 8 | 4 | 98 | 38 | 68 | P |
| 2. | Brentford FC (London) | 42 | 28 | 5 | 9 | 94 | 44 | 61 | |
| 3. | Queen's Park Rangers FC (London) | 42 | 21 | 9 | 12 | 80 | 68 | 51 | |
| 4. | Northampton Town FC (Northampton) | 42 | 21 | 8 | 13 | 82 | 58 | 50 | |
| 5. | Brighton & Hove Albion FC (Hove) | 42 | 21 | 8 | 13 | 87 | 63 | 50 | |
| 6. | Coventry City FC (Coventry) | 42 | 19 | 9 | 14 | 88 | 73 | 47 | |
| 7. | Fulham FC (London) | 42 | 18 | 11 | 13 | 87 | 83 | 47 | |
| 8. | Norwich City FC (Norwich) | 42 | 18 | 10 | 14 | 88 | 77 | 46 | |
| 9. | Crystal Palace FC (London) | 42 | 17 | 12 | 13 | 81 | 74 | 46 | |
| 10. | Bournemouth & Boscombe Athletic FC (Bournemouth) | 42 | 15 | 13 | 14 | 72 | 61 | 43 | |
| 11. | Southend United FC (Southend-on-Sea) | 42 | 15 | 13 | 14 | 69 | 59 | 43 | |
| 12. | Clapton Orient FC (London) | 42 | 14 | 13 | 15 | 55 | 62 | 41 | |
| 13. | Luton Town FC (Luton) | 42 | 14 | 12 | 16 | 64 | 78 | 40 | |
| 14. | Swindon Town FC (Swindon) | 42 | 13 | 12 | 17 | 73 | 83 | 38 | |
| 15. | Watford FC (Watford) | 42 | 15 | 8 | 19 | 60 | 73 | 38 | |
| 16. | Exeter City FC (Exeter) | 42 | 12 | 11 | 19 | 67 | 73 | 35 | |
| 17. | Walsall FC (Walsall) | 42 | 13 | 8 | 21 | 71 | 78 | 34 | |
| 18. | Newport County AFC (Newport) | 42 | 12 | 10 | 20 | 74 | 85 | 34 | |
| 19. | Torquay United FC (Torquay) | 42 | 10 | 11 | 21 | 64 | 94 | 31 | |
| 20. | Bristol Rovers FC (Bristol) | 42 | 11 | 8 | 23 | 67 | 93 | 30 | |
| 21. | Gillingham FC (Gillingham) | 42 | 11 | 8 | 23 | 51 | 80 | 30 | |
| 22. | Merthyr Town FC (Merthyr Tydfil) | 42 | 6 | 9 | 27 | 60 | 135 | 21 | # |
| | | 924 | 354 | 216 | 354 | 1632 | 1632 | 924 | |

# Merthyr Town FC (Merthyr Tydfil) were not re-elected to the league for the next season.

Elected: Thames FC (London)

## F.A. CUP FINAL    (Wembley Stadium, London – 26/04/1930 – 92,448)

ARSENAL FC (LONDON)　　　　　　　2-0　　　　　　　Huddersfield Town AFC (Huddersfield)

*James, Lambert*

Arsenal: Preedy, Parker, Hapgood, Baker, Seddon, John, Hulme, Jack, Lambert, James, Bastin.

Huddersfield: Turner, Goodall, Spence, Naylor, Wilson, Campbell, A.Jackson, Kelly, Davies, Raw, WH Smith.

## Semi-finals

| Arsenal FC (London) | 2-2, 1-0 | Hull City AFC (Kingston-upon-Hull) |
|---|---|---|
| Huddersfield Town AFC (Huddersfield) | 2-1 | Sheffield Wednesday FC (Sheffield) |

## Quarter-finals

| Aston Villa FC (Birmingham) | 1-2 | Huddersfield Town AFC (Huddersfield) |
|---|---|---|
| Newcastle United FC (Newcastle-upon-Tyne) | 1-1, 0-1 | Hull City AFC (Kingston-upon-Hull) |
| Nottingham Forest FC (Nottingham) | 2-2, 1-3 | Sheffield Wednesday FC (Sheffield) |
| West Ham United FC (London) | 0-3 | Arsenal FC (London) |

# 1930-31

| Football League Division 1 1930-1931 Season | Arsenal | Aston Villa | Birmingham | Blackburn Rovers | Blackpool | Bolton Wanderers | Chelsea | Derby County | Grimsby Town | Huddersfield Town | Leeds United | Leicester City | Liverpool | Manchester City | Manchester United | Middlesbrough | Newcastle United | Portsmouth | Sheffield United | Sheffield Wednesday | Sunderland | West Ham United |
|---|---|---|---|---|---|---|---|---|---|---|---|---|---|---|---|---|---|---|---|---|---|---|
| Arsenal FC | | 5-2 | 1-1 | 3-2 | 7-1 | 5-0 | 2-1 | 6-3 | 9-1 | 0-0 | 3-1 | 4-1 | 3-1 | 3-1 | 4-1 | 5-3 | 1-2 | 1-1 | 1-1 | 2-0 | 1-3 | 1-1 |
| Aston Villa FC | 5-1 | | 1-1 | 5-2 | 4-1 | 3-1 | 3-3 | 4-6 | 2-0 | 6-1 | 4-3 | 4-2 | 4-2 | 4-2 | 7-0 | 8-1 | 4-3 | 2-2 | 4-0 | 2-0 | 42 | 6-1 |
| Birmingham FC | 2-4 | 0-4 | | 4-1 | 1-1 | 0-2 | 6-2 | 1-2 | 4-1 | 2-0 | 0-1 | 2-1 | 2-0 | 3-2 | 0-0 | 1-2 | 1-1 | 2-1 | 3-1 | 2-0 | 1-0 | 0-2 |
| Blackburn Rovers FC | 2-2 | 0-2 | 2-1 | | 5-0 | 2-2 | 2-0 | 1-0 | 5-2 | 5-3 | 3-1 | 3-0 | 3-3 | 0-1 | 4-1 | 4-5 | 1-0 | 1-2 | 2-1 | 5-2 | 3-0 | 1-0 |
| Blackpool FC | 1-4 | 2-2 | 0-1 | 1-1 | | 3-3 | 2-1 | 1-0 | 3-1 | 1-1 | 3-7 | 5-4 | 1-3 | 2-2 | 5-1 | 3-2 | 0-0 | 2-2 | 2-1 | 0-4 | 3-1 | 1-3 |
| Bolton Wanderers FC | 1-4 | 1-1 | 2-0 | 1-1 | 1-0 | | 1-1 | 1-2 | 4-2 | 1-0 | 2-0 | 4-1 | 2-0 | 1-1 | 3-1 | 3-0 | 0-3 | 3-1 | 6-2 | 2-2 | 2-2 | 4-2 |
| Chelsea FC | 1-5 | 0-2 | 1-0 | 3-2 | 3-0 | 0-1 | | 1-1 | 5-0 | 1-2 | 1-0 | 1-0 | 2-2 | 2-0 | 6-2 | 4-0 | 1-1 | 2-0 | 1-0 | 0-0 | 5-0 | 2-1 |
| Derby County FC | 4-2 | 1-1 | 0-0 | 1-1 | 3-2 | 4-1 | 6-2 | | 1-0 | 4-1 | 4-1 | 1-0 | 2-2 | 1-1 | 6-1 | 1-2 | 1-5 | 5-1 | 4-3 | 2-3 | 4-1 | 1-1 |
| Grimsby Town FC | 0-1 | 1-2 | 4-1 | 2-0 | 6-2 | 4-1 | 0-1 | 5-3 | | 2-1 | 2-0 | 8-2 | 0-0 | 3-5 | 2-1 | 4-1 | 2-2 | 0-3 | 2-1 | 2-3 | 2-1 | 4-0 |
| Huddersfield Town AFC | 1-1 | 1-6 | 1-0 | 1-1 | 10-1 | 3-2 | 1-1 | 3-0 | 2-2 | | 3-0 | 4-1 | 2-1 | 1-1 | 3-0 | 2-2 | 0-3 | 1-3 | 1-1 | 1-1 | 2-0 | 2-0 |
| Leeds United AFC | 1-2 | 0-2 | 3-1 | 4-2 | 2-2 | 3-1 | 2-3 | 3-1 | 0-0 | 1-2 | | 1-3 | 1-2 | 4-2 | 5-0 | 7-0 | 1-0 | 2-2 | 4-0 | 2-3 | 0-3 | 3-0 |
| Leicester City FC | 2-7 | 4-1 | 2-1 | 3-1 | 6-0 | 2-1 | 2-1 | 1-1 | 0-1 | 1-2 | 4-0 | | 3-2 | 3-2 | 5-4 | 0-3 | 3-1 | 3-1 | 2-2 | 2-5 | 1-1 | 1-1 |
| Liverpool FC | 1-1 | 1-1 | 0-0 | 2-1 | 5-2 | 7-2 | 3-1 | 0-0 | 1-1 | 1-4 | 2-0 | 3-1 | | 0-2 | 1-3 | 4-2 | 3-1 | 6-1 | 1-2 | 2-4 | 2-0 | |
| Manchester City FC | 1-4 | 3-1 | 4-2 | 3-0 | 2-4 | 3-0 | 2-0 | 4-3 | 1-0 | 0-1 | 1-0 | 0-2 | 1-1 | | 4-1 | 4-2 | 2-0 | 1-3 | 0-4 | 2-0 | 2-0 | 1-1 |
| Manchester United FC | 1-2 | 3-4 | 2-0 | 0-1 | 0-0 | 1-1 | 1-0 | 2-1 | 0-2 | 0-6 | 0-0 | 0-0 | 4-1 | 1-3 | | 4-4 | 4-7 | 0-1 | 1-2 | 4-1 | 1-1 | 1-0 |
| Middlesbrough FC | 2-5 | 3-1 | 1-1 | 4-1 | 5-1 | 3-0 | 2-2 | 4-1 | 2-1 | -3 | 5-0 | 2-2 | 3-3 | 4-1 | 3-1 | | 3-1 | 0-1 | 4-1 | 2-0 | 1-0 | 2-2 |
| Newcastle United FC | 1-3 | 2-0 | 2-2 | 2-3 | 0-2 | 4-0 | 1-0 | 2-5 | 1-2 | 1-1 | 4-1 | 5-2 | 0-4 | 0-1 | 4-3 | 0-5 | | 4-7 | 1-0 | 1-2 | 2-0 | 4-2 |
| Portsmouth FC | 1-1 | 5-0 | 2-2 | 3-0 | 4-3 | 1-0 | 1-1 | 2-0 | 4-3 | 2-2 | 1-1 | 2-1 | 4-0 | 1-1 | 4-1 | 1-0 | 1-2 | | 2-3 | 2-4 | 1-1 | 2-0 |
| Sheffield United FC | 1-1 | 3-4 | 3-1 | 1-1 | 5-1 | 2-0 | 4-0 | 3-3 | 2-1 | 0-2 | 1-1 | 0-2 | 4-1 | 2-2 | 3-1 | 4-2 | 3-1 | 3-1 | | 1-1 | 3-3 | 1-2 |
| Sheffield Wednesday FC | 1-2 | 3-0 | 9-1 | 1-3 | 7-1 | 1-0 | 1-1 | 3-2 | 4-1 | 2-1 | 4-0 | 3-5 | 1-1 | 3-0 | 3-2 | 2-1 | 2-2 | 1-3 | | | 7-2 | 5-3 |
| Sunderland AFC | 1-4 | 1-1 | 1-0 | 8-2 | 2-4 | 3-1 | 2-0 | 1-3 | 3-2 | 4-2 | 4-0 | 2-5 | 6-5 | 3-3 | 1-2 | 1-1 | 5-0 | 0-0 | 2-1 | 5-1 | | 6-1 |
| West Ham United FC | 2-4 | 5-5 | 1-2 | 4-3 | 3-2 | 1-4 | 4-1 | 0-1 | 3-4 | 2-1 | 1-1 | 2-0 | 7-0 | 2-0 | 5-1 | 0-3 | 3-2 | 4-3 | 4-1 | 3-3 | 0-3 | |

| | Division 1 | Pd | Wn | Dw | Ls | GF | GA | Pts | |
|---|---|---|---|---|---|---|---|---|---|
| 1. | ARSENAL FC (LONDON) | 42 | 28 | 10 | 4 | 127 | 59 | 66 | |
| 2. | Aston Villa FC (Birmingham) | 42 | 25 | 9 | 8 | 128 | 78 | 59 | |
| 3. | Sheffield Wednesday FC (Sheffield) | 42 | 22 | 8 | 12 | 102 | 75 | 52 | |
| 4. | Portsmouth FC (Portsmouth) | 42 | 18 | 13 | 11 | 84 | 67 | 49 | |
| 5. | Huddersfield Town AFC (Huddersfield) | 42 | 18 | 12 | 12 | 81 | 65 | 48 | |
| 6. | Derby County FC (Derby) | 42 | 18 | 10 | 14 | 94 | 79 | 46 | |
| 7. | Middlesbrough FC (Middlesbrough) | 42 | 19 | 8 | 15 | 98 | 90 | 46 | |
| 8. | Manchester City FC (Manchester) | 42 | 18 | 10 | 14 | 75 | 70 | 46 | |
| 9. | Liverpool FC (Liverpool) | 42 | 15 | 12 | 15 | 86 | 85 | 42 | |
| 10. | Blackburn Rovers FC (Blackburn) | 42 | 17 | 8 | 17 | 83 | 84 | 42 | |
| 11. | Sunderland AFC (Sunderland) | 42 | 16 | 9 | 17 | 89 | 85 | 41 | |
| 12. | Chelsea FC (London) | 42 | 15 | 10 | 17 | 64 | 67 | 40 | |
| 13. | Grimsby Town FC (Cleethorpes) | 42 | 17 | 5 | 20 | 82 | 87 | 39 | |
| 14. | Bolton Wanderers FC (Bolton) | 42 | 15 | 9 | 18 | 68 | 81 | 39 | |
| 15. | Sheffield United FC (Sheffield) | 42 | 14 | 10 | 18 | 78 | 84 | 38 | |
| 16. | Leicester City FC (Leicester) | 42 | 16 | 6 | 20 | 80 | 95 | 38 | |
| 17. | Newcastle United FC (Newcastle-upon-Tyne) | 42 | 15 | 6 | 21 | 78 | 87 | 36 | |
| 18. | West Ham United FC (London) | 42 | 14 | 8 | 20 | 79 | 94 | 36 | |
| 19. | Birmingham FC (Birmingham) | 42 | 13 | 10 | 19 | 55 | 70 | 36 | |
| 20. | Blackpool FC (Blackpool) | 42 | 11 | 10 | 21 | 71 | 125 | 32 | |
| 21. | Leeds United AFC (Leeds) | 42 | 12 | 7 | 23 | 68 | 81 | 31 | R |
| 22. | Manchester United FC (Manchester) | 42 | 7 | 8 | 27 | 53 | 115 | 22 | R |
| | | 924 | 363 | 198 | 363 | 1823 | 1823 | 924 | |

## Top Goalscorer

1)  Tom WARING  (Aston Villa FC)  49

| Football League Division 2 1930-1931 Season | Barnsley | Bradford City | Bradford P.A. | Bristol City | Burnley | Bury | Cardiff City | Charlton Ath. | Everton | Millwall | Nottingham F. | Oldham Ath. | Plymouth Arg. | Port Vale | Preston N.E. | Reading | Southampton | Stoke City | Swansea T. | Tottenham H. | W.B.A. | Wolves |
|---|---|---|---|---|---|---|---|---|---|---|---|---|---|---|---|---|---|---|---|---|---|---|
| Barnsley FC | ■ | 2-1 | 1-0 | 1-0 | 0-1 | 2-1 | 4-0 | 5-0 | 11 | 2-3 | 3-1 | 1-2 | 0-4 | 5-2 | 1-1 | 3-2 | 3-1 | 4-2 | 1-0 | 0-1 | 0-0 | 3-0 |
| Bradford City AFC | 1-0 | ■ | 0-4 | 1-1 | 2-3 | 3-1 | 2-1 | 3-2 | 0-3 | 0-0 | 1-0 | 0-0 | 1-0 | 2-1 | 0-0 | 6-1 | 4-3 | 2-2 | 3-0 | 2-0 | 2-3 | 4-1 |
| Bradford Park Avenue | 1-0 | 1-2 | ■ | 5-2 | 4-1 | 5-1 | 3-0 | 3-2 | 4-1 | 6-0 | 4-1 | 4-0 | 7-1 | 5-1 | 2-2 | 1-3 | 1-1 | 2-2 | 5-1 | 4-1 | 3-1 | 1-1 |
| Bristol City FC | 2-1 | 0-1 | 2-0 | ■ | 1-1 | 4-2 | 1-0 | 3-0 | 0-1 | 1-2 | 1-4 | 1-0 | 2-1 | 1-1 | 1-1 | 1-0 | 2-1 | 1-1 | 2-1 | 2-1 | 1-1 | 0-3 |
| Burnley FC | 2-2 | 1-1 | 3-2 | 4-2 | ■ | 0-2 | 1-0 | 1-1 | 5-2 | 2-1 | 5-2 | 6-1 | 2-2 | 1-2 | 1-0 | 8-1 | 3-2 | 1-2 | 2-2 | 1-0 | 2-1 | 4-2 |
| Bury FC | 3-1 | 3-1 | 3-1 | 6-0 | 2-1 | ■ | 3-0 | 0-1 | 2-2 | 5-0 | 1-0 | 1-3 | 2-0 | 0-3 | 3-0 | 2-2 | 1-0 | 0-3 | 2-0 | 2-0 | 2-2 | 1-0 |
| Cardiff City AFC | 2-0 | 1-1 | 0-3 | 0-1 | 4-0 | 1-3 | ■ | 0-2 | 1-2 | 4-4 | 1-1 | 0-0 | 4-1 | 2-1 | 0-0 | 5-0 | 0-1 | 3-2 | 1-0 | 0-0 | 3-6 | 0-3 |
| Charlton Athletic FC | 1-1 | 2-1 | 3-1 | 0-0 | 2-1 | 3-2 | 4-1 | ■ | 0-7 | 2-0 | 1-1 | 1-1 | 1-3 | 3-1 | 1-3 | 2-1 | 3-1 | 1-2 | 3-0 | 1-0 | 0-4 | 1-2 |
| Everton FC | 5-2 | 4-2 | 4-2 | 1-3 | 3-2 | 3-2 | 1-1 | 7-1 | ■ | 2-0 | 2-0 | 6-4 | 9-1 | 2-3 | 2-1 | 3-2 | 2-1 | 5-0 | 5-1 | 4-2 | 2-1 | 4-0 |
| Millwall FC | 4-1 | 1-1 | 1-1 | 2-0 | 2-1 | 1-0 | 0-0 | 6-0 | 1-3 | ■ | 5-1 | 1-0 | 4-1 | 0-1 | 5-7 | 4-0 | 1-0 | 1-3 | 3-1 | 2-3 | 2-0 | 1-1 |
| Nottingham Forest FC | 3-3 | 4-1 | 1-0 | 6-1 | 3-3 | 3-0 | 3-1 | 4-3 | 2-2 | 2-1 | ■ | 4-1 | 1-1 | 1-0 | 1-4 | 1-1 | 3-1 | 3-0 | 3-0 | 2-2 | 1-6 | 3-4 |
| Oldham Athletic AFC | 0-0 | 3-0 | 2-0 | 1-3 | 3-1 | 3-2 | 4-2 | 0-3 | 3-3 | 3-1 | 3-1 | ■ | 2-1 | 3-3 | 2-0 | 1-1 | 2-1 | 3-1 | 2-1 | 1-2 | 2-2 | 2-0 |
| Plymouth Argyle FC | 4-0 | 0-2 | 0-0 | 5-3 | 1-2 | 3-6 | 5-1 | 1-3 | 2-3 | 5-0 | 1-0 | 1-1 | ■ | 2-1 | 1-2 | 3-1 | 2-3 | 1-2 | 0-0 | 2-0 | 5-1 | 3-2 |
| Port Vale FC | 5-2 | 1-0 | 8-2 | 1-0 | 0-0 | 0-1 | 2-0 | 1-1 | 1-3 | 3-2 | 3-2 | 2-0 | 2-1 | ■ | 2-1 | 1-0 | 0-0 | 2-0 | 3-0 |  | 1-0 | 0-1 |
| Preston North End FC | 1-1 | 4-2 | 1-1 | 2-2 | 2-0 | 3-0 | 7-0 | 4-1 | 2-1 | 1-3 | 2-4 | 1-0 | 2-1 | 1-3 | ■ | 3-3 | 5-0 | 5-1 | 0-0 | 2-1 | 2-3 | 5-4 |
| Reading FC | 6-1 | 0-0 | 3-0 | 4-1 | 3-1 | 3-4 | 3-0 | 2-0 | 0-2 | 2-1 | 5-2 | 1-3 | 1-2 | 0-3 | 1-4 | ■ | 1-1 | 7-3 | 1-0 | 1-2 | 0-3 | 3-0 |
| Southampton FC | 4-0 | 4-1 | 2-3 | 5-1 | 1-1 | 5-0 | 0-1 | 3-0 | 3-1 | 0-0 | 1-0 | 3-3 | 2-0 | 2-1 | 3-2 |  | ■ | 2-1 | 1-2 | 0-3 | 1-1 | 2-0 |
| Stoke City FC | 0-0 | 1-1 | 1-1 | 3-1 | 1-1 | 3-1 | 1-0 | 0-0 | 2-0 | 2-3 | 1-0 | 4-0 | 0-0 | 1-0 | 3-1 | 2-1 | 1-3 | ■ | 5-0 | 2-1 | 0-1 | 1-2 |
| Swansea Town AFC | 1-0 | 1-2 | 2-1 | 5-2 | 1-1 | 5-2 | 3-2 | 1-1 | 2-5 | 4-1 | 3-2 | 0-0 | 2-0 | 2-1 | 2-1 | 2-1 | 0-1 | 1-2 | ■ | 1-2 | 1-1 | 1-1 |
| Tottenham Hotspur FC | 4-2 | 3-1 | 3-2 | 4-1 | 8-1 | 3-1 | 2-2 | 5-0 | 1-0 | 4-1 | 2-1 | 4-0 | 4-1 | 1-0 | 5-0 | 0-0 | 7-1 | 1-3 | 3-0 | ■ | 2-2 | 1-0 |
| West Bromwich Albion FC | 5-0 | 1-0 | 1-1 | 3-0 | 2-0 | 2-0 | 3-2 | 3-2 | 1-2 | 0-0 | 2-1 | 2-0 | 1-2 | 4-1 | 2-0 | 1-0 | 1-2 | 4-0 | 0-0 | 0-2 | ■ | 2-1 |
| Wolverhampton Wanderers FC | 2-0 | 0-1 | 1-1 | 0-1 | 2-4 | 7-0 | 4-1 | 1-1 | 3-1 | 2-0 | 4-2 | 3-0 | 4-3 | 3-0 | 2-0 | 3-1 | 3-2 | 5-1 | 3-1 | 3-1 | 1-4 | ■ |

## Division 2

| | | Pd | Wn | Dw | Ls | GF | GA | Pts | |
|---|---|---|---|---|---|---|---|---|---|
| 1. | Everton FC (Liverpool) | 42 | 28 | 5 | 9 | 121 | 66 | 61 | P |
| 2. | West Bromwich Albion FC (West Bromwich) | 42 | 22 | 10 | 10 | 83 | 49 | 54 | P |
| 3. | Tottenham Hotspur FC (London) | 42 | 22 | 7 | 13 | 88 | 55 | 51 | |
| 4. | Wolverhampton Wanderers FC (Wolverhampton) | 42 | 21 | 5 | 16 | 84 | 67 | 47 | |
| 5. | Port Vale FC (Stoke-on-Trent) | 42 | 21 | 5 | 16 | 67 | 61 | 47 | |
| 6. | Bradford Park Avenue FC (Bradford) | 42 | 18 | 10 | 14 | 97 | 66 | 46 | |
| 7. | Preston North End FC (Preston) | 42 | 17 | 11 | 14 | 83 | 64 | 45 | |
| 8. | Burnley FC (Burnley) | 42 | 17 | 11 | 14 | 81 | 77 | 45 | |
| 9. | Southampton FC (Southampton) | 42 | 19 | 6 | 17 | 74 | 62 | 44 | |
| 10. | Bradford City AFC (Bradford) | 42 | 17 | 10 | 15 | 61 | 63 | 44 | |
| 11. | Stoke City FC (Stoke-on-Trent) | 42 | 17 | 10 | 15 | 64 | 71 | 44 | |
| 12. | Oldham Athletic AFC (Oldham) | 42 | 16 | 10 | 16 | 61 | 72 | 42 | |
| 13. | Bury FC (Bury) | 42 | 19 | 3 | 20 | 75 | 82 | 41 | |
| 14. | Millwall FC (London) | 42 | 16 | 7 | 19 | 71 | 80 | 39 | |
| 15. | Charlton Athletic FC (London) | 42 | 15 | 9 | 18 | 59 | 86 | 39 | |
| 16. | Bristol City FC (Bristol) | 42 | 15 | 8 | 19 | 54 | 82 | 38 | |
| 17. | Nottingham Forest FC (Nottingham) | 42 | 14 | 9 | 19 | 80 | 85 | 37 | |
| 18. | Plymouth Argyle FC (Plymouth) | 42 | 14 | 8 | 20 | 76 | 84 | 36 | |
| 19. | Barnsley FC (Barnsley) | 42 | 13 | 9 | 20 | 59 | 79 | 35 | |
| 20. | Swansea Town AFC (Swansea) | 42 | 12 | 10 | 20 | 51 | 74 | 34 | |
| 21. | Reading FC (Reading) | 42 | 12 | 6 | 24 | 72 | 96 | 30 | R |
| 22. | Cardiff City AFC (Cardiff) | 42 | 8 | 9 | 25 | 47 | 87 | 25 | R |
| | | 924 | 373 | 178 | 373 | 1608 | 1608 | 924 | |

| Football League Division 3 (N) 1930-1931 Season | Accrington St. | Barrow | Carlisle United | Chesterfield | Crewe Alex. | Darlington | Doncaster R. | Gateshead | Halifax Town | Hartlepools Utd. | Hull City | Lincoln City | Nelson | New Brighton | Rochdale | Rotherham Utd. | Southport | Stockport Co. | Tranmere R. | Wigan Borough | Wrexham | York City |
|---|---|---|---|---|---|---|---|---|---|---|---|---|---|---|---|---|---|---|---|---|---|---|
| Accrington Stanley FC | | 3-1 | 3-0 | 1-3 | 3-1 | 2-1 | 2-0 | 2-1 | 1-1 | 0-2 | 1-3 | 5-3 | 3-1 | 3-0 | 2-3 | 3-2 | 2-0 | 2-2 | 5-2 | 3-0 | 1-3 | 4-2 |
| Barrow AFC | 0-0 | | 7-2 | 0-3 | 2-0 | 3-2 | 3-1 | 0-0 | 3-1 | 4-0 | 3-0 | 3-2 | 2-1 | 4-1 | 0-0 | 1-0 | 1-1 | 1-0 | 1-3 | 4-1 | 2-3 | 1-2 |
| Carlisle United FC | 7-3 | 0-1 | | 0-0 | 4-1 | 2-1 | 1-1 | 2-2 | 6-2 | 3-0 | 1-5 | 3-6 | 8-1 | 2-0 | 7-1 | 1-2 | 4-3 | 5-1 | 3-0 | 6-1 | 1-1 | 2-0 |
| Chesterfield FC | 7-3 | 3-1 | 2-1 | | 2-0 | 2-1 | 2-1 | 8-1 | 7-0 | 3-0 | 0-4 | 3-2 | 2-1 | 1-0 | 4-1 | 2-1 | 2-1 | 1-1 | 5-1 | 3-1 | 4-0 | 3-1 |
| Crewe Alexandra FC | 2-1 | 6-2 | 3-5 | 2-1 | | 2-2 | 2-1 | 6-2 | 0-1 | 2-1 | 3-4 | 2-0 | 4-2 | 1-3 | 3-1 | 2-3 | 0-0 | 1-0 | 1-2 | 3-2 | 2-1 | 5-1 |
| Darlington FC | 1-1 | 3-2 | 3-0 | 5-1 | 1-2 | | 0-0 | 2-2 | 4-1 | 4-2 | 2-4 | 0-1 | 2-1 | 3-1 | 1-1 | 2-2 | 2-3 | 1-2 | 2-0 | 2-3 | 1-1 | 3-0 |
| Doncaster Rovers FC | 6-1 | 0-0 | 2-0 | 1-0 | 2-0 | 1-2 | | 1-1 | 3-3 | 1-1 | 0-2 | 0-1 | 2-0 | 0-0 | 4-0 | 3-3 | 0-0 | 2-0 | 6-0 | 5-1 | 1-1 | 0-2 |
| Gateshead FC | 4-0 | 4-1 | 1-0 | 3-3 | 2-2 | 1-1 | 2-1 | | 3-1 | 0-0 | 1-0 | 0-1 | 2-0 | 4-0 | 0-2 | 2-0 | 2-3 | 2-1 | 3-0 | 4-2 | 4-3 | 2-1 |
| Halifax Town AFC | 1-1 | 4-0 | 1-5 | 1-1 | 4-0 | 1-0 | 0-2 | 3-0 | | 3-1 | 1-1 | 3-2 | 1-0 | 1-0 | 1-0 | 0-1 | 0-0 | 3-0 | 2-1 | 0-1 | 0-0 | 0-0 |
| Hartlepools United FC | 3-3 | 3-2 | 3-5 | 1-3 | 2-0 | 1-1 | 0-2 | 2-3 | 2-1 | | 1-3 | 0-3 | 4-0 | 4-1 | 4-0 | 4-2 | 0-2 | 1-2 | 1-2 | 6-1 | 2-1 | 3-0 |
| Hull City AFC | 1-1 | 1-1 | 1-1 | 3-1 | 5-1 | 1-1 | 8-2 | 4-0 | 10-0 | 5-0 | | 1-3 | 4-0 | 3-0 | 3-1 | 2-2 | 5-1 | 1-1 | 1-0 | 0-0 | 2-3 | 3-1 |
| Lincoln City FC | 5-2 | 5-0 | 5-1 | 1-1 | 3-1 | 1-0 | 1-0 | 0-0 | 4-1 | 1-0 | 3-1 | | 2-0 | 4-0 | 5-0 | 1-3 | 3-3 | 6-1 | 1-3 | 2-0 | 3-2 | 4-1 |
| Nelson FC | 4-2 | 0-3 | 1-2 | 0-5 | 1-1 | 3-1 | 2-0 | 2-2 | 3-2 | 1-1 | 0-2 | 1-2 | | 2-2 | 0-0 | 0-0 | 1-4 | 1-1 | 0-4 | 2-1 | 2-0 | 2-5 |
| New Brighton FC | 0-0 | 3-1 | 2-0 | 3-1 | 3-0 | 1-5 | 2-1 | 0-0 | 3-0 | 1-0 | 1-1 | 2-1 | 2-0 | | 2-1 | 3-1 | 1-2 | 0-2 | 1-3 | 0-2 | 1-1 | 5-3 |
| Rochdale AFC | 1-6 | 4-2 | 1-3 | 2-3 | 1-0 | 1-2 | 3-5 | 0-1 | 2-3 | 1-2 | 1-0 | 4-2 | 5-4 | 2-0 | | 6-1 | 0-4 | 1-0 | 1-3 | 0-4 | 4-3 | 2-2 |
| Rotherham United FC | 8-1 | 6-0 | 1-0 | 0-1 | 1-1 | 0-2 | 3-0 | 1-1 | 2-1 | 1-1 | 1-1 | 2-2 | 3-0 | 2-0 | 1-3 | | 3-3 | 3-4 | 4-6 | 5-2 | 1-4 | 2-1 |
| Southport FC | 3-3 | 3-2 | 1-2 | 3-0 | 3-1 | 0-1 | 2-1 | 1-0 | 5-2 | 2-0 | 1-0 | 1-2 | 8-1 | 3-0 | 4-0 | 4-1 | | 2-0 | 1-1 | 3-1 | 1-1 | 1-0 |
| Stockport County FC | 4-1 | 6-0 | 3-0 | 2-1 | 2-0 | 0-1 | 2-2 | 3-1 | 3-0 | 3-1 | 3-2 | 4-2 | 1-0 | 2-0 | 2-2 | 5-2 | 2-0 | | 1-1 | 4-1 | 2-2 | 0-0 |
| Tranmere Rovers FC | 8-0 | 5-0 | 2-0 | 2-0 | 0-0 | 1-2 | 1-2 | 4-0 | 3-3 | 7-1 | 3-2 | 7-3 | 4-2 | 3-1 | 3-0 | 3-1 | 3-0 | 5-1 | | 5-1 | 2-1 | 3-1 |
| Wigan Borough FC | 3-2 | 2-1 | 1-2 | 1-5 | 6-0 | 2-0 | 3-0 | 3-3 | 3-0 | 3-2 | 3-1 | 0-1 | 3-1 | 1-1 | 3-0 | 0-0 | 1-0 | 2-1 | 4-3 | | 1-1 | 3-1 |
| Wrexham AFC | 6-1 | 1-1 | 2-1 | 2-1 | 7-0 | 2-0 | 4-1 | 5-1 | 3-2 | 2-0 | 2-0 | 2-2 | 5-1 | 2-1 | 1-1 | 3-2 | 2-4 | 3-2 | 2-2 | 2-0 | | 3-2 |
| York City FC | 3-1 | 4-2 | 4-0 | 2-2 | 4-3 | 2-1 | 4-2 | 4-3 | 4-1 | 4-2 | 3-2 | 1-1 | 3-0 | 4-1 | 3-0 | 1-1 | 3-1 | 1-2 | 3-1 | 2-3 | 0-1 | |

## Division 3 (North)

| | | Pd | Wn | Dw | Ls | GF | GA | Pts | |
|---|---|---|---|---|---|---|---|---|---|
| 1. | Chesterfield FC (Chesterfield) | 42 | 26 | 6 | 10 | 102 | 57 | 58 | P |
| 2. | Lincoln City FC (Lincoln) | 42 | 25 | 7 | 10 | 102 | 59 | 57 | |
| 3. | Tranmere Rovers FC (Birkenhead) | 42 | 24 | 6 | 12 | 111 | 74 | 54 | |
| 4. | Wrexham AFC (Wrexham) | 42 | 21 | 12 | 9 | 94 | 62 | 54 | |
| 5. | Southport FC (Southport) | 42 | 22 | 9 | 11 | 88 | 56 | 53 | |
| 6. | Hull City AFC (Kingston-upon-Hull) | 42 | 20 | 10 | 12 | 99 | 55 | 50 | |
| 7. | Stockport County FC (Stockport) | 42 | 20 | 9 | 13 | 77 | 61 | 49 | |
| 8. | Carlisle United FC (Carlisle) | 42 | 20 | 5 | 17 | 98 | 81 | 45 | |
| 9. | Gateshead FC (Gateshead) | 42 | 16 | 13 | 13 | 71 | 73 | 45 | |
| 10. | Wigan Borough FC (Wigan) | 42 | 19 | 5 | 18 | 76 | 86 | 43 | |
| 11. | Darlington FC (Darlington) | 42 | 16 | 10 | 16 | 71 | 59 | 42 | |
| 12. | York City FC (York) | 42 | 18 | 6 | 18 | 85 | 82 | 42 | |
| 13. | Accrington Stanley FC (Accrington) | 42 | 15 | 9 | 18 | 84 | 108 | 39 | |
| 14. | Rotherham United FC (Rotherham) | 42 | 13 | 12 | 17 | 81 | 83 | 38 | |
| 15. | Doncaster Rovers FC (Doncaster) | 42 | 13 | 11 | 18 | 65 | 65 | 37 | |
| 16. | Barrow AFC (Barrow-in-Furness) | 42 | 15 | 7 | 20 | 68 | 89 | 37 | |
| 17. | Halifax Town AFC (Halifax) | 42 | 13 | 9 | 20 | 55 | 89 | 35 | |
| 18. | Crewe Alexandra FC (Crewe) | 42 | 14 | 6 | 22 | 66 | 93 | 34 | |
| 19. | New Brighton FC (Wallasey) | 42 | 13 | 7 | 22 | 49 | 76 | 33 | |
| 20. | Hartlepools United FC (Hartlepool) | 42 | 12 | 6 | 24 | 67 | 86 | 30 | |
| 21. | Rochdale AFC (Rochdale) | 42 | 12 | 6 | 24 | 62 | 107 | 30 | |
| 22. | Nelson FC (Nelson) | 42 | 6 | 7 | 29 | 43 | 113 | 19 | # |
| | | 924 | 373 | 178 | 373 | 1714 | 1714 | 924 | |

# Nelson FC (Nelson) were not re-elected to the league for the next season.   Elected:  Chester FC (Chester)

| Football League Division 3 (S) 1930-1931 Season | Bournemouth | Brentford | Brighton | Bristol Rovers | Clapton Orient | Coventry City | Crystal Palace | Exeter City | Fulham | Gillingham | Luton Town | Newport Co. | Northampton | Norwich City | Notts County | Q.P.R. | Southend Utd. | Swindon Town | Thames | Torquay United | Walsall | Watford |
|---|---|---|---|---|---|---|---|---|---|---|---|---|---|---|---|---|---|---|---|---|---|---|
| Bournemouth & B. Athletic | | 1-0 | 1-2 | 4-0 | 1-1 | 2-0 | 0-0 | 3-1 | 2-1 | 2-1 | 0-0 | 4-2 | 1-3 | 4-1 | 2-1 | 2-0 | 0-0 | 4-1 | 3-3 | 2-2 | 0-2 | 1-1 |
| Brentford FC | 1-2 | | 3-2 | 4-0 | 3-0 | 1-2 | 8-2 | 2-1 | 4-1 | 11 | 0-1 | 3-2 | 0-4 | 3-1 | 2-2 | 5-3 | 3-1 | 5-2 | 6-1 | 0-0 | 6-1 | 2-1 |
| Brighton & Hove Albion | 3-1 | 1-0 | | 4-0 | 3-1 | 2-0 | 1-1 | 3-2 | 1-1 | 5-0 | 2-0 | 5-0 | 1-1 | 1-0 | 1-3 | 1-1 | 1-2 | 1-0 | 2-4 | 3-0 | 3-3 | 1-0 |
| Bristol Rovers FC | 2-5 | 2-5 | 3-3 | | 4-1 | 1-0 | 2-1 | 1-1 | 2-1 | 1-0 | 5-1 | 2-0 | 1-4 | 3-0 | 2-2 | 3-0 | 2-3 | 4-1 | 4-1 | 3-1 | 1-2 | 1-5 |
| Clapton Orient FC | 0-0 | 3-0 | 1-0 | 3-1 | | 3-3 | 3-2 | 2-3 | 2-0 | 0-2 | 3-2 | 3-1 | 2-2 | 2-0 | 1-4 | 2-3 | 3-1 | 2-3 | 2-1 | 4-0 | 2-5 | 4-0 |
| Coventry City FC | 3-3 | 0-1 | 0-0 | 5-1 | 4-0 | | 3-5 | 3-1 | 2-1 | 1-2 | 1-2 | 6-4 | 0-1 | 3-0 | 1-2 | 2-0 | 0-0 | 4-0 | 7-1 | 6-1 | 2-1 | 2-2 |
| Crystal Palace FC | 1-0 | 5-1 | 0-1 | 0-2 | 3-1 | 1-0 | | 7-2 | 5-2 | 5-0 | 5-1 | 7-1 | 0-0 | 2-1 | 1-1 | 4-0 | 3-1 | 3-1 | 2-1 | 5-0 | 6-3 | 6-1 |
| Exeter City FC | 4-1 | 4-0 | 2-2 | 0-3 | 6-1 | 2-3 | 4-3 | | 3-2 | 3-0 | 1-1 | 3-0 | 3-3 | 1-0 | 3-3 | 2-0 | 1-1 | 3-1 | 4-3 | 2-2 | 2-5 | 2-1 |
| Fulham FC | 1-0 | 1-1 | 0-1 | 6-2 | 2-0 | 0-0 | 2-0 | 4-2 | | 1-1 | 2-1 | 0-1 | 4-2 | 1-0 | 3-1 | 0-2 | 1-0 | 6-1 | 4-2 | 3-0 | 5-2 | 3-2 |
| Gillingham FC | 0-0 | 1-1 | 0-0 | 1-1 | 0-0 | 2-0 | 6-2 | 3-5 | 3-2 | | 4-0 | 4-1 | 0-2 | 2-1 | 0-5 | 2-2 | 1-0 | 0-1 | 3-1 | 2-3 | 2-0 | 4-2 |
| Luton Town FC | 2-3 | 1-1 | 2-2 | 4-1 | 0-1 | 2-0 | 1-2 | 3-1 | 5-0 | 4-1 | | 3-1 | 4-0 | 1-0 | 3-0 | 5-1 | 2-1 | 4-0 | 8-0 | 3-1 | 0-0 | 4-1 |
| Newport County AFC | 7-3 | 0-2 | 2-0 | 1-1 | 1-1 | 1-1 | 2-1 | 4-0 | 1-3 | 1-3 | 3-1 | | 5-2 | 3-0 | 2-3 | 2-3 | 3-1 | 3-1 | 1-1 | 2-1 | 1-1 | 0-2 |
| Northampton Town FC | 2-2 | 1-2 | 2-1 | 1-1 | 0-0 | 0-3 | 0-0 | 1-0 | 4-2 | 0-1 | 0-0 | 1-0 | | 3-1 | 0-0 | 6-0 | 4-0 | 3-0 | 4-1 | 0-3 | 3-0 | 2-3 |
| Norwich City FC | 2-1 | 3-0 | 2-2 | 1-3 | 2-0 | 2-2 | 2-1 | 1-2 | 1-1 | 4-0 | 1-0 | 4-1 | 1-1 | | 2-2 | 1-1 | 0-1 | 2-0 | 0-0 | 3-0 | 3-1 | 0-1 |
| Notts County FC | 2-0 | 1-0 | 2-2 | 3-0 | 5-0 | 4-1 | 2-2 | 1-2 | 6-1 | 2-1 | 1-0 | 5-0 | 2-2 | 4-0 | | 2-0 | 1-1 | 2-0 | 4-0 | 2-0 | 6-1 | 1-0 |
| Queen's Park Rangers FC | 3-0 | 3-1 | 4-1 | 2-0 | 4-2 | 2-0 | 4-0 | 7-2 | 0-2 | 1-0 | 3-1 | 7-1 | 0-2 | 3-1 | 4-1 | | 0-2 | 1-2 | 3-0 | 1-2 | 3-0 | 2-3 |
| Southend United FC | 4-0 | 0-1 | 0-2 | 4-0 | 2-0 | 2-0 | 2-4 | 5-1 | 2-4 | 3-2 | 0-2 | 6-2 | 2-1 | 2-0 | 2-1 | 2-0 | | 5-3 | 1-0 | 6-3 | 2-0 | 1-0 |
| Swindon Town FC | 4-1 | 3-2 | 1-1 | 3-1 | 5-1 | 4-0 | 4-4 | 2-1 | 4-1 | 5-2 | 0-0 | 4-4 | 5-1 | 5-2 | 1-2 | 4-1 | 1-1 | | 3-0 | 4-0 | 4-3 | 2-1 |
| Thames FC | 1-4 | 2-0 | 0-0 | 1-2 | 3-0 | 1-2 | 0-2 | 1-0 | 0-0 | 2-2 | 1-0 | 3-1 | 2-1 | 2-0 | 0-0 | 1-0 | 3-0 | 3-2 | | 1-1 | 4-1 | 3-2 |
| Torquay United FC | 4-4 | 0-3 | 3-1 | 3-3 | 5-2 | 0-0 | 3-1 | 0-0 | 3-1 | 3-0 | 1-1 | 3-0 | 2-0 | 1-4 | 6-2 | 3-1 | 5-0 | 5-1 | | | 0-1 | 3-1 |
| Walsall FC | 3-3 | 1-4 | 0-0 | 4-2 | 4-2 | 1-2 | 2-1 | 2-1 | 2-0 | 2-2 | 0-1 | 1-0 | 2-6 | 7-0 | 2-1 | 0-2 | 1-3 | 2-2 | 6-0 | 0-4 | | 2-2 |
| Watford FC | 2-0 | 1-3 | 5-0 | 2-2 | 1-2 | 4-1 | 0-2 | 0-1 | 2-2 | 1-0 | 1-0 | 6-2 | 1-2 | 2-2 | 0-1 | 0-4 | 1-3 | 3-0 | 1-0 | 6-0 | 2-2 | |

## Division 3  (South)

| | | Pd | Wn | Dw | Ls | GF | GA | Pts | |
|---|---|---|---|---|---|---|---|---|---|
| 1. | Notts County FC (Nottingham) | 42 | 24 | 11 | 7 | 97 | 46 | 59 | P |
| 2. | Crystal Palace FC (London) | 42 | 22 | 7 | 13 | 107 | 71 | 51 | |
| 3. | Brentford FC (London) | 42 | 22 | 6 | 14 | 90 | 64 | 50 | |
| 4. | Brighton & Hove Albion FC (Hove) | 42 | 17 | 15 | 10 | 68 | 53 | 49 | |
| 5. | Southend United FC (Southend-on-Sea) | 42 | 22 | 5 | 15 | 76 | 60 | 49 | |
| 6. | Northampton Town FC (Northampton) | 42 | 18 | 12 | 12 | 77 | 59 | 48 | |
| 7. | Luton Town FC (Luton) | 42 | 19 | 8 | 15 | 76 | 51 | 46 | |
| 8. | Queen's Park Rangers FC (London) | 42 | 20 | 3 | 19 | 82 | 75 | 43 | |
| 9. | Fulham FC (London) | 42 | 18 | 7 | 17 | 77 | 75 | 43 | |
| 10. | Bournemouth & Boscombe Athletic FC (Bournemouth) | 42 | 15 | 13 | 14 | 72 | 73 | 43 | |
| 11. | Torquay United FC (Torquay) | 42 | 17 | 9 | 16 | 80 | 84 | 43 | |
| 12. | Swindon Town FC (Swindon) | 42 | 18 | 6 | 18 | 89 | 94 | 42 | |
| 13. | Exeter City FC (Exeter) | 42 | 17 | 8 | 17 | 84 | 90 | 42 | |
| 14. | Coventry City FC (Coventry) | 42 | 16 | 9 | 17 | 75 | 65 | 41 | |
| 15. | Bristol Rovers FC (Bristol) | 42 | 16 | 8 | 18 | 75 | 92 | 40 | |
| 16. | Gillingham FC (Gillingham) | 42 | 14 | 10 | 18 | 61 | 76 | 38 | |
| 17. | Walsall FC (Walsall) | 42 | 14 | 9 | 19 | 78 | 95 | 37 | T |
| 18. | Watford FC (Watford) | 42 | 14 | 7 | 21 | 72 | 75 | 35 | |
| 19. | Clapton Orient FC (London) | 42 | 14 | 7 | 21 | 63 | 91 | 35 | |
| 20. | Thames FC (London) | 42 | 13 | 8 | 21 | 54 | 93 | 34 | |
| 21. | Norwich City FC (Norwich) | 42 | 10 | 8 | 24 | 47 | 76 | 28 | |
| 22. | Newport County AFC (Newport) | 42 | 11 | 6 | 25 | 69 | 111 | 28 | # |
| | | 924 | 371 | 182 | 371 | 1669 | 1669 | 924 | |

T: Walsall FC (Walsall) were transferred to Division 3 (North) from the next season.

\# Newport County AFC were not re-elected to the league for the next season.   Elected: Mansfield Town FC

## F.A. CUP FINAL   (Wembley Stadium, London – 25/04/1931 – 92,406)

WEST BROMWICH ALBION FC                    2-1                    Birmingham FC (Birmingham)
*WG Richardson 2*                                                                                      *Bradford*

West Bromwich: Pearson, Shaw, Trentham, Magee, W.Richardson, Edwards, Glidden, Carter, W.G. Richardson, Sandford, Wood.

Birmingham: Hibbs, Liddell, Barkas, Cringan, Morrall, Leslie, Briggs, Crosbie, Bradford, Gregg, Curtis.

## Semi-finals

Birmingham FC (Birmingham)                  2-0                    Sunderland AFC (Sunderland)
Everton FC (Liverpool)                            0-1                    West Bromwich Albion FC (West Bromwich)

## Quarter-finals

Birmingham FC (Birmingham)               2-2, 3-0                    Chelsea FC (London)
Everton FC (Liverpool)                           9-1                    Southport FC (Southport)
Sunderland AFC (Sunderland)               1-1, 4-2                    Exeter City FC (Exeter)
West Bromwich Albion FC (West Bromwich)   1-1, 2-1  Wolverhampton Wanderers FC (Wolverhampton)

# 1931-32

| Football League Division 1 1931-1932 Season | Arsenal | Aston Villa | Birmingham | Blackburn R. | Blackpool | Bolton Wands. | Chelsea | Derby County | Everton | Grimsby Town | Huddersfield T. | Leicester City | Liverpool | Manchester C. | Middlesbrough | Newcastle Utd. | Portsmouth | Sheffield Utd. | Sheffield Wed. | Sunderland | W.B.A. | West Ham Utd. |
|---|---|---|---|---|---|---|---|---|---|---|---|---|---|---|---|---|---|---|---|---|---|---|
| Arsenal FC | | 1-1 | 3-0 | 4-0 | 2-0 | 1-1 | 1-1 | 2-1 | 3-2 | 4-0 | 1-1 | 2-1 | 6-0 | 4-0 | 5-0 | 1-0 | 3-3 | 0-2 | 3-1 | 2-0 | 0-1 | 4-1 |
| Aston Villa FC | 1-1 | | 3-2 | 1-5 | 5-1 | 2-1 | 1-3 | 2-0 | 2-3 | 7-0 | 2-3 | 3-2 | 6-1 | 2-1 | 7-1 | 3-0 | 0-1 | 5-0 | 3-1 | 2-0 | 2-0 | 5-1 |
| Birmingham FC | 2-2 | 1-1 | | 2-1 | 3-0 | 2-2 | 4-0 | 1-1 | 4-0 | 2-1 | 5-0 | 2-0 | 3-1 | 1-5 | 3-0 | 4-1 | 2-1 | 1-3 | 1-2 | 0-0 | 1-0 | 4-1 |
| Blackburn Rovers FC | 1-1 | 2-0 | 1-2 | | 5-1 | 3-1 | 2-2 | 3-2 | 5-3 | 3-2 | 3-0 | 6-0 | 1-3 | 2-2 | 4-2 | 0-3 | 5-3 | 1-2 | 1-6 | 5-2 | 2-0 | 2-4 |
| Blackpool FC | 1-5 | 1-3 | 1-1 | 2-1 | | 0-3 | 2-4 | 2-1 | 2-0 | 4-3 | 2-0 | 2-3 | 2-2 | 2-2 | 1-2 | 3-1 | 1-1 | 2-0 | 1-2 | 3-2 | 1-2 | 7-2 |
| Bolton Wanderers FC | 1-0 | 2-1 | 5-1 | 3-1 | 1-2 | | 1-0 | 1-2 | 2-1 | 5-3 | 1-2 | 1-0 | 8-1 | 1-1 | 4-2 | 2-1 | 4-0 | 3-1 | 2-4 | 3-1 | 1-0 | 0-1 |
| Chelsea FC | 2-1 | 3-6 | 2-1 | 1-2 | 4-1 | 3-0 | | 2-1 | 0-0 | 4-1 | 0-1 | 1-0 | 2-0 | 3-2 | 4-0 | 4-1 | 0-0 | 1-1 | 2-3 | 2-2 | 0-2 | 3-2 |
| Derby County FC | 1-1 | 3-1 | 2-1 | 1-1 | 5-0 | 5-1 | 1-0 | | 3-0 | 3-3 | 3-2 | 1-1 | 1-2 | 2-1 | 5-2 | 1-1 | 2-1 | 1-3 | 0-1 | 3-1 | 3-1 | 5-1 |
| Everton FC | 1-3 | 4-2 | 3-2 | 5-0 | 3-2 | 1-0 | 7-2 | 2-1 | | 4-2 | 4-1 | 9-2 | 2-1 | 0-1 | 5-1 | 8-1 | 0-1 | 5-1 | 9-3 | 4-2 | 2-1 | 6-1 |
| Grimsby Town FC | 3-1 | 2-2 | 1-1 | 4-3 | 0-0 | 2-0 | 1-2 | 2-1 | 1-2 | | 1-4 | 3-0 | 5-1 | 2-1 | 2-0 | 1-2 | 3-1 | 0-2 | 3-1 | 1-3 | 0-0 | 2-1 |
| Huddersfield Town AFC | 1-2 | 1-1 | 1-1 | 1-1 | 5-0 | 2-0 | 2-1 | 6-0 | 0-0 | 1-1 | | 2-1 | 4-3 | 1-0 | 1-1 | 1-2 | 1-0 | 2-2 | 6-1 | 4-1 | 2-2 | 3-1 |
| Leicester City FC | 1-2 | 3-8 | 3-1 | 1-0 | 2-2 | 1-3 | 1-0 | 1-1 | 0-1 | 1-2 | 2-4 | | 2-1 | 4-0 | 2-2 | 4-2 | 2-1 | 4-3 | 3-2 | 5-0 | 2-3 | 2-1 |
| Liverpool FC | 2-1 | 2-0 | 4-3 | 4-2 | 3-2 | 2-2 | 2-1 | 1-1 | 1-3 | 4-0 | 0-3 | 3-3 | | 4-3 | 7-2 | 4-2 | 1-3 | 2-1 | 3-1 | 1-2 | 4-1 | 2-2 |
| Manchester City FC | 1-3 | 3-3 | 2-1 | 3-1 | 7-1 | 2-1 | 1-1 | 3-0 | 1-0 | 4-1 | 3-0 | 5-1 | 0-1 | | 1-2 | 5-1 | 3-3 | 1-1 | 1-2 | 1-1 | 2-5 | 0-1 |
| Middlesbrough FC | 2-5 | 1-1 | 2-0 | 0-2 | 0-3 | 3-1 | 0-2 | 5-2 | 1-0 | 4-0 | 1-0 | 1-1 | 4-1 | 3-3 | | 2-1 | 0-1 | 4-3 | 4-0 | 0-1 | 1-0 | 3-2 |
| Newcastle United FC | 3-2 | 3-1 | 0-3 | 5-3 | 2-2 | 3-1 | 4-1 | 3-3 | 0-0 | 2-0 | 2-1 | 3-2 | 0-1 | 2-1 | 3-1 | | 0-0 | 5-3 | 4-1 | 1-2 | 5-1 | 2-2 |
| Portsmouth FC | 0-3 | 0-3 | 2-1 | 2-0 | 2-2 | 3-2 | 1-0 | 2-0 | 0-3 | 2-0 | 3-2 | 0-1 | 2-0 | 3-2 | 2-0 | 6-0 | | 2-1 | 2-0 | 0-0 | 0-1 | 3-0 |
| Sheffield United FC | 4-1 | 5-4 | 1-0 | 3-2 | 1-3 | 4-0 | 4-2 | 3-1 | 1-5 | 2-1 | 0-2 | 2-2 | 3-0 | 2-1 | 2-1 | 0-3 | 1-2 | | 1-1 | 1-1 | 1-0 | 6-0 |
| Sheffield Wednesday FC | 1-3 | 1-0 | 5-1 | 5-1 | 3-0 | 7-1 | 2-2 | 3-1 | 1-3 | 4-1 | 4-1 | 3-1 | 1-1 | 1-1 | 1-1 | 2-0 | 3-1 | 2-1 | | 3-2 | 2-5 | 6-1 |
| Sunderland AFC | 2-0 | 1-1 | 2-3 | 2-2 | 4-0 | 3-0 | 2-1 | 0-0 | 2-3 | 2-0 | 1-3 | 4-1 | 1-3 | 2-5 | 0-0 | 1-4 | 5-1 | 1-0 | 3-1 | | 2-1 | 2-0 |
| West Bromwich Albion FC | 1-0 | 3-0 | 0-1 | 4-1 | 4-0 | 3-0 | 4-0 | 4-0 | 1-1 | 5-6 | 3-2 | 1-2 | 1-2 | 1-1 | 1-1 | 2-1 | 3-0 | 0-1 | 1-1 | 1-0 | | 3-1 |
| West Ham United FC | 1-1 | 2-1 | 2-4 | 1-3 | 1-1 | 3-1 | 3-1 | 2-1 | 4-2 | 3-1 | 1-1 | 1-4 | 1-0 | 1-1 | 0-2 | 2-1 | 2-1 | 1-2 | 1-2 | 2-2 | 1-5 | |

144

| | Division 1 | Pd | Wn | Dw | Ls | GF | GA | Pts | |
|---|---|---|---|---|---|---|---|---|---|
| 1. | EVERTON FC (LIVERPOOL) | 42 | 26 | 4 | 12 | 116 | 64 | 56 | |
| 2. | Arsenal FC (London) | 42 | 22 | 10 | 10 | 90 | 48 | 54 | |
| 3. | Sheffield Wednesday FC (Sheffield) | 42 | 22 | 6 | 14 | 96 | 82 | 50 | |
| 4. | Huddersfield Town AFC (Huddersfield) | 42 | 19 | 10 | 13 | 80 | 63 | 48 | |
| 5. | Aston Villa FC (Birmingham) | 42 | 19 | 8 | 15 | 104 | 72 | 46 | |
| 6. | West Bromwich Albion FC (West Bromwich) | 42 | 20 | 6 | 16 | 77 | 55 | 46 | |
| 7. | Sheffield United FC (Sheffield) | 42 | 20 | 6 | 16 | 80 | 75 | 46 | |
| 8. | Portsmouth FC (Portsmouth) | 42 | 19 | 7 | 16 | 62 | 62 | 45 | |
| 9. | Birmingham FC (Birmingham) | 42 | 18 | 8 | 16 | 78 | 67 | 44 | |
| 10. | Liverpool FC (Liverpool) | 42 | 19 | 6 | 17 | 81 | 93 | 44 | |
| 11. | Newcastle United FC (Newcastle-upon-Tyne) | 42 | 18 | 6 | 18 | 80 | 87 | 42 | |
| 12. | Chelsea FC (London) | 42 | 16 | 8 | 18 | 69 | 73 | 40 | |
| 13. | Sunderland AFC (Sunderland) | 42 | 15 | 10 | 17 | 67 | 73 | 40 | |
| 14. | Manchester City FC (Manchester) | 42 | 13 | 12 | 17 | 83 | 73 | 38 | |
| 15. | Derby County FC (Derby) | 42 | 14 | 10 | 18 | 71 | 75 | 38 | |
| 16. | Blackburn Rovers FC (Blackburn) | 42 | 16 | 6 | 20 | 89 | 95 | 38 | |
| 17. | Bolton Wanderers FC (Bolton) | 42 | 17 | 4 | 21 | 72 | 80 | 38 | |
| 18. | Middlesbrough FC (Middlesbrough) | 42 | 15 | 8 | 19 | 64 | 89 | 38 | |
| 19. | Leicester City FC (Leicester) | 42 | 15 | 7 | 20 | 74 | 94 | 37 | |
| 20. | Blackpool FC (Blackpool) | 42 | 12 | 9 | 21 | 65 | 102 | 33 | |
| 21. | Grimsby Town FC (Cleethorpes) | 42 | 13 | 6 | 23 | 67 | 98 | 32 | R |
| 22. | West Ham United FC (London) | 42 | 12 | 7 | 23 | 62 | 107 | 31 | R |
| | | 924 | 380 | 164 | 380 | 1727 | 1727 | 924 | |

## Top Goalscorer

1)  William "Dixie" DEAN          (Everton FC)      44

| Football League Division 2 1931-1932 Season | Barnsley | Bradford City | Bradford P.A. | Bristol City | Burnley | Bury | Charlton Ath. | Chesterfield | Leeds United | Man. United | Millwall | Nottingham F. | Notts County | Oldham Ath. | Plymouth Arg. | Port Vale | Preston N.E. | Southampton | Stoke City | Swansea Town | Tottenham H. | Wolves |
|---|---|---|---|---|---|---|---|---|---|---|---|---|---|---|---|---|---|---|---|---|---|---|
| Barnsley FC | ■ | 1-2 | 2-2 | 1-1 | 0-1 | 0-1 | 1-4 | 3-1 | 0-2 | 0-0 | 2-1 | 3-1 | 1-1 | 3-1 | 0-0 | 3-0 | 4-2 | 3-3 | 1-0 | 2-3 | 3-2 | 2-2 |
| Bradford City AFC | 9-1 | ■ | 0-0 | 3-0 | 1-2 | 1-3 | 1-1 | 3-0 | 4-1 | 4-3 | 0-0 | 2-2 | 0-2 | 2-0 | 3-3 | 4-0 | 0-1 | 5-2 | 2-2 | 5-1 | 2-0 | 2-2 |
| Bradford Park Avenue | 1-0 | 1-0 | ■ | 2-0 | 2-0 | 2-1 | 3-0 | 1-0 | 3-0 | 3-1 | 1-2 | 4-1 | 1-1 | 5-0 | 2-0 | 2-2 | 1-5 | 2-1 | 2-1 | 2-1 | 2-1 | 2-1 |
| Bristol City FC | 4-0 | 0-1 | 0-0 | ■ | 1-6 | 1-3 | 1-2 | 1-1 | 0-2 | 2-1 | 1-4 | 1-1 | 3-2 | 1-1 | 0-2 | 0-2 | 4-2 | 0-1 | 0-0 | 1-1 | 1-1 | 0-4 |
| Burnley FC | 5-3 | 1-1 | 3-2 | 1-2 | ■ | 2-2 | 0-1 | 2-2 | 0-5 | 2-0 | 1-1 | 1-0 | 1-1 | 1-4 | 1-1 | 2-2 | 2-2 | 1-3 | 3-0 | 4-1 | 2-0 | 1-3 |
| Bury FC | 7-1 | 0-2 | 4-2 | 2-1 | 1-0 | ■ | 6-0 | 0-1 | 1-4 | 0-0 | 2-0 | 2-2 | 2-1 | 2-1 | 2-2 | 2-0 | 4-1 | 3-0 | 0-1 | 2-1 | 1-1 | 1-0 |
| Charlton Athletic FC | 3-1 | 1-0 | 2-2 | 2-0 | 0-1 | 3-0 | ■ | 0-0 | 0-1 | 1-0 | 1-3 | 3-1 | 3-1 | 2-2 | 2-0 | 2-1 | 2-1 | 2-3 | 1-1 | 3-3 | 2-5 | 3-2 |
| Chesterfield FC | 2-2 | 2-2 | 3-2 | 3-1 | 5-1 | 4-1 | 3-2 | ■ | 1-1 | 1-3 | 1-0 | 1-0 | 1-4 | 0-2 | 1-2 | 4-0 | 3-1 | 1-0 | 1-3 | 1-2 | 4-2 | 1-2 |
| Leeds United AFC | 0-1 | 1-1 | 3-2 | 1-0 | 3-1 | 1-0 | 2-0 | 3-3 | ■ | 1-4 | 0-1 | 1-1 | 2-2 | 5-0 | 0-0 | 0-2 | 4-1 | 1-0 | 2-0 | 3-2 | 1-0 | 2-1 |
| Manchester United FC | 3-0 | 1-0 | 0-2 | 0-1 | 5-1 | 1-2 | 0-2 | 3-1 | 2-5 | ■ | 2-0 | 3-2 | 3-3 | 5-1 | 2-1 | 2-0 | 3-2 | 2-3 | 1-1 | 2-1 | 1-1 | 3-2 |
| Millwall FC | 2-0 | 6-1 | 3-0 | 1-0 | 2-0 | 2-1 | 1-0 | 5-0 | 2-3 | 1-1 | ■ | 1-0 | 4-3 | 0-0 | 1-3 | 2-2 | 4-1 | 0-1 | 1-0 | 3-1 | 1-2 | 1-2 |
| Nottingham Forest FC | 1-2 | 2-1 | 6-1 | 3-1 | 1-2 | 0-2 | 3-2 | 4-0 | 3-3 | 2-1 | 1-1 | ■ | 2-1 | 2-0 | 3-2 | 2-1 | 2-2 | 1-1 | 0-1 | 6-1 | 1-3 | 2-0 |
| Notts County FC | 2-3 | 1-1 | 2-2 | 3-0 | 5-0 | 0-1 | 2-2 | 1-1 | 1-1 | 1-2 | 2-0 | 2-6 | ■ | 1-0 | 3-0 | 4-2 | 1-4 | 5-0 | 2-1 | 1-2 | 3-1 | 3-1 |
| Oldham Athletic AFC | 2-2 | 1-1 | 2-1 | 2-1 | 3-1 | 1-2 | 1-0 | 6-1 | 2-1 | 1-5 | 1-1 | 2-4 | 5-2 | ■ | 1-3 | 3-0 | 2-2 | 2-0 | 1-3 | 2-0 | 1-2 | 0-2 |
| Plymouth Argyle FC | 3-0 | 3-3 | 4-1 | 2-1 | 4-0 | 5-1 | 1-1 | 4-0 | 3-2 | 3-1 | 8-1 | 5-1 | 3-4 | 5-0 | ■ | 1-3 | 2-1 | 1-2 | 1-1 | 4-2 | 4-1 | 3-3 |
| Port Vale FC | 3-0 | 2-0 | 1-3 | 4-2 | 1-3 | 1-1 | 0-1 | 2-1 | 1-2 | 1-2 | 2-2 | 2-0 | 2-0 | 1-1 | 2-0 | ■ | 0-1 | 0-0 | 3-0 | 0-4 | 1-3 | 1-7 |
| Preston North End FC | 1-2 | 5-2 | 1-0 | 1-1 | 2-1 | 0-2 | 3-2 | 2-2 | 0-0 | 0-0 | 2-0 | 1-1 | 0-0 | 2-3 | 5-2 | 1-4 | ■ | 2-1 | 2-0 | 1-0 | 2-0 | 4-2 |
| Southampton FC | 2-0 | 0-1 | 0-3 | 1-1 | 3-0 | 2-1 | 1-1 | 1-2 | 2-1 | 1-1 | 3-1 | 4-0 | 3-1 | 1-1 | 0-6 | 5-1 | 3-3 | ■ | 1-2 | 3-0 | 2-1 | 1-3 |
| Stoke City FC | 2-0 | 3-1 | 1-0 | 1-1 | 3-0 | 3-2 | 4-0 | 2-1 | 3-4 | 3-0 | 0-0 | 2-1 | 2-2 | 1-1 | 3-2 | 4-0 | 4-1 | 2-0 | ■ | 0-0 | 2-2 | 2-1 |
| Swansea Town AFC | 3-0 | 0-1 | 1-0 | 2-0 | 5-1 | 2-0 | 2-0 | 1-1 | 0-2 | 3-1 | 4-0 | 4-1 | 5-1 | 1-0 | 4-1 | 2-3 | 0-3 | 3-4 | 1-1 | ■ | 1-1 | 1-1 |
| Tottenham Hotspur FC | 4-2 | 1-5 | 3-3 | 2-1 | 1-1 | 0-0 | 0-1 | 3-3 | 3-1 | 4-1 | 1-0 | 1-3 | 2-0 | 3-2 | 0-1 | 9-3 | 4-0 | 5-2 | 3-3 | 6-2 | ■ | 3-3 |
| Wolverhampton Wanderers FC | 2-0 | 3-1 | 6-0 | 4-2 | 3-1 | 6-0 | 3-1 | 6-0 | 1-1 | 7-0 | 5-0 | 0-0 | 0-0 | 7-1 | 2-0 | 2-0 | 3-2 | 5-1 | 0-1 | 2-0 | 4-0 | ■ |

## Division 2

| | | Pd | Wn | Dw | Ls | GF | GA | Pts | |
|---|---|---|---|---|---|---|---|---|---|
| 1. | Wolverhampton Wanderers FC (Wolverhampton) | 42 | 24 | 8 | 10 | 115 | 49 | 56 | P |
| 2. | Leeds United AFC (Leeds) | 42 | 22 | 10 | 10 | 78 | 54 | 54 | P |
| 3. | Stoke City FC (Stoke-on-Trent) | 42 | 19 | 14 | 9 | 69 | 48 | 52 | |
| 4. | Plymouth Argyle FC (Plymouth) | 42 | 20 | 9 | 13 | 100 | 66 | 49 | |
| 5. | Bury FC (Bury) | 42 | 21 | 7 | 14 | 70 | 58 | 49 | |
| 6. | Bradford Park Avenue FC (Bradford) | 42 | 21 | 7 | 14 | 72 | 63 | 49 | |
| 7. | Bradford City AFC (Bradford) | 42 | 16 | 13 | 13 | 80 | 61 | 45 | |
| 8. | Tottenham Hotspur FC (London) | 42 | 16 | 11 | 15 | 87 | 78 | 43 | |
| 9. | Millwall FC (London) | 42 | 17 | 9 | 16 | 61 | 61 | 43 | |
| 10. | Charlton Athletic FC (London) | 42 | 17 | 9 | 16 | 61 | 66 | 43 | |
| 11. | Nottingham Forest FC (Nottingham) | 42 | 16 | 10 | 16 | 77 | 72 | 42 | |
| 12. | Manchester United FC (Manchester) | 42 | 17 | 8 | 17 | 71 | 72 | 42 | |
| 13. | Preston North End FC (Preston) | 42 | 16 | 10 | 16 | 75 | 77 | 42 | |
| 14. | Southampton FC (Southampton) | 42 | 17 | 7 | 18 | 66 | 77 | 41 | |
| 15. | Swansea Town AFC (Swansea) | 42 | 16 | 7 | 19 | 73 | 75 | 39 | |
| 16. | Notts County FC (Nottingham) | 42 | 13 | 12 | 17 | 75 | 75 | 38 | |
| 17. | Chesterfield FC (Chesterfield) | 42 | 13 | 11 | 18 | 64 | 86 | 37 | |
| 18. | Oldham Athletic AFC (Oldham) | 42 | 13 | 10 | 19 | 62 | 84 | 36 | |
| 19. | Burnley FC (Burnley) | 42 | 13 | 9 | 20 | 59 | 87 | 35 | |
| 20. | Port Vale FC (Stoke-on-Trent) | 42 | 13 | 7 | 22 | 58 | 89 | 33 | |
| 21. | Barnsley FC (Barnsley) | 42 | 12 | 9 | 21 | 55 | 91 | 33 | R |
| 22. | Bristol City FC (Bristol) | 42 | 6 | 11 | 25 | 39 | 78 | 23 | R |
| | | 924 | 358 | 208 | 358 | 1567 | 1567 | 924 | |

| Football League Division 3 (N) 1931-1932 Season | Accrington St. | Barrow | Carlisle United | Chester | Crewe Alexandra | Darlington | Doncaster R. | Gateshead | Halifax Town | Hartlepools Utd. | Hull City | Lincoln City | New Brighton | Rochdale | Rotherham Utd. | Southport | Stockport Co. | Tranmere Rovers | Walsall | Wigan Borough | Wrexham | York City |
|---|---|---|---|---|---|---|---|---|---|---|---|---|---|---|---|---|---|---|---|---|---|---|
| Accrington Stanley FC | ■ | 2-0 | 5-3 | 2-3 | 2-0 | 4-0 | 3-2 | 1-2 | 4-0 | 5-0 | 1-1 | 2-2 | 4-1 | 3-0 | 5-2 | 1-1 | 2-0 | 2-2 | 1-0 | --- | 5-0 | 2-1 |
| Barrow AFC | 3-0 | ■ | 4-1 | 4-0 | 2-1 | 3-4 | 3-2 | 3-1 | 3-1 | 4-1 | 0-2 | 0-2 | 4-1 | 4-1 | 3-0 | 1-1 | 4-2 | 3-1 | 7-1 | --- | 1-0 | 3-1 |
| Carlisle United FC | 3-0 | 3-1 | ■ | 4-3 | 2-1 | 0-2 | 5-1 | 0-0 | 4-0 | 3-2 | 0-1 | 0-3 | 0-0 | 4-0 | 1-2 | 2-2 | 1-1 | 1-1 | 4-0 | --- | 2-2 | 1-1 |
| Chester FC | 1-0 | 4-2 | 4-1 | ■ | 1-0 | 3-1 | 1-1 | 1-1 | 3-1 | 2-3 | 2-0 | 2-1 | 2-0 | 7-2 | 2-1 | 4-0 | 2-1 | 3-1 | 5-1 | 4-0 | 2-5 | 3-0 |
| Crewe Alexandra FC | 3-1 | 3-2 | 5-1 | 1-0 | ■ | 0-1 | 2-0 | 3-5 | 4-3 | 6-0 | 4-3 | 8-1 | 3-2 | 1-0 | 5-0 | 1-1 | 2-2 | 0-0 | 2-1 | 4-3 | 3-0 | 8-1 |
| Darlington FC | 4-1 | 0-2 | 0-1 | 4-1 | 1-0 | ■ | 2-3 | 1-2 | 3-0 | 6-3 | 2-1 | 0-6 | 3-0 | 3-1 | 2-1 | 0-1 | 2-0 | 1-2 | 2-0 | 5-0 | 1-1 | 4-1 |
| Doncaster Rovers FC | 3-1 | 0-1 | 3-3 | 3-0 | 2-1 | 3-2 | ■ | 1-2 | 3-1 | 1-3 | 2-1 | 0-3 | 2-1 | 2-0 | 2-0 | 3-0 | 1-1 | 2-2 | 2-1 | --- | 2-4 | 1-0 |
| Gateshead FC | 4-0 | 4-0 | 4-0 | 1-2 | 3-3 | 3-2 | 2-1 | ■ | 1-1 | 3-1 | 2-1 | 2-3 | 4-0 | 3-1 | 4-1 | 2-0 | 2-1 | 3-3 | 2-0 | --- | 4-0 | 6-0 |
| Halifax Town AFC | 1-0 | 1-0 | 1-1 | 2-1 | 4-1 | 0-3 | 4-0 | 1-2 | ■ | 2-0 | 2-2 | 3-0 | 0-0 | 3-2 | 1-1 | 3-0 | 2-2 | 0-0 | 1-2 | --- | 1-0 | 4-1 |
| Hartlepools United FC | 1-0 | 0-2 | 2-2 | 2-2 | 3-1 | 3-3 | 5-0 | 1-2 | 4-1 | ■ | 2-3 | 4-3 | 1-0 | 3-0 | 1-4 | 2-1 | 2-2 | 0-5 | 4-3 | --- | 0-1 | 7-2 |
| Hull City AFC | 3-0 | 3-0 | 2-0 | 0-2 | 2-4 | 4-1 | 4-1 | 0-1 | 1-0 | 3-1 | ■ | 4-1 | 4-1 | 4-1 | 0-1 | 1-0 | 4-4 | 3-0 | 3-0 | --- | 5-0 | 2-3 |
| Lincoln City FC | 5-1 | 3-1 | 3-1 | 4-0 | 5-1 | 2-0 | 1-2 | 1-0 | 9-1 | 6-0 | 1-0 | ■ | 3-0 | 3-0 | 3-1 | 7-0 | 1-2 | 4-2 | 3-3 | 3-0 | 0-0 | 1-1 |
| New Brighton FC | 2-1 | 0-3 | 4-1 | 0-1 | 0-1 | 0-0 | 1-0 | 1-3 | 2-0 | 1-1 | 1-2 | 2-1 | ■ | 1-1 | 3-1 | 3-1 | 2-1 | 1-1 | 0-1 | --- | 1-1 | 0-2 |
| Rochdale AFC | 2-2 | 0-6 | 4-3 | 0-3 | 2-3 | 1-1 | 3-1 | 0-3 | 1-4 | 1-3 | 3-6 | 3-5 | 3-2 | ■ | 1-4 | 0-1 | 1-0 | 3-6 | 0-1 | --- | 2-4 | 3-5 |
| Rotherham United FC | 2-3 | 0-2 | 4-1 | 3-0 | 0-2 | 2-4 | 6-3 | 2-1 | 5-0 | 1-2 | 2-0 | 0-1 | 2-2 | 5-0 | ■ | 2-0 | 1-1 | 3-0 | 0-0 | --- | 0-0 | 0-1 |
| Southport FC | 4-2 | 3-1 | 2-0 | 1-1 | 1-1 | 3-0 | 5-0 | 1-1 | 2-2 | 1-2 | 1-0 | 1-1 | 1-0 | 3-1 | 3-2 | ■ | 1-0 | 1-0 | 5-1 | --- | 2-0 | 3-0 |
| Stockport County FC | 3-0 | 2-0 | 0-0 | 0-0 | 1-2 | 1-0 | 1-0 | 1-1 | 2-1 | 3-2 | 0-1 | 3-1 | 3-1 | 1-0 | 0-1 | 1-0 | ■ | 0-1 | 0-1 | --- | 5-1 | 3-2 |
| Tranmere Rovers FC | 8-1 | 6-1 | 3-0 | 2-2 | 4-1 | 3-1 | 0-1 | 4-3 | 5-2 | 5-0 | 2-2 | 1-0 | 5-1 | 9-1 | 6-1 | 2-0 | 2-2 | ■ | 4-1 | --- | 3-1 | 2-2 |
| Walsall FC | 5-5 | 1-2 | 3-1 | 1-1 | 2-1 | 1-0 | 2-0 | 1-2 | 4-2 | 2-3 | 1-4 | 0-3 | 2-1 | 1-0 | 3-0 | 2-1 | 2-1 | 2-1 | ■ | --- | 3-0 | 2-2 |
| Wigan Borough FC | --- | --- | 3-2 | --- | --- | --- | --- | 2-1 | 0-1 | 1-1 | 3-1 | 0-3 | --- | --- | --- | --- | --- | --- | --- | ■ | --- | --- |
| Wrexham AFC | 2-1 | 0-1 | 1-0 | 1-1 | 2-4 | 3-0 | 2-1 | 2-1 | 2-3 | 5-3 | 2-1 | 1-3 | 2-1 | 4-0 | 1-0 | 1-1 | 2-1 | 2-1 | 5-1 | 5-0 | ■ | 2-1 |
| York City FC | 1-0 | 1-0 | 2-4 | 3-1 | 3-3 | 3-0 | 1-2 | 3-2 | 7-2 | 3-1 | 0-0 | 1-1 | 4-0 | 5-2 | 2-0 | 1-2 | 1-0 | 3-2 | 2-0 | --- | 3-2 | ■ |

### Division 3 (North)

| | | Pd | Wn | Dw | Ls | GF | GA | Pts | |
|---|---|---|---|---|---|---|---|---|---|
| 1. | Lincoln City FC (Lincoln) | 40 | 26 | 5 | 9 | 106 | 47 | 57 | P |
| 2. | Gateshead FC (Gateshead) | 40 | 25 | 7 | 8 | 94 | 48 | 57 | |
| 3. | Chester FC (Chester) | 40 | 21 | 8 | 11 | 78 | 60 | 50 | |
| 4. | Tranmere Rovers FC (Birkenhead) | 40 | 19 | 11 | 10 | 107 | 58 | 49 | |
| 5. | Barrow AFC (Barrow-in-Furness) | 40 | 24 | 1 | 15 | 86 | 59 | 49 | |
| 6. | Crewe Alexandra FC (Crewe) | 40 | 21 | 6 | 13 | 95 | 66 | 48 | |
| 7. | Southport FC (Southport) | 40 | 18 | 10 | 12 | 58 | 53 | 46 | |
| 8. | Hull City AFC (Kingston-upon-Hull) | 40 | 20 | 5 | 15 | 82 | 53 | 45 | |
| 9. | York City FC (York) | 40 | 18 | 7 | 15 | 76 | 81 | 43 | |
| 10. | Wrexham AFC (Wrexham) | 40 | 18 | 7 | 15 | 64 | 69 | 43 | |
| 11. | Darlington FC (Darlington) | 40 | 17 | 4 | 19 | 66 | 69 | 38 | |
| 12. | Stockport County FC (Stockport) | 40 | 13 | 11 | 16 | 55 | 53 | 37 | |
| 13. | Hartlepools United FC (Hartlepool) | 40 | 16 | 5 | 19 | 78 | 100 | 37 | |
| 14. | Accrington Stanley FC (Accrington) | 40 | 15 | 6 | 19 | 75 | 80 | 36 | |
| 15. | Doncaster Rovers FC (Doncaster) | 40 | 16 | 4 | 20 | 59 | 80 | 36 | |
| 16. | Walsall FC (Walsall) | 40 | 16 | 3 | 21 | 57 | 85 | 35 | |
| 17. | Halifax Town AFC (Halifax) | 40 | 13 | 8 | 19 | 61 | 87 | 34 | |
| 18. | Carlisle United FC (Carlisle) | 40 | 11 | 11 | 18 | 64 | 79 | 33 | |
| 19. | Rotherham United FC (Rotherham) | 40 | 14 | 4 | 22 | 63 | 72 | 32 | |
| 20. | New Brighton FC (Wallasey) | 40 | 8 | 8 | 24 | 38 | 76 | 24 | |
| 21. | Rochdale AFC (Rochdale) | 40 | 4 | 3 | 33 | 48 | 135 | 11 | |
| ---. | Wigan Borough FC (Wigan) | 12 | 3 | 1 | 8 | 12 | 33 | 7 | # |
| | | 840 | 353 | 134 | 353 | 1510 | 1510 | 840 | |

# Wigan Borough FC (Wigan) resigned from the league on 26th October 1931 and their playing record was deleted.

| Football League Division 3 (S) 1931-1932 Season | Bournemouth | Brentford | Brighton | Bristol Rovers | Cardiff City | Clapton Orient | Coventry City | Crystal Palace | Exeter City | Fulham | Gillingham | Luton Town | Mansfield T. | Northampton | Norwich City | Q.P.R. | Reading | Southend Utd. | Swindon T. | Thames | Torquay Utd. | Watford |
|---|---|---|---|---|---|---|---|---|---|---|---|---|---|---|---|---|---|---|---|---|---|---|
| Bournemouth & B. Athletic | ▓ | 1-3 | 1-2 | 2-2 | 3-0 | 0-1 | 2-2 | 4-1 | 5-2 | 0-3 | 0-2 | 1-1 | 3-2 | 1-1 | 1-0 | 2-2 | 2-2 | 0-0 | 2-1 | 4-2 | 5-0 | 3-3 |
| Brentford FC | 4-2 | ▓ | 2-2 | 4-2 | 2-3 | 3-0 | 4-2 | 1-1 | 2-2 | 0-0 | 1-1 | 1-0 | 1-1 | 2-0 | 0-1 | 1-0 | 3-0 | 2-3 | 2-0 | 1-0 | 3-0 | 1-2 |
| Brighton & Hove Albion | 4-1 | 1-2 | ▓ | 2-0 | 0-0 | 1-1 | 4-1 | 0-3 | 1-1 | 2-3 | 7-0 | 3-2 | 4-0 | 0-0 | 2-1 | 1-0 | 2-0 | 1-2 | 1-0 | 4-1 | 0-2 | 2-1 |
| Bristol Rovers FC | 4-1 | 2-0 | 0-4 | ▓ | 2-2 | 2-1 | 3-1 | 6-1 | 2-4 | 2-2 | 5-2 | 3-1 | 1-1 | 3-2 | 0-1 | 1-1 | 2-0 | 0-0 | 0-2 | 4-1 | 1-1 | 3-2 |
| Cardiff City AFC | 0-0 | 3-2 | 1-1 | 3-1 | ▓ | 5-0 | 6-1 | 1-3 | 5-2 | 0-3 | 1-0 | 4-1 | 2-0 | 5-0 | 0-2 | 0-4 | 5-1 | 2-3 | 3-0 | 9-2 | 5-2 | 2-1 |
| Clapton Orient FC | 1-2 | 2-2 | 2-2 | 1-0 | 1-1 | ▓ | 5-2 | 1-3 | 2-2 | 0-1 | 3-1 | 0-0 | 4-0 | 3-2 | 1-3 | 3-0 | 2-2 | 2-4 | 4-2 | 1-1 | 1-3 | 2-2 |
| Coventry City FC | 6-1 | 0-1 | 4-3 | 1-1 | 2-1 | 4-2 | ▓ | 8-0 | 4-0 | 5-5 | 6-4 | 3-2 | 5-1 | 4-1 | 3-0 | 1-0 | 5-1 | 0-2 | 3-2 | 2-0 | 3-1 | 5-0 |
| Crystal Palace FC | 1-1 | 1-0 | 2-0 | 5-0 | 5-0 | 0-0 | 2-2 | ▓ | 3-0 | 2-0 | 1-0 | 1-1 | 2-1 | 4-0 | 3-1 | 1-1 | 1-1 | 3-2 | 0-0 | 2-1 | 7-0 | 2-1 |
| Exeter City FC | 1-0 | 4-1 | 3-1 | 1-0 | 3-1 | 4-3 | 3-0 | 0-1 | ▓ | 0-3 | 4-0 | 1-1 | 3-0 | 0-0 | 3-0 | 6-2 | 4-0 | 3-0 | 1-1 | 4-1 | 3-1 | 2-0 |
| Fulham FC | 3-0 | 2-1 | 3-0 | 3-2 | 4-0 | 5-1 | 5-3 | 4-0 | 3-1 | ▓ | 0-2 | 3-2 | 2-1 | 1-3 | 4-0 | 1-3 | 3-3 | 1-1 | 2-2 | 8-0 | 10-2 | 5-0 |
| Gillingham FC | 1-4 | 0-2 | 0-0 | 1-0 | 1-1 | 0-2 | 1-3 | 0-0 | 0-1 | 2-1 | ▓ | 1-3 | 2-0 | 3-2 | 3-3 | 1-0 | 1-1 | 4-0 | 2-1 | 2-0 | 1-1 | 0-1 |
| Luton Town FC | 1-0 | 1-1 | 3-2 | 3-0 | 2-1 | 1-5 | 3-1 | 3-0 | 6-3 | 1-3 | 2-0 | ▓ | 3-1 | 1-0 | 7-1 | 4-1 | 6-1 | 1-3 | 6-0 | 2-0 | 6-1 | 0-1 |
| Mansfield Town FC | 2-1 | 2-0 | 3-3 | 0-3 | 1-2 | 4-3 | 3-3 | 1-1 | 3-1 | 1-2 | 3-1 | 5-2 | ▓ | 2-0 | 5-2 | 2-2 | 1-7 | 4-4 | 3-2 | 4-0 | 2-4 | 3-2 |
| Northampton Town FC | 1-1 | 3-0 | 0-1 | 6-0 | 4-3 | 2-2 | 5-0 | 2-1 | 0-1 | 1-0 | 1-2 | 3-0 |  | ▓ | 2-2 | 6-1 | 2-4 | 1-2 | 4-1 | 0-4 | 2-0 | 1-1 |
| Norwich City FC | 1-2 | 1-0 | 2-1 | 6-0 | 2-0 | 3-2 | 6-2 | 3-2 | 0-1 | 2-2 | 1-1 | 3-3 | 1-1 | 0-0 | ▓ | 2-1 | 0-0 | 1-1 | 4-2 | 7-0 | 2-0 | 4-1 |
| Queen's Park Rangers FC | 0-3 | 1-2 | 1-1 | 2-1 | 2-3 | 3-2 | 1-1 | 2-2 | 1-0 | 3-1 | 7-0 | 3-1 | 1-1 | 3-2 | 2-2 | ▓ | 2-0 | 2-1 | 1-2 | 6-0 | 3-1 | 4-4 |
| Reading FC | 3-1 | 1-2 | 3-1 | 3-0 | 5-1 | 5-0 | 2-1 | 3-0 | 2-0 | 4-2 | 2-0 | 2-1 | 4-1 | 3-2 | 1-1 | 3-2 | ▓ | 3-1 | 5-2 | 5-1 | 4-1 | 2-1 |
| Southend United FC | 1-3 | 1-0 | 2-0 | 4-1 | 1-1 | 1-3 | 4-0 | 1-0 | 0-1 | 4-1 | 2-0 | 1-1 | 5-2 | 0-1 | 2-0 | 0-0 | 1-1 | ▓ | 3-0 | 1-1 | 4-2 | 3-0 |
| Swindon Town FC | 3-0 | 1-3 | 1-2 | 2-1 | 1-4 | 2-3 | 2-2 | 3-2 | 2-2 | 4-0 | 3-2 | 5-2 | 3-0 | 2-0 | 1-2 | 0-2 | 1-2 |  | ▓ | 2-0 | 3-0 | 4-1 |
| Thames FC | 4-2 | 1-1 | 1-2 | 0-2 | 3-3 | 5-2 | 1-3 | 0-0 | 0-0 | 3-0 | 2-4 | 6-3 | 0-2 | 1-0 | 3-2 | 0-0 | 1-3 | 1-1 |  | ▓ | 1-1 | 1-2 |
| Torquay United FC | 1-1 | 1-1 | 1-1 | 8-1 | 2-2 | 3-0 | 3-3 | 3-1 | 2-1 | 2-3 | 1-0 | 1-2 | 2-2 | 4-1 | 2-4 | 2-3 | 1-4 | 2-1 | 2-1 | 3-1 | ▓ | 3-6 |
| Watford FC | 4-2 | 1-4 | 2-2 | 5-2 | 3-0 | 2-1 | 2-0 | 1-2 | 1-0 | 3-1 | 2-0 | 3-1 | 4-1 | 1-2 | 1-1 | 2-2 | 3-2 | 1-1 | 4-1 | 3-2 | 1-0 | ▓ |

| | Division 3 (South) | Pd | Wn | Dw | Ls | GF | GA | Pts | |
|---|---|---|---|---|---|---|---|---|---|
| 1. | Fulham FC (London) | 42 | 24 | 9 | 9 | 111 | 62 | 57 | P |
| 2. | Reading FC (Reading) | 42 | 23 | 9 | 10 | 97 | 67 | 55 | |
| 3. | Southend United FC (Southend-on-Sea) | 42 | 21 | 11 | 10 | 77 | 53 | 53 | |
| 4. | Crystal Palace FC (London) | 42 | 20 | 11 | 11 | 74 | 63 | 51 | |
| 5. | Brentford FC (London) | 42 | 19 | 10 | 13 | 68 | 52 | 48 | |
| 6. | Luton Town FC (Luton) | 42 | 20 | 7 | 15 | 95 | 70 | 47 | |
| 7. | Exeter City FC (Exeter) | 42 | 20 | 7 | 15 | 77 | 62 | 47 | |
| 8. | Brighton & Hove Albion FC (Hove) | 42 | 17 | 12 | 13 | 73 | 58 | 46 | |
| 9. | Cardiff City AFC (Cardiff) | 42 | 19 | 8 | 15 | 87 | 73 | 46 | |
| 10. | Norwich City FC (Norwich) | 42 | 17 | 12 | 13 | 76 | 67 | 46 | |
| 11. | Watford FC (Watford) | 42 | 19 | 8 | 15 | 81 | 79 | 46 | |
| 12. | Coventry City FC (Coventry) | 42 | 18 | 8 | 16 | 108 | 97 | 44 | |
| 13. | Queen's Park Rangers FC (London) | 42 | 15 | 12 | 15 | 79 | 73 | 42 | |
| 14. | Northampton Town FC (Northampton) | 42 | 16 | 7 | 19 | 69 | 69 | 39 | |
| 15. | Bournemouth & Boscombe Athletic FC (Bournemouth) | 42 | 13 | 12 | 17 | 70 | 78 | 38 | |
| 16. | Clapton Orient FC (London) | 42 | 12 | 11 | 19 | 77 | 90 | 35 | |
| 17. | Swindon Town FC (Swindon) | 42 | 14 | 6 | 22 | 70 | 84 | 34 | |
| 18. | Bristol Rovers FC (Bristol) | 42 | 13 | 8 | 21 | 65 | 92 | 34 | |
| 19. | Torquay United FC (Torquay) | 42 | 12 | 9 | 21 | 72 | 106 | 33 | |
| 20. | Mansfield Town FC (Mansfield) | 42 | 11 | 10 | 21 | 75 | 108 | 32 | T |
| 21. | Gillingham FC (Gillingham) | 42 | 10 | 8 | 24 | 40 | 82 | 28 | |
| 22. | Thames FC (London) | 42 | 7 | 9 | 26 | 53 | 109 | 23 | # |
| | | 924 | 360 | 204 | 360 | 1694 | 1694 | 924 | |

# Thames FC (London) did not seek re-election at the end of the season and were thus relegated from the league.

T: Mansfield Town FC (Mansfield) were transferred to Division 3 (North) from the next season.

Elected: Aldershot FC (Aldershot) and Newport County AFC (Newport)

## F.A. CUP FINAL   (Wembley Stadium, London – 23/04/1932 – 92,298)

| NEWCASTLE UNITED FC | 2-1 | Arsenal FC (London) |
|---|---|---|
| *Allen 2* | | *John* |

Newc.: McInroy, Nelson, Fairhurst, McKenzie, Davidson, Weaver, Boyd, Richardson, Allen, McMenemy, Lang.

Arsenal: Moss, Parker, Hapgood, C.Jones, Roberts, Male, Hulme, Jack, Lambert, Bastin, John.

## Semi-finals

| Arsenal FC (London) | 1-0 | Manchester City FC (Manchester) |
|---|---|---|
| Chelsea FC (London) | 1-2 | Newcastle United FC (Newcastle-upon-Tyne) |

## Quarter-finals

| Bury FC (Bury) | 3-4 | Manchester City FC (Manchester) |
|---|---|---|
| Huddersfield Town AFC (Huddersfield) | 0-1 | Arsenal FC (London) |
| Liverpool FC (Liverpool) | 0-2 | Chelsea FC (London) |
| Newcastle United FC (Newcastle-upon-Tyne) | 5-0 | Watford FC (Watford) |

# 1932-33

| Football League Division 1 1932-1933 Season | Arsenal | Aston Villa | Birmingham | Blackburn R. | Blackpool | Bolton Wands. | Chelsea | Derby County | Everton | Huddersfield T. | Leeds United | Leicester City | Liverpool | Man. City | Middlesbro' | Newcastle Utd. | Portsmouth | Sheffield Utd. | Sheffield Wed. | Sunderland | W.B.A. | Wolves |
|---|---|---|---|---|---|---|---|---|---|---|---|---|---|---|---|---|---|---|---|---|---|---|
| Arsenal FC | | 5-0 | 3-0 | 8-0 | 1-1 | 3-2 | 4-1 | 3-3 | 2-1 | 2-2 | 1-2 | 8-2 | 0-1 | 2-1 | 4-2 | 1-0 | 2-0 | 9-2 | 4-2 | 6-1 | 1-2 | 1-2 |
| Aston Villa FC | 5-3 | | 1-0 | 4-0 | 6-2 | 6-1 | 3-1 | 2-0 | 2-1 | 0-3 | 0-0 | 4-2 | 5-2 | 1-1 | 3-1 | 3-0 | 4-1 | 3-0 | 3-6 | 1-0 | 3-2 | 1-3 |
| Birmingham FC | 0-1 | 3-2 | | 3-1 | 2-1 | 2-1 | 0-0 | 3-1 | 4-0 | 0-2 | 2-1 | 0-4 | 3-0 | 3-0 | 1-4 | 1-2 | 4-0 | 4-1 | 2-1 | 2-0 | 1-1 | 0-0 |
| Blackburn Rovers FC | 2-3 | 0-5 | 2-0 | | 6-5 | 3-2 | 1-3 | 3-3 | 3-1 | 4-2 | 1-1 | 1-1 | 2-2 | 1-0 | 4-2 | 2-1 | 3-2 | 3-0 | 1-1 | 1-3 | 4-4 | 1-0 |
| Blackpool FC | 1-2 | 6-2 | 0-1 | 3-0 | | 1-3 | 4-0 | 4-1 | 2-1 | 1-1 | 2-1 | 2-1 | 4-1 | 1-0 | 3-1 | 0-4 | 0-2 | 0-3 | 3-4 | 3-1 | 2-4 | 2-2 |
| Bolton Wanderers FC | 0-4 | 0-1 | 2-2 | 4-2 | 1-0 | | 2-3 | 1-1 | 2-4 | 2-1 | 5-0 | 5-0 | 3-3 | 2-1 | 4-3 | 2-2 | 4-1 | 3-3 | 3-0 | 0-0 | 2-2 | 2-0 |
| Chelsea FC | 1-3 | 0-1 | 4-2 | 2-2 | 1-0 | 1-1 | | 1-3 | 1-0 | 0-1 | 6-0 | 4-1 | 0-2 | 3-1 | 2-1 | 0-1 | 4-4 | 3-0 | 0-2 | 1-1 | 1-2 | 3-1 |
| Derby County FC | 2-2 | 0-0 | 2-2 | 2-1 | 1-1 | 4-1 | 0-1 | | 2-0 | 2-3 | 5-1 | 3-2 | 1-1 | 4-0 | 2-2 | 3-2 | 2-0 | 3-0 | 2-0 | 3-0 | 2-2 | 4-4 |
| Everton FC | 1-1 | 3-3 | 4-1 | 6-1 | 2-0 | 2-2 | 3-2 | 4-2 | | 2-0 | 6-3 | 3-1 | 1-0 | 0-0 | 1-1 | 1-0 | 2-1 | 4-0 | 2-1 | 6-1 | 1-1 | 5-1 |
| Huddersfield Town AFC | 0-1 | 0-0 | 0-0 | 0-3 | 0-1 | 2-1 | 2-0 | 0-0 | 0-0 | | 2-2 | 4-1 | 3-1 | 1-0 | 0-1 | 4-0 | 2-2 | 1-0 | 4-0 | 2-1 | 2-1 | 3-2 |
| Leeds United AFC | 0-0 | 1-1 | 1-1 | 3-1 | 3-1 | 4-3 | 2-0 | 0-2 | 1-0 | 1-1 | | 1-1 | 5-0 | 2-1 | 0-1 | 6-1 | 0-1 | 1-3 | 3-2 | 2-3 | 1-1 | 2-0 |
| Leicester City FC | 1-1 | 3-0 | 2-2 | 1-1 | 3-0 | 2-0 | 1-1 | 4-0 | 2-2 | 3-1 | 3-1 | | 1-2 | 1-2 | 1-1 | 0-3 | 2-1 | 1-1 | 0-0 | 4-2 | 6-2 | 2-2 |
| Liverpool FC | 2-3 | 0-0 | 1-0 | 2-2 | 4-3 | 0-1 | 3-0 | 6-1 | 7-4 | 2-2 | 0-1 | 1-2 | | 1-1 | 1-3 | 3-0 | 4-3 | 2-2 | 4-1 | 3-3 | 2-0 | 5-1 |
| Manchester City FC | 2-3 | 5-2 | 1-0 | 2-3 | 5-1 | 2-1 | 1-4 | 2-1 | 3-0 | 3-0 | 0-0 | 4-1 | 1-1 | | 2-3 | 1-2 | 3-1 | 1-0 | 2-2 | 2-4 | 1-0 | 4-1 |
| Middlesbrough FC | 3-4 | 0-2 | 2-2 | 4-0 | 2-0 | 2-1 | 2-1 | 0-3 | 0-2 | 1-1 | 0-1 | 1-1 | 0-1 | 2-0 | | 2-3 | 5-4 | 2-2 | 1-1 | 1-2 | 3-1 | 2-1 |
| Newcastle United FC | 2-1 | 3-1 | 2-1 | 2-1 | 1-2 | 3-1 | 2-0 | 0-0 | 1-2 | 0-4 | 2-1 | 4-3 | 2-0 | 5-1 | 1-1 | | 1-1 | 2-0 | 3-1 | 0-1 | 3-0 | 3-2 |
| Portsmouth FC | 1-3 | 2-4 | 1-1 | 2-0 | 2-1 | 2-4 | 2-0 | 2-2 | 1-0 | 3-3 | 2-1 | 2-1 | 1-2 | 2-0 | 2-0 | 2-0 | | 1-0 | 3-0 | 1-3 | 3-0 | 2-0 |
| Sheffield United FC | 3-1 | 1-0 | 2-1 | 2-1 | 1-0 | 3-2 | 4-1 | 4-3 | 3-2 | 1-2 | 0-0 | 5-2 | 6-2 | 2-5 | 2-0 | 3-1 | 2-3 | | 2-3 | 3-0 | 1-1 | 0-0 |
| Sheffield Wednesday FC | 3-2 | 0-2 | 1-1 | 1-1 | 4-1 | 2-0 | 2-2 | 0-0 | 3-1 | 2-1 | 2-0 | 4-1 | 3-0 | 2-1 | 2-0 | 2-1 | 2-0 | 3-3 | | 3-1 | 3-1 | 2-0 |
| Sunderland AFC | 3-2 | 1-1 | 1-0 | 4-2 | 1-1 | 7-4 | 2-1 | 0-2 | 3-1 | 1-2 | 0-0 | 2-1 | 0-0 | 3-2 | 0-0 | 0-2 | 0-3 | 2-2 | 1-2 | | 2-2 | 0-1 |
| West Bromwich Albion FC | 1-1 | 3-1 | 1-0 | 1-3 | 2-1 | 4-0 | 3-2 | 2-0 | 3-1 | 2-1 | 0-1 | 4-3 | 2-1 | 4-0 | 0-1 | 3-2 | 4-2 | 0-1 | 2-0 | 5-1 | | 4-1 |
| Wolverhampton Wanderers FC | 1-7 | 2-4 | 1-0 | 5-3 | 2-3 | 4-1 | 1-2 | 3-1 | 4-2 | 6-4 | 3-3 | 1-1 | 3-1 | 1-2 | 2-0 | 1-1 | 5-2 | 5-1 | 3-5 | 0-2 | 3-3 | |

| | Division 1 | Pd | Wn | Dw | Ls | GF | GA | Pts | |
|---|---|---|---|---|---|---|---|---|---|
| 1. | ARSENAL FC (LONDON) | 42 | 25 | 8 | 9 | 118 | 61 | 58 | |
| 2. | Aston Villa FC (Birmingham) | 42 | 23 | 8 | 11 | 92 | 67 | 54 | |
| 3. | Sheffield Wednesday FC (Sheffield) | 42 | 21 | 9 | 12 | 80 | 68 | 51 | |
| 4. | West Bromwich Albion FC (West Bromwich) | 42 | 20 | 9 | 13 | 83 | 70 | 49 | |
| 5. | Newcastle United FC (Newcastle-upon-Tyne) | 42 | 22 | 5 | 15 | 71 | 63 | 49 | |
| 6. | Huddersfield Town AFC (Huddersfield) | 42 | 18 | 11 | 13 | 66 | 53 | 47 | |
| 7. | Derby County FC (Derby) | 42 | 15 | 14 | 13 | 76 | 69 | 44 | |
| 8. | Leeds United AFC (Leeds) | 42 | 15 | 14 | 13 | 59 | 62 | 44 | |
| 9. | Portsmouth FC (Portsmouth) | 42 | 18 | 7 | 17 | 74 | 76 | 43 | |
| 10. | Sheffield United FC (Sheffield) | 42 | 17 | 9 | 16 | 74 | 80 | 43 | |
| 11. | Everton FC (Liverpool) | 42 | 16 | 9 | 17 | 81 | 74 | 41 | |
| 12. | Sunderland AFC (Sunderland) | 42 | 15 | 10 | 17 | 63 | 80 | 40 | |
| 13. | Birmingham FC (Birmingham) | 42 | 14 | 11 | 17 | 57 | 57 | 39 | |
| 14. | Liverpool FC (Liverpool) | 42 | 14 | 11 | 17 | 79 | 84 | 39 | |
| 15. | Blackburn Rovers FC (Blackburn) | 42 | 14 | 10 | 18 | 76 | 102 | 38 | |
| 16. | Manchester City FC (Manchester) | 42 | 16 | 5 | 21 | 68 | 71 | 37 | |
| 17. | Middlesbrough FC (Middlesbrough) | 42 | 14 | 9 | 19 | 63 | 73 | 37 | |
| 18. | Chelsea FC (London) | 42 | 14 | 7 | 21 | 63 | 73 | 35 | |
| 19. | Leicester City FC (Leicester) | 42 | 11 | 13 | 18 | 75 | 89 | 35 | |
| 20. | Wolverhampton Wanderers FC (Wolverhampton) | 42 | 13 | 9 | 20 | 80 | 96 | 35 | |
| 21. | Bolton Wanderers FC (Bolton) | 42 | 12 | 9 | 21 | 78 | 92 | 33 | R |
| 22. | Blackpool FC (Blackpool) | 42 | 14 | 5 | 23 | 69 | 85 | 33 | R |
| | | 924 | 361 | 202 | 361 | 1645 | 1645 | 924 | |

## Top Goalscorer

| | | | |
|---|---|---|---|
| 1) | Jack BOWERS | (Derby County FC) | 35 |

## Football League Division 2 — 1932-1933 Season

| | Bradford City | Bradford P.A. | Burnley | Bury | Charlton Ath. | Chesterfield | Fulham | Grimsby Town | Lincoln City | Man. United | Millwall | Nottingham F. | Notts County | Oldham Ath. | Plymouth Arg. | Port Vale | Preston N.E. | Southampton | Stoke City | Swansea Town | Tottenham H. | West Ham Utd. |
|---|---|---|---|---|---|---|---|---|---|---|---|---|---|---|---|---|---|---|---|---|---|---|
| Bradford City AFC | | 1-0 | 2-1 | 3-0 | 3-0 | 4-2 | 2-0 | 2-2 | 2-2 | 1-2 | 1-5 | 2-2 | 1-2 | 3-0 | 2-3 | 7-0 | 0-0 | 1-0 | 1-1 | 1-1 | 0-1 | 5-1 |
| Bradford Park Avenue | 2-0 | | 0-4 | 4-0 | 3-0 | 5-1 | 1-4 | 1-1 | 6-0 | 1-1 | 3-0 | 3-1 | 3-4 | 1-3 | 1-0 | 4-2 | 2-0 | 2-1 | 2-2 | 1-0 | 3-3 | 3-0 |
| Burnley FC | 0-0 | 2-0 | | 1-0 | 0-1 | 1-1 | 3-3 | 2-0 | 0-0 | 2-3 | 3-0 | 3-3 | 2-1 | 1-1 | 1-1 | 1-1 | 4-0 | 2-0 | 1-2 | 1-2 | 1-1 | 4-0 |
| Bury FC | 1-1 | 0-0 | 5-3 | | 3-1 | 6-0 | 1-1 | 4-1 | 2-2 | 2-2 | 3-0 | 5-2 | 3-1 | 3-3 | 2-1 | 0-0 | 1-2 | 1-0 | 3-2 | 3-0 | 1-0 | 6-1 |
| Charlton Athletic FC | 0-0 | 0-2 | 2-2 | 1-3 | | 2-5 | 1-2 | 2-3 | 4-2 | 0-1 | 1-4 | 3-0 | 3-3 | 1-0 | 4-1 | 2-1 | 0-1 | 2-0 | 1-0 | 3-1 | 0-3 | 3-1 |
| Chesterfield FC | 1-2 | 2-1 | 6-0 | 1-3 | 2-3 | | 3-2 | 1-2 | 3-0 | 1-1 | 1-0 | 0-1 | 0-0 | 3-1 | 1-1 | 2-2 | 4-3 | 1-0 | 1-2 | 1-0 | 1-1 | 1-0 |
| Fulham FC | 1-0 | 5-2 | 2-1 | 3-3 | 3-1 | 2-2 | | 0-1 | 3-2 | 3-1 | 1-1 | 0-1 | 3-4 | 1-0 | 3-1 | 1-1 | 1-0 | 4-2 | 1-3 | 3-1 | 2-2 | 4-2 |
| Grimsby Town FC | 1-1 | 5-1 | 1-2 | 1-0 | 5-5 | 1-1 | 1-0 | | 3-3 | 1-1 | 1-1 | 1-1 | 1-1 | 5-1 | 2-3 | 6-1 | 5-5 | 2-2 | 0-1 | 2-1 | 3-2 | 2-1 |
| Lincoln City FC | 0-0 | 2-2 | 1-4 | 2-1 | 1-1 | 5-3 | 3-0 | 6-3 | | 3-2 | 3-0 | 1-1 | 1-1 | 1-3 | 2-0 | 0-1 | 2-1 | 1-0 | 2-3 | 2-0 | 2-2 | 6-0 |
| Manchester United FC | 0-1 | 2-1 | 2-1 | 1-3 | 1-1 | 2-1 | 4-3 | 1-1 | 4-1 | | 7-1 | 2-1 | 2-0 | 2-0 | 4-0 | 1-1 | 0-0 | 1-2 | 0-2 | 1-1 | | 1-2 |
| Millwall FC | 3-3 | 1-1 | 4-1 | 5-2 | 2-1 | 0-0 | 2-1 | 0-1 | 2-0 | 2-0 | | 1-1 | 1-1 | 6-1 | 2-0 | 0-1 | 1-1 | 3-0 | 0-0 | 3-1 | 1-4 | 1-0 |
| Nottingham Forest FC | 3-1 | 1-1 | 1-1 | 0-2 | 0-1 | 2-3 | 1-0 | 3-2 | 2-2 | 3-2 | 0-0 | | 3-0 | 2-3 | 1-1 | 1-1 | 2-1 | 4-2 | 1-0 | 2-2 | 3-1 | 2-2 |
| Notts County FC | 2-0 | 1-4 | 4-2 | 2-2 | 3-2 | 1-1 | 1-2 | 1-3 | 1-1 | 1-0 | 1-0 | 2-4 | | 2-1 | 4-1 | 5-0 | 0-0 | 1-2 | 3-4 | 1-2 | 3-0 | 2-0 |
| Oldham Athletic AFC | 6-1 | 1-3 | 2-2 | 2-1 | 0-0 | 2-0 | 1-3 | 0-1 | 5-2 | 1-1 | 1-0 | 1-2 | 5-0 | | 3-1 | 2-1 | 0-2 | 2-0 | 0-4 | 0-0 | 1-5 | 3-2 |
| Plymouth Argyle FC | 2-1 | 3-2 | 4-0 | 1-0 | 6-1 | 1-0 | 2-3 | 4-0 | 0-3 | 2-3 | 0-0 | 1-1 | 0-2 | 2-1 | | 3-1 | 5-0 | 1-1 | 1-0 | 1-0 | 2-2 | 4-1 |
| Port Vale FC | 2-0 | 3-1 | 1-1 | 1-0 | 2-1 | 9-1 | 1-2 | 4-2 | 3-2 | 3-3 | 2-0 | 0-1 | 4-0 | 2-4 | 4-1 | | 0-1 | 0-2 | 1-3 | 2-1 | 1-1 | 4-0 |
| Preston North End FC | 1-4 | 2-3 | 6-1 | 1-3 | 4-2 | 2-0 | 1-2 | 4-2 | 5-3 | 0-1 | 2-1 | 3-0 | 2-2 | 3-0 | 3-1 | | | 3-1 | 1-3 | 1-0 | 2-6 | 4-1 |
| Southampton FC | 3-1 | 2-0 | 3-1 | 1-0 | 3-0 | 2-1 | 2-2 | 3-0 | 4-0 | 4-2 | 2-3 | 0-2 | 6-2 | 0-2 | 2-0 | 2-2 | 1-0 | | 1-0 | 2-0 | 1-1 | 4-3 |
| Stoke City FC | 4-1 | 4-0 | 3-0 | 2-3 | 2-0 | 2-1 | 0-1 | 0-0 | 5-2 | 0-0 | 1-2 | 0-1 | 0-2 | 4-0 | 0-0 | 1-0 | 1-1 | 3-1 | | 2-0 | 2-0 | 0-0 |
| Swansea Town AFC | 2-0 | 3-1 | 2-0 | 2-1 | 2-0 | 3-0 | 3-0 | 1-0 | 3-1 | 2-1 | 1-0 | 0-1 | 2-0 | 2-0 | 0-1 | 2-0 | 3-1 | 2-1 | 0-2 | | 0-2 | 1-0 |
| Tottenham Hotspur FC | 1-1 | 2-0 | 4-1 | 2-1 | 4-1 | 4-1 | 0-0 | 4-3 | 3-2 | 6-1 | 2-1 | 0-0 | 3-1 | 1-1 | 0-0 | 4-0 | 1-1 | 5-0 | 3-2 | 7-0 | | 2-2 |
| West Ham United FC | 2-4 | 2-1 | 4-4 | 0-1 | 7-3 | 3-1 | 1-1 | 5-2 | 0-0 | 3-1 | 3-0 | 4-3 | 1-1 | 5-2 | 2-2 | 5-0 | 1-1 | 3-1 | 1-2 | 2-2 | 3-1 | |

### Division 2

| | | Pd | Wn | Dw | Ls | GF | GA | Pts | |
|---|---|---|---|---|---|---|---|---|---|
| 1. | Stoke City FC (Stoke-on-Trent) | 42 | 25 | 6 | 11 | 78 | 39 | 56 | P |
| 2. | Tottenham Hotspur FC (London) | 42 | 20 | 15 | 7 | 96 | 51 | 55 | P |
| 3. | Fulham FC (London) | 42 | 20 | 10 | 12 | 78 | 65 | 50 | |
| 4. | Bury FC (Bury) | 42 | 20 | 9 | 13 | 84 | 59 | 49 | |
| 5. | Nottingham Forest FC (Nottingham) | 42 | 17 | 15 | 10 | 67 | 59 | 49 | |
| 6. | Manchester United FC (Manchester) | 42 | 15 | 13 | 14 | 71 | 68 | 43 | |
| 7. | Millwall FC (London) | 42 | 16 | 11 | 15 | 59 | 57 | 43 | |
| 8. | Bradford Park Avenue FC (Bradford) | 42 | 17 | 8 | 17 | 77 | 71 | 42 | |
| 9. | Preston North End FC (Preston) | 42 | 16 | 10 | 16 | 74 | 70 | 42 | |
| 10. | Swansea Town AFC (Swansea) | 42 | 19 | 4 | 19 | 50 | 54 | 42 | |
| 11. | Bradford City AFC (Bradford) | 42 | 14 | 13 | 15 | 65 | 61 | 41 | |
| 12. | Southampton FC (Southampton) | 42 | 18 | 5 | 19 | 66 | 66 | 41 | |
| 13. | Grimsby Town FC (Cleethorpes) | 42 | 14 | 13 | 15 | 79 | 84 | 41 | |
| 14. | Plymouth Argyle FC (Plymouth) | 42 | 16 | 9 | 17 | 63 | 67 | 41 | |
| 15. | Notts County FC (Nottingham) | 42 | 15 | 10 | 17 | 67 | 78 | 40 | |
| 16. | Oldham Athletic AFC (Oldham) | 42 | 15 | 8 | 19 | 67 | 80 | 38 | |
| 17. | Port Vale FC (Stoke-on-Trent) | 42 | 14 | 10 | 18 | 66 | 79 | 38 | |
| 18. | Lincoln City FC (Lincoln) | 42 | 12 | 13 | 17 | 72 | 87 | 37 | |
| 19. | Burnley FC (Burnley) | 42 | 11 | 14 | 17 | 67 | 79 | 36 | |
| 20. | West Ham United FC (London) | 42 | 13 | 9 | 20 | 75 | 93 | 35 | |
| 21. | Chesterfield FC (Chesterfield) | 42 | 12 | 10 | 20 | 61 | 84 | 34 | R |
| 22. | Charlton Athletic FC (London) | 42 | 12 | 7 | 23 | 60 | 91 | 31 | R |
| | | 924 | 351 | 222 | 351 | 1542 | 1542 | 924 | |

| Football League Division 3 (N) 1932-1933 Season | Accrington Stan. | Barnsley | Barrow | Carlisle United | Chester | Crewe Alexandra | Darlington | Doncaster Rovers | Gateshead | Halifax Town | Hartlepools United | Hull City | Mansfield Town | New Brighton | Rochdale | Rotherham United | Southport | Stockport County | Tranmere Rovers | Walsall | Wrexham | York City |
|---|---|---|---|---|---|---|---|---|---|---|---|---|---|---|---|---|---|---|---|---|---|---|
| Accrington Stanley FC | — | 2-0 | 0-0 | 3-1 | 1-4 | 2-0 | 2-0 | 1-1 | 0-3 | 4-1 | 7-1 | 1-2 | 6-0 | 5-4 | 0-3 | 5-1 | 1-1 | 1-1 | 3-0 | 1-3 | 5-3 | 5-0 |
| Barnsley FC | 4-0 | — | 3-0 | 4-1 | 0-3 | 7-1 | 6-2 | 2-3 | 2-4 | 1-1 | 3-2 | 1-0 | 6-2 | 1-2 | 3-1 | 3-1 | 2-0 | 2-2 | 2-1 | 2-1 | 5-3 | 1-1 |
| Barrow AFC | 5-0 | 2-3 | — | 2-1 | 2-3 | 3-0 | 4-0 | 3-0 | 1-2 | 3-3 | 3-1 | 0-2 | 1-0 | 2-1 | 1-1 | 2-1 | 2-0 | 0-3 | 2-0 | 1-2 | 1-1 | 1-0 |
| Carlisle United FC | 2-2 | 0-1 | 0-1 | — | 1-1 | 2-0 | 3-0 | 0-2 | 1-2 | 5-3 | 3-1 | 1-1 | 3-1 | 1-3 | 2-2 | 0-0 | 0-0 | 2-1 | 0-1 | 1-1 | 2-1 | 5-1 |
| Chester FC | 4-2 | 3-1 | 2-1 | 4-0 | — | 3-1 | 5-2 | 2-0 | 3-1 | 6-3 | 3-3 | 1-1 | 5-2 | 3-0 | 2-0 | 1-0 | 1-1 | 2-2 | 1-2 | 1-0 | 0-3 | 5-0 |
| Crewe Alexandra FC | 3-1 | 2-2 | 2-0 | 1-0 | 0-1 | — | 2-4 | 4-0 | 2-0 | 2-1 | 6-2 | 1-1 | 7-0 | 4-0 | 3-1 | 8-0 | 1-1 | 2-1 | 2-0 | 2-1 | 2-0 | 1-0 |
| Darlington FC | 2-2 | 1-1 | 1-2 | 5-2 | 1-1 | 3-4 | — | 2-2 | 1-3 | 2-1 | 1-2 | 1-3 | 2-1 | 5-1 | 4-1 | 1-0 | 1-1 | 1-0 | 1-1 | 1-2 | | 3-0 |
| Doncaster Rovers FC | 2-2 | 3-1 | 1-1 | 4-2 | 3-3 | 5-1 | 3-1 | — | 3-1 | 5-1 | 4-1 | 1-1 | 2-2 | 2-0 | 1-0 | 1-0 | 2-1 | 1-1 | 2-2 | 3-2 | 1-1 | 3-2 |
| Gateshead FC | 1-0 | 1-1 | 2-3 | 1-0 | 3-0 | 2-1 | 3-0 | 4-0 | — | 3-0 | 3-1 | 2-3 | 3-2 | 2-0 | 3-0 | 1-1 | 4-1 | 0-3 | 0-2 | 1-1 | 4-4 | 2-2 |
| Halifax Town AFC | 0-0 | 2-1 | 2-0 | 0-1 | 0-2 | 1-5 | 4-2 | 0-0 | 1-0 | — | 4-0 | 1-3 | 5-1 | 3-3 | 2-0 | 2-1 | 1-0 | 1-3 | 4-1 | 4-0 | 0-0 | 2-0 |
| Hartlepools United FC | 3-1 | 6-4 | 0-1 | 2-1 | 3-1 | 3-2 | 2-1 | 4-0 | 2-2 | 1-1 | — | 0-1 | 6-3 | 3-2 | 3-0 | 2-0 | 4-2 | 1-1 | 2-3 | 2-0 | 3-1 | 4-2 |
| Hull City AFC | 4-2 | 5-1 | 3-0 | 6-1 | 2-0 | 3-0 | 3-1 | 6-1 | 1-1 | 3-1 | 3-0 | — | 4-1 | 5-0 | 1-1 | 4-2 | 4-0 | 3-0 | 3-0 | 0-0 | 4-1 | 2-1 |
| Mansfield Town FC | 1-3 | 0-1 | 2-1 | 3-1 | 1-0 | 4-0 | 3-3 | 2-2 | 1-2 | 2-2 | 7-1 | 2-1 | — | 5-0 | 4-1 | 9-2 | 4-0 | 1-2 | 2-0 | 2-0 | 0-0 | 2-0 |
| New Brighton FC | 2-2 | 3-5 | 1-2 | 2-0 | 3-1 | 1-2 | 7-1 | 4-4 | 1-1 | 0-3 | 5-2 | 1-0 | 1-0 | — | 0-3 | 5-2 | 2-1 | 1-1 | 1-1 | 2-2 | 0-2 | 0-1 |
| Rochdale AFC | 2-0 | 2-3 | 0-0 | 0-1 | 2-0 | 1-4 | 1-1 | 2-3 | 1-0 | 1-0 | 6-2 | 3-2 | 2-1 | 1-0 | — | 2-2 | 1-3 | 0-2 | 0-3 | 1-1 | 3-1 | 1-4 |
| Rotherham United FC | 2-3 | 0-0 | 1-0 | 1-0 | 0-5 | 5-0 | 3-1 | 1-1 | 1-2 | 6-1 | 1-1 | 3-2 | 3-0 | 1-0 | 2-0 | — | 3-1 | 2-1 | 2-0 | 4-1 | 0-2 | 1-0 |
| Southport FC | 2-3 | 2-0 | 3-0 | 4-0 | 2-1 | 4-1 | 5-1 | 1-0 | 4-1 | 1-2 | 6-3 | 0-1 | 5-2 | 1-1 | 2-0 | 2-0 | — | 2-1 | 1-1 | 2-1 | 0-0 | 5-1 |
| Stockport County FC | 2-0 | 5-4 | 4-1 | 0-1 | 8-5 | 1-0 | 5-1 | 5-1 | 4-3 | 6-0 | 6-2 | 3-5 | 2-2 | 1-1 | 2-3 | 1-0 | 3-1 | — | 3-0 | 5-0 | 1-0 | 2-0 |
| Tranmere Rovers FC | 4-0 | 3-0 | 1-3 | 1-2 | 2-2 | 5-0 | 3-1 | 3-2 | 4-2 | 2-3 | 3-3 | 2-0 | 3-0 | 2-3 | 3-1 | 1-0 | 2-1 | 2-2 | — | 1-3 | 0-0 | 2-3 |
| Walsall FC | 1-0 | 1-1 | 1-1 | 5-0 | 3-1 | 2-1 | 4-0 | 2-0 | 4-0 | 4-1 | 1-0 | 8-1 | 0-0 | 2-1 | 1-0 | 3-1 | 0-0 | 3-2 | | — | 2-3 | 4-2 |
| Wrexham AFC | 1-0 | 3-0 | 4-1 | 2-1 | 1-2 | 7-0 | 3-1 | 3-0 | 5-1 | 5-2 | 8-1 | 3-1 | 1-1 | 5-0 | 4-1 | 5-1 | 6-0 | 2-0 | 1-1 | 3-0 | — | 3-1 |
| York City FC | 0-0 | 3-2 | 3-1 | 0-1 | 3-1 | 4-0 | 6-1 | 2-3 | 2-2 | 5-3 | 1-1 | 1-2 | 4-3 | 3-0 | 2-6 | 4-3 | 0-1 | 2-2 | 0-1 | 4-2 | 2-3 | — |

## Division 3 (North)

| | | Pd | Wn | Dw | Ls | GF | GA | Pts | |
|---|---|---|---|---|---|---|---|---|---|
| 1. | Hull City AFC (Kingston-upon-Tyne) | 42 | 26 | 7 | 9 | 100 | 45 | 59 | P |
| 2. | Wrexham AFC (Wrexham) | 42 | 24 | 9 | 9 | 106 | 51 | 57 | |
| 3. | Stockport County FC (Stockport) | 42 | 21 | 12 | 9 | 99 | 58 | 54 | |
| 4. | Chester FC (Chester) | 42 | 22 | 8 | 12 | 94 | 66 | 52 | |
| 5. | Walsall FC (Walsall) | 42 | 19 | 10 | 13 | 75 | 58 | 48 | |
| 6. | Doncaster Rovers FC (Doncaster) | 42 | 17 | 14 | 11 | 77 | 79 | 48 | |
| 7. | Gateshead FC (Gateshead) | 42 | 19 | 9 | 14 | 78 | 67 | 47 | |
| 8. | Barnsley FC (Barnsley) | 42 | 19 | 8 | 15 | 92 | 80 | 46 | |
| 9. | Barrow AFC (Barrow-in-Furness) | 42 | 18 | 7 | 17 | 60 | 60 | 43 | |
| 10. | Crewe Alexandra FC (Crewe) | 42 | 20 | 3 | 19 | 80 | 84 | 43 | |
| 11. | Tranmere Rovers FC (Birkenhead) | 42 | 17 | 8 | 17 | 70 | 66 | 42 | |
| 12. | Southport FC (Southport) | 42 | 17 | 7 | 18 | 70 | 67 | 41 | |
| 13. | Accrington Stanley FC (Accrington) | 42 | 15 | 10 | 17 | 78 | 76 | 40 | |
| 14. | Hartlepools United FC (Hartlepool) | 42 | 16 | 7 | 19 | 87 | 116 | 39 | |
| 15. | Halifax Town AFC (Halifax) | 42 | 15 | 8 | 19 | 71 | 90 | 38 | |
| 16. | Mansfield Town FC (Mansfield) | 42 | 14 | 7 | 21 | 84 | 100 | 35 | |
| 17. | Rotherham United FC (Rotherham) | 42 | 14 | 6 | 22 | 60 | 84 | 34 | |
| 18. | Rochdale AFC (Rochdale) | 42 | 13 | 7 | 22 | 58 | 80 | 33 | |
| 19. | Carlisle United FC (Carlisle) | 42 | 13 | 7 | 22 | 51 | 75 | 33 | |
| 20. | York City FC (York) | 42 | 13 | 6 | 23 | 72 | 92 | 32 | |
| 21. | New Brighton FC (Wallasey) | 42 | 11 | 10 | 21 | 63 | 88 | 32 | |
| 22. | Darlington FC (Darlington) | 42 | 10 | 8 | 24 | 66 | 109 | 28 | |
| | | 924 | 373 | 178 | 373 | 1691 | 1691 | 924 | |

| Football League Division 3 (S) 1932-1933 Season | Aldershot | Bournemouth | Brentford | Brighton | Bristol City | Bristol Rovers | Cardiff City | Clapton Orient | Coventry City | Crystal Palace | Exeter City | Gillingham | Luton Town | Newport County | Northampton | Norwich City | Q.P.R. | Reading | Southend United | Swindon Town | Torquay United | Watford |
|---|---|---|---|---|---|---|---|---|---|---|---|---|---|---|---|---|---|---|---|---|---|---|
| Aldershot FC | | 1-1 | 1-1 | 1-1 | 1-0 | 1-0 | 1-0 | 4-0 | 1-1 | 3-1 | 4-1 | 3-0 | 2-2 | 2-1 | 0-1 | 1-3 | 2-0 | 4-4 | 1-2 | 0-1 | 2-0 | 2-1 |
| Bournemouth & B. Athletic | 1-0 | | 1-1 | 1-1 | 6-1 | 2-2 | 3-2 | 4-2 | 3-1 | 3-2 | 1-1 | 1-0 | 0-2 | 1-2 | 1-1 | 1-1 | 3-0 | 0-3 | 4-0 | 5-1 | 1-2 | 2-2 |
| Brentford FC | 2-0 | 1-1 | | 2-1 | 2-1 | 0-0 | 7-3 | 4-2 | 2-1 | 2-0 | 0-2 | 1-2 | 1-0 | 6-0 | 1-0 | 2-2 | 2-0 | 1-1 | 3-1 | 1-0 | 3-1 | 2-1 |
| Brighton & Hove Albion | 0-2 | 3-0 | 1-2 | | 7-0 | 0-3 | 1-0 | 0-0 | 1-0 | 1-2 | 2-1 | 1-0 | 2-0 | 1-0 | 2-1 | 1-1 | 4-1 | 5-3 | 1-2 | 5-1 | 1-1 | 3-0 |
| Bristol City FC | 2-2 | 1-1 | 1-2 | 3-4 | | 3-1 | 3-1 | 3-0 | 5-3 | 3-3 | 0-1 | 1-1 | 5-2 | 3-2 | 5-4 | 1-1 | 2-3 | 4-1 | 5-1 | 5-1 | 2-0 | 2-3 |
| Bristol Rovers FC | 4-1 | 1-0 | 2-4 | 5-3 | 1-1 | | 0-0 | 2-0 | 1-0 | 2-3 | 1-0 | 1-0 | 0-0 | 2-2 | 4-3 | 1-1 | 4-1 | 1-0 | 3-1 | 1-0 | 0-2 | 2-0 |
| Cardiff City AFC | 2-1 | 3-0 | 2-1 | 1-2 | 1-1 | 4-3 | | 6-1 | 2-2 | 1-1 | 1-3 | 1-0 | 3-2 | 1-3 | 6-0 | 4-2 | 2-5 | 0-1 | 2-0 | 3-0 | 2-1 | 1-1 |
| Clapton Orient FC | 2-3 | 1-1 | 1-5 | 2-0 | 2-2 | 0-3 | 3-0 | | 2-1 | 4-1 | 2-2 | 1-2 | 0-0 | 3-1 | 2-2 | 0-0 | 2-2 | 2-5 | 0-0 | 7-1 | 1-4 | 2-0 |
| Coventry City FC | 3-0 | 3-0 | 2-3 | 2-2 | 6-0 | 2-0 | 5-0 | 5-0 | | 6-2 | 4-0 | 4-2 | 4-0 | 3-1 | 3-1 | 3-5 | 7-0 | 3-1 | 2-3 | 2-1 | 5-0 | 1-3 |
| Crystal Palace FC | 3-0 | 3-0 | 2-1 | 5-0 | 2-2 | 2-0 | 4-1 | 2-1 | 1-3 | | 2-2 | 5-1 | 3-0 | 0-0 | 2-0 | 4-0 | 0-1 | 1-1 | 4-1 | 4-3 | 2-1 | 0-3 |
| Exeter City FC | 0-0 | 2-3 | 1-2 | 4-1 | 2-0 | 1-0 | 1-0 | 3-0 | 5-0 | 1-1 | | 2-1 | 2-0 | 4-0 | 3-1 | 2-1 | 2-0 | 4-1 | 3-0 | 5-0 | 5-0 | 5-2 |
| Gillingham FC | 5-2 | 4-0 | 1-3 | 2-0 | 4-2 | 2-0 | 1-1 | 3-1 | 3-0 | 2-0 | 1-2 | | 1-1 | 2-0 | 5-1 | 0-2 | 4-1 | 1-1 | 3-2 | 3-1 | 1-1 | 3-3 |
| Luton Town FC | 2-1 | 1-2 | 5-5 | 0-0 | 5-4 | 1-1 | 8-1 | 4-1 | 4-1 | 1-1 | 4-0 | 2-1 | | 2-2 | 2-1 | 1-1 | 3-1 | 1-1 | 3-3 | 6-2 | 2-1 | 3-2 |
| Newport County AFC | 2-1 | 1-1 | 1-6 | 5-2 | 1-1 | 3-1 | 4-2 | 0-2 | 2-1 | 1-3 | 1-1 | 0-2 | 3-2 | | 0-3 | 3-4 | 5-1 | 3-3 | 1-3 | 1-2 | 3-1 | 2-0 |
| Northampton Town FC | 5-2 | 6-0 | 1-0 | 0-0 | 2-1 | 1-1 | 2-0 | 3-0 | 5-1 | 1-0 | 5-3 | 1-0 | 1-0 | 8-0 | | 2-2 | 2-1 | 1-0 | 0-0 | 6-0 | 2-0 | 0-0 |
| Norwich City FC | 3-2 | 6-0 | 3-0 | 1-0 | 3-0 | 1-1 | 3-1 | 2-0 | 2-1 | 3-0 | 0-0 | 2-0 | 2-1 | 3-1 | 2-0 | | 3-2 | 2-2 | 1-0 | 5-2 | 1-2 | 1-2 |
| Queen's Park Rangers FC | 2-2 | 3-1 | 2-3 | 0-1 | 1-1 | 1-1 | 5-1 | 2-1 | 3-3 | 2-1 | 1-3 | 1-1 | 3-1 | 6-1 | 1-1 | 2-2 | | 0-3 | 6-1 | 4-2 | 1-1 | 2-1 |
| Reading FC | 2-2 | 6-2 | 1-3 | 3-0 | 2-2 | 3-1 | 4-2 | 3-1 | 3-3 | 2-3 | 2-2 | 4-0 | 4-1 | 4-1 | 4-0 | 3-2 | 3-1 | | 1-1 | 7-1 | 5-2 | 2-0 |
| Southend United FC | 5-1 | 2-1 | 0-1 | 2-1 | 3-1 | 2-2 | 2-2 | 3-3 | 1-3 | 1-2 | 1-2 | 2-2 | 2-1 | 3-0 | 1-0 | 2-1 | 0-1 | 3-1 | | 0-0 | 2-1 | 2-1 |
| Swindon Town FC | 3-2 | 2-0 | 0-0 | 5-1 | 1-4 | 1-1 | 6-2 | 3-3 | 1-2 | 1-0 | 2-2 | 1-1 | 1-1 | 2-0 | 2-1 | 2-4 | 0-0 | 0-1 | 2-2 | | 0-0 | 1-2 |
| Torquay United FC | 1-0 | 2-1 | 1-1 | 1-0 | 0-0 | 1-1 | 4-1 | 1-1 | 3-3 | 2-1 | 1-3 | 1-2 | 3-1 | 4-0 | 5-1 | 2-2 | 3-1 | 1-1 | 8-1 | 4-3 | | 3-2 |
| Watford FC | 2-0 | 2-1 | 1-1 | 0-4 | 1-0 | 3-1 | 2-1 | 1-1 | 3-1 | 1-0 | 0-0 | 2-0 | 4-1 | 3-2 | 4-0 | 1-2 | 2-2 | 1-1 | 2-2 | 2-2 | 0-0 | |

## Division 3 (South)

| | | Pd | Wn | Dw | Ls | GF | GA | Pts | |
|---|---|---|---|---|---|---|---|---|---|
| 1. | Brentford FC (London) | 42 | 26 | 10 | 6 | 90 | 49 | 62 | P |
| 2. | Exeter City FC (Exeter) | 42 | 24 | 10 | 8 | 88 | 48 | 58 | |
| 3. | Norwich City FC (Norwich) | 42 | 22 | 13 | 7 | 88 | 55 | 57 | |
| 4. | Reading FC (Reading) | 42 | 19 | 13 | 10 | 103 | 71 | 51 | |
| 5. | Crystal Palace FC (London) | 42 | 19 | 8 | 15 | 78 | 64 | 46 | |
| 6. | Coventry City FC (Coventry) | 42 | 19 | 6 | 17 | 106 | 77 | 44 | |
| 7. | Gillingham FC (Gillingham) | 42 | 18 | 8 | 16 | 72 | 61 | 44 | |
| 8. | Northampton Town FC (Northampton) | 42 | 18 | 8 | 16 | 76 | 66 | 44 | |
| 9. | Bristol Rovers FC (Bristol) | 42 | 15 | 14 | 13 | 61 | 56 | 44 | |
| 10. | Torquay United FC (Torquay) | 42 | 16 | 12 | 14 | 72 | 67 | 44 | |
| 11. | Watford FC (Watford) | 42 | 16 | 12 | 14 | 66 | 63 | 44 | |
| 12. | Brighton & Hove Albion FC (Hove) | 42 | 17 | 8 | 17 | 66 | 65 | 42 | |
| 13. | Southend United FC (Southend-on-Sea) | 42 | 15 | 11 | 16 | 65 | 82 | 41 | |
| 14. | Luton Town FC (Luton) | 42 | 13 | 13 | 16 | 78 | 78 | 39 | |
| 15. | Bristol City FC (Bristol) | 42 | 12 | 13 | 17 | 83 | 90 | 37 | |
| 16. | Queen's Park Rangers FC (London) | 42 | 13 | 11 | 18 | 72 | 87 | 37 | |
| 17. | Aldershot FC (Aldershot) | 42 | 13 | 10 | 19 | 61 | 72 | 36 | |
| 18. | Bournemouth & Boscombe Athletic FC (Bournemouth) | 42 | 12 | 12 | 18 | 60 | 81 | 36 | |
| 19. | Cardiff City AFC (Cardiff) | 42 | 12 | 7 | 23 | 69 | 99 | 31 | |
| 20. | Clapton Orient FC (London) | 42 | 8 | 13 | 21 | 59 | 93 | 29 | |
| 21. | Newport County AFC (Newport) | 42 | 11 | 7 | 24 | 61 | 105 | 29 | |
| 22. | Swindon Town FC (Swindon) | 42 | 9 | 11 | 22 | 60 | 105 | 29 | |
| | | 924 | 347 | 230 | 347 | 1634 | 1634 | 924 | |

# F.A. CUP FINAL  (Wembley Stadium, London – 29/04/1933 – 92,950)

| EVERTON FC (LIVERPOOL) | 3-0 | Manchester City FC (Manchester) |
|---|---|---|

*Stein, Dean, Dunn*

Everton: Sagar, Cook, Cresswell, Britton, White, Thompson, Geldard, Dunn, Dean, Johnson, Stein.
Man. City: Langford, Cann, Dale, Busby, Cowan, Bray, Toseland, Marshall, Herd, McMullan, Brook.

## Semi-finals

| Everton FC (Liverpool) | 2-1 | West Ham United FC (London) |
|---|---|---|
| Manchester City FC (Manchester) | 3-2 | Derby County FC (Derby) |

## Quarter-finals

| Burnley FC (Burnley) | 0-1 | Manchester City FC (Manchester) |
|---|---|---|
| Derby County FC (Derby) | 4-4, 1-0 (aet) | Sunderland AFC (Sunderland) |
| Everton FC (Liverpool) | 6-0 | Luton Town FC (Luton) |
| West Ham United FC (London) | 4-0 | Birmingham FC (Birmingham) |

# 1933-34

| Football League Division 1 1933-1934 Season | Arsenal | Aston Villa | Birmingham | Blackburn Rovers | Chelsea | Derby County | Everton | Huddersfield Town | Leeds United | Leicester City | Liverpool | Manchester City | Middlesbrough | Newcastle United | Portsmouth | Sheffield United | Sheffield Wednesday | Stoke City | Sunderland | Tottenham Hotspur | W.B.A. | Wolves |
|---|---|---|---|---|---|---|---|---|---|---|---|---|---|---|---|---|---|---|---|---|---|---|
| Arsenal FC | ■ | 3-2 | 1-1 | 2-1 | 2-1 | 1-0 | 1-2 | 3-1 | 2-0 | 2-0 | 2-1 | 1-1 | 6-0 | 3-0 | 1-1 | 2-0 | 1-1 | 3-0 | 2-1 | 1-3 | 3-1 | 3-2 |
| Aston Villa FC | 2-3 | ■ | 1-1 | 1-1 | 2-0 | 0-2 | 2-1 | 4-3 | 3-0 | 2-3 | 4-2 | 0-0 | 3-0 | 2-3 | 1-1 | 3-0 | 1-0 | 1-2 | 2-1 | 1-5 | 4-4 | 6-2 |
| Birmingham FC | 0-0 | 0-0 | ■ | 2-0 | 0-3 | 2-1 | 2-2 | 1-3 | 4-0 | 3-0 | 1-2 | 0-1 | 0-0 | 1-2 | 3-1 | 4-2 | 3-0 | 0-1 | 1-1 | 2-0 | 0-1 | 0-0 |
| Blackburn Rovers FC | 2-2 | 2-1 | 3-1 | ■ | 4-2 | 2-1 | 1-1 | 2-2 | 4-2 | 3-0 | 3-1 | 3-0 | 0-0 | 3-2 | 3-2 | 3-1 | 3-1 | 4-1 | 0-0 | 1-0 | 4-0 | 7-1 |
| Chelsea FC | 2-2 | 1-0 | 1-1 | 3-0 | ■ | 0-2 | 2-0 | 2-3 | 1-1 | 2-0 | 2-0 | 1-2 | 2-3 | 2-1 | 4-0 | 5-0 | 0-1 | 2-0 | 4-0 | 0-4 | 3-2 | 5-2 |
| Derby County FC | 2-4 | 1-1 | 4-0 | 1-1 | 1-0 | ■ | 1-1 | 1-1 | 3-1 | 2-1 | 3-1 | 4-1 | 2-0 | 1-1 | 0-1 | 5-1 | 1-1 | 5-1 | 0-0 | 4-3 | 1-1 | 3-1 |
| Everton FC | 3-1 | 2-2 | 2-0 | 7-1 | 2-1 | 0-3 | ■ | 0-1 | 2-0 | 1-1 | 0-0 | 2-0 | 1-1 | 3-7 | 1-1 | 4-0 | 2-3 | 2-2 | 1-0 | 1-1 | 1-0 | 1-2 |
| Huddersfield Town AFC | 0-1 | 2-1 | 0-0 | 5-3 | 6-1 | 2-0 | 1-0 | ■ | 0-0 | 5-1 | 0-2 | 1-0 | 2-1 | 4-1 | 4-0 | 6-1 | 3-2 | 2-2 | 2-1 | 2-0 | 3-1 | 3-1 |
| Leeds United AFC | 0-1 | 2-4 | 1-0 | 4-0 | 3-1 | 0-2 | 2-2 | 1-1 | ■ | 8-0 | 5-1 | 3-1 | 5-2 | 3-0 | 1-0 | 1-1 | 2-1 | 2-0 | 3-1 | 0-0 | 3-0 | 3-3 |
| Leicester City FC | 4-1 | 1-1 | 3-7 | 1-2 | 1-1 | 2-0 | 3-1 | 1-0 | 2-2 | ■ | 1-0 | 0-0 | 1-2 | 3-2 | 2-1 | 4-0 | 2-0 | 3-1 | 0-0 | 1-3 | 0-1 | 1-1 |
| Liverpool FC | 2-3 | 2-3 | 4-1 | 4-0 | 3-0 | 4-2 | 3-2 | 2-2 | 4-3 | 1-3 | ■ | 3-2 | 6-2 | 1-2 | 2-2 | 3-2 | 1-3 | 1-1 | 1-1 | 3-1 | 1-1 | 1-1 |
| Manchester City FC | 2-1 | 1-0 | 1-0 | 3-1 | 4-2 | 2-0 | 2-2 | 2-2 | 0-1 | 1-1 | 2-1 | ■ | 5-2 | 1-1 | 2-1 | 4-1 | 2-3 | 4-2 | 4-1 | 2-0 | 2-7 | 4-0 |
| Middlesbrough FC | 0-2 | 1-2 | 0-3 | 3-1 | 2-2 | 3-1 | 2-0 | 3-0 | 2-1 | 4-1 | 4-1 | 2-1 | ■ | 1-0 | 2-0 | 10-3 | 2-3 | 6-1 | 0-4 | 1-1 | 3-0 | 0-0 |
| Newcastle United FC | 0-1 | 1-1 | 0-0 | 3-1 | 2-2 | 1-1 | 1-2 | 3-3 | 2-0 | 1-1 | 9-2 | 2-2 | 1-1 | ■ | 2-2 | 3-1 | 0-0 | 2-2 | 2-1 | 1-3 | 1-2 | 5-1 |
| Portsmouth FC | 1-0 | 3-2 | 0-2 | 2-0 | 0-2 | 1-0 | 0-0 | 3-0 | 2-1 | 3-5 | 1-0 | 2-0 | 4-1 | 2-0 | ■ | 1-1 | 0-2 | 3-1 | 0-0 | 0-1 | 2-2 | 1-1 |
| Sheffield United FC | 1-3 | 3-3 | 2-1 | 1-0 | 4-1 | 2-0 | 1-1 | 1-4 | 2-1 | 2-1 | 2-2 | 1-1 | 3-1 | 4-0 | 0-1 | ■ | 5-1 | 1-2 | 2-0 | 0-0 | 0-1 | 3-1 |
| Sheffield Wednesday FC | 1-2 | 1-2 | 2-1 | 4-0 | 2-1 | 1-1 | 0-0 | 1-2 | 0-2 | 1-1 | 1-2 | 1-1 | 3-0 | 3-1 | 1-2 | 0-1 | ■ | 2-2 | 2-0 | 2-1 | 3-1 | 2-1 |
| Stoke City FC | 1-1 | 1-1 | 1-1 | 2-0 | 1-0 | 0-4 | 1-2 | 3-0 | 1-2 | 2-1 | 1-1 | 0-1 | 2-0 | 2-1 | 2-1 | 3-0 | 0-1 | ■ | 3-0 | 2-0 | 4-1 | 1-1 |
| Sunderland AFC | 3-0 | 5-1 | 4-1 | 3-0 | 0-0 | 0-0 | 3-2 | 1-1 | 4-2 | 2-1 | 4-1 | 0-0 | 2-0 | 0-2 | 5-0 | 4-0 | 4-1 | 3-0 | ■ | 6-0 | 2-2 | 3-3 |
| Tottenham Hotspur FC | 1-1 | 3-2 | 3-2 | 4-1 | 2-1 | 1-2 | 3-0 | 1-3 | 5-1 | 0-1 | 0-3 | 5-1 | 2-0 | 4-0 | 0-0 | 4-1 | 4-3 | 0-0 | 3-1 | ■ | 2-1 | 4-0 |
| West Bromwich Albion FC | 1-0 | 2-1 | 1-2 | 0-1 | 3-1 | 5-1 | 3-3 | 2-3 | 0-3 | 2-0 | 2-2 | 4-0 | 3-0 | 1-1 | 2-1 | 3-0 | 1-1 | 5-1 | 6-5 | 1-2 | ■ | 2-0 |
| Wolverhampton Wanderers FC | 0-1 | 4-3 | 2-0 | 5-3 | 1-1 | 3-0 | 2-0 | 5-2 | 2-0 | 1-1 | 3-2 | 8-0 | 0-1 | 2-1 | 1-1 | 3-2 | 6-2 | 0-2 | 1-6 | 1-0 | 0-0 | ■ |

| Division 1 | Pd | Wn | Dw | Ls | GF | GA | Pts | |
|---|---|---|---|---|---|---|---|---|
| 1. ARSENAL FC (LONDON) | 42 | 25 | 9 | 8 | 75 | 47 | 59 | |
| 2. Huddersfield Town AFC (Huddersfield) | 42 | 23 | 10 | 9 | 90 | 61 | 56 | |
| 3. Tottenham Hotspur FC (London) | 42 | 21 | 7 | 14 | 79 | 56 | 49 | |
| 4. Derby County FC (Derby) | 42 | 17 | 11 | 14 | 68 | 54 | 45 | |
| 5. Manchester City FC (Manchester) | 42 | 17 | 11 | 14 | 65 | 72 | 45 | |
| 6. Sunderland AFC (Sunderland) | 42 | 16 | 12 | 14 | 81 | 56 | 44 | |
| 7. West Bromwich Albion FC (West Bromwich) | 42 | 17 | 10 | 15 | 78 | 70 | 44 | |
| 8. Blackburn Rovers FC (Blackburn) | 42 | 18 | 7 | 17 | 74 | 81 | 43 | |
| 9. Leeds United AFC (Leeds) | 42 | 17 | 8 | 17 | 75 | 66 | 42 | |
| 10. Portsmouth FC (Portsmouth) | 42 | 15 | 12 | 15 | 52 | 55 | 42 | |
| 11. Sheffield Wednesday FC (Sheffield) | 42 | 16 | 9 | 17 | 62 | 67 | 41 | |
| 12. Stoke City FC (Stoke-on-Trent) | 42 | 15 | 11 | 16 | 58 | 71 | 41 | |
| 13. Aston Villa FC (Birmingham) | 42 | 14 | 12 | 16 | 78 | 75 | 40 | |
| 14. Everton FC (Liverpool) | 42 | 12 | 16 | 14 | 62 | 63 | 40 | |
| 15. Wolverhampton Wanderers FC (Wolverhampton) | 42 | 14 | 12 | 16 | 74 | 86 | 40 | |
| 16. Middlesbrough FC (Middlesbrough) | 42 | 16 | 7 | 19 | 68 | 80 | 39 | |
| 17. Leicester City FC (Leicester) | 42 | 14 | 11 | 17 | 59 | 74 | 39 | |
| 18. Liverpool FC (Liverpool) | 42 | 14 | 10 | 18 | 79 | 87 | 38 | |
| 19. Chelsea FC (London) | 42 | 14 | 8 | 20 | 67 | 69 | 36 | |
| 20. Birmingham FC (Birmingham) | 42 | 12 | 12 | 18 | 54 | 56 | 36 | |
| 21. Newcastle United FC (Newcastle-upon-Tyne) | 42 | 10 | 14 | 18 | 68 | 77 | 34 | R |
| 22. Sheffield United FC (Sheffield) | 42 | 12 | 7 | 23 | 58 | 101 | 31 | R |
| | 924 | 349 | 226 | 349 | 1524 | 1524 | 924 | |

# Top Goalscorer

1)   Jack BOWERS                    (Derby County FC)      34

| Football League Division 2 1933-1934 Season | Blackpool | Bolton Wands. | Bradford City | Bradford P.A. | Brentford | Burnley | Bury | Fulham | Grimsby Town | Hull City | Lincoln City | Man. United | Millwall | Nottingham F. | Notts County | Oldham Athletic | Plymouth Arg. | Port Vale | Preston N.E. | Southampton | Swansea Town | West Ham Utd. |
|---|---|---|---|---|---|---|---|---|---|---|---|---|---|---|---|---|---|---|---|---|---|---|
| Blackpool FC | | 1-1 | 3-2 | 1-1 | 3-1 | 1-1 | 2-0 | 4-3 | 3-4 | 0-0 | 2-0 | 3-1 | 2-2 | 2-3 | 2-1 | 0-0 | 1-1 | 1-0 | 1-2 | 4-2 | 2-1 | 1-1 |
| Bolton Wanderers FC | 1-2 | | 3-0 | 0-1 | 3-2 | 4-1 | 2-0 | 3-1 | 0-4 | 3-3 | 1-2 | 3-1 | 5-0 | 1-1 | 1-0 | 1-0 | 2-0 | 3-0 | 0-2 | 2-0 | 2-1 | 5-1 |
| Bradford City AFC | 1-0 | 5-1 | | 3-0 | 2-1 | 2-1 | 2-2 | 1-0 | 2-1 | 1-2 | 3-0 | 1-1 | 1-0 | 3-2 | 3-1 | 5-2 | 3-4 | 1-2 | 1-0 | 2-2 | 2-1 | 2-2 |
| Bradford Park Avenue | 1-2 | 1-4 | 2-1 | | 5-2 | 5-0 | 0-1 | 3-1 | 2-1 | 3-1 | 2-1 | 6-1 | 4-0 | 6-2 | 3-2 | 4-2 | 4-1 | 2-2 | 2-1 | 3-1 | 5-1 | 0-0 |
| Brentford FC | 1-0 | 3-1 | 2-1 | 2-0 | | 5-2 | 2-3 | 1-2 | 1-2 | 2-2 | 5-0 | 3-4 | 3-0 | 2-1 | 2-2 | 2-1 | 3-0 | 2-0 | 3-2 | 2-0 | 2-0 | 4-1 |
| Burnley FC | 3-2 | 1-3 | 4-2 | 1-0 | 3-1 | | 1-2 | 2-1 | 2-0 | 3-1 | 3-1 | 1-4 | 2-1 | 1-0 | 1-0 | 0-1 | 2-2 | 0-0 | 1-4 | 2-1 | 3-1 | 4-2 |
| Bury FC | 2-5 | 1-1 | 1-0 | 2-1 | 1-2 | 1-1 | | 3-3 | 1-3 | 3-1 | 0-2 | 2-1 | 5-1 | 4-2 | 3-1 | 1-1 | 4-0 | 0-3 | 2-1 | 1-0 | 4-1 | 2-1 |
| Fulham FC | 1-0 | 0-2 | 0-1 | 0-2 | 1-1 | 1-1 | 2-1 | | 1-0 | 1-1 | 1-0 | 0-2 | 2-0 | 3-1 | 3-0 | 1-2 | 3-2 | 3-0 | 1-0 | 1-0 | 1-0 | 3-1 |
| Grimsby Town FC | 7-0 | 2-3 | 1-4 | 3-2 | 2-2 | 1-0 | 2-0 | 3-1 | | 4-1 | 3-0 | 7-3 | 5-2 | 2-1 | 2-2 | 2-1 | 5-1 | 1-2 | 3-0 | 3-1 | 3-1 | 1-1 |
| Hull City AFC | 3-0 | 1-0 | 2-2 | 1-2 | 0-1 | 0-1 | 3-1 | 0-0 | 0-1 | | 2-0 | 4-1 | 3-2 | 2-2 | 0-1 | 2-0 | 5-4 | 2-1 | 0-1 | 1-0 | 0-0 | 2-0 |
| Lincoln City FC | 2-2 | 2-2 | 0-1 | 2-1 | 0-2 | 4-0 | 1-2 | 5-0 | 3-3 | 2-1 | | 5-1 | 0-1 | 0-0 | 0-1 | 1-1 | 1-1 | 1-0 | 0-1 | 1-1 | 1-0 | 0-2 |
| Manchester United FC | 2-0 | 1-5 | 2-1 | 0-4 | 1-3 | 5-2 | 2-1 | 1-0 | 1-0 | 4-1 | 1-1 | | 1-1 | 0-1 | 1-2 | 2-3 | 0-3 | 2-0 | 1-0 | 1-0 | 1-1 | 0-1 |
| Millwall FC | 0-0 | 2-1 | 1-1 | 0-1 | 2-0 | 0-0 | 0-0 | 0-1 | 0-1 | 2-0 | 4-1 | 0-2 | | 0-0 | 3-2 | 1-0 | 0-0 | 0-3 | 1-1 | 1-0 | 2-1 | 2-0 |
| Nottingham Forest FC | 0-0 | 2-2 | 1-2 | 3-0 | 1-1 | 0-2 | 7-2 | 2-0 | 4-2 | 0-1 | 6-2 | 1-1 | 2-0 | | 2-0 | 1-3 | 2-1 | 6-1 | 2-3 | 4-1 | 4-2 | 0-1 |
| Notts County FC | 1-1 | 1-2 | 3-0 | 1-0 | 1-2 | 3-1 | 2-1 | 4-1 | 1-2 | 0-0 | 2-0 | 0-0 | 1-0 | 2-0 | | 1-1 | 2-1 | 3-2 | 2-2 | 2-2 | 1-1 | 1-2 |
| Oldham Athletic AFC | 2-0 | 1-3 | 4-3 | 1-3 | 1-4 | 1-0 | 2-2 | 2-2 | 1-5 | 7-0 | 3-0 | 2-0 | 1-0 | 4-1 | 2-0 | | 1-1 | 5-1 | 3-1 | 1-1 | 0-0 | 4-1 |
| Plymouth Argyle FC | 0-3 | 3-0 | 3-0 | 4-1 | 1-1 | 1-0 | 3-3 | 4-0 | 0-2 | 1-1 | 3-0 | 4-0 | 1-0 | 4-3 | 1-0 | 1-0 | | 3-0 | 0-0 | 0-0 | 2-2 | 4-4 |
| Port Vale FC | 1-0 | 0-0 | 3-1 | 3-1 | 1-0 | 0-2 | 4-1 | 2-2 | 0-1 | 3-0 | 1-0 | 2-3 | 5-1 | 3-1 | 0-0 | 2-0 | 4-0 | | 2-0 | 2-1 | 1-0 | 0-0 |
| Preston North End FC | 3-0 | 1-1 | 0-1 | 3-1 | 3-2 | 3-2 | 0-3 | 2-0 | 1-2 | 5-0 | 2-1 | 3-2 | 4-2 | 4-0 | 2-0 | 1-0 | 0-1 | 0-0 | | 3-1 | 3-0 | 1-1 |
| Southampton FC | 3-2 | 1-0 | 4-1 | 5-0 | 0-0 | 2-1 | 1-0 | 2-0 | 4-2 | 1-1 | 3-1 | 1-0 | 2-3 | 2-0 | 3-2 | 1-0 | 0-1 | 1-4 | 0-1 | | 1-0 | 3-2 |
| Swansea Town AFC | 2-2 | 0-0 | 2-1 | 5-1 | 2-3 | 3-0 | 1-1 | 1-0 | 1-1 | 1-1 | 1-0 | 2-1 | 2-0 | 1-1 | 1-1 | 2-2 | 2-1 | 4-0 | 1-2 | 1-0 | | 1-1 |
| West Ham United FC | 1-2 | 4-2 | 1-2 | 0-1 | 3-2 | 1-2 | 3-1 | 5-1 | 3-1 | 2-1 | 4-1 | 2-1 | 1-1 | 2-1 | 5-3 | 1-4 | 5-1 | 1-0 | 6-0 | 0-0 | 1-1 | |

## Division 2

|  |  | Pd | Wn | Dw | Ls | GF | GA | Pts |  |
|---|---|---|---|---|---|---|---|---|---|
| 1. | Grimsby Town FC (Cleethorpes) | 42 | 27 | 5 | 10 | 103 | 59 | 59 | P |
| 2. | Preston North End FC (Preston) | 42 | 23 | 6 | 13 | 71 | 52 | 52 | P |
| 3. | Bolton Wanderers FC (Bolton) | 42 | 21 | 9 | 12 | 79 | 55 | 51 | |
| 4. | Brentford FC (London) | 42 | 22 | 7 | 13 | 85 | 60 | 51 | |
| 5. | Bradford Park Avenue FC (Bradford) | 42 | 23 | 3 | 16 | 86 | 67 | 49 | |
| 6. | Bradford City AFC (Bradford) | 42 | 20 | 6 | 16 | 73 | 67 | 46 | |
| 7. | West Ham United FC (London) | 42 | 17 | 11 | 14 | 78 | 70 | 45 | |
| 8. | Port Vale FC (Stoke-on-Trent) | 42 | 19 | 7 | 16 | 60 | 55 | 45 | |
| 9. | Oldham Athletic AFC (Oldham) | 42 | 17 | 10 | 15 | 72 | 60 | 44 | |
| 10. | Plymouth Argyle FC (Plymouth) | 42 | 15 | 13 | 14 | 69 | 70 | 43 | |
| 11. | Blackpool FC (Blackpool) | 42 | 15 | 13 | 14 | 62 | 64 | 43 | |
| 12. | Bury FC (Bury) | 42 | 17 | 9 | 16 | 70 | 73 | 43 | |
| 13. | Burnley FC (Burnley) | 42 | 18 | 6 | 18 | 60 | 72 | 42 | |
| 14. | Southampton FC (Southampton) | 42 | 15 | 8 | 19 | 54 | 58 | 38 | |
| 15. | Hull City AFC (Kingston-upon-Hull) | 42 | 13 | 12 | 17 | 52 | 68 | 38 | |
| 16. | Fulham FC (London) | 42 | 15 | 7 | 20 | 48 | 67 | 37 | |
| 17. | Nottingham Forest FC (Nottingham) | 42 | 13 | 9 | 20 | 73 | 74 | 35 | |
| 18. | Notts County FC (Nottingham) | 42 | 12 | 11 | 19 | 53 | 62 | 35 | |
| 19. | Swansea Town AFC (Swansea) | 42 | 10 | 15 | 17 | 51 | 60 | 35 | |
| 20. | Manchester United FC (Manchester) | 42 | 14 | 6 | 22 | 50 | 85 | 34 | |
| 21. | Millwall FC (London) | 42 | 11 | 11 | 20 | 39 | 68 | 33 | R |
| 22. | Lincoln City FC (Lincoln) | 42 | 9 | 8 | 25 | 44 | 75 | 26 | R |
|  |  | 924 | 366 | 192 | 366 | 1441 | 1441 | 924 | |

156

| | Accrington Stan. | Barnsley | Barrow | Carlisle United | Chester | Chesterfield | Crewe Alexandra | Darlington | Doncaster Rovers | Gateshead | Halifax Town | Hartlepools United | Mansfield Town | New Brighton | Rochdale | Rotherham United | Southport | Stockport County | Tranmere Rovers | Walsall | Wrexham | York City |
|---|---|---|---|---|---|---|---|---|---|---|---|---|---|---|---|---|---|---|---|---|---|---|
| Accrington Stanley FC | ■ | 0-9 | 0-4 | 2-1 | 4-1 | 1-0 | 0-2 | 2-0 | 4-1 | 5-2 | 1-1 | 2-2 | 1-1 | 8-0 | 1-3 | 2-2 | 3-2 | 0-3 | 2-2 | 1-0 | 1-1 | 4-1 |
| Barnsley FC | 6-0 | ■ | 3-1 | 1-0 | 2-0 | 3-2 | 5-2 | 4-0 | 2-2 | 0-0 | 1-0 | 5-4 | 6-1 | 2-0 | 4-1 | 5-1 | 3-2 | 2-0 | 5-1 | 1-1 | 3-0 | 1-0 |
| Barrow AFC | 2-6 | 3-4 | ■ | 2-0 | 9-0 | 2-0 | 0-3 | 5-2 | 2-1 | 12-1 | 5-2 | 2-2 | 6-3 | 3-3 | 5-3 | 4-1 | 3-3 | 2-0 | 1-3 | 5-5 | 3-1 | 2-2 |
| Carlisle United FC | 3-0 | 1-4 | 0-0 | ■ | 1-0 | 1-1 | 6-1 | 3-3 | 0-1 | 6-0 | 1-0 | 4-1 | 3-2 | 1-2 | 3-0 | 0-1 | 0-0 | 2-2 | 2-1 | 3-2 | 0-0 | 3-2 |
| Chester FC | 7-0 | 4-2 | 1-3 | 3-3 | ■ | 3-2 | 1-0 | 8-0 | 3-1 | 4-0 | 1-2 | 3-3 | 1-1 | 0-0 | 7-1 | 5-1 | 1-0 | 1-1 | 4-2 | 0-1 | 1-2 | 1-1 |
| Chesterfield FC | 1-0 | 3-0 | 2-1 | 4-0 | 6-1 | ■ | 3-2 | 0-1 | 1-1 | 6-2 | 4-2 | 3-1 | 3-2 | 4-0 | 3-0 | 2-1 | 2-1 | 1-0 | 1-0 | 1-2 | 4-0 | 2-0 |
| Crewe Alexandra FC | 4-2 | 4-2 | 1-3 | 4-0 | 3-5 | 1-2 | ■ | 2-3 | 4-0 | 3-2 | 1-1 | 1-0 | 2-1 | 6-2 | 4-1 | 0-2 | 2-2 | 2-2 | 3-1 | 1-4 | 1-0 | 5-3 |
| Darlington FC | 3-1 | 0-4 | 4-1 | 1-2 | 0-4 | 1-1 | 1-1 | ■ | 4-0 | 3-3 | 4-2 | 5-3 | 1-4 | 1-0 | 1-1 | 4-1 | 4-0 | 1-2 | 1-3 | 2-1 | 2-1 | 4-0 |
| Doncaster Rovers FC | 5-1 | 4-4 | 3-2 | 2-1 | 3-1 | 1-3 | 4-0 | 3-2 | ■ | 5-2 | 3-0 | 3-0 | 1-0 | 1-0 | 5-0 | 2-1 | 3-0 | 0-2 | 2-0 | 4-0 | 1-4 | 3-1 |
| Gateshead FC | 2-0 | 1-4 | 0-0 | 2-3 | 1-3 | 2-1 | 2-1 | 2-2 | 2-4 | ■ | 4-0 | 6-3 | 5-3 | 6-0 | 2-1 | 4-1 | 2-2 | 0-4 | 1-2 | 2-1 | 0-3 | 0-2 |
| Halifax Town AFC | 2-1 | 1-1 | 4-1 | 3-2 | 1-0 | 5-0 | 3-2 | 2-0 | 0-1 | 2-4 | ■ | 6-2 | 4-2 | 1-1 | 4-2 | 3-2 | 6-2 | 4-2 | 0-2 | 2-1 | 2-0 | 3-0 |
| Hartlepools United FC | 3-0 | 0-2 | 7-0 | 3-2 | 1-0 | 0-3 | 2-1 | 6-2 | 2-2 | 3-3 | 5-0 | ■ | 3-1 | 2-1 | 2-1 | 4-0 | 1-2 | 3-1 | 1-1 | 0-1 | 4-1 | 2-0 |
| Mansfield Town FC | 5-0 | 1-5 | 0-5 | 6-0 | 2-1 | 0-3 | 4-1 | 4-0 | 1-1 | 1-1 | 6-1 | 1-1 | ■ | 5-2 | 5-0 | 3-0 | 2-2 | 1-1 | 0-0 | 1-2 | 1-1 | 0-2 |
| New Brighton FC | 0-3 | 0-1 | 2-2 | 2-1 | 0-2 | 0-0 | 2-1 | 3-2 | 2-2 | 3-1 | 4-1 | 5-1 | 0-2 | ■ | 3-1 | 5-2 | 2-1 | 1-0 | 2-0 | 0-1 | 2-1 | |
| Rochdale AFC | 0-1 | 3-1 | 1-2 | 0-1 | 6-0 | 0-1 | 2-0 | 1-0 | 0-2 | 2-0 | 1-2 | 3-0 | 2-2 | 1-1 | ■ | 0-2 | 3-3 | 1-1 | 1-0 | 3-3 | 1-2 | 3-6 |
| Rotherham United FC | 3-1 | 0-2 | 1-1 | 0-1 | 0-3 | 1-3 | 3-4 | 0-0 | 0-0 | 3-2 | 1-2 | 4-2 | 1-2 | 2-2 | 4-0 | ■ | 0-1 | 1-1 | 2-2 | 1-1 | 1-3 | 3-2 |
| Southport FC | 1-1 | 2-2 | 1-3 | 1-1 | 3-1 | 0-0 | 1-1 | 3-2 | 0-0 | 1-1 | 1-4 | 0-2 | 3-3 | 4-0 | 3-0 | 4-0 | ■ | 1-4 | 2-2 | 3-1 | 1-1 | 0-0 |
| Stockport County FC | 3-0 | 1-1 | 4-1 | 4-0 | 4-2 | 0-0 | 1-1 | 6-0 | 4-3 | 1-0 | 13-0 | 5-2 | 3-1 | 5-1 | 4-1 | 3-1 | 9-2 | ■ | 2-1 | 3-2 | 7-3 | 2-1 |
| Tranmere Rovers FC | 2-0 | 5-2 | 4-1 | 3-1 | 6-1 | 0-1 | 5-1 | 2-2 | 2-0 | 2-1 | 3-2 | 3-2 | 3-2 | 1-0 | 4-0 | 1-2 | 5-0 | 1-1 | ■ | 1-0 | 1-2 | 3-0 |
| Walsall FC | 5-0 | 5-1 | 2-4 | 3-2 | 5-0 | 2-2 | 5-1 | 3-0 | 2-0 | 5-1 | 2-0 | 5-0 | 0-0 | 2-1 | 2-0 | 3-1 | 4-1 | 2-0 | 5-3 | ■ | 3-1 | 1-0 |
| Wrexham AFC | 3-2 | 4-2 | 3-2 | 8-1 | 0-3 | 2-3 | 5-1 | 6-1 | 1-1 | 2-3 | 0-2 | 3-1 | 5-0 | 5-4 | 4-1 | 4-0 | 2-1 | 0-1 | 5-1 | 4-2 | ■ | 2-3 |
| York City FC | 3-2 | 1-1 | 6-1 | 4-1 | 3-2 | 1-2 | 4-1 | 1-1 | 1-2 | 1-1 | 1-0 | 1-3 | 1-0 | 2-1 | 6-1 | 0-1 | 1-0 | 2-2 | 1-0 | 2-2 | 2-4 | ■ |

## Division 3 (North)

| | | Pd | Wn | Dw | Ls | GF | GA | Pts | |
|---|---|---|---|---|---|---|---|---|---|
| 1. | Barnsley FC (Barnsley) | 42 | 27 | 8 | 7 | 118 | 61 | 62 | P |
| 2. | Chesterfield FC (Chesterfield) | 42 | 27 | 7 | 8 | 86 | 43 | 61 | |
| 3. | Stockport County FC (Stockport) | 42 | 24 | 11 | 7 | 115 | 52 | 59 | |
| 4. | Walsall FC (Walsall) | 42 | 23 | 7 | 12 | 97 | 60 | 53 | |
| 5. | Doncaster Rovers FC (Doncaster) | 42 | 22 | 9 | 11 | 83 | 61 | 53 | |
| 6. | Wrexham AFC (Wrexham) | 42 | 23 | 5 | 14 | 102 | 73 | 51 | |
| 7. | Tranmere Rovers FC (Birkenhead) | 42 | 20 | 7 | 15 | 84 | 63 | 47 | |
| 8. | Barrow AFC (Barrow-in-Furness) | 42 | 19 | 9 | 14 | 116 | 94 | 47 | |
| 9. | Halifax Town AFC (Halifax) | 42 | 20 | 4 | 18 | 80 | 91 | 44 | |
| 10. | Chester FC (Chester) | 42 | 17 | 6 | 19 | 89 | 86 | 40 | |
| 11. | Hartlepools United FC (Hartlepool) | 42 | 16 | 7 | 19 | 89 | 93 | 39 | |
| 12. | York City FC (York) | 42 | 15 | 8 | 19 | 71 | 74 | 38 | |
| 13. | Carlisle United FC (Carlisle) | 42 | 15 | 8 | 19 | 66 | 81 | 38 | |
| 14. | Crewe Alexandra FC (Crewe) | 42 | 15 | 6 | 21 | 81 | 97 | 36 | |
| 15. | New Brighton FC (Wallasey) | 42 | 14 | 8 | 20 | 62 | 87 | 36 | |
| 16. | Darlington FC (Darlington) | 42 | 13 | 9 | 20 | 70 | 101 | 35 | |
| 17. | Mansfield Town FC (Mansfield) | 42 | 11 | 12 | 19 | 81 | 88 | 34 | |
| 18. | Southport FC (Southport) | 42 | 8 | 17 | 17 | 63 | 90 | 33 | |
| 19. | Gateshead FC (Gateshead) | 42 | 12 | 9 | 21 | 76 | 110 | 33 | |
| 20. | Accrington Stanley FC (Accrington) | 42 | 13 | 7 | 22 | 65 | 101 | 33 | |
| 21. | Rotherham United FC (Rotherham) | 42 | 10 | 8 | 24 | 53 | 91 | 28 | |
| 22. | Rochdale AFC (Rochdale) | 42 | 9 | 6 | 27 | 53 | 103 | 24 | |
| | | 924 | 373 | 178 | 373 | 1800 | 1800 | 924 | |

| Football League Division 3 (S) 1933-1934 Season | Aldershot | Bournemouth | Brighton | Bristol City | Bristol Rovers | Cardiff City | Charlton Athletic | Clapton Orient | Coventry City | Crystal Palace | Exeter City | Gillingham | Luton Town | Newport County | Northampton | Norwich City | Q.P.R. | Reading | Southend United | Swindon Town | Torquay United | Watford |
|---|---|---|---|---|---|---|---|---|---|---|---|---|---|---|---|---|---|---|---|---|---|---|
| Aldershot FC | | 0-0 | 0-1 | 2-2 | 0-1 | 1-3 | 3-2 | 0-0 | 1-1 | 0-4 | 0-2 | 0-2 | 0-0 | 3-2 | 1-1 | 2-1 | 3-1 | 3-0 | 2-0 | 1-2 | 3-0 | 3-2 |
| Bournemouth & B. Athletic | 1-2 | | 1-1 | 5-0 | 2-0 | 1-3 | 1-2 | 2-0 | 3-3 | 1-1 | 1-3 | 1-1 | 4-3 | 0-0 | 4-0 | 2-4 | 3-2 | 1-1 | 1-4 | 1-1 | 3-4 | 3-2 |
| Brighton & Hove Albion | 3-1 | 6-0 | | 5-1 | 0-2 | 4-0 | 1-0 | 1-1 | 1-1 | 4-1 | 2-1 | 5-2 | 1-1 | 1-1 | 3-3 | 1-1 | 0-1 | 1-1 | 1-0 | 3-0 | 3-1 | 2-0 |
| Bristol City FC | 1-1 | 3-1 | 5-0 | | 0-3 | 3-0 | 0-1 | 3-0 | 0-0 | 2-2 | 1-1 | 1-1 | 0-0 | 1-1 | 2-3 | 0-1 | 0-2 | 1-2 | 5-1 | 2-2 | 2-0 | 1-0 |
| Bristol Rovers FC | 4-1 | 3-0 | 1-1 | 5-1 | | 3-1 | 2-5 | 2-2 | 4-1 | 0-1 | 1-1 | 4-2 | 0-1 | 2-0 | 1-1 | 3-0 | 4-1 | 1-0 | 3-1 | 3-0 | 2-1 | 1-0 |
| Cardiff City AFC | 1-2 | 4-2 | 1-4 | 1-5 | 1-5 | | 1-1 | 1-2 | 3-3 | 4-0 | 2-1 | 1-3 | 0-4 | 1-1 | 1-3 | 0-2 | 3-1 | 2-0 | 1-1 | 0-1 | 0-1 | 4-1 |
| Charlton Athletic FC | 1-0 | 4-3 | 4-3 | 2-1 | 2-1 | 2-0 | | 1-1 | 2-0 | 4-2 | 4-1 | 2-2 | 2-0 | 6-1 | 1-1 | 3-3 | 1-2 | 0-0 | 1-3 | 1-0 | 6-0 | 4-3 |
| Clapton Orient FC | 9-2 | 4-1 | 2-1 | 4-0 | 0-0 | 4-2 | 1-3 | | 0-0 | 2-0 | 4-0 | 2-1 | 1-1 | 3-0 | 5-1 | 3-2 | 2-2 | 2-3 | 5-2 | 1-0 | 4-1 | 2-3 |
| Coventry City FC | 5-1 | 4-1 | 2-0 | 9-0 | 5-3 | 4-1 | 3-2 | 3-1 | | 5-1 | 1-3 | 7-1 | 2-2 | 5-2 | 3-1 | 0-0 | 0-1 | 0-0 | 2-0 | 5-1 | 3-1 | 2-0 |
| Crystal Palace FC | 4-1 | 4-1 | 2-1 | 0-1 | 1-2 | 3-2 | 1-0 | 3-2 | 2-1 | | 0-0 | 3-2 | 2-2 | 1-1 | 1-2 | 0-1 | 4-1 | 0-0 | 1-1 | 0-0 | 4-1 | 4-3 |
| Exeter City FC | 0-0 | 4-0 | 3-0 | 2-0 | 0-0 | 4-0 | 2-0 | 0-3 | 1-0 | 1-2 | | 2-0 | 4-2 | 1-1 | 0-2 | 3-4 | 1-1 | 4-1 | 2-0 | 2-2 | 4-0 | 3-1 |
| Gillingham FC | 1-2 | 5-1 | 3-0 | 2-1 | 3-2 | 6-2 | 1-1 | 1-1 | 3-7 | 0-5 | 1-1 | | 1-1 | 1-0 | 5-1 | 1-2 | 1-4 | 5-1 | 0-0 | 3-3 | 3-3 | 3-3 |
| Luton Town FC | 1-1 | 2-0 | 1-2 | 3-0 | 2-2 | 3-1 | 2-1 | 2-0 | 0-1 | 2-1 | 3-2 | 4-2 | | 1-1 | 3-1 | 2-3 | 4-2 | 3-1 | 3-1 | 2-3 | 10-2 | 2-1 |
| Newport County AFC | 1-2 | 1-1 | 2-2 | 2-2 | 1-0 | 2-2 | 1-1 | 1-1 | 0-0 | 1-0 | 1-0 | 3-1 | 1-2 | | 2-0 | 0-0 | 1-2 | 1-2 | 3-0 | 1-2 | 0-0 | 0-3 |
| Northampton Town FC | 0-0 | 4-1 | 1-1 | 2-3 | 1-2 | 2-0 | 1-2 | 3-0 | 2-2 | 4-2 | 5-3 | 1-0 | 2-3 | 5-3 | | 2-2 | 2-1 | 2-4 | 2-2 | 2-2 | 1-1 | 1-0 |
| Norwich City FC | 2-2 | 6-1 | 4-3 | 7-2 | 0-0 | 2-0 | 3-0 | 3-0 | 3-1 | 2-0 | 1-1 | 4-1 | 4-0 | 2-1 | 2-0 | | 1-0 | 3-2 | 0-0 | 3-2 | 0-2 | 3-1 |
| Queen's Park Rangers FC | 2-4 | 1-0 | 2-0 | 1-0 | 1-0 | 4-0 | 2-1 | 2-0 | 0-1 | 2-1 | 2-0 | 5-0 | 2-1 | 2-1 | 2-1 | 5-2 | | 0-0 | 4-0 | 1-0 | 2-0 | 0-0 |
| Reading FC | 3-2 | 4-0 | 2-0 | 1-1 | 2-2 | 3-1 | 1-0 | 4-1 | 0-0 | 3-1 | 2-0 | 4-1 | 4-0 | 2-2 | 1-0 | 5-0 | 5-0 | | 5-0 | 2-0 | 5-2 | 6-1 |
| Southend United FC | 1-0 | 1-2 | 0-0 | 3-0 | 2-1 | 1-1 | 2-0 | 1-2 | 2-1 | 0-4 | 1-2 | 0-1 | 3-5 | 2-0 | 0-0 | 0-2 | 2-2 | | | 4-1 | 3-1 | 1-0 |
| Swindon Town FC | 1-0 | 3-2 | 1-1 | 4-2 | 1-0 | 6-3 | 1-3 | 3-0 | 0-1 | 3-2 | 1-1 | 3-1 | 3-1 | 1-1 | 1-1 | 0-0 | 3-1 | 3-1 | 1-4 | | 2-0 | 1-0 |
| Torquay United FC | 0-0 | 1-0 | 0-1 | 2-2 | 2-1 | 3-1 | 1-4 | 2-1 | 1-3 | 0-2 | 0-2 | 2-1 | 1-2 | 3-2 | 1-2 | 1-1 | 1-1 | 3-0 | 2-0 | | | 1-3 |
| Watford FC | 3-0 | 1-2 | 2-0 | 1-1 | 0-0 | 1-2 | 0-1 | 6-0 | 3-3 | 3-1 | 2-0 | 2-1 | 0-1 | 3-0 | 2-0 | 1-3 | 0-0 | 2-0 | 2-1 | 4-0 | 5-0 | |

### Division 3 (South)

| | | Pd | Wn | Dw | Ls | GF | GA | Pts | |
|---|---|---|---|---|---|---|---|---|---|
| 1. | Norwich City FC (Norwich) | 42 | 25 | 11 | 6 | 88 | 49 | 61 | P |
| 2. | Coventry City FC (Coventry) | 42 | 21 | 12 | 9 | 100 | 54 | 54 | |
| 3. | Reading FC (Reading) | 42 | 21 | 12 | 9 | 82 | 50 | 54 | |
| 4. | Queen's Park Rangers FC (London) | 42 | 24 | 6 | 12 | 70 | 51 | 54 | |
| 5. | Charlton Athletic FC (London) | 42 | 22 | 8 | 12 | 83 | 56 | 52 | |
| 6. | Luton Town FC (Luton) | 42 | 21 | 10 | 11 | 83 | 61 | 52 | |
| 7. | Bristol Rovers FC (Bristol) | 42 | 20 | 11 | 11 | 77 | 47 | 51 | |
| 8. | Swindon Town FC (Swindon) | 42 | 17 | 11 | 14 | 64 | 68 | 45 | |
| 9. | Exeter City FC (Exeter) | 42 | 16 | 11 | 15 | 68 | 57 | 43 | |
| 10. | Brighton & Hove Albion FC (Hove) | 42 | 15 | 13 | 14 | 68 | 60 | 43 | |
| 11. | Clapton Orient FC (London) | 42 | 16 | 10 | 16 | 75 | 69 | 42 | |
| 12. | Crystal Palace FC (London) | 42 | 16 | 9 | 17 | 71 | 67 | 41 | |
| 13. | Northampton Town FC (Northampton) | 42 | 14 | 12 | 16 | 71 | 78 | 40 | |
| 14. | Aldershot FC (Aldershot) | 42 | 13 | 12 | 17 | 52 | 71 | 38 | |
| 15. | Watford FC (Watford) | 42 | 15 | 7 | 20 | 71 | 63 | 37 | |
| 16. | Southend United FC (Southend-on-Sea) | 42 | 12 | 10 | 20 | 51 | 74 | 34 | |
| 17. | Gillingham FC (Gillingham) | 42 | 11 | 11 | 20 | 75 | 96 | 33 | |
| 18. | Newport County AFC (Newport) | 42 | 8 | 17 | 17 | 49 | 70 | 33 | |
| 19. | Bristol City FC (Bristol) | 42 | 10 | 13 | 19 | 58 | 85 | 33 | |
| 20. | Torquay United FC (Torquay) | 42 | 13 | 7 | 22 | 53 | 93 | 33 | |
| 21. | Bournemouth & Boscombe Athletic FC (Bournemouth) | 42 | 9 | 9 | 24 | 60 | 102 | 27 | |
| 22. | Cardiff City AFC (Cardiff) | 42 | 9 | 6 | 27 | 57 | 105 | 24 | |
| | | 924 | 348 | 228 | 348 | 1526 | 1526 | 924 | |

# F.A. CUP FINAL   (Wembley Stadium, London – 28/04/1934 – 93,258)

MANCHESTER CITY FC (MANCHESTER)   2-1   Portsmouth FC (Portsmouth)

Tilson 2                                                                                          *Rutherford*

Man. City: Swift, Barnett, Dale, Busby, Cowan, Bray, Toseland, Marshall, Tilson, Herd, Brook.

Portsmouth: Gilfillan, Mackie, W.Smith, Nichol, Allen, Thackeray, Worrall, J.Smith, Weddle, Easson, Rutherford.

## Semi-finals

| Manchester City FC (Manchester) | 6-1 | Aston Villa FC (Birmingham) |
| Portsmouth FC (Portsmouth) | 4-1 | Leicester City FC (Leicester) |

## Quarter-finals

| Arsenal FC (London) | 1-2 | Aston Villa FC (Birmingham) |
| Bolton Wanderers FC (Bolton) | 0-3 | Portsmouth FC (Portsmouth) |
| Manchester City FC (Manchester) | 1-0 | Stoke City FC (Stoke-on-Trent) |
| Preston North End FC (Preston) | 0-1 | Leicester City FC (Leicester) |

# 1934-35

**Football League Division 1, 1934-1935 Season**

| | Ars | AV | Bir | Bla | Che | Der | Eve | Gri | Hud | Lee | Lei | Liv | MC | Mid | Por | PNE | SW | Sto | Sun | Tot | WBA | Wol |
|---|---|---|---|---|---|---|---|---|---|---|---|---|---|---|---|---|---|---|---|---|---|---|
| Arsenal FC | ■ | 1-2 | 5-1 | 4-0 | 2-2 | 0-1 | 2-0 | 1-1 | 1-0 | 3-0 | 8-0 | 8-1 | 3-0 | 8-0 | 1-1 | 5-3 | 4-1 | 2-0 | 0-0 | 5-1 | 4-3 | 7-0 |
| Aston Villa FC | 1-3 | ■ | 2-2 | 1-1 | 0-3 | 3-2 | 2-2 | 3-2 | 1-1 | 1-1 | 5-0 | 4-2 | 4-2 | 0-3 | 5-4 | 42 | 4-0 | 4-1 | 1-1 | 1-0 | 2-3 | 2-1 |
| Birmingham FC | 3-0 | 2-1 | ■ | 1-0 | 0-1 | 3-2 | 2-3 | 3-2 | 0-4 | 3-1 | 2-3 | 1-3 | 1-3 | 4-2 | 2-1 | 3-0 | 0-4 | 0-0 | 2-2 | 2-1 | 1-2 | 1-1 |
| Blackburn Rovers FC | 2-0 | 5-0 | 3-1 | ■ | 1-2 | 2-5 | 6-2 | 2-2 | 4-2 | 1-1 | 0-0 | 0-2 | 1-0 | 3-2 | 0-0 | 1-0 | 2-1 | 0-1 | 0-0 | 2-0 | 3-0 | 4-2 |
| Chelsea FC | 2-5 | 2-0 | 2-2 | 4-2 | ■ | 1-1 | 3-0 | 2-0 | 2-1 | 7-1 | 3-1 | 4-1 | 4-2 | 2-1 | 1-1 | 0-0 | 1-2 | 0-2 | 2-2 | 1-3 | 2-3 | 4-2 |
| Derby County FC | 3-1 | 1-1 | 1-1 | 1-1 | 3-0 | ■ | 4-1 | 1-4 | 4-1 | 1-2 | 1-1 | 1-2 | 1-2 | 2-0 | 0-1 | 0-3 | 4-0 | 0-2 | 3-1 | 2-1 | 9-3 | 2-0 |
| Everton FC | 0-2 | 2-2 | 2-0 | 5-2 | 3-2 | 2-2 | ■ | 3-1 | 4-2 | 4-4 | 2-1 | 1-0 | 1-2 | 1-1 | 3-2 | 4-1 | 2-2 | 5-0 | 6-2 | 5-2 | 4-0 | 5-2 |
| Grimsby Town FC | 2-2 | 5-1 | 4-3 | 1-2 | 3-1 | 1-3 | 0-0 | ■ | 1-1 | 3-2 | 3-1 | 3-2 | 1-1 | 2-2 | 3-0 | 3-1 | 3-1 | 3-1 | 0-0 | 3-0 | 3-0 | 2-1 |
| Huddersfield Town AFC | 1-1 | 1-1 | 2-2 | 6-0 | 3-0 | 1-0 | 1-1 | 1-5 | ■ | 3-1 | 2-3 | 8-0 | 3-0 | 3-1 | 2-0 | 3-4 | 4-0 | 1-4 | 0-3 | 0-0 | 3-0 | 4-1 |
| Leeds United AFC | 1-1 | 1-1 | 1-1 | 5-1 | 5-2 | 4-2 | 2-0 | 3-1 | 2-0 | ■ | 0-2 | 0-3 | 1-2 | 2-4 | 3-1 | 3-3 | 0-0 | 4-2 | 2-4 | 4-3 | 4-1 | 1-1 |
| Leicester City FC | 3-5 | 5-0 | 2-1 | 0-1 | 1-0 | 0-1 | 5-2 | 2-2 | 0-3 | 1-0 | ■ | 3-1 | 1-3 | 3-1 | 6-3 | 0-0 | 0-1 | 0-3 | 0-2 | 6-0 | 0-0 | 1-1 |
| Liverpool FC | 0-2 | 3-1 | 5-4 | 2-0 | 6-0 | 1-3 | 2-1 | 1-1 | 3-2 | 4-2 | 5-1 | ■ | 2-1 | 2-2 | 0-0 | 1-2 | 5-0 | 2-2 | 4-1 | 3-2 | 2-1 | |
| Manchester City FC | 1-1 | 4-1 | 0-0 | 3-3 | 2-0 | 0-1 | 2-2 | 1-0 | 3-0 | 6-3 | 3-1 | | ■ | 6-2 | 2-4 | 1-2 | 4-1 | 3-1 | 1-0 | 3-1 | 3-2 | 5-0 |
| Middlesbrough FC | 0-1 | 4-1 | 0-1 | 3-3 | 2-2 | 1-1 | 3-2 | 0-2 | 2-1 | 3-3 | 1-0 | 2-0 | 1-2 | ■ | 1-1 | 3-3 | 5-3 | 2-0 | 0-0 | 3-1 | 0-0 | 2-2 |
| Portsmouth FC | 3-3 | 0-1 | 2-1 | 3-1 | 1-1 | 5-1 | 5-1 | 1-0 | 5-0 | 0-0 | 1-1 | 1-2 | 4-2 | 1-0 | ■ | 4-0 | 2-1 | 0-1 | 2-4 | 1-1 | 0-2 | 0-1 |
| Preston North End FC | 2-1 | 0-0 | 0-1 | 3-1 | 2-0 | 0-1 | 2-2 | 1-0 | 2-0 | 0-2 | 2-0 | 2-2 | 2-4 | 2-0 | 1-1 | ■ | 2-1 | 5-2 | 1-1 | 1-0 | 1-2 | 2-1 |
| Sheffield Wednesday FC | 0-0 | 2-1 | 2-1 | 2-2 | 3-1 | 1-0 | 0-0 | 1-1 | 1-0 | 1-1 | 4-1 | 1-0 | 3-3 | 3-0 | 2-1 | | ■ | 4-1 | 2-2 | 4-0 | 2-1 | 3-1 |
| Stoke City FC | 2-2 | 4-1 | 2-0 | 3-1 | 0-1 | 1-1 | 3-2 | 0-0 | 2-0 | 8-1 | 3-0 | 1-1 | 2-0 | 2-0 | 1-2 | 3-1 | 1-1 | ■ | 0-3 | 4-1 | 3-0 | 1-2 |
| Sunderland AFC | 2-1 | 3-3 | 5-1 | 3-0 | 4-0 | 1-4 | 7-0 | 3-0 | 4-1 | 3-0 | 2-0 | 2-3 | 3-2 | 1-1 | 4-1 | 3-1 | 2-2 | 4-1 | ■ | 1-2 | 0-1 | 0-0 |
| Tottenham Hotspur FC | 0-6 | 0-2 | 1-1 | 1-0 | 1-3 | 2-2 | 1-1 | 2-1 | 0-0 | 1-1 | 2-2 | 5-1 | 0-0 | 3-1 | 4-1 | 1-2 | 3-2 | 3-2 | 1-1 | ■ | 0-1 | 3-1 |
| West Bromwich Albion FC | 0-3 | 2-2 | 1-2 | 2-2 | 2-2 | 4-3 | 0-1 | 4-2 | 4-1 | 6-3 | 4-1 | 1-1 | 1-1 | 6-3 | 4-0 | 0-0 | 1-1 | 3-0 | 1-1 | 4-0 | ■ | 5-2 |
| Wolverhampton Wanderers FC | 1-1 | 5-2 | 3-1 | 2-1 | 6-1 | 5-1 | 4-2 | 0-3 | 2-3 | 1-2 | 3-1 | 5-3 | 5-0 | 5-3 | 2-3 | 2-2 | 2-1 | 1-2 | 6-2 | 3-2 | | ■ |

| | Division 1 | Pd | Wn | Dw | Ls | GF | GA | Pts | |
|---|---|---|---|---|---|---|---|---|---|
| 1. | ARSENAL FC (LONDON) | 42 | 23 | 12 | 7 | 115 | 46 | 58 | |
| 2. | Sunderland AFC (Sunderland) | 42 | 19 | 16 | 7 | 90 | 51 | 54 | |
| 3. | Sheffield Wednesday FC (Sheffield) | 42 | 18 | 13 | 11 | 70 | 64 | 49 | |
| 4. | Manchester City FC (Manchester) | 42 | 20 | 8 | 14 | 82 | 67 | 48 | |
| 5. | Grimsby Town FC (Cleethorpes) | 42 | 17 | 11 | 14 | 78 | 60 | 45 | |
| 6. | Derby County FC (Derby) | 42 | 18 | 9 | 15 | 81 | 66 | 45 | |
| 7. | Liverpool FC (Liverpool) | 42 | 19 | 7 | 16 | 85 | 88 | 45 | |
| 8. | Everton FC (Liverpool) | 42 | 16 | 12 | 14 | 89 | 88 | 44 | |
| 9. | West Bromwich Albion FC (West Bromwich) | 42 | 17 | 10 | 15 | 83 | 83 | 44 | |
| 10. | Stoke City FC (Stoke-on-Trent) | 42 | 18 | 6 | 18 | 71 | 70 | 42 | |
| 11. | Preston North End FC (Preston) | 42 | 15 | 12 | 15 | 62 | 67 | 42 | |
| 12. | Chelsea FC (Chelsea) | 42 | 16 | 9 | 17 | 73 | 82 | 41 | |
| 13. | Aston Villa FC (Birmingham) | 42 | 14 | 13 | 15 | 74 | 88 | 41 | |
| 14. | Portsmouth FC (Portsmouth) | 42 | 15 | 10 | 17 | 71 | 72 | 40 | |
| 15. | Blackburn Rovers FC (Blackburn) | 42 | 14 | 11 | 17 | 66 | 78 | 39 | |
| 16. | Huddersfield Town AFC (Huddersfield) | 42 | 14 | 10 | 18 | 76 | 71 | 38 | |
| 17. | Wolverhampton Wanderers FC (Wolverhampton) | 42 | 15 | 8 | 19 | 88 | 94 | 38 | |
| 18. | Leeds United AFC (Leeds) | 42 | 13 | 12 | 17 | 75 | 92 | 38 | |
| 19. | Birmingham FC (Birmingham) | 42 | 13 | 10 | 19 | 63 | 81 | 36 | |
| 20. | Middlesbrough FC (Middlesbrough) | 42 | 10 | 14 | 18 | 70 | 90 | 34 | |
| 21. | Leicester City FC (Leicester) | 42 | 12 | 9 | 21 | 61 | 86 | 33 | R |
| 22. | Tottenham Hotspur FC (London) | 42 | 10 | 10 | 22 | 54 | 93 | 30 | R |
| | | 924 | 346 | 232 | 346 | 1677 | 1677 | 924 | |

## Top Goalscorer

1) Ted DRAKE　　　　　　　　　　(Arsenal FC)　　42

160

| Football League Division 2 1934-1935 Season | Barnsley | Blackpool | Bolton Wands. | Bradford City | Bradford P.A. | Brentford | Burnley | Bury | Fulham | Hull City | Man. United | Newcastle Utd. | Norwich City | Nottingham F. | Notts County | Oldham Athletic | Plymouth Arg. | Port Vale | Sheffield United | Southampton | Swansea Town | West Ham Utd. |
|---|---|---|---|---|---|---|---|---|---|---|---|---|---|---|---|---|---|---|---|---|---|---|
| Barnsley FC | ■ | 2-2 | 1-1 | 2-0 | 1-1 | 3-3 | 0-0 | 3-0 | 2-0 | 2-2 | 0-2 | 2-1 | 2-1 | 1-2 | 1-1 | 4-0 | 1-4 | 2-0 | 0-0 | 1-1 | 1-0 | 1-1 |
| Blackpool FC | 3-0 | ■ | 1-1 | 2-1 | 1-0 | 2-2 | 1-0 | 1-1 | 1-1 | 2-1 | 1-2 | 4-1 | 2-1 | 1-0 | 3-1 | 4-0 | 4-1 | 3-1 | 1-0 | 4-1 | 2-1 | 3-2 |
| Bolton Wanderers FC | 8-0 | 4-2 | ■ | 3-0 | 1-2 | 2-0 | 7-0 | 2-0 | 4-0 | 1-2 | 3-1 | 1-0 | 4-0 | 2-3 | 5-1 | 2-0 | 3-2 | 2-0 | 1-1 | 4-0 | 1-0 | 3-1 |
| Bradford City AFC | 1-0 | 0-2 | 1-1 | ■ | 3-1 | 3-0 | 1-1 | 0-0 | 0-0 | 3-2 | 2-0 | 3-3 | 1-1 | 4-0 | 2-0 | 2-0 | 0-1 | 3-0 | 2-5 | 1-1 | 2-0 | 0-2 |
| Bradford Park Avenue | 3-2 | 0-0 | 4-0 | 2-1 | ■ | 2-3 | 1-1 | 2-1 | 0-0 | 1-2 | 1-2 | 1-3 | 1-1 | 1-1 | 0-0 | 2-0 | 2-2 | 1-1 | 1-3 | 3-1 | 3-1 | 1-3 |
| Brentford FC | 8-1 | 2-1 | 1-0 | 2-0 | 1-0 | ■ | 6-1 | 2-1 | 1-0 | 2-1 | 3-1 | 3-0 | 2-1 | 1-1 | 4-1 | 2-1 | 0-0 | 8-0 | 3-1 | 3-2 | 1-0 | 4-1 |
| Burnley FC | 4-1 | 1-2 | 2-1 | 2-0 | 1-2 | 0-3 | ■ | 3-3 | 3-1 | 1-3 | 1-2 | 0-3 | 1-0 | 2-1 | 4-0 | 4-2 | 1-2 | 2-2 | 0-2 | 3-0 | 3-0 | 5-2 |
| Bury FC | 4-1 | 1-5 | 2-1 | 2-1 | 2-4 | 4-1 | 0-0 | ■ | 2-0 | 0-1 | 0-1 | 0-2 | 1-0 | 1-0 | 1-0 | 2-0 | 2-1 | 3-1 | 3-1 | 4-1 | 2-1 | 2-4 |
| Fulham FC | 1-3 | 4-1 | 2-1 | 3-1 | 2-2 | 2-2 | 2-0 | 1-2 | ■ | 4-0 | 3-1 | 3-2 | 1-3 | 2-1 | 7-0 | 3-1 | 3-0 | 2-0 | 7-2 | 3-3 | 4-1 | 3-0 |
| Hull City AFC | 1-1 | 2-2 | 0-2 | 1-0 | 2-0 | 2-1 | 1-3 | 0-1 | 1-2 | ■ | 3-2 | 1-1 | 5-0 | 5-1 | 1-1 | 1-1 | 1-0 | 0-3 | 0-0 | 0-0 | 0-1 | 4-0 |
| Manchester United FC | 4-1 | 3-2 | 0-3 | 2-0 | 2-0 | 0-0 | 3-4 | 1-0 | 1-0 | 3-0 | ■ | 0-1 | 5-0 | 3-2 | 2-1 | 4-0 | 3-1 | 2-1 | 3-3 | 3-0 | 3-1 | 3-1 |
| Newcastle United FC | 4-1 | 4-1 | 1-3 | 4-2 | 0-1 | 2-5 | 2-0 | 5-1 | 1-1 | 6-2 | 0-1 | ■ | 2-0 | 2-0 | 1-1 | 4-2 | 3-0 | 1-2 | 4-1 | 1-0 | 5-1 | 3-0 |
| Norwich City FC | 0-1 | 1-1 | 2-3 | 6-1 | 3-0 | 2-2 | 2-3 | 4-1 | 0-0 | 3-0 | 3-2 | 2-0 | ■ | 3-3 | 7-2 | 0-0 | 3-0 | 0-0 | 3-1 | 4-0 | 2-2 | 1-2 |
| Nottingham Forest FC | 4-1 | 0-0 | 0-1 | 2-0 | 2-2 | 0-0 | 5-0 | 1-4 | 1-1 | 2-1 | 2-2 | 5-1 | 5-2 | ■ | 2-3 | 4-0 | 1-3 | 2-0 | 2-1 | 3-1 | 1-0 | 2-0 |
| Notts County FC | 1-4 | 3-2 | 0-2 | 2-3 | 1-1 | 0-1 | 1-0 | 1-2 | 1-1 | 1-1 | 1-0 | 0-1 | 1-0 | 3-5 | ■ | 2-1 | 1-3 | 3-2 | 0-1 | 3-1 | 4-0 | 0-2 |
| Oldham Athletic AFC | 1-4 | 2-3 | 1-4 | 3-1 | 1-1 | 1-3 | 1-2 | 7-2 | 2-1 | 5-0 | 3-1 | 3-2 | 4-2 | 0-5 | 1-0 | ■ | 1-1 | 2-0 | 3-2 | 0-2 | 2-2 | 1-2 |
| Plymouth Argyle FC | 3-1 | 1-2 | 1-0 | 3-1 | 2-2 | 1-1 | 2-2 | 3-0 | 3-1 | 6-4 | 0-2 | 1-3 | 0-1 | 5-2 | 4-0 | 2-0 | ■ | 2-1 | 2-0 | 4-0 | 3-2 | 0-1 |
| Port Vale FC | 4-0 | 2-2 | 1-3 | 1-0 | 1-1 | 2-2 | 3-1 | 0-1 | 1-1 | 1-2 | 3-2 | 1-3 | 1-1 | 2-0 | 5-3 | 2-0 | 2-2 | ■ | 2-0 | 4-1 | 2-1 | 2-2 |
| Sheffield United FC | 2-1 | 1-1 | 6-2 | 1-2 | 3-1 | 1-2 | 0-0 | 5-3 | 1-2 | 3-4 | 3-2 | 5-1 | 1-1 | 2-1 | 3-0 | 1-2 | 3-0 | ■ | 6-1 | 1-1 | 1-2 |
| Southampton FC | 0-1 | 2-0 | 1-2 | 1-1 | 4-1 | 1-0 | 0-0 | 2-1 | 1-1 | 3-0 | 1-0 | 2-0 | 1-4 | 1-2 | 1-1 | 2-2 | 1-0 | 0-0 | 1-1 | ■ | 1-0 | 2-2 |
| Swansea Town AFC | 1-1 | 2-1 | 2-1 | 3-1 | 0-0 | 2-4 | 2-0 | 1-0 | 2-0 | 2-1 | 1-0 | 3-4 | 1-1 | 3-0 | 2-1 | 5-1 | 3-0 | 1-1 | 0-0 | 0-1 | ■ | 5-4 |
| West Ham United FC | 4-3 | 2-1 | 4-1 | 1-0 | 2-1 | 2-0 | 1-2 | 3-0 | 2-1 | 1-2 | 0-0 | 3-2 | 1-0 | 3-1 | 4-0 | 2-0 | 2-1 | 3-1 | 2-0 | 2-1 | 2-0 | ■ |

## Division 2

| | | Pd | Wn | Dw | Ls | GF | GA | Pts | |
|---|---|---|---|---|---|---|---|---|---|
| 1. | Brentford FC (London) | 42 | 26 | 9 | 7 | 93 | 48 | 61 | P |
| 2. | Bolton Wanderers FC (Bolton) | 42 | 26 | 4 | 12 | 96 | 48 | 56 | P |
| 3. | West Ham United FC (London) | 42 | 26 | 4 | 12 | 80 | 63 | 56 | |
| 4. | Blackpool FC (Blackpool) | 42 | 21 | 11 | 10 | 79 | 57 | 53 | |
| 5. | Manchester United FC (Manchester) | 42 | 23 | 4 | 15 | 76 | 55 | 50 | |
| 6. | Newcastle United FC (Newcastle-upon-Tyne) | 42 | 22 | 4 | 16 | 89 | 68 | 48 | |
| 7. | Fulham FC (London) | 42 | 17 | 12 | 13 | 76 | 56 | 46 | |
| 8. | Plymouth Argyle FC (Plymouth) | 42 | 19 | 8 | 15 | 75 | 64 | 46 | |
| 9. | Nottingham Forest FC (Nottingham) | 42 | 17 | 8 | 17 | 76 | 70 | 42 | |
| 10. | Bury FC (Bury) | 42 | 19 | 4 | 19 | 62 | 73 | 42 | |
| 11. | Sheffield United FC (Sheffield) | 42 | 16 | 9 | 17 | 79 | 70 | 41 | |
| 12. | Burnley FC (Burnley) | 42 | 16 | 9 | 17 | 63 | 73 | 41 | |
| 13. | Hull City AFC (Kingston-upon-Hull) | 42 | 16 | 8 | 18 | 63 | 74 | 40 | |
| 14. | Norwich City FC (Norwich) | 42 | 14 | 11 | 17 | 71 | 61 | 39 | |
| 15. | Bradford Park Avenue FC (Bradford) | 42 | 11 | 16 | 15 | 55 | 63 | 38 | |
| 16. | Barnsley FC (Barnsley) | 42 | 13 | 12 | 17 | 60 | 83 | 38 | |
| 17. | Swansea Town AFC (Swansea) | 42 | 14 | 8 | 20 | 56 | 67 | 36 | |
| 18. | Port Vale FC (Stoke-on-Trent) | 42 | 11 | 12 | 19 | 55 | 74 | 34 | |
| 19. | Southampton FC (Southampton) | 42 | 11 | 12 | 19 | 46 | 75 | 34 | |
| 20. | Bradford City AFC (Bradford) | 42 | 12 | 8 | 22 | 50 | 68 | 32 | |
| 21. | Oldham Athletic AFC (Oldham) | 42 | 10 | 6 | 26 | 56 | 95 | 26 | R |
| 22. | Notts County FC (Nottingham) | 42 | 9 | 7 | 26 | 46 | 97 | 25 | R |
| | | 924 | 369 | 186 | 369 | 1502 | 1502 | 924 | |

## Football League Division 3 (N) — 1934-1935 Season

| | Accrington Stan. | Barrow | Carlisle United | Chester | Chesterfield | Crewe Alexandra | Darlington | Doncaster Rovers | Gateshead | Halifax Town | Hartlepools United | Lincoln City | Mansfield Town | New Brighton | Rochdale | Rotherham United | Southport | Stockport County | Tranmere Rovers | Walsall | Wrexham | York City |
|---|---|---|---|---|---|---|---|---|---|---|---|---|---|---|---|---|---|---|---|---|---|---|
| Accrington Stanley FC | | 5-2 | 1-0 | 1-1 | 1-0 | 3-0 | 2-1 | 1-5 | 4-2 | 1-1 | 0-4 | 3-0 | 2-0 | 1-3 | 2-5 | 2-3 | 1-1 | 3-1 | 1-0 | 3-3 | 2-2 | 5-2 |
| Barrow AFC | 0-2 | | 2-1 | 4-2 | 1-1 | 1-1 | 4-4 | 2-1 | 3-2 | 2-0 | 2-0 | 1-1 | 3-0 | 1-2 | 1-1 | 2-1 | 2-1 | 1-4 | 1-0 | 3-1 | 1-3 | 0-3 |
| Carlisle United FC | 2-0 | 0-0 | | 1-3 | 3-1 | 1-3 | 1-2 | 1-1 | 5-4 | 2-4 | 2-2 | 2-1 | 1-1 | 4-1 | 0-0 | 2-1 | 0-1 | 1-2 | 1-1 | 1-6 | 0-2 | 4-0 |
| Chester FC | 4-0 | 6-2 | 3-0 | | 1-1 | 2-2 | 3-1 | 1-3 | 2-2 | 5-0 | 4-1 | 0-1 | 3-2 | 5-4 | 1-0 | 4-1 | 0-2 | 5-1 | 0-0 | 2-1 | 6-2 | 5-1 |
| Chesterfield FC | 0-0 | 3-0 | 3-0 | 1-2 | | 1-2 | 2-2 | 3-2 | 3-1 | 4-0 | 4-0 | 3-1 | 0-0 | 1-0 | 2-0 | 2-1 | 3-3 | 5-0 | 0-2 | 2-0 | 1-4 | 3-1 |
| Crewe Alexandra FC | 4-2 | 4-3 | 1-1 | 1-1 | 1-0 | | 4-1 | 1-1 | 2-1 | 3-1 | 1-1 | 1-0 | 1-1 | 2-3 | 4-1 | 0-0 | 2-1 | 2-3 | 1-2 | 1-0 | 2-0 | 3-2 |
| Darlington FC | 5-0 | 3-1 | 5-0 | 1-0 | 2-1 | 6-2 | | 1-1 | 2-1 | 0-1 | 3-0 | 4-1 | 1-0 | 2-2 | 4-0 | 0-0 | 0-0 | 2-2 | 3-2 | 3-1 | | 2-0 |
| Doncaster Rovers FC | 2-1 | 2-0 | 3-0 | 3-0 | 0-2 | 2-0 | 2-0 | | 5-0 | 0-1 | 3-1 | 1-3 | 2-1 | 7-1 | 1-0 | 3-5 | 2-0 | 3-4 | 2-0 | 4-0 | 2-1 | 4-1 |
| Gateshead FC | 1-1 | 1-0 | 3-2 | 2-4 | 1-4 | 5-2 | 3-0 | 0-0 | | 3-1 | 2-1 | 0-2 | 2-2 | 2-1 | 2-0 | 1-1 | 1-2 | 3-2 | 0-2 | 1-0 | 1-0 | 2-1 |
| Halifax Town AFC | 2-1 | 2-1 | 4-0 | 1-0 | 0-2 | 1-0 | 2-1 | 1-0 | 4-0 | | 4-1 | 2-1 | 2-1 | 6-2 | 1-1 | 2-1 | 4-3 | 2-1 | 1-2 | 1-1 | 3-2 | 5-3 |
| Hartlepools United FC | 4-2 | 5-2 | 5-2 | 0-2 | 1-1 | 4-2 | 0-1 | 2-1 | 1-2 | 0-3 | | 1-5 | 1-1 | 2-2 | 0-0 | 3-1 | 4-1 | 4-0 | 6-1 | 2-1 | 4-3 | 3-1 |
| Lincoln City FC | 1-0 | 6-0 | 4-2 | 0-0 | 2-0 | 1-1 | 2-4 | 0-2 | 5-0 | 2-3 | 2-1 | | 4-0 | 1-0 | 3-0 | 4-0 | 4-1 | 3-0 | 2-2 | 5-1 | 1-3 | 3-1 |
| Mansfield Town FC | 2-1 | 3-2 | 3-0 | 1-1 | 1-0 | 4-1 | 2-2 | 2-0 | 1-1 | 4-0 | 2-1 | 3-4 | | 2-1 | 1-0 | 2-1 | 2-3 | 3-2 | 4-2 | 4-2 | 4-0 | 5-1 |
| New Brighton FC | 2-1 | 3-1 | 5-1 | 0-2 | 3-1 | 1-1 | 0-1 | 1-1 | 3-0 | 0-0 | 1-4 | 0-2 | 2-1 | | 1-0 | 3-2 | 0-0 | 1-2 | 0-1 | 2-2 | 0-0 | 4-2 |
| Rochdale AFC | 2-2 | 0-1 | 3-1 | 3-3 | 0-2 | 3-0 | 1-3 | 0-1 | 6-1 | 2-4 | 3-2 | 2-0 | 1-0 | 3-1 | | 1-3 | 2-2 | 0-5 | 1-1 | 1-0 | 3-3 | 2-0 |
| Rotherham United FC | 2-0 | 0-0 | 4-1 | 6-1 | 2-2 | 2-2 | 2-1 | 1-3 | 3-0 | 2-2 | 0-1 | 5-0 | 3-0 | 1-2 | 4-0 | | 4-2 | 2-0 | 3-1 | 4-2 | 2-0 | 4-1 |
| Southport FC | 0-0 | 0-2 | 0-3 | 1-1 | 1-1 | 2-1 | 1-4 | 1-2 | 1-1 | 1-2 | 3-3 | 1-2 | 2-1 | 2-1 | 0-3 | | 1-2 | 4-0 | 3-2 | 2-1 | 0-3 | |
| Stockport County FC | 5-1 | 4-1 | 2-0 | 0-1 | 4-2 | 4-0 | 3-0 | 3-2 | 5-1 | 2-1 | 3-2 | 1-2 | 0-2 | 1-1 | 3-1 | 4-0 | 6-1 | | 1-0 | 0-3 | 6-1 | 0-0 |
| Tranmere Rovers FC | 2-1 | 2-1 | 3-1 | 1-1 | 2-1 | 5-1 | 4-1 | 0-2 | 2-2 | 1-0 | 3-0 | 2-1 | 3-0 | 0-1 | 4-1 | 3-3 | 4-1 | 3-1 | | 4-0 | 1-1 | 4-0 |
| Walsall FC | 6-0 | 5-0 | 1-0 | 1-1 | 4-0 | 4-0 | 0-2 | 5-0 | 4-1 | 1-2 | 0-0 | 2-2 | 5-1 | 0-0 | 5-2 | 2-2 | 3-1 | 3-0 | 0-0 | | 0-0 | 2-3 |
| Wrexham AFC | 2-2 | 1-1 | 4-2 | 2-2 | 2-1 | 2-1 | 4-0 | 1-2 | 3-1 | 5-0 | 0-2 | 2-2 | 1-3 | 3-0 | 2-0 | 0-1 | 3-0 | 2-1 | 2-2 | 4-2 | | 2-0 |
| York City FC | 5-2 | 1-1 | 7-0 | 1-1 | 1-1 | 7-3 | 2-1 | 1-2 | 3-0 | 0-1 | 3-1 | 1-2 | 2-1 | 1-0 | 0-1 | 5-0 | 3-1 | 3-1 | 0-0 | 4-1 | 0-0 | |

## Division 3 (North)

| | | Pd | Wn | Dw | Ls | GF | GA | Pts | |
|---|---|---|---|---|---|---|---|---|---|
| 1. | Doncaster Rovers FC (Doncaster) | 42 | 26 | 5 | 11 | 87 | 44 | 57 | P |
| 2. | Halifax Town AFC (Halifax) | 42 | 25 | 5 | 12 | 76 | 67 | 55 | |
| 3. | Chester FC (Chester) | 42 | 20 | 14 | 8 | 91 | 58 | 54 | |
| 4. | Lincoln City FC (Lincoln) | 42 | 22 | 7 | 13 | 87 | 58 | 51 | |
| 5. | Darlington FC (Darlington) | 42 | 21 | 9 | 12 | 80 | 59 | 51 | |
| 6. | Tranmere Rovers FC (Birkenhead) | 42 | 20 | 11 | 11 | 74 | 55 | 51 | |
| 7. | Stockport County FC (Stockport) | 42 | 22 | 3 | 17 | 90 | 72 | 47 | |
| 8. | Mansfield Town FC (Mansfield) | 42 | 19 | 9 | 14 | 75 | 62 | 47 | |
| 9. | Rotherham United FC (Rotherham) | 42 | 19 | 7 | 16 | 86 | 73 | 45 | |
| 10. | Chesterfield FC (Chesterfield) | 42 | 17 | 10 | 15 | 71 | 52 | 44 | |
| 11. | Wrexham AFC (Wrexham) | 42 | 16 | 11 | 15 | 76 | 69 | 43 | |
| 12. | Hartlepools United FC (Hartlepool) | 42 | 17 | 7 | 18 | 80 | 78 | 41 | |
| 13. | Crewe Alexandra FC (Crewe) | 42 | 14 | 11 | 17 | 66 | 86 | 39 | |
| 14. | Walsall FC (Walsall) | 42 | 13 | 10 | 19 | 81 | 72 | 36 | |
| 15. | York City FC (York) | 42 | 15 | 6 | 21 | 76 | 82 | 36 | |
| 16. | New Brighton FC (Wallasey) | 42 | 14 | 8 | 20 | 59 | 76 | 36 | |
| 17. | Barrow AFC (Barrow-in-Furness) | 42 | 13 | 9 | 20 | 58 | 87 | 35 | |
| 18. | Accrington Stanley FC (Accrington) | 42 | 12 | 10 | 20 | 63 | 89 | 34 | |
| 19. | Gateshead FC (Gateshead) | 42 | 13 | 8 | 21 | 58 | 96 | 34 | |
| 20. | Rochdale AFC (Rochdale) | 42 | 11 | 11 | 20 | 53 | 71 | 33 | |
| 21. | Southport FC (Southport) | 42 | 10 | 12 | 20 | 55 | 85 | 32 | |
| 22. | Carlisle United FC (Carlisle) | 42 | 8 | 7 | 27 | 51 | 102 | 23 | |
| | | 924 | 367 | 190 | 367 | 1593 | 1593 | 924 | |

| Football League Division 3 (S) 1934-1935 Season | Aldershot | Bournemouth | Brighton | Bristol City | Bristol Rovers | Cardiff City | Charlton Athletic | Clapton Orient | Coventry City | Crystal Palace | Exeter City | Gillingham | Luton Town | Millwall | Newport County | Northampton | Q.P.R. | Reading | Southend United | Swindon Town | Torquay United | Watford |
|---|---|---|---|---|---|---|---|---|---|---|---|---|---|---|---|---|---|---|---|---|---|---|
| Aldershot FC | | 1-1 | 1-0 | 1-0 | 1-2 | 2-0 | 3-2 | 1-1 | 3-1 | 2-2 | 0-0 | 4-1 | 0-1 | 0-0 | 3-2 | 2-0 | 1-0 | 2-5 | 3-2 | 3-0 | 2-0 | 0-0 |
| Bournemouth & B. Athletic | 4-1 | | 1-0 | 1-1 | 3-0 | 3-1 | 2-2 | 1-0 | 0-2 | 1-1 | 3-2 | 1-1 | 1-3 | 3-1 | 3-1 | 0-1 | 0-2 | 4-1 | 2-1 | 1-1 | 1-2 | 1-2 |
| Brighton & Hove Albion | 3-0 | 2-0 | | 2-0 | 3-1 | 3-1 | 2-1 | 3-0 | 2-0 | 3-0 | 6-0 | 1-1 | 4-1 | 0-2 | 3-1 | 2-3 | 5-1 | 1-0 | 2-2 | 2-2 | 0-0 | 2-0 |
| Bristol City FC | 2-0 | 2-1 | 1-0 | | 1-1 | 4-0 | 1-4 | 0-0 | 0-2 | 0-1 | 2-0 | 3-1 | 0-2 | 4-2 | 2-1 | 1-1 | 5-1 | 1-0 | 2-0 | 2-0 | 1-0 | 3-1 |
| Bristol Rovers FC | 1-0 | 4-1 | 0-0 | 2-2 | | 3-2 | 0-0 | 1-2 | 2-1 | 5-3 | 5-5 | 4-3 | 1-1 | 2-0 | 5-3 | 7-1 | 2-0 | 3-0 | 2-1 | 2-2 | 1-0 | 2-0 |
| Cardiff City AFC | 1-1 | 2-1 | 0-0 | 3-3 | 4-1 | | 2-1 | 3-0 | 2-4 | 2-0 | 5-0 | 0-2 | 1-0 | 3-1 | 3-4 | 2-2 | 2-1 | 1-1 | 2-0 | 1-3 | 1-1 | 2-1 |
| Charlton Athletic FC | 4-0 | 0-1 | 3-1 | 4-1 | 2-0 | 3-1 | | 2-1 | 3-3 | 2-2 | 1-0 | 2-0 | 4-2 | 3-1 | 6-0 | 0-1 | 3-1 | 3-1 | 3-0 | 6-0 | 3-2 | 5-2 |
| Clapton Orient FC | 3-1 | 0-1 | 6-0 | 4-0 | 5-2 | 0-1 | 1-2 | | 0-1 | 2-0 | 0-3 | 2-2 | 1-1 | 2-1 | 4-0 | 3-2 | 3-1 | 2-1 | 3-0 | 2-0 | 3-1 | 1-1 |
| Coventry City FC | 0-0 | 4-1 | 0-2 | 1-1 | 1-0 | 2-0 | 4-0 | 4-0 | | 1-1 | 1-1 | 4-0 | 1-0 | 5-1 | 5-0 | 2-0 | 4-1 | 1-2 | 6-3 | 3-0 | 6-0 | 1-1 |
| Crystal Palace FC | 3-0 | 1-0 | 3-0 | 3-1 | 2-0 | 6-1 | 1-2 | 1-0 | 3-1 | | 0-1 | 2-0 | 2-1 | 1-1 | 6-0 | 2-0 | 2-3 | 3-1 | 1-0 | 7-0 | 2-2 | 0-0 |
| Exeter City FC | 8-1 | 4-1 | 3-1 | 3-0 | 2-2 | 2-1 | 3-1 | 1-1 | 2-0 | 0-6 | | 2-0 | 1-2 | 0-1 | 0-1 | 3-0 | 3-0 | 2-3 | 4-3 | 3-3 | 1-1 | 1-1 |
| Gillingham FC | 1-1 | 3-1 | 0-0 | 1-0 | 1-1 | 1-0 | 3-6 | 1-0 | 2-5 | 2-0 | 2-1 | | 1-1 | 1-3 | 5-0 | 3-1 | 0-0 | 1-1 | 2-2 | 2-0 | 3-0 | 1-2 |
| Luton Town FC | 6-1 | 4-0 | 4-0 | 1-1 | 6-2 | 4-0 | 1-2 | 3-0 | 4-0 | 2-2 | 4-0 | 2-2 | | 2-1 | 4-1 | 2-2 | 1-1 | 2-4 | 1-1 | 2-0 | 3-1 | 2-2 |
| Millwall FC | 3-0 | 2-0 | 3-1 | 0-1 | 0-2 | 2-2 | 1-3 | 1-1 | 1-3 | 3-2 | 1-0 | 3-2 | 1-4 | | 2-0 | 0-1 | 2-0 | 2-2 | 1-0 | 1-0 | 4-2 | 0-0 |
| Newport County AFC | 2-0 | 6-1 | 1-0 | 2-0 | 1-1 | 4-0 | 0-2 | 3-3 | 2-1 | 2-3 | 1-3 | 2-2 | 2-4 | 1-2 | | 1-3 | 2-1 | 2-2 | 0-5 | 1-2 | 1-4 | 0-1 |
| Northampton Town FC | 0-0 | 0-1 | 4-1 | 2-2 | 1-0 | 3-0 | 1-1 | 3-1 | 3-4 | 3-2 | 2-1 | 2-1 | 2-1 | 1-0 | 2-0 | | 1-0 | 1-3 | 4-2 | 3-0 | 1-0 | 1-0 |
| Queen's Park Rangers FC | 2-0 | 2-1 | 2-1 | 4-1 | 2-0 | 2-2 | 0-3 | 6-3 | 1-1 | 3-3 | 1-1 | 2-0 | 3-0 | 1-0 | 4-1 | 3-1 | | 2-0 | 1-1 | 1-1 | 5-1 | 2-1 |
| Reading FC | 5-4 | 4-1 | 4-4 | 2-0 | 5-1 | 1-1 | 2-2 | 0-0 | 2-0 | 6-1 | 2-0 | 3-0 | 1-0 | 2-1 | 6-1 | 3-1 | 0-0 | | 3-2 | 2-1 | 3-1 | 3-2 |
| Southend United FC | 2-1 | 0-0 | 3-2 | 6-0 | 2-1 | 5-1 | 0-3 | 0-2 | 1-1 | 1-4 | 1-2 | 0-0 | 3-3 | 2-1 | 1-0 | 2-1 | 2-0 | 6-1 | | 2-0 | 2-3 | 0-2 |
| Swindon Town FC | 3-2 | 0-2 | 4-4 | 1-0 | 1-0 | 2-1 | 2-2 | 1-1 | 0-0 | 1-1 | 6-1 | 3-0 | 0-1 | 0-1 | 0-0 | 5-3 | 3-1 | 1-1 | 5-0 | | 5-0 | 2-1 |
| Torquay United FC | 2-1 | 1-2 | 3-0 | 3-1 | 1-2 | 5-2 | 1-2 | 4-2 | 1-0 | 7-1 | 3-0 | 5-0 | 6-2 | 1-1 | 2-1 | 2-0 | 7-0 | 1-1 | 2-0 | 2-1 | | 1-3 |
| Watford FC | 0-1 | 3-1 | 0-1 | 4-0 | 3-0 | 1-3 | 2-0 | 5-0 | 2-0 | 2-0 | 0-1 | 3-1 | 2-2 | 2-3 | 7-0 | 1-1 | 2-0 | 1-0 | 3-1 | 7-4 | 3-0 | |

### Division 3 (South)

| | | Pd | Wn | Dw | Ls | GF | GA | Pts | |
|---|---|---|---|---|---|---|---|---|---|
| 1. | Charlton Athletic FC (London) | 42 | 27 | 7 | 8 | 103 | 52 | 61 | P |
| 2. | Reading FC (Reading) | 42 | 21 | 11 | 10 | 89 | 65 | 53 | |
| 3. | Coventry City FC (Coventry) | 42 | 21 | 9 | 12 | 86 | 50 | 51 | |
| 4. | Luton Town FC (Luton) | 42 | 19 | 12 | 11 | 92 | 60 | 50 | |
| 5. | Crystal Palace FC (London) | 42 | 19 | 10 | 13 | 86 | 64 | 48 | |
| 6. | Watford FC (Watford) | 42 | 19 | 9 | 14 | 76 | 49 | 47 | |
| 7. | Northampton Town FC (Northampton) | 42 | 19 | 8 | 15 | 65 | 67 | 46 | |
| 8. | Bristol Rovers FC (Bristol) | 42 | 17 | 10 | 15 | 73 | 77 | 44 | |
| 9. | Brighton & Hove Albion FC (Hove) | 42 | 17 | 9 | 16 | 69 | 62 | 43 | |
| 10. | Torquay United FC (Torquay) | 42 | 18 | 6 | 18 | 81 | 75 | 42 | |
| 11. | Exeter City FC (Exeter) | 42 | 16 | 9 | 17 | 70 | 75 | 41 | |
| 12. | Millwall FC (London) | 42 | 17 | 7 | 18 | 57 | 62 | 41 | |
| 13. | Queen's Park Rangers FC (London) | 42 | 16 | 9 | 17 | 63 | 72 | 41 | |
| 14. | Clapton Orient FC (London) | 42 | 15 | 10 | 17 | 65 | 65 | 40 | |
| 15. | Bristol City FC (Bristol) | 42 | 15 | 9 | 18 | 52 | 68 | 39 | |
| 16. | Swindon Town FC (Swindon) | 42 | 13 | 12 | 17 | 67 | 78 | 38 | |
| 17. | Bournemouth & Boscombe Athletic FC (Bournemouth) | 42 | 15 | 7 | 20 | 54 | 71 | 37 | |
| 18. | Aldershot FC (Aldershot) | 42 | 13 | 10 | 19 | 50 | 75 | 36 | |
| 19. | Cardiff City AFC (Cardiff) | 42 | 13 | 9 | 20 | 62 | 82 | 35 | |
| 20. | Gillingham FC (Gillingham) | 42 | 11 | 13 | 18 | 55 | 75 | 35 | |
| 21. | Southend United FC (Southend-on-Sea) | 42 | 11 | 9 | 22 | 65 | 78 | 31 | |
| 22. | Newport County AFC (Newport) | 42 | 10 | 5 | 27 | 54 | 112 | 25 | |
| | | 924 | 362 | 200 | 362 | 1534 | 1534 | 924 | |

## F.A. CUP FINAL  (Wembley Stadium, London – 27/04/1935 – 93,204)

**SHEFFIELD WEDNESDAY FC (SHEFFIELD)**　　4-2　　West Bromwich Albion FC (West Bromwich)

*Palethorpe, Hooper, Rimmer 2*　　　　　　　　　　　　　　　　　　　　　　　　　*Boyes, Sandford*

Wednesday: Brown, Nibloe, Catlin, Sharp, Millership, Burrows, Hooper, Surtees, Palethorpe, Starling, Rimmer.

West Bromwich: Pearson, Shaw, Trentham, Murphy, W.Richardson, Edwards, Glidden, Carter, W.G. Richardson, Sandford, Boyes.

### Semi-finals

| | | |
|---|---|---|
| Bolton Wanderers FC (Bolton) | 1-1,  0-2 | West Bromwich Albion FC (West Bromwich) |
| Sheffield Wednesday FC (Sheffield) | 3-0 | Burnley FC (Burnley) |

### Quarter-finals

| | | |
|---|---|---|
| Burnley FC (Burnley) | 3-2 | Birmingham FC (Birmingham) |
| Everton FC (Liverpool) | 1-2 | Bolton Wanderers FC (Bolton) |
| Sheffield Wednesday FC (Sheffield) | 2-1 | Arsenal FC (London) |
| West Bromwich Albion FC (West Bromwich) | 1-0 | Preston North End FC (Preston) |

# 1935-36

| Football League Division 1 1935-1936 Season | Arsenal | Aston Villa | Birmingham | Blackburn Rovers | Bolton Wanderers | Brentford | Chelsea | Derby County | Everton | Grimsby Town | Huddersfield Town | Leeds United | Liverpool | Manchester City | Middlesbrough | Portsmouth | Preston North End | Sheffield Wednesday | Stoke City | Sunderland | W.B.A. | Wolves |
|---|---|---|---|---|---|---|---|---|---|---|---|---|---|---|---|---|---|---|---|---|---|---|
| Arsenal FC | ■ | 1-0 | 1-1 | 5-1 | 1-1 | 1-1 | 1-1 | 1-1 | 1-1 | 6-0 | 1-1 | 2-2 | 1-2 | 2-3 | 2-0 | 2-3 | 2-1 | 2-2 | 1-0 | 3-1 | 4-0 | 4-0 |
| Aston Villa FC | 1-7 | ■ | 2-1 | 2-4 | 1-2 | 2-2 | 2-2 | 0-2 | 1-1 | 2-6 | 4-1 | 3-3 | 3-0 | 2-2 | 2-7 | 4-2 | 5-1 | 1-2 | 4-0 | 2-2 | 0-7 | 4-2 |
| Birmingham FC | 1-1 | 2-2 | ■ | 4-2 | 0-0 | 2-1 | 2-1 | 2-3 | 4-2 | 1-1 | 4-1 | 2-0 | 2-0 | 0-1 | 1-0 | 4-0 | 0-0 | 4-1 | 0-5 | 2-7 | 1-3 | 0-0 |
| Blackburn Rovers FC | 0-1 | 5-1 | 1-2 | ■ | 0-3 | 1-0 | 1-0 | 0-0 | 1-1 | 1-0 | 2-1 | 0-3 | 2-2 | 4-1 | 2-2 | 3-1 | 1-1 | 3-2 | 0-1 | 1-1 | 3-1 | 1-0 |
| Bolton Wanderers FC | 2-1 | 4-3 | 2-0 | 3-1 | ■ | 0-2 | 2-3 | 0-2 | 2-0 | 4-0 | 1-2 | 3-0 | 0-0 | 3-3 | 3-1 | 4-0 | 1-1 | 1-1 | 1-2 | 2-1 | 3-1 | 0-3 |
| Brentford FC | 2-1 | 1-2 | 0-1 | 3-1 | 4-0 | ■ | 2-1 | 6-0 | 4-1 | 3-0 | 1-2 | 2-2 | 1-2 | 0-0 | 1-0 | 3-1 | 5-2 | 2-2 | 0-0 | 1-5 | 2-2 | 5-0 |
| Chelsea FC | 1-1 | 1-0 | 0-0 | 5-1 | 2-1 | 2-1 | ■ | 1-1 | 2-2 | 0-2 | 1-0 | 1-0 | 2-2 | 2-1 | 2-1 | 1-0 | 5-2 | 1-2 | 3-5 | 3-1 | 2-2 | 2-2 |
| Derby County FC | 0-4 | 1-3 | 2-2 | 1-0 | 4-0 | 2-1 | 1-1 | ■ | 3-3 | 2-0 | 2-0 | 2-1 | 2-2 | 3-0 | 3-2 | 1-1 | 2-0 | 3-1 | 0-1 | 4-0 | 2-0 | 3-1 |
| Everton FC | 0-2 | 2-2 | 4-3 | 4-0 | 3-3 | 1-2 | 5-1 | 4-0 | ■ | 4-0 | 1-3 | 0-0 | 0-0 | 2-2 | 5-2 | 3-0 | 5-0 | 4-3 | 5-1 | 0-3 | 5-3 | 4-1 |
| Grimsby Town FC | 1-0 | 4-1 | 1-0 | 1-1 | 3-1 | 6-1 | 1-3 | 4-1 | 0-4 | ■ | 1-1 | 0-1 | 0-0 | 3-1 | 1-0 | 1-2 | 0-0 | 4-0 | 3-0 | 4-0 | 4-2 | 2-1 |
| Huddersfield Town AFC | 0-0 | 4-1 | 1-0 | 1-1 | 0-0 | 2-2 | 2-0 | 1-1 | 2-1 | 1-0 | ■ | 1-2 | 1-0 | 1-1 | 4-1 | 1-1 | 1-0 | 1-0 | 2-1 | 1-0 | 2-3 | 3-0 |
| Leeds United AFC | 1-1 | 4-2 | 0-0 | 1-4 | 5-2 | 1-2 | 2-0 | 1-0 | 3-1 | 1-2 | 2-2 | ■ | 1-0 | 1-1 | 0-1 | 1-0 | 0-1 | 7-2 | 4-1 | 3-0 | 1-1 | 2-0 |
| Liverpool FC | 0-1 | 3-2 | 1-2 | 4-1 | 1-1 | 0-0 | 2-3 | 0-0 | 6-0 | 7-2 | 3-0 | 2-1 | ■ | 0-2 | 2-2 | 2-0 | 1-0 | 2-0 | 0-3 | 5-0 | 0-0 | 0-0 |
| Manchester City FC | 1-0 | 5-0 | 3-1 | 2-0 | 7-0 | 2-1 | 0-0 | 1-0 | 1-0 | 0-3 | 1-2 | 1-3 | 6-0 | ■ | 6-0 | 0-0 | 1-3 | 3-0 | 1-2 | 0-1 | 1-0 | 2-1 |
| Middlesbrough FC | 2-2 | 1-2 | 0-2 | 6-1 | 0-0 | 0-0 | 4-1 | 0-3 | 6-1 | 5-1 | 4-2 | 1-1 | 2-2 | 2-0 | ■ | 3-2 | 2-0 | 5-0 | 0-0 | 6-0 | 3-1 | 4-2 |
| Portsmouth FC | 2-1 | 3-0 | 0-3 | 3-1 | 2-1 | 1-3 | 2-0 | 3-0 | 2-0 | 3-2 | 0-0 | 2-2 | 2-1 | 1-2 | 1-0 | ■ | 1-1 | 3-2 | 2-0 | 2-2 | 3-1 | 1-0 |
| Preston North End FC | 1-0 | 3-0 | 3-1 | 2-0 | 1-0 | 2-4 | 2-2 | 1-0 | 2-2 | 1-0 | 4-5 | 3-1 | 4-0 | 0-5 | 1-1 | 1-1 | ■ | 0-1 | 1-1 | 3-2 | 3-0 | 2-0 |
| Sheffield Wednesday FC | 3-2 | 5-2 | 3-1 | 0-0 | 2-2 | 3-3 | 4-1 | 1-0 | 3-3 | 3-0 | 1-2 | 3-0 | 0-0 | 1-0 | 0-0 | 0-1 | 1-0 | ■ | 0-1 | 0-0 | 2-5 | 0-0 |
| Stoke City FC | 0-3 | 2-3 | 3-1 | 2-0 | 1-2 | 2-2 | 3-0 | 0-0 | 2-1 | 1-0 | 1-0 | 3-1 | 2-1 | 1-0 | 1-1 | 2-0 | 2-1 | 0-3 | ■ | 0-2 | 3-2 | 4-1 |
| Sunderland AFC | 5-4 | 1-3 | 2-1 | 7-2 | 7-2 | 1-3 | 3-3 | 3-1 | 3-3 | 3-1 | 4-3 | 2-1 | 2-0 | 2-0 | 2-1 | 5-0 | 4-2 | 5-1 | 1-0 | ■ | 6-1 | 3-1 |
| West Bromwich Albion FC | 1-0 | 0-3 | 0-0 | 8-1 | 2-2 | 1-0 | 1-2 | 0-3 | 6-1 | 4-1 | 1-2 | 3-2 | 6-1 | 5-1 | 5-2 | 2-0 | 2-4 | 2-2 | 2-0 | 1-3 | ■ | 2-1 |
| Wolverhampton Wanderers FC | 2-2 | 2-2 | 3-1 | 8-1 | 3-3 | 3-2 | 3-3 | 0-0 | 4-0 | 1-0 | 2-2 | 3-0 | 3-1 | 4-3 | 4-0 | 2-0 | 4-2 | 2-1 | 1-1 | 3-4 | 2-0 | ■ |

| | Division 1 | Pd | Wn | Dw | Ls | GF | GA | Pts | |
|---|---|---|---|---|---|---|---|---|---|
| 1. | SUNDERLAND AFC (SUNDERLAND) | 42 | 25 | 6 | 11 | 109 | 74 | 56 | |
| 2. | Derby County FC (Derby) | 42 | 18 | 12 | 12 | 61 | 52 | 48 | |
| 3. | Huddersfield Town AFC (Huddersfield) | 42 | 18 | 12 | 12 | 59 | 56 | 48 | |
| 4. | Stoke City FC (Stoke-on-Trent) | 42 | 20 | 7 | 15 | 57 | 57 | 47 | |
| 5. | Brentford FC (London) | 42 | 17 | 12 | 13 | 81 | 60 | 46 | |
| 6. | Arsenal FC (London) | 42 | 15 | 15 | 12 | 78 | 48 | 45 | |
| 7. | Preston North End FC (Preston) | 42 | 18 | 8 | 16 | 67 | 64 | 44 | |
| 8. | Chelsea FC (London) | 42 | 15 | 13 | 14 | 65 | 72 | 43 | |
| 9. | Manchester City FC (Manchester) | 42 | 17 | 8 | 17 | 68 | 60 | 42 | |
| 10. | Portsmouth FC (Portsmouth) | 42 | 17 | 8 | 17 | 54 | 67 | 42 | |
| 11. | Leeds United AFC Leeds) | 42 | 15 | 11 | 16 | 66 | 64 | 41 | |
| 12. | Birmingham FC (Birmingham) | 42 | 15 | 11 | 16 | 61 | 63 | 41 | |
| 13. | Bolton Wanderers FC (Bolton) | 42 | 14 | 13 | 15 | 67 | 76 | 41 | |
| 14. | Middlesbrough FC (Middlesbrough) | 42 | 15 | 10 | 17 | 84 | 70 | 40 | |
| 15. | Wolverhampton Wanderers FC (Wolverhampton) | 42 | 15 | 10 | 17 | 77 | 76 | 40 | |
| 16. | Everton FC (Liverpool) | 42 | 13 | 13 | 16 | 89 | 89 | 39 | |
| 17. | Grimsby Town FC (Cleethorpes) | 42 | 17 | 5 | 20 | 65 | 73 | 39 | |
| 18. | West Bromwich Albion FC (West Bromwich) | 42 | 16 | 6 | 20 | 89 | 88 | 38 | |
| 19. | Liverpool FC (Liverpool) | 42 | 13 | 12 | 17 | 60 | 64 | 38 | |
| 20. | Sheffield Wednesday FC (Sheffield) | 42 | 13 | 12 | 17 | 63 | 77 | 38 | |
| 21. | Aston Villa FC (Birmingham) | 42 | 13 | 9 | 20 | 81 | 110 | 35 | R |
| 22. | Blackburn Rovers FC (Blackburn) | 42 | 12 | 9 | 21 | 55 | 96 | 33 | R |
| | | 924 | 351 | 122 | 351 | 1556 | 1556 | 924 | |

## Top Goalscorers

| | | | |
|---|---|---|---|
| 1) | W.G. RICHARDSON | (West Bromwich Albion FC) | 39 |
| 2) | Raich CARTER | (Sunderland AFC) | 31 |
| | Pat GLOVER | (Grimsby Town FC) | 31 |
| | Robert GURNEY | (Sunderland AFC) | 31 |

| Football League Division 2 1935-1936 Season | Barnsley | Blackpool | Bradford City | Bradford P.A. | Burnley | Bury | Charlton Ath. | Doncaster R. | Fulham | Hull City | Leicester City | Man. United | Newcastle Utd. | Norwich City | Nottingham F. | Plymouth Arg. | Port Vale | Sheffield United | Southampton | Swansea Town | Tottenham H. | West Ham Utd. |
|---|---|---|---|---|---|---|---|---|---|---|---|---|---|---|---|---|---|---|---|---|---|---|
| Barnsley FC | | 1-2 | 0-1 | 5-1 | 3-1 | 1-1 | 1-2 | 2-1 | 2-0 | 5-1 | 3-3 | 0-3 | 3-2 | 2-3 | 0-2 | 1-2 | 4-2 | 3-2 | 3-1 | 0-0 | 0-0 | 1-2 |
| Blackpool FC | 3-0 | | 3-3 | 4-2 | 2-0 | 2-3 | 6-1 | 5-2 | 1-1 | 4-1 | 3-5 | 4-1 | 6-0 | 2-1 | 1-4 | 3-1 | 3-1 | 3-0 | 2-1 | 1-1 | 2-4 | 4-1 |
| Bradford City AFC | 1-1 | 2-1 | | 2-1 | 0-0 | 2-0 | 2-1 | 3-1 | 1-0 | 1-1 | 2-0 | 1-0 | 3-2 | 0-1 | 0-0 | 2-2 | 1-1 | 2-1 | 2-1 | 2-2 | 0-1 | 3-1 |
| Bradford Park Avenue | 3-0 | 3-2 | 1-1 | | 2-0 | 1-1 | 3-0 | 3-1 | 1-1 | 2-1 | 3-1 | 1-0 | 3-2 | 1-0 | 1-4 | 22 | 3-0 | 3-3 | 2-1 | 1-1 | 2-5 | 2-0 |
| Burnley FC | 3-0 | 3-2 | 3-0 | 1-1 | | 1-1 | 0-2 | 1-1 | 0-2 | 2-0 | 2-2 | 2-2 | 1-2 | 1-1 | 1-0 | 0-1 | 5-1 | 1-1 | 2-0 | 5-2 | 0-0 | 1-0 |
| Bury FC | 3-0 | 1-1 | 1-1 | 1-0 | 0-4 | | 1-1 | 5-1 | 0-0 | 3-1 | 3-0 | 2-3 | 3-4 | 0-1 | 2-6 | 2-0 | 5-0 | 3-2 | 0-0 | 2-1 | 1-1 | 3-0 |
| Charlton Athletic FC | 3-0 | 1-1 | 2-1 | 3-1 | 4-0 | 5-2 | | 3-0 | 2-1 | 4-1 | 1-0 | 0-0 | 4-2 | 4-1 | 4-0 | 1-1 | 1-1 | 1-1 | 2-0 | 4-1 | 2-1 | 2-2 |
| Doncaster Rovers FC | 1-1 | 0-3 | 2-1 | 3-2 | 1-0 | 1-0 | 2-0 | | 0-0 | 6-1 | 1-0 | 0-0 | 2-2 | 3-0 | 0-0 | 1-2 | 2-0 | 0-0 | 0-1 | 1-1 | 2-1 | 0-2 |
| Fulham FC | 1-1 | 4-2 | 5-1 | 4-1 | 2-2 | 7-0 | 0-0 | 1-3 | | 3-0 | 2-0 | 2-2 | 3-1 | 1-1 | 6-0 | 2-2 | 7-0 | 3-1 | 0-2 | 0-1 | 1-2 | 4-2 |
| Hull City AFC | 1-3 | 0-3 | 2-5 | 1-1 | 1-2 | 2-3 | 2-4 | 2-3 | 1-1 | | 3-3 | 1-1 | 2-3 | 0-0 | 2-1 | 2-1 | 1-2 | 2-2 | 2-2 | 3-2 | 1-0 | 2-3 |
| Leicester City FC | 2-0 | 4-1 | 2-1 | 5-0 | 2-0 | 1-2 | 4-1 | 60 | 5-2 | 2-2 | | 1-1 | 1-0 | 1-1 | 2-1 | 2-0 | 2-0 | 1-3 | 1-1 | 4-1 | 4-1 | 1-1 |
| Manchester United FC | 1-1 | 3-2 | 3-1 | 4-0 | 4-0 | 2-1 | 3-0 | 0-0 | 1-0 | 2-0 | 0-1 | | 3-1 | 2-1 | 5-0 | 3-2 | 7-2 | 3-1 | 4-0 | 3-0 | 0-0 | 2-3 |
| Newcastle United FC | 3-0 | 1-0 | 3-2 | 3-3 | 1-1 | 3-0 | 1-2 | 2-1 | 6-2 | 4-1 | 3-1 | 0-2 | | 1-1 | 5-1 | 5-0 | 2-2 | 3-0 | 4-1 | 2-0 | 1-4 | 3-3 |
| Norwich City FC | 3-1 | 0-1 | 1-1 | 4-1 | 2-0 | 5-3 | 3-1 | 2-1 | 1-0 | 3-0 | 1-2 | 3-5 | 1-0 | | 4-0 | 0-0 | 4-2 | 0-1 | 5-1 | 0-1 | 1-0 | 4-3 |
| Nottingham Forest FC | 6-0 | 2-2 | 1-0 | 2-0 | 2-0 | 2-2 | 0-0 | 6-2 | 1-1 | 0-0 | 0-1 | 1-1 | 1-2 | 2-2 | | 0-1 | 9-2 | 0-1 | 2-0 | 2-2 | 4-1 | 0-2 |
| Plymouth Argyle FC | 7-1 | 3-2 | 0-1 | 2-0 | 3-0 | 4-2 | 1-3 | 2-0 | 0-1 | 2-1 | 3-1 | 1-0 | 5-1 | 3-1 | | | 4-1 | 1-1 | 0-0 | 1-2 | 2-1 | 4-1 |
| Port Vale FC | 0-4 | 2-2 | 2-1 | 3-2 | 1-1 | 2-2 | 2-1 | 2-0 | 1-0 | 4-0 | 1-1 | 0-3 | 3-0 | 3-1 | 2-0 | 2-0 | | 1-1 | 0-2 | 0-1 | 1-5 | 2-3 |
| Sheffield United FC | 2-0 | 1-0 | 3-0 | 2-1 | 2-0 | 3-0 | 2-2 | 3-0 | 0-1 | 7-0 | 1-2 | 1-1 | 5-1 | 3-2 | 1-0 | 0-0 | 4-0 | | 2-1 | 4-1 | 1-1 | 4-2 |
| Southampton FC | 0-1 | 1-0 | 1-0 | 3-0 | 1-0 | 0-0 | 2-5 | 1-0 | 1-2 | 1-0 | 1-0 | 2-1 | 1-3 | 1-1 | 7-2 | 2-0 | 0-1 | 0-1 | | 4-3 | 2-0 | 2-4 |
| Swansea Town AFC | 0-0 | 1-0 | 8-1 | 1-2 | 1-3 | 4-1 | 1-2 | 2-0 | 0-2 | 6-1 | 2-0 | 2-1 | 1-2 | 4-3 | 2-1 | 2-0 | 3-2 | 1-3 | 0-0 | | 1-1 | 0-1 |
| Tottenham Hotspur FC | 3-0 | 3-1 | 4-0 | 4-0 | 5-1 | 4-3 | 1-1 | 3-1 | 2-2 | 3-1 | 1-1 | 0-0 | 1-2 | 2-1 | 1-1 | 1-2 | 5-2 | 1-1 | 8-0 | 7-2 | | 1-3 |
| West Ham United FC | 2-0 | 2-1 | 1-1 | 1-0 | 0-0 | 6-0 | 1-3 | 1-2 | 0-0 | 4-1 | 3-2 | 1-2 | 4-1 | 3-2 | 5-2 | 4-2 | 4-0 | 3-2 | 0-0 | 4-0 | 2-2 | |

## Division 2

| | | Pd | Wn | Dw | Ls | GF | GA | Pts | |
|---|---|---|---|---|---|---|---|---|---|
| 1. | Manchester United FC (Manchester) | 42 | 22 | 12 | 8 | 85 | 43 | 56 | P |
| 2. | Charlton Athletic FC (London) | 42 | 22 | 11 | 9 | 85 | 58 | 55 | P |
| 3. | Sheffield United FC (Sheffield) | 42 | 20 | 12 | 10 | 79 | 50 | 52 | |
| 4. | West Ham United FC (London) | 42 | 22 | 8 | 12 | 90 | 68 | 52 | |
| 5. | Tottenham Hotspur FC (London) | 42 | 18 | 13 | 11 | 91 | 55 | 49 | |
| 6. | Leicester City FC (Leicester) | 42 | 19 | 10 | 13 | 79 | 57 | 48 | |
| 7. | Plymouth Argyle FC (Plymouth) | 42 | 20 | 8 | 14 | 71 | 57 | 48 | |
| 8. | Newcastle United FC (Newcastle-upon-Tyne) | 42 | 20 | 6 | 16 | 88 | 79 | 46 | |
| 9. | Fulham FC (London) | 42 | 15 | 14 | 13 | 76 | 52 | 44 | |
| 10. | Blackpool FC (Blackpool) | 42 | 18 | 7 | 17 | 93 | 72 | 43 | |
| 11. | Norwich City FC (Norwich) | 42 | 17 | 9 | 16 | 72 | 65 | 43 | |
| 12. | Bradford City AFC (Bradford) | 42 | 15 | 13 | 14 | 55 | 65 | 43 | |
| 13. | Swansea Town AFC (Swansea) | 42 | 15 | 9 | 18 | 67 | 76 | 39 | |
| 14. | Bury FC (Bury) | 42 | 13 | 12 | 17 | 66 | 84 | 38 | |
| 15. | Burnley FC (Burnley) | 42 | 12 | 13 | 17 | 50 | 59 | 37 | |
| 16. | Bradford Park Avenue FC (Bradford) | 42 | 14 | 9 | 19 | 62 | 84 | 37 | |
| 17. | Southampton FC (Southampton) | 42 | 14 | 9 | 19 | 47 | 65 | 37 | |
| 18. | Doncaster Rovers FC (Doncaster) | 42 | 14 | 9 | 19 | 51 | 71 | 37 | |
| 19. | Nottingham Forest FC (Nottingham) | 42 | 12 | 11 | 19 | 69 | 76 | 35 | |
| 20. | Barnsley FC (Barnsley) | 42 | 12 | 9 | 21 | 54 | 80 | 33 | |
| 21. | Port Vale FC (Stoke-on-Trent) | 42 | 12 | 8 | 22 | 56 | 106 | 32 | R |
| 22. | Hull City AFC (Kingston-upon-Hull) | 42 | 5 | 10 | 27 | 47 | 111 | 20 | R |
| | | 924 | 351 | 222 | 351 | 1533 | 1533 | 924 | |

| Football League Division 3 (N) 1935-1936 Season | Accrington Stan. | Barrow | Carlisle United | Chester | Chesterfield | Crewe Alexandra | Darlington | Gateshead | Halifax Town | Hartlepools Utd. | Lincoln City | Mansfield Town | New Brighton | Oldham Athletic | Rochdale | Rotherham Utd. | Southport | Stockport Co. | Tranmere R. | Walsall | Wrexham | York City |
|---|---|---|---|---|---|---|---|---|---|---|---|---|---|---|---|---|---|---|---|---|---|---|
| Accrington Stanley FC | | 2-0 | 0-0 | 0-3 | 0-1 | 2-1 | 1-0 | 6-1 | 2-0 | 3-2 | 2-2 | 1-1 | 5-2 | 1-0 | 2-4 | 1-1 | 1-0 | 1-1 | 3-1 | 3-1 | 0-1 | 7-2 |
| Barrow AFC | 0-1 | | 1-1 | 2-4 | 1-1 | 1-1 | 2-0 | 3-0 | 0-0 | 1-1 | 0-0 | 2-2 | 3-0 | 3-0 | 6-2 | 3-0 | 0-1 | 1-0 | 0-0 | 1-0 | 2-1 | 1-1 |
| Carlisle United FC | 3-1 | 2-2 | | 1-3 | 2-1 | 1-2 | 3-0 | 2-0 | 0-0 | 0-0 | 4-1 | 3-0 | 3-0 | 2-1 | 4-3 | 1-1 | 4-0 | 2-1 | 0-1 | 2-1 | 5-1 | 0-0 |
| Chester FC | 4-0 | 1-2 | 3-2 | | 1-1 | 0-1 | 4-1 | 4-0 | 3-1 | 4-0 | 4-2 | 4-0 | 8-2 | 1-1 | 5-2 | 0-0 | 5-1 | 2-0 | 1-1 | 2-0 | 1-1 | 12-0 |
| Chesterfield FC | 0-3 | 6-1 | 5-0 | 1-0 | | 6-0 | 5-1 | 2-0 | 3-1 | 2-0 | 0-1 | 2-1 | 3-1 | 3-0 | 2-2 | 5-0 | 5-0 | 0-0 | 0-1 | 3-0 | 5-0 | 2-2 |
| Crewe Alexandra FC | 4-0 | 3-1 | 2-0 | 1-1 | 5-6 | | 2-0 | 2-4 | 3-2 | 3-2 | 2-1 | 1-1 | 5-1 | 2-2 | 3-1 | 4-1 | 4-1 | 0-1 | 0-0 | 4-3 | 3-2 | 2-1 |
| Darlington FC | 2-1 | 4-1 | 4-1 | 1-1 | 1-2 | 2-2 | | 5-2 | 3-2 | 4-2 | 1-0 | 2-1 | 4-1 | 5-0 | 4-0 | 3-1 | 3-2 | 3-1 | 1-3 | 1-1 | 4-2 | 3-0 |
| Gateshead FC | 0-0 | 4-3 | 1-1 | 2-0 | 3-3 | 2-1 | 1-1 | | 2-2 | 1-0 | 4-0 | 3-1 | 3-1 | 0-0 | 1-0 | 1-1 | 3-1 | 1-0 | 1-1 | 2-2 | 2-0 | 0-0 |
| Halifax Town AFC | 1-0 | 3-2 | 1-0 | 2-3 | 2-3 | 2-4 | 0-1 | 1-1 | | 0-1 | 2-1 | 1-0 | 3-0 | 4-2 | 2-0 | 1-0 | 1-2 | 0-0 | 1-0 | 1-1 | 4-1 | 2-0 |
| Hartlepools United FC | 2-1 | 0-0 | 1-1 | 0-2 | 2-1 | 1-0 | 2-1 | 2-0 | 1-0 | | 1-1 | 4-1 | 4-1 | 0-1 | 1-0 | 5-1 | 2-1 | 1-1 | 2-2 | 5-0 | 1-1 | 4-2 |
| Lincoln City FC | 6-0 | 2-0 | 2-0 | 1-1 | 0-1 | 6-2 | 2-1 | 5-0 | 3-1 | 1-0 | | 1-2 | 2-0 | 2-1 | 5-1 | 4-0 | 4-0 | 3-0 | 5-0 | 4-1 | 3-1 | 3-2 |
| Mansfield Town FC | 3-1 | 1-3 | 1-1 | 0-0 | 0-1 | 1-1 | 4-2 | 3-1 | 3-2 | 4-0 | 2-2 | | 2-0 | 1-0 | 3-0 | 8-2 | 5-1 | 2-1 | 2-3 | 2-2 | 3-2 | 5-0 |
| New Brighton FC | 2-3 | 2-3 | 3-0 | 3-3 | 1-2 | 3-1 | 1-1 | 1-0 | 1-4 | 0-0 | 0-5 | 1-0 | | 1-3 | 2-0 | 3-0 | 2-1 | 2-0 | 0-0 | 1-1 | 0-4 | 0-2 |
| Oldham Athletic AFC | 3-0 | 3-1 | 3-0 | 1-3 | 0-0 | 0-0 | 2-0 | 2-2 | 3-0 | 2-2 | 2-3 | 4-1 | 6-0 | | 3-3 | 4-1 | 4-0 | 1-3 | 4-1 | 2-1 | 5-2 | 6-2 |
| Rochdale AFC | 2-2 | 1-1 | 0-0 | 1-1 | 1-1 | 2-1 | 1-1 | 5-0 | 5-0 | 0-1 | 0-0 | 3-1 | 1-0 | 2-6 | | 1-1 | 2-1 | 1-1 | 0-0 | 6-4 | 2-1 | 2-3 |
| Rotherham United FC | 1-3 | 1-0 | 4-0 | 1-2 | 0-0 | 3-1 | 4-0 | 3-0 | 2-0 | 3-0 | 1-1 | 2-1 | 5-0 | 1-0 | 6-0 | | 5-0 | 1-1 | 1-2 | 2-0 | 1-2 | 5-0 |
| Southport FC | 2-1 | 3-1 | 0-3 | 2-1 | 1-0 | 1-1 | 4-1 | 1-1 | 2-0 | 1-1 | 0-3 | 3-3 | 2-1 | 1-1 | 1-1 | 2-1 | | 2-3 | 1-1 | 1-0 | 1-1 | 0-1 |
| Stockport County FC | 1-2 | 2-1 | 2-0 | 2-0 | 2-2 | 0-1 | 2-0 | 3-1 | 1-0 | 2-1 | 4-0 | 6-1 | 1-1 | 2-0 | 4-0 | 1-2 | 2-0 | | 2-1 | 0-1 | 3-2 | 3-2 |
| Tranmere Rovers FC | 6-0 | 1-0 | 4-1 | 3-1 | 1-3 | 4-2 | 2-0 | 2-0 | 0-2 | 3-1 | 1-1 | 4-2 | 3-1 | 13-4 | 5-2 | 2-2 | 5-2 | 4-1 | | 3-1 | 6-1 | 3-1 |
| Walsall FC | 2-0 | 5-1 | 3-0 | 1-0 | 1-1 | 4-1 | 4-1 | 2-0 | 2-1 | 6-0 | 4-1 | 7-0 | 1-2 | 1-2 | 1-0 | 0-1 | 3-1 | 0-1 | 0-0 | | 5-0 | 6-0 |
| Wrexham AFC | 3-0 | 2-0 | 1-1 | 1-0 | 0-1 | 0-1 | 3-1 | 2-4 | 1-3 | 1-0 | 1-1 | 5-1 | 3-0 | 0-1 | 0-1 | 2-0 | 4-2 | 4-0 | 4-0 | 1-1 | | 1-0 |
| York City FC | 1-1 | 1-2 | 2-0 | 1-2 | 1-1 | 4-1 | 4-1 | 2-2 | 2-2 | 2-2 | 2-1 | 7-5 | 2-0 | 3-1 | 2-1 | 2-1 | 0-0 | 0-4 | 2-0 | 0-0 | 1-1 | |

### Division 3 (North)

| | | Pd | Wn | Dw | Ls | GF | GA | Pts | |
|---|---|---|---|---|---|---|---|---|---|
| 1. | Chesterfield FC (Chesterfield) | 42 | 24 | 12 | 6 | 92 | 39 | 60 | P |
| 2. | Chester FC (Chester) | 42 | 22 | 11 | 9 | 100 | 45 | 55 | |
| 3. | Tranmere Rovers FC (Birkenhead) | 42 | 22 | 11 | 9 | 93 | 58 | 55 | |
| 4. | Lincoln City FC (Lincoln) | 42 | 22 | 9 | 11 | 91 | 51 | 53 | |
| 5. | Stockport County FC (Stockport) | 42 | 20 | 8 | 14 | 65 | 49 | 48 | |
| 6. | Crewe Alexandra FC (Crewe) | 42 | 19 | 9 | 14 | 80 | 76 | 47 | |
| 7. | Oldham Athletic AFC (Oldham) | 42 | 18 | 9 | 15 | 86 | 73 | 45 | |
| 8. | Hartlepools United FC (Hartlepool) | 42 | 15 | 12 | 15 | 57 | 61 | 42 | |
| 9. | Accrington Stanley FC (Accrington) | 42 | 17 | 8 | 17 | 63 | 72 | 42 | |
| 10. | Walsall FC (Walsall) | 42 | 16 | 9 | 17 | 79 | 59 | 41 | T |
| 11. | Rotherham United FC (Rotherham) | 42 | 16 | 9 | 17 | 69 | 66 | 41 | |
| 12. | Darlington FC (Darlington) | 42 | 17 | 6 | 19 | 74 | 79 | 40 | |
| 13. | Carlisle United FC (Carlisle) | 42 | 14 | 12 | 16 | 56 | 62 | 40 | |
| 14. | Gateshead FC (Gateshead) | 42 | 13 | 14 | 15 | 56 | 76 | 40 | |
| 15. | Barrow AFC (Barrow-in-Furness) | 42 | 13 | 12 | 17 | 58 | 65 | 38 | |
| 16. | York City FC (York) | 42 | 13 | 12 | 17 | 62 | 95 | 38 | |
| 17. | Halifax Town AFC (Halifax) | 42 | 15 | 7 | 20 | 57 | 61 | 37 | |
| 18. | Wrexham AFC (Wrexham) | 42 | 15 | 7 | 20 | 66 | 75 | 37 | |
| 19. | Mansfield Town FC (Mansfield) | 42 | 14 | 9 | 19 | 80 | 91 | 37 | |
| 20. | Rochdale AFC (Rochdale) | 42 | 10 | 13 | 19 | 58 | 88 | 33 | |
| 21. | Southport FC (Southport) | 42 | 11 | 9 | 22 | 48 | 90 | 31 | |
| 22. | New Brighton FC (Wallasey) | 42 | 9 | 6 | 27 | 43 | 102 | 24 | |
| | | 924 | 355 | 214 | 355 | 1533 | 1533 | 924 | |

T: Walsall FC (Walsall) were transferred to Division 3 (South) from the next season.

**Football League Division 3 (S) 1935-1936 Season**

| | Aldershot | Bournemouth | Brighton | Bristol City | Bristol Rovers | Cardiff City | Clapton Orient | Coventry City | Crystal Palace | Exeter City | Gillingham | Luton Town | Millwall | Newport County | Northampton | Notts County | Q.P.R. | Reading | Southend United | Swindon Town | Torquay United | Watford |
|---|---|---|---|---|---|---|---|---|---|---|---|---|---|---|---|---|---|---|---|---|---|---|
| Aldershot FC | | 2-0 | 1-0 | 0-0 | 6-1 | 1-1 | 1-0 | 1-2 | 1-3 | 3-0 | 0-2 | 0-1 | 1-1 | 1-1 | 2-0 | 3-1 | 1-3 | 1-0 | 1-1 | 1-3 | 1-0 | 1-1 |
| Bournemouth & B. Athletic | 0-0 | | 1-2 | 3-0 | 2-1 | 4-4 | 2-0 | 1-1 | 2-5 | 1-1 | 1-2 | 2-1 | 1-2 | 2-0 | 4-0 | 0-1 | 0-1 | 4-1 | 2-1 | 1-0 | 1-1 | 2-2 |
| Brighton & Hove Albion | 2-1 | 0-1 | | 3-0 | 4-1 | 1-0 | 1-3 | 2-1 | 2-1 | 3-1 | 1-1 | 1-1 | 0-0 | 7-1 | 5-1 | 5-1 | 1-1 | 4-2 | 1-3 | 0-2 | 3-2 | 2-1 |
| Bristol City FC | 1-0 | 1-0 | 0-3 | | 0-2 | 0-2 | 2-0 | 0-0 | 2-0 | 2-1 | 2-1 | 1-2 | 4-1 | 1-2 | 3-2 | 1-1 | 0-0 | 1-1 | 2-1 | 5-0 | 2-0 | 2-2 |
| Bristol Rovers FC | 2-2 | 2-1 | 5-2 | 1-1 | | 1-1 | 1-1 | 3-2 | 2-4 | 6-1 | 4-3 | 2-2 | 2-0 | 3-0 | 5-2 | 0-0 | 0-1 | 1-4 | 3-2 | 2-1 | 3-0 | 0-1 |
| Cardiff City AFC | 0-1 | 1-1 | 1-0 | 1-0 | 0-0 | | 4-1 | 1-0 | 1-1 | 5-2 | 4-0 | 2-3 | 3-1 | 2-0 | 0-0 | 3-2 | 3-2 | 2-3 | 1-1 | 2-1 | 1-2 | 0-2 |
| Clapton Orient FC | 0-1 | 1-1 | 3-1 | 2-0 | 2-0 | 2-1 | | 0-1 | 1-0 | 1-2 | 3-1 | 3-0 | 1-0 | 4-0 | 4-0 | 0-2 | 1-0 | 1-0 | 3-0 | 1-2 | 1-1 | 0-2 |
| Coventry City FC | 0-2 | 2-0 | 5-0 | 3-1 | 3-1 | 5-1 | 2-0 | | 8-1 | 3-0 | 4-0 | 0-0 | 5-0 | 7-1 | 4-0 | 5-1 | 6-1 | 3-1 | 3-0 | 3-1 | 2-1 | 2-0 |
| Crystal Palace FC | 2-1 | 2-0 | 4-0 | 6-1 | 5-3 | 3-2 | 2-2 | 3-1 | | 2-2 | 1-1 | 5-1 | 5-0 | 6-0 | 6-1 | 0-0 | 0-2 | 2-0 | 3-0 | 5-1 | 1-0 | 1-2 |
| Exeter City FC | 5-1 | 1-3 | 3-3 | 0-1 | 3-1 | 2-0 | 2-3 | 1-3 | 1-0 | | 2-5 | 1-2 | 4-3 | 3-3 | 3-1 | 0-0 | 0-0 | 4-5 | 1-0 | 0-3 | 1-1 | 1-3 |
| Gillingham FC | 4-2 | 1-2 | 1-2 | 2-1 | 1-2 | 3-0 | 3-0 | 1-1 | 0-2 | 2-2 | | 0-1 | 1-3 | 3-0 | 2-3 | 0-0 | 2-2 | 2-0 | 2-1 | 3-1 | 1-0 | 0-0 |
| Luton Town FC | 2-2 | 0-0 | 2-1 | 1-0 | 12-0 | 2-2 | 5-3 | 1-1 | 6-0 | 3-1 | 1-2 | | 0-0 | 7-0 | 3-3 | 1-0 | 2-0 | 2-1 | 1-2 | 2-1 | 1-0 | 2-1 |
| Millwall FC | 1-2 | 3-0 | 0-0 | 1-1 | 2-1 | 2-4 | 1-0 | 2-2 | 4-0 | 2-2 | 4-1 | 0-0 | | 2-2 | 2-1 | 2-1 | 2-0 | 0-1 | 1-2 | 1-0 | 1-1 | 0-0 |
| Newport County AFC | 1-1 | 0-0 | 0-2 | 2-0 | 1-0 | 0-0 | 2-3 | 2-1 | 2-5 | 2-1 | 4-2 | 0-2 | 4-1 | | 5-1 | 1-2 | 3-4 | 1-5 | 3-1 | 2-2 | 1-6 | 0-5 |
| Northampton Town FC | 3-0 | 2-1 | 1-0 | 0-2 | 3-3 | 2-0 | 2-0 | 2-4 | 3-1 | 1-1 | 0-0 | 0-0 | 2-4 | 3-0 | | 3-1 | 1-4 | 4-2 | 0-0 | | 2-1 | 2-0 |
| Notts County FC | 1-2 | 1-3 | 1-1 | 1-1 | 6-0 | 2-0 | 2-0 | 2-1 | 3-1 | 3-1 | 3-3 | 0-3 | 0-0 | 6-2 | 3-0 | | 3-0 | 1-3 | 1-2 | 0-0 | 1-0 | 0-2 |
| Queen's Park Rangers FC | 5-0 | 2-0 | 3-2 | 4-1 | 4-0 | 5-1 | 4-0 | 0-0 | 3-0 | 3-1 | 5-2 | 0-0 | 2-3 | 1-1 | 0-1 | 2-2 | | 0-1 | 2-1 | 5-1 | 2-1 | 3-1 |
| Reading FC | 3-1 | 0-2 | 3-0 | 5-2 | 3-2 | 4-1 | 4-1 | 2-1 | 0-1 | 2-0 | 1-0 | 2-1 | 3-1 | 5-2 | 3-1 | 1-2 | | | 2-1 | 2-0 | 2-0 | 3-0 |
| Southend United FC | 2-2 | 3-3 | 0-0 | 0-1 | 1-1 | 3-1 | 2-1 | 0-0 | 7-1 | 4-0 | 4-2 | 0-1 | 6-0 | 1-2 | 0-1 | 0-0 | 0-1 | 1-2 | | 1-0 | 2-1 | 1-1 |
| Swindon Town FC | 3-2 | 2-3 | 1-2 | 1-1 | 3-0 | 2-1 | 2-2 | 1-2 | 0-2 | 1-1 | 3-0 | 3-0 | 3-1 | 1-1 | 3-1 | 2-1 | 2-2 | 4-1 | 1-3 | | 4-1 | 1-6 |
| Torquay United FC | 3-1 | 0-2 | 1-0 | 2-0 | 2-0 | 2-1 | 1-0 | 3-3 | 3-2 | 2-1 | 4-2 | 2-1 | 1-3 | 3-2 | 3-3 | 0-1 | 4-2 | 0-0 | 1-1 | 2-1 | | 2-1 |
| Watford FC | 0-0 | 4-1 | 2-1 | 0-2 | 1-2 | 4-0 | 1-1 | 5-0 | 3-2 | 1-0 | 1-2 | 1-3 | 2-1 | 2-5 | 4-1 | 1-2 | 2-1 | 4-2 | 5-0 | 2-1 | 2-2 | |

## Division 3 (South)

| | | Pd | Wn | Dw | Ls | GF | GA | Pts | |
|---|---|---|---|---|---|---|---|---|---|
| 1. | Coventry City FC (Coventry) | 42 | 24 | 9 | 9 | 102 | 45 | 57 | P |
| 2. | Luton Town FC (Luton) | 42 | 22 | 12 | 8 | 81 | 45 | 56 | |
| 3. | Reading FC (Reading) | 42 | 26 | 2 | 14 | 87 | 62 | 54 | |
| 4. | Queen's Park Rangers FC (London) | 42 | 22 | 9 | 11 | 84 | 53 | 53 | |
| 5. | Watford FC (Watford) | 42 | 20 | 9 | 13 | 80 | 54 | 49 | |
| 6. | Crystal Palace FC (London) | 42 | 22 | 5 | 15 | 96 | 74 | 49 | |
| 7. | Brighton & Hove Albion FC (Hove) | 42 | 18 | 8 | 16 | 70 | 63 | 44 | |
| 8. | Bournemouth & Boscombe Athletic FC (Bournemouth) | 42 | 16 | 11 | 15 | 60 | 56 | 43 | |
| 9. | Notts County FC (Nottingham) | 42 | 15 | 12 | 15 | 60 | 57 | 42 | |
| 10. | Torquay United FC (Torquay) | 42 | 16 | 9 | 17 | 62 | 62 | 41 | |
| 11. | Aldershot FC (Aldershot) | 42 | 14 | 12 | 16 | 53 | 61 | 40 | |
| 12. | Millwall FC (London) | 42 | 14 | 12 | 16 | 58 | 71 | 40 | |
| 13. | Bristol City FC (Bristol) | 42 | 15 | 10 | 17 | 48 | 59 | 40 | |
| 14. | Clapton Orient FC (London) | 42 | 16 | 6 | 20 | 55 | 61 | 38 | |
| 15. | Northampton Town FC (Northampton) | 42 | 15 | 8 | 19 | 62 | 90 | 38 | |
| 16. | Gillingham FC (Gillingham) | 42 | 14 | 9 | 19 | 66 | 77 | 37 | |
| 17. | Bristol Rovers FC (Bristol) | 42 | 14 | 9 | 19 | 69 | 95 | 37 | |
| 18. | Southend United FC (Southend-on-Sea) | 42 | 13 | 10 | 19 | 61 | 62 | 36 | |
| 19. | Swindon Town FC (Swindon) | 42 | 14 | 8 | 20 | 64 | 73 | 36 | |
| 20. | Cardiff City AFC (Cardiff) | 42 | 13 | 10 | 19 | 60 | 73 | 36 | |
| 21. | Newport County AFC (Newport) | 42 | 11 | 9 | 22 | 60 | 111 | 31 | |
| 22. | Exeter City FC (Exeter) | 42 | 8 | 11 | 23 | 59 | 93 | 27 | |
| | | 924 | 362 | 200 | 362 | 1497 | 1497 | 924 | |

# F.A. CUP FINAL   (Wembley Stadium, London – 25/04/1936 – 93,384)

| ARSENAL FC (LONDON) | 1-0 | Sheffield United FC (Sheffield) |
|---|---|---|

*Drake*

Arsenal: Wilson, Male, Hapgood, Crayston, Roberts, Copping, Hulme, Bowden, Drake, James, Bastin.

Sheffield United: Smith, Hooper, Wilkinson, Jackson, Johnson, McPherson, Barton, Barclay, Dodds, Pickering, Williams.

## Semi-finals

| Arsenal FC (London) | 1-0 | Grimsby Town FC (Cleethorpes) |
|---|---|---|
| Fulham FC (London) | 1-2 | Sheffield United FC (Sheffield) |

## Quarter-finals

| Arsenal FC (London) | 4-1 | Barnsley FC (Barnsley) |
|---|---|---|
| Fulham FC (London) | 3-0 | Derby County FC (Derby) |
| Grimsby Town FC (Cleethorpes) | 3-1 | Middlesbrough FC (Middlesbrough) |
| Sheffield United FC (Sheffield) | 3-1 | Tottenham Hotspur FC (London) |

## 1936-37

| Football League Division 1 1936-1937 Season | Arsenal | Birmingham | Bolton Wanderers | Brentford | Charlton Athletic | Chelsea | Derby County | Everton | Grimsby Town | Huddersfield Town | Leeds United | Liverpool | Manchester City | Manchester United | Middlesbrough | Portsmouth | Preston North End | Sheffield Wednesday | Stoke City | Sunderland | W.B.A. | Wolves |
|---|---|---|---|---|---|---|---|---|---|---|---|---|---|---|---|---|---|---|---|---|---|---|
| Arsenal FC | | 1-1 | 0-0 | 1-1 | 1-1 | 4-1 | 2-2 | 3-2 | 0-0 | 1-1 | 4-1 | 1-0 | 1-3 | 1-1 | 5-3 | 4-0 | 4-1 | 1-1 | 0-0 | 4-1 | 2-0 | 3-0 |
| Birmingham FC | 1-3 | | 1-1 | 4-0 | 1-2 | 0-0 | 0-1 | 2-0 | 2-3 | 4-2 | 2-1 | 5-0 | 2-2 | 2-2 | 0-0 | 2-1 | 1-0 | 1-1 | 2-4 | 2-0 | 1-1 | 1-0 |
| Bolton Wanderers FC | 0-5 | 0-0 | | 2-2 | 2-1 | 2-1 | 1-3 | 1-2 | 1-2 | 2-2 | 2-1 | 0-1 | 0-2 | 0-4 | 1-3 | 1-0 | 0-0 | 1-0 | 0-0 | 1-1 | 4-1 | 1-2 |
| Brentford FC | 2-0 | 2-1 | 2-2 | | 4-2 | 1-0 | 6-2 | 2-2 | 2-3 | 1-1 | 4-1 | 5-2 | 2-6 | 4-0 | 4-1 | 4-0 | 1-1 | 2-1 | 2-1 | 3-3 | 2-1 | 3-2 |
| Charlton Athletic FC | 0-2 | 2-2 | 1-0 | 2-1 | | 1-0 | 2-0 | 2-0 | 1-0 | 1-0 | 1-0 | 1-1 | 1-1 | 3-0 | 2-2 | 0-0 | 3-1 | 1-0 | 2-0 | 3-1 | 4-2 | 4-0 |
| Chelsea FC | 2-0 | 1-3 | 0-1 | 2-1 | 3-0 | | 1-1 | 4-0 | 3-2 | 0-0 | 2-1 | 2-0 | 4-4 | 4-2 | 1-0 | 1-1 | 0-0 | 1-1 | 1-0 | 1-3 | 3-0 | 0-1 |
| Derby County FC | 5-4 | 3-1 | 3-0 | 2-3 | 5-0 | 1-1 | | 3-1 | 3-1 | 3-3 | 5-3 | 4-1 | 0-5 | 5-4 | 0-2 | 1-3 | 1-2 | 3-2 | 2-2 | 3-0 | 1-0 | 5-1 |
| Everton FC | 1-1 | 3-3 | 3-2 | 3-0 | 2-2 | 0-0 | 7-0 | | 3-0 | 2-1 | 7-1 | 2-0 | 1-1 | 2-3 | 2-3 | 4-0 | 2-2 | 3-1 | 1-1 | 3-0 | 4-2 | 1-0 |
| Grimsby Town FC | 1-3 | 1-1 | 3-1 | 0-1 | 3-0 | 3-4 | 1-0 | 3-0 | | 2-2 | 4-1 | 2-1 | 5-3 | 6-2 | 5-1 | 1-0 | 6-4 | 5-1 | 1-3 | 6-0 | 2-3 | 1-1 |
| Huddersfield Town AFC | 0-0 | 1-1 | 2-0 | 1-1 | 1-2 | 4-2 | 2-0 | 0-3 | 0-3 | | 3-0 | 4-0 | 1-1 | 3-1 | 2-0 | 1-2 | 4-2 | 1-0 | 2-1 | 2-1 | 1-1 | 4-0 |
| Leeds United AFC | 3-4 | 0-2 | 2-2 | 3-1 | 2-0 | 2-3 | 2-0 | 3-0 | 2-0 | 2-1 | | 2-0 | 1-1 | 2-1 | 5-0 | 3-1 | 1-0 | 1-1 | 1-2 | 3-0 | 3-1 | 0-1 |
| Liverpool FC | 2-1 | 2-0 | 0-0 | 2-2 | 1-2 | 1-1 | 3-3 | 3-2 | 7-1 | 1-1 | 3-0 | | 0-5 | 2-0 | 0-2 | 0-0 | 1-1 | 2-2 | 2-1 | 4-0 | 1-2 | 1-0 |
| Manchester City FC | 2-0 | 1-1 | 2-2 | 2-1 | 1-1 | 0-0 | 3-2 | 4-1 | 1-1 | 3-0 | 4-0 | 5-1 | | 1-0 | 2-1 | 3-1 | 4-1 | 4-1 | 2-1 | 2-4 | 6-2 | 4-1 |
| Manchester United FC | 2-0 | 1-2 | 1-0 | 1-3 | 0-0 | 0-0 | 2-2 | 2-1 | 1-1 | 3-1 | 0-0 | 2-5 | 3-2 | | 2-1 | 0-1 | 1-1 | 1-1 | 2-1 | 2-1 | 2-2 | 1-1 |
| Middlesbrough FC | 1-1 | 3-1 | 2-0 | 3-0 | 1-1 | 2-0 | 1-3 | 2-0 | 0-0 | 5-0 | 4-2 | 3-3 | 2-0 | 3-2 | | 2-2 | 2-1 | 2-0 | 1-0 | 5-5 | 4-1 | 1-0 |
| Portsmouth FC | 1-5 | 2-1 | 1-1 | 1-3 | 0-1 | 4-1 | 1-2 | 2-2 | 2-1 | 1-0 | 3-0 | 6-2 | 2-1 | 2-1 | 2-1 | | 0-1 | 1-0 | 1-0 | 3-2 | 5-3 | 1-1 |
| Preston North End FC | 1-3 | 2-2 | 1-2 | 1-1 | 0-0 | 1-0 | 5-2 | 1-0 | 3-2 | 1-1 | 1-0 | 3-1 | 2-5 | 3-1 | 2-0 | 1-1 | | 1-1 | 0-1 | 0-1 | 3-2 | 1-3 |
| Sheffield Wednesday FC | 0-0 | 0-3 | 2-0 | 0-2 | 3-1 | 1-1 | 2-3 | 6-4 | 2-1 | 2-2 | 1-2 | 1-2 | 5-1 | 1-0 | 1-0 | 0-0 | 0-1 | | 0-0 | 2-0 | 2-3 | 1-3 |
| Stoke City FC | 0-0 | 2-0 | 2-2 | 5-1 | 1-1 | 2-0 | 1-2 | 2-1 | 2-0 | 1-1 | 2-1 | 1-1 | 2-2 | 3-0 | 6-2 | 2-4 | 0-2 | 1-0 | | 5-3 | 10-3 | 2-1 |
| Sunderland AFC | 1-1 | 4-0 | 3-0 | 4-1 | 1-0 | 2-3 | 3-2 | 3-1 | 5-1 | 3-2 | 2-1 | 4-2 | 1-3 | 1-1 | 4-1 | 3-2 | 3-0 | 2-1 | 3-0 | | 1-0 | 6-2 |
| West Bromwich Albion FC | 2-4 | 3-2 | 0-2 | 1-0 | 1-2 | 2-0 | 1-3 | 2-1 | 4-2 | 2-1 | 3-0 | 3-1 | 2-2 | 1-0 | 3-1 | 3-1 | 0-0 | 2-3 | 2-2 | 6-4 | | 2-1 |
| Wolverhampton Wanderers FC | 2-0 | 2-1 | 2-3 | 4-0 | 6-1 | 1-2 | 3-1 | 7-2 | 5-2 | 3-1 | 3-0 | 2-0 | 2-1 | 3-1 | 0-1 | 1-1 | 5-0 | 4-3 | 2-1 | 1-1 | 5-2 | |

## Division 1

| | | Pd | Wn | Dw | Ls | GF | GA | Pts | |
|---|---|---|---|---|---|---|---|---|---|
| 1. | MANCHESTER CITY FC (MANCHESTER) | 42 | 22 | 13 | 7 | 107 | 61 | 57 | |
| 2. | Charlton Athletic FC (London) | 42 | 21 | 12 | 9 | 58 | 49 | 54 | |
| 3. | Arsenal FC (London) | 42 | 18 | 16 | 8 | 80 | 49 | 52 | |
| 4. | Derby County FC (Derby) | 42 | 21 | 7 | 14 | 96 | 90 | 49 | |
| 5. | Wolverhampton Wanderers FC (Wolverhampton) | 42 | 21 | 5 | 16 | 84 | 67 | 47 | |
| 6. | Brentford FC (London) | 42 | 18 | 10 | 14 | 82 | 78 | 46 | |
| 7. | Middlesbrough FC (Middlesbrough) | 42 | 19 | 8 | 15 | 74 | 71 | 46 | |
| 8. | Sunderland AFC (Sunderland) | 42 | 19 | 6 | 17 | 89 | 87 | 44 | |
| 9. | Portsmouth FC (Portsmouth) | 42 | 17 | 10 | 15 | 62 | 66 | 44 | |
| 10. | Stoke City FC (Stoke-on-Trent) | 42 | 15 | 12 | 15 | 72 | 57 | 42 | |
| 11. | Birmingham FC (Birmingham) | 42 | 13 | 15 | 14 | 64 | 60 | 41 | |
| 12. | Grimsby Town FC (Cleethorpes) | 42 | 17 | 7 | 18 | 86 | 81 | 41 | |
| 13. | Chelsea FC (London) | 42 | 14 | 13 | 15 | 52 | 55 | 41 | |
| 14. | Preston North End FC (Preston) | 42 | 14 | 13 | 15 | 56 | 67 | 41 | |
| 15. | Huddersfield Town AFC (Huddersfield) | 42 | 12 | 15 | 15 | 62 | 64 | 39 | |
| 16. | West Bromwich Albion FC (West Bromwich) | 42 | 16 | 6 | 20 | 77 | 98 | 38 | |
| 17. | Everton FC (Liverpool) | 42 | 14 | 9 | 19 | 81 | 78 | 37 | |
| 18. | Liverpool FC (Liverpool) | 42 | 12 | 11 | 19 | 62 | 84 | 35 | |
| 19. | Leeds United AFC (Leeds) | 42 | 15 | 4 | 23 | 60 | 80 | 34 | |
| 20. | Bolton Wanderers FC (Bolton) | 42 | 10 | 14 | 18 | 43 | 66 | 34 | |
| 21. | Manchester United FC (Manchester) | 42 | 10 | 12 | 20 | 55 | 78 | 32 | R |
| 22. | Sheffield Wednesday FC (Sheffield) | 42 | 9 | 12 | 21 | 53 | 69 | 30 | R |
| | | 924 | 347 | 230 | 347 | 1555 | 1555 | 924 | |

## Top Goalscorer

1)  Freddie STEELE                              (Stoke City FC)     33

| Football League Division 2 1936-1937 Season | Aston Villa | Barnsley | Blackburn R. | Blackpool | Bradford City | Bradford P.A. | Burnley | Bury | Chesterfield | Coventry City | Doncaster R. | Fulham | Leicester City | Newcastle Utd. | Norwich City | Nottingham F. | Plymouth Arg. | Sheffield United | Southampton | Swansea Town | Tottenham H. | West Ham Utd. |
|---|---|---|---|---|---|---|---|---|---|---|---|---|---|---|---|---|---|---|---|---|---|---|
| Aston Villa FC | | 4-2 | 2-2 | 4-0 | 5-1 | 4-1 | 0-0 | 0-4 | 6-2 | 0-0 | 1-1 | 0-3 | 1-3 | 0-2 | 3-0 | 1-1 | 5-4 | 2-1 | 4-0 | 4-0 | 1-1 | 0-2 |
| Barnsley FC | 0-4 | | 3-2 | 2-1 | 1-1 | 2-1 | 1-1 | 2-2 | 1-1 | 3-0 | 4-1 | 1-0 | 1-2 | 1-0 | 2-1 | 1-0 | 1-3 | 1-1 | 2-1 | 0-1 | 1-0 | 0-0 |
| Blackburn Rovers FC | 3-4 | 1-1 | | 2-0 | 3-0 | 1-1 | 3-1 | 2-3 | 5-2 | 2-5 | 2-0 | 0-2 | 0-0 | 6-1 | 1-0 | 9-1 | 2-3 | 3-1 | 1-0 | 2-1 | 0-4 | 1-2 |
| Blackpool FC | 2-3 | 1-1 | 2-0 | | 4-2 | 6-0 | 2-0 | 1-2 | 0-1 | 3-0 | 1-1 | 3-1 | 6-2 | 3-0 | 0-2 | 7-1 | 1-1 | 1-0 | 2-0 | 3-2 | 0-0 | 1-0 |
| Bradford City AFC | 2-2 | 3-2 | 2-2 | 1-4 | | 2-3 | 1-3 | 0-1 | 2-2 | 1-0 | 0-0 | 1-1 | 1-2 | 2-0 | 2-0 | 2-1 | 1-1 | 3-2 | 2-2 | 4-0 | 2-2 | 2-1 |
| Bradford Park Avenue | 3-3 | 2-1 | 1-2 | 2-1 | 2-1 | | 2-0 | 0-1 | 4-5 | 1-3 | 1-0 | 1-1 | 1-2 | 0-3 | 1-0 | 3-2 | 0-0 | 0-3 | 3-1 | 1-1 | 3-2 | 2-1 |
| Burnley FC | 1-2 | 3-0 | 0-0 | 3-0 | 3-0 | 2-2 | | 1-2 | 3-1 | 3-3 | 3-0 | 0-2 | 0-0 | 0-3 | 3-0 | 3-0 | 2-0 | 1-0 | 1-3 | 0-0 | 3-1 | 2-1 |
| Bury FC | 2-1 | 2-1 | 1-1 | 2-3 | 5-0 | 3-1 | 3-1 | | 4-0 | 0-4 | 4-2 | 1-1 | 0-1 | 1-2 | 3-2 | 1-1 | 2-0 | 2-0 | 2-1 | 2-0 | 5-3 | 1-1 |
| Chesterfield FC | 1-0 | 2-1 | 0-4 | 0-4 | 7-1 | 4-2 | 4-1 | 1-1 | | 2-3 | 5-1 | 4-1 | 2-5 | 4-0 | 3-1 | 4-2 | 0-1 | 2-2 | 3-0 | 4-0 | 1-3 | 1-1 |
| Coventry City FC | 1-0 | 3-0 | 0-1 | 1-2 | 3-1 | 4-0 | 0-1 | 1-3 | 2-1 | | 1-1 | 1-1 | 0-2 | 2-2 | 1-1 | 2-2 | 2-0 | 2-0 | 2-0 | 2-1 | 1-0 | 4-0 |
| Doncaster Rovers FC | 1-0 | 0-1 | 0-1 | 0-4 | 1-1 | 1-3 | 2-0 | 1-0 | 0-4 | 1-1 | | 2-1 | 0-0 | 1-2 | 1-2 | 0-2 | 2-1 | 1-1 | 2-0 | 0-0 | 1-1 | 1-4 |
| Fulham FC | 3-2 | 1-0 | 1-1 | 0-3 | 0-1 | 0-0 | 2-0 | 1-1 | 1-0 | 0-2 | 1-0 | | 2-0 | 3-4 | 2-3 | 5-2 | 2-2 | 4-0 | 2-0 | 5-0 | 3-3 | 5-0 |
| Leicester City FC | 1-0 | 5-1 | 1-0 | 1-2 | 4-1 | 5-0 | 7-3 | 0-3 | 3-1 | 1-0 | 7-1 | 2-0 | | 3-2 | 2-2 | 2-1 | 3-2 | 1-2 | 2-2 | 0-0 | 4-1 | 2-2 |
| Newcastle United FC | 0-2 | 0-1 | 2-0 | 1-2 | 2-0 | 1-1 | 3-0 | 1-3 | 1-2 | 4-2 | 7-0 | 1-1 | 1-0 | | 0-1 | 3-2 | 1-1 | 4-0 | 3-0 | 5-1 | 0-1 | 5-3 |
| Norwich City FC | 5-1 | 0-1 | 0-0 | 1-2 | 0-0 | 3-1 | 2-2 | 0-0 | 2-0 | 0-3 | 2-1 | 3-0 | 1-2 | 1-5 | | 4-0 | 1-2 | 1-1 | 4-2 | 3-0 | 2-3 | 3-3 |
| Nottingham Forest FC | 1-1 | 4-1 | 2-0 | 1-1 | 2-1 | 3-2 | 1-2 | 1-0 | 2-2 | 1-1 | 2-1 | 5-3 | 0-3 | 0-2 | 3-4 | | 2-3 | 1-1 | 1-1 | 6-1 | 3-0 | 1-0 |
| Plymouth Argyle FC | 2-2 | 1-2 | 2-0 | 1-3 | 4-4 | 2-0 | 0-1 | 3-0 | 1-1 | 1-0 | 7-0 | 0-3 | 2-1 | 1-1 | 2-0 | 4-1 | | 2-0 | 3-1 | 0-0 | 2-2 | 2-0 |
| Sheffield United FC | 5-1 | 2-0 | 0-1 | 2-2 | 3-1 | 3-0 | 1-1 | 1-1 | 5-0 | 2-2 | 3-1 | 2-0 | 3-1 | 2-1 | 2-0 | 4-1 | 2-0 | | 0-0 | 1-0 | 3-2 | 2-0 |
| Southampton FC | 2-2 | 1-3 | 2-2 | 5-2 | 2-0 | 0-0 | 1-1 | 4-1 | 3-2 | 1-1 | 1-0 | 3-3 | 1-1 | 2-0 | 3-1 | 0-3 | 0-0 | 4-0 | | 2-1 | 1-0 | 0-2 |
| Swansea Town AFC | 1-2 | 3-1 | 1-0 | 1-1 | 3-0 | 3-0 | 3-0 | 2-0 | 4-1 | 2-0 | 0-1 | 3-0 | 1-3 | 1-2 | 1-0 | 0-1 | 2-1 | 5-1 | | | 2-1 | 0-0 |
| Tottenham Hotspur FC | 2-2 | 3-0 | 5-1 | 1-2 | 5-1 | 5-1 | 3-0 | 2-0 | 5-1 | 3-1 | 2-0 | 1-1 | 4-2 | 0-1 | 2-3 | 2-1 | 1-3 | 2-2 | 4-0 | 3-1 | | 2-3 |
| West Ham United FC | 2-1 | 0-0 | 3-1 | 3-0 | 4-1 | 1-0 | 0-2 | 5-1 | 1-1 | 4-0 | 1-0 | 3-3 | 4-1 | 0-2 | 4-1 | 2-2 | 1-1 | 1-0 | 4-0 | 2-0 | 2-1 | |

| | **Division 2** | **Pd** | **Wn** | **Dw** | **Ls** | **GF** | **GA** | **Pts** | |
|---|---|---|---|---|---|---|---|---|---|
| 1. | Leicester City FC (Leicester) | 42 | 24 | 8 | 10 | 89 | 57 | 56 | P |
| 2. | Blackpool FC (Blackpool) | 42 | 24 | 7 | 11 | 88 | 53 | 55 | P |
| 3. | Bury FC (Bury) | 42 | 22 | 8 | 12 | 74 | 55 | 52 | |
| 4. | Newcastle United FC (Newcastle-upon-Tyne) | 42 | 22 | 5 | 15 | 80 | 56 | 49 | |
| 5. | Plymouth Argyle FC (Plymouth) | 42 | 18 | 13 | 11 | 71 | 53 | 49 | |
| 6. | West Ham United FC (London) | 42 | 19 | 11 | 12 | 73 | 55 | 49 | |
| 7. | Sheffield United FC (Sheffield) | 42 | 18 | 10 | 14 | 66 | 54 | 46 | |
| 8. | Coventry City FC (Coventry) | 42 | 17 | 11 | 14 | 66 | 54 | 45 | |
| 9. | Aston Villa FC (Birmingham) | 42 | 16 | 12 | 14 | 82 | 70 | 44 | |
| 10. | Tottenham Hotspur FC (London) | 42 | 17 | 9 | 16 | 88 | 66 | 43 | |
| 11. | Fulham FC (London) | 42 | 15 | 13 | 14 | 71 | 61 | 43 | |
| 12. | Blackburn Rovers FC (Blackburn) | 42 | 16 | 10 | 16 | 70 | 62 | 42 | |
| 13. | Burnley FC (Burnley) | 42 | 16 | 10 | 16 | 57 | 61 | 42 | |
| 14. | Barnsley FC (Barnsley) | 42 | 16 | 9 | 17 | 50 | 64 | 41 | |
| 15. | Chesterfield FC (Chesterfield) | 42 | 16 | 8 | 18 | 84 | 89 | 40 | |
| 16. | Swansea Town AFC (Swansea) | 42 | 15 | 7 | 20 | 50 | 65 | 37 | |
| 17. | Norwich City FC (Norwich) | 42 | 14 | 8 | 20 | 63 | 71 | 36 | |
| 18. | Nottingham Forest FC (Nottingham) | 42 | 12 | 10 | 20 | 68 | 90 | 34 | |
| 19. | Southampton FC (Southampton) | 42 | 11 | 12 | 19 | 53 | 77 | 34 | |
| 20. | Bradford Park Avenue FC (Bradford) | 42 | 12 | 9 | 21 | 52 | 88 | 33 | |
| 21. | Bradford City AFC (Bradford) | 42 | 9 | 12 | 21 | 54 | 94 | 30 | R |
| 22. | Doncaster Rovers FC (Doncaster) | 42 | 7 | 10 | 25 | 30 | 84 | 24 | R |
| | | 924 | 356 | 212 | 356 | 1479 | 1479 | 924 | |

| Football League Division 3 (N) 1936-1937 Season | Accrington St. | Barrow | Carlisle United | Chester | Crewe Alex. | Darlington | Gateshead | Halifax Town | Hartlepools Utd. | Hull City | Lincoln City | Mansfield Town | New Brighton | Oldham Athletic | Port Vale | Rochdale | Rotherham Utd. | Southport | Stockport Co. | Tranmere R. | Wrexham | York City |
|---|---|---|---|---|---|---|---|---|---|---|---|---|---|---|---|---|---|---|---|---|---|---|
| Accrington Stanley FC | ■ | 5-0 | 2-1 | 2-1 | 4-1 | 1-0 | 2-1 | 3-2 | 1-2 | 0-1 | 1-2 | 0-3 | 5-0 | 1-1 | 2-3 | 3-1 | 3-0 | 6-3 | 2-1 | 4-0 | 2-2 | 2-1 |
| Barrow AFC | 1-0 | ■ | 5-0 | 1-2 | 2-2 | 1-0 | 3-0 | 1-2 | 3-1 | 2-3 | 0-4 | 2-2 | 2-1 | 1-2 | 3-1 | 3-0 | 5-1 | 2-1 | 0-0 | 2-0 | 1-1 | 2-2 |
| Carlisle United FC | 2-0 | 2-2 | ■ | 1-1 | 4-0 | 2-0 | 2-1 | 1-2 | 2-0 | 1-1 | 3-1 | 1-2 | 1-1 | 2-1 | 5-2 | 10 | 4-1 | 1-1 | 1-0 | 3-1 | 2-1 | 1-1 |
| Chester FC | 1-1 | 6-0 | 4-0 | ■ | 5-0 | 2-1 | 6-0 | 1-1 | 3-0 | 3-1 | 7-3 | 5-1 | 4-1 | 2-1 | 0-0 | 2-2 | 2-1 | 2-3 | 1-1 | 5-2 | 4-1 | 3-1 |
| Crewe Alexandra FC | 2-2 | 4-1 | 1-2 | 1-1 | ■ | 1-1 | 3-1 | 0-1 | 1-1 | 2-1 | 2-1 | 2-1 | 0-2 | 1-2 | 0-1 | 2-2 | 0-2 | 3-2 | 1-2 | 2-2 | 1-1 | 2-2 |
| Darlington FC | 4-1 | 2-4 | 1-5 | 1-3 | 0-3 | ■ | 0-2 | 3-3 | 5-5 | 2-2 | 2-2 | 0-0 | 1-2 | 0-3 | 1-0 | 4-1 | 6-3 | 4-2 | 1-1 | 3-2 | 1-1 | 1-1 |
| Gateshead FC | 1-1 | 1-1 | 1-0 | 1-1 | 2-0 | 5-0 | ■ | 0-2 | 2-2 | 6-3 | 0-5 | 3-3 | 1-1 | 0-0 | 3-1 | 2-1 | 5-4 | 0-0 | 4-0 | -00 | | 3-2 |
| Halifax Town AFC | 3-0 | 2-1 | 6-1 | 1-0 | 4-1 | 4-1 | 2-1 | ■ | 2-0 | 1-0 | 2-3 | 0-0 | 0-0 | 0-1 | 0-1 | 3-2 | 4-1 | 1-1 | 1-1 | 2-1 | 1-2 | 1-2 |
| Hartlepools United FC | 1-0 | 3-1 | 3-0 | 0-1 | 4-1 | 1-3 | 6-1 | 5-3 | ■ | 2-2 | 3-1 | 3-0 | 5-0 | 1-0 | 2-0 | 4-1 | 0-2 | 2-0 | 2-4 | 2-1 | 2-0 | 2-0 |
| Hull City AFC | 0-3 | 3-2 | 1-1 | 1-1 | 2-0 | 4-3 | 3-2 | 0-0 | 1-0 | ■ | 1-1 | 3-0 | 4-1 | 2-0 | 1-1 | 1-1 | 2-1 | 3-2 | 0-1 | 5-2 | 1-0 | 1-0 |
| Lincoln City FC | 3-3 | 6-0 | 3-0 | 3-0 | 2-4 | 4-3 | 4-0 | 4-1 | 3-0 | 5-0 | ■ | 2-0 | 2-0 | 1-0 | 5-3 | 3-0 | 4-1 | 0-2 | 1-0 | 6-2 | 3-1 | |
| Mansfield Town FC | 2-1 | 2-1 | 1-4 | 5-0 | 1-4 | 3-1 | 3-2 | 3-0 | 8-2 | 5-2 | 2-2 | ■ | 2-3 | 1-2 | 7-1 | 6-2 | 4-1 | 3-0 | 0-2 | 2-3 | 3-0 | 1-2 |
| New Brighton FC | 1-1 | 1-1 | 1-1 | 1-0 | 1-0 | 2-0 | 1-1 | 1-1 | 4-0 | 1-1 | 1-2 | 0-0 | ■ | 0-2 | 2-0 | 5-1 | 4-0 | 3-1 | 1-1 | 1-2 | 1-0 | 4-1 |
| Oldham Athletic AFC | 3-1 | 4-3 | 2-1 | 1-1 | 1-1 | 1-1 | 4-4 | 1-0 | 2-0 | 3-1 | 1-0 | 1-1 | 3-1 | ■ | 5-1 | 3-0 | 3-3 | 0-2 | 3-0 | 2-2 | 2-2 | |
| Port Vale FC | 1-1 | 3-2 | 1-0 | 4-0 | 0-0 | 2-2 | 4-2 | 3-1 | 1-0 | 1-3 | 1-1 | 5-1 | 3-1 | 1-0 | ■ | 1-1 | 2-1 | 0-2 | 3-0 | 2-1 | 0-3 | 1-1 |
| Rochdale AFC | 4-1 | 3-1 | 3-0 | 0-1 | 2-0 | 4-0 | 0-2 | 3-5 | 1-1 | 4-0 | 2-3 | 1-3 | 4-0 | 3-0 | 0-0 | ■ | 1-0 | 2-1 | 2-2 | 2-1 | 0-6 | 3-0 |
| Rotherham United FC | 2-2 | 4-1 | 0-1 | 2-1 | 3-2 | 2-4 | 3-0 | 6-0 | 2-4 | 0-0 | 3-1 | 4-1 | 3-0 | 4-4 | 2-0 | 1-1 | ■ | 3-0 | 1-1 | 3-1 | 2-2 | 2-2 |
| Southport FC | 3-1 | 3-3 | 2-1 | 1-2 | 1-1 | 0-0 | 3-0 | 2-1 | 1-1 | 1-4 | 2-1 | 3-2 | 3-0 | 2-0 | 3-1 | 4-1 | | ■ | 1-1 | 1-0 | 1-1 | 1-4 |
| Stockport County FC | 3-2 | 4-1 | 1-2 | 4-0 | 1-0 | 3-3 | 4-2 | 0-0 | 1-1 | 3-1 | 2-0 | 3-1 | 4-1 | 1-0 | 3-0 | 4-2 | 2-1 | | ■ | 5-0 | 2-0 | 6-0 |
| Tranmere Rovers FC | 1-2 | 0-0 | 5-1 | 5-0 | 6-1 | 1-1 | 6-1 | 2-1 | 1-0 | 2-1 | 2-2 | 0-2 | 3-2 | 3-3 | 4-2 | 4-3 | 1-2 | 3-3 | 2-2 | ■ | 1-1 | 0-0 |
| Wrexham AFC | 1-0 | 2-1 | 1-0 | 1-2 | 5-0 | 4-0 | 6-0 | 0-2 | 0-1 | 2-1 | 0-3 | 2-3 | 4-1 | 1-1 | 1-0 | 0-1 | 4-2 | 3-3 | 0-0 | 2-0 | ■ | 2-0 |
| York City FC | 4-2 | 1-2 | 5-2 | 0-2 | 2-3 | 3-0 | 2-0 | 4-0 | 4-1 | 1-1 | 0-0 | 1-1 | 2-1 | 3-1 | 1-2 | 4-1 | 4-3 | 4-0 | 2-1 | 4-0 | 3-4 | ■ |

## Division 3 (North)

| | | Pd | Wn | Dw | Ls | GF | GA | Pts | |
|---|---|---|---|---|---|---|---|---|---|
| 1. | Stockport County FC (Stockport) | 42 | 23 | 14 | 5 | 84 | 39 | 60 | P |
| 2. | Lincoln City FC (Lincoln) | 42 | 25 | 7 | 10 | 103 | 57 | 57 | |
| 3. | Chester FC (Chester) | 42 | 22 | 9 | 11 | 87 | 57 | 53 | |
| 4. | Oldham Athletic AFC (Oldham) | 42 | 20 | 11 | 11 | 77 | 59 | 51 | |
| 5. | Hull City AFC (Kingston-upon-Hull) | 42 | 17 | 12 | 13 | 68 | 69 | 46 | |
| 6. | Hartlepools United FC (Hartlepool) | 42 | 19 | 7 | 16 | 75 | 69 | 45 | |
| 7. | Halifax Town AFC (Halifax) | 42 | 18 | 9 | 15 | 68 | 63 | 45 | |
| 8. | Wrexham AFC (Wrexham) | 42 | 16 | 12 | 14 | 71 | 57 | 44 | |
| 9. | Mansfield Town FC (Mansfield) | 42 | 18 | 8 | 16 | 91 | 76 | 44 | T |
| 10. | Carlisle United FC (Carlisle) | 42 | 18 | 8 | 16 | 65 | 68 | 44 | |
| 11. | Port Vale FC (Stoke-on-Trent) | 42 | 17 | 10 | 15 | 58 | 64 | 44 | |
| 12. | York City FC (York) | 42 | 16 | 11 | 15 | 79 | 70 | 43 | |
| 13. | Accrington Stanley FC (Accrington) | 42 | 16 | 9 | 17 | 76 | 69 | 41 | |
| 14. | Southport FC (Southport) | 42 | 12 | 13 | 17 | 73 | 87 | 37 | |
| 15. | New Brighton FC (Wallasey) | 42 | 13 | 11 | 18 | 55 | 70 | 37 | |
| 16. | Barrow AFC (Barrow-in-Furness) | 42 | 13 | 10 | 19 | 70 | 86 | 36 | |
| 17. | Rotherham United FC (Rotherham) | 42 | 14 | 7 | 21 | 78 | 91 | 35 | |
| 18. | Rochdale AFC (Rochdale) | 42 | 13 | 9 | 20 | 69 | 86 | 35 | |
| 19. | Tranmere Rovers FC (Birkenhead) | 42 | 12 | 9 | 21 | 71 | 88 | 33 | |
| 20. | Crewe Alexandra FC (Crewe) | 42 | 10 | 12 | 20 | 55 | 83 | 32 | |
| 21. | Gateshead FC (Gateshead) | 42 | 11 | 10 | 21 | 63 | 98 | 32 | |
| 22. | Darlington FC (Darlington) | 42 | 8 | 14 | 20 | 66 | 96 | 30 | |
| | | 924 | 351 | 222 | 351 | 1602 | 1602 | 924 | |

T: Mansfield Town FC (Mansfield) were transferred to Division 3 (South) from the next season.

**Football League Division 3 (S) 1936-1937 Season**

| | Aldershot | Bournemouth | Brighton | Bristol City | Bristol Rovers | Cardiff City | Clapton Orient | Crystal Palace | Exeter City | Gillingham | Luton Town | Millwall | Newport County | Northampton | Notts County | Q.P.R. | Reading | Southend United | Swindon Town | Torquay United | Walsall | Watford |
|---|---|---|---|---|---|---|---|---|---|---|---|---|---|---|---|---|---|---|---|---|---|---|
| Aldershot FC | | 1-3 | 0-1 | 3-0 | 4-0 | 0-1 | 1-1 | 2-2 | 1-1 | 3-0 | 2-3 | 1-2 | 2-0 | 0-2 | 0-1 | 0-0 | 0-2 | 1-2 | 2-1 | 0-1 | 4-4 | 2-2 |
| Bournemouth & B. Athletic | 2-1 | | 1-0 | 0-0 | 3-0 | 0-2 | 2-1 | 3-1 | 0-0 | 1-0 | 2-1 | 2-1 | 5-0 | 3-2 | 1-0 | 3-1 | 2-1 | 1-0 | 5-2 | 3-3 | 3-2 | 3-2 |
| Brighton & Hove Albion | 1-0 | 1-0 | | 2-0 | 5-2 | 7-2 | 1-1 | 1-0 | 1-0 | 4-0 | 2-1 | 2-2 | 2-0 | 1-2 | 2-2 | 4-1 | 1-1 | 1-0 | 2-0 | 5-1 | 3-0 | 1-1 |
| Bristol City FC | 3-0 | 4-1 | 1-0 | | 4-1 | 2-1 | 4-0 | 1-0 | 2-1 | 2-0 | 2-3 | 2-0 | 3-1 | 0-1 | 1-1 | 3-2 | 1-2 | 0-1 | 1-2 | 4-1 | 0-0 | 2-2 |
| Bristol Rovers FC | 1-0 | 4-0 | 2-0 | 3-1 | | 5-1 | 4-0 | 1-0 | 4-2 | 0-3 | 4-0 | 2-1 | 1-1 | 2-0 | 2-3 | 1-1 | 2-2 | 1-2 | 2-1 | 5-1 | 3-0 | 0-1 |
| Cardiff City AFC | 4-1 | 2-1 | 1-2 | 3-1 | 3-1 | | 2-1 | 1-1 | 3-1 | 2-0 | 3-0 | 0-1 | 0-1 | 2-1 | 0-2 | 2-0 | 1-1 | 1-1 | 1-2 | 0-2 | 2-2 | 2-2 |
| Clapton Orient FC | 1-1 | 2-1 | 2-0 | 0-0 | 2-1 | 0-1 | | 1-1 | 1-0 | 2-0 | 0-2 | 1-0 | 1-2 | 3-1 | 1-1 | 0-0 | 3-2 | 3-0 | 1-1 | 2-0 | 2-2 | 1-1 |
| Crystal Palace FC | 3-0 | 2-2 | 2-0 | 1-0 | 3-0 | 2-2 | 2-3 | | 8-0 | 1-1 | 0-4 | 1-0 | 6-1 | 2-2 | 1-2 | 0-0 | 3-1 | 1-1 | 2-0 | 0-0 | 3-1 | 2-0 |
| Exeter City FC | 1-2 | 1-1 | 0-4 | 3-0 | 3-2 | 3-1 | 0-2 | 3-2 | | 1-1 | 2-4 | 1-1 | 3-1 | 2-5 | 1-3 | 0-3 | 2-0 | 2-2 | 1-1 | 2-1 | 3-0 | 2-1 |
| Gillingham FC | 1-2 | 1-0 | 1-0 | 5-3 | 1-0 | 0-0 | 0-2 | 2-0 | 2-2 | | 1-0 | 1-0 | 4-4 | 2-0 | 3-0 | 0-0 | 2-1 | 1-0 | 4-1 | 1-0 | 2-2 | 2-1 |
| Luton Town FC | 5-2 | 1-0 | 2-1 | 4-0 | 2-0 | 8-1 | 2-0 | 5-2 | 2-2 | 5-2 | | 5-0 | 5-0 | 3-2 | 2-1 | 0-1 | 4-0 | 1-0 | 5-1 | 2-0 | 2-0 | 4-1 |
| Millwall FC | 4-2 | 0-2 | 3-0 | 3-1 | 1-2 | 3-1 | 2-1 | 3-0 | 3-3 | 3-0 | 0-2 | | 7-2 | 1-0 | 0-0 | 2-0 | 0-2 | 1-2 | 1-1 | 1-1 | 3-1 | 2-1 |
| Newport County AFC | 4-0 | 4-0 | 1-4 | 0-0 | 2-2 | 2-3 | 1-1 | 1-1 | 2-0 | 0-0 | 2-1 | 1-2 | | 1-3 | 2-0 | 1-2 | 3-0 | 6-2 | 1-1 | 1-1 | 1-2 | 1-3 |
| Northampton Town FC | 5-3 | 0-0 | 2-0 | 5-1 | 4-1 | 2-0 | 1-1 | 2-0 | 2-1 | 5-0 | 3-1 | 2-2 | 3-2 | | 1-1 | 0-1 | 2-1 | 4-3 | 4-0 | 3-0 | 6-3 | 0-1 |
| Notts County FC | 3-0 | 4-3 | 0-1 | 1-0 | 4-3 | 4-0 | 0-0 | 0-1 | 3-1 | 2-0 | 2-1 | 1-1 | 3-1 | 3-2 | | 1-2 | 1-0 | 2-1 | 3-2 | 2-0 | 3-3 | 2-1 |
| Queen's Park Rangers FC | 3-0 | -2 | 2-3 | 5-0 | 2-1 | 6-0 | 2-1 | 1-3 | 4-0 | 0-1 | 2-1 | 0-1 | 6-2 | 3-2 | 0-2 | | 0-0 | 7-2 | 1-1 | 3-0 | 2-0 | 1-2 |
| Reading FC | 2-0 | 3-2 | 2-0 | 2-1 | 2-0 | 3-0 | 1-1 | 1-1 | 1-0 | 6-2 | 2-2 | 3-0 | 4-4 | 3-1 | 4-1 | 2-0 | | 2-3 | 2-2 | 5-1 | 0-2 | 3-0 |
| Southend United FC | 2-2 | 0-0 | 2-1 | 3-0 | 2-3 | 8-1 | 0-0 | 2-1 | 4-4 | 0-2 | 3-0 | 0-0 | 9-2 | 2-0 | 2-3 | 3-2 | 1-1 | | 2-0 | 0-0 | 3-0 | 1-1 |
| Swindon Town FC | 5-1 | 3-1 | 1-2 | 0-1 | 4-1 | 4-2 | 1-3 | 4-0 | 3-1 | 3-0 | 2-2 | 3-0 | 1-2 | 2-0 | 2-2 | 1-1 | 1-2 | 4-0 | | 4-2 | 3-0 | 1-1 |
| Torquay United FC | 5-1 | 0-0 | 0-2 | 5-2 | 1-0 | 1-0 | 4-1 | 3-0 | 0-1 | 0-2 | 2-2 | 1-2 | 0-2 | 1-2 | 5-0 | 2-2 | 1-1 | 2-2 | 1-4 | | 3-1 | 4-7 |
| Walsall FC | 0-0 | 1-1 | 1-4 | 1-5 | 5-2 | 1-0 | 3-2 | 1-0 | 4-2 | 2-1 | 0-1 | 0-3 | 1-2 | 2-2 | 2-1 | 2-4 | 0-1 | 3-0 | 5-2 | 1-0 | | 3-1 |
| Watford FC | 5-3 | 4-0 | 1-0 | 1-0 | 3-0 | 2-0 | 2-1 | 3-1 | 1-1 | 6-1 | 1-3 | 2-2 | 3-0 | 4-1 | 0-2 | 2-0 | 6-1 | 1-3 | 2-2 | 4-0 | 0-0 | |

## Division 3 (South)

| | | Pd | Wn | Dw | Ls | GF | GA | Pts | |
|---|---|---|---|---|---|---|---|---|---|
| 1. | Luton Town FC (Luton) | 42 | 27 | 4 | 11 | 103 | 53 | 58 | P |
| 2. | Notts County FC (Nottingham) | 42 | 23 | 10 | 9 | 74 | 52 | 56 | |
| 3. | Brighton & Hove Albion FC (Hove) | 42 | 24 | 5 | 13 | 74 | 43 | 53 | |
| 4. | Watford FC (Watford) | 42 | 19 | 11 | 12 | 85 | 60 | 49 | |
| 5. | Reading FC (Reading) | 42 | 19 | 11 | 12 | 76 | 60 | 49 | |
| 6. | Bournemouth & Boscombe Athletic FC (Bournemouth) | 42 | 20 | 9 | 13 | 65 | 59 | 49 | |
| 7. | Northampton Town FC (Northampton) | 42 | 20 | 6 | 16 | 85 | 68 | 46 | |
| 8. | Millwall FC (London) | 42 | 18 | 10 | 14 | 64 | 54 | 46 | |
| 9. | Queen's Park Rangers FC (London) | 42 | 18 | 9 | 15 | 73 | 52 | 45 | |
| 10. | Southend United FC (Southend-on-Sea) | 42 | 17 | 11 | 14 | 78 | 67 | 45 | |
| 11. | Gillingham FC (Gillingham) | 42 | 18 | 8 | 16 | 52 | 66 | 44 | |
| 12. | Clapton Orient FC (London) | 42 | 14 | 15 | 13 | 52 | 52 | 43 | |
| 13. | Swindon Town FC (Swindon) | 42 | 14 | 11 | 17 | 75 | 73 | 39 | |
| 14. | Crystal Palace FC (London) | 42 | 13 | 12 | 17 | 62 | 61 | 38 | |
| 15. | Bristol Rovers FC (Bristol) | 42 | 16 | 4 | 22 | 71 | 80 | 36 | |
| 16. | Bristol City FC (Bristol) | 42 | 15 | 6 | 21 | 58 | 70 | 36 | |
| 17. | Walsall FC (Walsall) | 42 | 13 | 10 | 19 | 62 | 84 | 36 | |
| 18. | Cardiff City AFC (Cardiff) | 42 | 14 | 7 | 21 | 54 | 87 | 35 | |
| 19. | Newport County AFC (Newport) | 42 | 12 | 10 | 20 | 67 | 98 | 34 | |
| 20. | Torquay United FC (Torquay) | 42 | 11 | 10 | 21 | 57 | 80 | 32 | |
| 21. | Exeter City FC (Exeter) | 42 | 10 | 12 | 20 | 59 | 88 | 32 | |
| 22. | Aldershot FC (Aldershot) | 42 | 7 | 9 | 26 | 50 | 89 | 23 | |
| | | 924 | 362 | 200 | 362 | 1496 | 1496 | 924 | |

## F.A. CUP FINAL  (Wembley Stadium, London – 01/05/1937 – 93,495)

SUNDERLAND AFC (SUNDERLAND)　　　3-1　　　Preston North End FC (Preston)

*Gurney, Carter, Burbanks*　　　　　　　　　　　　　　　　　　*F.O'Donnell*

Sunderland: Mapson, Gorman, Hall, Thomson, Johnson, McNab, Duns, Carter, Gurney, Gallacher, Burbanks.

Preston: Burns, Gallimore, A.Beattie, Shankly, Tremelling, Milne, Dougal, Beresford, F.O'Donnell, Fagan, H.O'Donnell.

## Semi-finals

| | | |
|---|---|---|
| Preston North End FC (Preston) | 4-1 | West Bromwich Albion FC (West Bromwich) |
| Sunderland AFC (Sunderland) | 2-1 | Millwall FC (London) |

## Quarter-finals

| | | |
|---|---|---|
| Millwall FC (London) | 2-0 | Manchester City FC (Manchester) |
| Tottenham Hotspur FC (London) | 1-3 | Preston North End FC (Preston) |
| West Bromwich Albion FC (West Bromwich) | 3-1 | Arsenal FC (London) |
| Wolverhampton Wanderers FC | 1-1, 2-2 (aet), 0-4 (aet) | Sunderland AFC (Sunderland) |

# 1937-38

| Football League Division 1 1937-1938 Season | Arsenal | Birmingham | Blackpool | Bolton Wanderers | Brentford | Charlton Athletic | Chelsea | Derby County | Everton | Grimsby Town | Huddersfield Town | Leeds United | Leicester City | Liverpool | Manchester City | Middlesbrough | Portsmouth | Preston North End | Stoke City | Sunderland | W.B.A. | Wolves |
|---|---|---|---|---|---|---|---|---|---|---|---|---|---|---|---|---|---|---|---|---|---|---|
| Arsenal FC | ■ | 0-0 | 2-1 | 5-0 | 0-2 | 2-2 | 2-0 | 3-0 | 2-1 | 5-1 | 3-1 | 4-1 | 3-1 | 1-0 | 2-1 | 1-2 | 1-1 | 2-0 | 4-0 | 4-1 | 1-1 | 5-0 |
| Birmingham FC | 1-2 | ■ | 1-1 | 2-0 | 0-0 | 1-1 | 1-1 | 1-0 | 0-3 | 2-2 | 2-2 | 3-2 | 4-1 | 2-2 | 2-2 | 3-1 | 2-2 | 0-2 | 1-1 | 2-2 | 2-1 | 2-0 |
| Blackpool FC | 2-1 | 0-3 | ■ | 2-2 | 1-1 | 1-0 | 0-2 | 1-1 | 1-0 | 2-2 | 4-0 | 5-2 | 2-4 | 0-1 | 2-1 | 4-2 | 2-0 | 1-0 | 0-1 | 0-0 | 3-1 | 0-2 |
| Bolton Wanderers FC | 1-0 | 1-1 | 3-0 | ■ | 2-0 | 1-0 | 5-5 | 0-2 | 1-2 | 3-1 | 2-0 | 0-0 | 6-1 | 0-0 | 2-1 | 3-1 | 1-1 | 1-4 | 1-0 | 1-1 | 3-0 | 1-2 |
| Brentford FC | 3-0 | 1-2 | 2-4 | 1-1 | ■ | 5-2 | 1-1 | 2-3 | 3-0 | 6-1 | 2-0 | 1-1 | 1-1 | 1-3 | 2-1 | 3-3 | 2-0 | 2-1 | 0-0 | 4-0 | 0-2 | 2-1 |
| Charlton Athletic FC | 0-3 | 2-0 | 4-1 | 1-1 | 1-0 | ■ | 3-1 | 1-2 | 3-1 | 0-0 | 4-0 | 1-1 | 2-0 | 3-0 | 0-0 | 1-0 | 5-1 | 0-0 | 3-0 | 2-1 | 3-1 | 4-1 |
| Chelsea FC | 2-2 | 2-0 | 1-3 | 0-0 | 2-1 | 1-1 | ■ | 3-0 | 2-0 | 1-0 | 3-1 | 4-1 | 4-1 | 6-1 | 2-2 | 0-1 | 3-1 | 0-2 | 2-1 | 0-0 | 2-2 | 0-2 |
| Derby County FC | 2-0 | 0-0 | 3-1 | 4-2 | 1-3 | 3-2 | 4-0 | ■ | 2-1 | 1-2 | 0-4 | 2-2 | 0-1 | 4-1 | 1-7 | 1-1 | 1-0 | 1-1 | 4-1 | 2-2 | 5-3 | 1-2 |
| Everton FC | 1-4 | 1-1 | 3-1 | 4-1 | 3-0 | 3-0 | 4-1 | 1-1 | ■ | 3-2 | 1-2 | 1-1 | 3-0 | 1-3 | 4-1 | 2-2 | 5-2 | 3-5 | 3-0 | 3-3 | 5-3 | 0-1 |
| Grimsby Town FC | 2-1 | 4-0 | 1-0 | 0-1 | 0-1 | 1-1 | 2-0 | 0-0 | 2-1 | ■ | 4-2 | 1-1 | 2-1 | 0-0 | 3-1 | 2-1 | 1-0 | 1-1 | 1-5 | 0-2 | 1-4 | 1-0 |
| Huddersfield Town AFC | 2-1 | 2-1 | 3-1 | 1-0 | 0-3 | 1-1 | 1-2 | 2-0 | 1-3 | 1-2 | ■ | 0-3 | 0-0 | 1-2 | 1-0 | 3-0 | 2-0 | 1-3 | 3-0 | 1-1 | 2-1 | 1-0 |
| Leeds United AFC | 0-1 | 1-0 | 1-1 | 1-1 | 4-0 | 2-2 | 0-0 | 0-2 | 4-4 | 1-1 | 2-1 | ■ | 0-2 | 2-0 | 2-1 | 5-3 | 3-1 | 0-0 | 2-1 | 4-3 | 1-0 | 1-1 |
| Leicester City FC | 1-1 | 1-4 | 0-1 | 1-1 | 0-1 | 1-0 | 1-0 | 0-0 | 3-1 | 1-0 | 2-1 | 2-4 | ■ | 2-2 | 1-4 | 0-1 | 3-3 | 1-0 | 2-0 | 4-0 | 4-1 | 1-1 |
| Liverpool FC | 2-0 | 3-2 | 4-2 | 2-1 | 3-4 | 1-2 | 2-2 | 3-4 | 1-2 | 2-1 | 0-1 | 1-1 | 1-1 | ■ | 2-0 | 1-1 | 3-2 | 2-2 | 3-0 | 4-0 | 0-1 | 0-1 |
| Manchester City FC | 1-2 | 2-0 | 2-1 | 1-2 | 0-2 | 5-3 | 1-0 | 6-1 | 2-0 | 3-1 | 3-2 | 6-2 | 3-0 | 1-3 | ■ | 1-6 | 2-1 | 1-2 | 0-0 | 0-0 | 7-1 | 2-4 |
| Middlesbrough FC | 2-1 | 1-1 | 2-2 | 1-2 | 0-1 | 3-1 | 4-3 | 4-2 | 1-2 | 1-0 | 0-1 | 2-0 | 4-2 | 1-1 | 4-0 | ■ | 0-0 | 2-1 | 2-1 | 2-1 | 4-1 | 0-3 |
| Portsmouth FC | 0-0 | 1-1 | 1-2 | 1-1 | 4-1 | 2-1 | 2-4 | 4-0 | 3-1 | 3-0 | 3-0 | 4-0 | 1-1 | 1-1 | 2-2 | 0-2 | ■ | 3-2 | 2-0 | 1-0 | 2-3 | 1-0 |
| Preston North End FC | 1-3 | 2-1 | 2-0 | 2-2 | 1-1 | 0-1 | 0-0 | 4-1 | 2-1 | 4-1 | 1-1 | 3-1 | 0-0 | 4-1 | 2-2 | 0-2 | 1-1 | ■ | 2-1 | 0-0 | 1-1 | 2-0 |
| Stoke City FC | 1-1 | 2-2 | 1-3 | 3-2 | 3-0 | 2-0 | 2-1 | 8-1 | 1-1 | 1-1 | 0-1 | 1-2 | 2-0 | 0-1 | 3-2 | 3-0 | 3-1 | 1-1 | ■ | 0-0 | 4-0 | 1-1 |
| Sunderland AFC | 1-1 | 1-0 | 2-1 | 3-1 | 1-0 | 1-1 | 1-1 | 2-0 | 2-0 | 2-2 | 2-1 | 0-0 | 1-0 | 2-3 | 3-1 | 3-1 | 0-2 | 0-2 | 1-1 | ■ | 3-0 | 1-0 |
| West Bromwich Albion FC | 0-0 | 4-3 | 1-2 | 2-4 | 4-3 | 0-0 | 4-0 | 4-2 | 3-1 | 2-1 | 5-1 | 2-1 | 1-3 | 5-1 | 1-1 | 3-1 | 1-2 | 1-1 | 0-1 | 1-6 | ■ | 2-2 |
| Wolverhampton Wanderers FC | 3-1 | 3-2 | 1-0 | 1-1 | 2-1 | 1-1 | 1-1 | 2-2 | 2-0 | 1-1 | 1-4 | 1-1 | 10-1 | 2-0 | 3-1 | 0-1 | 5-0 | 0-0 | 2-2 | 4-0 | 2-1 | ■ |

| Division 1 | Pd | Wn | Dw | Ls | GF | GA | Pts | |
|---|---|---|---|---|---|---|---|---|
| 1. ARSENAL FC (LONDON) | 42 | 21 | 10 | 11 | 77 | 44 | 52 | |
| 2. Wolverhampton Wanderers FC (Wolverhampton) | 42 | 20 | 11 | 11 | 72 | 49 | 51 | |
| 3. Preston North End FC (Preston) | 42 | 16 | 17 | 9 | 64 | 44 | 49 | |
| 4. Charlton Athletic FC (London) | 42 | 16 | 14 | 12 | 65 | 51 | 46 | |
| 5. Middlesbrough FC (Middlesbrough) | 42 | 19 | 8 | 15 | 72 | 65 | 46 | |
| 6. Brentford FC (London) | 42 | 18 | 9 | 15 | 69 | 59 | 45 | |
| 7. Bolton Wanderers FC (Bolton) | 42 | 15 | 15 | 12 | 64 | 60 | 45 | |
| 8. Sunderland AFC (Sunderland) | 42 | 14 | 16 | 12 | 55 | 57 | 44 | |
| 9. Leeds United AFC (Leeds) | 42 | 14 | 15 | 13 | 64 | 69 | 43 | |
| 10. Chelsea FC (London) | 42 | 14 | 13 | 15 | 65 | 65 | 41 | |
| 11. Liverpool FC (Liverpool) | 42 | 15 | 11 | 16 | 65 | 71 | 41 | |
| 12. Blackpool FC (Blackpool) | 42 | 16 | 8 | 18 | 61 | 66 | 40 | |
| 13. Derby County FC (Derby) | 42 | 15 | 10 | 17 | 66 | 87 | 40 | |
| 14. Everton FC (Liverpool) | 42 | 16 | 7 | 19 | 79 | 75 | 39 | |
| 15. Huddersfield Town AFC (Huddersfield) | 42 | 17 | 5 | 20 | 55 | 68 | 39 | |
| 16. Leicester City FC (Leicester) | 42 | 14 | 11 | 17 | 54 | 75 | 39 | |
| 17. Stoke City FC (Stoke-on-Trent) | 42 | 13 | 12 | 17 | 58 | 59 | 38 | |
| 18. Birmingham FC (Birmingham) | 42 | 10 | 18 | 14 | 58 | 62 | 38 | |
| 19. Portsmouth FC (Portsmouth) | 42 | 13 | 12 | 17 | 62 | 68 | 38 | |
| 20. Grimsby Town FC (Cleethorpes) | 42 | 13 | 12 | 17 | 51 | 68 | 38 | |
| 21. Manchester City FC (Manchester) | 42 | 14 | 8 | 20 | 80 | 77 | 36 | R |
| 22. West Bromwich Albion FC (West Bromwich) | 42 | 14 | 8 | 20 | 74 | 91 | 36 | R |
| | 924 | 337 | 250 | 337 | 1430 | 1430 | 924 | |

# Top Goalscorer

1)  Tommy LAWTON          (Everton FC)    28

| Football League Division 2 1937-1938 Season | Aston Villa | Barnsley | Blackburn R. | Bradford P.A. | Burnley | Bury | Chesterfield | Coventry City | Fulham | Luton Town | Man. United | Newcastle Utd. | Norwich City | Nottingham F. | Plymouth Arg. | Sheffield United | Sheffield Wed. | Southampton | Stockport Co. | Swansea Town | Tottenham H. | West Ham Utd. |
|---|---|---|---|---|---|---|---|---|---|---|---|---|---|---|---|---|---|---|---|---|---|---|
| Aston Villa FC | | 3-0 | 2-1 | 2-0 | 0-0 | 2-1 | 0-2 | 1-1 | 2-0 | 4-1 | 3-0 | 2-0 | 2-0 | 1-2 | 3-0 | 1-0 | 4-3 | 3-0 | 7-1 | 4-0 | 2-0 | 2-0 |
| Barnsley FC | 0-1 | | 0-0 | 0-1 | 2-2 | 2-2 | 1-1 | 1-1 | 0-0 | 3-1 | 2-2 | 3-0 | 0-0 | 2-2 | 3-2 | 1-1 | 4-1 | 0-2 | 2-0 | 2-0 | 1-1 | 1-0 |
| Blackburn Rovers FC | 1-0 | 5-3 | | 0-0 | 3-3 | 2-1 | 3-3 | 1-3 | 2-2 | 2-2 | 1-1 | 2-1 | 5-3 | 5-1 | 2-1 | 2-3 | 1-0 | 4-0 | 3-0 | 3-1 | 2-1 | 2-1 |
| Bradford Park Avenue | 1-2 | 4-3 | 7-1 | | 3-1 | 1-1 | 3-2 | 0-1 | 1-2 | 1-1 | 4-0 | 2-0 | 3-0 | 2-2 | 2-0 | 5-1 | 1-1 | 2-0 | 4-1 | 0-1 | 3-1 | 2-1 |
| Burnley FC | 3-0 | 1-0 | 3-1 | 1-1 | | 2-0 | 0-2 | 2-0 | 1-0 | 3-2 | 1-0 | 2-1 | 3-0 | 0-0 | 0-2 | 2-0 | 1-1 | 4-0 | 0-0 | 2-0 | 2-1 | 2-0 |
| Bury FC | 1-1 | 0-2 | 2-1 | 5-1 | 4-0 | | 4-0 | 0-2 | 4-2 | 3-4 | 1-2 | 1-1 | 3-1 | 2-0 | 2-0 | 1-0 | 2-0 | 2-1 | 1-3 | 0-0 | 1-2 | 4-3 |
| Chesterfield FC | 0-1 | 0-0 | 3-0 | 0-3 | 0-1 | 1-2 | | 4-0 | 0-2 | 5-2 | 1-7 | 2-0 | 6-2 | 1-0 | 2-0 | 1-0 | 1-0 | 5-0 | 1-0 | 4-1 | 2-2 | 0-1 |
| Coventry City FC | 0-1 | 1-0 | 3-2 | 0-0 | 1-0 | 0-2 | 2-2 | | 0-1 | 2-1 | 1-0 | 1-0 | 2-0 | 1-1 | 4-0 | 2-2 | 0-1 | 2-0 | 1-0 | 5-0 | 2-1 | 1-1 |
| Fulham FC | 1-1 | 0-0 | 3-1 | 1-1 | 2-1 | 4-0 | 1-1 | 3-4 | | 4-1 | 1-0 | 1-2 | 3-4 | 2-0 | 2-3 | 1-1 | 0-0 | 1-0 | 2-0 | 8-1 | 3-1 | 1-1 |
| Luton Town FC | 3-2 | 4-0 | 4-1 | 4-2 | 3-1 | 0-1 | 1-1 | 1-4 | 4-0 | | 1-0 | 4-1 | 1-1 | 2-2 | 1-1 | 2-3 | 2-2 | 1-3 | 6-4 | 5-1 | 2-4 | 2-2 |
| Manchester United FC | 3-1 | 4-1 | 2-1 | 3-1 | 4-0 | 2-0 | 4-1 | 2-2 | 1-0 | 4-2 | | 3-0 | 0-0 | 4-3 | 0-0 | 0-1 | 1-0 | 1-2 | 3-1 | 5-1 | 0-1 | 4-0 |
| Newcastle United FC | 2-0 | 0-1 | 2-0 | 3-0 | 2-2 | 1-0 | 3-1 | 1-2 | 1-2 | 1-3 | 2-2 | | 0-1 | 3-1 | 3-1 | 6-0 | 1-0 | 3-0 | 0-0 | 1-0 | 1-0 | 2-2 |
| Norwich City FC | 1-0 | 1-0 | 3-2 | 1-1 | 1-0 | 1-2 | 2-1 | 0-2 | 0-4 | 2-3 | 1-1 | 2-0 | | 2-0 | 2-0 | 2-2 | 3-1 | 4-3 | 1-0 | 1-1 | 2-1 | 1-2 |
| Nottingham Forest FC | 0-2 | 2-1 | 3-1 | 1-0 | 1-1 | 1-0 | 4-2 | 2-1 | 0-1 | 1-0 | 2-3 | 0-0 | 1-2 | | 1-0 | 2-1 | 0-1 | 2-1 | 1-2 | 2-1 | 3-1 | 0-0 |
| Plymouth Argyle FC | 0-3 | 2-2 | 2-2 | 1-0 | 2-3 | 2-1 | 1-1 | 3-1 | 4-0 | 2-4 | 1-1 | 2-1 | 1-1 | 1-0 | | 2-0 | 2-4 | 4-0 | 2-1 | 2-2 | 2-2 | 2-1 |
| Sheffield United FC | 0-0 | 6-3 | 1-1 | 3-1 | 2-1 | 2-1 | 0-2 | 3-2 | 2-1 | 2-0 | 1-2 | 4-0 | 4-1 | 2-1 | 0-0 | | 2-1 | 5-0 | 2-0 | 1-1 | 1-0 | 3-1 |
| Sheffield Wednesday FC | 1-2 | 0-1 | 1-1 | 1-1 | 2-1 | 2-0 | 2-1 | 2-1 | 4-0 | 1-3 | 3-0 | 1-0 | 0-2 | 1-1 | 0-1 | 1-0 | | 0-0 | 3-3 | 1-1 | 0-3 | 1-0 |
| Southampton FC | 0-0 | 2-0 | 1-0 | 2-1 | 0-0 | 4-1 | 0-1 | 0-4 | 4-0 | 3-6 | 3-3 | 1-0 | 3-1 | 2-0 | 0-0 | 2-1 | 5-2 | | 4-1 | 1-1 | 2-1 | 3-3 |
| Stockport County FC | 1-3 | 1-2 | 0-1 | 1-2 | 3-1 | 0-1 | 1-1 | 1-1 | 2-0 | 2-1 | 1-0 | 1-3 | 1-1 | 1-0 | 1-3 | 1-1 | 2-1 | 0-0 | | 1-0 | 3-2 | 0-0 |
| Swansea Town AFC | 2-1 | 1-0 | 3-2 | 0-1 | 3-1 | 1-0 | 1-0 | 3-3 | 1-1 | 2-2 | 1-0 | 1-0 | 1-0 | 2-1 | 1-0 | 3-5 | 1-1 | 0-0 | 0-2 | | 3-2 | 0-0 |
| Tottenham Hotspur FC | 2-1 | 3-0 | 3-1 | 2-1 | 4-0 | 1-3 | 2-0 | 0-0 | 1-1 | 3-0 | 0-1 | 2-2 | 4-0 | 3-2 | 1-2 | 1-2 | 5-0 | 2-0 | 2-0 | 2-0 | | 2-0 |
| West Ham United FC | 1-1 | 4-1 | 2-0 | 3-1 | 1-0 | 3-1 | 5-0 | 0-0 | 0-0 | 0-0 | 1-0 | 1-0 | 3-3 | 2-1 | 0-1 | 0-2 | 1-0 | 3-1 | 1-0 | 2-1 | 1-3 | |

## Division 2

| | | Pd | Wn | Dw | Ls | GF | GA | Pts | |
|---|---|---|---|---|---|---|---|---|---|
| 1. | Aston Villa FC (Birmingham) | 42 | 25 | 7 | 10 | 73 | 35 | 57 | P |
| 2. | Manchester United FC (Manchester) | 42 | 22 | 9 | 11 | 82 | 50 | 53 | P |
| 3. | Sheffield United FC (Sheffield) | 42 | 22 | 9 | 11 | 73 | 56 | 53 | |
| 4. | Coventry City FC (Coventry) | 42 | 20 | 12 | 10 | 66 | 45 | 52 | |
| 5. | Tottenham Hotspur FC (London) | 42 | 19 | 6 | 17 | 76 | 54 | 44 | |
| 6. | Burnley FC (Burnley) | 42 | 17 | 10 | 15 | 54 | 54 | 44 | |
| 7. | Bradford Park Avenue FC (Bradford) | 42 | 17 | 9 | 16 | 69 | 56 | 43 | |
| 8. | Fulham FC (London) | 42 | 16 | 11 | 15 | 61 | 57 | 43 | |
| 9. | West Ham United FC (London) | 42 | 14 | 14 | 14 | 53 | 52 | 42 | |
| 10. | Bury FC (Bury) | 42 | 18 | 5 | 19 | 63 | 60 | 41 | |
| 11. | Chesterfield FC (Chesterfield) | 42 | 16 | 9 | 17 | 63 | 63 | 41 | |
| 12. | Luton Town FC (Luton) | 42 | 15 | 10 | 17 | 89 | 86 | 40 | |
| 13. | Plymouth Argyle FC (Plymouth) | 42 | 14 | 12 | 16 | 57 | 65 | 40 | |
| 14. | Norwich City FC (Norwich) | 42 | 14 | 11 | 17 | 56 | 75 | 39 | |
| 15. | Southampton FC (Southampton) | 42 | 15 | 9 | 18 | 55 | 77 | 39 | |
| 16. | Blackburn Rovers FC (Blackburn) | 42 | 14 | 10 | 18 | 71 | 80 | 38 | |
| 17. | Sheffield Wednesday FC (Sheffield) | 42 | 14 | 10 | 18 | 49 | 56 | 38 | |
| 18. | Swansea Town AFC (Swansea) | 42 | 13 | 12 | 17 | 45 | 73 | 38 | |
| 19. | Newcastle United FC (Newcastle-upon-Tyne) | 42 | 14 | 8 | 20 | 51 | 58 | 36 | |
| 20. | Nottingham Forest FC (Nottingham) | 42 | 14 | 8 | 20 | 47 | 60 | 36 | |
| 21. | Barnsley FC (Barnsley) | 42 | 11 | 14 | 17 | 50 | 64 | 36 | R |
| 22. | Stockport County FC (Stockport) | 42 | 11 | 9 | 22 | 43 | 70 | 31 | R |
| | | 924 | 355 | 214 | 355 | 1346 | 1346 | 924 | |

**Football League Division 3 (N) 1937-1938 Season**

| | Accrington St. | Barrow | Bradford City | Carlisle United | Chester | Crewe Alex. | Darlington | Doncaster R. | Gateshead | Halifax Town | Hartlepools Utd. | Hull City | Lincoln City | New Brighton | Oldham Athletic | Port Vale | Rochdale | Rotherham Utd. | Southport | Tranmere R. | Wrexham | York City |
|---|---|---|---|---|---|---|---|---|---|---|---|---|---|---|---|---|---|---|---|---|---|---|
| Accrington Stanley FC | | 2-0 | 3-1 | 1-4 | 0-0 | 3-2 | 2-1 | 0-1 | 1-5 | 3-4 | 2-1 | 0-2 | 0-3 | 3-1 | 1-2 | 2-1 | 0-1 | 0-0 | 3-0 | 0-1 | 4-0 | 1-2 |
| Barrow AFC | 0-0 | | 0-0 | 4-2 | 0-2 | 1-0 | 1-1 | 1-1 | 1-3 | 2-1 | 0-0 | 1-0 | 4-1 | 3-0 | 2-1 | 3-0 | 0-1 | 1-0 | 1-2 | 2-2 | 0-1 | 1-2 |
| Bradford City AFC | 2-2 | 1-0 | | 4-0 | 2-2 | 3-1 | 2-1 | 2-0 | 1-1 | 3-0 | 4-1 | 1-2 | 2-0 | 3-0 | 1-1 | 5-0 | 3-1 | 3-2 | 1-1 | 1-3 | 2-2 | 0-1 |
| Carlisle United FC | 3-1 | 2-1 | 2-0 | | 1-3 | 5-1 | 3-0 | 2-2 | 1-0 | 5-2 | 3-1 | 0-1 | 0-1 | 1-1 | 1-1 | 3-1 | 0-1 | 0-1 | 1-0 | 0-0 | 0-0 | 2-1 |
| Chester FC | 3-1 | 3-1 | 3-1 | 1-0 | | 0-3 | 3-2 | 4-0 | 2-1 | 1-1 | 6-0 | 1-3 | 1-1 | 1-2 | 3-3 | 7-2 | 4-1 | 2-3 | 2-1 | 1-1 | 2-1 | 4-3 |
| Crewe Alexandra FC | 3-1 | 4-0 | 3-1 | 4-1 | 1-0 | | 2-2 | 0-0 | 1-3 | 4-0 | 2-0 | 0-1 | 2-0 | 1-0 | 0-1 | 1-2 | 5-1 | 3-1 | 5-0 | 1-0 | 1-1 | 4-2 |
| Darlington FC | 3-0 | 0-1 | 4-2 | 3-1 | 2-1 | 0-1 | | 1-1 | 1-2 | 3-0 | 2-0 | 1-3 | 1-4 | 1-0 | 1-0 | 2-2 | 2-4 | 2-1 | 1-1 | 0-2 | 5-3 | 2-2 |
| Doncaster Rovers FC | 5-1 | 1-0 | 4-0 | 1-3 | 2-1 | 0-0 | 4-0 | | 1-0 | 2-2 | 3-3 | 2-1 | 3-0 | 3-0 | 1-0 | 3-2 | 5-0 | 0-1 | 3-0 | 1-1 | 2-0 | 2-1 |
| Gateshead FC | 1-0 | 6-0 | 3-0 | 2-1 | 3-1 | 2-0 | 5-2 | 2-3 | | 4-1 | 2-1 | 3-2 | 1-1 | 3-1 | 0-0 | 2-1 | 3-1 | 0-0 | 5-0 | 2-2 | 2-2 | 2-2 |
| Halifax Town AFC | 1-2 | 1-1 | 0-2 | 0-0 | 1-1 | 2-1 | 1-0 | 0-1 | 2-0 | | 0-0 | 1-0 | 2-0 | 2-0 | 2-1 | 2-1 | 2-3 | 1-3 | 1-1 | 1-0 | 0-0 | 2-2 |
| Hartlepools United FC | 2-0 | 1-1 | 1-1 | 4-1 | 0-1 | 2-2 | 2-1 | 0-0 | 1-3 | 2-0 | | 2-2 | 2-0 | 1-0 | 2-0 | 3-3 | 4-0 | 1-2 | 2-2 | 2-0 | 2-0 | 0-0 |
| Hull City AFC | 0-0 | 4-0 | 2-2 | 2-1 | 2-2 | 1-1 | 4-0 | 2-1 | 3-1 | 0-1 | 4-0 | | 1-1 | 1-1 | 4-1 | 0-0 | 4-1 | 1-1 | 10-1 | 0-1 | 3-2 | 3-1 |
| Lincoln City FC | 2-0 | 5-0 | 4-0 | 0-1 | 1-1 | 3-2 | 0-0 | 2-2 | 3-2 | 2-0 | 2-1 | 2-1 | | 4-1 | 0-1 | 1-0 | 2-0 | 5-0 | 1-3 | 0-1 | 7-1 | 2-0 |
| New Brighton FC | 2-1 | 2-1 | 1-1 | 5-1 | 4-0 | 4-0 | 3-0 | 1-2 | 4-1 | 2-0 | 4-1 | 0-0 | 0-1 | | 1-0 | 1-1 | 2-0 | 2-3 | 2-2 | 0-1 | 1-1 | 2-1 |
| Oldham Athletic AFC | 1-0 | 0-0 | 1-2 | 3-0 | 3-2 | 0-0 | 3-0 | 2-1 | 3-1 | 2-1 | 3-1 | 1-1 | 2-2 | 2-1 | | 3-0 | 4-2 | 3-1 | 2-0 | 2-1 | 2-0 | 6-2 |
| Port Vale FC | 4-1 | 4-0 | 4-3 | 2-2 | 2-2 | 1-1 | 1-0 | 1-1 | 2-2 | 0-2 | 5-1 | 2-4 | 1-0 | 3-2 | 2-2 | | 4-1 | 0-0 | 1-1 | 1-0 | 2-0 | 3-2 |
| Rochdale AFC | 0-1 | 3-3 | 2-0 | 3-1 | 4-0 | 1-4 | 1-1 | 4-5 | 2-2 | 1-1 | 2-2 | 0-0 | 0-1 | 2-1 | 1-1 | 1-1 | | 2-0 | 3-2 | 0-0 | 6-1 | 0-0 |
| Rotherham United FC | 1-1 | 3-0 | 2-1 | 0-1 | 4-1 | 1-0 | 4-2 | 2-2 | 1-1 | 4-1 | 3-1 | 2-2 | 4-0 | 1-2 | 2-1 | 3-2 | 1-0 | | 1-1 | 2-1 | 1-1 | 3-0 |
| Southport FC | 2-1 | 2-0 | 2-0 | 1-1 | 2-1 | 3-1 | 1-1 | 1-3 | 0-0 | 2-2 | 2-2 | 1-0 | 0-0 | 2-2 | 1-0 | 2-1 | 2-0 | 0-3 | | 1-3 | 1-2 | 2-3 |
| Tranmere Rovers FC | 5-0 | 3-0 | 2-1 | 5-0 | 0-0 | 2-2 | 1-1 | 2-0 | 4-2 | 2-0 | 4-0 | 3-1 | 2-0 | 5-2 | 1-1 | 2-1 | 3-2 | 0-2 | 7-2 | | 3-2 | 1-2 |
| Wrexham AFC | 2-0 | 3-2 | 2-1 | 0-0 | 3-1 | 1-0 | 4-0 | 2-0 | 0-0 | 2-0 | 6-3 | 0-1 | 1-0 | 0-1 | 1-0 | 0-0 | 2-1 | 2-0 | 4-1 | 1-3 | | 1-1 |
| York City FC | 1-1 | 1-2 | 3-1 | 3-1 | 4-0 | 1-2 | 1-2 | 2-0 | 5-1 | 1-1 | 1-0 | 0-1 | 3-1 | 3-1 | 0-0 | 2-2 | 0-5 | 4-1 | 1-2 | 2-0 | 2-1 | |

### Division 3 (North)

| | | Pd | Wn | Dw | Ls | GF | GA | Pts | |
|---|---|---|---|---|---|---|---|---|---|
| 1. | Tranmere Rovers FC (Birkenhead) | 42 | 23 | 10 | 9 | 81 | 41 | 56 | P |
| 2. | Doncaster Rovers FC (Doncaster) | 42 | 21 | 12 | 9 | 74 | 49 | 54 | |
| 3. | Hull City AFC (Kingston-upon-Hull) | 42 | 20 | 13 | 9 | 80 | 43 | 53 | |
| 4. | Oldham Athletic AFC (Oldham) | 42 | 19 | 13 | 10 | 67 | 46 | 51 | |
| 5. | Gateshead FC (Gateshead) | 42 | 20 | 11 | 11 | 84 | 59 | 51 | |
| 6. | Rotherham United FC (Rotherham) | 42 | 20 | 10 | 12 | 68 | 56 | 50 | |
| 7. | Lincoln City FC (Lincoln) | 42 | 19 | 8 | 15 | 66 | 50 | 46 | |
| 8. | Crewe Alexandra FC (Crewe) | 42 | 18 | 9 | 15 | 71 | 53 | 45 | |
| 9. | Chester FC (Chester) | 42 | 16 | 12 | 14 | 77 | 72 | 44 | |
| 10. | Wrexham AFC (Wrexham) | 42 | 16 | 11 | 15 | 58 | 63 | 43 | |
| 11. | York City FC (York) | 42 | 16 | 10 | 16 | 70 | 68 | 42 | |
| 12. | Carlisle United FC (Carlisle) | 42 | 15 | 9 | 18 | 57 | 67 | 39 | |
| 13. | New Brighton FC (Wallasey) | 42 | 15 | 8 | 19 | 60 | 61 | 38 | |
| 14. | Bradford City AFC (Bradford) | 42 | 14 | 10 | 18 | 66 | 69 | 38 | |
| 15. | Port Vale FC (Stoke-on-Trent) | 42 | 12 | 14 | 16 | 65 | 73 | 38 | T |
| 16. | Southport FC (Southport) | 42 | 12 | 14 | 16 | 53 | 82 | 38 | |
| 17. | Rochdale AFC (Rochdale) | 42 | 13 | 11 | 18 | 67 | 78 | 37 | |
| 18. | Halifax Town AFC (Halifax) | 42 | 12 | 12 | 18 | 44 | 66 | 36 | |
| 19. | Darlington FC (Darlington) | 42 | 11 | 10 | 21 | 54 | 79 | 32 | |
| 20. | Hartlepools United FC (Hartlepool) | 42 | 10 | 12 | 20 | 53 | 80 | 32 | |
| 21. | Barrow AFC (Barrow-in-Furness) | 42 | 11 | 10 | 21 | 41 | 71 | 32 | |
| 22. | Accrington Stanley FC (Accrington) | 42 | 11 | 7 | 24 | 45 | 75 | 29 | |
| | | 924 | 344 | 236 | 344 | 1401 | 1401 | 924 | |

T: Port Vale FC (Stoke-on-Trent) were transferred to Division 3 (South) from the next season.

| Football League Division 3 (S) 1937-1938 Season | Aldershot | Bournemouth | Brighton | Bristol City | Bristol Rovers | Cardiff City | Clapton Orient | Crystal Palace | Exeter City | Gillingham | Mansfield Town | Millwall | Newport County | Northampton | Notts County | Q.P.R. | Reading | Southend United | Swindon Town | Torquay United | Walsall | Watford |
|---|---|---|---|---|---|---|---|---|---|---|---|---|---|---|---|---|---|---|---|---|---|---|
| Aldershot FC | | 2-0 | 1-2 | 1-1 | 0-2 | 1-1 | 1-2 | 1-0 | 0-1 | 2-0 | 1-0 | 2-1 | 5-0 | 0-2 | 0-1 | 1-0 | 0-0 | 1-0 | 1-1 | 1-0 | 1-0 | 1-0 |
| Bournemouth & B. Athletic | 3-0 | | 0-0 | 0-0 | 1-3 | 3-0 | 2-1 | 1-0 | 2-2 | 2-0 | 5-4 | 0-3 | 1-1 | 0-0 | 1-1 | 1-1 | 1-1 | 7-1 | 1-2 | 0-0 | 5-0 | 0-0 |
| Brighton & Hove Albion | 2-1 | 3-1 | | 1-1 | 3-0 | 2-1 | 2-1 | 2-1 | 6-0 | 1-0 | 2-0 | 1-0 | 1-0 | 1-2 | 0-1 | 3-1 | 1-1 | 3-1 | 3-1 | 1-1 | 1-0 | 1-2 |
| Bristol City FC | 3-1 | 2-1 | 1-1 | | 0-0 | 0-1 | 2-0 | 0-0 | 4-1 | 3-1 | 2-1 | 0-0 | 0-0 | 1-0 | 3-1 | 2-0 | 1-0 | 4-2 | 1-1 | 2-0 | 3-1 | 3-1 |
| Bristol Rovers FC | 0-1 | 2-1 | 0-0 | 1-0 | | 2-1 | 3-2 | 1-0 | 1-1 | 2-1 | 0-0 | 0-2 | 2-0 | 1-1 | 1-1 | 1-1 | 2-2 | 2-1 | 1-2 | 2-0 | 5-2 | 0-2 |
| Cardiff City AFC | 0-1 | 3-0 | 4-1 | 0-0 | 1-1 | | 2-0 | 4-2 | 1-1 | 4-0 | 4-1 | 3-2 | 3-1 | 4-1 | 2-2 | 2-2 | 4-1 | 5-0 | 2-2 | 5-2 | 3-1 | 1-1 |
| Clapton Orient FC | 2-1 | 3-0 | 0-3 | 0-0 | 1-0 | 1-1 | | 0-2 | 2-1 | 3-0 | 1-2 | 2-1 | 0-2 | 1-0 | 2-0 | 1-1 | 1-1 | 1-1 | 1-0 | 2-0 | 2-2 | 1-1 |
| Crystal Palace FC | 1-1 | 0-1 | 3-2 | 1-1 | 3-2 | 1-0 | 1-0 | | 2-2 | 3-0 | 4-0 | 0-0 | 3-0 | 0-1 | 3-1 | 4-0 | 3-1 | 2-1 | 0-1 | 4-1 | 3-1 | 4-1 |
| Exeter City FC | 0-1 | 3-1 | 4-0 | 3-2 | 0-0 | 2-1 | 2-0 | 2-2 | | 3-5 | 4-0 | 1-5 | 2-0 | 4-1 | 0-3 | 0-4 | 0-2 | 1-1 | 0-0 | 2-0 | 3-2 | 1-2 |
| Gillingham FC | 2-0 | 0-2 | 1-1 | 1-0 | 0-1 | 1-0 | 1-2 | 2-4 | 2-1 | | 0-0 | 2-3 | 1-0 | 2-1 | 2-1 | 1-5 | 1-2 | 2-1 | 0-0 | 1-1 | 3-0 | 0-0 |
| Mansfield Town FC | 2-0 | 3-2 | 1-1 | 3-5 | 1-0 | 3-0 | 3-1 | 2-0 | 2-3 | 3-1 | | 1-1 | 1-1 | 4-1 | 1-2 | 3-2 | 5-1 | 2-2 | 2-0 | 1-1 | 3-1 | 0-1 |
| Millwall FC | 4-0 | 4-0 | 2-0 | 0-3 | 2-1 | 1-0 | 3-0 | 2-2 | 5-0 | 1-0 | 4-0 | | 4-0 | 3-0 | 5-0 | 1-4 | 1-1 | 1-0 | 0-0 | 7-0 | 4-0 | 1-0 |
| Newport County AFC | 4-0 | 1-1 | 1-0 | 0-0 | 2-2 | 1-1 | 3-1 | 0-0 | 2-2 | 2-0 | 1-0 | 3-1 | | 0-0 | 3-0 | 1-1 | 2-2 | 2-0 | 2-0 | 0-2 | 1-2 | 1-0 |
| Northampton Town FC | 1-0 | 1-3 | 3-1 | 1-0 | 2-0 | 0-0 | 2-0 | 1-1 | 1-0 | 4-1 | 3-0 | 0-1 | 2-0 | | 2-0 | 0-2 | 2-2 | 0-2 | 1-0 | 0-3 | 1-1 | 3-2 |
| Notts County FC | 1-0 | 1-2 | 0-3 | 2-0 | 1-1 | 2-0 | 1-0 | 0-1 | 0-0 | 1-0 | 2-0 | 1-1 | 1-1 | 5-0 | | 2-2 | 2-1 | 0-2 | 3-0 | 0-0 | 3-1 | 1-2 |
| Queen's Park Rangers FC | 3-0 | 1-2 | 2-1 | 0-2 | 4-0 | 2-1 | 3-2 | 1-0 | 4-0 | 2-1 | 1-1 | 0-2 | 0-0 | 1-1 | 2-1 | | 3-0 | 1-0 | 3-0 | 6-3 | 3-1 | 1-0 |
| Reading FC | 3-2 | 4-1 | 2-1 | 0-1 | 4-0 | 0-0 | 2-0 | 3-2 | 1-0 | 2-0 | 3-2 | 1-0 | 2-1 | 4-3 | 0-2 | 1-0 | | 3-2 | 2-1 | 1-1 | 2-1 | 4-1 |
| Southend United FC | 4-1 | 1-0 | 2-1 | 5-0 | 1-1 | 3-1 | 1-2 | 2-2 | 1-1 | 2-0 | 0-1 | 1-2 | 0-2 | 4-2 | 2-1 | 2-1 | 4-2 | | 0-0 | 5-1 | 1-0 | 2-2 |
| Swindon Town FC | 2-0 | 1-0 | 0-1 | 2-3 | 2-1 | 2-0 | 1-0 | 4-0 | 3-0 | 3-3 | 3-2 | 1-0 | 1-0 | 1-0 | 1-3 | 0-0 | 1-1 | 0-0 | | 1-0 | 1-1 | 0-2 |
| Torquay United FC | 1-5 | 0-0 | 0-1 | 1-3 | 4-1 | 0-1 | 3-1 | 0-0 | 2-1 | 1-0 | 0-1 | 1-1 | 0-0 | 1-2 | 0-3 | 0-2 | 3-2 | 3-3 | 1-0 | | 1-0 | 0-1 |
| Walsall FC | 2-0 | 2-0 | 0-3 | 2-8 | 5-2 | 1-0 | 2-0 | 1-1 | 0-2 | 3-1 | 2-0 | 1-1 | 3-1 | 1-1 | 1-0 | 0-3 | 2-5 | 1-5 | 2-3 | 0-0 | | 3-1 |
| Watford FC | 5-1 | 0-2 | 1-1 | 3-1 | 4-0 | 4-0 | 2-0 | 1-2 | 0-0 | 1-1 | 2-0 | 1-1 | 3-0 | 1-3 | 2-0 | 3-1 | 4-0 | 3-1 | 4-0 | 4-0 | 2-1 | |

## Division 3 (South)

| | | Pd | Wn | Dw | Ls | GF | GA | Pts | |
|---|---|---|---|---|---|---|---|---|---|
| 1. | Millwall FC (London) | 42 | 23 | 10 | 9 | 83 | 37 | 56 | P |
| 2. | Bristol City FC (Bristol) | 42 | 21 | 13 | 8 | 68 | 40 | 55 | |
| 3. | Queen's Park Rangers FC (London) | 42 | 22 | 9 | 11 | 80 | 47 | 53 | |
| 4. | Watford FC (Watford) | 42 | 21 | 11 | 10 | 73 | 43 | 53 | |
| 5. | Brighton & Hove Albion FC (Hove) | 42 | 21 | 9 | 12 | 64 | 44 | 51 | |
| 6. | Reading FC (Reading) | 42 | 20 | 11 | 11 | 71 | 63 | 51 | |
| 7. | Crystal Palace FC (London) | 42 | 18 | 12 | 12 | 67 | 47 | 48 | |
| 8. | Swindon Town FC (Swindon) | 42 | 17 | 10 | 15 | 49 | 49 | 44 | |
| 9. | Northampton Town FC (Northampton) | 42 | 17 | 9 | 16 | 51 | 57 | 43 | |
| 10. | Cardiff City AFC (Cardiff) | 42 | 15 | 12 | 15 | 67 | 54 | 42 | |
| 11. | Notts County FC (Nottingham) | 42 | 16 | 9 | 17 | 50 | 50 | 41 | |
| 12. | Southend United FC (Southend-on-Sea) | 42 | 15 | 10 | 17 | 70 | 68 | 40 | |
| 13. | Bournemouth & Boscombe Athletic FC (Bournemouth) | 42 | 14 | 12 | 16 | 56 | 57 | 40 | |
| 14. | Mansfield Town FC (Mansfield) | 42 | 15 | 9 | 18 | 62 | 67 | 39 | |
| 15. | Bristol Rovers FC (Bristol) | 42 | 13 | 13 | 16 | 46 | 61 | 39 | |
| 16. | Newport County AFC (Newport) | 42 | 11 | 16 | 15 | 43 | 52 | 38 | |
| 17. | Exeter City FC (Exeter) | 42 | 13 | 12 | 17 | 57 | 70 | 38 | |
| 18. | Aldershot FC (Aldershot) | 42 | 15 | 5 | 22 | 39 | 59 | 35 | |
| 19. | Clapton Orient FC (London) | 42 | 13 | 7 | 22 | 42 | 61 | 33 | |
| 20. | Torquay United FC (Torquay) | 42 | 9 | 12 | 21 | 38 | 73 | 30 | |
| 21. | Walsall FC (Walsall) | 42 | 11 | 7 | 24 | 52 | 88 | 29 | |
| 22. | Gillingham FC (Gillingham) | 42 | 10 | 6 | 26 | 36 | 77 | 26 | # |
| | | 924 | 350 | 224 | 350 | 1264 | 1264 | 924 | |

# Gillingham FC were not re-elected to the league for next season.     Elected: Ipswich Town FC (Ipswich)

## F.A. CUP FINAL   (Wembley Stadium, London – 30/04/1938 – 93,497)

PRESTON NORTH END FC (PRESTON)     1-0  (aet)     Huddersfield Town AFC (Huddersfield)

*Mutch pen.*

Preston: Holdcroft, Gallimore, A.Beattie, Shankly, Smith, Batey, Watmough, Mutch, Maxwell, R.Beattie, H.O'Donnell.

Huddersfield: Hesford, Craig, Mountford, Willingham, Young, Boot, Hulme, Isaac, McFadyen, Barclay, Beasley.

## Semi-finals

| Preston North End FC (Preston) | 2-1 | Aston Villa FC (Birmingham) |
| Sunderland AFC (Sunderland) | 1-3 | Huddersfield Town AFC (Huddersfield) |

## Quarter-finals

| Aston Villa FC (Birmingham) | 3-2 | Manchester City FC (Manchester) |
| Brentford FC (London) | 0-3 | Preston North End FC (Preston) |
| Tottenham Hotspur FC (London) | 0-1 | Sunderland AFC (Sunderland) |
| York City FC (York) | 0-0,  1-2 | Huddersfield Town AFC (Huddersfield) |

# 1938-39

| Football League Division 1 1938-1939 Season | Arsenal | Aston Villa | Birmingham | Blackpool | Bolton Wands. | Brentford | Charlton Athletic | Chelsea | Derby County | Everton | Grimsby Town | Huddersfield T. | Leeds United | Leicester City | Liverpool | Man. United | Middlesbrough | Portsmouth | Preston N.E. | Stoke City | Sunderland | Wolves |
|---|---|---|---|---|---|---|---|---|---|---|---|---|---|---|---|---|---|---|---|---|---|---|
| Arsenal FC | | 0-0 | 3-1 | 2-1 | 3-1 | 2-0 | 2-0 | 1-0 | 1-2 | 1-2 | 2-0 | 1-0 | 2-3 | 0-0 | 2-0 | 2-1 | 1-2 | 2-0 | 1-0 | 4-1 | 2-0 | 0-0 |
| Aston Villa FC | 1-3 | | 5-1 | 3-1 | 1-3 | 5-0 | 2-0 | 6-2 | 0-1 | 0-3 | 0-2 | 4-0 | 2-1 | 1-2 | 2-0 | 0-2 | 1-1 | 2-0 | 3-0 | 3-0 | 1-1 | 2-2 |
| Birmingham FC | 1-2 | 3-0 | | 2-1 | 0-2 | 5-1 | 3-4 | 1-1 | 3-0 | 1-0 | 1-1 | 1-1 | 4-0 | 2-1 | 0-0 | 3-3 | 2-1 | 2-0 | 1-3 | 1-2 | 1-2 | 3-2 |
| Blackpool FC | 1-0 | 2-4 | 2-1 | | 0-0 | 4-1 | 0-0 | 5-1 | 2-2 | 0-2 | 3-1 | 1-1 | 1-2 | 1-1 | 1-1 | 3-5 | 4-0 | 2-1 | 2-1 | 1-1 | 1-1 | 1-0 |
| Bolton Wanderers FC | 1-1 | 1-2 | 3-0 | 0-1 | | 1-1 | 2-1 | 0-2 | 2-1 | 4-2 | 1-1 | 3-2 | 2-2 | 4-0 | 3-1 | 0-0 | 4-1 | 5-1 | 0-2 | 1-3 | 2-1 | 0-0 |
| Brentford FC | 1-0 | 2-4 | 0-1 | 1-1 | 2-2 | | 1-0 | 1-0 | 1-3 | 2-0 | 1-2 | 2-1 | 0-1 | 2-0 | 2-1 | 2-5 | 2-1 | 2-0 | 3-1 | 1-0 | 2-3 | 0-1 |
| Charlton Athletic FC | 1-0 | 1-0 | 4-4 | 3-1 | 2-1 | 1-1 | | 2-0 | 1-0 | 2-1 | 3-1 | 2-1 | 2-0 | 1-0 | 1-3 | 7-1 | 3-0 | 3-3 | 3-1 | 4-2 | 3-0 | 0-4 |
| Chelsea FC | 4-2 | 2-1 | 2-2 | 1-1 | 1-1 | 1-3 | 1-3 | | 0-2 | 0-2 | 5-1 | 3-0 | 2-2 | 3-0 | 4-1 | 0-1 | 4-2 | 1-0 | 3-1 | 1-1 | 4-0 | 1-3 |
| Derby County FC | 1-2 | 2-1 | 0-1 | 2-1 | 3-0 | 1-2 | 3-1 | 0-1 | | 2-1 | 4-1 | 1-0 | 1-0 | 1-1 | 2-2 | 5-1 | 1-4 | 0-1 | 2-0 | 5-0 | 1-0 | 2-2 |
| Everton FC | 2-0 | 3-0 | 4-2 | 4-0 | 2-1 | 2-1 | 1-4 | 4-1 | 2-2 | | 3-0 | 3-2 | 4-0 | 4-0 | 2-1 | 3-0 | 4-0 | 5-1 | 0-0 | 1-1 | 6-2 | 1-0 |
| Grimsby Town FC | 2-1 | 1-2 | 1-0 | 2-0 | 1-1 | 0-0 | 1-1 | 2-1 | 1-1 | 3-0 | | 3-3 | 3-2 | 6-1 | 2-1 | 1-0 | 0-2 | 2-1 | 1-1 | 3-1 | 1-3 | 2-4 |
| Huddersfield Town AFC | 1-1 | 1-1 | 3-1 | 3-0 | 2-1 | 1-2 | 4-0 | 3-1 | 3-0 | 3-0 | 2-0 | | 0-1 | 2-0 | 1-1 | 1-1 | 0-1 | 3-0 | 3-0 | 1-4 | 0-1 | 1-2 |
| Leeds United AFC | 4-2 | 2-0 | 2-0 | 1-0 | 1-2 | 3-2 | 2-1 | 1-1 | 1-4 | 1-2 | 0-1 | 2-1 | | 8-2 | 1-1 | 3-1 | 0-1 | 2-2 | 2-1 | 0-0 | 3-3 | 1-0 |
| Leicester City FC | 0-2 | 1-1 | 2-1 | 3-4 | 0-0 | 1-1 | 1-5 | 3-2 | 2-3 | 3-0 | 0-2 | 0-1 | 2-0 | | 2-2 | 1-1 | 5-3 | 5-0 | 2-1 | 2-2 | 0-2 | 0-2 |
| Liverpool FC | 2-2 | 3-0 | 4-0 | 1-0 | 1-2 | 1-0 | 1-0 | 2-1 | 2-1 | 0-3 | 2-2 | 3-3 | 3-0 | 1-1 | | 1-0 | 3-1 | 4-4 | 4-1 | 1-0 | 1-1 | 0-2 |
| Manchester United FC | 1-0 | 1-1 | 4-1 | 0-0 | 2-2 | 3-0 | 0-2 | 5-1 | 1-1 | 0-2 | 3-1 | 1-1 | 0-0 | 3-0 | 2-0 | | 1-1 | 1-1 | 1-1 | 0-1 | 0-1 | 1-3 |
| Middlesbrough FC | 1-1 | 1-1 | 2-2 | 9-2 | 1-2 | 3-1 | 4-0 | 1-1 | 2-0 | 4-4 | 3-2 | 4-1 | 1-2 | 3-2 | 3-0 | 3-1 | | 8-2 | 2-2 | 5-1 | 3-0 | 1-0 |
| Portsmouth FC | 0-0 | 0-0 | 2-0 | 1-0 | 2-1 | 2-2 | 0-2 | 2-1 | 1-3 | 0-1 | 2-1 | 4-0 | 2-0 | 0-1 | 1-1 | 0-0 | 1-1 | | 0-0 | 2-0 | 2-1 | 1-0 |
| Preston North End FC | 2-1 | 3-2 | 5-0 | 1-1 | 2-2 | 2-0 | 2-0 | 1-1 | 4-1 | 0-1 | 1-1 | 3-0 | 2-0 | 2-1 | 1-0 | 1-1 | 3-1 | 2-2 | | 1-1 | 2-1 | 4-2 |
| Stoke City FC | 1-0 | 3-1 | 6-3 | 1-1 | 4-1 | 3-2 | 1-0 | 6-1 | 3-0 | 0-0 | 1-2 | 2-2 | 1-1 | 1-0 | 3-1 | 1-1 | 1-3 | 1-1 | 3-1 | | 3-1 | 5-3 |
| Sunderland AFC | 0-0 | 1-5 | 1-0 | 1-2 | 2-2 | 1-1 | 1-1 | 3-2 | 1-0 | 1-2 | 1-1 | 0-0 | 2-1 | 2-0 | 2-3 | 5-2 | 1-2 | 0-2 | 1-2 | 3-0 | | 1-1 |
| Wolverhampton Wanderers FC | 0-1 | 2-1 | 2-1 | 1-1 | 1-1 | 5-2 | 3-1 | 2-0 | 0-0 | 7-0 | 5-0 | 3-0 | 4-1 | 0-0 | 2-2 | 3-0 | 6-1 | 3-0 | 3-0 | 3-0 | 0-0 | |

| | Division 1 | Pd | Wn | Dw | Ls | GF | GA | Pts | |
|---|---|---|---|---|---|---|---|---|---|
| 1. | EVERTON FC (LIVERPOOL) | 42 | 27 | 5 | 10 | 88 | 52 | 59 | |
| 2. | Wolverhampton Wanderers FC (Wolverhampton) | 42 | 22 | 11 | 9 | 88 | 39 | 55 | |
| 3. | Charlton Athletic FC (London) | 42 | 22 | 6 | 14 | 75 | 59 | 50 | |
| 4. | Middlesbrough FC (Middlesbrough) | 42 | 20 | 9 | 13 | 93 | 74 | 49 | |
| 5. | Arsenal FC (London) | 42 | 19 | 9 | 14 | 55 | 41 | 47 | |
| 6. | Derby County FC (Derby) | 42 | 19 | 8 | 15 | 66 | 55 | 46 | |
| 7. | Stoke City FC (Stoke-on-Trent) | 42 | 17 | 12 | 13 | 71 | 68 | 46 | |
| 8. | Bolton Wanderers FC (Bolton) | 42 | 15 | 15 | 12 | 67 | 58 | 45 | |
| 9. | Preston North End FC (Preston) | 42 | 16 | 12 | 14 | 63 | 59 | 44 | |
| 10. | Grimsby Town FC (Cleethorpes) | 42 | 16 | 11 | 15 | 61 | 69 | 43 | |
| 11. | Liverpool FC (Liverpool) | 42 | 14 | 14 | 14 | 62 | 63 | 42 | |
| 12. | Aston Villa FC (Birmingham) | 42 | 16 | 9 | 17 | 71 | 60 | 41 | |
| 13. | Leeds United AFC (Leeds) | 42 | 16 | 9 | 17 | 59 | 67 | 41 | |
| 14. | Manchester United FC (Manchester) | 42 | 11 | 16 | 15 | 57 | 65 | 38 | |
| 15. | Blackpool FC (Blackpool) | 42 | 12 | 14 | 16 | 56 | 68 | 38 | |
| 16. | Sunderland AFC (Sunderland) | 42 | 13 | 12 | 17 | 54 | 67 | 38 | |
| 17. | Portsmouth FC (Portsmouth) | 42 | 12 | 13 | 17 | 47 | 70 | 37 | |
| 18. | Brentford FC (London) | 42 | 14 | 8 | 20 | 53 | 74 | 36 | |
| 19. | Huddersfield Town AFC (Huddersfield) | 42 | 12 | 11 | 19 | 58 | 64 | 35 | |
| 20. | Chelsea FC (London) | 42 | 12 | 9 | 21 | 64 | 80 | 33 | |
| 21. | Birmingham FC (Birmingham) | 42 | 12 | 8 | 22 | 62 | 84 | 32 | R |
| 22. | Leicester City FC (Leicester) | 42 | 9 | 11 | 22 | 48 | 82 | 29 | R |
| | | 924 | 345 | 234 | 345 | 1418 | 1418 | 924 | |

## Top Goalscorer

1) Tommy LAWTON       (Everton FC)   35

| Football League Division 2 1938-1939 Season | Blackburn Rovers | Bradford P.A. | Burnley | Bury | Chesterfield | Coventry City | Fulham | Luton Town | Manchester City | Millwall | Newcastle United | Norwich City | Nottingham F. | Plymouth Argyle | Sheffield United | Sheffield Wed. | Southampton | Swansea Town | Tottenham H. | Tranmere Rovers | W.B.A. | West Ham United |
|---|---|---|---|---|---|---|---|---|---|---|---|---|---|---|---|---|---|---|---|---|---|---|
| Blackburn Rovers FC | | 6-4 | 1-0 | 1-0 | 3-0 | 0-2 | 2-1 | 2-0 | 3-3 | 3-1 | 3-0 | 6-0 | 3-2 | 4-0 | 1-2 | 2-4 | 3-0 | 4-0 | 3-1 | 3-2 | 3-0 | 3-1 |
| Bradford Park Avenue | 0-4 | | 2-2 | 3-2 | 0-0 | 0-2 | 1-5 | 2-1 | 4-2 | 1-0 | 0-1 | 3-0 | 1-2 | 2-2 | 0-3 | 3-1 | 2-1 | 1-1 | 0-0 | 3-0 | 4-4 | 1-2 |
| Burnley FC | 3-2 | 0-0 | | 0-1 | 1-2 | 1-0 | 2-0 | 3-2 | 1-1 | 2-0 | 2-0 | 3-0 | 2-1 | 1-0 | 2-3 | 1-2 | 2-1 | 1-1 | 1-0 | 3-1 | 0-3 | 1-0 |
| Bury FC | 2-4 | 0-1 | 1-0 | | 3-1 | 5-0 | 0-2 | 2-5 | 1-5 | 1-1 | 1-1 | 2-3 | 2-1 | 3-0 | 2-2 | 2-3 | 5-2 | 4-0 | 3-1 | 5-0 | 3-3 | 1-1 |
| Chesterfield FC | 0-2 | 2-2 | 3-2 | 2-1 | | 3-0 | 0-1 | 1-2 | 0-3 | 3-0 | 2-0 | 2-0 | 7-1 | 3-1 | 1-0 | 3-1 | 6-1 | 6-1 | 3-1 | 3-0 | 3-1 | 1-0 |
| Coventry City FC | 0-1 | 3-1 | 1-1 | 0-0 | 2-0 | | 3-1 | 1-0 | 0-1 | 2-1 | 1-0 | 2-0 | 5-1 | 1-2 | 0-3 | 1-0 | 3-0 | 3-0 | 4-0 | 2-0 | 1-1 | 0-0 |
| Fulham FC | 2-3 | 4-0 | 0-0 | 1-2 | 2-0 | 1-0 | | 2-1 | 2-1 | 2-1 | 1-0 | 2-0 | 2-2 | 1-2 | 1-2 | 2-2 | 1-1 | 1-0 | 1-0 | 1-1 | 3-0 | 3-2 |
| Luton Town FC | 1-1 | 2-2 | 1-0 | 2-1 | 5-0 | 1-3 | 2-1 | | 3-0 | 0-0 | 2-1 | 2-1 | 1-0 | 3-4 | 2-0 | 1-5 | 6-2 | 6-3 | 0-0 | 3-0 | 3-1 | 1-2 |
| Manchester City FC | 3-2 | 5-1 | 2-0 | 0-0 | 3-1 | 3-0 | 3-5 | 1-2 | | 1-6 | 4-1 | 4-1 | 3-0 | 1-3 | 3-2 | 1-1 | 2-1 | 5-0 | 2-0 | 5-2 | 3-3 | 2-4 |
| Millwall FC | 4-1 | 3-1 | 1-1 | 0-0 | 3-1 | 0-0 | 1-1 | 2-1 | 3-1 | | 1-1 | 6-0 | 5-0 | 3-0 | 4-0 | 2-0 | 0-1 | 1-1 | 2-0 | 2-1 | 1-5 | 0-2 |
| Newcastle United FC | 2-2 | 1-0 | 3-2 | 6-0 | 0-1 | 0-4 | 2-1 | 2-0 | 0-2 | 2-2 | | 4-0 | 4-0 | 2-1 | 0-0 | 2-1 | 1-0 | 1-2 | 0-1 | 5-1 | 5-1 | 2-0 |
| Norwich City FC | 4-0 | 1-3 | 4-0 | 3-1 | 2-0 | 1-1 | 3-3 | 2-1 | 0-0 | 0-2 | 1-1 | | 1-0 | 2-1 | 1-2 | 2-2 | 2-1 | 3-0 | 1-2 | 2-0 | 2-3 | 2-6 |
| Nottingham Forest FC | 1-3 | 2-0 | 2-2 | 1-1 | 0-1 | 3-0 | 1-1 | 2-4 | 3-4 | 3-0 | 2-0 | 1-0 | | 2-1 | 0-2 | 3-3 | 0-2 | 1-2 | 2-1 | 2-2 | 2-0 | 0-0 |
| Plymouth Argyle FC | 1-0 | 4-1 | 1-0 | 0-1 | 0-0 | 0-2 | 0-0 | 4-1 | 0-0 | 2-2 | 0-1 | 1-0 | 3-0 | | 0-1 | 1-1 | 2-0 | 0-0 | 0-1 | 3-1 | 0-1 | 0-0 |
| Sheffield United FC | 0-0 | 3-1 | 1-1 | 1-1 | 1-1 | 0-0 | 2-0 | 2-2 | 1-0 | 2-1 | 0-0 | 4-0 | 0-1 | 0-1 | | 0-0 | 5-1 | 1-2 | 6-1 | 2-0 | 1-1 | 3-1 |
| Sheffield Wednesday FC | 3-0 | 2-0 | 4-1 | 2-0 | 0-0 | 2-2 | 5-1 | 4-1 | 3-1 | 3-1 | 0-2 | 7-0 | 1-1 | 1-2 | 1-0 | | 2-0 | 1-1 | 1-0 | 2-0 | 2-1 | 1-4 |
| Southampton FC | 1-3 | 3-2 | 2-1 | 0-0 | 2-2 | 0-2 | 2-1 | 0-4 | 1-2 | 1-1 | 0-0 | 3-1 | 2-2 | 2-1 | 2-2 | 4-3 | | 4-1 | 1-2 | 3-1 | 2-1 | 0-2 |
| Swansea Town AFC | 2-1 | 2-2 | 4-0 | 3-3 | 1-1 | 2-4 | 1-1 | 2-3 | 2-0 | 1-1 | 0-1 | 0-1 | 1-0 | 2-1 | 1-2 | 0-1 | 1-3 | | 1-1 | 1-0 | 3-2 | 3-2 |
| Tottenham Hotspur FC | 4-3 | 2-2 | 1-0 | 4-3 | 2-2 | 2-1 | 1-0 | 1-0 | 2-3 | 4-0 | 1-0 | 4-1 | 4-1 | 1-0 | 2-2 | 3-3 | 1-1 | 3-0 | | 3-1 | 2-2 | 2-1 |
| Tranmere Rovers FC | 1-1 | 2-1 | 0-3 | 3-0 | 0-1 | 1-2 | 0-1 | 2-3 | 3-9 | 0-0 | 0-3 | 0-1 | 1-1 | 2-0 | 0-2 | 1-4 | 1-1 | 2-0 | 0-2 | | 3-1 | 2-2 |
| West Bromwich Albion FC | 2-0 | 0-2 | 1-2 | 6-0 | 1-0 | 3-1 | 3-0 | 3-0 | 3-1 | 0-0 | 5-2 | 4-2 | 0-0 | 4-2 | 3-4 | 5-1 | 2-0 | 0-0 | 4-3 | 2-0 | | 3-2 |
| West Ham United FC | 1-2 | 0-2 | 1-0 | 0-0 | 1-1 | 4-1 | 1-0 | 0-1 | 2-1 | 0-0 | 1-1 | 2-0 | 5-0 | 2-1 | 0-0 | 2-3 | 1-2 | 5-2 | 0-2 | 6-1 | 2-1 | |

## Division 2

| | | Pd | Wn | Dw | Ls | GF | GA | Pts | |
|---|---|---|---|---|---|---|---|---|---|
| 1. | Blackburn Rovers FC (Blackburn) | 42 | 25 | 5 | 12 | 94 | 60 | 55 | P |
| 2. | Sheffield United FC (Sheffield) | 42 | 20 | 14 | 8 | 69 | 41 | 54 | P |
| 3. | Sheffield Wednesday FC (Sheffield) | 42 | 21 | 11 | 10 | 88 | 59 | 53 | |
| 4. | Coventry City FC (Coventry) | 42 | 21 | 8 | 13 | 62 | 45 | 50 | |
| 5. | Manchester City FC (Manchester) | 42 | 21 | 7 | 14 | 96 | 72 | 49 | |
| 6. | Chesterfield FC (Chesterfield) | 42 | 20 | 9 | 13 | 69 | 52 | 49 | |
| 7. | Luton Town FC (Luton) | 42 | 22 | 5 | 15 | 82 | 66 | 49 | |
| 8. | Tottenham Hotspur FC (London) | 42 | 19 | 9 | 14 | 67 | 62 | 47 | |
| 9. | Newcastle United FC (Newcastle-upon-Tyne) | 42 | 18 | 10 | 14 | 61 | 48 | 46 | |
| 10. | West Bromwich Albion FC (West Bromwich) | 42 | 18 | 9 | 15 | 89 | 72 | 45 | |
| 11. | West Ham United FC (London) | 42 | 17 | 10 | 15 | 70 | 52 | 44 | |
| 12. | Fulham FC (London) | 42 | 17 | 10 | 15 | 61 | 55 | 44 | |
| 13. | Millwall FC (London) | 42 | 14 | 14 | 14 | 64 | 53 | 42 | |
| 14. | Burnley FC (Burnley) | 42 | 15 | 9 | 18 | 50 | 56 | 39 | |
| 15. | Plymouth Argyle FC (Plymouth) | 42 | 15 | 8 | 19 | 49 | 55 | 38 | |
| 16. | Bury FC (Bury) | 42 | 12 | 13 | 17 | 65 | 74 | 37 | |
| 17. | Bradford Park Avenue FC (Bradford) | 42 | 12 | 11 | 19 | 61 | 82 | 35 | |
| 18. | Southampton FC (Southampton) | 42 | 13 | 9 | 20 | 56 | 82 | 35 | |
| 19. | Swansea Town AFC (Swansea) | 42 | 11 | 12 | 19 | 50 | 83 | 34 | |
| 20. | Nottingham Forest FC (Nottingham) | 42 | 10 | 11 | 21 | 49 | 82 | 31 | |
| 21. | Norwich City FC (Norwich) | 42 | 13 | 5 | 24 | 50 | 91 | 31 | R |
| 22. | Tranmere Rovers FC (Birkenhead) | 42 | 6 | 5 | 31 | 39 | 99 | 17 | R |
| | | 924 | 360 | 204 | 360 | 1441 | 1441 | 924 | |

## Football League Division 3 (N) — 1938-1939 Season

| | Accrington Stanley | Barnsley | Barrow | Bradford City | Carlisle United | Chester | Crewe Alexandra | Darlington | Doncaster Rovers | Gateshead | Halifax Town | Hartlepools United | Hull City | Lincoln City | New Brighton | Oldham Athletic | Rochdale | Rotherham United | Southport | Stockport County | Wrexham | York City |
|---|---|---|---|---|---|---|---|---|---|---|---|---|---|---|---|---|---|---|---|---|---|---|
| Accrington Stanley FC | | 0-2 | 0-2 | 2-3 | 1-1 | 2-3 | 2-1 | 3-0 | 0-0 | 1-1 | 1-2 | 0-0 | 1-1 | 3-4 | 1-2 | 1-3 | 0-5 | 2-1 | 1-4 | 3-2 | 3-1 | 3-1 |
| Barnsley FC | 4-1 | | 4-0 | 5-2 | 3-0 | 3-0 | 5-2 | 7-1 | 1-1 | 2-0 | 1-0 | 2-0 | 5-1 | 4-0 | 1-1 | 3-0 | 2-0 | 2-0 | 3-1 | 0-1 | 2-1 | 1-0 |
| Barrow AFC | 2-3 | 1-2 | | 2-1 | 5-0 | 0-1 | 1-2 | 2-0 | 4-4 | 1-1 | 0-0 | 1-1 | 3-1 | 2-2 | 3-0 | 2-0 | 3-1 | 4-1 | 4-0 | 0-2 | 4-0 | 2-0 |
| Bradford City AFC | 2-1 | 0-2 | 3-0 | | 2-0 | 1-0 | 4-1 | 6-2 | 2-1 | 1-1 | 1-0 | 0-1 | 6-2 | 3-0 | 3-3 | 1-4 | 3-0 | 5-2 | 2-1 | 4-0 | 4-0 | 6-0 |
| Carlisle United FC | 6-4 | 3-1 | 3-0 | 0-2 | | 1-3 | 1-0 | 1-1 | 2-3 | 2-2 | 1-2 | 2-0 | 1-2 | 4-3 | 1-1 | 2-0 | 5-1 | 3-1 | 1-1 | 3-2 | 1-1 | 1-3 |
| Chester FC | 1-0 | 2-1 | 1-2 | 3-2 | 6-1 | | 4-0 | 0-0 | 0-4 | 2-2 | 5-1 | 8-2 | 1-1 | 0-0 | 1-3 | 4-2 | 0-0 | 1-4 | 2-0 | 4-3 | 4-2 | 5-1 |
| Crewe Alexandra FC | 2-1 | 0-0 | 1-1 | 0-0 | 7-1 | 0-2 | | 2-0 | 1-2 | 3-2 | 2-2 | 0-1 | 6-0 | 7-1 | 1-2 | 4-1 | 0-0 | 4-2 | 2-1 | 1-0 | 8-2 | |
| Darlington FC | 3-0 | 0-1 | 3-1 | 0-4 | 2-1 | 3-3 | 1-0 | | 1-2 | 5-2 | 1-0 | 3-0 | 0-1 | 3-1 | 3-0 | 3-3 | 1-2 | 3-1 | 0-2 | 4-3 | 3-1 | 1-2 |
| Doncaster Rovers FC | 7-1 | 1-3 | 1-1 | 1-2 | 1-0 | 4-1 | 1-2 | 4-1 | | 2-3 | 0-0 | 3-1 | 1-0 | 4-1 | 4-1 | 3-2 | 5-0 | 1-1 | 0-0 | 3-1 | 0-0 | 1-0 |
| Gateshead FC | 4-1 | 1-1 | 2-1 | 0-0 | 1-1 | 3-0 | 0-5 | 0-2 | 2-0 | | 2-0 | 2-0 | 2-2 | 4-0 | 0-3 | 2-0 | 2-2 | 7-1 | 0-0 | 4-1 | 5-1 | 2-3 |
| Halifax Town AFC | 2-0 | 1-4 | 1-0 | 2-2 | 5-1 | 1-1 | 0-0 | 1-1 | 0-0 | 3-3 | | 2-0 | 1-0 | 2-0 | 3-1 | 0-0 | 2-1 | 1-1 | 1-1 | 3-3 | 0-2 | 2-1 |
| Hartlepools United FC | 2-1 | 0-1 | 1-2 | 1-3 | 2-1 | 2-5 | 0-1 | 3-0 | 1-3 | 3-1 | 1-0 | | 3-3 | 2-1 | 3-2 | 0-0 | 4-2 | 1-1 | 0-2 | 4-2 | 0-0 | 3-2 |
| Hull City AFC | 6-1 | 0-1 | 4-0 | 3-2 | 11-1 | 3-0 | 2-1 | 3-2 | 0-0 | 1-0 | 1-1 | 4-1 | | 4-2 | 3-0 | 0-2 | 3-3 | 0-2 | 2-1 | 4-4 | 1-1 | 2-0 |
| Lincoln City FC | 3-0 | 2-4 | 1-1 | 4-0 | 2-1 | 0-3 | 3-2 | 3-0 | 2-5 | 1-0 | 0-0 | 2-2 | 0-3 | | | | 1-0 | 2-2 | 0-1 | 3-2 | 8-3 | 3-3 |
| New Brighton FC | 4-1 | 1-2 | 2-0 | 2-1 | 2-3 | 1-3 | 1-2 | 3-0 | 3-6 | 0-1 | 1-0 | 5-2 | 6-1 | 3-2 | | 0-1 | 3-1 | 3-0 | 1-1 | 0-0 | 2-3 | 3-2 |
| Oldham Athletic AFC | 2-0 | 4-2 | 1-0 | 2-1 | 6-0 | 1-3 | 3-0 | 2-0 | 0-0 | 1-3 | 1-0 | 4-2 | 4-1 | 1-0 | 1-0 | | 1-2 | 2-0 | 2-4 | 3-1 | 4-2 | 6-0 |
| Rochdale AFC | 4-1 | 2-1 | 2-2 | 1-1 | 2-3 | 5-2 | 5-0 | 6-1 | 1-1 | 5-2 | 4-5 | 3-4 | 4-0 | 4-0 | 2-0 | 1-2 | | 0-1 | 5-0 | 0-1 | 0-0 | 2-2 |
| Rotherham United FC | 2-1 | 0-1 | 1-2 | 2-0 | 4-0 | 2-0 | 4-1 | 3-3 | 0-0 | 2-2 | 0-1 | 5-1 | 0-2 | 1-3 | 0-0 | 3-1 | 7-1 | | 1-0 | 3-2 | 3-0 | 2-0 |
| Southport FC | 1-0 | 0-0 | 4-1 | 2-2 | 7-1 | 2-0 | 1-2 | 4-1 | 0-4 | 2-0 | 1-0 | 2-0 | 4-0 | 4-1 | 1-1 | 0-0 | 4-1 | 1-0 | | 3-0 | 3-1 | 1-1 |
| Stockport County FC | 3-0 | 1-1 | 3-1 | 2-0 | 3-0 | 0-0 | 5-1 | 5-2 | 1-2 | 3-2 | 3-3 | 5-0 | 2-2 | 3-3 | 1-1 | 3-1 | 1-2 | 5-0 | 3-1 | | 2-1 | 3-1 |
| Wrexham AFC | 2-0 | 1-1 | 3-0 | 1-1 | 2-5 | 3-2 | 0-4 | 3-1 | 3-0 | 2-0 | 3-2 | 3-0 | 4-2 | 1-2 | 4-1 | 1-0 | 2-0 | 4-3 | 2-1 | | | 1-3 |
| York City FC | 2-2 | 2-3 | 2-3 | 0-1 | 4-1 | 2-2 | 4-1 | 1-1 | 2-2 | 1-1 | 3-0 | 2-0 | 1-0 | 1-3 | 2-0 | 4-1 | 0-7 | 0-1 | 2-3 | 1-2 | 1-0 | |

## Division 3 (North)

| | | Pd | Wn | Dw | Ls | GF | GA | Pts | |
|---|---|---|---|---|---|---|---|---|---|
| 1. | Barnsley FC (Barnsley) | 42 | 30 | 7 | 5 | 94 | 34 | 67 | P |
| 2. | Doncaster Rovers FC (Doncaster) | 42 | 21 | 14 | 7 | 87 | 47 | 56 | |
| 3. | Bradford City AFC (Bradford) | 42 | 22 | 8 | 12 | 89 | 56 | 52 | |
| 4. | Southport FC (Southport) | 42 | 20 | 10 | 12 | 75 | 54 | 50 | |
| 5. | Oldham Athletic AFC (Oldham) | 42 | 22 | 5 | 15 | 76 | 59 | 49 | |
| 6. | Chester FC (Chester) | 42 | 20 | 9 | 13 | 88 | 70 | 49 | |
| 7. | Hull City AFC (Kingston-upon-Hull) | 42 | 18 | 10 | 14 | 83 | 74 | 46 | |
| 8. | Crewe Alexandra FC (Crewe) | 42 | 19 | 6 | 17 | 82 | 70 | 44 | |
| 9. | Stockport County FC (Stockport) | 42 | 17 | 9 | 16 | 91 | 77 | 43 | |
| 10. | Gateshead FC (Gateshead) | 42 | 14 | 14 | 14 | 74 | 67 | 42 | |
| 11. | Rotherham United FC (Rotherham) | 42 | 17 | 8 | 17 | 64 | 64 | 42 | |
| 12. | Halifax Town AFC (Halifax) | 42 | 13 | 16 | 13 | 52 | 54 | 42 | |
| 13. | Barrow AFC (Barrow-in-Furness) | 42 | 16 | 9 | 17 | 66 | 65 | 41 | |
| 14. | Wrexham AFC (Wrexham) | 42 | 17 | 7 | 18 | 66 | 79 | 41 | |
| 15. | Rochdale AFC (Rochdale) | 42 | 15 | 9 | 18 | 92 | 82 | 39 | |
| 16. | New Brighton FC (Wallasey) | 42 | 15 | 9 | 18 | 68 | 73 | 39 | |
| 17. | Lincoln City FC (Lincoln) | 42 | 12 | 9 | 21 | 66 | 92 | 33 | |
| 18. | Darlington FC (Darlington) | 42 | 13 | 7 | 22 | 62 | 92 | 33 | |
| 19. | Carlisle United FC (Carlisle) | 42 | 13 | 7 | 22 | 64 | 111 | 33 | |
| 20. | York City FC (York) | 42 | 12 | 8 | 22 | 66 | 92 | 32 | |
| 21. | Hartlepools United FC (Hartlepool) | 42 | 12 | 7 | 23 | 55 | 94 | 31 | |
| 22. | Accrington Stanley FC (Accrington) | 42 | 7 | 6 | 29 | 49 | 103 | 20 | |
| | | 924 | 365 | 194 | 365 | 1609 | 1609 | 924 | |

## Football League Division 3 (S) — 1938-1939 Season

| | Aldershot | Bournemouth | Brighton | Bristol City | Bristol Rovers | Cardiff City | Clapton Orient | Crystal Palace | Exeter City | Ipswich Town | Mansfield Town | Newport County | Northampton | Notts County | Port Vale | Q.P.R. | Reading | Southend United | Swindon Town | Torquay United | Walsall | Watford |
|---|---|---|---|---|---|---|---|---|---|---|---|---|---|---|---|---|---|---|---|---|---|---|
| Aldershot FC | ■ | 2-1 | 1-1 | 0-1 | 1-0 | 1-1 | 1-0 | 2-1 | 2-0 | 3-1 | 3-0 | 1-0 | 3-0 | 0-3 | 1-0 | 2-0 | 1-1 | 1-0 | 1-0 | 1-1 | 3-3 | 1-1 |
| Bournemouth & B. Athletic | 4-0 | ■ | 2-0 | 4-0 | 5-2 | 0-0 | 0-0 | 1-1 | 2-0 | 0-0 | 1-1 | 0-1 | 3-1 | 3-2 | 1-1 | 4-2 | 0-0 | 0-4 | 2-0 | 2-5 | 3-1 | 1-1 |
| Brighton & Hove Albion | 0-3 | 1-1 | ■ | 1-0 | 6-3 | 1-2 | 2-0 | 0-0 | 6-1 | 2-0 | 3-0 | 0-0 | 1-0 | 2-0 | 1-0 | 3-1 | 2-2 | 3-0 | 4-0 | 2-0 | 3-1 | 0-0 |
| Bristol City FC | 1-0 | 2-0 | 2-0 | ■ | 2-1 | 1-1 | 3-1 | 1-1 | 4-1 | 3-2 | 2-0 | 0-2 | 0-0 | 2-1 | 5-1 | 2-2 | 5-1 | 1-0 | 1-1 | 1-3 | 2-1 | 2-0 |
| Bristol Rovers FC | 0-0 | 1-0 | 0-1 | 1-1 | ■ | 1-1 | 1-0 | 1-2 | 4-1 | 3-3 | 3-0 | 0-0 | 1-0 | 0-0 | 0-1 | 0-0 | 2-4 | 4-1 | 5-0 | 0-1 | 2-0 | 1-1 |
| Cardiff City AFC | 2-4 | 5-0 | 4-1 | 2-1 | 0-2 | ■ | 1-2 | 0-1 | 1-2 | 2-1 | 0-0 | 1-2 | 2-0 | 4-1 | 2-4 | 1-0 | 0-1 | 1-0 | 2-1 | 3-1 | 2-1 | 5-3 |
| Clapton Orient FC | 2-0 | 1-1 | 2-0 | 1-1 | 2-1 | 1-1 | ■ | 4-0 | 3-3 | 1-1 | 0-0 | 1-3 | 3-0 | 1-1 | 1-0 | 2-1 | 1-2 | 5-0 | 5-0 | 3-0 | 1-1 | 0-0 |
| Crystal Palace FC | 3-0 | 3-0 | 1-0 | 3-2 | 0-0 | 2-0 | 4-2 | ■ | 3-2 | 3-0 | 6-2 | 1-1 | 2-0 | 5-1 | 1-0 | 0-0 | 4-3 | 1-1 | 1-3 | 4-0 | 2-0 | |
| Exeter City FC | 3-3 | 0-0 | 2-2 | 1-1 | 2-1 | 1-1 | 2-1 | 4-4 | ■ | 3-0 | 2-0 | 3-1 | 3-2 | 1-0 | 1-3 | 1-1 | 3-2 | 3-3 | 0-0 | 1-2 | 3-2 | 1-3 |
| Ipswich Town FC | 7-2 | 0-2 | 0-0 | 4-0 | 0-0 | 1-2 | 3-0 | 2-1 | 2-2 | ■ | 5-1 | 1-4 | 2-0 | 0-2 | 2-0 | 1-0 | 2-1 | 4-2 | 3-1 | 1-0 | 1-0 | 5-1 |
| Mansfield Town FC | 1-0 | 2-0 | 4-2 | 3-2 | 1-3 | 2-2 | 1-0 | 0-0 | 4-2 | 0-1 | ■ | 0-2 | 1-1 | 2-0 | 2-2 | 0-0 | 3-1 | 1-1 | 4-0 | 0-0 | 0-0 | |
| Newport County AFC | 1-0 | 2-2 | 2-0 | 0-2 | 2-0 | 3-0 | 2-1 | 2-0 | 0-0 | 3-2 | 0-0 | ■ | 1-1 | 2-1 | 0-2 | 2-0 | 2-0 | 3-0 | 6-4 | 1-0 | 2-1 | 1-0 |
| Northampton Town FC | 5-0 | 2-0 | 1-4 | 2-2 | 2-1 | 2-1 | 3-0 | 0-0 | 0-0 | 2-0 | 3-4 | 1-0 | ■ | 2-1 | 2-0 | 1-0 | 1-1 | 2-2 | 0-2 | 4-1 | 4-1 | 2-0 |
| Notts County FC | 1-1 | 0-1 | 4-3 | 0-0 | 3-1 | 1-1 | 1-0 | 0-1 | 3-1 | 2-1 | 1-1 | 2-0 | 1-0 | ■ | 4-0 | 0-0 | 2-0 | 4-1 | 2-0 | 5-1 | 0-0 | 0-3 |
| Port Vale FC | 1-3 | 2-0 | 1-1 | 4-0 | 2-1 | 1-1 | 1-1 | 2-0 | 3-2 | 0-0 | 3-0 | 2-1 | 0-2 | 3-1 | ■ | 1-2 | 0-2 | 2-2 | 2-2 | 0-1 | 5-1 | 1-2 |
| Queen's Park Rangers FC | 7-0 | 2-0 | 1-2 | 3-1 | 1-1 | 5-0 | 1-1 | 1-2 | 5-0 | 0-0 | 3-0 | 0-0 | 3-0 | 0-1 | 2-2 | ■ | 2-2 | 1-1 | 2-1 | 1-1 | 3-0 | 1-0 |
| Reading FC | 5-0 | 1-0 | 3-0 | 2-2 | 2-0 | 0-0 | 2-2 | 3-1 | 1-1 | 2-1 | 0-0 | 0-1 | 5-1 | 3-1 | 2-1 | 2-4 | ■ | 3-0 | 3-0 | 3-5 | 1-1 | 3-2 |
| Southend United FC | 2-1 | 2-2 | 1-1 | 2-0 | 3-2 | 2-0 | 1-0 | 3-1 | 0-1 | 0-0 | 2-0 | 5-0 | 2-0 | 1-0 | 0-0 | 2-1 | 2-0 | ■ | 2-3 | 1-1 | 2-0 | 3-0 |
| Swindon Town FC | 2-1 | 4-2 | 3-2 | 1-0 | 2-1 | 4-1 | 2-0 | 2-2 | 2-1 | 1-1 | 1-2 | 8-0 | 1-0 | 4-1 | 1-2 | 2-2 | 4-2 | 2-1 | ■ | 3-1 | 1-4 | 3-0 |
| Torquay United FC | 1-1 | 2-0 | 0-2 | 3-1 | 2-2 | 1-3 | 2-1 | 1-2 | 0-1 | 1-1 | 3-0 | 1-1 | 1-2 | 0-2 | 1-0 | 0-2 | 2-3 | 1-1 | 2-0 | ■ | 0-1 | 2-1 |
| Walsall FC | 2-2 | 1-2 | 0-2 | 5-0 | 2-2 | 6-3 | 5-1 | 1-1 | 1-2 | 0-1 | 0-0 | 1-1 | 1-0 | 3-3 | 4-0 | 0-1 | 3-0 | 0-2 | 5-0 | 5-0 | ■ | 2-0 |
| Watford FC | 1-1 | 1-0 | 1-1 | 2-2 | 4-1 | 1-0 | 1-0 | 4-1 | 4-2 | 0-0 | 2-0 | 1-1 | 2-0 | 0-1 | 2-0 | 4-1 | 3-1 | 3-0 | 4-1 | 0-0 | 4-2 | ■ |

| | Division 3 (South) | Pd | Wn | Dw | Ls | GF | GA | Pts | |
|---|---|---|---|---|---|---|---|---|---|
| 1. | Newport County AFC (Newport) | 42 | 22 | 11 | 9 | 58 | 45 | 55 | P |
| 2. | Crystal Palace FC (London) | 42 | 20 | 12 | 10 | 71 | 52 | 52 | |
| 3. | Brighton & Hove Albion FC (Hove) | 42 | 19 | 11 | 12 | 68 | 49 | 49 | |
| 4. | Watford FC (Watford) | 42 | 17 | 12 | 13 | 62 | 51 | 46 | |
| 5. | Reading FC (Reading) | 42 | 16 | 14 | 12 | 69 | 59 | 46 | |
| 6. | Queen's Park Rangers FC (London) | 42 | 15 | 14 | 13 | 68 | 49 | 44 | |
| 7. | Ipswich Town FC (Ipswich) | 42 | 16 | 12 | 14 | 62 | 52 | 44 | |
| 8. | Bristol City FC (Bristol) | 42 | 16 | 12 | 14 | 61 | 63 | 44 | |
| 9. | Swindon Town FC (Swindon) | 42 | 18 | 8 | 16 | 72 | 77 | 44 | |
| 10. | Aldershot FC (Aldershot) | 42 | 16 | 12 | 14 | 53 | 66 | 44 | |
| 11. | Notts County FC (Nottingham) | 42 | 17 | 9 | 16 | 59 | 54 | 43 | |
| 12. | Southend United FC (Southend-on-Sea) | 42 | 16 | 9 | 17 | 61 | 64 | 41 | |
| 13. | Cardiff City AFC (Cardiff) | 42 | 15 | 11 | 16 | 61 | 65 | 41 | |
| 14. | Exeter City FC (Exeter) | 42 | 13 | 14 | 15 | 65 | 82 | 40 | |
| 15. | Bournemouth & Boscombe Athletic FC (Bournemouth) | 42 | 13 | 13 | 16 | 52 | 58 | 39 | |
| 16. | Mansfield Town FC (Mansfield) | 42 | 12 | 15 | 15 | 44 | 62 | 39 | |
| 17. | Northampton Town FC (Northampton) | 42 | 15 | 8 | 19 | 51 | 58 | 38 | |
| 18. | Port Vale FC (Stoke-on-Trent) | 42 | 14 | 9 | 19 | 52 | 58 | 37 | |
| 19. | Torquay United FC (Torquay) | 42 | 14 | 9 | 19 | 54 | 70 | 37 | |
| 20. | Clapton Orient FC (London) | 42 | 11 | 13 | 18 | 53 | 55 | 35 | |
| 21. | Walsall FC (Walsall) | 42 | 11 | 11 | 20 | 68 | 69 | 33 | |
| 22. | Bristol Rovers FC (Bristol) | 42 | 10 | 13 | 19 | 55 | 61 | 22 | |
| | | 924 | 336 | 252 | 336 | 1319 | 1319 | 924 | |

## F.A. CUP FINAL   (Wembley Stadium, London – 29/04/1939 – 99,370)

PORTSMOUTH FC (PORTSMOUTH)          4-1          Wolverhampton Wanderers FC
*Barlow 2, Anderson, Parker*                                                    *Dorsett*

Portsmouth:  Walker, Morgan, Rochford, Guthrie, Rowe, Wharton, Worrall, McAlinden, Anderson, Barlow, Parker.

Wolves:  Scott, Morris, Taylor, Galley, Cullis, Gardiner, Burton, McIntosh, Westcott, Dorsett, Maguire.

## Semi-finals

| | | |
|---|---|---|
| Portsmouth FC (Portsmouth) | 2-1 | Huddersfield Town AFC (Huddersfield) |
| Wolverhampton Wanderers FC (Wolverhampton) | 5-0 | Grimsby Town AFC (Cleethorpes) |

## Quarter-finals

| | | |
|---|---|---|
| Chelsea FC (London) | 0-1 | Grimsby Town FC (Cleethorpes) |
| Huddersfield Town AFC (Huddersfield) | 1-1, 2-1 | Blackburn Rovers FC (Blackburn) |
| Portsmouth FC (Portsmouth) | 1-0 | Preston North End FC (Preston) |
| Wolverhampton Wanderers FC (Wolverhampton) | 2-0 | Everton FC (Liverpool) |

# 1939-40

Football League Division 1 1939-1940 Season

| | Arsenal | Aston Villa | Blackburn Rovers | Blackpool | Bolton Wanderers | Brentford | Charlton Athletic | Chelsea | Derby County | Everton | Grimsby Town | Huddersfield Town | Leeds United | Liverpool | Manchester United | Middlesbrough | Portsmouth | Preston North End | Sheffield United | Stoke City | Sunderland | Wolves |
|---|---|---|---|---|---|---|---|---|---|---|---|---|---|---|---|---|---|---|---|---|---|---|
| Arsenal FC | | -- | 1-0 | -- | -- | -- | -- | -- | -- | -- | -- | -- | -- | -- | -- | -- | -- | -- | -- | -- | 5-2 | -- |
| Aston Villa FC | -- | | -- | -- | -- | -- | -- | -- | -- | 1-2 | -- | -- | -- | -- | 2-0 | -- | -- | -- | -- | -- | -- | -- |
| Blackburn Rovers FC | -- | -- | | -- | -- | -- | -- | -- | -- | 2-2 | -- | -- | -- | -- | -- | -- | -- | -- | -- | -- | -- | -- |
| Blackpool FC | -- | -- | -- | | -- | 2-1 | -- | -- | -- | -- | -- | -- | -- | -- | -- | -- | -- | -- | -- | -- | -- | 2-1 |
| Bolton Wanderers FC | -- | -- | -- | -- | | -- | -- | -- | -- | -- | -- | -- | -- | -- | -- | 2-1 | -- | -- | -- | -- | -- | -- |
| Brentford FC | -- | -- | -- | -- | -- | | -- | -- | -- | -- | 1-0 | -- | -- | -- | -- | -- | -- | -- | -- | -- | -- | -- |
| Charlton Athletic FC | -- | -- | -- | -- | -- | -- | | -- | -- | -- | -- | -- | -- | -- | 2-0 | -- | -- | -- | -- | -- | -- | -- |
| Chelsea FC | -- | -- | -- | -- | 3-2 | -- | -- | | -- | -- | -- | -- | -- | -- | 1-1 | -- | -- | -- | -- | -- | -- | -- |
| Derby County FC | -- | 1-0 | -- | -- | -- | -- | -- | -- | | -- | -- | -- | -- | -- | -- | -- | 2-0 | -- | -- | -- | -- | -- |
| Everton FC | -- | -- | -- | -- | -- | 1-1 | -- | -- | -- | | -- | -- | -- | -- | -- | -- | -- | -- | -- | -- | -- | -- |
| Grimsby Town FC | -- | -- | -- | -- | -- | -- | -- | -- | -- | -- | | -- | -- | -- | -- | -- | -- | 2-0 | -- | -- | -- | 0-0 |
| Huddersfield Town AFC | -- | -- | -- | 0-1 | -- | -- | -- | -- | -- | -- | -- | | -- | -- | -- | -- | -- | -- | -- | -- | -- | -- |
| Leeds United AFC | -- | -- | -- | -- | -- | -- | 0-1 | -- | -- | -- | -- | -- | | -- | -- | -- | -- | -- | 0-1 | -- | -- | -- |
| Liverpool FC | -- | -- | -- | -- | -- | -- | -- | 1-0 | -- | -- | -- | -- | -- | | 4-1 | -- | -- | -- | -- | -- | -- | -- |
| Manchester United FC | -- | -- | -- | -- | -- | -- | -- | -- | -- | 4-0 | -- | -- | -- | -- | | -- | -- | -- | -- | -- | -- | -- |
| Middlesbrough FC | -- | -- | -- | -- | -- | -- | -- | -- | -- | -- | -- | -- | -- | -- | -- | | -- | -- | -- | -- | 2-2 | -- |
| Portsmouth FC | -- | -- | 2-1 | -- | -- | -- | -- | -- | -- | -- | -- | -- | -- | -- | -- | -- | | -- | -- | -- | -- | -- |
| Preston North End FC | -- | -- | -- | -- | -- | -- | -- | -- | -- | -- | -- | -- | 0-0 | -- | -- | -- | -- | | 0-0 | -- | -- | -- |
| Sheffield United FC | -- | -- | -- | -- | -- | -- | -- | -- | -- | -- | -- | -- | -- | 2-1 | -- | -- | -- | -- | | -- | -- | -- |
| Stoke City FC | -- | -- | -- | -- | 1-2 | -- | 4-0 | -- | -- | -- | -- | -- | -- | -- | -- | -- | -- | -- | -- | | -- | -- |
| Sunderland AFC | -- | -- | -- | -- | -- | -- | -- | -- | -- | 3-0 | -- | 1-2 | -- | -- | -- | -- | -- | -- | -- | -- | | -- |
| Wolverhampton Wanderers FC | 2-2 | -- | -- | -- | -- | -- | -- | -- | -- | -- | -- | -- | -- | -- | -- | -- | -- | -- | -- | -- | -- | |

| Division 1 | Pd | Wn | Dw | Ls | GF | GA | Pts |
|---|---|---|---|---|---|---|---|
| 1. Blackpool FC (Blackpool) | 3 | 3 | - | - | 5 | 2 | 6 |
| 2. Sheffield United FC (Sheffield) | 3 | 2 | 1 | - | 3 | 1 | 5 |
| 3. Arsenal FC (London) | 3 | 2 | 1 | - | 8 | 4 | 5 |
| 4. Liverpool FC (Liverpool) | 3 | 2 | - | 1 | 6 | 3 | 4 |
| 5. Everton FC (Liverpool) | 3 | 1 | 2 | - | 5 | 4 | 4 |
| 6. Bolton Wanderers FC (Bolton) | 3 | 2 | - | 1 | 6 | 5 | 4 |
| 7. Derby County FC (Derby) | 3 | 2 | - | 1 | 3 | 3 | 4 |
| 7. Charlton Athletic FC (London) | 3 | 2 | - | 1 | 3 | 3 | 4 |
| 9. Stoke City FC (Stoke-on-Trent) | 3 | 1 | 1 | 1 | 7 | 4 | 3 |
| 10. Manchester United FC (Manchester) | 3 | 1 | 1 | 1 | 5 | 3 | 3 |
| 11. Chelsea FC (London) | 3 | 1 | 1 | 1 | 4 | 4 | 3 |
| 11. Brentford FC (London) | 3 | 1 | 1 | 1 | 3 | 3 | 3 |
| 13. Grimsby Town FC (Cleethorpes) | 3 | 1 | 1 | 1 | 2 | 4 | 3 |
| 14. Aston Villa FC (Birmingham) | 3 | 1 | - | 2 | 3 | 3 | 2 |
| 15. Sunderland AFC (Sunderland) | 3 | 1 | - | 2 | 6 | 7 | 2 |
| 16. Wolverhampton Wanderers FC (Wolverhampton) | 3 | - | 2 | 1 | 3 | 4 | 2 |
| 17. Huddersfield Town AFC (Huddersfield) | 3 | 1 | - | 2 | 2 | 3 | 2 |
| 18. Portsmouth FC (Portsmouth) | 3 | 1 | - | 2 | 3 | 5 | 2 |
| 19. Preston North End FC (Preston) | 3 | - | 2 | 1 | - | 2 | 2 |
| 20. Blackburn Rovers FC (Blackburn) | 3 | - | 1 | 2 | 3 | 5 | 1 |
| 21. Middlesbrough FC (Middlesbrough) | 3 | - | 1 | 2 | 3 | 8 | 1 |
| 22. Leeds United AFC (Leeds) | 3 | - | 1 | 2 | - | 2 | 1 |
| | 66 | 25 | 16 | 25 | 83 | 83 | 66 |

The League was suspended due to World War 2 conditions and did not resume until the 1946-47 season. However, regional competitions were played during the intervening years.

| Football League Division 2 1939-1940 Season | Barnsley | Birmingham | Bradford Park Avenue | Burnley | Bury | Chesterfield | Coventry City | Fulham | Leicester City | Luton Town | Manchester City | Millwall | Newcastle United | Newport County | Nottingham Forest | Plymouth Argyle | Sheffield Wednesday | Southampton | Swansea Town | Tottenham Hotspur | W.B.A. | West Ham United |
|---|---|---|---|---|---|---|---|---|---|---|---|---|---|---|---|---|---|---|---|---|---|---|
| Barnsley FC | ▓ | -- | -- | -- | -- | -- | -- | -- | -- | -- | -- | -- | -- | -- | 4-1 | -- | -- | -- | -- | -- | -- | -- |
| Birmingham FC | -- | ▓ | -- | 2-0 | -- | -- | -- | -- | 2-0 | -- | -- | -- | -- | -- | -- | -- | -- | -- | -- | -- | -- | -- |
| Bradford Park Avenue | -- | -- | ▓ | -- | -- | -- | -- | -- | -- | 0-3 | -- | 2-2 | -- | -- | -- | -- | -- | -- | -- | -- | -- | -- |
| Burnley FC | -- | -- | -- | ▓ | -- | -- | 1-1 | -- | -- | -- | -- | -- | -- | -- | -- | -- | -- | -- | -- | -- | -- | -- |
| Bury FC | -- | -- | -- | -- | ▓ | -- | -- | 3-1 | -- | -- | -- | -- | -- | -- | -- | -- | -- | -- | -- | -- | -- | -- |
| Chesterfield FC | -- | -- | 2-0 | -- | -- | ▓ | -- | -- | -- | -- | -- | -- | -- | -- | -- | -- | -- | -- | -- | -- | -- | -- |
| Coventry City FC | 4-2 | -- | -- | -- | -- | -- | ▓ | -- | -- | -- | -- | -- | -- | -- | -- | -- | -- | -- | -- | -- | 3-3 | -- |
| Fulham FC | -- | -- | -- | -- | -- | -- | -- | ▓ | -- | 1-1 | -- | -- | -- | -- | -- | -- | -- | -- | -- | -- | -- | -- |
| Leicester City FC | -- | -- | -- | -- | -- | -- | -- | -- | ▓ | -- | 4-3 | -- | -- | -- | -- | -- | -- | -- | -- | -- | -- | -- |
| Luton Town FC | -- | -- | -- | -- | -- | -- | -- | -- | -- | ▓ | -- | -- | -- | -- | -- | -- | 3-0 | -- | -- | -- | -- | -- |
| Manchester City FC | -- | -- | -- | -- | 1-1 | 2-0 | -- | -- | -- | -- | ▓ | -- | -- | -- | -- | -- | -- | -- | -- | -- | -- | -- |
| Millwall FC | -- | -- | -- | -- | -- | -- | -- | -- | -- | -- | -- | ▓ | 3-0 | -- | -- | 0-2 | -- | -- | -- | -- | -- | -- |
| Newcastle United FC | -- | -- | -- | -- | -- | -- | -- | -- | -- | -- | -- | -- | ▓ | -- | -- | -- | -- | -- | 8-1 | -- | -- | -- |
| Newport County AFC | -- | -- | -- | -- | -- | -- | -- | -- | -- | -- | -- | -- | -- | ▓ | -- | -- | -- | 3-1 | -- | 1-1 | -- | -- |
| Nottingham Forest FC | -- | -- | -- | -- | -- | -- | -- | -- | -- | -- | -- | -- | 2-0 | 2-1 | ▓ | -- | -- | -- | -- | -- | -- | -- |
| Plymouth Argyle FC | -- | -- | -- | -- | -- | -- | -- | -- | -- | -- | -- | -- | -- | -- | -- | ▓ | -- | -- | -- | -- | -- | 1-3 |
| Sheffield Wednesday FC | 3-1 | -- | -- | -- | -- | -- | -- | -- | -- | -- | -- | -- | -- | -- | -- | 0-1 | ▓ | -- | -- | -- | -- | -- |
| Southampton FC | -- | -- | -- | -- | 3-0 | -- | -- | -- | -- | -- | -- | -- | -- | -- | -- | -- | -- | ▓ | 1-3 | -- | -- | -- |
| Swansea Town AFC | -- | -- | -- | -- | -- | -- | -- | -- | -- | -- | -- | -- | -- | -- | -- | -- | -- | -- | ▓ | -- | 1-2 | -- |
| Tottenham Hotspur FC | -- | 1-1 | -- | -- | -- | -- | -- | -- | -- | -- | -- | -- | -- | -- | -- | -- | -- | -- | -- | ▓ | -- | -- |
| West Bromwich Albion FC | -- | -- | -- | -- | -- | -- | -- | -- | -- | -- | -- | -- | -- | -- | -- | -- | -- | -- | -- | 3-4 | ▓ | -- |
| West Ham United FC | -- | -- | -- | -- | -- | -- | -- | 2-1 | 0-2 | -- | -- | -- | -- | -- | -- | -- | -- | -- | -- | -- | -- | ▓ |

## Division 2

| | | Pd | Wn | Dw | Ls | GF | GA | Pts |
|---|---|---|---|---|---|---|---|---|
| 1. | Luton Town FC (Luton) | 3 | 2 | 1 | - | 7 | 1 | 5 |
| 2. | Birmingham FC (Birmingham) | 3 | 2 | 1 | - | 5 | 1 | 5 |
| 3. | Coventry City FC (Coventry) | 3 | 1 | 2 | - | 8 | 6 | 4 |
| 3. | Plymouth Argyle FC (Plymouth) | 3 | 2 | - | 1 | 4 | 3 | 4 |
| 5. | West Ham United FC (London) | 3 | 2 | - | 1 | 5 | 4 | 4 |
| 6. | Leicester City FC (Leicester) | 3 | 2 | - | 1 | 6 | 5 | 4 |
| 6. | Tottenham Hotspur FC (London) | 3 | 1 | 2 | - | 6 | 5 | 4 |
| 8. | Nottingham Forest FC (Nottingham) | 3 | 2 | - | 1 | 5 | 5 | 4 |
| 9. | Millwall FC (London) | 3 | 1 | 1 | 1 | 5 | 4 | 3 |
| 9. | Newport County AFC (Newport) | 3 | 1 | 1 | 1 | 5 | 4 | 3 |
| 11. | Manchester City FC (Manchester) | 3 | 1 | 1 | 1 | 6 | 5 | 3 |
| 12. | West Bromwich Albion FC (West Bromwich) | 3 | 1 | 1 | 1 | 8 | 8 | 3 |
| 13. | Bury FC (Bury) | 3 | 1 | 1 | 1 | 4 | 5 | 3 |
| 14. | Newcastle United FC (Newcastle-upon-Tyne) | 3 | 1 | - | 2 | 8 | 6 | 2 |
| 15. | Chesterfield FC (Chesterfield) | 2 | 1 | - | 1 | 2 | 2 | 2 |
| 16. | Barnsley FC (Barnsley) | 3 | 1 | - | 2 | 7 | 8 | 2 |
| 17. | Southampton FC (Southampton) | 3 | 1 | - | 2 | 5 | 6 | 2 |
| 18. | Sheffield Wednesday FC (Sheffield) | 3 | 1 | - | 2 | 3 | 5 | 2 |
| 19. | Swansea Town AFC (Swansea) | 3 | 1 | - | 2 | 5 | 11 | 2 |
| 20. | Fulham FC (London) | 3 | - | 1 | 2 | 3 | 6 | 1 |
| 21. | Burnley FC (Burnley) | 2 | - | 1 | 1 | 1 | 3 | 1 |
| 22. | Bradford Park Avenue FC (Bradford) | 3 | - | 1 | 2 | 2 | 7 | 1 |
| | | 64 | 25 | 14 | 25 | 110 | 110 | 64 |

| Football League Division 3 (N) 1939-1940 Season | Accrington Stanley | Barrow | Bradford City | Carlisle United | Chester | Crewe Alexandra | Darlington | Doncaster Rovers | Gateshead | Halifax Town | Hartlepools United | Hull City | Lincoln City | New Brighton | Oldham Athletic | Rochdale | Rotherham United | Southport | Stockport County | Tranmere Rovers | Wrexham | York City |
|---|---|---|---|---|---|---|---|---|---|---|---|---|---|---|---|---|---|---|---|---|---|---|
| Accrington Stanley FC | ■ | -- | -- | -- | -- | -- | -- | -- | -- | -- | -- | -- | -- | -- | 2-0 | -- | -- | -- | -- | -- | -- | -- |
| Barrow AFC | 1-2 | ■ | 2-2 | -- | -- | -- | -- | -- | -- | -- | -- | -- | -- | -- | -- | -- | -- | -- | -- | -- | -- | -- |
| Bradford City AFC | 0-2 | -- | ■ | -- | -- | -- | -- | -- | -- | -- | -- | -- | -- | -- | -- | -- | -- | -- | -- | -- | -- | -- |
| Carlisle United FC | -- | -- | -- | ■ | -- | -- | -- | -- | -- | -- | -- | -- | -- | -- | -- | -- | 2-0 | -- | -- | -- | -- | -- |
| Chester FC | -- | -- | -- | -- | ■ | -- | -- | 1-0 | -- | -- | -- | -- | -- | -- | -- | -- | -- | -- | -- | 2-0 | -- | -- |
| Crewe Alexandra FC | -- | -- | -- | -- | -- | ■ | -- | -- | -- | -- | 0-0 | -- | -- | -- | -- | -- | -- | -- | -- | -- | -- | -- |
| Darlington FC | -- | -- | -- | -- | -- | -- | ■ | -- | -- | -- | -- | -- | -- | -- | -- | -- | -- | -- | 1-0 | -- | -- | -- |
| Doncaster Rovers FC | -- | -- | -- | -- | -- | -- | -- | ■ | -- | -- | -- | -- | -- | -- | -- | 2-0 | -- | -- | -- | -- | -- | -- |
| Gateshead FC | -- | -- | -- | -- | -- | 0-3 | -- | -- | ■ | -- | 3-0 | -- | -- | -- | -- | -- | -- | -- | -- | -- | -- | -- |
| Halifax Town AFC | -- | -- | -- | -- | -- | -- | -- | -- | -- | ■ | -- | -- | -- | -- | 2-0 | -- | -- | -- | -- | -- | 1-1 | -- |
| Hartlepools United FC | -- | 1-1 | -- | -- | -- | -- | -- | -- | -- | -- | ■ | -- | -- | -- | -- | -- | -- | -- | -- | -- | -- | -- |
| Hull City AFC | -- | -- | -- | -- | -- | -- | -- | -- | -- | -- | -- | ■ | 2-2 | -- | -- | -- | -- | -- | -- | -- | -- | -- |
| Lincoln City FC | -- | -- | -- | -- | -- | -- | 0-2 | -- | 4-3 | -- | -- | -- | ■ | -- | -- | -- | -- | -- | -- | -- | -- | -- |
| New Brighton FC | -- | -- | 2-1 | -- | -- | -- | -- | 4-2 | -- | -- | -- | -- | -- | ■ | -- | -- | -- | -- | -- | -- | -- | -- |
| Oldham Athletic AFC | -- | -- | -- | 3-1 | -- | -- | -- | -- | -- | -- | -- | -- | -- | -- | ■ | -- | -- | -- | -- | -- | -- | -- |
| Rochdale AFC | -- | -- | -- | -- | -- | -- | -- | -- | -- | -- | -- | -- | -- | -- | -- | ■ | -- | -- | -- | -- | 1-0 | 1-0 |
| Rotherham United FC | -- | -- | -- | -- | -- | -- | 2-2 | -- | -- | -- | -- | -- | -- | -- | -- | -- | ■ | -- | -- | -- | -- | 2-1 |
| Southport FC | -- | -- | -- | -- | -- | -- | -- | -- | -- | -- | -- | 1-1 | -- | -- | -- | -- | -- | ■ | -- | 3-3 | -- | -- |
| Stockport County FC | -- | -- | -- | -- | -- | -- | -- | 0-3 | -- | -- | -- | -- | -- | -- | -- | -- | -- | -- | ■ | -- | -- | -- |
| Tranmere Rovers FC | -- | -- | -- | -- | -- | -- | -- | -- | -- | -- | -- | -- | -- | -- | -- | -- | -- | 3-1 | -- | ■ | -- | -- |
| Wrexham AFC | -- | -- | -- | -- | -- | -- | -- | -- | -- | -- | -- | -- | -- | -- | 2-0 | -- | -- | -- | -- | -- | ■ | -- |
| York City FC | -- | -- | -- | -- | 2-2 | -- | -- | -- | -- | -- | -- | -- | -- | -- | -- | -- | -- | -- | -- | -- | -- | ■ |

## Division 3 (North)

| | | Pd | Wn | Dw | Ls | GF | GA | Pts |
|---|---|---|---|---|---|---|---|---|
| 1. | Accrington Stanley FC (Accrington) | 3 | 3 | - | - | 6 | 1 | 6 |
| 2. | Halifax Town AFC (Halifax) | 3 | 2 | 1 | - | 6 | 1 | 5 |
| 3. | Darlington FC (Darlington) | 3 | 2 | 1 | - | 5 | 2 | 5 |
| 3. | Chester FC (Chester) | 3 | 2 | 1 | - | 5 | 2 | 5 |
| 5. | New Brighton FC (Wallasey) | 3 | 2 | - | 1 | 6 | 5 | 4 |
| 6. | Rochdale AFC (Rochdale) | 3 | 2 | - | 1 | 2 | 2 | 4 |
| 7. | Crewe Alexandra FC (Crewe) | 2 | 1 | 1 | - | 3 | - | 3 |
| 8. | Wrexham AFC (Wrexham) | 3 | 1 | 1 | 1 | 3 | 2 | 3 |
| 9. | Tranmere Rovers FC (Birkenhead) | 3 | 1 | 1 | 1 | 6 | 6 | 3 |
| 10. | Lincoln City FC (Lincoln) | 3 | 1 | 1 | 1 | 6 | 7 | 3 |
| 11. | Rotherham United FC (Rotherham) | 3 | 1 | 1 | 1 | 5 | 6 | 3 |
| 12. | Carlisle United FC (Carlisle) | 2 | 1 | - | 1 | 3 | 3 | 2 |
| 12. | Hull City AFC (Kingston-upon-Hull) | 2 | - | 2 | - | 3 | 3 | 2 |
| 14. | Gateshead FC (Gateshead) | 3 | 1 | - | 2 | 6 | 7 | 2 |
| 15. | Barrow AFC (Barrow-in-Furness) | 3 | - | 2 | 1 | 4 | 5 | 2 |
| 15. | Doncaster Rovers FC (Doncaster) | 3 | 1 | - | 2 | 4 | 5 | 2 |
| 15. | Southport FC (Southport) | 3 | - | 2 | 1 | 4 | 5 | 2 |
| 18. | Oldham Athletic AFC (Oldham) | 3 | 1 | - | 2 | 3 | 5 | 2 |
| 19. | Hartlepools United FC (Hartlepool) | 3 | - | 2 | 1 | 1 | 4 | 2 |
| 20. | York City FC (York) | 3 | - | 1 | 2 | 3 | 5 | 1 |
| 21. | Bradford City AFC (Bradford) | 3 | - | 1 | 2 | 3 | 6 | 1 |
| 22. | Stockport County FC (Stockport) | 2 | - | - | 2 | - | 5 | 1 |
| | | 62 | 22 | 18 | 22 | 87 | 87 | 62 |

**Football League Division 3 (S) — 1939-1940 Season**

| | Aldershot | Bournemouth | Brighton | Bristol City | Bristol Rovers | Cardiff City | Clapton Orient | Crystal Palace | Exeter City | Ipswich Town | Mansfield Town | Northampton | Norwich City | Notts County | Port Vale | Q.P.R. | Reading | Southend United | Swindon Town | Torquay United | Walsall | Watford |
|---|---|---|---|---|---|---|---|---|---|---|---|---|---|---|---|---|---|---|---|---|---|---|
| Aldershot FC | ███ | -- | -- | 0-1 | -- | -- | -- | -- | -- | -- | -- | -- | -- | -- | -- | -- | -- | -- | -- | -- | -- | -- |
| Bournemouth & B. Athletic | -- | ███ | -- | -- | -- | -- | -- | -- | -- | -- | -- | 10-0 | -- | -- | -- | 2-2 | -- | -- | -- | -- | -- | -- |
| Brighton & Hove Albion | 2-1 | -- | ███ | -- | -- | -- | -- | -- | -- | -- | -- | -- | -- | -- | 0-0 | -- | -- | -- | -- | -- | -- | -- |
| Bristol City FC | -- | -- | 3-3 | ███ | -- | -- | -- | -- | -- | -- | -- | -- | 1-2 | -- | -- | -- | -- | -- | -- | -- | -- | -- |
| Bristol Rovers FC | -- | -- | -- | -- | ███ | -- | -- | -- | -- | -- | -- | -- | -- | -- | -- | -- | -- | 2-2 | -- | -- | -- | -- |
| Cardiff City AFC | -- | -- | -- | -- | -- | ███ | -- | -- | -- | -- | -- | -- | -- | 2-4 | -- | -- | -- | -- | -- | -- | -- | -- |
| Clapton Orient FC | -- | -- | -- | -- | -- | -- | ███ | -- | -- | 2-2 | -- | -- | -- | -- | -- | -- | -- | 0-0 | -- | -- | -- | -- |
| Crystal Palace FC | -- | -- | -- | -- | 3-0 | -- | -- | ███ | -- | -- | -- | -- | -- | -- | -- | -- | -- | -- | -- | -- | -- | -- |
| Exeter City FC | -- | -- | -- | -- | -- | -- | -- | -- | ███ | -- | -- | -- | -- | -- | -- | -- | -- | -- | -- | 2-2 | -- | -- |
| Ipswich Town FC | -- | -- | -- | -- | 2-0 | -- | -- | -- | -- | ███ | -- | 1-1 | -- | -- | -- | -- | -- | -- | -- | -- | -- | -- |
| Mansfield Town FC | -- | -- | -- | -- | -- | -- | 4-5 | -- | -- | -- | ███ | -- | -- | -- | -- | -- | -- | -- | -- | -- | -- | -- |
| Northampton Town FC | -- | -- | -- | -- | -- | -- | -- | 1-2 | -- | -- | -- | ███ | -- | -- | -- | -- | -- | -- | 1-0 | -- | -- | -- |
| Norwich City FC | -- | -- | -- | -- | -- | 1-2 | -- | -- | -- | -- | -- | -- | ███ | -- | -- | -- | -- | -- | -- | -- | -- | -- |
| Notts County FC | -- | 2-1 | -- | -- | -- | -- | -- | -- | -- | -- | -- | -- | -- | ███ | -- | -- | -- | -- | -- | -- | -- | -- |
| Port Vale FC | -- | -- | -- | -- | -- | -- | -- | 0-1 | -- | -- | -- | -- | -- | -- | ███ | -- | -- | -- | -- | -- | -- | -- |
| Queen's Park Rangers FC | -- | -- | -- | -- | -- | -- | -- | -- | -- | -- | -- | -- | -- | -- | -- | ███ | -- | -- | -- | -- | -- | 2-2 |
| Reading FC | -- | -- | -- | -- | -- | -- | -- | 5-0 | -- | -- | -- | -- | -- | -- | -- | -- | ███ | 1-0 | -- | -- | -- | -- |
| Southend United FC | -- | -- | -- | -- | -- | -- | -- | -- | -- | -- | -- | -- | -- | -- | -- | -- | -- | ███ | -- | 3-2 | -- | -- |
| Swindon Town FC | 2-2 | -- | -- | -- | -- | 0-1 | -- | -- | -- | -- | -- | -- | -- | -- | -- | -- | -- | -- | ███ | -- | -- | -- |
| Torquay United FC | -- | -- | -- | -- | -- | -- | -- | -- | -- | 2-2 | -- | -- | -- | -- | -- | -- | -- | -- | -- | ███ | 0-0 | -- |
| Walsall FC | -- | -- | -- | -- | -- | -- | -- | -- | -- | -- | -- | -- | -- | -- | -- | 1-0 | -- | -- | -- | -- | ███ | -- |
| Watford FC | -- | -- | -- | -- | -- | -- | 1-1 | -- | -- | 1-2 | -- | -- | -- | -- | -- | -- | -- | -- | -- | -- | -- | ███ |

## Division 3 (South)

| | | Pd | Wn | Dw | Ls | GF | GA | Pts |
|---|---|---|---|---|---|---|---|---|
| 1. | Reading FC (Reading) | 3 | 2 | 1 | - | 8 | 2 | 5 |
| 2. | Exeter City FC (Exeter) | 3 | 2 | 1 | - | 5 | 3 | 5 |
| 3. | Notts County FC (Nottingham) | 2 | 2 | - | - | 6 | 3 | 4 |
| 4. | Ipswich Town FC (Ipswich) | 3 | 1 | 2 | - | 5 | 3 | 4 |
| 5. | Brighton & Hove Albion FC (Hove) | 3 | 1 | 2 | - | 5 | 4 | 4 |
| 6. | Cardiff City AFC (Cardiff) | 3 | 2 | - | 1 | 5 | 5 | 4 |
| 7. | Crystal Palace FC (London) | 3 | 2 | - | 1 | 8 | 9 | 4 |
| 8. | Bournemouth & Boscombe Athletic FC (Bournemouth) | 3 | 1 | 1 | 1 | 13 | 4 | 3 |
| 9. | Mansfield Town FC (Mansfield) | 3 | 1 | 1 | 1 | 8 | 8 | 3 |
| 9. | Bristol City FC (Bristol) | 3 | 1 | 1 | 1 | 5 | 5 | 3 |
| 9. | Norwich City FC (Norwich) | 3 | 1 | 1 | 1 | 4 | 4 | 3 |
| 9. | Torquay United FC (Torquay) | 3 | - | 3 | - | 4 | 4 | 3 |
| 9. | Clapton Orient FC (London) | 3 | - | 3 | - | 3 | 3 | 3 |
| 9. | Southend United FC (Southend-on-Sea) | 3 | 1 | 1 | 1 | 3 | 3 | 3 |
| 9. | Walsall FC (Walsall) | 3 | 1 | 1 | 1 | 3 | 3 | 3 |
| 16. | Queen's Park Rangers FC (London) | 3 | - | 2 | 1 | 4 | 5 | 2 |
| 16. | Watford FC (Watford) | 3 | - | 2 | 1 | 4 | 5 | 2 |
| 18. | Northampton Town FC (Northampton) | 3 | 1 | - | 2 | 2 | 12 | 2 |
| 19. | Aldershot FC (Aldershot) | 3 | - | 1 | 2 | 3 | 5 | 1 |
| 20. | Swindon Town FC (Swindon) | 3 | - | 1 | 2 | 2 | 4 | 1 |
| 21. | Bristol Rovers FC (Bristol) | 3 | - | 1 | 2 | 2 | 7 | 1 |
| 22. | Port Vale FC (Stoke-on-Trent) | 2 | - | 1 | 1 | - | 1 | 1 |
| | | 64 | 19 | 26 | 19 | 102 | 102 | 64 |

## South League (Group "A")

| | | Pd | Wn | Dw | Ls | GF | GA | Pts |
|---|---|---|---|---|---|---|---|---|
| 1. | Arsenal FC (London) | 18 | 13 | 4 | 1 | 62 | 22 | 30 |
| 2. | West Ham United FC (London) | 18 | 12 | 1 | 5 | 57 | 33 | 25 |
| 3. | Millwall FC (London) | 18 | 8 | 5 | 5 | 46 | 38 | 21 |
| 4. | Watford FC (Watford) | 18 | 9 | 3 | 6 | 44 | 38 | 21 |
| 5. | Norwich City FC (Norwich) | 18 | 7 | 6 | 5 | 41 | 36 | 20 |
| 6. | Charlton Athletic FC (London) | 18 | 8 | 1 | 9 | 61 | 58 | 17 |
| 7. | Crystal Palace FC (London) | 18 | 5 | 3 | 10 | 39 | 56 | 13 |
| 8. | Clapton Orient FC (London) | 18 | 5 | 3 | 10 | 28 | 60 | 13 |
| 9. | Tottenham Hotspur FC (London) | 18 | 5 | 2 | 11 | 37 | 43 | 12 |
| 10. | Southend United FC (Southend-on-Sea) | 18 | 4 | - | 14 | 30 | 61 | 8 |
| | | 180 | 76 | 28 | 76 | 445 | 445 | 180 |

## South League (Group "B")

| | | Pd | Wn | Dw | Ls | GF | GA | Pts |
|---|---|---|---|---|---|---|---|---|
| 1. | Queen's Park Rangers FC (London) | 18 | 12 | 2 | 4 | 49 | 26 | 26 |
| 2. | Bournemouth & Boscombe Athletic FC (Bournemouth) | 18 | 11 | 2 | 5 | 52 | 37 | 24 |
| 3. | Chelsea FC (London) | 18 | 9 | 5 | 4 | 43 | 37 | 23 |
| 4. | Reading FC (Reading) | 18 | 10 | 2 | 6 | 47 | 42 | 22 |
| 5. | Fulham FC (London) | 18 | 7 | 4 | 7 | 42 | 41 | 18 |
| 6. | Portsmouth FC (Portsmouth) | 18 | 7 | 2 | 9 | 37 | 42 | 16 |
| 7. | Aldershot FC (Aldershot) | 18 | 5 | 4 | 9 | 38 | 49 | 14 |
| 8. | Brighton & Hove Albion FC (Hove) | 18 | 5 | 1 | 12 | 42 | 53 | 11 |
| 9. | Southampton FC (Southampton) | 18 | 4 | - | 14 | 41 | 63 | 8 |
| | | 162 | 70 | 22 | 70 | 391 | 390 | 162 |

## South League (Group "C")

| | | Pd | Wn | Dw | Ls | GF | GA | Pts |
|---|---|---|---|---|---|---|---|---|
| 1. | Tottenham Hotspur FC (London) | 18 | 11 | 4 | 3 | 43 | 30 | 26 |
| 2. | West Ham United FC (London) | 18 | 10 | 4 | 4 | 53 | 28 | 24 |
| 3. | Arsenal FC (London) | 18 | 9 | 5 | 4 | 41 | 26 | 23 |
| 4. | Brentford FC (London) | 18 | 8 | 4 | 6 | 42 | 34 | 20 |
| 5. | Millwall FC (London) | 18 | 7 | 5 | 6 | 36 | 30 | 19 |
| 6. | Charlton Athletic FC (London) | 18 | 7 | 4 | 7 | 39 | 56 | 18 |
| 7. | Fulham FC (London) | 18 | 8 | 1 | 9 | 38 | 42 | 17 |
| 8. | Southampton FC (Southampton) | 18 | 5 | 3 | 10 | 28 | 55 | 13 |
| 9. | Chelsea FC (London) | 18 | 4 | 3 | 11 | 33 | 53 | 11 |
| 10. | Portsmouth FC (Portsmouth) | 18 | 3 | 3 | 12 | 26 | 45 | 9 |
| | | 180 | 72 | 36 | 72 | 379 | 399 | 180 |

## South League (Group "D")

| | | Pd | Wn | Dw | Ls | GF | GA | Pts |
|---|---|---|---|---|---|---|---|---|
| 1. | Crystal Palace FC (London) | 18 | 13 | 1 | 4 | 64 | 30 | 27 |
| 2. | Queen's park Rangers FC (London) | 18 | 10 | 3 | 5 | 38 | 28 | 23 |
| 3. | Watford FC (Watford) | 18 | 7 | 7 | 4 | 41 | 29 | 21 |
| 4. | Southend United FC (Southend-on-Sea) | 18 | 8 | 3 | 7 | 41 | 37 | 19 |
| 5. | Aldershot FC (Aldershot) | 18 | 7 | 3 | 8 | 38 | 36 | 17 |
| 6. | Clapton Orient FC (London) | 18 | 7 | 3 | 8 | 33 | 45 | 17 |
| 7. | Norwich City FC (Norwich) | 17 | 6 | 4 | 7 | 31 | 31 | 16 |
| 8. | Bournemouth & Boscombe Athletic FC (Bournemouth) | 17 | 7 | 2 | 8 | 38 | 40 | 16 |
| 9. | Reading FC (Reading) | 18 | 6 | 2 | 10 | 31 | 42 | 14 |
| 10. | Brighton & Hove Albion FC (Hove) | 18 | 2 | 4 | 12 | 30 | 65 | 8 |
| | | 178 | 73 | 32 | 73 | 385 | 383 | 178 |

## West League

| | | Pd | Wn | Dw | Ls | GF | GA | Pts |
|---|---|---|---|---|---|---|---|---|
| 1. | Stoke City FC (Stoke-on-Trent) | 22 | 13 | 5 | 4 | 57 | 41 | 31 |
| 2. | Liverpool FC (Liverpool) | 22 | 12 | 5 | 5 | 66 | 40 | 29 |
| 3. | Everton FC (Liverpool) | 22 | 12 | 4 | 6 | 64 | 33 | 28 |
| 4. | Manchester United FC (Manchester) | 22 | 14 | - | 8 | 74 | 41 | 28 |
| 5. | Manchester City FC (Manchester) | 22 | 12 | 4 | 6 | 73 | 41 | 28 |
| 6. | Wrexham AFC (Wrexham) | 22 | 10 | 5 | 7 | 45 | 50 | 25 |
| 7. | New Brighton FC (Wallasey) | 22 | 10 | 3 | 9 | 55 | 52 | 23 |
| 8. | Port Vale FC (Stoke-on-Trent) | 22 | 10 | 2 | 10 | 52 | 56 | 22 |
| 9. | Chester FC (Chester) | 22 | 7 | 5 | 10 | 40 | 51 | 19 |
| 10. | Crewe Alexandra FC (Crewe) | 22 | 6 | 1 | 15 | 44 | 79 | 13 |
| 11. | Stockport County FC (Stockport) | 22 | 4 | 3 | 15 | 45 | 79 | 11 |
| 12. | Tranmere Rovers FC (Birkenhead) | 22 | 2 | 3 | 17 | 41 | 93 | 7 |
| | | 264 | 112 | 40 | 112 | 656 | 656 | 264 |

## North-East League

| | | Pd | Wn | Dw | Ls | GF | GA | Pts |
|---|---|---|---|---|---|---|---|---|
| 1. | Huddersfield Town AFC (Huddersfield) | 20 | 15 | 4 | 1 | 54 | 22 | 34 |
| 2. | Newcastle United FC (Newcastle-upon-Tyne) | 20 | 12 | 1 | 7 | 59 | 42 | 25 |
| 3. | Bradford Park Avenue FC (Bradford) | 19 | 10 | 2 | 7 | 47 | 38 | 22 |
| 4. | Middlesbrough FC (Middlesbrough) | 20 | 9 | 4 | 7 | 49 | 42 | 22 |
| 5. | Leeds United AFC (Leeds) | 18 | 9 | 3 | 6 | 36 | 27 | 21 |
| 6. | Bradford City AFC (Bradford) | 19 | 8 | 4 | 7 | 41 | 37 | 20 |
| 7. | Hull City AFC (Kingston-upon-Hull) | 20 | 8 | 1 | 11 | 35 | 41 | 17 |
| 8. | York City FC (York) | 20 | 8 | 1 | 11 | 36 | 51 | 17 |
| 9. | Darlington FC (Darlington) | 19 | 6 | 3 | 10 | 44 | 56 | 15 |
| 10. | Hartlepools United FC (Hartlepool) | 20 | 6 | 1 | 13 | 27 | 47 | 13 |
| 11. | Halifax Town AFC (Halifax) | 19 | 3 | 2 | 14 | 28 | 53 | 8 |
| | | 214 | 94 | 26 | 94 | 456 | 456 | 214 |

## North-West League

| | | Pd | Wn | Dw | Ls | GF | GA | Pts |
|---|---|---|---|---|---|---|---|---|
| 1. | Bury FC (Bury) | 22 | 16 | 2 | 4 | 64 | 30 | 34 |
| 2. | Preston North End FC (Preston) | 22 | 15 | 2 | 5 | 63 | 27 | 32 |
| 3. | Blackpool FC (Blackpool) | 22 | 13 | 6 | 3 | 75 | 36 | 32 |
| 4. | Bolton Wanderers FC (Bolton) | 22 | 13 | 4 | 5 | 55 | 30 | 30 |
| 5. | Oldham Athletic AFC (Oldham) | 22 | 11 | 2 | 9 | 55 | 61 | 24 |
| 6. | Burnley FC (Burnley) | 22 | 9 | 5 | 8 | 48 | 43 | 23 |
| 7. | Barrow AFC (Barrow-in-Furness) | 22 | 8 | 4 | 10 | 54 | 57 | 20 |
| 8. | Blackburn Rovers FC (Blackburn) | 22 | 7 | 4 | 11 | 37 | 40 | 18 |
| 9. | Rochdale AFC (Rochdale) | 22 | 5 | 5 | 12 | 38 | 58 | 15 |
| 10. | Southport FC (Southport) | 22 | 5 | 4 | 13 | 34 | 62 | 14 |
| 11. | Carlisle United FC (Carlisle) | 22 | 4 | 4 | 14 | 38 | 68 | 12 |
| 12. | Accrington Stanley FC (Accrington) | 22 | 2 | 6 | 14 | 31 | 78 | 10 |
| | | 264 | 108 | 48 | 108 | 592 | 590 | 264 |

## South-West League

| | | Pd | Wn | Dw | Ls | GF | GA | Pts |
|---|---|---|---|---|---|---|---|---|
| 1. | Plymouth Argyle FC (Plymouth) | 28 | 16 | 4 | 8 | 72 | 41 | 36 |
| 2. | Torquay United FC (Torquay) | 28 | 14 | 6 | 8 | 73 | 62 | 34 |
| 3. | Bristol Rovers FC (Bristol) | 28 | 9 | 10 | 9 | 62 | 55 | 28 |
| 4. | Newport County AFC (Newport) | 28 | 12 | 4 | 12 | 70 | 63 | 28 |
| 5. | Swindon Town FC (Swindon) | 28 | 10 | 8 | 10 | 66 | 63 | 28 |
| 6. | Swansea Town AFC (Swansea) | 28 | 10 | 6 | 12 | 54 | 60 | 26 |
| 7. | Cardiff City AFC (Cardiff) | 28 | 6 | 13 | 9 | 45 | 63 | 25 |
| 8. | Bristol City FC (Bristol) | 28 | 7 | 5 | 16 | 57 | 92 | 19 |
| | | 224 | 84 | 56 | 84 | 499 | 499 | 224 |

| Midlands League | Pd | Wn | Dw | Ls | GF | GA | Pts |
|---|---|---|---|---|---|---|---|
| 1. Wolverhampton Wanderers FC (Wolverhampton) | 28 | 19 | 3 | 6 | 76 | 44 | 41 |
| 2. West Bromwich Albion FC (West Bromwich) | 28 | 18 | 4 | 6 | 87 | 51 | 40 |
| 3. Birmingham FC (Birmingham) | 28 | 12 | 5 | 11 | 56 | 60 | 29 |
| 4. Coventry City FC (Coventry) | 28 | 13 | 3 | 12 | 68 | 57 | 29 |
| 5. Luton Town FC (Luton) | 28 | 10 | 4 | 14 | 76 | 88 | 24 |
| 6. Northampton Town FC (Northampton) | 28 | 7 | 8 | 13 | 48 | 59 | 22 |
| 7. Leicester City FC (Leicester) | 28 | 7 | 6 | 15 | 51 | 71 | 20 |
| 8. Walsall FC (Walsall) | 28 | 7 | 5 | 16 | 51 | 83 | 19 |
| | 224 | 93 | 38 | 93 | 513 | 513 | 224 |

| East Midlands League | Pd | Wn | Dw | Ls | GF | GA | Pts |
|---|---|---|---|---|---|---|---|
| 1. Chesterfield FC (Chesterfield) | 20 | 14 | 2 | 4 | 69 | 23 | 30 |
| 2. Sheffield United FC (Sheffield) | 20 | 12 | 1 | 7 | 46 | 34 | 25 |
| 3. Barnsley FC (Barnsley) | 20 | 10 | 5 | 5 | 43 | 39 | 25 |
| 4. Grimsby Town FC (Cleethorpes) | 20 | 10 | 2 | 8 | 40 | 44 | 22 |
| 5. Mansfield Town FC (Mansfield) | 20 | 9 | 3 | 8 | 49 | 48 | 21 |
| 6. Doncaster Rovers FC (Doncaster) | 20 | 7 | 4 | 9 | 37 | 45 | 18 |
| 7. Lincoln City FC (Lincoln) | 20 | 9 | - | 11 | 42 | 53 | 18 |
| 8. Rotherham United FC (Rotherham) | 20 | 7 | 4 | 9 | 24 | 42 | 18 |
| 9. Sheffield Wednesday FC (Sheffield) | 20 | 5 | 5 | 10 | 33 | 42 | 15 |
| 10. Nottingham Forest FC (Nottingham) | 20 | 5 | 4 | 11 | 37 | 43 | 14 |
| 11. Notts County FC (Nottingham) | 20 | 6 | 2 | 12 | 40 | 57 | 14 |
| | 220 | 94 | 32 | 94 | 460 | 470 | 220 |

# 1940-41

| North | Pd | Wn | Dw | Ls | GF | GA | Pts | Gl. Av. |
|---|---|---|---|---|---|---|---|---|
| 1. Preston North End FC (Preston) | 29 | 18 | 7 | 4 | 81 | 37 | 43 | 2.189 |
| 2. Chesterfield FC (Chesterfield) | 35 | 20 | 6 | 9 | 76 | 40 | 46 | 1.900 |
| 3. Manchester City FC (Manchester) | 35 | 18 | 10 | 7 | 104 | 55 | 46 | 1.890 |
| 4. Barnsley FC (Barnsley) | 30 | 18 | 4 | 8 | 86 | 49 | 40 | 1.775 |
| 5. Everton FC (Liverpool) | 34 | 19 | 7 | 8 | 85 | 51 | 45 | 1.666 |
| 6. Blackpool FC (Blackpool) | 20 | 13 | 3 | 4 | 56 | 34 | 29 | 1.646 |
| 7. Halifax Town AFC (Halifax) | 30 | 10 | 13 | 7 | 64 | 51 | 33 | 1.254 |
| 8. Manchester United FC (Manchester) | 35 | 14 | 8 | 13 | 80 | 65 | 36 | 1.249 |
| 9. Lincoln City FC (Lincoln) | 27 | 13 | 7 | 7 | 65 | 53 | 33 | 1.226 |
| 10. Newcastle United FC (Newcastle-upon-Tyne) | 23 | 12 | - | 11 | 49 | 41 | 24 | 1.195 |
| 11. Huddersfield Town AFC (Huddersfield) | 33 | 11 | 6 | 16 | 69 | 58 | 28 | 1.189 |
| 12. Middlesbrough FC (Middlesbrough) | 27 | 16 | 1 | 10 | 84 | 71 | 33 | 1.183 |
| 13. New Brighton FC (Wallasey) | 26 | 15 | 1 | 10 | 97 | 82 | 31 | 1.182 |
| 14. Burnley FC (Burnley) | 35 | 17 | 7 | 11 | 62 | 53 | 41 | 1.169 |
| 15. Leeds United AFC (Leeds) | 30 | 13 | 8 | 9 | 62 | 54 | 34 | 1.148 |
| 16. Liverpool FC (Liverpool) | 37 | 15 | 6 | 16 | 91 | 82 | 36 | 1.102 |
| 17. Wrexham AFC (Wrexham) | 29 | 15 | 5 | 9 | 78 | 71 | 35 | 1.098 |
| 18. Chester FC (Chester) | 35 | 14 | 6 | 15 | 94 | 89 | 34 | 1.056 |
| 19. Doncaster Rovers FC (Doncaster) | 32 | 15 | 7 | 10 | 77 | 74 | 37 | 1.040 |
| 20. Oldham Athletic AFC (Oldham) | 37 | 17 | 4 | 16 | 78 | 77 | 38 | 1.012 |
| 21. Grimsby Town FC (Cleethorpes) | 27 | 12 | 2 | 13 | 60 | 63 | 26 | .952 |

## North (continued)

| | | Pd | Wn | Dw | Ls | GF | GA | Pts | Gl. Av. |
|---|---|---|---|---|---|---|---|---|---|
| 22. | Bradford Park Avenue FC (Bradford) | 31 | 9 | 7 | 15 | 64 | 74 | 25 | .864 |
| 23. | Rotherham United FC (Rotherham) | 29 | 12 | 5 | 12 | 48 | 57 | 29 | .842 |
| 24. | Blackburn Rovers FC (Blackburn) | 32 | 9 | 10 | 13 | 49 | 60 | 28 | .816 |
| 25. | Bury FC (Bury) | 38 | 10 | 9 | 19 | 80 | 100 | 29 | .800 |
| 26. | Bolton Wanderers FC (Bolton) | 16 | 6 | 2 | 8 | 31 | 40 | 14 | .775 |
| 27. | Tranmere Rovers FC (Birkenhead) | 25 | 9 | 5 | 11 | 67 | 90 | 23 | .744 |
| 28. | Sheffield United FC (Sheffield) | 25 | 6 | 6 | 13 | 44 | 60 | 18 | .733 |
| 29. | Bradford City AFC (Bradford) | 24 | 8 | 3 | 13 | 71 | 99 | 19 | .727 |
| 30. | Rochdale AFC (Rochdale) | 32 | 12 | 5 | 15 | 64 | 92 | 29 | .695 |
| 31. | Southport FC (Southport) | 28 | 7 | 2 | 19 | 61 | 88 | 16 | .693 |
| 32. | York City FC (York) | 25 | 7 | 4 | 14 | 49 | 71 | 18 | .690 |
| 33. | Hull City AFC (Kingston-upon-Hull) | 23 | 8 | 3 | 12 | 44 | 67 | 19 | .656 |
| 34. | Sheffield Wednesday FC (Sheffield) | 30 | 9 | 6 | 15 | 50 | 78 | 24 | .641 |
| 35. | Stockport County FC (Stockport) | 29 | 9 | 5 | 15 | 54 | 93 | 23 | .580 |
| 36. | Crewe Alexandra FC (Crewe) | 24 | 2 | 3 | 19 | 32 | 84 | 7 | .380 |

## South

| | | Pd | Wn | Dw | Ls | GF | GA | Pts | Gl. Av. |
|---|---|---|---|---|---|---|---|---|---|
| 1. | Crystal Palace FC (London) | 27 | 16 | 4 | 7 | 86 | 44 | 36 | 1.954 |
| 2. | West Ham United FC (London) | 25 | 14 | 6 | 5 | 70 | 39 | 34 | 1.794 |
| 3. | Coventry City FC (Coventry) | 10 | 5 | 3 | 2 | 28 | 16 | 13 | 1.750 |
| 4. | Arsenal FC (London) | 19 | 10 | 5 | 4 | 66 | 38 | 25 | 1.736 |
| 5. | Cardiff City AFC (Cardiff) | 24 | 12 | 5 | 7 | 75 | 50 | 29 | 1.500 |
| 6. | Reading FC (Reading) | 26 | 14 | 5 | 7 | 73 | 51 | 33 | 1.431 |
| 7. | Norwich City FC (Norwich) | 19 | 9 | 2 | 8 | 73 | 55 | 20 | 1.327 |
| 8. | Watford FC (Watford) | 35 | 15 | 6 | 14 | 96 | 73 | 36 | 1.315 |
| 9. | Portsmouth FC (Portsmouth) | 31 | 16 | 2 | 13 | 92 | 71 | 34 | 1.296 |
| 10. | Tottenham Hotspur FC (London) | 23 | 9 | 5 | 9 | 53 | 41 | 23 | 1.292 |
| 11. | Millwall FC (London) | 31 | 16 | 5 | 10 | 73 | 57 | 37 | 1.280 |
| 12. | Walsall FC (Walsall) | 32 | 14 | 7 | 11 | 100 | 80 | 35 | 1.250 |
| 13. | West Bromwich Albion FC (West Bromwich) | 28 | 13 | 5 | 10 | 83 | 69 | 31 | 1.202 |
| 14. | Leicester City FC (Leicester) | 33 | 17 | 5 | 11 | 87 | 73 | 39 | 1.191 |
| 15. | Northampton Town FC (Northampton) | 30 | 14 | 3 | 13 | 84 | 71 | 31 | 1.183 |
| 16. | Bristol City FC (Bristol) | 20 | 10 | 2 | 8 | 55 | 48 | 22 | 1.145 |
| 17. | Mansfield Town FC (Mansfield) | 29 | 12 | 6 | 11 | 77 | 68 | 30 | 1.132 |
| 18. | Charlton Athletic FC (London) | 19 | 7 | 4 | 8 | 37 | 34 | 18 | 1.088 |
| 19. | Aldershot FC (Aldershot) | 24 | 14 | 2 | 8 | 73 | 68 | 30 | 1.073 |
| 20. | Brentford FC (London) | 23 | 9 | 3 | 11 | 51 | 51 | 21 | 1.000 |
| 21. | Chelsea FC (London) | 23 | 10 | 4 | 9 | 57 | 58 | 24 | .981 |
| 22. | Birmingham FC (Birmingham) | 16 | 7 | 1 | 8 | 38 | 43 | 15 | .883 |
| 23. | Fulham FC (London) | 30 | 10 | 7 | 13 | 62 | 73 | 27 | .849 |
| 24. | Luton Town FC (Luton) | 35 | 11 | 7 | 17 | 82 | 100 | 29 | .820 |
| 25. | Stoke City FC (Stoke-on-Trent) | 36 | 9 | 9 | 18 | 76 | 96 | 27 | .791 |
| 26. | Queen's Park Rangers FC (London) | 23 | 8 | 3 | 12 | 47 | 60 | 19 | .783 |
| 27. | Brighton & Hove Albion FC (Hove) | 25 | 8 | 7 | 10 | 51 | 75 | 23 | .680 |
| 28. | Nottingham Forest FC (Nottingham) | 25 | 7 | 3 | 15 | 50 | 77 | 17 | .649 |
| 29. | Bournemouth & Boscombe Athletic FC | 27 | 9 | 3 | 15 | 59 | 92 | 21 | .641 |
| 30. | Notts County FC (Nottingham) | 21 | 8 | 3 | 10 | 42 | 66 | 19 | .636 |
| 31. | Southend United FC (Southend-on-Sea) | 29 | 12 | 4 | 13 | 64 | 101 | 28 | .633 |
| 32. | Southampton FC (Southampton) | 31 | 4 | 4 | 23 | 53 | 111 | 12 | .477 |
| 33. | Swansea Town AFC (Swansea) | 10 | 2 | 1 | 7 | 12 | 33 | 5 | .363 |
| 34. | Clapton Orient FC (London) | 15 | 1 | 3 | 11 | 19 | 66 | 5 | .287 |

# 1941-42

## London League

| | | Pd | Wn | Dw | Ls | GF | GA | Pts |
|---|---|---|---|---|---|---|---|---|
| 1. | Arsenal FC (London) | 30 | 23 | 2 | 5 | 108 | 43 | 48 |
| 2. | Portsmouth FC (Portsmouth) | 30 | 20 | 2 | 8 | 105 | 59 | 42 |
| 3. | West Ham United FC (London) | 30 | 17 | 5 | 8 | 81 | 44 | 39 |
| 4. | Aldershot FC (Aldershot) | 30 | 17 | 5 | 8 | 85 | 56 | 39 |
| 5. | Tottenham Hotspur FC (London) | 30 | 15 | 8 | 7 | 61 | 41 | 38 |
| 6. | Crystal Palace FC (London) | 30 | 14 | 6 | 10 | 70 | 53 | 34 |
| 7. | Reading FC (Reading) | 30 | 13 | 8 | 9 | 76 | 58 | 34 |
| 8. | Charlton Athletic FC (London) | 30 | 14 | 5 | 11 | 72 | 64 | 33 |
| 9. | Brentford FC (London) | 30 | 14 | 2 | 14 | 80 | 76 | 30 |
| 10. | Queen's Park Rangers FC (London) | 30 | 11 | 3 | 16 | 52 | 59 | 25 |
| 11. | Fulham FC (London) | 30 | 10 | 4 | 16 | 79 | 99 | 24 |
| 12. | Brighton & Hove Albion FC (Hove) | 30 | 9 | 4 | 17 | 71 | 108 | 22 |
| 13. | Chelsea FC (London) | 30 | 8 | 4 | 18 | 56 | 88 | 20 |
| 14. | Millwall FC (London) | 30 | 7 | 5 | 18 | 53 | 82 | 19 |
| 15. | Clapton Orient FC (London) | 30 | 5 | 7 | 18 | 42 | 94 | 17 |
| 16. | Watford FC (Watford) | 30 | 6 | 4 | 20 | 47 | 114 | 16 |
| | | 480 | 203 | 74 | 203 | 1138 | 1138 | 480 |

## North Regional Championship

| | | Pd | Wn | Dw | Ls | GF | GA | Pts |
|---|---|---|---|---|---|---|---|---|
| 1. | Blackpool FC (Blackpool) | 18 | 14 | 1 | 3 | 75 | 19 | 29 |
| 2. | Lincoln City FC (Lincoln) | 18 | 13 | 3 | 2 | 54 | 28 | 29 |
| 3. | Preston North End FC (Preston) | 18 | 13 | 1 | 4 | 58 | 18 | 27 |
| 4. | Manchester United FC (Manchester) | 18 | 10 | 6 | 2 | 79 | 27 | 26 |
| 5. | Stoke City FC (Stoke-on-Trent) | 18 | 12 | 2 | 4 | 75 | 36 | 26 |
| 6. | Everton FC (Liverpool) | 18 | 12 | 2 | 4 | 61 | 31 | 26 |
| 7. | Blackburn Rovers FC (Blackburn) | 18 | 10 | 6 | 2 | 40 | 24 | 26 |
| 8. | Liverpool FC (Liverpool) | 18 | 11 | 4 | 3 | 66 | 44 | 26 |
| 9. | Gateshead FC (Gateshead) | 18 | 9 | 5 | 4 | 39 | 35 | 23 |
| 10. | Sunderland AFC (Sunderland) | 18 | 9 | 4 | 5 | 50 | 30 | 22 |
| 11. | Huddersfield Town AFC (Huddersfield) | 18 | 10 | 1 | 7 | 48 | 33 | 21 |
| 12. | Bradford Park Avenue FC (Bradford) | 18 | 8 | 5 | 5 | 33 | 28 | 21 |
| 13. | Grimsby Town FC (Cleethorpes) | 18 | 7 | 6 | 5 | 41 | 31 | 20 |
| 14. | Barnsley FC (Barnsley) | 18 | 8 | 4 | 6 | 39 | 31 | 20 |
| 15. | Newcastle United FC (Newcastle-upon-Tyne) | 18 | 7 | 6 | 5 | 46 | 39 | 20 |
| 16. | Sheffield Wednesday FC (Sheffield) | 18 | 8 | 3 | 7 | 48 | 54 | 19 |
| 16. | Manchester City FC (Manchester) | 18 | 8 | 3 | 7 | 48 | 54 | 19 |
| 18. | Sheffield United FC (Sheffield) | 18 | 7 | 4 | 7 | 39 | 38 | 18 |
| 19. | Burnley FC (Burnley) | 18 | 6 | 6 | 6 | 36 | 40 | 18 |
| 20. | Halifax Town AFC (Halifax) | 18 | 7 | 3 | 8 | 29 | 41 | 17 |
| 21. | Oldham Athletic AFC (Oldham) | 18 | 6 | 4 | 8 | 40 | 49 | 16 |
| 22. | Rochdale AFC (Rochdale) | 18 | 6 | 4 | 8 | 28 | 52 | 16 |
| 23. | Chesterfield FC (Chesterfield) | 18 | 5 | 5 | 8 | 27 | 31 | 15 |
| 24. | Chester FC (Chester) | 18 | 6 | 3 | 9 | 45 | 53 | 15 |
| 25. | Middlesbrough FC (Middlesbrough) | 18 | 6 | 3 | 9 | 44 | 56 | 15 |
| 26. | Leeds United AFC (Leeds) | 18 | 7 | 1 | 10 | 36 | 46 | 15 |
| 27. | Doncaster Rovers FC (Doncaster) | 18 | 6 | 2 | 10 | 39 | 46 | 14 |
| 28. | Bradford City AFC (Bradford) | 18 | 5 | 4 | 9 | 32 | 42 | 14 |
| 29. | Rotherham United FC (Rotherham) | 18 | 6 | 2 | 10 | 33 | 47 | 14 |
| 30. | New Brighton FC (Wallasey) | 18 | 4 | 6 | 8 | 39 | 75 | 14 |
| 31. | Tranmere Rovers FC (Birkenhead) | 18 | 5 | 3 | 10 | 35 | 60 | 13 |

## North Regional Championship (continued)

| | | Pd | Wn | Dw | Ls | GF | GA | Pts |
|---|---|---|---|---|---|---|---|---|
| 32. | York City FC (York) | 18 | 4 | 4 | 10 | 41 | 55 | 12 |
| 33. | Mansfield Town FC (Mansfield) | 18 | 6 | - | 12 | 29 | 50 | 12 |
| 34. | Bolton Wanderers FC (Bolton) | 18 | 3 | 5 | 10 | 35 | 48 | 11 |
| 35. | Southport FC (Southport) | 18 | 5 | 1 | 12 | 33 | 61 | 11 |
| 36. | Bury FC (Bury) | 18 | 3 | 3 | 12 | 37 | 59 | 9 |
| 37. | Wrexham AFC (Wrexham) | 18 | 2 | 5 | 11 | 40 | 69 | 9 |
| 38. | Stockport County FC (Stockport) | 18 | 2 | 2 | 14 | 34 | 73 | 6 |

The North Regional Championship was played between August 1941 and 25th December 1941.

In the South Regional Championship, the "Average" was calculated over 18 matches.

The "League Championship" was played between 27/12/41 and 30/05/42. The "Average" was based on 23 matches but clubs which had not played a minimum of 18 matches were not included in the classification (i.e. clubs from positions 23 – 51).

## South Regional League

| | | Pd | Wn | Dw | Ls | GF | GA | Pts | Average |
|---|---|---|---|---|---|---|---|---|---|
| 1. | Leicester City FC (Leicester) | 17 | 11 | 3 | 3 | 40 | 17 | 25 | 26.471 |
| 2. | West Bromwich Albion FC (West Bromwich) | 13 | 9 | 1 | 3 | 62 | 26 | 19 | 26.308 |
| 3. | Cardiff City AFC (Cardiff) | 15 | 9 | 1 | 5 | 43 | 28 | 19 | 22.800 |
| 4. | Norwich City FC (Norwich) | 8 | 4 | 2 | 2 | 20 | 13 | 10 | 22.500 |
| 5. | Bournemouth & Boscombe Athletic FC (B'mouth) | 10 | 6 | - | 4 | 26 | 18 | 12 | 21.600 |
| 5. | Bristol City FC (Bristol) | 15 | 9 | - | 6 | 46 | 45 | 18 | 21.600 |
| 7. | Walsall FC (Walsall) | 18 | 9 | 1 | 8 | 49 | 45 | 19 | 19.000 |
| 8. | Northampton Town FC (Northampton) | 16 | 7 | 2 | 7 | 39 | 38 | 16 | 18.000 |
| 9. | Wolverhampton Wanderers FC (Wolverhampton) | 16 | 6 | 2 | 8 | 27 | 36 | 14 | 15.750 |
| 10. | Southampton FC (Southampton) | 10 | 4 | - | 6 | 27 | 32 | 8 | 14.400 |
| 11. | Luton Town FC (Luton) | 18 | 5 | 1 | 12 | 34 | 73 | 11 | 11.000 |
| 12. | Nottingham Forest FC (Nottingham) | 13 | 2 | 1 | 10 | 18 | 39 | 5 | 6.923 |
| 13. | Swansea Town AFC (Swansea) | 9 | 1 | - | 8 | 18 | 39 | 2 | 4.000 |
| | | 178 | 82 | 14 | 82 | 449 | 449 | 178 | |

## "League Championship"

| | | Pd | Wn | Dw | Ls | GF | GA | Pts | Average |
|---|---|---|---|---|---|---|---|---|---|
| 1. | Manchester United FC (Manchester) | 19 | 12 | 4 | 3 | 44 | 25 | 28 | 33.895 |
| 2. | Blackpool FC (Blackpool) | 22 | 14 | 4 | 4 | 108 | 34 | 32 | 33.455 |
| 3. | Northampton Town FC (Northampton) | 21 | 14 | 2 | 5 | 70 | 31 | 30 | 32.857 |
| 3. | Liverpool FC (Liverpool) | 21 | 14 | 2 | 5 | 57 | 39 | 30 | 32.857 |
| 5. | Wolverhampton Wanderers FC | 20 | 13 | 1 | 6 | 52 | 29 | 27 | 31.050 |
| 6. | Huddersfield Town AFC (Huddersfield) | 20 | 9 | 6 | 5 | 42 | 33 | 24 | 27.600 |
| 7. | Blackburn Rovers FC (Blackburn) | 22 | 10 | 6 | 6 | 40 | 31 | 26 | 27.182 |
| 8. | West Bromwich Albion FC (West Bromwich) | 18 | 9 | 3 | 6 | 53 | 43 | 21 | 26.833 |
| 8. | Grimsby Town FC (Cleethorpes) | 18 | 8 | 5 | 5 | 31 | 22 | 21 | 26.833 |
| 10. | Sunderland AFC (Sunderland) | 22 | 9 | 7 | 6 | 53 | 42 | 25 | 26.136 |
| 11. | Cardiff City AFC (Cardiff) | 20 | 9 | 4 | 7 | 59 | 38 | 22 | 25.300 |
| 12. | Preston North End FC (Preston) | 19 | 6 | 7 | 6 | 41 | 30 | 19 | 23.000 |
| 12. | Chesterfield FC (Chesterfield) | 18 | 8 | 2 | 8 | 32 | 31 | 18 | 23.000 |
| 12. | Middlesbrough FC (Middlesbrough) | 18 | 7 | 4 | 7 | 37 | 36 | 18 | 23.000 |
| 12. | Everton FC (Liverpool) | 23 | 9 | 5 | 9 | 37 | 41 | 23 | 23.000 |
| 12. | Stoke City FC (Stoke-on-Trent) | 20 | 9 | 2 | 9 | 41 | 49 | 20 | 23.000 |
| 17. | Leicester City FC (Leicester) | 18 | 6 | 4 | 8 | 39 | 38 | 16 | 20.444 |

| "League Championship" (continued) | Pd | Wn | Dw | Ls | GF | GA | Pts | Average |
|---|---|---|---|---|---|---|---|---|
| 18. Bradford Park Avenue FC (Bradford) | 19 | 5 | 6 | 8 | 35 | 40 | 16 | 19.368 |
| 19. Halifax Town AFC (Halifax) | 19 | 4 | 7 | 8 | 30 | 40 | 15 | 18.158 |
| 19. Burnley FC (Burnley) | 19 | 7 | 1 | 11 | 29 | 53 | 15 | 18.158 |
| 21. Chester FC (Chester) | 20 | 6 | 3 | 11 | 34 | 41 | 15 | 17.250 |
| 22. Oldham Athletic AFC (Oldham) | 18 | 4 | 3 | 11 | 30 | 43 | 11 | 14.056 |
| 23. Barnsley FC (Barnsley) | 15 | 9 | 3 | 3 | 48 | 23 | 21 | 32.200 |
| 24. Norwich City FC (Norwich) | 12 | 7 | 1 | 4 | 27 | 19 | 15 | 28.750 |
| 25. Bristol City FC (Bristol) | 17 | 9 | 3 | 5 | 55 | 29 | 21 | 28.412 |
| 26. Sheffield United FC (Sheffield) | 17 | 8 | 4 | 5 | 39 | 33 | 20 | 27.059 |
| 27. Lincoln City FC (Lincoln) | 13 | 7 | 1 | 5 | 45 | 33 | 15 | 26.538 |
| 28. Manchester City FC (Manchester) | 17 | 9 | 1 | 7 | 33 | 26 | 19 | 25.706 |
| 28. York City FC (York) | 17 | 6 | 7 | 4 | 39 | 37 | 19 | 25.706 |
| 30. Nottingham Forest FC (Nottingham) | 16 | 8 | 1 | 7 | 32 | 30 | 17 | 24.438 |
| 31. Southampton FC (Southampton) | 12 | 5 | 2 | 5 | 27 | 32 | 12 | 23.000 |
| 32. Newcastle United FC (Newcastle-upon-Tyne) | 17 | 5 | 6 | 6 | 33 | 40 | 16 | 21.647 |
| 33. Bury FC (Bury) | 15 | 6 | 2 | 7 | 46 | 39 | 14 | 21.467 |
| 33. Rotherham United FC (Rotherham) | 15 | 6 | 2 | 7 | 32 | 34 | 14 | 21.467 |
| 33. Bolton Wanderers FC (Bolton) | 15 | 5 | 4 | 6 | 26 | 33 | 14 | 21.467 |
| 36. Bradford City AFC (Bradford) | 14 | 6 | 1 | 7 | 28 | 25 | 13 | 21.357 |
| 37. New Brighton FC (Wallasey) | 11 | 5 | - | 6 | 23 | 38 | 10 | 20.909 |
| 38. Southport FC (Southport) | 16 | 6 | 2 | 8 | 30 | 38 | 14 | 20.125 |
| 39. Wrexham AFC (Wrexham) | 12 | 4 | 2 | 6 | 26 | 32 | 10 | 19.167 |
| 40. Leeds United AFC (Leeds) | 17 | 7 | - | 10 | 33 | 33 | 14 | 18.941 |
| 41. Sheffield Wednesday FC (Sheffield) | 15 | 5 | 2 | 8 | 22 | 36 | 12 | 18.400 |
| 42. Gateshead FC (Gateshead) | 13 | 4 | 2 | 7 | 23 | 36 | 10 | 17.692 |
| 43. Rochdale AFC (Rochdale) | 13 | 5 | - | 8 | 23 | 39 | 10 | 17.692 |
| 44. Bournemouth & Boscombe Athletic FC | 8 | 2 | 2 | 4 | 11 | 21 | 6 | 17.250 |
| 45. Tranmere Rovers FC (Birkenhead) | 15 | 4 | 3 | 8 | 24 | 55 | 11 | 16.867 |
| 46. Luton Town FC (Luton) | 16 | 4 | 2 | 10 | 20 | 54 | 10 | 14.375 |
| 47. Walsall FC (Walsall) | 13 | 4 | - | 9 | 14 | 34 | 8 | 14.154 |
| 48. Swansea Town AFC (Swansea) | 11 | 1 | 4 | 6 | 11 | 39 | 6 | 12.545 |
| 49. Stockport County FC (Stockport) | 10 | 1 | 3 | 6 | 12 | 38 | 5 | 11.500 |
| 50. Doncaster Rovers FC (Doncaster) | 9 | 2 | - | 7 | 10 | 30 | 4 | 10.222 |
| 51. Mansfield Town FC (Mansfield) | 11 | 1 | 2 | 8 | 15 | 36 | 4 | 8.364 |

# 1942-43

| North Regional (1st Championship) | Pd | Wn | Dw | Ls | GF | GA | Pts |
|---|---|---|---|---|---|---|---|
| 1. Blackpool FC (Blackpool) | 18 | 16 | 1 | 1 | 93 | 28 | 33 |
| 2. Liverpool FC (Liverpool) | 18 | 14 | 1 | 3 | 70 | 34 | 29 |
| 3. Sheffield Wednesday FC (Sheffield) | 18 | 12 | 3 | 3 | 61 | 26 | 27 |
| 4. Manchester United FC (Manchester) | 18 | 12 | 2 | 4 | 58 | 26 | 26 |
| 5. Huddersfield Town AFC (Huddersfield) | 18 | 10 | 6 | 2 | 52 | 32 | 26 |
| 6. Stoke City FC (Stoke-on-Trent) | 18 | 11 | 3 | 4 | 46 | 25 | 25 |
| 7. Coventry City FC (Coventry) | 18 | 10 | 5 | 3 | 28 | 16 | 25 |
| 8. Southport FC (Southport) | 18 | 11 | 3 | 4 | 64 | 42 | 25 |
| 9. Derby County FC (Derby) | 18 | 11 | 2 | 5 | 51 | 37 | 24 |
| 10. Bradford Park Avenue FC (Bradford) | 18 | 8 | 7 | 3 | 46 | 21 | 23 |
| 11. Lincoln City FC (Lincoln) | 18 | 9 | 5 | 4 | 58 | 36 | 23 |
| 12. Halifax Town AFC (Halifax) | 18 | 10 | 3 | 5 | 39 | 27 | 23 |
| 13. Gateshead FC (Gateshead) | 18 | 10 | 3 | 5 | 52 | 45 | 23 |
| 14. Aston Villa FC (Birmingham) | 18 | 10 | 2 | 6 | 47 | 33 | 23 |

## North Regional (1st Championship) (cont.)

| | | Pd | Wn | Dw | Ls | GF | GA | Pts |
|---|---|---|---|---|---|---|---|---|
| 15. | Everton FC (Liverpool) | 18 | 10 | 2 | 6 | 52 | 41 | 22 |
| 16. | Grimsby Town FC (Cleethorpes) | 17 | 8 | 5 | 4 | 42 | 31 | 21 |
| 17. | York City FC (York) | 18 | 9 | 3 | 6 | 47 | 36 | 21 |
| 18. | Blackburn Rovers FC (Blackburn) | 18 | 9 | 3 | 6 | 56 | 43 | 21 |
| 19. | Barnsley FC (Barnsley) | 18 | 8 | 5 | 5 | 39 | 30 | 21 |
| 20. | Sheffield United FC (Sheffield) | 18 | 7 | 6 | 5 | 45 | 35 | 20 |
| 21. | Birmingham FC (Birmingham) | 18 | 9 | 2 | 7 | 27 | 30 | 20 |
| 22. | Sunderland AFC (Sunderland) | 18 | 8 | 3 | 7 | 46 | 40 | 19 |
| 23. | Chester FC (Chester) | 18 | 7 | 4 | 7 | 43 | 40 | 18 |
| 24. | Walsall FC (Walsall) | 18 | 6 | 5 | 7 | 33 | 31 | 17 |
| 25. | Northampton Town FC (Northampton) | 18 | 8 | 1 | 9 | 38 | 44 | 17 |
| 26. | Newcastle United FC (Newcastle-upon-Tyne) | 18 | 6 | 4 | 8 | 51 | 52 | 16 |
| 27. | Chesterfield FC (Chesterfield) | 18 | 5 | 6 | 7 | 30 | 34 | 16 |
| 28. | West Bromwich Albion FC (West Bromwich) | 18 | 6 | 4 | 8 | 35 | 43 | 16 |
| 29. | Notts County FC (Nottingham) | 18 | 7 | 2 | 9 | 34 | 57 | 16 |
| 30. | Manchester City FC (Manchester) | 18 | 7 | 1 | 10 | 46 | 47 | 15 |
| 31. | Nottingham Forest FC (Nottingham) | 18 | 6 | 3 | 9 | 38 | 39 | 15 |
| 32. | Burnley FC (Burnley) | 18 | 5 | 5 | 8 | 35 | 45 | 15 |
| 33. | Leicester City FC (Leicester) | 18 | 5 | 4 | 9 | 32 | 37 | 14 |
| 34. | Bury FC (Bury) | 18 | 6 | 2 | 10 | 53 | 81 | 14 |
| 35. | Stockport County FC (Stockport) | 18 | 5 | 3 | 10 | 34 | 55 | 13 |
| 36. | Rotherham United FC (Rotherham) | 18 | 4 | 5 | 9 | 28 | 48 | 13 |
| 37. | Tranmere Rovers FC (Birkenhead) | 18 | 5 | 3 | 10 | 36 | 63 | 13 |
| 38. | Wolverhampton Wanderers FC (Wolverhampton) | 18 | 5 | 2 | 11 | 28 | 41 | 12 |
| 39. | Crewe Alexandra FC (Crewe) | 18 | 5 | 2 | 11 | 43 | 64 | 12 |
| 40. | Middlesbrough FC (Middlesbrough) | 18 | 4 | 4 | 10 | 30 | 50 | 12 |
| 41. | Rochdale AFC (Rochdale) | 18 | 5 | 2 | 11 | 34 | 57 | 12 |
| 42. | Wrexham AFC (Wrexham) | 18 | 5 | 1 | 12 | 43 | 67 | 11 |
| 43. | Leeds United AFC (Leeds) | 18 | 3 | 4 | 11 | 28 | 45 | 10 |
| 44. | Oldham Athletic AFC (Oldham) | 18 | 4 | 2 | 12 | 29 | 54 | 10 |
| 45. | Bradford City AFC (Bradford) | 18 | 4 | 2 | 12 | 30 | 63 | 10 |
| 46. | Bolton Wanderers FC (Bolton) | 18 | 3 | 3 | 12 | 31 | 52 | 9 |
| 47. | Doncaster Rovers FC (Doncaster) | 17 | 3 | 3 | 11 | 23 | 41 | 9 |
| 48. | Mansfield Town FC (Mansfield) | 18 | 2 | 4 | 12 | 25 | 65 | 8 |

## London & South League

| | | Pd | Wn | Dw | Ls | GF | GA | Pts |
|---|---|---|---|---|---|---|---|---|
| 1. | Arsenal FC (London) | 28 | 21 | 1 | 6 | 102 | 40 | 43 |
| 2. | Tottenham Hotspur FC (London) | 28 | 16 | 6 | 6 | 68 | 28 | 38 |
| 3. | Queen's Park Rangers FC (London) | 28 | 18 | 2 | 8 | 64 | 49 | 38 |
| 4. | Portsmouth FC (Portsmouth) | 28 | 16 | 3 | 9 | 66 | 52 | 35 |
| 5. | Southampton FC (Southampton) | 28 | 14 | 5 | 9 | 86 | 58 | 33 |
| 6. | West Ham United FC (London) | 28 | 14 | 5 | 9 | 80 | 66 | 33 |
| 7. | Chelsea FC (London) | 28 | 14 | 4 | 10 | 52 | 45 | 32 |
| 8. | Aldershot FC (Aldershot) | 28 | 14 | 2 | 12 | 87 | 77 | 30 |
| 9. | Brentford FC (London) | 28 | 12 | 5 | 11 | 64 | 63 | 29 |
| 10. | Charlton Athletic FC (London) | 28 | 13 | 3 | 12 | 68 | 75 | 29 |
| 11. | Clapton Orient FC (London) | 28 | 11 | 5 | 12 | 54 | 72 | 27 |
| 12. | Brighton & Hove Albion FC (Hove) | 28 | 10 | 5 | 13 | 65 | 73 | 25 |
| 13. | Reading FC (Reading) | 28 | 9 | 6 | 13 | 67 | 74 | 24 |
| 14. | Fulham FC (London) | 28 | 10 | 2 | 16 | 69 | 78 | 22 |
| 15. | Crystal Palace FC (London) | 28 | 7 | 5 | 16 | 49 | 75 | 19 |
| 16. | Millwall FC (London) | 28 | 6 | 5 | 17 | 66 | 88 | 17 |
| 17. | Watford FC (Watford) | 28 | 7 | 2 | 19 | 51 | 88 | 16 |
| 18. | Luton Town FC (Luton) | 28 | 4 | 6 | 18 | 43 | 100 | 14 |

| North Regional (2nd Championship) | Pd | Wn | Dw | Ls | GF | GA | Pts |
|---|---|---|---|---|---|---|---|
| 1. Liverpool FC (Liverpool) | 20 | 15 | 2 | 3 | 64 | 32 | 32 |
| 2. Lovell's Athletic FC (Newport) | 20 | 11 | 5 | 4 | 63 | 32 | 27 |
| 3. Manchester City FC (Manchester) | 19 | 11 | 5 | 4 | 43 | 24 | 27 |
| 4. Aston Villa FC (Birmingham) | 20 | 13 | 1 | 6 | 44 | 30 | 27 |
| 5. Sheffield Wednesday FC (Sheffield) | 20 | 9 | 8 | 3 | 43 | 26 | 26 |
| 6. Manchester United FC (Manchester) | 19 | 11 | 3 | 5 | 52 | 26 | 25 |
| 7. York City FC (York) | 18 | 11 | 3 | 4 | 52 | 30 | 25 |
| 8. Huddersfield Town AFC (Huddersfield) | 19 | 11 | 3 | 5 | 48 | 28 | 25 |
| 9. Coventry City FC (Coventry) | 20 | 11 | 3 | 6 | 33 | 21 | 25 |
| 10. Stoke City FC (Stoke-on-Trent) | 20 | 10 | 4 | 6 | 42 | 34 | 24 |
| 11. West Bromwich Albion FC (West Bromwich) | 20 | 11 | 7 | 2 | 49 | 40 | 24 |
| 12. Notts County FC (Nottingham) | 20 | 9 | 6 | 5 | 37 | 34 | 24 |
| 13. Blackpool FC (Blackpool) | 19 | 8 | 7 | 4 | 49 | 31 | 23 |
| 14. Newcastle United FC (Newcastle-upon-Tyne) | 19 | 10 | 3 | 6 | 62 | 42 | 23 |
| 15. Blackburn Rovers FC (Blackburn) | 18 | 9 | 4 | 5 | 45 | 35 | 22 |
| 16. Bristol City FC (Bristol) | 19 | 8 | 6 | 5 | 41 | 33 | 22 |
| 17. Chesterfield FC (Chesterfield) | 20 | 9 | 4 | 7 | 35 | 30 | 22 |
| 18. Derby County FC (Derby) | 20 | 8 | 5 | 7 | 41 | 34 | 21 |
| 19. Aberaman AFC (Aberaman) | 18 | 10 | 1 | 7 | 39 | 41 | 21 |
| 20. Sunderland AFC (Sunderland) | 19 | 8 | 4 | 7 | 58 | 40 | 20 |
| 21. Rochdale AFC (Rochdale) | 16 | 9 | 2 | 5 | 39 | 26 | 20 |
| 22. Leicester City FC (Leicester) | 20 | 9 | 2 | 9 | 40 | 37 | 20 |
| 23. Sheffield United FC (Sheffield) | 19 | 8 | 4 | 7 | 43 | 42 | 20 |
| 24. Bradford Park Avenue FC (Bradford) | 19 | 7 | 5 | 7 | 35 | 31 | 19 |
| 25. Everton FC (Liverpool) | 19 | 9 | 1 | 9 | 51 | 46 | 19 |
| 26. Bath City FC (Bath) | 18 | 7 | 4 | 7 | 49 | 46 | 18 |
| 27. Birmingham FC (Birmingham) | 20 | 8 | 2 | 10 | 32 | 29 | 18 |
| 28. Barnsley FC (Barnsley) | 17 | 8 | 2 | 7 | 34 | 37 | 18 |
| 29. Nottingham Forest FC (Nottingham) | 18 | 7 | 4 | 7 | 30 | 34 | 18 |
| 30. Crewe Alexandra FC (Crewe) | 20 | 7 | 4 | 9 | 44 | 57 | 18 |
| 31. Bradford City AFC (Bradford) | 16 | 7 | 2 | 7 | 29 | 29 | 16 |
| 32. Wrexham AFC (Wrexham) | 17 | 7 | 3 | 7 | 36 | 37 | 17 |
| 33. Bolton Wanderers FC (Bolton) | 17 | 7 | 2 | 8 | 34 | 42 | 16 |
| 34. Tranmere Rovers FC (Birkenhead) | 20 | 6 | 4 | 10 | 37 | 48 | 16 |
| 35. Halifax Town AFC (Halifax) | 18 | 7 | 2 | 9 | 30 | 39 | 16 |
| 36. Chester FC (Chester) | 20 | 6 | 3 | 11 | 40 | 49 | 15 |
| 37. Northampton Town FC (Northampton) | 17 | 6 | 2 | 9 | 30 | 37 | 14 |
| 38. Wolverhampton Wanderers FC (Wolverhampton) | 17 | 5 | 4 | 8 | 38 | 45 | 14 |
| 39. Swansea Town AFC (Swansea) | 18 | 4 | 6 | 8 | 36 | 52 | 14 |
| 40. Grimsby Town FC (Cleethorpes) | 13 | 4 | 4 | 5 | 30 | 27 | 13 |
| 41. Bury FC (Bury) | 16 | 5 | 3 | 8 | 44 | 42 | 13 |
| 42. Doncaster Rovers FC (Doncaster) | 17 | 5 | 3 | 9 | 27 | 41 | 13 |
| 43. Rotherham United FC (Rotherham) | 18 | 4 | 5 | 9 | 28 | 43 | 13 |
| 44. Gateshead FC (Gateshead) | 13 | 6 | - | 7 | 29 | 36 | 12 |
| 45. Stockport County FC (Stockport) | 19 | 4 | 4 | 11 | 37 | 76 | 12 |
| 46. Southport FC (Southport) | 18 | 4 | 3 | 11 | 38 | 58 | 11 |
| 47. Leeds United AFC (Leeds) | 16 | 5 | 1 | 10 | 32 | 50 | 11 |
| 48. Oldham Athletic AFC (Oldham) | 18 | 4 | 3 | 11 | 28 | 47 | 11 |
| 49. Middlesbrough FC (Middlesbrough) | 18 | 5 | - | 13 | 31 | 69 | 10 |
| 50. Lincoln City FC (Lincoln) | 10 | 4 | 1 | 5 | 23 | 18 | 9 |
| 51. Burnley FC (Burnley) | 14 | 3 | 3 | 8 | 17 | 31 | 9 |
| 52. Walsall FC (Walsall) | 16 | 3 | 2 | 11 | 22 | 35 | 8 |
| 53. Cardiff City AFC (Cardiff) | 17 | 2 | 3 | 12 | 22 | 47 | 7 |
| 54. Mansfield Town FC (Mansfield) | 10 | 1 | 1 | 8 | 12 | 41 | 3 |

| West Regional League | | Pd | Wn | Dw | Ls | GF | GA | Pts |
|---|---|---|---|---|---|---|---|---|
| 1. | Lovell's Athletic FC (Newport) | 18 | 14 | 2 | 2 | 59 | 21 | 30 |
| 2. | Bath City FC (Bath) | 18 | 14 | - | 4 | 66 | 26 | 28 |
| 3. | Cardiff City AFC (Cardiff) | 18 | 8 | 3 | 7 | 41 | 45 | 19 |
| 4. | Bristol City FC (Bristol) | 17 | 7 | 3 | 7 | 59 | 37 | 17 |
| 5. | Swansea Town AFC (Swansea) | 18 | 3 | 1 | 14 | 27 | 77 | 7 |
| 6. | Aberaman AFC (Aberaman) | 17 | 2 | 1 | 14 | 29 | 75 | 5 |

# 1943-44

| North Regional (1st Championship) | | Pd | Wn | Dw | Ls | GF | GA | Pts |
|---|---|---|---|---|---|---|---|---|
| 1. | Blackpool FC (Blackpool) | 18 | 12 | 4 | 2 | 56 | 20 | 28 |
| 2. | Manchester United FC (Manchester) | 18 | 13 | 2 | 3 | 56 | 30 | 28 |
| 3. | Liverpool FC (Liverpool) | 18 | 13 | 1 | 4 | 72 | 26 | 27 |
| 4. | Doncaster Rovers FC (Doncaster) | 18 | 11 | 5 | 2 | 45 | 25 | 27 |
| 5. | Bradford Park Avenue FC (Bradford) | 18 | 11 | 4 | 3 | 65 | 28 | 26 |
| 6. | Huddersfield Town AFC (Huddersfield) | 18 | 12 | 2 | 4 | 48 | 25 | 26 |
| 7. | Northampton Town FC (Northampton) | 18 | 10 | 5 | 3 | 43 | 25 | 25 |
| 8. | Aston Villa FC (Birmingham) | 18 | 11 | 3 | 4 | 43 | 27 | 25 |
| 9. | Sunderland AFC (Sunderland) | 18 | 10 | 3 | 5 | 46 | 30 | 23 |
| 10. | Hartlepools United FC (Hartlepool) | 18 | 10 | 3 | 5 | 44 | 31 | 23 |
| 11. | Everton FC (Liverpool) | 18 | 9 | 4 | 5 | 60 | 34 | 22 |
| 12. | Blackburn Rovers FC (Blackburn) | 18 | 10 | 2 | 6 | 47 | 32 | 22 |
| 13. | Rochdale AFC (Rochdale) | 18 | 10 | 2 | 6 | 43 | 41 | 22 |
| 14. | Sheffield United FC (Sheffield) | 18 | 8 | 5 | 5 | 30 | 26 | 21 |
| 15. | Lincoln City FC (Lincoln) | 18 | 8 | 4 | 6 | 51 | 40 | 20 |
| 16. | Birmingham FC (Birmingham) | 18 | 8 | 4 | 6 | 38 | 31 | 20 |
| 17. | Manchester City FC (Manchester) | 18 | 9 | 2 | 7 | 38 | 35 | 20 |
| 18. | Mansfield Town FC (Mansfield) | 18 | 9 | 2 | 7 | 32 | 33 | 20 |
| 19. | Derby County FC (Derby) | 18 | 8 | 4 | 6 | 43 | 45 | 20 |
| 20. | Chester FC (Chester) | 18 | 9 | 2 | 7 | 40 | 43 | 20 |
| 21. | Grimsby Town FC (Cleethorpes) | 18 | 8 | 3 | 7 | 32 | 36 | 19 |
| 22. | West Bromwich Albion FC (West Bromwich) | 18 | 8 | 3 | 7 | 42 | 44 | 19 |
| 23. | Gateshead FC (Gateshead) | 18 | 8 | 2 | 8 | 40 | 51 | 18 |
| 24. | Burnley FC (Burnley) | 18 | 5 | 7 | 6 | 24 | 22 | 17 |
| 25. | Walsall FC (Walsall) | 18 | 5 | 7 | 6 | 27 | 31 | 17 |
| 26. | Nottingham Forest FC (Nottingham) | 18 | 6 | 5 | 7 | 33 | 39 | 17 |
| 27. | Leeds United AFC (Leeds) | 18 | 6 | 5 | 7 | 38 | 50 | 17 |
| 28. | Leicester City FC (Leicester) | 18 | 6 | 4 | 8 | 33 | 30 | 16 |
| 29. | Darlington FC (Darlington) | 18 | 6 | 4 | 8 | 49 | 48 | 16 |
| 30. | Rotherham United FC (Rotherham) | 18 | 7 | 2 | 9 | 38 | 42 | 16 |
| 31. | York City FC (York) | 18 | 7 | 2 | 9 | 35 | 40 | 16 |
| 32. | Halifax Town AFC (Halifax) | 18 | 6 | 4 | 8 | 27 | 36 | 16 |
| 33. | Southport FC (Southport) | 18 | 7 | 2 | 9 | 33 | 51 | 16 |
| 34. | Stoke City FC (Stoke-on-Trent) | 18 | 6 | 3 | 9 | 40 | 35 | 15 |
| 35. | Chesterfield FC (Chesterfield) | 18 | 7 | 1 | 10 | 29 | 31 | 15 |
| 36. | Oldham Athletic AFC (Oldham) | 18 | 7 | 1 | 10 | 30 | 44 | 15 |
| 37. | Stockport County FC (Stockport) | 18 | 5 | 5 | 8 | 24 | 43 | 15 |
| 38. | Coventry City FC (Coventry) | 18 | 4 | 6 | 8 | 25 | 23 | 14 |
| 39. | Newcastle United FC (Newcastle-upon-Tyne) | 18 | 5 | 4 | 9 | 32 | 37 | 14 |
| 40. | Sheffield Wednesday FC (Sheffield) | 18 | 5 | 4 | 9 | 29 | 34 | 14 |
| 41. | Middlesbrough FC (Middlesbrough) | 18 | 4 | 6 | 8 | 35 | 52 | 14 |

| North Regional (1st Championship) (cont.) | Pd | Wn | Dw | Ls | GF | GA | Pts |
|---|---|---|---|---|---|---|---|
| 42. Wolverhampton Wanderers FC (Wolverhampton) | 18 | 5 | 3 | 10 | 30 | 42 | 13 |
| 43. Bury FC (Bury) | 18 | 6 | 1 | 11 | 31 | 44 | 13 |
| 44. Barnsley FC (Barnsley) | 18 | 5 | 2 | 11 | 32 | 42 | 12 |
| 45. Bradford City AFC (Bradford) | 18 | 4 | 3 | 11 | 27 | 47 | 11 |
| 46. Wrexham AFC (Wrexham) | 18 | 5 | 1 | 12 | 43 | 63 | 11 |
| 47. Notts County FC (Nottingham) | 18 | 4 | 3 | 11 | 26 | 53 | 11 |
| 48. Bolton Wanderers FC (Bolton) | 18 | 5 | - | 13 | 24 | 46 | 10 |
| 49. Tranmere Rovers FC (Birkenhead) | 18 | 4 | 1 | 13 | 39 | 71 | 9 |
| 50. Crewe Alexandra FC (Crewe) | 18 | 4 | 1 | 13 | 29 | 62 | 9 |

| London & South League | Pd | Wn | Dw | Ls | GF | GA | Pts |
|---|---|---|---|---|---|---|---|
| 1. Tottenham Hotspur FC (London) | 30 | 19 | 8 | 3 | 71 | 36 | 46 |
| 2. West Ham United FC (London) | 30 | 17 | 7 | 6 | 74 | 39 | 41 |
| 3. Queen's Park Rangers FC (London) | 30 | 14 | 12 | 4 | 69 | 54 | 40 |
| 4. Arsenal FC (London) | 30 | 14 | 10 | 6 | 72 | 42 | 38 |
| 5. Crystal Palace FC (London) | 30 | 16 | 5 | 9 | 75 | 53 | 37 |
| 6. Portsmouth FC (Portsmouth) | 30 | 16 | 5 | 9 | 68 | 59 | 37 |
| 7. Brentford FC (London) | 30 | 14 | 7 | 9 | 71 | 51 | 35 |
| 8. Chelsea FC (London) | 30 | 16 | 2 | 12 | 79 | 55 | 34 |
| 9. Fulham FC (London) | 30 | 11 | 9 | 10 | 80 | 73 | 31 |
| 10. Millwall FC (London) | 30 | 13 | 4 | 13 | 70 | 66 | 30 |
| 11. Aldershot FC (Aldershot) | 30 | 12 | 6 | 12 | 64 | 73 | 30 |
| 12. Reading FC (Reading) | 30 | 12 | 3 | 15 | 73 | 62 | 27 |
| 13. Southampton FC (Southampton) | 30 | 10 | 7 | 13 | 67 | 88 | 27 |
| 14. Charlton Athletic FC (London) | 30 | 9 | 7 | 14 | 57 | 73 | 25 |
| 15. Watford FC (Watford) | 30 | 6 | 8 | 16 | 58 | 80 | 20 |
| 16. Brighton & Hove Albion FC (Hove) | 30 | 9 | 2 | 19 | 55 | 82 | 20 |
| 17. Luton Town FC (Luton) | 30 | 3 | 5 | 22 | 41 | 104 | 11 |
| 18. Clapton Orient FC (London) | 30 | 4 | 3 | 23 | 32 | 87 | 11 |

| North Regional (2nd Championship) | Pd | Wn | Dw | Ls | GF | GA | Pts |
|---|---|---|---|---|---|---|---|
| 1. Bath City FC (Bath) | 21 | 16 | 2 | 3 | 78 | 26 | 34 |
| 2. Wrexham AFC (Wrexham) | 21 | 15 | 4 | 2 | 62 | 29 | 34 |
| 3. Liverpool FC (Liverpool) | 21 | 14 | 2 | 5 | 71 | 38 | 30 |
| 4. Birmingham FC (Birmingham) | 20 | 12 | 5 | 3 | 47 | 19 | 29 |
| 5. Rotherham United FC (Rotherham) | 21 | 12 | 5 | 4 | 54 | 30 | 29 |
| 6. Aston Villa FC (Birmingham) | 21 | 13 | 3 | 5 | 50 | 34 | 29 |
| 7. Blackpool FC (Blackpool) | 20 | 12 | 3 | 5 | 53 | 27 | 27 |
| 8. Cardiff City AFC (Cardiff) | 21 | 13 | 1 | 7 | 53 | 28 | 27 |
| 9. Manchester United FC (Manchester) | 21 | 10 | 7 | 4 | 55 | 38 | 27 |
| 10. Bradford Park Avenue FC (Bradford) | 20 | 11 | 4 | 5 | 50 | 30 | 26 |
| 11. Newcastle United FC (Newcastle-upon-Tyne) | 20 | 13 | - | 7 | 47 | 36 | 26 |
| 12. Everton FC (Liverpool) | 21 | 12 | 1 | 8 | 73 | 39 | 25 |
| 13. Stoke City FC (Stoke-on-Trent) | 21 | 10 | 5 | 6 | 66 | 45 | 25 |
| 14. Leicester City FC (Leicester) | 21 | 10 | 5 | 6 | 40 | 32 | 25 |
| 15. Darlington FC (Darlington) | 21 | 11 | 2 | 8 | 50 | 30 | 24 |
| 16. Nottingham Forest FC (Nottingham) | 20 | 9 | 6 | 5 | 32 | 20 | 24 |
| 17. Sheffield United FC (Sheffield) | 21 | 11 | 2 | 8 | 53 | 35 | 24 |
| 18. Coventry City FC (Coventry) | 21 | 10 | 4 | 7 | 48 | 37 | 24 |
| 19. Manchester City FC (Manchester) | 21 | 9 | 6 | 6 | 42 | 35 | 24 |
| 20. Lovell's Athletic FC (Newport) | 20 | 10 | 2 | 8 | 48 | 30 | 22 |
| 21. Gateshead FC (Gateshead) | 21 | 9 | 4 | 8 | 45 | 53 | 22 |
| 22. Doncaster Rovers FC (Doncaster) | 17 | 9 | 3 | 5 | 42 | 33 | 21 |
| 23. Derby County FC (Derby) | 21 | 8 | 5 | 8 | 33 | 28 | 21 |

| North Regional (2nd Championship) (cont.) | Pd | Wn | Dw | Ls | GF | GA | Pts |
|---|---|---|---|---|---|---|---|
| 24. Rochdale AFC (Rochdale) | 20 | 8 | 5 | 7 | 40 | 36 | 21 |
| 25. Barnsley FC (Barnsley) | 17 | 8 | 4 | 5 | 34 | 30 | 20 |
| 26. Halifax Town AFC (Halifax) | 20 | 8 | 4 | 8 | 44 | 42 | 20 |
| 27. Chester FC (Chester) | 20 | 9 | 2 | 9 | 65 | 65 | 20 |
| 28. Hartlepools United FC (Hartlepool) | 20 | 8 | 4 | 8 | 49 | 50 | 20 |
| 29. Stockport County FC (Stockport) | 19 | 10 | - | 9 | 44 | 49 | 20 |
| 30. Sheffield Wednesday FC (Sheffield) | 20 | 8 | 4 | 8 | 32 | 36 | 20 |
| 31. Blackburn Rovers FC (Blackburn) | 16 | 8 | 3 | 5 | 30 | 27 | 19 |
| 32. Huddersfield Town AFC (Huddersfield) | 21 | 8 | 3 | 10 | 41 | 40 | 19 |
| 33. West Bromwich Albion FC (West Bromwich) | 21 | 5 | 9 | 7 | 46 | 48 | 19 |
| 34. Bolton Wanderers FC (Bolton) | 21 | 8 | 3 | 10 | 42 | 49 | 19 |
| 35. Leeds United AFC (Leeds) | 18 | 8 | 3 | 7 | 34 | 40 | 19 |
| 36. Northampton Town FC (Northampton) | 19 | 9 | - | 10 | 37 | 39 | 18 |
| 37. Burnley FC (Burnley) | 18 | 6 | 6 | 6 | 39 | 42 | 18 |
| 38. Bristol City FC (Bristol) | 20 | 6 | 5 | 9 | 38 | 42 | 17 |
| 39. York City FC (York) | 20 | 7 | 11 | 2 | 37 | 40 | 16 |
| 40. Middlesbrough FC (Middlesbrough) | 21 | 6 | 4 | 11 | 41 | 51 | 16 |
| 41. Swansea Town AFC (Swansea) | 20 | 7 | 2 | 11 | 42 | 67 | 16 |
| 42. Grimsby Town FC (Cleethorpes) | 15 | 6 | 3 | 6 | 23 | 28 | 15 |
| 43. Bury FC (Bury) | 20 | 6 | 3 | 11 | 38 | 55 | 15 |
| 44. Oldham Athletic AFC (Oldham) | 18 | 5 | 4 | 9 | 28 | 36 | 14 |
| 45. Sunderland AFC (Sunderland) | 19 | 6 | 2 | 11 | 44 | 58 | 14 |
| 46. Chesterfield FC (Chesterfield) | 19 | 5 | 4 | 10 | 31 | 41 | 14 |
| 47. Mansfield Town FC (Mansfield) | 14 | 6 | 1 | 7 | 23 | 25 | 13 |
| 48. Wolverhampton Wanderers FC (Wolverhampton) | 20 | 3 | 6 | 11 | 28 | 56 | 12 |
| 49. Walsall FC (Walsall) | 17 | 3 | 6 | 8 | 17 | 35 | 12 |
| 50. Tranmere Rovers FC (Birkenhead) | 20 | 6 | - | 14 | 29 | 62 | 12 |
| 51. Bradford City AFC (Bradford) | 18 | 4 | 2 | 12 | 27 | 47 | 10 |
| 52. Southport FC (Southport) | 20 | 3 | 3 | 14 | 35 | 67 | 9 |
| 53. Lincoln City FC (Lincoln) | 18 | 3 | 2 | 13 | 25 | 56 | 8 |
| 54. Notts County FC (Nottingham) | 20 | 3 | - | 17 | 23 | 68 | 6 |
| 55. Crewe Alexandra FC (Crewe) | 18 | 2 | 1 | 15 | 31 | 83 | 5 |
| 56. Aberaman AFC (Aberaman) | 18 | 1 | 1 | 16 | 20 | 87 | 3 |

| West Regional League | Pd | Wn | Dw | Ls | GF | GA | Pts |
|---|---|---|---|---|---|---|---|
| 1. Lovell's Athletic FC (Newport) | 18 | 12 | 6 | 6 | 62 | 30 | 24 |
| 2. Cardiff City AFC (Cardiff) | 18 | 11 | 1 | 6 | 45 | 28 | 23 |
| 3. Bath City FC (Bath) | 18 | 9 | 1 | 8 | 41 | 42 | 19 |
| 4. Aberaman AFC (Aberaman) | 18 | 8 | 2 | 8 | 32 | 35 | 18 |
| 5. Bristol City FC (Bristol) | 18 | 8 | 1 | 9 | 32 | 36 | 17 |
| 6. Swansea Town AFC (Swansea) | 18 | 3 | 1 | 14 | 25 | 66 | 7 |

# 1944-45

| North Regional (1st Championship) | Pd | Wn | Dw | Ls | GF | GA | Pts |
|---|---|---|---|---|---|---|---|
| 1. Huddersfield Town AFC (Huddersfield) | 18 | 14 | 3 | 1 | 50 | 22 | 31 |
| 2. Derby County FC (Derby) | 18 | 14 | 1 | 3 | 54 | 19 | 29 |
| 3. Sunderland AFC (Sunderland) | 18 | 12 | 4 | 2 | 52 | 25 | 28 |
| 4. Aston Villa FC (Birmingham) | 18 | 12 | 3 | 3 | 54 | 19 | 27 |
| 5. Everton FC (Liverpool) | 18 | 12 | 2 | 4 | 58 | 25 | 26 |
| 6. Wrexham AFC (Wrexham) | 18 | 11 | 3 | 4 | 40 | 18 | 25 |
| 7. Doncaster Rovers FC (Doncaster) | 18 | 12 | - | 6 | 48 | 27 | 24 |
| 8. Bradford Park Avenue FC (Bradford) | 18 | 10 | 4 | 4 | 45 | 31 | 24 |

| North Regional (1st Championship) (cont.) | Pd | Wn | Dw | Ls | GF | GA | Pts | |
|---|---|---|---|---|---|---|---|---|
| 9. Bolton Wanderers FC (Bolton) | 18 | 9 | 6 | 3 | 34 | 22 | 24 | |
| 10. Manchester City FC (Manchester) | 18 | 9 | 4 | 5 | 53 | 31 | 22 | |
| 11. Stoke City FC (Stoke-on-Trent) | 18 | 9 | 4 | 5 | 37 | 25 | 22 | |
| 12. Birmingham FC (Birmingham) | 18 | 8 | 4 | 6 | 30 | 21 | 22 | * |
| 13. Barnsley FC (Barnsley) | 18 | 10 | 2 | 6 | 42 | 32 | 22 | |
| 14. Rotherham United FC (Rotherham) | 18 | 9 | 4 | 5 | 31 | 25 | 22 | |
| 15. West Bromwich Albion FC (West Bromwich) | 18 | 9 | 4 | 5 | 36 | 30 | 22 | |
| 16. Liverpool FC (Liverpool) | 18 | 9 | 3 | 6 | 41 | 30 | 21 | |
| 17. Grimsby Town FC (Cleethorpes) | 18 | 9 | 3 | 6 | 37 | 29 | 21 | |
| 18. Halifax Town AFC (Halifax) | 18 | 8 | 5 | 5 | 30 | 29 | 21 | |
| 19. Chester FC (Chester) | 18 | 9 | 3 | 6 | 45 | 45 | 21 | |
| 20. Blackpool FC (Blackpool) | 18 | 9 | 2 | 7 | 53 | 38 | 20 | |
| 21. Burnley FC (Burnley) | 18 | 8 | 4 | 6 | 39 | 27 | 20 | |
| 22. Leeds United AFC (Leeds) | 18 | 9 | 2 | 7 | 53 | 42 | 20 | |
| 23. Sheffield Wednesday FC (Sheffield) | 18 | 9 | 2 | 7 | 34 | 30 | 20 | |
| 24. Chesterfield FC (Chesterfield) | 18 | 8 | 3 | 7 | 30 | 19 | 19 | |
| 25. Darlington FC (Darlington) | 18 | 9 | 1 | 8 | 52 | 45 | 19 | |
| 26. Wolverhampton Wanderers FC (Wolverhampton) | 18 | 7 | 5 | 6 | 31 | 27 | 19 | |
| 27. Rochdale AFC (Rochdale) | 18 | 7 | 5 | 6 | 35 | 33 | 19 | |
| 28. Crewe Alexandra FC (Crewe) | 18 | 9 | 1 | 8 | 43 | 41 | 19 | |
| 29. Blackburn Rovers FC (Blackburn) | 18 | 7 | 4 | 7 | 30 | 29 | 18 | |
| 30. Manchester United FC (Manchester) | 18 | 8 | 2 | 8 | 40 | 40 | 18 | |
| 31. Preston North End FC (Preston) | 18 | 7 | 4 | 7 | 26 | 28 | 18 | |
| 32. Walsall FC (Walsall) | 18 | 5 | 6 | 7 | 27 | 29 | 16 | |
| 33. Gateshead FC (Gateshead) | 18 | 7 | 2 | 9 | 45 | 53 | 16 | |
| 34. Northampton Town FC (Northampton) | 18 | 5 | 6 | 7 | 30 | 38 | 16 | |
| 35. Newcastle United FC (Newcastle-upon-Tyne) | 18 | 7 | 1 | 10 | 51 | 38 | 15 | |
| 36. Sheffield United FC (Sheffield) | 18 | 6 | 3 | 9 | 27 | 25 | 15 | |
| 37. Hartlepools United FC (Hartlepool) | 18 | 7 | 1 | 10 | 41 | 47 | 15 | |
| 38. Oldham Athletic AFC (Oldham) | 18 | 7 | 1 | 10 | 28 | 36 | 15 | |
| 39. Mansfield Town FC (Mansfield) | 18 | 6 | 3 | 9 | 31 | 40 | 15 | |
| 40. Nottingham Forest FC (Nottingham) | 18 | 5 | 5 | 8 | 22 | 34 | 15 | |
| 41. Coventry City FC (Coventry) | 18 | 6 | 2 | 10 | 23 | 42 | 14 | |
| 42. York City FC (York) | 18 | 6 | 1 | 11 | 49 | 52 | 13 | |
| 43. Middlesbrough FC (Middlesbrough) | 18 | 5 | 3 | 10 | 34 | 57 | 13 | |
| 44. Bradford City AFC (Bradford) | 18 | 6 | 1 | 11 | 35 | 60 | 13 | |
| 45. Accrington Stanley FC (Accrington) | 18 | 5 | 2 | 11 | 29 | 46 | 12 | |
| 46. Port Vale FC (Stoke-on-Trent) | 18 | 5 | 2 | 11 | 22 | 36 | 12 | |
| 47. Bury FC (Bury) | 18 | 5 | 2 | 11 | 28 | 48 | 12 | |
| 48. Stockport County FC (Stockport) | 18 | 5 | 1 | 12 | 33 | 70 | 11 | |
| 49. Hull City AFC (Kingston-upon-Hull) | 18 | 4 | 3 | 11 | 23 | 60 | 11 | |
| 50. Southport FC (Southport) | 18 | 3 | 4 | 11 | 32 | 55 | 10 | |
| 51. Lincoln City FC (Lincoln) | 18 | 4 | 2 | 14 | 32 | 56 | 10 | |
| 52. Leicester City FC (Leicester) | 18 | 3 | 4 | 11 | 23 | 46 | 10 | |
| 53. Tranmere Rovers FC (Birkenhead) | 18 | 2 | 1 | 15 | 20 | 53 | 5 | |
| 54. Notts County FC (Nottingham) | 18 | 2 | 1 | 15 | 19 | 62 | 5 | |

| West Regional League | Pd | Wn | Dw | Ls | GF | GA | Pts |
|---|---|---|---|---|---|---|---|
| 1. Cardiff City AFC (Cardiff) | 18 | 12 | 3 | 3 | 54 | 24 | 27 |
| 2. Bristol City FC (Bristol) | 18 | 13 | 1 | 4 | 59 | 30 | 27 |
| 3. Lovell's Athletic FC (Newport) | 18 | 10 | 3 | 5 | 40 | 31 | 23 |
| 4. Bath City FC (Bath) | 18 | 8 | 3 | 7 | 47 | 46 | 19 |
| 5. Aberaman AFC (Aberaman) | 18 | 3 | 1 | 14 | 34 | 71 | 7 |
| 6. Swansea Town AFC (Swansea) | 18 | 2 | 1 | 15 | 32 | 63 | 5 |

* Birmingham FC (Birmingham) changed their club name to Birmingham City FC from the next season.

| | North Regional (2nd Championship) | Pd | Wn | Dw | Ls | GF | GA | Pts | |
|---|---|---|---|---|---|---|---|---|---|
| 1. | Derby County FC (Derby) | 26 | 19 | 3 | 4 | 78 | 28 | 41 | |
| 2. | Everton FC (Liverpool) | 27 | 17 | 3 | 7 | 79 | 43 | 37 | |
| 3. | Liverpool FC (Liverpool) | 24 | 16 | 3 | 5 | 67 | 26 | 35 | |
| 4. | Burnley FC (Burnley) | 26 | 15 | 3 | 8 | 56 | 36 | 33 | |
| 5. | Newcastle United FC (Newcastle-upon-Tyne) | 23 | 15 | 1 | 7 | 71 | 38 | 31 | |
| 6. | Aston Villa FC (Birmingham) | 25 | 14 | 2 | 9 | 70 | 45 | 30 | |
| 7. | Chesterfield FC (Chesterfield) | 24 | 10 | 9 | 5 | 40 | 24 | 29 | |
| 8. | Wolverhampton Wanderers FC (Wolverhampton) | 24 | 11 | 7 | 6 | 45 | 31 | 29 | |
| 9. | Manchester United FC (Manchester) | 22 | 13 | 3 | 6 | 47 | 33 | 29 | |
| 10. | Darlington FC (Darlington) | 24 | 13 | 3 | 8 | 61 | 45 | 29 | |
| 11. | Bristol City FC (Bristol) | 22 | 13 | 7 | 2 | 55 | 33 | 28 | |
| 12. | Blackburn Rovers FC (Blackburn) | 24 | 13 | 2 | 9 | 62 | 51 | 28 | |
| 13. | Huddersfield Town AFC (Huddersfield) | 27 | 12 | 4 | 11 | 52 | 49 | 28 | |
| 14. | Wrexham AFC (Wrexham) | 22 | 10 | 7 | 5 | 55 | 36 | 27 | |
| 15. | Bolton Wanderers FC (Bolton) | 23 | 11 | 5 | 7 | 52 | 35 | 27 | |
| 16. | Blackpool FC (Blackpool) | 24 | 12 | 3 | 9 | 58 | 42 | 27 | |
| 17. | Stoke City FC (Stoke-on-Trent) | 23 | 12 | 2 | 9 | 67 | 42 | 26 | |
| 18. | Lovell's Athletic FC (Newport) | 19 | 12 | 2 | 5 | 44 | 27 | 26 | |
| 19. | Cardiff City AFC (Cardiff) | 20 | 12 | 2 | 6 | 41 | 27 | 26 | |
| 20. | Grimsby Town FC (Cleethorpes) | 21 | 10 | 6 | 5 | 51 | 37 | 26 | |
| 21. | Birmingham FC (Birmingham) | 24 | 9 | 7 | 8 | 38 | 34 | 25 | * |
| 22. | Crewe Alexandra FC (Crewe) | 23 | 11 | 3 | 9 | 50 | 50 | 25 | |
| 23. | Doncaster Rovers FC (Doncaster) | 20 | 11 | 2 | 7 | 44 | 26 | 24 | |
| 24. | Bradford Park Avenue FC (Bradford) | 22 | 10 | 4 | 8 | 49 | 39 | 24 | |
| 25. | Accrington Stanley FC (Accrington) | 24 | 9 | 6 | 9 | 39 | 41 | 24 | |
| 26. | Barnsley FC (Barnsley) | 24 | 11 | 2 | 11 | 39 | 42 | 24 | |
| 27. | Rotherham United FC (Rotherham) | 20 | 10 | 3 | 7 | 41 | 37 | 23 | |
| 28. | Gateshead FC (Gateshead) | 21 | 9 | 5 | 7 | 46 | 42 | 23 | |
| 29. | Preston North End FC (Preston) | 25 | 9 | 4 | 12 | 41 | 56 | 22 | |
| 30. | Sheffield United FC (Sheffield) | 24 | 9 | 3 | 12 | 56 | 48 | 21 | |
| 31. | Sunderland AFC (Sunderland) | 25 | 9 | 3 | 13 | 53 | 54 | 21 | |
| 32. | Leeds United AFC (Leeds) | 22 | 9 | 3 | 10 | 53 | 55 | 21 | |
| 33. | Sheffield Wednesday FC (Sheffield) | 25 | 8 | 5 | 12 | 53 | 56 | 21 | |
| 34. | Leicester City FC (Leicester) | 21 | 7 | 6 | 8 | 40 | 38 | 20 | |
| 35. | Bath City FC (Bath) | 20 | 10 | - | 10 | 50 | 48 | 20 | |
| 36. | Bury FC (Bury) | 20 | 8 | 4 | 8 | 38 | 43 | 20 | |
| 37. | York City FC (York) | 22 | 8 | 4 | 10 | 48 | 56 | 20 | |
| 38. | Chester FC (Chester) | 22 | 9 | 2 | 11 | 49 | 61 | 20 | |
| 39. | Bradford City AFC (Bradford) | 20 | 8 | 3 | 9 | 43 | 46 | 19 | |
| 40. | West Bromwich Albion FC (West Bromwich) | 22 | 6 | 7 | 9 | 39 | 44 | 19 | |
| 41. | Hartlepools United FC (Hartlepool) | 21 | 8 | 3 | 10 | 34 | 54 | 19 | |
| 42. | Coventry City FC (Coventry) | 21 | 6 | 6 | 9 | 36 | 53 | 18 | |
| 43. | Nottingham Forest FC (Nottingham) | 17 | 5 | 7 | 5 | 23 | 25 | 17 | |
| 44. | Tranmere Rovers AFC (Birkenhead) | 23 | 8 | 1 | 14 | 40 | 56 | 17 | |
| 45. | Halifax Town AFC (Halifax) | 18 | 6 | 5 | 7 | 22 | 35 | 17 | |
| 46. | Lincoln City FC (Lincoln) | 17 | 6 | 4 | 7 | 42 | 51 | 16 | |
| 47. | Manchester City FC (Manchester) | 19 | 7 | 2 | 10 | 32 | 43 | 16 | |
| 48. | Northampton Town FC (Northampton) | 14 | 6 | 3 | 5 | 23 | 30 | 15 | |
| 49. | Oldham Athletic AFC (Oldham) | 21 | 7 | 1 | 13 | 39 | 56 | 15 | |
| 50. | Stockport County FC (Stockport) | 19 | 7 | - | 12 | 31 | 50 | 14 | |
| 51. | Middlesbrough FC (Middlesbrough) | 24 | 6 | 2 | 16 | 40 | 73 | 14 | |
| 52. | Walsall FC (Walsall) | 18 | 5 | 3 | 10 | 24 | 33 | 13 | |
| 53. | Swansea Town AFC (Swansea) | 20 | 6 | 1 | 13 | 42 | 63 | 13 | |
| 54. | Port Vale FC (Stoke-on-Trent) | 21 | 5 | 2 | 14 | 27 | 60 | 12 | |
| 55. | Mansfield Town FC (Mansfield) | 12 | 5 | 6 | 1 | 22 | 38 | 11 | |
| 56. | Hull City AFC (Kingston-upon-Hull) | 18 | 5 | 1 | 12 | 30 | 54 | 11 | |

| North Regional (2nd Championship) (cont.) | Pd | Wn | Dw | Ls | GF | GA | Pts |
|---|---|---|---|---|---|---|---|
| 57. Rochdale AFC (Rochdale) | 20 | 4 | 3 | 13 | 17 | 49 | 11 |
| 58. Southport FC (Southport) | 22 | 3 | 3 | 16 | 33 | 82 | 9 |
| 59. Notts County FC (Nottingham) | 21 | 4 | - | 17 | 29 | 62 | 8 |
| 60. Aberaman AFC (Aberaman) | 17 | 2 | 2 | 13 | 36 | 69 | 6 |

| London & South League | Pd | Wn | Dw | Ls | GF | GA | Pts |
|---|---|---|---|---|---|---|---|
| 1. Tottenham Hotspur FC (London) | 30 | 23 | 6 | 1 | 81 | 30 | 52 |
| 2. West Ham United FC (London) | 30 | 22 | 3 | 5 | 96 | 47 | 47 |
| 3. Brentford FC (London) | 30 | 17 | 4 | 9 | 87 | 57 | 38 |
| 4. Chelsea FC (London) | 30 | 16 | 5 | 9 | 100 | 55 | 37 |
| 5. Southampton FC (Southampton) | 30 | 17 | 3 | 10 | 96 | 69 | 37 |
| 6. Crystal Palace FC (London) | 30 | 15 | 5 | 10 | 74 | 70 | 35 |
| 7. Reading FC (Reading) | 30 | 14 | 6 | 10 | 78 | 68 | 34 |
| 8. Arsenal FC (London) | 30 | 14 | 3 | 13 | 77 | 67 | 31 |
| 9. Queen's Park Rangers FC (London) | 30 | 10 | 10 | 10 | 70 | 61 | 30 |
| 10. Watford FC (Watford) | 30 | 11 | 6 | 13 | 66 | 84 | 28 |
| 11. Fulham FC (London) | 30 | 11 | 4 | 15 | 79 | 83 | 26 |
| 12. Portsmouth FC (Portsmouth) | 30 | 11 | 4 | 15 | 56 | 61 | 26 |
| 13. Charlton Athletic FC (London) | 30 | 12 | 2 | 16 | 72 | 81 | 26 |
| 14. Brighton & Hove Albion FC (Hove) | 30 | 10 | 2 | 18 | 66 | 95 | 22 |
| 15. Luton Town FC (Luton) | 30 | 6 | 7 | 17 | 56 | 104 | 19 |
| 16. Aldershot FC (Aldershot) | 30 | 7 | 4 | 19 | 44 | 85 | 18 |
| 17. Millwall FC (London) | 30 | 5 | 7 | 18 | 50 | 84 | 17 |
| 18. Clapton Orient FC (London) | 30 | 5 | 7 | 18 | 39 | 86 | 17 |

# 1945-46

| North League | Pd | Wn | Dw | Ls | GF | GA | Pts |
|---|---|---|---|---|---|---|---|
| 1. Sheffield United FC (Sheffield) | 42 | 27 | 6 | 9 | 112 | 62 | 60 |
| 2. Everton FC (Liverpool) | 42 | 23 | 9 | 10 | 88 | 54 | 55 |
| 3. Bolton Wanderers FC (Bolton) | 42 | 20 | 11 | 11 | 67 | 45 | 51 |
| 4. Manchester United FC (Manchester) | 42 | 19 | 11 | 12 | 98 | 62 | 49 |
| 5. Sheffield Wednesday FC (Sheffield) | 42 | 20 | 8 | 14 | 67 | 60 | 48 |
| 6. Newcastle United FC (Newcastle-upon-Tyne) | 42 | 21 | 5 | 16 | 106 | 70 | 47 |
| 7. Chesterfield FC (Chesterfield) | 42 | 17 | 12 | 13 | 68 | 49 | 46 |
| 8. Barnsley FC (Barnsley) | 42 | 17 | 11 | 14 | 76 | 68 | 45 |
| 9. Blackpool FC (Blackpool) | 42 | 18 | 9 | 15 | 94 | 92 | 45 |
| 10. Manchester City FC (Manchester) | 42 | 20 | 4 | 18 | 78 | 75 | 44 |
| 11. Liverpool FC (Liverpool) | 42 | 17 | 9 | 16 | 80 | 70 | 43 |
| 12. Middlesbrough FC (Middlesbrough) | 42 | 17 | 9 | 16 | 75 | 87 | 43 |
| 13. Stoke City FC (Stoke-on-Trent) | 42 | 18 | 6 | 18 | 88 | 79 | 42 |
| 14. Bradford Park Avenue FC (Bradford) | 42 | 17 | 6 | 19 | 71 | 84 | 40 |
| 15. Huddersfield Town AFC (Huddersfield) | 42 | 17 | 4 | 21 | 90 | 89 | 38 |
| 16. Burnley FC (Burnley) | 42 | 13 | 10 | 19 | 63 | 84 | 36 |
| 17. Grimsby Town FC (Cleethorpes) | 42 | 13 | 9 | 20 | 61 | 89 | 35 |
| 18. Sunderland AFC (Sunderland) | 42 | 15 | 5 | 22 | 55 | 83 | 35 |
| 19. Preston North End FC (Preston) | 42 | 14 | 6 | 22 | 70 | 77 | 34 |
| 20. Bury FC (Bury) | 42 | 12 | 10 | 20 | 60 | 85 | 34 |
| 21. Blackburn Rovers FC (Blackburn) | 42 | 11 | 7 | 24 | 60 | 111 | 29 |
| 22. Leeds United AFC (Leeds) | 42 | 9 | 7 | 26 | 66 | 118 | 25 |
| | 924 | 375 | 174 | 375 | 1693 | 1693 | 924 |

## Division 3 (North – East Region)

| | | Pd | Wn | Dw | Ls | GF | GA | Pts |
|---|---|---|---|---|---|---|---|---|
| 1. | Rotherham United FC (Rotherham) | 18 | 12 | 2 | 4 | 56 | 28 | 26 |
| 2. | Darlington FC (Darlington) | 18 | 12 | 2 | 4 | 61 | 36 | 26 |
| 3. | Gateshead FC (Gateshead) | 18 | 11 | 2 | 5 | 51 | 34 | 24 |
| 4. | Doncaster Rovers FC (Doncaster) | 18 | 8 | 4 | 6 | 34 | 35 | 20 |
| 5. | York City FC (York) | 18 | 6 | 6 | 6 | 34 | 34 | 18 |
| 6. | Halifax Town AFC (Halifax) | 18 | 7 | 4 | 7 | 39 | 46 | 18 |
| 7. | Bradford City AFC (Bradford) | 18 | 6 | 4 | 8 | 45 | 40 | 16 |
| 8. | Carlisle United FC (Carlisle) | 18 | 5 | 3 | 10 | 34 | 58 | 13 |
| 9. | Lincoln City FC (Lincoln) | 18 | 4 | 2 | 12 | 34 | 54 | 10 |
| 10. | Hartlepools United FC (Hartlepool) | 18 | 3 | 3 | 12 | 22 | 45 | 9 |
| | | 180 | 74 | 32 | 74 | 410 | 410 | 180 |

## Division 3 (North – West Region)

| | | Pd | Wn | Dw | Ls | GF | GA | Pts |
|---|---|---|---|---|---|---|---|---|
| 1. | Accrington Stanley FC (Accrington) | 18 | 10 | 4 | 4 | 37 | 19 | 24 |
| 2. | Rochdale AFC (Rochdale) | 18 | 10 | 2 | 6 | 43 | 35 | 22 |
| 3. | Crewe Alexandra FC (Crewe) | 18 | 9 | 3 | 6 | 43 | 31 | 21 |
| 4. | Chester FC (Chester) | 18 | 8 | 5 | 5 | 44 | 38 | 21 |
| 5. | Wrexham AFC (Wrexham) | 18 | 8 | 4 | 6 | 30 | 25 | 20 |
| 6. | Tranmere Rovers FC (Birkenhead) | 18 | 9 | 2 | 7 | 33 | 31 | 20 |
| 7. | Stockport County FC (Stockport) | 18 | 6 | 3 | 9 | 38 | 38 | 15 |
| 8. | Oldham Athletic AFC (Oldham) | 18 | 5 | 5 | 8 | 29 | 32 | 15 |
| 9. | Barrow AFC (Barrow-in-Furness) | 18 | 4 | 4 | 10 | 21 | 44 | 12 |
| 10. | Southport FC (Southport) | 18 | 3 | 4 | 11 | 22 | 47 | 10 |
| | | 180 | 72 | 36 | 72 | 340 | 340 | 180 |

## South League

| | | Pd | Wn | Dw | Ls | GF | GA | Pts |
|---|---|---|---|---|---|---|---|---|
| 1. | Birmingham City FC (Birmingham) | 42 | 28 | 5 | 9 | 96 | 45 | 61 |
| 2. | Aston Villa FC (Birmingham) | 42 | 25 | 11 | 6 | 106 | 58 | 61 |
| 3. | Charlton Athletic FC (London) | 42 | 25 | 10 | 7 | 92 | 45 | 60 |
| 4. | Derby County FC (Derby) | 42 | 24 | 7 | 11 | 101 | 62 | 55 |
| 5. | West Bromwich Albion FC (West Bromwich) | 42 | 22 | 8 | 12 | 104 | 69 | 52 |
| 6. | Wolverhampton Wanderers FC (Wolverhampton) | 42 | 20 | 11 | 11 | 75 | 48 | 51 |
| 7. | West Ham United FC (London) | 42 | 20 | 11 | 11 | 94 | 76 | 51 |
| 8. | Fulham FC (London) | 42 | 20 | 10 | 12 | 93 | 73 | 50 |
| 9. | Tottenham Hotspur FC (London) | 42 | 22 | 3 | 17 | 78 | 81 | 47 |
| 10. | Chelsea FC (London) | 42 | 19 | 6 | 17 | 92 | 80 | 44 |
| 11. | Arsenal FC (London) | 42 | 16 | 11 | 15 | 76 | 73 | 43 |
| 12. | Millwall FC (London) | 42 | 17 | 8 | 17 | 79 | 105 | 42 |
| 13. | Coventry City FC (Coventry) | 42 | 15 | 10 | 17 | 70 | 69 | 40 |
| 14. | Brentford FC (London) | 42 | 14 | 10 | 18 | 82 | 72 | 38 |
| 15. | Nottingham Forest FC (Nottingham) | 42 | 12 | 13 | 17 | 72 | 73 | 37 |
| 16. | Southampton FC (Southampton) | 42 | 14 | 9 | 19 | 97 | 105 | 37 |
| 17. | Swansea Town AFC (Swansea) | 42 | 15 | 7 | 20 | 90 | 112 | 37 |
| 18. | Luton Town FC (Luton) | 42 | 13 | 7 | 22 | 60 | 92 | 33 |
| 19. | Portsmouth FC (Portsmouth) | 42 | 11 | 6 | 25 | 66 | 87 | 28 |
| 20. | Leicester City FC (Leicester) | 42 | 8 | 7 | 27 | 57 | 101 | 23 |
| 21. | Newport County AFC (Newport) | 42 | 9 | 2 | 31 | 52 | 125 | 20 |
| 22. | Plymouth Argyle FC (Plymouth) | 42 | 3 | 8 | 31 | 39 | 120 | 14 |
| | | 924 | 372 | 180 | 372 | 1771 | 1771 | 924 |

| Division 3 (South – North Region) | Pd | Wn | Dw | Ls | GF | GA | Pts | |
|---|---|---|---|---|---|---|---|---|
| 1. Queen's Park Rangers FC (London) | 20 | 14 | 4 | 2 | 50 | 15 | 32 | |
| 2. Norwich City FC (Norwich) | 20 | 11 | 4 | 5 | 54 | 31 | 26 | |
| 3. Port Vale FC (Stoke-on-Trent) | 20 | 9 | 6 | 5 | 34 | 25 | 24 | |
| 4. Watford FC (Watford) | 20 | 10 | 2 | 8 | 42 | 47 | 22 | |
| 5. Ipswich Town FC (Ipswich) | 20 | 8 | 4 | 8 | 33 | 36 | 20 | |
| 6. Notts County FC (Nottingham) | 20 | 8 | 4 | 8 | 39 | 47 | 20 | |
| 7. Northampton Town FC (Northampton) | 20 | 8 | 3 | 9 | 37 | 34 | 19 | |
| 8. Clapton Orient FC (London) | 20 | 5 | 6 | 9 | 28 | 42 | 16 | * |
| 9. Walsall FC (Walsall) | 20 | 6 | 3 | 11 | 31 | 42 | 15 | |
| 10. Southend United FC (Southend-on-Sea) | 20 | 5 | 5 | 10 | 33 | 49 | 15 | |
| 11. Mansfield Town FC (Mansfield) | 20 | 3 | 5 | 12 | 29 | 42 | 11 | |
| | 220 | 87 | 46 | 87 | 410 | 410 | 220 | |

| Division 3 (South – South Region) | Pd | Wn | Dw | Ls | GF | GA | Pts |
|---|---|---|---|---|---|---|---|
| 1. Crystal Palace FC (London) | 20 | 13 | 3 | 4 | 55 | 31 | 29 |
| 2. Cardiff City AFC (Cardiff) | 20 | 13 | 2 | 5 | 69 | 31 | 28 |
| 3. Bristol City FC (Bristol) | 20 | 11 | 2 | 7 | 51 | 40 | 24 |
| 4. Brighton & Hove Albion FC (Hove) | 20 | 10 | 1 | 9 | 49 | 50 | 21 |
| 5. Bristol Rovers FC (Bristol) | 20 | 7 | 6 | 7 | 44 | 44 | 20 |
| 6. Swindon Town FC (Swindon) | 20 | 8 | 3 | 9 | 35 | 47 | 19 |
| 7. Bournemouth & Boscombe Athletic FC (Bournemouth) | 20 | 7 | 3 | 10 | 52 | 50 | 17 |
| 8. Aldershot FC (Aldershot) | 20 | 6 | 5 | 9 | 38 | 56 | 17 |
| 9. Exeter City FC (Exeter) | 20 | 6 | 4 | 10 | 33 | 41 | 16 |
| 10. Reading FC (Reading) | 20 | 5 | 5 | 10 | 43 | 49 | 15 |
| 11. Torquay United FC (Torquay) | 20 | 5 | 4 | 11 | 22 | 52 | 14 |
| | 220 | 91 | 38 | 91 | 491 | 491 | 220 |

* Clapton Orient FC (London) changed their club name to Leyton Orient FC (London) from the next season.

**F.A. CUP FINAL** (Wembley Stadium, London – 27/04/1946 – 98,215)

DERBY COUNTY FC (DERBY)       4-1       Charlton Athletic FC (London)

*H.Turner o.g., Doherty, Stamps 2*       *H.Turner*

Derby: Woodley, Nicholas, Howe, Bullions, Leuty, Musson, Harrison, Carter, Stamps, Doherty, Duncan.

Charlton: Bartram, Phipps, Shreeve, H.Turner, Oakes, Johnson, Fell, Brown, AA Turner, Welsh, Duffy.

## Semi-finals

| | | |
|---|---|---|
| Bolton Wanderers FC (Bolton) | 0-2 | Charlton Athletic FC (London) |
| Derby County FC (Derby) | 1-1, 4-0 | Birmingham City FC (Birmingham) |

## Quarter-finals

| | | |
|---|---|---|
| Aston Villa FC (Birmingham) | 3-4, 1-1 | Derby County FC (Derby) |
| Bradford Park Avenue FC (Bradford) | 2-2, 0-6 | Birmingham City FC (Birmingham) |
| Charlton Athletic FC (London) | 6-3, 3-1 | Brentford FC (London) |
| Stoke City FC (Stoke-on-Trent) | 0-2, 0-0 | Bolton Wanderers FC (Bolton) |

# 1946-47

| Football League Division 1 1946-1947 Season | Arsenal | Aston Villa | Blackburn Rovers | Blackpool | Bolton Wanderers | Brentford | Charlton Athletic | Chelsea | Derby County | Everton | Grimsby Town | Huddersfield Town | Leeds United | Liverpool | Manchester United | Middlesbrough | Portsmouth | Preston North End | Sheffield United | Stoke City | Sunderland | Wolves |
|---|---|---|---|---|---|---|---|---|---|---|---|---|---|---|---|---|---|---|---|---|---|---|
| Arsenal FC | | 0-2 | 1-3 | 1-1 | 2-2 | 2-2 | 1-0 | 1-2 | 0-1 | 2-1 | 5-3 | 1-2 | 4-2 | 1-2 | 6-2 | 4-0 | 21 | 4-1 | 2-3 | 1-0 | 2-2 | 1-1 |
| Aston Villa FC | 0-2 | | 2-1 | 1-1 | 1-1 | 5-2 | 4-0 | 2-0 | 2-0 | 0-1 | 3-3 | 2-2 | 2-1 | 1-2 | 0-0 | 0-1 | 1-1 | 4-2 | 2-3 | 0-1 | 4-0 | 3-0 |
| Blackburn Rovers FC | 1-2 | 0-1 | | 1-1 | 2-1 | 0-3 | 1-0 | 1-2 | 1-1 | 4-1 | 1-1 | 2-2 | 1-0 | 0-0 | 2-1 | 1-2 | 0-1 | 1-2 | 2-0 | 0-2 | 1-2 | 1-2 |
| Blackpool FC | 2-1 | 1-0 | 1-0 | | 0-1 | 4-2 | 0-0 | 1-0 | 2-1 | 0-3 | 2-3 | 2-1 | 3-0 | 3-2 | 3-1 | 0-5 | 4-3 | 4-0 | 4-2 | 0-2 | 0-5 | 2-0 |
| Bolton Wanderers FC | 1-3 | 2-1 | 0-0 | 1-1 | | 1-0 | 0-1 | 1-1 | 5-1 | 0-2 | 1-2 | 4-0 | 2-0 | 1-3 | 2-2 | 1-1 | 1-0 | 1-2 | 3-2 | 3-2 | 0-1 | 0-3 |
| Brentford FC | 0-1 | 0-2 | 0-3 | 2-1 | 1-0 | | 1-4 | 0-2 | 0-3 | 1-1 | 0-1 | 2-0 | 1-1 | 1-1 | 0-0 | 0-0 | 1-3 | 2-3 | 2-1 | 1-4 | 0-3 | 4-1 |
| Charlton Athletic FC | 2-2 | 1-1 | 0-2 | 0-1 | 2-0 | 3-0 | | 2-3 | 2-4 | 4-1 | 0-0 | 0-3 | 5-0 | 1-3 | 1-3 | 3-3 | 0-0 | 0-0 | 1-2 | 1-0 | 5-0 | 1-4 |
| Chelsea FC | 2-1 | 1-3 | 0-2 | 1-4 | 4-3 | 3-2 | 2-2 | | 3-0 | 1-1 | 0-0 | 1-0 | 3-0 | 3-1 | 0-3 | 2-0 | 0-3 | 1-2 | 1-4 | 2-5 | 2-1 | 1-2 |
| Derby County FC | 0-1 | 1-2 | 2-1 | 1-2 | 1-3 | 2-1 | 1-0 | 3-1 | | 5-1 | 4-1 | 1-0 | 2-1 | 1-4 | 4-3 | 1-1 | 2-0 | 2-2 | 1-2 | 3-0 | 5-1 | 2-1 |
| Everton FC | 3-2 | 2-0 | 1-0 | 1-1 | 2-1 | 0-2 | 1-1 | 2-0 | 4-1 | | 3-3 | 1-0 | 4-1 | 1-0 | 2-2 | 2-1 | 1-0 | 2-0 | 2-3 | 2-2 | 4-2 | 0-2 |
| Grimsby Town FC | 0-0 | 0-3 | 2-1 | 2-3 | 2-2 | 2-2 | 3-1 | 2-1 | 2-0 | 2-2 | | 1-0 | 4-1 | 1-6 | 0-0 | 4-0 | 3-2 | 2-3 | 2-1 | 2-5 | 1-2 | 0-0 |
| Huddersfield Town AFC | 0-0 | 1-0 | 0-1 | 1-3 | 1-0 | 3-0 | 5-1 | 1-4 | 5-2 | 1-0 | 3-2 | | 1-0 | 1-4 | 2-2 | 3-1 | 1-2 | 3-0 | 1-1 | 1-0 | 0-0 | 0-1 |
| Leeds United AFC | 1-1 | 1-1 | 0-1 | 4-2 | 4-0 | 1-2 | 0-2 | 2-1 | 1-2 | 2-1 | 1-0 | 5-0 | | 1-2 | 0-2 | 3-3 | 0-1 | 0-3 | 2-2 | 1-2 | 1-1 | 0-1 |
| Liverpool FC | 4-2 | 4-1 | 2-1 | 2-3 | 0-3 | 1-0 | 1-1 | 7-4 | 1-1 | 0-0 | 5-0 | 1-0 | 2-0 | | 1-0 | 0-1 | 3-0 | 3-0 | 1-2 | 2-0 | 1-0 | 1-5 |
| Manchester United FC | 5-2 | 2-1 | 4-0 | 3-0 | 1-0 | 4-1 | 4-1 | 1-1 | 4-1 | 3-0 | 2-1 | 5-2 | 3-1 | 5-0 | | 1-0 | 3-0 | 1-1 | 6-2 | 1-1 | 0-3 | 3-1 |
| Middlesbrough FC | 2-0 | 1-2 | 0-1 | 1-2 | 3-1 | 2-0 | 1-2 | 3-2 | 1-0 | 4-0 | 3-0 | 4-1 | 3-0 | 2-2 | 2-4 | | 3-3 | 2-0 | 2-4 | 5-4 | 1-3 | 1-1 |
| Portsmouth FC | 0-2 | 3-2 | 3-1 | 0-1 | 2-0 | 3-0 | 3-0 | 0-2 | 1-2 | 2-1 | 4-1 | 3-1 | 4-1 | 1-2 | 0-1 | 3-1 | | 4-4 | 0-0 | 1-3 | 4-1 | 1-1 |
| Preston North End FC | 2-0 | 3-1 | 4-0 | 2-0 | 0-4 | 5-2 | 5-1 | 1-1 | 1-1 | 2-1 | 3-0 | 6-2 | 3-2 | 0-0 | 1-1 | 0-1 | 1-1 | | 1-2 | 1-3 | 2-2 | 2-2 |
| Sheffield United FC | 2-1 | 1-2 | 0-1 | 4-2 | 4-2 | 6-1 | 1-3 | 2-2 | 3-2 | 2-0 | 1-1 | 2-2 | 6-2 | 0-1 | 2-2 | 2-1 | 3-1 | 2-3 | | 2-1 | 4-2 | 2-0 |
| Stoke City FC | 3-1 | 0-0 | 0-0 | 4-1 | 1-2 | 3-1 | 2-2 | 6-1 | 3-2 | 2-1 | 3-0 | 3-0 | 5-2 | 2-1 | 3-2 | 3-1 | 1-1 | 5-0 | 3-0 | | 0-0 | 0-3 |
| Sunderland AFC | 1-4 | 4-1 | 1-0 | 3-2 | 3-1 | 2-1 | 1-1 | 1-2 | 3-2 | 4-1 | 1-2 | 3-0 | 1-0 | 1-4 | 1-1 | 1-0 | 0-0 | 0-2 | 2-1 | 0-1 | | 0-1 |
| Wolverhampton Wanderers FC | 6-1 | 1-2 | 3-3 | 3-1 | 5-0 | 1-2 | 2-0 | 6-4 | 7-2 | 2-3 | 2-0 | 6-1 | 1-0 | 1-2 | 3-2 | 2-4 | 3-1 | 4-1 | 3-1 | 3-0 | 2-1 | |

| Division 1 | Pd | Wn | Dw | Ls | GF | GA | Pts | |
|---|---|---|---|---|---|---|---|---|
| 1. LIVERPOOL FC (LIVERPOOL) | 42 | 25 | 7 | 10 | 84 | 52 | 57 | |
| 2. Manchester United FC (Manchester) | 42 | 22 | 12 | 8 | 95 | 54 | 56 | |
| 3. Wolverhampton Wanderers FC (Wolverhampton) | 42 | 25 | 6 | 11 | 98 | 56 | 56 | |
| 4. Stoke City FC (Stoke-on-Trent) | 42 | 24 | 7 | 11 | 90 | 53 | 55 | |
| 5. Blackpool FC (Blackpool) | 42 | 22 | 6 | 14 | 71 | 70 | 50 | |
| 6. Sheffield United FC (Sheffield) | 42 | 21 | 7 | 14 | 89 | 75 | 49 | |
| 7. Preston North End FC (Preston) | 42 | 18 | 11 | 13 | 76 | 74 | 47 | |
| 8. Aston Villa FC (Birmingham) | 42 | 18 | 9 | 15 | 67 | 53 | 45 | |
| 9. Sunderland AFC (Sunderland) | 42 | 18 | 8 | 16 | 65 | 66 | 44 | |
| 10. Everton FC (Liverpool) | 42 | 17 | 9 | 16 | 62 | 67 | 43 | |
| 11. Middlesbrough FC (Middlesbrough) | 42 | 17 | 8 | 17 | 73 | 68 | 42 | |
| 12. Portsmouth FC (Portsmouth) | 42 | 16 | 9 | 17 | 66 | 60 | 41 | |
| 13. Arsenal FC (London) | 42 | 16 | 9 | 17 | 72 | 70 | 41 | |
| 14. Derby County FC (Derby) | 42 | 18 | 5 | 19 | 73 | 79 | 41 | |
| 15. Chelsea FC (London) | 42 | 16 | 7 | 19 | 69 | 84 | 39 | |
| 16. Grimsby Town FC (Cleethorpes) | 42 | 13 | 12 | 17 | 61 | 82 | 38 | |
| 17. Blackburn Rovers FC (Blackburn) | 42 | 14 | 8 | 20 | 45 | 53 | 36 | |
| 18. Bolton Wanderers FC (Bolton) | 42 | 13 | 8 | 21 | 57 | 69 | 34 | |
| 19. Charlton Athletic FC (London) | 42 | 11 | 12 | 19 | 57 | 71 | 34 | |
| 20. Huddersfield Town AFC (Huddersfield) | 42 | 13 | 7 | 22 | 53 | 79 | 33 | |
| 21. Brentford FC (London) | 42 | 9 | 7 | 26 | 45 | 88 | 25 | R |
| 22. Leeds United AFC (Leeds) | 42 | 6 | 6 | 30 | 45 | 90 | 18 | R |
| | 924 | 372 | 180 | 372 | 1513 | 1513 | 924 | |

## Top Goalscorer

| 1) | Dennis WESTCOTT | (Wolverhampton Wanderers FC) | 37 |
|---|---|---|---|

## Football League Division 2 — 1946-1947 Season

| | Barnsley | Birmingham City | Bradford P.A. | Burnley | Bury | Chesterfield | Coventry City | Fulham | Leicester City | Luton Town | Manchester City | Millwall | Newcastle United | Newport County | Nottingham F. | Plymouth Argyle | Sheffield Wed. | Southampton | Swansea Town | Tottenham H. | W.B.A. | West Ham United |
|---|---|---|---|---|---|---|---|---|---|---|---|---|---|---|---|---|---|---|---|---|---|---|
| Barnsley FC | ■ | 3-1 | 3-1 | 1-0 | 4-0 | 1-2 | 0-2 | 4-1 | 1-0 | 4-0 | 0-2 | 4-1 | 1-1 | 3-1 | 3-2 | 1-3 | 4-1 | 4-4 | 3-1 | 1-3 | 2-1 | 1-2 |
| Birmingham City FC | 1-2 | ■ | 4-0 | 0-2 | 3-0 | 0-0 | 2-0 | 2-1 | 4-0 | 1-0 | 3-1 | 4-0 | 2-0 | 1-1 | 4-0 | 6-1 | 3-1 | 3-1 | 3-1 | 1-0 | 1-0 | 3-0 |
| Bradford Park Avenue | 1-3 | 2-0 | ■ | 0-1 | 2-2 | 0-0 | 5-1 | 1-2 | 1-2 | 2-1 | 1-1 | 0-0 | 2-1 | 2-1 | 0-1 | 3-2 | 1-1 | 2-3 | 0-0 | 2-1 | 2-4 | 0-1 |
| Burnley FC | 2-2 | 1-0 | 1-2 | ■ | 1-1 | 1-1 | 1-1 | 2-0 | 0-0 | 1-1 | 0-0 | 3-0 | 3-0 | 3-2 | 3-0 | 2-1 | 2-0 | 1-0 | 1-0 | 0-0 | 0-2 | 2-1 |
| Bury FC | 4-4 | 2-0 | 6-3 | 2-2 | ■ | 0-2 | 1-0 | 7-2 | 2-3 | 3-0 | 2-2 | 5-2 | 2-2 | 0-1 | 5-0 | 3-3 | 4-2 | 2-1 | 3-3 | 1-2 | 4-0 | 4-0 |
| Chesterfield FC | 2-1 | 0-1 | 1-1 | 0-0 | 3-1 | ■ | 2-1 | 1-1 | 2-0 | 2-1 | 0-1 | 2-3 | 1-0 | 2-0 | 1-1 | 4-1 | 4-2 | 5-0 | 1-0 | 0-0 | 1-1 | 3-1 |
| Coventry City FC | 1-1 | 0-0 | 0-0 | 0-3 | 3-1 | 1-1 | ■ | 1-0 | 2-1 | 0-0 | 1-1 | 4-0 | 1-1 | 6-0 | 1-1 | 1-0 | 5-1 | 2-0 | 3-2 | 3-1 | 3-2 | 2-1 |
| Fulham FC | 6-1 | 0-1 | 0-3 | 1-0 | 2-0 | 2-1 | 2-0 | ■ | 4-2 | 2-1 | 2-2 | 3-2 | 0-3 | 4-1 | 1-1 | 3-1 | 1-2 | 0-0 | 3-0 | 1-1 | 0-1 | 3-2 |
| Leicester City FC | 6-0 | 2-1 | 2-1 | 1-4 | 0-0 | 0-1 | 1-0 | 2-0 | ■ | 2-1 | 0-3 | 5-0 | 2-4 | 3-0 | 1-1 | 4-1 | 3-5 | 2-0 | 0-1 | 1-1 | 1-1 | 4-0 |
| Luton Town FC | 3-1 | 1-3 | 3-0 | 1-3 | 2-0 | 1-1 | 1-1 | 2-0 | 1-2 | ■ | 0-0 | 3-0 | 4-3 | 6-3 | 3-2 | 3-4 | 4-1 | 2-2 | 3-0 | 3-2 | 2-0 | 2-1 |
| Manchester City FC | 5-1 | 1-0 | 7-2 | 1-0 | 3-1 | 0-0 | 1-0 | 4-0 | 1-0 | 2-0 | ■ | 1-0 | 0-2 | 5-1 | 2-1 | 4-3 | 2-1 | 1-1 | 1-1 | 1-1 | 5-0 | 2-0 |
| Millwall FC | 3-1 | 0-2 | 0-1 | 1-1 | 1-0 | 1-1 | 3-5 | 1-1 | 1-0 | 2-0 | 1-3 | ■ | 1-4 | 3-1 | 4-0 | 1-1 | 2-2 | 3-1 | 1-1 | 0-3 | 1-2 | 0-0 |
| Newcastle United FC | 4-2 | 2-2 | 5-0 | 1-2 | 1-1 | 2-1 | 3-1 | 1-3 | 1-1 | 7-2 | 3-2 | 0-2 | ■ | 13-0 | 3-0 | 3-2 | 4-0 | 1-3 | 1-1 | 1-0 | 2-4 | 2-3 |
| Newport County AFC | 2-1 | 0-3 | 1-3 | 0-3 | 2-0 | 1-1 | 4-2 | 4-2 | 2-3 | 0-3 | 0-3 | 3-1 | 4-2 | ■ | 2-5 | 1-0 | 4-3 | 1-2 | 2-4 | 2-4 | 2-7 | 1-1 |
| Nottingham Forest FC | 2-1 | 1-1 | 4-0 | 1-0 | 2-0 | 1-0 | 1-0 | 2-1 | 2-0 | 4-2 | 0-1 | 1-2 | 0-2 | 6-1 | ■ | 5-1 | 2-2 | 6-0 | 1-1 | 1-1 | 1-1 | 4-3 |
| Plymouth Argyle FC | 3-2 | 0-2 | 2-4 | 2-2 | 3-1 | 1-0 | 2-2 | 2-2 | 4-0 | 2-1 | 2-3 | 0-2 | 0-1 | 4-1 | 2-0 | ■ | 4-1 | 2-3 | 2-1 | 3-4 | 2-1 | 3-1 |
| Sheffield Wednesday FC | 2-4 | 1-0 | 1-2 | 1-2 | 2-5 | 0-1 | 4-2 | 1-1 | 1-3 | 1-1 | 1-0 | 3-0 | 1-1 | 2-1 | 2-0 | 2-1 | ■ | 3-0 | 3-0 | 5-1 | 2-2 | 1-1 |
| Southampton FC | 1-1 | 1-0 | 3-2 | 0-1 | 1-1 | 1-1 | 5-2 | 2-0 | 1-1 | 1-3 | 0-1 | 1-2 | 1-1 | 5-1 | 5-2 | 5-1 | 3-1 | ■ | 4-0 | 1-0 | 0-1 | 4-2 |
| Swansea Town AFC | 2-2 | 1-0 | 1-6 | 0-2 | 1-0 | 1-2 | 2-3 | 0-2 | 3-4 | 2-0 | 0-3 | 1-2 | 5-1 | 3-2 | 3-1 | 2-0 | 4-2 | | ■ | 0-2 | 2-3 | 2-1 |
| Tottenham Hotspur FC | 1-1 | 1-2 | 3-3 | 1-1 | 2-1 | 3-4 | 0-0 | 1-1 | 2-1 | 0-0 | 2-1 | 1-1 | 3-1 | 2-1 | 2-0 | 2-1 | 2-0 | 2-1 | 3-1 | ■ | 2-0 | 0-0 |
| West Bromwich Albion FC | 2-5 | 3-0 | 1-1 | 1-1 | 3-0 | 3-2 | 1-1 | 6-1 | 4-2 | 1-2 | 31 | 2-4 | 3-2 | 2-2 | 5-1 | 2-1 | 2-5 | 2-1 | 2-0 | 2-1 | ■ | 2-3 |
| West Ham United FC | 4-0 | 0-4 | 1-1 | 0-5 | 3-3 | 5-0 | 1-2 | 3-2 | 0-2 | 2-1 | 1-0 | 3-1 | 0-2 | 3-0 | 2-2 | 4-1 | 2-1 | 4-0 | 3-0 | 2-2 | 3-2 | ■ |

### Division 2

| | Club | Pd | Wn | Dw | Ls | GF | GA | Pts | |
|---|---|---|---|---|---|---|---|---|---|
| 1. | Manchester City FC (Manchester) | 42 | 26 | 10 | 6 | 78 | 35 | 62 | P |
| 2. | Burnley FC (Burnley) | 42 | 22 | 14 | 6 | 65 | 29 | 58 | P |
| 3. | Birmingham City FC (Birmingham) | 42 | 25 | 5 | 12 | 74 | 33 | 55 | |
| 4. | Chesterfield FC (Chesterfield) | 42 | 18 | 14 | 10 | 58 | 44 | 50 | |
| 5. | Newcastle United FC (Newcastle-upon-Tyne) | 42 | 19 | 10 | 13 | 95 | 62 | 48 | |
| 6. | Tottenham Hotspur FC (London) | 42 | 17 | 14 | 11 | 65 | 53 | 48 | |
| 7. | West Bromwich Albion FC (West Bromwich) | 42 | 20 | 8 | 14 | 88 | 75 | 48 | |
| 8. | Coventry City FC (Coventry) | 42 | 16 | 13 | 13 | 66 | 59 | 45 | |
| 9. | Leicester City FC (Leicester) | 42 | 18 | 7 | 17 | 69 | 64 | 43 | |
| 10. | Barnsley FC (Barnsley) | 42 | 17 | 8 | 17 | 84 | 86 | 42 | |
| 11. | Nottingham Forest FC (Nottingham) | 42 | 15 | 10 | 17 | 69 | 74 | 40 | |
| 12. | West Ham United FC (London) | 42 | 16 | 8 | 18 | 70 | 76 | 40 | |
| 13. | Luton Town FC (Luton) | 42 | 16 | 7 | 19 | 71 | 73 | 39 | |
| 14. | Southampton FC (Southampton) | 42 | 15 | 9 | 18 | 69 | 76 | 39 | |
| 15. | Fulham FC (London) | 42 | 15 | 9 | 18 | 63 | 74 | 39 | |
| 16. | Bradford Park Avenue FC (Bradford) | 42 | 14 | 11 | 17 | 65 | 77 | 39 | |
| 17. | Bury FC (Bury) | 42 | 12 | 12 | 18 | 80 | 78 | 36 | |
| 18. | Millwall FC (London) | 42 | 14 | 8 | 20 | 56 | 79 | 36 | |
| 19. | Plymouth Argyle FC (Plymouth) | 42 | 14 | 5 | 23 | 79 | 96 | 33 | |
| 20. | Sheffield Wednesday FC (Sheffield) | 42 | 12 | 8 | 22 | 67 | 88 | 32 | |
| 21. | Swansea Town AFC (Swansea) | 42 | 11 | 7 | 24 | 55 | 83 | 29 | R |
| 22. | Newport County AFC (Newport) | 42 | 10 | 3 | 29 | 61 | 133 | 23 | R |
| | | 924 | 362 | 200 | 362 | 1547 | 1547 | 924 | |

| Football League Division 3 (N) 1946-1947 Season | Accrington Stanley | Barrow | Bradford City | Carlisle United | Chester | Crewe Alexandra | Darlington | Doncaster Rovers | Gateshead | Halifax Town | Hartlepools United | Hull City | Lincoln City | New Brighton | Oldham Athletic | Rochdale | Rotherham United | Southport | Stockport County | Tranmere | Wrexham | York City |
|---|---|---|---|---|---|---|---|---|---|---|---|---|---|---|---|---|---|---|---|---|---|---|
| Accrington Stanley FC | | 1-3 | 0-0 | 4-3 | 1-4 | 2-3 | 3-0 | 0-1 | 0-3 | 1-1 | 2-1 | 0-0 | 8-4 | 3-1 | 2-3 | 2-3 | 2-3 | 1-0 | 2-1 | 2-1 | 0-1 | 1-2 |
| Barrow AFC | 1-3 | | 0-0 | 3-1 | 1-0 | 0-2 | 2-3 | 0-1 | 1-0 | 3-0 | 2-0 | 1-0 | 1-3 | 0-1 | 5-2 | 2-2 | 2-3 | 2-1 | 1-0 | 0-1 | 1-0 | 0-1 |
| Bradford City AFC | 3-1 | 5-0 | | 2-2 | 0-0 | 1-0 | 2-0 | 0-1 | 2-2 | 3-1 | 1-2 | 1-1 | 3-0 | 2-1 | 1-0 | 0-1 | 2-0 | 5-1 | 0-2 | 2-2 | 2-1 | 3-2 |
| Carlisle United FC | 4-2 | 4-1 | 4-3 | | 3-2 | 33 | 1-5 | 2-3 | 3-1 | 1-0 | 5-1 | 0-2 | 1-0 | 3-2 | 1-2 | 1-3 | 1-1 | 1-1 | 1-1 | 4-2 | 1-1 | 1-2 |
| Chester FC | 3-1 | 3-0 | 3-0 | 4-0 | | 2-0 | 1-1 | 1-3 | 0-1 | 2-0 | 2-1 | 5-1 | 3-0 | 2-1 | 2-0 | 1-0 | 2-2 | 2-1 | 3-0 | 4-1 | 2-0 | 6-0 |
| Crewe Alexandra FC | 5-0 | 0-1 | 2-2 | 2-0 | 0-2 | | 3-2 | 0-3 | 1-1 | 2-0 | 1-1 | 2-0 | 0-5 | 3-0 | 3-0 | 2-2 | 1-2 | 2-0 | 3-2 | 4-3 | 1-0 | 2-0 |
| Darlington FC | 5-0 | 0-1 | 2-0 | 2-1 | 3-3 | 4-0 | | 1-1 | 2-0 | 0-1 | 2-1 | 0-2 | 4-3 | 4-0 | 1-1 | 4-1 | 4-3 | 4-2 | 1-2 | 1-2 | 1-1 | 3-1 |
| Doncaster Rovers FC | 5-0 | 8-0 | 4-3 | 9-2 | 3-0 | 1-1 | 5-0 | | 3-0 | 2-0 | 5-1 | 4-1 | 1-1 | 0-0 | 4-2 | 2-1 | 1-1 | 2-0 | 1-3 | 2-0 | 5-0 | 0-0 |
| Gateshead FC | 2-1 | 0-5 | 1-2 | 1-3 | 3-4 | 2-1 | 1-0 | 1-3 | | 6-1 | 0-1 | 1-0 | 3-0 | 3-0 | 1-0 | 2-2 | 2-0 | 2-2 | 1-2 | 3-1 | 3-3 | 1-2 |
| Halifax Town AFC | 2-1 | 3-2 | 1-2 | 0-1 | 1-2 | 1-2 | 0-2 | 4-2 | 2-1 | | 1-4 | 2-0 | 2-3 | 0-1 | 1-1 | 3-0 | 2-3 | 1-1 | 1-2 | 1-3 | 0-0 | 0-3 |
| Hartlepools United FC | 0-2 | 1-1 | 0-0 | 4-1 | 5-1 | 5-2 | 4-1 | 0-2 | 1-3 | 1-4 | | 0-0 | 2-0 | 3-0 | 1-1 | 0-3 | 2-1 | 3-0 | 1-0 | 1-0 | 1-3 | 1-1 |
| Hull City AFC | 3-0 | 1-0 | 0-2 | 2-0 | 1-0 | 2-2 | 2-1 | 0-1 | 1-2 | 3-0 | 1-1 | | 0-0 | 1-1 | 0-1 | 0-1 | 0-2 | 4-0 | 0-3 | 1-0 | 1-0 | 2-2 |
| Lincoln City FC | 1-1 | 1-0 | 0-1 | 3-1 | 2-2 | 1-3 | 2-0 | 3-5 | 4-0 | 3-1 | 5-2 | 0-3 | | 5-1 | 1-3 | 2-3 | 4-0 | 4-2 | 4-0 | 2-1 | 3-1 | 2-2 |
| New Brighton FC | 4-0 | 0-1 | 0-0 | 2-2 | 0-3 | 4-0 | 4-1 | 2-5 | 2-3 | 1-1 | 2-1 | 1-5 | 4-2 | | 4-0 | 1-2 | 1-0 | 1-0 | 1-0 | 2-1 | 1-0 | 0-3 |
| Oldham Athletic AFC | 1-2 | 0-1 | 0-1 | 0-2 | 1-0 | 3-1 | 2-0 | 0-1 | 1-1 | 6-1 | 0-0 | 1-2 | 3-1 | 2-2 | | 3-2 | 0-1 | 2-4 | 0-0 | 1-2 | 1-5 | 2-2 |
| Rochdale AFC | 5-1 | 1-1 | 0-1 | 6-0 | 2-1 | 1-1 | 3-0 | 2-3 | 2-3 | 1-0 | 1-0 | 5-2 | 2-0 | 2-2 | 1-3 | | 1-1 | 0-0 | 1-4 | 3-0 | 0-1 | 0-1 |
| Rotherham United FC | 4-1 | 4-3 | 2-1 | 4-0 | 3-1 | 5-1 | 4-1 | 3-2 | 4-0 | 6-1 | 4-0 | 2-0 | 3-0 | 3-0 | 8-0 | 3-3 | | 2-1 | 2-1 | 6-0 | 3-2 | 6-1 |
| Southport FC | 0-1 | 2-2 | 0-1 | 0-2 | 2-4 | 2-2 | 2-2 | 0-5 | 2-1 | 6-1 | 3-3 | 3-1 | 1-3 | 2-0 | 2-4 | 0-2 | 2-0 | | 4-1 | 1-2 | 1-1 | 0-3 |
| Stockport County FC | 2-0 | 2-0 | 4-0 | 2-0 | 0-3 | 3-2 | 1-0 | 1-3 | 2-0 | 4-1 | 1-2 | 2-0 | 3-2 | 2-0 | 4-0 | 5-2 | 1-2 | 2-0 | | 4-0 | 1-0 | 4-2 |
| Tranmere Rovers FC | 0-1 | 1-1 | 2-0 | 1-1 | 3-2 | 3-2 | 2-0 | 3-5 | 1-0 | 1-1 | 4-1 | 1-3 | 5-2 | 3-3 | 2-3 | 1-4 | 2-0 | 2-1 | | | 0-0 | 2-1 |
| Wrexham AFC | 4-0 | 1-1 | 2-0 | 2-1 | 0-4 | 1-0 | 7-1 | 0-2 | 2-0 | 2-0 | 4-1 | 0-1 | 4-1 | 3-2 | 2-1 | 2-2 | 1-1 | 1-1 | 2-1 | 0-0 | | 3-1 |
| York City FC | 0-1 | 0-2 | 0-3 | 2-2 | 4-4 | 2-3 | 3-0 | 1-4 | 3-1 | 2-0 | 1-4 | 3-0 | 2-4 | 1-2 | 1-0 | 2-3 | 2-3 | 1-1 | 3-2 | 0-1 | 2-2 | |

### Division 3 (North)

|   |   | Pd | Wn | Dw | Ls | GF | GA | Pts |   |
|---|---|---|---|---|---|---|---|---|---|
| 1. | Doncaster Rovers FC (Doncaster) | 42 | 33 | 6 | 3 | 123 | 40 | 72 | P |
| 2. | Rotherham United FC (Rotherham) | 42 | 29 | 6 | 7 | 114 | 53 | 64 | |
| 3. | Chester FC (Chester) | 42 | 25 | 6 | 11 | 95 | 51 | 56 | |
| 4. | Stockport County FC (Stockport) | 42 | 24 | 2 | 16 | 78 | 53 | 50 | |
| 5. | Bradford City AFC (Bradford) | 42 | 20 | 10 | 12 | 62 | 47 | 50 | |
| 6. | Rochdale AFC (Rochdale) | 42 | 19 | 10 | 13 | 80 | 64 | 48 | |
| 7. | Wrexham AFC (Wrexham) | 42 | 17 | 12 | 13 | 65 | 51 | 46 | |
| 8. | Crewe Alexandra FC (Crewe) | 42 | 17 | 8 | 16 | 70 | 74 | 43 | |
| 9. | Barrow AFC (Barrow-in-Furness) | 42 | 17 | 7 | 18 | 54 | 62 | 41 | |
| 10. | Tranmere Rovers FC (Birkenhead) | 42 | 17 | 7 | 18 | 66 | 77 | 41 | |
| 11. | Hull City AFC (Kingston-upon-Hull) | 42 | 16 | 8 | 18 | 49 | 53 | 40 | |
| 12. | Lincoln City FC (Lincoln) | 42 | 17 | 5 | 20 | 86 | 87 | 39 | |
| 13. | Hartlepools United FC (Hartlepool) | 42 | 15 | 9 | 18 | 64 | 73 | 39 | |
| 14. | Gateshead FC (Gateshead) | 42 | 16 | 6 | 20 | 62 | 72 | 38 | |
| 15. | York City FC (York) | 42 | 14 | 9 | 19 | 67 | 81 | 37 | |
| 16. | Carlisle United FC (Carlisle) | 42 | 14 | 9 | 19 | 70 | 93 | 37 | |
| 17. | Darlington FC (Darlington) | 42 | 15 | 6 | 21 | 68 | 80 | 36 | |
| 18. | New Brighton FC (Wallasey) | 42 | 14 | 8 | 20 | 57 | 77 | 36 | |
| 19. | Oldham Athletic AFC (Oldham) | 42 | 12 | 8 | 22 | 55 | 80 | 32 | |
| 20. | Accrington Stanley FC (Accrington) | 42 | 14 | 4 | 24 | 56 | 92 | 32 | |
| 21. | Southport FC (Southport) | 42 | 7 | 11 | 24 | 53 | 85 | 25 | |
| 22. | Halifax Town AFC (Halifax) | 42 | 8 | 6 | 28 | 43 | 92 | 22 | |
| | | 924 | 380 | 164 | 380 | 1537 | 1537 | 924 | |

**Football League Division 3 (S) — 1946-1947 Season**

| | Aldershot | Bournemouth | Brighton | Bristol City | Bristol Rovers | Cardiff City | Crystal Palace | Exeter City | Ipswich Town | Leyton Orient | Mansfield T. | Northampton | Norwich City | Notts County | Port Vale | Q.P.R. | Reading | Southend Utd. | Swindon Town | Torquay United | Walsall | Watford |
|---|---|---|---|---|---|---|---|---|---|---|---|---|---|---|---|---|---|---|---|---|---|---|
| Aldershot FC | | 2-1 | 1-3 | 4-3 | 0-2 | 0-1 | 0-2 | 2-0 | 4-1 | 0-0 | 1-1 | 1-1 | 3-1 | 1-1 | 0-0 | 1-2 | 1-3 | 0-0 | 2-0 | 0-0 | 1-2 | 1-2 |
| Bournemouth & B. Athletic | 2-2 | | 1-0 | 0-0 | 1-3 | 2-0 | 4-0 | 4-1 | 1-1 | 2-0 | 3-1 | 2-1 | 0-1 | 1-2 | 3-0 | 1-1 | 1-0 | 3-1 | 5-2 | 5-0 | 2-3 | 0-1 |
| Brighton & Hove Albion | 2-1 | 1-1 | | 1-1 | 1-2 | 0-4 | 1-0 | 1-6 | 0-0 | 2-1 | 5-0 | 2-2 | 3-3 | 3-2 | 0-0 | 0-2 | 1-4 | 2-1 | 1-4 | 2-0 | 2-0 | 1-1 |
| Bristol City FC | 9-0 | 1-0 | 0-0 | | 4-0 | 2-1 | 3-0 | 2-2 | 1-2 | 3-0 | 5-2 | 2-3 | 2-1 | 1-1 | 3-0 | 1-1 | 5-2 | 2-0 | 3-1 | 5-0 | 1-2 | 1-2 |
| Bristol Rovers FC | 0-0 | 0-2 | 0-0 | 0-3 | | 1-0 | 2-1 | 1-0 | 1-1 | 6-1 | 1-0 | 0-3 | 1-2 | 4-1 | 0-0 | 3-1 | 2-2 | 1-3 | 3-0 | 3-0 | 2-2 | 3-1 |
| Cardiff City AFC | 2-1 | 2-0 | 4-0 | 1-1 | 4-0 | | 0-0 | 5-0 | 3-2 | 1-0 | 5-0 | 6-2 | 6-1 | 2-1 | 1-0 | 2-2 | 3-0 | 3-1 | 5-0 | 1-0 | 3-0 | 1-0 |
| Crystal Palace FC | 0-0 | 0-1 | 1-0 | 0-0 | 2-1 | 1-2 | | 1-0 | 1-1 | 2-0 | 1-1 | 2-2 | 0-1 | 2-1 | 1-2 | 0-0 | 2-1 | 0-3 | 4-1 | 6-1 | 1-1 | 2-0 |
| Exeter City FC | 4-1 | 4-1 | 2-1 | 1-3 | 3-2 | 0-2 | 2-1 | | 0-0 | 3-1 | 1-0 | 1-0 | 3-0 | 2-2 | 1-1 | 3-0 | 1-3 | 1-5 | 1-1 | 1-1 | 2-2 | 1-0 |
| Ipswich Town FC | 1-1 | 2-1 | 1-2 | 3-2 | 0-2 | 0-1 | 1-1 | 2-1 | | 0-0 | 2-1 | 1-2 | 5-0 | 1-2 | 2-1 | 1-1 | 2-0 | 1-0 | 3-1 | 1-1 | 2-1 | 2-0 |
| Leyton Orient FC | 1-3 | 2-3 | 2-1 | 4-1 | 3-0 | 0-1 | 0-1 | 3-1 | 2-2 | | 3-1 | 2-1 | 3-0 | 1-3 | 5-3 | 1-1 | 3-3 | 1-1 | 0-0 | 0-1 | 1-0 | 3-1 |
| Mansfield Town FC | 1-3 | 1-1 | 0-3 | 1-3 | 3-1 | 1-3 | 3-1 | 1-0 | 4-3 | 1-3 | | 3-2 | 4-4 | 1-0 | 0-3 | 0-3 | 2-2 | 0-1 | 1-1 | 1-0 | 1-1 | 2-0 |
| Northampton Town FC | 2-2 | 2-1 | 6-1 | 2-2 | 1-2 | 0-2 | 1-0 | 1-2 | 2-2 | 4-1 | 3-0 | | 1-0 | 2-1 | 1-0 | 4-4 | 4-0 | 2-3 | 4-1 | 0-0 | 0-8 | 4-1 |
| Norwich City FC | 2-3 | 1-6 | 2-3 | 2-2 | 3-3 | 2-1 | 2-3 | 1-3 | 0-1 | 5-0 | 3-1 | 2-3 | | 2-2 | 3-0 | 0-1 | 0-2 | 1-5 | 1-5 | 2-0 | 0-2 | 4-2 |
| Notts County FC | 2-0 | 1-0 | 2-0 | 0-3 | 6-0 | 1-1 | 0-0 | 0-0 | 1-2 | 1-2 | 5-1 | 1-0 | 3-0 | | 3-2 | 1-2 | 1-0 | 0-2 | 0-0 | 0-2 | 3-1 | 4-1 |
| Port Vale FC | 4-2 | 1-0 | 4-1 | 2-1 | 2-1 | 0-4 | 4-2 | 1-2 | 1-0 | 2-1 | 4-1 | 1-1 | 1-3 | 4-1 | | 2-2 | 5-1 | 5-1 | 1-1 | 2-1 | 2-2 | 3-0 |
| Queen's Park Rangers FC | 4-1 | 3-0 | 2-0 | 1-0 | 0-2 | 2-3 | 1-2 | 2-0 | 1-3 | 2-0 | 3-1 | 1-0 | 1-1 | 4-1 | 2-0 | | 2-0 | 1-0 | 7-0 | 0-0 | 1-0 | 2-1 |
| Reading FC | 1-0 | 3-2 | 2-0 | 2-5 | 1-1 | 0-0 | 10-2 | 4-0 | 1-3 | 2-0 | 3-0 | 3-0 | 4-3 | 1-1 | 0-2 | 1-0 | | 7-2 | 3-3 | 2-2 | 1-1 | 2-3 |
| Southend United FC | 2-1 | 2-2 | 0-0 | 4-1 | 2-3 | 0-2 | 2-0 | 2-2 | 1-1 | 0-1 | 4-0 | 3-0 | 3-0 | 1-1 | 1-3 | 0-2 | | | 2-0 | 0-2 | 3-1 | 5-0 |
| Swindon Town FC | 7-0 | 1-3 | 2-2 | 1-1 | 1-0 | 3-2 | 1-0 | 2-0 | 2-1 | 2-0 | 6-1 | 3-1 | 1-1 | 4-2 | 3-2 | 2-2 | 2-1 | | | 2-4 | 4-1 | |
| Torquay United FC | 0-1 | 2-2 | 3-1 | 2-3 | 3-0 | 0-0 | 2-1 | 2-1 | 0-0 | 3-2 | 2-2 | 2-1 | 2-1 | 1-2 | 1-0 | 0-0 | 3-0 | 0-1 | 1-5 | | 2-0 | 2-0 |
| Walsall FC | 2-0 | 3-0 | 1-1 | 3-0 | 2-0 | 2-3 | 3-3 | 2-1 | 4-2 | 3-1 | 0-0 | 2-0 | 2-2 | 2-0 | 4-1 | 0-2 | 2-2 | 2-2 | 0-1 | 2-1 | | 1-3 |
| Watford FC | 4-1 | 0-2 | 1-4 | 2-3 | 1-0 | 2-0 | 1-0 | 3-1 | 2-0 | 3-1 | 1-2 | 1-1 | 4-1 | 2-2 | 2-0 | 0-2 | 2-1 | 4-0 | 1-1 | 3-3 | 0-2 | |

## Division 3 (South)

| | | Pd | Wn | Dw | Ls | GF | GA | Pts | |
|---|---|---|---|---|---|---|---|---|---|
| 1. | Cardiff City AFC (Cardiff) | 42 | 30 | 6 | 6 | 93 | 30 | 66 | P |
| 2. | Queen's Park Rangers FC (London) | 42 | 23 | 11 | 8 | 74 | 40 | 57 | |
| 3. | Bristol City FC (Bristol) | 42 | 20 | 11 | 11 | 94 | 56 | 51 | |
| 4. | Swindon Town FC (Swindon) | 42 | 19 | 11 | 12 | 84 | 73 | 49 | |
| 5. | Walsall FC (Walsall) | 42 | 17 | 12 | 13 | 74 | 59 | 46 | |
| 6. | Ipswich Town FC (Ipswich) | 42 | 16 | 14 | 12 | 61 | 53 | 46 | |
| 7. | Bournemouth & Boscombe Athletic FC (Bournemouth) | 42 | 18 | 8 | 16 | 72 | 54 | 44 | |
| 8. | Southend United FC (Southend-on-Sea) | 42 | 17 | 10 | 15 | 71 | 60 | 44 | |
| 9. | Reading FC (Reading) | 42 | 16 | 11 | 15 | 83 | 74 | 43 | |
| 10. | Port Vale FC (Stoke-on-Trent) | 42 | 17 | 9 | 16 | 68 | 63 | 43 | |
| 11. | Torquay United FC (Torquay) | 42 | 15 | 12 | 15 | 52 | 61 | 42 | |
| 12. | Notts County FC (Nottingham) | 42 | 15 | 10 | 17 | 63 | 63 | 40 | |
| 13. | Northampton Town FC (Northampton) | 42 | 15 | 10 | 17 | 72 | 75 | 40 | |
| 14. | Bristol Rovers FC (Bristol) | 42 | 16 | 8 | 18 | 59 | 69 | 40 | |
| 15. | Exeter City FC (Exeter) | 42 | 15 | 9 | 18 | 60 | 69 | 39 | |
| 16. | Watford FC (Watford) | 42 | 17 | 5 | 20 | 61 | 76 | 39 | |
| 17. | Brighton & Hove Albion FC (Hove) | 42 | 13 | 12 | 17 | 54 | 72 | 38 | |
| 18. | Crystal Palace FC (London) | 42 | 13 | 11 | 18 | 49 | 62 | 37 | |
| 19. | Leyton Orient FC (London) | 42 | 12 | 8 | 22 | 54 | 75 | 32 | |
| 20. | Aldershot FC (Aldershot) | 42 | 10 | 12 | 20 | 48 | 78 | 32 | |
| 21. | Norwich City FC (Norwich) | 42 | 10 | 8 | 24 | 64 | 100 | 28 | |
| 22. | Mansfield Town FC (Mansfield) | 42 | 9 | 10 | 23 | 48 | 96 | 28 | T |
| | | 924 | 353 | 218 | 353 | 1458 | 1458 | 924 | |

T: Mansfield Town FC (Mansfield) were transferred to Division 3 (North) from the next season.

**F.A. CUP FINAL**   (Wembley Stadium, London – 26/04/1947 – 99,000)

CHARLTON ATHLETIC FC (LONDON)        1-0  (aet)                    Burnley FC (Burnley)

*Duffy*

Charlton: Bartram, Croker, Shreeve, Johnson, Phipps, Whittaker, Hurst, Dawson, W.Robinson, Welsh, Duffy.

Burnley: Strong, Woodruff, Mather, Attwell, Brown, Bray, Chew, Morris, Harrison, Potts, Kippax.

## Semi-finals

| Charlton Athletic FC (London) | 4-0 | Newcastle United FC (Newcastle-upon-Tyne) |
| Liverpool FC (Liverpool) | 0-0, 0-1 | Burnley FC (Burnley) |

## Quarter-finals

| Charlton Athletic FC (London) | 2-1 | Preston North End FC (Preston) |
| Liverpool FC (Liverpool) | 4-1 | Birmingham City FC (Birmingham) |
| Middlesbrough FC (Middlesbrough) | 1-1, 0-1 | Burnley FC (Burnley) |
| Sheffield United FC (Sheffield) | 0-2 | Newcastle United FC (Newcastle-upon-Tyne) |

# 1947-48

| Football League Division 1 1947-1948 Season | Arsenal | Aston Villa | Blackburn Rovers | Blackpool | Bolton Wanderers | Burnley | Charlton Athletic | Chelsea | Derby County | Everton | Grimsby Town | Huddersfield Town | Liverpool | Manchester City | Manchester United | Middlesbrough | Portsmouth | Preston North End | Sheffield United | Stoke City | Sunderland | Wolves |
|---|---|---|---|---|---|---|---|---|---|---|---|---|---|---|---|---|---|---|---|---|---|---|
| Arsenal FC | | 1-0 | 2-0 | 2-1 | 2-0 | 3-0 | 6-0 | 0-2 | 1-2 | 1-1 | 8-0 | 2-0 | 1-2 | 1-1 | 2-1 | 7-0 | 0-0 | 3-0 | 3-2 | 3-0 | 3-1 | 5-2 |
| Aston Villa FC | 4-2 | | 3-2 | 0-1 | 3-1 | 2-2 | 2-1 | 3-0 | 2-2 | 3-0 | 2-2 | 2-1 | 2-1 | 1-1 | 0-1 | 1-1 | 2-1 | 4-1 | 2-0 | 1-0 | 2-0 | 1-2 |
| Blackburn Rovers FC | 0-1 | 0-0 | | 1-1 | 4-0 | 1-2 | 0-0 | 1-1 | 3-4 | 2-3 | 4-0 | 1-2 | 1-2 | 1-0 | 1-1 | 1-7 | 1-0 | 2-3 | 4-0 | 2-0 | 4-3 | 1-0 |
| Blackpool FC | 3-0 | 1-0 | 1-0 | | 1-1 | 0-1 | 3-1 | 3-0 | 2-2 | 5-0 | 3-1 | 4-0 | 2-0 | 1-1 | 1-0 | 1-0 | 1-0 | 0-1 | 2-1 | 1-2 | 0-1 | 2-2 |
| Bolton Wanderers FC | 0-1 | 1-0 | 1-0 | 1-0 | | 1-1 | 1-0 | 2-1 | 0-3 | 0-0 | 2-0 | 1-5 | 3-0 | 2-1 | 0-1 | 1-3 | 4-0 | 1-2 | 2-3 | 0-1 | 3-1 | 3-2 |
| Burnley FC | 0-1 | 1-0 | 0-0 | 1-0 | 2-0 | | 0-2 | 1-0 | 0-2 | 0-1 | 4-1 | 2-1 | 3-0 | 1-1 | 0-0 | 3-0 | 3-2 | 1-0 | 0-0 | 4-0 | 4-0 | 1-1 |
| Charlton Athletic FC | 2-4 | 1-1 | 0-1 | 2-0 | 2-1 | 1-1 | | 3-1 | 1-5 | 2-3 | 2-3 | 0-0 | 2-0 | 0-1 | 1-2 | 1-0 | 2-2 | 1-2 | 4-0 | 0-1 | 1-0 | 5-1 |
| Chelsea FC | 0-0 | 4-2 | 1-0 | 2-2 | 1-1 | 0-2 | 3-0 | | 1-0 | 3-1 | 2-3 | 2-4 | 3-1 | 2-2 | 0-4 | 4-2 | 1-0 | 2-0 | 1-0 | 4-1 | 1-1 | 1-1 |
| Derby County FC | 1-0 | 1-3 | 5-0 | 1-0 | 2-1 | 1-1 | 0-3 | 5-1 | | 1-0 | 4-1 | 0-0 | 0-4 | 0-0 | 1-1 | 4-2 | 2-1 | 2-1 | 1-1 | 1-1 | 5-1 | 1-2 |
| Everton FC | 0-2 | 3-0 | 4-1 | 1-2 | 2-0 | 0-3 | 0-1 | 2-3 | 1-3 | | 3-1 | 1-1 | 0-3 | 1-0 | 2-0 | 2-1 | 2-1 | 2-0 | 0-1 | 0-1 | 3-0 | 1-1 |
| Grimsby Town FC | 0-4 | 3-0 | 2-2 | 0-1 | 0-2 | 1-2 | 1-3 | 0-0 | 2-3 | 3-0 | | 3-0 | 0-2 | 1-0 | 1-1 | 0-5 | 1-0 | 1-1 | 0-3 | 0-0 | 1-2 | 0-4 |
| Huddersfield Town AFC | 1-1 | 0-1 | 1-1 | 2-0 | 1-2 | 0-1 | 0-1 | 3-1 | 2-1 | 1-3 | 5-1 | | 1-1 | 1-1 | 0-2 | 2-1 | 0-2 | 1-0 | 2-1 | 0-0 | 2-2 | 0-1 |
| Liverpool FC | 1-3 | 3-3 | 2-1 | 2-0 | 0-0 | 1-1 | 2-3 | 3-0 | 2-2 | 4-0 | 3-1 | 4-0 | | 1-1 | 2-2 | 0-1 | 0-3 | 3-1 | 4-0 | 0-0 | 0-0 | 2-1 |
| Manchester City FC | 0-0 | 0-2 | 1-3 | 1-0 | 0-2 | 4-1 | 4-0 | 1-0 | 3-2 | 0-1 | 3-1 | 1-1 | 2-0 | | 0-0 | 2-0 | 1-0 | 0-3 | 4-3 | 3-0 | 3-0 | 4-3 |
| Manchester United FC | 1-1 | 2-0 | 4-1 | 1-1 | 0-2 | 5-0 | 6-2 | 5-0 | 1-0 | 2-2 | 3-4 | 4-4 | 2-0 | 1-1 | | 2-1 | 3-2 | 1-1 | 0-1 | 1-1 | 3-1 | 3-2 |
| Middlesbrough FC | 1-1 | 1-3 | 1-1 | 4-0 | 4-1 | 1-2 | 1-2 | 0-0 | 1-1 | 0-1 | 4-1 | 1-0 | 3-1 | 2-1 | 2-2 | | 1-2 | 1-1 | 3-0 | 2-1 | 2-2 | 2-4 |
| Portsmouth FC | 0-0 | 2-4 | 1-1 | 1-1 | 2-0 | 0-1 | 3-1 | 2-1 | 0-0 | 3-0 | 4-0 | 3-2 | 1-0 | 1-0 | 1-3 | 6-1 | | 1-0 | 6-0 | 3-0 | 2-2 | 2-0 |
| Preston North End FC | 0-0 | 3-0 | 2-1 | 0-7 | 1-0 | 3-2 | 2-1 | 2-0 | 7-4 | 3-0 | 2-1 | 0-2 | 3-3 | 2-1 | 2-1 | 2-1 | 1-2 | | 3-3 | 2-1 | 2-2 | 1-3 |
| Sheffield United FC | 1-2 | 3-1 | 4-1 | 2-1 | 2-1 | 1-1 | 1-1 | 3-1 | 1-2 | 2-1 | 4-0 | 0-1 | 3-1 | 2-1 | 2-1 | 1-1 | 1-2 | 3-1 | | 3-0 | 3-2 | 2-2 |
| Stoke City FC | 0-0 | 1-2 | 2-1 | 1-1 | 2-0 | 3-0 | 0-1 | 2-0 | 1-0 | 1-1 | 2-1 | 1-1 | 0-2 | 3-0 | 0-2 | 2-4 | 2-1 | 0-1 | 1-1 | | 3-1 | 2-3 |
| Sunderland AFC | 1-1 | 0-0 | 0-1 | 1-0 | 1-2 | 2-0 | 0-1 | 2-3 | 1-1 | 2-0 | 4-2 | 2-0 | 5-1 | 0-1 | 1-0 | 3-0 | 4-1 | 0-2 | 1-1 | 1-0 | | 2-1 |
| Wolverhampton Wanderers FC | 1-1 | 4-1 | 5-1 | 1-1 | 1-0 | 1-1 | 2-0 | 1-0 | 1-0 | 2-4 | 8-1 | 2-1 | 1-2 | 1-0 | 2-6 | 1-3 | 3-1 | 4-2 | 1-1 | 1-2 | 2-1 | |

211

| | Division 1 | Pd | Wn | Dw | Ls | GF | GA | Pts | |
|---|---|---|---|---|---|---|---|---|---|
| 1. | ARSENAL FC (LONDON) | 42 | 23 | 13 | 6 | 81 | 32 | 59 | |
| 2. | Manchester United FC (Manchester) | 42 | 19 | 14 | 9 | 81 | 48 | 52 | |
| 3. | Burnley FC (Burnley) | 42 | 20 | 12 | 10 | 56 | 43 | 52 | |
| 4. | Derby County FC (Derby) | 42 | 19 | 12 | 11 | 77 | 57 | 50 | |
| 5. | Wolverhampton Wanderers FC (Wolverhampton) | 42 | 19 | 9 | 14 | 83 | 70 | 47 | |
| 6. | Aston Villa FC (Birmingham) | 42 | 19 | 9 | 14 | 65 | 57 | 47 | |
| 7. | Preston North End FC (Preston) | 42 | 20 | 7 | 15 | 67 | 68 | 47 | |
| 8. | Portsmouth FC (Portsmouth) | 42 | 19 | 7 | 16 | 68 | 50 | 45 | |
| 9. | Blackpool FC (Blackpool) | 42 | 17 | 10 | 15 | 57 | 41 | 44 | |
| 10. | Manchester City FC (Manchester) | 42 | 15 | 12 | 15 | 52 | 47 | 42 | |
| 11. | Liverpool FC (Liverpool) | 42 | 16 | 10 | 16 | 65 | 61 | 42 | |
| 12. | Sheffield United FC (Sheffield) | 42 | 16 | 10 | 16 | 65 | 70 | 42 | |
| 13. | Charlton Athletic FC (London) | 42 | 17 | 6 | 19 | 57 | 66 | 40 | |
| 14. | Everton FC (Liverpool) | 42 | 17 | 6 | 19 | 52 | 66 | 40 | |
| 15. | Stoke City FC (Stoke-on-Trent) | 42 | 14 | 10 | 18 | 41 | 55 | 38 | |
| 16. | Middlesbrough FC (Middlesbrough) | 42 | 14 | 9 | 19 | 71 | 73 | 37 | |
| 17. | Bolton Wanderers FC (Bolton) | 42 | 16 | 5 | 21 | 46 | 58 | 37 | |
| 18. | Chelsea FC (London) | 42 | 14 | 9 | 19 | 53 | 71 | 37 | |
| 19. | Huddersfield Town AFC (Huddersfield) | 42 | 12 | 12 | 18 | 51 | 60 | 36 | |
| 20. | Sunderland AFC (Sunderland) | 42 | 13 | 10 | 19 | 56 | 67 | 36 | |
| 21. | Blackburn Rovers FC (Blackburn) | 42 | 11 | 10 | 21 | 54 | 72 | 32 | R |
| 22. | Grimsby Town FC (Cleethorpes) | 42 | 8 | 6 | 28 | 45 | 111 | 22 | R |
| | | 924 | 358 | 208 | 358 | 1343 | 1343 | 924 | |

## Top Goalscorer

1) Ronnie ROOKE       (Arsenal FC)    33

| Football League Division 2 1947-1948 Season | Barnsley | Birmingham City | Bradford P.A. | Brentford | Bury | Cardiff City | Chesterfield | Coventry City | Doncaster Rovers | Fulham | Leeds United | Leicester City | Luton Town | Millwall | Newcastle United | Nottingham Forest | Plymouth Argyle | Sheffield Wed. | Southampton | Tottenham H. | W.B.A. | West Ham United |
|---|---|---|---|---|---|---|---|---|---|---|---|---|---|---|---|---|---|---|---|---|---|---|
| Barnsley FC | | 0-1 | 2-2 | 1-1 | 2-1 | 1-2 | 0-3 | 0-1 | 2-0 | 1-2 | 3-0 | 2-0 | 3-0 | 1-0 | 1-1 | 2-2 | 2-1 | 3-1 | 2-1 | 2-1 | 0-1 | 1-1 |
| Birmingham City FC | 2-3 | | 4-3 | 0-0 | 2-0 | 2-0 | 0-0 | 1-1 | 3-0 | 3-1 | 5-1 | 1-0 | 2-1 | 1-0 | 0-0 | 2-1 | 1-1 | 1-0 | 0-0 | 0-0 | 4-0 | 0-1 |
| Bradford Park Avenue | 3-2 | 1-2 | | 1-1 | 5-3 | 0-1 | 1-3 | 2-2 | 4-0 | 3-0 | 3-1 | 0-2 | 2-2 | 4-0 | 0-3 | 3-1 | 3-0 | 2-0 | 1-3 | 0-2 | 3-1 | 4-1 |
| Brentford FC | 3-3 | 1-2 | 2-1 | | 4-1 | 0-0 | 0-3 | 1-4 | 2-0 | 0-2 | 3-0 | 2-2 | 0-3 | 2-1 | 1-0 | 3-1 | 0-0 | 1-0 | 2-2 | 2-0 | 1-0 | 1-1 |
| Bury FC | 1-1 | 1-1 | 0-4 | 2-2 | | 1-2 | 2-0 | 0-0 | 4-2 | 1-0 | 1-1 | 0-2 | 2-2 | 0-0 | 3-5 | 1-0 | 0-0 | 1-2 | 3-0 | 2-0 | 1-2 | 1-2 |
| Cardiff City AFC | 1-0 | 2-0 | 1-0 | 1-0 | 2-2 | | 0-0 | 1-1 | 3-0 | 0-0 | 0-0 | 3-0 | 1-0 | 6-0 | 1-1 | 4-1 | 3-0 | 2-1 | 5-1 | 0-3 | 0-5 | 0-3 |
| Chesterfield FC | 1-1 | 0-3 | 0-1 | 4-0 | 1-2 | 2-2 | | 4-3 | 0-3 | 1-0 | 3-0 | 2-3 | 2-0 | 2-0 | 0-1 | 0-0 | 1-1 | 0-2 | 0-1 | 3-1 | 0-2 | 6-0 |
| Coventry City FC | 3-2 | 0-1 | 5-0 | 3-0 | 0-0 | 1-0 | 3-0 | | 1-0 | 5-2 | 1-2 | 0-1 | 4-1 | 0-1 | 1-1 | 1-1 | 0-0 | 3-1 | 0-1 | 1-1 | 1-0 | 0-1 |
| Doncaster Rovers FC | 1-2 | 0-0 | 3-0 | 0-0 | 1-3 | 2-2 | 1-0 | 0-0 | | 0-1 | 3-0 | 1-1 | 0-2 | 2-2 | 0-3 | 2-0 | 2-0 | 0-1 | 1-1 | 1-1 | 2-1 | 1-0 |
| Fulham FC | 0-1 | 1-1 | 0-0 | 5-0 | 1-1 | 4-1 | 0-0 | 0-2 | 0-0 | | 3-2 | 3-1 | 1-1 | 1-0 | 3-0 | 0-0 | 1-1 | 0-2 | 0-2 | 0-2 | 1-1 | 1-1 |
| Leeds United AFC | 4-1 | 0-1 | 2-0 | 1-1 | 5-1 | 4-0 | 3-0 | 2-1 | 0-0 | 0-1 | | 3-1 | 0-2 | 2-1 | 3-1 | 2-2 | 5-0 | 2-2 | 0-0 | 1-3 | 3-1 | 2-1 |
| Leicester City FC | 4-1 | 0-0 | 1-2 | 2-1 | 2-1 | 2-1 | 1-2 | 2-2 | 3-2 | 0-2 | 2-0 | | 3-2 | 3-0 | 2-2 | 3-1 | 2-1 | 2-3 | 0-0 | 0-3 | 1-1 | 1-3 |
| Luton Town FC | 2-1 | 0-1 | 3-3 | 3-0 | 1-1 | 1-1 | 2-1 | 2-3 | 2-1 | 0-3 | 6-1 | 2-1 | | 1-2 | 2-1 | 2-1 | 0-0 | 1-1 | 0-0 | 2-0 | 1-1 | 0-0 |
| Millwall FC | 3-3 | 0-0 | 0-1 | 0-1 | 1-7 | 0-1 | 0-2 | 6-2 | 1-0 | 1-2 | 1-1 | 0-4 | 3-1 | | 2-1 | 2-0 | 2-0 | 0-0 | 3-0 | 0-0 | 1-1 | 1-1 |
| Newcastle United FC | 1-0 | 1-0 | 2-0 | 1-0 | 1-0 | 4-1 | 2-3 | 0-0 | 2-0 | 1-0 | 4-2 | 2-0 | 4-1 | 1-0 | | 0-2 | 6-1 | 4-2 | 5-0 | 1-0 | 3-1 | 1-0 |
| Nottingham Forest FC | 1-1 | 0-2 | 1-2 | 2-0 | 2-1 | 1-2 | 1-3 | 4-0 | 4-2 | 0-2 | 1-0 | 1-0 | 1-2 | 5-2 | 0-0 | | 1-1 | 0-0 | 1-1 | 1-0 | 3-1 | 2-1 |
| Plymouth Argyle FC | 1-0 | 0-3 | 2-2 | 0-0 | 0-0 | 3-0 | 1-2 | 1-0 | 2-2 | 1-0 | 0-0 | 1-3 | 1-1 | 3-0 | 1-1 | 1-1 | | 0-2 | 3-1 | 1-1 | 2-1 | 1-1 |
| Sheffield Wednesday FC | 5-2 | 0-0 | 3-1 | 1-1 | 2-2 | 2-1 | 1-0 | 1-1 | 2-0 | 2-0 | 3-1 | 1-1 | 1-0 | 3-2 | 1-0 | 2-1 | 1-1 | | 1-2 | 1-0 | 1-2 | 5-3 |
| Southampton FC | 4-1 | 2-0 | 1-2 | 2-1 | 1-0 | 2-2 | 3-0 | 3-1 | 6-1 | 1-0 | 1-2 | 3-1 | 3-1 | 5-1 | 4-2 | 2-1 | 2-3 | 3-1 | | 1-1 | 1-1 | 3-1 |
| Tottenham Hotspur FC | 0-3 | 1-2 | 3-1 | 4-0 | 2-2 | 2-1 | 3-1 | 2-0 | 2-0 | 0-2 | 3-0 | 0-1 | 3-2 | 1-1 | 0-3 | 2-0 | 5-1 | 0-0 | 0-0 | | 1-1 | 2-2 |
| West Bromwich Albion FC | 0-2 | 1-1 | 6-0 | 3-2 | 3-3 | 2-3 | 1-0 | 3-1 | 1-3 | 2-1 | 3-2 | 1-3 | 1-0 | 2-1 | 0-1 | 3-2 | 1-1 | 1-1 | 1-0 | 1-0 | | 1-2 |
| West Ham United FC | 2-1 | 0-0 | 0-0 | 0-1 | 2-0 | 4-2 | 4-0 | 1-0 | 2-1 | 3-0 | 2-1 | 1-1 | 0-0 | 1-1 | 0-2 | 2-1 | 1-1 | 1-4 | 2-0 | 1-1 | 0-2 | |

## Division 2

| | | Pd | Wn | Dw | Ls | GF | GA | Pts | |
|---|---|---|---|---|---|---|---|---|---|
| 1. | Birmingham City FC (Birmingham) | 42 | 22 | 15 | 5 | 55 | 24 | 59 | P |
| 2. | Newcastle United FC (Newcastle-upon-Tyne) | 42 | 24 | 8 | 10 | 72 | 41 | 56 | P |
| 3. | Southampton FC (Southampton) | 42 | 21 | 10 | 11 | 71 | 53 | 52 | |
| 4. | Sheffield Wednesday FC (Sheffield) | 42 | 20 | 11 | 11 | 66 | 53 | 51 | |
| 5. | Cardiff City AFC (Cardiff) | 42 | 18 | 11 | 13 | 61 | 58 | 47 | |
| 6. | West Ham United FC (London) | 42 | 16 | 14 | 12 | 55 | 53 | 46 | |
| 7. | West Bromwich Albion FC (West Bromwich) | 42 | 18 | 9 | 15 | 63 | 58 | 45 | |
| 8. | Tottenham Hotspur FC (London) | 42 | 15 | 14 | 13 | 56 | 43 | 44 | |
| 9. | Leicester City FC (Leicester) | 42 | 16 | 11 | 15 | 60 | 57 | 43 | |
| 10. | Coventry City FC (Coventry) | 42 | 14 | 13 | 15 | 59 | 52 | 41 | |
| 11. | Fulham FC (London) | 42 | 15 | 10 | 17 | 47 | 46 | 40 | |
| 12. | Barnsley FC (Barnsley) | 42 | 15 | 10 | 17 | 62 | 64 | 40 | |
| 13. | Luton Town FC (Luton) | 42 | 14 | 12 | 16 | 56 | 59 | 40 | |
| 14. | Bradford Park Avenue FC (Bradford) | 42 | 16 | 8 | 18 | 68 | 72 | 40 | |
| 15. | Brentford FC (London) | 42 | 13 | 14 | 15 | 44 | 61 | 40 | |
| 16. | Chesterfield FC (Chesterfield) | 42 | 16 | 7 | 19 | 54 | 55 | 39 | |
| 17. | Plymouth Argyle FC (Plymouth) | 42 | 9 | 20 | 13 | 40 | 58 | 38 | |
| 18. | Leeds United AFC (Leeds) | 42 | 14 | 8 | 20 | 62 | 72 | 36 | |
| 19. | Nottingham Forest FC (Nottingham) | 42 | 12 | 11 | 19 | 54 | 60 | 35 | |
| 20. | Bury FC (Bury) | 42 | 9 | 16 | 17 | 58 | 68 | 34 | |
| 21. | Doncaster Rovers FC (Doncaster) | 42 | 9 | 11 | 22 | 40 | 66 | 29 | R |
| 22. | Millwall FC (London) | 42 | 9 | 11 | 22 | 44 | 74 | 29 | R |
| | | 924 | 335 | 254 | 335 | 1247 | 1247 | 924 | |

**Football League Division 3 (N) 1947-1948 Season**

| | Accrington Stanley | Barrow | Bradford City | Carlisle United | Chester | Crewe Alexandra | Darlington | Gateshead | Halifax Town | Hartlepools United | Hull City | Lincoln City | Mansfield Town | New Brighton | Oldham Athletic | Rochdale | Rotherham United | Southport | Stockport County | Tranmere Rovers | Wrexham | York City |
|---|---|---|---|---|---|---|---|---|---|---|---|---|---|---|---|---|---|---|---|---|---|---|
| Accrington Stanley FC | | 0-1 | 2-0 | 1-2 | 1-0 | 2-1 | 3-0 | 1-0 | 2-0 | 4-2 | 2-4 | 2-1 | 1-0 | 5-3 | 2-3 | 1-2 | 0-1 | 0-0 | 5-2 | 1-0 | 0-2 | 1-0 |
| Barrow AFC | 3-0 | | 0-1 | 2-0 | 1-0 | 2-0 | 0-0 | 1-2 | 2-1 | 1-2 | 0-2 | 0-1 | 1-0 | 1-1 | 2-4 | 0-1 | 1-3 | 2-0 | 0-0 | 3-0 | 1-1 | 1-0 |
| Bradford City AFC | 1-2 | 1-1 | | 1-1 | 3-2 | 1-2 | 4-0 | 2-2 | 2-1 | 3-1 | 2-0 | 2-4 | 0-1 | 1-1 | 0-2 | 4-0 | 0-1 | 4-2 | 1-0 | 4-1 | 1-0 | 1-3 |
| Carlisle United FC | 2-3 | 1-2 | 1-2 | | 2-0 | 5-2 | 4-1 | 1-1 | 5-2 | 1-1 | 0-0 | 2-5 | 3-1 | 2-1 | 4-1 | 5-0 | 0-3 | 2-3 | 4-0 | 4-3 | 1-2 | 1-1 |
| Chester FC | 1-0 | 0-0 | 2-1 | 4-1 | | 4-2 | 1-1 | 2-3 | 0-0 | 2-0 | 4-1 | 1-1 | 1-2 | 4-2 | 2-1 | 2-1 | 2-3 | 0-0 | 2-2 | 4-0 | 4-1 | 2-3 |
| Crewe Alexandra FC | 0-0 | 1-2 | 3-2 | 0-2 | 1-0 | | 4-1 | 0-1 | 0-1 | 2-0 | 3-1 | 3-0 | 0-0 | 4-0 | 2-2 | 2-1 | 3-3 | 4-1 | 4-2 | 3-2 | 1-0 | 1-3 |
| Darlington FC | 3-1 | 2-2 | 1-1 | 4-3 | 1-1 | 0-1 | | 1-1 | 4-1 | 1-0 | 2-0 | 1-3 | 1-2 | 3-1 | 0-6 | 0-0 | 1-1 | 1-3 | 0-0 | 0-2 | 3-1 | 1-1 |
| Gateshead FC | 4-2 | 0-2 | 2-2 | 1-3 | 2-1 | 2-0 | 1-2 | | 3-0 | 7-0 | 0-1 | 3-2 | 2-1 | 3-1 | 3-5 | 5-0 | 1-1 | 3-2 | 1-1 | 3-0 | 2-2 | 0-0 |
| Halifax Town AFC | 3-3 | 1-1 | 0-0 | 2-1 | 1-1 | 4-1 | 1-1 | 0-0 | | 0-0 | 0-2 | 0-1 | 1-1 | 1-2 | 1-5 | 2-3 | 2-1 | 0-0 | 4-0 | 2-2 | 0-1 | 0-1 |
| Hartlepools United FC | 4-0 | 0-3 | 0-2 | 1-1 | 2-1 | 0-1 | 3-0 | 3-2 | 1-1 | | 3-1 | 1-2 | 1-0 | 1-0 | 3-1 | 4-1 | 2-2 | 2-0 | 0-0 | 1-1 | 0-2 | 2-2 |
| Hull City AFC | 4-2 | 0-0 | 2-1 | 3-1 | 2-1 | 2-1 | 0-3 | 2-3 | 1-2 | 5-0 | | 0-1 | 1-1 | 3-0 | 1-0 | 0-0 | 5-3 | 1-0 | 1-0 | 3-0 | 1-1 | 1-1 |
| Lincoln City FC | 2-3 | 2-1 | 3-0 | 3-0 | 4-2 | 0-0 | 3-1 | 3-0 | 3-1 | 5-0 | 2-3 | | 0-0 | 1-2 | 0-2 | 3-0 | 3-1 | 3-1 | 3-0 | 2-0 | 2-1 | 0-0 |
| Mansfield Town FC | 1-0 | 1-0 | 1-1 | 2-3 | 2-1 | 3-1 | 4-0 | 1-2 | 3-1 | 3-2 | 1-1 | 0-2 | | 5-0 | 1-1 | 1-1 | 2-1 | 2-0 | 1-2 | 1-3 | 1-0 | 1-2 |
| New Brighton FC | 0-1 | 1-1 | 0-2 | 1-3 | 0-1 | 1-2 | 2-1 | 1-2 | 1-0 | 1-2 | 1-0 | 0-1 | 2-2 | | 2-2 | 0-0 | 1-2 | 2-2 | 1-0 | 0-2 | 1-1 | 2-1 |
| Oldham Athletic AFC | 1-0 | 2-1 | 3-0 | 2-1 | 3-1 | 0-0 | 3-3 | 0-1 | 1-1 | 0-2 | 0-0 | 0-0 | 1-1 | 3-0 | | 1-1 | 1-5 | 1-1 | 0-0 | 0-1 | 1-4 | 2-2 |
| Rochdale AFC | 1-3 | 2-2 | 2-0 | 2-1 | 2-2 | 1-2 | 2-1 | 2-1 | 2-1 | 0-2 | 1-0 | 1-1 | 1-2 | 1-0 | 2-0 | | 1-0 | 2-1 | 1-2 | 1-1 | 2-1 | 3-0 |
| Rotherham United FC | 1-0 | 0-0 | 4-1 | 7-2 | 2-1 | 5-1 | 0-0 | 0-0 | 3-0 | 3-2 | 0-0 | 0-2 | 2-1 | 6-1 | 4-1 | 4-1 | | 0-2 | 4-1 | 2-0 | 6-0 | 3-2 |
| Southport FC | 1-1 | 1-2 | 1-2 | 0-4 | 3-0 | 2-0 | 2-0 | 2-1 | 2-0 | 2-0 | 1-2 | 1-1 | 1-1 | 4-0 | 4-0 | 2-2 | 1-2 | | 0-4 | 1-4 | 1-0 | 2-1 |
| Stockport County FC | 1-1 | 2-3 | 3-3 | 2-3 | 4-1 | 2-1 | 1-3 | 1-1 | 2-1 | 2-0 | 0-1 | 5-0 | 1-2 | 3-0 | 4-0 | 2-2 | 0-3 | | | 2-0 | 0-1 | 4-2 |
| Tranmere Rovers FC | 0-1 | 1-0 | 2-1 | 0-3 | 2-3 | 2-0 | 0-1 | 3-0 | 0-1 | 1-0 | 2-1 | 1-4 | 0-1 | 1-0 | 1-0 | 4-1 | 0-1 | 2-2 | 2-3 | | 2-3 | 4-2 |
| Wrexham AFC | 1-1 | 3-1 | 4-2 | 2-1 | 2-1 | 1-1 | 1-2 | 0-3 | 6-3 | 3-1 | 1-0 | 3-0 | 2-1 | 0-0 | 1-2 | 5-1 | 1-3 | 2-0 | 2-0 | 6-0 | | 3-0 |
| York City FC | 1-2 | 0-0 | 3-3 | 2-2 | 2-0 | 0-1 | 0-2 | 3-1 | 6-0 | 4-0 | 2-2 | 0-1 | 1-2 | 3-1 | 1-0 | 0-0 | 2-0 | 3-3 | 3-2 | 1-2 | 1-1 | |

## Division 3 (North)

| | | Pd | Wn | Dw | Ls | GF | GA | Pts | |
|---|---|---|---|---|---|---|---|---|---|
| 1. | Lincoln City FC (Lincoln) | 42 | 26 | 8 | 8 | 81 | 40 | 60 | P |
| 2. | Rotherham United FC (Rotherham) | 42 | 25 | 9 | 8 | 95 | 49 | 59 | |
| 3. | Wrexham AFC (Wrexham) | 42 | 21 | 8 | 13 | 74 | 54 | 50 | |
| 4. | Gateshead FC (Gateshead) | 42 | 19 | 11 | 12 | 75 | 57 | 49 | |
| 5. | Hull City AFC (Kingston-upon-Hull) | 42 | 18 | 11 | 13 | 59 | 48 | 47 | |
| 6. | Accrington Stanley FC (Accrington) | 42 | 20 | 6 | 16 | 62 | 59 | 46 | |
| 7. | Barrow AFC (Barrow-in-Furness) | 42 | 16 | 13 | 13 | 49 | 40 | 45 | |
| 8. | Mansfield Town FC (Mansfield) | 42 | 17 | 11 | 14 | 57 | 51 | 45 | |
| 9. | Carlisle United FC (Carlisle) | 42 | 18 | 7 | 17 | 88 | 77 | 43 | |
| 10. | Crewe Alexandra FC (Crewe) | 42 | 18 | 7 | 17 | 61 | 63 | 43 | |
| 11. | Oldham Athletic AFC (Oldham) | 42 | 14 | 13 | 15 | 63 | 64 | 41 | |
| 12. | Rochdale AFC (Rochdale) | 42 | 15 | 11 | 16 | 48 | 72 | 41 | |
| 13. | York City FC (York) | 42 | 13 | 14 | 15 | 65 | 60 | 40 | |
| 14. | Bradford City AFC (Bradford) | 42 | 15 | 10 | 17 | 65 | 66 | 40 | |
| 15. | Southport FC (Southport) | 42 | 14 | 11 | 17 | 60 | 63 | 39 | |
| 16. | Darlington FC (Darlington) | 42 | 13 | 13 | 16 | 54 | 70 | 39 | |
| 17. | Stockport County FC (Stockport) | 42 | 13 | 12 | 17 | 63 | 67 | 38 | |
| 18. | Tranmere Rovers FC (Birkenhead) | 42 | 16 | 4 | 22 | 54 | 72 | 36 | |
| 19. | Hartlepools United FC (Hartlepool) | 42 | 14 | 8 | 20 | 51 | 73 | 36 | |
| 20. | Chester FC (Chester) | 42 | 13 | 9 | 20 | 64 | 67 | 35 | |
| 21. | Halifax Town AFC (Halifax) | 42 | 7 | 13 | 22 | 43 | 76 | 27 | |
| 22. | New Brighton FC (Wallasey) | 42 | 8 | 9 | 25 | 38 | 81 | 25 | |
| | | 924 | 353 | 218 | 353 | 1369 | 1369 | 924 | |

| Football League Division 3 (S) 1947-1948 Season | Aldershot | Bournemouth | Brighton | Bristol City | Bristol Rovers | Crystal Palace | Exeter City | Ipswich Town | Leyton Orient | Newport County | Northampton | Norwich City | Notts County | Port Vale | Q.P.R. | Reading | Southend United | Swansea Town | Swindon Town | Torquay United | Walsall | Watford |
|---|---|---|---|---|---|---|---|---|---|---|---|---|---|---|---|---|---|---|---|---|---|---|
| Aldershot FC | █ | 0-3 | 1-1 | 1-1 | 2-0 | 2-0 | 0-0 | 0-1 | 0-0 | 1-2 | 1-1 | 2-2 | 1-0 | 1-1 | 1-4 | 1-2 | 1-1 | 0-3 | 2-2 | 1-0 | 3-1 | 1-1 |
| Bournemouth & B. Athletic | 1-1 | █ | 4-1 | 2-0 | 3-0 | 0-0 | 2-1 | 4-0 | 1-1 | 5-0 | 2-0 | 1-3 | 2-0 | 3-0 | 0-1 | 2-0 | 0-1 | 1-0 | 1-0 | 6-2 | 1-1 | 1-1 |
| Brighton & Hove Albion | 1-1 | 0-2 | █ | 0-2 | 3-1 | 1-1 | 0-1 | 4-1 | 0-0 | 3-0 | 2-3 | 2-0 | 1-3 | 2-2 | 0-5 | 2-0 | 1-0 | 0-1 | 1-0 | 2-1 | 0-4 | 1-3 |
| Bristol City FC | 2-4 | 0-4 | 1-2 | █ | 5-2 | 2-0 | 1-1 | 4-0 | 6-0 | 1-0 | 1-1 | 6-0 | 1-0 | 2-1 | 2-1 | 0-2 | 6-0 | 3-2 | 2-2 | 1-2 | 0-0 | 1-2 |
| Bristol Rovers FC | 7-1 | 1-2 | 4-1 | 0-2 | █ | 1-1 | 2-2 | 2-0 | 0-2 | 2-3 | 1-2 | 2-3 | 2-0 | 2-1 | 0-1 | 2-3 | 1-2 | 2-2 | 3-1 | 0-2 | 2-3 | 3-0 |
| Crystal Palace FC | 1-0 | 2-0 | 0-0 | 4-0 | 0-0 | █ | 1-2 | 2-1 | 2-0 | 2-1 | 1-0 | 2-0 | 1-1 | 2-0 | 0-1 | 2-1 | 0-0 | 4-0 | 1-1 | 2-1 | 2-3 | 1-2 |
| Exeter City FC | 4-0 | 1-1 | 1-0 | 3-1 | 4-0 | 2-0 | █ | 1-0 | 1-1 | 4-4 | 1-1 | 2-0 | 0-1 | 0-0 | 1-2 | 1-0 | 0-0 | 3-1 | 2-1 | 0-2 | 0-6 | 3-1 |
| Ipswich Town FC | 2-0 | 1-1 | 4-0 | 1-0 | 0-4 | 3-0 | 2-0 | █ | 1-0 | 3-0 | 5-2 | 1-2 | 2-0 | 2-1 | 1-0 | 4-0 | 3-2 | 0-1 | 2-1 | 3-1 | 1-3 |  |
| Leyton Orient FC | 0-3 | 2-0 | 2-1 | 0-2 | 2-4 | 1-1 | 2-4 | 1-1 | █ | 2-2 | 5-0 | 2-1 | 2-1 | 0-0 | 1-3 | 2-2 | 2-0 | 1-0 | 0-3 | 4-1 | 0-1 | 0-2 |
| Newport County AFC | 2-2 | 2-2 | 1-1 | 1-0 | 2-2 | 3-1 | 3-0 | 3-1 | 3-2 | █ | 1-2 | 1-1 | 3-1 | 0-0 | 0-0 | 2-0 | 1-5 | 1-1 | 2-0 | 0-1 | 4-2 | 3-4 |
| Northampton Town FC | 2-1 | 3-6 | 4-0 | 0-4 | 1-3 | 3-1 | 3-1 | 4-2 | 1-1 | 1-1 | █ | 1-0 | 1-2 | 4-1 | 1-1 | 1-1 | 2-0 | 0-1 | 0-0 | 1-0 | 1-0 | 0-1 |
| Norwich City FC | 0-1 | 0-1 | 2-2 | 2-3 | 1-5 | 3-1 | 3-0 | 1-5 | 3-0 | 1-2 | 2-3 | █ | 0-1 | 1-2 | 5-2 | 2-1 | 1-0 | 1-2 | 2-2 | 1-1 | 1-0 | 1-0 |
| Notts County FC | 0-2 | 1-2 | 4-0 | 3-1 | 4-2 | 1-0 | 1-1 | 0-1 | 1-4 | 4-1 | 3-2 | 1-2 | █ | 2-1 | 1-1 | 5-1 | 2-1 | 5-1 | 2-1 | 0-0 | 1-0 | 3-3 |
| Port Vale FC | 6-4 | 2-1 | 5-0 | 1-0 | 1-1 | 4-1 | 1-1 | 4-1 | 3-0 | 4-1 | 1-0 | 2-0 | 1-2 | █ | 0-2 | 1-0 | 2-1 | 1-1 | 1-0 | 1-1 | 0-1 | 7-0 |
| Queen's Park Rangers FC | 0-0 | 1-0 | 2-0 | 2-0 | 5-2 | 1-0 | 3-1 | 2-0 | 1-2 | 1-0 | 2-0 | 3-1 | 4-1 | 2-1 | █ | 2-0 | 3-2 | 0-0 | 0-2 | 3-3 | 2-1 | 5-1 |
| Reading FC | 0-0 | 3-0 | 1-0 | 2-7 | 0-0 | 0-0 | 2-1 | 1-2 | 6-2 | 0-0 | 1-1 | 2-4 | 3-1 | 2-0 | 3-2 | █ | 1-3 | 4-1 | 2-3 | 2-0 | 0-1 | 2-0 |
| Southend United FC | 4-0 | 0-2 | 2-2 | 4-0 | 1-0 | 2-1 | 2-0 | 3-2 | 2-1 | 1-0 | 3-1 | 0-0 | 1-2 | 1-1 | 0-0 | 1-1 | █ | 1-1 | 1-0 | 1-0 | 1-1 | 1-1 |
| Swansea Town AFC | 2-1 | 3-2 | 0-0 | 6-1 | 0-1 | 2-0 | 2-0 | 1-1 | 5-0 | 3-0 | 5-1 | 3-2 | 2-0 | 3-1 | 1-1 | 3-0 |  | █ | 1-0 | 1-1 | 1-1 | 1-1 |
| Swindon Town FC | 1-0 | 0-1 | 1-1 | 2-2 | 1-1 | 0-0 | 3-2 | 0-1 | 0-1 | 1-2 | 0-0 | 3-2 | 1-1 | 1-0 | 0-0 | 1-1 | 0-0 | 1-0 | █ | 2-2 | 0-3 | 3-0 |
| Torquay United FC | 2-0 | 0-1 | 1-2 | 2-3 | 1-2 | 3-3 | 1-2 | 3-0 | 0-1 | 4-1 | 4-2 | 1-1 | 2-2 | 5-0 | 1-1 | 1-2 | 4-1 | 1-1 | 1-1 | █ | 3-2 | 0-1 |
| Walsall FC | 3-0 | 0-0 | 0-0 | 2-0 | 2-0 | 1-1 | 4-0 | 1-2 | 3-1 | 1-1 | 2-0 | 1-2 | 0-1 | 1-2 | 0-1 | 0-0 | 6-0 | 2-1 | 1-0 | 1-0 | █ | 2-0 |
| Watford FC | 1-2 | 0-3 | 2-3 | 1-1 | 3-2 | 0-5 | 3-1 | 2-3 | 2-1 | 1-2 | 1-1 | 2-2 | 1-3 | 1-1 | 0-1 | 0-1 | 2-2 | 4-1 | 1-0 | 2-2 | 2-0 | █ |

## Division 3 (South)

| | | Pd | Wn | Dw | Ls | GF | GA | Pts | |
|---|---|---|---|---|---|---|---|---|---|
| 1. | Queen's Park Rangers FC (London) | 42 | 26 | 9 | 7 | 74 | 37 | 61 | P |
| 2. | Bournemouth & Boscombe Athletic FC (Bournemouth) | 42 | 24 | 9 | 9 | 76 | 35 | 57 | |
| 3. | Walsall FC (Walsall) | 42 | 21 | 9 | 12 | 70 | 40 | 51 | |
| 4. | Ipswich Town FC (Ipswich) | 42 | 23 | 3 | 16 | 67 | 61 | 49 | |
| 5. | Swansea Town AFC (Swansea) | 42 | 18 | 12 | 12 | 70 | 52 | 48 | |
| 6. | Notts County FC (Nottingham) | 42 | 19 | 8 | 15 | 68 | 59 | 46 | |
| 7. | Bristol City FC (Bristol) | 42 | 18 | 7 | 17 | 77 | 65 | 43 | |
| 8. | Port Vale FC (Stoke-on-Trent) | 42 | 16 | 11 | 15 | 63 | 54 | 43 | |
| 9. | Southend United FC (Southend-on-Sea) | 42 | 15 | 13 | 14 | 51 | 58 | 43 | |
| 10. | Reading FC (Reading) | 42 | 15 | 11 | 16 | 56 | 58 | 41 | |
| 11. | Exeter City FC (Exeter) | 42 | 15 | 11 | 16 | 55 | 63 | 41 | |
| 12. | Newport County AFC (Newport) | 42 | 14 | 13 | 15 | 61 | 73 | 41 | |
| 13. | Crystal Palace FC (London) | 42 | 13 | 13 | 16 | 49 | 49 | 39 | |
| 14. | Northampton Town FC (Northampton) | 42 | 14 | 11 | 17 | 58 | 72 | 39 | |
| 15. | Watford FC (Watford) | 42 | 14 | 10 | 18 | 57 | 79 | 38 | |
| 16. | Swindon Town FC (Swindon) | 42 | 10 | 16 | 16 | 41 | 46 | 36 | |
| 17. | Leyton Orient FC (London) | 42 | 13 | 10 | 19 | 51 | 73 | 36 | |
| 18. | Torquay United FC (Torquay) | 42 | 11 | 13 | 18 | 63 | 62 | 35 | |
| 19. | Aldershot FC (Aldershot) | 42 | 10 | 15 | 17 | 45 | 67 | 35 | |
| 20. | Bristol Rovers FC (Bristol) | 42 | 13 | 8 | 21 | 71 | 75 | 34 | |
| 21. | Norwich City FC (Norwich) | 42 | 13 | 8 | 21 | 61 | 76 | 34 | |
| 22. | Brighton & Hove Albion FC (Hove) | 42 | 11 | 12 | 19 | 43 | 73 | 34 | |
| | | 924 | 346 | 232 | 346 | 1327 | 1327 | 924 | |

## F.A. CUP FINAL   (Wembley Stadium, London – 24/04/1948 – 99,000)

**MANCHESTER UNITED FC (MANCHESTER)   4-2**      Blackpool FC (Blackpool)

*Rowley 2, Pearson, Anderson*      *Shimwell pen., Mortensen*

Man. United: Crompton, Carey, Aston, Anderson, Chilton, Cockburn, Delaney, Morris, Rowley, Pearson, Mitten.

Blackburn: Robinson, Shimwell, Crosland, Johnston, Hayward, Kelly, Matthews, Munro, Mortensen, Dick, Rickett.

## Semi-finals

| | | |
|---|---|---|
| Blackpool FC (Blackpool) | 3-1 | Tottenham Hotspur FC (London) |
| Derby County FC (Derby) | 1-3 | Manchester United FC (Manchester) |

## Quarter-finals

| | | |
|---|---|---|
| Fulham FC (London) | 0-2 | Blackpool FC (Blackpool) |
| Manchester United FC (Manchester) | 4-1 | Preston North End FC (Preston) |
| Queen's Park Rangers FC (London) | 1-1, 0-5 | Derby County FC (Derby) |
| Southampton FC (Southampton) | 0-1 | Tottenham Hotspur FC (London) |

# 1948-49

Football League Division 1 1948-1949 Season

| | Arsenal | Aston Villa | Birmingham City | Blackpool | Bolton Wanderers | Burnley | Charlton Athletic | Chelsea | Derby County | Everton | Huddersfield Town | Liverpool | Manchester City | Manchester United | Middlesbrough | Newcastle United | Portsmouth | Preston North End | Sheffield United | Stoke City | Sunderland | Wolves |
|---|---|---|---|---|---|---|---|---|---|---|---|---|---|---|---|---|---|---|---|---|---|---|
| Arsenal FC | | 3-1 | 2-0 | 2-0 | 5-0 | 3-1 | 2-0 | 1-2 | 3-3 | 5-0 | 3-0 | 1-1 | 1-1 | 0-1 | 1-1 | 0-1 | 3-2 | 0-0 | 5-3 | 3-0 | 5-0 | 3-1 |
| Aston Villa FC | 1-0 | | 0-3 | 2-5 | 2-4 | 3-1 | 4-3 | 1-1 | 1-1 | 0-1 | 3-3 | 2-1 | 1-0 | 2-1 | 1-1 | 2-4 | 1-1 | 2-0 | 4-3 | 2-1 | 1-1 | 5-1 |
| Birmingham City FC | 1-1 | 0-1 | | 1-1 | 0-0 | 0-0 | 1-0 | 1-0 | 0-1 | 1-0 | 1-0 | 0-1 | 4-1 | 1-0 | 0-0 | 2-0 | 3-0 | 1-0 | 1-2 | 2-1 | 0-0 | 0-1 |
| Blackpool FC | 1-1 | 1-0 | 1-0 | | 1-0 | 1-1 | 0-1 | 2-1 | 1-1 | 3-0 | 0-0 | 1-0 | 1-1 | 0-3 | 1-1 | 1-3 | 1-0 | 2-2 | 0-3 | 2-1 | 3-3 | 1-3 |
| Bolton Wanderers FC | 1-0 | 3-0 | 0-0 | 2-2 | | 0-1 | 2-2 | 1-1 | 4-0 | 1-0 | 1-2 | 0-3 | 5-1 | 0-1 | 4-1 | 1-5 | 1-2 | 5-3 | 6-1 | 2-1 | 4-1 | 0-5 |
| Burnley FC | 1-1 | 1-1 | 2-2 | 2-0 | 3-0 | | 0-0 | 3-0 | 3-1 | 1-0 | 1-2 | 0-2 | 1-0 | 0-2 | 0-0 | 0-3 | 2-1 | 1-0 | 2-0 | 1-3 | 3-1 | 0-0 |
| Charlton Athletic FC | 4-3 | 0-2 | 1-1 | 0-0 | 1-4 | 3-1 | | 1-1 | 1-5 | 3-1 | 3-1 | 2-1 | 3-2 | 2-3 | 2-0 | 0-0 | 0-1 | 0-0 | 2-1 | 4-1 | 4-0 | 2-3 |
| Chelsea FC | 0-1 | 2-1 | 2-0 | 3-3 | 2-2 | 1-0 | 2-2 | | 0-3 | 6-0 | 5-0 | 2-1 | 1-1 | 1-1 | 1-0 | 2-3 | 1-2 | 5-3 | 1-0 | 2-2 | 0-1 | 4-1 |
| Derby County FC | 2-1 | 2-2 | 1-0 | 3-1 | 1-0 | 2-0 | 5-1 | 2-1 | | 3-2 | 4-1 | 3-0 | 2-0 | 1-3 | 2-0 | 2-4 | 1-0 | 1-0 | 2-1 | 4-1 | 2-2 | 3-2 |
| Everton FC | 0-0 | 1-3 | 0-5 | 5-0 | 1-0 | 2-1 | 1-1 | 2-1 | 0-1 | | 2-0 | 1-1 | 0-0 | 2-0 | 3-1 | 3-3 | 0-5 | 4-1 | 2-1 | 2-1 | 1-0 | 1-0 |
| Huddersfield Town AFC | 1-1 | 0-1 | 0-0 | 1-0 | 0-2 | 1-0 | 1-2 | 3-4 | 1-1 | 1-1 | | 0-4 | 1-0 | 2-1 | 0-0 | 0-2 | 0-0 | 0-2 | 0-0 | 1-3 | 2-0 | 4-0 |
| Liverpool FC | 0-1 | 1-1 | 1-0 | 1-1 | 0-1 | 1-1 | 1-1 | 1-1 | 0-0 | 0-0 | 0-1 | | 0-1 | 0-2 | 4-0 | 1-1 | 3-1 | 0-2 | 3-3 | 4-0 | 4-0 | 1-0 |
| Manchester City FC | 0-3 | 4-1 | 1-0 | 1-1 | 1-0 | 2-2 | 0-1 | 1-0 | 2-1 | 0-0 | 3-1 | 2-4 | | 0-0 | 1-0 | 1-1 | 3-2 | 1-0 | 0-0 | 1-1 | 3-3 | |
| Manchester United FC | 2-0 | 3-1 | 3-0 | 3-4 | 3-0 | 1-1 | 1-1 | 1-1 | 1-2 | 2-0 | 4-1 | 0-0 | 0-0 | | 1-0 | 1-1 | 3-2 | 2-2 | 3-2 | 3-0 | 1-2 | 2-0 |
| Middlesbrough FC | 0-1 | 6-0 | 1-1 | 1-0 | 5-0 | 4-1 | 2-4 | 1-1 | 1-0 | 1-0 | 1-0 | 0-1 | 0-1 | 1-4 | | 3-2 | 1-1 | 1-0 | 3-1 | 1-1 | 0-0 | 4-4 |
| Newcastle United FC | 3-2 | 2-1 | 1-0 | 3-1 | 1-1 | 1-1 | 2-0 | 2-2 | 3-0 | 1-0 | 2-4 | 1-0 | 0-0 | 0-1 | 1-0 | | 0-5 | 2-5 | 3-2 | 2-2 | 2-1 | 3-1 |
| Portsmouth FC | 4-1 | 3-0 | 3-1 | 1-1 | 0-0 | 1-0 | 3-1 | 5-2 | 1-0 | 4-0 | 2-0 | 3-2 | 3-1 | 2-2 | 1-0 | 1-0 | | 3-1 | 3-0 | 1-0 | 3-0 | 5-0 |
| Preston North End FC | 1-1 | 0-1 | 0-0 | 1-3 | 1-1 | 0-3 | 2-3 | 3-2 | 0-0 | 3-1 | 2-0 | 3-2 | 1-3 | 1-6 | 6-1 | 2-1 | 2-2 | | 4-1 | 2-1 | 1-3 | 1-1 |
| Sheffield United FC | 1-1 | 0-1 | 4-0 | 3-2 | 1-1 | 0-0 | 2-0 | 2-1 | 3-1 | 1-1 | 0-0 | 1-2 | 0-2 | 2-2 | 1-0 | 0-0 | 3-1 | 3-2 | | 2-2 | 2-5 | 1-1 |
| Stoke City FC | 1-0 | 4-2 | 2-1 | 3-2 | 4-0 | 2-1 | 2-2 | 4-3 | 4-2 | 1-0 | 1-2 | 3-0 | 2-3 | 2-1 | 3-0 | 1-1 | 0-1 | 2-0 | 0-1 | | 0-0 | 2-1 |
| Sunderland AFC | 1-1 | 0-0 | 1-1 | 2-2 | 2-0 | 0-0 | 1-0 | 3-0 | 2-1 | 1-1 | 0-1 | 0-2 | 3-0 | 2-1 | 1-0 | 1-1 | 1-4 | 0-0 | 2-0 | 1-1 | | 3-3 |
| Wolverhampton Wanderers FC | 1-3 | 4-0 | 2-2 | 2-1 | 2-0 | 3-0 | 2-0 | 1-1 | 2-2 | 1-0 | 7-1 | 0-0 | 1-1 | 3-2 | 0-3 | 3-0 | 3-0 | 2-1 | 6-0 | 3-1 | 0-1 | |

## Division 1

| | | Pd | Wn | Dw | Ls | GF | GA | Pts | |
|---|---|---|---|---|---|---|---|---|---|
| 1. | PORTSMOUTH FC (PORTSMOUTH) | 42 | 25 | 8 | 9 | 84 | 42 | 58 | |
| 2. | Manchester United FC (Manchester) | 42 | 21 | 11 | 10 | 77 | 44 | 53 | |
| 3. | Derby County FC (Derby) | 42 | 22 | 9 | 11 | 74 | 55 | 53 | |
| 4. | Newcastle United FC (Newcastle-upon-Tyne) | 42 | 20 | 12 | 10 | 70 | 56 | 52 | |
| 5. | Arsenal FC (London) | 42 | 18 | 13 | 11 | 74 | 44 | 49 | |
| 6. | Wolverhampton Wanderers FC (Wolverhampton) | 42 | 17 | 12 | 13 | 79 | 66 | 46 | |
| 7. | Manchester City FC (Manchester) | 42 | 15 | 15 | 12 | 47 | 51 | 45 | |
| 8. | Sunderland AFC (Sunderland) | 42 | 13 | 17 | 12 | 49 | 58 | 43 | |
| 9. | Charlton Athletic FC (London) | 42 | 15 | 12 | 15 | 63 | 67 | 42 | |
| 10. | Aston Ville FC (Birmingham) | 42 | 16 | 10 | 16 | 60 | 76 | 42 | |
| 11. | Stoke City FC (Stoke-on-Trent) | 42 | 16 | 9 | 17 | 66 | 68 | 41 | |
| 12. | Liverpool FC (Liverpool) | 42 | 13 | 14 | 15 | 53 | 43 | 40 | |
| 13. | Chelsea FC (Chelsea) | 42 | 12 | 14 | 16 | 69 | 68 | 38 | |
| 14. | Bolton Wanderers FC (Bolton) | 42 | 14 | 10 | 18 | 59 | 68 | 38 | |
| 15. | Burnley FC (Burnley) | 42 | 12 | 14 | 16 | 43 | 50 | 38 | |
| 16. | Blackpool FC (Blackpool) | 42 | 11 | 16 | 15 | 54 | 67 | 38 | |
| 17. | Birmingham City FC (Birmingham) | 42 | 11 | 15 | 16 | 36 | 38 | 37 | |
| 18. | Everton FC (Liverpool) | 42 | 13 | 11 | 18 | 41 | 63 | 37 | |
| 19. | Middlesbrough FC (Middlesbrough) | 42 | 11 | 12 | 19 | 46 | 57 | 34 | |
| 20. | Huddersfield Town AFC (Huddersfield) | 42 | 12 | 10 | 20 | 40 | 69 | 34 | |
| 21. | Preston North End FC (Preston) | 42 | 11 | 11 | 20 | 62 | 75 | 33 | R |
| 22. | Sheffield United FC (Sheffield) | 42 | 11 | 11 | 20 | 57 | 78 | 33 | R |
| | | 924 | 329 | 266 | 329 | 1303 | 1303 | 924 | |

## Top Goalscorer

1)  William MOIR          (Bolton Wanderers FC)     25

## Football League Division 2 — 1948-1949 Season

| | Barnsley | Blackburn Rovers | Bradford P.A. | Brentford | Bury | Cardiff City | Chesterfield | Coventry City | Fulham | Grimsby Town | Leeds United | Leicester City | Lincoln City | Luton Town | Nottingham Forest | Plymouth Argyle | Q.P.R. | Sheffield Wed. | Southampton | Tottenham Hotspur | W.B.A. | West Ham United |
|---|---|---|---|---|---|---|---|---|---|---|---|---|---|---|---|---|---|---|---|---|---|---|
| Barnsley FC | ■ | 1-1 | 0-0 | 1-2 | 3-2 | 1-1 | 0-1 | 1-1 | 1-1 | 2-1 | 1-1 | 3-1 | 2-0 | 1-2 | 4-0 | 0-0 | 4-0 | 4-0 | 3-0 | 4-1 | 2-0 | 2-3 |
| Blackburn Rovers FC | 5-3 | ■ | 2-3 | 2-1 | 1-2 | 2-1 | 0-2 | 2-0 | 1-0 | 3-3 | 0-0 | 2-0 | 7-1 | 4-1 | 2-1 | 2-1 | 2-0 | 2-1 | 1-2 | 1-1 | 0-0 | 0-0 |
| Bradford Park Avenue | 0-2 | 2-0 | ■ | 3-1 | 4-1 | 3-0 | 1-1 | 2-1 | 1-1 | 0-1 | 1-1 | 3-3 | 0-3 | 4-1 | 1-2 | 2-2 | 0-1 | 1-1 | 2-0 | 1-1 | 4-1 | 2-3 |
| Brentford FC | 0-0 | 0-1 | 1-0 | ■ | 8-2 | 1-1 | 1-1 | 2-2 | 0-0 | 2-0 | 1-3 | 1-2 | 2-1 | 2-0 | 2-1 | 2-2 | 0-3 | 2-1 | 0-0 | 1-1 | 0-0 | 0-0 |
| Bury FC | 4-2 | 3-1 | 2-1 | 1-2 | ■ | 0-3 | 2-2 | 0-2 | 2-0 | 5-1 | 3-1 | 1-2 | 3-1 | 3-1 | 1-1 | 1-1 | 0-0 | 2-1 | 1-0 | 1-1 | 4-0 | 2-0 |
| Cardiff City AFC | 0-3 | 1-0 | 6-1 | 2-0 | 2-1 | ■ | 3-4 | 3-0 | 2-1 | 3-0 | 2-1 | 1-1 | 3-1 | 3-3 | 1-0 | 1-0 | 3-0 | 1-1 | 2-1 | 0-1 | 2-2 | 4-0 |
| Chesterfield FC | 3-2 | 0-0 | 2-3 | 0-1 | 4-0 | 0-2 | ■ | 0-0 | 0-1 | 0-3 | 3-1 | 1-1 | 1-0 | 2-1 | 0-0 | 2-1 | 1-1 | 1-0 | 1-0 | 0-0 | 2-1 | 2-1 |
| Coventry City FC | 4-0 | 0-1 | 2-0 | 2-1 | 2-1 | 0-1 | 0-2 | ■ | 1-0 | 4-1 | 4-1 | 1-2 | 1-0 | 2-0 | 1-2 | 1-1 | 1-1 | 3-4 | 2-2 | 2-0 | 1-0 | 1-0 |
| Fulham FC | 1-1 | 1-1 | 2-0 | 2-1 | 7-2 | 4-0 | 2-1 | 1-0 | ■ | 3-1 | 1-0 | 1-0 | 2-1 | 4-1 | 4-0 | 6-1 | 5-0 | 1-1 | 1-0 | 1-1 | 1-2 | 2-0 |
| Grimsby Town AFC | 3-0 | 1-2 | 0-3 | 3-0 | 2-3 | 2-2 | 3-3 | 4-1 | 2-3 | ■ | 5-1 | 1-0 | 2-2 | 2-1 | 1-2 | 2-2 | 4-1 | 2-0 | 0-1 | 1-1 | 1-0 | 3-0 |
| Leeds United AFC | 4-1 | 1-0 | 4-2 | 0-0 | 0-1 | 0-0 | 1-0 | 4-1 | 1-1 | 6-3 | ■ | 3-1 | 3-1 | 2-0 | 1-0 | 1-0 | 1-2 | 1-1 | 1-1 | 0-0 | 1-3 | 1-3 |
| Leicester City FC | 1-1 | 3-1 | 2-2 | 0-0 | 3-2 | 2-2 | 2-2 | 3-1 | 0-3 | 1-1 | 6-2 | ■ | 5-3 | 1-1 | 4-2 | 1-1 | 2-3 | 2-2 | 1-3 | 1-2 | 0-3 | 1-1 |
| Lincoln City FC | 0-1 | 3-0 | 3-6 | 3-1 | 1-1 | 0-0 | 2-2 | 1-0 | 0-3 | 2-3 | 0-0 | 2-0 | ■ | 4-4 | 1-3 | 1-2 | 0-0 | 3-1 | 1-2 | 0-0 | 1-2 | 4-3 |
| Luton Town FC | 1-0 | 2-0 | 0-1 | 2-1 | 1-0 | 3-0 | 1-0 | 2-0 | 1-3 | 1-1 | 0-0 | 1-1 | 6-0 | ■ | 4-3 | 3-1 | 0-0 | 2-1 | 1-1 | 1-1 | 0-1 | 0-1 |
| Nottingham Forest FC | 0-1 | 1-0 | 2-0 | 1-2 | 1-0 | 0-0 | 0-1 | 3-0 | 0-2 | 0-0 | 0-0 | 2-1 | 1-1 | 2-0 | ■ | 1-0 | 0-0 | 1-2 | 2-1 | 2-2 | 0-1 | 3-0 |
| Plymouth Argyle FC | 3-1 | 3-0 | 3-0 | 1-0 | 1-0 | 0-1 | 2-2 | 2-3 | 3-1 | 0-2 | 2-1 | 1-1 | 0-0 | 1-1 | 1-0 | ■ | 3-1 | 3-2 | 1-2 | 0-5 | 1-2 | 2-0 |
| Queen's Park Rangers FC | 2-2 | 4-2 | 1-0 | 2-0 | 3-1 | 0-0 | 1-1 | 0-3 | 1-0 | 1-2 | 2-0 | 4-1 | 0-3 | 2-1 | 2-1 | 2-1 | ■ | 1-3 | 1-3 | 0-0 | 0-2 | 2-1 |
| Sheffield Wednesday FC | 1-1 | 3-0 | 2-1 | 0-0 | 1-2 | 1-1 | 0-0 | 2-1 | 1-2 | 4-1 | 3-1 | 0-1 | 2-2 | 0-0 | 2-1 | 2-1 | 2-0 | ■ | 2-0 | 3-1 | 2-1 | 3-0 |
| Southampton FC | 3-0 | 3-0 | 2-2 | 2-0 | 2-0 | 2-0 | 1-0 | 5-2 | 3-0 | 0-0 | 2-1 | 6-0 | 4-0 | 1-1 | 2-1 | 2-0 | 3-0 | 1-0 | ■ | 3-1 | 1-1 | 0-1 |
| Tottenham Hotspur FC | 4-1 | 4-0 | 5-1 | 2-0 | 3-1 | 0-1 | 4-0 | 4-0 | 1-1 | 5-2 | 2-2 | 1-1 | 2-1 | 2-1 | 3-0 | 1-0 | 3-2 | 0-1 | 1-1 | ■ | 2-0 | 1-1 |
| West Bromwich Albion FC | 2-0 | 2-1 | 7-1 | 2-0 | 2-3 | 2-0 | 0-0 | 1-0 | 1-2 | 5-2 | 1-0 | 2-1 | 5-0 | 2-1 | 3-0 | 1-1 | 1-0 | 2-0 | 2-2 | 1-1 | ■ | 2-1 |
| West Ham United FC | 2-0 | 2-1 | 4-1 | 1-1 | 2-1 | 3-1 | 1-2 | 2-2 | 1-0 | 1-0 | 3-2 | 4-1 | 2-2 | 0-1 | 0-5 | 3-0 | 2-0 | 2-2 | 1-1 | 1-0 | 1-0 | ■ |

### Division 2

| | | Pd | Wn | Dw | Ls | GF | GA | Pts | |
|---|---|---|---|---|---|---|---|---|---|
| 1. | Fulham FC (London) | 42 | 24 | 9 | 9 | 77 | 37 | 57 | P |
| 2. | West Bromwich Albion FC (West Bromwich) | 42 | 24 | 8 | 10 | 69 | 39 | 56 | P |
| 3. | Southampton FC (Southampton) | 42 | 23 | 9 | 10 | 69 | 36 | 55 | |
| 4. | Cardiff City AFC (Cardiff) | 42 | 19 | 13 | 10 | 62 | 47 | 51 | |
| 5. | Tottenham Hotspur FC (London) | 42 | 17 | 16 | 9 | 72 | 44 | 50 | |
| 6. | Chesterfield FC (Chesterfield) | 42 | 15 | 17 | 10 | 51 | 45 | 47 | |
| 7. | West Ham United FC (London) | 42 | 18 | 10 | 14 | 56 | 58 | 46 | |
| 8. | Sheffield Wednesday FC (Sheffield) | 42 | 15 | 13 | 14 | 63 | 56 | 43 | |
| 9. | Barnsley FC (Barnsley) | 42 | 14 | 12 | 16 | 62 | 61 | 40 | |
| 10. | Luton Town FC (Luton) | 42 | 14 | 12 | 16 | 55 | 57 | 40 | |
| 11. | Grimsby Town FC (Cleethorpes) | 42 | 15 | 10 | 17 | 72 | 76 | 40 | |
| 12. | Bury FC (Bury) | 42 | 17 | 6 | 19 | 67 | 76 | 40 | |
| 13. | Queen's Park Rangers FC (London) | 42 | 14 | 11 | 17 | 44 | 62 | 39 | |
| 14. | Blackburn Rovers FC (Blackburn) | 42 | 15 | 8 | 19 | 53 | 63 | 38 | |
| 15. | Leeds United AFC (Leeds) | 42 | 12 | 13 | 17 | 55 | 63 | 37 | |
| 16. | Coventry City FC (Coventry) | 42 | 15 | 7 | 20 | 55 | 64 | 37 | |
| 17. | Bradford Park Avenue FC (Bradford) | 42 | 13 | 11 | 18 | 65 | 78 | 37 | |
| 18. | Brentford FC (London) | 42 | 11 | 14 | 17 | 42 | 53 | 36 | |
| 19. | Leicester City FC (Leicester) | 42 | 10 | 16 | 16 | 62 | 79 | 36 | |
| 20. | Plymouth Argyle FC (Plymouth) | 42 | 12 | 12 | 18 | 49 | 64 | 36 | |
| 21. | Nottingham Forest FC (Nottingham) | 42 | 14 | 7 | 21 | 50 | 54 | 35 | R |
| 22. | Lincoln City FC (Lincoln) | 42 | 8 | 12 | 22 | 53 | 91 | 28 | R |
| | | 924 | 339 | 246 | 339 | 1303 | 1303 | 924 | |

**Football League Division 3 (N) 1948-1949 Season** — Results Grid

| | ACC | BAR | BRA | CAR | CHE | CRE | DAR | DON | GAT | HAL | HAR | HUL | MAN | NEW | OLD | ROC | ROT | SOU | STO | TRA | WRE | YOR |
|---|---|---|---|---|---|---|---|---|---|---|---|---|---|---|---|---|---|---|---|---|---|---|
| Accrington Stanley FC | ■ | 1-1 | 6-0 | 2-1 | 3-1 | 2-0 | 3-2 | 2-0 | 1-2 | 1-0 | 1-2 | 1-2 | 1-1 | 5-1 | 1-1 | 0-0 | 2-3 | 3-1 | 2-1 | 0-2 | 0-1 | 2-1 |
| Barrow AFC | 0-0 | ■ | 0-0 | 0-0 | 1-1 | 1-0 | 1-1 | 3-1 | 3-0 | 0-0 | 2-0 | 1-2 | 1-0 | 2-1 | 2-1 | 0-1 | 0-2 | 2-1 | 2-1 | 0-0 | 1-1 | 5-0 |
| Bradford City AFC | 2-2 | 0-2 | ■ | 1-2 | 3-2 | 1-2 | 0-2 | 0-1 | 1-1 | 2-1 | 0-0 | 4-2 | 1-0 | 1-1 | 2-1 | 1-0 | 1-2 | 4-2 | 1-1 | 1-3 | 1-2 | 2-2 |
| Carlisle United FC | 4-1 | 2-0 | 3-2 | ■ | 2-1 | 6-2 | 0-2 | 3-0 | 2-1 | 0-0 | 0-0 | 1-1 | 3-1 | 2-2 | 2-0 | 1-1 | 1-8 | 4-2 | 2-1 | 2-2 | 3-2 | 3-3 |
| Chester FC | 3-0 | 4-1 | 3-0 | 2-1 | ■ | 1-1 | 1-2 | 1-2 | 1-1 | 0-1 | 0-0 | 0-2 | 1-1 | 2-0 | 2-2 | 2-1 | 1-1 | 2-0 | 2-0 | 2-2 | 2-0 | 4-1 |
| Crewe Alexandra FC | 2-0 | 0-1 | 2-1 | 3-0 | 1-0 | ■ | 3-1 | 0-0 | 2-1 | 0-0 | 3-0 | 0-0 | 3-1 | 2-1 | 0-4 | 1-2 | 0-3 | 1-0 | 3-3 | 2-0 | 1-0 | 2-0 |
| Darlington FC | 3-0 | 2-3 | 1-5 | 2-2 | 3-3 | 4-1 | ■ | 1-5 | 1-3 | 2-1 | 2-0 | 0-2 | 1-2 | 0-2 | 2-1 | 6-1 | 2-0 | 0-1 | 1-1 | 3-2 | 3-1 | 3-1 |
| Doncaster Rovers FC | 0-0 | 0-0 | 2-0 | 2-0 | 0-0 | 0-1 | 1-1 | ■ | 2-1 | 1-2 | 0-0 | 0-0 | 1-1 | 2-1 | 3-0 | 1-0 | 0-0 | 1-2 | 3-1 | 2-0 | 4-2 | 1-0 |
| Gateshead FC | 1-1 | 3-0 | 6-2 | 3-0 | 2-1 | 4-1 | 1-3 | 0-3 | ■ | 1-2 | 2-1 | 0-2 | 0-0 | 3-0 | 2-2 | 2-1 | 3-2 | 2-2 | 0-1 | 3-3 | 2-0 | 1-1 |
| Halifax Town AFC | 1-0 | 1-0 | 1-1 | 3-4 | 1-2 | 0-0 | 0-3 | 1-0 | 2-2 | ■ | 2-0 | 2-4 | 2-2 | 0-2 | 3-1 | 2-1 | 2-0 | 0-1 | 0-1 | 0-1 | 2-0 | 1-2 |
| Hartlepools United FC | 1-0 | 1-0 | 1-0 | 1-0 | 2-1 | 4-1 | 0-1 | 2-1 | 1-3 | 0-0 | ■ | 0-2 | 1-1 | 3-1 | 1-2 | 6-1 | 1-4 | 2-2 | 0-0 | 3-0 | 2-2 | 2-3 |
| Hull City AFC | 3-1 | 3-0 | 2-0 | 3-0 | 3-2 | 5-0 | 0-1 | 0-1 | 2-0 | 6-0 | 2-0 | ■ | 4-0 | 4-1 | 6-0 | 1-1 | 3-2 | 5-1 | 6-1 | 2-0 | 3-0 | 2-3 |
| Mansfield Town FC | 2-0 | 2-0 | 1-0 | 2-0 | 1-0 | 5-1 | 2-2 | 2-2 | 1-1 | 2-1 | 1-0 | 1-1 | ■ | 2-0 | 3-2 | 2-0 | 1-2 | 1-1 | 4-0 | 0-0 | 1-2 | 3-0 |
| New Brighton FC | 1-3 | 3-1 | 1-0 | 2-0 | 1-1 | 2-1 | 1-0 | 0-1 | 2-2 | 2-0 | 1-1 | 0-0 | 1-0 | ■ | 0-1 | 1-2 | 0-1 | 0-1 | 0-2 | 2-1 | 2-0 | 3-1 |
| Oldham Athletic AFC | 4-3 | 2-1 | 1-2 | 1-0 | 2-1 | 3-2 | 7-1 | 0-2 | 0-0 | 2-2 | 5-1 | 1-1 | 4-0 | 4-2 | ■ | 0-1 | 1-3 | 2-1 | 5-2 | 0-2 | 1-1 | 4-0 |
| Rochdale AFC | 4-1 | 3-0 | 1-1 | 1-0 | 3-1 | 3-0 | 3-4 | 0-2 | 3-0 | 1-0 | 0-1 | 1-1 | 1-0 | 1-1 | 1-2 | ■ | 2-0 | 1-0 | 2-0 | 2-1 | 2-1 | 2-0 |
| Rotherham United FC | 1-0 | 2-2 | 2-0 | 1-1 | 2-1 | 6-1 | 4-3 | 2-0 | 1-0 | 4-0 | 2-1 | 0-0 | 1-1 | 2-1 | 3-1 | | ■ | 1-0 | 2-1 | 7-0 | 1-3 | 2-1 |
| Southport FC | 3-0 | 0-0 | 2-1 | 2-2 | 2-1 | 0-0 | 1-3 | 0-2 | 0-3 | 2-3 | 1-2 | 0-0 | 1-1 | 0-1 | 0-1 | 3-1 | 1-3 | ■ | 1-0 | 2-3 | 3-0 | 0-2 |
| Stockport County FC | 2-1 | 1-2 | 5-2 | 2-0 | 1-1 | 4-0 | 2-0 | 5-1 | 3-1 | 3-1 | 4-0 | 0-0 | 2-0 | 1-0 | 1-2 | 2-2 | 0-1 | 0-0 | ■ | 4-1 | 1-0 | 1-1 |
| Tranmere Rovers FC | 2-2 | 2-0 | 1-0 | 2-1 | 1-1 | 2-2 | 2-1 | 2-0 | 1-1 | 2-2 | 0-2 | 1-2 | 1-0 | 1-1 | 0-1 | 1-1 | 1-0 | 0-0 | 2-1 | ■ | 0-2 | 0-0 |
| Wrexham AFC | 1-0 | 1-0 | 5-0 | 4-0 | 1-0 | 2-2 | 4-3 | 2-0 | 1-4 | 2-1 | 1-0 | 0-2 | 1-1 | 2-1 | 1-1 | 2-0 | 0-4 | 2-0 | 0-0 | 0-0 | ■ | 3-3 |
| York City FC | 1-1 | 2-0 | 0-2 | 6-0 | 2-0 | 1-3 | 2-5 | 2-3 | 0-1 | 2-2 | 4-0 | 1-3 | 2-1 | 2-1 | 4-0 | 1-1 | 6-1 | 1-3 | 4-0 | 1-0 | 5-1 | ■ |

## Division 3 (North)

| | | Pd | Wn | Dw | Ls | GF | GA | Pts | |
|---|---|---|---|---|---|---|---|---|---|
| 1. | Hull City AFC (Kingston-upon-Hull) | 42 | 27 | 11 | 4 | 93 | 28 | 65 | P |
| 2. | Rotherham United FC (Rotherham) | 42 | 28 | 6 | 8 | 90 | 46 | 62 | |
| 3. | Doncaster Rovers FC (Doncaster) | 42 | 20 | 10 | 12 | 53 | 40 | 50 | |
| 4. | Darlington FC (Darlington) | 42 | 20 | 6 | 16 | 83 | 74 | 46 | |
| 5. | Gateshead FC (Gateshead) | 42 | 16 | 13 | 13 | 69 | 58 | 45 | |
| 6. | Oldham Athletic AFC (Oldham) | 42 | 18 | 9 | 15 | 75 | 67 | 45 | |
| 7. | Rochdale AFC (Rochdale) | 42 | 18 | 9 | 15 | 55 | 53 | 45 | |
| 8. | Stockport County FC (Stockport) | 42 | 16 | 11 | 15 | 61 | 56 | 43 | |
| 9. | Wrexham AFC (Wrexham) | 42 | 17 | 9 | 16 | 56 | 62 | 43 | |
| 10. | Mansfield Town FC (Mansfield) | 42 | 14 | 14 | 14 | 52 | 48 | 42 | |
| 11. | Tranmere Rovers FC (Birkenhead) | 42 | 13 | 15 | 14 | 46 | 57 | 41 | |
| 12. | Crewe Alexandra FC (Crewe) | 42 | 16 | 9 | 17 | 52 | 74 | 41 | |
| 13. | Barrow AFC (Barrow-in-Furness) | 42 | 14 | 12 | 16 | 41 | 48 | 40 | |
| 14. | York City FC (York) | 42 | 15 | 9 | 18 | 74 | 74 | 39 | |
| 15. | Carlisle United FC (Carlisle) | 42 | 14 | 11 | 17 | 60 | 77 | 39 | |
| 16. | Hartlepools United FC (Hartlepool) | 42 | 14 | 10 | 18 | 45 | 58 | 38 | |
| 17. | New Brighton FC (Wallasey) | 42 | 14 | 8 | 20 | 46 | 58 | 36 | |
| 18. | Chester FC (Chester) | 42 | 11 | 13 | 18 | 57 | 56 | 35 | |
| 19. | Halifax Town AFC (Halifax) | 42 | 12 | 11 | 19 | 45 | 62 | 35 | |
| 20. | Accrington Stanley FC (Accrington) | 42 | 12 | 10 | 20 | 55 | 64 | 34 | |
| 21. | Southport FC (Southport) | 42 | 11 | 9 | 22 | 45 | 64 | 31 | |
| 22. | Bradford City AFC (Bradford) | 42 | 10 | 9 | 23 | 48 | 77 | 29 | |
| | | 924 | 350 | 224 | 350 | 1301 | 1301 | 924 | |

| Football League Division 3 (S) 1948-1949 Season | Aldershot | Bournemouth | Brighton | Bristol City | Bristol Rovers | Crystal Palace | Exeter City | Ipswich Town | Leyton Orient | Millwall | Newport County | Northampton | Norwich City | Notts County | Port Vale | Reading | Southend United | Swansea Town | Swindon Town | Torquay United | Walsall | Watford |
|---|---|---|---|---|---|---|---|---|---|---|---|---|---|---|---|---|---|---|---|---|---|---|
| Aldershot FC |  | 0-0 | 1-1 | 0-0 | 1-5 | 3-0 | 1-2 | 2-0 | 1-1 | 5-0 | 1-2 | 3-1 | 4-1 | 0-1 | 0-1 | 0-6 | 1-0 | 1-2 | 1-2 | 1-3 | 0-1 | 0-0 |
| Bournemouth & B. Athletic | 1-0 |  | 0-1 | 0-0 | 1-0 | 2-0 | 1-0 | 4-2 | 3-0 | 2-0 | 1-2 | 5-2 | 1-2 | 2-1 | 2-0 | 1-3 | 3-2 | 1-1 | 3-0 | 5-0 | 2-0 | 2-1 |
| Brighton & Hove Albion | 0-4 | 1-6 |  | 0-0 | 2-1 | 1-1 | 2-0 | 6-1 | 3-1 | 1-2 | 3-2 | 0-0 | 1-0 | 3-2 | 1-0 | 2-0 | 1-0 | 0-2 | 1-1 | 3-1 | 1-2 | 0-0 |
| Bristol City FC | 1-1 | 2-1 | 1-1 |  | 1-1 | 2-0 | 1-0 | 2-0 | 3-0 | 0-0 | 1-1 | 3-0 | 1-6 | 3-1 | 1-1 | 0-2 | 2-1 | 0-0 | 1-3 | 0-2 | 2-2 | 1-1 |
| Bristol Rovers FC | 0-2 | 4-0 | 0-0 | 3-1 |  | 1-0 | 3-1 | 1-6 | 2-3 | 2-0 | 3-1 | 1-0 | 2-2 | 3-2 | 4-1 | 4-1 | 0-0 | 1-1 | 1-1 | 1-0 | 3-0 | 3-1 |
| Crystal Palace FC | 2-1 | 2-1 | 0-2 | 4-0 | 1-0 |  | 1-1 | 1-1 | 2-1 | 1-1 | 0-1 | 2-2 | 1-1 | 1-5 | 1-1 | 0-1 | 2-1 | 1-1 | 1-1 | 0-1 | 1-3 | 3-1 |
| Exeter City FC | 3-3 | 2-3 | 1-1 | 1-1 | 2-1 | 3-1 |  | 1-3 | 3-1 | 3-0 | 1-2 | 5-1 | 4-1 | 3-1 | 2-1 | 1-2 | 0-0 | 1-1 | 3-1 | 2-0 | 2-1 | 2-1 |
| Ipswich Town FC | 4-1 | 1-0 | 2-2 | 2-0 | 0-1 | 3-2 | 2-2 |  | 2-2 | 1-0 | 5-1 | 4-2 | 1-2 | 3-2 | 4-1 | 3-2 | 1-3 | 2-0 | 4-2 | 5-1 | 3-2 | 1-2 |
| Leyton Orient FC | 1-2 | 1-2 | 0-3 | 3-1 | 1-1 | 1-1 | 5-2 | 1-1 |  | 2-2 | 5-2 | 0-3 | 0-3 | 3-1 | 2-0 | 0-1 | 2-0 | 3-1 | 1-1 | 3-1 | 1-1 | 1-0 |
| Millwall FC | 1-1 | 4-0 | 6-2 | 4-1 | 1-1 | 1-0 | 2-1 | 0-0 | 0-0 |  | 3-1 | 3-2 | 1-3 | 3-2 | 1-1 | 1-1 | 1-0 | 2-0 | 3-1 | 1-3 | 2-1 | 2-2 |
| Newport County AFC | 0-2 | 1-2 | 1-1 | 0-2 | 2-1 | 5-0 | 0-2 | 3-0 | 3-2 | 1-2 |  | 2-0 | 4-3 | 3-3 | 2-2 | 1-1 | 4-2 | 2-5 | 4-1 | 1-2 | 1-1 | 1-1 |
| Northampton Town FC | 2-0 | 1-0 | 1-1 | 3-1 | 0-1 | 3-2 | 4-0 | 1-1 | 4-1 | 4-0 | 2-1 |  | 1-0 | 1-2 | 2-2 | 1-2 | 2-2 | 0-1 | 0-1 | 0-0 | 0-1 | 1-1 |
| Norwich City FC | 0-0 | 1-1 | 2-1 | 4-0 | 3-0 | 3-0 | 3-0 | 2-0 | 0-0 | 1-2 | 0-0 | 2-1 |  | 3-0 | 2-0 | 1-2 | 3-0 | 1-0 | 0-0 | 0-0 | 1-2 | 0-1 |
| Notts County FC | 2-0 | 2-3 | 1-1 | 2-1 | 4-1 | 5-1 | 9-0 | 9-2 | 2-1 | 1-3 | 11-1 | 2-0 | 2-1 |  | 2-1 | 1-0 | 0-0 | 1-1 | 1-2 | 5-0 | 2-0 | 4-0 |
| Port Vale FC | 3-0 | 0-2 | 3-4 | 4-2 | 2-0 | 0-0 | 1-1 | 1-2 | 3-0 | 1-0 | 1-2 | 1-0 | 0-0 | 1-0 |  | 3-0 | 0-2 | 0-2 | 2-0 | 3-1 | 0-2 | 3-1 |
| Reading FC | 2-0 | 4-2 | 6-1 | 2-1 | 1-0 | 5-1 | 2-0 | 2-1 | 3-0 | 2-0 | 4-1 | 1-0 | 2-1 | 1-4 | 1-2 |  | 2-1 | 0-2 | 0-0 | 4-0 | 1-0 | 3-1 |
| Southend United FC | 1-0 | 0-0 | 0-0 | 1-0 | 0-1 | 0-1 | 0-0 | 1-1 | 2-2 | 2-1 | 0-1 | 0-1 | 2-2 | 3-2 | 0-0 | 0-0 |  | 0-0 | 3-4 | 1-1 | 2-0 | 0-1 |
| Swansea Town AFC | 2-1 | 2-0 | 3-0 | 2-0 | 5-0 | 3-0 | 6-0 | 2-0 | 3-1 | 2-0 | 2-1 | 1-0 | 2-1 | 3-1 | 3-1 | 2-1 | 2-2 |  | 4-0 | 6-1 | 3-1 | 2-0 |
| Swindon Town FC | 3-1 | 2-2 | 0-0 | 2-1 | 1-1 | 1-0 | 1-1 | 4-0 | 1-1 | 2-0 | 5-2 | 2-2 | 3-3 | 3-0 | 0-2 | 1-1 | 2-1 | 1-0 |  | 1-1 | 2-1 | 1-1 |
| Torquay United FC | 2-2 | 1-1 | 1-1 | 0-2 | 0-2 | 2-0 | 2-1 | 1-1 | 7-1 | 2-1 | 4-0 | 3-0 | 2-1 | 3-1 | 0-0 | 4-2 | 0-3 | 0-4 | 3-1 |  | 5-1 | 3-1 |
| Walsall FC | 0-0 | 0-0 | 0-0 | 0-1 | 0-1 | 3-1 | 4-3 | 2-1 | 2-3 | 5-6 | 3-1 | 2-0 | 4-1 | 3-2 | 1-1 | 2-0 | 0-3 | 2-1 | 0-1 | 1-1 |  | 0-1 |
| Watford FC | 0-1 | 0-1 | 0-0 | 1-1 | 0-0 | 2-0 | 0-1 | 1-2 | 2-1 | 1-1 | 2-2 | 0-1 | 1-1 | 1-1 | 2-1 | 4-1 | 0-0 | 4-2 | 0-3 | 1-1 | 2-0 |  |

## Division 3 (South)

| | | Pd | Wn | Dw | Ls | GF | GA | Pts | |
|---|---|---|---|---|---|---|---|---|---|
| 1. | Swansea Town AFC (Swansea) | 42 | 27 | 8 | 7 | 87 | 34 | 62 | P |
| 2. | Reading FC (Reading) | 42 | 25 | 5 | 12 | 77 | 50 | 55 | |
| 3. | Bournemouth & Boscombe Athletic FC (Bournemouth) | 42 | 22 | 8 | 12 | 69 | 48 | 52 | |
| 4. | Swindon Town FC (Swindon) | 42 | 18 | 15 | 9 | 64 | 56 | 51 | |
| 5. | Bristol Rovers FC (Bristol) | 42 | 19 | 10 | 13 | 61 | 51 | 48 | |
| 6. | Brighton & Hove Albion FC (Hove) | 42 | 15 | 18 | 9 | 55 | 55 | 48 | |
| 7. | Ipswich Town FC (Ipswich) | 42 | 18 | 9 | 15 | 78 | 77 | 45 | |
| 8. | Millwall FC (London) | 42 | 17 | 11 | 14 | 63 | 64 | 45 | |
| 9. | Torquay United FC (Torquay) | 42 | 17 | 11 | 14 | 65 | 70 | 45 | |
| 10. | Norwich City FC (Norwich) | 42 | 16 | 12 | 14 | 67 | 49 | 44 | |
| 11. | Notts County FC (Nottingham) | 42 | 19 | 5 | 18 | 102 | 68 | 43 | |
| 12. | Exeter City FC (Exeter) | 42 | 15 | 10 | 17 | 63 | 76 | 40 | |
| 13. | Port Vale FC (Stoke-on-Trent) | 42 | 14 | 11 | 17 | 51 | 54 | 39 | |
| 14. | Walsall FC (Walsall) | 42 | 15 | 8 | 19 | 56 | 64 | 38 | |
| 15. | Newport County AFC (Newport) | 42 | 14 | 9 | 19 | 68 | 92 | 37 | |
| 16. | Bristol City FC (Bristol) | 42 | 11 | 14 | 17 | 44 | 62 | 36 | |
| 17. | Watford FC (Watford) | 42 | 10 | 15 | 17 | 41 | 54 | 35 | |
| 18. | Southend United FC (Southend-on-Sea) | 42 | 9 | 16 | 17 | 41 | 46 | 34 | |
| 19. | Leyton Orient FC (London) | 42 | 11 | 12 | 19 | 58 | 80 | 34 | |
| 20. | Northampton Town FC (Northampton) | 42 | 12 | 9 | 21 | 51 | 62 | 33 | |
| 21. | Aldershot FC (Aldershot) | 42 | 11 | 11 | 20 | 48 | 59 | 33 | |
| 22. | Crystal Palace FC (London) | 42 | 8 | 11 | 23 | 38 | 76 | 27 | |
| | | 924 | 343 | 238 | 343 | 1347 | 1347 | 924 | |

# F.A. CUP FINAL    (Wembley Stadium, London – 30/04/1949 – 99,500)

WOLVERHAMPTON WANDERERS FC        3-1                    Leicester City FC (Leicester)

*Pye 2, Smyth*                                                                  *Griffiths*

Wolves: Williams, Pritchard, Springthorpe, Crook, Shorthouse, Wright, Hancocks, Smyth, Pye, Dunn, Mullen.

Leicester: Bradley, Jelly, Scott, W.Harrison, Plummer, King, Griffiths, Lee, J.Harrison, Chisholm, Adam.

## Semi-finals

| Leicester City FC (Leicester) | 3-1 | Portsmouth FC Portsmouth) |
| Manchester United FC (Manchester) | 1-1, 0-1 | Wolverhampton Wanderers FC (Wolverhampton) |

## Quarter-finals

| Hull City AFC (Kingston-upon-Hull) | 0-1 | Manchester United FC (Manchester) |
| Leicester City FC (Leicester) | 2-0 | Brentford FC (London) |
| Portsmouth FC (Portsmouth) | 2-1 | Derby County FC (Derby) |
| Wolverhampton Wanderers FC (Wolverhampton) | 1-0 | West Bromwich Albion FC (West Bromwich) |

# 1949-50

| Football League Division 1 1949-1950 Season | Arsenal | Aston Villa | Birmingham City | Blackpool | Bolton Wanderers | Burnley | Charlton Athletic | Chelsea | Derby County | Everton | Fulham | Huddersfield Town | Liverpool | Manchester City | Manchester United | Middlesbrough | Newcastle United | Portsmouth | Stoke City | Sunderland | W.B.A. | Wolves |
|---|---|---|---|---|---|---|---|---|---|---|---|---|---|---|---|---|---|---|---|---|---|---|
| Arsenal FC | | 1-3 | 4-2 | 1-0 | 1-1 | 0-1 | 2-3 | 2-3 | 1-0 | 5-2 | 2-1 | 1-0 | 1-2 | 4-1 | 0-0 | 1-1 | 4-2 | 2-0 | 6-0 | 5-0 | 4-1 | 1-1 |
| Aston Villa FC | 1-1 | | 1-1 | 0-0 | 3-0 | 0-1 | 1-1 | 4-0 | 1-1 | 2-2 | 3-1 | 2-1 | 2-0 | 1-0 | 0-4 | 4-0 | 0-1 | 1-0 | 1-1 | 2-0 | 1-0 | 1-4 |
| Birmingham City FC | 2-1 | 2-2 | | 0-2 | 0-0 | 0-1 | 2-0 | 0-3 | 2-2 | 0-0 | 1-1 | 2-1 | 2-3 | 1-0 | 0-0 | 0-0 | 0-2 | 0-3 | 1-0 | 1-2 | 2-0 | 1-1 |
| Blackpool FC | 2-1 | 1-0 | 1-1 | | 2-0 | 2-0 | 2-0 | 0-0 | 1-0 | 0-1 | 0-0 | 4-1 | 0-0 | 0-0 | 3-3 | 1-1 | 0-0 | 2-1 | 4-2 | 0-1 | 3-0 | 1-2 |
| Bolton Wanderers FC | 2-2 | 1-1 | 1-0 | 0-0 | | 0-1 | 3-0 | 1-0 | 0-0 | 1-2 | 2-1 | 1-2 | 3-2 | 3-0 | 1-2 | 1-2 | 2-2 | 1-0 | 4-0 | 2-1 | 3-0 | 2-4 |
| Burnley FC | 0-0 | 1-0 | 1-1 | 0-0 | 2-1 | | 1-0 | 1-2 | 0-1 | 5-1 | 0-0 | 1-0 | 0-2 | 0-0 | 1-0 | 3-2 | 1-2 | 2-1 | 2-1 | 2-2 | 0-0 | 0-1 |
| Charlton Athletic FC | 1-1 | 1-4 | 2-0 | 1-2 | 0-0 | 1-1 | | 1-0 | 1-3 | 2-0 | 2-1 | 2-2 | 1-3 | 3-1 | 1-2 | 0-3 | 6-3 | 1-2 | 2-0 | 2-2 | 1-2 | 2-3 |
| Chelsea FC | 1-2 | 1-3 | 3-0 | 1-1 | 1-1 | 0-1 | 1-3 | | 1-2 | 3-2 | 0-0 | 3-1 | 1-1 | 3-0 | 1-1 | 2-1 | 1-3 | 1-4 | 2-2 | 3-1 | 2-1 | 0-0 |
| Derby County FC | 1-2 | 3-2 | 4-1 | 0-0 | 4-0 | 1-1 | 1-2 | 2-2 | | 2-0 | 2-1 | 4-2 | 2-2 | 7-0 | 0-1 | 1-0 | 1-1 | 2-3 | 2-3 | 3-2 | 3-1 | 1-2 |
| Everton FC | 0-1 | 1-1 | 0-0 | 3-0 | 0-0 | 1-1 | 0-1 | 1-1 | 1-2 | | 1-1 | 3-0 | 0-1 | 3-1 | 0-0 | 3-1 | 2-1 | 1-2 | 2-1 | 0-2 | 1-2 | 1-2 |
| Fulham FC | 2-2 | 3-0 | 1-0 | 1-0 | 3-0 | 1-0 | 1-2 | 1-1 | 0-0 | 0-0 | | 4-1 | 0-1 | 1-0 | 1-0 | 1-2 | 2-1 | 0-1 | 2-2 | 0-3 | 0-1 | 1-2 |
| Huddersfield Town AFC | 2-2 | 1-0 | 1-0 | 0-1 | 2-0 | 1-2 | 2-1 | 1-2 | 2-0 | 1-2 | 2-2 | | 3-2 | 1-0 | 3-1 | 2-2 | 1-2 | 0-1 | 4-0 | 3-1 | 1-1 | 1-0 |
| Liverpool FC | 2-0 | 2-1 | 2-0 | 0-1 | 1-1 | 0-1 | 1-0 | 2-2 | 3-1 | 3-1 | 1-1 | 2-3 | | 4-0 | 1-1 | 2-0 | 2-2 | 1-1 | 4-2 | 2-1 | 0-2 | |
| Manchester City FC | 0-2 | 3-3 | 4-0 | 0-3 | 1-1 | 1-0 | 2-0 | 1-1 | 2-2 | 0-0 | 2-0 | 1-2 | 1-2 | | 1-2 | 0-1 | 1-1 | 1-0 | 1-1 | 2-1 | 1-1 | 2-1 |
| Manchester United FC | 2-0 | 7-0 | 0-2 | 1-2 | 3-0 | 3-2 | 3-2 | 1-0 | 0-1 | 1-1 | 3-0 | 6-0 | 0-0 | 2-1 | | 2-0 | 1-1 | 0-2 | 2-2 | 1-3 | 1-1 | 3-0 |
| Middlesbrough FC | 1-1 | 0-2 | 1-0 | 2-0 | 2-0 | 4-1 | 1-0 | 2-1 | 3-1 | 0-1 | 1-2 | 3-0 | 4-1 | 0-0 | 2-3 | | 1-0 | 1-5 | 2-0 | 2-0 | 3-0 | 2-0 |
| Newcastle United FC | 0-3 | 3-2 | 3-1 | 3-0 | 3-1 | 0-0 | 1-0 | 2-2 | 2-1 | 4-0 | 3-1 | 0-0 | 5-1 | 4-2 | 2-1 | 0-1 | | 1-3 | 4-1 | 2-2 | 5-1 | 2-0 |
| Portsmouth FC | 2-1 | 5-1 | 2-0 | 2-3 | 1-1 | 2-1 | 1-0 | 4-0 | 3-1 | 7-0 | 3-0 | 4-0 | 2-1 | 1-1 | 0-0 | 1-1 | 1-0 | | 0-0 | 2-2 | 0-1 | 1-1 |
| Stoke City FC | 2-5 | 1-0 | 3-1 | 1-1 | 3-2 | 1-1 | 0-3 | 2-3 | 1-3 | 1-0 | 0-2 | 0-0 | 0-0 | 2-0 | 3-1 | 1-0 | 1-0 | 0-1 | | 2-1 | 1-3 | 2-1 |
| Sunderland AFC | 4-2 | 2-1 | 1-1 | 1-1 | 2-0 | 2-1 | 2-1 | 4-1 | 6-1 | 4-2 | 2-0 | 1-1 | 3-2 | 1-2 | 2-2 | 2-0 | 2-2 | 1-1 | 3-0 | | 2-1 | 3-1 |
| West Bromwich Albion FC | 1-2 | 1-1 | 3-0 | 1-0 | 2-1 | 3-0 | 1-0 | 1-1 | 1-0 | 4-0 | 4-1 | 0-0 | 0-1 | 0-0 | 1-2 | 0-3 | 1-1 | 3-0 | 0-0 | 0-2 | | 1-1 |
| Wolverhampton Wanderers FC | 3-0 | 2-3 | 6-1 | 3-0 | 1-1 | 0-0 | 2-1 | 2-2 | 4-1 | 1-1 | 1-1 | 7-1 | 1-1 | 3-0 | 1-1 | 3-1 | 2-1 | 1-0 | 2-1 | 1-3 | 1-1 | |

## Division 1

| | | Pd | Wn | Dw | Ls | GF | GA | Pts | |
|---|---|---|---|---|---|---|---|---|---|
| 1. | PORTSMOUTH FC (PORTSMOUTH) | 42 | 22 | 9 | 11 | 74 | 38 | 52 | |
| 2. | Wolverhampton Wanderers FC (Wolverhampton) | 42 | 20 | 13 | 9 | 76 | 49 | 53 | |
| 3. | Sunderland AFC (Sunderland) | 42 | 21 | 10 | 11 | 83 | 62 | 52 | |
| 4. | Manchester United FC (Manchester) | 42 | 18 | 14 | 10 | 69 | 44 | 50 | |
| 5. | Newcastle United FC (Newcastle-upon-Tyne) | 42 | 19 | 12 | 11 | 77 | 55 | 50 | |
| 6. | Arsenal FC (London) | 42 | 19 | 11 | 12 | 79 | 55 | 49 | |
| 7. | Blackpool FC (Blackpool) | 42 | 17 | 15 | 10 | 46 | 35 | 49 | |
| 8. | Liverpool FC (Liverpool) | 42 | 17 | 14 | 11 | 64 | 54 | 48 | |
| 9. | Middlesbrough FC (Middlesbrough) | 42 | 20 | 7 | 15 | 59 | 48 | 47 | |
| 10. | Burnley FC (Burnley) | 42 | 16 | 13 | 13 | 40 | 40 | 45 | |
| 11. | Derby County FC (Derby) | 42 | 17 | 10 | 15 | 69 | 61 | 44 | |
| 12. | Aston Villa FC (Birmingham) | 42 | 15 | 12 | 15 | 61 | 61 | 42 | |
| 13. | Chelsea FC (London) | 42 | 12 | 16 | 14 | 58 | 65 | 40 | |
| 14. | West Bromwich Albion FC (West Bromwich) | 42 | 14 | 12 | 16 | 47 | 53 | 40 | |
| 15. | Huddersfield Town AFC (Huddersfield) | 42 | 14 | 9 | 19 | 52 | 73 | 37 | |
| 16. | Bolton Wanderers FC (Bolton) | 42 | 10 | 14 | 18 | 45 | 59 | 34 | |
| 17. | Fulham FC (London) | 42 | 10 | 14 | 18 | 41 | 54 | 34 | |
| 18. | Everton FC (Liverpool) | 42 | 10 | 14 | 18 | 42 | 66 | 34 | |
| 19. | Stoke City FC (Stoke-on-Trent) | 42 | 11 | 12 | 19 | 45 | 75 | 34 | |
| 20. | Charlton Athletic FC (London) | 42 | 13 | 6 | 23 | 53 | 65 | 32 | |
| 21. | Manchester City FC (Manchester) | 42 | 8 | 13 | 21 | 36 | 68 | 29 | R |
| 22. | Birmingham City FC (Birmingham) | 42 | 7 | 14 | 21 | 31 | 67 | 28 | R |
| | | 924 | 330 | 264 | 330 | 1247 | 1247 | 924 | |

## Top Goalscorer

1)  Richard DAVIS  (Sunderland AFC)  25

222

| Football League Division 2 1949-1950 Season | Barnsley | Blackburn Rovers | Bradford P.A. | Brentford | Bury | Cardiff City | Chesterfield | Coventry City | Grimsby Town | Hull City | Leeds United | Leicester City | Luton Town | Plymouth Argyle | Preston N.E. | Q.P.R. | Sheffield United | Sheffield Wed. | Southampton | Swansea Town | Tottenham H. | West Ham United |
|---|---|---|---|---|---|---|---|---|---|---|---|---|---|---|---|---|---|---|---|---|---|---|
| Barnsley FC | ■ | 1-1 | 3-2 | 0-1 | 1-0 | 1-0 | 1-2 | 4-3 | 7-2 | 1-1 | 1-1 | 2-2 | 1-0 | 4-1 | 0-1 | 3-1 | 2-2 | 3-4 | 2-1 | 5-2 | 2-0 | 1-1 |
| Blackburn Rovers FC | 4-0 | ■ | 0-1 | 4-1 | 2-1 | 1-0 | 1-1 | 0-1 | 3-0 | 4-2 | 0-1 | 3-0 | 0-0 | 1-0 | 2-3 | 0-0 | 0-2 | 0-0 | 0-0 | 2-0 | 1-2 | 2-0 |
| Bradford Park Avenue | 1-3 | 2-2 | ■ | 0-2 | 1-2 | 3-3 | 2-0 | 2-2 | 4-1 | 5-1 | 1-2 | 2-2 | 1-0 | 3-2 | 1-2 | 1-0 | 1-1 | 1-3 | 0-0 | 0-2 | 1-3 | 2-1 |
| Brentford FC | 3-0 | 2-0 | 2-0 | ■ | 2-0 | 1-0 | 0-0 | 2-0 | 1-0 | 3-1 | 0-0 | 0-1 | 1-0 | 0-0 | 1-0 | 0-2 | 1-0 | 1-1 | 0-1 | 0-0 | 1-4 | 0-2 |
| Bury FC | 2-0 | 3-0 | 1-0 | 1-2 | ■ | 2-2 | 2-0 | 0-0 | 3-1 | 0-0 | 2-0 | 3-0 | 5-2 | 5-1 | 1-1 | 0-0 | 1-5 | 0-0 | 1-1 | 1-1 | 1-2 | 3-1 |
| Cardiff City AFC | 3-0 | 2-1 | 1-2 | 0-0 | 1-0 | ■ | 2-0 | 1-0 | 1-0 | 2-0 | 1-0 | 2-4 | 0-0 | 1-0 | 3-2 | 4-0 | 1-2 | 1-1 | 1-1 | 1-0 | 0-1 | 0-1 |
| Chesterfield FC | 1-0 | 2-1 | 1-1 | 3-1 | 2-1 | 0-1 | ■ | 0-1 | 2-1 | 0-1 | 3-1 | 1-0 | 0-1 | 2-0 | 2-0 | 2-1 | 0-1 | 1-2 | 0-0 | 4-1 | 1-1 | 1-0 |
| Coventry City FC | 1-1 | 1-1 | 3-1 | 1-1 | 1-2 | 2-1 | 3-0 | ■ | 1-1 | 2-0 | 0-4 | 1-2 | 1-0 | 3-0 | 0-0 | 0-0 | 2-4 | 3-0 | 1-2 | 1-2 | 0-1 | 5-1 |
| Grimsby Town AFC | 2-2 | 1-2 | 4-0 | 4-1 | 4-2 | 0-0 | 5-2 | 3-2 | ■ | 1-0 | 2-0 | 2-1 | 6-1 | 2-2 | 1-3 | 1-1 | 4-0 | 4-1 | 1-1 | 2-1 | 2-3 | 2-0 |
| Hull City AFC | 2-0 | 3-1 | 3-3 | 2-0 | 3-2 | 1-1 | 1-0 | 2-1 | 2-2 | ■ | 1-0 | 4-0 | 1-1 | 4-2 | 4-2 | 1-1 | 1-2 | 0-4 | 1-1 | 1-2 | 0-0 | 2-2 |
| Leeds United AFC | 1-0 | 2-1 | 0-0 | 1-0 | 4-1 | 2-0 | 0-0 | 3-3 | 1-0 | 3-0 | ■ | 1-1 | 2-1 | 1-1 | 3-1 | 1-1 | 0-1 | 1-1 | 1-0 | 1-2 | 3-0 | 2-2 |
| Leicester City FC | 2-2 | 3-3 | 4-1 | 1-1 | 0-2 | 1-0 | 0-1 | 1-0 | 1-0 | 1-2 | 1-1 | ■ | 3-2 | 0-0 | 1-0 | 3-2 | 1-1 | 2-2 | 2-2 | 0-0 | 1-2 | 2-1 |
| Luton Town FC | 3-1 | 5-2 | 3-1 | 1-0 | 2-1 | 0-0 | 1-1 | 2-0 | 0-0 | 0-3 | 1-0 | 1-0 | ■ | 1-1 | 1-1 | 1-2 | 1-3 | 0-0 | 1-1 | 1-2 | 1-1 | 2-2 |
| Plymouth Argyle FC | 2-2 | 0-0 | 1-1 | 2-0 | 2-0 | 0-0 | 2-1 | 1-2 | 4-2 | 1-3 | 1-2 | 2-1 | 0-0 | ■ | 1-0 | 0-2 | 0-1 | 0-1 | 0-0 | 0-2 | 0-2 | 0-3 |
| Preston North End FC | 1-1 | 3-1 | 3-0 | 2-0 | 3-1 | 3-0 | 0-0 | 1-1 | 2-0 | 4-2 | 1-1 | 2-1 | 0-1 | 0-0 | ■ | 3-2 | 4-1 | 0-1 | 0-3 | 2-1 | 1-3 | 2-1 |
| Queen's Park Rangers FC | 0-5 | 2-3 | 0-1 | 3-3 | 1-0 | 0-1 | 3-2 | 2-0 | 1-2 | 1-4 | 1-1 | 2-0 | 3-0 | 0-2 | 0-0 | ■ | 1-3 | 0-0 | 1-0 | 0-0 | 0-2 | 0-1 |
| Sheffield United FC | 1-1 | 4-0 | 2-1 | 1-1 | 4-4 | 2-0 | 1-0 | 1-1 | 3-1 | 5-0 | 0-1 | 2-2 | 2-2 | 1-1 | 1-0 | 1-1 | ■ | 2-0 | 0-1 | 1-1 | 2-1 | 0-0 |
| Sheffield Wednesday FC | 2-0 | 2-0 | 1-1 | 3-3 | 1-0 | 1-1 | 4-2 | 1-1 | 4-0 | 6-2 | 5-2 | 3-1 | 1-1 | 2-4 | 0-1 | 1-0 | 2-1 | ■ | 2-2 | 3-0 | 0-0 | 2-1 |
| Southampton FC | 0-0 | 3-1 | 3-1 | 2-3 | 4-1 | 3-1 | 1-1 | 1-2 | 5-0 | 2-1 | 5-3 | 2-1 | 3-3 | 1-0 | 1-2 | 1-0 | 1-0 | 1-0 | ■ | 1-2 | 1-1 | 3-2 |
| Swansea Town AFC | 4-0 | 2-0 | 2-0 | 3-0 | 1-2 | 5-1 | 0-2 | 1-2 | 2-1 | 1-2 | 1-2 | 0-0 | 0-0 | 2-2 | 2-1 | 0-1 | 1-0 | 1-2 | 4-0 | ■ | 1-0 | 1-0 |
| Tottenham Hotspur FC | 2-0 | 2-3 | 5-0 | 1-1 | 3-1 | 2-0 | 1-0 | 3-1 | 1-2 | 0-0 | 2-0 | 0-2 | 0-0 | 4-1 | 3-2 | 3-0 | 7-0 | 1-0 | 4-0 | 3-1 | ■ | 4-1 |
| West Ham United FC | 2-1 | 0-2 | 1-0 | 2-2 | 4-0 | 0-1 | 1-1 | 0-1 | 4-3 | 2-1 | 3-1 | 2-2 | 0-0 | 2-2 | 0-3 | 1-0 | 0-0 | 2-2 | 1-2 | 3-0 | 0-1 | ■ |

## Division 2

| | | Pd | Wn | Dw | Ls | GF | GA | Pts | |
|---|---|---|---|---|---|---|---|---|---|
| 1. | Tottenham Hotspur FC (London) | 42 | 27 | 7 | 8 | 81 | 35 | 61 | P |
| 2. | Sheffield Wednesday FC (Sheffield) | 42 | 18 | 16 | 8 | 67 | 48 | 52 | P |
| 3. | Sheffield United FC (Sheffield) | 42 | 19 | 14 | 9 | 68 | 49 | 52 | |
| 4. | Southampton FC (Southampton) | 42 | 19 | 14 | 9 | 64 | 48 | 52 | |
| 5. | Leeds United AFC (Leeds) | 42 | 17 | 13 | 12 | 54 | 45 | 47 | |
| 6. | Preston North End FC (Preston) | 42 | 18 | 9 | 15 | 60 | 49 | 45 | |
| 7. | Hull City AFC (Kingston-upon-Tyne) | 42 | 17 | 11 | 14 | 64 | 72 | 45 | |
| 8. | Swansea Town AFC (Swansea) | 42 | 17 | 9 | 16 | 53 | 49 | 43 | |
| 9. | Brentford FC (London) | 42 | 15 | 13 | 14 | 44 | 49 | 43 | |
| 10. | Cardiff City AFC (Cardiff) | 42 | 16 | 10 | 16 | 41 | 44 | 42 | |
| 11. | Grimsby Town FC (Cleethorpes) | 42 | 16 | 8 | 18 | 74 | 73 | 40 | |
| 12. | Coventry City FC (Coventry) | 42 | 13 | 13 | 16 | 55 | 55 | 39 | |
| 13. | Barnsley FC (Barnsley) | 42 | 13 | 13 | 16 | 64 | 67 | 39 | |
| 14. | Chesterfield FC (Chesterfield) | 42 | 15 | 9 | 18 | 43 | 47 | 39 | |
| 15. | Leicester City FC (Leicester) | 42 | 12 | 15 | 15 | 55 | 65 | 39 | |
| 16. | Blackburn Rovers FC (Blackburn) | 42 | 14 | 10 | 18 | 55 | 60 | 38 | |
| 17. | Luton Town FC (Luton) | 42 | 10 | 18 | 14 | 41 | 51 | 38 | |
| 18. | Bury FC (Bury) | 42 | 14 | 9 | 19 | 60 | 65 | 37 | |
| 19. | West Ham United FC (London) | 42 | 12 | 12 | 18 | 53 | 61 | 36 | |
| 20. | Queen's Park Rangers FC (London) | 42 | 11 | 12 | 19 | 40 | 57 | 34 | |
| 21. | Plymouth Argyle FC (Plymouth) | 42 | 8 | 16 | 18 | 44 | 65 | 32 | R |
| 22. | Bradford Park Avenue FC (Bradford) | 42 | 10 | 11 | 21 | 51 | 77 | 31 | R |
| | | 924 | 331 | 262 | 331 | 1231 | 1231 | 924 | |

## Football League Division 3 (N) — 1949-1950 Season

| | ACC | BAR | BRA | CAR | CHE | CRE | DAR | DON | GAT | HAL | HAR | LIN | MAN | NEW | OLD | ROC | ROT | SOU | STO | TRA | WRE | YOR |
|---|---|---|---|---|---|---|---|---|---|---|---|---|---|---|---|---|---|---|---|---|---|---|
| Accrington Stanley FC | ▓ | 1-0 | 3-2 | 1-1 | 4-0 | 1-1 | 3-0 | 2-2 | 0-1 | 1-0 | 1-2 | 2-0 | 2-2 | 3-0 | 3-4 | 1-0 | 1-4 | 4-0 | 4-2 | 2-0 | 2-0 | 0-0 |
| Barrow AFC | 2-1 | ▓ | 1-0 | 1-3 | 3-1 | 0-1 | 2-1 | 1-1 | 1-1 | 4-0 | -0 | 0-0 | 0-1 | 1-1 | 3-1 | 0-1 | 1-1 | 1-0 | 0-1 | 1-2 | 2-1 | 3-2 |
| Bradford City AFC | 5-2 | 3-2 | ▓ | 3-2 | 1-0 | 0-2 | 4-1 | 1-2 | 2-1 | 1-3 | 1-3 | 0-1 | 2-1 | 2-1 | 1-1 | 2-1 | 1-2 | 6-0 | 0-1 | 2-4 | 1-0 | 0-2 |
| Carlisle United FC | 2-1 | 2-0 | 3-0 | ▓ | 5-1 | 2-2 | 0-1 | 0-0 | 4-2 | 0-2 | 2-1 | 0-2 | 1-1 | 0-0 | 3-0 | 2-0 | 3-1 | 3-3 | 2-0 | 0-0 | 1-0 | 4-3 |
| Chester FC | 1-0 | 1-0 | 4-1 | 2-4 | ▓ | 0-1 | 4-4 | 3-1 | 0-3 | 5-1 | 3-0 | 3-1 | 6-3 | 2-0 | 1-1 | 0-2 | 4-2 | 4-1 | 0-4 | 0-0 | 2-1 | 2-3 |
| Crewe Alexandra FC | 2-1 | 1-1 | 2-2 | 2-1 | 1-2 | ▓ | 2-0 | 0-2 | 3-1 | 6-3 | 1-0 | 3-2 | 1-1 | 1-2 | 1-1 | 0-1 | 4-1 | 1-2 | 1-0 | 2-0 | 1-1 | 3-3 |
| Darlington FC | 0-2 | 1-1 | 4-3 | 1-1 | 2-1 | 1-1 | ▓ | 2-1 | 2-3 | 5-1 | 1-0 | 2-0 | 2-2 | 3-1 | 1-1 | 1-1 | 2-1 | 0-2 | 1-1 | 0-2 | 3-1 | 1-1 |
| Doncaster Rovers FC | 4-1 | 1-0 | 1-1 | 0-0 | 2-0 | 0-2 | 2-1 | ▓ | 1-1 | 4-0 | 0-0 | 1-4 | 0-1 | 0-0 | 1-1 | 0-0 | 1-0 | 5-1 | 3-0 | 1-1 | 2-0 | 1-1 |
| Gateshead FC | 5-0 | 3-1 | 4-2 | 2-1 | 4-0 | 1-1 | 3-3 | 1-1 | ▓ | 7-1 | 2-0 | 2-1 | 0-1 | 2-1 | 2-0 | 1-3 | 2-2 | 3-2 | 1-0 | 5-1 | 0-1 | 1-1 |
| Halifax Town AFC | 1-4 | 1-0 | 3-1 | 1-1 | 2-1 | 3-1 | 1-3 | 2-2 | 5-2 | ▓ | 1-2 | 0-1 | 0-3 | 3-0 | 1-1 | 3-2 | 4-3 | 0-0 | 3-1 | 0-1 | 0-0 | 1-2 |
| Hartlepools United FC | 0-0 | 2-3 | 3-0 | 1-5 | 5-1 | 1-6 | 2-0 | 1-1 | 3-5 | 3-3 | ▓ | 2-1 | 1-3 | 2-0 | 0-2 | 1-2 | 1-2 | 1-0 | 1-0 | 2-0 | 3-1 | 2-0 |
| Lincoln City FC | 1-0 | 4-0 | 2-2 | 2-1 | 2-0 | 2-0 | 2-0 | 1-0 | 2-0 | 1-0 | 6-0 | ▓ | 1-0 | 1-2 | 1-2 | 2-0 | 0-0 | 1-1 | 1-1 | 0-0 | 2-0 | 1-0 |
| Mansfield Town FC | 2-0 | 1-1 | 0-2 | 4-1 | 0-2 | 3-0 | 2-1 | 1-2 | 1-0 | 7-1 | 2-1 | 1-1 | ▓ | 2-2 | 3-1 | 1-1 | 2-2 | 1-2 | 3-0 | 1-1 | 1-0 | 1-0 |
| New Brighton FC | 3-0 | 2-0 | 1-0 | 3-2 | 3-3 | 0-2 | 1-0 | 2-2 | 0-1 | 1-1 | 1-0 | 1-0 | 1-2 | ▓ | 0-0 | 0-4 | 0-3 | 1-0 | 1-3 | 0-0 | 3-1 | 3-1 |
| Oldham Athletic AFC | 0-1 | 1-3 | 2-1 | 1-1 | 0-2 | 2-1 | 2-0 | 1-4 | 1-0 | 2-1 | 3-1 | 0-2 | 1-0 | 3-0 | ▓ | 0-0 | 2-2 | 2-5 | 3-3 | 2-1 | 2-3 | 2-0 |
| Rochdale AFC | 2-0 | 2-1 | 2-2 | 1-0 | 0-1 | 2-1 | 2-0 | 0-1 | 1-3 | 1-0 | 4-0 | 2-0 | 7-1 | 4-0 | 1-0 | ▓ | 1-0 | 2-0 | 1-1 | 3-0 | 1-1 | 3-1 |
| Rotherham United FC | 6-0 | 1-2 | 5-2 | 1-1 | 3-2 | 0-0 | 1-1 | 0-2 | 1-2 | 5-1 | 1-3 | 2-2 | 3-0 | 0-1 | 4-3 | 1-0 | ▓ | 4-0 | 2-1 | 1-1 | 2-2 | 1-1 |
| Southport FC | 1-0 | 0-1 | 1-1 | 1-2 | 1-1 | 2-2 | 1-1 | 3-3 | 0-3 | 1-1 | 2-1 | 1-1 | 1-1 | 0-2 | 3-2 | 3-2 | 4-0 | ▓ | 1-0 | 2-1 | 0-0 | 1-1 |
| Stockport County FC | 1-0 | 1-3 | 1-0 | 2-0 | 3-0 | 4-1 | 2-1 | 0-1 | 2-1 | 2-0 | 1-0 | 1-1 | 1-0 | 0-2 | 1-3 | 1-1 | 0-2 | 3-2 | ▓ | 2-1 | 2-1 | 3-1 |
| Tranmere Rovers FC | 0-1 | 2-1 | 1-0 | 0-0 | 2-3 | 2-2 | 3-1 | 2-4 | 1-0 | 2-1 | 2-1 | 2-2 | 2-1 | 4-2 | 1-0 | 0-2 | 2-0 | 2-0 | 2-0 | ▓ | 2-1 | 1-0 |
| Wrexham AFC | 1-1 | 1-0 | 0-0 | 1-1 | 1-1 | 1-2 | 2-1 | 0-1 | 0-1 | 2-3 | 1-0 | 4-0 | 0-0 | 2-2 | 2-1 | 3-0 | 0-1 | 1-0 | 0-2 | 0-0 | ▓ | 2-0 |
| York City FC | 2-1 | 2-0 | 1-1 | 1-1 | 2-3 | 1-1 | 1-1 | 0-3 | 1-5 | 3-1 | 0-2 | 1-2 | 3-3 | 2-1 | 0-1 | 2-2 | 0-3 | 0-1 | 1-1 | 1-0 | 5-0 | ▓ |

## Division 3 (North)

| | | Pd | Wn | Dw | Ls | GF | GA | Pts | |
|---|---|---|---|---|---|---|---|---|---|
| 1. | Doncaster Rovers FC (Doncaster) | 42 | 19 | 17 | 6 | 66 | 38 | 55 | P |
| 2. | Gateshead FC (Gateshead) | 42 | 23 | 7 | 12 | 87 | 54 | 53 | |
| 3. | Rochdale AFC (Rochdale) | 42 | 21 | 9 | 12 | 68 | 41 | 51 | |
| 4. | Lincoln City FC (Lincoln) | 42 | 21 | 9 | 12 | 60 | 39 | 51 | |
| 5. | Tranmere Rovers FC (Tranmere) | 42 | 19 | 11 | 12 | 51 | 48 | 49 | |
| 6. | Rotherham United FC (Rotherham) | 42 | 19 | 10 | 13 | 80 | 59 | 48 | |
| 7. | Crewe Alexandra FC (Crewe) | 42 | 17 | 14 | 11 | 68 | 55 | 48 | |
| 8. | Mansfield Town FC (Mansfield) | 42 | 18 | 12 | 12 | 66 | 54 | 48 | |
| 9. | Carlisle United FC (Carlisle) | 42 | 16 | 15 | 11 | 68 | 51 | 47 | |
| 10. | Stockport County FC (Stockport) | 42 | 19 | 7 | 16 | 55 | 52 | 45 | |
| 11. | Oldham Athletic AFC (Oldham) | 42 | 16 | 11 | 15 | 58 | 63 | 43 | |
| 12. | Chester FC (Chester) | 42 | 17 | 6 | 19 | 70 | 79 | 40 | |
| 13. | Accrington Stanley FC (Accrington) | 42 | 16 | 7 | 19 | 57 | 62 | 39 | |
| 14. | New Brighton FC (Wallasey) | 42 | 14 | 10 | 18 | 45 | 63 | 38 | |
| 15. | Barrow AFC (Barrow-in-Furness) | 42 | 14 | 9 | 19 | 47 | 53 | 37 | |
| 16. | Southport FC (Southport) | 42 | 12 | 13 | 17 | 51 | 71 | 37 | |
| 17. | Darlington FC (Darlington) | 42 | 11 | 13 | 18 | 56 | 69 | 35 | |
| 18. | Hartlepools United FC (Hartlepool) | 42 | 14 | 5 | 23 | 52 | 79 | 33 | |
| 19. | Bradford City AFC (Bradford) | 42 | 12 | 8 | 22 | 61 | 76 | 32 | |
| 20. | Wrexham AFC (Wrexham) | 42 | 10 | 12 | 20 | 39 | 54 | 32 | |
| 21. | Halifax Town AFC (Halifax) | 42 | 12 | 8 | 22 | 58 | 85 | 32 | |
| 22. | York City FC (York) | 42 | 9 | 13 | 20 | 52 | 70 | 31 | |
| | | 924 | 349 | 226 | 349 | 1315 | 1315 | 924 | |

Elected: Scunthorpe & Lindsey United FC (Scunthorpe) and Shrewsbury Town FC (Shrewsbury)

Division 3 (North) was extended to 24 clubs from the next season

| Football League Division 3 (S) 1949-1950 Season | Aldershot | Bournemouth | Brighton | Bristol City | Bristol Rovers | Crystal Palace | Exeter City | Ipswich Town | Leyton Orient | Millwall | Newport County | Northampton | Norwich City | Nottingham Forest | Notts County | Port Vale | Reading | Southend United | Swindon Town | Torquay United | Walsall | Watford |
|---|---|---|---|---|---|---|---|---|---|---|---|---|---|---|---|---|---|---|---|---|---|---|
| Aldershot FC | ■ | 0-1 | 0-1 | 0-1 | 3-1 | 0-0 | 1-2 | 5-0 | 2-0 | 2-1 | 4-1 | 0-0 | 2-0 | 1-1 | 2-0 | 1-0 | 2-0 | 1-1 | 0-0 | 3-5 | 1-0 | 0-1 |
| Bournemouth & B. Athletic | 2-1 | ■ | 2-2 | 3-1 | 0-2 | 2-0 | 2-0 | 4-0 | 4-1 | 1-0 | 1-1 | 1-2 | 2-0 | 1-2 | 3-0 | 2-2 | 2-1 | 3-0 | 1-1 | 1-2 | 1-1 | 0-0 |
| Brighton & Hove Albion | 1-1 | 1-1 | ■ | 2-1 | 1-2 | 0-0 | 0-0 | 2-1 | 2-2 | 1-0 | 5-0 | 1-1 | 1-3 | 2-2 | 2-3 | 2-1 | 2-1 | 2-1 | 0-1 | 2-1 | 1-1 | 2-1 |
| Bristol City FC | 2-0 | 3-2 | 1-2 | ■ | 1-2 | 2-0 | 1-0 | 4-2 | 0-0 | 2-1 | 6-0 | 3-1 | 1-2 | 0-2 | 4-0 | 2-0 | 2-2 | 1-1 | 1-0 | 0-0 | 2-1 | 0-1 |
| Bristol Rovers FC | 2-1 | 0-0 | 3-0 | 2-3 | ■ | 0-0 | 1-0 | 2-0 | 3-0 | 3-1 | 3-0 | 0-0 | 5-1 | 0-3 | 0-3 | 2-1 | 2-1 | 1-1 | 2-0 | 2-0 | 1-1 | 0-2 |
| Crystal Palace FC | 2-1 | 1-0 | 6-0 | 1-1 | 1-0 | ■ | 5-3 | 2-0 | 1-1 | 1-0 | 1-0 | 0-4 | 2-0 | 1-1 | 1-2 | 0-1 | 1-1 | 2-1 | 2-2 | 1-3 | 2-0 | 2-0 |
| Exeter City FC | 1-0 | 1-2 | 2-3 | 0-0 | 2-0 | 2-1 | ■ | 1-1 | 1-1 | 2-1 | 3-3 | 1-3 | 3-1 | 0-0 | 2-2 | 3-1 | 3-4 | 1-1 | 3-0 | 1-1 | 2-1 | 3-1 |
| Ipswich Town FC | 1-0 | 1-2 | 2-2 | 0-0 | 3-1 | 4-4 | 1-0 | ■ | 4-4 | 0-3 | 1-0 | 2-2 | 3-0 | 1-2 | 0-4 | 2-1 | 2-0 | 1-3 | 3-1 | 3-1 | 1-5 | 1-1 |
| Leyton Orient FC | 2-7 | 2-1 | 0-1 | 1-0 | 1-0 | 2-2 | 4-1 | 4-0 | ■ | 1-1 | 2-1 | 1-0 | 1-2 | 1-1 | 1-4 | 1-0 | 2-1 | 2-2 | 1-3 | 2-1 | 2-2 | 0-0 |
| Millwall FC | 3-0 | 1-0 | 5-1 | 3-1 | 0-1 | 2-3 | 3-1 | 3-1 | 3-1 | ■ | 1-2 | 0-2 | 1-2 | 2-1 | 1-3 | 3-0 | 3-1 | 1-2 | 1-0 | 1-3 | 1-1 | 1-3 |
| Newport County AFC | 6-0 | 5-0 | 0-1 | 6-4 | 2-3 | 2-2 | 1-2 | 1-0 | 3-2 | 4-3 | ■ | 1-4 | 3-2 | 4-1 | 1-1 | 1-1 | 1-1 | 2-1 | 1-2 | 1-0 | 2-1 | 3-3 |
| Northampton Town FC | 1-1 | 2-3 | 2-1 | 4-2 | 2-0 | 2-2 | 3-3 | 1-2 | 3-0 | 1-0 | 4-3 | ■ | 3-1 | 0-0 | 5-1 | 1-1 | 2-0 | 2-0 | 0-1 | 3-0 | 2-0 | 0-0 |
| Norwich City FC | 4-0 | 0-1 | 1-2 | 3-0 | 4-0 | 2-0 | 1-2 | 1-1 | 4-0 | 0-2 | 4-0 | 2-1 | ■ | 1-1 | 4-3 | 0-1 | 1-1 | 0-0 | 4-0 | 3-3 | 3-2 | 2-1 |
| Nottingham Forest FC | 3-0 | 3-0 | 0-1 | 3-0 | 2-0 | 2-0 | 5-0 | 2-0 | 2-1 | 3-1 | 3-0 | 0-1 | 0-1 | ■ | 1-2 | 2-0 | 1-2 | 1-2 | 2-1 | 1-2 | 1-0 | 0-1 |
| Notts County FC | 3-1 | 2-0 | 4-2 | 4-1 | 2-0 | 0-1 | 3-3 | 2-0 | 7-1 | 2-0 | 7-0 | 2-0 | 5-0 | 2-0 | ■ | 3-1 | 4-0 | 2-0 | 3-0 | 1-1 | 1-1 | 1-0 |
| Port Vale FC | 0-1 | 1-1 | 3-0 | 0-2 | 1-0 | 2-0 | 1-0 | 2-2 | 2-0 | 4-0 | 1-0 | 3-1 | 2-2 | 1-1 | 3-1 | ■ | 1-1 | 0-0 | 0-1 | 2-0 | 2-0 | 2-0 |
| Reading FC | 1-3 | 2-1 | 3-0 | 1-0 | 0-1 | 1-2 | 3-2 | 3-1 | 5-1 | 2-0 | 4-1 | 3-1 | 4-1 | 1-1 | 0-1 | 2-1 | ■ | 5-0 | 4-3 | 2-0 | 1-1 | 1-0 |
| Southend United FC | 3-0 | 1-0 | 3-2 | 2-0 | 3-1 | 0-0 | 1-0 | 2-2 | 2-0 | 3-0 | 6-0 | 1-2 | 1-0 | 2-3 | 2-0 | 1-0 | 3-2 | ■ | 2-0 | 2-0 | 2-2 | 1-1 |
| Swindon Town FC | 2-1 | 3-1 | 4-2 | 1-1 | 1-0 | 4-2 | 7-1 | 0-3 | 0-1 | 1-1 | 1-1 | 6-1 | 1-1 | 0-5 | 1-1 | 0-0 | 2-0 | 2-2 | ■ | 1-2 | 4-3 | 0-1 |
| Torquay United FC | 4-0 | 3-1 | 0-0 | 3-3 | 1-0 | 1-0 | 1-4 | 2-2 | 4-1 | 1-0 | 5-3 | 1-0 | 1-1 | 2-0 | 0-0 | 0-0 | 4-2 | 2-4 | 1-0 | ■ | 2-1 | 2-1 |
| Walsall FC | 0-0 | 1-1 | 4-2 | 1-1 | 3-1 | 3-1 | 3-0 | 1-3 | 1-2 | 0-1 | 2-0 | 1-3 | 1-1 | 1-3 | 3-3 | 1-0 | 2-0 | 1-1 | 0-0 | 7-1 | ■ | 1-1 |
| Watford FC | 1-0 | 4-1 | 0-0 | 2-0 | 0-2 | 0-0 | 1-2 | 6-0 | 2-1 | 0-0 | 0-1 | 0-0 | 0-0 | 1-0 | 2-1 | 0-2 | 1-1 | 1-0 | 1-2 | 1-0 | 3-0 | ■ |

| Division 3 (South) | Pd | Wn | Dw | Ls | GF | GA | Pts | |
|---|---|---|---|---|---|---|---|---|
| 1. Notts County FC (Nottingham) | 42 | 25 | 8 | 9 | 95 | 50 | 58 | P |
| 2. Northampton Town FC (Northampton) | 42 | 20 | 11 | 11 | 72 | 50 | 51 | |
| 3. Southend United FC (Southend-on-Sea) | 42 | 19 | 13 | 10 | 66 | 48 | 51 | |
| 4. Nottingham Forest FC (Nottingham) | 42 | 20 | 9 | 13 | 67 | 39 | 49 | |
| 5. Torquay United FC (Torquay) | 42 | 19 | 10 | 13 | 66 | 63 | 48 | |
| 6. Watford FC (Watford) | 42 | 16 | 13 | 13 | 45 | 35 | 45 | |
| 7. Crystal Palace FC (London) | 42 | 15 | 14 | 13 | 55 | 54 | 44 | |
| 8. Brighton & Hove Albion FC (Hove) | 42 | 16 | 12 | 14 | 57 | 69 | 44 | |
| 9. Bristol Rovers FC (Bristol) | 42 | 19 | 5 | 18 | 51 | 51 | 43 | |
| 10. Reading FC (Reading) | 42 | 17 | 8 | 17 | 70 | 64 | 42 | |
| 11. Norwich City FC (Norwich) | 42 | 16 | 10 | 16 | 65 | 63 | 42 | |
| 12. Bournemouth & Boscombe Athletic FC (Bournemouth) | 42 | 16 | 10 | 16 | 57 | 56 | 42 | |
| 13. Port Vale FC (Stoke-on-Trent) | 42 | 15 | 11 | 16 | 47 | 42 | 41 | |
| 14. Swindon Town FC (Swindon) | 42 | 15 | 11 | 16 | 59 | 62 | 41 | |
| 15. Bristol City FC (Bristol) | 42 | 15 | 10 | 17 | 60 | 61 | 40 | |
| 16. Exeter City FC (Exeter) | 42 | 14 | 11 | 17 | 63 | 75 | 39 | |
| 17. Ipswich Town FC (Ipswich) | 42 | 12 | 11 | 19 | 57 | 86 | 35 | |
| 18. Leyton Orient FC (London) | 42 | 12 | 11 | 19 | 53 | 85 | 35 | |
| 19. Walsall FC (Walsall) | 42 | 9 | 16 | 17 | 61 | 62 | 34 | |
| 20. Aldershot FC (Aldershot) | 42 | 13 | 8 | 21 | 48 | 60 | 34 | |
| 21. Newport County AFC (Newport) | 42 | 13 | 8 | 21 | 67 | 98 | 34 | |
| 22. Millwall FC (London) | 42 | 14 | 4 | 24 | 55 | 63 | 32 | |
| | 924 | 350 | 224 | 350 | 1336 | 1336 | 924 | |

Elected: Colchester United FC (Colchester) and Gillingham FC (Gillingham)

Division 3 (South) was extended to 24 clubs from the next season.


## F.A. CUP FINAL   (Wembley Stadium, London – 29/04/1950 – 100,000)

ARSENAL FC (LONDON)                    2-0                    Liverpool FC (Liverpool)

*Lewis 2*

Arsenal: Swindin, Scott, Barnes, Forbes, L.Compton, Mercer, Cox, Logie, Goring, Lewis, D.Compton.

Liverpool: Sidlow, Lambert, Spicer, Taylor, Hughes, Jones, Payne, Barron, Stubbins, Fagan, Liddell.


## Semi-finals

| Arsenal FC (London) | 2-2, 1-0 | Chelsea FC (London) |
|---|---|---|
| Liverpool FC (Liverpool) | 2-0 | Everton FC (Liverpool) |


## Quarter-finals

| Arsenal FC (London) | 1-0 | Leeds United AFC (Leeds) |
|---|---|---|
| Chelsea FC (London) | 2-0 | Manchester United FC (Manchester) |
| Derby County FC (Derby) | 1-2 | Everton FC (Liverpool) |
| Liverpool FC (Liverpool) | 2-1 | Blackpool FC (Blackpool) |